HANDBOOK

OF

Family Therapy

Edited by

Alan S. Gurman, Ph.D.

Professor,
Department of Psychiatry,
University of Wisconsin Medical School

and

David P. Kniskern, Psy.D.

Associate Professor,
Department of Psychiatry,
University of Cincinnati College of Medicine

BRUNNER/MAZEL, *Publishers* • New York

Library of Congress Cataloging—in Publication Data
Main entry under title:
Handbook of family therapy.

    Includes bibliographies.
    Includes indexes.
    1. Family psychotherapy. I. Gurman, Alan S.
II. Kniskern, David P., 1948-
RC488.5.H33   616.89′156   80-20357
ISBN 0-87630-242-8

Published by
BRUNNER/MAZEL, INC.
19 Union Square
New York, NY 10003

MANUFACTURED IN THE UNITED STATES OF AMERICA

10 9 8 7

To Our Families:

Gerri, Jesse and Theodore Gurman

and

Rebecca, Jonathan and Ethan Kniskern

Foreword

This volume is unique. No previous book, and no collection of papers one could assemble from the literature, addresses or achieves for the field of family therapy what is accomplished in the *Handbook*. It responds to a pressing need for a comprehensive source that will enable students, practitioners and researchers to compare and assess critically for themselves an array of major current clinical concepts in family therapy. And, I must add, this achievement comes just in time, before the task would have become unmanageable.

During the last 25 years, the concept of family therapy and the scope of the field have evolved with startling rapidity. Especially during the past decade, family-oriented clinicians have been flooded with books and journals, with workshops and courses. Although agreement on a number of principles has gradually emerged, enthusiastic and persuasive advocates have informed and, quite expectably, polarized their readers and audiences. Concepts and techniques that have seemed intriguing when considered separately have been perplexing when juxtaposed. Quite often, spokesmen have persisted in clinging to viewpoints that were distinctive in the past and have failed to acknowledge that their beliefs now converge with those of others. A mystique for the faithful is thus sustained but a muddle is created for the field as a whole.

In some instances, allegations of difference appear to reflect terminologic preferences that have obscured similarities of clinical practice. Still other competing "schools" have used the same terms but appear to practice and teach quite differently. Consequently, even though many of the core ideas of family therapy are now incorporated into the thinking and practice of numerous clinicians, including many who do not call themselves family therapists, the "schools" and models of family therapy frequently have been perceived as competing ideologies.

Fortunately, in recent years a number of second and third generation family therapists have begun to clarify and compare approaches. In facilitating such comparisons, the *Handbook of Family Therapy* is a generative and invaluable accomplishment. Until now, systematic and detailed comparisons across the field of family therapy, with representatives of divergent approaches speaking for themselves, simply had not been attempted. The editors wisely forego spoonfeeding the reader with a blenderized reconciliation of viewpoints. But the ingredients are here, both for partial reconciliations and for specifying researchable hypotheses and differences.

Several editorial features of the *Handbook* aid but do not supplant the reader's integrative task. Gurman and Kniskern requested that all of the contributors attempt to follow the same guidelines, specified in the Preface, that could provide a comparative frame of reference. For some approaches, a number of the issues listed in the guidelines are not conceptually relevant, or may not have been considered (yet). Several issues in the guidelines have stimulated some of the authors to clarify here for the first time previously unstated premises and assumptions. Additionally, I personally was usefully jarred, as most readers no doubt will be, by the exercise of formulating and comparing my own views of therapy within the framework of the editorial guidelines.

Perhaps the most thought-provoking passages in this volume are the abundant and astute Editors' Notes. Sometimes the editors forthrightly express a contrary opinion, at other times they cite either confirmatory or challenging evidence, and at still other times they pointedly compare or contrast the concepts, terminologies, and methods of the various authors.

In selecting the models of family therapy to be presented in the *Handbook*, the editors acknowledge that the choices were difficult and that they differ from those that others might have preferred. Also, their clustering of the models of therapy into general categories was necessarily somewhat arbitrary. While thinking about alternative groupings, I concluded that current family therapy approaches do in fact have far more in common than has generally been recognized. For example, the concept of the family as a system is so widely accepted that it no longer differentiates family therapy approaches from one another. Skynner, who began with a "psychoanalytic" approach, emphasizes strongly a systems framework (Chapter 2), and so does the approach of Barton and Alexander (Chapter 11), who began with behavioral- learning theory. On the other hand, the meaning

attributed to the term "system" is not always the same. Specifically, the Kerr (Bowen) emphasis on the family as *the* system, versus the individual (Chapter 7), needs to be distinguished with care from the *general* systems theory of most other family theorists in which the family, the individual, and other systems as well (biological to societal) are conceptualized in complementary hierarchical relationships with one another.

Another example of overlap is that nowadays nearly all family therapists are problem-focused, at least initially; but more clarification is needed as to what constitutes a "problem" that is relevant to therapy. Similarly, nearly all family therapists claim to give detailed attention to observable behavior and interaction.

For me, a meaningful continuum on which family therapists still do differ is the degree to which the therapist's subjective experience with the family is used as a significant and explicit source of data that influences treatment moves. Such an emphasis characterizes, by and large, the approaches categorized as the "psychoanalytic and object-relations approaches," and the "intergenerational approaches," but not Kerr (Bowen). The therapist's experience also has been given considerable attention by Virginia Satir (discussed by Bodin), the Selvini-Palazzoli group (discussed by Stanton), and the Duhls. But most of the other authors listed under "systems theory approaches" and "behavioral approaches" exclude or minimize use of the therapist's "craziness," as Whitaker calls it, as an agency for facilitating change, and they put relatively more effort into organizing data collection and directing the family in structured, specified tasks. Attention to the experiential dimension reflects the interest of some therapists in facilitating personal growth (for both themselves and the family members). But this goal, with rare exceptions, is pursued by family therapists today in addition to (not instead of) behavioral change and symptom relief.

Because of the widespread tendency of many family therapists to try out, incorporate and adapt concepts, goals, and techniques from many different sources, it is difficult to characterize the family therapy "model" that I believe is most widespread in actual practice, and which the editors in the final chapter label the "pragmatic psychodynamic therapies." This term implies that dynamic principles are acknowledged and accepted, but are conceptualized within a general systems rather than a psychoanalytic framework, and that this framework is used in selecting whatever variety of techniques and strategies appear most likely to resolve rapidly the presenting problems of the family. This "model" is represented in the *Handbook*, in highly individualized versions, by Epstein, Framo, Skynner, and Sager, and outside of this volume by such therapists as Donald Bloch, Ira Glick, Michael Goldstein, Henry Grunebaum, Norman Paul, Fred Sander, Roger Shapiro, Margaret Singer, Helm Stierlin, Lyman Wynne, and Izrael Zwerling.

These pragmatic psychodynamic "models" are most directly descended from the approach of Nathan Ackerman, who above all was interested in therapy that works. He freely drew upon dynamic and systems concepts and strategic directives in a tradition that was as coextensive as he could make it with the whole field of family therapy. Hence, he resisted throughout his lifetime, as he would today, the delineation of family therapy organizations and narrowly circumscribed schools or models of thought that could strangulate future change and growth. Although the impact of recent political and organizational developments in family therapy is still uncertain, I am reassured, as I believe Ackerman would be, by the evidence of this volume: while family therapists are reaching a consensus about many broad principles, the field retains the vitality and energy of the pioneering years and continues to generate innovative and provocative ideas.

It is a tribute to the diversity and quality of the contributions included in the *Handbook* that one is induced to compare not only current family therapy approaches with one another, but also to consider how they fit in with other theories of the family and of therapy. Models of the family deriving from sociologic-anthropologic traditions, and those used in research on family interaction, family development, and familial risk factors in psychopathology, are understandably not included, since their clinical implications have not yet been clearly developed or applied.

A few of the authors in this volume, especially Boszormenyi-Nagy, explicitly go beyond family therapy to models that can become relevant to general health care delivery, in which the family is a subsystem and family therapy is a component of treatment planning, but not necessarily the centerpiece. Such proposals for a broadened framework for the family therapy field are likely to be increasingly important in the future, but it must be conceded that these extensions are currently more theoretical potentialities than widely practiced actualities. In still another sphere, multiple family therapy, most frequently used with families of patients in hospital and day treatment programs, is a highly pragmatic, mostly nontheoretical approach that goes beyond treating one family at a time. Years ago family therapists agreed that families are distinctively different from *ad hoc* groups of individuals. Except for Ross Speck, the late Peter Laqueur, and in a different way, Murray Bowen, the field has mostly neglected trying to conceptualize how and when therapy is desirable with *ad hoc* groups and with "natural" networks in which couples or nuclear families are the components.

A special strength of this volume is that the editors repeatedly identify hypotheses that can and should be tested. They especially raise questions about the effectiveness of methods (for example, co-therapy) which are held in sharply contrasting regard by different therapists. The concluding two chapters on research on the process and outcome of family therapy are splendidly integrated with the rest of the volume. Building upon their previous reviews of the literature, Gurman and Kniskern summarize provocatively but persuasively the evidence on the crucial outcome issues of efficacy, safety, and efficiency of family therapy. Considerably more is now established about the efficacy of outcome than most clinicians and treatment researchers probably assume, given the dour attitude toward psychotherapy that is widely held at present. For example, in the treatment of marital problems, it is now established that individual psychotherapy has fewer positive outcomes and a strikingly higher rate of negative outcomes than does conjoint marital therapy.

On the other hand, the outcome questions that can and should be answered remain dismayingly numerous. Hopefully, the suggestions in this volume will goad at least some readers into further thought and action leading to outcome research. For example, Gurman and Kniskern point out, and I strongly concur, that "the comparative study of two or more treatment methods is virtually useless unless a specific patient population has been well defined." Family therapists, preoccupied with valid objections to defining populations in terms of individual psychiatric diagnoses, have not agreed upon an alternative, family-based approach. Various suggestions for a family diagnostic typology do not yet appear to be treatment relevant, while clinical "situations" and developmental problems that should be specified and related directly to treatment strategies have been introduced only recently and have been identified mainly in the marital sphere. With families, an example of such a clinical "situation" is the family at the time of an adolescent leaving home; alternative therapeutic approaches can readily be compared at such a point in individual and family development.

There appears to be almost a uniform assertion by family therapists that each of their approaches is *potentially* "applicable" to almost any problem. Such beliefs are not responsive to the crucial questions of *comparative* applicability, in which controlled clinical trials, both with alternative family approaches and with other kinds of intervention altogether, badly need to be carried out. Especially relevant to the "real world" of simultaneous and combined treatments is the issue of how and when treatments may interact synergistically and positively, or cancel each other out. It is all very well to "require," for example, that the strategic family therapist be in charge of "all" the therapy, including medication, individual therapy, hospitalization decisions, etc. But such assertions of leadership are apt to be unrealistic in many settings because of institutional power politics, or at least made difficult by the sheer complexity of current therapeutic, social, and educational agencies and institutions, as well as by the diversity of individual modes of practice. A major question for the family therapy of the future that concerns me greatly is whether and how family therapists can gain the competence and the willingness to assume collaborative and integrative relationships with colleagues that will insure more comprehensive health care. Meanwhile, the *Handbook of Family Therapy* provides a splendid documentation of the state of the art to which we can turn for years to come. The evidence is there, I believe, that the field has now matured to the point of being open to a thorough scrutiny of its premises and its effectiveness, and to a reassessment of its scope and applicability.

LYMAN C. WYNNE, M.D., Ph.D.
*Professor of Psychiatry and
Director of Family Programs,
University of Rochester Medical Center,
Rochester, New York*

About the Editors

Alan S. Gurman received his B.A. from Boston University (1967) and his M.A. (1970) and Ph.D. (1971) from Columbia University. After a two-year Postdoctoral Fellowship in the Department of Psychiatry at the University of Wisconsin Medical School, he joined the faculty there. Currently a Professor of Psychiatry, he is also the Director of the Psychiatric Outpatient Clinic and Co-Director of the Couples-Family Clinic. Dr. Gurman is a former Secretary-Treasurer and member of the Executive Committee of the Society for Psychotherapy Research, and member of the Board of Directors of the American Family Therapy Association. In 1978 he was co-recipient (with David P. Kniskern) of the award for "Outstanding Research Contribution in Marital and Family Therapy" of the American Association for Marriage and Family Therapy (AAMFT). He has also served as a member of the AAMFT's National Advisory Committee on Standards for Education and Training, and as a Member of the Commission on Accreditation for Marriage and Family Therapy Education. The author of over 60 professional articles and book chapters, he has also edited *Couples in Conflict: New Directions in Marital Therapy* (with D. Rice), *Effective Psychotherapy: A Handbook of Research* (with A. Razin), and *Questions and Answers in the Practice of Family Therapy*. Dr. Gurman is a member of the editorial boards of *Family Process*, the *Journal of Marital and Family Therapy*, the *American Journal of Family Therapy*, the *Journal of Consulting and Clinical Psychology*, and several other professional journals. He also maintains a private practice of psychotherapy.

David P. Kniskern received his Psy.D. degree from the University of Illinois. After a predoctoral and postdoctoral fellowship in the Department of Psychiatry at the University of Wisconsin Medical School, he joined the faculty of the Department of Psychiatry at the University of Cincinnati College of Medicine. He is currently an Associate Professor of Psychology in that Department, where he coordinates the outpatient marital/family therapy training. The author of numerous articles and chapters about clinical and research aspects of marital/family therapy, in 1978 he was co-recipient (with Alan S. Gurman) of the award for "Outstanding Research Contribution in Marital and Family Therapy" of the American Association for Marital and Family Therapy. Dr. Kniskern also maintains a private practice of psychotherapy.

Preface

Consider the following: (a) Whereas in 1973 there existed only one professional journal (*Family Process*) devoted in large part to family therapy, there now exist almost one dozen English language family therapy journals and almost as many foreign language journals; (b) there now exist over 300 free-standing family institutes in the United States; (c) the membership of the American Association for Marriage and Family Therapy increased from 973 in 1970, to 3,373 in 1975, to 7,565 in 1979—this represents an increase of 777% during the decade; and (d) in 1977, a second major national family therapy organization, the American Family Therapy Association, was established. By these, or any of several other meaningful criteria, it is clear that the growth of family therapy in the last decade has been extraordinary. It was within this context that our own teaching, clinical and research experience in family therapy led us to conclude that, although a great deal of clearly valuable theory and practice had developed in the field, this had occurred in widely varying centers and had proceeded in widely varying directions. As probably every teacher of family therapy would agree, until now there has existed no single book in the field that is adequate to the task of serving as a primary reference source for a comprehensive analysis of the truly significant conceptual and clinical influences on the field.

Thus, this *Handbook* was conceived and planned to fill this significant gap in the family therapy literature. Our primary goal was to develop a comprehensive presentation of all the major models of family therapy, with original contributions from prominent representatives of each of the approaches represented. We have been unusually fortunate in having many of the first and second generation leaders in the field join us in this project.

Any book attempting to present a comprehensive view of a field must, nonetheless, be selective about what is included. Despite the length of this volume, some readers may be disappointed to find certain approaches to family therapy missing, and perhaps surprised to find certain others included. For example, while cognitive, rational-emotive, client-centered, and Adlerian therapy, Gestalt therapy, and transactional analysis certainly have exerted salient influences on the practice of individual and group therapy, and while some family clinicians adopt aspects of these methods in their work, it is our judgment that these therapeutic approaches have not yet exerted a significant impact on the field of family therapy. In a related vein, there are a number of individuals, such as Virginia Satir, John Elderkin Bell, Lyman Wynne and Theodore Lidz, whose personal and/or historical influence on the field has been enormous, yet whose work is not represented by separate chapters because, in these cases, no discernible "school" or therapeutic method has evolved from their contributions.

In general, then, this *Handbook* is focused on the major theories of family and marital therapy, with the obvious exceptions of the chapters on the history of family therapy and on research in family therapy. In addition, we have included three chapters on "special areas" of the family field, two of which (marital and family enrichment, divorce and divorce therapy) are not dominated by any single theoretical orientation, and one of which (the treatment of sexual dysfunction) focuses on a particular domain of common, relationship-related clinical disorders. Such approaches as multifamily group therapy and network therapy are not included here. While important developments have taken place within each of these approaches, we concluded that, given space limitations, they were not in sufficiently widespread use to justify inclusion, whereas the issues involved in enrichment, sexual dysfunction and divorce touch virtually every practitioner of family and marital therapy. Therapeutic intervention with families in other areas of increasing social concern, such as stepfamilies and violence and the family, while clearly deserving of continued clinical and research innovation and experimentation, could not be accommodated for similar practical reasons.

Admittedly, our categorization of the various models of therapy included in this *Handbook* (i.e., Psychoanalytic-Object Relations, Intergenerational, Systems Theory and Behavioral) is somewhat arbitrary, though it was arrived at after a great deal of thought on our part. Just as, in our view, the boundaries between the intrapersonal and the interpersonal domains of experience are subtle, so, too, are the bound-

aries between the various family therapies often unclear. Recognition of this lack of clarity among schools reflects the beginnings of the process of synthesis and integration which we hope this volume will further.

The crucial problem in the planning of this *Handbook* was to develop a method by which authors could be encouraged to present a comprehensive statement of their theoretical assumptions and clinical methods in a way that would facilitate comparison and understanding by the reader. Without some structure, we feared that the contributions would be presented in such different ways that the writing styles and personalities of the authors would obscure "real" similarities among schools. Too rigid a structure, and we feared that the spirit and "feel" of a school's approach would be squeezed from each chapter. We adopted two strategies to steer us between these undesirable extremes. First, we have added to each chapter critical Editors' Notes. The purposes of these Notes are 1) to point out the similarities and differences between an author's thinking and the views of other contributors to this volume; 2) to take issue occasionally with a contributor's idea or conclusion on the basis of our own thinking or clinical experience, or to refer the reader to relevant ideas or data published elsewhere; and 3) to offer our own views on certain fundamental clinical issues. We have devoted a good deal of thought to these Notes and hope they serve to stimulate the reader's own critical thinking; also, in some cases we hope they will stimulate useful empirical study.

The second method we have used to achieve a consistency across the contributions to this volume was to offer a set of "Guidelines for Contributors" to each author. These Guidelines address what we consider to be a comprehensive enumeration of the central aspects of *any* method of family or marital therapy (the authors of the chapters on the history of family therapy, on family therapy research, and on enrichment and divorce were exempted from following these guidelines for reasons that should be self-evident). Most of the authors followed these Guidelines religiously, while a few varied somewhat the format of their exposition. Variations notwithstanding, it is clear to us that providing these Guidelines to contributors accomplished its fundamental purpose, i.e., to facilitate the comparative study of different family therapy approaches and insure comprehensiveness in each of the contributions. The contributors to this *Handbook* were never expected to address each point under each main heading; rather, these more focal points were suggested as illustrative of the kinds of issues pertinent to each section of the Guidelines.

We have received enormously positive reactions about the utility of these Guidelines for studying and teaching the various theories of family and marital therapy and include them here as a guide to the reader:

I. BACKGROUND OF THE APPROACH

Purpose: To place the approach in historical perspective both within the field of psychotherapy in general and within the area of marital/family therapy in particular.

1) The major influences that contributed to the development of the approach, e.g., people, books, theories, conferences.
2) The therapeutic forms that were forerunners of the approach, e.g., play therapy, psychoanalysis, desensitization, etc.
3) Types of patients with which the approach was initially developed.
4) Early theoretical speculations and/or therapy techniques.

II. THE HEALTHY OR WELL-FUNCTIONING MARRIAGE OR FAMILY

Purpose: To describe within your theoretical framework how a healthy family/marriage operates, or what is indicative of smooth operation.

1) How are roles defined within a healthy family/marriage?
2) How are problems solved?
3) What markers are characteristic of the family life-cycle?
4) Describe how a healthy family changes over time.
5) How is affection/sexuality handled?
6) What levels of intimacy and separateness are found?
7) How dependent or autonomous are family members?
8) Relationships with extended family.
9) Relationships with non-family members.

III. THE PATHOLOGICAL OR DYSFUNCTIONAL MARRIAGE OR FAMILY

Purpose: To describe the way in which pathological functioning is conceptualized within the approach.

1) Describe any formal or informal system for diagnosing or typing families.
2) What leads to family or marital dysfunction?
3) How do symptoms develop?
4) What determines the type of symptom to appear?
5) Why are some people symptomatic and not others? Alternatively, what is the role of the "identified patient"?
6) Are there "well" members in pathological marriages/families?

IV. THE ASSESSMENT OF SYSTEM DYSFUNCTION

Purpose: To describe the methods, whether formal or informal, used to gain an understanding of a particular marriage's or family's style or pattern of interaction, symptomatology and adaptive resources.

1) At what *unit* levels is assessment made (e.g., individual, dyadic, triadic, system)?
2) At what *psychological* levels is assessment made (e.g., intrapsychic, behavioral)?
3) Are any tests, devices, questionnaires, or observations used?
4) Is assessment separate from treatment or integrated with it? E.g., what is the temporal relation between assessment and treatment?
5) What is the role of the verbal interview as contrasted, e.g., with home visits, structured interaction tasks, etc.

V. GOAL-SETTING

Purpose: To describe the nature of therapeutic goals established and the process by which they are established.

1) Are there treatment goals that apply to *all* cases for which the treatment is appropriate (see VI. Treatment Applicability) regardless of between-family differences?

2) Of the number of possible goals for a given family/couple, how are the central goals selected for this couple/family?

3) Do you distinguish between intermediate or mediating goals and ultimate goals?

4) *Who* determines the goals of treatment? Therapist, family, other? Both? How are differences in goals resolved?

5) Is it important that treatment goals be discussed with the family/couple explicitly? If yes, why? If no, why not?

6) At what level of psychological experience are goals established, e.g., are they described in overt, motoric terms, in affective-cognitive terms, etc.?

VI. TREATMENT APPLICABILITY

Purpose: To describe those families/couples for whom your approach is particularly relevant.

1) For what families/couples is your approach particularly relevant?

2) For what families/couples is your approach either not appropriate or of uncertain relevance?

3) When, if ever, would a referral be made for either another (i.e., different) type of family/marital therapy, or for an entirely different treatment, e.g., hypnotherapy, chemotherapy?

4) When would *no* treatment (of any sort) be recommended? For 1) and 2), discussion in terms of syndromes, family "types," identified patient types, symptom severity, etc. would be appropriate.

VII. THE STRUCTURE OF THE THERAPY PROCESS

Purpose: To describe the treatment setting, frequency, and duration of treatment characteristic of your approach.

1) Is treatment conjoint, concurrent, three-generational, individual, etc.? Why? Are combined therapies used, e.g., individual psychotherapy plus family therapy?

2) How many therapists are usually involved? From your perspective, what are the advantages (or disadvantages) of using co-therapists?

3) What is the spatial arrangement within the therapy room? Is it a significant structural aspect of therapy?

4) Is therapy time-limited or unlimited? Why? Ideal models aside, how long does therapy *typically* last?

5) How often are sessions held?

6) How are decisions about therapy structure made? Who makes these decisions?

VIII. THE ROLE OF THE THERAPIST

Purpose: To describe the stance the therapist takes with the family/couple.

1) To what degree does the therapist overtly control sessions? How active/directive is the therapist?

2) Do patients talk predominantly to the therapist or to each other?

3) Does the therapist use self-disclosure? What limits are imposed on therapist self-disclosure?

4) Does the therapist "join" the family or remain outside?

5) Does the therapist's role change as therapy progresses? Does it change as termination approaches?

IX. TECHNIQUES OF MARITAL-FAMILY THERAPY

Purpose: To describe techniques always or frequently used in a particular approach to marital/family therapy, and their tactical purposes.

1) How structured are therapy sessions?

2) What techniques are used to join the family or to create a treatment alliance?

3) What techniques lead to changes in structure or transactional pattern?

4) Is "homework" used?

5) What techniques lead to disen-

gagement of the therapist? On what basis is termination decided?

6) How is the decision made to use a particular technique at a particular time? Are different techniques used for different family/marital problems?

7) How are resistances to change dealt with, e.g., differential motivation among family members?

8) What are both the most common *and* the most serious technical errors a therapist can make operating within your therapeutic approach?

9) On what basis is termination decided and how is termination effected?

X. CURATIVE FACTORS IN MARITAL/FAMILY THERAPY

Purpose: To describe the factors that lead to change in families/couples and to assess their relative importance.

1) Do patients need insight or understanding in order to change? Differentiate between historical-genetic insight and interactional insight.

2) Are interpretations important and, if so, do they take history (genetics) into account?

3) Is the learning of new skills seen as important? If so, are these skills taught in didactic fashion or are they shaped as approximations occur naturalistically in treatment?

4) Does the therapist's personality or psychological health play an important part?

5) What other therapist factors influence the course and outcome of the treatment?

6) How important are techniques?

7) Is transference utilized?

8) Is countertransference utilized? Is it seen as a major risk in marital/family therapy?

9) Must each family member change?

10) What patient (family) factors or variables enhance or limit the probability of successful treatment?

11) What characterizes "good/ successful" *vs*. "bad/unsuccessful" termination of therapy?

XI. EFFECTIVENESS OF THE APPROACH

Purpose: To summarize briefly the existing status of empirical and/or clinical research on your approach, and to point to future research needs.

1) What evidence exists for the efficacy of your approach?

2) Given the research that exists (whatever its amount), what theoretical *and* practical questions about your approach are most pressing in terms of future empirical study?

XIII. TRAINING OF MARITAL-FAMILY THERAPISTS

Purpose: To describe the proper training and qualifications for a marital/family therapist.

1) Should a therapist learn individual therapy? Should he avoid it? If she/he should learn it, should this be before or concurrent with the learning of family/marital therapy?

2) Is previous personal therapy important? If yes, what kind—individual, family?

3) Can paraprofessionals do marital/family therapy as taught by your approach?

4) Is co-therapy useful as a training device?

5) What is an ideal program and sequence of training, especially in light of the therapeutic approach you represent?

As Editors, we have found the preparation of this volume to be a demanding but intellectually stimulating and personally rewarding experience. We are impressed by the vitality and optimism that exist among the leaders of the family therapy field. In this volume, as a group, they have articulated the existing theoretical base and intuitive/experiential understanding of family process and family therapy. They have also honestly and responsibly described areas of mystery and non-understanding. We hope that this *Handbook* will serve for the present as a "state of the art" look at family theory, as a textbook for the student of family therapy, and as a resource for the practicing family therapist to be stimulated by multiple views of family therapy. For the future, we hope this *Handbook* will become a conceptual "staging area" for family therapists, a place to push off from and further the growth and development of the field.

Finally, we want to thank Pat Mings for her able and reliable secretarial contributions at every stage in the development of this *Handbook*.

Madison, Wisconsin   ALAN S. GURMAN
Cincinnati, Ohio   DAVID P. KNISKERN
July, 1980

Contents

Contributors

JAMES F. ALEXANDER, Ph.D.
Professor and Director of Clinical Training
Department of Psychology
University of Utah
Salt Lake City, UT

HARRY J. APONTE, A.C.S.W.
Private Practice
Philadelphia, PA

COLE BARTON, Ph.D.
University of Utah and Western States Youth
    and Family Institute
Salt Lake City, UT

DUANE S. BISHOP, M.D.
Associate Professor
Section of Psychiatry and Human Behavior
Brown University Medical School
    and
Clinical Director
Butler Hospital
Providence, RI

ARTHUR M. BODIN, Ph.D.
Research Associate and
Senior Clinical Psychologist
Emergency Treatment Center
Palo Alto, CA

IVAN BOSZORMENYI-NAGY, M.D.
Director, Department of Family Psychiatry
Eastern Pennsylvania Psychiatric Institute
    and
Clinical Professor of Psychiatry
Hahnemann Medical College
Philadelphia, PA

CARLFRED B. BRODERICK, Ph.D.
Professor and Director, Marriage
and Family Counseling Program
Department of Sociology and Anthropology
    and
Co-Director
The Human Relations Center
University of Southern California
Los Angeles, CA

NANCY DAVIDSON, Ph.D.
Department of Psychology
University of Missouri
Columbia, MO

BUNNY S. DUHL, M. Ed.
Co-Director
Boston Family Institute
Brookline, MA

FREDERICK J. DUHL, M.D.
Co-Director
Boston Family Institute
Brookline, MA

NATHAN B. EPSTEIN, M.D.
Professor and Chairman
Section of Psychiatry and Human Behavior
Brown University Medical School
    and
Medical Director/Psychiatrist-in-Chief
Butler Hospital
Providence, RI

JAMES L. FRAMO, Ph.D.
Professor
Department of Psychology
Temple University
Philadelphia, PA

STEVEN B. GORDON, Ph.D.
Child and Family Center
Institute for Behavior Therapy
New York, NY

ALAN S. GURMAN, Ph.D.
Professor and Director, Outpatient Clinic
Department of Psychiatry
University of Wisconsin Medical School
Madison, WI

JULIA R. HEIMAN, Ph.D.
Research Scientist
Long Island Research Institute and
Research Assistant Professor
Department of Psychiatry
State University of New York
Stony Brook, NY

NEIL S. JACOBSON, Ph.D.
Assistant Professor
Department of Psychology
University of Washington
Seattle, WA

FLORENCE W. KASLOW, Ph.D.
Dean and Professor
Florida School of Professional Psychology
Miami, FL

DAVID V. KEITH, M.D.
Assistant Professor and Director, Advanced
    Training Program in Family Psychiatry
Department of Psychiatry
University of Wisconsin Medical School
Madison, WI

MICHAEL E. KERR, M.D.
Clinical Assistant Professor and Director of
    Training
The Family Center
Georgetown University Hospital
Washington, D.C.

DAVID P. KNISKERN, Psy.D.
Associate Professor and Coordinator of
    Outpatient Family Therapy Training
Department of Psychiatry
University of Cincinnati College of Medicine
Cincinnati, OH

LUCIANO L'ABATE, Ph.D.
Professor and Director, Family Study Center
Department of Psychology
Georgia State University
Atlanta, GA

JOSEPH LoPICCOLO, Ph.D.
Professor and Director, Sex Therapy Center
Department of Psychiatry and Behavioral
    Sciences
Health Sciences Center
State University of New York
Stony Brook, NY

LESLIE LoPICCOLO, M.S.
Sex Therapist in Private Practice
San Francisco, CA

WILLIAM M. PINSOF, Ph.D.
Assistant Professor
Center for Family Studies/Family Institute of
    Chicago *and*
Department of Psychiatry and Behavioral
    Sciences
Northwestern University Medical School
Chicago, IL

CLIFFORD J. SAGER, M.D.
Director of Family Psychiatry
Jewish Board of Family and Children's
    Services
    and
Clinical Professor of Psychiatry
Mt. Sinai School of Medicine
City University of New York
New York, NY

SANDRA S. SCHRADER, Ph.D.
Assistant Professor
School of Home Economics and Family
    Studies
University of Connecticut
Storrs, CT

**A.C. ROBIN SKYNNER, M.B., F.R.C.
Psych., D.P.M.**
Private Practice
The Group-Analytic Practice
    and
Chairman, Institute of Family Therapy
London, England

M. DUNCAN STANTON, Ph.D.
Associate Professor of Psychology in
    Psychiatry
University of Pennsylvania School of Medicine
    and
Director, Addicts and Families Program
Philadelphia Child Guidance Clinic
Philadelphia, PA

DAVID N. ULRICH, Ph.D.
Chief Psychologist
Child Guidance Clinic of Greater Stamford
Stamford, CT

JOHN M. VANDEUSEN, Ph.D.
Director, Indochinese Mental Health Project
Pennsylvania Office of Mental Health
Philadelphia, PA

CARL A. WHITAKER, M.D.
Professor
Department of Psychiatry
University of Wisconsin Medical School
Madison, WI

PART I

Historical

Perspective

CHAPTER 1

The History of Professional Marriage and Family Therapy

Carlfred B. Broderick, Ph.D.

and Sandra S. Schrader, Ph.D.

It seems likely that people have been listening to each other's family problems and responding with commiseration and advice as long as there have been families. It seems equally likely that as soon as mankind became prosperous enough to develop specialized professions (the chief, the priest, the physician, the prostitute) many of these worthies included giving advice on family matters among their duties and prerogatives. Only in our own century and our own culture, however, has a profession developed whose sole purpose is to deal with problems between family members. Doubtless it was an inevitable development. The temper of the times was such as to encourage attempts to intervene in every social problem. From Prohibition to Social Security, from the Community Mental Health Movement to the Women's Rights Movement, we have been a nation boldly (if not always wisely) committed to finding cures for new and old social ills. The family received particular attention as the divorce and juvenile delinquency rates rose dramatically decade after decade. Indeed, as we shall see, marital therapy and family

therapy are only two of the many related movements which grew up in response to evident social needs. The social hygiene movement, the family life education movement, the child guidance and parent education movements, and an array of new psychotherapeutic modalities such as group, brief, and behavioral approaches all emerged within a narrow span of decades in response to the same compelling historic currents.

The present cluster of cross-borrowing, overlapping professions which deal with the relationships among family members began as at least four largely independent movements.[1] The oldest of these is the marriage counseling move-

---

[1] *Editors' Note.* The issue of whether marriage and family therapy are a profession (or, according to some, two distinct professions) is currently loaded with controversy, political machinations and, indeed, a solid dose of narcissism. In any case, Broderick has indicated to us elsewhere (Broderick, 1979) three criteria that define a profession: 1) self-awareness and the identity of a body of experts; 2) a set of skills requiring advanced training and established standards of performance; and 3) a recognition of this body of experts and the utility of their expert service by the larger society.

ment. It differs from the others in that it developed initially as a part-time, second profession for physicians, ministers, psychologists, lawyers, social workers and educators who became involved in people's marital problems as a spin-off of their primary vocations. A much later and originally quite separate movement toward conjoint marital therapy developed within the psychiatric community. A third major group, the family therapists, emerged from the joining of several independent-minded pioneers, many of them working with children. Finally, last on the scene (although with roots as deep as any of the others), a new profession of sex therapists has sprung up, building particularly upon the foundation laid by Masters and Johnson in their 1970 book, *Human Sexual Inadequacy*.

In this chapter we shall attempt to trace the evolution of each of these movements and their progressive amalgamation in contemporary training and practice. Before doing so, however, it may be helpful to sketch some of the closely related historic developments.

THE SOCIAL WORK MOVEMENT

The history of social work has been inextricably interwoven with the history of marriage and family therapy from the beginning. Social workers have by turns been the most daring pioneers and the most passive "Johnny come lately's" in the whole parade of professionals.

Social historians date the beginning of social work in this country with the founding of the first city-wide charity organization in Buffalo, New York in 1877 (Rich, 1956). Modeling themselves on similar organizations in Great Britain, early American societies concerned themselves primarily with aiding the poor at a time when there was little government investment in what has since come to be called "welfare." From the beginning it was observed, however, that the proper unit of concern for these societies was not the single client but the family. "Work with families" was the phrase used in the earliest descriptions of the casework activities of these organizations (Rich, 1956, p. 13). As Robert Treat Paine, president of the Boston Associated Charities, put it in his first annual report, "Each one of the 7,716 cases reported is a human family

with human lives, cares, and woes (Paine, 1899, p. 355).

One of the early pioneers in the conversion of a volunteer service into a profession requiring advanced training was Zilpha D. Smith. In 1890 she wrote of her colleagues, "Most of you deal with poor persons or defective *individuals,* removed from family relationships. We deal with the *family* as a whole, usually working to keep it together, but sometimes helping to break it up into units and to place them in your care" (Smith, 1890).

But perhaps the greatest champion of looking at the whole family and its need was Mary Richmond, originally the General Secretary of the Baltimore Charity Organization Society, and eventually one of the main organizers of the profession at the national level. Her 1908 publication of a case record of a widow and four children followed over nine years (she entitled it *A Real Story of A Real Family*) set a new standard of family-oriented case record keeping among social workers (Rich, 1956). In her influential book *Social Diagnosis* (Richmond, 1917), she quoted the Swiss neuropathologist Paul Dubois as referring "to this necessity of not confining one's therapeutic efforts to the patient alone, but extending it to those who live with them. This is often the one way to obtain complete and lasting results" (Dubois, 1907). Then she elaborated, "In some forms of social work, notably family rebuilding, a client's social relations are so likely to be all important that family case workers welcome the opportunity to see at the very beginning of intercourse several of the members of the family assembled in their own home environment, acting and reacting upon one another, each taking a share in the development of the client's story, each revealing in ways other than words social facts of real significance" (Richmond, 1917, p. 137). In 1928 she wrote a paper "Concern of the Community with Marriage" (Richmond, 1928), which further stressed the importance of dealing with relationships as well as individual problems.

With these strong beginnings i' seems possible that the field of social work might well have brought forth the fields of marriage and family counseling as mere subspecialities within the broader field of family casework. Without question, work of this nature did go on in social agencies from these earliest times forward. It seems to have been so taken for granted, however, that it was seldom deemed worthy of note in print. A second and probably more important reason that the field of marriage and family counseling did not find more of its impetus from the social work profession was the salient impact of the field of psychiatry on social work beginning in the 1920s and continuing to the present. The orthopsychiatric team of psychiatrist (at the head), psychologists and social workers (at the bottom) all but submerged the independent thrust toward the whole family therapy which had been evident in the early years. The proceedings of the first round table discussions of the American Orthopsychiatric Association in 1930 were a harbinger of the decades to follow. In their discussion of that occasion John Spiegel and Norman Bell (1959, p. 116) have written:

A psychiatrist, a social worker and a clinical psychologist spoke in this panel discussion, about treatment of behavior and personality problems in children. Alone among the three discussants, the social worker, Charlotte Towle, dealt with the problems and the family in dynamic fashion. She was articulate and direct concerning the family, saying in part "Treatment cannot be given to any member of the family without affecting the entire group. In some cases the entire family must be drawn into treatment. Approach to this or that member or centering treatment on a certain individual cannot be a random thing" (Towle, 1948).

The prolonged discussion that followed dealt largely in whether notes should be made in front of the patient. No reference to Towle's ideas was made at all. The whole issue of the dynamic formulation and handling of family relationships simply dropped out of sight.

The point may be further documented by Florence T. Waite's summary of 50 years of casework practice published in 1941. She pointed out that:

. . .family casework had moved beyond the older emphasis on trying to know and be in touch with several family members. It had developed a clinical orientation and tended to concentrate on the individual because: 1) competitiveness and jealousy existed among family members; 2) seeing the whole family blurred the autonomy of the individual and the worker was apt to take over the family too completely and overpoweringly; 3) society has increased its emphasis on the individual even at the expense of his membership in the family and society at large (as summarized in Sherman, 1961, pp. 19-20).

While that view doubtless overstates the retreat of social workers from relationship counseling for this period, it does appear to be true that from the decades of the '30s forward they have never, as a profession, taken the lead in the marriage and family therapy movements. They have, however, at every point, provided a substantial part of the professional cadre actually seeing couples and families in the various pioneering programs which we shall describe later. It seems likely that their actual contribution is much greater than present accounts give them credit for (cf. Guerin, 1976; Kaslow, 1979).

THE DEVELOPMENT OF SOCIAL PSYCHIATRY[2]

Psychoanalysis, as it was initially propounded by Freud, placed instinctual libidinal drive at the center of its explanation of human behavior. Although Freud recognized the importance of early familial relationships in shaping the personality (the prime example being the Oedipal rivalry), still, several of his students felt he underemphasized social elements. Among the most outspoken were Alfred Adler and Carl Jung.

About 1910 Adler became the first of Freud's pupils to openly challenge him on these matters, offering an alternative and more socially rooted theory of psychodynamics (Adler, 1917). He held that the driving dynamic of life was the deeply internalized sense of inferiority which we all fell heir to by virtue of being born small and helpless. Rather than sexual drive, we were motivated by a compulsion to achieve feelings of adequacy and power. In this struggle we might follow one of two paths. We might flee into illness from which we dominate and manipulate those around us through weakness (a strategy later theorists called meta-complementarity (Watzlawick, Beavin and Jackson, 1967). Alternatively, we might engage those around us

---

[2]This discussion is heavily indebted to the treatment of this subject by Thompson (1951).

in a more open struggle for power. In this second case, Adler foreshadowed the theories of most contemporary family therapists who also attempt to explain individual pathology as a by-product of family conflict.

In 1910 Jung spelled out this concept in more contemporary sounding terms:

> The concealed discord between the parents, the secret worry, the regressed hidden wishes, all of these produce in the individual a certain affective state which slowly but severely, though unconsciously, works its way into the child's mind, producing therein the same conditions and hence the same reactions to external stimuli. . . The more sensitive and moldable the child, the deeper the impression (Jung, 1910. pp. 246-247).

Another Jungian concept which places the role of social expectations in sharp focus is the *persona* (or *mask*) which each person assumes in social situations in order to meet the expectations of others. This concept is closely allied with those being developed independently by the influential social psychologists Mead (1934) and Cooley (1909) in this same general period.

In the 1920s, Rank introduced innovations in style which were more appropriate to family therapy than traditional techniques had been. He focused more on what was happening in the session itself and less on what had happened years before; he introduced his own personality and feelings into sessions rather than remaining detached and fostering idealization, and he set a definite time to limit treatment (Thompson, 1951).

In the 1930s, as Hitler gradually forced analysts to leave continental Europe, a strong community of analysts developed in America. These men and women were more in touch with the work of anthropologists and sociologists than their predecessors had been and these influences were manifest in varying degrees in their theories and therapeutic approaches. Among the most influential to emerge from this cross-fertilization were Erich Fromm (1941, 1947) and Harry Stack Sullivan (1947, 1953).

Fromm's emphasis was upon the interaction between man and his society. He echoed Jung's insights into social *customs:* "The most beautiful as well as the most ugly inclinations of man are not a part of a fixed and biologically given human nature but result from the social process which creates man" (Fromm, 1941, p. 12). His emphasis in the development of individuality foreshadowed the work of Bowen and others on the importance of differentiation from the family.

Sullivan was the most interpersonally oriented of all of the American analysts. He was definitely influenced by early social psychologists such as Mead and Cooley. For example, one of his central concepts is the notion that, before the child had learned to communicate in symbols, he experiences his mother's emotions through "empathy." Maternal anger or disapproval of any kind is transmitted to the child as anxiety and insecurity. The concept of self is shaped by the parts of one's behavior that others respond to, positively or negatively. Sullivan uses the term "reflected appraisals" to indicate much the same process as "looking glass self" (Cooley, 1909) or "generalized other" (Mead, 1934) referred to in social psychology. His theory of child development, far more than Freud's or any other analyst's at that time, reflected the child as growing in response to shifting social situations as he matures.

Two other aspects of Sullivan's work provided important precedents and foundations for the innovators who were to follow. First, he was among the first to assert and to demonstrate that schizophrenia could be treated by psychotherapy. Several of the founders of family therapy were initially engaged in a Sullivanian approach to the treatment of schizophrenia (e.g., Bowen and Jackson). Secondly, he was first and foremost a clinician rather than a theorist; that is, he refused to be impressed with any theory which could not be demonstrated in practical work with patients (Thompson, 1951). Without doubt, *this disposition to trust one's experience instead of the reigning dogma characterizes the founders of all of the movements discussed in this chapter.*

Other analysts made important contributions toward the establishment of a social emphasis in psychiatry and by mid-century, when the family therapy pioneers were beginning to experiment, there was a well-established bias in that direction among American analysts. The work of Fromm-Reichmann (1950), Horney (1937, 1939), and Thompson (1951), in particular, led to greater understanding of the relationship between a patient's behavior and his/her familial experiences and interactions.

THE EARLY SEXOLOGISTS

If social work and psychiatry provided the main precedents and techniques which latter-day relationship therapists have built upon, we are nevertheless greatly indebted to the special contributions of two men who, though M.D.'s, were associated with neither profession. We refer to the pioneering sexologists, Havelock Ellis of Great Britain and Magnus Hirschfeld of Germany. More than any others, they paved the way for working with couples in a practical way on the sexual problems of everyday life.

Havelock Ellis was a remarkable man. He was a physician who also produced some of the most widely acclaimed translations of the Greek dramatic poets. Raised in Victorian prudery, largely without a father's influence, he vowed to do all within his power to spare others the ignorance and discomfort in sexual matters which he experienced as a young man. In all, he produced seven volumes covering almost every imaginable aspect of sexual behavior. His writing was literate, well reasoned and well documented, but beyond that he was remarkably free from the moralizing that previous sexual scholars had indulged in, and he livened up his text with literally hundreds of excerpts from sexual histories he collected over the years. Decades in advance of his time he worked personally with individuals (mostly women) in helping them overcome their sexual fears. He developed his own version of non-demand pleasuring about which we will have more to say later in the section on sex therapy.

His German counterpart, Magnus Hirschfeld, founded the Institute of Sexual Science in Berlin in 1918 and together with Ellis and August Forel founded the World League for Sexual Reform. Between 1921 and 1932 this group convened five meetings of the International Congress for Sexual Reform on a Scientific Basis. Literally thousands of physicians from all over the world visited his center in the 15 years of its existence. He culminated his career with a five-volume work, *Geschlechtskunde* (1930, in English *Sex Education*), which reported his conclusions

based on analyzing 10,000 questionnaires filled out by men and women who came to him for advice.

As part of his wide-ranging interest in sexual reform, he instituted the first German Marriage Consultation Bureau (Hirschfeld, 1940) and was instrumental in influencing his Austrian colleague, Dr. Karl Kautsky, to set up the first publicly funded "Center for Sexual Advice" in Vienna (Stone, 1949). The movement grew and by 1932 there were hundreds of centers throughout Germany, Austria, Switzerland, The Netherlands, and the Scandinavian countries. Although it appears that the emphasis in these centers was on contraceptive and eugenic counseling, it is clear that psychological and relational matters were routinely discussed (Hoenig, 1978).

When Hitler took over first Germany and then Austria and then most of Europe, one of his earliest actions was to destroy Hirschfeld's original center (he was a Jew) and to convert the publicly owned centers to "Health and Racial Hygiene Bureaus." Their revised function was to interview all applicants for marriage licenses as to their emotional, intellectual, physical and genealogical fitness for marriage and reproduction. It must be counted one of the bitter ironies of that era that the movement which began as an idealistic effort to assist couples and families with information and counseling ended as the instrumentality through which the Nazis prevented intermarriage between "Aryans" and "non-Aryans" and implemented the sterilization of "mental and physical defectives" and, as the world was eventually to learn, of Jews.

Some insight into the murky thinking of those times may be gained by a few excerpts from an article by the American eugenicist Marie Kopp, writing in the *Journal of Heredity* in 1938, six years into the new program.

The European approach to the counseling of individuals, couples, and families differs fundamentally from the American attitude toward these functions. In the United States of America, marriage counseling to date has in the main been concerned with the solution of the problems related to the psychology and physiology of sex, reproduction, family, and racial relationships. In Europe, on the other hand, the main objectives are the betterment of the biological stock. To accomplish this purpose, those most unfit for marriage are dissuaded or prevented from marriage and procreation and those most fit are encouraged to shoulder the responsibilities of parenthood (p. 154). . .

The contemporary marital counseling in Germany typifies the new European service in its concern with the biological improvement of its people. The counseling of individuals presenting psychological or socio-medical problems of adjustment, on the other hand, is no longer a major concern of services operating under municipal and state auspices (p. 158) . . .

The counseling bureaus formerly sponsored by the various German municipalities and by political, social, and commercial groups have ceased to exist (p. 159) . . .

As we shall see below, the concept developed by Hirschfeld and others did survive, but in America and England rather than in the lands of its first flowering.

Meanwhile, another development was taking place in America, which, while having no direct clinical aspect, nevertheless played an important role in paving the way for eventual establishment of modern sex therapy; sex was becoming a legitimate arena for scientific research. Kinsey, Pomeroy and Martin (1948) list 16 studies of human sexuality published in America before 1940. These, together with the published works of Ellis, Hirschfeld and others, constituted a pool of scientific knowledge upon which physicians, social hygienists, and other could draw in counseling couples with sexual problems.

THE FAMILY LIFE EDUCATION MOVEMENT

As a nation, Americans tend to have great faith in education as a vehicle for addressing social problems. As early as 1883 mothers' groups had begun to come together to discuss how to incorporate the best pedagogic principles into their own parenting (Groves and Groves, 1947). In 1908 in Washington, D.C., the constitutional convention, so to speak, of the American Home Economics Association took place and courses began increasingly to be instituted in high schools and colleges which were calculated to improve American homemaking. It is true that at first emphasis was heavily upon cooking, sewing, and money management but

relational aspects of the married woman's role were always there as an explicit (though often neglected) category within the discipline. With the passage of the Smith-Lever Act of 1914 and the Smith-Hughes Act of 1917, the home economics perspective was given further visibility. These acts provided federal grants to establish and maintain county home demonstration agents as part of the state agricultural extension programs, and vocational home economics instruction in high schools throughout the country.

In 1923, Vassar College introduced the first preparation for parenthood course at the college level (Groves and Groves, 1947). The following year Ernst Groves began a similar course for credit at Boston University. That year he also agreed to teach a non-credit course on marriage in response to a petition from the senior class for such instruction (Stone, 1949).

Beginning in 1930, Paul Popenoe set up a series of all day workshops that toured university campuses and churches in Southern California and elsewhere with a wide list of lecture-discussion topics available in serial or concurrent sessions. For example, the following typical program was offered on the University of Southern California campus on March 3, 1934 (American Institute of Family Relations, 1934).

Morning Addresses:

Women's Jobs or Women's Homes, The Family in a Changing Social Situation;

Afternoon Roundtables:

Guiding Youth in the Ethics of Sex, Getting Acquainted, Premarital Examinations, What Makes Personality, Sex Education of Children in the Home, Voluntary Sterilization, Extra-curricular Activities, Current Family Literature, Shall Parenthood Be Penalized?, The Problem of Movies, The Technique of Counseling, The Choice of a Mate, Improving Divorce Courts, Teaching Family Relations, Censorship, Social Hygiene;

Evening Sessions:

Love before Marriage, Love in Early Married Life, and Love after 40.

Popenoe and his colleagues conducted 100 such workshops between 1930 and 1940 in what must have been one of the most active family life education efforts in the country (AIFR, 1940).

In 1936, Ernest R. Groves, having moved from Boston to the University of North Carolina, instituted the first "functional" Marriage and Family Relations course for college credit. Institutionally oriented courses on the family had been offered at U.S. universities at least since 1893 when Charles R. Henderson taught a course on the family at the University of Chicago (Mudd, 1951, p. 6). By 1908 a survey by Bernard had determined that about 20 such courses were being offered across the nation (Bernard, 1908). Groves' new "functional" approach differed from traditional approaches in several important ways: 1) It was eclectic, drawing upon law, biology, medicine, home economics, and psychology as well as sociology; 2) it was practical, being shaped to the needs of the students rather than to the theoretical or empirical investments of the academic profession; and 3) it was unabashedly intended to be remedial and cautionary; that is its intent was not only to analyze and describe but to *improve* the courtship and marriage of the students involved. In this, its goals were very similar to those of early marriage counselors.

In fact, from the beginning those teaching functional courses found themselves doing premarital and marital counseling with their students. This was done almost always without fee and usually without any professional training in the techniques of counseling. A survey of those who taught such courses in 1948 (by then functional courses were taught in 632 colleges and universities) showed that they were mainly either home economists who had expanded their definition of their discipline or sociologists who had risked being identified with a non-traditional (and some said non-academic) approach to the family. A few psychologists, notably Cliff Adams at Pennsylvania State University, also joined in (Bowman, 1949).

By that time there were also a growing number of functional textbooks to choose from (e.g., Baber, 1939; Bowman, 1949; Duvall, 1946; Duvall and Hill, 1948; Folsom, 1943; Groves and Groves, 1947; Landis and Landis, 1948; P. Landis, 1946; Waller, 1938), a professional association to belong to (The National Council of Family Relations (NCFR), founded in 1938 by Paul Sayre) and a professional journal, *Marriage and Family Living*[3] (founded in 1939, as an organ of NCFR).

As we shall see in greater detail below, the founders of the family life education movement were among the pioneers also of the marriage counseling movement in America. In particular, Ernest Groves played a key role in the establishment of each profession.

THE HISTORY OF THE MARRIAGE COUNSELING PROFESSION

Initially marriage counselors were physicians, lawyers, educators and social workers with a very partial commitment to dealing face to face with people's marital problems. We have already noted the importance of the burgeoning of functional marriage courses for the development of the movement. If one raised pragmatic, immediate, significant life questions with people, it was inevitable that they would wish to discuss them further with their instructor. Another equally important development was the growth of the specialty of gynecology and obstetrics in medicine. This resulted in a vastly increased pool of readily accessible "experts" on sexual and related matters. At least one, Robert L. Dickinson, had made major research contributions to the field, collecting careful notes on the sexual anatomy and also on the sexual histories of thousands of patients over a period of 25 years (Dickinson, 1949; Dickinson and Beam, 1931). Many gynecologists saw sexual and marital counseling as one important aspect of their profession. As late as 1950, over one-quarter of the members of the American Association of Marriage Counselors were gynecologists and an almost equal proportion were in other medical specialties.

Phase I: 1929-1932, The Pioneers

Two different marriage counseling centers, one on each coast, claim to have been the first in America. Both were influenced by Hirschfeld

---

[3]In 1964 this became the *Journal of Marriage and the Family*.

and his pioneering work in Germany. One claimant was Paul Popenoe, who uncontestedly opened the doors of the American Institute of Family Relations in Los Angeles in February of 1930. He was initially the sole member of the staff, supported by a committee of 40 local backers and by the three dollar per hour fee which he charged for consultation (not a trivial amount in that year of the Great Depression) and $100 per workshop program.

Popenoe, a biologist specializing in human heredity, came to this new enterprise from the social hygiene movement, having been the executive secretary of that organization in New York City. A eugenics activist, he was a member of the American Genetic Association and became the editor of the *Journal of Heredity* (Peacock, 1977; Popenoe, 1975). (In fact, he was editor when Ms. Kopp published her piece on the new approaches to counseling in Nazi Germany.) He claims the distinction of being the first to introduce the phrase "marriage counseling" into the English language, that being his translation from the German "Eheberatungsstellen," the term used for marital consultation centers in Vienna and elsewhere on the continent (Popenoe, 1975). Probably more than any other person, he promoted public recognition of the marriage counseling profession through such means as the monthly article in *Ladies Home Journal*, "Can This Marriage Be Saved?" (begun in 1945 and still continuing) and on early television, providing case materials for "Divorce Court," a popular semi-documentary of the 1940s and 1950s.

The other claimants, Abraham and Hannah Stone, date their beginning differently in different places. In 1949, Abraham Stone published a short history of the field, listing his New York City clinic as commencing operating in 1929 just a few months prior to Popenoe. About the same time, his clinic filled out a survey form for Emily Mudd's book on marriage counseling which lists a 1930 opening date (several months after Popenoe) (Mudd, 1951, p. 293). Doubtless, a case could be made for either date since the Stones had been doing marriage counseling in their roles as physicians for some years prior to this. In any case, whether in 1929 or 1930, and whether first or second by a few months, it is agreed that they began operations in the New

York Labor Temple and in 1932 moved to the Community Church of New York where they ran an ecumenical marriage center for many years.

A third pioneer, Emily Hartshorne Mudd, opened the Marriage Council of Philadelphia in 1932. Dr. Mudd was committed to research on the marriage counseling process and in 1939 was the first, so far as we know, to develop a continuing program of evaluative studies (Mudd, 1951). She was among the first to publish a book in the field (1951) and she collaborated in the first case book (Mudd et al., 1958) She was also one of the three or four people most responsible for the founding of the American Association of Marriage Counselors.

Phase II: 1934-1945, The Establishment of the American Association of Marriage Counselors

In 1934, Lester Dearborn, a social hygienist and sex counselor with the Boston Y.M.C.A., invited Dr. Mudd to Boston to discuss the formation of a professional organization whose goals would be "to establish standards, exchange information and special knowledge about marital and family relations" (Humphrey, 1978). Nothing came of the meeting at that time and Dearborn later approached Abraham Stone on the matter but again without results. Finally, he got in touch with Ernest Groves, who took hold of the idea and, in April of 1942 at the annual invitational Conference on Conservation of Marriage and the Family which he had instigated at Chapel Hill, N.C., Groves proposed the establishment of a professional association for marriage counselors (Humphrey, 1978). Later that year, Dearborn and a colleague, psychiatrist Dr. Robert Laidlaw, invited six others to join them in an organizational meeting on June 20, 1942. Besides the conveners, attending were Drs. Ernest and Gladys Groves, Emily (Stuart) Mudd, Dr. Abraham Stone, Dr. Robert L. Dickenson, and Dr. Valerie Parker (Mudd and Fowler, 1976).

For the next three years they met annually but informally under the chairmanship of Lester Dearborn. Then, in April 1945, they formally elected Ernest Groves the first president, Lester Dearborn first vice-president, Emily Mudd second vice-president, and Robert W. Laidlaw secretary-treasurer (Mudd and Fowler, 1976). The purpose of the organization was stated as follows:

The American Association of Marriage Counselors is a professional organization which concentrates its work specifically on marriage counseling. It has this stated purpose in the bylaws: to establish and maintain professional standards in marriage counseling. This purpose shall be furthered by meetings, clinical sessions, publications and research. Membership in it is open to those who meet its detailed requirements for clinicians in the field or for affiliates whose work in this or related fields is outstanding and for associates whose background, training, and beginning practice are sufficiently advanced to enable them to gain professionally by meeting with the more experienced counselors (Mudd and Fowler, 1976, p. 433).

Meanwhile, in England, in the midst of World War II, David Mace, in 1943, founded the National Marriage Guidance Council of Great Britain on a quite different premise. His idea was for a few professionals to train and supervise a much larger number of lay people. These paraprofessionals (as we would call them today) would be able to provide counseling at a much reduced cost which would bring the service into the earning range of the English working-class couple. By 1944 they had developed a syllabus for training marriage counselors and had established a system which still operates today not only in Great Britain but in many of the British Commonwealth countries (Mace, 1945, 1948).

Phase III: 1946-1963, The Construction of a Profession

In 1932 there were three functioning centers for marriage counseling. Fifteen years later, in 1947, Ernest Groves listed 15 which he felt were "representative and nationally recognized." In addition to the original three in Los Angeles, Philadelphia, and New York, there were four additional New York centers plus others in Boston, Chicago, Detroit, Cincinnati, Cleveland, Washington, D.C., Chapel Hill, N.C., and San Francisco (Groves and Groves, 1947).

In 1948 a joint committee of the American Association of Marriage Counselors and the National Council on Family Relations, under the chairmanship of Abraham Stone, proposed a set of standards for marriage counselors (see Table 1).

As Nichols (1979) has noted, the course of development from a more or less naively service-oriented group to a fledgling profession can be traced in the sequence of standards for training issued by the organization over the years. Their first target of concern was standards for marriage counselors (1949), next their concern shifted to standards for marriage counseling centers (1953), then for training centers for postgraduate professional marriage counselors (1959), and related doctoral programs with a major in marriage counseling (1962). It is perhaps also a sign of maturity that in 1962 a code of ethics was formally adopted (Mudd and Fowler, 1976).

In 1956 the association accredited three training centers: Marriage Council of Philadelphia, The Merrill-Palmer School in Detroit, and the Menninger Clinic in Topeka, Kansas.

Perhaps the most propitious event of this span of years is the one that marks the end of it. In 1963 California became the first state to pass a licensing law for marriage and family counselors. With this act the profession might be said to have come of age.

Phase IV: 1964-Present, The Formative Years

It might be supposed that by 1963 the practice of marriage counseling would have established a reasonably clear identity. Yet it has been characteristic of the field that it was always richer in enthusiasm and commitment than in consensus or clarity as to its nature.

One study by Michaelson (1963) found some slight evidence of convergence toward a conjoint treatment approach over time. Taking samples of case records from one marriage counseling center in the East, one in the Midwest, and one in the Far West, she determined that in 1940 they had seen 89% of their clients individually, in 1950 88%, and in 1960 83%. Conjoint interviews had increased steadily if not dramatically from 5% in 1940 to 9% in 1950 and 15% in 1960. Whole family conferences, on the other hand, had dropped from 5% to 3% to 1% over the same interval. The shifts were statistically significant because of the large number of cases, but not very impressive.

TABLE 1
Marriage Counseling
Report of the
Joint Subcommittee on Standards for Marriage
Counselors
of the
National Council on Family Relations
and
The American Association of Marriage Counselors

Abraham Stone, M.D., Chairman
Janet Fowler Nelson, Secretary

Gladys H. Groves	Emily Hartshorne Mudd
Sophia J. Kleegman, M.D.	Reverend Otis R. Rice
Robert W. Laidlaw, M.D.	Anna Budd Ware
Herbert D. Lamson	

Marriage counseling is here regarded as a specialized field of family counseling which centers largely on the interpersonal relationship between husband and wife. It involves many disciplines and is interprofessional in character. Those who wish to enter this field, however, whether physician, clergyman, psychiatrist or social worker, require a common body of scientific knowledge, techniques and qualifications.

Standards for acceptable and recognized marriage counselors, are herewith presented in terms of academic training, professional experience and qualifications, and personal qualifications.

1. Academic Training
    a. Every marriage counselor shall have a graduate or professional degree from an approved institution as a minimum qualification. This degree shall be in one of the following fields: education, home economics, law, medicine, nursing, psychology, religion, social anthropology, social work, and sociology.
    b. Whatever the field of major emphasis, there shall be included accredited training in: psychology of personality development; elements of psychiatry; human biology, including the fundamentals of sex anatomy, physiology and genetics; sociology of marriage and the family; legal aspects of marriage and the family; and counseling techniques.
2. Professional Experience and Qualifications
    a. The candidate shall have had at least three years of recognized professional experience subsequent to obtaining his degree. In addition, he shall have had actual experience as a clinical assistant in marriage counseling under approved supervision.
    b. A candidate's qualifications shall include:
    • Diagnostic skill in differentiating between the superficial and the deeper level types of maladjustment, and the ability to recognize

when the latter type requires referral to other specialists.
    • A scientific attitude toward individual variation and deviation, especially in the field of human sex behavior, and the ability to discuss sexual problems objectively.
3. Personal Qualifications
    a. The candidate shall possess personal and professional integrity in accordance with accepted ethical standards.
    b. The candidate shall have an attitude of interest, warmth, and kindness toward people, combined with a high degree of integration and emotional maturity.
    c. The personal experience of marriage and parenthood is a decided asset.

Marriage and Family Living, 1949, Vol. 11, p. 5.

In 1965 Alexander surveyed AAMC members and found that only 25% of them identified themselves primarily as marriage counselors. For the remainder it was an auxiliary profession. There was some difference between those who found their primary identity as marriage therapists, those who found their primary identity as some other type of clinician (psychologist, psychiatrist, social worker) and those whose primary identification was as an educator or some other nonclinical profession.[4] Table 2 shows the results. It will be seen that those who saw themselves primarily as marriage counselors treated clients individually only 11% of the time, while therapists from older traditions saw 47% of their clients individually, and the academics, etc., 19%. Thus, it appears that seeing couples and families is at least in part a function of the degree of identification one makes with the developing field as against traditional approaches.[5] Ultimately, though, the effects of specific training experiences, rather than mere disciplinary iden-

[4]*Editors' Note.* Since Alexander's (1968) data are now almost two decades old, it would be interesting and informative to know whether the same trends currently characterize the AAMFT membership, and whether they also characterize non-AAMFT members who practice family therapy.

[5]*Editors' Note.* Elsewhere (Gurman and Kniskern, 1979) we have argued that family therapy is better characterized by its perspectives on human behavior than by its clinical practices alone. Moreover, another possibility, beyond that offered by Broderick and Schrader, for why therapists have turned in increasing numbers to treating couples and families is simply that doing so may be the best treatment for certain problems (Gurman and Kniskern, 1978).

tification, are likely to exert a more profound influence.

TABLE 2

Percent of AAMC Members in 1965 by Primary Professional Identification and Treatment Modality

| | Primary Professional Identification | | |
Treatment Modality	Marriage Counselor (N = 75)	Other Therapist (N = 114)	Nonclinical Professional (N = 93)
Individual	11%	46%	19%
Marriage	63%	30%	56%
Family	23%	23%	17%
Other*	3%	1%	8%
Total	100%	100%	100%

*Modified to absorb rounding percents.
From Alexander, 1968, Table 15, p. 157.

Another evidence of the scattered loyalties of the marriage counselors during these early decades is revealed in Gurman's (1973) comprehensive survey of all professional articles on marriage counseling and therapy done from the beginning through 1972 (see Table 3).

TABLE 3

Frequency of Publications on Marital Therapy in Selected Time Periods

Time Period	Number of Publications[a]		Cumulative Frequency
	N	%	
Pre-1940	5	(1.2)	5
1940-1948	11	(2.7)	16
1949-1951	16	(3.8)	32
1952-1954	16	(3.8)	48
1955-1957	21	(5.0)	69
1958-1960	29	(7.0)	98
1961-1963	45	(10.9)	143
1964-1966	68	(16.4)	211
1967-1969	119	(28.7)	330
1970-1972[b]	85	(20.5)	415
Total	415	(100.0)	

[a]Numbers in parentheses indicate the percent of the total number of publications occurring in each time period.
[b]This time period extends through August, 1972, only; hence, the number of publications in this period will need to be adjusted upward later.
From Gurman, 1973, Table 1, p. 49.

It can be seen that the growth of a body of clinical literature was very slow prior to 1960 and that all of the literature prior to 1963 constituted fewer items than were published in the following six years (1964-1969). Two other observations about literature in the field are ap-

propriate. First, when Gurman examined the journals in which these articles (through 1972) appeared, he noted "the heterogeneity of the professional discipline represented. . .is striking: psychiatric, psychological, social work, and sociological journals are all included" (Gurman, 1973, p. 49). He found over 50 journals represented among these professions.

Even more disconcerting is Goodman's (1973) analysis of that subset of 170 marriage counseling articles published between 1931 and 1968 which present research findings. She noted that 28% contained no references, while this occurred in only 9.5% of the articles she drew from the scientific literature in more academic fields.[6] The average number of references per marriage counseling article is six (compared to 15 among the scientific articles). Cross-referencing was minimal.

Only 54 of the 170 papers were cited by other papers within the population. In other words 68% of the papers constituting the field received no citations in the relevant research literature. . . . There were only 116 instances of cross-referencing and a fifth of them were self-citations. . . . Only fifteen of the papers were cited three or more times, seven being the highest number of citations received by any paper in the population (Goodman, 1973, p. 112).

What these data make apparent is that as recently as a decade ago there was no cohesive body of professionals who followed each other's work, built upon each other's experience, critiqued each other's theories, evaluated each other's contributions.[7] Rather, each practitioner played to his own home discipline, blissfully unmoved by the, to him or her, largely irrelevant work of marriage counselors from different backgrounds. The AAMC had no journal of its

[6]Goodman's "more academic fields" are identified as "fields based on the classical scientific model: emphasizing elemental analysis, using extensive controls, and directed toward producing prediction based on universal laws deduced from empirical findings" (Goodman, 1973, p. 111). They are not specified beyond this definition.

[7]Editors' Note. Clearly, the scientific status of marital and family therapy has changed enormously since Goodman's depressing report (cf, Gurman and Kniskern, 1978; Gurman and Kniskern, Chapter 20; Pinsof, Chapter 19). There now exist at least 300 empirical studies of the outcomes of marital and family therapy, and the quality of these studies is improving substantially as well.

own at this point in history,[8,9] partly because its diverse members preferred to publish in the journals of their primary professions. Moreover, in those early years the organization contained only a small fraction of those who counted themselves engaged in marital therapy of one sort or another.

We will return to the more recent history of this movement in the final section, which recounts the growing cross-fertilization and integration of the four movements we chronicle in this chapter.

FROM CLASSICAL ANALYSIS TO CONJOINT MARITAL THERAPY

Psychoanalysis by its very nature is concerned with the internal dynamics of the human psyche, and with an analysis of the patient-therapist relationship. Freud left a legacy of conviction that it was counter-productive and dangerous for a therapist to become involved with more than one member of the same family. It is not clear from his writing what exactly prompted him to feel so strongly on the matter. It is known that on at least one occasion he did undertake the analysis of a husband and wife simultaneously. The couple were James and Alex Strachey, who later became his English translators (Stone, 1971). Perhaps the experience was a difficult one for him. In any case, he wrote:

When it comes to the treatment of relationships I must confess myself utterly at a loss and I have altogether little faith in any individual therapy of them (Freud, 1912).

and later he commented further:

When the husband's resistance is added to that of the wife, efforts are made fruitless and therapy is

[8]That deficit was not corrected until 1975 with the launching of the *Journal of Marriage and Family Counseling* (renamed the *Journal of Marital and Family Therapy* in 1979) with William C. Nichols as its first editor.
[9]*Editors' Note.* At the time this *Handbook* was being prepared, there existed almost a dozen English language family therapy journals and at least a half-dozen foreign language journals, e.g., *Family Process, Journal of Marital and Family Therapy, American Journal of Family Therapy, Journal of Family Therapy, Journal of Sex and Marital Therapy, Family Therapy, Journal of Sex Education and Therapy,* and *Journal of Divorce*.

prematurely broken off,. . .We had undertaken something which under existing conditions was impossible to carry out (Freud, 1915).

This negative assessment became virtually a doctrine among analysts. In 1938 a survey of British analysts found that nearly without exception they accepted the prohibition against analyzing members of the same family (Glover, 1955).

On the other hand, it should be noted that a minority felt that there were extenuating circumstances under which this might be permissible (for the most part when families insisted) and we must assume that some had attempted it without reaping the dire consequences others feared would attend such a practice. As late as 1956, even such a forward-looking analyst as Kubie wrote:

The concurrent analysis of husband and wife. . .may be of great value when conducted independently by two psychoanalysts; but experienced psychoanalysts generally regard as unwise the simultaneous treatment of both husband and wife by one analyst. . .it makes the task of both patients harder. In the end one or the other is likely to lose his confidence in the impartiality of the analyst and the analysis of the patient will suffer accordingly. Therefore, since it is usually wise not to postpone the analysis of one until after the other is finished, it is well to send the second patient to another psychoanalyst as soon as possible (Kubie, 1956, pp. 36-37)

In addition to concern about impartiality, analysts were centrally concerned with the complications of multiple transference and countertransference problems. Mittlemann (1956) further cautioned that the concurrent analysis of both members of a marriage by the same analyst required a good memory to keep straight what had been learned from each. In the even more radical modality of conjoint therapy, the concern was that neither would be willing to deal candidly with sensitive material in the presence of the other spouse. It is probable that none of these objections could have been successfully met on theoretical grounds. However, as increasing numbers of analysts found occasions to break the rules for special cases, it became clear that in practice these problems could be overcome and that therapy sometimes actually went faster.

It appears that the first report on the psychoanalysis of married couples was made by Clarence Oberndorf, a New York analyst, at a meeting of the American Psychiatric Association in 1931 (Sager, 1966). The paper was published in expanded form in 1938 and described the sequential analysis of five married couples (Oberndorf, 1938). In 1933 he read a paper "Folie à Deux" before the New York Neurological Society (published the following year as Oberndorf, 1934), which attempted to spell out a theory of interactive or emergent neuroses in a marriage.

In 1936 the Ninth International Congress of Psychoanalysis met in Nyon, Switzerland with the theme, "Family Neuroses and the Neurotic Family." Sager's summary of the conference and its impact is succinct:

Laforgue, the main speaker, reported on his experience in analyzing simultaneously several members of one family. He showed how two partners in a marriage unconsciously communicate how they support their complementary neurosis. . . . Leuba, at the same Congress, discussed his analytic experience with 14 families and made the first attempt at a systematic "family diagnosis." These early reports unfortunately got sidetracked in the subsequent development of psychoanalysis. . . (Sager, 1966, p. 459).

Perhaps the intervention of the Second World War deflected the attention of the psychoanalytic community from the issue. In any case, soon after the end of that conflict in 1948 Bela Mittlemann of the New York Psychoanalytic Institute published the first accounts of concurrent marital therapies in America. Earlier (1944) he had contributed a theoretical paper elaborating on Oberndorf's concept of *folie à deux*. He wrote, "Because of the continuous and intimate nature of marriage every neurosis in a married person is strongly anchored in the married relationship." Mittlemann continued, "It is a useful and at times indispensable therapeutic measure to concentrate the analytic discussions on these complementary patterns and, if necessary, to have both mates treated" (Mittlemann, 1944, p. 491).

About this time Henry Dicks and his colleagues at Tavistock Clinic in England had set up a Family Psychiatric Unit, staffed by psychiatric social workers who worked toward the reconciliation of couples referred by the divorce courts. They soon after brought under the Tavistock umbrella the Family Discussion Bureau, a marital casework agency directed by Dr. Michael and Enid Balint. Although these clinics were modeled after the American marriage counseling centers discussed in the previous section, their inclusion in the services of a respected psychiatric facility such as the Tavistock Clinic added impetus to the movement among psychiatrists (Dicks, 1964). Another milestone was passed in 1956 with the publication by Victor Eisenstein, Director of the New Jersey Neuropsychiatric Institute, of an edited book titled *Neurotic Interaction in Marriage*. In 1959 Don Jackson coined the term "conjoint therapy" to describe a therapist meeting conjointly with a husband and wife (Jackson, 1959).

The movement continued as a force among psychoanalysts into the 1960s with major articles appearing in psychiatric texts (e.g., Green, 1965; Green et al., 1965; Laidlaw, 1956), and journals (e.g., Rodgers, 1965; Watson, 1963) and even in the new journal, *Family Process* (Carroll et al., 1963). In 1965 the Society of Medical Psychoanalysis held a symposium on Psychoanalysis and Marriage (Sager, 1966). Nevertheless, increasingly in the 1960s and 1970s the movement has been absorbed into the more broadly based family therapy movement. Probably Sager's excellent 1966 history of the movement (upon which we have drawn shamelessly) was written at the very zenith of its independent development.

THE FAMILY THERAPY MOVEMENT

Precursors

The family therapy movement, like the marital therapy movement, grew out of the general field of psychiatry. Within that broad discipline we have already outlined some of the major elements which prepared the way for what was to follow. Certain published works seem to have been particularly seminal if we are to credit the footnotes in the writings of the earliest pioneers. A series of papers over the years emphasized the importance of the family in the etiology and management of serious emotional difficulties. In addition to some of Freud's early work on the Oedipal complex and related ideas, some of the most frequently cited were: 1) Flugel's (1921) *The Psychoanalytic Study of the Family*, which discussed the individual analysis of various family members; 2) Moreno's work over the decades of the 1930s and 1940s with group psychodrama methods, including work with married couples and other family members (Moreno, 1934, 1940, 1952); 3) Ackerman's (1938) article, "The Unity of the Family," and 4) Richardson's (1945) influential book, *Patients Have Families*.

In 1949 John Bowlby published an article, "The Study and Reduction of Group Tension in the Family," in which he described conjoint family interviews used as auxiliary to individual interviews at the Tavistock Child Guidance Clinic. Apparently this technique developed out of frustration with a young teenager he had in treatment who was making very little progress.

After two years of weekly treatment sessions, very many of which were missed, I decided to confront the main actors with the problem as I saw it. Thus I planned a session in which I could see father, mother and boy together. This proved a very interesting and valuable session. . .and a turning point in the case (1949, pp. 19-20).

Noting that this approach was really only an adaptation of group therapy techniques already developed by others, he went on to reassure his readers that he and his colleagues at Tavistock considered the family application of these techniques still experimental. "Though we rarely employ it more than once or twice in a particular case, we are coming to use it almost as a routine after the initial examination and before treatment is inaugurated" (p. 20).

There is no contemporary evidence that this paper, published in a new, and at that time not very widely read, journal, was seen by any of the Americans who were active in founding the family therapy movement. As we shall see, however, by an odd quirk, the work at Tavistock served as a major stimulus to the development of this new approach in the United States.

There is some evidence that other European therapists in Hungary and elsewhere were also beginning to see whole families at this time, but none of this information made its way across the Atlantic until years later (Silverman and Silverman, 1962). In the United States, Rudolf Dreikurs of the Community Child Guidance Center of Chicago seems to have developed a program very similar to the one at Tavistock in this same time period. We have found very few references to his work, however, aside from a footnote in Bell (1967), and it appears that his innovative approaches also contributed less than they might have to the movement as it actually emerged (see Dreikurs, 1948, 1949a, 1949b, 1950, and 1951).

The Founding Decade: 1952-1961

As every historian of the family therapy movement has noted (e.g., Guerin, 1976; Kaslow, 1979), it began in a dozen places at once among independent-minded therapists and researchers in many parts of the country. By the end of the 1950s, however, it had emerged as a connected movement whose members exchanged correspondence and visits and began to cite one another in footnotes. We have arbitrarily chosen the decade 1952 to 1961 as the founding decade because 1952 seems to be the year in which a number of the pioneers made major steps toward establishing conjoint family therapy as an approach of treatment and because 1961 is the year that nearly all of them finally met together in a body to prepare the way for the first "state of the art" joint handbook (Ackerman, Beatman and Sherman, 1967) and to found a common journal, *Family Process*, which first appeared in 1962.

John Bell

Among the many claimants for the title "father of family therapy," perhaps none has better credentials than John Bell. By all odds the best statement on how he got into the business was reported in a *Saturday Evening Post* Interview with him.

In August of 1951, Dr. John Bell—then a professor of psychology at Clark University in Worcester, Massachusetts—had been staying as a house guest at the home of Dr. John Sutherland, medical director of the famed Tavistock Clinic in London. One afternoon, while Mrs. Sutherland and Mrs. Bell were preparing tea and the Sutherland and Bell children were playing in a nearby room, the British doctor started describing some recent studies in his institution.

"I've been meaning to tell you about the work of one of our psychiatrists" [Bowlby], he said. "He's been having the whole family of the patient come in."

At that moment the two wives entered with the tea tray, and the conversation changed. But a few days later, sailing home to the United States, Dr. Bell recalled the idea of "having the whole family of the patient come in."

"Long afterward," he said a few months ago, "I learned I'd misunderstood Jock Sutherland. He was actually talking about seeing all the family members individually, with an occasional conference with the whole family. But it was my impression that his colleague was seeing the entire family together at each session. It was a startling thought to me—after all, nobody was doing a thing like that—but it sounded appealing. I decided to try it myself."

Back at Clark University Doctor Bell was asked to consult on the case of a 13-year-old boy who had been expelled from a Western Massachusetts school because of "violent behavioral problems." He decided to work not only with the patient, but also with his parents and his two sisters. The father, a bank official, took a dim view of the proposal, but finally agreed to participate.

"It's a lot of nonsense," he said. "It's Billy who has the trouble. The rest of the family is fine."

By the second session it became clear that the rest of the family was far from fine. The mother was revealed as a rigid perfectionist with strong feelings of hostility towards her son, an adopted child. The father, unable to cope with his wife, had taken to drinking. As the parents drifted apart, the son developed problems.

"The basic problem involved the entire family unit," Doctor Bell reported, "and it was with this entire unit that I decided to work."

Early in 1953 he made his first report to a group of fellow psychologists, describing the successful use of the new family approach on this and nine other families. Unfortunately his preliminary account wasn't published in a national scientific journal. Dr. Bell—now an official of the National Institute of Mental Health in San Francisco—continued his pioneering work, but most psychotherapists were unaware of it (Silverman and Silverman, 1962).

Something of Bell's character and of his relation to the rest of the field are reflected in his preface to the 1972 paperback version of Ackerman's early landmark publication, *The Psychodynamics of Family Life*. He wrote, in part,

When Arthur Rosenthal asked me to write a foreword to this new paperback edition of the late Nat Ackerman's classic book, I accepted immediately and without reservation.

Why had I reacted so fast? Out of the past came painful memories. I recalled how this book, when I first confronted it in 1958, had provoked in me sharply hostile reactions. My own ideas of the family and family therapy seemed to me to have gone beyond those of Ackerman, and to have been more revolutionary. As our differences emerged in public and were followed by years of competitive sparring, they raised barriers to professional and personal openness. Was I now really welcoming a public chance to expose old wounds?

But the later years brought about a change in our relations. The publication of *Family Process* threw us together as colleagues. A friendship of growing closeness and trust began and deepened, terminated too soon by his sudden death. This mutual respect and affection led us to reconsider our differences and contentions (Bell, 1972).

Among Bell's most respected contributions is his monograph, *Family Group Therapy* (1961). Together with the 1958 Ackerman volume, it constituted one of the founding documents of the profession. Its wide circulation, especially in the western part of the United States, had an immediate and immense impact. From 1956 to 1961, Bell gave several hundred lectures and workshops on family therapy. To an important degree because of Bell's work, family therapy gained prominence rapidly and was far in advance in the western United States at the end of the founding decade.

Nathan W. Ackerman

Ackerman came to family therapy from the field of child psychiatry. He had also been interested in group psychotherapy and was much influenced by the work of Moreno. Perhaps most important for Ackerman, as for many psychiatrists of his generation, was the experience of the Holocaust and World War II, which had a profound effect, turning his attention to the relationship of social contexts and the fate of individual persons. Some appreciation for the distance he came in his career can be gained from his description of his own training.

During the nineteen thirties, while I was undergoing medical and speciality training, the worst chore for the resident physician in neurology and psychiatry was a weekly duty to visit with the patient's relatives and to report progress. In those days, this was felt to be an unmitigated bore, an inescapable nuisance, having no bearing whatever on the medical care and treatment of the patient. It was tacitly understood among young physicians that the main incentive for contact with the family was gently to prepare the way for obtaining ultimately from the family, on the decease of the patient, a signed authorization for autopsy. This is a backward glance on the then dominant emphasis on brain pathology as connected with mental illness, also on the extraordinary transformation of the medical attitude toward relatives (Ackerman, 1967, p. 126).

His own view was sharply revised when, soon after finishing his residency, he became involved in an extensive study of mental health problems among the unemployed in a depression-struck mining town in Western Pennsylvania.

I went to see, first hand, the mental health effects on the families of unemployed miners. This experience was a shocker; I was startlingly awakened to the limitless, unexplored territory in the relations of family life and health. I studied 25 families in which the father, the sole breadwinner in the mining community, had been without work for between two and five years. The miners, long habituated to unemployment, idled away their empty hours on the street corner, or in the neighborhood saloon. They felt defeated and degraded. They clung to one another to give and take comfort and to pass away the endless days of inactivity. Humiliated by their failure as providers, they stayed away from home; they felt shamed before their wives. The wives and mothers, harassed by insecurity and want from day to day, irritably rejected their husbands; they punished them by refusing sexual relations. The man who could no longer bring home his pay envelope was no longer the head of the family. He lost his position of respect and authority in the family; the woman drove him into the streets. Often, she turned for comfort to her first son. Mother and son then usurped the leadership position within the family. Among these unemployed miners, there were guilty depressions, hypochondriacal fears, psychosomatic crises, sexual disorders, and crippled self-esteem. Not infrequently, these men were publicly condemned as deserters. The configuration for family life was radically altered by the miner's inability to fulfill his habitual role as provider (Ackerman, 1967, p. 126).

This experience plus others convinced him that emotional problems could be generated by the immediate environment as well as by the dynamics of the psyche. He carried this perception with him when he joined the psychiatric staff at Southard School, which was a facility for disturbed children associated with the Menninger Clinic in Topeka, Kansas. By 1937 he was the chief psychiatrist of the Child Guidance Clinic. While he adopted the prevailing orthopsychiatric principle that the psychiatrist saw the patient and the social worker saw the mother, by the mid-1940s he noted a growing flexibility in the field and a single therapist would sometimes see both. In his own private practice he began to experiment with this procedure and in a few cases he independently discovered, as Bowlby had, that an interview with the entire family could be exceptionally helpful in breaking through an impasse with a difficult child. His special contribution, however, was that he did not leave it at the level of a daring pragmatic innovation. For four years he conducted seminars around the issue of the relationship between the illness of the child and the mothering and fathering the child received. He began to see the family as the proper unit of diagnosis and treatment and began sending his staff on home visits to study the family (Guerin, 1976).

In 1955 he organized and chaired the first session on family diagnosis held at the meetings of the American Orthopsychiatric Association. In 1957 he opened the Family Mental Health Clinic at Jewish Family Services in New York City. This led, in 1960, to the founding of the Family Institute (after his death renamed the Ackerman Institute). Meanwhile, in 1958 he had published the first book-length treatment of diagnosis and treatment of family relationships, *The Psychodynamics of Family Life*.

In 1961 he joined with Don Jackson of Palo Alto to found the most influential and unifying journal in the field, *Family Process*.

Christian F. Midelfort

Christian Midelfort is an interesting example of what happens to a pioneer who remains largely isolated from a developing movement. Few have stronger claims as founding fathers. In the preface to his 1957 book, *The Family in Psychotherapy*, he writes:

As a participant in today's development of psychiatry, I have reported in this book my own results with family therapy in various types of mental illness. My development of this approach was first based on techniques I observed in my father's practice. . . .

To my knowledge the first place in this country to make use of this type of family therapy was the Lutheran Hospital in LaCrosse, Wisconsin. At this hospital relatives of psychiatric patients stayed as nurses aides and companions in consistent attendance to supervise occupational, recreational, and insulin therapies, to minimize suicidal risk, fear, aggression, and insecurity and to take part in therapeutic interviews with patient and psychiatrist. . . . Family treatment is also extended to the out-patient department for all types of mental illness (Midelfort, 1957, pp. v-vi).

He delivered a paper on the use of family therapy techniques at the American Psychiatric Association meetings in 1952, possibly the first such paper ever presented to a professional psychiatric meeting in the United States. Nevertheless, his situation as a staff psychiatrist in a small Wisconsin community did not lend itself to his taking part in the network of innovators which began to exchange visits, tapes, and materials in the 1957 to 1962 period. He was never on the Board of *Family Process*, never participated in the seminal meetings throughout the '60s and he did not operate a training center which might have produced disciples. As a result, his influence has been minimal and few contemporary family therapists are aware of his vastly underrated contributions.

Theodore Lidz

Lidz was another of the founders who was analytically trained. In the early '40s, while on the staff of Johns Hopkins University, he became interested in the families of schizophrenics. When he moved to Yale in 1951, he sharpened his focus and together with a colleague began studying a group of 17 young hospitalized schizophrenics and their families intensively. Following analytic concepts more closely than some of the others, he became es-

pecially concerned with the failure of these families to develop adequate boundaries and with their intense symbiotic needs derived from a parent's need for and inability to differentiate himself or herself from the patient. In some cases the parents were distant and hostile toward each other (the condition he labeled "schism"). In others there was a tendency for the mother to become domineering in a destructive way (the condition he labeled "skew"). He felt that the first condition was hardest on male children and the second on females (Lidz et al., 1957).

Lidz' interest remained focused essentially on the understanding and treatment of schizophrenic disorders rather than on the development of family therapy as a discipline. However, Lidz' group was probably the first, or among the first, to treat families, treating the parents and siblings of their hospitalized schizophrenic patients or in marital pairs and occasionally in conjoint family therapy.

Lidz reported his work in 1955 in Washington and in national meetings in 1956 and 1957. The clinical research of both Bowen and Wynne followed upon Lidz' research on the role of the family in the etiology and treatment of schizophrenic disorders. In 1961 he was one of those who agreed to be a consulting editor of *Family Process*.

Lyman C. Wynne[10]

Of all the pioneers, perhaps none was so fully prepared by formal training to become a family researcher and therapist as Lyman Wynne. In 1948, after having received his medical training at Harvard, he entered the graduate Department of Social Relations for a Ph.D. Those four years brought him into interaction with many of the leaders in the field of sociology, social psychology, and social anthropology. Among them he found himself most intrigued with the ideas of Talcott Parsons, including his view of personality as a subsystem within a large family system. Concurrently, he was working with Erich Lindemann at the Massachusetts General Hospital and the Human Relations Service at

---

[10]Much of this material is based on an interview with Wynne, January 26, 1979, in Los Angeles, California.

Wellesley, one of the earliest full service mental health clinics in America. He saw several patients with severe psychoses and with the further complication of ulcerative colitis. It became evident to Lindemann's team that family events were almost always at the root of colitis attacks in this population. Wynne saw his first whole families in 1947 as ancillary to the treatment of these seriously afflicted patients. Lindemann's work on grief in families and his theories of family structure, complete with social orbits, family splits, and many other concepts, seemed to fit right in with what Wynne was learning academically.

In 1952, he took a position as a psychiatrist with John Clauson's Laboratory of Socioenvironmental Studies at the National Institute of Mental Health (NIMH) in Bethesda, Maryland. It was there and at the Prince George County, Maryland, Mental Health Clinic that he began working intensively with the families of mental patients. Initially he saw whole families only when individual treatment or joint interviews with the mother and patient were not effective. Gradually, however, he began to apply Parsons' notion of family systems to the situations he faced and eventually worked out his own theory of family structure of schizophrenic patients (Wynne, 1961; Wynne et al., 1958).

About this time (1954), Murray Bowen joined the staff of the NIMH and in him Wynne found a colleague who was struggling with the same basic problems. But Wynne's first real indication that this approach was more widely practiced came at the 1956 and 1957 meetings of the American Psychiatric Association in Chicago. There he and Bowen met with Don Jackson, Theodore Lidz, and Ackerman. One of the immediate results of this encounter was the exchange, in 1959, of videotapes of family counseling sessions between Jackson and Wynne (see Jackson, Riskin and Satir (1961) for the Palo Alto reviews of the Wynne tapes). It took several close viewings of the tape Jackson sent before the Bethesda group finally concluded that they had been swindled. The tape from Palo Alto was a simulated session (starring Virginia Satir as mother). When confronted with this deception, Jackson confessed but pleaded that this was just like the families they actually saw and illustrated the double-bind especially well. Wynne contin-

ued interchange with Palo Alto and several of the other centers in the following years and was on the first board of editors of *Family Process*. Eventually (1971), he moved from the NIMH to the University of Rochester Medical School where he has continued his work with the families of schizophrenics.

Murray Bowen

Like the majority of the pioneers, Bowen was a psychiatrist who specialized in treating psychotic children. Like Ackerman, he got started toward family therapy while working at Menninger. Like Midelfort, he felt the parents, and especially mothers, should be required to live in the hospital with their disturbed child and in 1951 he requested the use of a cottage on the grounds at Menninger for this purpose (Guerin, 1976). It soon became evident that it would be still more helpful if fathers could be added, but after a few attempts he abandoned that approach as too complicated at that time. Instead, he concentrated on the "symbiosis," as he termed it, between the ill child and the mother.

In 1954 he joined Lyman Wynne at the NIMH and began a research project which involved having the families of schizophrenic youngsters come and live in the hospital. A pair of journalists with the *Saturday Evening Post* interviewed Bowen about his project and reported:

Seven complete families participated in the project, which ran from 1954 to 1959. Usually there were two or three families in the hospital's special unit at the same time. Husband and wife occupied one room, and the children were in other rooms nearby. All families ate in a common dining room and shared the same lounge and recreation room. In some instances the father went to work each morning and returned to the hospital at night. In others, the father took a leave of absence from his job. The subjects were under the observation of a 20-member team of psychiatrists, social workers, nurses and attendants, some of them working seven days a week in eight-hour shifts. Family privacy was respected but nurses were nearby and on call (Silverman and Silverman, 1962).

Initially the project provided separate therapists for the various family members. However, quoting from his own account of events:

After a year, all families were started in family psychotherapy, the only form of therapy for newly admitted families. The old families continued their already-established individual therapy and began going to family psychotherapy sessions, too. Family therapy for the new families was alive and fast moving, and progress was more rapid than with any other therapy. The other families were not making progress in either individual or family psychotherapy. In family sessions their attitude was, "I'll take up my problems with *my* therapist." But their individual therapy was also slow, both patients and parents expecting the other to deal with significant issues. After a few months, all individual psychotherapy was discontinued (Bowen, 1976, p. 228).

The new procedure was soon adopted in his private practice. His first patient to be switched over:

. . .was a bright young husband with a phobic reaction in a compulsive personality who was making steady progress after six months of psychoanalysis for four hours a week. The dilemma was discussed with the project consultant, who was a senior psychoanalyst. The therapist said:
"This man has a good chance for one of the better psychoanalytic results in three to four years with a total of 600 to 700 hours. There is also a good chance his wife will develop enough problems in two years to refer her to another analyst for three to four years. About six years from now, after 1,000 or more combined psychoanalytic hours, they should have their lives in reasonable order. How can I in good conscience continue this long and expensive course when I know within me that I can accomplish far more in less time with different approach? On the other hand, how can I in good conscious take a chance and suggest something new and untried when I know the chances are good with the proved psychoanalytic method?"
The consultant mused about analysts who hold onto patients too long and wondered how the husband and wife would react to the questions. The issue was discussed with the patient, and one week later his wife accompanied him to her first session. The clinical method used was analysis of the intrapsychic process in one and then the analysis of the corresponding emotional reaction in the other. They continued the family therapy sessions three times a week for 18 months for a total of 203 hours. The result was far better than would ordinarily be expected with 600 hours of psychoanalysis for each (Bowen, 1976, p. 230).

Already in 1956, however, Bowen began to feel that the administration of the NIMH was not supportive of his new approach. He attributed this to their being wary of his flouting the conventions of traditional psychiatric practice (Guerin, 1976). In any case, he finally moved to Georgetown University, only a few miles away, with the hope of continuing his project there. As it turned out, his sponsor there died in the midst of the transfer and he was never able to get his staff moved over. He has continued at Georgetown for many years and, since the spring of 1957 (when he presented reports of his research at both the family session of Orthopsychiatric meetings in March and the American Psychiatric Association meetings in May), he has been a major influence in the field.

Carl A. Whitaker

From the beginning Carl Whitaker has been noted as the most irreverent and whimsical of the founding fathers. In recent years he has developed this approach into a finely honed therapy of the absurd—a therapy in which he often seems to drive a family sane by appearing more mad than they. It was in keeping with this character, then, to be one of those who early risked violating the conventions of traditional psychotherapy. In 1944 he and John Warkentin, then practicing psychiatry in Oak Ridge, Tennessee, began bringing spouses and eventually children into sessions with their patients. In 1946 he moved to Atlanta (as Chief of Psychiatry at Emory) and partly shifted his emphasis to work with schizophrenics (Guerin, 1976). Here, too, he found that involving the families was useful. At the same time he embarked on a project of what he called "multiple therapy," and in 1958 published a report on 30 couples he had seen between 1955 and 1957 (Whitaker, 1958).

Whitaker might well be credited with having called the first formal meeting in the family therapy movement. In 1953 he invited Gregory Bateson from Palo Alto, Don Jackson (at that time a resident at Chestnut Lodge, Rockville, Maryland), and John Rosen from Pennsylvania to join him and his Atlanta colleagues for a four-day get-together in Sea Island, Georgia. The exact topics dicussed are not a matter of record.[11] There had been nine previous informal meetings held at Emory University, at which each took turns demonstrating his own approaches to therapy with individuals and also with families in Atlanta, while the others observed and then discussed and debated the issues which emerged (Guerin, 1976). Those nine meetings did not include Bateson or Jackson, but did include Ed Taylor and Michael Hayward from Philadelphia, and John Warkentin, Thomas Malone and Richard Felder from Atlanta.

As the family therapy movement developed, Whitaker was part of the central network from the beginning, in evidence of which he was on the first board of editors for *Family Process*. He was one of the first to extend the clinical definition of family to include grandparents, as well as collateral kin, all of whom he would invite for weekend workshops around a particular individual's or nuclear family's problem. In 1965 he moved from Atlanta to become a professor in the Department of Psychiatry at the University of Wisconsin Medical School.

The Palo Alto Group: Gregory Bateson, Jay Haley, John Weakland, Don D. Jackson, and Virginia Satir

It would be hard to imagine five more richly individual persons than those listed in this group. Yet their early contributions are so intertwined that it is impossible to outline the history of one without introducing the others.

In the beginning was Gregory Bateson. He was not a psychiatrist but rather an anthropologist and philosopher on the faculty of Stanford University. He had done anthropological field work in the South Pacific and elsewhere and had also studied the social systems of animals such as otters. As a philosopher he was interested in general systems theory and in hierarchies of classification. One of the several aspects of the later subject that fascinated him was the hierarchy of logical types (Whitehead and Russell, 1910) which produced paradoxical statements such as the classic "I am lying." Like all paradoxes, the harder one thinks about it the more disoriented one feels. It is true only if it is false and false only if it is true. Using the theory of logical types, however, it becomes clear that the paradox consists of two contradictory statements which elude comparison because they are at different logical levels. There is the evident content of the statement, "I am lying," and there is also the framing statement (or meta-statement as it came to be called) which is not spelled out explicitly but is inherent in all human discourse, namely, "I expect you to believe what I say to you." When the meta-message is made explicit, the original statement loses some of its mind-boggling paradoxical qualities and assumes the qualities of a mere pair of contradictory statements (A is true/A is not true).

Bateson was impressed with the number of situations in which similar paradoxes were present. Among his otters the meta-message "this is only play" made it possible for the animals to participate in realistic mock fights without fear or error. The apparently absurd verbalizations of mongoloid children and of schizophrenics had some of this same quality. Humor, especially certain types of humor such as repartée between a ventriloquist and his dummy or between puppets, seemed rich with paradoxical material, as also did hypnosis. In 1952 Bateson succeeded in getting a Rockefeller Foundation grant to pursue his studies in this area, and with this money he assembled a staff of variegated backgrounds and talents.

Among his earliest appointments were Jay Haley and John Weakland. Haley's background was in communication. He had most recently been engaged in analyzing fantasy sequences in popular movies using a logical model somewhat similar to that which intrigued Bateson. Weakland had begun his career as a chemical engineer but had turned to anthropology, with special interest in Chinese families.

One of Haley's early assignments was to go to a workshop offered by Milton Erickson, the remarkable hypnotherapist (Haley, 1976). That

---

[11]*Editors' Note.* While there is no published record of the 1953 conference referred to by Broderick and Schrader, a second Sea Island, Georgia meeting, October 15-17, 1955, produced a complete published transcript of the proceedings (see Whitaker, 1955).

fateful meeting resulted in a relationship which led finally to Haley's becoming Erickson's chief expositor and intellectual biographer. Erickson's methods, in turn, provided one of the foundations of the paradoxical approach to family therapy which became the trademark of the Palo Alto branch of the movement.

In 1954 the Rockefeller grant ran out and it became clear that it would not be renewed. The pragmatics of finding alternative funding pushed the team to narrow their focus to a more glamorous sub-issue and they chose schizophrenia. The application proposed the investigation of the premise that schizophrenia was the product of children's being caught in paradoxical binds by a mother who "is driven not only to punish the children's demand for love, but also to punish any indication which the child may give that he knows that he is not loved" (Haley, 1976, p. 67).

The reformulated research project was funded by a Macy Foundation grant and one of the first expenditures was to bring Don Jackson, a psychiatrist, into the project as clinical consultant. Jackson had spent the previous three years as a psychiatric resident at Chestnut Lodge in Rockville, Maryland (Guerin, 1976), where he was influenced by the philosophy of Sullivan and others who emphasized the interpersonal aspects of psychiatric problems. His own work had emphasized the importance of the family homeostatic mechanisms.

In 1956 the team of Bateson, Jackson, Haley and Weakland generated one of the most discussed papers in the history of psychiatry, "Toward a Theory of Schizophrenia." In it they introduced the concept of the *double-bind* as the crucial familial determinant of schizophrenia in children. Initially, the team had depended upon the clinical experience of Jackson to provide examples and correctives, but in 1956 they started having sessions with the families of schizophrenics videotaped and analyzed in detail as part of the research project (Haley, 1976).

In 1957 Jackson reported on the project at the American Psychiatric Association meetings in Chicago, where he met Wynne, Bowen, Lidz, and Ackerman (Guerin, 1976).

The year 1959 was pivotal for Jackson and for the movement. He published his paper on conjoint family therapy, arguing that it was more effective than seeing family members individually (Jackson, 1959). While remaining on as a consultant to the Bateson project, he set up the Mental Research Institute, which was much more sharply focused on family therapy per se. And he brought Virginia Satir from Chicago to work with him in the new institute. Actually, Satir had sought him out. She had become interested in family work while on the staff of the Chicago Psychiatric Institute and had heard about Bowen's project in Washington. When she finally met Bowen, he told her she should get to know Jackson, and so in 1959 she joined the staff at MRI (Guerin, 1976).

In 1961 Jackson attended the seminal meeting of family therapists in New York and agreed with Nathan Ackerman to have MRI and the Family Institute jointly sponsor a new journal, *Family Process*. Jay Haley was appointed the first editor and the first issue came out the following year. As we have noted before, this publication has been the chief unifying influence in the movement ever since. Satir, as her later writing shows, was greatly influenced by the Palo Alto Group, although she was not at all intimidated by it. For example, she could borrow a useful concept such as "meta-message" and give it a freer interpretation which fit more easily into her own view of family interaction. (Compare, for example, her use of the concept in *Conjoint Family Therapy* (1964) with other publications of the group such as Watzlawick, Beavin, and Jackson (1967).) During the mid-sixties she gradually disengaged from the MRI as she became more and more involved with the human growth movement. Probably more than any other early founder, she was responsible for popularizing the movement. She had a flair for clear, nontechnical exposition and charismatic presentation that led her to address tens of thousands in person, hundreds of thousands through her books, and millions through the media.

In 1962, at the close of the Bateson project, Haley and Weakland joined MRI. Then in 1967 Haley left to join Minuchin in Philadelphia at the Philadelphia Child Guidance Clinic.

In January of 1968 Don Jackson died, thereby depriving the field of one of its most articulate and creative forces. Watzlawick and Weakland remain at the MRI. A fuller history of the MRI can be found in Chapter 8.

The Philadelphia Group: Ivan Boszormenyi-Nagy and Associates

The Department of Family Psychiatry at the Eastern Pennsylvania Psychiatric Institute (EPPI) was one of the chief centers of research and training in the family therapy movement. Nagy, like several of the other founding fathers, was a psychiatrist devoted to the therapy of psychotics, and to the integration of family therapy with psychotherapy as a whole. As administrator of an interprofessional, interacademic center, he was able to assemble an impressive group of associates who helped to make Philadelphia a major early center of family therapy. James Framo, Gerald Zuk, Geraldine Spark, David Rubinstein, Barbara Krasner, Margaret Cotroneo, Leon Robinson, Geraldine Lincoln-Grossman, and Oscar Weiner were among them. This group was instrumental in the founding of the Family Institute of Philadelphia, with Nagy as its first full-term president. Members of the Department were also responsible for the first organized training program held in a European country (Holland, 1967), and for a number of early national conferences in family therapy in the United States. Literally thousands of professionals were trained at this center before the Commonwealth of Pennsylvania abruptly closed this leading psychiatric research and training institution (EPPI) in 1980. Among this group's earlier contributions was the volume entitled *Intensive Family Therapy* (Boszormenyi-Nagy and Framo, 1965). Nagy's major position statement on the premises of what has later become contextual therapy (see Chapter 5, this volume), an integrative approach, is *Invisible Loyalties* (Boszormenyi-Nagy and Spark, 1973). Nagy and some of his associates continue to be affiliated with both Hahnemann Medical College and their private training institutes, locally and nationally.

THE HISTORY OF SEX THERAPY

To Freud and his successors, sexual problems were symptoms of underlying neuroses which needed to be exorcised through intensive, long-term analytic reshaping of the psyche. There is another therapeutic tradition, however, almost as old, which treats sexual disorders as practical problems that ought to yield to specific remedies. We do not refer here to the general medical practitioner who might suggest that a premature ejaculator use a condom or a numbing cream to reduce stimulation or count backward from 2,000 by 7's to take his mind off sexual matters. Rather, we refer to the approaches used by early pioneers such as Ellis and Hirschfeld.

Ellis saw himself as something of a secular high priest of sex and refused to charge for consultations. Yet he saw scores of sexually unhappy people and was in correspondence with hundreds more. His approach varied from patient to patient, but two elements were common to most of his encounters: 1) He listened with acceptance and personal supportiveness, reassuring the individual that his or her personal experiences and fears were not unique; and 2) he recommended reading (usually of his own published work) to help further allay anxiety and to give a scientific and informed perspective on the matter.

Because he wrote the first major work on homosexuality (or sexual inversion as he prefered to call it), many of his clients were homosexuals of both sexes. Among his heterosexual clientele, most were women who were attracted, apparently, not only by his scientific scholarship and liberated views, but also by his striking leonine appearance coupled with a gentle personal style. When he felt it would be accepted, he sometimes personally introduced these women into his own version of non-demand sexual pleasuring. He considered himself impotent through most of his adult life and this awareness contributed to his confidence that these approaches would not be misconstrued as mere seduction. It is curious by contemporary standards that he never saw couples as clients, nor, so far as is recorded, instructed husbands and wives in how to enlarge their mutual repertoire of sexual approaches. (See his biography, *The Sage of Sex*, by Calder-Marshall (1959), especially pp. 173-174 and 238-243 for a fuller description of his approach.)

Meanwhile, on the continent, Hirschfeld and his colleagues were approaching these problems in a more systematic and professional manner. These sex and marital counselors also listened to problems empathically, gave reassurances as to normality, information on contraceptive and sexual practices, and assigned readings (including Ellis').

In general, sexual counseling in America closely followed the patterns set in Europe. Most practitioners came to the field from the social hygiene movement (for example, Paul Popenoe in Los Angeles and Lester Dearborn in Boston) or from medicine (for example, Abraham Stone in New York or Robert L. Dickinson). Without a doubt, special note should be given to the work of Dickinson. He was an extraordinary scientist and counselor in the area of human sexuality. A gynecologist, he systematically sketched the pelvic anatomy of each of his thousands of patients and of many males as well. His 1933 publication, *Human Sexual Anatomy*, and its 1949 expansion and revision illustrate and document the anatomy of the human pelvis in its most diverse manifestations. He even anticipated Masters by using a penis-sized test tube to simulate intercourse from various angles and depths of penetration, thus permitting a clear correlation between what could be observed internally and the sensation reported by the patient. Beyond his observational data, as noted in an earlier section, he interviewed thousands of his patients on their sex histories and current practices (Dickinson and Beam, 1931, 1934). It is doubtful that anyone before him was in a position to counsel couples on their sexual problems with more authority.

Thus, when he became one of the founding members of the American Association of Marriage Counselors, he brought a wealth of sophisticated knowledge on the sexual aspects of marriage to that small group of professionals. It is not surprising that the third meeting of the AAMC in the mid-1940s had as its topic "Clinical Techniques in the Treatment of Frigidity" (Humphrey, 1978).

The American with sexual problems in the 1930s and 1940s thus had some chance of finding a counselor who was at least informed as to the scientific knowledge available at that time. By modern standards these were, perhaps, not very effective sex therapists. Still, it seems probable that individuals or couples consulting one of these specialists would have received a great deal better help than if they had consulted their pastor or family doctor, or even their psycho-

therapist, if the professional in question lacked specialized training in this field.

The monumental work of Alfred Kinsey and his associates (1948, 1953) added immeasurably to the knowledge base which sex therapists had to draw upon. That research team took comprehensive lifetime sex histories from literally thousands of American men and women across a broad spectrum of social background. Their findings and the publicity which attended the publication of those findings raised the consciousness of Americans concerning their own sexual biases and behavior as nothing before or since has done.

As important as Kinsey's work was in the development of the field, it was, however, overshadowed by the contributions of Masters and Johnson (1966, 1970). William H. Masters was a research-oriented gynecologist who had been interested in the physiology of sexual functioning since his medical school days. He had apprenticed, in effect, in the laboratory of one of the outstanding authorities on pelvic anatomy in the world at that time, George Washington Carver of the University of Rochester School of Medicine. Carver advised him that if he was serious about this interest he owed it to himself first to wait until he was at least 40 before getting involved in sex research, second to earn first a reputation as a scientist in some other, less controversial field, and third, not to consider pursuing such research until he had the support of a major medical school or university (Brecher, 1971).

Masters came close to keeping this counsel. By 1954, when he entered into the project that was to make him famous, he had, indeed, achieved prominence in his profession through his research on hormone replacement in older women and the development of a non-surgical procedure for creating a vagina in women who had been born without one; also, he was a research professor at the Washington University School of Medicine. He did lack two years of being 40, but he was encouraged to hasten his project by the positive reception of Kinsey's work *Sexual Behavior in the Human Female* the year before (1953).

He began by interviewing 118 female and 27 male prostitutes. Eight of the women and three of the men also became experimental subjects and helped him to develop his instrumentation and technique. As it turned out, prostitutes were not good subjects from a physiological point of view. Their profession led to the development of various degrees of pelvic damage due to chronic congestion of the region. However, they were invaluable sources of information and experience about human arousal and sexual performance and he learned a great deal from them (Brecher, 1971).

In 1955 he decided it would be important to add a female co-investigator to the project. He applied to the University Placement Bureau and they sent over a Virginia Johnson, recently divorced and looking for a way to support her young family. She seemed serious-minded and mature and had a manner about her that he felt would put female subjects at ease. He hired her and they have remained partners in research and therapy and eventually in marriage.

To their surprise, it turned out not to be difficult at all to recruit subjects for the experiment. In the name of science (and for $10 an hour) there were any number of hospital technicians, nurses, and others who were willing to be photographed and monitored while masturbating or during intercourse. In all, between 1955 and 1966 the project recorded over 10,000 complete sexual response cycles, utilizing 694 subjects in the process (Masters and Johnson, 1966).

The results of their work began to be published in the late '50s and early '60s and reprints were quickly circulated among the network of those doing couple counseling. The articles were purposely written in the most obtuse medical jargon so as to certify the intent to write for a medical audience and not for popular consumption. Their book, *Human Sexual Response* (1966), followed the same format. Both the authors and the publishers were astonished at the sales volume. It is difficult to believe that many of the 300,000 who bought the book were able to understand what they read. If they found it difficult, however, they got a great deal of help from the media. Popularizations appeared in a number of widely used magazines and the authors were interviewed on popular talk shows. More importantly for this history, Masters and Johnson did literally dozens of presentations at various professional meetings explaining their findings to physicians, therapists and educators of all kinds.

The key contribution of their research was their organization of the human response cycle into four stages: excitement, plateau, orgasm, and resolution. But beyond this, their findings challenged many folk beliefs and cherished psychological dogmas, also. For example, they found no indication that a "vaginal" orgasm was better than or in any way different from a "clitoral" orgasm, despite Freud's (1938) doctrine to the contrary. Other widely held beliefs were also modified. The clitoris, touted by some leading sex counselors of the day as the "magic button" a man should stick with if he wanted to bring his partner pleasure, turned out to be a sensitive and even elusive organ. Women most often avoided direct contact with it when masturbating and it disappeared altogether into a protective sheath when sexual feelings became intense. They concluded from their studies that penis size was much overrated as an issue in giving women satisfaction and that, in fact, women rarely put anything into their vaginas, large or small, when masturbating, contrary to masculine fantasies. It was even discovered that diaphragms, at that time considered one of the most reliable forms of birth control, were only safely used with a gell or cream since the back of the vagina tented at the height of sexual arousal, leaving the diaphragm to slip and slide about in a most ineffective way.

These findings provided sex counselors with a whole new set of scientifically documented facts. Had that been their sole contribution, Masters' and Johnson's impact upon the field would have been enormous. But it was their second book, *Human Sexual Inadequacy* (1970), that set forth their clinical applications of their earlier findings and revolutionized the field.

The clinical work upon which it was based was initiated in 1959 as an effort separate from the research they were doing at the medical school. They decided that they would treat all sexual dysfunctions as a problem of the pair rather than of the individual and that they would operate as a male-female team in all cases. Initially they required the couples to come to St. Louis for three weeks, but eventually discovered that two were enough. Their techniques are sufficiently well-known to need no review here, but the remarkable thing was the apparent effectiveness of this intense brief therapy approach. They were successful in over 80% of their 790 cases and a five-year follow-up of 313 cases showed only about 5% long-term attrition.

Masters and Johnson began to train other couples in their methods at their center in St. Louis, but within months many others had begun to offer training in their own derivative versions of the new approach.

Actually, the approaches utilized by Masters and Johnson were not entirely new. A technique very similar to the one they recommended for dealing with premature ejaculation had been put forth by J.H. Semans in 1956. In 1958, a systematic behavioral approach (of individual, not conjoint, treatment) based on many of the same principles they used had been spelled out in a book by Wolpe, *Psychotherapy by Reciprocal Inhibition*. Neither of these innovative works had the impact on the field that *Human Sexual Inadequacy* had. In recent years, however, sex therapists have turned to those earlier contributions and found them helpful. Many prefer the Semans approach to the "squeeze" technique of Masters and Johnson, and one whole wing of the sex therapy movement that is represented by behavior therapists find more to model in Wolpe than in the St. Louis approach (LoPiccolo and LoPiccolo, 1978).

Since 1970 a veritable deluge of workshops, short courses, and the like have been offered, scores of sex clinics have been opened, books have proliferated, two journals have been founded (*Journal of Sex and Marital Therapy; Journal of Sex Education and Therapy*) and the American Association of Sex Educators and Counselors has set up standards for certifying qualified sex therapists. Although the youngest of the four therapeutic movements we have discussed, it is clear that the impact of sex therapy upon the broader profession has been no less than the others.

THE PROLIFERATION, SECULARIZATION AND AMALGAMATION OF THE FOUR MOVEMENTS

The decades of the 1960s and 1970s were periods in which the pioneers were joined by dozens of their own trainees and ultimately by thousands who had never really met them except, perhaps, in a weekend workshop or through their books. Many of the pioneers in each area continued to elaborate upon their earlier work. New names became prominent as innovators of every background joined the movements.

Proliferation

Although it would not be possible to note all of the important contributions of these decades, several within the family therapy movement deserve at least passing mention. Robert MacGregor and his colleagues in Galveston, Texas hit upon the technique of virtually storming the family with a team of professionals (prototypically a social worker, a psychologist, and a psychiatric intern, each accompanied by a trainee from his/her own discipline). In a fast-paced two-day intervention with both conjoint and divided sessions, this team attempted to have a lasting impact upon a delinquent child and his family. They called their approach Multiple Impact Therapy (MacGregor, 1967; Richie, 1960).

Another massive short-term intervention is Network Therapy, pioneered by Ross Speck (1967; Speck and Ohlan, 1967) and others. In this approach, the extended family, friends, neighbors, school counselors, probation officers, and anyone else who impinged upon the family are all brought together on a single occasion. Again, they may meet partly together and partly in subgroups. It is undeniably impossible to ignore the impact of such a gathering on the family being helped.

Bernard Guerney and his associates, first at Rutgers University and then at Pennsylvania State University, developed a still different approach to relationship counseling. Guerney trained parents in groups to become therapists to their own disturbed children (Guerney, 1964). Later, he expanded this technique to include training married couples and others in what he called "relationship enhancement" (Guerney, 1977).

One innovator who has virtually taken his place among the founders as one of the most influential of all family therapists is Salvador Minuchin. He grew up and was trained as a psychiatrist in Argentina, but in the early '60s he came to work at the Wiltwyck School for Boys, a psychiatric facility in New York City. While there, he became involved in a research project developed to determine if psychotherapeutic techniques could be adapted to help urban slum families with their overwhelming range of problems. The project resulted in a book (Minuchin et al., 1967) and in the opportunity for Minuchin to become director of the Philadelphia Child Guidance Clinic with the directive to institute a similar program for the urban poor there. He brought Braulio Montalvo with him from New York and convinced Jay Haley to join him also. Together these men and their associates developed a unique program for training members of the local black community as paraprofessional family therapists. Part of their success in this endeavor was due to the innovative training and "on line" supervision programs they developed. It was their modus operandi to have a supervisor (or more often a supervisory team composed of other trainees plus senior staff) interrupt a therapy session with suggestions for redirection. Initially they simply came to the door, but eventually they used phones and even "bugs" in the ear, modeling their approach after the techniques used by football coaching staffs in calling plays to their quarterbacks.

The contributions of the Minuchin-Haley team were substantive as well as methodological. The therapeutic approach which came to be known as "Structural Therapy" emerged out of their interaction. In addition to carrying over the communications and systems elements developed earlier at MRI, they gave added emphasis to the realignment of counterproductive family coaltions and tied their theory also to a family developmental framework (Haley, 1971; Minuchin, 1974). Minuchin also pursued his special interest in family-induced psychosomatic disorders including, especially, anorexia (Minuchin et al., 1978).

In the marriage counseling area, also, a great variety of new approaches came to the fore. Among them were the behavioral approaches developed by therapists such as Stuart (1969, 1975, 1976), Knox (1971) and the Oregon group (Jacobson and Margolin, 1979; Jacobson and Martin, 1976; Weiss, Hops and Patterson, 1973;

Weiss and Margolin, 1977). One of the most widely adopted techniques of these innovators has been the reciprocal behavioral contract or "quid pro quo," first outlined as a principle by Lederer and Jackson in 1968. Even insight-oriented therapists have found the concept adaptable to their approaches (see, for example, Sager, 1976).[12]

Couples communications workshops proliferated as a sort of short-term group approach to marital problems. Among the most carefully developed of these were the Minnesota Couples Communications Program (Miller, Nunnally and Wackman, 1975, 1976) and the conjugal therapy groups developed by Guerney and his colleagues at Pennsylvania State (Guerney, 1977).

Still another variant which focuses on prevention rather than cure is the marital enrichment movement in its many manifestations (Mace and Mace, 1976; Otto, 1975).

Within the sex therapy movement, we have earlier noted some of the development since Masters and Johnson established the field in 1970. One important social movement which we did not mention but which has had a powerful effect in some quarters is the Women's Movement. Feminists have repudiated the view that the best unit of diagnosis and treatment is the couple. Rather, they encourage women to meet together in groups and through discussion and the assignment of mastubatory exercises to take responsibility for their own sexuality. Hite (1976) and others have also objected to the view that women who cannot have an orgasm in intercourse (that is, without direct clitorial stimulation) are other than typical and normal. They insist that it is sexist to suppose that women should find intercourse as enjoyable as the more direct forms of stimulation. In these emphases, they follow behavioral approaches to sexual therapy rather than Masters and Johnson's approach.

Secularization and Amalgamation

Although there are still strong networks of

---

[12]*Editors' Note*. While behavior therapists exerted virtually no influence on the early development of *family* therapy, their contributions in the past decade have been enormous and their influence pervasive (see, e.g., Barton and Alexander, Chapter 11; Gordon and Davidson, Chapter 14).

therapists loyal to one or another pioneer, particularly in the family therapy and sex therapy areas, the enormous majority of marriage, family, and sex therapists today are trained in secular settings—that is, in programs which impartially have them read all of the current books rather than only one set. Perhaps the university or agency will invite Haley or Bowen or Satir or Stuart or Masters for a special workshop and for a period of weeks everyone is a convert to that philosophy. These men and women are charismatic and articulate. But after a series of such appearances there tends to be a general leveling out.

One of the major agents of secularization has been the American Association of Marriage Counselors. From its inception it was multidisciplinary and eclectic. In the early '60s many of the movers and shakers in the family therapy movement were invited to address the annual meetings of the organization. Ackerman, Bell, Satir, Sherman, Warkentin, and others made clinical presentations. So also did Masters and Johnson, although the cause of general amalgamation with the sex therapy field was set back at least a decade by AAMC's short-sighted rejection of the application of these two giants for membership. It seems that neither of them had received any training as relationship counselors and the committee on membership could not see any reason to make an exception in their case. (This was prior to the publication of their 1970 book and resulted in their refusing to make any further presentations to the group or to respond to later invitations to resubmit their applications.)

On the other hand, several of the leading family therapists did join, including Ackerman, Jackson, and Wynne. In October of 1964 discussions were held with the board of *Family Process* concerning an amalgamation which would involve the AAMC joining as a third co-sponsor of the journal. The offer was refused and it became clear that while a few of the board of the organization were free to join AAMC if they wished, the majority could see no reason to do so (Humphrey, 1978).

In 1970 AAMC decided to change its name to reflect the increasing interest of its members in family therapy and became the American Association of Marriage and Family Counselors

(AAMFC).

Meanwhile, the American Association of Sex Educators and Counselors (AASEC) was formed in 1967 with Patricia Schiller as its head. It became the first organization to set up standards of certification for sex therapists in 1972 (AASEC, 1973) and granted the first certificates the following year. In 1975 AASEC expanded its name and its image by becoming the American Association of Sex Educators, Counselors, Therapists (AASECT). This name change was of symbolic significance in that many from psychiatry and psychology saw themselves as *therapists* and found the term "counselor" to have connotations which evoked images of folksy advice givers.

Not to be outdone, in 1978 the American Association of Marriage and Family Counselors became the American Association for Marriage and Family Therapy.

In the midst of all of this organizing and relabeling, in 1977 a subgroup of the *Family Process* editors and friends organized (presumably in self-defense) into the American Family Therapy Association (AFTA). Its first officers were Murray Bowen, president; John Spiegel, vice-president; Gerald Berenson, executive vice-president; James Framo, secretary; Geraldine Spark, treasurer. At the present writing it is suffering birth pangs related to the fact that many of the group it seeks to represent feel that no such organization is needed, having got along without one for so many years.[13]

It is not clear as to what he future will bring, but AAMFT made a major breakthrough when it became recognized by the United States Department of Health, Education, and Welfare as the official agency designated to establish standards for certification of training programs in the

---

[13]*Editors' Note*. If we had to identify *the* single major issue that provoked the most heated controversy at the first meeting of AFTA in Chicago, April, 1979, it was whether AFTA should aim, in part, toward becoming a standard-setting, accreditation-conferring body or exist merely as a professional interest group. In fact, at least one straw vote on this issue showed that the approximately 150 charter members attending the meeting were split somewhat, though the majority opinion clearly favored the interest group option. At the second meeting of AFTA, March 1980, this group leaning was even more pronounced.

field of marriage and family therapy.[14]

Whether or not any of these organizations amalgamate, the field itself is coalescing. Specialities remain and may even proliferate, but it is increasingly true that the core curricula in training programs of all kinds will require competence in marriage, in family, and in sexual areas. As the number of states requiring licenses to practice marriage and family therapy spreads, the standards will become even more uniform.

In 1970 Olson broke new ground by surveying the history and status of both marriage counseling and family therapy in a single article. So far as we know, the present chapter is the first to survey marriage counseling, marital therapy, family therapy, and sexual therapy in a single treatment. Our view is that the present volume signifies an important stage in the continuing integration of these major historical forces at both theoretical and pragmatic levels.

REFERENCES

Ackerman, N.W. The unity of the family. *Archives of Pediatrics*, 1938, 55, 51-62.

Ackerman, N.W. *The Psychodynamics of Family Life*. New York: Basic Books, 1958.

Ackerman, N.W. The emergence of family diagnosis and treatment: a personal view. *Psychotherapy* 1967, 4, 125-129.

Ackerman, N.W., Beatman, F.L., & Sherman, S.N. (Eds.). *Expanding Theory and Practice in Family Therapy*. New York: Family Service Association of America, 1967.

Adler, A. The Neurotic Constitution (authorized translation by Bernard Blueck and John E. Lind). New York: Mofatt, Yard and Co., 1917.

Alexander, F. *An Empirical Study on the Differential Influence of Self-Concept on the Professional Behavior of Marriage Counselors*. Unpublished doctoral Dissertation, University of Southern California, 1968.

American Association of Sex Educators and Counselors, *Professional Training and Preparation of Sex Counselors and Sex Therapists*. Washington, D.C.: The American Association of Sex Educators and Counselors, 1973.

American Institute of Family Relations. Program for Southern California Conference on Education for Family Life at the University of Southern California, March 3, 1934. (From the Archives of the Institute)

American Institute of Family Relations. *Final Program: The 100th Conference of the American Institute of Family Relations on the Successful Family*. Oct 4 and 5, 1940 at Occidental College, Los Angeles. (From the Archives of the Institute)

American Institute of Family Relations. *Fact Sheet,* 1970. (From the Archives of the Institute)

Baber, R.E. *Marriage and the Family*. New York: McGraw-Hill Book Co., 1939.

Bateson, G., Jackson, D.D., Haley, J., & Weakland, J.H. Toward a Theory of Schizophrenia. *Behavioral Science,* 1956, 251-264.

Bell, J.E. *Family Group Therapy*. (Public Health Monograph #64, U.S. Department of Health, Education and Welfare). Washington, D.C.: U.S. Government Printing Office, 1961.

Bell, J.E. Family Group Therapy—A new treatment method for children. *Family Process,* 1967, 6, 254-263.

Bell, J.E. Preface. In N.W. Ackerman, *The Psychodynamics of Family Life*. New York: Basic Books, 1972. (Originally published in 1958.)

Bernard, L.L. The teaching of sociology in the United States. *American Journal of Sociology*, 1908, 15, 164-213.

Boszormenyi-Nagy, I., & Framo, J. (Eds.) *Intensive Family Therapy* New York: Harper and Row, 1965.

Boszormenyi-Nagy, I., & Spark, G. *Invisible Loyalties*. New York: Harper and Row, 1973.

Bowen, M. Family therapy and family group therapy. In D.H.L. Olson (Ed.) *Treating Relationships*. Lake Mills, Iowa: Graphic Publ. Co., 1976.

Bowlby, J. The Study and Reduction of Group Tension in the Family. *Human Relations,* 1949, 2, 123-128.

Bowman, H. *Marriage for Moderns*. New York: McGraw-Hill, 1942.

Bowman, H. *Marriage Education in College*. New York: Social Hygiene Association, 1949.

Brecher, E.M. *The Sex Researchers*. New York: The New American Library, 1971.

Calder-Marshall, A. *The Sage of Sex*. New York: Putnam, 1959.

Carroll, E.J., Cambor, C.G., Leopold, J.V., Miller, M.D., & Reis, W.J. Psychotherapy of Marital Couples. *Family Process,* 1963, 2, 25-33.

Clark, R. *Ellen Swallow: The Woman Who Founded Ecology*. Chicago: Follett Publishing Co., 1973.

Cooley, C.H. *Human Nature and the Social Order*. Glencoe, Ill.: Free Press, 1956. (Originally published, 1909.)

Cooley, C.H. *Social Organization*. New York: Scribner's, 1909.

Dickinson, R.L. *Human Sex Anatomy*. Baltimore: Williams and Wilkins, 1933. (Revised and expanded, 1949.)

Dickinson, R.L. & Beam, L. *A Thousand Marriages*. Baltimore: Williams and Wilkins, 1931.

Dickinson, R.L. & Beam, L. *The Single Women*. Baltimore: Williams and Wilkins, 1934.

Dicks, H.V. Concepts of Marital Diagnosis and Therapy as Developed at the Tavistock Family Psychiatric Clinic, London, England. In E.M. Nash, L. Jessner, D.W. Abse (Eds.), *Marriage Counseling in Medical Practice*. Chapel Hill: University of North Carolina Press, 1964.

Dreikurs, R. *The Challenge of Parenthood*. New York: Duell, Sloan, and Pearce, 1948.

Dreikurs, R. Counseling for family adjustment. *Individual*

[14]*Editors' Note*. In 1978, the American Association for Marriage and Family Therapy (AAMFT) established a ten-member Commission on Accreditation for Marriage and Family Therapy Education. To aid in the Commission's work, the AAMFT also created a National Advisory Committee on Standards for Education and Training. Of the 21 members of this Advisory Committee, as of October 1979, ten were charter members of the American Family Therapy Association (AFTA). This active and extremely significant collaboration between nationally eminent members of these two organizations hopefully will facilitate a major ongoing impact upon the future direction and substance of training in the field of marriage and family therapy.

Psychology Bulletin, 1949a, 7, 119-137.

Dreikurs, R. Psychotherapy through child guidance. *Nervous Child,* 1949b, *8,* 311-328.

Dreikurs, R. Technique and dynamics of multiple psychotherapy. *Psychiatric Quarterly,* 1950, *24,* 788-799.

Dreikurs, R. Family Group Therapy in the Chicago Community Child Guidance Center. *Mental Hygiene,* 1951, 35, 291-301.

Dubois, P. [*The Psychoneuroses and Their Moral Treatment*] (S.E. Jelliffe and W.A. White Eds. and trans.). New York: Funk and Wagnalls Co., 1907.

Duvall, E.M. *Building your Marriage.* (Public Affairs Pamphlet No. 113). New York: Public Affairs Committee, Inc., 1946.

Eisenstein, V.W. (Ed.), *Neurotic Interaction in Marriage.* New York: Basic Books, 1956.

Ellis, H. *Studies in the Psychology of Sex.* New York: Random House, 1936.

Flugel, J.C. *The Psycho-analytic Study of the Family.* London: Hogarth Press, 1921.

Folsom, J.K. *The Family and Democratic Society.* New York: John Wiley and Sons, 1943.

Freud, S. [*Recommendations for Physicians on the Psychoanalytic Method of Treatment*] (J. Riviere, trans.), Zentralblatt, Bd. II. Reprinted in Sammlung, Vierte Folge, 1912.

Freud, S. *General Introduction to Psychoanalysis.* New York: Liveright, 1915.

Freud, S. [The transformation of puberty] In A.A. Brill (Ed. and trans.). *The Basic Writings.* New York: The Modern Library, 1938.

Fromm, E. *Escape from Freedom.* New York: Farrar and Rinehart, 1941.

Fromm, E. *Man for Himself.* New York: Rinehart and Co., 1947.

Fromm-Reichmann, F. *Principles of Intensive Psychotherapy.* Chicago: University of Chicago Press, 1950.

Glover, E. *The Technique of Psycho-Analysis.* New York: International Universities Press, 1955.

Goodman, E.S. Marriage Counseling a Science: Some Research Considerations. *The Family Coordinator,* 1973, *22,* 111-116.

Green, B.L. Introduction: A multi-operational approach to marital problems. In B.L. Green (Ed.), *The Psychotherapies of Marital Disharmony.* New York: The Free Press, 1965.

Green, B.L., Broadhurst, B.P., & Lustig, N. Treatment of Marital Disharmony: The Use of Individual, Concurrent, and Cojoint Sessions as a "Combined Approach." In B.L. Green (Ed.), *The Psychotherapies of Marital Disharmony.* New York: The Free Press, 1965.

Groves, E.R. & Groves, G.H. *The Contemporary American Family.* Chicago: J.B. Lippincott Co., 1947.

Guerin, P.J., Jr., Family therapy: the first twenty-five years. In P.J. Guerin, Jr. (Ed.), *Family Therapy: Theory and Practice.* New York: Gardner, 1976.

Guerney, B.G., Jr., Filial Therapy: Description and Rational. *Journal of Consulting Psychology,* 1964, *28,* 303-310.

Guerney, B.G., Jr., *Relationship Enhancement.* San Francisco: Josey-Bass, 1977.

Gurman, A.S. Marital Therapy: Emerging Trends in Research and Practice. *Family Process,* 1973, *12,* 45-54.

Haley, J. Toward a theory of pathological systems. In G. H. Zuk and I. Boszormenyi-Nagy (Eds.), *Family Theory and Disturbed Families.* Palo Alto: Science and Behavior Books, 1971.

Haley, J. Development of theory: a history of a research project (Original, 1961). In C.E. Sluzki, and D.C. Ransom (Eds.), *Double Bind: The Foundation of a Communicational Approach to the Family.* New York: Grune and Stratton, 1976.

Hirschfeld, Magnus *Geschlechtskunde.* (5 Volumes). Stuttgart: J. Püttman Verlag, 1930.

Hirschfeld, Magnus, *Sexual Pathology: A Study of Derangements of the Sexual Instinct* (Original in 1932). (Authorized Translation by Jerome Gibbs.) New York: Emerson Books, Inc. 1940.

Hite, S. *The Hite Report.* New York: Macmillan, 1976.

Horney, K. *The Neurotic Personality of Our Time.* New York: Norton, 1937.

Horney, K. *New Ways In Psychoanalysis.* New York: Norton, 1939.

Hoenig, J. Dramatic personae: Selected biographical sketches of 19th century pioneers in sexology. In J. Money and H. Musaph (Eds.), *Handbook of Sexology Vol. I.* New York: Elsevier, 1978.

Humphrey, F.G. Presidential Address for American Association for Marriage and Family Therapy. Houston, Texas, (Oct.), 1978.

Jackson, D.D. Family interaction, family homeostasis, and some implications for cojoint family therapy. In J. Masserman (Ed.), *Individual and Family Dynamics.* New York: Grune and Stratton, 1959.

Jackson, D.D., Riskin, J., & Satir, V.M. A Method of Analysis of a Family Interview. *Archives of General Psychiatry,* 1961, *5,* 321-339.

Jacobson, N.S. & Margolin, G. *Marital Therapy: Strategies Based on Social Learning and Behavioral Exchange Principles.* New York: Brunner/Mazel, 1979.

Jacobson, N.S. & Martin, B. Behavioral marriage therapy: current status. *Psychological Bulletin,* 1976, *83,* 540-556.

Jung, C. The Association Method. *The American Journal of Psychology,* 1910, *21,* 219-269.

Kaslow, F.W. The history of family therapy: A kaleidiscopic overview. *Marriage and Family Review,* 1979, in press.

Kinsey, A.C., Pomeroy, W.E., & Martin, C.E. *Sexual Behavior in the Human Male.* Philadelphia: W.B. Saunders Co., 1948.

Kinsey, A.C., Pomeroy, W.B., Martin, C.F., & Gebhard, P.H. *Sexual Behavior in the Human Female.* Philadelphia: W.B. Saunders Co., 1953.

Kopp, M.E. Marriage Counseling in European Countries: present status and trends. *Journal of Heredity,* 1938, *29,* 153-160.

Knox, D. *Marriage Happiness: A Behavioral Approach to Counseling.* Champaign, Ill.: Research Press, 1971.

Kubie, L.S. Psychoanalysis and marriage: Practical and theoretical issues. In V.W. Eisenstein (Ed.), *Neurotic Interaction in Marriage.* New York: Basic Books, 1956.

Laidlaw, R.W. The psychotherapy of marital problems. In V.W. Eisenstein (Ed.), *Neurotic Interaction in Marriage.* New York: Basic Books, 1956.

Landis, J.T. & Landis, M.G. *The Marriage Handbook.* New York: Prentice-Hall, 1948.

Landis, P.H. *Your Marriage and Family Living.* New York: McGraw Hill Book Co., 1946.

Lederer, W.J. & Jackson, D.D. *The Mirages of Marriage.* New York: Norton, 1968.

Lidz, T., Cornelison, A., Fleck, S., & Terry, D. The intrafamilial environment of schizophrenic patients: II marital schism and marital skew. *American Journal of Psychiatry,* 1957, *114,* 241-248.

LoPiccolo, J., & LoPiccolo, L. *Handbook of Sex Therapy.* New York: Plenum Press, 1978.

Mace, D.R. Marriage guidance in England. *Marriage and*

Family Living, 1945, 7, 1-2, 5.

Mace, D.R. *Marriage Counseling*. London: Churchill, 1948.

Mace, D. & Mace, V. Marriage Enrichment—a preventative group approach for couples. In D.H.L. Olson (Ed.), *Treating Relationships*. Lake Mills, Iowa: Graphic Publishing Co., 1976.

MacGregor, R. Progress in Multiple Impact Theory. In N.W. Ackerman, F.L. Beatman, & S.N. Sherman (Eds.), *Expanding Theory and Practice in Family Therapy*. New York: Family Service Association of America, 1967.

Masters, W.H., & Johnson, V.E. *Human Sexual Response*. Boston: Little, Brown, 1966.

Masters, W.H., & Johnson, V.E. *Human Sexual Inadequacy*. Boston: Little, Brown, 1970.

Mead, G.H. *Mind, Self and Society* (C.W. Morris, Ed.). Chicago: University of Chicago Press, 1934.

Michaelson, R. *An Analysis of the Changing Focus of Marriage Counseling*. Unpublished doctoral dissertation, University of Southern California, 1963.

Midelfort, C.F. *The Family in Psychotherapy*. New York: The Blakiston Division, McGraw-Hill Book Co., Inc., 1957.

Miller, S., Nunnally, E.W., & Wackman, D.B. *Alive and Aware: Improving Communication in Relationships*. Minneapolis: Interpersonal Communication Programs, Inc., 1975.

Miller, S., Nunnally, E.W. & Wackman, D.B. Minnesota Couples Communication Program (MCCP): Premarital and Marital Groups. In D.H.L. Olson (Ed.), *Treating Relationships*. Lake Mills, Iowa: Graphic Publishing Co., 1976.

Minuchin, S. *Families and Family Therapy*. Cambridge: Harvard University Press, 1974.

Minuchin, S., Rosman, B.L., & Baker, L. *Psychosomatic Families: Anorexia Nervosa In Context*. Cambridge, Mass.: Harvard University Press, 1978.

Minuchin, S., Montalvo, B., Guerney, B.G., Rosman, B.L. & Schumer, F. *Families of the Slums*. New York: Basic Books, 1967.

Mittlemann, B. Complementary Neurotic Reactions in Intimate Relationships. *Psychoanalytic Quarterly*, 1944, 13, 479-491.

Mittlemann, B. The Concurrent Analysis of Married Couples. *Psychoanalytic Quarterly*, 1948, 17, 182-197.

Mittlemann, B. Analysis of neurotic patterns in family relationships. In V.W. Eisenstein (Ed.), *Neurotic Interaction in Marriage*. New York: Basic Books, 1956.

Moreno, J.L. *Who Shall Survive?* Washington, D.C.: Nervous and Mental Diseases Publishing Co., 1934.

Moreno, J.L. Psychodramatic Treatment of Marriage Problems. *Sociometry*, 1940, 3, 1.

Moreno, J.L. Psychodrama of a Family Conflict. *Group Psychotherapy*, 1952, 5, 20-37.

Mudd, E.H. *The Practice of Marriage Counseling*. New York: Association Press, 1951.

Mudd, E.H., Stone, A., Karpf, M.J., & Nelson, J.F. (Eds.), *Marriage Counseling: A Casebook*. New York: Association Press, 1958.

Mudd, E.H., & Fowler, C.R. The AAMC and AAMFC: Nearly Forty Years of Form and Function. In B.N. Ard, Jr., (Ed.), *Handbook of Marriage Counseling* (2nd Edition), Palo Alto: Science and Behavior Books, Inc., 1976.

Nichols, W. Doctoral Programs in Marital and Family Therapy. *Journal of Marital and Family Therapy*, 1979, 5, 23-28.

Oberndorf, C.P., Folie à Deux, *International Journal of Psychoanalysis*, 1934, 15, 14.

Oberndorf, C.P. Psychoanalysis of Married Couples. *Psychoanalytic Review*, 1938, 25, 453-475.

Olson, D.H. Marital and family therapy: Integrative review and critique. *Journal of Marriage and the Family*, 1970, 32, 501-538.

Olson, D.H. (Ed.) *Treating Relationships*. Lake Mills, Iowa: Graphic Publishing Co., Inc., 1976.

Otto, H. Marriage and family enrichment programs in North America—report and analysis. *Family Coordinator*, 1975, 24, 137-142.

Paine, R.T. *Proceedings of the National Conference on Charities and Corrections*, 1899, p. 355 (as cited in Rich, 1956, p. 18).

Peacock, E.C. The giant rests. *Family Life*, 1977, 37, 1:1.

Popenoe, P. The Foreword. In American Institute of Family Relations (Ed.), *Techniques of Marriage and Family Counseling, Vol. IV*. Los Angeles: American Institute of Family Relations, 1975.

Rich, M.E. *A Belief in People: A History of Family Social Work*. New York: Family Service Association of America, 1956.

Richie, A. Multiple Impact Therapy: An experiment. *Social Work*, 1960, 5, 16-21.

Richardson, H.B. *Patients Have Families*. New York: Commonwealth Fund, 1945.

Richmond, M.E. *Social Diagnosis*. New York: Russel Sage, 1917.

Richmond, M.E. Concern of the community with marriage. In M.E. Rich (Ed.), *Family Life Today: Papers Presented at the Fiftieth Anniversary of Family Social Casework in America*. Boston: Houghton Mifflin Co., 1928.

Rodgers, T.C. A specific parameter: concurrent psychotherapy of the spouse of analysand by the same analyst. *International Journal of Psychoanalysis*, 1965, 46, 237-243.

Sager, C.J. The Treatment of Married Couples. In S. Arieti (Ed.) *American Handbook of Psychiatry*, Vol. III. New York: Basic Books, Inc., 1966.

Sager, C.J. *Marriage Contracts and Couple Therapy*. New York: Brunner/Mazel, 1976.

Satir, V. *Conjoint Family Therapy*. Palo Alto: Science and Behavior Books, Inc., 1964.

Semans, J.H. Premature ejaculation: A new approach. *Southern Medical Journal*, 1956, 49, 353-358.

Sherman, S.N. The concept of the family in casework theory. In N.W. Ackerman, F.L. Beatman, and S.N. Sherman (Eds.), *Exploring the Base for Family Therapy*. New York: Family Service Association of America, 1961.

Silverman, M., & Silverman, M. Psychiatry inside the family circle. *Saturday Evening Post*, November, 1962, pp. 46-51.

Smith, Z.D. *Proceedings of the National Conference in Charities and Corrections*, 1890, p. 377 (as cited in Rich, 1956, p. 95).

Speck, R.V. Psychotherapy of the social network of a schizophrenic family. *Family Process*, 1967, 6, 208-214.

Speck, R.V. & Ohlan, J.L. The social networks of the family of schizophrenics. *American Journal of Orthopsychiatry*, 1967, 37, 206.

Spiegel, J.P. & Bell, N.W. The family of the psychiatric patient. In S. Arieti (Ed.), *American Handbook of Psychiatry Vol. 1*. New York: Basic Books, Inc., 1959.

Stone, A. Marriage Education and Marriage Counseling in the United States. *Marriage and Family Living*, 1949, 11, 38-39, 50.

Stone, I. *The Passions of The Mind*. New York: Doubleday and Co., 1971.

Stuart, R.B. Operant interpersonal treatment for marital

discord. *Journal of Consulting and Clinical Psychology*, 1969, *33*, 675-682.

Stuart, R.B. Behavioral remedies for marital ills. In A.S. Gurman, & D.G. Rice (Eds.), *Couples in Conflict*. New York: Jason Aronson, 1975.

Stuart, R.B. An operant interpersonal program for couples. In D.H.L. Olson (Ed.), *Treating Relationships*. Lake Mills, Iowa: Graphic Publishing Co., 1976.

Sullivan, H.S. *Conceptions of Modern Psychiatry*. Washington, D.C.: The William Alanson White Psychiatric Foundation, 1947.

Sullivan, H.S. *Interpersonal Theory of Psychiatry*. New York: Norton, 1953.

Thompson, C. *Psychoanalysis: Evolution and Development*. New York: Hermitage House, Inc., 1951.

Towle, C. Treatment of Behavior and Personality Problems in Children. The 1930 Symposium: The Social Worker. *Orthopsychiatry 1927-1948*. New York: American Orthopsychiatric Association, 1948.

Waite, F.T. Casework: Today and fifty years ago. *The Family*, 1941, *21*, 315-322.

Waller, W.W. *The Family: A Dynamic Interpretation*. New York: Dial Press, 1938.

Watson, A.S. The conjoint psychotherapy of marriage partners. *American Journal of Orthopsychiatry*, 1963, *33*, 912-922.

Watzlawick, P., Beavin, J.H., & Jackson, D.D. *Pragmatics of Human Communication*. New York: W.W. Norton, 1967.

Weiss, R.L., Hops, H., & Patterson, G.R. A framework for conceptualizing marital conflict: A technology for altering it, some data for evaluating it. In L.A. Hamerlynck, L.C. Handy, and E.J. Mash (Eds.), *Behavior Change: Methodology, Concepts and Practice*. Champaign, Ill.: Research Press, 1973.

Weiss, R.L. & Margolin, G. Assessment of marital conflict and accord. In A.R. Ciminero, K.S. Calhoun, and H.E. Adams (Eds.), *Handbook of Behavioral Assessment*. New York: Wiley, 1977.

Whitehead, A.N. & Russell, B. *Principia Mathematica*, Cambridge: Cambridge University Press, 1910.

Whitaker, C.A. Psychotherapy with couples. *American Journal of Psychotherapy*, 1958, *12*, 18-23.

Wolpe, J. *Psychotherapy by Reciprocal Inhibition*. Stanford: Stanford University Press, 1958.

Wynne, L. The study of intrafamilial alignments and splits in exploratory family therapy. In N.W. Ackerman, F.L. Beatman and S.N. Sherman (Eds.), *Exploring the Base for Family Therapy*. New York: Family Service Association of America, 1961.

Wynne, L., Ryckoff, I., Day, J. & Hirsch, S. Pseudo mutuality in the family relations of schizophrenics. *Psychiatry*, 1958, *21*, 205-220.

EDITORS' REFERENCES

Broderick, C.B. Personal communication, June, 1979.

Gurman, A.S. & Kniskern, D.P. Research on marital and family therapy: Progress, perspective and prospect. In S. Garfield & A. Bergin (Eds.), *Handbook of Psychotherapy and Behavior Change*. Second edition. New York: Wiley, 1978.

Gurman, A.S. & Kniskern, D.P. Marriage and/or family therapy: What's in a name? *American Association for Marital and Family Therapy Newsletter*, 1979, *10*, 1, 5-8.

Whitaker, C.A. *Psychotherapy of Chronic Schizophrenic Patients*. Boston: Little-Brown, 1955.

PART II

Psychoanalytic and
Object-Relations Approaches

CHAPTER 2

An Open-Systems, Group-Analytic Approach to Family Therapy

A. C. Robin Skynner, M.B., F.R.C. Psych., D.P.M.

DEVELOPMENT OF THE GROUP-ANALYTIC APPROACH

The form of my approach has many roots in a wide range of other theories and techniques. I have recently described the historical development of my work with families (Skynner, 1979a) and will only outline the sources here.

My extended family of origin includes a member diagnosed as having suffered from reactive schizophrenia. The good fortune of a greater balance of positive than negative influences in my nuclear family has led me to become a family therapist, to escape from the position in which this other member became locked. This family background is the major source of my understanding, from direct experience of dysfunction and its causes. Whether such a family history is necessary in order to practice with full effectiveness the method I shall describe remains an important and unanswered question. There is evidence for the hopeful possibility that many professionals do, in fact, possess this difficult but professionally advantageous background, but maintain an attitude of denial also characteristic

of such families, which cuts them off from this source of knowledge.

In early adulthood I became interested in the philosophy of science and in the relationship of language and thought to reality, being deeply influenced at first by Korzybski's (1933) *General Semantics*. A fortunate contact led to my being invited to join a small group of about a dozen of the most brilliant philosophers (including Russell, Ayer, Popper and Hampshire) and scientists (including Medawar, J. Z. Young, F. G. Young, and Penrose) to study the relationship between science and philosophy. Crawshay-Williams (1970), in his biography of Russell, describes me as one of the philosophers, though "a psychiatrist by profession," but at the time I was, in fact, a second-year medical student. This participation in the Metalogical Society, as it was called, provided a tremendous stimulus and clarification to my thinking. It also convinced me, by bringing me so early into contact with some of the most outstanding thinkers of the time, that the understanding I was seeking of human behavior was not already available and was not likely to be found without radical change in our whole way of thinking. Though I naturally did not understand then how important they were later to prove to our understanding of the functioning of family systems, the ideas underlying Russell's (Whitehead and Russell, 1910) "Theory of Types" (which I had already encountered in Korzybski's similar idea of "levels of abstraction") particularly intrigued me. Also, I was deeply impressed with the way in which the limitations of the observer had been "included in the equation" in modern physics (as in Einstein's Theories of Relativity and Heisenberg's Uncertainty Principle), yet neglected so completely in psychology and psychiatry, where the prejudices and personality limitations of the professionals seemed in large measure to determine their theoretical positions.

Basic training in both adult and child psychiatry, following on from medical qualification, led naturally towards an interest in the family as a whole. I have always worked in the fields of both adult and child psychiatry and psychotherapy and found that each illuminated the other.

An early interest in the group psychotherapy of adults, under the influence of S. H. Foulkes at the Maudsley Hospital (with whom I later underwent a group analysis and joined in practice), led to attempts to apply group methods to children, adolescents and parents (at first separately). This obliged me to face issues of hierarchy, control and the educative function of the therapist when working with children or severely disturbed persons, at a time when a neutral, interpretive stance was fashionable.

Also, while working with these artificially constituted groups, I learned to develop a constant awareness and use of the *group dynamic process*. This is perhaps the greatest difference between my own approach and schools of family therapy in the U.S.A. where, as Bowen (1978) has acknowledged, group and family therapy have developed along separate lines.

In 1962 John Elderkin Bell published a paper in a British journal which stimulated me to begin seeing families the same year. Extremely rapid change was often observed even with widely-spaced interviews. I have since read all I could regarding American family work and have taken much from all the schools there, but have received no training in family therapy. I did not visit the U.S.A. until ten years after beginning to practice family therapy. My ideas were therefore developed independently and the period of isolation may have led to a different line of evolution. Since about 1972 contact with American colleagues has led to an attempt to integrate their ideas and methods with my own.

My early interest in dynamic psychotherapy was very wide, beginning with the American neo-Freudians (Horney, Fromm, Sullivan, Thompson), and leading on to increasing acceptance of the ideas of Jung, Adler, Freud, Klein and Janet. The British object-relations school has been a particularly powerful source of understanding, and in the marital field the work of Dicks (1967) and publications of the Institute of Marital Studies (Lyons, 1973; Pincus, 1960) had developed these in a form suitable for conjoint work which it was easy to extend from the couple to the family.

During psychiatric training I also became interested in hypnosis, as well as in learning theory and the behavior modification techniques then being introduced into psychiatric treatment by the psychology department at the Maudsley. Though I soon rejected hypnosis and the naive use of a formal behavioral approach, I perceived the need for an *active* element in psychotherapy, and have always been interested in the relationship of psychodynamic ideas to learning theory, being influenced at the start by Dollard and Miller (1950) and Mowrer (1950), particularly.

When setting up the Course in Family and Marital Therapy, which later developed into the Institute of Family Therapy (London), this wide interest led me to invite, as other members of staff, a group of colleagues with an unusually broad range of orientations—psychoanalysts from the Tavistock Clinic, behaviorists from the Maudsley Hospital, group analysts from the Institute of Group Analysis, as well as two members who brought from the U.S.A. "action" techniques like "family sculpting" and "simulated families" and experience in exploring one's family of origin. The intensive work of this group together over seven years has provided an immense stimulus and help towards finding common ground and integrating the different concepts and methods. Visits to Britain of staff of the Ackerman Institute and the Philadelphia Child

Guidance Clinic, from 1972 onwards, also helped us absorb much of what we lacked of the American contributions, and visits to the U.S.A. since then have furthered this growth.

For over 20 years I have been interested in Eastern psychological ideas, with their focus on levels of attention and consciousness, techniques of meditation, etc., and have tried to find a relationship between these and Western concepts. Both my wife[1] and I have been particularly influenced by the ideas of Gurdjieff, and latterly Krishnamurti. Recent contact with the latter, which helped me to see how we constantly avoid new experience by holding onto the past, has been a crucial influence towards the greater integration of ideas I hope I have achieved in this chapter.

Contact with the Alexander Technique, in which I received lessons during my medical and psychiatric training from Wilfred Barlow (1973), a principal exponent and teacher, led to an early interest in the relationship of bodily movement to emotion, and in nonverbal communication, both so fundamental in understanding family interaction.

In the Second World War I was a pilot in the Royal Air Force and ended my active service in a Mosquito Squadron specializing in low level attacks. Watching a recent film (633 Squadron) combining elements of a number of missions by this squadron, I became aware that the experience of low-level bombing, with the need for high alertness, precise timing and accuracy, and getting in and out as quickly as possible, had profoundly influenced my family work, since I recognized the same feeling of arousal and intense alertness when leading up to a crucial intervention during therapy. (The fact that the Squadron's other function was concerned with night attacks, including dive-bombing in the dark where a navigator watched the altimeter and slapped the pilot's knee to prevent his diving into the ground, may also have been good preparation for co-therapy!)

This may have encouraged a certain style of rapid intervention and disengagement with families, whereas the different experience of maintaining a long, steady bombing run despite intense counterattack, needed for the American

high-level daylight raids, might have been better preparation for the more difficult long-term work with families producing psychotics (in which my experience is, in fact, weakest, even though indirect experience through supervision of others has helped to compensate). But I believe the *principles* enunciated here can be applied more broadly than I have been led to employ them by the peculiarities of my personality and past experience, and this should be acknowledged lest the brevity of my typical interventions be regarded as an essential feature.

HEALTH AND DYSFUNCTION IN FAMILIES

My views on the nature of healthy and unhealthy families are based on clinical and general experience, supplemented and corrected by the research studies we have available at the present time. As regards the latter, I rely particularly upon Westley and Epstein (1970), Mishler and Waxler (1968), MacGregor et al. (1964), Stabenau et al. (1965), and in particular Lewis et al. (1976).

Clinical work suggested to me the idea that families can be classified helpfully in terms of general *developmental level*. If children mature by the family facing them with, and supporting them through, a sequence of social challenges, then failure is likely to be perpetuated over generations unless there is help from outside the family. A mother lacking mothering herself, or a father lacking a firm but kindly fathering experience, will be likely to behave inappropriately when required to play these roles to which they have not been exposed, and for which they have not internalized an adequate model. Thus, families are seen as suffering from characteristic developmental failures over generations, in similar fashion to the idea of "fixation" at, or "regression" to, developmental levels in the Freudian schema.

This *by itself* is not seen as producing problems needing professional help, at least most of the time. To produce a *symptomatic* family there needs to be some stress, in addition, which the family cannot cope with because its limited level of development has not equipped it with necessary models or learning experiences.

Thus, "pathology" can have two meanings.

---

[1] Prudence Skynner, M. Inst. Fam. Ther. (London).

The first is similar to the psychoanalytic understanding of psychopathology, describing the dynamics of the family system. The second describes the decompensation of that particular system in the face of stress. Needless to say, *the family will be most likely to decompensate when faced with stresses corresponding to the multigenerational family failure in the developmental process.* And by contrast, the more completely the family has coped with the sequence of developmental challenges, the wider the range of responses it will possess and the less likelihood there will be of members' breaking down unless confronted with exceptional stresses.

This schema, developed by clinical experience, seems to guide clinical work in a useful manner, and I find this developmental concept the most valuable of all the ideas guiding my practice. The criteria to which it naturally leads are also in accordance with research findings on healthy and dysfunctional families, if one allows for the fact that the "normal" or "healthy" contrast groups in most research studies investigating mental dysfunction are not selected for optimal health in the same way that problem families are selected for evidence of disorder, but instead contain a large proportion of "midrange" families, with no evidence of being either especially healthy or especially sick. An exception to this criticism is the Timberlawn Research Foundation study (Lewis et al., 1976). As both Lewis and I were struck by the similarities between their research findings and my clinical observations at the time of publication of our books, I will summarize their conclusions, adding some details from the other studies mentioned, and just note the areas where their research corrected my own impressions.[2]

Table 1 outlines the Timberlawn findings, while Tables 2 and 3 attempt to sketch out the results of a more detailed examination of families towards the "healthy" end of the spectrum. None of these contained dysfunctional children at the time of the study but there were striking differences between the "adequate" families, who showed some "midrange" functioning but believed in the value of the family and achieved good results by much effort and struggle, and the "optimal" families, which seemed more effortless, spontaneous and joyful.

It will be seen that the characteristics of the three levels in Table 1 correspond in many ways to the three-stage process I have outlined elsewhere (Skynner, 1976), with fusion in the first stage, leading through preoccupation with boundaries and identity in the second, and an ability to move easily back and forth from closeness to distance in the third because individual identity is by then firmly established. Similarly, a parent-child coalition (usually between mother and index patient) at the first level leads on to a rigid hierarchy in the second, but develops into a flexible hierarchy in the third level, with sharing of power between the parents and with decisions reached by negotiation among all the family members.

Severely dysfunctional, chaotic, mother-centered families therefore need an activation of the father and more control and structure, even if rigid at first. Midrange families already possess structure of this kind, and need help in introducing more negotiation and sharing of parental power in their functioning.

One central feature of optimal function noted by the Timberlawn team was an *affiliative* rather than an *oppositional* attitude to others, that is, one based on trust and friendliness which evokes positive responses from others, rather than a distrustful, paranoid stance which evokes the opposite reaction. Another key observation from the research was the close association between healthy function in families and the ability to deal constructively with separation, loss and death. Indeed, this was found to be one of the most crucial distinguishing characteristics between the most healthy and all the unhealthy families; difficulty in this area was associated not only with emotional and social dysfunction, but also with physical illness of all kinds.

---

[2] *Editors' Note.* While the Timberlawn project has attracted a good deal of attention, it was not without methodological flaws and limitations. First, the sample was drawn from a white, upper-middle-class group of urban Protestants, so that generalization to other samples must be limited. Second, the Timberlawn results have not yet been replicated, making generalization even more dangerous. Third, all that the Timberlawn study in fact demonstrated were *correlations* between eight family variables and *global* measures of psychological health. To state the obvious, correlation (almost) never implies causation. Finally, the measures used in the project were, in fact, only marginally interactive, being based on rather subjective ratings of family behavior, and the Timberlawn study offered no *sequential* analyses of such behavior.

As the summary of the research shows, healthy families have an accurate perception of reality, so that their projected expectations of the behavior of others will lead them to predict accurately what others actually do. Moreover, because of the ability to deal with loss so effectively, the old expectations can be discarded easily, enabling members of healthy families to learn readily and grow through the experience of disillusion and disappointment. Because of their secure sense of identity, they will not be vulnerable to the false projected expectations of others, nor will they, having a positive attitude to loss, feel a need to bolster the illusions of others.

When the developmental level is more limited, *diffuseness of boundaries, unclear identity stance, reliance on the satisfactions of fantasy rather than reality, and difficulty in coping with loss all lead to the development of powerful projective systems that seek to preserve in unchanging form some past state of relationships, real or phantasied, and to manipulate others into behavior which will confirm this rigidly-held view of the world.*

While highly differentiated families are not vulnerable to such manipulative pressure (though they may *deliberately* pretend to conform to it for their own reasons, as where a mental health professional "humors" the psychotic who claims to be God, or bolsters the weak self-esteem of a deprived family), less differentiated individuals are readily "invaded" by such projective systems and unwittingly become part of them. In family therapy, this occurs when therapists get "sucked into the family system" (rather than joining it deliberately and consciously, keeping one foot outside it), or where co-therapists begin to reflect the marital conflict in their own behavior without insight into what is happening to them. The lower down the scale of differentiation one goes, the less value is placed on separateness, individuality, difference and growth, and the more is placed on sameness, conformity, and avoidance of change. The greatest compliments in such undifferentiated families are "you haven't changed a bit" or "he's always the same."

The main difference between "chaotic" and "midrange" families lies in this area. The former try to avoid perception of loss, change or growth altogether, locking all members in a timeless, static frozen pattern; the latter accept time and change, can move on, but only at the cost of burdening the children with the images and attachments of dead or departed relatives. Children born close to the time when grandparents die are especially likely to experience this emotional burden.

It is convenient at this point to introduce the subject of marital choice since, though social factors and such crucial personal values as mutual sexual attractiveness and shared interests obviously play a part, the mutual "fit" of the projective systems of the two partners plays an increasing role as one examines less and less differentiated families. *Each partner brings to the union expectations and fears corresponding to the level at which some aspect of their developmental process was blocked, and will seek to recreate a situation where the needed experience can be reencountered and grown through. This is the source of the tremendous potentiality of marriage, and of marital therapy, for growth.* But since both partners will be making similar demands (even if one does so covertly and the other more openly), each wanting the other to function in a perpetually gratifying parental role, the situation is fraught with difficulty, since neither can fully perform this role simultaneously even if he or she knew how to do so. And, in addition, layers of defensive function protecting against reencountering the pain originally experienced at the time of the developmental failure are acting in both parties in opposition to the straightforward revelation and gratification of the unmet needs.

This struggle of the two projective systems, both similar in some basic sense though incompatible in that each is trying to gain control of the other, will destroy the fruitful possibilities of the relationship if one system prevails too completely. The situation may be made more workable if part of the demands can be relieved by off-loading some aspect onto a child of the union, thereby transmitting the "pathology" and saving the marriage at the cost of the next generation. Or, alternatively, problems may be dealt with by projecting them out into an aspect of the suprasystem, preserving the marriage and family unit from disintegration at the cost of conflict with the environment. For example,

TABLE 1

Main differences found by Timberlawn Psychiatric Research Foundation Study (Lewis et al., 1976) in Structure and Function of Families Producing Mentally Healthy, Midrange, and Severely Dysfunctional Children

LEVEL OF FUNCTION OF CHILDREN	SEVERE DYSFUNCTION	MIDRANGE FUNCTION	HEALTHY FUNCTION
TYPES OF DISORDER	"Process" (chronic) schizophrenia; psychopathy (sociopathy)	Reactive psychosis; behavior disorders; neurosis	No evidence of psychiatric disorder; effective functioning
POWER STRUCTURE	CHAOTIC Parent-child coalition (usually between mother and index patient, father ineffective and excluded)	STRUCTURED/RIGID Rigid control, little negotiation. Parents either competing for dominance (behavior disorders) or dominant-submissive relationship (neuroses)	STRUCTURED/ FLEXIBLE Strong, equal-powered parental coalition, but children consulted and decisions through negotiation. Clear hierarchy with mutual respect
DIFFERENTIA-TION	FUSION Blurred boundaries, unclear identities, shifting roles; blaming, scapegoating, evasion of responsibility; invasiveness	SEPARATENESS THROUGH DISTANCING Identities more defined but at cost of emotional distancing, restriction of potential and of spontaneity; role stereotyping, including male/ female	CLEAR IDENTITY AND INTIMACY Identities highly defined and secure, permitting also high levels of closeness and intimacy; high individual responsibility
COMMMUNICA-TION	Vague, confused, evasive, contradictory; double-binds; mystification, imperviousness	Clearer than in severely dysfunctional, but in rigid, stereotyped way (so often superficially clearer than in healthy); impervious to new ideas; non-mutual	Open, clear, direct, frank. Lively and spontaneous; receptive and responsive to new ideas
RELATIONSHIP	OPPOSITIONAL DISTRUST, expectation of evil (betrayal, desertion); ambivalent feelings unintegrated, swings between extremes; inconsistency dealt with by denial; marriage highly unsatisfactory; split by parent/child coalition	OPPOSITIONAL Relative DISTRUST; human nature seen as basically evil, needing rigid control of self and others; repression, suppression; ambivalence not accepted, dealt with by repression and reaction formation against "bad" impulses; lack of marital satisfaction; competing or dominant/submissive roles	AFFILIATIVE TRUST; basic expectation of positive response to positive approach; warm, caring, mutual regard and responsibility. Ambivalent feelings accepted as normal. Both sides included and integrated. Mutually satisfying, complementary marital roles; sexuality mutually satisfying also

TABLE 1 (continued)			
LEVEL OF FUNCTION OF CHILDREN	SEVERE DYSFUNCTION	MIDRANGE FUNCTION	HEALTHY FUNCTION
REALITY SENSE	Reality denied; escape into fantasy satisfactions	Adequate reality sense to function effectively, but with some distortion and incongruent family "myths"	Image of self and family congruent with reality
AFFECT	Cynicism; hostility; sadism; hopelessness and despair	Hostility (behavior disorders) but without the degree of sadism in severely dysfunctional; subdued, joyless, restricted (neurotic disturbance)	Warmth, enjoyment; humor, wit; tenderness, empathy
ATTITUDE TO CHANGE, LOSS	Unable to cope with change and loss. Timeless, repetitive quality, with denial of separation and death, escape into fantasy	Change and loss faced, but with great pain and difficulty. Separation and death not really worked through; substitutes found for lost persons and feelings transferred, instead of internalization of lost person	Change, growth, separation and death all accepted realistically and losses worked through, due to: 1) strong parental coalition (in relation to older and younger generations); 2) strong, varied relationships outside family; 3) transcendent value system

TABLE 2

Main Characteristics of "Optimal" Families, in
Order of Apparent Importance

1. *Affiliative attitude* to human encounter—open, reaching-out, basically trusting (as contrasted with *oppositional*—distrust, withdrawal etc.)
2. *High respect for separateness, individuality*, autonomy, privacy (as contrasted with expectation of agreement, conformity, "speaking for others").
3. *Open, clear, frank communication* (as contrasted with confusion, evasion, restriction, etc.).
4. *Firm parental coalition*, egalitarian with shared power between parents (as contrasted with parental splits and parent/child coalitions).
5. *Control flexible, by negotiation*, within basic parent/child hierarchy (as contrasted with rigid, inflexible control and unchangeable rules).
6. *Highly spontaneous interaction*, with considerable humor and wit—"three-ring circus, but all under control" (as contrasted with rigid, stereotyped interaction).
7. *High levels of initiative* (as contrasted to passivity).
8. *Uniqueness and difference encouraged* and appreciated—liveliness, strong "characters" (as contrasted with bland, stereotyped, conformist types).

"Optimal" families could be differentiated from "adequate" families on all these characteristics except No. 7 (Initiative) to level of statistical significance. Both produced healthy children but "adequates" showed many "midrange" features.

TABLE 3
Differences in Marital and Sexual Function
Between "Adequate" and "Optimal" Families, All
Producing Healthy Children

	ADEQUATE	OPTIMAL
ROLES	Generally traditional gender roles but in rigid, stereotyped, highly role-segregated way.	Generally traditional gender roles but seemingly from choice, with rewarding, mutually pleasurable complementarity and reciprocity.
RELATION-SHIP	*Husbands* successful, aggressively work-oriented. More satisfied with lives than wives—distant and providing material but not emotional support. *Wives* generally unhappy, needy, lonely, feeling isolated from husbands and overwhelmed by children. Tending to obesity, depression and fatigue. Interests outside home limited.	*Both husbands and wives* express mutual pleasure and enjoyment with relationship and life generally. Husbands involved in work, but responsive to wife's needs, supportive and emotionally aware. Wives feel appreciated, cherished. Many, active interests outside home, though role of mother and wife central and satisfying.
SEXUALITY	Regular, generally similar frequency (about twice-weekly). Mostly satisfying to husbands. Wives generally dissatisfied (too much, too little, unpleasurable, etc.).	More variable in frequency between couples (several times weekly to twice a month) but highly, mutually pleasurable and satisfying to both partners. Pattern of long-term marital fidelity.
LEISURE	Limited involvement of couple with community.	More involvement of couple outside the home and family alone.
	Both "adequate" and "optimal" families shared very high belief and involvement in the idea of the family, and their children's activities.	

some couples avoid marital conflict by projecting a controlling, "paternal" role onto the school, subsequently collaborating to fight the school instead of each other, while the child plays parents off against the school instead of father against mother.

In either case, *therapy requires identification of the projective systems and bringing them back from whoever presents with the "complaint," whether the symptomatic child, the suffering school, or whatever, into the marriage, where help can be given towards a more constructive resolution.*

Many of the concepts outlined above help to explain why symptoms develop in one individual at a particular time, though the details are incompletely worked out. Usually they occur when parents cannot cope with a particular emotion which has been denied and excluded from awareness in a family over generations (Fisher and Mendell, 1956), when its intensity increases to a degree which threatens their defenses and so the marriage, and this overload is externalized through the projective system onto one or more other members, who then develop "symptoms." The "sick" member is usually chosen because of some special characteristic (similarity to parent or grandparent, birth at a time of stress, weakness compared with siblings, particular attachment to a parent producing vulnerability to that parent's projected emotions etc.). The individual concerned colludes in the process out of a deep, if unconscious, recognition that he is preserving the parent, the marriage or the family as a whole from disintegration, out of a motive of attachment as well as guilt. *The symptom will often be symbolic of the denied emotion* (fears of broken glass in food, expressing in a disguised way a recognition that the mother's love is mixed with a denied murderous hate), but I believe there are multiple determinants which are imperfectly understood. Many symptoms are "release" phenomena, due to breakdown of higher level control mechanisms. A "symptom" in one family ("disobedience," "violence") may be a virtue in another ("spiritedness," "toughness").

The so-called "well" siblings will be found to share the level of differentiation of the family as a whole (though they may be somewhat more differentiated, the index patient somewhat less differentiated, than the parents). *They may be nonsymptomatic because they possess more rigid defenses and so are more "sick" than the index patient in the sense of not being as open to the possibility of therapy and growth.* They are usually burdened with other projections which are high in the family hierarchy of values, but which limit their individuality and autonomy—e.g., to be successful for the family, to look after others and neglect their own lives (the latter is a particularly common pattern among mental health professionals), etc.

Severely dysfunctional families also show gender confusion, while midrange families often demonstrate gender role stereotyping. In healthy families children are perceived more accurately and allowed to develop as individuals. They do not have to carry burdens for the parents, who can function adequately without them, and indeed without each other. For healthy families, the pleasures of marriage and family life are a bonus, not an imperative need.

For the healthy family, relationships with the extended family and the outside world are like those between its members, with clear boundaries and the possibility of moving back and forth between close involvement and aloneness. Dysfunctional families tend to be overdependent on the extended family and vulnerable to disturbance in relatives, or they may maintain a rigid boundary, isolating themselves from relatives or the community (Bowen, 1978; Minuchin, 1974).

Barnhill and Longo (1978) have recently reviewed concepts regarding the family life-cycle and differences in the form of intervention demanded of the family therapist at each stage. They use a modification of Duvall's (1957) nine-stage schema as a basis. Pincus and Dare (1978) and Dare (1979) supplement these admirably from a more thoroughgoing psychoanalytic object-relations viewpoint. These are all in broad agreement with and complementary to each other, as well as being similar to my own views about the different needs of families during their life cycles (Skynner, 1976). Briefly, the first stage is one of mutual encounter, enjoyment, exploration and testing, beginning with the mutual idealization of courtship and followed by struggle and negotiation as real differences and conflicts between values are negotiated during the close contact of early marriage. During this period the partners often make good some of each other's deficits of early nurturance (or fail to meet such needs, if they are excessive, heralding increasing dissatisfaction and bitterness). The arrival of the first child profoundly changes the relationship, for instead of the former mutual nurturance and freedom both must nurture a helpless and dependent infant, the mother usually taking prime responsibility for the child, the father supporting and nurturing the mother as she does so, but whatever the arrangement both losing each other's exclusive attention.

The transition of baby to toddler, towards greater rebellion and independence, demands capacities for independence, as well as tolerance for separation, in the parents, tasks which have to be repeated in greater degree as children begin school and finally when they leave home. Similarly, at the oedipal period, as well as later at the burgeoning of adolescent sexuality and finally with courtship and marriage, the parents reencounter their own sexual conflicts and inhibitions; their ability to sustain their own sexual enjoyment as a couple, to develop new interests and turn back towards each other, as well as outwards to the wider social world, will help ensure smooth transitions of these stages for the children and the marriage.

Finally, after departure of children and retirement from employment, the final years can be as rich as any if the partners have both developed their relationship, as well as their individuality as separate persons, throughout the career-building and child-rearing period, avoiding individual or joint impoverishment by excessive investment in any one stage or task. The family and marital therapist can do much, even through simple and brief interventions, to help parents remain aware of the process as a whole, to perceive and cope with the different requirements at each stage, and to maintain a sense of balance and wholeness in their lives.

The main concepts I have emphasized are the role of the father and of a recurrent three-stage dialectical pattern in the process, beginning with the sequence of the Freudian oral/anal/genital stages (or dependency/control/sharing) in childhood, repeated in adolescence and also in early marriage, where the couple begins with a period of mutual dependency, next, faces issues of control, authority and hierarchy when the first child arrives, and, if fortunate, ends with an ability to share power. A confusion I was unable to resolve in my family book (Skynner, 1976), where I concluded from clinical experience that healthy function in families required *both* a clear hierarchy with father accorded the final power decision (a view confirmed by all previous research studies) *and* shared power between the parents, has been corrected by the Timberlawn research, demonstrating that both the views expressed in my book are correct but that they apply to families beginning from different levels of differentiation. The severely dysfunctional need the introduction of structure to bring them to midrange function, while midrange families may need the already existing structure loosened to bring about more power-sharing and negotiation with children regarding decisions.

The experience of my wife and myself working with couples groups confirms a similar sequence in the family life-cycle. Initially, the problem is dominance by the female and passivity in the male, who has to be helped to take control. The females almost invariably express a fundamental wish for this but also use every strategy to maintain control. If the outcome is successful, a period of male dominance and responsibility, reversing the earlier pattern of female dominance, leads finally on to cooperation and sharing of power between them.[3]

BASIC CONCEPTS

General Systems Theory

S. H. Foulkes (1948, 1964, 1965), a teacher who has been a major influence in the development of my own approach, worked with groups (in one of which I had my own personal group analysis) as if he understood open-systems concepts. However, he failed to communicate this understanding through his writings because he attempted to formulate it in terms of the Freudian conceptual framework to which he continued to pay formal allegiance, but which, as Beavers (1977) has pointed out, is inconsistent with open-systems ideas. My own techniques derive from this, but are based more explicitly on general systems theory.

Von Bertalanffy (1968), the main pioneer of general systems theory, helps to explain Foulkes' failure to find an adequate formulation of his methods through psychoanalytic language when he says, "American psychology in the first half of the 20th century was dominated by the concept of the reactive organism or, more dramatically, by the model of man as a robot. This conception was common to all major schools of American psychology, classical, and neo-behaviorism, learning and motivation theories, psychoanalysis, cybernetics, the concept of the brain as a computer and so forth" (p. 205).

Miller (1965) has given one of the clearest expositions of general systems theory as it applies to living systems. Like the rest of the universe, from galaxies to sub-atomic particles, living organisms are seen as part of a sequence of larger systems—family, group, community, nation, etc.—and composed of a series of ever-smaller subsystems (e.g., organs, tissues, cells, etc.). Each system has a measure of independ-

---

[3]*Editors' Note.* It is very important to emphasize here that the reader should not interpret Skynner's preceding comments as sexist or gender-biased. He is describing a healthy, evolutionary process of change in marital roles and of a balanced husband-wife power distribution. The stages in this process which he describes are based on his experience of *normative* (but obviously not, to Skynner, desirable) relationship patterns, i.e., what *typically* is true of men and women in dysfunctional marriages.

ence from the *suprasystem* of which it is a part (e.g., the individual from the family, the family from the community) but only within certain limits beyond which it must comply or suffer. The individuality of each system is maintained by its *boundary*, a region which contains and protects the parts of the system and where the transfer of information and matter/energy is restricted relative to regions internal and external to it. The communication across this boundary, as well as the coordination of the subsystems within it, is controlled by the *decider subsystem* (e.g., the government of a nation, the parents of a family, Freud's "censor," etc). Just as the boundary maintains a degree of autonomy for the system despite a general control by the suprasystem of which it is a part, so feedback loops, adjusting the functioning of the system according to its performance (like a thermostat in a heating system), maintain a general continuity of structure and function despite being "loose" enough to permit change and growth within permissible limits.

The focus in recent years on the family and its relationship to the individuals within it, as well as to the community and the helping professions outside it, has led to a recognition of the way such concepts can help us remember to visualize the *total* situation and avoid becoming lost in detail. To be effective, the family therapist must stand at the *boundary* of the family and the community or the *boundary* between the individual and the family, avoiding identification with one or the other side. From this position he can modify communication across the boundary, or the characteristics of the decider subsystem, or the feedback maintaining homeostasis so as to avoid self-destructive extremes of deviance and rebellion on the one hand or of conformity on the other, seeking to negotiate new compromise solutions which work better for the individual, the family and the community.[4]

This is perhaps only another way of saying

that, to be effective, a therapist must *remain aware of the total system and of his current place in it*. If he does not penetrate the boundary of a family or individual he can have no contact and so no understanding; yet, if he becomes "lost," identified with the projective system of the individual or the myths or paranoid fantasies of the family, he is as helpless to improve their adaptation as they are themselves. A systems approach does not necessarily involve bringing people into physical proximity, though working with actual groups does indeed have great advantages through the therapeutic potential a well-managed group session can manifest; the essential feature lies in the therapist's awareness and attitude, whereby he never gets completely lost in detail but constantly remembers, with part of his mind, the interconnectedness of the whole—individuals, family and community —thereby straddling the boundaries of all of them. In a systems approach the only new system present is in the mind of the therapist, a "model" of the interrelated systems which has been there before him all the time, but which the "tunnel vision" caused by his theoretical stance has made him neglect.[5]

Developmental Process

The concepts already outlined would apply to a universe of endless, repetitive process in perpetual motion where, in the long run, nothing changed. But one certain fact about living organisms is that they are programmed to self-destruct and cease existence as separate entities after a limited duration, if not destroyed by the environment earlier. Only the *group* can perpetuate itself, not the individual, though it does so through parts of some of the individuals detaching themselves and beginning the process again.

This continual reproductive process requires that the information needed to organize the new individual and render it capable of functioning with the relative independence of a system and in relation to its environment be programmed

[4]*Editors' Note.* In addition to the concept of boundaries, the core concepts of general systems theory (GST) also include the notions of: (a) *organization* (wholeness, boundaries and hierarchies); (b) *control* (homeostasis, feedback); (c) *energy* (entropy, negentropy); and (d) *time and space* (structure, process/function). As Steinglass (1978) has made clear, GST concepts emerge with different degrees of emphasis in the major theories of family therapy.

[5]*Editors' Note.* As this discussion suggests, general systems theory has produced some clinically useful *principles* for working with families. On the other hand, GST has led to the development of few, if any, specific technical innovations.

into its structure. The basic information is, of course, provided by the genetic program and if I say no more about this it is only because one can do nothing about it as regards an individual in trouble who comes to a professional for help. The second source of information is by modification of this basic program through *direct* interaction with the environment, whereby the responses come to fit the latter more closely through the process we call "learning." This second process increases in importance as we ascend the evolutionary ladder, giving a greater plasticity to behavior. Man has the further possibility of transmitting information by *symbolic* communication and storing it in permanent form available to the group independently of the decay and dissolution of the individual systems composing it, permitting thereby an exponential growth in the total store of information available to mankind.

The principal source from which each individual receives all three of these inputs is the family, which provides all of the genetic program, much of the second and a good deal of the third, the second and especially the third coming increasingly from the school and wider aspects of the social suprasystem after the first five years of the individual's life. The conditions governing the modifiable parts of this transmission process within the matrix of the family are, therefore, of fundamental importance to anyone seeking to have a beneficial effect upon the developmental process or to remedy deficiencies at a later date.

Some avoidable dangers at the genetic level of transmission are prevented by the prohibition of incestuous relationships, which would increase the likelihood of the appearance of disorders controlled by recessive genes.

The second form of transmission, that of nonsymbolic learning, requires some awareness in the family therapist of developmental stages through which the child passes, since aid can be given towards mastering the sequence of developmental tasks only if they are presented when his biological growth has reached the right stage, where attainment of preceding tasks has been successfully completed, and where parents and others give the right kind of help and support.

The first challenge, occupying the first year

or so, demands a transition from the stage where both the self and others are experienced in fragmented form and are not distinguished clearly (the Kleinian "paranoid-schizoid position" of "part-objects," "splitting" and "projection") to the beginnings of a more integrated existence where the infant distinguishes a boundary between itself and others, becomes aware of and able to cope with the conflict and pain of love and hate experienced simultaneously, and has the first experiences of the caring figure as a *whole* person towards whom concern, rather than wholly selfish demands, can be felt (Klein's "depressive position" of "whole-object relationships," containment of ambivalence, and the beginning of gratitude rather than greed and envy).

During this period the main care-giving figure needs to maintain a consistent, reliable presence and to be sensitively attuned and responsive to the child's needs, if the child is to develop a basic trust and confidence in itself and others. The appropriate gratification and support need to be maintained to a lessening degree through later stages since the awareness of separateness and differentiation of the "depressive position" brings with it a recognition of being vulnerable, precarious and dependent, necessarily absent from the previous omnipotent undifferentiated state.

Increasing appropriate "failure" of the caregiver is necessary for differentiation to proceed; too little frustration gives no incentive towards growth and independence; too much too soon can bring a catastrophic sense of inadequacy and depression or, ultimately, a retreat to the illusory safety of fusion and chaos.

A second developmental task, requiring the acceptance of a suprasystem which is not there just to gratify, but which demands in return a measure of social conformity, occupies roughly the second and third year, and is played out in the areas of sphincter control (hence the Freudian "anal" stage), speech and muscular activity—all functions through which the child is developing the possibility of control and choice. This stage requires a setting of firm boundaries whereby new powers and possibilities can be safely tested out within limits requiring that the wider social system be heeded and adapted to. If the mother (or primary care-giving figure) is central in the first stage, the father (or first rival for the original care-giver's attention) is central to the second, so that the traditional family roles of male and female parent are appropriate to the fulfillment of these developmental tasks.[6]

The fourth and fifth years show an increasing preoccupation with the sexuality of the self and of others and with the Freudian "oedipal" romance. It is played out in relation to the *couple* rather than to father or mother alone, and its successful resolution requires that the parental couple has a satisfying marital and sexual relationship which is relatively harmonious and not vulnerable to the child's jealousy and attempts to disrupt it. This makes it possible for the child to have a safe flirtation with the parent of the opposite sex, confirming it to gender-appropriate responses and a feeling of sexual worth. The child also learns to cope with jealousy and exclusion, to witness a balance of true sharing and separateness between the couple and eventu-

ally, around the age of six, to see that it cannot mate with the parent. This leads the child to aim, coinciding with the move to school, for substitute satisfactions in the wider social world and the ultimate attainment of a mate of its own.

In outline, failures in the *first* stage are associated, when they occur earlier, before paranoid-schizoid functioning is transcended, with schizophrenic or borderline states, and when they occur later, with problems around attachment and separation or depressive and manic-depressive functioning. The *second* stage is associated more with obsessional-compulsive states and other disorders where there is endless preoccupation with control, such as tics, stuttering, soiling and so on. The third stage is associated more with hysterical disorders and problems of potency and achievement, both sexual and otherwise.

The relationships with others the child internalizes during this sequence provide "models" for dealing with its social world. By "computing" with these recorded data, predictions are made regarding new situations, which, in normal circumstances, are constantly revised in the light of increasing actual experience, though in ordinary life we are not usually aware of this as an internal process any more than we are conscious of the cerebral processes mediating our vision. We simply have expectations that people will behave in certain ways in certain circumstances and are surprised and disappointed when they do not. Unless something goes wrong with the process, the expectations are modified through learning so that the predictions are more accurate at the next encounter.

Projective Systems

This set of learned expectations regarding the social behavior of others, as well as the expectations others are assumed to have of ourselves, comprises at any given time the projective system of each individual. This is experienced not as something internal being projected outwards but rather as the way the world is or should be.

From this point of view, the projective systems of individuals showing "psychopathology" differ in that they have not completed the sequence of developmental tasks outlined above, and instead of moving step-by-step towards so-

---

[6]The careful wording of this sentence has been chosen to indicate that *at least* as long as the child begins its life within the mother's body and is suckled by her, the biological, physical facts determine the mother's role as the *primary* attachment figure and the father's role as the first intruder into this exclusive dyad, the initial protector of both and guardian of the family boundary, and later a bridge for the child between its initial attachment to the mother and its final independent role in the community. Nevertheless, this situation would not necessarily apply with an adopted child, and both nurturant and controlling functions are obviously mediated by both sexes even if in different proportions by different couples. Such evidence as we have suggests that the mental health and effective development of children are best facilitated where there is a balance between clear differentiation of the two parental roles, on the one hand, and overlap and sharing between them, on the other (Westley and Epstein, 1970). But as I have discussed elsewhere (Skynner, 1976), the conflict and uncertainty among present evidence about which male/female, maternal/paternal characteristics are biologically determined, which are "shaped" by differential parental encouragement, and which are accentuated by general imitation of cultural patterns, are such that we must await, and remain open to, further evidence. My own views on this matter have changed so rapidly in recent years that I usually find myself disagreeing with what I write almost before the ink is dry, but the benefit that this changed understanding has brought to me personally, to my marriage and family relationships, and to my professional work has been so great that I believe present social changes herald the possibility of a new and more effective balance between the sexes which will enrich both. *Perhaps our main mistake lies in the very attempt to define these roles in some stable, permanent way rather than, as in a healthy marriage and family, to remain permanently (and uncomfortably!) open to the developmental experience and expansion of consciousness that these relationships automatically make available to us, if we can bear to accept them.*

cial expectations which correspond to the real adult world have got stuck with inappropriate expectations, or rather with expectations that may have been appropriate in childhood. Thus, the mentally disordered adult may still expect that mother (and so the world) will always gratify (or will never gratify); that father (and so the world) will always be punitive (or will always be outwitted and defeated); that the parental couple (and so the world, and so also his or her children) cannot tolerate a relationship that excludes others and so cannot experience commitment and full gratification and so on.

Moreover, the person so afflicted has not been able to find the experience to help him complete his developmental tasks from some other source and, as the gap widens with age between what he has learned to cope with socially and what society expects of him at each stage, attempts to relate socially become increasingly unsuccessful, frustrating and painful, leading towards increasing withdrawal from real involvement and layer upon layer of defensive functioning to protect the self-esteem and secure alternative gratifications, particularly through fantasy.

Thus, any form of therapy derived from psychoanalytic principles must *at least* include the provision of a social situation where the patient can develop sufficient trust in the safety of the situation and in the intentions of the therapist to help him find, face and surmount unfinished developmental tasks, for him to stop sheltering behind the defensive system and expose the expectations of self and others he originally learned and never transcended. This is the development of transference in individual therapy, the development of multiple transferential relationships in group psychotherapy, and the opening up of deeper levels of mutual expectation and demand in conjoint marital and family therapy, where the projective systems are already fully developed but hidden and denied.

Sexuality

A further complication is introduced by the fact of sexuality whereby, in man as in all more complex forms of life, male and female varieties of the species must combine to create new organisms to replace those that die, and so maintain the species as a group.

From this sexual fusion of the parents comes difference and separateness, since the fact that children derive half their genetic programming from each parent ensures diversity despite continuance of the basic pattern. Where the child is cared for by two parental figures, psychological diversity is also ensured by the internalization of parts of the two parental psyches to form a new combination in the psyche of the child, which will be harmonious if the parental relationship is positive or, alternatively, perpetuate parental struggles in neurotic conflict.

Developmentally, sexuality seems central to the formation, growth and differentiation of the family in various ways:

(a) It draws a couple together to reproduce.
(b) It triggers the production of children.
(c) It facilitates bonding of the parental pair, making their relationship *primary* and so, by excluding the children and making parent-child relationships secondary, motivates the children to mature and leave home since their exclusion and consequent jealousy lead them ultimately to reject the parents as hoped-for sexual partners and determine them to have the same pleasure themselves outside the family.

In this way infantile sexuality, oedipal jealousy, and the incest taboo combine to facilitate separation and individuation. For this process to function there must clearly be a "right amount of sex" between parents and children. Too much (overt incest) allows the donkey to eat the carrot, as it were, while too little (parental anxiety over, and so denial of, sexual attraction between parent and child) takes the carrot away altogether. In either case the motivation towards maturation is removed.

For a father to desire his daughter sexually and vice versa (or a mother her son), yet also to keep the boundary and feel the pain that they cannot marry, is also a constant reminder of mortality. By contrast, overt incest, and complete denial of oedipal sexuality are partially motivated by denial of the facts of growth, separation and death. Thus, an inability on the part of the parents to deal with loss may lead to excessive sexual involvement between parent and child, or unrealistic denial of its presence; in either case this makes a smooth transition towards enjoyable adult sexuality difficult. Since the choice of mate is strongly influenced by similarities to the parents or siblings, whether at a conscious or unconscious level, and since excessive anxiety surrounding the oedipal romance will thereby be associated with sexuality with the spouse, inhibitions and repressions set up to deal with problematic aspects of the parent-child sexual attraction will lead to avoidance of sexual feelings in the marriage as well. Those who have experienced a pleasurable and safe sexual responsiveness towards and from their parents are, by contrast, free to choose a mate with all the desirable and erotic characteristics of each or both parents, of attractive siblings or other relatives, without confusing this with incest.

Lastly, the fact of *two* parents raises additional possible problems and potentialities, since ways have to be found to handle decision-making in the family system. Miller (1965) describes the decider subsystem as "the essential critical subsystem which controls the entire system, causing its subsystem and components to co-act, without which there is no system" (p. 204), and later, "if there are multiple parallel deciders, without a hierarchy that has subordinate and superordinate deciders, there is not one system but multiple ones" (p. 218). Thus, if the family is to exist as an integrated system, as a whole rather than as two fragments, either some hierarchy is essential as between male and female parent (as well as between parents and children) *or* some capacity to share authority in some kind of effective collaboration has to be developed, and the child will internalize whatever solution is found as part of its own inner organization. We will return to this issue when we come to consider what determines "normality" and "abnormality" in family systems.

All that I have said refers to a "family" in the usual biological sense of that term as a reproductive unit of human society. But obviously many of these developmental functions can occur in other social units concerned with the upbringing of children, such as families where the children are all adopted, or single-parent families where other relatives or family contacts are used in fact or fantasy to replace the function of the missing parent. I have described elsewhere (Skynner, 1976, pp. 62-63) an interesting example of the working out of an unresolved oedipal conflict by a boy in a children's home, where the house-parents were helped to understand the roles they needed to play. But what I have said does imply that engagement in the functions required by the child-rearing task are vital to the psychological growth of a couple, as individuals as well as in their capacity for relationship. The so-called "child-free" couple, where that is a deliberate option, risks remaining a "couple of children."[7]

GENERAL PRINCIPLES OF THERAPY

Clarification and Change of Structure

This factor must be considered first because it may be relevant even to determining who should be invited to attend the first interview, as well as to persuading them to come and to setting up the structure in the interview room itself. The referral letter or other first contact may, for example, indicate that the father is being excluded or is excluding himself, or that a grandparent living with the family is a crucially powerful influence. In such situations it is vital to include, or to work towards including, the dominant and the excluded figures when the preliminary arrangements are made by letter, telephone or home visit, if encouragement of communication between key figures is to be possible at all.

Having brought the key figures together, sometimes it may be enough merely to facilitate communication among them. But even this process will usually involve some change in structure of the established hierarchy and rules of family interaction. The therapist may have to interrupt a parent who speaks for others, draw out a withdrawn and silent member, or control (or stimulate the parents to control) a disruptive child who is making constructive discussion impossible. Such interventions will not only reflect features in the family structure contributing to

---

[7]*Editors' Note.* We want to emphasize that what Skynner is saying here should be taken literally, i.e., that such couples *risk* "remaining a 'couple of children,' " but that being child-free does not *ipso facto* mean that a married couple *is* a "couple of children."

the dysfunction, but will often tend to change family functioning for the better in the long-term, even if such interventions are made only to improve communications in the interview.

Interventions may also be aimed more deliberately and systematically at changing the family structure, making this the main feature of the process, as in the work of Minuchin (1974) or Bowen (1978). Intergenerational boundaries may be more clearly drawn, giving parental and sibling subgroups the right to separate lives; an overly dominating mother may be silenced in order to activate a too-passive father, or vice versa; a referral agency seeking to impose its values on a family inappropriately may be corrected by declining to accept its judgment of the situation. In all such decisions the actual authority of the therapist and of the agency, their place in the hierarchy vis-à-vis the family and referrer, will be relevant to success or failure.

Clarifying Communication

Beyond considering structural issues sufficiently to ensure that the family attend together, often little more will be necessary than to facilitate communication among the members, loosening the boundaries so that a freer exchange is possible, or sometimes establishing clearer boundaries so that privacy is respected and separateness is allowed.

Teaching New Skills, Educating and Providing New Learning Experiences

In addition to changing the structure and improving communication, the therapist may note that some abilities have not been acquired in the course of development. The mother may have lacked mothering in her own childhood; the father may have had no father himself and be unable to take a position of authority; both parents may be unable to share with one another or children may be unable to play. The therapist may in such cases provide the appropriate missing experience, sometimes by formal behavioral techniques, more often by providing a "model" of nurturance, authority, sharing or playing which the family members can experience and

internalize by identification. Such modeling may occur sometimes by conscious demonstration, sometimes automatically through the natural and spontaneous behavior of the therapist's just being the kind of person he or she is. Three simple examples have been given elsewhere (Skynner, 1979). However, I believe one may often be not only teaching new skills during such transactions, but also helping patients reconnect internally with good experiences they have actually received earlier but dissociated themselves from out of anxiety or fear of pain (e.g., fear of acknowledging the good mothering they received because it is connected with the pain of the mother's inadequately mourned death; anxiety over sexual pleasure because it was associated with parental jealousy and rejection). The model provided by the therapist may reassure and support the patient towards reconnection with such vital experiences which appear to be missing but are in fact already internalized, though unavailable because denied.[8]

Teaching new skills gives the family *specific* abilities members lack. But families may also be helped towards learning from experience in a more general way, perhaps by seeing the value of questioning established patterns and by sharing the therapist's pleasure and enjoyment at learning and encountering new experiences.

Facilitating Differentiation

The above therapeutic mechanisms may involve only slight changes in a family's functioning, sufficient to prevent a symptom or change a vicious, descending spiral into an ascending one, even though the new pattern, once achieved, may remain as static as the old. Most types of short-term intervention, particularly behavioral methods, are aimed at limited results of this kind which, in my experience, are all that the majority of patients are seeking if one is dealing equally with the whole range of socioeconomic status.

A smaller proportion is, however, interested

---

[8]*Editors' Note.* Skynner is making an enormously important and provocative point here: that even apparently limited "behavioral" changes may produce profound intrapsychic change. While we are inclined to agree with Skynner, most psychoanalysts, we trust, would not. In any case, this hypothesis represents an exciting and researchable issue.

more in growth and development in a general sense than in relief of discomfort and distress alone, and these more reflective families may welcome longer-term psychotherapy (more often analytic in character) aimed at *facilitating differentiation.* This is perhaps less generally popular because it tends to involve additional suffering, even if temporary, rather than a mere increase of comfort. Couples who venture beyond therapy aimed at the presenting problems alone are likely to encounter periods of increased conflict, painful feelings of loss and aloneness, perhaps actual temporary separation or plans to divorce, sometimes even extramarital affairs threatening their relationship, which only a detached outsider can recognize as steps towards their differentiation as separate, independent persons, enjoying but no longer simply "needing" each other.

No effort is made to encourage the first type of family towards the growth orientation characteristic of the second, except to the extent that the achievement of limited goals is impossible without some measure of "growth" they would otherwise not seek. If anything, my attitude towards deeper exploration than is required for the task is quite discouraging and, unlike many psychoanalytic colleagues who tend to see psychotherapy as a good thing in itself, I tend if anything to push people away from therapy, to make them fight for it and prove their motivation. Nevertheless, the fact that I am *personally* committed to growth and use all situations, including my professional work, for this purpose may *indirectly* stimulate a growth perspective even when I am overtly discouraging it. Indeed, like other forms of "modeling" influence, it may have a more profound effect than deliberate attempts to promote the value of insight.

Fostering Affiliative Rather Than Oppositional Attitudes

Persons and families persistently troubled or in trouble tend to show a history of real deprivation, even if superficially "over-indulged" or "spoiled." The deprivation leads to what I call a "philosophy of scarcity," with expectations that there will not be enough for everyone, that one must hang on tightly to what one possesses, grab as much as one can and defend oneself fiercely against others who are trying to do the same.

In psychotherapy, particularly when it is long-term and aimed at growth and differentiation rather than amelioration of symptoms alone, there occurs in successful cases a quite sudden "flip" when it becomes recognized that the attitude described above is a self-fulfilling prophecy, and that reality can be totally different if one chooses to view it differently. Patients suddenly begin to operate, when this happens, according to what I call a "philosophy of plenty," a similarly self-fulfilling prophecy where there is more than enough for everyone and one may as well give everything away since one will get even more back, automatically. Trust replaces distrust. Envy, meanness and angry demand give way to generosity, kindness and giving others room to be, space to move and time to change. The person, marriage or family changes totally overnight.

The Timberlawn research team, which found these attitudes to be basic discriminating factors between healthy and unhealthy families, proposed the useful labels of "affiliative" and "oppositional" for these two basic social attitudes, which I have since adopted. The similarity of these ideas to fundamental ethical and moral principles in the main religious systems, and to the sudden "flip" or "catastrophe" (Zeeman, 1977) characterizing religious conversion, is only too obvious.

The ideas expressed by Boszormenyi-Nagy and Spark (1973) regarding loyalties and obligations among family members need mentioning here. Though I believe these authors have done family therapy a service by reminding us of the need to face and accept responsibility for these issues rather than to avoid them by denial and distancing, truly healthy families do not operate on the basis of "ledgers" of obligation, "contracts" or "giving to get." In the second state for which I have borrowed the word "affiliative," everything is given freely, without demand or expectation of return, and members are truly free because they are not bargaining or manipulating to get their love returned.[9]

---

[9]*Editors' Note.* While this may be a cogent criticism of behavior therapy, it misrepresents Nagy's position (see Chapter 5).

TECHNIQUE

Mode of Approach

Beels and Ferber (1969) describe three principal positions from which the family therapist can intervene and, as they are all used in the method being described here, even if with differing emphases, they need to be mentioned. I refer to these positions as interventions "from above," "from the side," and "from below."

Intervention "from above"

In this mode, the therapist acts as a "conductor," a "super-parent," or grandparental figure, adopting an authoritative, directive role and seeking to change the structure and function of the family by active intervention, giving advice, instruction, praise and criticism, or educating by role-playing or deliberately "modeling" the new behavior considered more effective. The control may be more open and direct at one extreme, or covert, subtle and manipulative at the other. All behavioral methods clearly come into this category, but such methods will also include those advocated by Minuchin (1974), Bowen (1978) and Satir (1964), among others.

Intervention "from the side"

Another method, labeled by Beels and Ferber that of the "systems-purists," also seeks to change the family towards modes of functioning considered more healthy by the therapist, whether the family agrees or not, but does so from a detached position where the therapist's values are not made explicit. Instead, the "tricks" or "games" used in the family system to limit communication and to maintain a form of operation giving advantage to the dominant subgroup at the expense of others, or of a scapegoat, are first carefully studied. Once grasped by the therapists, instructions or tasks are devised which will make it impossible for these dysfunctional interactions to continue without their becoming obvious to all concerned.

In this approach the therapists seek to outwit the family at their devious, manipulative modes of control, through using the dishonest forms of interaction characteristic of the family to their ultimate benefit, like a kind of "psychological judo." The use of paradox and of "therapeutic double-binds" is prominent in this type of approach.

Understandably, these methods have been developed most fully in trying to deal with the most severely dysfunctional and devious families, particularly those producing schizophrenics. Some representative clinicians working in this mode are Haley (1976), Watzlawick et al. (1967), and Palazzoli et al. (1978).

Intervention "from below"

The third approach, exemplified by therapists such as Napier and Whitaker (1978), Boszormenyi-Nagy (1965), and Sonne and Lincoln (1965), does not appear to involve any attempt at control. Rather, the therapist appears to *submit* to the control of the family, accepting exposure to and absorption of the family dynamics and so becoming affected by them. The intervention is, therefore, more from the role of the "child," "patient," or "scapegoat."

However, to be effective the therapist must avoid "joining" the family system completely, but must maintain some part of his/her personality (unless this function is carried out by the other member of a co-therapy team) outside it and aware of the effect the family is producing. The therapist's role will differ from that of an actual child or patient in retaining the right to *describe* what is being experienced, thereby obliging the family to face the truth about their effect on each other. This method has the advantage that it not only confronts the family members with their pathological functioning, but keeps responsibility squarely on them to do something about it. Also, it can produce a vastly more powerful emotional impact when the family perceives that it is actually hurting and harming someone whom they respect and like and whom they see as trying to be positive and helpful to them. It is "for real."

Intervention "from above" or "from the side" (modes which are increasingly combined today by many therapists) both enable the professional to escape suffering any personal involvement in the family's pathology (unless they outwit him), partly because a position of superiority and control is maintained throughout, and also because the therapist relies on intellectual knowledge and thought to determine his actions, whereby he can keep an inner distance from any emotional reverberations. There is, for instance, much use in both approaches of the word "strategy," indicating an intellectual, adversarial stance.[10] The word "systems" is also much used, though by definition neither can be considered truly open-system approaches since the observer is excluded from consideration within the total dynamic. Therapists operating exclusively and predominantly from these positions tend to focus their attention on the family and on their own therapeutic techniques to avoid consideration of their personal dynamics and motivations. They also tend to be "loners," who do not readily share in co-therapy relationships, in learning experiences with colleagues of equal status, or in other *mutual* interactions. Their students tend to have difficulty in developing independently unless they detach themselves and, as it were, "leave home."

Intervention "from below" can also be carried out from a relatively detached, protected posture using reliance on the intellect, through history-taking and other information-gathering, through emphasis on intellectual formulation of dynamics according to psychoanalytic hypotheses, and above all through verbal interpretation. Those with much experience in an individual psychoanalytic approach are more likely to maintain this detached position in their emotional responses to the family, but will be likely to make use of countertransference responses as an importance source of information, even if this is kept under tight intellectual control and is not openly reported to the family or exposed to the constructive criticism of colleagues as information about the *therapist's* residual problems rather than those of the family. Therapists with this background tend also to have difficulty in using systematic manipulative strategies, forceful control, or behavioral methods.

A Group-Analytic or Open-Systems Technique

We now have a basis from which to consider the method I favor. The interview begins as a variant of intervention from "below," but it can

make use of intervention from "above" and "the side," depending on the circumstances. A main difference from all three approaches so far described is the involvement of the therapist *as a person*, considered as engaging with the family system through a semipermeable interface permitting mutual exchange of personal information. The therapist and family interact to facilitate a process of growth and development on *both* sides. The family is considered as a subsystem of the extended family, this in turn of the wider relationship network, and next of the class or culture to which it belongs. As much of this broader system as necessary is involved in therapy in each case.

The therapist also has a semipermeable boundary with his professional suprasystem, so that information passes to and fro to inform him of his deficiencies and correct his blind spots, at the same time enabling other colleagues to benefit from his professional and personal growth in a similar mutual learning process.

All three systems—the family being treated and their network; the therapist's personal life, his family of origin, family of procreation, and other personal relationships; and the therapist's professional life, colleagues and professional

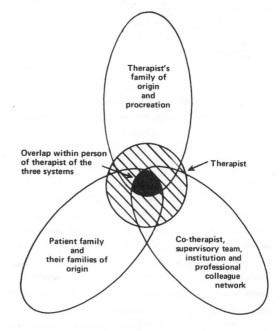

Figure 1: Interaction within the person of the therapist of the three social systems—personal, professional and patient/client family.

[10]*Editors' Note*. See Stanton (Chapter 10) for a detailed discussion of the role of the family therapist in "strategic" family therapy.

world—must interact within the person of the therapist in an optimal way if he is to be as effective as possible professionally and grow and learn from his experience (Figure 1). One consequence of this is that the criteria of "health," which influence the goals of treatment, are not based on an assumption that the therapist, his colleagues and profession, or his family of origin and family of procreation, or for that matter his own social class or culture, necessarily embody these. Rather, such values will be determined at any time by the best and broadest research available and by mutually corrective experience among therapist, colleagues and others. We will return to this issue under the heading of "Training."

It will be seen that this open-systems approach has many features resembling the Timberlawn description of healthy families, as compared with many other methods from "above," "the side" and "below," which often suggest at best "midrange" or "adequate" functioning in their emphasis on rigidity of roles, of values and of authority structure, their imperviousness to new ideas, their lack of the idea of mutality of influence between therapists and patients, their lack of spontaneity and (underlying this) their relative distrust, oppositional attitude and competitiveness in relation to other schools of thought.

Coming to *procedure*, one begins with a careful consideration of referral information to determine the group one will try to meet with. At the Woodberry Down Child Guidance Unit, where many of these ideas were worked out, a Referral Committee representing different disciplines met regularly to perform this task, using the principles I have described elsewhere (Skynner, 1976) as the "minimum sufficient network." Briefly, this means that one tries to bring together the smallest system likely to be capable of autonomous function and change. In terms of Freudian structural ideas, ego, superego and id functions must all be represented. Or, put another way, not only the *problem*, but the *motivation* to do something about the problem and the *capacity* to do something about it must all be brought together, if these functions reside in different persons. Thus, a child who complains of panic attacks or depression *can* be understood and treated separately by individual

or stranger-group methods, if old enough to move and cope outside the family system (though I would try routinely, nevertheless, to see the family for a first interview, to gather information and explore the possibility of clarifying the family system as well). By contrast, where the *parents* complain of a behavior disorder in a child, one must see the family if one is to get the motivation, the power and the symptom together "geographically." On the other hand, if the *school* is complaining and the parents seem unconcerned or ineffective, we would usually agree to see the family only at the school (which is suffering, not ourselves or the family), with the headmaster (who has the power) and the class teacher or housemaster (who has the information about the problem) present at the interview. Since it has both the motivation and some power, the school is made responsible for securing the attendance of the family.

Similarly, if the motivation for referral seems to lie in the unrealistic expectations of the referral agency (e.g., a middle-class assumption that working-class children should not be aggressive), or if the family has successfully manipulated the referral agency into an unrealistic acceptance of responsibility, or if several agencies are in conflict with one another, then the referral agent(s) should be included in the interview too.

It will be evident that the first step, in fact, is to educate referral agencies regarding the systems approach, securing their cooperation by demonstrating its effectiveness (and also declining to take over their responsibilities). Gradually, referrers learn that it is helpful to provide some outline of the family structure, including relations or other persons having a powerful influence, so that this may be considered in setting up the first interview. If such information is not available at the start, it may be obtained by letter or telephone from the referral agency; failing this, a brief interview can be arranged with one family member, usually the mother, to secure facts needed to determine the best arrangements.

Though it is valuable to have such information about the family structure and the reason for referral, if too much is discussed at the preliminary interview, the family members will often assume that they have performed their part of the therapeutic task and so take a passive role, putting responsibility on the therapist to provide answers and advice. Moreover, although it is, in fact, possible to use my methods even if one has received much previous information, it is far more difficult to avoid clinging to the comfort of intellectual understanding of the problem rather than letting oneself be affected by the family dynamics, especially when experience of this approach is limited and there is anxiety that it will fail. In addition, conflicts over confidentiality are far more likely to arise. Ideally, one should have only enough information to set the interview up with the "minimum sufficient network" adequately established (as far as one can judge this at the beginning of the intervention—one may see the need to expand it later).

The therapist should begin with an open mind, free of expectations which might tend to impose a structure on the information the family provide, so the setting is best kept as simple and unstructured as possible too. Unless there are young children, only a circle of chairs is provided, perhaps with a central table. If young children are present, the circle of chairs is all that is provided at first, to see how the children behave and how the parents manage them when they become restive, but play materials are available, out of sight, to be produced when their limited capacity for sitting still is exceeded (materials readily expressive of fantasy, without needing much supervision, are best; I favor soft, flexible family figures, and paper and crayons). These materials are placed in the center of the circle (on the table or on the floor), so that the children's play can be observed and linked to the verbal discussion.

The procedure that follows is absolutely simple in its outward form, and indeed often rather boring or unexciting, at least at first, to onlookers. The complexity lies in what is evoked in the therapist's inner experience and the difficulty rests in maintaining a quiet, open attentiveness without being pressured into prematurely "doing something." I open by asking about the problem, looking from one to another without catching any one person's gaze in order to indicate that all are free to speak. I listen to what is said, and I try to understand it. That is, I become aware of *not* understanding

some aspects and I quite straightforwardly ask questions to clarify these—nothing more. This position conveys to the family members that it is their task to explain the problem to me, not my task (at the start) to explain anything to them, and this position is maintained despite questions, demands, silences or any other attempt to provoke me into a premature response.

One has only to maintain an interested, questioning attitude, without hesitating to express puzzlement or bewilderment if one feels it, for the process to continue quite automatically. Usually the power-bearers in the family will begin and do most of the talking, but as one explores the problem one will start to feel the need to invite others to join in, in order to help one understand what is missing in the first account. Sometimes this happens quite naturally, without any particular effort on the part of the therapist beyond interest, curiosity and encouragement to continue. The problem complained of—rebelliousness in a child, for example—may actually begin to occur during the therapy session. Where this is not the case, I find that a few extremely simple principles quickly enable one to draw the whole family into the discussion in a way that is particularly acceptable and arouses no anxiety. Having started with a clear description of the *problem* as first presented, I invite others to give their views as well, agreeing or disagreeing with the first account. Then I ask questions about the social *context* of the symptomatic behavior, including its *effects* on others and the *effects of others upon it*—what makes it better or worse and what they do to try to *manage* it. This leads on naturally to explorations of *unexpressed feelings* about the problem as presented and, by asking everyone, including the children, what would most help to improve it, to *exposure of disagreements* and other material about the family dynamics.

This focus on the symptom is reassuring to the family members, since one is beginning with the problem they came about and widening out from this in a way they can readily understand, allaying their fears that one is going to blame some person or subgroup or spring some alarming interpretation upon them. Indeed, one can convey this reassuring message before they arrive by making it clear that therapy is intended to "help" the therapist through providing information, while also enabling him to "help" the whole family to "help" the designated patient through the increased understanding gained. Movement away from this early symptom-focused stage takes place naturally by steps that everyone can understand, and indeed by steps initiated by the family members as often as not, so that *they* discover the family systems viewpoint for themselves and begin to look at the symptom in a family context.

During this first stage the responsibility of the therapist is to be as fully *responsive* as possible, simply receiving verbal and nonverbal impressions of the family and avoiding "closure" towards any explanation, plan or goal too soon. The aim is to be *receptive* to all members of the family, to get to know them *individually* as well as remaining aware of their interaction. The *active* aspect of the therapist's role is to maintain this open, wide and clear attention, allowing the information to come in continuously without blocking it by trying to "understand" it prematurely in an intellectual way or, where glimpses of such "understanding" do occur, avoiding clinging to these in order that such thoughts will not interfere with the open and formless attentiveness required. This is really a continuation of the way I look from one to another when I open the session, maintaining an awareness of all the individuals present and according value to each one's presence and contribution.

This first stage is always painful for the therapist, in the sense that one has a sense of confusion and chaos, of being overwhelmed by unrelated fragments of information and by feelings of likely failure.

The first stage merges into a second (I have noticed no consistent time relation—it may occur on first seeing the family or after 20 minutes), in which I become aware of puzzling emotional responses or fantasies in myself, at first as fragmented and meaningless as the impression made by the family. These gain in clarity and insistence and, though at first appearing to arise "from nowhere," unrelated to the interview and perhaps personal in origin, they begin to *feel* increasingly as if they are somehow information about the family rather than about oneself alone, even though no rational connection can be made at first. (Of

course, such impressions are *also* information about the therapist, in the sense that for one tuning fork to resonate to another both must be similar, designed to resonate to the same frequency—the therapist is using his human commonality to understand other members of his species.)

This awareness of the effect on the family therapist's inner experience is associated with an increasing sense of *conflict*, at first a vague discomfort, gradually crystallizing into an impulse towards some active response, whether a statement, an expression of emotion, or movement, which at the same time is somehow felt to be inappropriate and better kept concealed.

Finally, there is a conviction that the response aroused is perhaps exactly what the therapist needs to put into the family system, since one realizes on reflecting on the interview that it is exactly what has been missing throughout it—some emotional attitude conspicuous by its absence—and that one is feeling inhibited because one is resonating to the family's taboos on expressing this particular aspect of human nature.

My experience in every case, as far as I can recall, is that this understanding of family problems occurs suddenly, unexpectedly, unpredictably. The period preceding it is *never* experienced as a logical, step-by-step process where one is aiming at, and has a sense of getting steadily closer to, a goal by some systematic, understandable process. Only after the sudden flash of insight, the instant falling into place of the formerly disconnected fragments of information to form an ordered and meaningful whole, does the early period of confusion become suddenly meaningful and understandable.

In my book on family therapy (Skynner, 1976, p. 178) I have suggested that: "I think the explanation must lie in a figure/ground type of phenomenon. *The real family problem is always contained in what is* not *communicated, what is* missing *from the content of the session.* To begin with, it therefore cannot be located, and one feels a sense of frustration and inadequacy. Only when a good deal of conscious or 'public' information has been accumulated, providing a 'ground,' can the 'figure'—an empty space in the pattern of facts, what is missing from the facts—be observed against this. And as in visual

pattern-recognition problems of this kind, recognition is sudden, even though once seen it
appears so obvious that one finds it hard to grasp
why one did not observe it earlier" (emphasis
added).

The *form* in which the therapist casts his intervention varies according to the understanding, educational level, capacity for reflection and
autonomous function, defensiveness and motivation of the family concerned. More intelligent, reflective and insightful families may be
best served by an interpretive, explanatory type
of feedback, whereby the therapist both provides them with the kind of information they
can work out themselves in detail later, and
gives them the opportunity to grasp some general principles of exploring family dysfunction
they can utilize to tackle future difficulties without professional help. Other families may lack
the capacity for reflection and insight, or be
deficient in ego-strength or social skills, and the
therapist's understanding may be more effective
if translated into a more behavioral, educative
approach, using advice, task-setting, restructuring, or communication of skills by example
and modeling.

But the most powerful intervention, having
the most rapid and dramatic effects (hence also
the most risky and needing the most careful
judgment as to timing) is for the therapist to *act*
upon his understanding of the family dynamic,
in such a way that the therapist virtually enacts
the scapegoat role; that is, he voluntarily and
consciously personifies the very emotion(s) the
family disowns. Viewed in this way, the experience to which the family is subjected is so
shocking, so horrifying, that the rapid and dramatic changes which frequently follow are scarcely
surprising. It is as if the family members have
been fleeing from a monster and finally find refuge in the safety of the therapist's room only to
discover, as they begin to feel secure and to
trust him, that he turns into the monster himself!

Needless to say, much effort, energy and skill
must go into building a relationship of warmth
and trust with the family to enable them to tolerate this experience. And this is best done
by—indeed follows automatically upon—the
earlier period where one seeks to understand,
identifies with, and builds a relationship with

each separate member of the family. To the extent that this is accomplished, the final phrasing
of the intervention will take the needs and fears
of *all* members into account, will allow for defenses and resistance, as well as revelations and
exposure of secrets. The therapist does not become *just* a scapegoat, but rather contains and
expresses the collusively denied or repressed
emotions, *as well as* representing and expressing the anxieties that led these emotions to be
denied and rejected in the first place. By absorbing the projective system of a disturbed family, the therapist suffers from their dilemma
himself first, but the solution, if found, is inevitably tailored to that particular family's exact
defensive structure. If the therapist succeeds in
escaping, he does so by a route that the family
can follow.

I think it will be easier to convey this process
and elaborate the details if at this point we can
take an actual example and study it in some
detail. It is, in fact, a family I saw for the second
time just after I began writing the last few pages
and with whom I tried in consequence to follow
and note my inner experience with a view to
describing it more carefully, rather than just
using it to treat the family.

CASE EXAMPLE

The X family telephoned for an appointment
on the suggestion of a medical colleague. Since
he had gone abroad, I had received, and sought,
no previous information about them.

Session One

The family was middle-class and consisted of
the parents, Alan, aged 12, and Sacha, aged 8.
After I had introduced myself in the waiting
room, they entered my room and sat in the pattern shown in Figure 2A. My seat was "reserved" as the notes lay upon it, so that they
could choose their positions in relation to me.

The mother did most of the talking. She explained that the psychiatrist who suggested they
contact me had seen her and her husband two
years earlier for treatment for a marital problem.
The therapy had to be terminated when this
colleague left Britain to return to his country of

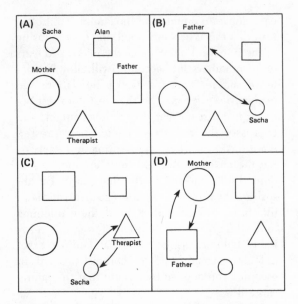

Figure 2. Positions taken up by family members at first and subsequent sessions (persons changing position indicated in latter). See text for details of sequence.

origin, but both parents agreed that the marital problems were now "sorted out" (I thought they passed over this rather quickly, however). The problem now was Alan, they said, who had been stealing from mother and not fulfilling his potential at school. Following complaints from his teacher, the headmaster had recommended psychotherapy, and Alan had attended a well-known clinic for Freudian psychoanalysis four times weekly, over about four or five months. But he had disliked going, had finally refused, and they reported that there had been no improvement.

Alan, on enquiry, said that he was unhappy at school, that he often started arguments at home after which he would walk out of the house, and that he had been stealing.

Sacha, when asked, said she had no problem except that "she could not write stories," a statement which (though not explored) gave the impression of fears of fantasizing.

I returned to the parents and the previous marital difficulties. They both acknowledged but then dismissed these as being no longer important (I did not learn what the problems were until the follow-up). But the children gave the impression of still being anxious about the parental relationship. Alan volunteered that they

had told him a year earlier that they would get divorced. Mother spontaneously emphasized the intensity of the relationship between herself and the children, explaining this by saying that it was because father was at work all day and "out of it," but father, when asked, said that the situation was no different when he was there.

I asked them to detail a typical incident, and they reported a sequence of stealing by Alan, reproof by mother, Alan walking out of the house, both parents feeling very anxious about him and much relieved when he returned late at night, so that they, and father in particular, did not reprove or punish him.

Following this, an argument developed between mother and Alan, in which Alan just held his own as her aggressive criticism mounted and both looked flushed and animated. Father took little part and he and Sacha, who said almost nothing spontaneously, looked like spectators on either side of a tennis court watching a singles match (an image which I expressed).

I queried the father's lack of participation, and suggested that the improvement in the marriage had perhaps meant that the boy had lost special and powerful relationships he had in the family before. Mother said, "Yes, he was master of the house when his father was away."

I suggested that he had, in fact, lost a special relationship with his mother when the marriage improved, but somehow hadn't yet found a new relationship with his father as a replacement. This seemed to make some sense to them all.

(All this was rather intellectual, and I can recall no particular feelings during this session, but I was taking things slowly and concentrating on forming good relationships with them all in view of the boy's hostility to the previous therapy.)

They all seemed to enjoy the session and I felt I had established a positive relationship with them. At the end, Alan said he would be willing to come for further family sessions, though he refused to have any further psychotherapy by himself.

Session Two

(This session occurred five weeks later—the Christmas holiday had intervened. During this interval I had begun to write this chapter and had resolved, just before this interview, to study my reactions more carefully when I next met with a family. This was the next family.)

They entered and sat in the same formation (Figure 2A). Father began, reporting that they had not understood anything from the first discussion but that it had left them all feeling more relaxed, open and "together" for a few days after it. Mother agreed, and then began an attack on Alan, escalating steadily in intensity, mainly over Alan's failure to fulfill his potential (and, obviously more important, her expectations) in his school work, music classes, and taking of exercise. Alan stood his ground again and father began to be more active in supporting Alan, who said mother was as bad as he was about not taking exercise and letting herself get fat. Father agreed that both mother and Alan were similar in being self-conscious about their bodies, feeling they were too fat, and that mother had an "anorexic problem, always overeating and then dieting." On enquiry, father said he had lost his own interest in food in childhood, and "liked to avoid eating between meals." This provoked the mother and developed into an argument between the parents, where mother asked him, "Why can't you bear people enjoying themselves?"

(About 25 minutes of the hour had elapsed and I wrote in my notes during this discussion about food: "No feeling in me except frustration. Not clear at all whether I will be able to do anything with this session." I realized that I might have to rewrite the chapter for the Handbook of Family Therapy, *admit I am a fraud and emigrate to a third world country where there is no psychotherapy. Shortly after this I became aware that I was having, or rather having a conflict about, enjoyable sexual responses to the mother's vibrant sexuality. I was preventing my thoughts from proceeding towards the idea of what she would be like in bed, felt embarrassed at myself, struggled to keep my attention on the whole family and at first treated this distraction of my attention as personal and unrelated to the family problem, so that I did not report it or use it.)*

The aggressive exchange switched back from between the parents to between mother and Alan. After this sequence occurred two or three times, I spotted it and pointed out how Alan

"drew the fire" on himself when his parents began fighting. Alan agreed with this and Sacha, when asked how she felt about being excluded from the interaction, said she was glad that Alan stopped the parents' fighting in this way.

(I was still preoccupied with my sexual awareness of the mother, and can still vividly remember the pattern of the folds of her dress across her thigh. I was also still feeling ashamed of myself for not paying proper attention to my work when they were paying me to do so. But suddenly I realized that these responses were related in some way to the family problem, though I could not see how.)

I now reported these feelings frankly, saying, "I often find my own feelings during an interview tell me something about the family problem, as if I am tuning in to it. At first I was concerned at feeling nothing, but *(to the mother)* I have just realized how aware I have been of what an attractive woman you are sexually and *(to the father, balancing things up and passing her back to him)* what a lucky man you are to have chosen her." I added that I had no idea what all this meant and that I had also felt very embarrassed at my sexual response, but wondered whether the parents were letting the children jealously interrupt their sexuality as well as their arguments? I suggested that the sex was not "earthed" between the parents but was floating about and getting into the children, and into me.

The children hotly denied that they were jealous about the parents' sexual relationship, but the parents felt it made sense. Sacha said, "I am worried that they do it," but quickly added that she meant the fighting. *(As the session ended I felt that no one seemed to like the ideas I was putting forward much. I felt I had made a mess of the session, gone too quickly and made them reject me).*

Session Three

(This session occurred two weeks later.) My worse fears were confirmed when I found the waiting room empty when I went to fetch them. (They had been early each time before.) Fifteen minutes later they had still not arrived, but then the father phoned to say that they were waiting for Alan, who was supposed to meet them at a rendezvous. I suggested they come anyway, as he would know how to get here. Shortly after this all four arrived, as Alan had turned up as father rang off. We all sat in the same places (Figure 2A). Mother attacked Alan for his "typical" non-cooperation, but he said the bus from the sports field had been late back to school and that mother had not given him a note to excuse him and make sure he was not delayed. It sounded as if mother might be in the wrong and father defended Alan more strongly from her attack.

As this argument subsided, mother turned to me and said "something *did* change last time. . . . You remember you said I was attractive?" I said I did. Mother then pointed to Alan and said, "Well, all the way from here to the station Alan was saying that I wasn't attractive at all, that I had crooked teeth, a big backside . . ." (Mother detailed a list of Alan's criticisms). "And as for *him* (*she turned and stabbed a finger at father*) he ignored it completely! Immediately there was a *retreat* from what you said by *everybody*! There was a sexual tension that each one was terrified to admit!"

(*Eureka! I experienced great relief that the theory was being confirmed, not only as regards the therapist's experiencing the "missing" emotion but also regarding the family's resistance to it.*)

Mother continued to recount how, the next day when Alan was looking at a picture of a nude girl in a newspaper (such pictures are a regular feature of some popular British newspapers) and she had asked him if he liked it, he began "screaming at her and denying he was interested." The session continued with a battle over this issue between mother and Alan, with father and Sacha on the sidelines again, mother saying that a lot of pictures in Alan's photograph album were of subjects suggesting a great deal of sexual tension.

I increasingly felt that the arguments between mother and Alan were both expressing and avoiding a kind of sexual engagement, and suggested this, adding that all the sex in the family seemed to be between mother and Alan. Where was the real marriage? At this point father cut in to say that he missed his previous good relationship with Alan. "I have lost him the last few years."

(*I suddenly experienced the seating pattern as a manifestation of the family problem, and felt a strong wish to change it, with an impulse to put father in Sacha's place and so next to mother and to Alan, but also in between them.*)

I reported these feelings to them, and asked father and Sacha if they would change places as an experiment (Figure 2B). The new arrangement felt very much more "right" to me. Father said he felt it made him "prominent" and therefore uncomfortable, even though he liked it. Following this, father turned towards Alan and confronted him for the first time, in a warm and quiet but very firm and authoritative voice, saying that he (father) was quite a jealous and possessive person, so that he wanted mother for himself and resented the way Alan constantly managed to get all her attention.

As father finished, mother had a sudden association to Alan once stealing £30. She added that at the time father "hadn't said much and had stood aside. Now he is taking a clear position to Alan for the first time."

Far from being upset, Alan looked pleased at his father's new firmness with him and I commented on this. As the session ended, I was aware that Sacha had been excluded from the whole interaction. I said I wondered how she fitted into it all, and that I felt I had made no progress with her.

Fourth Session

(The next session occurred after a two-week interval. Since the last session I had described this case to illustrate a point at a seminar, ending by saying that Sacha was still a mystery to me. At this, a female student had said, with a teasing twinkle in her eye, "well, you called her a little sweetie!", as if suggesting that I was not recognizing some sexual attraction. I usually feel quite comfortable with such sexual feelings and, as the outline of my concepts indicates, believe that a right measure of sexual attraction between adults and children is beneficial, *but I found myself once again embarrassed as I had been over my feelings towards the mother. However, on reflection, I wondered if in some way I was "filling a vacuum" with Sacha as I had done with the mother, that is, having father's unfulfilled oedipal romance with Sacha, or feeling her need for it. As will be seen, the interview* bore this out strikingly.)

They all looked cheerful and eager to begin. Sacha looked lively and bright instead of withdrawn and apathetic, and began by saying she had made a Valentine card for father (it was St. Valentine's Day). A general improvement was reported by everyone. The parents reported that everything felt lighter, easier, and that they were going out more often together on their own. Sacha said that she and Alan were getting on better, with fewer fights when the parents were absent and Alan added that he not only felt more alive and energetic himself, but that problems were solved as soon as they arose because "all the family tried to talk about them right away when they came up."

After this positive report, father turned to Alan and in a kindly but firm way criticized him for his lack of generosity and unwillingness to involve himself by joining the family "give and take." Mother continued the criticism in a more attacking way, and I pointed out how she kept breaking up the developing relationship between Alan and father. A good deal of the discussion centered around Alan's having spoiled mother's birthday by turning up late and worrying her.

(*I suddenly felt very strongly that he was jealous of Sacha's having been born.*)

I reported this to them, but it was completely avoided as mother and Alan once again began arguing. Alan stood his ground more firmly and quietly against her, saying he wished to be independent and separate, to think his own thoughts. The father also took a firmer position, telling both the children that he would like to be alone with the mother after 9:00 p.m. and that the children should go to bed and stop trying to interfere with their relationship.

Once again I became aware of how Sacha was still excluded from the interaction. In response to my pointing this out, she asked for help with her inability to stop blinking. She said it began when the father returned to the family from a period abroad, and this statement was followed by mother's saying that she felt guilty that sometimes she could not bear Sacha's presence and wished she didn't exist at all.

The parents focused again on Alan's neglect and spoiling of mother's birthday, and *I became increasingly aware of mother's own need for mothering*, which she was getting vicariously

through the children and which they in turn resented. This was confirmed by mother's remembering how much she had needed and enjoyed the company of Alan when she was alone with him, before Sacha was born. When he had gone to school, Sacha had replaced him.

Throughout all these sessions I had been waiting for some mention of the parents' families of origin. The first came at this point, as mother spontaneously said that Sacha had replaced her *sister*.

The time was up, and father asked to have the last word. He said he recalled Alan as a baby until the age of four, but could not remember Sacha during that early period.

(*I wondered again if father had missed out on his oedipal romance with her, and vice versa, but somehow we had not reached this yet.*)

Fifth Session

The parents had wanted more frequent sessions, as they were going abroad soon. As I met them, eight days later, *my attention was caught and held throughout the session by a very large and beautiful blue patterned tie the mother was wearing.*

Looking very lively and eager, the family entered and sat as before, except that Sacha chose the chair she occupied at the first session (between mother and father (Figure 2A) Father pointed this out and she moved to the position she occupied at the previous session (Figure 2B) When I explored her motives, she said she felt unhappy being so far from mother (I was between them). I offered to change with her and she readily accepted (Figure 2C).

The new position felt "right." The parents seemed more "together"; I had given mother back to father; and I was separated from them by the children, who needed support at losing their previous fusion with the parents. I felt and expressed pleasure at sitting next to Alan.

Father expressed his anxiety and distress at going abroad and leaving the children behind, and mother said of him: "I think he really has great difficulty in leaving the children and being able to be with his wife alone!" Father agreed, saying that he "would miss the warmth of home," and particularly his relationship with Sacha, which was "a gift from one day to the other."

Mother reported that Alan was arguing less with her and drawing fire from father instead. Next, Alan made them argue by comparing them adversely with each other, stimulating rivalry, but this stopped as soon as I pointed it out.

Mother expressed her more differentiated attitude by saying to the children: "I would like to be able to wash my mind of you, empty my brains of both of you, have a rest from you. What about my life!" She said she had realized that they had always been able to control her by making her feel a bad mother, making her feel guilty. This was expressed forcibly, putting them in their place and establishing a distance, but calmly and without anger.

Sacha had once again been left out. Her blinking had increased throughout the session. Noting this, I recounted to the family my presentation of their problem at a seminar to illustrate the use of my sexual response to the mother, adding that when I had mentioned my puzzlement about Sacha's role to my colleagues, someone had implied that I was denying my sexual attraction to Sacha. I then told them, amusingly, that I had felt embarrassed by this—was I flirting with *all* the females in the family, and if so what did it mean? This went home to mother, who turned suddenly to Sacha and said with a grin: "Would you like to take off with father on holiday in my place?" Sacha nodded, grinning too.

The focus turned to father's feelings about Sacha. The sexual father/daughter aspect did indeed seem to be lacking; the relationship was clearly based more on father's vicarious infantile gratification. He said, "I enjoyed my early childhood when I was happy, when I was very small, and I may have tried to relive this through Sacha." Father also made a connection between his hostility to his father following this period and Alan's hostility to him.

Sacha's blinking was still increasing. *At this stage I was feeling increasingly isolated and rejected by the family for the views I was expressing about the desirability of sexual feelings between father and daughter, and the fact that I had felt attraction of this kind myself.* Mother clearly understood and agreed, but I felt her basic loyalty had to be to the family denial.

My attention was still caught by mother's prominent tie and I felt impelled to mention it.

Mother grinned and said, "You mean I am the man in the family?" (Father had on a black polo-neck sweater.) Mother suggested another possible sexual link we had not explored—that between the males. This was avoided by them, but the relevance seemed confirmed when it was next revealed that Alan did up mother's tie for her. Alan looked uncomfortable and, suddenly, in a breakthrough, the mother said she had realized vividly how the sexual pattern between herself and her husband was always dictated by the children: "We like to make love on Saturday and Sunday but they barge in whenever they feel like it. There is always some excuse to disturb us and we are fools; we pretend we are doing something quite different altogether when they enter the room. The one thing I am longing to get away on holiday for is so we can make love as often as we like, without worrying about the children at all." Father nodded agreement, but though mother and the children seemed quite at ease during this discussion, father appeared much more embarrassed. He said, "Do you want us to have a notice on the door saying 'vacant' or 'engaged,' to tell you what we are doing? Why can't you knock?" I suggested that it was genuinely difficult for everybody if there were not some clear indication, such as a locked door, and Alan said to the parents, "Why don't you tell us? What's the problem about telling us, so we know when to stay away?"

Challenged by mother, father acknowledged his embarrassment about sex, which he linked to the embarrassment of his own parents, but said he already felt relieved by the discussion. He asked the children if either of them minded that he and mother still made love together? They seemed accepting, indeed pleased to hear it, and Alan asked if they were going to have another baby. Mother said they made love just because it was so enjoyable and I explained to Alan, without detail, that people could make love if they wished without needing to make a baby.

The incestuous sexual theme I had introduced earlier, for which I feared I would be rejected, now seemed increasingly accepted. Mother, smiling, said to the children, "I can see it now, goodness knows why I didn't see it before. You two feel the sexual tensions between us, you like to smell it, you like to come in and intrude upon it. That is why Sacha is always staying up late and disturbing us and finding excuses. I see that we have never drawn our boundary clearly between you children and ourselves. We have never made it clear."

Time was up. As they left I found myself chatting with father in a man-to-man way about the business trip on which he would shortly be taking his wife. I felt as if I was offering the supportive "homosexual" relationship he had lacked with his father.

I was left feeling that all was now well between the parents, or well enough for them to develop the relationship, but that I still needed to help the children to cope with this change.

Sixth Session

I began the session two weeks later still feeling I had to do something to help the children to cope with the loss of their parents, who were closer to each other sexually. Sacha's unusual liveliness, animation and confidence were striking. After we were seated, I asked if anyone wished to change places, and mother said she would like to change with father. He reluctantly complied (Figure 2D).

Mother began by saying that Sacha would probably do all the talking, as she had been very lively, woken up first and got the rest of the family up. Mother continued by saying that since moving her chair she had realized she wanted to put more space between herself and Sacha, that she resented Sacha's attachment and dependency. (Alan said that was mother's fault, implying the dependency was mutual.) Mother expressed increasing anger at Sacha's dependence, and said she wished Sacha would fight back instead of denying her hostility. Sacha was blinking steadily with a hostile stare, which I described as "stopping the daggers from flying out of her eyes." Soon we were again like spectators watching a tennis match, but now between mother and Sacha.

I found myself thinking Sacha could not grow away from mother because father would not accept her oedipal attachment, and I expressed this in simple language. Father complained again that both children stayed up late and interfered with his relationship with his wife.

I felt again that I had enabled the parents to be comfortable about their sexuality and to be closer, but that somehow the children were stranded. Reporting this, I confessed that I did not yet see how to help the children cope with the new situation, and particularly with their own sexuality.

Sacha responded to my mention of "the children's sexuality" by complaining that Alan's anger and teasing prevented a good relationship between them, as if the aggressiveness were a defense against enjoyable sexual feeling.

Still feeling blocked by the father's reluctance to acknowledge his side of the oedipal romance with Sacha, I mentioned that I had a beautiful daughter who obviously enjoyed her sexual feelings to me as much as I did mine towards her. I mentioned also how skillful she was at playing my wife and I off against each other, and commented that Sacha seemed unable to do this. Mother confirmed this, saying of Sacha, "She always failed to pull her father on her side against me" and of father, "he was never really ready to be her white knight on a charger."

The family next discussed an incident where Sacha had gone home to seek father's support when a rough boy had pushed her off a swing. Father had gone with her to the playground, but had spoken to the boy mildly, disappointing Sacha, who had screamed repeatedly that father was "a coward." As the story unfolded, it was Sacha who disclosed that, returning home to seek father's protection, she had become aware that her parents were "upstairs making love." Despite her feeling that she should not interrupt them, she had intruded and father had got up and gone with her, leaving mother. As the discussion continued, it became obvious that the motives for Sacha's interruption were mixed, and that neither female was pleased with the way father dealt with the situation!

(At this point I experienced a strong feeling that these children, and children in general, must find it difficult to lose the bodily intimacy of babyhood and also accept exclusion from their parents' intimate sexuality, unless they could find a substitute in their own sexuality.)

Reporting this, I acknowledged I still could not understand it well enough to help them. *I was also strongly feeling the lack of some normal sexual attraction and enjoyment between Alan and Sacha.*

I did not report this, but the relevance of my feelings was verified when mother immediately continued, "There is a terrific sexual tension between the children when they are left alone, but (*teasingly*) they are too afraid to have a good time like mum and dad."

Following this the parents continued to talk in terms of adult sexuality, while the children responded appropriately to each statement, but as if translating into another language where nonsexual games and play substituted for sex. Sacha said, "The difference is that when they like each other men and women can say they want to be with each other, but children can't." I suggested that she was speaking about intercourse, and this led to a relaxed discussion of what it meant. Alan confirmed his knowledge about it, but Sacha blocked as if she knew but was denying her knowledge. I explained the details, and said it was exciting and enjoyable. The children said they did not wish to do anything like that yet.

The theme changed to complaints about father's inhibitions over being aggressive, forceful and potent. Sacha, in particular, angrily protested to father, "You never even shout at me, let alone hit me," as if greatly deprived.

Father repeatedly avoided this confrontation, but Sacha pursued the subject, shouting angrily, "I am asking for you to hit me and you keep trying to change the subject!" Father finally acknowledged that he was realizing he did not want to feel "sexual overtones coming towards him from Sacha." Mother said teasingly to her, "Oh, she is faithful to Daddy only, and to prove it she doesn't show interest in any other boy, but Daddy doesn't care and she is angry with him for it!" Mother went on to describe her awareness in childhood of her own father's strong sexual feelings for her, and his jealousy of any other males, "It made me feel good, but it was really very bad for me. I felt that somehow I could get my father though really I couldn't."

I was struck by the father's fear of violent, animal feelings, including sexuality and aggression. Drawing attention to this, I pointed out that father could have "been a beast" and enjoyed himself three times over in the incident described earlier; he could have finished making love to his wife, smacked Sacha for interrupting,

and shouted at the boy who bullied her. Everyone found this hugely amusing.

They continued on the theme of the desire of all other members that father should be the strongest in the family. Mother described how the children wanted him to win when they all played games together and how upset they got when he once suggested that in the future he would let mother win. Mother continued, "When the father is the strongest in the family, everything comes back to peace and quiet; there is order, harmony, no wars. But in reality I am the strongest." An argument developed between the children and mother about who was the strongest, and Alan said to father, "If you didn't have a son, you'd have no one to bully," as if he had to "put himself down" to keep his father above him.

(*Throughout the interview I had been preoccupied with a family therapy session carried out by a colleague at the Institute of Family Therapy, which was part of a program our Institute was making for BBC television. The family concerned also contained a dominant mother, withdrawn father and a stealing boy whose rivalry was not being adequately contested. The staff at the Institute, which had watched the film, had seemed to me as inhibited about discussing the sexual, oedipal problems as the therapist had been with the family. I had found this intensely frustrating and had almost exploded. At the same time, I had admired the fact that this colleague paid real attention to the children's needs, and realized that I tended to neglect this aspect.*

I recognized for the first time that this was connected with the fact that while I had become relaxed and comfortable at talking about parental sexuality in front of children, I was much more embarrassed about talking about children's sexuality in front of adults. Although more in a "parental" role in the Institute, as its "founder" and first Chairman, I suddenly found myself identifying with the children in the family being watched, and taking a "child" role in relation to the Institute "family" as if it were my own. I had reported this to my colleagues, saying that watching the film had made me identify with the children and have the fantasy that "I shall masturbate as much as I like, any time I like, and no one will stop me." I had not under-

stood the significance of this at the time, but felt sure it was the key to the television family interview.)

I reported all this to the family I was treating, saying it kept coming to my mind as if it had some connection. I then realized, and reported, that the fathers in both families were like my own father, fearful of their own potency, and that perhaps as a child I had also been frightened of my own developing sexual potency, and embarrassed over masturbation because of a need to be weaker than my father and keep him strong, and out of fear that my parents would allow me to inhibit their sexuality if mine was too strongly experienced.

As I was reporting this, I had a profound feeling that many things I had not previously understood, in my personal life, my family of origin, my theoretical conceptions and my professional work, had fallen into place and become connected together. I said to the family that I had perhaps brought myself in more personally than usual because I had been learning something important about my own family of origin and myself. They left looking quiet and thoughtful. There was no time for further discussion but I felt a deep assurance that I had given the children what they needed, and that the main work was done.

Final Three Sessions

A six-week interval followed, since a visit by the parents abroad—the first without the children—overlapped with my teaching visit to the U.S. As the deadline of delivery for this chapter had arrived, I took it with me, including the report as summarized so far. I did not realize until my return the extent to which "the chips were down," since my firm prediction, now in the editor's hands, was still to be tested.

The family came for three more sessions at intervals of two weeks. The seating remained unchanged except that mother and father changed places with each other twice. At the first of these (Session 7), father took an authoritative position for the first time, criticizing Alan for lack of effort at school. Alan said the school was too permissive and that he wanted to change to another with more discipline and educational "stretching," which I personally also thought he needed.

The females "sat this one out," looking relaxed, but when mother tried once to dominate, father told her to "keep out of it . . . you take too much territory." *I still felt some lack of connection between Alan and father, and found myself thinking repeatedly that the father's father had failed in his relationship with the father in some way, and that the males in the family were uncomfortable with their homoerotic feelings.* I said this and while father showed discomfort, mother and Sacha agreed, saying the females, by contrast, were getting along famously. *I felt myself to be occupying paternal grandfather's role, giving the males permission for a more comfortable attitude to their homosexual feelings.*

At the next (8th) session, the father looked much more manly, showing a new quiet firmness, as well as an obviously sexual enjoyment of his wife, moving his chair close and leaning towards her. Both expressed feelings of increasing differentiation, mother saying she "had her own universe instead of seeing the family as an extension of herself," the father agreeing. The children, rather bored, asked why they were still coming for therapy.

The final (9th) session began with the parents' saying that on the way to the interview they had both found themselves having the same thought—that this would be the last visit. Sadness at parting was expressed, together with pleasure at the changes. Mother reported that Alan had "changed drastically," was a "pleasure to be with" and could "express his pain instead of keeping it inside him." The changes in Alan and the family were confirmed by other members.

However, Alan was obviously finding the termination more difficult, showing obvious envy of my role which, as I pointed out, made him both deny it ("You only sit there and write") and also want to continue to see me ("We're not perfect, not everything is cleared up, though most things are"). I confronted him with this difficulty in accepting what I had to give him, while I kicked his shoe and punched his arm gently in a friendly fight.

He then expressed more clearly his remaining discomfort in his relationships with girls, where he seemed unable to distinguish real hostility from the aggressiveness and provocation which were really adolescent sexual behavior. Though I felt he might at some time need and accept some separate therapy, I suggested that he should talk to his father about this first, to see if he could help him.

I had been waiting throughout the treatment for some family history to emerge, and had been surprised that so little had come earlier. Then, in the last ten minutes, mother reported that her mother, who had suffered all her life from "troubles with her uterus," had telephoned to say she had finally been told by her new doctor that her problem was just that "she needed a man." Mother said that her mother obviously felt relieved and released by "being given permission to have sex" for the first time, but that "it would cause trouble" with her father, "who is inhibited." Mother now said that her parents had never had a fulfilling sex life because of their inhibitions. This was in contrast to the mother's grandfather, who had "screwed around until he was 70."

This discussion of the sexual attitudes of grandparental figures led mother to speak of how physically attractive her husband had recently become. He had begun leading a keep-fit class and she enjoyed seeing how attractive he was to the women attending it. Father laughed and acknowledged he enjoyed it too and was going to "end up playing for Europe."

The family left with expressions of warmth and gratitude, as well as sadness.

The interval between sessions was in this case often less than I normally use (three weeks or more), because of the pressure I was under to deliver this chapter by the deadline. This may have increased the number of sessions beyond the amount required when following the normal procedure.

Follow-up

As this *Handbook* goes to press a ten-month follow-up is available: Two weeks after termination, a confrontation between Alan and his head-teacher resulted in acceptance by the parents that the school was unsuitable for him (as had become apparent in Session 7 and which I was now able to confirm directly for myself); he was therefore moved, as he had previously requested, to the local state school where he found the academic "stretching," the more robust attitude to boisterous behavior, and the firmer structure that he both needed and desired. He settled well there, while at home the improvement noted during the therapy had steadily continued throughout. The presenting problems have not recurred. The lives of, and relationships among, all the family members have continued to become more rich and satisfying.

There was one individual session with Alan, at the time of the change of school, to ensure that he had not relapsed, and also partly for the purpose of clarifying whether he needed separate therapy—in fact he did not desire it and the joint sessions appeared to have dealt sufficiently with his problems. In addition, there were three further sessions, six months later, for the parental couple without the children, to help them deal with a longstanding problem presented by the father's elder brother who had regularly intruded into, and tried to disrupt, their marriage. As the final draft of this chapter had been dispatched, it was no longer necessary to keep the technique "pure" for the sake of clarity; the approach at this family of origin level could therefore be eclectic and so more swift—enabling the entanglement of the brother in this marital system to be dealt with in one final session where an essentially psychoanalytic understanding (that he had displaced into his brother's marriage the oedipal conflict which had never been resolved in relation to his parents) was presented in systemic, paradoxical form (namely, that his attempt to disrupt his parents' marriage, and now that of his brother, had the positive purpose of stimulating father and brother towards greater potency, and so strengthening the marital bonds in each case by provoking and "testing" them; further, as the effect was clearly most beneficial, he should continue to intrude between them as much as possible, even though it was recognized that this required a generous sacrifice of his own life and freedom). A spate of international phone calls and letters from this brother, both to the couple and to myself—sometimes several within an hour and each canceling the one before —indicated that the medicine had been internalized and was operating effectively. The couple confirmed that they now felt able to exclude him from the marital relationship.

During these further interviews, the family histories were explored and a genogram was constructed. The sexual histories and relationships were also explored in a more explicit way than had seemed appropriate while the children were present. Though the information was fascinating in the light it threw on the previous interaction and the reasons for my "countertransference" responses, the previous therapy nevertheless appeared complete in itself. The additional information supported the view that the same basic pattern or structure is repeated at different levels of organization—i.e., extended family, family, marital, and intrapersonal systems. Therapeutic interventions may therefore be based adequately on information obtained from only one of these levels, though the redundancy provided by use of several levels simultaneously will decrease the possibility of important factors being overlooked.

* * * * *

This understanding of the family "from inside," achieved by opening oneself to the projective system so that one internalizes the individuals separately through identification and begins to suffer from the struggle with the family conflict oneself, can be combined with the methods of approach already described and emphasized by other schools of family therapy. To understand "from inside," one needs to approach "from below," abandoning a *defensive* use of one's professional role and power. Conceptual thought must not be allowed to dominate and obscure the faint emotional responses generated by the family projective system. But the requisite quiet and open attentiveness can eventually be maintained while thought processes continue to register data and suggest possible explanations in the light of theory. This additional source of understanding of the family "from outside," reached by routes "from above" and "from the side," may be extended and used to explore and initiate change while a deeper emotional interaction is proceeding. Such interventions may be particularly necessary to remove blocks to communication which would prevent the therapist's gaining adequate exposure to the family dynamics. For example, it may be necessary at the start to insist that the

father or "healthy" children attend, despite resistance; to refuse to see parents and children separately until the therapist judges this desirable; to break up communication patterns that exclude or restrict the contributions of some members; or in other ways to use professional authority to change the family structure or the ground rules of the interview.

So far, I have attempted to formulate my experience and behavior when interviewing a family within the framework of Western psychology, particularly psychoanalysis, group analysis and social learning, even though general systems theory is, in fact, a return to the more holistic view still preserved in the East. But, to be truthful, I believe these approaches are really inadequate to describe my methods, for I have little doubt that *the key requirement in the therapist is a deep awareness of his own identity which he is able to sustain in the face of overwhelming, if transient, emotional arousal engendered by encounter with profoundly disturbed family systems seeking to externalize their pathology.* This does not mean clinging to a professional role, to a particular theory or technique, or even to one's personality in the ordinary, superficial sense (though this is indeed what most therapists do, and it is what determines their limitations).

If I were to try to express this essential requirement in a sentence, I would say that it entails a more intense consciousness of both one's inner and outer experience, such that reality is completely distinguishable from fantasy whether the latter originates within oneself or is stimulated in response to the projective (fantasy) systems of others.

Where this heightened consciousness exists, there is no need to cling to anything static (necessarily some sort of fantasy, including rational thought), since reality (necessarily ever-new and changing) is so vivid and fulfilling. Reality *IS* reality and fantasy *IS NOT* reality, in the sense that a real dinner *is not* a menu.

By this ability to maintain a heightened consciousness of reality, and so to avoid being hypnotized by the fantasies engendered by the projective system of the individuals or family, the therapist is to them a landmark or beacon by which they can find and orientate themselves. He need, in fact, do nothing but *BE* with them, in the sense of maintaining his identity and integrity.

By *being* with them the therapist constantly contradicts their projected expectations, startles them into a new awareness of reality by also dissipating, briefly at least, the fantasy that constantly engulfs and controls them, by showing them how unreal and shadowy it is just as sunshine dissipates a fog and dispels the terrors imagination conjures up to fill its shadows, merely by revealing the quiet countryside. Paradox, "therapeutic double-binds," koan-like questions, the "crazy" statements and "zany" interventions that characterize so much of the work of Carl Whitaker (see Chapter 6) and which I make much use of myself, tasks and suggestions that break up established structures—all have as their common underlying effect (whatever explanation the therapist may use to justify it) the function of *shocking* the family into a level of heightened awareness and so out of their dreams and self-fulfilling negative prophesies.

Western thought, including psychoanalysis and academic psychology, has particularly neglected the issues of intensity of attention and level of consciousness, so central in Eastern approaches. But once this is taken into account, many seemingly diverse techniques readily find an explanation and a place within the concepts put forward here. If consciousness is equated to light, both Freudian and Jungian methods of analysis are akin to searching for objects in a darkened room one by one, striking match after match; the paradoxical and task-setting techniques are akin to setting off a photographic flash bulb, momentarily illuminating the whole room in a vision which it is subsequently difficult to deny one has seen, even if one forgets the details. The various meditative techniques all seek to generate a more powerful and reliable source of light to replace the flickering "matches" and occasional "flash bulbs" which comprise our ordinary waking consciousness, thereby illuminating reality and dissipating fantasy just as awakening from ordinary sleep dissipates the reality of sleeping dreams, or at least alters our conviction of their truth.

The point of view I am proposing can also embrace and give added meaning to the *attachment* concepts of Bowlby (1969, 1973) and the ideas of Winnicott (1971) regarding the significance of *play* and *transitional objects* in enabling the child to move gradually from the security of the first attachment figure into the wider world. Heard (1978) has recently proposed a most interesting integration of the ideas of these two writers, and though the language she uses makes her proposals at first appear rather complicated, she appears to be suggesting that what both Bowlby and Winnicott have in common is the view that new, experimental behavior, whether exploring the internal or the external world (both forms of "play"), can feel safe only within a sufficiently constant, reliable, predictable context (Winnicott's "held" situation, or the goal of the "proximity-seeking" behavior in Bowlby's scheme).

The tendency of severely dysfunctional and midrange individuals and families to cling to the known, to fear loss and change, to be unable to learn from experience because they order their lives in such a way that projected expectations, based on the internalized models, are never contradicted or threatened with change—for example, by choosing a spouse whose inner world will mesh smoothly and confirm past experience; by selecting friends who will not recognize and challenge defenses and denials of reality; by embracing political, religious and ethical codes which will avoid new experience which might demand change and growth—can thus be seen as equivalent to proximity-seeking behavior, a clinging to security because enough safety was not provided in early life to make the excitement of exploration outweigh the corresponding fear. At root, it is a clinging to mother.

Translated into these terms, what I am saying in this chapter is that to use my approach the therapist must simultaneously (or at least in rapidly alternating fashion) *both* maintain a parental, "holding" role (keeping the situation constant and safe) *and* provide a model of "play" (explore, open up, risk, venture out into the unknown). To the extent that the therapist cannot do this (be parent *and* child, therapist *and* patient, at once) he will need a co-therapist or colleague-support-system to handle one side of the polarity when he gets stuck in the other. But in whatever way this dual function can be accomplished, the therapist must lead the family members towards the exploratory attitudes they previously turned away from, in a context of safety, support and encouragement.

The approach I favor, therefore, links equally both with the most modern psychoanalytic concepts just described and also with the oldest known form of mental healing, that of Shamanism, and offers a possible mechanism explaining the similar internalization and partial resolution of the patient's problems described by Jung (1954). The relationship to Shamanism—the need for the therapist's internalization of the projective system, and the fundamental requirement of an absolute trust in one's own identity and an abandonment of all clinging to technique—is expressed most beautifully in the ritual song of a Pacific North West Indian Shaman, entitled "The Song of Tom the Shaman":

I know thee. My name is Tom. I want to find thy sickness. I know thy sickness. I will take thy sickness. My name is Tom. I am a strong doctor. If I take thy sickness, thou wilt see thy sickness. My name is Tom. I don't lie. My name is Tom. I don't talk shit. I am a doctor. Many days I haven't eaten. Ten days maybe I haven't eaten. I don't have my tools with me. I don't have my sack with me. My name is Tom. I will take thy sickness now and thou wilt see it (Rothenberg, 1972).

SOME FURTHER COMMENTS ON THE GROUP-ANALYTIC METHOD

Though the questions raised by the Editors of this *Handbook* (see Preface) need to be put and answered, many of them are irrelevant to the *practice* of my approach, in the sense that a knowledge of knots is irrelevant to the task of cutting the Gordian knot. What is needed is an understanding of how to keep a sharp edge on one's sword—a wide, deep and still attention.

I hope it will be clear, from the description of the method and the example just given, that assessment and treatment are fully integrated and that both begin the moment the therapist and family encounter each other. Also, assessment and treatment aspects of the interaction are proceeding at a variety of levels—individual, dyadic, triadic and system—though the balance of these may change in different cases and in the course of therapy. A longer-term treatment is likely to present as an "individual" problem, to move to examining this as part of a pattern

in the nuclear family system and this in turn as a product of unresolved problems in the marital dyad. Exploration of the dyadic relationship will lead on naturally to study of the complementary character difficulties in each member of the couple, bringing the study to the individual, intrapsychic level and to the beginnings of these individual difficulties in developmental failures in the families of origin. This brings us to the systems level again, either intrapsychically or by bringing in the grandparental generation to the interview, but the object will be to help the differentiation of each member of the couple from these systems from which they sprang, as well as from each other and from their children.

However, the emphasis may vary. Some "primitive" families may be best worked with mainly at the level of producing a small structural change in the whole system, sufficient to turn a descending into an ascending spiral. With others it may be better for all if one individual is helped to differentiate and separate, while the "treatment" of the others is aimed at distancing them from this individual and so avoiding threatening their defenses by exposure to more insight and change than they can bear (e.g., by arranging placement of a child in a boarding school). Since the unconscious or unexpressed inner worlds of each person are read mainly through nonverbal communication, and the therapist's understanding is fed back to the family as often by "modeling" and action as by symbolic communication, it is obviously meaningless to classify the method as either "behavioral" or "intrapsychic"; both, like assessment and treatment, are as integrated as inspiration and expiration in breathing.

Because of the desirability to keep the therapist's attention open, clear and free of preformed judgments and thoughts, I prefer if possible to avoid tests, questionnaires or other structured devices. I find it hard to imagine any that would not complicate and prolong the process, but if time and cost were not important they could probably be included for research purposes. There is also no reason in principle why the method cannot be used at home, at school or anywhere else—provided the different circumstances are allowed for (Skynner, 1976). It should also be clear that there is a constant concern with clarifying "goals," though the word is not one I customarily use, either in my work or my writings, because of its associations with the idea of a *therapist's making plans or decisions* in order to *do something to or for* a patient or family. But from the moment the family members are encountered they are brought up constantly against the question of what they want, and this is reformulated and clarified over and over again throughout treatment, right to the end. Responsibility is thrown back onto the family at the beginning of each meeting. The therapist's task is to help *clarify* what the family wants, to help expose conflicts and inconsistencies regarding incompatible desires both between and within members, to help them negotiate more generally acceptable compromises, to help them see what stands in the way of their getting what they want and to help them discuss how the wishes might be achieved. It will be evident, too, that I want the answer (or "goal") to come if possible *from the family*, even if it is obvious to me from the moment I meet them, for if all collaborate in achieving a solution they are more likely to have reached a real joint decision where hidden resistances which might sabotage a therapist-imposed solution have already been exposed and allowed for. Moreover, the family will have had the opportunity to learn about *problem-solving in general* (i.e., second-order learning), which they may be able to use without external aid when they meet future problems; such a benefit obviously cannot follow if the therapist does the thinking for them.

Using the method described, a step-by-step process of clarifying a destination and how to get there automatically follows. In this sense there will obviously be intermediate goals (what they think they need when they come) and ultimate goals (the different things they may discover they want by the time they leave), though again I feel this kind of jargon complicates rather than elucidates a simple and obvious process.[11]

_____

[11]*Editors' Note.* We view intermediate (or mediating) and ultimate goals somewhat differently, following Parloff's (1976) distinction, i.e., "mediating goals are those which reflect the clinician's assumptions regarding the necessary steps and stages through which a patient must progress if the treatment is to be effective . . . (these goals) permit the attainment of the ultimate goals . . . (which) go beyond such . . . mediating variables as inferences regarding the resolution of neurotic conflicts . . ." (p. 317). Also note our discussion (Gurman & Kniskern, Chapter 20) in this volume of the importance of this distinction for outcome research on family therapy.

It is also often counterproductive for the therapist to formulate plans or goals *explicitly*, since this will enable a resistant, aggressive family to sabotage them. Supervising trainees, I find behaviorally-oriented therapists fall incessantly into this trap. If, instead, one throws responsibility for decisions and for changing (or for not changing—it is their choice) back onto the family or couple, they can only defeat *themselves* and the therapist can make it quite clear that the self-defeat is their problem, not his. "Goals" are established in a language and at a level the particular family can grasp—motoric, conceptual or whatever. The idea of a treatment goal so general as to apply to *all* families would be so broad as to be almost meaningless. However, "to clarify the situation" would satisfy me and if that did not satisfy the family I would tell them it is their problem to put the understanding into practice, not mine.

Many other questions put by the editors to guide the contributors to this volume (see Preface) are similarly difficult to respond to without my answers seeming ambiguous and unsatisfactory, precisely because of the flexibility and potential complexity of the approach. Essential decisions about therapy structure (whether or not to see the family, who must come, how much disturbance they can make) are *absolutely* under the control of the therapist if it comes to the crunch, but despite the therapist's ultimate veto the structure is as far as possible negotiated and is used to offer maximum freedom of communication. The family members are encouraged to talk to each other and to do all the work, *but* the therapist will intervene as forcefully and as often as may be necessary. A violent verbal confrontation may, for example, be necessary to establish control or break a defensive pattern. The therapist both joins the family and remains outside, oscillating between one and the other position in order to pick up the projections and then to reflect on and analyze or act from them.

The treatment alliance is aimed at by being basically warm, friendly, interested, sympathetic, helpful, humorous and absolutely natural, yet without abrogating responsibility and authority. The therapist also seeks to see the situation through the eyes of each individual in turn.

The equivalent of "transference" in the individual psychoanalytic technique, which I am describing here in terms of *systems of projected expectations* (more briefly "*projective systems*"), and its recognition by the "countertransference" activation of corresponding "irrational" emotional reactions in the therapist are obviously the cornerstone of what is most specific in my method. This use of countertransference has never appeared to present a risk to anyone but the therapist, *provided* it is used in the manner described, by the therapist *expressing* his irrational feelings as information the family can either accept as being about themselves, or reject as being about the therapist (rather than as "interpretations" lobbed into the family like hand-grenades from the bunkered safety of "blank screen anonymity"). The degree of self-disclosure required of the therapist is necessarily high, and I see no necessity for any limits to this provided that it is aimed to be ultimately in the service of the therapeutic task rather than solely for the therapist's benefit, which certainly means the therapist must stay within the limits of what he can cope with emotionally. However, it must be added that, using this approach, crucial breakthroughs in insight and change tend to take place when the therapist feels *at* those limits and even fears he is out of control and is breaking them (the theory underlying the technique explains why this is so and the case example illustrates it well.)

This process being central to the method, the therapist's psychological health (together with his objective and open acceptance of his remaining ill-health, which is all part of the same thing) is the most crucial attribute in the therapist. Other important factors are related to this—he must be at ease with himself, able to enjoy himself, relatively satisfied with his life, his marriage, his sexuality and his family (or be able to accept objectively and openly, and to use therapeutically, what he lacks or what cannot be changed).

There are no *serious* technical errors I have encountered or witnessed in using this method, in the sense of *harming* families.[12] The com-

monest errors we have noted are (a) underestimation of its subtlety and complexity because of its outward simplicity and (b) attempts to make it into a "technique," i.e., a set of principles which can be manipulated intellectually without requiring personal involvement and fresh exposure, learning and risk each time. People who want to "find out how to do it," for example, have not only missed the point completely, but also failed to see that they have missed it.

Regarding the relationship between "insight" and "change," I doubt if anyone can change his habitual behavior without some change in the way he perceives the world. A fine for speeding not only reduces the average speed of my automobile but also increases my awareness of the police and my attention to my rearview mirror. In this unusually *broad* sense, "insight" and change would go together. But I have not found that an ability to recognize or verbalize such alterations in habitual perception that accompany change is in any way essential to that change, even though it may be necessary to second-order change (the ability independently to continue to change). In general, interactional insight has appeared more important than historico-genetic insight, but the latter nevertheless often facilitates change because it makes the patients' behavior both *meaningful* and obviously *inappropriate* to present circumstances. For example, it may for the first time open the real possibility to the patient that he is not just "naturally" or "born" miserable or hostile, but that he has developed negative emotional *habits*. Thus, curiously, analytic historico-genetic insight may actually make a person receptive to the idea that change based on relearning is possible and so open him to a behavioral approach. Moreover, by relieving guilt, it may also permit more objectivity and ability to face the facts of current behavior, i.e., increase interactional insight. However, it is also my impression that (a) insight follows change as much as the reverse—that they are parts of a cyclic process; and (b) that a combination of historico-genetic and interactional insight is powerful not so much

---

[12]*Editors' Note.* Elsewhere (Gurman and Kniskern, 1978), we have critically examined the evidence of deterioration or the so-called "negative effects" of family therapy. Contrary to Skynner's view here, our analysis suggested that there *are* some serious technical errors that can be made in family therapy in general, and some of which are especially pertinent to a psychodynamically-oriented family therapy,

---

e.g., if the therapist "directly attacks 'loaded' issues and family members' defenses very early in treatment . . . (and) does little to structure and guide the opening of therapy or to support family members" (p. 14).

through a process of "rational understanding" as by making the person aware of the habitual and unvarying nature of his perception and behavior over long duration and under different circumstances. This provides a "shock" of increased awareness through a sudden perception that his usual behavior, which formerly felt "natural," suddenly appears ludicrous, totally inappropriate to his present life, "crazy," and so motivates change.

"Paradoxical" interventions are particularly relevant to this issue of stimulating a more vivid awareness of contradictions in the patient's thought and behavior. Though the "systems purists" tend to treat the individual as a "black box" best left unexplored and seek to change its function only by understanding the pattern of relationships between its "inputs" and "outputs," a glance inside the "black box" might reveal the very simple fact that *all* double-binds and other paradoxical communications are attempts to maintain a fantasy world, different from reality, by expressing *both* fantasy and reality at the same time in a form which conceals the discrepancy between the two, and also by conveying at the same time a "command" to others to collude with the "self-deception" and so preserve the speaker's fantasy world (or the joint fantasy of the marriage or family). Paradoxical *therapeutic* interventions can then be seen not as "tricks" but as expressions of the most essential truth, which subtly break the rule that fantasy and reality must be kept apart, by relating the two in a disguised, seemingly innocent fashion which expresses only the positive aspects. Once the family or couple accept the bait, they cannot avoid seeing more than appeared to be implied in the original paradoxical intervention. And when the essential conflict or contradiction is located, by the therapist exposing himself to the projective system in the manner described above, the therapeutic intervention may be formulated in paradoxical form as readily as any other.

"Techniques," in the sense of detached manipulation of the behavior of others (something you can know how to do before you do it, plans, strategies, etc.), are not an important part of my approach and the whole idea is antithetical to it. Nevertheless, most "techniques" *can* be used at some point in the therapy, if the method described fails, and I have personally learned all I can from other more "technical" schools of family therapy, using any methods that seem helpful. New *skills* are certainly transmitted as part of therapy, usually more by a gradual "shaping" and mainly through "modeling," but didactic methods are used at times, especially with sexual problems.

If one member of the family changes and stays in contact with the rest, then probably all family members change, just as all the solar system is presumably affected by the passage of a comet. But in both cases some changes may be large, others so small as to be immeasurable and irrelevant to practical astronomy, in the one case, or to the handling of the family in the other. The concept of the "minimum sufficient network," described elsewhere in this chapter, is concerned with this issue. The problem of differential motivation has also been addressed. In summary, it is handled as far as possible by constant negotiation and then by addition of separate therapies if the aims of some members go further than others.

My method is not time-limited. When the presenting problem is a complaint about a child, the duration tends to vary between a total of one and six sessions, with an average of around three, if one excludes follow-ups. I do not think a time limit would speed this up particularly, and I personally could not cope with an even briefer exposure to a greater number of families without losing my present enjoyment of my work. Sessions are normally held every three to four weeks, except where more extensive support and supervision are needed, as I have described elsewhere. Bowen (1978) and the Palazzoli group (1978) have found similar advantages to this spacing, which throws responsibility onto the family members and gives them time to digest the experience generated at each interview. The standard length of the session is one hour.

The above comments apply to cases where the marital relationship is basically positive and such problems as exist can be dealt with indirectly through discussions of the management of the referred patient. Where the therapy leads naturally to uncovering serious dissatisfactions in the marriage, or where a couple present initially with severe marital problems, even short-term therapy is likely to be longer than this, ranging between three and twelve sessions. For more resistant problems of all kinds, particularly where a marriage is reproducing serious difficulties due to powerful unresolved attachments to the families of origin of the couple, we routinely employ couples groups led by my wife and myself as co-therapists, not only for their economy but also for their much greater effectiveness, impact and speed of change, as compared with work with one couple at a time. Couples groups are particularly effective with those marital partners who employ defensive mutual projective systems which are particularly intense and highly resistant to insight and change, as well as with those couples seeking growth and differentiation as individuals rather than resolution of a specific problem. Couples groups therefore tend to be used by us for both the healthiest and the sickest patients, though naturally the two extremes will not normally be mixed together, but selected for different groups.

Since in both cases the aim is *differentiation* of the individuals rather than change in the marital system alone, with either an improved marriage (in about four out of five cases) or amicable divorce with cooperation over care of the children (in about one in five cases) as equally acceptable alternatives, therapy is much more prolonged than with the short-term "system-change" interventions. The groups meet weekly with a duration of attendance for successful resolution ranging usually between one and two-and-a-half years (this is about half the time we have found to be needed for similar degrees of individual growth in "stranger" groups run along similar lines).

Termination occurs naturally, usually by some members of the family wondering whether they need to continue coming. This often occurs as the therapist is having similar thoughts, and wondering what else needs to be done. The presenting complaint will have disappeared or diminished to a satisfactory degree, and usually other aspects of functioning will have improved, too.

Termination is ideally a joint decision in this manner, which would be regarded as good/successful. Some families terminate prematurely, i.e., before the presenting problems are solved to the degree thought possible by the therapist, and against advice (such termination

is not always appropriately considered bad/unsuccessful, since if the parting is amicable and a good relationship has been established, some such families return and achieve a good/successful result later). Bad/unsuccessful results would be those cases which were not screened out in the first two interviews as unlikely to benefit for one reason or another, and which receive further family interviews without noticeable benefit.

Treatment Applicability

The methods that I have described were developed in a number of settings ranging, at one extreme, from public hospitals and clinics situated in parts of East and Northeast London with the highest rates of psychosis, delinquency, drug addiction, housing and other social problems in the country, to private practice mainly with intelligent, professional patients including a proportion of the gifted, rich and famous. One striking feature of the methods described here is that they have all appeared to work about equally well right across the social scale, from the most gifted families with members of "genius" intelligence level to the most deprived, disadvantaged, multiproblem families.

However, as noted earlier, this wide applicability is partly due to the fact that the approach is both highly flexible and compatible with at least some aspects of most other approaches, and partly to the fact that no difficulty has been found in combining it with individual, separate "stranger" group or other forms of psychotherapy, medication, etc.

Such problems as my colleagues and I have encountered in these variations of my approach or combinations of it with other methods have almost always proved to be problems in the therapist rather than in the technique. For example, those accustomed to individual work can sometimes be possessive or jealous over patients. Those with a psychoanalytic background often demand to "understand" and have access to all available information, rather than to work with the information immediately available in the interview and trust collaborating colleagues to carry out their separate share of the intervention.

Used in a flexible, highly sensitive way, with

respect for defenses, the method seems particularly valuable with highly defended, "borderline" families, since the therapist can "carry"
the pathology in the early stages and take the
lead in anxiety-provoking areas, leaving the family members free to follow if they wish or to
disown him temporarily if their defenses become too threatened. Apart from this, I have
found no special indications or contraindications
for my approach compared with other family
techniques.

Regarding comparison with other types of
therapy generally, we have also found no contraindication to this family approach for preliminary diagnosis and assessment, even though
individual, stranger group, therapeutic community or other modes of intervention might
then be recommended, perhaps with periodic
joint family sessions to review progress and integrate the work.

Separate psychotherapy for spouses or other
family members is sometimes recommended
when it is vital to establish some measure of
separate identity in members whose personalities are very fused, and where they are too
threatened to attempt this in each other's company. However, in such cases conjoint sessions
can be added beneficially and the combination
of treatments may fruitfully lead on to placement
in multifamily or couples groups. Separate
group or individual treatments of one or more
family members may also be indicated when
conjoint family or couple therapy has produced
as much change as one or more members desire,
but others wish to go further in order to explore
their inner world more deeply and differentiate
themselves more fully from the family system.
Such additional separate treatment is more often
desired and appropriate when couple therapy
has led to agreed separation or divorce, or where
family therapy has enabled an adolescent to become disentangled from parents who wish to
remain in a state of relative fusion. The separate
individual or group psychotherapy is sometimes
carried out by myself or my wife, but many are
referred to psychoanalyst and psychotherapist
colleagues. Where conjoint sessions continue
with one of us, it has appeared best to have
therapists other than ourselves doing the separate treatment with one or more family members. We have found no difficulty where a good

relationship exists with such colleagues, even
when they take sides or are overpossessive,
since our focus is on the interactions among the
family members, or among them and the ther-
apist(s), and on the responses of the latter to the
interactions and (in co-therapy) to each other.
A combination of four-way interviewing and separate sessions with two co-therapists does, however, seem an especially powerful means of
intervention though, because of its high demand
on the therapists' time, we tend to use it only
where there is a risk of psychotic decompensation with any therapy less intensive, supportive and coherent.

"Active" methods of treatment of sexual dysfunction, influenced particularly by the combined behavioral/analytic techniques developed
by Helen Singer Kaplan (1974), are regularly
employed in the course of the conjoint methods
described here, with couples who present with
relationship or sexual problems or, in the case
of family therapy, after the problems displaced
into the children have been brought back into
the marriage, which then becomes the focus,
with the children excluded. In situations where
a dynamic understanding is not of great importance, referral might be made to a behaviorist
or sex therapist.

Referral to a behaviorist or sex therapist might
be made where the initial investigation indicated that the main need was for information,
education, training in skills or techniques, or
where deficient performance seemed due to cultural attitudes or family prohibitions, relatively
uncomplicated by the defenses described in the
psychoanalytic literature which, through their
function of distorting or obliterating the patients' *awareness* of the problem, make reedu-
cation impossible until the defense is reduced.
In particular, one would avoid referring to a
therapist with limited psychodynamic understanding a patient or couple whose defensive
system relied especially on projective mechanisms by which they induced those involved
with them to absorb their problem (e.g., the
impotent man who relieves his feelings of inadequacy by inducing feelings of incompetence
in his therapist), or where the symptoms themselves serve a defensive function (e.g., constant
fighting between a couple as a defense against
(as well as a disguised gratification of) genital or

pregenital intimacy.

Medication would be employed as required to control the more severe depressive states or other emotional reactions interfering with relationship and communication, though this is avoided as far as possible since it generally strengthens defenses opposing change.

Apart from these situations, it is rare to refer patients to other forms of therapy because they are, at least in my experience, slow and inefficient as compared with the methods described here.

A decision not to recommend any treatment at all is generally made when the family makes impossible demands which do not permit a viable contract (e.g., that a child shall behave well even when the parents intend to continue to treat it badly), though even here the door is left open for the family to return should they change their views. Confronting, exploratory approaches are also avoided where a "borderline" parent is functioning as well as can be expected in the community, though we would ensure that a good support system or "safety net" existed, or provide this ourselves, in case of future crises and decompensation. Economic considerations, relating the resources of the clinic to the demand upon them, might lead one to avoid therapy in less severe problems if services are already overburdened by those in more urgent need. But in all these cases, one or two family interviews, which are really a "trial of treatment," usually provide the most economical and accurate method of screening out those families where intervention should be cautious or minimal, where motivation is inadequate to sustain the effort required to bring about change, or where pathology is too limited to justify intervention, given the resources available.

Co-therapy

Economic considerations also influence decisions regarding co-therapy. Following the simple principle that one should not use an expensive or time-consuming procedure where a simpler or less expensive one will do, most treatment is carried out by one therapist. A second is added where the system is so chaotic and confusing that one therapist cannot readily cope alone; where there are gender identity confu-

sions or conflicts which make the presence of male and female role models or advocates of sufficient advantage; where important information may be gained by co-therapists absorbing the projective system of a marriage when other methods of understanding have failed; or where the combination of a more experienced and a less experienced therapist has teaching advantages.

Team therapy using the one-way screen is usually reserved for continued learning through peer-group supervision, for research, or for assistance in cases where treatment has become blocked.

In general, either inability to work alone or inability to work with a co-therapist is regarded as an undesirable limitation in the therapist. Co-therapy is regarded as akin to marriage—an advantage if the partners are well matched and work together harmoniously; a disaster if not, but nevertheless still providing an opportunity for each therapist to learn and grown.

EFFECTIVENESS OF THE APPROACH

It should be said at once that no controlled or otherwise scientifically valid research study exists regarding the effectiveness of the approach described here. An attempt was made by Crowe (1978), a former student of mine and present colleague, who began with, and has retained, a basically behavioral orientation, to compare the results of three forms of conjoint marital interviewing: support only, strict behavioral methods, and a mixture of "systems" and what he describes as "group-analytic" methods learned from me. The research, painstaking and thorough, demonstrates a greater efficacy for behavioral intervention than for support only, with the third group intermediate. But with this third "group-analytic" group he eschewed any form of directive intervention (which is very frequent in my own approach) and made no use of the projective systems information which, as will have become clear, is such a central part of my own work. Together with the fact that almost all the therapy was done by Crowe himself, highly skilled in behavioral methods but with no psychoanalytic training, the research unfortunately sheds little light on the efficacy of methods like my own, which seek to combine analytic and behavioral modes and to gain the best of both worlds.

Clinical experience indicates unusually rapid and dramatic change using my methods, even compared with most other types of family therapy, and this has been confirmed at least by counting of clinical impressions. At the Queen Elizabeth Hospital for Children, a psychiatric social worker, the late Miss P. A. Brierley, made a study (unpublished) of the outcome of all cases seen in the psychiatric department during the year of 1969, some results of which I have detailed elsewhere (Skynner, 1976). Improvement satisfactory to the family was achieved in about one-fifth of all cases in one session, in about one-third in two sessions, and in nearly half within five sessions, in response (as far as could be judged) to the joint family discussions. A further one-fifth of cases referred were judged to be improved or improving due to other forms of intervention, such as boarding school and other special school placement, individual psychotherapy, etc.

About one-third of all referrals were screened out within two interviews as unsuitable for treatment, for reasons given later, and it is of interest that of the total number of referrals seen, only about 2% of those continuing beyond two sessions failed to show beneficial change. Conjoint interviewing therefore appeared to save as much time by showing quickly where therapy would be wasted, as by speeding up change where this was possible. As a result of these two factors, cases dealt with by the psychiatric department of the hospital almost quadrupled over a four-year period, with no increase whatever in staff, and with seemingly better results than had been achieved with traditional methods.

However, it should be emphasized that there was no routine period between the end of treatment and follow-up, and assessment was often based on reports from the school, from referral agencies and from the follow-up notes of the referring pediatricians, rather than on further interviews with the families. Also, with longer durations of treatment, other kinds of therapy (individual, play groups for children, groups for mothers, special schools for children) would often be added. Nevertheless, the figures for rapid results after one or two sessions are less affected by this and are much more likely to be attributable to the family sessions alone.

I did systematically follow up the 20 cases in Miss Brierley's study referred with the complaint of school phobia, through enquiry to the schools between two and three years after termination of treatment. The results, reported in a paper (Skynner, 1974a), show excellent and enduring results, usually after only one or two treatment sessions, even in children who had been off school for over a year. The exceptions were a truant misdiagnosed as school phobic and where advice to the school was not followed, a hallucinated schizophrenic, and two true cases of school phobia who changed to the care of colleagues using conventional approaches.

It should be added that the types of referral to the hospital psychiatric department were predisposed to better results, since they contained high proportions of neurotic, psychosomatic and habit disorders, and attendance was supported by the exclusively medical referrers. A similar study at the neighboring Woodberry Down Child Guidance Unit, a local authority clinic receiving mainly nonmedical referrals from schools with high proportions of antisocial behavior, minor delinquency etc., and where the families were likely to be less cooperative, would almost certainly have produced lower rates of success. But the increased efficiency of treatment, the greater number of cases helped, and the consequent diminution in waiting time, whereby families were seen early when most receptive, appeared to be roughly in proportion when compared with conventional methods used previously, even with this more difficult population.

I have quoted here only studies which have involved some measures, even though only clinical judgments, of a representative group of referrals. There has, however, been very painstaking follow-up of particular families where the outcome seemed likely to throw light on broader issues, and such follow-ups, during the past 18 years, have confirmed the impression given above of rapid and dramatic change in a considerable proportion of cases.

In my view, the most pressing needs for future research into the approach described here are: (a) Does it *in fact* work unusually quickly and if so (b) is the specific mechanism responsible for the rapid change the one put forward here—the therapist's manifesting the "denied" emotions in a supportive context? A third line of research, if the first two beliefs were supported, would be to examine the possibility that a considerable proportion of more experienced family therapists, who seem to achieve rapid results through intuitive rather than rational and carefully planned interventions, may be making use of the projective mechanisms described without realizing it (as I had done until the need to write this chapter stimulated me to study the process, particularly my subjective experience during interviews, more carefully).[13]

TRAINING FOR THE GROUP-ANALYTIC APPROACH

No systematic and comprehensive training program embodying the central principles which set my approach off from others so far exists, so what I have to say here is extrapolated from the teaching programs that I have initiated and colleagues have developed and extended; it is also extrapolated, in a negative sense, from what I have seen of programs lacking the open-systems design I believe to be essential.

The cornerstone of a full "training," as opposed to an introductory or supportive program, must be the treatment of actual families under supervision. In view of the vital importance of nonverbal communication, this is best carried out by observation through a one-way screen, where the clearest and broadest impression of the family's nonverbal responses can be obtained, or, failing this, by closed-circuit television or videotape. Nevertheless, the quality of the supervision is obviously more important than the "hardware" and a second-rate supervisor may produce less competent students with the most sophisticated aids than a first-class supervisor using case discussion alone. If I overemphasize this, it is perhaps because I see so many therapists overvaluing the "hardware" and hoping that technical "gimmicks" will somehow substitute for hard-earned understanding, experience and skill. Apart from this, I would like to see students exposed to as many theories and

techniques as possible, though within a sequence of presentation and of accompanying coordinated discussion which would limit confusion and help them build an approach to suit their individual capacities. The family therapy teaching programs I initiated within the Institute of Group Analysis, now run within the Institute of Family Therapy, have always had this broadly-based character, including psychoanalytic, group-analytic, behavioral, systems, "action" and psycho-dramatic methods, active techniques of treating sexual dysfunction and so on. I think no major disagreement would be likely to arise about the value of any form of teaching advocated by other contributors to this volume, except insofar as they might advocate their own methods at the expense of others rather than in addition to them.

I will now concentrate on what is essential and perhaps more specific for training in the methods I am advocating.

When I put some questions to my wife, who shared with me the task of setting up the first courses in what has now become the Institute of Family Therapy (London), as to what was most essential, her replies were so concise and clear that I would like to quote them. In contrast to our own methods, which she experienced as simple and direct, she had noted that many colleagues she had observed both in Britain and the U.S.A. seemed often unable to see the obvious and simple issues staring them in the face and to lose sight of the essence of the problems through introducing unnecessarily complicated concepts and techniques. Highly involved analytic interpretations and complicated "strategies" and activities like sculpting or task-setting seemed to her more often used by professionals to escape their own anxiety and personal problems than to reveal those of the family. She felt that all techniques could be useful but that their misuse seemed always to arise from the professional's reluctance to face his own personal problems and motivations clearly. She had also been impressed by the slowness of most approaches, by the fears that so many people expressed regarding direct and painful confrontation, and by the apparent anxiety over trusting nonverbal information and spontaneous response.

Whatever technical training is provided, it will be of limited value (though certainly of some

---

[13]*Editors' Note.* These are, indeed, very researchable predictions which, if confirmed, would shed a great deal of light on the nature of the salient mechanisms by which family therapy produces (or fails to produce) positive effects.

value nevertheless) unless the professional is put through experiences which clarify his motivation in taking up his work, put him more deeply in touch with the limitations and deficiencies in himself, his family of origin, his marriage and family of procreation or alternative current personal relationships.

It will be clear that the most essential feature of my approach lies in a very direct, open involvement with patients where it is taken for granted by the therapist that communication is two-way, that a learning process is set in motion whereby the therapist will change and grow if the patients are to have the best chance of growing too. The therapist's personality and values, marriage and family life must *actually* be in question every time he engages with the family. He must demonstrate the possibility of facing loss, growth, change and death by the way he functions himself and by the way he changes and learns from one session to another. This sounds a tall order, but it is more a principle that the therapist should be like a mountain guide who goes ahead and tests the footholds first himself, then helps others up behind him, rather than that he should be like a perfect climber familiar with every detail of the mountain. There is no more problem (and no less!) in teaching from this position than there is in practicing from it in therapy, for if the right model is provided by the teacher it has the same rapid effect on the trainee as modeling by the therapist has on families. This type of rapid (yet apparently relatively enduring) change is worth emphasizing, because I believe that the essence of the requisite training experience lies in this kind of modeling, encouraging, supporting interaction. Obviously more can be learned over a longer period, but the crucial aspect of what is needed to teach my approach is totally different from the slow, dogged attempt to accumulate knowledge sequentially through increasing experience, which many family therapists equate with training. The transmission process is not accomplished all at once, of course, but each new understanding is suddenly "caught" in a flash of illumination, if it is grasped at all.

Besides helping people to learn about themselves through supervision of their work, where the focus will be more on those personal difficulties which interfere with the task, most methods of increasing self-knowledge are likely to be beneficial unless they are misused in defensive fashion. My experience of students with prior individual or group therapy greatly favors the latter, and though individual therapy may be desirable for trainees with problems over intimacy and separation, rigid classical analysis tends to give trainees a therapeutic experience that appears, more often than not, to make it *more* difficult for them to learn family therapy subsequently. This is because of the excessive preoccupation they develop with intellectual "understanding" and control of the situation, with focus on detail, with emphasis on therapist passivity and neutrality, with fear of personal exposure, and with a generally rather precious and over-exquisite preoccupation with the importance of the therapist's role. I believe that couples groups composed of trainees and their spouses would be better than separate therapy alone, perhaps together with some sessions with the trainees' children as well as their spouses. This we have not done, except "accidentally" where the trainees sought assistance with marital or family difficulties directly, but Bowen (1978) has attempted it beneficially.

We have, however, made very full use of encouraging trainees in systematic studies of their families of origin, following closely the ideas of Bowen (1978) and Framo (1976). We have found this invaluable and I would regard it as an indispensable part of any family therapist's training, whatever other form of personal psychotherapy is advocated in addition.

Finally, the constant study and monitoring of the group dynamics of both staff and student groups, particularly the interaction between these and the way in which the professional systems reproduce typical family dynamics (e.g., casting of leaders or subgroups into "father" and "mother" roles, provoking conflict between them, etc.), and the feeding back of this information to the staff-student groups have appeared to me the most powerful learning experience of all, providing both firsthand experience of pathological "family" dynamics and simultaneous opportunities to learn and move towards more healthy forms of structure and communication. In such studies of the professional system, there is a particular need to focus on (since there is a strong tendency to avoid) issues of loss, separation and death; sexuality; and competition. I have described the application of this method in a number of papers (Skynner 1965, 1968, 1974b, 1975), and last of which (Skynner and Skynner, 1979) reports on its use in our introductory teaching program at the Institute of Family Therapy. Ideally, an expert in group dynamics not involved in the hierarchy of the institution being studied should be brought in for crucial meetings of this kind at least from time to time, acting as "family therapist" to the "institutional family." Difficult though this may appear, it seems to me that senior members of institutions might be able to perform this role effectively with institutions other than their own; indeed, the meeting together of different staff groups in conference conditions often has a liberating and facilitating effect of this kind.

Needless to say, the level and extent of self-knowledge needed will depend on the general level of skill required. Simple behavioral methods have the advantage of demanding little of the personality and self-knowledge of the therapist, and are adequate for many cases. Paraprofessionals could use some of the simpler concepts presented here, under supervision, but should obviously not be encouraged to try to work with the projective system in the manner described. Nevertheless, the ideas used here can be extremely valuable in the supervision of paraprofessionals or less highly experienced therapists, if the supervisor makes use of his awareness of the projective process in a manner similar to that described by Caplan (1964), where the supervisor avoids confronting the supervisee with his own psychopathology but uses the supervisee's "countertransference" responses to help him understand and identify with the family.

Whatever form of personal psychotherapeutic experience is recommended, an open-systems training demands that the trainee's motives for taking up his work be made a constant focus throughout. Since the professional roles of mental health professionals form a central part of their defensive systems (Skynner, 1964, 1968, 1976), which maintain a split between "parental" and "infantile" aspects of the personality, failure to explore this crucial area adequately must lead to limited self-understanding and a tendency to burden patients and students with infantile aspects of the therapist's or teacher's projective system, restricting the growth of those with whom they work. Also, since the therapy of trainee therapists is inevitably carried out by other mental health professionals sharing a similar defensive system, some collusion in avoiding such exploration is inevitable. This is one reason why an open-systems attitude to a joint exploration of the group process of training institutes, including the interaction of teachers, students and patients, is so essential. To the extent that its authority is accepted (and only to that extent) the group process provides information which can enable all individuals, including the leadership group, to grow beyond the limitations of their shared defense system.

REFERENCES

Barlow, W. *The Alexander Principle*. London, Gollancz, 1973.

Barnhill, L. R. & Longo, D. Fixation and regression in the family life cycle. *Family Process*, 1978, *17*, 469-478.

Beavers, W. H. *Psychotherapy and Growth: A Family Systems Perspective*. New York: Brunner/Mazel, 1977.

Beels, C. C. & Ferber, A. Family therapy: A view. *Family Process*. 1969, *9*, 280-318.

Bell, J. E. Recent advances in family group therapy. *Journal of Child Psychology and Psychiatry*, 1962, *3*, 1-21.

Bertalanffy, L. V. *General System Theory*. New York: Braziller, 1968.

Boszormenyi-Nagy, I. Intensive family therapy as process. In: I. Boszormenyi-Nagy & J. Framo (Eds.) *Intensive Family Therapy*. New York: Harper and Row, 1965.

Boszormenyi-Nagy, I. and Spark, G. M. *Invisible Loyalties*. New York: Harper and Row, 1973.

Bowen, M. *Family Therapy in Clinical Practice*. New York: Jason Aronson, 1978.

Bowlby, J. *Attachment and Loss*. Vols I and II. New York: Basic Books, 1969 and 1973.

Caplan, G. *Principles of Preventive Psychiatry*. London: Tavistock, 1964.

Crawshay-Williams, R. *Russell Remembered*. London: Oxford University Press, 1970.

Crowe, M. J. Conjoint marital therapy: A controlled outcome study. *Psychological Medicine*, 1978, *8*, 623-636.

Dare, C. Psychoanalysis and systems in family therapy. *Journal of Family Therapy*, 1979, *1*, 137-152.

Dicks, H. V. *Marital Tensions*. Boston and London: Routledge and Kegan Paul, 1967.

Dollard, J. & Miller, N. E. *Personality and Psychotherapy*. New York: McGraw-Hill, 1950.

Duvall, E. *Family Development*. Chicago: Lippincott, 1957.

Fisher, S. & Mendell, D. The communication of neurotic patterns over two and three generations. *Psychiatry*, 1956, *19*, 41-46.

Foulkes, S. H. *Introduction to Group-Analytic Psychotherapy*. London: Heinemann, 1948.

Foulkes, S. H. *Therapeutic Group Analysis*. London: Allen and Unwin, 1964.

Foulkes, S. H. & Anthony, E. J. *Group Psychotherapy: The Psycho-analytic Approach.* Harmondsworth, England: Penguin Books, 1957; 2nd Edition 1965.

Framo, J. L. Family of origin as a therapeutic resource for adults in family and marital therapy: You can and should go home again. *Family Process.* 1976, *15*, 193-210.

Groesbeck, C. J. and Taylor, B. The psychiatrist as wounded physician, *American Journal of Psychoanalysis*, 1979, *37*, 131-139.

Haley, J. *Problem-Solving Therapy.* San Francisco: Jossey-Bass, 1976.

Heard, D. H. From object relations to attachment theory: A basis for family therapy. *British Journal of Medical Psychology,* 1978, *51*, 67-76.

Jung, C. G. *The Practice of Psychotherapy.* Collected Works, Vol. 16, Routledge & Kegan Paul, 1954.

Kaplan, H. S. *The New Sex Therapy.* New York: Brunner/Mazel, 1974.

Korzybski, A. *General Semantics.* Lancaster, Penn.: Science Press, 1933.

Lewis, J. M., Beavers, W. R., Gossett, J. T., & Phillips, V. A. *No Single Thread: Psychological Health in Family Systems.* New York: Brunner/Mazel, 1976.

Lyons, L. Therapeutic intervention in relation to the institution of marriage. In: R. Gosling (Ed.) *Support, Innovation and Autonomy.* New York: Harper and Row, 1973.

Miller, J. G. Living systems: basic concepts. *Behavioural Science,* 1965, *10*, 193-245.

MacGregor, R., Ritchie, A. M., Serrano, A. C., Schuster, F. P., McDanald, E. C., & Goolishian, H. A. *Multiple Impact Therapy with Families.* New York: McGraw-Hill, 1964.

Minuchin, S. *Families and Family Therapy.* Cambridge, MA: Harvard University Press, 1974.

Mishler, E. & Waxler, N. *Interaction in Families.* New York: John Wiley and Sons, 1968.

Mowrer, O. H. *Learning Theory and Personality Dynamics,* New York: Ronald Press, 1950.

Napier, A. Y. & Whitaker, C. A. *The Family Crucible.* New York: Harper and Row, 1978.

Palazzoli, M. S., Cecchin, G., Prata, G., & Boscolo, L. *Paradox and Counter Paradox.* New York: Jason Aronson, 1978.

Pincus, L. (Ed.) *Marriage: Studies in Emotional Conflict and Growth.* London: Methuen, 1960.

Pincus, L. & Dare, C. *Secrets in the Family.* Boston and London: Faber and Faber, 1978.

Rothenberg, J. The archaic song of Dr. Tom the Shaman. Song 99 in H. Roberts & M. Swadsesh (Eds.), *Songs of the Nootka Indians of Western Vancouver Island: Transactions of the American Philosophical Society,* Vol. 45, Part 3. New York: Doubleday, 1972.

Satir, V. *Conjoint Family Therapy.* Palo Alto, CA: Science and Behavior Books, 1964.

Skynner, A. C. R. Group-analytic themes in training and case-discussion groups. In: *Selected Lectures: 6th International Congress of Psychotherapy.* New York: Karger, 1965.

Skynner, A. C. R. A family of family casework agencies. *International Journal of Group Psychotherapy,* 1968, *18*, 352-361.

Skynner, A. C. R. School phobia: A reappraisal. *British Journal of Medical Psychology.* 1974 (a), *47*, 1-16.

Skynner, A. C. R. An experiment in group consultation with the staff of a comprehensive school. *Group Process,* 1974 (b), *6*, 99-114.

Skynner, A. C. R. The large group in training. In: L. C. Kreeger (Ed.) *The Large Group; Dynamics and Therapy.* London: Constable, 1975.

Skynner, A. C. R. *Systems of Family and Marital Psychotherapy.* New York: Brunner/Mazel, 1976. (British Edition entitled *One Flesh: Separate Persons.* London, Constable 1976).

Skynner, A. C. R. The physician as family therapist. In: G. Usdin & J. M. Lewis (Eds.) *Psychiatry in General Medical Practice.* New York: McGraw-Hill, 1979.

Skynner, A. C. R. & Skynner, P. M. An open-systems approach to teaching family therapy. *Journal of Marital and Family Therapy.* 1979, *5*, 5-16.

Sonne, J. C. & Lincoln, G. Heterosexual co-therapy relationship and it's significance in family therapy. In: S. Friedman, *Psychotherapy for the Whole Family.* New York: Springer, 1965.

Stabenau, J. R., Tupin, J., Werner, M., & Pollin, W. A. A comparative study of families of schizophrenics, delinquents, and normals. *Psychiatry,* 1965, *28*, 45-59.

Watzlawick, P., Beavin, J. & Jackson, D. *Pragmatics of Human Communication.* New York: Norton, 1967.

Westley, W. A. & Epstein, N. B. *The Silent Majority.* San Francisco: Jossey-Bass, 1970.

Whitehead, A. N. & Russell, B. *Principia Mathematica.* Cambridge, England: Cambridge University Press, 1910.

Winnicott, D. W. *Therapeutic Consultations in Child Psychiatry.* London: Hogarth Press, 1971.

Zeeman, E. C. Catastrophe Theory. *Scientific American,* 1977 (January) *236* (1), 65-83.

EDITORS' REFERENCES

Gurman, A. S. & Kniskern, D. P. Deterioration in marital and family therapy: Empirical, clinical and conceptual issues. *Family Process,* 1978, *17*, 3-20.

Parloff, M. B. The narcissism of small differences—and some big ones. *International Journal of Group Psychotherapy,* 1976, *26*, 311-319.

Steinglass, P. The conceptualization of marriage from a systems theory perspective. In: T. Paolino & B. McCrady (Eds.), *Marriage and marital therapy.* New York: Brunner/Mazel, 1978.

CHAPTER 3

Couples Therapy and
Marriage Contracts

Clifford J. Sager, M.D.

Marriage contracts have existed at least since the beginning of recorded history. The term is used now to refer to a variety of actual contracts as well as to more nebulous "understandings" and assumptions. Ancient marriage contracts usually set forth economic stipulations for the couple as well as certain responsibilities and duties. These still exist both in legal and religious forms. Clear definition and agreement to terms by both parties lessen the likelihood of problems, but such a document cannot deal with emotional reactions, desires, expectations or with changed conditions over a long period of time. In recent years, recognizing their own credo and feelings, some couples have written their own marriage contracts, which may even include a clause providing for reexamination of the contract and an opportunity for redecision regarding maintenance of the marriage after a designated period. *All these contracts presuppose that it is possible for both mates to know all the terms of their contracts and that there are no secret clauses, fine print or hidden expectations or agendas.*

Some behavior therapists have helped cou-

ples to work out marriage contracts that stress the behavior of the spouses (Patterson, 1971). They then use their therapeusis to reinforce the positive behavior and discourage negative behavior that the mates have defined for themselves. This approach has been helpful to many.

The expectations that individuals have of their mates and what they themselves wish to give to the relationship and to the partner are little discussed by most potential mates. In fact, aspects of these expectations are even unknown to the person who has them. *It is these unexpressed and often unconscious and contradictory expectations that have been inadequately explored and not brought to the full awareness of both partners.* We even fail to teach young adults about the existence of the area of these needs (How much distance do I need? Should or can I share power? and so on). Within one's own family life and education for life we offer some preparation for other aspects of marriage. What training is offered most commonly deals with concrete matters, rarely with more subtle emotional needs and expectations. Yet it is just these latter that may determine whether a relationship succeeds or founders, whether it produces a measure of happiness or of misery.

In developing the marriage contract concept I have tried to arrive at some of the factors that are decisive in determining the quality of intimate relationships. I originally started this exploration with the hope of finding a way to organize the flood of data that married individuals would lay at my couch, so that I could develop a skeleton that could be fleshed out and give clues to developing a flexible therapeutic plan for each couple. This search, over many years of clinical work and with the help of numerous colleagues, has led to the development of a theoretical structure regarding dyadic system interaction. This schema considers individual intrapsychic factors that help to determine the system and in turn are affected by the dyadic system, some understanding of determinants of interactions, a typology of marriages, and an eclectic therapeutic approach. The approach is not complete or without its flaws. It is ever in transition and development as it is tested, utilized and critically examined by others.[1]

The goals of this chapter are 1) to offer a series of hypotheses that will contribute to an understanding of why people behave as they do in marriage—and in other committed relationships[2]; 2) to offer a flexible, eclectic approach to therapy that is based on those hypotheses; and 3) to suggest that marital therapy can be valuable for treating the married individual in distress, as well as for those couples with marital dysfunction.

THE CONTRACTS

The term "marriage contracts" used in the title of this chapter is a purposeful misnomer. As I use the term, I am not referring to formal contracts in which both contracting parties

---

[1]I urge you, as you read what follows, to think of yourself and your most intimate relationships. Try to see if the picture I draw fits together and makes sense for you and your partner before you distance yourself from the material by thinking of "cases." If it does make sense, then I urge you to test it out in your own clinical work.

[2]In this chapter I refer to all couples in a committed relationship. Whether couples are married or not, heterosexual or homosexual, similar systemic interactional and intrapsychic phenomena pertain.

clearly see the terms written out, have carefully negotiated, or have had others negotiate for them, and then agreed to and signed the same document. In the "contracts" I refer to each mate has his/her own terms that often differ in important respects. Not only does the mate not know parts of the other's terms, but each is also unaware of important aspects of his/her own terms. Some terms, within the same person, may be contradictory and the source of inconsistent behavior and/or ambivalent feelings. Each person thinks he/she gives what he/she "contracts" to give and expects his/her partner *to give in exchange* what the first wants. Clinical experience has convinced me that many of the terms are based not only on current styles of philosophy and mores, but also on earlier introjected childhood influences. With this understanding, one begins to appreciate some of the reasons for the instability currently characterizing marriage now that institutional, ideological, technological and economic changes have made it relatively easy to break the union.

Clinical experience suggests that the emotional and behavioral problems of women and men can be treated effectively by utilizing the power of the marital interaction, even when the individual's symptoms are not manifested primarily within the marital relationship. *Conjoint treatment need not be reserved solely for the treatment of marital disharmony.* Manifestations of distorted perceptions, repressions, transferentially determined feelings and actions, mechanisms of defense and unrealistic expectations of one's spouse that exist in many marriages can rapidly provide a source of excellent therapeutic leverage. Working with the couple together often provides an opportunity to treat individual symptomatology and its etiological sources as well as marital disharmony.

The central concept in this approach is that each partner in a marriage brings to it an individual, unwritten "contract," a set of expectations and promises, conscious and unconscious. These individual contracts may be modified during the marriage but will remain separate unless the two partners are fortunate enough to arrive at a single joint contract that is "felt" and agreed to at all levels of awareness, or unless they work toward a single contract with professional help.

In a sense, the work of therapy can be seen

as helping a couple arrive at one functioning contract the terms of which both partners are aware of and can subscribe to. Each partner can then give and get a fair measure in exchange. Expectations and fears are out front. Not all terms need be fully in accord with both partners' optimal desires, but crucial terms for each do have to be close enough so that compromises can be made if necessary. Often, where one or two crucial areas are worked through in moving towards a single contract, others readily fall into place. For some mates, of course, the effort will demonstrate that the partners cannot give each what he or she wants or needs and that there is no possibility for these two people to arrive at a viable agreement. Compromise, quid pro quo arrangements, allaying of anxiety (and hence defensive reactions), and improved communication skills will be prime forces in helping couples to arrive at a single contract.

A corollary of this central concept is that every committed couple develops an operational, interactional contract or script. This script is the creation of their marital system, the conscious and unconscious ways in which the two people work together, or against each other, to try to fulfill the terms of their individual contracts. This is a joint script or "contract" because each partner usually unconsciously colludes in the marital system's activity, that is, tacitly acting out a variety of games with each other, each intuitively knowing how far he or she can go in any direction before having to change course before destroying the system.

The interactional script, or the "rules of the game," of a couple is the basis on which each mate interacts with the other in a characteristic style to attempt to fulfill his/her own contract. The major thrust of one's adaptation in this "game" is his/her behavioral profile. That is, the profile is a description of a partner's behavior with his spouse as he attempts to get what he wants in any way possible to him, and how he "protects" himself or collaborates with his spouse in the other's endeavors to fulfill her contract. These profiles provide an easily comprehensible topography of that couple's relationship. Later I shall make clear how the concept of the marriage contract, along with the interactional contract, provides the basic information and dynamic framework for determining therapeutic inter-

ventions. Along with the behavioral profiles and the interactional contract, the marriage contract provides a basis for the therapist to utilize therapeutic approaches that are consistent with his own predilections and prejudices. To develop a meaningful holistic theory of this most complex of human relationships still eludes us because there are so many independent variables that are operative in mate selection and maintenance of a couple relationship over time.

THE TWO INDIVIDUAL MARRIAGE CONTRACTS

The marriage contract is a concept, not an entity, yet partners react as if it were a true contract, one that is commonly breached by the mate, but not by oneself. The breach may occur of course, because the mate is unaware that his/her partner has a set of terms that differ from his/her own. For example, partner X has not fully expressed that he/she expects partner Y to protect X from loneliness at all times. Y, unaware of this expectation, for the first time in their marriage goes away for a routine business trip for three days, calling briefly each evening. On Y's return both partners are perplexed by X's angered and hurt feelings. Y had violated X's contract but was unaware of having done so, as was X, too, because X was unaware of the expectation he/she had. The short-term bonding stage of "being in love" is usually the stage in which one enters into a marriage. This period has among its characteristics an unconscious desire to please the beloved and to see him/her unrealistically, that is, as we wish that person to be. Hence, it is easy for one to assume in this period that one's beloved subscribes to the same unspoken set of terms. Evidence to the contrary is pushed aside and denied, the warning signs suppressed and repressed.

Each "contract" has terms on three levels of awareness: *verbalized*—these terms are discussed with each other, although not always heard by the receiver; *conscious but not verbalized*—these are the parts of one's own contract of which one is aware but which are not verbalized to the mate, usually out of fear of anger or disapproval; *beyond awareness or unconscious*—these aspects are beyond one's usual awareness. One may have an idea of what some of these are. They are often sensed as a passing internal caution, impulse or a fleeting feeling of concern that gets pushed away. Stopping to think often brings some of these to light. Each mate can help the other surface these, as does the therapist. Some of these contractual terms are often inconsistent with one's conscious self-image. A reminder list (Table 1) for patients defines the nature of these three levels of awareness.

Individual marriage contracts contain clauses that cover most aspects of feelings, needs, activities and relationships. *Not all areas need to be dealt with clinically, since disharmony within a marriage is usually determined and characterized by a few major issues.* Some issues may be important to one partner but not to the other and can readily become the basis for quid pro quo exchanges when they come out into the open. The most common subjects for contractual clauses are listed here and organized into three categories for the therapist's consideration, so that one may select the areas that pertain most to an individual or particular couple.

An almost unlimited number of areas might be included in a marital contract, but to attempt to include all possibilities would be unnecessary. Therapists or partners may add additional subjects that may be important for them. The contractual terms can be divided into these three categories: 1) parameters based on expectations of the marriage; 2) those based on intrapsychic and biological needs; and 3) those based on external foci.

Category 1. Expectations of the Marriage

The act of becoming married, whether or not actually licensed by state or clergy, denotes an important level of commitment of self to the mate and to a new entity, the marriage. Each partner marries for certain purposes and with specific goals, bringing to the marriage the expectations he/she has of the institution itself. Generally, not all of these purposes and goals are fully conscious.

In addition to the expectations each partner has of what marriage will give him/her and what he/she is willing to give to it, the marital system itself, like any other system, may modify existing goals or create new ones. The most common

TABLE 1
Reminder List for Marriage or Couple Contracts

"Marriage contract" is a misnomer as the term is used here because we are not referring to formal contracts. These are not legally written contracts or agreements that both mates write out and subscribe to openly. You each have your own "contract" that probably differs from the other. Do not be surprised if your own contract is inconsistent because you simultaneously may have strong contradictory wishes or needs. For example, you may have the desire to be independent and yet at the same time also require your mate's approval of your actions. Contradictions are common for most of us.

Each "contract" has three levels of awareness:

1) *Verbalized*—these are discussed with each other, although not always heard by the receiver.
2) *Conscious but not verbalized*—the parts of your contract that you are aware of but do not verbalize to your spouse because you fear his/her anger, disapproval, you feel embarrassed, etc.
3) *Beyond awareness or unconscious*—aspects that are beyond your usual awareness. You may have an idea of what some of these are. They are often felt as a warning light in your head or a fleeting feeling of concern that gets pushed away. Do the best you can with these.

Each person acts as if the other knew the terms of the "contract" (which were never really agreed upon) and feels angered, hurt, betrayed, etc. when he/she believes the spouse did not fulfill his/her part of the "contract." In each area, note down where you believe your partner did not keep his/her part of the bargain. Do not worry about being fair. How do you *really feel* about it? How about your own lack of keeping your part of the agreement?

"Contractual" terms, i.e., desires, expectations and what you are *willing to give* as well as want from marriage and your mate, fall into three general categories. This reminder list consists of these three categories; following under each are listed several common areas that are sources of marital and personal trouble. Some you may have thought of before, others not.

Leave plenty of time, two or three hours, for both of you to talk together about how each one feels about the terms. Really get into it—examine yourself and your partner carefully. Write down where you disagree. Do not attempt to resolve differences the first time around—just see what each of you wants, expects and understands. Sometimes a few questions can use up the discussion period—do not rush. If you can complete one section a week that is a fine pace.

Respond to all areas that are meaningful to you. Skip the others—but think it through first. Improvise others that are meaningful to you if they are not listed.

Read through the reminder list together first, then go back and start with Category I, item a.

---

initial expectations are that marriage may provide:

1) A mate who will be loyal, devoted, loving and exclusive—someone with whom to grow and develop.
2) A constant support against the rest of the world. Spouses are expected to stand by each other in times of need, whether the adversity derives from external sources, such as loss of a job or an encounter with the law, or from within, as in the case of physical or mental illness.
3) Companionship and insurance against loneliness.
4) Achievement of one's ultimate relationship goal. Instead of regarding marriage as one point along the continuum of a relationship that is constantly evolving new goals, some people assume that, in some magical fashion, they will live happily ever after once they are married.
5) A panacea for the chaos and strife in one's life. All will now be calm and orderly.
6) A relationship that must last "until death do us part." Marriage has traditionally been viewed as a lifelong commitment. This concept has now changed for many.
7) Sanctioned and readily available sex.
8) A family and the experience of reproducing and participating in the growth and development of children.
9) A relationship that emphasizes the family rather than just a mate. This concept is somewhat akin to that of the "good corporation team member." We have contradictory mainstreams in the United States today, one stressing the primacy of the individual, another that of the dyad, and a third (and the most traditional) the primacy of the family unit.
10) Others to be included in or excluded from the new family—parents, children, friends, even pets.

11) A home, a refuge from the world.
12) A respectable position and status in society. Many people feel that there is a certain status in being married, in being or having a wife or husband.
13) Economic security.
14) A social unit. The family as an economic and social unit contributes to a sense of continuity, of building and planning for the future, which in itself gives meaning and purpose to a person's life. Marriage lends purpose to the lives of most people. Without it, many believe (correctly or not) that they do not have a purpose.
15) An umbrella image to sanctify one's desire to work, build and accumulate wealth, power and position.
16) A respectable cover for aggressive drives. Competitive and hostile characteristics are rationalized as being for the good of the family. Marriage supplies a socially acceptable channel for aggressive impulses, since providing for and protecting one's family, home and possessions are socially sanctioned and encouraged.

Category 2. Intrapsychic and Biological Determinants

Items in Category 2 are based on the needs and desires that arise from within the individual. These items are determined in large part by intrapsychic and biological factors rather than by the marital system per se, although the latter may have a great modifying effect. Thus, these parameters derive from the individual as a system, while those discussed in the first category are related to marriage as the system. These "individual" parameters are important because the mate, as distinguished from the institution of marriage itself, is the subsystem that is expected to fulfill the needs of the other subsystem. Some of the individual's needs are of biological origin and others develop from the familial and the broader cultural environment. As I describe areas in this category, I am not concerned with the etiology of particular needs. Some such factors may have been part of the personality of the individual for a long time; others have been only potential and required interaction with a particular mate to become realized. There is usually no sharp line but a shading, an area of overlap, that separates the category of intrapsychic and biological needs from the other two. Much of the material is beyond awareness and becomes clear through deduction from the patient's total productions and actions and those of the spouse. Although the descriptions of what we see in this category will vary somewhat with the therapist's orientation, some aspects will be perceived similarly by the clinician and the patients themselves, regardless of biases.

The reciprocal nature of the individual contracts, both conscious and beyond awareness, is especially important: "I want so-and-so and in *exchange* I am willing to give such-and-such." It is the latent emotional charge in this dialectic that touches off a great proportion of marital dysfunction when one mate feels he/she has fulfilled his/her end of the bargain, but the other has failed to fulfill his/her part. Each partner tends to feel self-righteous as the other is condemned as a contract- or promise-breaker.

1) *Independence-dependence*. This crucial area involves the individual's ability to take care of and function for himself. Does he or she require a spouse to complete the sense of self or to initiate what he cannot do himself? Is there a feeling of inability to survive without the mate? Is one's sense of worth dependent on the spouse's attitude or feeling toward him/her? Is he/she dependent on the mate to initiate plans, to set their taste, pace and style?

2) *Activity-passivity*. This parameter concerns the individual's desire and ability to take action necessary to bring about what he or she wants. Can he be active in deed as well as in idea? If passive, is he hostile to an active mate? For example, will he exercise veto power without suggesting alternative proposals?

3) *Closeness-distance*. Does anxiety increase with closeness or exposure of feelings, thoughts and acts to one's mate? Communication patterns and problems are frequently related to the ability or inability to tolerate closeness. Is communication open enough to make needs known, to solve prob-

lems, to share feelings and experiences? "Tell me what you are thinking" can be an intrusive, controlling inquiry or an invitation to an open, intimate and honest dialogue. What defenses against closeness does each mate exhibit? How imperative is the need for one's own living space? How strongly will one resist intrusion upon it?

4) *Use-abuse of power*. The relationship to power and the need for it color most marriages. Can power be shared in the marriage or can one partner only delegate to the other? Once acquired, power can be employed directly or indirectly, delegated or abdicated. Can the individual accept and use power without ambivalence and anxiety? Is he or she so fearful of not having power that he must be in control, or is he even paranoid about his mate's having power? Conversely, does he have a need to renounce his own desire for power and an expectation that the partner's power will be used in his behalf?

5) *Dominance-submission* ("the seesaw configuration"—if one is up, the other must be down). This may be consistent with the independence-dependence area. Who submits? Who dominates? Or are matters resolved in other ways by this couple? This parameter overlaps with the power parameter just as the independence and power parameters overlap each other.

6) *Fear of loneliness or abandonment*. To what extent is "love" for the mate motivated by fear of being alone? What is the mate expected to do to prevent loneliness and to alleviate the spouse's fear of desertion? How do such fears make the individual function in the relationship? Has he chosen a mate who is likely to stay with him or someone who is bound to feed on his fears about desertion?

7) *Need to possess and control*. Does the individual have to control or possess his/her mate in order to feel secure? This area could be subsumed under the parameter of power but, used separately, it elicits much additional useful information.

8) *Level of anxiety*. This domain and mechanisms of defense are often neglected areas

of consideration in work with couples. For physiological and/or psychological reasons, some people experience a higher level of anxiety than others. Anxiety may be revealed openly or indirectly via the defenses against its awareness or overt manifestation. How does the overt anxiety or defense against anxiety affect the mate? Can the mate accept the partner's anxiety without accepting blame for it? Does he or she respond in a way that decreases or increases the anxiety?

9) *Mechanisms of defense.* What are each mate's characteristic ways of dealing with anxiety? How does his or her style affect the mate? The therapist should look for the most common mechanisms of defense: sublimation, altruistic surrender, repression, regression, reaction formation, perceptual defense (and/or denial), inhibition of impulses and affect, introjection (incorporation and identification), reversal (turning against self), displacement, projection, isolation and intellectualization, undoing (magic), and fantasy (to sustain denial).

10) *Love.* Does each partner have to love the other? How is love understood? Is it short-term bonding with its intensity of "being in love" or long-term bonding? Is there anxiety over the end of short-term bonding, and can each accept the shift to long-term bonding without feeling that the shift threatens the foundation of the relationship?

11) *Gender identity.* "Gender identity," according to Money and Ehrhardt (1972), "is the sameness, unity and persistence of one's individuality as male or female (or ambivalent) in greater or lesser degree, especially as it is experienced in self-awareness and behavior. Gender identity is the private experience of gender role and gender role is the public expression of gender identity" (p. 284). Is the individual secure in gender identity? Does he depend on his wife to reassure him that he is a man? Does she need him to make her feel like a woman? How defensive and aggressive is each in affirming gender?

12) *Characteristics desired in one's sex partner.* These include, for example, gender, per-

sonality, physical characteristics and grace, and role requirements: need to receive and give love; feelings, attitudes, ability to function sexually and to enjoy sex with the mate; level of achievement of mate, survival ability and skills, etc.

13) *Acceptance of self and other.* Does each partner have the ability to love himself as well as the other? Does narcissism interfere with object love? Is love equated with vulnerability and therefore to be eschewed?

14) *Cognitive style.* Cognitive style may be defined as the characteristic way a person selects information to take in, how he processes it and the way he communicates the outcome to others. Spouses often approach and work on problems differently or view situations differently. They select or perceive a variety of data and may come up with very different conclusions; direct argument between them rarely resolves the difference. All too often they do not respect the value of the mate's style and of their having two sets of perceptions or processes to work with as a couple. Difference in cognitive styles, which includes sensory intake differences and thought process differences, is the source of a great deal of marital conflict and unhappiness. Instead of exclaiming, "Vive la difference!", as we are prone to do when referring to gonads, few couples learn how to capitalize on differences in cognitive style.

Category 3. External Foci Of Marital Problems

After examining 750 couples who came for help with their marital situations, Greene (1970) found 12 complaints to be the most common. In order of frequency, these were: lack of communication, constant arguments, unfulfilled emotional needs, sexual dissatisfaction, financial disagreements, in-law trouble, infidelity, conflicts about children, domineering spouse, suspicious spouse, alcoholism, and physical attack. These complaints belong in the third category because they are not the etiological factor but the symptoms of underlying problems. They describe disturbances of transactional behavior patterns. Hence, *the complaints that most commonly cause couples to seek help are derivative and in treatment we often have to seek the underlying difficulties* that originate among the expectations of the marriage or the biologic and intrapsychic parameters.

1) *Communication.* To what degree is there openness and clarity in the giving and receiving of information and "messages"? Can there be overt expressions of love, understanding, anxiety, anger, desires and so forth?

2) *Life-style.* Do the similarities pave the way to compatibility or, conversely, do the differences and one's perception of differences lead to constant strife or subjugation? Do these trivial examples reflect more basic differences?

3) *Families of origin.* One partner may harbor resentment toward the mate's family or toward particular members of that family (mother, father, or a sibling). How does the couple handle family visits? How successful are they in making decisions that involve their current relationships with both families of origin?

4) *Child-rearing.* The philosophy of child-rearing is not as important as actual practice on a daily basis. Who has authority with the children? How are decisions made about values, upbringing and child care?

5) *Relationship with children.* What alliances are made with the children? For what purposes? Are particular children identified as belonging more to one parent than the other?

6) *Family myths.* Do the partners collaborate in the maintenance of myths? Do they strive to present a certain image of their marriage, their family, themselves?

7) *Money.* Who makes how much? How are expenditures controlled? Who does the bookkeeping? Is money viewed as power, as love?

8) *Sex.* Attitudes may differ on such fundamental considerations as frequency of sexual relations, who initiates sex, alternative sex objects (homosexual, heterosexual, bisexual, fetishistic, or group sex), means of achieving or heightening gratification (fantasy, playing out of fantasy), and fidelity. How do feelings of love, commitment and consideration interrelate with the sex drive and its fulfillment?

9) *Values.* Is there general agreement on priorities, such as money, culture, school, home, clothes, personal moral code, religion, politics, other relationships? Values are reflected in most of the other areas listed here but they also merit specific consideration.

10) *Friends.* What is the attitude of each toward his mate's friends? What does each partner seek from friends? Can both spouses understand that each cannot (and need not) try to fulfill all of the other's emotional and recreational needs?

11) *Roles.* What tasks and responsibilities are expected of each partner? Who will do the housework, cooking, shopping? Are roles narrowly gender-determined, or shared, or flexible in accordance with time and proclivities?

12) *Interests.* When interested in an activity, do spouses insist that their mates share the interest? Are differences in interests respected or resented? Which interest is an expression of individuality and which an expression of a need for distance, or, conversely, for clinging and dependence?

This is, of necessity, a partial listing. Every couple, like every individual, has problems specific to the particular relationship. For example, differences in race, religion, or social class are relevant parameters for some couples but not for others. The list is, however, complete enough to provide both couples and professionals with an awareness of the most common areas of difficulty encountered in marital therapy. Others may be added as specific situations indicate. Tables 2, 3 and 4 serve as convenient summaries of these three categories for patients and can be used to guide the course of therapy.

LEVELS OF AWARENESS OF THE INDIVIDUAL MARRIAGE CONTRACT

For clinical purposes, it is useful to consider each partner's awareness of the individual marriage contract on three levels:

TABLE 2
Category of Marital Contracts Based on Expectations of Marriage or Living Together

Each partner marries for his/her own purposes and goals. The marital system itself generates other purposes of which the individuals may have originally been unaware. Keep in mind that this list is meant only to remind you to consider these possibilities. Others may be important for you; if so, put them in.

Among the more common expectations (a person may have several) of marriages are:

(a) Those for a mate who will be loyal, devoted, loving and exclusive, one with whom you may grow and develop together.
(b) To provide constant support against the rest of the world.
(c) Insurance against loneliness.
(d) Marriage as a goal in itself rather than a beginning.
(e) Panacea against chaos and strife in life.
(f) A relationship that must last "until death do us part."
(g) To provide sanctioned and readily available sex.
(h) To create a family.
(i) Others to be included.
(j) A relationship that emphasizes the family rather than just a mate.
(k) A refuge from the world.
(l) A respectable position and status in society.
(m) An economic unit; a social unit.
(n) An umbrella image to inspire me to work, build, accumulate.
(o) A respectable cover for aggressive drives (everything I do is only for my family, not for me).
(p) Others, list.
(q) Have you included those areas where you feel your mate let you down? Please do so and add how you feel.
(r) Please write out a summary of what you *want* from your marriage that relates to the above areas and what *in exchange* you will give.

TABLE 3
Category of Marital Contracts Based on Psychological and Biological needs

These areas are determined in large part by psychological and biological factors rather than by the marital system as such. They arise largely from within the person but can be greatly influenced by partner interaction. The needs and desires by which these factors may be expressed often are beyond your awareness; yet you do have some ideas about them. Among the areas that may be important are:

(a) Independence-dependence: This has to do with feelings, the general conduct of yourself in relation to your mate; do you set the style and pattern for yourself?
(b) Activity-Passivity: This has to do with initiative and action.
(c) Closeness-distance: How much closeness and intimacy do you really want? Your mate? How much do you want to include each other in what you think and do? How does either pull away when you want or feel you have to? Are you aware of putting distance between you?
(d) Use and abuse of power: Who controls what? How do you feel about who is in charge? Are you competitive with your spouse? Do you abdicate power?
(e) Dominance and submission: Who submits, who dominates in the relationships? Is there an equal give and take of leadership in the relationship? Rate yourself and your mate on a 1-9 scale where 1 = complete submission to the other and 9 = complete domination. 5 = more or less equal give and take or allocating of leadership roles.
(f) Fear of loneliness or abandonment.
(g) Need to possess and control spouse or vice versa.
(h) Level of anxiety, what triggers it and what are your main coping or defensive patterns to reduce anxiety; answer for self and mate.
(i) How do you feel about yourself as a man or woman?
(j) Physical and personality characteristics desired or required in your mate: How does he/she measure up? Does he/she turn you on sexually? If not what is lacking? Do you like his/her attitudes about sex? How do they compare to your own? Are there any sex problems?
(k) Ability to love and to accept yourself and your mate. Do you?
(l) How do you and your mate approach problems—are your styles of thinking the same or

(*continued*)

TABLE 3 (*continued*)

different? How does this affect your relationship?

(m) Are your interests and those of your mate the same? Do you feel that most interests should be the same?

(n) Any other areas not mentioned.

(o) Please write out a summary of what you *want* from your mate that relates to the above area and what *in exchange* you will give.

TABLE 4

Category of Marital Contracts Based on the External Foci of Problems Rooted in Categories 1 and 2

These areas usually are the apparent cause of marital trouble, but in reality they are often the symptoms of something wrong in an area of Category 1 or 2. These most common problem areas and stimuli of marital disharmony are:

(a) Communication: Is there openness and clarity in the sending as well as the receiving; can you talk and listen to each other? Do you feel isolated, one from the other?

(b) Are there intellectual differences between you and your spouse?

(c) Do you feel that your spouse has some mental problem or block that prevents your working together?

(d) Life-style; work and recreational interests.

(e) Do you fight about your families of origin: What is involved?

(f) Difference in child-rearing practices and philosophy.

(g) Children: Are children used in alliance against either parent? Is any child identified particularly as yours or your mate's? Specify.

(h) Are there family or personal myths or pretensions that are important to maintain? Specify.

(i) Are there differences over control, spending, saving or the making of money?

(j) Sex: What turns you on; who initiates, frequency, alternative sex partners, practices, etc., feeling desired and loved. Is sex pleasurable, fun, gratifying? Why so and why not if it isn't?

(k) Values, including priority systems and those related to gender, equality, cultural, economic and social class, etc.

(l) Friends: Do you share and does each have their own? Do you and mate each have friends of the opposite gender as well as the same?

(m) Gender- and interest-determined roles and responsibilities at home, socially, making and spending money, leisure time, etc.

(n) Include those areas where you feel your mate let you down or caused trouble. Be specific; include your feelings.

(o) How do you most often react when you feel you have been let down or deceived? How does your mate?

(p) Other areas not mentioned.

(q) Please write out a summary of what you *want* that relates to the above areas from your mate and what in exchange you will *give*:

FINAL QUESTION—add any additional comments or thoughts about yourself, your mate and your marriage that have occurred to you. A summarizing paragraph would be a good idea as the questions above may have missed important areas or did not get to how you really see things. Be as lengthy and detailed as you care to.

TABLE 5

Marital Expectations Questionnaire

(The following Marital Expectations questionnaire was developed by a staff member, Ilona Sena, for use in the Quick Response Service of Jewish Family Service in New York City. It has proved to be most helpful in getting couples to focus quickly on crucial system areas and to prepare the way for the reminder list, if evaluation indicates significant couple therapy is indicated.)

This is to be completed in private by each person and to be shared at a later date. Please be as specific as possible and if you need more space for any category use additional paper.

1) What are your expectations from marriage and/or a long-term relationship?

2) Which of your expectations do you feel are being met?

3) Which expectations do you feel are *not* being met?

4) What personality traits or behavior would you like to see changed in your partner?

5) What do you feel you would like to change about yourself so as to improve the relationship?

6) Are there any private hopes or plans that you've always wanted to share with your spouse/partner, but have been reluctant to do so? If so, please indicate.

7) How do you make decisions and resolve differences or fights?

8) Is there anything else you would like to add?

Level 1. Conscious, Verbalized

This would include what each partner tells the mate about his or her expectations in clearly understandable language. Although a spouse may express himself clearly to the other, the second may shut out the communication and not hear or allow to register what has been stated. The reciprocal aspects of the stated expectations are not usually verbalized or recognized. The statement is usually made as a wish, desire, or loosely defined plan, but not in terms of "What I expect you to do for me in exchange is . . ."

Level 2. Conscious But Not Verbalized

This refers to each partner's expectations, plans, beliefs and fantasies, which differ from the content at Level 1 only in that they are not verbalized to the mate, usually because of fear of the other's anger, rejection or a feeling of shame at what the disclosure will reveal to the other. Uncertainties about entering a fuller relationship, incipient conflicts and disappointments may enter awareness but are not discussed and aired openly. Occasionally, willful deception for manipulative or narrow self-gain purposes may be involved. This happens less frequently than might be anticipated. It is more common in brief-encounter relationships than in committed ones.

Level 3. Beyond Awareness

This third level comprises desires, needs and expectations, often contradictory and unrealistic, of which the contractor has no awareness. They may be similar to or in conflict with the needs and expectations that are operative at Levels 1 and 2, depending on how well integrated the individual is. Some of the contractual clauses in the third level may be preconscious and close to the surface; others may be further from awareness. This is the area of power and control needs, closeness-distance, contradictory active-passive impulses, child-adult conflicts, gender identity conflicts and so on. *In many respects this is the most significant contractual level, because of the behavior-determining parameters that are included and their widespread*

effects on so many of the subtleties of relating.[3]

The aspects of individual marriage contracts that are not accessible to conscious awareness may be regarded for clinical purposes as working hypotheses inferred from the behavior, fantasies and other productions of each spouse. Contracts on this level may have the irrational, contradictory and primitive characteristics that are attributed to "the unconscious" in accordance with psychoanalytic theory. As a rule, not all the terms of the contract can possibly be fulfilled because of their mutually contradictory and unrealistic aspects. Nonfulfillment of unconscious expectations tends to evoke intense emotional reactions that are puzzling and disturbing to both spouses. The affect may be displaced so that the reaction appears to be inappropriate to the reality of the immediate stimulus.[4]

Contracts on any or all levels are dynamic and may change at any point in the marital relationship. As might be expected, such changes frequently take place when there is a significant modification of needs, expectations, or role demands of one or both partners, or when a new force enters the marital system. Interestingly, *spouses are often more aware of their partner's third level needs than of their own.* They can be helpful in shedding light on each other's terms. A wife will not infrequently say, "I know he likes to act so strong and possessive, but I also realize how dependent he is on me and how like a little boy he is in so many ways." On the other hand, a husband may say, "She is in such conflict—she really wants to be independent and to do her own thing, and at the same time she wants me to be Big Daddy and take care of her."

Having described the common themes of the

---

[3]*Editors' Note.* Of course, conflicts and clauses at Level 3 which are *preconscious* will yield more readily to cognitive understanding (insight through interpretation) than will those that are *unconscious*. Therapists need to be careful in their assessment of Level 3 clauses not to confuse these different levels of consciousness lest they interpret too quickly in treatment material which may arouse too much anxiety and lead to early termination of therapy and/or other undesirable consequences.

[4]*Editors' Note.* Sager's point here is well-taken and his argument that highly specific complaints by marital partners often are *derivative* of unconscious conflict is repeated at many points in this chapter. Such a model is especially useful in understanding why simple behavioral techniques to modify overt behavior may, at times, fail. For a contrasting view, see Jacobson's chapter in this volume.

individual marriage contract, and having seen that all contract clauses are exercised at three levels of awareness, we are ready to examine the third "unwritten document" that is present in all marital arrangements: the operational or interactional contract through which the marriage functions.

THE INTERACTIONAL CONTRACT

In marriage, a man and a woman come together with their individual contracts and create a new system. Marital systems often serve purposes of which neither partner is aware. The newly created system usually continues to take on additional purposes and functions, while earlier ones may be discarded. It may become invested in these functions to the detriment of its original functions as conceived by the individuals involved. The new functions may differ from, if not conflict with, the contract of one or both partners, or with the original implicit or explicit contracts for their union. An example might be the husband who becomes so preoccupied with making money for his family and maintaining a high standard of living for them that he virtually cuts himself off emotionally from his wife and children. Here, one function of the union has superseded other functions, frustrating the fulfillment of needs that his wife may have for companionship and affectionate exchange with him.

In addition to each partner's own marriage contract, every couple has a common, single, largely nonverbalized interactional contract or "game." Parts of this interaction are collusive in that partners intuitively or unconsciously "agree" to avoid certain areas, deny particular problems or aspects of one another's attitudes or behavior, share unexpressed fantasies and act upon them, or play "games" that test the limits of their system's homeostasis. The collusion represents the unexpressed rules of the game both have "agreed" upon. This third contract is not at all the same as the single contract that evolves naturally or during therapy as the disparate terms of the two individual contracts are resolved. That single contract deals with desires, what one is willing to give, the goals and purposes of the relationship for each person and for the marital system itself. The interactional con-

tract *is the operational one* which describes *how* the two mates try to achieve fulfillment of the terms of their separate contracts. It is the set of conventions and implicit rules of behavior, of maneuvers, strategies and tactics that have developed in their dealings with each other. The two partners collaborate to establish and maintain a method of achieving sufficient gratification of their biological needs, as well as of their adult and remaining infantile wishes. To remain viable, the marital system must accomplish this without arousing enough defensive anxiety tension to destroy the marital unit or to make it totally dysfunctional. The interactional contract deals with how the partners try together to fulfill their separate goals and purposes. It is the *how*, not the *what*.

Each individual marriage contract is modified by interaction with the partner and often new "clauses" are added to "correct" the behavior of the mate or to provide another facet of adaptation to the relationship. In their interaction, both partners are usually unaware of the nonverbal cues, as well as the verbal expressions, that contribute to the quality of their interaction. This interactive contract provides the operational field in which each struggles with the other to achieve fulfillment of his own individual contract, including the realistic, unrealistic and ambivalent clauses that it contains. It is the interface where each partner tries to achieve his own objectives and to force the other to behave in accordance with his design of the marriage. The couple's interaction and interactional patterning are the structure of their relationship.

The interactional contract is unique for each couple because it evolves from the most basic wishes and strivings, as well as the defensive maneuvers, of each partner. Each spouse stimulates defensive maneuvers in the other that may or may not be characteristic of that partner in another relationship.[5]

Each partner's behavioral style in the relationship can be assessed by means of the clini-

---

[5] *Editors' Note.* We are reminded here of Dicks' (1967) articulate view of this matter: "The special feature of such apparent hate-relationships in marriage is that they occur within the framework of a compelling sense of belonging. The spouses are clear in their minds that they would not dream of treating anyone else but each other in this way" (p. 70).

cian's observations of how he relates to his spouse. Certain patterns of the biological and intrapsychic parameters of Category 2 correlate, in a general fashion, with each of the seven behavioral profiles. These parameters and the defense mechanisms employed appear to be motivating and modifying forces. However, we depend largely on the spouses' description of their behavior and our own observation to designate the major behavioral pattern (profile) for each partner in the interactional system. These profiles are a summary of the basic quality and flavor of each mate's interaction with the other. Behavioral profiles are not absolute; they can be modified as the relationship continues. Each mate has many other behavioral characteristics, but we prefer to choose the main thrust of the current mode of interacting with the partner. In the course of an interaction, partners may exchange roles with each other or switch to another profile as the interactional cycle or sequence proceeds.

Much of therapy consists of altering the interactional contract and the partners' behavior by a variety of methods. Some techniques are designed to increase awareness. This consciousness, for example, can then be used to work toward some clauses of a new single contract that then, in turn, provides the basis for healthier interactions, interactions that will fulfill reasonable objectives and purposes, and provide as full a measure as possible of adult goals for each individual and for the couple. Since the goals of the marriage are determined by the couple, the clauses of each individual contract come into the foreground and have to be dealt with, if they have not already been altered in the process. Early in treatment I try to clarify the salient positive and negative aspects of the separate contracts, so that with awareness each partner often can resolve some of the conflicting and ambivalent clauses of his or her contract and move on to do the same with the partner. *Awareness is not necessarily a prerequisite for change, but the motivation to make the effort to change is necessary.*

A lack of motivation to work on improving the marriage on the part of one mate may signal that person's conviction to terminate the marriage, may be a manifestation of righteousness and a feeling that it is the mate that must do the work,

or is a function of his/her anxiety. It is crucial for the therapist to make an accurate differentiation among these alternate factors. When in doubt, it is wise to resist premature termination of therapy or the marriage on the part of the apparently poorly motivated partner. Individual therapy or exploration may be appropriate to determine the etiology of the apparent lack of motivation.

TOWARD A TYPOLOGY OF COUPLES

Earlier in this chapter, I described the concept of the two partners' individual marital contracts with their unspoken elements and those beyond awareness and the interactional contract. The latter is the unconscious system two partners have developed to deal with each other in their attempts to fulfill their individual contracts. These concepts provide the basis for a fresh approach to classifying dyadic committed relationships, marital or otherwise. The typological system described here considers data from a large number of parameters. It is descriptive as well as dynamic and considers various aspects of etiology that affect the ongoing dyad. It tries to avoid the pitfall of attempting to explain the remote origin of an individual's behavior, yet it considers intrapsychic as well as transactional and system components. Any typology of human interactions must be an oversimplification and have its limitations.

I will describe the seven major behavioral profiles that are descriptions of how a mate can react to his or her partner, and the various partner combinations that are based on these behavioral profiles. These combinations comprise the typology.

Behavioral Profiles

Within committed couples, each partner adopts a characteristic way of relating to the other. There may be some fluidity and change in various situations, but for any period of time each has a major mode of relating with the other. With another partner, even one similar to the first, the slight variances that exist can evoke different behavioral patterns for each partner. It is this particular style of interacting with the other and the meaning attributed to it that determine the quality of the marriage.

Seven major styles of relating that individuals have with their mates are delineated. I refer to them as behavioral profiles. Each of these partner types describes a way of relating that has broad general characteristics. They are not rigid categories, and most people show some characteristics of different profiles or may shift from one to another in a short time. In working with couples, I try to determine the profile that is most frequently used in decisive interactions and that best reflects the style and quality of each partner's relationship with the other. But I am also alert to the variations that each individual is bound to display.

Those mates who have a particular behavioral patterning also have a somewhat particular patterning of their needs, as reflected in 12 areas of biological and intrapsychic parameters that we look for in the individual marriage contracts. In the following descriptions of the profiles, these 12 areas of needs and expectations are summarized for each behavioral profile.[6]

Clinical observation suggests that each partner acts with the other in their relationship as a certain "type," in accordance with one of the seven behavioral profiles. In considering these profiles, three important points should be kept in mind. First, the seven behavioral profiles do not comprise all of the possible types, although other identifiable qualities could probably be subsumed under one of the seven descriptions. Second, one's choice of mate may have been guided by one's perception of that mate as a particular type, but one's perception may not be accurate; it may be colored by one's own realistic or neurotic needs, including the need to deny positive or negative attributes in terms of one's own value system and unconscious needs and fears. What evolves is often quite different from what each mate may have anticipated or is currently aware of. Third, as experiences and circumstances alter the dynamics of each partner and of their marital system, each spouse may suddenly or gradually behave as a different type from what he or she was at another time in the relationship.

An individual's behavioral profile is determined in part by his personality structure and prior life experiences. However, another important determinant is his or her mate. The interaction with the latter may draw or force the first partner to use different means of relating (behavioral profile) than he had been accustomed to in the past. Although self-esteem, cultural determinants and rigidity of defenses may combine to set the limits of change for some people, many are able to adapt differently with sequential partners, as their partner changes or as events in the marriage life-cycle change the two partners' system. Thus, a profile is not immutable, nor is it determined by past experience or biology alone. It is a product of interaction and other multiple determinants.

The profiles described here typify the normal as well as the mildly to moderately pathological behavior constellations. Any of the profiles, extrapolated to an extreme, could be reflected in grossly pathological behavior.

The seven profiles to be discussed in detail are the equal, romantic, parental, childlike, rational, companionate and parallel partner.

I) Equal partner

The equal partner seeks a relationship on equal terms for himself and his spouse (whether or not the partner wants equality). The equal partner expects that both will have the same rights, privileges and obligations, without any overt or covert double-standard clauses. The equal partner expects each to be a complete person in his or her own right, largely self-activating, with his own work and friends, but responsive to the needs of the mate and emotionally interdependent with him or her.

The equal partner must be reasonably able to welcome and tolerate a mature peer relationship, to be relatively noncompetitive with the spouse and to take pleasure in the other's accomplishments. He/she understands and respects gender differences so that these are not used to the disadvantage of either mate. The equal partner must be relatively free of urgency to have infantile needs fulfilled and aware that his own lovability cannot be dependent on how effectively he fulfills the infantile needs of his mate. Yet, at the same time, there is a capacity sometimes to be the child and be taken care of

[6]More complete descriptions of these profiles and their intrapsychic parameters are described in Sager (1976a, 1977) and Sager and Hunt (1979).

or sometimes to be parental to one's partner when that is needed.

Summary of Equal Partner Behavior Based on Inner Needs:

1) Tends to independence; is cooperative and interdependent with mate.
2) Is more active than passive.
3) Is capable of close, sustained intimacy without clinging.
4) Is able to show strength—to share, or assume decision-making and to allow mate to do the same. Is neither submissive nor dominating. May be mildly competitive with mate, yet is pleased by the other's success and is not threatened.
5) Has no great fear of abandonment.
6) Does not seek to possess or to be possessed by mate. Does give and accept commitment.
7) Has a low to moderate level of anxiety.
8) Sexual response to mate varies from moderate to high.
9) Has an excellent capacity to love self and mate.
10) Has a well-developed and defined style[7] but also respects mate's.

II) Romantic partner

Just as the equal partner is the societal ideal of today, the romantic was the societal ideal of the most recent past. The romantic partner concept still prevails widely, even among many of those who now aspire to be equal partners. The exciting and polymorphous element of love is paramount for the romantic partner.

The romantic partner behaves as if he wants and expects his partner to be his soul mate and as if together they will be one entity. Such a person acts as if he were incomplete—only with his partner can he become whole.

The romantic may be seeking fulfillment of his childhood aspiration to be the sole object of the love, adoration and support of his mother

or father. This need is frequently rooted in the desire for exclusive rights to the services and love of the parent of the opposite sex. Consequently, the romantic is often insatiable and cannot receive enough proof of love. When reasonably secure in a romantic relationship, that individual may then flower and exploit his potential more fully. Because of the romantic's great overvaluation of his partner and lack of sense of completion without his mate, he tends to be very jealous and protective of their relationship. Love and sexual passion are usually very important and intensity of passion is often used as a litmus paper to test the current quality of the relationship.

Summary of Romantic Partner Behavior Based on Inner Needs:

1) Tends to be dependent on mate.
2) Is extremely fearful of abandonment, a significant factor in determining behavior.
3) Very possessive and controlling, even when appearing to be submissive.
4) Has a high level of anxiety; often feels incomplete and incapable of dealing with a hostile world.
5) Needs to use many defense mechanisms.
6) May have some mild problems of gender identity.
7) Usually has a very intense sexual response to mate.
8) Often confuses love with fear of losing mate.
9) Style ranges from intuitive to moderately well-organized; usually wants to respect the other's style.

III) Parental partner

The parental partner at the extreme may be considered a master, that is, a controlling and authoritarian parent. Many variations and modifications along the good-parent-to-master continuum do occur.

The prototype of the parental partner is Torvold, Nora's husband in Ibsen's "A Doll's House." The parental partner exercises governing and caretaking control over the mate and infantilizes him or her. He or she may do so from his own proclivities, or be maneuvered into being parental by the mate, or through a combination

---

[7]Style refers to cognitive style. It may be defined as the way people approach and deal with situations and problems. Some like to gather information, then proceed to act logically; others act intuitively or impulsively. Each person has his or her own style of solving problems and in expressing his/her conclusions.

of both. The parental partner's role may be a benign and loving one that fosters, within limits, the "child's" need for growth and independence. The script requires that the child continue either to feel sufficiently insecure to accept being "bought off," seduced and overpowered or to feel masochistic enough to give up individualism or freedom. On the other hand, rather than assume the role of the protective parent, the parental partner may behave as a punitive, authoritarian parent and seek to elicit from his mate the counterpart role of the obedient child held in psychological bondage.

The essence of the dynamics of the parental partner is the need to shore up his/her sense of adult self by being parent to an obedient child-spouse. The parent's word is law and an important cornerstone of this type of dyad. Transgressions may be tolerated as long as these are the actions of a mildly rebellious or foolish child whose irresponsible foibles may be forgiven by the understanding, benevolent, patronizing parent. The parent's underlying lack of self-esteem is defended against by a rigid structure designed to prove that he is adult, competent, lovable, just and kind. Closeness may exist but it must be on the parent's terms.

Summary of Parental Partner Behavior Based on Inner Needs:

1) Tends to be somewhat independent, but may be very dependent on the other's remaining childlike; will go to great lengths to keep him or her that way.
2) Tends to be more active than passive.
3) Needs to be powerful, to dominate mate. Is competitive and must constantly demonstrate own superior competence.
4) Has a great fear of abandonment. Cannot afford to lose mate.
5) Has a great need to possess and control although, ultimately, a childlike partner often has greater control.
6) Usually tends to be sexually responsive.
7) Deprecates or patronizes mate's style. Own style is well organized and leads to prompt problem-solving.

IV) Childlike partner

The childlike partner is the counterpart of the parental partner. The childlike partner may have a predisposition to interact as a child and may maneuver his mate into the parental role. In the interaction he aims to be cared for, protected, disciplined, guided and free of responsibility. In exchange, the child offers the parental partner the right to feel more adult, to be needed and to have his defense system supported.

The childlike partner often becomes the true wielder of power. His power derives from the parent's overwhelming need to keep the child in a childlike role so that he can define his own sense of self as an adult. Many child partners sense their power and are able to exploit the situation by threatening to leave.

Most men and women retain aspects of childhood dependence regardless of what realistic competence they have achieved. It is the ability to bring forth the creative child in oneself that adds to the charm of many partners. However, the creative and playful child in everyone is not to be confused with the person who utilizes childlike dependence and pseudoinnocence as a major adaptation with his mate. The demanding or "helpless" child can put a strain on any relationship.

Summary of Childlike Partner Behavior Based on Inner Needs:

1) Tends to be dependent.
2) Is largely passive.
3) Does not seek much power and generally submits to partner. May, however, use power (threaten to withdraw or leave) to dominate when mate is emotionally dependent.
4) Has a great fear of abandonment which often motivates behavior.
5) Has a high level of anxiety.
6) Requires many defense mechanisms.
7) Sexual response to mate is positive to enthusiastic.
8) Style is somewhat chaotic and intuitive. Often ridicules partner's more organized style, but deeply appreciates its benefits.

V) Rational partner

The rational partner, as the appellation implies, defends himself against admitting that emotions may influence his behavior. He tries to establish a reasoned, logical, well-ordered relationship with his mate. Duties and responsibilities between mates are clearly delineated by the rational partner. He fulfills his responsibilities. Although the rational partner often does not demonstrate a high level of affection or passion, he is capable of deep feelings of love and can experience a great sense of pain and emptiness if he loses the person he loves. He tends to be "economic" in his approach to matters having to do with life with his partner. He is pragmatic and down-to-earth, understands the rules of the system and inherently tends to play the game of life according to the rules. Rarely does he create new rules or change the given ones. On matters of a factual nature he assumes he is correct; on matters of taste, style and culture he will often defer to his mate.

The rational partner often has social grace, kindness and consideration and is usually there when needed, even if he does not appear to be sensitive to all of the nuances of his mate's feelings. He is not to be confused with a narcissistic person who is essentially incapable of object-love. Once he is committed, the rational mate tends to be loyal and to devote himself to making the relationship work. He depends on his partner to bring spontaneity and emotional expression into their system, while he acts as the governor when he believes his partner goes "too far."

The rational partner is to be differentiated from the parallel partner, who lives without close emotional touch with his mate. Often the rational partner has a close and intimate partner relationship. Whether he has such a relationship or not, the essence of his behavior is the cool logic by which decisions appear to be made, the balance sheet always being automatically updated. Unless he loses his partner, he and his intimates may never fully realize the truly interdependent roles that the rational partner and his spouse play out with one another.

Summary of Rational Partner Behavior Based on Inner Needs:

1) Often more dependent than is apparent. Forms close and emotionally dependent relationships but hides many emotional needs and remains in charge of the practical, administrative side of the relationship.

2) While very active in practical matters, leaves to mate those aspects of their common existence that have greater emotional content. There is, therefore, a division of responsibilities which may or may not be satisfactory.

3) Can be quite close, but tends to avoid deep, continued expressions of motivation and analysis of feelings; may actually appear to be distant and removed in demeanor.

4) Tends to assume and use power and to appear dominant. Often, however, appearance is deceptive and the mate has the ultimate power. Usually not competitive with partner.

5) Is well defended against fear of abandonment.

6) Anxiety level is low, rarely exceeding average.

7) Generally capable of a deep and lasting love relationship.

8) Own style is highly organized; collects all data, then arrives at "correct" and logical conclusions. Expects others to conform to these conclusions because they are "obviously right." Not likely to accept any other style except in a condescending way or in any areas in which he is not threatened, such as matters of taste or culture.

VI) Companionate partner

The companionate partner's operations are designed primarily to ward off aloneness. The companionate partner can usually accept closeness. He-she does not expect love but does seek thoughtfulness and kindness, for which he/she believes he/she is willing to give the same in return, perhaps in conjunction with economic security. Essentially, the companionate partner wants a companion with whom to share daily living; he/she does not aspire to romantic love (although this may be a deep desire) and readily accepts the quid pro quo necessities of conjugal living. Some companionate partners could be described as "burned-out" romantics.

The companionate partner's arrangement can be very gratifying when it fulfills the major needs of persons who are no longer uncompromising about their ideals. It is seen increasingly among older couples who live together in or out of marriage. The companionate partner considers the relationship to be a realistic arrangement between people who no longer have illusions, who know their needs and what they are willing to give in exchange for having those needs fulfilled.

The companionate partner's style, as he interrelates, is based on genuine deep needs plus consciously made compromises that are acceptable to him/her on all levels of awareness. The companionate partner is not to be confused with other partner behavioral types who may enter a relationship for fear of being alone or unloved, where the wish is still for romantic love, rather than for companionship.

Summary of Companionate Partner Behavior Based on Inner Needs:

1) Often shows a mixture of independence and dependence without an extreme amount of either one.
2) Tends to be somewhat more active than passive.
3) Is neither very close nor very distant.
4) Exercises power, but moderately. Usually not competitive.
5) Prefers life with a partner, but has no great fear of abandonment.
6) Love in the usual sense, which includes passion, is of no great importance, but acceptance, consideration, caring, commitment and kindness are essential.
7) Style tends to be well-ordered and rational. Can accept mate's style if it does not undergo (or seem to undergo) change.

VII) Parallel partner

The parallel partner interacts so as to avoid an intimate sharing relationship. Despite any protests to the contrary, he/she wants the partner to respect his emotional distance and independence. The paralleler may be responding to the mate's unconscious attempts to elicit this response from him/her or may have his/her own imperative need to remain emotionally removed, or there may be a combination of both factors. A parallel partner desires the conventional appurtenances of marriage, including home, children, dog, slippers and washing machine, but does not wish to be intimate. He/she prefers separate beds or bedrooms and sometimes even separate residences.

For the parallel partner, it is of paramount importance to maneuver the mate so that the two keep their distance and do not move closer than the perigee that keeps him/her comfortable. The contract of the parallel partner is predicated on a fear of losing his/her integrity as a person and being controlled. He/she struggles against being merged in any way. The defensive system of parallel partners is emphatically demonstrated by their emotional distance; they appear as cool and guarded people but may be extremely charming.

The parallel partner's need for distance is often a reaction formation to a great dependency need that is inadmissible for him/her to acknowledge with awareness. Such a person is often reactively ultra-independent. If successfully penetrated, he/she may melt into a romantic with a need for a partner with whom to complete him/herself. This would leave him/her extremely vulnerable to the mate. The struggle of the paralleler is never to allow him/herself to care "too much" emotionally for his/her mate, so that he avoids becoming aware of his/her own vulnerability and his/her unconscious desire for dependency.

Summary of Parallel Partner Behavior Based on Inner Needs:

1) Tends to be somewhat independent and doesn't mind if mate is. The important thing is that mate must be able to respect the basic ground rule of emotional distance.
2) Is generally more active than passive.
3) Is incapable of sustained closeness.
4) Tends to be in charge of him/herself and of setting the fundamental style of the relationship. Prefers mate to have power in his or her own areas of daily life and work. Is usually not very competitive.
5) Has an intense fear of abandonment, but is well guarded against it by the defense of maintaining distance.
6) On one level, does not want to possess or be possessed; on another, must exert extreme control to keep mate from violating the requisite distance boundary.
7) Sexual response to mate varies, but, when

intense, it is usually on a purely physical level with few (admitted) emotional components. Can be a technically competent but otherwise ungiving sexual partner.

8) No great love of self or mate since love must be inhibited. Is commonly narcissistic.

9) Tends to be fairly well organized and to have a rigid style. Is rarely able to incorporate mate's style to complement his own since that would require closeness.

Partner Combinations

The seven partner behavioral profiles allow for 28 possible combinations of two partners when we hyphenate the two descriptors. I shall briefly delineate the major partnership combinations, as well as indicate why some combinations are more likely to make for a fulfilling and/or stable relationship than others. Some partner combinations appear to be destined for disaster (these will be discussed below); nevertheless, they may prosper when both partners have the ability to shift into a secondary behavioral profile at crucial moments or as a continuing subtheme. It is important for the therapist to look for these secondary, and even tertiary, interactive themes as he follows the couple. Instant videotape playback offers an excellent technique (Berger 1978) for observing and enlightening the couple about these profile shifts. These are similar phenomena to Berne's (1961) changes in ego states. The couple may be aware of the shifts to a secondary theme, but the changes often remain subliminal. Shifting to another behavioral profile need not always be positive. A shift to a profile that produces negative interaction may occur when either or both mates find continued positive feelings to be anxiety-producing.

As noted earlier, any profile when extrapolated to its extreme may make for pathological behavior on the part of that individual. However, this does not necessarily lead to marital system dysfunction, since the quality of relationships is multidetermined. The pathological behavior of one spouse may be an unconscious response to the need of the other to take over (be parental) or to calm with rationality (rational partner). Or, the partner may be flexible, able and loving and react to the "pathological" behaving partner in a way that will shortly remove

the need for pathological behavior, e.g., by not becoming anxious in response. Some partners enter into a folie à deux which allows their system to remain functional for them, or they may exquisitely complement one another. Then, too, their system may avoid incipient entropy or explosion by switching to a secondary set of profiles at these crucial times. It is the great number of variables at play within a couple system that makes it impossible to state how any particular combination of profiles of two mates "should" best be treated—treatment must vary with each couple and each therapist's evaluation and biases—at least for the present. Where possible I shall give clues to how I might intervene. These generalizations should be used as a backdrop to approach these system constellations—the specificity for any case, or classes of cases, cannot be conveyed as one might describe a surgical procedure.[8]

In general, therapeutic intervention should take place at the point of the source of underlying problems, and in such a way as to most expeditiously make a significant change. Pointing out to partners their behavioral profiles with each other is usually a good start for using the concept therapeutically. It is readily understandable to most couples, though sometimes resisted, as it may differ with one's self-image or an invested image of one's partner. We may then set out to explore alternative ways of behaving to get what one wants. Once agreed upon, behavioral goals are established, tasks can be set to help foster the desired change. Knowledge of underlying contractual terms is essential to determining what are really the desired changes.[9] Simultaneously, the individual contracts are worked with to move towards a single contract. Obstacles to acceptance of a single con-

---

[8]*Editors' Note.* On the other hand, if Sager's typology is to continue to evolve and to guide therapeutic assessment and inform treatment planning, empirically reliable and specific methods of classifying couples will be required.

[9]*Editors' Note.* Note the *major* difference here between Sager's requirements for comprehensive clinical assessment with couples and those put forth by Jacobson (Chapter 15). Both models direct the clinician's attention to the rules and processes of dyadic "exchange." The major difference between these models, however, is Sager's conviction, and Jacobson's denial, that there exist "underlying" contractual terms. In clinical practice, then, Jacobson is much more willing to accept the couple's stated change desires at face value.

tract may arise on any level. I prefer, in general, to work with behavioral goals and tasks as a first approach, falling back to more time-consuming insight approaches when these are necessary. In all couple relationships, love, commitment and the motivation to make the relationship work often cause spouses to seek out necessary compromises and shifts to less egocentric modes of adaptation.

Equal partner combinations

1) Equal-Equal Partners. When two persons interact as equal partners, they may or may not be able to establish and maintain a good relationship. Some seem to fall into this relationship naturally, without much thought, soul-searching, or ideological discussion about it; others consciously work very hard at it, trying to overcome the shaping of their behavior and values by a lifetime of training devoted to concepts of sharply defined gender roles and differences, as well as defensive posturing. The equal-equal partner ideal, although espoused by many, is achieved by few. It cannot be achieved mechanistically but has to come from a deep sense of respect for oneself and one's mate. Some interpret the equal partner concept too literally and fear they will lose a partner who is independent, or that their own dependence needs will not be tolerated.

When both mates function as equal partners, they tend to do well together, but problems may arise when either partner is ambivalent about the equal relationship. A common manifestation of this is the difficulties that arise when one partner cannot accept equality. Relationships founder if either stops loving the other partner, or if one turns to someone else for major emotional and/or sexual gratification or decides not to be committed to anyone at all for a while. Equal partners, with their relatively good self-security, need not act out in other relationships; they take their commitments seriously and do not lightly terminate a relationship. Conversely, they may also feel relatively secure about leaving a marriage that is no longer productive or loving for them.

Equal-equal partners remain together after the early passion (short-term bonding phase) of their relationship has ended presumably because they want to be together, not because either is afraid not to be. Secure in who they are, equal partners are not threatened by recognition of their own dependent needs or those of their partner. They are flexible with one another and can accept being parent or child to each other when the need arises. They can ask for help, care or clarification of an issue. They tend not to allow important issues to smolder between them and conversely do not have to be anticipatory or overreact to every possible infringement of their equality. The paranoid stance is absent between them, but each, while self-assertive, is respectful of the others' needs and sensitivities. For most couples, an equal relationship is the most difficult to maintain because it is not as dependent on forces outside the couple, such as social institutions, to keep the two people together. The equal-equal partnership is not a relationship that is dull or necessarily low key, and it rarely has the flatness that we often see with two compliant or peace-at-any-price mates who are afraid (or just have no desire) to rock the boat. They do not avoid an argument that is necessary to resolve an issue. They generally communicate well with one another concerning emotional as well as concrete issues.

Many couples who are striving for equal relationships founder on different interpretations of equality and sometimes the "equality" issue is a smoke screen for other aspects of their individual marriage contracts—possibly a desire to be taken care of, a fear of responsibility or a sense of inadequacy at the idea of having to compete in the "real world" with others. These anxieties and fears are normal for women and men. We cannot expect ourselves or others to have developed equally and simultaneously in all the various emotional and cognitive parameters. Often we are "advanced" or "mature" in one area, childlike in another.

Many attempts at equal partnerships fail because the emotional need of one partner is actually to create distance by using the guise of independence, rather than to achieve equality. The outward manifestations of a partner's need to avoid closeness and interdependence can be strikingly similar to those of the more mature person working toward equality, but the emotional driving force behind each is very different, as must be the relationship that ensues.

The above discussion gives some clues to intervention. In general, when working with couples who are striving to be equal partners, as with any couples, it becomes important to determine the major underlying cause of their dissension. Aside from their history, complaints and individual contracts, it is of utmost importance to explore the differences between each partner's idealized concept of their equal-equal relationship and their internal conflicts of not wanting to be so equal themselves or their anxiety about their partner's independence. The difference between intellectual credo and emotional needs often is the cause of marital discomfort in these people. Equality must be understood in humanistic terms. Couples often need assistance in accepting their own and their partner's ambivalence in this regard.

2) Equal-Romantic Partnership. This combination often leads to a good relationship, provided neither partner demands that the other change his or her basic interactional profile. The romantic who requires a great deal of togetherness may be threatened by his mate's desire for his own space. If his mate remains independent, the romantic may cling, may become more dependent or may feel angry and betrayed because his partner is not keeping the (unilateral) contract to be a romantic. The equal partner may want to thrust egalitarianism upon the romantic, who feels threatened and rejected by this. Simultaneously, the romantic partner, calling on the name of love in vain, demands greater closeness and open communication, which is felt by his mate to be a controlling as well as an anachronistic maneuver. The equal partner may feel hemmed in by the demand that he change and hence may react negatively to his romantic partner's pressures.

In varying degrees the equal partner can accommodate and be complementary to several other partner profiles—provided his own freedom is not too circumscribed. The equal partner wishes to respect the individuality of his mate and might react adversely to a partner who would be his sycophant or a childlike partner. On the other hand, equality is an elastic concept and the equal partner is often satisfied to have a partner who is a little less equal.

In treatment of the equal-romantic couple, intervention takes place in such a way as to get to the equal partner's need for or insistence on full equality of his partner. Or, if the pressure comes from the romantic partner's need to be reassured of love in a way that he/she can accept, this will be the focus of intervention. In the latter case, we may deal first with the romantic partner's unsureness of lovability, of, if love is given by the equal partner but not perceived by the romantic, work with them on understanding one another's communications.

3) Equal-Rational Partnership. Some equal-rational partnerships begin as an equal-equal relationship, in keeping with the couple's expressed or implied philosophy, but the interaction may change gradually as one partner becomes anxious at the other's independence (which becomes defined as irresponsibility, thoughtlessness, irrationality) and becomes more and more rational in his/her attempt to control the relationship by keeping his/her partner's and his/her own behavior within "reasonable" bounds that ease his/her anxiety. This partner becomes less free and open as his/her efforts are increasingly determined by defensive impulses and he/she becomes excessively logical and reasonable. The rational partner is able to accept equal partnerism intellectually, but, because of his anxiety, he lacks the emotional commitment and ability to follow through. The equal partner in such an interaction often unconsciously presses a little too far in stirring up his mate's anxiety. The latter responds negatively, is then accused by the equal partner of being too restrictive, and they find themselves in a bitter struggle.

In treatment, one must be alert to chinks in the equal partner's behavior that cause him/her to stimulate the rational partner's anxiety. Emphasis may then shift to system intervention that will allay the rational partner's anxiety about partner loss—an anxiety that can become a self-fulfilling prophesy if both partners do not work together in therapy. Therapy should include helping the rational partner to be more emotionally expressive.

4) Equal-Companionate Partnership. The equal-companionate partnership usually works quite well. Although superficially the equal and the companionate may appear to be the same, they are very different. The equal partner believes both mates should have equal status and opportunity and each should be his/her own person. He-she usually loves his/her partner and tries to live out his ideal relationship. The companionate partner makes a realistic compromise and gives up love in exchange for consideration, kindness, devotion. The companionate partner does not believe mates need be equals; in fact, there is often a conventional male-female division of work and responsibilities, as well as activities.

Difficulty may arise in the equal-companionate partnership when either mate begins to want more from the other than was originally contracted for and is unable to accept something different. The equal partner may want love or want the mate to be more equal to him, as inequality makes him guilty, interferes with his independent activities and makes his partner less of a person. The companionate person may regard his partner's demand that he be equal or that he love as a cause for anger and exasperation because he did not agree to such a contract and does not feel capable of fulfilling it. The companionate partner may become anxious as he comes to realize that the equal partner really is his own person and is not dependent on him, or anxiety may develop when the equal partner will not support the companionate partner's dependence.

Clarification of contractual terms and attempting to arrive at a single viable contract are of prime importance in this combination. If one wants love (equal) and the other is unable to give it (companionate), the threat to the relationship may make it possible for the companionate partner to drop defensiveness (which pushes the equal partner away) and move closer to his/her mate. The therapist must always be alert to underlying needs of the equal partner, who may not be so equal and might fear being loved and loving in return.

5) *Equal-Parallel Partnership.* This, too, may work out satisfactorily so long as the equal partner does not make too many demands for intimacy. However, the odds are against its viability without severe compromises being made. The distance of the parallel partner is often the carrot

in front of the equal partner, who wants greater closeness; the pull-push involved in their interactive process may make for a stormy but lively relationship or may eventually destroy it. The equality may fit in well with the parallel partner's needs as he perceives them. To the extent that each partner can be constructive in the relationship, they may collaborate living out a kind of pseudo equal-equal partner combination.

Therapy may hinge on the sincerity of the equal partner's desire for love and intimacy. This must be explored and clarified. If we are dealing with a pseudo-equal partner, his defensiveness and denial of his anxiety about closeness must be clarified. Sometimes therapy can preserve the relationship if the equal partner is willing to accept some emotional distance. In therapy the stress can be taken off the original parallel partner and be shifted, via tasks, to an agreed upon goal of helping both partners accept a level of intimacy that is comfortable for both. Sometimes, we see a shift to a reasonably healthy equal-equal partnership that might even have a romantic flavor to it. If the equal is truly equal and neither partner can or is willing to shift closer to the other's intimacy distance or closeness level, the relationship is likely to founder or continue as ungratifying.

6) *Equal-Parental Partnership.* This combination is likely to be an unstable one. The parental partner is driven to try to dominate the equal one. The latter, if sufficiently strong as an individual, need not be pushed into a power struggle, but this is a common sequel. If he is unable to shift the relationship to a more equitable modus vivendi, the equal partner may terminate the relationship, or the parental one, realizing there is a mismatch and needing to appear to be in charge, may force the issue of termination.

The sooner it is possible to start to work on elucidation of individual contracts the better. The causes of disharmony quickly become apparent and the spouses are then able to decide whether they wish to work towards a viable contract or not. This decision to work through a new set of basic assumptions must take priority. The process often requires deep-seated changes in the parental partner's dynamics that may be too threatening.

7) *Equal-Childlike Partnership*. This too is likely to be an unstable equation that must change if the couple is to stay together in reasonable harmony. The equal partner in this instance may be a "reformed parent" who feels uneasy as a parent or rescuer. The childlike partner of the duo may once have been an equal partner whose dependency needs have become ascendant. The childlike partner may do well with the equal partner for a while, until he fails to meet his own or his partner's expectations of equality in a variety of situations. While he uses every bit of his ingenuity to press the equal into a parental role, the equal mate may come to feel exploited or lose respect for his partner over time because he finds the childlike behavior distasteful and nongratifying. The childlike partner does not want to be equal. The equal partner does not want responsibility for a child and finds that not only are the latter's needs burdensome but that he does not want a love relationship with someone who is not adult.

In this combination, too, clarification of contracts and the decision to work on a viable interactional contract become important. If this duo is to have a chance of success, the therapist has to be on guard against his own collusion with the equal partner to pressure the childlike into more equal behavior.

Romantic partner combinations

1) *Romantic-Romantic Partners*. Superficially, the romantic partner tends to be most complementary with another romantic. Romantic-romantic partners fit together like two pieces of a jigsaw puzzle, two parts that are incomplete by themselves but together constitute a whole.

Many romantic-romantic partner combinations continue their romantic relationship indefinitely. These are fortunate couples who are rarely seen in clinical practice. They have usually developed the ability to complement each other well and to shift into supportive or dependent roles in relation to one another as needed. Power may shift back and forth in an appropriate fashion, always with the emphasis on functioning as a unit. Fear of abandonment rarely emerges as a source of anxiety because each feels secure in the love and continuance of the other. Only death of the mate is feared.

Such couples are not free of problems but manage to cope with them and to survive as a unit as they go through the marital cycle.

However, the "high" of the consummated short-term bonded romantic-romantic partnership, with its passion, openness, intimacy and pervasive interdependence, tends to run downhill after a few years. Because the diminution of intensity is often regarded as a loss of love, many couples are unable to make the transition to a satisfactory long-term bonded relationship. Since the change in intensity rarely occurs simultaneously in both partners, the one who still is more passionate often reacts strongly to changes in the other partner's subtle and overt behavior. These reactions, in turn, usually arouse guilt in the partner, a sense of being fenced in, or a desire to withdraw from an intimacy now regarded as controlling, engulfing or too limiting. The former romantic may have changed into an equal, companionate or parallel partner or may now wish to establish a new romantic-romantic partnership with someone else in order to experience again the intense high of being "in love." The activity and frustration involved in this endeavor can devastate the remaining partner, since the "soul mate" quality of mutual exclusivity and understanding is needed by the romantic partner to provide the security and sense of belonging and passion that he strives for. Some romantics, after an intense romantic-romantic relationship, move towards becoming an equal partner in that or another subsequent partnership.

Therapeutically, if both partners want to work on the relationship, there is a fair chance for its survival. To turn the clock back to recapture the intensity of the love of early days is a goal I do not accept, but I try to shift the couple to the goal of long-term bonding, possibly to an equal-equal partnership with romantic coloring. Again, expectations and underlying needs of Category 2 have to be explored and attempts made to work towards a new viable single contract. Intellectual approaches are of little value; tasks are more helpful, as well as insight methods, to strengthen the clinging partner's self-esteem and to help both partners stay within the bounds of realistic expectations.

2) *Romantic-Rational Partnership*. This is

often a difficult relationship because the romantic partner feels the rational one is not close enough, does not express feelings, is too logical and so on. The rational partner is glad to have the romantic be his emotional expressor, because he can absolve himself of responsibility when he feels uncomfortable about his partner's expression. Nevertheless, many of these endure through a lifetime, often because the relationship has a childlike-parent partnership subtheme that is rewarding to both. There is an unconscious collusion in which the romantic can feel superior as the "more sensitive" partner, while he berates his "insensitive" mate and both make believe that the second theme of the duet does not exist. This unconscious arrangement is often satisfactory to the rational partner, who indulges his "child" despite the put-downs to which he is frequently subjected.

For treatment suggestions for this pairing, see number 1 in this section.

3) Romantic-Companionate Partnership. This combination is rare in a new relationship, but it is not unusual in a former romantic-romantic relationship. When one partner's passion has cooled, he may still like or love his mate though he no longer experiences his former intense sexual reactions or need for constant sharing. Often the feeling changes to a sister-brother or parental-childlike relationship. This may be transitional to another form of interactional contract or to the demise of the marriage. For some couples it ushers in a difficult period during which the companionate partner distances himself in response to the romantic's attempts to reconstitute a romantic-romantic interaction.

For therapy suggestions, see number 1 in this section.

4) Romantic-Parallel Partnership. Much the same pertains here as for the romantic-rational partnership. This combination is even more unstable, however, because the romantic feels the greater impact and rigidity of a more definite need for distance. One reason for the romantic's demands for greater closeness may, paradoxically, be a defense (reaction formation) against his own need for distance, which can now be claimed to be his partner's desire instead of his own, as his parallel partner predictably pushes

him away. The romantic protests too much about his desire for a warm, close and intimate mate. Clinically, we must be alert as we view such interactions to see if the romantic does not first cue the paralleler to increase the distance between them. The childlike-parental or any other secondary theme is not as likely to serve as a balancing factor. What does often keep the couple together, however, is the romantic's game involvement with his partner. In this game, the romantic, or, if he is defending against closeness, we might call him a pseudo-romantic—does not really want his partner to be a romantic too, as that would expose his own fear of closeness. He is satisfied to criticize his partner for being distant, but he does not push too hard, thus allowing the couple to sink back into their usual modus operandi until the next round of the game.

Therapeutic intervention must focus first on diagnosis because differentiation must be made as to whether the romantic partner is truly such a pseudo. Careful observation of their interaction is helpful—hence we might give tasks first while the partners also talk through their contracts. The task should be designed to elicit giving and receiving intimacy. The sensate focus or pleasuring exercise (without genital touching) of Masters and Johnson (1970) is excellent for this purpose as a diagnostic instrument to determine intimacy in the marital interaction, not as sex therapy.

5) Romantic-Parental Partnership. This combination may work well. Many romantics do fall into a childlike stance with a parental partner who is not too demanding a parent. This is one of the few combinations that is effectively complementary for the romantic. For both partners the sense of completion comes through the living out of a romantic child-good parent relationship.

There are no specific recommendations for therapy, as these will depend on the sources of the problems and defensive systems. Attention to contractual differences will give ample clues for intervention.

6) Romantic-Childlike Partnership. This partnership tends to be quite unstable. The childlike partner's stances may have been or appeared to be those of a romantic partner in the couple's early interactions but changed later into the childlike role. However, the romantic tends to become uneasy and anxious when his mate persists in being childlike; he prefers a more equal romantic to quell his own anxiety. He wants and needs someone responsible to complement the childlike qualities he senses in himself. A little childishness in his mate is okay, but a really childlike partner arouses a defensive reaction in him. At the same time, of course, the child is struggling to make his romantic partner into a parental one. This type of complementary partnership is a very uneasy one, unless a saving secondary behavioral theme is brought into play.

Therapy should lead to early elucidation of contracts and defenses. Confrontation of their behavior and its eventual consequences often mobilizes motivation to work on change of self for both.

Parental partner combinations

1) Parental-Childlike Partners. The parental partner finds his or her complementary person in someone who will interact with him as a child. The interaction elicits the complementary profile from the other. When neither parent nor child is ambivalent about his own or his spouse's role, the two tend to do quite well; many good relationships are based on this combination. When there is ambivalence, disharmony is likely.

Parental partners often refuse to admit dependency needs and hide behind their reaction formation maneuvers. These maneuvers are similar to the masculine-protest maneuvers of the man who is unsure of his masculinity. This defense against normal dependency needs is destructive to efforts to have the relationship progress to another phase. It sets up the basis for eventual revolt by the childlike partner, who no longer wishes to act as the immature one and experiences the effects of his partner's unacknowledged dependency needs.

Therapy should seek out ambivalence within each spouse regarding his own and partner's behavior. With this as an entry point, the therapist must be on guard against projecting his own values and must be sure that the goals of therapy are the patients'.

2) Parent-Parent Partnership. Sometimes two parents, each of whom has some childlike components, become mates. The sameness and ambivalence in each usually lead to a poor and stormy relationship, unless they shift into parallel living or one truly "conquers" the other and the latter assumes a more constant childlike stance. A more constructive development would be a modus operandi of shifting roles and dividing responsibilities for different areas of marital duties.

Essentially, the parent-parent partnership is an unstable one. There is a common misconception that is based on this observation and on the concept that marriage inevitably is a war of the sexes, that is, that in a "good" marriage one partner must be dominant and the other submissive. This common generalization is not consistent with my observations.

Therapy usually proceeds best on the basis of searching for positive aspects of the relationship. Working towards a single contract rapidly makes clear whether either or both can or wish to shift from their parental positions.

There are other significant profile types with which the parental interactor connects. The examples given provide an adequate conceptual approach to understanding how other behavioral types may interact with the parental-acting partner.

Childlike partner combinations

Several facets of the childlike-parental partnership, which is a naturally complementary one, have been described in the preceding discussion of the parental-childlike partnership. I shall add only a few ramifications.

The childlike partner, as in some actual parent-child relationships, may sometimes become the true wielder of power. Without the child the parent's fears of his own anomie and lack of sense of worth roil up, leading to anxiety and an intense need to force the other into a childlike position. Most childlike partners sense their power and may sometimes use it by threatening to leave. This struggle for control is the basis for much negative interaction.

The sooner contract work begins, along with

tasks such as to set forth alternating periods of who is in charge, the sooner the couple can arrive at whether they wish to attempt to change their interactions or not.

Childlike-Childlike Partnership. Such two partners are like playmates or children who live within a matrix of a child's world that has no tomorrow and requires no significant responsibility. For a while all may go on well as play and fun. But when crises and frustrations develop, each then wants the other to be a parent. Disruption and breakdown of each one's individual marriage contract occur with the disappointment of each at not being able to make the other into a parent. They compete at being the child and hostilities ensue. Couples who can adopt flexibly alternating parental roles often lead a good life. Others wrap themselves in the cotton wadding of their relationship as protection from the rest of the world. Some go through life much like brothers and sisters playing house together—incest without guilt.

A therapeutic approach that was successful is illustrated by two actors, each a childlike partner, who came to see me. They had made a good sandbox relationship by developing the ability literally to act the role of parent to the other mate when he or she needed a parent. As long as he could feel that he was playing a role temporarily, as if he were a parent, the parental-acting mate often was able to handle the role and successfully accomplish what the reality of the situation required. But when either thought he actually had to be parental, he would become anxious at the realization and would abdicate. In therapy I encouraged them to play-act as parents when a parent was needed for one mate, and we even rehearsed several situations. One such episode involved the anxiety aroused in the wife, who had an audition coming up with a director and a producer whom she feared. I asked the husband to be her father. His role was to be a "good father"—to evaluate the situation objectively, support his daughter, reassure her, and advise her how to handle the situation. He first embraced her, held her for a while and was then truly supporting and constructive. Later, at home, they played out the parenting scene several times, so that the line between acting and reality became nonexistent in this circum-scribed context. The audition went well.

Rational partner combinations

The rational partner often forms a complementary relationship with someone who will supply the emotion and spontaneity that he or she is afraid to experience directly. He will often choose a partner who has the potential to act as a romantic or childlike partner. Occasionally, a relationship with an equal or companionate partner works out well. In therapy, what has appeared to be *rational-rational partnership* often turns out to be a parallel-parallel partnership. Unlike the parallel partner, the rational partner has the capacity for closeness and passionate love—but he has to deny passion in himself—and he likes his partner to struggle to move in and stay close with him. He can then vicariously enjoy his partner's passion and any "mishaps" can be blamed on the mate's emotionality.

A *rational-equal partnership* may go well if both wish to establish equality and adhere to their contracts. A rational partner becomes perplexed and upset at what he considers a breach of contract. A *rational-parental combination* can work well, too. Some rational partners accept parental direction from a partner whose judgment they can respect. The rational partner can also do well with a companionate or parallel partner. All depends on clarity and bilateral acceptance of the contractual terms. An important clause must specify that the spouse of a rational partner not demand that he give what he cannot give. Further, the mate should take care not to injure his self-esteem. In other words, the game is to be played by the rules. A change of rules by either party may, of course, either precipitate problems or move the relationship to a different and perhaps more satisfying steady state.

The rational partner may mate constructively with almost any of the other partner types, provided that the contracts are reasonably consonant and that his self-esteem is not violated by the partner. He is vulnerable because he loves and cares but finds it difficult to be in touch with his feelings.

In therapy it is important not to push the rational partner to be more in touch and expressive of feelings than he can tolerate. Sometimes, if the therapist joins him and is very intellectual, the rational partner will then move more out of himself.

Companionate partner combinations

The companionate's contract is based on genuine deep needs plus consciously made compromises with reality that are acceptable on all levels of awareness. It is not to be confused with the unilateral contract of a person who rushes into an ill-considered relationship out of fear of being alone or unloved or of one who still demands romantic love and is not prepared to accept a considerate, mutually companionable relationship.

The *companionate-companionate partnership* is the most common and most satisfactory for the companionate partner. The two partners have a contract to be good companions, to respect and take care of each other. Love is not expected, but kindness and consideration are. Each partner asks and offers the same.

Problems arise when there are hidden clauses in the companionate partners' contract; for example, a man acting as a companionate partner may at first offer his spouse economic security, but after a while this may be withdrawn. Sometimes the unbargained-for invalidism of the mate puts an unbearable strain on the companionate partner. More subtle sources of disharmony arise from one partner's need to be loved or to be unique. If a low level of sexual activity was a clause in either or both contracts and this changes to a desire for better or more frequent sex, or vice versa, this, too, can become a focus for disharmony. Invidious comparisons to a former mate can be disastrous.

Living in the past, rather than for the present and the future, is often the most destructive element of companionate interactions among couples who marry at middle age or later. Spouses may compete for who had a better life before or who is now more loved and catered to by their children or grandchildren. Or money, emotional support and consideration may be offered more readily to one's children in opposition to one's spouse. Adult children often motivated by selfishness, are too often allowed to play a decisive role in the quality of the parents' new marriage.

Therapy often proceeds best with compa-nionate partners by working with contracts very early, as this is close to their own style.

Parallel partner combinations

The parallel partner does best with another parallel interactor. If both respect each other's defenses and are compatible in other areas, as they often are, they can have a comfortable and satisfactory relationship.

A *parallel-rational partnership* may also work well, provided each is at ease with the accommodations that are being made. But either of them—and especially the rational partner, who needs warmth to warm him up—may use the interaction to demand more (or to demand by withholding) because he or she needs more from the partner. Similarly, a *parallel-companionate partnership* may work out well if the companionate partner does not demand greater closeness.

Parallel partners can also be involved in therapy readily through the negotiation of contracts, especially of the concrete items. Extension to Category 2 is often possible. However, change is difficult because of the paralleler's need for rigid defensiveness. Rational approaches should not be spurned by the therapist if he wants to have a patient with whom to work. Thus, tasks are particularly useful if they are designed to avoid too much anxiety.

With a *parental or childlike partner*, the parallel partner is likely to be involved in a difficult struggle. Either of these two will try to maneuver the parallel interactor into the role that meets the child's or parent's needs, which, in turn, the parallel partner will vigorously resist. He must be accepted as is! A childlike partner who originally had parallel-acting parents (or whose contra-gender parent was distant to him as a child) might find a parallel partner just right because the paralleler fits into the childlike partner's unconscious needs. If the childlike one must then continually try to win close, intimate love from the "distant parent," they can have a superficially stormy relationship that actually meets deep psychological needs of both partners.

It is not uncommon for a paralleler to marry someone who perceives the former's need for distance but believes that love will bring him/her closer in time. The need for distance not only is perceived but is the essential challenge. To give love to a parallel partner with the expectation of reciprocity produces anguish. The paralleler cannot reciprocate and is put further on guard to remain aloof. The romantic, who must push for closeness, feels unloved when the desired response is not forthcoming and reacts with his defensive system, bewildered and perplexed by forces he cannot understand or control.

Putting the Pieces Together

Behavioral profiles change as partners continue to interact and as forces outside their relationship impinge on them. The system is not static and always has potential for change. How two partners relate to each other depends on several factors: their individual contracts; their interactional contracts and mechanisms of defense and how the latter affect their mates; the drive, energy and purpose they have to win in marital contests; the amount and quality of their love, affection, commitment and consideration for each other; their desire to maintain the relationship and to make it work; their physical health; influences outside the couple, including their family systems; and a host of other variables, some of which we have discussed and will review briefly. With our present state of knowledge we cannot accurately predict interactional behavior or explain all that we do observe. Behavior within the couple system is complex and of multiple origins. Each individual brings the genetic and environmental history that has molded his/her personality; further, as his/her relationship with the mate continues, he/she changes further. His reactions within their dyadic system are determined by remote factors from earlier periods of his life, as well as by immediate and current factors. Other determinants impinge from outside the marital system. When the couple has children, they, too, become additional determinants that can deeply affect the marital system's functioning, as do the necessities of each period of the marital- and life-cycle.

The biological and intrapsychic parameters of the marriage contract terms are the most significant determining variables of the quality of the marriage. Only recently have we begun to see more clearly the significance of each partner's defense mechanisms. We have long been able to discover and describe each individual's defense mechanisms, but we have not seen clearly how these contribute to determining the quality of the partners' interactions and, thus, the essence of the relationship. The detailed interactions elicit defenses that, in turn, color the interaction further. The qualities of a partner and of the particular relationship may elicit defenses that have not been used by a partner since an earlier epoch in his life-cycle, or perhaps had never been elicited before.

The seven behavioral profiles describe the basic behavioral style of each individual in the particular couple relationship. It is not how he *thinks he behaves* or what he professes to be his credo or his image of himself that is paramount. It is how he actually behaves with his mate that is decisive. Clearly, no behavioral profile exists in pure form. There are secondary and tertiary subthemes that modify the relationship. These subthemes act to provide gratifications as well as safety valves when the negative pressures become too great.

In their interaction, each partner is attempting to achieve fulfillment of his or her individual contract, including ambivalences and even self-imposed deterrents to fulfillment. Each wants more from the partner than from anyone else in the world, and each is willing to give something in exchange for what he wants. And so they play games based on testing, faith, teasing, love, suspicion, coercion, threats, manipulation and a thousand other ways of attempting to get what each believes he wants or to see to it that he or his partner does not get what is wanted. Thus, partners try to elicit from each other reactions that will fulfill their fondest wishes, as well as prove the truth of their worst fears and suspicions.

Nuances and complexities of interrelationships are the spice, passion, anguish and joy of dyadic love partnerships. With understanding and compassion, abetted by the skilled therapist who comprehends the couple's life-style and is not hampered by countertransference, many relationships heading for destruction have a chance to be constructively redirected.

Congruence, Complementarity, and Conflict

General objectives of therapy are to improve the relationship and to facilitate the growth of each partner. Couple and therapist work together toward a single marriage contract that will reflect, in increasing measure, the individual's as well as the marital system's goals and purposes. The *process* of working together toward achievement of these goals and purposes as a couple and for each individual is the essence of their relationship.

A marriage contract can be alive and meaningful only in terms of a specific other person with whom there is an intimate, meaningful and committed relationship. One's desire for particular qualities in a mate or marriage is usually altered significantly from one's fantasy or projection as one becomes involved with a particular person and the relationship evolves.

Most people function somewhat differently in each relationship: Even those who have been married previously and believe they know what they want in a new mate are often surprised by the extent to which they modify their terms in the crucible of the new partnership.

The various terms of each partner's individual marriage contract may be congruent, complementary, or in conflict with terms in his or her partner's contract. In addition, some clauses of an individual's contract may be internally congruent or conflictual with other terms, commonly producing internal conflict and ambivalent messages and behavior.

Ideally, each person's contract should be consistent within itself and congruent with or complementary to the partner's contract. Contracts that approach this ideal evolve into a single effective contract that both spouses can subscribe to consciously and freely. However, it is not necessary or even desirable for all terms to be identical, so long as the partners know where differences exist respect the other's right to differ, and are able to negotiate compromises in a way that either resolves or prevents serious disharmony or dissatisfaction. When dissatisfaction does occur, as it inevitably will, mates must be able to identify their expectations and their feelings, communicate well and verbally fight through differences to some equitable solution within an ambience of mutual respect.

Therapists help the couples to eliminate hidden terms, "fine print," and implicit clauses from their marriage contracts, but we do not expect two people to adhere invariably to the letter and spirit of their newly emerging single joint contract. We hope instead to teach partners how to negotiate with each other, since the terms of their contract and goals of their marriage will constantly evolve to reflect changes in life situations. Most therapeutic time is spent in changing the *need* for a counterproductive clause, not in examining and talking directly about contracts necessarily. When necessary to do so, we deal with remote etiological factors that can alter intrapsychic forces in either or both partners that have lead to unrealistic expectations or perceptions.

USE OF CONTRACTS IN THERAPY

The marriage contract is a dyadic and individual phenomenon, as well as a therapeutic and educational concept that tries to spell out the vague and intuitive. It penetrates to the core of any significant dyadic relationship and rapidly unmasks what makes the relationship good, poor or impossible. The individual contracts are the products of two people and are real; they have existed in reality even if they had not been fully verbalized before. Unlike a complicated x-ray scan, the two contracts are not only intelligible to the trained professional, but they can also be easily "read" and understood by the spouses themselves.

How the Data Are Collected

There need not, nor can there be, a rigid method of collecting the necessary information. Data on the first (conscious, verbalized) and second (conscious, not verbalized) levels of awareness can be supplied by the couple during the sessions, as well as by their responses to the therapist's request that they each write out their contracts or else discuss the items together. Explaining the concept of the two contracts and giving them a reminder list of topics (see Appendix A) often facilitates the spouses' understanding of what is expected of them, and at the same time lessens some of the fear of putting their thoughts into writing. I have found that the reminder list is usually well received by couples in all socioeconomic and cultural groups. The contracts need not necessarily be written out by the patients, a procedure I rarely use today. It took me a long time to realize that the original research procedure of having spouses separately write out their contracts interfered with a primary concern of treatment—to get spouses to talk with each other. Hence, I now most frequently give only one reminder list to a couple. When spouses are not able to talk together without fighting or when they have schedule difficulties that keep them from coming together frequently for long enough periods to do the necessary talking through, I may ask them to write out their individual contracts separately first. In a few instances, it is apparent that one or both partners will be measurably less guarded if they write out their contracts separately. In these instances I also continue to utilize the writing approach.

The therapist must be flexible and, if necessary, ingenious, to get the couple to eventually work together. The guiding principle is the sooner they work together and get their terms out in the open, the better. I ask them to read the reminder list (Table 1) together. They are then to arrange two to three hour periods of time when they can discuss the reminder list items. Each is to tell the other what he/she wants to give and what he/she wants in exchange from the other or from the relationship. Defensiveness, as much as is possible, must be put aside, as well as monosyllabic answers. Each searches deeply within him/herself and need not be surprised to find that he or she may hold contradictory ideas or feelings. Each is to make clear in the discussion how he/she feels about each item, one by one. The couple is not to try to resolve all differences at this point—just write down the significant differences that have emerged.

This process begins to clarify the individual contracts and to start the couple simultaneously working towards the single, common contract which is a central therapeutic focus, as mentioned earlier. They are told to expect to spend at least three hours on each of the three sections—one section a week is sufficient. The material is then brought back to the next session. Not only are the partners' responses, but also

how resistance was expressed and what feelings were evoked by the discussion, are important.

Some of the problems and resistances to carrying out the discussion procedure have been mentioned. The task requires a good deal of motivation, interpersonal skill and trust in opening up to one another. *A significant part of the therapist's role, as in the giving of any task, is to determine the resistances, to try to bypass or work them through.* Often, as much is learned that is therapeutically useful by a failure to carry out a task as by its completion. If motivation of one or both partners is inadequate to carry out or even to start the task, this should be recognized by the therapist and contracts should then not be worked on at that time. Often pressing immediate problems, anger, floods of complaints, and other interferences with getting to the primary task must be dealt with first. For some, the problems or the goals they have may be circumscribed and it might be counterproductive or unnecessary to work with the contract concept.

If I recognize that the task will not be carried out when I first suggest it, I may then withdraw my suggestion. Not finding time to talk together but going to two movies or watching the television late show together, and similar excuses reveals resistances to be explored. The mobilization of anxiety involved in examining one's self and one's relationship is tremendous. This must be recognized and the patients helped. Talking through some contractual terms during the conjoint sessions is often helpful. It is here that one's therapeutic skill becomes important in the evaluation and overcoming of resistance. Similarly, lack of communication skills in the couple may indicate that these skills will have to be taught and accepted by them before meaningful contractual work can begin. Often, I will stimulate discussion in the session on a salient contract point that appears to be a source of difficulty for the two. In the process, I teach them how to talk and listen to each other. We might even have to first spend time on learning how to fight fairly verbally, using constructive rules.[10] Lack of trust is easy to determine—one

---

[10]*Editors' Note.* A creative application of couples therapy based on social learning theory has recently been proposed by Margolin (1979) in the context of teaching spouse-abusing couples how to resolve conflicts.

spouse will tell us how whatever he/she has revealed of him/herself in the past the other has used against him/her—or by a dozen other clues. We then have to deal with the lack of trust first before the partners can talk through their contracts. Writing out the contracts separately without disclosure to the other is sometimes a better procedure, at least as a start for such a couple.

The above discussion indicates that the contract approach, like any other in therapeutic approach, cannot be employed in a cookbook fashion—adaptability on the part of the therapist is the crucial factor. *A single contract will not be arrived at easily.* For some, it may require time-consuming periods of individual therapy to work through a particular impasse produced by a remote source of anxiety. The contract keeps the therapist and the mates focused on a direction and goals.

The therapist can use the reminder list as a guide to himself in obtaining contractual information during conjoint sessions. This is an effective use of the list, although time-consuming, and may tend to infantilize the couple. For these reasons my preference is to use what the patients can produce on their own at home as well as material elicited during sessions.

A request that the couple talk about or write out the contracts is contraindicated if: 1) The partners see their problem as confined to one specific area and will not consider further exploration at this time; 2) one mate has a secret of major proportions, whose maintenance would negate the entire process; or 3) one mate is so paranoid and/or destructive that the technique would be counterproductive. Some couples are never asked to write out their contracts because I surmise that they will be resistant and find it impossible to look within themselves. Others would be unable to talk to each other without using the information in a hostile way. Others lack motivation to improve the relationship, while some see the need only for the partner to change.

Sessions are usually conjoint. Within the first three sessions I spend a few minutes alone with each spouse to try to make sure there are no obvious "secrets" that are likely to impede or be contraindicative of conjoint marital therapy.

As treatment proceeds further, data are gathered during sessions with the therapist. Questions along the lines of "What do you wish, want, need, expect or fantasy to be ideal?" with regard to various aspects of the relationship are addressed to each partner. Reversing the question and asking one spouse what he/she believes the other wants or expects is also fruitful because it elicits cross-discussion and corroboration or disagreement, as well as exposing misconceptions.

Data on the third level of awareness are naturally the most difficult to obtain and are more controversial, since often they depend on theoretical constructs or suppositions. The first step is to take a brief history of each spouse and his/her parents' relationship and attempt to reconstruct latent content from conscious interactions. Dream material may also be requested and used; further, the individual's understanding of his own parents' relationship and his guesses about his own parents' contracts are helpful pieces of information.

In the short run, the greatest aid in getting to unconscious material is each spouse's understanding of the other's deepest needs. The extent to which spouses are sensitive to each other's psychological needs and conflicts is both astonishing and understandable.[11] People know more about themselves and those close to them than they admit until pressed to do so. Seemingly unsophisticated people can reveal insight into their own and their partners' deep conflicts over gender identity, power, dependency, passivity versus activity and so on. Clues are the thoughts, fears and misgivings that one has hitherto pushed away.

I frequently offer tentative hypotheses about the third level of the couple's contracts, which may then be confirmed or negated by the reactions of the spouses. These hypotheses are often interpretations, and, although exploratory and diagnostic, they are also part of the therapeutic work. For example, in a conjoint session I said to a woman who was very acerbic and defensive, "I am sitting here trying to imagine how you must have been hurt for you to be so sharp with David and to hold him off at such a

---

[11]*Editors' Note.* Moreover, in contrast to individual psychodynamic psychotherapy, the opportunity to use the patient-therapist transference as the primary vehicle for understanding the patient's "deepest needs" is severely limited in couples therapy since, in effect, the major "transference" relationship is that which exists between husband and wife. See Gurman (1978) for a fuller discussion of this issue.

distance. You appear to be afraid to let him see aspects of you he will like." This combination of hypothesis, observation and interpretation released a flood of feelings that allowed her to be more open and less bristly.

Early Sessions

In the first session, the contracts may begin to emerge. The therapist can then proceed to order the data immediately, with the three classifications of contractual terms as reference points. As the two individual contracts emerge, so too does the interactional contract—the rules, strategies and tactics of the relationship. I begin immediately to speculate to myself about each partner's contract and how congruent, complementary or mutually exclusive different parts of the two contracts may be. The data are tentatively organized as they surface. I am ready to reorder information quickly as the picture continues to develop. I try not to have an investment in maintaining an early hypothesis. I do not put top priority in the first session on gathering a specific amount of contract information. What has brought the spouses to treatment and what they urgently want to deal with or communicate to each other and to me comes first. The history unfolds dynamically, as does contractual information.

After the pressure of the spouses' urgency is reduced by catharsis and the realization that they are heard, I begin to flesh out the picture by determining how loving and considerate they are to each other, the extent of the investment they have in staying together, background material, observation of their interactive, communicative and cognitive styles, their values, respect for each other, the reality stresses in their lives, effects of other family members, and so on. I regard as significant the factors and incidents that arouse feelings of conflict, disharmony, non-caring and pain, as well as those that fulfill the purpose of the marital system and/or expressions of love, concern, caring and tenderness. Structuring of the individual and interactional contracts can be developed from the partners' interaction—what they say and how they say it, their body language, and my hypotheses deduced from the history of their parents' marriages and how each related as a

child and relates now to parents and siblings. Each spouse's view of the mate's current relationship with his own parents is often illuminating. I inquire further into what each spouse expected of the marriage and of the partner and what each wished to give in return at the time of courtship and how these expectations have worked out since.

Exactly when to introduce the concept of the marriage contract to patients cannot be rigidly determined. First, the therapist must be convinced of its value if he is to employ it effectively. Second, no questionnaires or forms should be used on a routine basis. Whether the reminder list is responded to at home or worked out in conjoint sessions with the therapist, the contracts should not be introduced routinely on the first, second or any other visit. The proper timing is when the pressure of immediate complaints is alleviated, as evidenced by the spouses' feeling less intense about their complaints. I often try to show the couple how complaints in Category 3 of the reminder list relate to problems in Category 1 or 2—*thus shifting attention to the fire and away from the smoke.* This usually has a salutary effect and tends to calm anger. I may give simple quid pro quo tasks designed to dissipate anger or helplessness. For example, a wife complains her husband never compliments her cooking despite her efforts. He refuses to eat out, says she cooks okay but never makes what he likes. I set for the wife the task of asking her husband what he likes and how he likes it prepared and then preparing what he wants. He, in turn, is to compliment her on her cooking *regardless* of what he feels about it, and he is to take her out to dinner once during the week to a restaurant of her choice. Both partners usually cooperate on a task of this nature and it decompresses the immediate situation. Lack of compliance to the task, of course, becomes grist for the therapeutic mill, as do the feelings and reactions that are elicited.

I often introduce the contract concept by discussing with the couple that they are two closely interdependent persons but that the dreams, hopes and expectations that each had of the other, of himself and of the marriage have somehow turned into something that had not been anticipated. I then elaborate on the contracts, extracting from what they have already expressed some of their contractual understandings and misunderstandings. I try to illustrate to them the sources of some of their feelings of disappointment, anger, depression, or self-pity. If the evidence is present in the data, I show them how each feels cheated because he/she believes he/she has kept his/her part of the bargain but the mate has not fulfilled some terms of a contract that was never overtly agreed upon. The impulse to point the finger at who violated "The Contract" first is almost universal; self-righteousness and self-justification are often the first hurdles to be overcome.

At this point I may give the couple the reminder list of the contractual parameters to help them clarify their present contract. Some couples may have already touched on some of the salient points during the session and have already begun to develop their individual contracts.

One couple, after two months of stormy therapy during which they separated and moved back together twice, wrote out their individual contracts. When they returned with them they said they had now decided to separate. The process of writing on paper what each wanted made each independently know he/she did not want to be married and that the marriage had been a mismatch from the start. In this case, the result was positive—it had been clear to me for several weeks that divorce was inevitable for this couple. I had asked them to write out their contracts in the hope that each would arrive independently at the same conclusion. In many similar cases, using the contracts as a confrontation technique has been very useful. This confrontation of one's own feelings is a common source of anxiety that the therapist needs to be aware of and to deal with.

The interactional contract is determined by observing how the partners interact together in the conjoint session, by their own reportage of their transactions and by the way they carry out their duties and responsibilities as a couple. Videotaping or audiotaping of sessions is an excellent way to observe the interactional patterns at work. Instant playback confronts the couple directly with how they deal with each other (Berger, 1978). With these techniques, we can often help patients turn more quickly to less injurious transactions.

How the Data Are Assessed

The assessment process begins with the couple's and the therapist's noting where the partners' contracts agree or complement each other and where they conflict. The connections among complaints, interactions and contract terms have to be made by the therapist in his assessment. If one spouse has given considerable weight to an issue not mentioned by the other, the therapist can ask about the point and note the response.

I frequently start arbitration or negotiation of one or two areas at once, to test the give-and-take potential and motivation of each spouse. *Areas that resist simple quid pro quo solutions often derive from significant intrapsychic factors and a basic distrust of self and/or the other.* These become the basis for multifaceted therapeutic work and may require teaching communication skills or working through unrealistic concepts of love, e.g., "If I were loved he/she would give me what I want . . . he/she would know without my having to ask!" Quid pro quo, without resentment, is a basic part of all good long-term relationships. It should not be compared with a crass materialistic attitude—which is often offered as a resistance. A nonresponse to a particular subject on the list can often be indicative of a troublesome area. If the partners have written out their contracts, it is a simple task to mark off with a colored pencil the problem areas of each contract, as well as where there are meaningful differences and similarities between the two.

The therapist can use the three sets of contractual terms to help organize the data he seeks and receives from couples. Whether expressed in these particular terms or not, the essence of most marital therapy, by whatever means it is practiced, moves the partners towards eliminating the two covert contracts and working collaboratively with the therapist to establish an up-front single, mutually acceptable contract. *Removing the blocks in the way of achieving a workable single contract, along with setting up mechanisms for review of it when necessary, constitutes the process of therapy and in itself becomes a goal of treatment.* Consequently, it is necessary for the therapist to possess a knowledge of dyadic dynamics, systems theory, individual psychology and psychodynamics, and a wide range of techniques deriving from behavior therapy, transactional analysis, Gestalt therapy, psychoanalysis and marital therapy. Anything that will help to produce planned and desired change, and that will give the couple the necessary insight and equipment to function together as a system and as individuals can and must be called into play by the therapist.

Ideally, the contract approach becomes a lifelong project, initiated with the help of the therapist and sustained by the partners themselves. Contracts do exist operationally for all couples. Our job as therapists is to try to call them forth into full consciousness and to teach couples to use them constructively.

THERAPEUTIC PRINCIPLES AND TECHNIQUES

The individual and interactional contracts can be useful with any theoretical approach or modality of treatment. We can now focus more directly on those aspects of treatment that have not been emphasized or made sufficiently explicit.

One point bears repetition: The individual marriage contracts and the interactional contract help make sense of the wealth of material we collect from patients. We are free to work therapeutically in keeping with our own bias. Mine is eclectic and, I hope, flexible. The following therapeutic approaches are suggested for the therapist to reflect on, test out, incorporate, modify or reject as he/she pleases. Each therapist can work most effectively by developing his or her own style. He/she should, however, give him/herself and his patients the benefit of becoming familiar with new developments of theory and technique so that he/she is able to make his/her own choices and not be bound by the limited number of therapeutic alternatives that were made available at the time of his/her training.

I do have some general preference for procedure, provided I see no necessity for a variance, which does occur frequently. I like to determine both partners' desire to improve the relationship, whether they expect only the other to change or if one or both wish to end the relationship. Ambivalence is to be expected, but some commitment to work on the relationship and recognition of the necessity to contribute to change are imperative. We then together set immediate goals and I may assign tasks that are designed to move the couple towards their goals. Tasks and emotional reactions are dealt with in the next session. I question the partners on their expectations of the relationship and of one another, and how these expectations have been realized. This opens the way to introduction of the concept of the two individual marriage contracts and the need for the partners to work together towards a single contract. I will use emotional insight methods, such as a probing hypothesis or Gestalt technique, or will relate present behavior to childhood and parental behavior, as well as employing other insight-producing methods as I see opportunities for these, or I may pursue another approach when one has failed or brought us to an impasse. Although most sessions are conjoint, I may split a session, seeing each partner alone for a while, or have a few individual sessions to attempt to work through a remote behavioral determinant that cannot be bypassed. When I do this both partners know why and are not likely to use the fact of the individual session against the other.

Using the marital contract concept makes it relatively easy to pinpoint the significant factors responsible for marital discord. The individual contracts facilitate deciding where, how and when to intervene therapeutically. In addition, the contracts provide the spouses themselves with a frame of reference with which they, as well as the therapist, can periodically examine themselves and their relationship.

The Diagnosis-Therapy Dialectic

Correct diagnosis is essential for planning the best treatment program. The individual marriage contracts and interactional behavioral profiles suggest a fresh approach toward an eventual diagnostic and classification system of marriage. The typology I have suggested and the other constructs described earlier deal with a large number of parameters. They do avoid the pitfall of trying to explain the remote origins of an individual's behavior, yet they consider significant elements of intrapsychic as well as transactional components. A diagnosis of marital dysfunction cannot be a static label but should be a dynamic evaluation of how the couple functions as a unit or system to fulfill the marital system's and the two individuals' goals and purposes. As such, it is always in flux. Together, these elements still do not quite constitute a satisfactory diagnostic system, but they are a definite step in that direction. They do constitute a nearly complete descriptive and dynamic entity, but without pinpointing etiological factors, which still elude us because of the complexity of dealing with so many variables, many of which still remain unknown.

On the basis of the congruence, complementarity and conflict of the individual marriage contract terms, we have a complex of intrapsychic and transactional manifestations that highlights the problems and their immediate causes (even if it does not attempt to evaluate in greater detail remote etiological factors), as well as the strengths of the couple and their system. We are, thus, in a position to use these factors knowledgeably in the treatment program, although *all* etiological input remains incomplete.

When the concepts of the two individual contracts, the two behavioral profiles hyphenated as typology, and the interaction contract are used together, diagnosis and treatment become intertwined as two interpenetrating factors that eventually create a new unity. Diagnosis determines treatment. Treatment, to the extent that it produces change, alters diagnosis. This dialectic between diagnosis and treatment goes on continually. This is exemplified in the two marriage contracts that provide the basis for the interactional or operational contract. Change in the two individual contracts towards a single one alters the couple's interactional behavior. The dynamics of the system have changed and, therefore, the diagnosis will have changed too. This, in turn, may necessitate a change in treatment goals, strategy and/or tactics. This back-and-forth process, which is measured by progress towards achieving a single contract and by change in the system and its component subsystems, continues until the spouses arrive at their single joint marriage contract. Such a state of single contractedness between partners can only be approximated. Except in rare instances, even its approximation cannot be maintained as a steady state without being worked on.

The dictum "diagnosis determines treatment" is a truism that presupposes we have an excellent nosology based on etiological and descriptive components and that our therapy is specific for each diagnosis. We are far from this ideal state and I question if it will be attained in the near future. Clinical pragmatism and bias far outdistance research; theory often follows practice and we move ahead slowly.

The diagnostic schema developed here and elaborated elsewhere (Sager, 1976a, 1977) is complex and still it is incomplete. The elements of the diagnostic schema are the behavioral profiles and interactional scripts, the individual marriage contracts and the flexibility and motivation evidenced by the desire, will and ability of each partner to work towards a single contract. The individual defenses elicited in each partner as a function of and determinant of their dyadic system are of fundamental importance. Major psychological problems such as thought disorders, primary affective disorders and marked discrepancies in intelligence between partners are all considerations. The rigidity and type of defenses of a partner reflect his/her intrapsychic dynamics. We have simultaneously to evaluate and take into cognizance individual dynamics and the system.

The contracts reflect, among other factors, each individual's intrapsychic needs. When these change, a shift has taken place intrapsychically and, therefore, the marital interactional system will be altered too. In general, those individuals and couples who are most defended tend to do most poorly when treated first with insight approaches. The first steps usually should enlist couple support in goal-setting and then utilize tasks or other behavioral approaches. Those couples who are better in touch with feelings and have less rigid defensive systems can profit from the interjection of more insight-producing procedures and the eliciting of feelings. The talking through of individual contracts must be delayed for some couples because of their inability to talk or listen to each other due to anger or poor communication skills. In these instances, such skills have to be developed first. One approach is to use the *Marital Expectations Questionnaire* (Appendix E). Their answers to these eight questions can then be read to each other at the next session or at home.

Other couples may have to be taught how to fight fairly and constructively before they can proceed to work on their contracts.

The therapist gets clues from the couple systems and the individual behavioral and intrapsychic changes that in turn help to determine the next intervention procedure. Decisions to continue the relationship or not must rest with the couple. The therapist is guided by their decisions. On the other hand, the therapist must be firm to deal with talk of divorce from a partner who uses this threat as a weapon. I may have to ask each spouse to write out his/her individual contract in private if one partner overpowers the other when they talk together.

Ideally, when a single contract state is approximated and lived out, the diagnosis is then "no dysfunction" and there is no further need for treatment.

Prophylactic attention to the couple's interaction and maintenance of congruent goals and purposes should go on indefinitely. Most couples discontinue treatment when their distress no longer outweighs their gratification and pleasure. As couples come to understand the terms of their own contracts, usually employed quite explicitly in treatment, they tend to use the contract concept and work on their contract together, even after major obstacles have been overcome in treatment. The major therapeutic role in this period should not be to compulsively ferret out every conflict, but to teach the partners themselves how to deal with conflicts and goal changes, to prepare for the next phase of their life cycle, and to maintain cultural and sexual interests together. Thus, near the end of treatment there is a shift for a short time to emphasis on how to use for preventive purposes what has been learned in therapy. The therapist's first therapeutic task is to gain inclusion into the couple's system so that he can help to change it. The last is to withdraw from the system, leaving the couple with their own means to prevent trouble in the future and to cope early with counterproductive trends.

Treatment Modalities

There are many different methods of working with couples. Berman and Lief (1975) report that at present 80% of marital therapy is conducted

with both spouses seen conjointly by the same therapist or therapists. I, too, prefer conjoint sessions and elect not to work with a co-therapist except briefly for training purposes.[12] In the vast majority of instances, the cost of co-therapy to the individuals or the institution is doubled without a commensurate gain in the quality of treatment. All therapists are expected to be alert to countertransferential, as well as cultural and gender-determined, biases. I ask my patients to help me in this endeavor and this is most helpful. In my teaching and staff work I see patients in the presence of my colleagues. This assures me of supervision and criticism that helps to keep me from becoming grandiose and keeps my self-critical faculties alive. Occasionally, I find it is wise to invite a colleague to join me in a session when a patient believes that my being male, white, middle-class or whatever has made me biased. Sometimes the patient is correct. Usually the decision to include a colleague for a session has been a constructive one. I also am in a peer group with colleagues every week which furthers my critical self-awareness. I recommend peer groups for all who have completed their training.

Couples groups can also be a very helpful modality. I utilize a flexible approach to loosely structured theme-centered couples groups, based on subject parameters from the contracts of couples in the group that are pertinent for those particular couples. Sufficient communality of contractual problems and motivation to work on their relationship are criteria for selection. I do not elect to put couples who clearly want to separate in the same group as those who wish to try to stay together. The objectives are too different. I prefer separate groups for divorcing couples and married couples. I now also have groups where one or both partners are in their second or third marriage. This is one additional application of the multitheoretical and multi-technique approach with which I am most comfortable. Couples in groups see one another's problems and are helpful to one another in terms

---

[12]*Editors' Note.* Indeed, there is very little empirical research on the comparative clinical efficacy of co-therapy vs. single therapist treatment, and what little research does exist seems to support Sager's position (Gurman and Kniskern, 1978). In addition, as Sager argues, the cost-effectiveness of such a clinical practice requires careful study.

of perceptiveness and insight and of assisting other group members to work toward their single contract. An individual can see his own behavior or his spouse's in someone else more clearly than in himself. I find that four couples in a group, five at most, are optimal for the way I work. More than one depressed couple in the group often deadens the group and is to be avoided. I usually do not see couples privately during the time (10-12 sessions) they are in the group.

Berman and Lief (1975) believe that treatment in individual sessions is necessary if therapy is not to remain on the behavioral level. My experience differs from theirs. In conjoint sessions, I am able to deal with and to affect determinants of current behavior, when it is necessary to deal with these in order to help produce change (Sager, 1966, 1967a,b,c). I often use intrapsychic and historical material concurrently with the here-and-now data and the more directly behavioral and interactional approaches. Psychoanalytic knowledge of dynamics can be drawn upon without necessarily using the techniques of psychoanalysis. Mates are seen individually when one needs to work through an intrapsychic aspect that would seem to yield best to individual therapy before resuming work together. However, the use of individual sessions occurs less frequently as I have come to appreciate the therapeutic power and leverage of the conjoint session.

Having the freedom to work with couples conjointly, individually, in group, in sex therapy, and with other family members enables the therapist to use whatever modality will be most effective for a particular couple at a particular point. However, for me, the major form of treatment delivery remains the conjoint session.

I do bring in other family members when I find indications for doing so. Sometimes it may be the parents of one or both partners. Almost invariably I want to see the couple's children with them at least once. Not to do so when treating couples with children misses the input of the couple's larger system. Even if they are asymptomatic, they are part of a troubled system. Their presence, at least for one session, can be helpful. Children see and understand a great deal. It is reassuring for them to meet their parents' therapist and to have the scene de-mystified. Having parents in therapy is a threat to children—even when the parents think the children are unaware of their treatment, the children are acutely aware of their parent's disharmony. To see the family system together can give us important clues, as well as help us to spot evidence of problems in the children of a troubled system.

The need for sex therapy can play an important role in the treatment of some couples. At the very least, the therapist cannot be satisfied with a response to, "How is sex for the two of you?", such as "It's okay," or "It was fair but it's no good now." It is important to learn the specifics of sex now and in the past.

The sexual relationship of two people can give us important insights into the totality of their relationship. Although we can no longer say that sex reflects the degree and type of closeness, love, ability to function, consideration, ability to share and a host of other factors do relate to other parameters. Often, too, sex therapy can be helpful in removing an irritating problem for the couple and its removal may have a salutary effect on the rest of their relationship. For a more detailed discussion of sex therapy in marital therapy see my earlier papers (Sager, 1974, 1977).

In the first session almost every couple demonstrates behavior that is determined by transferential and regressive dynamics toward each other. I will not argue with anyone who cares to call this behavior a manifestation of parataxic distortions (Sullivan, 1953), the introject-projection system of Dicks (1967), or any other term the therapist wishes to hypothesize the etiology of these observable phenomena. We often see evidence of childhood neurosis and regressive behavior in the first conjoint session that might otherwise have required many months or years to elicit in psychoanalysis. It would be a terrible waste of leverage and clinical knowledge if we were not to utilize these phenomena in the conjoint session, along with the theoretical and technical approaches that are based on systems, communication and learning theories. Interpretations that are offered as hypotheses, as well as tasks based on our awareness of psychodynamics, are important tools in conjoint treatment.

The systems approach to conjoint therapy can

even be adapted to deal with dream and unconscious material. Goldstein (1974) has partners speculate about the meaning of each other's dreams but avoids making interpretations himself. I, too, often have the partners speculate about their own and their partner's dreams, but may also use Gestalt methods of having the individual work with his/her dreams, or suggest connections and offer interpretations myself (Sager, 1966). Dreams are helpful in determining contractual terms on the third level of awareness and in assaying interactional components. They may be used in a wide variety of ways that relate to current and remote factors.

Spouses' interactions are very much determined by their acute subliminal awareness of each other's unconscious contractual terms and desires. Transferential phenomena play a significant role because of the many unconsciously determined factors that influence mate selection and ways of perceiving and relating to one's mate. The therapist who can be theoretically eclectic and technically pragmatic has the advantage of being able to move back and forth between focusing on the interactional system of the couple and on the intrapsychic component of each individual, to see how one affects and helps to determine the content and manifestations of the other.

Theoretical Approaches

Good introductions to marital therapy, for both theory and practice can be found in Sager and Kaplan (1972) and in Martin (1976). The three major theoretical approaches to marital theory are developed in detail and critically examined by various authors in Paolino and McCrady's (1978) volume. Gurman's (1978) evaluative and comparative chapter on contemporary marital therapies in that book is particularly useful.

Modalities may be utilized in a way that is consistent with any of the three major psychological theoretical approaches. A biological approach along with the psychological, such as the use of psychotropic drugs, should be utilized when appropriate. Most therapists employ a mix of two or more theoretical approaches, although they may place major emphasis on one. Our selection is in large part made in terms of what we find to be comfortable and compatible with our own personalities, what training and experience we have had, which teachers we identify with and our biases from other sources.

The major theoretical approaches are:

1) The *biological*, which uses methods based on treating physically determined etiological factors or their manifestations.
2) *General systems theory*, which uses various means to alter the dyadic system's functioning in a way designed to fulfill the couple's therapeutic goals.
3) *Psychodynamic theory*, which employs insight-producing methods based on classical and other schools of psychoanalysis, psychoanalytic psychotherapy, Gestalt therapy, transactional analysis and so on.
4) *Learning theory*, the theoretical base for the techniques of behavior therapy and behavior modification.

The organic approach emphasizes physically determined etiological and secondary factors, including somatopsychic effects. It is important for these determinants to be diagnosed and treated with the best of medical knowledge and to use remedial methods where these are applicable. When indicated, psychotropic drugs should be employed judiciously. For example, a partner who is in a serious depression cannot work productively in any form of psychotherapy, let alone explore his own and his partner's contract. Antidepressive medication might be the first order of the day, while also exploring dyadic factors and individual factors that may have precipitated or help to maintain the depression.

The systems approach, based on general systems theory, views the marital system as composed of two individual subsystems, husband and wife. It is hypothesized that any intervention that affects a subsystem will affect the entire system. The work of the therapist is to devise interventions that are likely to produce the effect on the system that the therapist and the patients desire. This concept allows for a wide latitude of types of intervention as well as a variety of points at which to intervene. This systems concept is able to incorporate in its general theory most theoretical and technical efforts to understand and change the behavior of the human dyad. This approach is widely used in family therapy, as in Minuchin's (1974) method of restructuring the family.

Many marital transactions become patterns that often require only a partial stimulus, as the result of experience and conditioning, to set off a predictable reaction. The origins of these set patterns are often lost in the couple's ancient history. To try to pursue who did what to whom first is a fruitless task, although it is carried on with gusto and glee by many couples. The transactions that have become set patterns and the feelings that they arouse may be altered by a number of methods. These include: restructuring the system or shaping the behavior of spouses so that the motivations, defenses or impulses of either spouse are altered in a positive way; observing and being confronted with the current transaction itself (including video playback confrontation methods [Berger, 1978]); altering the means and effectiveness of communication; prescribing tasks that are designed to change behavior; and other techniques.

The following is an illustration of a systems theory-based intervention at a point of contract negotiation impasse. A couple, working on their contracts, were hung up on two crucial issues, which were closely interrelated, although they appeared to be unaware of this. The husband insisted (on conscious and unconscious levels) that he must control all facets of their life. The woman was resentful and could no longer accept compliance. In the sexual parts of their contracts, she wanted more pleasure and variety of sex play and positions—"more spontaneity." She had been orgastic during coitus early in their marriage, but rarely was for several years now. Her husband insisted on using only the male superior position during coitus and was angry and upset because she "couldn't or wouldn't" have orgasms. I instructed them to have coitus the next two times with the wife in the superior position. The second time they did so she had an orgasm. Her husband was exhilarated by her excitement and both felt closer afterwards than they had for years. The change in the system, by the wife "controlling" sex, allowed the husband to realize that he, as well as she, could profit from her exercise of some control. This proved to be a turning point that

then allowed them to include in their single contract a freer flow of power. The terms were set forth and they increasingly (not always smoothly) worked towards a relationship of greater equality.

Psychodynamics and insight theories now include much more than our heritage from classical psychoanalysis. The latter encompasses important aspects that should not be discarded when their validity and therapeutic usefulness remain pertinent. There are numerous additional theoretical and technical methods that are also psychodynamic, such as transactional analysis, Gestalt theory, the more interpersonal and cultural theories of psychoanalysis, such as those originated by Horney (1939, 1950) and Sullivan (1945, 1953) and a host of others. Fairbairn's (1952, 1963) object relations concepts, along with Dicks' (1967) adaptation of these to work with couples and Ackerman's contributions (1958, 1966) to the theory of family therapy may also be included among insight approaches.

An individual's psychodynamics are determined by the interplay of his biology and environment, which includes more than the influence of parents and siblings or environmental events occurring in the early years of life. Intrapsychic dynamics can always be altered and influenced by new experiences, including transactions with a spouse. Because we are open systems that keep changing with our variegated input, the marital system takes on the coloring not only of what each individual brings to it, but also of the spouses' social environment and the way their world impinges on them.

As the marital system has its input, so in turn the marital relationship feeds back to and changes the intrapsychic dynamics of each person. For example, we frequently observe changes over a period of time in which dominance has passed from one partner to the other, or it is not uncommon for a man who has been fearful of women to become reassured in a relationship. He then is no longer fearful, nor need he be dominated or dominating after marriage. Presumably his new experience with a particular woman has changed his intrapsychic dynamics as the two arrived at a workable modus vivendi.

An insight-producing approach was utilized with a couple when their contracts indicated he wanted his wife to be more in charge of things and not to be so submissive to him. She persisted that a couple got along best when the woman played second fiddle and that she had no desire to have it otherwise. She assumed a good child profile and wanted her husband to be a benevolent parent. In our first meeting her description of her parents' relationship was one of constant battle because her mother always took over and tried to control her father. A little more questioning revealed that she knew her father loved and admired his older sister who was submissive to her husband and "had a good marriage." She now recognized she subliminally had modeled her own behavior after her image of her aunt's. We followed the vein of this insight further, including aspects of her oedipal feelings and her counterphobic defense, which had been aroused by her impulses to be more assertive, much as her mother had been. Her impulses made her afraid and suspicious of her husband's desire for her to be more of an equal partner. The insights gained allowed her to move towards greater assertiveness in an appropriate fashion as she became convinced her archaic coping behavior was no longer constructive. Her intrapsychic and behavior changes then in turn affected the couple's interactions.

Behavior modification and *behavior therapy* techniques are the clinical applications of learning theory (O'Leary and Turkewitz, 1978). The interdependence of the two adults in the marital system leaves them ample opportunity to learn to reinforce each other's positive and negative behavior. Therapy based on aspects of learning theory plays an increasingly important role in couple therapy, both marital and sexual. Many therapists now use some techniques borrowed from behavior therapy—for example, tasks to carry out at home, the use of reward systems and so on. The results of the tasks, the feelings aroused and the use of those feelings in therapy become part of the multifaceted and integrated technical approach to help couples work towards a single operational contract. Utilizing tasks designed to change behavior and then dealing with resistance to carrying out the tasks and emotional reactions engendered by the tasks (whether successfully carried out or not) means utilization of insight and/or system interventions in combination with behavioral techniques. The insight therapy approaches can be used to deal with the resistances and emotional reactions to the task assignments. Another approach could be the behavioral approach of stepwise desensitization. The purist approach to behavior therapy has matured so that some behavior therapy innovators have begun to soften their positions to combine behavioral, insight and system theory methods, as have some psychoanalytically oriented therapists and previously rigid systems adherents.

The three basic theoretical and psychotherapeutic approaches—psychoanalytic, systems and learning theory—are each subdivided into a vast number of approaches to marital therapy. I prefer to remain fluid and try to add to my therapeutic endeavors whatever may be useful. I rarely discard anything totally since I find that sooner or later an opportunity arises to utilize a theoretical approach or technique learned long ago. As healers we must take from wherever we can. The *organic approaches* are beyond the scope of this chapter except to caution the therapist to be alert to the new developments and possibilities that are constantly emerging in this important area.

Therapist's Role

The therapist's role is somewhat similar to that of an experienced fishing guide who has contracted with his clients to help them catch fish but has not guaranteed success. The guide tries to set up the most feasible and expeditious conditions for them to accomplish their goal. He uses all his accumulated knowledge and experience. He knows the habits of the fish in his locale. He tries to make his clients as comfortable as possible on the journey but they must realize that fish cannot be caught from the terrace of a tenth-floor suite of the local Hilton hotel and that the trip may be arduous and rough, inconvenient and even painful at times but that the rewards are worth it—if they really do want to catch fish. It is the guide's duty not to steer the boat into white water that is too dangerous for his clients to handle. Sometimes the guide is in conflict because he knows the fish may be in a deep pool past the rapids. Then he must make a choice. Usually he does not choose to take his clients through rapids that will endanger their lives. There may be other fish in safer pools, or perhaps this couple will find that their expedition together should end.

Goals

Goal specificity is essential in treatment and also offers an approach to the rapid initiation of therapy. One way of proceeding in an ordered, stepwise fashion is to set simple achievable goals and then proceed to others equally simple and achievable when the first have been attained. The therapist must be flexible enough to allow interruptions in the program. The contract information helps to guide the couple and the therapist in goal-setting and involves the patients as full participants in deciding upon the goals they want. It helps to assure, too, that their priorities, values, standards, and purposes are being met, not just the therapist's.

Goals voiced at the start of treatment do not have to be the ultimate ones. Almost any goal or purpose that husband, wife and therapist agree upon is acceptable if it is plausible and possible to achieve. As therapy continues, unexpected goals or problems may come to the fore that must be dealt with. The therapist has to separate the valid goals from those that are distractions or resistance. For example, if one spouse is firm, clear and not ambivalent about wanting to separate, for the therapist to accept the other spouse's goal to improve the marriage would not be valid. Likewise, a goal both spouses may claim they want, to never argue again, would not be a valid one. Such a goal is impossible to achieve in a good relationship and may well be a resistance to dealing with genuine issues.

Some couples, or at least one spouse, may come to treatment with the goal to separate. If one partner irrevocably wants to leave the other, then the task of the therapist, with the concurrence of the two spouses, is to facilitate a separation with as little destructiveness as possible. However, some couples seem unable to arrive at a workable modus vivendi until their marriage is threatened with termination; one or both partners may use the threat of separation in an attempt to improve the relationship or to force the couple to seek therapy.

My objective is to try to help the couple continue their marriage if they wish to. I make clear to them that the separation or divorce of two persons who loved at one time represents a disappointment, a blow to each partner's self-esteem, and the end of a hope and dream that is painful to accept. It may deeply affect their children and their relationships with them; it is likely to cause economic hardships. At the very least, if they decide it is best to separate, the couple should understand why they are doing so and learn from the experience they have had together. What can each learn that will enhance the chances for greater self-fulfillment and for the next relationship to work out better (if another relationship is wanted)?

The therapist often has to provide firm leadership to establish whether both spouses want to remain together and to improve the quality of their relationship. Couples who at the outset are not sure whether they want to stay together can be helped to use the therapeutic process to clarify their contracts and make a decision.

Sometimes one or both mates may have covert goals in seeking professional help. For example, one partner may want his spouse to be in the "protective hands" of the therapist as a "guarantee" against the spouse's developing a depression or psychotic episode, or a soon-to-depart spouse may fear his spouse's rage when the separation is announced. In such instances therapy may be used by one spouse as an attempt to shift responsibility for the mate to the therapist. Some mates go through the motions of therapy to tell themselves, their mate, children, friends, relatives and even God, that they have tried everything before actually separating. The inevitability of divorce or separation when both mates do not want to stay together is best respected by the therapist.

Patients often define their goals at first in terms of their immediate complaints: "We are always fighting. If he would only not jump on me all the time, we would be okay." Or, "I feel she no longer loves me. I can't get overtime work anymore and so money is tight. The minute I come in the door now, she wants me to fix things. She doesn't think about me." or, a third, "I have trouble with sex, that is, in keeping my erection and I never used to until these past six months when she found out I had a one-night stand." Or, "I'm stuck here with this house, the kids and a station wagon. He's never home. He's married more to that company than to me."

These complaints would be viewed very simplistically if we were to believe that all that is needed to remedy each situation would be: for the first woman, that we instruct her husband to stop jumping on her; for the second, that the man just make more money and his wife give him time to relax; for the third, that the man be relieved of guilt about his extramarital sexual experience, and that his wife "forgive" him, and then he immediately would be returned to his sexual competence and all would be fine between them; and, for the fourth, that the husband be urged to spend more time with his family and give more directly of himself. Of course, no such simple solutions exist.

These Category 3 complaints are derivative symptoms, rather than etiological agents. Obviously, much more is involved in each instance than can be significantly changed by a common-sense suggestion. If it could be done that easily it would have been, and professional help would not have been sought.

More sophisticated couples may state their immediate goals differently but they may still arise from the third category of the derivative complaints, as the four previous examples do. More subtle versions might be, "My wife and I don't communicate meaningfully anymore—we can talk about things, but not feelings." Or, "Yes, I can write checks, too, but we really don't have equal responsibility and rights when it comes to making decisions about significant expenditures. He can decide to buy a new suit for himself, but if I want a coat I have to ask him if it's okay to spend the money now." The presumed goals in response to these two complaints would be to "improve communication" in the first instance and to arrive at a suitable modus operandi for money management in the second. In pursuing these two goals, we shortly discover that these complaints are derivative. The first instance, that of poor communication, is a manifestation of the wife's need to maintain distance. In the second example, the use of money is but one among many manifestations of these mates' pervasive struggle for control.

The therapist has the responsibility to help the couple establish goals that will help them get what they really want. For the patients, this is often best defined in behavioral terms, even when insight may be required to help produce the change, because insight-producing measures often are time-consuming. The more rapidly we can achieve the desired goals, the better. It may be important for the partners to learn that the overt expression of their complaint is rooted in fundamental differences that must be solved if the power struggle is to become less crucial in their daily interactions. Or, the therapist may elect to bypass the immediate problem and help them work more directly on power, leaving money conflicts to be returned to later if the spouses have not, by then, resolved the problems themselves. When marriage contracts are used to clarify the underlying sources that produce the marital system's malfunction, the appropriate immediate goals become clearer.

Goal-setting may proceed on a step-by-step basis. Some couples are satisfied with traveling a short distance down the road to the infinity of their ideal of the perfect relationship; others want to go the whole route—or almost. The partners have to make the decision of how far they wish to go, while the therapist controls his compulsive need to achieve perfection. In either case, goals must be attainable if their use is to be effective, as Ferber and Ranz (1972) emphasize in their work on goal-reaching and tasks in family therapy. The therapist cannot allow a common goal to be set that one of the partners cannot possibly fulfill or does not wish to.

Tasks

Tasks that are designed to achieve goals must consider the marital system's dynamics and the needs and psychodynamics of each spouse. Tasks have to be designed that will teach and facilitate change through experience, but that will not arouse so much anxiety or resentment that they are certain to be rejected (unless it is our plan to have the task rejected for predictable therapeutic purposes). By making clear the problem areas and the underlying dynamics, the marriage contracts greatly facilitate our devising suitable tasks. In fact, the contracts serve as a guide for setting tasks that will help spouses fulfill each other's unconscious needs, or probe their areas of anxiety and resistance.

For example, the sensate focus or pleasuring exercises of sex therapy can be used as an x-ray or therapeutic test in marital therapy to explore with a couple their readiness to accept closeness, their capacity to collaborate, to give to and receive from the mate, to communicate with each other, and to ask for what they want and to give and accept directions from each other.

Tasks may include individual ones for one mate, quid pro quo tasks in which each does something for the other, or those that are done together. They are carried out at home or in the course of the day. All are designed to produce behavioral changes; some are expected to produce insight, some are not. An example of an insight-producing task is the paradoxical task, which makes ego-syntonic behavior ego-alien. This usually entails having a mate carry out to an absurd extent a behavioral pattern that is disturbing to his spouse (Haley, 1963).

For example, a wife complained that her husband was untidy at home, which he confirmed. His wife unsuccessfully tried to change his ways, alternately yelling at him and picking up after him, much as his mother had done. The man was instructed to be as untidy as he could possibly be—to really mess things up; at the same time the woman was instructed to keep yelling at him and berating him but *not* to clean up after him. Even if she did not feel inclined to do so, she was to yell at him if he left anything untidy or messy about the house. Each spouse heard the instructions to the other in the conjoint session. (The therapist must give such instructions with a straight face and must convincingly convey that he really does want his instructions to be followed.)

When carried to such an extrapolated extent, the behavior of each spouse becomes ridiculously clear to the other; insight into the effects of one's own behavior is almost immediate, and frequently both change their behavior of their own accord. In this case the husband realized sheepishly that he was acting like a spoiled brat and the wife saw herself as the proverbial shrew, which she did not wish to be. Both laughed ruefully at what had happened. Each realized that the exaggeration of his/her usual behavior was ego-alien. By means of this simple task we had changed ego-syntonic behavior to ego-alien

behavior. It also was sufficient to make both spouses change their irritating behavior of their own accord.

In the conjoint session following a task assignment, the spouses describe what they did and their reactions to the task. We are concerned with how the assignments were carried out and what the spouses felt. What was good about it, what was not? How did each cope with the other's task as well as his own? Failure—why a task was not carried out—is as important to learn about as is success. Failures, resistances, and emotional reactions form the grist for the therapeutic session. To deal with these requires all our skill, calling on our technical and theoretical knowledge to deal with the immediate (interactive and system) and the remote (intrapsychic, earlier life experiences) etiological aspects.

A fascinating challenge for the therapist is to develop tasks that will tap into the unconscious desires and needs of each spouse. The therapist has to assay rapidly the unconscious terms of the contracts so that they can serve as a guide. This was done, for example in the Smith case, when each of these childlike partners was trying to make the other a strong but benevolent and giving parent. Each partner's need to be both dependent and in charge was dealt with by putting each spouse in charge of family decisions for alternating periods of three days each, so that the conflict over who was in charge and how to appear to abdicate control while having the mate consider one's needs was worked through via the task.

Problems that originate primarily in the first and second contract categories—expectations of marriage and the biological and intrapsychic determinants—can frequently be dealt with by means of tasks combined with techniques of brief psychotherapy, which are used to bypass or work through the sources of the reactions and feelings that are brought to light in the following session.

Overcoming Resistance to Change

Removing blocks to working toward a single contract is the crucial work of treatment. Some problems are of such a nature that at times individual sessions or more intensive insight therapy may be indicated. Possibly conjoint and concurrent marital sessions, family therapy (with the spouse's children, siblings and/or parents as indicated), group therapy or psychopharmacology may be appropriate at a particular time.

All the therapist's skill, artistry, creativity and training are required to overcome or circumvent resistance to change. To achieve the necessary interactional behavior changes by whatever means are at his/her disposal—systems methods, psychodynamic and insight approaches, behavior modification, or any other theoretical approach—is the central task of the therapist. The therapist usually has to work back and forth, utilizing those methods that he believes will be the most effective. A multifaceted approach allows for greater therapeutic flexibility.

The authority of the therapist is an important therapeutic instrument. It is a powerful force that should be used consciously, judiciously and with the full knowledge of its possibilities and limitations. This brings us to the problem of the therapist's countertransferences. These are the same in any form of marital therapy, wherein the therapist is exposed to all the stresses of the triangular relationship with two patients (Sager, 1967b). The therapist may discover that, in subtle ways, he is sometimes competitive with the husband or that he is taking sides with the husband against the wife or that he is prone to male chauvinistic thinking or to feminist or anti-male thinking. He has to check his value system constantly, so that it is not imposed on the couple. On the other hand, no therapist should attempt to treat people he actively dislikes or fears. Except for family therapy when children are also included in the group, there is no form of psychotherapy that is so prone to touch the hidden sources of the therapist's emotions and value systems and to threaten to overwhelm his objectivity.

Because the marriage contract is a concept and not a psychological or interpersonal test, its application and the methodology for using the contract concept must remain flexible. It has to be adapted or modified by each clinician to his or her own needs and also for the needs and capabilities of each couple. To develop a quantitative "score" for the two individual contracts or the behavioral profiles would be to miss the dynamic essence of the concept. The two contracts that move toward becoming one with the participation of both spouses and therapist cannot be specified in terms of a predictable sequence of therapeutic events. Therapist and patients must remain free to use techniques within their perception of their necessities and the treatment situation, with the therapist remaining alert to what the couple wants. The desire of two people to remain together out of strength, affection and love is the best motivational force the therapist can have to work with and the therapist himself is limited only by his own perceptiveness and ingenuity.

TRAINING TO USE THE CONTRACT MODEL

Beyond one's basic training in his/her professional discipline, the more exposure to a variety of theoretical approaches and experiences in working with couples that one has had, the better will he or she be prepared to utilize a flexible approach with the contract concept. The most important single factor is having lived long enough (this is not a function of age) to have been in love and to have lived with or been married to someone for a few years. It is of prime importance to work on your own individual contracts with your mate and to go through the self-search and risk-taking in exposing yourself as you both work towards a single contract. More than an intellectual commitment is necessary to employ contracts in treatment; you have to be able to convey to your couple patients that this method can be helpful to them. Until you have confronted yourself with your own anxieties and resistances to working with your partner on your own contracts, you cannot appreciate the quality and quantity of the feelings it can elicit. An exercise that I use in teaching the contract approach is to ask students to write out their own and their partner's contracts from a past relationship, and designate the congruence, complementarity and conflict. This bit of distance makes the process easier the first time—but it is then important to examine your current relationship. After you have done your own with your partner, you are then ready to ask your couples to respond to the reminder list. Supervision by a therapist who has worked with the contracts, as well as exchanges of experiences with peers who are trying it at the same time, is important in getting the support and help you may need at the start.

RESEARCH

A great deal of research remains to be done to test the hypotheses on which the theoretical models of the marital contracts are based. Outcome studies that measure the quality of a marriage, as well as the functioning of the two individuals, remain to be done. Studies of the outcome of this approach compared to other treatment methods will be even more difficult to do. Such comparative outcome studies are difficult. See Gurman and Kniskern (1978) for a number of creative models and approaches to the study of marital therapy outcome that have been suggested and implemented.

The individual and single couple contracts themselves can be useful as research instruments. For example, it would be useful to compare individual contracts of the same person in different relationships, as in sequential marriages. Does one want the same or appear willing to give the same? Does one mature? Are one's expectations consistent with where he/she is in his/her life-cycle? The behavioral profiles have not been researched to determine if my description of each profile and its correlations with items from Category 2 of the reminder list can be replicated by researchers who do not have the same investment in this material as I.

The reminder list has been used and revised several times over a 14-year period. Some items may be redundant, other parameters perhaps should be included. But no research, just clinical empiricism, has determined its present form.

The interactional script, a contract which is hypothesized to be the dynamic description of how each partner reacts with the other to attempt to fulfill his/her individual contract, offers many questions for research. As a construct that attempts to describe how and why two interdependent people act as a system, the complexity resulting from the many variables involved may not allow for the system to be tested scientifically. It may have to stand as a theoretical construct (subject to modification) so long as it is the most parsimonious explanation for observable data and provides a means to improve

our therapeutic and prophylactic approaches.[13]

The concept of the two individual contracts providing the basis for a working-through process to a single contract can be tested in terms of individual and dyadic system changes. Crucial parameters would be tested at the beginning, along the way if desired, and at the conclusion of treatment. The degree of achievement of the single contract could also be measured. Follow-up at stated periods would be important. A longitudinal study over many years' use of the single contract and its periodic updating could be a very fruitful endeavor. Such a study should include not only couples who have sought help but also those who consider themselves to have an excellent relationship and had not sought help.

A study comparing contractual terms of couples at different ages, from a variety of ethnic, class and educational levels would be interesting and less difficult than these other suggestions.

The difficulties of such studies are obvious. I hope that some workers will have the motivation and energy to research some of these crucial areas.

REFERENCES

Ackerman, N. W. *The Psychodynamics of Family Life*. New York: Basic Books, 1958.

Ackerman, N. W. *Treating the Troubled Family*. New York: Basic Books 1966.

Berger, M. *Videotape Techniques in Psychiatric Training and Treatment*. New York: Brunner/Mazel, 1978.

Berman, E. & Lief, H. Marital therapy from a psychiatric perspective: An overview. *American Journal of Psychiatry*, 1975, *132*, 583-592.

Berne, E. *Transactional Analysis in Psychotherapy*. New York: Grove Press, 1961.

Dicks, H. V. *Marital Tensions*. New York: Basic Books, 1967.

Dicks, H. V. Object relations theory and marital studies. *British Journal of Medical Psychology*, 1963, 37, 125.

Fairbairn, W. R. Synopsis of an object relations theory of the personality. *International Journal of Psychoanalysis*, 1963, *44*, 224.

---

[13]*Editors' Note.* In our view, it is not the inherent *complexity* of the phenomena at hand that makes scientific study difficult (witness the advances in physics, neurobiology, etc.), but the *non-disconfirmability* of many psychodynamic and systems theory principles. That is, many of these principles are stated in a manner that preclude the possibility of their being operationalized in a way that would allow them to be disproven. This problem does, of course, severely limit the extent to which treatments based on these principles can be improved and refined through empirical study.

Fairbairn, W. R. *Psychoanalytic Studies of the Personality.* London: Tavistock, 1952.

Ferber, A. & Ranz, J. How to succeed in family therapy: Set reachable goals—Give workable tasks. In: A. Ferber (Ed.), *The Book of Family Therapy.* New York: Science House, 1972.

Goldstein, M. The uses of dreams in conjoint marital therapy. *Journal of Sex and Marital Therapy,* 1974, *1,* 75-81.

Greene, B. L. *A Clinical Approach to Marital Problems.* Springfield, Ill.: Thomas, 1970.

Gurman, A. S. Contemporary Marital Therapies: A critical and comparative analysis of psychoanalytic, behavioral and systems theory approaches. In: T. J. Paolino, Jr. & B. S. McCrady (Eds.), *Marriage and Marital Therapy.* New York: Brunner/Mazel, 1978.

Haley, J. *Strategies of Psychotherapy.* New York: Grune & Stratton, 1963.

Horney, K. *Neurosis and Human Growth.* New York: Norton, 1950.

Horney, K. *New Ways in Psychoanalysis.* New York: Norton, 1939.

Masters, W. & Johnson V. *Human Sexual Inadequacy.* Boston: Little, Brown, 1970.

Martin, P. A. *A Marital Therapy Manual.* New York: Brunner/Mazel, 1976.

Minuchin, S. *Families and Family Therapy.* Cambridge: Harvard University Press, 1974.

Money, J. & Ehrhardt, A. A. *Man & Woman, Boy & Girl.* Baltimore: Johns Hopkins University Press, 1972.

O'Leary, K. D. & Turkewitz, H. Marital therapy from a behavioral perspective. In: T. J. Paolino, Jr. and B. S. McCrady (Eds.) *Marriage and Marital Therapy,* New York: Brunner/Mazel, 1978.

O'Neill, N. & O'Neill, G. *Open Marriage.* New York: Avon, 1972.

Paolino, T. J., Jr. & McCrady, B. S. *Marriage and Marital Therapy.* New York: Brunner/Mazel, 1978.

Patterson, G. R. *Families.* Champaign, Illinois: Research Press, 1971.

Sager, C. J. The treatment of married couples. In: S. Arieti (Ed.), *The American Handbook of Psychiatry,* New York: Basic Books, 1966.

Sager, C. J. The diagnosis and treatment of marital complaints. *American Journal of Psychoanalysis,* 1967a, *27,* 139-156.

Sager, C. J. Transference in conjoint treatment of married couples. *Archives of General Psychiatry,* 1967b, *16,* 185-193.

Sager, C. J. Marital psychotherapy. In: J. Masserman (Ed.), *Current Psychiatric Therapies,* New York: Grune and Stratton, 1967c.

Sager, C. J. Sexual dysfunctions and marital discord. In: H. S. Kaplan, *The New Sex Therapy.* New York: Brunner/Mazel, 1974.

Sager, C. J. *Marriage Contracts and Couple Therapy.* New York: Brunner/Mazel, 1976(a).

Sager, C. J. The role of sex therapy in marital therapy. *American Journal of Psychiatry,* 1976, *133:5,* 555-558. (b)

Sager, C. J. A typology of intimate relationships. *Journal of Sex and Marital Therapy,* 1977, *3,* 83-112.

Sager, C. J. & Hunt, B. *Intimate Partners.* New York: McGraw-Hill, 1979.

Sager, C. J. & Kaplan, H. S. (Eds.) *Progress in Group and Family Therapy.* New York: Brunner/Mazel, 1972.

Sager, C. J., Kaplan, H. S., Gundlach, R. H., Kremer, M., Lenz, R. & Royce, J. The marriage contract. *Family Process,* 1971, *10,* 311-326.

Sullivan, H. S. *The Interpersonal Theory of Psychiatry.* New York: Norton, 1953.

Sullivan, H. S. Conceptions of modern psychiatry. Reprinted from *Psychiatry,* 1940, 3:2 and 8:2, 1945. Distributed by New York: Norton, 1945.

Tiger, L. & Fox, R. *The Imperial Animal.* New York: Holt, Rinehart and Winston, 1971.

EDITORS' REFERENCES

Dicks, H. V. *Marital Tensions.* New York: Basic Books, 1967.

Gurman, A. S. Contemporary marital therapies: A critique and comparative analysis of psychoanalytic, behavioral and systems theory approaches. In: T. Paolino & B. McCrady (Eds.), *Marriage and Marital Therapy.* New York: Brunner/Mazel, 1978.

Gurman, A. S. & Kniskern, D. P. Research on marital and family therapy: Progress, perspective and prospect. In: S. Garfield & A. Bergin (Eds.) *Handbook of Psychotherapy and Behavior Change.* Second edition. New York: Wiley, 1978.

Margolin, G. Conjoint marital therapy to enhance anger management and reduce spouse abuse. *American Journal of Family Therapy,* 1979, 7, 13-23.

PART III

Intergenerational Approaches

CHAPTER 4

The Integration of Marital Therapy with Sessions with Family of Origin

James L. Framo, Ph.D.

Anyone who treats families and couples knows of the deep satisfactions and measureless sacrifices of family life, and also of the hurts and emotional injuries that closely related people can inflict on one another. In most families children are treasured and cared for, yet in some families children are neglected, over-indulged, discriminated against, exploited, seduced, persecuted, and occasionally killed. Some marriages encourage growth and enrich peoples' lives, yet husbands and wives are also capable of creating a whole range of miseries for each other, ranging from loneliness in marriage, bitter frustration, cruelty, degrading conflicts, to spouse murder or waiting for each other to die. Whitaker has said, ". . . marriages end up driving some people mad, pushing others into homicidal and suicidal acts, producing hateful demons out of perfectly nice people, and inducing alcoholism in others" (Whitaker and Keith, 1977, p. 69).

Professional therapists have developed many theories and techniques for understanding and treating such problems, most of which are quite resistant to change. When one considers the billions of pieces of input that have gone into individuals over many years, and the fact that therapy effects can occur only during a relatively fleeting moment of time, inducing change is a formidable task indeed.[1] I believe it is very difficult to alter attitudes and behavior in individuals, much less change systems. Of all the forces that impinge on people (culture, society, work, neighborhood, friends, etc.), the family by far has the greatest imprinting influence. And, as every family therapist knows, a family or marital system is a well-oiled machine that often musters all its resources to neutralize and impede change, while yearning for something better.

I started seeing families and couples in 1958, and since the publication of *Intensive Family Therapy* (Boszormenyi-Nagy and Framo, 1965), my work has undergone various changes as I

---

[1]*Editors' Note.* Though he does not state it in this way, Framo is really raising two very interesting and researchable ideas here: first, that there are only select times in the development of the family (e.g., crises) when major lasting change is possible; and second, that in psychotherapy, the change process is discontinuous, i.e., there are especially favorable moments in the process when change may occur.

refined and modified my conceptual thinking and techniques in order to get the most favorable results. The treatment methods to be described herein represent the culmination and direction toward which those 21 years of experience have led me. I have streamlined my approach from the early days of long-term family therapy to a more efficient short-term treatment progression.

This chapter will describe a treatment sequence (starting with conventional family or marital therapy, utilizing the couples group format, and aiming toward the adults having sessions with their parents and siblings) which can have powerful effects on the original problems for which the families or couples entered treatment. Although these methods do not always work and are not easy to use, I have found them, through trial and error, to be the most effective in producing lasting change. These procedures are the clinical application of my depth theoretical orientation, which postulates that current family and marital difficulties largely stem from attempts to master earlier conflicts from the original family; these conflicts and transference distortions from the past are being lived anachronistically through the spouse and children (Framo, 1965a, 1970). When these adults are able to go back to deal directly with their parents and brothers and sisters about the previously avoided issues that have existed between them, an opportunity exists for reconstructive changes to come about in their marital relationship and in the relationship between these adults and *their* children. The great resistances of adult clients toward bringing in family of origin testifies to the great power of this approach.[2] Because of my conviction that even one session with original family can accomplish more than many regular individual, family or marital therapy sessions, I have developed techniques for dealing with client resistances and for preparing clients in special kinds of ways for these sessions. This procedure has general applicability and serves diagnostic as well as therapeutic purposes. Not only can clients discover what from the original family is being worked out through

the spouse and children, but these adults are also being given the chance to come to terms with parents before the parents die.

The methods to be described in this chapter are largely oriented toward marital theory and conjoint marital therapy rather than toward the two-generational situation of family therapy. Although I still do see whole families, including the children, from the beginning of therapy to the end, most of the family therapy I do these days is converted to conjoint marital therapy when the originally symptomatic children have been defocused. Those couples who enter therapy specifically for marital problems either do not have children or do not present their children as the primary focus of concern. The major reason for this strategy is that, in my judgment, most children's problems are metaphors about the quality of the relationship between the parents. In a previous publication I wrote, "Whenever there are disturbed children there is a disturbed marriage, although all disturbed marriages do not create disturbed children" (Framo, 1965a, p. 154).[3] Consequently, it is suggested that the best way to help children is to help their parents. The greatest gift parents can give their children is a viable marriage relationship based on each parent having a strong sense of self. My treatment sequence does not consist only of orienting clients toward working things out with the previous generation. Much of the therapy that goes on with the couple alone or in the couples group consists of dealing with the current marital issues. Consequently, I will be describing my marital assessment methods as well as marital treatment techniques, in both the early and later phases of therapy.

In the rest of this chapter I will attempt to follow the guidelines offered by the editors of this *Handbook* (see Preface) but will not be able to adhere to them strictly. For instance, my treatment model involves different settings and interventions at different stages of treatment, and since therapy goals may change accordingly, it is not possible to comply strictly with the guidelines on goal-setting.

---

[2] *Editors' Note.* Of course, this power has the potential to be for better or for worse, as is true of any therapeutic method. Moreover, "resistance" is not necessarily "bad"; there are times when people resist therapists' change efforts wisely!

[3] *Editors' Note.* While this notion is common among clinicians, empirical evidence bearing on the issue is clearly inconclusive. Note also that a "disturbed" child's behavior may help to cause marital disturbance, as well as be a consequence of it.

BACKGROUND OF THE APPROACH

Those who write textbooks on family therapy have had difficulty classifying my work as a readily identifiable "Framo" theory, in the way that there is Bowen Theory or Minuchin's Structural Family Therapy. Every family therapy student knows that there are a number of family therapy "schools," classified variously as communication, systems, brief/strategic, structural, psychodynamic, experiential, Gestalt, behavioral, intergenerational, problem-solving, etc. The history of various movements reveals a repetitive pattern of initial unity and then separation into various factions, sometimes resulting in denunciations between the "true believers" and the revisionists. The bitterness among Freud, Jung, Adler, and other factions within the psychoanalytic movement is well known.

The family therapy movement is no exception to this historical sequence of events, except that the rivalries are more or less friendly ones. The early workers in the family therapy field are like a family; they are sometimes jealous of each other and they compete for preeminence, but they also care for each other. It is always difficult to separate ideological, theoretical differences from issues of territoriality, however. The family therapy pioneers were highly creative, charismatic individuals who, being mavericks within their own profession, needed to establish their unique professional identity and stake out their domain.[4] One unfortunate consequence has been the politicization of the field, which sometimes resulted in one or other of the family therapy schools using pejorative labels about the other schools. I wince, for example, when I see myself categorized in the textbooks as a "psychoanalytic family therapist," not only because the word "psychoanalytic" has fallen into disrepute, but also because that characterization is largely inaccurate. I would like to take this opportunity, as a family therapist, to briefly state my views on psychoanalytic theory.

In recent years it has become fashionable to attack psychoanalysis, both as a theory and as a method of treatment. It is difficult today to take a long perspective and appreciate the truly profound nature of Freud's discoveries. For the first time in human history, explanatory concepts were applied to disorders of behavior, experience, and feeling. He brought the *person* into the study of emotional disorder by tying in mental phenomena with the substance of human existence. With Freud, mental processes began to make sense and become lawful: An emotional disorder was not just something that happened, or the result of Satanic influence or a diseased body organ, but came to be understood as part and parcel of being biological and human, of being aggressive, of needing, hoping, fearing, loving and hating in a world which required socialization in order to survive. Freud's concept of the unconscious and the principle of psychological determinism aroused intense fear and hostility, however. Even today there are mental health professionals who disavow or give lip service to the unconscious and cannot emotionally accept the idea, partially because the unconscious, by definition, is not acceptable.[5] The phenomenon of ready aversion to the unconscious is similar, I have found, to the automatic repulsion and denial to which the family system approach is subject, by professionals as well as families. (In one family I evaluated, referred by the court, in which consummated incest had occurred between father and daughter, the fear of family exploration was so intense—especially mother's role in the incest—that the father and his wife preferred for the father to accept the possibility of a 30-year prison sentence rather than to continue with the family sessions.)

Psychoanalytic theory in its comprehensiveness deals with a staggering range of phenomena. If we wiped out all knowledge which psychoanalysis has given us, how much would be left to explain human motivation and *why* people feel and behave as they do? Although some psychoanalytic constructs have not stood the test of time, and others are so mystical that

---

[4]*Editors' Note.* See Broderick and Schrader's (Chapter 1) history of family therapy for a fuller discussion of the maverick role of early family therapists.

[5]*Editors' Note.* In fairness, it must be noted that therapists who "reject the unconscious" do so for one or more of several quite defensible reasons: 1) It is a concept which largely defies quantification and disconfirmability; 2) theories of unconscious psychological functioning very often are linked in only very uncertain manners to therapeutic technique; 3) use of the concept has led to the development of few techniques whose clinical efficacy has been convincingly demonstrated.

they are untestable, few seriously question the validity of such concepts as defense mechanisms, narcissism, the repetition compulsion, mourning and the like. Insofar as therapy is concerned, it must be kept in mind that psychoanalysis was never intended as a treatment for the masses; its real value lies in the insights that its depth, long-term, clinical-laboratory work can give to basic knowledge of human psychology. Psychoanalysis is not suitable for reality problems; it is not a good idea, for example, to be in analysis when one's marriage is falling apart.

I have my own criticisms of psychoanalysis. One gets the curious feeling in reading the psychoanalytic literature that the patient lives in a vacuum, that the intrapsychic world is almost a closed system, that life stops when one is in analysis, and that the environment is largely treated as a constant. With characteristic perceptive genius, Freud identified the fundamental extrinsic determinants of human distress when he classified the external dangers as loss of the object, loss of the penis (castration), loss of the object's love, and loss of the superego's love. There are also occasional references to such exogenous factors as the primal scene, or the effects of poor mothering upon ego development, or some unusual circumstance in the patient's life, and there is even recognition that neurotic parents bring up neurotic children. Most psychoanalysts, however, operationally function from the assumption that it is not the environment that makes people sick (even though Freud in his philosophical writings on applied psychoanalysis does discuss the deleterious effects of society on human adjustment), but that *people do it to themselves* via fantasy and intrapsychic work and elaboration of what goes on outside.

Experience in family therapy has indicated that symptoms or disordered behavior can be viewed as adaptive, nay, necessary, responses to the intimate social contexts of a person's life. The most powerful social influence is, perforce, the family, yet psychoanalytic theory has been ambiguous and contradictory about the role of the family in the etiology and maintenance of emotional disturbance. Freud, admittedly, was the first person to recognize in a systematic way the part that love, hate, jealousy, rivalry, am-

bivalence, and generational differences which arise from the inherent nature of family relationships play in the development of psychopathology. He was certainly not oblivious to the actual reality of the family environment. In his case histories, he described his involvement with the families of his patients, such as in the cases of Dora and Little Hans.[6] Despite all this understanding, however, Freud set the model that psychotherapy should consist of a one-to-one confidential relationship between patient and therapist, and that the family should be kept out because the transference field would be contaminated. Psychoanalytic theory, which utilizes a family dynamic in its nuclear concept of the oedipus complex, either deals with the intrapsychic struggle over the oedipal wishes or leaps to its wider social aspects in the culture at large. In *Totem and Taboo (1913)*, *Civilization and its Discontents (1930)*, and *Group Psychology (1921)*, Freud proposed that the function of the oedipus complex was to protect the family from disruption—for only if incest and patricide were outlawed could the family and thus society survive. Yet, though in one sense psychoanalytic thought sees the survival of man as dependent on the preservation of the family, the lack of focus on the transactional dynamics of the family itself represents a real gap in the theory.

Over the years since the heyday of psychoanalysis, a series of developments in many different fields (ego psychology, group dynamics, child development, sociology of the family, communication theory, general systems theory, etc.) has blended into a family transactional approach. Jackson (1967) gave explicit recognition to this movement when he stated, "We are on the edge of a new era in psychiatry, and the related disciplines of psychology, social work, anthropology and sociology. In this new era we will come to look at human nature in a much more complex way than ever before. From this threshold the view is not of the individual *in vitro* but of the small or larger group within

---

[6]Even in Freud's case histories there were some notable omissions. For example, he did not mention that during the course of Little Hans' treatment Hans' parents were in the process of getting a divorce and indeed did divorce when treatment was over. For a reexamination of the case of Little Hans from the standpoint of family dynamics, see Strean (1967).

which any particular individual's behavior is adaptive. We will move from individual assessment to analysis of contexts, or more precisely, the *system* from which individual conduct is inseparable" (p. 139). To be sure, as Zilboorg and Henry (1941) have pointed out, for each stage of history emotional disturbances have been defined in a manner which is congruent with the spirit and ethos of the age. It may well be that the family movement reflects, in part, an American emphasis on environmental reform, as Spiegel and Bell (1959) have noted.

There is a major theoretical controversy within the family field. There are the so-called family systems "purists" like Haley (1975), who polarize the intrapsychic and the interactional, claiming that family theory and therapy should only be concerned with what goes on *between* people. For these family therapists, intrapsychic phenomena and the past are irrelevant for producing change. My own point of view is that, while I believe that psychoanalytic theory cannot explain family system phenomena, I do not agree that in understanding and treating family relationships we should discard everything we have known about dynamic psychology. What goes on inside people's heads is just as important as what goes on between them in their interpersonal relationships. *Neither level can be reduced to the other; one does not have to make a choice as to which is more important.*

More technically, the core of my theoretical approach is the *relationship* between the intrapsychic and the transactional. That is to say, I see insoluble intrapsychic conflicts, derived from the original family, being acted out, replicated, mastered or defended against with the current intimates, via some very complicated processes that are poorly understood. Not only do spouses have transference distortions of each other, giving rise sometimes to outlandish expectations of marriage and of their partners, but the children can also be caught up in bizarre "transference fixes" that are impervious to reality considerations (e.g., that the small child should mother the parent, or that the child is inherently a "bad seed" that needs to be repaired or exterminated). Indeed, the interpersonal resolution of inner conflict is what creates the kind of profound human distress that we see clinically in troubled families and couples.

Whenever people are closely related to each other, as in a family, they reciprocally carry part of each other's psychology and form a feedback system, which in turn patterns and regulates their individual behaviors. The creative leap of this family system theory was recognition of this interlocking, multiperson motivational system whereby family members collusively carry psychic functions for each other. Exploration of this phenomenon, in which dynamic and systems concepts are amalgamated, can provide a conceptual bridge from the personal to the social. The foregoing perhaps explains why Foley (1974), in his classification of family theorists, refers to me as an "integrationist."

A summary of the main tenets of the theory of intergenerational transmission of beliefs, attitudes and symptoms, expanded from Fairbairn's (1952) object-relations theory and elaborated by Framo (1970, 1976a), follows:

(a) Fairbairn (1952) has postulated that man's need for a satisfactory object relationship constitutes the fundamental motive of life. His object-relationship approach is contrasted with Freud's theory of instinctual gratification as being primary in man.

(b) Since they are unable to give up the maternal object or change it in outer reality, infants incorporate the frustrating aspects of their relational world. These internalized objects are retained as introjects, psychological representatives of the external objects.

(c) These introjects form part of the structure of the personality and undergo various splits. During the course of development of the individual, external real figures may be assimilated in successive strata or by fusion into the existing bad object situations.

(d) Intrapsychic conflicts arise from experiences in the original family, and reparative efforts to deal with these conflicts impel the individual to force close relations into fitting the internal role models.

(e) One's mate or children are perceived largely in terms of the individual's own needs, or as carrying for him his own denied, split-off traits. Mates select each other on the basis of rediscovering lost aspects of their primary object relations, which they had split off and which, in their involvement with the spouse, they reexperience by projective identification (Dicks, 1967). A main source of marital disharmony is that spouses project disowned aspects of themselves onto the mate and then fight them in the mate.

(f) Children are especially prone to these projections; some children could not get their parents to love them even if they sacrificed their life. One's current intimates, one's spouse and children, are shadowy stand-ins for old ghosts, the embodiments of old introjects.

(g) The adult, by having sessions with his or her family of origin, takes the problems back to their original sources, thereby making available a direct route to etiological factors. These sessions serve diagnostic as well as therapeutic purposes in that both the old and new families can be cross-referenced for similar patterns.

(h) Dealing with the real, external figures loosens the grip of the internalized representatives of these figures and exposes them to current realities. The parents and siblings of today are not the parents and siblings of the past; indeed, they never were. The original transference figures can also be the objects of transference today; few adults ever get to see their parents as real people.

(i) Having gone backward in time, the individual can then move forward in behaving toward the spouse and children in more appropriate fashion, as persons in their own right, since their transference meaning has changed.

(j) Not only do family of origin sessions help resolve problems in the current family, but coming to terms with parents and siblings before they die can also be a profoundly liberating experience.

In addition to basing my work on the intrapsychic object-relations theory of Fairbairn and the marital interaction theory of Dicks, I have been influenced by theories of family therapists as well. A theoretical debt is owed to Bowen (1978), who was the first to relate present family difficulties to multigenerational processes. The professional world is still reverberating to the

account of his study of his own family, reported at a family conference under the title of "Toward the Differentiation of a Self in One's Own Family" (Anonymous, 1972). Boszormenyi-Nagy and Spark (1973), Whitaker (1976), Haas (1968), Paul and Paul (1975) and Headley (1977) have dealt with related concepts in work with family of origin. My approach to marital therapy, based originally on my family therapy experiences (Framo, 1965a), has been more recently described in Framo (1980).

I would like to clarify one other misconception about my approach. As I stated previously (Framo, 1975), changing a family system is for me the ultimate professional challenge, and my therapeutic philosophy is to learn as many kinds of treatment approaches as possible in order to have a full repertoire of techniques available to shift a system. Consequently, I have attended workshops on transactional analysis, Gestalt therapy, encounter groups, behavior therapy, rational-emotive, EST, existential therapy, etc. I have used methods of working with families from a number of different schools (communicational, paradoxical, strategic, sculpting, etc.) and believe it is necessary to be eclectic in dealing with the tremendous variety and kinds of difficulties presented by families and couples. It takes years of experience to be appropriately and selectively eclectic in the sense of choosing a specific method for a particular problem.[7] One cannot apply one's theory to all problems.

I do not use object-relations theory and family of origin sessions with all my couples. There are aspects of marriages and families that are unrelated to problems hanging over from families of origin, such as those reflecting social and cultural changes. Furthermore, some uncomplicated marital problems can be treated by "conventional" marital therapy techniques, focusing on the marital interaction in the here and now. These couples' marital difficulties are temporary, not deep-seated, largely situational, a function of the stage of marriage they are in, and for the most part based on misunderstandings which can be untangled in a few sessions. (In a later section, when I specify different types of marital problems, this point will be further

----

[7]Every therapist comes up against unique kinds of problem situations for which there are no known techniques; the art of psychotherapy often consists of on-the-spot improvisation.

elaborated upon.) It is the more serious marital problems which require depth exploration of the conflict paradigms from each spouse's original family and how they get played out in the marriage. Having said that, however, I believe that everyone can profit from meeting with his/her parents and brothers and sisters; the family members get to know each other better and can work toward more differentiated intimacy.

THE HEALTHY OR WELL-FUNCTIONING MARRIAGE AND FAMILY

There are a number of considerations to be taken into account in determining what is a healthy or well-functioning marriage or family. Firstly, most clinicians have been trained to recognize or deal with abnormality and therefore have a tendency to miss the adaptive features of individuals' personalities or family/marital relationships. Little is known about the self-corrective mechanisms that all families have. Since family therapists usually see families and couples when they are under stress and behaving at their worst, therapists often get distorted views of the positive sides of the relationships. Besides, most people think of therapy as the place where one talks about what goes wrong rather than what goes right. (I have observed couples being intensely hostile to each other during treatment sessions, and then, as soon as they leave the office, walking away arm in arm.) Finally, under the intensive scrutiny of the therapy microscope almost every individual, family, or couple can look sick. I believe that nearly every person, family, and marriage, over the course of a lifetime, go through periods of turmoil and disorganization that at the time appear pathological.

Little systematic work has been done on the so-called normal family (Lewis, Beavers, Gossett, and Phillips, 1976). I am not aware of any family theoretician or family therapist who has developed a comprehensive theory of healthy marital or family functioning. Most family researchers have used minimal operational criteria for defining normal families, such as—a normal family is one that has not come to community attention for a problem (been arrested, in therapy, school problem, etc.). Most family therapists, myself included, however, have indirectly alluded to aspects of healthy functioning, largely

in contrast to descriptions of pathological families and couples. Accordingly, I have gleaned out of my various writings some *ideal* principles of healthy or normal family and marital functioning:

1) That parents each be well-differentiated, having developed a sense of self before separating from their families of origin.
2) Clear separation of generational boundaries within the family. The children should be free of the role of saving a parent or the parental marriage.
3) Realistic perceptions and expectations by parents of each other and of their children.
4) The loyalty to the family of procreation is greater than to the family of origin.
5) The spouses put themselves and each other before anyone else, including the children; the marriage, however, is not a symbiotic one which excludes the children. The children do not feel that to be close to one parent means they are alienating the other.
6) Encouragement of identity development and autonomy for all family members. Successful development in the children will mean that they will leave home at some point to start families of their own.
7) Nonpossessive warmth and affection expressed between parents, between parents and children, and among the siblings.
8) The capacity to have open, honest, and clear communication and to deal with issues with each other.
9) A realistic, adult-to-adult, caring relationship between each parent and his/her parents and siblings.
10) An open family in the sense of involvement with others outside the family, including extended family and friends. Outsiders are allowed inside the family.

Insofar as the marital relationship is concerned, in a recent publication (Framo, 1980), I specified criteria for improvement in marital therapy; these criteria have implications for a healthy marriage:

1) The partners are more personally differentiated, and dependency on each other is voluntary.
2) They have come to terms with the roots of

their irrational expectations of marriage and of the spouse derived from the family of origin.

3) They have developed a more empathic understanding of their mate.

4) They can meet each other's realistic needs in the face of their differentness.

5) They can communicate more clearly and openly.

6) They like each other more and they enjoy sex with each other.

7) They have learned to deal with the issues between them.

8) They can enjoy life more, and get pleasure from work and from their children.

9) They have developed flexibility in dealing with situational stresses and crises.

10) They have adjusted to the disenchantment of romantic love and have more realistic appraisals of the vicissitudes of mature, deidealized love.

As I said, the foregoing criteria are ideal ones; I am sure no family or marriage meets all of them. In addition, in light of the fact that 40% of new marriages are likely to end in divorce, I should make a statement about families that break up. In my judgment, some divorces are steps of growth, whereas others I perceive as manifestations of unresolved problems from original family. In a paper on divorce therapy (Framo, 1978a), I specified its goals as helping the couple to disengage from their relationship with a minimum of destructiveness to self, the partner, and the children, and with the freedom to form new relationships. I do believe that, though difficult, it is possible for divorce and remarriage to occur without enduring cost to the children or parents. In other words, a stepfamily can be a healthy, well-functioning family (Visher and Visher, 1979).

THE PATHOLOGICAL OR DYSFUNCTIONAL MARRIAGE OR FAMILY

My main conceptualizations and ideas about dysfunctional families and couples are contained in previous publications (Framo, 1965a, 1970). I postulated that symptoms are formed, selected, faked, exchanged, maintained, and reduced or extinguished as a function of the relationship context in which they are naturally embedded. Children's symptoms are frequently the outcome of irrational role assignments which one or both parents ascribe to the child; these designations usually have nothing to do with the inherent nature of the child. Children who are assigned the role of "the troublemaker," "the crazy one," "mother's protector," or "the stupid one" may incorporate and *become* their assigned role, may spend a lifetime disputing the role, or may play-act at the role. Such a child may, on the other hand, learn to become his own person, independent of the role.

Examples of other factors which create or affect symptoms are: blurring of generational boundaries (e.g., mother goes to son to complain about her husband); family traumas (e.g., death or absence of parent, divorce, unemployment of parent); maintenance of symptoms for system purposes (e.g., the child's being sick so mother will have someone to take care of); scapegoating (e.g., "Our marriage would be fine if it weren't for that kid."); emotional overburdening of the child (e.g., the child being expected to be marriage counselor for his parents); and overt/covert rejection or infantilization of the child. The particular type of symptom developed depends, in general, on what the system requires. Some dangerous symptoms of children are ignored by parents, although the school or others may recognize their seriousness. On the other hand, a child's "symptom" may be trivial as seen by outsiders, yet the parents may exaggerate its importance and may want to use drastic measures for handling it (e.g., parents wanting to institutionalize a child because "he lies").

Among the factors that enable some children to survive and be relatively untouched by the family pathology are the following:

1) These children, for reasons having to do with the parents' backgrounds, did not become the focus of concern. Even their physical appearance could play a role in not being selected as special.

2) These siblings used the identified patient as a model of what to avoid.

3) These children may have had resources outside the family (e.g., aunt, friend, teacher),

and therefore established wider emotional investments.

4) These children were more successful at utilizing defenses of isolation, but paid a price by having constricted personalities.

I have not developed any system for typing or classifying families, although I have recently (Framo, 1980) devised an informal scheme for classifying marriages. This very crude classification system is based on responsiveness to therapy; that is, those at the beginning of the list I find, in general, less difficult to treat than those toward the end. The scheme is not precise enough to call it "marital diagnosis." Diagnosis suggests that specific treatment strategies have been devised for each discrete category, which is certainly not the case.[8]

1) Couples whose marriage relationships are basically sound and whose problems largely stem from communicational misunderstandings. These couples essentially rehabilitate their own marriage, needing only a couple of therapy sessions.

2) Marriages where the partners love each other, are committed to the marriage, but "can't get along." Some of these couples are responding to the impact of parenthood, while others have in-law complications; some argue a lot, and others avoid conflict.

3) Brother-sister marriages where the spouses care a great deal for each other, but there is little excitement in the relationship. Sex is routine and marital life is comfortable but dull.

4) Conflictual marriages where the spouses feel markedly ambivalent about each other. The partners are engaged in a power struggle and are in conflict over a variety of issues, ranging from feminist issues, to sex, disciplining of the children, dual-career conflicts, in-laws, money, and all the other "cover" issues.

5) Marriages in which one partner is symptomatic. Involving both partners in conjoint treatment can move this kind of marriage

into the "conflict" category. The symptoms (e.g., depression) may become unnecessary as the partners begin to deal with their issues.

6) Marriages whose problems are a consequence of incomplete marital maturation. These partners have never really left home and are overinvolved with one or both families of origin.

7) Marriages of mental health professionals or of "professional patients" are not easy to change. For some of these couples, being in therapy is a way of life. The professional therapist-spouses have been doing bad therapy on each other, sometimes for years; each is an expert on the partner's dynamics.

8) Second or third marriages are usually complicated by ghosts of the previous marriages, children, and obligations to the former spouses. Loyalty rearrangements, problems of stepparenting, financial stresses, and grandparents all present difficulties.

9) Older couples whose relationship problems have calcified and whose options are limited. These couples have come to therapy too late.

10) "Pseudo-mutual" couples who deny all problems in the marriage and present a child as the problem. These couples cannot admit to the ordinary difficulties all couples can acknowledge. The therapist may reach these couples indirectly by accepting the child as the problem (Montalvo and Haley, 1973). An alternative method of working with child-focused families is offered by Bradt and Moynihan (1971).

11) The marriage that is in extremis, where the couple come to therapy as a last resort before seeing lawyers. One partner may be finished with the marriage and the other is trying to hold on. Some of these couples can be engaged in divorce therapy.

12) Finally, there is the kind of chronically unhappy marriage where the partners "can't live with and can't live without." These couples may have had many unsuccessful individual or marital therapy experiences; they should have divorced and could not because permanent separation means psychic death.

---

[8]*Editors' Note.* Of course, diagnostic categories may also be used to *develop* and refine specific treatments.

THE ASSESSMENT OF SYSTEM DYSFUNCTION

My unit of treatment is the whole family when there are problems involving the children. As I stated earlier, sometimes I do *family* therapy (i.e., parents and children together) from beginning to end. Other times, when the problems in the children have been alleviated, I dismiss the children and work with the parents' marriage. Still other couples enter therapy explicitly for marital problems and either do not have children or state that their marital relationship is the problem.

I no longer do individual therapy. When I treat a couple, I insist on seeing them together, usually with a female co-therapist. If one spouse wants to be seen alone first or wants the partner to be seen alone, or either one refuses to come in for a conjoint interview, I will refer elsewhere. During therapy I refuse interviews with a single individual, although during ongoing couples group therapy I will see a couple unit for emergencies. I am aware that there are therapists who find it diagnostically valuable to have separate interviews with a single spouse, but in my experience the advantages of individual sessions (such as learning about secrets, affairs, etc.) are not worth the suspicions of the absent partner, the temporary relief of the confiding spouse, or the conflicts of loyalty and confidentiality in the therapist that such sessions promulgate. Furthermore, each spouse lives in the context of an intimate relationship, and separating the partners for private sessions negates the context, obscures the interactional collusiveness, and violates the integrity of the marital unit. The only exception made to my own rule is when I may separate divorcing spouses in the later stages of divorce therapy, although even in this circumstance I consider that the person who cannot tolerate the presence of the partner has not emotionally divorced that partner.

The only method of assessment I use is the clinical interview, which I find far superior to any formal questionnaire, guided interview schedule, situational test, or experimental procedure. Questionnaires and formal tasks do not give an observer the opportunity to follow up on leads or observe reactions. It is much easier to deceive a questionnaire than it is to fool an experienced clinician. Besides, questionnaires tell you nothing about how partners typically behave with each other, because people do not know how they interact with their intimates. Previously, I have stated my objections to the use of questionnaires in family research (Framo, 1965b).

Initial interviews, on the other hand, can also be misleading; it takes several interviews to get a fairly clear picture of what is going on.[9] Generally speaking, I do not make interventions in the first few sessions, as my co-therapist and I assess the couple, and while they, to be sure, assess us. The reason for early non-intervention is that I want to get maximum information without deliberately affecting the process. To be sure, assessment and treatment are inseparable, even when the therapist does not make a purposeful intervention. Among the factors that have therapeutic or antitherapeutic effects in the initial interviews are: history of previous therapies, therapy expectations, reputation of the therapist, the basis for the decision to come to therapy, the physical setting of the office, the physical appearance of the therapist(s), the kinds of questions asked, how they are asked, amount of the fee, degree of "connectedness" between clients and therapist(s), a sense of hope or despair stimulated by the first interview, etc.

When I see a couple, I consider there are three main areas of inquiry: the husband and wife as individuals, and their relationship, i.e., how their intrapsychic spheres intermesh. More specifically, I attempt to cover such topics as the following in the early interviews: referral source, brief statement of problems from each spouse, age, occupation, length of marriage, ages and gender of children, previous therapies, prior marriages, basis of mate selection, family's reactions to choice of partner, the partners' fight styles, whether the spouses basically love each other, whether they ever had a good relationship, commitment to the marriage, the quality and quantity of their sexual relationship, a brief history of each family of origin, current relationship with parents and siblings, how they relate to each other in the interview, motivation for therapy, and so forth.

---

[9] I have had the experience of thinking in the first interview that a husband was crazy or unreachable, and wondering to myself why this lovely woman ever married a guy like that. By the end of the second interview he would seem reasonable and she would turn out to be impossible to deal with.

GOAL-SETTING

One of the ways that family and marital therapy differ from all other psychotherapies is that there are varied and sometimes competing vested interests at play during treatment sessions. In individual therapy the therapist is dealing with warring elements within one person, but when there are issues *between* people, their goals of therapy will vary. For instance, a wife's goal might be to get out of the marriage without guilt, whereas the husband's goal might be to make the marriage relationship better; if the marriage ends in divorce, the wife may consider the therapy a great success, and the husband may consider it to be a failure and may refuse to pay for the treatment. In family therapy, a divorced woman who feels she has a second chance for happiness with a man who does not want her child may have the goal of institutionalizing the child with the blessing of a mental health professional; the child, of course, has the goal of staying with the mother.

In the first interview, I routinely ask each person what his or her goals of therapy are: "What would you like to accomplish in therapy?" One complication surrounding treatment goals is that the husband and wife may openly state goals that are at variance with their secret agendas for therapy outcome. For example, the husband may profess interest in saving his marriage, yet all the while be hoping the therapist will pronounce that the marriage is over. Some of the secret agendas are unconscious: A wife may unwittingly be attempting to prove to the therapist how cruel and heartless her husband really is, while praising his generosity. A husband may punish his wife for each step she takes toward autonomy (e.g., not speak to her for several days when she goes back to school), yet state that he wants a wife who is independent. Finally, clients' goals almost always change as therapy progresses. They shift goals to accommodate to their widening awareness and changing perception of their problems.[10] For instance, in the early part of therapy a couple may state as their problem the cliché, "We do not communicate," and later they may realize not only that their problems are more complicated than communication ones, but also that they have entirely different values about the meaning of marriage.

Further, while the husband and wife may clash over the goals of therapy, their goals may also be at variance with the goals of the therapist. Perhaps part of the skill of a therapist resides in finding the appropriate balance between the conflict of goals and expectations of all the family members as well as those of the therapist. I have often wondered whether, in some situations, it is not necessary for someone in the family to lose if someone is to gain. For instance, if a 40-year-old man finally gets to the point where he can leave his suffocating, widowed mother and get married, from his and the therapist's point of view he is better, but from his mother's point of view he is worse.

Since my treatment model involves different settings and interventions at different stages, as the typical couple progress through single couple therapy, couples groups therapy, and family of origin sessions, my own goals of therapy change from one sequence to the next. My long-range goals of marital therapy were stated earlier in this chapter. In the early phases the first goal is the establishment of a working relationship between the couple and co-therapists; without trust, therapy will never get off the ground.

The great majority of couples that I see enter a couples group following several diagnostic interviews (Framo, 1973). My goal during the couples group sessions consists primarily of utilizing the group process to further the therapy of the couple. The feedback the members get from each other is quite therapeutic; feedback from group members often has more impact than the statements of the therapists. Some other benefits of the group format are: The partners come to recognize the universality of certain marital problems and do not feel so different from other couples; the couples usually develop trust in each other and consequently become more open; in a "good" group even deep secrets will be revealed; problems across couples are contrasted or are found to be similar, so couples use each other as models of what to imitate or avoid; observations of each other become sharper as treatment progresses; the couples usually come to care for each other, and caring is always

---

[10]*Editors' Note.* We agree completely and have argued, in the final chapter of this *Handbook*, that such "emergent goals" must be accommodated in family therapy outcome research designs.

therapeutic; the goals of the spouses usually undergo modification in response to therapists' activity and feedback from the group, etc. Consequently, during the couples group sessions, the spouses become much more aware of their unrealistic expectations of marriage and of their spouse. These realizations bring about curiosity as to the genesis of their irrational expectations—which provides the opening for me to suggest anew that working things out with original family is one way of getting beyond the marital impasse.

The group process helps individuals to become less resistant to bringing in their family, especially since this goal of mine becomes the group goal; family of origin sessions come to be perceived by the group as a sort of final examination or graduation ceremony. The two major goals for the family of origin sessions are discovering what from the old family is being projected onto the spouse, and having a corrective experience with parents and siblings. The ultimate payoff or goal is a more differentiated self with consequent improvement in the marital or family relationships.

TREATMENT APPLICABILITY

Most of the couples I have treated were seen in my private practice and therefore were, economically at least, upper-middle class. However, I have used these methods in a community mental health center where the social classes of the clients spanned the entire spectrum. I have seen couples conjointly, done couples group therapy, and had family of origin sessions with clients who were severely disadvantaged, poor, and nearly illiterate.

There are certain universals of family and marital life that exist with all human beings, in all classes and cultures. One family problem has been mentioned as being universal among those seeking treatment—namely, that the loyalty of a spouse to the family of origin was greater than to the spouse and children. Almost everybody has a peer intimate relationship and has a parent, brother, or sister, and whenever there are intimates there are going to be relationship difficulties. Interestingly, those people who are not psychologically-minded and who want something concrete, like a pill, when they are in distress often do not resist meeting with a spouse or with parents or siblings, although they have no concept of psychotherapy. Their very nonsophistication makes them more open to conjoint family or marital therapy since they do not know enough about therapy to know that a session with the family of origin is not what is usually done.

In one sense I think everyone, people in treatment or not, can profit from family of origin sessions. Few people ever get to know their parents as real people, few families ever share, all together as a family, the really meaningful thoughts and feelings, and few people get to that last stage with parents, that of forgiving them and telling them that they are loved. So I see family of origin sessions as not being just a therapy method but as a kind of pandemic experience for people in general. As a matter of fact, in recent years I have been meeting the requests of family therapists to have one-time sessions with their original families. These sessions have been most productive.

Clinically, however, there are some marital situations where the family of origin sessions are more necessary, and still others where, although they are needed, there are certain unique circumstances which preclude their being held. Everyone transfers irrational attitudes and projects onto their spouse, including prominent people and professional marriage therapists; this phenomenon is part of being human and is a byproduct of the nature of intimate relationships. However, some people, who are more differentiated in Bowen's (1978) sense, have less need of fusion and can more accurately perceive the spouse as a person in his/her own right. These are the couples seen in marital therapy for relatively superficial problems and for whom family of origin sessions are not necessarily indicated. At the other extreme are those people who view their spouses as plasticene objects to be molded to their own needs, who do not really know where they end and the spouse begins, who are overdependent (e.g., the spouse can't go to the bathroom without the other asking, "Where are you going?"), and who may exhibit intense transference rage toward the mate (culminating sometimes in spouse murder). These people are unable to commit themselves to anyone because the deeper involvement is with the parents (e.g., the only time they may come alive during treatment sessions is when they discuss their parents). Their marital relationship is unreal, shadowy, and dreamlike because where they "live" is in the old family. For these kinds of couples, family of origin sessions are a must, but, as might be expected, they are also the most difficult to set up, to conduct, and to handle from the standpoint of subsequent emotional fallout.

From time to time, when I have given workshops, I have been asked whether there are couples who should *not* be seen in a couples group. I have never had the experience of having a couple in a group and thinking they would have done better as a single couple. There are couples who are reluctant to enter a group, but once in the group their apprehensions vanish. I am usually able to get them to come into a group by telling them that in the group they will accomplish their goals more quickly—which is true. The only couples I see as a single couple are those who need only a few sessions or those who are unable to arrange for the times that the groups meet. Although I have not yet met such a marital situation, it is possible that there may be some unique combination of circumstances and dynamics that would make couples group therapy contraindicated for a given couple. For instance, it is possible that a couple where incest with their children had occurred might not be able to deal with that event in the group. On the other hand, I have seen some pretty heavy secrets revealed in that setting, such as the man whose father was in jail for child-molesting.

Contraindications for family of origin sessions is a topic that we know little about, largely because there have only been a few years' experience with the method. I consider family of origin therapy as the major surgery of family therapy, and, like major surgery, there are risks and possible complications, especially short-term emotional upsets.

I have referred various family members for specific therapies, such as sex therapy, vocational guidance, behavior therapy, remediation of learning disabilities, group therapy, marathons, and even individual psychotherapy. I prefer that an individual in marital therapy with me not be in individual therapy with someone else while the marital therapy is going on. The main reason for this stance is that these clients will frequently reserve important material for their individual sessions; besides, the outside therapist and I could be working at cross-purposes, especially if that other therapist is an adherent of the illness model. I do not feel that I have a right to tell clients to terminate their individual therapy or analysis before starting marital therapy, but I do inform them of the handicaps that their separate therapy could impose on the marital therapy. When the desire for more extensive work on self is expressed, or when I think it advisable, however, I do refer clients for individual therapy when the marital therapy has terminated.

The final point on treatment applicability concerns the question as to whether *no* treatment of any sort is ever recommended. There are couples, especially those who have had too much therapy, to whom I make the recommendation that the best thing they can do for themselves is not to be in treatment. I have also dismissed some couples from ongoing therapy who have been using therapy as a substitute for living. I tell them, "Go out and live your lives and stop examining yourselves."

THE STRUCTURE OF THE THERAPY PROCESS

As stated earlier, couples are seen only conjointly, and almost all couples are seen in a couples group format after a few diagnostic sessions with the couple alone. There are no sessions with individuals. One major goal of the couples group setting is to prepare clients for the family of origin (intergenerational) sessions, which usually occur toward the end of therapy. The reasons for having the family of origin sessions late in therapy is that those sessions are more productive when the clients have changed in therapy and are ready to deal with the difficult issues with their parents and siblings.

Occasionally, I have family sessions with couples and their children, particularly if the partners in marital therapy express some concern about their children. These sessions are, of course, held outside the group. These family sessions have been valuable on several counts: The children are given the message that they are no longer responsible for handling their parents' problems because that job has been taken over by the therapists; the children give the kind of ingenuous, truthful accounts of what is going on at home that only children can give; and if the session occurs toward the end of therapy, the children can give a reading on how they preceive changes in their parents' relationship. Many couples at the end of successful marital therapy report "improvement" in their children, even when I have never seen the children.

Insofar as combined therapies are concerned, the one form of treatment that I find does not interfere with family therapy is for adolescents to be in peer group therapy concurrent with the family therapy. The separate adolescent group and family settings seem to enhance each other. (I do not conduct the adolescent group therapy; that is done by someone to whom I refer the adolescent.)

Although I have had to work as a solo therapist at times, I prefer to work with a co-therapist, particularly a female. Through the years I have worked with many co-therapists and I have come to see the value of having someone there to share responsibility, to notice things I do not see, to fight with me about what's going on, to provide more therapeutic leverage, to protect my flank, to make observations I do not think of, to allow me to remove myself psychologically, and to provide a reassuring presence during the kinds of chaotic or frightening events which can occur during family or marital therapy. Families and couples always respond more favorably to being seen by co-therapists, especially male-female teams, rather than a single therapist.[11] Women, especially, are pleased that another woman is present to understand a woman's point of view. Over the past seven years, in addition to working with other co-therapists, I have worked with my wife[12] in our evening private practice. The subject of husband-wife co-therapy is a large, rather complicated one that must await a separate publication. The only disadvantages I have seen with co-therapy is when there is a poor match between the per-

sonalities of the therapists. A co-therapy team can become like a marriage, and differences will inevitably arise—about strategy, interruptions, status, and who is chief honcho. If the co-therapists do not have the mechanisms for working out their differences, then they should "divorce," because couples and families will exploit their alienation, try to cure the co-therapy rift, or terminate prematurely.

The physical arrangement of sessions is as follows: Swivel chairs are used (so partners can turn and face each other) and the chairs are arranged in a circle. I cannot imagine conducting family or marital therapy sessions from behind a desk. All my sessions are audiotaped, and clients are free at any time to borrow the tapes to listen to at home. Many people take advantage of this offer, or bring their own cassette recorders to sessions. Listening to sessions at home can add an important dimension to the treatment, in that, with anxiety being less, the observing ego is more operative at that time. Many clients report that while listening to sessions at home they noticed aspects of themselves (anger, sulking, conning, phoniness, obsequiousness, contempt, etc.) that their defensiveness during sessions blocked them from seeing. I make no apologies about taping; the microphone is clearly present, and I communicate, in effect, "This is the way I work." Almost never does anyone object to being taped. (In those early days, when we used to ask permission and apologize for taping, there were many objections.) After every session a summary of the session is written up; if this is not done, one will never remember what is on the tape, and the tape will be useless.

Marital or family therapy, as I conduct it, is not time-limited; it does not seem appropriate to me to specify arbitrarily how many sessions are needed for a given problem. However, when I calculated the average number of sessions that couples come for marital therapy, it turned out to be 15 sessions.[13] This figure is an average one;

---

[11]*Editors' Note.* Indeed, in psychotherapy of any kind we know of no such "always" conditions. Moreover, there is little empirical evidence of the inherent superiority of co-therapy (Gurman and Kniskern, 1978a).

[12]Mary D. Framo, M.S.S., social worker-family therapist.

[13]*Editors' Note.* We have additional data from a variety of family therapists that confirms Framo's experience. In addition to the mean length of our own family therapy cases being about 15 sessions, colleagues in Italy (Andolfi, 1978) offer similar data, and our own extensive review of the research literature also shows three to four months' time to be the modal length of marital and family treatment (Gurman, 1973; Gurman and Kniskern, 1978a).

the range was from one session to about 50 sessions. Sessions are generally held once a week; with interruptions for holidays and vacations, the average length of treatment is about five months. Occasionally, some families and couples are seen on an irregular basis; some people seem to profit more when there is more than one week between sessions, whereas others come irregularly because they cannot afford to come more frequently. Decisions about therapy structure are made explicitly by the co-therapists, subject to occasional negotiation with the clients.

THE ROLE OF THE THERAPIST

Like practically all family therapists, I am rather active in therapy sessions; I cannot conceive of doing marital or family therapy in a passive, non-directive way. Because of the multiplicity of events on numerous levels, some degree of control of sessions by the therapist is necessary. For instance, since there is such deep and abiding resistance to bringing in family of origin, and because of my convictions about its value, I tend to come down rather hard on that subject; that is the one area where I am most directive.

Following the initial diagnostic sessions, where I abstain from making interventions, my conversational style usually consists of a fluid blend of questioning, empathizing, challenging, stage-directing, avoiding snares, confronting, balancing, supporting, reflecting, disagreeing, and, when relevant, judicious sharing of some of my own life experiences. On the subject of self-disclosure, I think it important that the therapist convey in some form that he has experienced pain and loss, shame, guilt and disappointment, as well as the exhilaration and joys of living. I even think it is helpful at times to communicate the reality of one's own parenting difficulties, as well as of one's own marriage as going through up and down phases. It is just as unwise to support the fantasy of the therapist's life as ideal as it is to overburden clients with one's own problems.

In our efforts to read the punctuation of the couple and raise concealed intrapsychic and interpersonal conflicts into open interactional expression, I and my co-therapist will move in and out of their orbit and emotional field. While one therapist is "inside," it is better for the other to be "outside," in a position to rescue the one who got caught up in the couple's or the group's irrationality. When partners will not talk to each other and only want to talk to the therapist(s), I insist they talk to each other; when they only will talk to each other, I insist they talk to me. Any behavior can be used as a defense.

My role as a therapist is fairly consistent throughout the course of treatment, although there may be times when the co-therapists will flexibly alternate roles. That is, the one who has usually been the rescuer may become the confronter, and vice versa. By the time the end of therapy has approached, I have noticed there is a tendency for me to become more personal and social with clients. Some couples groups after termination have had parties in one of the couples' homes, and although there was a time when I would never mix with clients socially, these days I do go with my wife, on a selected basis, to some of these social events. While it would be risky or inappropriate to mix socially with some clients, I have found no problems arising from social contact of this sort with the great majority of couples following termination. Family therapists have tended to break down a number of traditional professional taboos without the sky falling in.

TECHNIQUES OF MARITAL-FAMILY THERAPY

In my earlier writings on therapy techniques in *Intensive Family Therapy* (1965a), I dealt with the phases of family therapy as well as such technical problems as resistance, marriage problems, the "well sibling," transference/countertransference, and co-therapy. At that time most of my experience was with families with a schizophrenic member. Although some of those observations and techniques have held up over time, others have been modified; an update on my techniques can be found in an informal paper written ten years later (Framo, 1975).

My techniques vary according to whether I am seeing a couple, couples group, or family of origin, not only because of the number and kind of people in the room but because of the variation in goals, the nature of the therapy contract, and the psychological set of the clients. When couples first enter therapy, they are intensely preoccupied with the fate of their relationship. Standard marital therapy techniques are used to deal with the relationship itself, such as: accepting the couple, both as individuals and as a relationship, no matter how strange or unusual they seem at first; helping them develop congruent communications; the feedback technique (partners repeating back to each other what they think they heard); quid pro quo negotiations; work on differentiation; changing the rules of the relationship; teaching the couple how to "fight" or deal with issues with each other (Bach and Wyden, 1969); audiotape playback; as well as such conventional techniques as reflection, confrontation, interpretations, eliciting of affect, and so forth. On occasion, paradoxical tasks are assigned, but this sort of "homework," as well as some Masters and Johnson sex therapy exercises, is used sparingly.[14]

Techniques will differ according to the kind of marital problem being presented (see the earlier section of this chapter regarding types of marital problems). The greatest mistake made by beginning marital therapists, in my judgment, is that they are often misled by spouses' rage or apparent indifference toward each other, and they conclude that the marriage is unworkable. I have learned to respect the integrity and the tenaciousness of bonds in marital relationships, even in the most alienated couples or unlikely matches.

The Couples Group

I originally put couples together in a group in order to free myself from the transference/countertransference logjam that occurs with certain kinds of couples (Framo, 1973). While some couples are a pleasure to work with, there are others who triangle in the therapist as judge or prosecutor, those who are incapable of hearing anyone but themselves, those who become overdependent and helpless, and still others who try to solve their marital

problems by joining in an attack on the therapist. In order to handle my own reactions of frustration, impotence, or exasperation, I began putting my difficult couples together. It was only later, after experience with the couples group format, that I recognized the power of this form of treatment. I now believe that couples group therapy is the treatment of choice for premarital, living together, marital, and separation or divorce relationship problems. Indeed, all the couples I see come into a couples group unless there are scheduling difficulties or the relationship problem does not require more than a couple of sessions.

The group contains three couples, and the method, in brief, consists of focusing on one couple at a time while the other two couples observe, and then eliciting feedback from everyone in the group; then the next couple is attended to, and then the next, all of the individuals getting and giving feedback. Sessions last for two hours and are conducted with a female cotherapist. The couples groups are open-ended in that as couples terminate new ones are added. The focus is on the marital pair within the group context; it is recognized that other therapists conduct couples groups more like conventional peer group therapy where anyone can talk at any time. My primary focus is on the couple rather than the group, because that pair had a history before the group started and is likely to have a future together long after the group has disbanded. I am particularly interested in the transference distortions which occur between partners, not so much in the transference reactions across couples. Although I place the group as secondary to the couple, a group process is inevitable and must be managed and utilized to therapeutic advantage.

I find that couples do better when they are with couples who are not too far removed from them by age or stage of the life-cycle. That is, I tend to put together couples recently married or with young children, and have other groups with older couples whose children are grown. It has not worked too well when I have put, say, a young couple with two older couples; the latter would often lecture the young couple about the troubles that lay ahead. The couples are usually seen alone for several sessions before coming into a group. Some people are fearful of entering

---

[14]Most sexual problems disappear as a function of working on the relationship difficulties of the couple. Those couples who still have a sexual dysfunction after their relationship improves are referred elsewhere for sex therapy.

the group, and I am usually able to get them in by saying, truthfully in my experience, that whatever goals of therapy they have they will accomplish faster in the group.

The rules of the couples group are stated in the first session: Violence is not permitted; partners are not to discuss the other couples outside of the group where they can be overheard by others; when one partner cannot attend, the other should come to sessions; terminations should never occur on the telephone and should be announced a week in advance; and individuals should try to give feedback in a constructive way. Unlike most therapists, I do not discourage the couples from having social contact with each other outside the sessions; during the ten years I have conducted couples groups I have seen only benefits arising from the couples' becoming friends with each other. Indeed, one of the curative factors in couples groups is the caring that the participants come to have for each other. I once had in a class a psychiatric resident from Ghana who said that in his country, when a couple had a serious marital problem, the two extended families would gather together in a circle and help the couple work it out. It is unfortunate that in our country people have to pay for supportive networks. One resource rarely used by therapists in treating marital problems is the extended family of each partner; my work with family of origin is designed, in part, for this purpose.

When the couple is seen in the context of the couples group, the presence of other couples and the group process add another dimension to the therapy. Now there is a wider audience for the interactional behavior; in this atmosphere, there is less blaming of each other and more focus on self. At a certain stage in the course of a couples group, each individual usually hits a plateau and starts questioning his/her own behavior or attitude toward the spouse; some even start wondering about the source of their irrational perceptions and beliefs. There is considerable variation in the readiness of people to get to this point, depending not only on the differentiating capacity of the individual for insight, but on what is happening in the marital relationship as well. Some people, of course, never get beyond blaming the spouse; some couples become stalemated this way and treatment

can only progress by avoiding their interaction and focusing on the individuals. In any event, the person starting to examine self provides my entry into trying to get the client to bring in the family of origin as a way of dealing with his/her unrealistic expectations of the partner or the marriage.

Family of Origin Sessions

Early in the work with a couple, I indicate that I make it a practice to have each individual meet with his or her own family of origin, without the spouse being present. Anticipating the anxiety that this statement precipitates, I state that the sessions are usually held toward the end of therapy, after the clients have been prepared for the family conference and can see its value. During the couples group sessions, while working directly on the marital problems, I will occasionally ask direct questions about what is happening between a spouse and his or her parents and siblings. I have noticed that although all sorts of important things may be going on in the family of origin, if you do not directly ask, clients do not tell you; they consider those events to be extrinsic to their marital problems. (I recall one fellow who said, "I don't see why you ask about my stopping at my mother's house everyday. What does that have to do with my relationship to my wife?") In addition to asking about current relationships to family of origin members or about in-law relationships, from time to time I remind group members that everyone is expected to bring in his/her original family.

There are usually members of the group who, although frightened at the prospect, plan to follow through and bring in their family. Some of them report that they have even mentioned the session to selected family members who might be receptive to the idea. There are other members of the group who firmly rule out ever bringing in their family of origin. The therapists' expectations along these lines and the varying degrees of readiness to meet that expectation on the part of the couples group members become part of the culture of each group. Usually, the more willing members ally themselves with the therapists and attempt to persuade the reluctant ones to consider doing it. Some individuals become strongly motivated to work things out with a parent or sibling. After some clients have had their family of origin sessions, they can present more convincing evidence of their value; some of the most intransigent clients have reconsidered their negative positions upon hearing these accounts.

Over the years, I have developed certain techniques for dealing with the aversive response of most people to the prospect of sitting with their parents and brothers and sisters and discussing openly the heretofore avoided hard issues. The resistances assume manifold forms. An early one is when clients state that they get along fine with their family and there are no issues to be dealt with. When I get a detailed family of origin history, however, which disassembles the global characterization, issues become apparent in nearly every sentence.

Gradually, most clients begin to see that the family of origin sessions have the potential of benefiting themselves or the marriage; also, other reasons begin to emerge for having the sessions. As the agenda for the session is prepared, the marital problems recede in importance and clients gradually are induced to deal with past and present issues with their family. It is fascinating to observe how the marital conflicts, which totally preoccupied the client several weeks earlier, fade away and are replaced by the dawning realization that maybe something can be done about that long-standing guilty overcloseness or alienation from a mother, father or sibling. Working out a better relationship with family of origin frequently becomes a goal in its own right. Some clients, however, resist the endeavor to the end, either saying that their family situation is hopeless or indicating that meeting with the family could make things much worse by "opening up a Pandora's Box." Especially difficult to deal with is the client who describes his/her family as "close and extremely loving," with the implication that it is not possible for people to love too much. Spouses' reactions to their mates' account of their family history frequently reveal undisclosed facts. For instance, one client never mentioned the suicide of her father until her spouse brought it up.

On the basis of the family histories, the client is assisted in developing an agenda of issues to bring up with each and every member of the family. Each concrete issue becomes anxiety-laden. When the adult male says he always longed for affection from his father and I suggest he tell father that in the session, his apprehensive reaction is predictable. An adult daughter preparing to tell her mother that she can no longer be responsible for mother's happiness approaches that confrontation with great fear.

I do not have spouses present in the family of origin session because the focus is on what transpired in a given individual's family as that person was growing up, long before the spouse was met. If the spouse were present, the incoming family would be inhibited from discussing sensitive issues in the presence of an "outsider," or could not resist triangling in the client's marriage instead of dealing with the relationships in *this* family. (There are occasions when I have included the spouse in order to deal with problems in the in-law relationships, but I do not consider these sessions "family of origin" work in the sense in which I use it.) Usually one spouse is more ready to deal with his/her family than is the other. Most of the time, partners urge each other to do it even if they themselves are unwilling; as a matter of fact, I have seen some partners threaten divorce if the spouses do not attempt to work things out with their family. Only once did I have a spouse oppose the partner's meeting with his family.

Most of the resistance to bringing in the family of origin resides in the client, because usually when he/she becomes motivated the family follows. The reasons given by clients for not wanting to bring in original family are infinite, each one sounding most convincing and legitimate to the therapist unfamiliar with family of origin work ("They live too far away," "I know they would never come," "My mother is in bad health," "My father doesn't believe in psychiatrists or psychologists," etc.). Occasionally, despite all the efforts of a client to get his/her family in, some families refuse; some of these refusals are based on clients' sabotaging the session by implicitly presenting it to the family as punishment, whereas other times there are circumstances peculiar to a given family situation that preclude such a session.

I have the clients themselves take responsibility for writing and phoning and gathering their family members together to come in. Some families are scattered around the country, but in this age of jet travel geographical distance does not present a serious barrier. Family members come in from all parts of the country, and some have traveled from overseas. The emotional barriers are far more critical; when these are overcome, the reality problems are not difficult to deal with.

As the session approaches, anxiety starts building up in the client and usually starts spreading to the family outside. I begin to get calls from various family members about a parent's poor health and whether the emotional strain of such a session could bring about a medical disaster. One message I attempt to communicate, both to the client and the family members, is that the parents or siblings themselves have issues they might like to bring up with the client or other family members.

Techniques must be modified for the family of origin sessions, inasmuch as the parents and siblings are usually not coming in with an acknowledged need for help. Similar to when I interview a family at a workshop in front of an audience, I find it necessary to tread a fine line between dealing with meaningful things and yet not explicitly treating the incoming family members like patients. In my experience in working with many families of origin, I have found that there are certain tactical and strategic errors which should be avoided. Historically, one of the earliest identified resistances in family therapy was that of the "absent member maneuver," a process whereby the family members collude to keep a significant member out of the session (Sonne, Speck and Jungreis, 1962). This resistance is especially likely to come into play when planning family of origin sessions. For instance, sometimes the client is willing to bring in parents, but refuses to bring in a brother or sister. Or, sometimes the family shows up without an important member, despite assurances that everyone would be there. Generally speaking, I will not hold the session without a significant family member; the session is postponed until that person can make it. The presence of siblings is especially critical in family of origin sessions, and they are the ones most likely to be absent.

I believe that a male-female co-therapy team that is congruent is a potent therapeutic force;

this is especially true in working with families of origin. Whenever, by necessity, I have had to conduct these sessions alone, I have felt undefended and powerless. Part of the reason for this is that family of origin sessions are so unpredictable; you can never tell what they are going to be like. Families described by clients as docile and passive sometimes turn out to be hostile and difficult, and families described as impossible sometimes create a "love-in." The incoming families find it reassuring that a man and woman are seeing them, not only because both sexes are represented, but also because that arrangement seems to remove the session from the stereotype of psychiatry, which most people distrust. The co-therapy arrangement allows the initial human contact to take place more easily and then, throughout the session, can bring to bear the kinds of bilateral, complementary, and opposing interventions that only a well functioning co-therapy team can do.

There is considerable variation in these family of origin sessions; they differ in intensity, time focus, issues, degree of relatedness, amount of fusion, content, pace, awkwardness, defensiveness, and every other dimension that can occur when family members are brought together for the purpose of getting to know each other better and dealing openly with each other. One error that can be made is to accept the client's anger toward the parents or siblings at face value, missing the positive feelings and yearnings. The natural feeling toward parents is one of ambivalence, and if the therapists support the client's bitterness toward parents, the session will rapidly go downhill. Indeed, the anger in these sessions sometimes goes in all directions (parents to their children, siblings to each other, parents to their own siblings or parents), but the deeper levels of caring almost always eventually emerge in these sessions.

The sessions are audiotaped and it is suggested that they be listened to later by all the family members, including those who could not be present, as well as the spouse. Although most of these sessions are one-shot ones (lasting now for four hours in two separate periods with a break in between), some families return for several sessions. A detailed account of a full length case study of a couple, including couples group and family of origin therapy, is contained in

Framo (1978b).

Following the family of origin sessions of both partners, most marriage relationships improve since some of the mythologies have been cleared away and the transference distortions diminished. My theoretical formulation of change, based on the object-relation inner and outer interchanges, is in the earliest stage of hypothesis formation. Empirically speaking, however, these sessions usually work; there is something about facing and dealing with old issues with one's original family that seems to take the charge out of the negative reactions to the spouse. Some partners, however, following the family of origin sessions, having discovered more clearly whom they were really married to, begin to consider seriously whether or not to stay in their marriage. They agonize over such questions as the effects on their children, what a single life would be like, financial issues, and all the other difficult reality consequences of divorce. Some of these couples then become engaged in divorce therapy (Framo, 1978a).

The best terminations, to be sure, are those that are mutually agreed upon. Some couples terminate prematurely for various reasons, whereas I have had to terminate others unilaterally when I estimated that the couple was going nowhere in therapy. Terminations are always prepared for, and all clients are told that my door is always open for needed sessions in the future.

CURATIVE FACTORS

Despite the thousands of articles written on how and why psychotherapy works, when it does, definitive answers have not been established. Many ideas have been put forth about the root therapeutic factors, depending on the theoretical orientation of the proponent. Among the various curative elements which the more than a hundred kinds of psychotherapies have proposed are the following: the relationship to the therapist, acceptance and sensing that someone cares, emotional insight, modeling, power influences, unconditional positive regard, conditioning, systematic desensitization, corrective emotional experience, awareness of body sensations, analysis of the transference, game-free training, restructuring, paradoxical or "illogical" problem resolution and so forth. I can only speculate about what is curative in my methods of treatment; independent observers might arrive at quite different hypotheses. In the second section of this chapter I stated some criteria for marital improvement, and in the first section I suggested some ideas as to why family of origin sessions are usually helpful. I will now elaborate on a few of those points.

Insofar as marital therapy is concerned, spouses who report a successful therapy experience seem to have become more separate as persons, have higher self-esteem, are more tolerant of each other's regressive features and idiosyncrasies, can communicate more clearly about formerly anxiety-laden topics, can fight less destructively, can treat formerly loaded issues with humor, have more realistic expectations of marriage and of each other, are more affectionate and sexual with each other, manifest less hostility (in its various forms) to each other, are more accepting of the zigzag course that intimate relationships take, and are not deeply disappointed that they are not wildly, romantically "in love." (At the end of marital therapy one woman said incredulously about her marriage relationship, "You mean this is it?") Just how the couples arrive at this final stage is not clear to me in terms of what I do or do not do. Usually clients perceive therapist(s)' interventions differently than they were intended. Greater understanding of what happens in the therapy is not always achieved by asking clients either. Jay Efran, a colleague of mine, is fond of telling this story: He asked a client at the end of therapy what really helped him the most in all those months, expecting to hear some profound insight. Instead, the client replied, "It was that time when I was feeling low and you said something like, 'Behind every cloud there is a silver lining.'" Carl Whitaker says that one of his clients reported his most successful session as being one in which "nobody was up to anything." As someone once put it, the damndest things help people.

One of the things which seems to help marriages, as I stated previously, is that the partners have a more empathic understanding of each other. Having been given the opportunity to hear each other's life history and now knowing what the spouse had to struggle with, partners find each other's behavior more understandable.[15] (One wife said, "I still don't like my husband's rages, but after learning what his father did to him, I know where they come from and I don't take them personally anymore.") Furthermore, I have noticed that most married people do not really listen to each other; they are like amateur actors who wait for their cue to recite memorized lines and do not listen to the meaning of the words of the other actors. In marital therapy, the partners have learned to listen and to really hear each other, thereby diminishing their own preoccupations, righteousness, and self-centeredness.

I do not fully understand why an adult meeting with his/her family of origin in the special way I have described should frequently produce such profound changes, particularly the way such sessions often affect the problems for which the couple or family originally entered therapy. Most psychotherapies focus on unscrambling the inner life of a client and then leave it up to that person to work things out with the parents or siblings on his/her own. Individual therapy or analysis may help a man gain insight into the unconscious reasons why he cannot get close to his father, yet in actuality he and father may remain distant. Psychoanalysts and other individual therapists will not get involved with healing the real problems in family relationships. Some otherwise very mature adults are currently enslaved in their relationship with their parents (e.g., the executive who must call his mother every day), or are completely cut off from a hated brother or sister. The family of origin method is designed to deal with these kinds of problems—which certainly have their effects on the marital or parental functioning.

In addition to adults hurting from difficulties with their parents and siblings in the present, they are also locked into the fantasy family of the past. As a matter of fact, the real source of marital conflicts of today, in my view, has to do with unconscious attempts to deal with and master that fantasy family, using the current intimates as stand-ins.[16] Something happens to that repressed fantasy family when the adult meets with his/her actual, real original family and confronts them with the heretofore avoided issues which had existed between them. Dealing with the real, external figures seems to loosen the grip of the introjects of those figures and exposes the past to current realities.

Following the sessions, the old family can never go back to the way it used to be, and the adult client frequently begins to perceive the spouse and children in a more realistic way. Family of origin sessions change marital relationships in many different ways. For instance, the wife whose husband complained of her being "bossy, super-independent, and not seeming to need me," in her family of origin session told her parents she was giving up her role of taking care of them and instead wanted them to take care of her. When her parents at least tried to meet this need, she could allow herself to be more vulnerable with her husband. See the case history in Framo (1978b) for a more complete account of how working things out with the family of origin directly can help a marriage.

My interpretations to a couple do take historical factors into account, but in vivo. That is to say, since I have seen the actual parents and siblings, I am in a better position to point out how patterns and behaviors from the old family are being inappropriately played out with the spouse and children. Some of these interpretations catch hold on the basis of what is customarily called "insight." Insight is a much abused term, particularly under attack by those who claim that "understanding" never really changed anybody. Insight, as I see it, is an extraordinarily complicated phenomenon combining cognitive, emotional, and motoric elements. From my viewpoint, unless insight leads to behavioral or attitudinal change, it is not insight.

Although ideally it is best if each member of

---

[15]*Editors' Note.* And such a basis for empathy often precludes the necessity of formal marital skill training, as we point out in Editors' Note number 15 in Jacobson's Chapter 15 in this volume.

[16]It is not surprising that among the anger-provoking insults spouses will hurl at their partner during an argument are such statements as the following: "You're just like your mother," or, "You're not going to treat me the way your father treated your mother," or, "You keep forgetting I'm your husband, not your father."

a family or both marital partners change, it is not necessary for each individual, *qua* individual, to change if there are to be relational alterations. Small system or interactional changes can have powerful effects, such as an excluded father being more involved in the family, or a couple's fight style not having such deadly intensity, or the children being able to deal with mother directly instead of having to go through grandmother, etc.

Transference is a ubiquitous human phenomenon and will develop over time in any significant relationship. Over the years, as my experience has accumulated, however, I have come to deemphasize the transference to the therapist(s). Instead, I now focus attention on the transference distortions which occur between the intimates. While transference to the therapist(s) will always be present, a therapist can choose not to deal with it explicitly unless it is seriously getting in the way of therapy.[17] For example, when spouses insist on my telling them how I feel about them, I indicate that my feelings are not as important as their feelings about each other, since they will be dealing with each other long after I have been forgotten. One of the reasons I started doing couples groups was to dilute the transference to me, since some couples had such strong needs to view me as judge, rescuer or persecutor that they were unable to move in treatment.

Family or marital therapy is much more likely to elicit countertransference feelings than is individual or group therapy, because of the ways in which the ghosts of the therapist's own family intrude into the treatment room (Framo, 1968).[18] I agree with Bowen (1978) that the best safeguard against inappropriate reactions to a family or couple is for the therapist to get his/her own house in order and improve his/her own functioning. This goal can best be accomplished by working out problems with one's own original family, as well as family of procreation.

---

[17]*Editors' Note.* Indeed, most psychodynamically-oriented marriage therapists do not often directly address their couples' transference reactions (Gurman, 1978).

[18]*Editors' Note.* Coché (1978) has addressed how this issue of what she calls "personal spill" can even influence the conduct of family therapy research.

EFFECTIVENESS OF THE APPROACH

Any theoretician always feels somewhat abashed when he has to admit that concrete, hard data have not been provided as evidence for the effectiveness of his conceptual approach to psychotherapy. The discipline of psychology is more committed to research than any of the other mental health disciplines; as a matter of fact, in some quarters, any psychologist who does not do numerical studies with proper experimental design and probability statistics is regarded as not really a psychologist. Having been originally trained as a clinical psychologist, my mortification should be complete because I have done no systematic research on my treatment methods. In a recent paper, Wells and Dezen stated, ". . . a number of these [family therapy] schools (in some instances led by major figures in the family therapy movement, the very role models for the aspiring practitioner) have never submitted their methods to empirical testing and, indeed, seem oblivious to such a need" (1978, p. 266).

Still, I am not yet deserving of being drummed out of the corps. In demonstration of my not being oblivious to research needs, not only did I prepare a lengthy survey of family interaction research in the early days of family therapy (Framo, 1965b), but in 1967 I organized the first national conference on family interaction research with 29 family researchers and family therapists, the proceedings of which were published in a book (Framo, 1972). In the introduction to that book, I stated the perennial basic conflict between the clinician and the researcher: ". . . systematic researchers would argue that, while clinicians can provide vital information and inspiration for the formulation of hypotheses via hunches and impressions, opinions are still opinions, unable to be proved or refuted by any scientific standard. . . . there is general agreement that observations must be organized into theory, that theories should be operationally stated and put in the form of testable hypotheses, and that variables should be manipulated by certain rules so as to permit the data to confirm or disprove the hypotheses by other than personal means. Only in this way, the researchers state, can laws of broad applicability be abstracted from the individual instance. The clinicians dispute this thesis, saying that problems are defined by researchers in terms that are most convenient to research, and that experimentalists, in their quest for scientific objectivity, end up measuring pallid, trivial variables and distill all humanity from their investigations" (pp. 3-4). The dilemma between studying "the significant or the exact," as someone put it, keeps many clinician-theoreticians from doing research. As soon as one starts converting theory to operational definitions, much is lost in translation, and one ends up measuring something that bears little resemblance to the original.[19]

There are many other intricate problems associated with doing research in this area, particularly therapy outcome research. There are such technical problems as adequacy of control groups, how to handle no-treatment groups who seek help on their own, the homogeneity of samples, the size of a sample, finding sophisticated measuring instruments, etc. It seems to me that the field needs some creative designs for studies that will take into account the unique features of marital and family therapy.[20] From whose vantage point do we evaluate success or failure? Marital and family therapy differs from all other psychotherapies; each person has a different agenda for therapy goals, both stated and secret, and the goal usually is that someone else should change. How can client satisfaction be the sole criterion of change? If a divorced woman feels she has a second chance for happiness with a man, but if the man says he wants to marry her and does not want her child, would the therapy be successful if the clients were pleased that the family therapist went along with institutionalizing the child?[21]

In addition to the enormous complexity of the treatment situation, which can create formidable barriers to systematic investigation, there are also the practical obstacles to doing research in clinical settings, especially the problem of staff cooperation. There are very few clinical settings where the clinical director will allow interference in the routine; psychotherapists generally do not want any researcher examining ("tampering with"?) their treatment. Gurman and Kniskern (1978), in a comprehensive review of over 200 marital and family therapy outcome studies, have performed a valuable service by specifying criteria for evaluating the adequacy of outcome studies. The problem with those criteria is that they would be nearly impossible to meet in a clinical setting (such as random assignment of families and couples, or, more difficult to meet, random assignment of therapists—a criterion which would require a huge clinic).[22]

A problem exists in communicating about systems in an academic clinical psychology setting, as in most psychiatric settings (Framo, 1976b), where the study of the individual is paramount. More traditional studies in clinical psychology are favored by students over family interaction research because, frankly, the latter are more difficult to do and take more time. A few motivated students have done their dissertations in this area, but they are exceptional and, besides, they selected the kinds of studies that were feasible within their doctoral time frame.

I am the kind of clinician who needs to step back from his practice and conceptualize about what has been observed. One quandary of a theoretician-clinician is how to treat and conceptualize, teach, give workshops, write, and still have time to do systematic studies. I have had fantasies of having a support staff to handle all the inquiries and requests that I get, and a large group of research assistants who would study and evaluate my treatment methods. There are very few family therapists in the country who work with family of origin as I do, and

---

[19]*Editors' Note.* But, then, of course, one can never test *all* of a theory in a single investigation. It is the aggregate testing of this series of predictions that is the essence of the empirical approach and which, in toto, allows for the testing of a theory by examining its power to make specific predictions.

[20]*Editors' Note.* These certainly are fundamental issues in evaluating the outcomes of family therapy, but are not quite as insoluble or unaddressed as Framo seems to imply here. See, e.g., Gurman and Kniskern (1978a), and the Editors' final chapter in this *Handbook.*

[21]*Editors' Note.* Again, we offer some specific guidelines for the choice of vantage point in assessing family therapy outcome in the last chapter of this volume, and in Gurman and Kniskern (1978a).

[22]*Editors' Note.* The criteria we suggest are goals to strive for, not, in our view, criteria for publication. In fact, we have championed the instructiveness and utility of significantly less rigorous designs under some conditions (see Gurman and Kniskern, 1978b; and the last chapter of this volume).

I think it necessary to confirm with hard data my clinical impressions on how powerful such sessions can be in producing change. Not only treatment results need to be examined, utilizing systematic follow-up, but greater understanding is needed on why and how sessions with family of origin can break up deep-seated attitudes and behavior patterns.

TRAINING OF MARITAL-FAMILY THERAPISTS

I believe that family therapists were "trained" by their original families, and the formal training they get today refines that lifelong process. In my judgment, while there are certain kinds of family problems that can be handled by any reasonably intelligent person or paraprofessional trained in the problem-solving method, there are other, more complex situations, which require the kind of "natural" who has been trained as a general psychotherapist first and later as a family therapist. That is to say, I believe that every family therapist should have had individual and peer group therapy experience, as well as experience with the whole range of emotional disturbances in varied clinical settings. Intensive supervision by a supervisor who knows what he/she is doing is also a must in the training of any therapist. Whether or not those individual or group therapy experiences should occur prior to or concurrent with the learning of marital or family therapy is a question open to study. This viewpoint of prior individual and group therapy experience is consistent with my theoretical perspective of exploring the relationship between the intrapsychic and the transactional. There is something about working through people's internal and interpersonal defenses, it seems to me, that helps one know how to deal with the intimate system operations. If, for example, a man has an internalized fear of women which he handles by projection of anticipated attack from his wife, we are in a position not only to understand why he beats up his wife, but also to help him deal directly with his mother about his earlier fear of her.

It is interesting that several family therapists have recommended that family therapy trainees have a personal therapy experience (meaning individual therapy), but no one recommends that trainees should have marital or family therapy with his/her spouse, family of origin, or family of procreation. While I do not think it should be a requirement, I personally believe such experiences to be among the best preparations for becoming a family therapist (Framo, 1979). Bowen's method of training includes having trainees conduct genealogical searches in the quest for self, an extremely valuable method of training.

In my classes there are no formal examinations; the only requirement is the writing of a family biography. Students have reported that this was the most painful and difficult, yet the most meaningful assignment of their lives. I have become aware, further, of the high rate of divorce among family therapy trainees, a phenomenon insufficiently studied. One could speculate that the trainee and the spouse are living in such different worlds that they lose touch with each other. The foregoing is one of the reasons I encourage trainees to include their spouse or other family member in certain aspects of my training program.

There is insufficient space to go into detail on the didactic and experiential aspects of my training program. I believe that trainees should be exposed to the various theories and methods of working with families so that eventually they will develop a style that is comfortable for them. In addition to becoming familiar with the classical literature in the field, trainees can learn a lot about marital and family dynamics from plays, movies, and novels. Another area that is neglected in family therapy training programs is knowledge about ethnic family cultures. Other aspects of training, such as group supervision, live supervision, simulated families, videotape, program evaluation, and so forth, would each require separate treatment, a task beyond the purposes of this chapter. Although I stress the value of students' working things out with their own families, I do believe that they must learn skills. Overall, however, it is the personal development of trainees, rather than *just* their technical skills, which will determine their effectiveness as family therapists in dealing with what I have called the "gut" issues of family life—the passions, hates, loves, injustices, sacrifices, comforts, disappointments, frustrations, ambivalences, and gratifications. These are the universals with which everyone raised in a family has had to struggle.

REFERENCES

Anonymous. Toward the differentiation of a self in one's own family. In J. L. Framo (Ed.), *Family Interaction: A Dialogue between Family Researchers and Family Therapists*. New York: Springer, 1972.

Bach, G. R. & Wyden, P. *The Intimate Enemy: How to Fight Fair in Love and Marriage*. New York: Morrow, 1969.

Boszormenyi-Nagy, I. & Framo, J. L. (Eds.) *Intensive Family Therapy*. New York: Harper & Row Medical Dept., 1965.

Boszormenyi-Nagy, I. & Spark, G. M. *Invisible Loyalties*. New York: Harper & Row Medical Dept., 1973.

Bowen, M. *Family Therapy in Clinical Practice*. New York: Aronson, 1978.

Bradt, J. O. & Moynihan, C. J. A study of child-focused families. In J. O. Bradt & C. J. Moynihan (Eds.) *Systems Therapy*, 1971. Available from Groome Child Guidance Clinic, 5225 Loughboro Rd., N.W., Washington, D.C. 20016.

Dicks, H. V. *Marital Tensions*. New York: Basic Books, 1967.

Fairbairn, W. R. D. *An Object-Relations Theory of the Personality*. New York: Basic Books, 1952.

Foley, V. D. *An Introduction to Family Therapy*. New York: Grune & Stratton, 1974.

Framo, J. L. Rationale and techniques of intensive family therapy. In I. Boszormenyi-Nagy & J. L. Framo (Eds.) *Intensive Family Therapy*. New York: Harper & Row Medical Dept., 1965. (a)

Framo, J. L. Systematic research on family dynamics. In I. Boszormenyi-Nagy & J. L. Framo (Eds.) *Intensive Family Therapy*. New York: Harper & Row Medical Dept., 1965. (b)

Framo, J. L. My families, my family. *Voices*, 1968, *4*, 18-27.

Framo, J. L. Symptoms from a family transactional viewpoint. In: N. W. Ackerman, J. Lieb, & J. K. Pearce (Eds.) *Family Therapy in Transition*. Boston: Little, Brown, 1970.

Framo, J. L. *Family Interaction: A Dialogue between Family Researchers and Family Therapists*. New York: Springer, 1972.

Framo, J. L. Marriage therapy in a couples group. In D. A. Bloch (Ed.) *Techniques of Family Psychotherapy: A Primer*. New York: Grune & Stratton, 1973.

Framo, J. L. Personal reflections of a family therapist. *Journal of Marriage and Family Counseling*, 1975, *1*, 15-28.

Framo, J. L. Family of origin as a therapeutic resource for adults in marital and family therapy: You can and should go home again. *Family Process*, 1976, *15*, 193-210. (a)

Framo, J. L. Chronicle of a struggle to establish a family unit within a community mental health center. In P. Guerin (Ed.) *Family Therapy*. New York: Gardner Press, 1976. (b)

Framo, J. L. The friendly divorce. *Psychology Today*. Feb., 1978. (a)

Framo, J. L. In-laws and out-laws: A marital case of kinship confusion. In P. Papp (Ed.) *Family Therapy: Full Length Case Studies*. New York: Gardner Press, 1978. (b)

Framo, J. L. A personal viewpoint on training in marital and family therapy. *Professional Psychology*, 1979, *10*, 868-875.

Framo, J. L. Marriage and marital therapy: Issues and initial interview techniques. In M. Andolfi and I. Zwerling (Eds.) *Dimensions of Family Therapy*. New York: Guilford Press, 1980.

Freud, S. Totem and taboo (1913). In J. Strachey (Ed.), *The Standard Edition of the Complete Works of Sigmund Freud*, London: Hogarth Press, Vol. 13, 1955.

Freud, S. Group psychology and the analysis of the ego (1921). In J. Strachey (Ed.), *The Standard Edition of the Complete Works of Sigmund Freud*. London: Hogarth Press, Vol. 18, 1955.

Freud, S. Civilization and its discontents (1930). In J. Strachey (Ed.), *The Standard Edition of the Complete Works of Sigmund Freud*. London: Hogarth Press, Vol. 21, 1961.

Gurman, A. S. & Kniskern, D. P. Research on marital and family therapy: Progress, perspective and prospect. In S. Garfield & A. Bergin (Eds.) *Handbook of Psychotherapy and Behavior Change*. Second edition. New York: Wiley, 1978.

Haas, W. The intergenerational encounter: A method in treatment. *Social Work*, 1968, *13*, 91-101.

Haley, J. Why a mental health clinic should avoid family therapy. *Journal of Marriage and Family Counseling*, 1975, *1*, 3-13.

Headley, L. *Adults and Their Parents in Family Therapy*. New York: Plenum Press, 1977.

Jackson, D. D. The individual and the larger contexts. *Family Process*, 1967, *6*, 139-147.

Lewis, J. M., Beavers, W. R., Gossett, J. T., & Phillips, V. A. *No Single Thread: Psychological Health in Family Systems*. New York: Brunner/Mazel, 1976.

Montalvo, B. & Haley, J. In defense of child therapy. *Family Process*, 1973, *12*, 227-244.

Paul, N. L. & Paul, B. B. *A Marital Puzzle*. New York: Norton, 1975.

Sonne, J. C., Speck, R. V., & Jungreis, J. E. The absent-member maneuver as a resistance in family therapy of schizophrenia. *Family Process*, 1962, *1*, 44-62.

Spiegel, J. P. & Bell, N. W. The family of the psychiatric patient. In S. Arieti (Ed.) *American Handbook of Psychiatry*. Vol. 1. New York: Basic Books, 1959.

Strean, H. S. A family therapist looks at Little Hans. *Family Process*, 1967, *6*, 227-234.

Visher, E. B. & Visher, J. S. *Stepfamilies: A Guide to Working with Stepparents and Stepchildren*. New York: Brunner/Mazel, 1979.

Wells, R. A. & Dezen, A. E. The results of family therapy revisited: The non-behavioral methods. *Family Process*, 1978, *3*, 251-274.

Whitaker, C. A. A family is a four dimensional relationship. In P. J. Guerin (Ed.) *Family Therapy*. New York: Gardner Press, 1976.

Whitaker, C. & Keith, D. V. Counseling the dissolving marriage. In R. F. Stahmann & W. J. Hiebert (Eds.) *Klemer's Counseling in Marital and Sexual Problems*. Baltimore: Williams & Wilkins, 1977

Zilboorg, G. & Henry G. W. *A History of Medical Psychology*. New York: Norton, 1941.

EDITORS' REFERENCES

Andolfi, M. Personal communication, December, 1978.

Coché, J. M. *The uniqueness of family therapy outcome research: Critical research issues*. Paper presented at the Ninth Annual Meeting of the Society for Psychotherapy Research, Toronto, June, 1978.

Gurman, A. S. The effects and effectiveness of marital therapy: A review of outcome research. *Family Process*, 1973, *12*, 145-170.

Gurman, A. S. Contemporary marital therapies: A critique and comparative analysis of psychoanalytic, behavioral and systems theory approaches. In T. J. Paolino & B. S. McCrady (Eds.), *Marriage and Marital Therapy*. New York: Brunner/Mazel, 1978.

Gurman, A. S. & Kniskern, D. P. Research on marital and family therapy: Progress, perspective and prospect. In S. Garfield & A. Bergin (Eds.), *Handbook of Psychotherapy and Behavior Change*. Second edition. New York: Wiley, 1978. (a).

Gurman, A. S. & Kniskern, D. P. Technolatry, methodolatry and the results of family therapy. *Family Process*, 1978, *17*, 275-281. (b).

CHAPTER 5

Contextual Family Therapy

Ivan Boszormenyi-Nagy, M.D.

and David N. Ulrich, Ph.D.

THE CONTEXTUAL ORIENTATION

Contextual therapy[1] is a comprehensive relational approach, whose ultimate goal is to integrate the significant premises of all approaches to psychotherapy, provided that they are ethically concerned and contractually responsible in the sense that they take into account the interests of all the persons whom the therapy potentially affects. The goal is also to arrive at the most effective preventive design. Contextual therapy integrates the systemic view of classical family therapy with a multiple individual level of dynamics.

At present these goals are obscured by infinite divergence in conceptual points of view about psychotherapy. We suggest that through a mul-

tilateral contractual approach, i.e., giving balanced consideration to all responsible points of view, the present trend toward divergence can eventually be reversed.

The contextual orientation assumes that the leverages of all psychotherapeutic interventions are anchored in relational determinants, and that a comprehensive approach must consider these determinants in terms of four interlocking dimensions.

While we speak of relational determinants for therapy, the contextual approach never loses sight of the goal of benefiting persons, not systems. The entry point of intervention can be one individual's "complaints" or symptoms, as well as relational problems.

Four Dimensions

The first dimension of a comprehensive approach to assessment and treatment planning has to do with *facts*, with what is provided by destiny. For example, the ethnic identity of one's roots, illness, adoption, survivorship—are all given facts; they are parts of a configuration

---

[1]This chapter reflects a major recasting of the approach of the senior author, including the premises contained in *Invisible Loyalties* (Boszormenyi-Nagy and Spark, 1973), reflecting the developments that have taken place since the publication of that book and since the article, "Behavior change through family change" (Boszormenyi-Nagy, 1976). The second author has contributed to the tasks of selecting, condensing, providing clinical illustrations, and giving the present written form to the materials of this chapter.

of destiny. The existence of a split between the parents becomes a fateful fact for the child. The obligation to consider the welfare interests of others becomes a fact.

The second dimension may be given the general heading of *psychology*, or what happens within the person. That a child grows up with a physical or emotionally-induced developmental handicap is a fact. The psychological context contains the attitudes of the child, parents, and others toward the handicap. A significant aspect of psychological phenomena is that one component may be substituted for another without loss of symbolic meaning, as in therapeutic transference. There is no theoretical parsimony in trying to invalidate the significance of drives, psychic development, and inner experience. On the contrary, it appears that the intensive, in-depth relational implications of psychoanalytic theory need to be explored, expanded, and integrated with the other contextual dimensions.

The third dimension may be characterized as the dimension of *transactions or power alignments*. These events are superimposed on, but can never invalidate, the other three dimensions. The fulfillment of need complementarity, for instance, may appear as a power struggle. A therapist may be drawn into a covertly exploitative power alignment, for instance, binding one family member into the "identified patient" role.

The fourth dimension, which we regard as the cornerstone of contextual therapy, is concerned with *relational ethics*. Here "ethics" carries no implication of a specific set of moral priorities or criteria of right vs. wrong. It is concerned with the balance of equitable fairness between people. By "fairness" we mean neither the mechanistic rigidity of giving all three children bicycles for Christmas, nor a barter system in which each item is part of a trade-off, but rather the long-term preservation of an oscillating balance among family members, whereby the basic interests of each are taken into account by the others.[2] What one person experiences is not the criterion of fairness. To gauge the balance, it is necessary to employ multilateral criteria, i.e., consideration by each family member of the interests of all family members, including his or her own and a reciprocal exchange of these considerations. Relational ethics are founded on the principle of equitability, i.e., that everyone is entitled to have his or her welfare interests considered in a way that is fair from a multilateral perspective. Aside from its fundamental implications for autonomy and health, this is a safeguard against the intrusion of the values of the therapist, in that the therapist must acquire the disciplined openness to consider the interests of each family member from the vantage point of every family member, not merely from the vantage point of one family member or from the therapist's own perspective. This is reflected in the methodological principle of multidirectional partiality.

Issues of entitlement and indebtedness vis-à-vis others are existentially given, whether acknowledged or not. Relationships become trustworthy to the degree that they permit the facing of these issues of who owes whom. Such issues cannot be reduced to a subcategory of the psychological dimension or in any way be accounted for by the pleasure-pain principle. They do not originate from any individual's mental characteristics. Yet facing them is prerequisite to the most effective ways of personal fulfillment. One's satisfaction from relationships is determined not only by needs and ego strengths but also by how one's existentially given debts and entitlements accrue.

We consider relational ethics to be a fundamental dynamic force, holding family and societal relationships together through mutuality and trustworthiness of relationship. According to multilateral logic, the balance of fairness between people is the most profound and inclusive context. This is the context to which the term "contextual therapy" applies.

Unlike symbolic or transactional phenomena, relational ethics allow no valid substitution. A debt incurred vis-à-vis mother through her merit can be repaid only to the mother. Working through one's rage toward father in displacement on the person of the therapist is not a payment of a relational debt. It may turn out to be a preparation for payment, or it may not. In a therapy based on relational ethics, action or

---

[2]*Editors' Note.* While the origins and basic assumptions of contextual family therapy and behavioral family methods are enormously different, it is fascinating to note the essential similarity of the position taken, within each model, of the relative importance of the "long-term oscillating balance" among the family members (what behaviorists call the "bank account" of exchanges) and the "barter system trade-off" (what behaviorists call "contingency contracting").

consideration of action toward payment of the debt, or toward realization of an entitlement, is seen as a fundamental move toward building trust or health. Contextual therapy thus differs radically from therapy based solely on psychological or transactional premises.

The Development of Contextual Therapy

In the medical origins of psychotherapy, there was hope for a scientific method providing "cure" of symptoms or pathology with minimal reference to ethical resources such as trust-building relationships. But with Freud's theory of the object-relatedness of human instinctual drives, an implicit turn toward the relational occurred, to become even more explicit in the teachings of Sullivan (1953) and Fairbairn (1954). On the philosophical side, meanwhile, the relational reality of human life was being confirmed by Buber (1958).

During the 1950s, as they gradually recognized the limitations of individual therapy primarily with children or with psychotics, a small number of clinicians began to explore conjoint therapy, initially for the nuclear family. In 1957, Boszormenyi-Nagy and his co-workers introduced family therapy into a research project at the Eastern Pennsylvania Psychiatric Institute in Philadelphia involving intensive psychotherapy of hospitalized psychotics. The initial orientation was psychoanalytic ego psychology, with existential and experiential aspects added. From these orientations developed a phase of classical, systemic or transactionally-structuring family therapy, with increasing dialectical understanding of depth relational dynamics. Emphasis was placed on total attendance, communications, and behavior patterns. In conjoint family therapy, naturally, treatment was no longer restricted to the diagnosed member. The work was rapidly expanded to people with a wide spectrum of nonpsychotic symptoms and their family members.

Intrinsically, but for long time unrecognized, the paradigm entering the field was that of a multilateral therapeutic contract. Thus, an implicitly ethical contractual reorientation was getting underway, but it was obscured by a side-tracking into general systems theory which left no room for dynamic concepts such as balances of entitlement or indebtedness.

During the 1960s, a number of family therapists began to feel that work should not be limited to the nuclear family or to transactions in the here and now, and multigenerational linkages began to find their way into various conceptual systems. Subsequently, in the late 1960s, Boszormenyi-Nagy and his associates started to explore the therapeutic leverages to be found in the ethics of transgenerational relationships (Boszormenyi-Nagy and Spark, 1973).

The evolution of the contextual approach since 1958—first family therapy, then extended family and intergenerational, then the contextual view of all therapy—has been an organic evolution. Its impetus has been the societal background of ripped-off, overburdened, abandoned nuclear families. The conditions under which the family as a social institution is trying to survive are visible to everyone. We submit that the family is trying to exist in the vacuum that was left when the connection between visible relationships and intergenerational rootedness broke down and the ethical implications of that connection were lost. In this social context, such ethical aspects as loyalty and legacy cannot be reduced to functions of the superego. Multilateral determination transcends the individual, as part of relational reality.

Our multilateral concern is not, however, limited to intergenerational connections as such. Whether one person or several are present at the session, the goal of contextual therapy is to achieve a responsible orientation to intermember issues of fairness and trust on the part of both participant and therapist.

The very use of the term "patient" has to be dissolved when the multilaterality of the relational ethical dynamic becomes the guiding principle. On the other hand, in contrast with the systemic view, the contextual approach retains interest in each individual's subjective vantage point, not just psychologically but in terms of relational merits, claims and obligations.

The development of the multilateral perspective has progressed to the point where it appears unavoidable to challenge reductionistic psychological or transactional-systemic assumptions about the determination of human behavior. Moreover, a distinction can now be drawn between those therapies which propose strategies within substitutive relational contexts (e.g., behavior modification, or encounter, or utilization of therapeutic transference) and those that offer assistance within the participants' original relational context.[3] We propose that the second avenue offers the higher therapeutic leverage.

Yet, from our point of view, much remains to be done to define the key dynamic points of the human context.

The Basic Relational Context

From the multigenerational perspective, it would appear artificial ever to assume that all of the family variables crucial to a child's development could be found within the parents or within the parental relationship. Instead, it becomes habitual to use a framework of at least three generations. At any point in time, at least three generations overlap. Even if the grandparents are absent or dead, their influence continues. Psychological, transactional, and ethical aspects lose crucial meanings if they are not seen in this perspective. *The struggle of countless preceding generations survives in the structure of the nuclear family.* Overtly disparate sequences of transactional behavior, sometimes separated by generations, may have invisible dynamic linkages. A husband's abusive act toward his wife may have far more dynamic connection to a behavioral sequence of 30 or 60 years ago than to the act of hers that triggered his abuse.

We consider a basic dynamic substrate to be the wish for trustworthy relationships among family members, based on reciprocal consideration of each other's basic welfare interests, having to do with survival, growth, and relatedness. One who contributes to the balance by regarding and supporting the interests of the other may be said to acquire *merit*. In terms of relational ethics, merit is the unit that counts. The ethical dimension thus transcends such issues as "need complementarity" and "convergence of interests," which are psychological and transactional.

The family is strengthened by moves toward

trustworthiness and weakened by moves away. Moves toward trustworthy relatedness we call *rejunctive*; moves away from such relatedness we call *disjunctive*. A family context is never enhanced by moves away from trust. A husband, for instance, will not improve his marital relationship by trying to destroy his wife's residual trust in her parents. The descriptive term *relational stagnation* (Boszormenyi-Nagy and Spark, 1973) is used for any instance of familial disengagement from concern about fairness. In a stagnating family, moves toward rejunction are blocked or cancelled out.

Depending on their integrity and on the complementarity of their needs (Boszormenyi-Nagy, 1965), marital partners can develop a degree of trustworthy convergence. But if their welfare interests clash, they may drift toward exploitative maneuvers and divorce.

Thus, an ethical dimension exists in any relationship. An even deeper source of relational ethics is provided when the relationships stem from intergenerational rootedness. Such rootedness provides an inherent synergism. Those who are linked by membership in successive generations have an intrinsic coincidence of interests that works deep ultimate effects upon them.

We consider an anchor point of the multigenerational linkage of trustworthiness to be the responsibility for parenting, which is a structure basic to all lives. If a person has no children, the parenting component can come through the commitment to relieve one's own parents' difficulties. Through dynamic linkages, parental accountability will affect the basic potential for trust in future generations. Parental responsibility could even include the decision not to have children.

In our view, the responsibility of the parents has a reciprocal anchor point in the child's loyalty to its roots. We see *loyalty* as a factual relational dynamic, central to the child's functioning even into adulthood. The child has a reservoir of trust out of which he or she can initiate repayment of trust toward the parents. Originally, this reserve of trust derives from the legacy of intergenerational relatedness. Additionally, it derives from the human concern for fairness of give and take. To the degree that the parents are able to maintain a balance of fairness, they

---

[3]*Editors' Note.* In its ideal form of practice, of course, behavior therapy strongly emphasizes the importance of treating behavior in its natural environment (roughly equivalent to what Boszormenyi-Nagy and Ulrich call the "original relational context") in order to promote generalization and, hence, maintenance of treatment effects.

acquire a merit that reinforces the child's basic loyalty commitment.

No matter how damaging the relationships have become, it is safe to assume that on the child's part there is some natural reserve of trust and a desire to extend it. The child will keep trying until utterly depleted. In a conjoint session, a child may show trust through a willingness to come forward with a human response even when the parents are acting like stones. Thus, the child is parentified. Yet the child's response can provide the leverage needed to get a rejunctive move from the parents.

No matter how monstrous the parents' attitudes may be or how hateful and attacking the child, a therapist will only become entrapped by taking for granted that the deepest or primary level in the family is adversary. One adolescent observed that he had a terrible childhood for two reasons. His mother was a monster and he was constantly fighting with other kids. Why? "They said things about my mother." Filial resentment is secondary to wished-for filial love and existential indebtedness. The ultimate linkages of trust hinge more on accounts of merit than on emotional states of positive or negative content.

The fact that common rootedness creates an interlocking of vital interests is often obscured by divergence at the level of attitudes. Violent conflict can erupt when an adolescent challenges his parents' view of how fast he should grow up. Yet, except in the most pathological instance, all three concur that growing up is one of the child's basic welfare interests. The interweaving of convergent and divergent attitudes as the members pass through various phases of family life may actually show little about the underlying legacies of parental accountability and filial loyalty.

We cannot stress too much that, in calling for recognition of the ethical dimension, we are not engaging in moralistic judgment in any direction. Nor are we referring in any way to the noble altruistic or self-sacrificial postures that are customarily regarded as costly to the self. We wish also to stress that we are not lending weight to any process opposed to individuation. Bowen (1978) implies that "differentiation of self" can occur only in a context of responsibility to others. When Moses negotiated the Cove-

nants, he did not slip in any loopholes such as, "Provided I enjoy it," or, "Provided I asked to be born."

Legacy and the Ledger of Merit and Indebtedness

The term "legacy" has been introduced to denote the specific configuration of expectations that originate from rootedness and impinge on the offspring (Boszormenyi-Nagy, 1976). Certain basic contextual expectations convey an intrinsic imperative stemming not from the merit of the parents but from the universal implication of being born of parents. The roots of the individual's very existence become a source of systemic legacies that affect his or her personal entitlements and indebtedness. The origins are multigenerational; there is a chain of destiny anchored in every generative relationship.

In referring to personal entitlements and indebtedness, we approach the concept of ledger. In the contextual approach, ledger has to do with an accumulation of the accounts of what has been given and what is owed. We are not dealing with ledger in the sense of barter, balancing of power alignments, or behavioral contracts that specify something for her and something for him. Here, ledger is a statement about two ethical components. The first has to do with the debts and entitlements dictated by *legacy*. These may vary greatly even between two siblings; e.g., it may be imperative for one to become a success, the other to become a failure. According to the legacy of this family, the son may be entitled to approval, the daughter only to shame. Thus, the legacy may fall with gross unfairness on the two. But whatever the specific terms, they derive their weight from the fact that the children were born of the parents. The children are ethically bound to accommodate their lives somehow to their legacies.

The other ethical component of ledger has to do with accumulation of merit through *contribution to the welfare of the other*. Thus, "entitlement" may combine what is due as a parent or child and what one has come to merit. A natural mother who abandons her child may have earned no merit, yet the legacy of filial loyalty puts the child into a special ledger position vis-à-vis the mother, who still retains some entitlement. Thus, it becomes inevitable that the child's loyalty will be split between the natural and substitute parents.

The individual may pay legacy obligations only in the way he or she has been taught to pay, e.g., the beaten child may become the child-beating parent. Stierlin (1976) used the term "delegated." In that case, the person's hands may, indeed, be tied by the chains of destiny. But for those able to look, there are options that meet their own terms. Then the repayment can merge with those human strivings related to the person's own needs, wishes, and motivations. A therapist can help creatively define such options. Levinson (1978) draws attention to the range of creative options available even within the most conventional of life-styles.[4] While Levinson was not addressing himself to legacy issues, his findings suggest that the individual seeking options for legacy payments is likely to have some degree of choice.

Legacy expectations cannot be reduced to the pleasure-pain principle. They are in the realm of ethical imperatives: "I ought to do this"; "It behooves me to do this." Payment can be postponed, but refusal or failure means stagnation, loss of trust and entitlement, and the violation of the basic imperative of fairness to the merits of previous generations.

The individual's own investment in trustworthiness and fairness of relationships compels observance of legacy. A split between parents might involve only an issue of loyalty for the child. But in the case where the child observes, "We only go with my mother's side of the family," a chain of legacy is at work. If grandfather violated a cultural taboo by leaving the farm to work in the city and his son became an entrepreneur, the grandson may be caught in conflicting legacies of individual enterprise and attachment to the clan. He may spend his life in a futile pursuit of collective causes, while hating his career, no matter how successful. Or he may find creative options for fulfilling his obligations to both legacies, while keeping his own life intact, e.g., by winning recognition for his expertise on the economic development of "third world" nations.

The lineage of expectations enables (confers entitlement), but also may bind (impose debt upon) the individual in various ways. The failure or shame of the predecessors can set up the expectation of failure for the offspring. The unconscious premises may be, e.g., "I cannot respond to my wife in ways my father and grandfather did not respond to theirs"; "Even if I try to reverse it, I remain committed to doing what my parents did"; "If I fail elsewhere, I will remain available to my family"; "I will not advance trust to my husband"; "I will abandon my child"; "I will destroy myself"; "I will destroy my child"; "I cannot relate except as my parents did, and what they did was corrupt"; "I will be bad, I will be shameful."

If two spouses achieve intimacy and then lose it, a legacy dynamic would not appear to be involved in the loss. But the loss could be associated with some guilt-inducing event such as the death of a father to whom, or through whom, a debt was still owed. What had been merely a postponement now becomes an irreversible failure of repayment. The loss of intimacy can then be seen as a result.

If, however, the legacies of the marital couple are such as to leave them free to consider each other's needs, and they are not encumbered by excessive filial loyalties, the couple and their children may keep the ledger in good shape.[5]

No family member can alone judge whether the ledger is in balance. When each family member is making an honest effort to state his or her own subjective vantage point, to take into account what is said by the others, and to avoid exploiting the others, it is safe to assume that issues of real indebtedness will emerge. Only through the antithesis of such subjectively stated vantage points can anything like an "objective" balance of multilaterally-considered justice be arrived at. The subjective vantage points include factual, ethical, transactional, and psychological (perceptual-emotional) dimensions.

The ledger carries a statement of entitlement and indebtedness for each individual in the family. The parent-child relationship is asymmet-

[4]*Editors' Note.* The reader should bear in mind, however, that Levinson's research is based entirely on male samples.

[5]*Editors' Note.* Note how these legacies of "excessive filial loyalties" may emerge as conflict-laden "clauses" in Sager's (Chapter 3) third (i.e., preconscious and unconscious) level of marriage contracts.

rical in that the child's entitlement naturally exceeds its indebtedness. The imbalance gradually shifts as the child moves toward adulthood and power. But the initial asymmetry of the power context intensifies the significance of the ethical context. If parental behavior becomes exploitative, this will have a dual impact on the young child's life. Its first impact is in the present, as the child responds with tears, rage, or self-destructive behavior. Its future impact comes through defective character formation, impaired learning ability, etc. It is the impact on the future that weights the ledger more heavily. The more powerful party of the here and now who exploits that power, i.e., the adult, may eventually pay the compensatory ethical cost of "existential guilt" (Buber, 1958) and indebtedness.

In these terms, the exploitative parents are "drawing on" the child as they would draw on a bank account, instead of making the investment necessary for responsible parenthood. What they draw from the child may help to make up for what they dissipate through infinite overpayment to the generation preceding them. For this reason, though existentially guilty, they may feel very little guilt.

In the natural course of events, as a child gains in growth and power, he or she becomes increasingly accountable for taking action to preserve the ledger balance. A parent who consistently declines to claim an entitlement and persists in a pattern of overpayment may reflect, and eventually create, as much developmental detriment as one who constantly demands too much. A psychotic or delinquent member may see the reasonable request of another as an intolerable demand. This represents a collapse of accountability, unless, at a deeper level, it is the psychotic one who is better attuned to the unfairness of the long-range imbalances between the two. The therapist who ignores this possibility may never recognize his own collusion against the psychotic "patient."

It is hard to imagine a first interview or even an ordinary conversation about people that stays away from premises about fairness or implicit ledger concepts. Ledger issues permeate our daily lives and relationships, not just the Old and New Testaments. It is only our efforts at scientific theory-building that have heretofore been impermeable to these issues.

Split Loyalty

One of the most salient points of connection between individual and relational theory, and the point of greatest relational tension, occurs when one person becomes involved with a legacy of split filial loyalty, that is, when the parents set up conflicting claims so that the child can offer loyalty to one parent only at the cost of his or her loyalty to the other. Whereas the term "loyalty conflict" indicates a breach between a trustworthy filial loyalty and a competing peer (spouse) loyalty, "split loyalty" connotes a fragmented primary loyalty or trust base.

A split between parents is not in itself the issue. The fact that a child seems closer to one parent or the other does not have to cause concern. The issue is the unconditional nature of the child's involvement in the split. The clinical clues may be subtle, e.g., mother "explains" father to the children. Or they may be more blatant. One parent confides to the children about the other. Or, the parents lack sexual contact and draw the children in as libidinal substitutes. Or, mother and father engage in angry, hungry outbursts and the child takes on the job of calming and feeding them. But the child cannot, it does not work, so what remains to the child is a more and more desperate use of symptoms to bring them together. An anorexic girl reported a dream in which her parents were lying near death on adjoining gravesites. In the time it would take her to feed one, the other would die.

A heavy impact on the child occurs when, for instance, the mother and her parents are aligned against the father, and the child is expected to join this alignment. Thus, the child is charged with being loyal to one parent at the cost of his or her loyalty to the other. But the child cannot give up the commitment to father's side. "I can and have to side with my father." (The dilemma for the child would be the same, of course, if the alignment were against the mother.) This impact gets deeper because the child's commitment includes not only father but also the excluded paternal grandparents. Then for the child the question may become, "Which way can I move—other than saying, 'I don't care'?" This is a costly thing. Thirty years later, when father is dead and mother is suffering bereavement and illness, the grown child's response to the mother is still, "I don't care." This is one way of balancing the loyalties, by punishing the surviving parent. Another cost is a crippling ambivalence to the grown child's spouse and children. Therapeutic leverage occurs not by highlighting the ambivalence toward each parent but by centering on the split in loyalties. In concrete terms, "When you have to stand up for father against mother, what do you do with that? That is a tremendous trap—what do you do about it?" At this point, where the triangle connects, the individual suffers the greatest tension. It is emotionally costly for the young child to play the rejunctive role of: "If you are going to take me away, then I am going to stay with Mommy; if she is going to take me away, then I am going to stay with you."

Invisible Loyalty

We conceive of filial loyalty as a universal and central relational dynamic, originating from both rootedness and parental merit and taking either overt or covert forms. One of its overt forms is the sometimes deeply anguished efforts of adults to keep their lines open to aging and difficult parents. In its covert forms, it may provide a far more powerful leverage for pathology, and for resistance to health, than has yet been fully realized.

Laing (1965) and Stierlin (1976) have described the mystification of the child. The child may have no way of getting access to direct knowledge of the multigenerational ledger terms to which his or her own life has been subordinated. In developmental terms, the child is vulnerable. He or she may "buy into" the expectation that the debt to the parents is endless and that its payment takes priority over every other human concern. The parents' unwillingness to accept "installment" payments on the indebtedness can make the obligations boundless. The covert linkages may be infinite, though unconsciously perpetrated. If, for instance, mother scorns weakness, the son's fear of weakness may repeatedly immobilize his efforts. To give up the fear would seem unconsciously to be a repudia-

tion of mother's priorities. Or, if mother is an obsessive housekeeper, the grown daughter, following a rupture with her parents, may erupt into a housecleaning binge of manic proportions that alienates her husband. Here, the intrapsychic process could be one of unconscious incorporation; the ethical dynamic is that of invisible loyalty. Neither of these dynamics excludes the other or can be reduced to the other. For purposes of therapeutic leverage, we consider the latter to be the more inclusive.

If there is a destructive stagnation going on in the family, i.e., extreme parental disengagement from relational accountability, a child whose trust has not died and whose human concern is still very much alive may go to desperate lengths to exert some kind of leverage against that process. Such action might eventually take the form of anorexia or of acting-out in the community. Whether by recurrent shoplifting or by refusing to eat, the child is making an intrinsic loyalty contribution. He or she is forcing into the open an issue of human balance. Meanwhile, if the parents continue to play an evasive game, they can draw the blood out of the one who is human enough to bring in the issue.

The therapist of a delinquent boy repeatedly threatened him with removal from the community. Finally, the therapist announced, "I am giving you one more chance." From the vantage point of relational ethics, it would have been equally correct to say that the adolescent was giving the therapist one more chance to realize what so desperately needed attention. The opposite model, of collusion with child against parent, would have been no more productive. But it is not colluding with the child to acknowledge the ethical merit of the fact that his actions stem from his own distress over what is happening to his family.

The "Revolving Slate"

Plays, novels, professional writings, and daily experience all call attention to an extraordinary aspect of the human condition. This is the fateful mandate of legacy that patterns shall be repeated, against unavailing struggle, from one generation to the next; e.g., a young man was deciding against parenthood because, "I see too much of my father in myself, and I don't want to pass it on." An ambivalent father abandons his wife, who, in turn, abandons their child. The father rescues the child, then abandons his second wife and the child along with her. The stepmother is the only one with whom the child can have a relationship of trust. To exonerate his mother, the child can only put his father down: "You are no better than she is." To exonerate either father or mother, he can only put his stepmother down: "You are no better than they are." To exonerate her, he can only put down his therapist: "You are no better than any of us." Much more is involved here than an unconscious displacement of hostility. The child is caught in a vicious self-destructive chain reaction. He tries to balance the ledger by substituting father as a monster instead of mother, and so on. As the child matures, his vindictive behavior may extend to his own spouse and children. This intergenerational linkage of substitutive balancing is ethically invalid. The child is caught in a revolving slate of vindictive behavior.

To behave otherwise would require the grown child to step out of the context of his generative rootedness. Consciously, he may struggle to give his children a better life. But the unconscious, binding premise is: "How can I treat my children better than my father treated me, without being disloyal to my father?" So, while there are grounds for existential guilt, the child turned parent may actually feel little guilt over his unfairness to his own children.

We hold that *this "revolving slate" aspect of invisible filial loyalties is the chief factor in family and marital dysfunction.* The grown child of the stagnant family will be disengaged from the ongoing task of weighing what is fair in his or her relationships to spouse, children, and significant others. The disengagement may take symptomatic forms such as contempt, hatred, avoidance, coldness, indifference, or cruelty. A 20-year old girl broke off repeatedly from her fiance. At age ten, she had given the following TAT story:

David and Jane just got married. When Dave came home, Jane wouldn't talk to him. Dave said, "Aren't you going to talk to me?"
"No."
"Why not?"

"My sister just ran away." So everybody went out to look for her.

This projective fragment provides a clue to what was becoming apparent in the clinical situation ten years later. Indeed, the girl presented herself as immature, fixated at a preoedipal level, etc. But from the contextual point of view, she was bound to a legacy which compelled her to preserve her commitment to her family at the cost of new relationships. Helping her to face the intrinsically unfair expectations of this "revolving slate" would offer the best chance for therapeutic leverage.

Liberation from the revolving cycle of destructive action can take place only through discovery of resources of trustworthiness. If they are to get free, individuals must discover rejunctive ways of preserving loyalty and exonerating the generations before. If society does not illuminate such a path, the therapist can make the attempt. In the previously described case of the abandoned son, it is essential first to somehow help him reach the realization that, however deep their failures, neither father nor mother was a monster. Therefore, it is not necessary to call either a monster to exonerate the other, or to make of oneself or one's child a monster in order to exonerate both. To restore whatever is good and human in the images of the parents; to find new, more positive ways of making appropriate loyalty payments; to move on toward the reinvestment of other aspects of his life experience with trust—these are almost unbearably difficult tasks for the son, and the therapist may wonder if he or she has the right to call for such an undertaking. Yet the son will be the main beneficiary of the effort; he is not just performing a noble altruistic mission.

Exploitation

In the broadest sense, the term "exploitation" may cover most of what is ethically stagnant or "pathological" between people. If people's actions lack merit, there is an inequitability of give and take; then trustworthiness of relationship breaks down, interactions become ethically stagnant or "pathological," and there is no support left for future acts of merit. When trust has deteriorated, intention is diverted from the effort to balance the ledger in universal terms of human decency and concern. When a wife complains that her husband is incapable of intimacy, she is usually referring not only to sex but also to an absence of the everyday actions that are indicative of genuine concern for her and the children's interests. Instead, each of the family members may be acting on partly unconscious convictions associated with lack of trust, e.g., "I did not receive trust from my parents, therefore I cannot advance it to you." Or, "Because of my legacy, I owe in an alien coin whose value is in success, or failure, or abandonment, or destruction." These interpersonally validated convictions may lead to a vast array of exploitative arrangements. Some are transient games; others warp the growth prospects of the family and sap its health.

We collude to the extent that we regard as "normal" the pattern of the commuting father who believes he is "living his life by the book," doing what is expected of a man and keeping his accounts in balance when he goes out to an untrustworthy competitive world and spends himself finding money. In turn, he expects his wife and children to feed him trust and emotions. Such a father may be acutely uncomfortable with any attempt to hold him accountable in human terms. "You're asking me to change the rules!" Instead, on the ground that he can apply his business rules at home, he confines his effort to an intrusive and accusing scrutiny of every detail of his children's behavior. If his "book" compels him to withhold and demand too much, his daughter can become anorexic.

Interlocking need templates

The husband and wife may be joined in collusive arrangements through their "interlocking need templates" (Boszormenyi-Nagy, 1962, 1965). The wife who complains that her husband is incapable of intimacy may be acting to forestall him. The wife's obsession with her husband's coldness or anger enables her to disown whatever craziness she has. They may be locked into a tightly over-utilized relationship in which each serves as the monstrous part of the other.[6] They

---

[6]*Editors' Note.* Again, we are struck by the relevance of Boszormenyi-Nagy and Ulrich's comments to Sager's (Chapter 3) emphasis on the ways in which bilaterally internally inconsistent needs, or "contractual clauses," lead to marital conflict.

can act out this substitutive victimization for years. One may then go under. They may try to salvage the relationship by drawing on their child, whose burden may then become enormous.

While providing a reservoir of trust, the child is vulnerable to the family's definition of what is fair. This gives the parents a wide margin for exploitation, much of which can go unnoticed by outsiders. The most neatly tended suburban house can contain a jungle. The one who appears to the world as the "good sibling," meeting all outward criteria of health, may be the worst exploited and the most vulnerable. When social agencies do become involved with a family, they may collude in the scapegoating of the "bad" child, whose "badness" may be the final move of any family member to bind the chaos.

Scapegoating or substitutive blaming

In the case of the scapegoated child, one or both parents may be engaging in projective identification, dumping the legacy of badness on the child instead of on themselves or each other. Even when a daughter is in the very act of defending mother from father's wrath, mother's intervention may be designed to bring his wrath down on the daughter instead. This sort of thing gives the parents enough relief so they can survive themselves and each other. But the child, who gets blame instead of thanks for her devotion, is placed in a crippling bind.

In such an instance, projection is not the only mechanism at work. The circumstances of relational unfairness and exploitation are factual. The parents see themselves as entitled to draw from the child because they are engaged in some kind of eternal effort at overpayment elsewhere. Usually this is directed toward their parents. In many cases, it has been the guilt of immigrants who did not find the streets paved with gold and could not make restitution to the relatives whom they had left behind. The scapegoated child finally learns that his or her only remaining source of leverage is in the manipulation of the parents' guilt.

Parentification

It is in the child's interest to have a good parent. If the parent falls short, the child will try to make up the deficit. Thus, the legacy of filial loyalty tends to make the child parentified. In a healthy family, to the extent a child supplements the parents' resources, this can be an avenue of growth and enrichment, e.g., the child who comforts mother when mother has suffered a loss. Yet, when parents are set to draw heavily on a child, its whole life can get sucked into the captive devotion to becoming a parental figure. There is not much chance for normal growth. The damaging feature is not the transactional reversal of adult managerial role performance, but the unilateral depletion of the child's trust resources.

To an outsider, the child might appear narcissistic, unwilling to yield its place at center stage. To the child, however, being in the center may represent an intrinsic command, to which it loyally responds. Or, the child's oedipal strivings may mask the underlying care. As one six-year-old put it, "I am an overconcerned child."

The parentified child may be the "good sibling" who sacrifices all self-strivings so as to preserve the family balance. Abrupt collapse during adolescence may terminate the effort. At the other extreme is the "black sheep," a psychotic, delinquent, or otherwise failing member without whom the parents could not survive. Or, a son may drive himself to win glittering but empty successes to dispel the gloom of his parents. One result is predictable: Unless the pattern can be resolved, the parentified child will not be able to give freely to spouse or children. In therapy, one of the first steps toward deparentification consists in helping the family to acknowledge the trust advances drawn from the parentified child.

Relational corruption

The term "corruption" cannot be used precisely, but no other word appears to serve for the quality that sometimes surfaces in close relationships. It is clearly discernible during a treatment session when one person is lured into giving a caring response and the other cuts it down in an elusive, slippery, mocking way. This kind of barbed hollowness may be the person's usual response to others. In terms of relational ethics, it may signify a person so bound to a legacy of familial corruption that he is entitled to be unfair with anyone. The original traumatic injustices that led the family to this state may long since have been obscured. Now, it is a choice between being corrupt or really deserting the roots of one's whole humanity. It is hard to conceive of the cost of such a desertion.

We submit that, in all of these aspects of exploitation, neither an exclusively intrapsychic nor a transactional-systemic model can get to the fundamental issue. This is the balance of fairness between people, the collapse of trust that comes with the failure of that balance, and the myriad sequelae of the collapse.

Family Typology via the Concept of Stagnation

Stagnation is the world of ethically invalid attempts at solving life's problems. "The only one you owe anything is yourself," as if self-realization could occur without responsibility. Or, there may be a hollow effort at materially "right" ledger-balancing: Father will provide the house and station wagon, mother will provide the meals and make the drapes, while the children will clean the garage and bring home honor grades that show good money potential, all of it without awareness of what anyone's basic life interests might be. Other forms of stagnation involve unilateral or inequitable pseudo-solutions.

The following typology is determined partly by criteria inside the psychology of the participant individuals and partly by criteria relating to multigenerational chains of loyalty, legacy, and merit ledgers. A fuller account of forms of relational stagnation appears in Boszormenyi-Nagy and Spark (1973).

The child of constantly battling parents may feel hurt, rejected, overstimulated, or depressed. On a relational commitment level, however, the child will tend to feel obligated to save the parents and their marriage from the threat of destruction. The child may overtly fail in all outside social involvements in order to safeguard loyal adherence to the family, whether through psychosis, school phobia, delinquency, etc. Such failure may represent the child's loyal execution of the mandates of legacy.

Loyalty to the excessive expectations of one's family of origin may preclude deep commitment to anyone in a close relationship and lead to an unconscious freezing of the inner self. This successful martyrdom may, at the same time, give the martyr a controlling influence in the family of origin.

On leaving the family through selection of a partner or activity that falls far short of one's own intellectual and social capacities and is unacceptable by family standards, disloyalty to the family is only temporarily offset by sacrificial giving to the handicapped mate or the menial task. Likewise, a marital couple may collusively share their denial of the importance of ties with the two families of origin. In a mixed religious marriage, the spouses may give promise of unusually stable loyalty commitments to each other, as though both parties, by becoming outcasts from their ingroups, could form a new ingroup. Such promises, however, may mask their unresolved individuation within the families of origin, and the new commitment may be to a commonly shared "cause" rather than to each other. The more passionately the family of origin rejects the traitorous member, the more likely it is that he or she will remain tied to the early loyalty system, albeit in the form of negative loyalty, i.e., by remaining tightly bound in the posture of opposition, thereby posing an example of that which is unacceptable to the family. The disloyal member may hold the rest of the family together at his or her expense.

Such occurrences as self-defeating choice of a partner, endless fighting, sexual dysfunction, etc., tend to amount to a functional attitude of rejection of the mate to underline the invisible loyalty to one's family of origin. Even when other dynamics are operating, we believe that this ethical dynamic influences the outcome.

Long-suppressed and subjectively justified anger about being given up for adoption or abandoned in other ways by parents may erupt through displacement upon adoptive parents or a mate.

In some instances, avoidance of growth in family relationships may be masked by the overt personal achievements of one family member. The achiever and the psychiatrically ill spouse or sibling represent two components of the same homeostatic system of stagnation.

Finally, the "well sibling," who, it appears, has successfully escaped the pathogenic system, may often be caught in a guilt-laden paralyzed commitment to overavailability. He or she may be commissioned to take care of the entire fam-

ily's needs for manifest reason and organization, thus allowing the others to enjoy their regressive gratifications in safety.

Clinical manifestations

Stagnation can be expressed in many ways: "We never fight" may conceal the ledger more effectively than, "We always fight." A father may sum up a daughter's shoplifting episode with, "Well, now that she has learned her lesson, we can close the book on it." Or, "I wash my hands of this. From now on she can do as she pleases." Either way, he closes the book on the question of what is owing to the child. The same is done by the father of the delinquent adopted son who says, "I don't expect anything of him, and I don't expect any thanks of him. I just hope we can make it until he gets out."

If an adolescent says, "I give up," this can signify a realistic, if painful, acceptance of parental limitations. Or it can mean that his fingers have finally slipped off the last rung of the ladder of trust and hope, and his moves from now on will be dominated by the wish for escape.

Treating oneself or another as a clinical specimen is a guarantee of stagnation. "That's just the way I am, I was always like that," disclaims any active effort at engagement in a rejunctive process. Or, "My wife is paranoid"; "My child is lazy"; "My husband is a workaholic." This labeling brings live give and take to a halt. The expert, of course, can assist by making the diagnosis official.[7]

"Let's just forget about the past and get on with the present," is a blanket denial of the ledger, as if the mortgage could be burned as soon as the furniture was moved in. Here, too, the expert is sometimes willing to assist.

Stagnation vs autonomy

In the extreme case, when ethical stagnation takes the form of a total rupture of parent-child

---

[7]*Editors' Note.* Note the similarity of Boszormenyi-Nagy and Ulrich's view with what Hurvitz (1970) calls "terminal" vs. "instrumental" hypotheses family members use to explain each other's (or their own) behavior. Terminal hypotheses interpret behavior, meanings or feelings in such ways that nothing can be done to change the existing situation, while instrumental hypotheses offer the basis for some action that may be taken. Note also how a behaviorist deals with such stagnating labels by avoiding trait attributions and requiring operational definitions of global constructs.

relationships, the unresolved issues can become enormously costly in terms of the autonomous growth of all parties to the break. If it is a parent who has left, the child will never give up the search for the parent or the hope of restoring balance. As Tessman (1978) discovered in her study of the children of parting parents, the paradigm of loss and mourning does not fit here. The parent is not dead. An attempt to extrapolate from psychoanalytic theory to custody issues (Goldstein, Freud and Solnit, 1973) has led to the notion that a child can relinquish one parent without traumatic effect. Relational theory, supported by massive clinical evidence, points in the opposite direction. To assume that the child can relinquish the parent is to prescribe stagnation and failure of autonomy for the child.

In his theory of differentiation, Bowen (1978) makes "immaturity" a central concept. We suggest that the concept of immaturity may itself be differentiated. In many cases, the dynamic is not one of deprivation or emotional overinvolvement but rather the ethical dynamics of covertly substitutive entitlement. If one has ceased to try to collect from the original debtor, the result may be stagnation, and the stagnant one may seem very immature, indeed, as he or she presses demands on substitute debtors. Conversely, it is the claim of the contextual approach that there is a dynamic linkage between steps toward differentiation and an engagement in the process of balancing one's debts and entitlements.

Implications for the Well-Functioning Family

Imbalances of fairness are inevitable. The criterion of functioning is the flexibility displayed in the multilateral oscillation of the imbalances. Parental responsibility is considered the essential anchoring point, while the child's accountability increases as its capacity to reciprocate increases. Role definitions are arrived at through a sensitive engagement in the intrinsic fairness of relationship. Tendencies toward exploiting and scapegoating are noticed and corrected. Problem-solving occurs through intention to achieve ledger balancing by honest give and take.

Trustworthy relationships function to en-

hance autonomy in problem-solving. Such relationships increase all members' entitlements, including the entitlement to take responsible action on one's own. This requires, of course, that no one has been so indulged or deprived as to lack the capacity to become autonomous. It means that the legacy is such as to permit autonomy. And it means that there is no hidden ledger of unpaid debts, real or imaginary, that keeps some family members in bondage to others. Failure of autonomy is a signal to the therapist to explore for those conditions and to take the kinds of enabling actions we describe later in this chapter.

The family life-cycle is characterized by open negotiation of transitions such as adolescence, separation, marriage, and death. Each change brings new demands, both for new commitments and new freedom of choice. Ideally, the changing loyalty commitments are negotiated with due awareness of legacy expectations.

Affection and sexuality are natural concomitants of an open and reciprocal relationship. However, *it is the essential tenet of contextual therapy that the capacity for affection, warmth, closeness, etc., cannot be preserved if no honest effort is being made to balance the ledger.*

In the well-functioning family, separateness does not contradict intimacy. Genuine autonomy can be reached only through consideration of relational equitability. This leaves room for dependencies, which should be reciprocal so they do not become exploitative.

Without actively extending concern for the multigenerational extended family, the crucial issues of ledger, loyalty, and legacy could be neither understood nor resolved. Yet, family relationship must be neither so tight that flexibility of outside contact is impaired, nor so stagnant that outside contacts serve only as an escape.

Symptom Development

The breakdown of trustworthiness of relationship through disengagement from multilateral caring and accountability sets the stage for symptom development. The kind of symptom to appear is determined by many factors, e.g., constitutional factors, sibling rank, identification with a parent or relative, and vicissitudes such as the death of an older sibling. To these we add: imperatives of loyalty and legacy; limitation of freedom for engagement in friendship, sexuality, or achievement of any kind; the nature of the stagnation; the areas of relational corruption. The role of the "identified patient" includes making a contribution by trying to break through the stagnation.

Pathology can also be asymptomatic, e.g., the "good child" who is parentified. At times, the most overburdened, depleted, parentified one shows symptoms; other times, the symptoms appear in the most resourceful. Those who are engaged in trustworthy accountability function best for the time being. But whether symptomatic or not, nobody stands outside the demands of loyalty, legacy, and ledger.

Intrapsychic Aspects

We conclude this discussion of the contextual orientation with a note on our present understanding of psychodynamics vis-à-vis contextual theory. In our view, the contextual is the more comprehensive structure, encompassing but not superseding the other. At the same time, there seems to be a discontinuity between the two. The obvious difference in therapeutic approach is that one uses the patient-therapist relationship as the therapeutic tool, whereas the other seeks to work within the context of the original relationships, and transference elements may intrude into this effort. In terms of assessment of what is happening in treatment, we have already noted a number of points where it appeared that psychodynamics and the dynamics of legacy and loyalty were operating side by side. One of the most significant immediate theoretical linkages is that which exists between the relational concept of trustworthiness and the individual psychological emphasis on basic trust as a keystone of development.

Material from dreams, projective tests, etc., can provide clues to the relational process, but only as experienced from one side. It would require a degree of sophistication and new language we now lack to correlate the projective materials of two related persons in multilateral balance or ledger terms.

The contextual approach does, of course, take affects, drives, defenses, ego states, transference elements, etc., into account. The effort to reopen issues of trust may provoke responses such as rage or despair, without acknowledgment of which the contextual therapist will not proceed far. Indeed, such responses may be intensified by the contextual approach because they are experienced in vivo rather than in the substitutive context of the therapeutic transference.[8]

In our framework, affects have to be utilized as *contextual indicators* for therapeutic strategy. They are usually associated with ledger issues and serve as signals that those issues are present. Rage at one's wife may be prompted by a revolving slate dynamic; the husband rages even while grieving that he cannot help his parents because they will not take the help he offers. His grief may mean there is still some possibility of open loyalty and caring for his parents.

CONTEXTUAL THERAPY

Method and Purpose

It is our proposition that the contextual approach offers the most direct and economical route to the goals of autonomy and satisfaction for the person. We are daily testing this proposition in clinical practice. If we are correct, an hour spent working on basic dynamic leverages of relational trustworthiness can do more than hours spent unraveling symptomatic difficulties between spouses or even pursuing associations and dreams.[9]

The goal of contextual therapy is to enable the participants to take rejunctive action. The approach aims at activity of the highest degree,

---

[8]*Editors' Note.* Despite the internal consistency of Boszormenyi-Nagy and Ulrich's view, there exists no empirical evidence of the superiority of family therapy conducted "in vivo" vs. that conducted in substitutive relationships. See Skynner's (Chapter 2) discussion of the power of "substitutive family therapy" for a contrasting view. In any case, Boszormenyi-Nagy and Ulrich's hypothesis is quite testable empirically.

[9]*Editors' Note.* Again, another highly researchable view which might be examined by studying whether contextual family therapy achieves equivalent (or superior) clinical outcomes to family therapy based on "substitutive" treatment relationships.

in that the therapist leads the family members toward a self-motivated search of relational integrity. Whether they talk to each other or to the therapist, they are guided toward working on their own relational commitments and balances of fairness. This is a many-faceted task. To begin, we will describe the essential methods and purposes of contextual family therapy.

The therapist encourages the partners to open up a multilateral perspective of fairness. This means clearly asserting their own view of things and beginning to hear the other sides. As each item of information about anybody comes into view, the therapist may ask, e.g., "When that happened, how did you see your father acting? How would he explain it, how would he think about what you did? How would your sister think about it? How would you have wanted it different?"

This means that attention is broadened to include the original context, the roots that never became a static "past history." The therapist may ask how everybody thinks that what he or she is talking about now relates to something that has a timeless reference. Or, "What comes to my mind is your mother when she refused to accept any gifts from your father. How do you relate to that?" In other words, relational roots and ethical balances remain active guidelines for therapeutic strategy and course of action.

The therapist guides and makes connections by being interested and curious. But the focus is not simply on cognitive exploration or insight. From the outset, regardless of symptom type, family developmental stage, treatment motivation, etc., *the goal is always one of getting all partners to shift their intentions in the direction of a rejunctive effort.* In this sense, their first reluctant struggle to overcome their own ambivalence enough to look at another side of something represents a shift of intention. At this point, active therapeutic engagement has begun.

One can conceive of rejunctive actions as following a gradient. At the beginning, there may be only the shift of intention, the beginnings of a willingness to imagine what the other persons might think from their side of the scene. Further along, if the significant other is not available to share the therapeutic process, there might be a letter, a telephone call, a visit with the inten-

tion of beginning to reopen a relational exploration. Later, there might be more substantive exchanges. The therapist has such a gradient in mind when he or she asks the person to consider: "I do wonder what more you can do at that point. Your mother calls you, but she doesn't hear what you're saying. What do you think about this? What else can you do?" As the person responds to this encouragement, the therapist endorses the response. Although it may sometimes be the therapist's task to point out the risks of inaction, it is not necessary to criticize people for what they have so far been unable to do. The goal is to enable the family members to gain trust from one another's increasingly trustworthy input.

The gradient may never lift anyone as high as he or she would wish. Family members sometimes report that it has been years since they tried to have an open conversation with a parent and the result then was a disaster. The parent would only lay blame, stir guilt, or withdraw. The person may ask: "What can be accomplished now? How can I change such a parent? Why should I hurt myself again?" The goal can be spelled out, not in terms of how to change the parent, but in terms of what the person is willing to invest in making the attempt to change the relationship, whether this attempt is successful or not. As a wife said after her husband's offer to go to his parents' home for Passover for the first time in years had been rejected, "At least now he can live with himself."

In some respects, this therapeutic approach may appear similar to the ego-supportive work of individual psychotherapy. The distinction is that the therapist offers support to the patient not for all aspects of self-serving effort but specifically for the actions that, through consideration of relational merits, will elicit the remaining resources of trust and concern.

The therapist may use self-disclosure to the degree that this facilitates movement toward re-engagement. It is limited to what is appropriate in the sense that it does not arouse anxiety or embarrassment.

From the outset, the therapeutic task is set up as one that belongs to the family members. As past and present items come up for review, it is the son or daughter, for instance, who has to figure out how father would explain what he did, or else actually to go and ask father about it. Thus, instead of prescribing the right kinds of transactions, the therapist holds everyone selectively accountable for a multilateral perspective. This is, in effect, a "practice in accountability" for self and others, leading up to the responsibility for dealing with the vicissitudes in the person's total life situation, including the future interests of his or her offspring.

As one person explores the perspectives of the various family members whose lives have impinged significantly on his or hers, the therapist can build, and revise, an estimate of the legacies, invisible loyalties, and ledger balances. The therapist will guide all partners toward those rejunctive tasks that are needed and available for the restoration of some kind of ledger balance. This job has to get quite specific. An analogy might sometimes be finding the "window in the sky" through which a space shot must pass if it is to attain a stable orbit. The question is, how can any person design a way to relate to the other as a human being, on terms that may for the first time in his or her life be acceptable to the self and still carry value for the other? If such a point of ethical joining is found, there will, of course, be later deviations from it. But as long as there is a possibility of finding this point of convergence, there is still hope for restoring a degree of trustworthiness in the relationship. If the attempt fails, the therapist will have to help people find reserves of strength to weather the failure. The therapist needs a solid conviction of the value of trying again and again with better and better plans for action.

Going to the original context and enabling each person to get some kind of mastery of the disjunctive issues has a quite specific aim. *This aim is to loosen the chains of invisible loyalty and legacy, so each person can give up symptomatic behaviors and explore new options.*

Application of these basic premises to particular situations, e.g., the dying or dead parent, the dying child, suicide, etc., will require of the therapist concern and specialized knowledge and experience of the meaning of these events to all of the family members involved in them, including the ledger issues that may remain unfaced when death removes a family member.

Once some momentum has been acquired in the therapy sessions, the universal hunger for trust will lead the members to want to return, although in the extreme case their resistance may be too great to permit them to do so. It may not be long before their efforts with family members outside the therapy sessions will begin to produce a feedback effect, so that the therapist begins to be aware that he or she is, in fact, treating an extended family.

Based on his or her conviction about the basic rules of contextual therapy, the therapist is actively guiding from the beginning. As trust deepens, the therapist can be more openly confronting. Once the family members have adopted a positive attitude toward the goals of re-engagement and rejunction, the need arises to explore concrete behavioral options toward achieving them. But since from the outset the participants' role has been one of an exercise in responsibility, the therapist need make no major shift in role as termination approaches.

Therapy is not time-limited. The therapist takes no rigid position about how far the family can go, or how fast, toward rejunctive goals. Once re-engagement in the fundamental dynamics of trust has occurred, they have reached their initial goal. The point of termination that is most desirable is the point at which the family members have restored enough trustworthiness so they are willing to undertake further rebalancing efforts on their own. Then the family members and the therapist may more or less simultaneously arrive at a sense that enough work has been done.

In practice, families sometimes terminate as soon as they have achieved symptom relief. This could be a "bad" termination in the sense that disjunctive implications for this and future generations remain unaltered. But an honest facing of not pushing beyond where the family wants to stop is preferable to the therapist's taking over responsibility and setting terminal points for the family's progress. Even a vigorous early refusal to continue treatment could be a "good" termination if it means that someone has faced the issues, recognized the ethical implications, and reorganized their attitudes toward children and spouse accordingly.

There is no typical length of treatment. It can vary from one or two sessions to two or three years, or more. It is usually weekly or biweekly, but it can be less frequent.

Who Sees Whom

Often in this brief account of method and purpose, we have focused on the person as if there might be only one present in the therapy session. This can be the case. Contextual therapy is an orientation in which theoretical and clinical aspects are closely meshed and rely for their effectiveness on the commitment of the therapist to the multilateral contract. This orientation has nothing to do with how many people are seen at once. Whether the arrangements are individual, conjoint, concurrent, three-generational, etc., depends on their optimal utility for rejunctive movement.

For the purposes of family therapy, we consider it desirable to begin with all family members present, but we would seldom insist that a meeting of the full family is absolutely required. The decision about whom to see belongs to the therapist and will, of course, to some degree reflect the style of the therapist. "Optimal utility" means bringing together as many people as can work with one another toward restoration of trustworthiness. For example, the legitimate privacy of an adolescent requires consideration. The shame of one parent's origins should not be expected to be divulged in the presence of the vindictively inclined spouse.

At any time, any family member may be seen singly if there is something that requires discussion in private. The privacy of what was discussed may be preserved; it is not our intention as family therapists to dissolve all privacies, and we no longer push for the unconditional disclosure of all "secrets". Automatic "confidentiality" of everything covered in separate sessions, however, is seen as inconsistent with the multilateral contractual context of therapy.

If a couple comes for marital treatment, this is in no way considered a separate modality. Since parenting is an essential component of marriage, the therapist will at the outset make it clear that he or she expects to include the children, if any, in the treatment contract if not the process, insofar as the children's and parents' interests require this to be done. If there are no children, the work is done in the context of responsibility for potential parenting and consideration of the spouse's legacies of filial loyalty. If the couple does not intend to have children, their parenting responsibility toward their own parents and all those who invest them with trust becomes the issue.

Likewise, if an individual asks for treatment and has not yet given any consideration to involving the family, we do not see this in terms of a separate treatment modality. Even if the therapist is working with individuals, new explanations for individual symptoms and their recurrence will emerge as the symptoms are put into a relational context. But far more is involved than good history-taking or a cognitive understanding of the connections between symptoms and context. If the therapist is committed to the multilateral approach, the essence of the implicit and explicit therapeutic contract is to benefit not only the person in treatment but also the others to whom that individual is linked through interlocking basic welfare interests. Some people immediately and intuitively appreciate this approach. For those who want to know why they are being asked to talk about their families, the therapist can state the conviction that consideration of the others' interests is integral to the approach. In the examination of legacy and balance aspects, the issue is not just, "what is good for you," but, "what rejunctive impact can your actions have upon the welfare of those with whom you have intergenerational or other deep relational ties?" Thus, multilateral contractual ethics are not simply a set of cognitive guidelines. They engage every individual at the level of action and concern for the interests of the other members, while to the therapist they provide the strategic master plan for all therapeutic tactics and the basis for leverage. From this vantage point, *to suggest a combination of "individual psychotherapy plus family therapy" would be simply a contradiction in terms, since any individual work is done in the same context as if more than one person were being seen.*

Since we regard mutual accountability and individuation as corollaries, there is no attempt at an artificial "cutting off" of family members connected through shared rootedness. The multilateral perspective requires a single therapeutic contract for the family. This means either one therapist or co-therapists who can operate together on the same contract with no contradictions. We do not, for example, seek to restore a school-phobic child to functioning without regard for the mother who may decompensate if the child leaves the house.

The principal advantage of co-therapists is that one can learn from the vantage point of the other, especially if they are of opposite sexes. The decision to use co-therapists may also turn on practical considerations, e.g., if one family member needs separate sessions, one therapist may not be able to schedule them. The possible disadvantage is that, unless the co-therapists are working from the same contextual premises, they may reinforce disjunctive efforts by differing family members.

Assessment of Dysfunction

Through one or more members, the capacity for engagement in an accountable, i.e., trustworthy, context is explored. Thus, assessment follows from the therapist's expectation of courageous facing of the balances of fairness. The exploration is conducted at all levels available to the therapist. These include the intrapsychic, behavioral, transactional, etc., but the relational criteria of balanced reciprocity transcend the other levels. Any methods such as tests, questionnaires, tasks, etc., can be useful if they serve the purposes of a multidirected therapeutic investment through better understanding of all members as individuals also. We do not set up a separate category of "evaluation" interviews; assessment of trust resources occurs as part of the initial efforts to restore trust.

What We Don't Do; What We Do Instead

Pointing out the inherent imbalances of fairness has inherent risks, because the person will either reject the idea or wait for the therapist to work on it. Nor is it the therapist's task to decide the ultimate justice of the issue of why mother, father, or grandparent behaved as they did. The therapist makes the members accountable for asserting the merits of their own positions regarding the fairness of each side. *There is no relabeling; it is not the therapist's task to try to put things in a better light. Relabeling belongs to a prescriptive rather than elicitory approach to therapy. Our aim is to elicit the*

family members' thinking about and recognition of unused trust resources.[10]

The therapist guides but does not take a rigid position on any issue. If the therapist gets rigid, the family members can leave him or her holding the bag. Instead, the task is to apply multidirectional partiality, a flexible, sequential side-taking for everybody's entitlements and also their obligations. However, the contextual therapist should be persistent about the basic principle of rejunctive work to be done, even if he allows for moratoria as needed by the family members.

We do not prescribe tasks on a transactional or power basis. While recognizing much that is systemic, we do not follow the premise that manipulation of the transactional or communicational system, without effort by individuals to be accountable for themselves and for their relationships, will bring lasting change. If the person cannot discover what to do, the therapist may suggest that the person consider an action, or the therapist may encourage action, e.g., "Is there any way I can help you to get this done?" The underlying assumption is that the essence of therapy is action leading to a balance of individuation and fair accountability. The more experienced and skillful the therapist, the more he or she can help with options for personal action.

If a parent's failure to help a child results from honest lack of knowledge, there is nothing to prevent the therapist from instructing the parent. But the context is not one of prescribing for anyone how to "manage" anyone else, in the sense of using or possessing. Instead, it is to help with a deeper commitment to learning about multilaterality and equitability of the parent-child relationship.[11]

---

[10]*Editors' Note.* By way of contrast, the most predominant use of relabeling occurs in the various "strategic" family therapies discussed by Stanton (Chapter 10). But note that the purposes of relabeling are quite varied and are not always to "put things in a better light."

[11]*Editors' Note.* Behavioral family therapists, by contrast, seem to generally view (assume) all such skill deficits as deriving from a lack of knowledge, hence, "honest." While we consider the behavioral view rather naive, it is still unclear *how* the therapist should determine the "honesty" of a knowledge/skill deficit. In any case, by whatever implicit criteria a therapist makes such a judgment, his/her methods of therapy will be enormously influenced by his judgments in this realm.

It should be clear by now that the goal is not to explore pathology. If one person appears to have done something sadistic, the focus is not on the sadism but on how this action affected the balances between people and where the resources are for building increased trust.

Generally speaking, the conventional kind of interpretation is not sufficient. Making accountable is different from making aware. Rarely are the members of a family seeking help ready to be candidates for analytic therapy. At best, unilateral interpretations may only interrupt the momentum of the dialogue. Since the focus is on the original, rather than the substitutive therapeutic context, there is no primary need to deal with derivative symbolic materials. Likewise, the focus is not on "What are your needs?", which can reveal a bottomless pit. Instead, "What do you want, what do you want to do about it, what should you do about it?" Nor is there any implication that once people have achieved insight, they are on their own with it outside the therapist's office. Instead, what they intend to do about it is the issue that generates therapeutic leverage.

Seldom is the focus on "why?" in individual terms. Nothing could get more stagnant than two parents drawing on their own expertise to confront a child with the reasons why she lifted a sweater from a shop. The focus needs to be broadened to the relational context of the event. If the child's act was a move to break the parents' stagnation, the therapist does not condone the theft, but the stagnation becomes the focus of treatment.[12]

As for transference, the therapist ignores it at his or her peril, as when a family colludes to have the therapist stranded or a wife sets up a male therapist as the benevolent father who makes her husband look like a nothing. In such instances, *the therapist moves not to interpret the action but to offset it*, e.g., by calling on the wife to adopt a parenting role herself vis-à-vis her children, or by showing that he or she does not side against the husband. The more the therapist pushes, the greater the risk of being cast

as the bad parent. Sometimes this risk has to be balanced against the risk of stagnation.

Thus, the therapist's awareness of transference, projection, etc., serves as a guide to intervention, but these phenomena are not viewed in their intrapsychic aspect alone. It is advisable, for instance, to examine how, within the transference, for each person the therapist may become a competitor for loyalty vis-à-vis the person's family of origin (Boszormenyi-Nagy, 1972).

Goals and Goal-Setting

In all cases, the basic goal is rejunctive effort, e.g., through encouragement of open negotiation on ledger issues, exploration of loyalty and legacy aspects where these impinge, undoing of stagnation, re-examination of "cut-offs," balancing of parentification, etc., and search for evidences of corruption. The ultimate rejunctive goal provides leverage for any intermediate goals.

The members of the couple or family are made accountable for their own possible goals, with insistent expectations and creative assistance by the therapist. The goals are action designs, trial actions, and attitudinal re-adaptations based on new convictions. Since it is fundamental to the contextual approach that family members are all affected by one another's moves and attitudes, changes made by any family member will not leave the others unchanged. The therapist's guidelines follow from the conviction gained from his or her own experiences with relationships, as well as from the degree of personal liberation already achieved through his or her own rejunctive effort.

No claim is intended that the goals of contextual therapy are somehow so esoteric that they have nothing in common with other approaches. On the contrary, the contextual approach seeks to incorporate all useful knowledge. As in "uncovering" therapies, we do consider the importance of ego strength for commitment to the attempt at improved relationships. We aim for integration of the defensive structure. We share the assumption that growth occurs through facing of avoided emotional processes when their facing will promote relational commitment and trustworthiness.

---

[12]*Editors' Note.* While Boszormenyi-Nagy and Ulrich do not explicitly discuss outcome criteria on which to judge the efficacy of contextual family therapy, certainly resolution of the presenting problem must constitute a *minimal* requirement for "successful" treatment.

We want family members to learn to stand up against guilt and for their own entitlements. Yet we actively base our strategy on utilizing dormant resources for trustworthiness. The enhancement of trustworthiness requires mutuality of effort among members. As they work at this mutuality, as they become more multilaterally fair, each changes and improves the nature of his or her own entitlement. This is a different and deeper way of standing up for one's self. We have found that this strategy is especially effective with persons whose ego functions show little strength.

As in transactional and restructuring approaches, we aim for age-appropriate power and role structure in the family, as well as for constructive complementarity of male-female roles in a flexible context of trust-building. We address difficulties in communication and problem-solving, too. But all this takes place within our own context. For example, there are times when transactional considerations might be subordinate to the requirements of fairness, as when a wife expects repayment for her sacrifice in caring for her husband through a long illness.

Treatment Applicability

We consider the contextual approach relevant to all human issues. It can reach people of "weak ego" at the point where otherwise only supportive help would be possible. Due to its comprehensive, synthetic nature, the approach possesses the combined relevance of psychological and transactional approaches.

We can find no contraindication of a thoughtful, responsible, synthetically informed therapeutic approach, if therapy is indicated at all. We regard the litany of contraindications of family therapy to be an exercise in fallacy, e.g., "valid family secret," "unyielding prejudices," "rigid defenses," adolescent members, organic disease, partial absenteeism, etc. The limitations on what therapy can accomplish should not be confused with contraindications.

One session might be sufficient to meet the family's need. It is also conceivable that their need might lie in a different direction than treatment, e.g., assessment of a child's learning disability.

Major Aspects of Therapeutic Method

Multidirectional partiality

The therapist becomes advocate for all within the basic relational context, i.e., the multigenerational extended family, including the dead. This position sounds simplistically logical and easy. However, it is one of the sources of the greatest resistance against the contextual approach. Everybody is inclined to see the world in terms of subjectively prejudicial, implicitly scapegoating attitudes. It is never easy to exonerate a seeming monster. To earn the position of multidirectional advocate, the therapist offers his or her commitment to finding and utilizing the resources of trust in the family. The commitment is not made in words; it is made by acting from the first moment with this rejunctive goal in mind and by refraining from any action that would work against it, while allowing family members time to gain in multilateral fairness.

To accomplish this end, the contextual therapist does not proceed primarily on the basis of his or her intuition or own values or any single technical guideline. Instead, consideration is given to the interests of all involved in all their dimensions—factual, psychological, and transactional as well as ethical. This requires systematic spelling out in the therapist's own mind.

Toward the participants, the therapist does not adopt a stance of impartial contemplation of all competing interests. We hold that "impartiality" or "neutrality," if it can actually be achieved, is an undesirable goal, and its pursuit can be deadening. The therapist is multidirectionally partial, i.e., directing empathy, endorsement, listening to one person, then in turn to that person's adversary. This reinforces the multilaterality that exists between them, but from the therapist's point of view it is an ongoing choice of direction, a sequence of sidings to which the term "multidirectional partiality" has been applied (Boszormenyi-Nagy, 1966).

The therapist has little investment in family controversy. Time is not allotted to vague, chaotic manipulations; the therapist does not join in collusive battles from which he or she may emerge only as the target. Of course, the family may erupt in controversy, and the therapist may momentarily get thrown off balance. The return to solid ground comes with the demand, "Wait a minute. I want this one to make a clear point, and then that one." When an honest statement from one becomes ammunition for his victimization, the therapist moves at once to block this disjunctive effort.

The therapist sets the family members the task of defining the issues that have depleted trust between them. At the outset, it is not a matter of asking, "Now, let's see what's fair about this," because the term "fairness" can trigger resistance and polarize attitudes. To elicit articulate, authentic adversary positions, i.e., to get positions defined in as clear a subjective meaning as possible, we start with one member's complaint, treat it as something deserving of respect, and develop it by asking for specific concrete descriptions. Even the act of restating one's position in front of the therapist can enhance trust. Once the statement is made, the therapist invites the other to respond. As the process unfolds, the therapist puts increasing demand on each to really make the point. If the therapist allows anyone to water it down or giggle it off, this is condescending. If the therapist allows people to bury their point under a flurry of recriminations and counterattacks, the therapist has been taken. The thrust is toward requiring each to be accountable to the other.

Helping each member clarify something may prevent the dialogue from breaking down. But if the therapist steps in to make the point for a person, the therapist may feel relief while the work stops.

As the context deepens, the first clues as to multigenerational dynamic linkages may emerge. When this happens, the therapist expresses interest and curiosity and thus brings the linkages to the surface.

The issues on which family members are able to take an adversary stand may at first be derivative. The wife may question her husband's commitment to finding a better job, when the implicit issue is whether he will leave his mother. Or the husband may allege that the wife does not care what happens to the children at school. The therapist may move by stages to the central issue: "Are you saying that your wife lacks sensitivity to the children's suffering?" Later, "Are you two struggling with what you give to and receive from each other?"

As this kind of dialogue builds, it has to acquire a momentum of its own, into which any interpretation or proffering of the therapist's own values is only an intrusion. Within this context, affect can surge spontaneously. What emerges is more pointed and more genuine than if the therapist merely gave permission for diffuse and fragmented kinds of outpourings. At the end of such a session, there may be a mood of quiet elation among people who have advanced enough trust both to speak and to hear one another.

This cannot happen if the therapist is afraid or unable to permit the issue to be joined. If the same issue exists in his or her family and it remains unfaced, the therapist may not be ready to let others deal with it.

As the dialogue unfolds, the therapist assesses the inter-individual ledgers of the family. This is a guide for the therapist, but nothing is gained by explaining their accounts to the family members. The more the therapist takes a prescriptive, structuring role regarding relational commitments and accountability, the more he or she can be used for manipulative and avoidant measures regarding their relational attitudes.[13]

Siding

By doing so, the therapist earns trust that he or she will side with each family member in turn. We consider the therapist free to relate actively to each family member, as long as the therapist is alert to the risks of transference and countertransference. Siding with one after another family member is not the same as "joining" the family.

The therapist balances the siding. Siding with someone is also balanced by the therapist's demand for accountability from that person. This is, first, the demand to define one's own point of view as responsibly as possible. "You made a point, it probably has some truth in it or you

---

[13]*Editors' Note.* Again, we view this as an important hypothesis rather than as a fact. Contrary to Boszormenyi-Nagy and Ulrich's concerns about the therapist's assuming a prescriptive and structuring role, there exists a growing body of outcome research which suggests that prescriptive and highly structured interventions may yield quite positive clinical outcomes (see, e.g., Barton and Alexander, Chapter 11; Jacobson, Chapter 15; Stanton, Chapter 10; L'Abate, Chapter 17).

wouldn't have said it. So let's look at this now. When you say your husband put his work ahead of you from the beginning, what is the meaning of this? From the point of view of a wife, how would you measure it?" In the extreme case, "I have the feeling that if I were your wife at this point I would feel you were unfair. Can you account for that?" If mother holds back in a slippery way and lets daughter defend her from father at the cost of incurring father's rage, the therapist asks mother to comment. The essence of the question is, "How do you account for your part here?" Next, the demand is to listen to and consider the interests of the other. "You have heard what she said—now I would like you to consider it."

The effort requires a high degree of sensitivity to the immediate status of each person's relational ledger. Does he or she feel that his/her side is being overlooked? If it is, the reaction will be swift and predictable. The person is still too deeply hurt to be able to consider someone else's interests and entitlements. The therapist may need first to engage in deeper siding. If the issue is one involving a parent, the therapist says, "You haven't told me many of those things where you were victimized." Or, "When your parents brought you into this thing between them, you were in the heaviest kind of trap for a child." In making such statements, the therapist is not leading the offspring into either simple dependency cravings or a loyalty trap, because it has already been made clear that the therapist will act as the parents' advocate as well.

The siding moves apace with the demand for accountability. The therapist may ask a person to consider the merit of a child, spouse, or parent: "What is the ledger and what can you do about it?" This will trigger whatever ambivalence there is. Some aspect of disloyalty or hostility will emerge as negative items on the ledger. Then the therapist may from moment to moment be in and out of siding with the one who is undergoing the stress. Acknowledgement may be given to the affect: "I feel you're protecting your mother. As a loyal daughter, you should. That's the big burden—being a child who's trying to make allowances, extending extra amounts, giving payment in advance, like most children do. You are an overpaying

daughter who's angry because you've paid so much."

If the siding becomes soft and undemanding of effort, then the therapeutic progress stops. If, on the other hand, the therapist confronts too much, the confrontation may change the affect. Therefore, a moratorium principle is in order: "If you can't make a clear point now, we'll come to it later." Carefully balanced siding may make it possible for the individual with "weak ego" to progress in treatment.

Effective siding requires discrimination about ledger balances. A daughter may provoke an insult from her father. At the transactional level, her annoyance at the insult may seem out of place; after all, she did provoke it, what does she expect? But both the provocation and the annoyance may be related to the intensity of her anger because she has been a parentified and exploited child. If the therapist attempts to deal only at the surface level, the daughter will somehow circumvent the therapist. Here, the pressure of primary process, which overrides what may seem rational on the surface at the moment, could actually be a better guide to the true state of the ledger.

Or, the therapist assumes the task of decoding a mixed message from father to child about mother, hoping this will help the child see the parents in a better light. But the child does not want to be burdened with the intolerable accountability for reconciling the parents.

The therapist who sides strongly with a child through acknowledging the child's efforts at holding the family together may appear to side against a mother whose attitude to the child is one of complaint. But at a deeper relational level, the therapist is still siding with the mother by congratulating her on the quality of her child. This attitude is based not on mere playing of paradoxes, but on deep convictions about how important it is to people to find trustworthiness in relationships.

At some point, the momentum of multidirectional siding may collapse. The wife who has clearly stated her distress at her husband's coldness may, every time he advances genuine warmth to her, advance a lack of trust to him by shooting him down. Then the therapist will restore leverage by deepening the concern for what is happening between them and turning toward the legacy and loyalty aspects on the wife's side that have led to the bind.

Loyalty framing

Especially when working with children, from the first contact on the therapist frames the work as a process in which loyalties will be respected and disloyalties laid open to question. Invalid overgiving based on willingness to be exploited will also come under challenge. The therapist does not enter into the process of blaming. Instead, "I have never seen a family in which there is a genuine monster. If she is bad, what have you done to help? What could you do? What is good in this family?" In a bad situation, "What is best to do? If it doesn't work now, did it ever?" "If you can't give to her, could your children give to her?"

When a parent lodges a complaint against a child, the therapist asks the child, "Tell us what you have tried to do about this. I am sure you can think of having tried to be helpful." Likewise, when the parents bring in a complaint about each other, the therapist may address the child: "Are you worried about your parents? Do you think this family needs help? How have you been trying to help them?" Such questions are based on our clinical experience that in any family the child's loyalty leads to helping efforts. Almost invariably these can be openly elicited. A process of dialectical reversal is continually involved. The parent says the child is bad; the therapist listens but then asks what is good about the child.

When this loyalty framework has been firmly set, the exploration of grievances can be measured against it. The child is not asked to report on what is going on in the family or to denounce the parents in the presence of a therapist who is still a stranger. If the child brings a dramatic accusation against the parents, it becomes their task to show what concern they have about the child's complaint.

In the ultimate case, when the child says, "You don't love me," and the parent's reply shows that the child is right, the therapist can ask the child, "Do you think your parents are happy about this?" And to the parents, "Now where do you go from here?" But also, "Tell me how was it when you were your child's age."

When the therapist is engaged in siding with one person, "Tell me more about how you were hurt," this is always within an established loyalty framework. The goal is not, "I am going to teach you how to take your hate off your husband and children and put it back where it belongs." Instead, the context is one of working to exonerate the other. If the therapist acknowledges that the person's life was messed up, it does not have to follow that the parents deserve all the blame. Most likely, they were at least as much victims as victimizers themselves.

Loyalty framing is based on the conviction that to leave the person in a condition of unresolved hate or resentment toward a parent is damaging to the offspring and can have multigenerationally damaging sequelae. We have encountered some people whose therapists have taught or allowed them to learn about their feelings by focussing their hatred on their parents. Neither the therapist nor the client will find deliverance if this is the end goal. Such a move goes against people's most deeply sensed loyalty. It drives the invisible loyalties deeper underground, where their symptomatic effects will be all the more pernicious. And it leads the offspring to an unbearable conclusion: If they were no good, I can't be any better. Furthermore, I have no entitlement to be any better. At this point the vital interests of the parents are synergistic with their children's interests.

The therapist can give the screw another turn by implying that he or she would be the better parent. Some child psychiatrists make the comparison explicit, when they suggest that the therapists' flexibility might be "redemptive evidence" to the patients that their parents were not the only kind of people in the world. If we compel the person under our care to add a split between therapist and parents to the split between parents, we are not relieving the burden.

Exoneration

Reopening of questions about parents takes place in a context of fair exoneration. The goal is not merely to obtain information, achieve better cognitive understanding, or even find more closeness and warmth, although all these are worth having. The task set up for the offspring is to begin to dispel the cloud of shame, blame, and implicit contempt that hangs over the parents' lives and thus envelops the children, too.

If this sounds like a ponderous or unpalatable therapeutic task, it might be worth considering that everybody is engaging in it anyway. The offspring who demands that the therapist accept him or her as a monster is also insisting that it cannot be the parents that are the monsters. A newly-wed wife who will not be diverted from her narrative of all her husband's unfairness is saying, in effect, "Compared to this, my father was not so bad." The challenge for her therapist is to help her find a better way to exonerate her father, a way that will not destroy her prospects for a decent marriage.

The goal has less to do with insight than with intention and commitment. "I don't want to live in the past. My father and I let it alone and that's the way we both like it." Here the intent is only to preserve stagnation and postpone debts whose pressure may be felt only after the chance for repayment has irrevocably passed. The therapist encourages the person instead to face his or her ambivalence and move on to at least consider the ethical balances. The action can begin with a willingness to examine why he or she doesn't want to think about it. Such an examination may turn up curious discoveries, e.g., "Aunt Molly kept a scorecard and she would turn over in her grave if I should take sides with mother against father. From there, what do I think about it. How do I really feel about it? From there, what more can I do about it?" This leads to, "What would be important for you to know to convince you they have some good things in their lives? Could you find out more? What do you imagine could happen if you began to talk to them about it?" Later, "Could you ask them about never seeming to care how well you did? How would you do this?"

If the commitment to explore is carried out fully, an actual confrontation with the parent may never need occur. Instead, the therapist might ask, "What would it be like? What do you think would happen?" If a confrontation does occur, it can be in a context of shared concern rather than hate. "This means something to me—I know it must mean something to you."

Either way, the exonerative effort is carried out with due regard for the person's ambiva-lence, the rage or resentment, shame or guilt, grief or mourning that intrude on the road to discovery. There may have to be many revolutions of this wheel of multidirectional partiality.

The essential task is to try, from the vantage point of parent and grandparent, to think what the oncoming events of their lives meant to them and so to experience how it came about that they did what they did, and thereby to see their actions in a human context, instead of looking backward at whatever disastrous consequences their actions may have led to.

Giving to the parent can also be a move toward exoneration. If I can give, I am not so weak after all. If I am not so weak, then I was not so deprived after all. The giving might consist of finding something the person can say on his or her own terms that the parent will be willing to hear.

The task can get done even if the parent never responds to it. The goal has to do with learning to face the balances. This may seem very hard, for a child who has been abandoned. It may also be very hard for the therapist. Yet this is the most active therapeutic stance possible. Even the dependent person is guided to turn his self-commiserative attitude into an active pursuit. He cannot change his parents but he does not have to remain passive either.

Bringing Children into Treatment

The implicit loyalty conflict

Introduction of children into any therapeutic setting requires sensitivity to a major pitfall. The very fact that the therapist shows adult concern for the child creates a situation in which there is some implicit disloyalty for the child. This cannot be avoided; therefore, an effort is needed to avoid its consequences insofar as possible.

The hazard is greater if the child is being seen alone. In the traditional child guidance approach, the child therapist and caseworker sometimes took sides with their respective clients. Their fights with each other would neatly parallel the fights in the client family. Another aspect of the split approach was the therapist's effort to build a relationship with the child that might set up a loyalty conflict with the parents. It was also considered good technique to assure the child that, in this setting, whatever he or she said about the parents would reflect no disloyalty. If the parents tried to pull the child's loyalty back to them, they were accused of "undermining" treatment. Thus, the child was bound and double-bound, within a deepening loyalty conflict, unless the therapist had maturity enough to acknowledge the merit of a multilateral context of trustworthiness.

The question becomes: What is a child therapist? Clearly the therapist can protect the child's interest only by taking into account the interests of that child's parents. We have heard of cases where family members have been parceled out to as many as four independent therapists. In doing this, there is no allowance for a multilateral view of anybody's interests.

In working with the child, this means meticulous attention to the process of "loyalty framing."

Inclusion of children

Work with children is an integral part of the contextual approach. Even when the spouses present themselves with a marital problem, the therapist makes it clear from the outset that he or she expects to see the children at a very early stage of the treatment, if only for a few times. This puts the marital problem into an intergenerational context. Parenting is an essential and inseparable part of the marital considerations, and it is ethically the heaviest issue in its demands on human concern. The future life prospects of young and even yet unborn children represent the highest ethical priority.

Asking the parents to report on their children's status yields only an outside view. The therapist cannot bring life into the children's side of things or get a direct sense of the relational balances. Time is going by, the children are developing, and they as well as the parents may need help. If there is severe marital difficulty, the therapist needs to see how the burden of this situation leads to the children's being intrinsically parentified by the marital discord, how the parents are taking unilaterally from children, and how the children struggle and suffer with this. When the children speak up from the vantage point of their position in life, the therapist can ask the parents to respond to the children and thus put what they are saying about the children together with what the children are saying to them.

Even if the focus is on the marital situation, the greatest therapeutic leverage comes through what happens to the children. This is leverage in the ethical realm, stressing the children's entitlements for a trustworthy climate for growth, and the parents' accountability for seeing that the children's entitlements are examined in a fair light. We have come to the core of trustworthiness in relationships and the formation of basic trust. As a mother remarked of her son, "When he saw that his children were being hurt, he started doing something about his marriage." This holds equally true if there is a divorce pending. What happens to the children then becomes even more a focus of concern.

Parental refusal to bring children into treatment is seen in terms of disengagement from ethical considerations. The therapist is persistent. "I really want you to be accountable for doing the best possible work. I will help you if I can. But let me tell you, your parenting is an inseparable part of your marriage. I want to know more about the children. Let's see if you can do better by them. Every day counts in their development, and they may urgently need help now. You have a parental duty to look at this." Even if the parents enter a hard denial that the children need to come in, the therapist does not compromise regarding this principle. The matter is one in which there can be no game playing. Meanwhile, the therapist may be considering what factors give the parents an immunity from guilt and concern for their children.

Introduction of the children is on the basis of a therapeutic contract with the parents. The therapist is not bringing the children in so the parents can sit back as judges while he or she does child therapy. Instead, the therapist prepares the way by asking, "How will you handle it with the children while they are here?" If the therapist takes over from the parents, they are no longer accountable and the therapist is implicitly acting as the better parent.

Once the parents have brought out an item of their tension in relation to the child, whether it has to do with the impact of their marital dispute on the child or an issue between them and the child, this opens the way for the therapist to ask for a response to the parents from the child in a loyalty framework. "Are you trying to help?" If before this context has been established the child erupts with accusations, they are better postponed. Once the parents have given permission, the child is freer to speak, and it becomes the parents' task to respond.

Almost without exception, the child will advance enough trust to respond with some openness about what is going on in the family and what the child has tried to do about it. Almost invariably, the parents are shocked at the degree of the child's awareness and pain. At this point, the therapist moves to acknowledge the child's contribution and to urge the parents likewise to acknowledge it. The format is one of enabling and trust-building. The focus is not on the child's burden but on the fact that the child is trying to do something about it. This is a profoundly positive event, and the therapist insures that the child is not left to congratulate him/herself.

Whatever acknowledgment the parents can give the child, at this point, is a first step toward balancing of accounts. It is a step toward deparentification, because the parents are now encouraged to respond to the child at an adult level. The child sees that the parents are working with another adult, and this diminishes the pressure on the child to preserve the marriage, as well as relieving whatever blame the child feels about the marriage. The parents are also encouraged to clarify for the child what they intend to do to make things better. If the therapist can exercise enough leadership to establish this kind of context, there is little risk that the introduction of the children into the sessions will be an act of exploitation.

Resistance

If there are invisible loyalties, anyone who wants to grow and thereby induce change is a traitor to them. Paradoxically, the process of looking for what is good about the other encounters great resistance. The projection of blame serves, of course, the end of self-justification. Pushing people to explore the good triggers ambivalence—rage, resentment, and, ultimately, hopelessness. At a deeper relational level, the aim is to preserve the invisible loyalties: These matters were meant to remain hidden. If I speak well of my wife, I am disloyal to mother. If I speak well of mother, I desecrate the memory of father. Finally, there is the preservation of legacy: I do not deserve better; my place is within the shame of the family. So, why bother with the past, why can't you just let me go on from here? The resistance to the past is the voice of the past.

There is no less resistance encountered here than in the psychoanalytic approach. Avoidance, denial, repression, disassociation, withdrawal, evasiveness, disengagement, failing to face or connect, escape from accountability—by whatever label they are called, these old familiar processes are hard at work in the context of exploring loyalty and legacy. Also, as people are encouraged to begin an examination of respective positions, the resistances are revealed even faster.

The therapeutic approach is neither to interpret such resistance nor to try to bypass it. Instead, the participants are encouraged to face, in the original context rather than in the substitutive context of therapeutic transference, the ethical issues from which their resistance derives, to define their adversary positions vis-à-vis these issues, and to move toward multilateral consideration of each other's interests. The multidirectional partiality of the therapist both supports and directs the participants' facing of the relational issues. This device is not available in traditional individual therapy.

Such an approach generates anxiety. Stirring up anxiety is not the goal; neither is the immediate goal to reduce anxiety. The objective is to lead everyone through the anxiety to considerations that will begin to restore trust. In this process, of course, timing must be taken carefully into account. If the therapist becomes a harsh adjudicator, if family members are held accountable or pushed into taking stands too soon, the ongoing dynamic of the treatment process can collapse. Rather than taking a rigid position, the therapist can take an unyielding interest in the possibility of change. Finally, if there is no movement, the therapist can give the option: "You decide if you can work this way, looking at all sides. Not everyone can. If not, there are other ways to seek help." Even if this stage is reached, the participants are still given the task of facing the issue and making a responsible choice.

Efficacy of the Approach

The openness of the approach to the incorporation of all helpful leverages of all other therapeutic approaches is the first guarantee of its effectiveness. Evidence of its power is coming in through a variety of channels: clinical practice, applications as in abortion and custody counseling, depth of response generated in presentations to other professionals, and effects in the lives of contextual therapists. The evidence from professionals engaged in all these activities is that they find new avenues of hope to work with difficult client populations.

Issues for Future Study[14]

The most pressing theoretical and practical issues for future study include the following: 1) further substantiating and clarifying the dynamic significance of balance and legacy aspects, in particular, ascertaining at what points the therapist can best use the basic dynamic leverages of relational trustworthiness to bypass the exploration of interactional sequences or intrapsychic events and thereby speed the therapeutic process; 2) refining therapeutic method to enhance the leverage obtained through these dynamics; 3) spelling out of the operational implications of a multilateral, multicentered ethical view of dynamics; 4) defining the optimal composition of concepts and techniques for the training of contextual therapists; 5) in support of the above objectives, expanding the psychoanalytic approach to connect with the relational dynamics; 6) reduction of the chaos in the field, exploration of points of convergence with Bowen and others, seeking out the common

basic premises inherent in the variety of techniques; 7) exploration of adaptations in related fields when preventive work in its global, positively enabling sense can be done, e.g., the legal aspects of divorce and custody proceedings.[15]

As we move out on these broad fronts, we will define specific empirical issues, as they arise, and address their solution by whatever means is appropriate.

Training

We are currently exploring what would constitute an ideal training program for contextual therapists. The essential task for the trainee is a progressive deepening of commitment to the mandate of multidirectional partiality, with reference both to the family members' lives and to the therapist's. To carry out this commitment, the therapist needs depth of experience and understanding concerning the four basic dimensions of the human context, how to differentiate them, how they interact, and what leverages they provide.

To accomplish these aims, certain components are essential. We do not prescribe training in "individual" therapy as such; however, either through a traditional psychodynamic or through a contextual approach, the trainee must acquire a clinical awareness of intrapsychic events, including transference phenomena. The dimension of psychological dynamics is one of the important components of the relational context. Personal therapy is important, preferably in a multilateral context, whether alone or with other family members. Either as an aspect of the therapy or as a separate venture, the trainee must engage in guided exploration of self in relation to own family, in a multilateral perspective.

---

[14]*Editors' Note.* The reader should note that the issues raised here by Boszormenyi-Nagy and Ulrich are entirely conceptual and practical and do not address explicitly any empirical questions regarding treatment outcome, etc. At several earlier points in this chapter we have offered research questions which have an important bearing on the treatment model presented in this chapter, and we suggest that these be reviewed.

[15]*Editors' Note.* In our view, contextual family therapy is most usefully thought of not so much as a theory of family therapy as a *theory of family therapy theories*, i.e., a meta-theory. Therefore, it seems difficult for the model to describe explicitly the range of specific techniques allowed to contextual therapists. We suggest, therefore, that a very useful contribution to the further growth of contextual therapy would be to explicate which therapist behaviors are consistent with the model and affect the outcome of contextual therapy.

The academic aspect of the program would need to include adequate instruction in the psychological and transactional dimensions. "Adequate" would be defined by a fresh, thorough approach to judging what materials are relevant to the preparation of a therapist. Possession of a Ph.D. or M.D. would not be considered prima facie evidence that a person had covered these materials. This issue highlights the need for an integrative understanding of the essential dimensions of psychodynamic, developmental and "systemic," and transactional knowledge.

Major emphasis would be placed on combined didactic-clinical training in the contextual approach, including seminars and workshops, as well as individual and group supervision utilizing appropriate equipment. Co-therapy would have value for learning because it provides multilaterality of vantage points.

The program would be reinforced by practica in applied settings, such as family relations court and the protective services branch of state welfare, or any setting where momentous decisions about people's lives are being made and where a multilateral perspective is called for.

The program would need to balance the requirements of specificity and breadth well enough so that a trainee could select a subspecialization, such as child or marital therapy, without sacrificing options for leverage, such as ability to deal with parenting issues. There must also be enough depth to enable the trainee to deal with heavy situations, such as suicidal efforts or psychotic "crises," incest, or despair.

A basic criterion of progress is whether the trainee has a growing conviction of the value of the offer of professional accountability and fairness in return for all participants' accountable attitude toward engaging in a joint effort.

CONCLUSION

We hold that the basic principles of the contextual approach should permeate all psychotherapy, regardless of whether it is concerned with adult, child, marriage, family, group, etc., and regardless of whether the theoretical approach deals primarily with intrapsychic, behavioral, or transactional phenomena.

We have not worked out the applicability of the contextual principles to specific psychody-namic and transactional principles. What we stress now is the ultimate relevance of the ethical dimension and the comprehensive inclusion of the other dimensions. We cannot yet offer specific guidelines, but we do offer the conviction that *it is important to know solidly the ethical dimension and never to violate its requirements or subordinate them to other considerations*. Within this framework, there is plenty of room for any approach to operate according to its tactical rules of the game.

REFERENCES

Boszormenyi-Nagy, I. The concept of schizophrenia from the point of view of family treatment. *Family Process*, 1962, *1*, 103-113.

Boszormenyi-Nagy, I. A theory of relationships: Experience and transaction. In: I. Boszormenyi-Nagy & J. Framo (Eds.), *Intensive Family Therapy: Theoretical and Practical Aspects*. New York: Harper and Row, 1965.

Boszormenyi-Nagy, I. From family therapy to a psychology of relationships; fictions of the individual and fictions of the family. *Comprehensive Psychiatry*, 1966, 7, 408-423.

Boszormenyi-Nagy, I. Loyalty implications of the transference model in psychotherapy. *Archives of General Psychiatry*, 1972, 27, 374-380.

Boszormenyi-Nagy, I. & Spark, G. *Invisible Loyalties: Reciprocity in Intergenerational Family Therapy*. New York: Harper and Row, 1973.

Boszormenyi-Nagy, I. Behavior change through family change. In: A. Burton (Ed.), *What Makes Behavior Change Possible?* New York: Brunner/Mazel, 1976.

Bowen, M. *Family Therapy in Clinical Practice*. New York: Jason Aronson, 1978.

Buber, M. *I and thou*. New York: Charles Scribner's Sons, 1958.

Fairbairn, W. R. D. *An Object-Relations Theory of the Personality*. New York: Basic Books, 1954.

Goldstein, J., Freud, A., & Solnit, A. *Beyond the Best Interests of the Child*. New York: Macmillan, 1973.

Laing, R. D. Mystification, confusion, and conflict. In: I. Boszormenyi-Nagy & J. Framo (Eds.), *Intensive Family Therapy: Theoretical and Practical Aspects*. New York: Harper and Row, 1965.

Levinson, D. *The Seasons of a Man's Life*. New York: Alfred A. Knopf, 1978.

Stierlin, H. *Separating Parents and Adolescents, a Perspective on Running Away, Schizophrenia, and Waywardness*. New York: Quadrangle, 1974.

Stierlin, H. The dynamics of owning and disowning: Psychoanalytic and family perspectives. *Family Process*, 1976, *15*, 277-288.

Sullivan, H. S. *The Interpersonal Theory of Psychiatry*. New York: W. W. Norton & Co., 1953.

Tessman, L. *Children of Parting Parents*. New York: Jason Aronson, 1978.

EDITORS' REFERENCE

Hurvitz, N. Interaction hypotheses in marriage counseling. *Family Coordinator*, 1970, *19*, 64-75.

CHAPTER 6

Symbolic-Experiential
Family Therapy

Carl A. Whitaker, M.D.

and David V. Keith, M.D.[1]

BACKGROUND OF THE APPROACH[2]

The background of our style of family therapy is defined by a particular, personal pattern. My development as a psychotherapist was associated with a deficit in the formal training in psychiatry. Due to my previous training as an obstetrician/gynecologist, I was granted board credit in psychiatry. The World War II personnel demands left little psychiatric training available. I then (1938) worked for two years as the resident psychiatric administrator in a small diagnostic hospital operated under an antiquated custodial care system. I was taught nothing about dynamic or psychoanalytic psychiatry. Rather, I learned hospital care maneuvers and, thereby, escaped the fear of insanity which was so prevalent among those who learned psychiatry in the midst of the big state hospital masses

of "deteriorating" patients.

My subsequent training was in a child guidance clinic. I learned play therapy and was supervised by the chief social worker who had been trained in the Rankian tradition. She interviewed each mother, while I interviewed the child. The two interviews were handled separately and then reviewed. No effort was made to involve the father, and there was no co-therapy. I was steeped in the power dynamics of experiences that result from interacting with children as the process of change is lived out in the playroom. The use of symbols and nonverbal communication is dominant in child therapy, and playing on the floor, playing with toys, talking Melanie Klein (1932) talk, struggling with problems of discipline and boundary control—all encouraged a learning of process talk. The child who was bored with toys was obviously ending his psychotherapy; the child who talked about the little boy next door who needed help was ready to leave therapy.

In addition to learning from patients, I was forced to learn by teaching. The psychiatry faculty at the University of Louisville were over-

[1]Preparation of this chapter was supported in part by NIMH Grant No. MH14971-03.

[2]*Editors' Note.* The first section of this chapter was written by Whitaker alone; the rest of the chapter was written by both Whitaker and Keith.

seas and this young child psychiatry resident became a "faculty member" who taught medical students to do psychotherapy. I knew nothing about psychotherapy, and not much about psychiatric patients, but medical student interviews with emotionally disturbed patients pressured me to adapt child therapy to work with neurotic adolescent and adult psychosomatic patients.

A subsequent three years with delinquent teenagers in an inpatient home and an outpatient clinic again focused on behavior problems. Play therapy with these teenagers included the use of toys, amputation dolls, clay, checkers and many joint games. I kept compulsive reports and my written notes usually included every word from the beginning to the end of the entire psychotherapy.

During the next two years (1944-1946) at the pre-atom bomb Oak Ridge Hospital, we seven staff psychiatrists were under massive pressure from the Army and from the 75,000 industrial workers in the huge atomic plant. The entire three plants and the living city were fenced. There were only three gates and only those with a pass could enter or leave. We saw 20 patients a day in half-hour interviews, back-to-back. This kind of intensity led to an absence of meta-discussion, of intellectual formulation, or of learning adroit ways of talking *about* therapy.

My inexperience and the psychological stress of the setting led to the use of co-therapy. Dr. John Warkentin and I began to see patients conjointly so we could talk to each other. We were both psychologically rather naive, given my surgical and play therapy experience and his Ph.D. in psychophysiology. We taught each other and we learned with patients.

One unique experience changed my orientation in a most forceful way. I had been seeing a five-year-old and using a baby bottle with warm milk. The next patient was an acute manic psychotic brought from our ten-bed inpatient ward. He spied the bottle and became tremendously excited. Sucking it was an orgastic experience. The next 12 daily interviews, each one preoccupied with the intense bottle feeding experience, pulled him out of his psychosis and he was discharged back to his job. For the next three years, I was convinced that every patient could benefit by sucking on a baby bottle. Most patients accepted the offer and a large percent-

age rocked in my lap. I became their play therapy or primary process mother. It made no difference whether they were psychotic, neurotic or in trouble with psychosomatic problems. However, once I had developed my own capacity to be a symbolic "mother," the technique became useless—like an old joke. The patients would not accept it, apparently because it was not consonant with my then (1950) current emotional state. However, the technique was adopted by several of the clinic staff. In time it also became sterile and useless in their psychotherapy.

During the subsequent two years, our group, supported by co-therapy and constant consultation, evolved an interactive pattern including an aggressive give and take with patients—arm wrestling, leg wrestling and confrontation episodes. It was as if I was now developing my paternal competence. After two years, that pattern also became nonfunctional for our group. These experiences convinced me that each technique is a process whereby the therapist is developing himself and using the patient as an intermediary, that is, the therapist is interacting in a primary process mode, as Slavson (1971) did with his group therapy with delinquents.

Concurrent with the emergence of these techniques was the development of a kind of functional pyknolepsy. I would fall asleep in the middle of an interview and dream about my relationship with the patient who was in front of me. As I shared the dream with the patient, it became a part of our interview. It took years to get over my embarrassment, but I became more and more certain that a therapeutic process was taking place between us. This technique also spread within the group but was not sustained by most of them.

By 1954, one member of the faculty, Dr. Richard Felder, quite routinely slept once or twice during each group therapy meeting. He would wake and report two or sometimes three dreams. The group would protest whenever the number of dreams dropped back to one. I have been able to continue this dream technique over the years, although it seems less frequent of late. It happens now only when I'm under pressure, when therapy is not succeeding, and when I care deeply about the family I am working with.

Dr. Warkentin and I moved to Emory University in 1946 and Dr. Thomas Malone joined in 1948. This new Department of Psychiatry group was in full-time medical school teaching and concurrent practice of individual psychotherapy and occasionally couples and family therapy, although it was very rudimentary and unstructured by any cogent theory. However, we were pressing for a core theory to explain the process of individual therapy. In 1953, we published *The Roots of Psychotherapy* (Whitaker and Malone, 1953).

The move to establish a medical school department at Emory University in Atlanta was very carefully preplanned. There had been no previous department of psychiatry, and we were allowed to inaugurate our own system. It was organized around the process of being successful in interpersonal relationships and a process psychotherapy which followed the Rankian brief therapy model (Rank, 1936), rather than around models focused on insight or psychopathology. All medical students had group psychotherapy throughout their first two years. Our seven staff members each met with his group each week. During the second year of training, the group became the collective psychotherapist for a patient. Thus, the medical students were taught to be people during their first and second years in relationship to each other, and taught to be physicians doing psychotherapy in their second year. In their third year, they functioned as though they were resident psychotherapists for three patients each afternoon, two afternoons a week for six weeks. John Warkentin's background in psychophysiology helped us to remain aware of the somatic correlates of our work. Dr. Thomas Malone joined our group in 1948. His Ph.D. in psychoanalytic psychology and his analytic training with Dr. Ernst Simmel added another facet to our group orientation. We deliberately taught the process of psychotherapy rather than psychodynamics during the nine years of our developing a department of psychiatry.

During these same years, 1946-1955, my involvement in treating schizophrenia with an aggressive kind of play therapy was expanding. The addition of co-therapy made the experience of treating individual schizophrenics in a rented home with a recovered schizophrenic as live-in attendant a creative and exciting process. Two therapists, who functioned as "co-parents," helped reactivate a regressive process in the schizophrenic. We strove to induce a full-fledged infantile state and disrupt the pseudo-infantile state of the schizophrenia. As an infant, he could be nourished, his affect hunger satiated, and the psychotic transference used to facilitate recovery.

The development of our methodology also rested on a pragmatic approach to psychotherapy as a symbolic experience. In Atlanta, the medical students were trained to take everything said by the patient as symbolically important as well as realistically factual. The use of co-therapy with students allowed for open communication about the experience going on between the two therapists and the single patient.

Our staff work with schizophrenic patients eventuated in a series of ten four-day weekend conferences on the treatment of schizophrenia involving four of our group and several from Philadelphia, including Ed Taylor, John Rosen, Mike Hayward, and, on some occasions, an anthropologist, George Devereux. The conferences centered on intensive treatment of one schizophrenic, or a schizophrenic and his family, for the four days. Two interviews were carried out each day by a subgroup, while the rest watched through the one-way mirror. We spent the rest of the day and night discussing the interviews. The tenth conference was held at Sea Island, Georgia (1955), and included Gregory Bateson and Don Jackson. This meeting led to the publication of *Psychotherapy of Chronic Schizophrenic Patients* (Whitaker, 1958).

While I can think of no profound specific influences in the development of my approach to psychotherapy, personal conversations with Gregory Bateson, Alan Watts and Alan Gregg were important in validating my personal experience with patients. Klein's writings on psychoanalysis with children (e.g., Klein, 1932) and Fred Allen's (1942) *Psychotherapy with Children* were influential. The works of Benedict (1934), Langer (1951), Angyal (1941) and Jung (1961) also had an impact on my growth as a therapist and the development of a conceptual pattern.[3]

---

[3]*Editors' Note.* For a more detailed examination of the background of the approach described in this chapter, see Neill and Kniskern (1981).

THE HEALTHY OR WELL-FUNCTIONING MARRIAGE OR FAMILY

Health is a process of perpetual becoming. When John Warkentin coined the term "growing edge therapy," he pictured an open wound healing in from both sides. The operation of a family, healthy or not, is covert and implicit. The rules and regulations are not expressed in a formal manner; they develop out of the operation of the family. They are largely expressed in living rather than in words. Health has neither a past or future. Most important in the healthy family is the sense of an integrated whole. The healthy family is not a fragmented group nor a congealed group. The whole functions as the leader and the control system, both in supporting the family's security and in inducing change. The healthy family will utilize constructive input and handle negative feedback with power and comfort. The group is also therapist to the individuals, rotating the security blanket and serving as goad when needed by persons or subgroups.

The family as a three to four generational whole is longitudinally integrated. That is, the family and the subgroups and the individual members relate to an intrapsychic family of three plus generations. Interaction within the extended family is related to this sense of their historical ethos.

The healthy family maintains a separation of the generations. Mother and father are not children and the children are not parents. The two generations function in these two separate role categories. Members of the same generation have equal rank. However, there is a massive freedom of choice in periodic role selection and each role is available to any member. Father can be a five-year-old, mother can be a three-year-old, the three-year-old can be a father, the father can be a mother, depending upon the situation, with each family member protected by an implicit "as if" clause.

The power distribution within the healthy family is flexible, with a casualness evolved through the freedom to express individual difference and to renegotiate role structure and role expectations and to reevaluate past experience.

There is a great freedom of choice in each individual's right to be himself. He may develop his own uniqueness with encouragement and very little counterpressure. This freedom for aloneness or belongingness is protected by the group.

A basic characteristic of all healthy families is the availability of this "as if" structure. Play characterizes all metacommunication. For example, the six-year-old son says to daddy, "Can I serve the meat tonight?" and daddy says, "Sure, you sit over on this chair and serve the meat and the potatoes and I'll sit over in your place and complain." Daddy does this and probably gets more out of making believe he's six than son does out of the great experience of making believe he's mother's husband, and father of the family and an adult man. Metacommunication is considered to be an experimental process, an offer of participation that implies the clear freedom to return to an established role security rather than be caught in the "as if" tongue-in-cheek micro-theater. That trap is the context that pushes son into stealing cars or daughter into incest with father while mother plays the madame. The whimsy and creativity of the family can even be exaggerated to where family subgroups or individuals are free to be nonrational or crazy.[4]

The normal family does not reify stress. Some families stay connected by the evening meal fight. The healthy family is one that continues to grow in spite of whatever troubles come its way. The family lives with the fact of its inconsistency. It acknowledges the passing of time. The healthy family always seeks to expand its experience. All families have myths; myths are part of the definition of a family. One of the problems for dysfunctional families is that they are unable to tolerate changes in their myths, i.e., they have demythologized themselves. Sonne (1973) has a lovely descriptive term, metaphorolytic. In contrast, the healthy family has an evolving myth. The evolving myth permits

---

[4]*Editors' Note.* It is our impression from having worked closely with Whitaker for several years that his notion of the importance of an individual's or a family's "craziness" is frequently misunderstood by family therapists. He is *not* endorsing the value of "craziness" in the traditional diagnostic (e.g., DSM-III) sense, but rather is arguing for the value of having *access to psychotic and other irrational aspects of psychological experience.*

them to travel through the cycles of regression and reintegration. Symptoms are not absent from the healthy family, but they are a way to increase the family's experience and thereby its growth.

Roles are defined by a panorama of conditions in the family: past history (the family of origin), present history (age of kids), and ideas about the future (mother's plan to return to teaching). The family roles are further defined by interactions with each family member, with the extended family demands, and with the culture. The roles are also defined by the individual's own growth experiences. The guiding myth evolves; it is not fixed. The same, by the way, is true for schools of psychotherapy. Sometimes roles are defined by covert needs of parents established before the child's birth in order to reestablish for the parents a sense of being back at home in their family of origin, whether that was a good or a bad world; home is home. We believe roles are defined interactionally in vivo, not by deliberate decision-making. Mother's need for the comforting of her mother may establish the role of the first child or the role of the first child may be defined by mother's need to care for the real live dolly of her three-year-old fantasy with daddy. As mother becomes more involved with taking care of the later children, the third child or the fourth child may be given the role of father's girlfriend or father's mother as his need and mother's need are integrated. A friend of ours, Barbara Joosse, says, "We get the children we need."

Problems are solved in the normal family by marshalling customs, myths, family rules, hopes, taboos and facts. There are many covert assumptions and some overt rationalizations but basically problems develop as impasses, i.e., go to resolution by the standard process of thesis, antithesis and synthesis. Father wants a new convertible, mother says we can't afford it, time resolves this by their buying a less expensive car with a tape deck in it.

Problem-solving is often accomplished by realigning the gestalt. The realigning is accomplished in a complex systems way. The family's process of deciding is similar to that of each of us. Decisions are based on those factual realities brought to bear on the situation and the methodologies that worked in the past. These may

be impulsive, irrational, ambivalent and dependent, strongly influenced on a covert level by watching mother and father make decisions, by watching school teachers or others who have been important to them. Living problems are like calculus problems with multiple variables. The constants are the long-term family values of both spouses. The decisions include influences from the next door neighbor, the work situation of the parents and the school situation of each of the children. These cultural bound influences, language bound limitations, restrictions and processes from the families of origin of the two parents result in a compromise end point with many pressures of varying quantitative effect in an algebraic summation of taboos, rules, mythologies and realities. All of this sounds complex and ponderous, but the human mind and its combinations in the family operate with computer-like precision, handling an infinite variety of stimuli.

The family life-cycle is a great model of evolution in a system, changing while simultaneously maintaining its integrity. The clearest markers in the family life-cycle are birth, death and marriage. The developmental periods of the children in large part define family process, e.g., the new baby pulls all three generations together. (Can a parent be middle aged before the children reach adolescence?) Some other life-cycle markers include changes in income, family moves, the time when father quit drinking, or mother turned religious. These are important events that the family therapist must listen and watch for. They are frequently understated and underestimated in importance; however, it is common for important life events to cluster in the family history. We learn from families that life-cycle stress is cumulative within the system as a whole. For example, father's fight with his mother may produce tension in the marriage, which causes the mother to be depressed, but the symptom is a school phobia in the nine-year-old. The clearest example of cumulative stress in the family life-cycle is usually in the family with adolescent children. The kids are individuating and in an identity crisis, the parents are frequently into a mid-life crisis while the grandparents are in an old-age crisis related to retirement, illness or other change in self-image. The healthy family acknowledges the stress in all of its members and does not concretize it in one of them.

Another way to look at the family life-cycle is as serial impasses. The primary "we" of courtship is ruptured, the secondary "we" of living together emerges and develops stress. The stress is resolved by repression, by struggling through it in the open, or by various other means such as accidents or change of focus, and the we-ness is reestablished. The stress between unification and separation of the individuals is repeatedly erupting and resolving.

The healthy family becomes increasingly strong as a group, therapeutic in its role to itself and its components, increasingly flexible and casual, and increasingly covert. Organic functioning of the whole resembles physical skills like the psychomotor stage of cognitive development. Coordination is confused by the long circuiting of awareness. The high level of affect that is established in the beginning gradually becomes part of the fiber of the family and individual freedom to separate and return crystalizes an increasing wholeness within the family. The component parts contribute to the whole and the whole contributes to the component parts.

The healthy family changes through identity crisis (self-doubt, illness, struggling with the children). Frustration is a useful enzyme for accelerating change. The processes are assimilation and accommodation. On another scale, the process is regression and reintegration, falling apart and then reorganizing. Laughing and crying serve that function in individuals.

Passion and sexuality are the voltage in a family system. When the flow is free, things go well. When the flow is impeded, the system heats up and there is always the possibility of damage. Affection implies a moderate emotion. Passion describes our sense of the feeling juices in the family. "Passion" arises out of a Greek word which means to struggle. Thus, it defines a process and not a state. It includes sadism and hatred as well as lovingness. The kernel of affective energy at the center of family living process is the core of psychosomatic living, an undifferentiated germ plasm. The behavior in the family is an emanation, always with interpersonal and metaphorical components. In effect, we assume the biological basis of family therapy. The culture thinks of a healthy family as one with a lot of positive affect. We agree. We also think that children hate and ought to know that they are hated (Winnicott, 1949). The failure to have an easy flow of affect results in at least migraine headaches.

Feelings in the family in whatever form or degree are handled in nonverbal and symbolic pulses. The family has a natural "as if" clause in its living. The "as if" clause makes it possible for mother and child or father and child to play out quasi-sexual roles. Mother and son go on a date and dad stays home, complaining jealously and insisting that junior bring mom home before 10:00. Father and daughter go to the grade school dance. Father catches himself being absurd in a temper tantrum and switches to playing a roaring buffoon. The healthy family knows the difference between murder and play murder, between sexual play and intercourse. This "as if" clause was demonstrated dramatically when one child-abusing family began to play fight with rubber bats in our office. The whole family had great fun with a symbolic slugfest, transcending the danger of real murder.

Love, sexuality and hatred are lived out through touching, nonverbal intimacy, fighting and making up, subgrouping and resubgrouping, triangulation and detriangulation, teaming and fantasies.

Case Example

Bob and Harriett completed therapy just before the birth of their first child. They asked for another appointment when the baby was four months old. He felt that she had grown cold toward him and she said he was too distant and mechanical with her. He was frustrated with her constant refusal to have sex. He was sympathetic with her feelings about herself and her fatigue and her attachment to the new baby. One Sunday afternoon, he attempted to turn her on, but she stayed cold. He went to the kitchen to substitute something to eat but returned to the bedroom. She was sitting on the bed, thumbing through a magazine. He had a visual image of himself bashing her ribs in with his fist. He relaxed, changed his shirt and went out to mow the lawn. His conscious experience of this fantasy had somehow facilitated an existential shift in his head. It permitted him a more open, less demanding lovingness.

It is the physical sexuality combined with lifetime commitment that makes marriage a unique, clearly biological relationship. We think the whole family is involved in the family sex life in one way or another. Sex is more open and fun if it involves all the generations. One of the best ways is by sexual joking. In the early marital years half of the couple's sex life is fighting about it. Unfortunately, we don't learn that until after we are married. Family sexuality is obviously conveyed in a preverbal, experiential manner. Midelfort (1976) says that sex education does not occur in the schools; it is not a vocabulary course. Real sex education is in the parents' eyes. When the mother in a pseudo-mutual family declares their sex life is "just lovely," the therapist thinks of a funeral parlor visitation where the lady is saying that the corpse is "just lovely."

In this section on the healthy family, we have emphasized that family process is covert and nonverbal. In our method of doing psychotherapy, we distrust communication training methods because they often cool (act out) rather than increase (act in) interpersonal stress. In our method of therapy, affective expression is a natural process which is *allowed* rather than taught.

Increases in intimacy and separateness must go hand in hand. Neither can increase without an increase in the other. One can only be as close as one can be separate, and one can only be as separate as one can be close. Family rules define the degree of this pressure tolerated, and the unspoken family barometer is very accurate. In a healthy family, a wide range of intimacy and separateness levels are found. The levels are also movable without inducing panic in a healthy family. The size of the family space bubble and each individual's space bubble is determined by experience and the historical perspective that the family members have inherited via their "social genes" (Grinker, 1971).

Real dependency is linked to real autonomy in the same way that intimacy and separateness are linked. A symbiotic relationship is one in which there is a fixed emotional distance. Each member is dependent upon the other to not alter the distance. The relationship controls the two persons. Thus, two married persons may appear to be quite autonomous, but if the relationship heats up in some way, such as having a child or one member's becoming ill, it may cause quite a bit of stress in the other member because they are dependent upon this relationship remaining distant. In a marriage, the wife may appear dependent, while the husband appears autonomous and independent. However, on the covert side it may be quite different; the wife carries a lot of power while the husband is really a little boy and his power is in his tantrums and/or his good behavior.

Case Example

Bob and Gloria had been married for 23 years. The marriage had been unsatisfactory but fairly stable. Gloria stayed at home, took care of the kids and seemed quite dependent. Bob was a successful businessman who spent a lot of time away from home and characterized himself as being strongly independent. During the marriage he maintained a close relationship with his mother who lived nearby. The couple was divorced one year after his mother's death. We assume that the marriage was not able to absorb his dependency needs.

The healthy family is a subculture established over several generations. The power of this subculture is well structured and the struggle between that subculture filtering down from the mother's family of origin is gradually integrated with the power of the subculture handed down from the father's family of origin.

Relationships with extended families, however, are secondary to the healthy nuclear family. It is possible to visit the extended family of origin without double-crossing the nuclear family. Troubles develop when there is a fixed relationship with someone in the extended family, e.g., two sisters have a closer relationship between themselves than either has with her husband. In the healthy family, the relationships are also variable and responsive to specific needs. Grandma may be able to take care of the kids once in a while if the second generation needs it, but she is also free to turn them down. The 40-year-old son is able to go home to take care of his mother after she falls and strains her hip. He does not double-cross his wife in doing this.

Extended family relationships are troublesome when they are not updated. In other words, the extended family relationships are in-the-head projections left over from age five or 15.

The boundaries of the family are flexible and here the custom and historical perspective are as important as they are in the family dynamics. Who is allowed in, when, under what conditions, for how long, on whose okay—all are programmed covertly. The interdigitating of the two family cultures evolves over time and endless experiences in vivo. The family is in a constant flux between the culture of the two families, modified by reality stresses and their resolution.

The healthy family has a capacity for outside relationships and the ability to move in and out without being a counterbalance to family struggles. That is, the wife may choose to play bridge on Wednesday evenings because she likes to play bridge, not just to get even with husband. Members need not have joint access to non-family members. The husband need not share in all of his wife's relationships and vice versa.

THE PATHOLOGICAL OR DYSFUNCTIONAL FAMILY

Our general orientation toward pathological functioning is related to the concept of craziness, which can be colored pink by calling it creativity. We include both of Minuchin's (1974) concepts of disengaged families and enmeshed families in this category, that is, the family which has excessive callouses and no craziness but is massively inhibited, or the family with "nobody-in-it" in which the family members live back-to-back. The dysfunctional family is characterized by a very limited sense of the whole. In a more specific way, it is frequently true that the only person who believes in the "spirit of the family" is the family scapegoat who may, of course, be either the "black sheep," the delinquent, or the member who is crazy or disorganized in some way that stresses the family, or the "white knight," the socially overadapted family hero, who is often a workaholic and whom the family utilizes to cover up its anxiety and extol its health. Family craziness is denoted in the same way as the craziness of the individual, that is, a nonrational functioning process which may show up as silliness or as chaos. The schizo-

phrenogenic family we think of as being dedicated to a state of chaos. In general, the degree of craziness is measured by an integration of the creative, nonrational impulsiveness in the family and psychosocial adaptability. Some families are highly creative, but, like individuals who are crazy, they disconnect themselves from the social structure. Some others are creatively exciting and are more socially adapted and integrated. The summation of these two is one way of measuring the dysfunction. Indications of that are expressed by way of fixed triangles and fixed subgroups. When the family has unresolved oedipal triangles or a feud between the males and females, the functioning of the family as a whole is disrupted. It disrupts the marriage and many times, even more, the relationship of the two extended families from which it originated. Pathological functioning in a family is largely a nonverbal process and we assume that the verbalization is mostly a façade, a kind of sociopolitical sop to the culture.

Craziness in the family may be compared to several of the individual diagnostic categories. The catatonic family imitates the New England patterns of rigidity and emotional constriction; there are paranoid families who are profoundly suspicious, feeling very much like the lower socioeconomic "have nots" feel about the "haves." A surprising number of families operate like the simple schizophrenic in that they make decisions without any content and in a very fogbound manner. They roam into decisions and their behavior apparently has no basic understructure that is perceptible or even intellectually available to them.

The craziness of the individual can be divided easily into three general categories. First, there is the *driven crazy*, who has been driven outside the family and is trying to find a primary process mother in the community. Another type of craziness we call *going crazy*, that is, craziness that emerges out of the profound acceptance, or unconditional positive regard, that Carl Rogers spoke of. Falling in love can be a metaphor for this process. This is identical with a therapeutic psychosis, a kind of intensified version of the therapeutic neurosis. A third variety of craziness, many times misidentified, is *acting crazy*. This pattern comes about when one who has been crazy is faced with an intolerable anxiety and regresses into crazy behavior. It is not a process craziness but a reactive craziness, in the same sense that there is process schizophrenia and reactive schizophrenia.

Diagnosing Families

Our system for diagnosing is basically informal. On the most fundamental level, we assay the quality of the intimacy or quality of the esprit de corps. We try to evaluate the interactional aspects of the two cultures of the families of origin and the situational dynamics in the present, as well as historical residuals from situational stress, whether physical illness, death of family members, divorce or other shifts in family function. We look for ghost members, symbiotic interactions across the generations in the past, and cultural residuals, such as ethnic or religious differences, from the two families of origin.

The interactional aspects of the family include such things as the lonely father syndrome, the battle fatigue mother syndrome, and the infidelity syndrome, which is always bilaterally established by the two partners. For example, mother falls in love with the children and gives her heart to them, and father then gives his heart to his business, to a girlfriend on the outside, or to an intensive hobby pattern, such as golf or poker. We look for the parentified child, which is probably a variant of the unchanged infantile delusion of grandeur, expanded, intensified and escalated because of mother's need for something to worship. The newborn child ordinarily occupies a kind of Christ-like role and if mother is in deep need of such, Christ can be kept alive for some time. Mother then becomes one of the apostles or even the Virgin Mary. We try to spot the several black sheep or the white knights so that we can plan to deliberately detumesce each. We make considerable effort also to search for the David and Goliath syndrome in which the mother fears father physically and raises her son, or daughter, to kill off the giant in the home. This may actually come about when the boy is 15 and father makes one more threat to mother, whereupon son assaults him. We also look for the prodigal son syndrome, a process in which the umbilical cord is allowed to stretch: The child goes out to discover that the big bad world is dangerous and, having discovered this, comes running back to mother and father's knee, giving them each the hoped-for regression.

Causes and Development of Family Dysfunction

We assume that dysfunction is related to the struggle over whose family of origin this new family is going to model itself after. One way to view etiology asserts that there is no such thing as marriage; it is merely the two scapegoats sent out by families to perpetuate themselves. There are also family growth impasses which lead to dysfunction—the arrival of a new child, the death of a family member, invasion from the outside culture, developmental dynamics relating to the growth of children, aging of parents, or other natural phenomena related to time.

Dysfunction also arises following father's retirement or one child's leaving for college, or other time or space wars. Time and space conflicts can produce stress without its becoming apparent to those involved. Who gets the nicest bedroom as the children come along, who occupies the living room or the parents' bedroom, to what degree do friends belong in the family living space, and the struggle between parents and children over who has territorial rights to the car, the garage, etc., may be important literally and as symbolic expressions of family power dynamics.

Families may develop dysfunction from situational stress. For example, pregnancy develops a new triangle between mother and father; mother turns to the intrauterine teammate and father may or may not be able to handle the sense of isolation and may turn to his mother or some other compensatory support system. This may begin an ever expanding dysfunction. If three or four serious stresses develop in one year, the tendency to develop dysfunction is greatly increased.

The effort to maintain a homeostatic quality or a pseudo-mutual cover-up counters the effort to change. The family, on a covert level, develops a compromise resolution of this push-pull for change and homeostasis. For example, children may try to teach mother and father how to fight and how to love as they model by fighting and loving each other.

The type of symptom is usually related to pre-set roles for family members and by pre-set fixation of triangles in an interaction between the functional determinants of the two families of origin. For example, if a man from a family of isolates marries a woman from a family of social activists, the marriage may become the scapegoat or the two families of origin may carefully avoid each other for many years as a way of mitigating the nuclear family's stress. The weakest link or the person most impregnated with the family mythology, for example, the oldest son or daughter, who is assumed to be a potential United States President or international beauty queen, or the nun that's to get the family into heaven, may determine the symptom. If the oldest son is in college and the youngest son in high school when father dies, it may evolve that the youngest son will take over the family farm. His anger at the older brother's escape and at father's death and mother's putting him in the position of being the new father may create a family situation where symptoms are all but inevitable. If mother is guilty about her early sex life, she may pressure the oldest son to be a priest or the oldest daughter to be a nun. If mother was frustrated in her effort to go to medical school, she may pressure son to become a family doctor. This symptom-developing stress may precipitate the entire family into making this young doctor a white knight victim so that he gradually self-destructs in his effort to be a hero for mother and his family. In similar fashion, a father who barely maintains his law-abiding status may raise a son who picks up the impulse for rebellion and begins to steal cars because of the gleam in father's eye around the excitement of defying the power structure of society.

It is important to consider why some family members are symptomatic, when others are not. Members of the family may become pre-assigned a role such that situational dynamics precipitate a heroic symptom. If father's mother dies, father may go into a depression and the nuclear family dynamics may compensate. The genetic set of the family member may also precipitate symptoms. For example, if father is a stimulus activator and is chronically hyperkinetic, while mother is a stimulus repressor,

father may go into a manic pattern to activate mother and mother may then go into a kind of catatonic withdrawal to tolerate father's stress.

Social genes may also precipitate family pathology. If father is successful in five different roles, then the eldest son may feel pressured into matching his father's drive or his mother's adoration of father. If father is a physician and a workaholic, son also may decide that he does not want that kind of slavery and thus evolve pathology in his professional choice or escalate to a failure in medical school. The choice of symptom is like any other political choice. Mark Twain said, "The town drunk is an elected office." The family scapegoat is also an elected office. Somebody has to run for it, other people have to "vote," and gradually the choice is made by the family as a whole. The symptom choice includes not only both the families of origin and, of course, some of the family network, but also the historical family of previous generations. If three generations have been doctors, it's very difficult for the first son not to become a physician. Symptom choice may even result from projected demands. The oldest daughter may become pathologically parentified because of mother's need for her mother or because of father's need for his mother, his wife being too immature to carry that role even in a substitute way. One daughter may become hysterical because father and mother have drifted apart, father needs a girlfriend and daughter applies for the job.

We do not believe that there are well members in a pathologized family. If there are several children, it is possible for the youngest one to have very little role pressure because demands of the nuclear family and the two extended families have been projected into the older children. Family members who look well are often pathologized by teaming roles. If there is a schizoid member, there is apt to be a counter-schizoid member. If there is a covert, repressed person, there is apt to be a symbiotic partner who is expressive, outgoing, and more overt, just as husband-wife choices are apt to be operationally symbiotic. The labeled "well" person we assume is a white knight. He is similar to a professional psychotherapist—dedicated to earning the family's place in heaven, to helping the family wipe out its historical sinfulness or to polishing the family coat of arms within the social structure. The white knight usually does not believe he is a victim of his family. He believes mother is the center of his world. His dedication may, however, have the quality of religious fanaticism and include a disregard for self. It is a question in our minds as to whether all workaholics are either white knights to their family or to the culture as a whole, planning to do all they can to advance Georgia or the blacks or God's Kingdom, the Church, etc.

In sum, then, diagnosis of the family, like diagnosis of the individual, is an administrative system that results in dissociation. Either shredding or lumping of interactional signals is grossly contaminated by the observer as participant. Creative therapy should be carefully protected by couching all designations in metaphorical schemes that do not allow cross-sectional maps. The map is not the territory and the territory is not the interactional choreography.

FAMILY ASSESSMENT

Assessment is implicit with us. Assessment is equated with the first interview process, which begins with the first telephone call and continues into the first interview. With families that are rigid, cautious and self-protective, the first interview process may continue for two or three interviews. Two components operate in parallel. The first is related to our attempt to get acquainted, to develop an empathic relationship and to identify the anxiety components needed to pressure the family into change. We ask each family member to describe the family and how it works. The second component is a trial of labor, an old obstetrical method. When the pregnant mother is ready to deliver but unable to spontaneously begin labor, the obstetrician will attempt to induce labor. If uterine contractions do not continue spontaneously, then the trial is interrupted and mother urged to wait. Our "trial of labor" takes many forms (to be described later in the chaper) and always gives us a clue as to the ability of the family to change.

We try to include the largest system possible in our initial assessment. We do an informal assessment of the whole system, the subsystems of each generation, the triadic patterns the dyadic collusions and teaming, and the individual dynamics. If the grandparents are not available for the first interview, we examine the relationship of this generation to the rest of the family whole. We move from interaction with the total system to an in vivo interactive give and take.

Thus, at the end of the assessment, we have a feel for the family and they have an experiential orientation to our way of working. If the family or someone else seeks a concrete assessment, we put it in both real and symbolic language. Usually, we attempt a double-bind. The father may be told that he ought to know that we won't be able to trust him. The wife of the alcoholic may be told that she is hopelessly dependent on her husband's alcoholism and we think that change is unlikely. The delinquent son is reframed so that the problem is the child's being driven out of his family.

There are three problems with making concrete diagnoses. The first is that our language is not structured to describe process. The result is that a diagnosis may have iatrogenic effects on the life of the family by reifying the problems. The second is that diagnostic terms are extended metaphors, an attempt to make one kind of reality conform to another kind of reality. The third problem is that each family has a private culture and language system to which the therapist has only partial access. In our view, therapy is the family's trip. We are like guides. The diagnostic process may be crippling to the family and/or mystifying.

We make multiple process assumptions about families and how they work. As we listen to the family story, we question in terms of our experiential symbolic model. For example, we assume that the father is farthest out of the family and ask him to tell his story about the family first. Then we proceed through the rest of the family and save mother for last because we assume that she is the one who does most of the gatekeeping in the family. We assume that the father is lonesome and question the family about it. We assume that the family has a form of teaming and ask about that. We look for emotional distance methods for deflecting or decreasing intimacy, the amount of subjectivity available, how the balance of power works, and whether it is covert or overt.

There are a number of perspectives from which to examine any family. Usually, we begin by assuming that the family is a biologically intact whole. This means that every family member is involved with the presenting stress. The first interview usually focuses on involvement rather than on how people are disenfranchised. Creating an interpersonal network is also an important part of the first interview. In this way we carefully implicate the whole family in the trouble. Where is the family in the family lifecycle? We assume in family therapy that all pathology is interpersonal. What are the interpersonal components of the pathology present?

The emotional age of each of the family members is informally assessed. This is a clinical impression. For example, there is a period of preoedipal innocence, then the conscientious, responsible, fact-oriented world of the five- to eight-year-old, the presexual stage of seven to nine, the homosocial period of 12 to 15, and the heterosocial exploration period of 15 to 18. This may be assayed by verbalizations or estimating the relationship to the other members of the family. A depressed, dependent father of 50 may be labeled a post-weaning five-year-old. A nonsexual mother who has never had an orgasm may be labeled as a nine-year-old and just premenstrual. The psychotic schizophrenic is assumed to be emotionally one-and-a-half or two, the manic psychotic a three-year-old, and the psychopath about the same age. One family with a rigid father and teasy cute wife were like two eight-year-olds playing house. The five-year-old son, in complaining about his father's workshop, sounds like a mother-in-law.

In the early part of therapy, assessment is mainly behavioral and interpersonal. After the family members adopt the assumption of themselves as a biologically cohesive unit, we work backwards toward the intrapsychic world. The separation of intrapsychic, behavioral and interpersonal is regarded as arbitrary. It is useful semantically and for theoretical examination, but in our reality there is no difference. Another way of thinking about patients is to compare them with well-known public figures, cartoon or fictional characters, e.g., Archie Bunker, Johnny Carson, Richard Nixon. These picture images stick with the patients and they use and change them.

We look for and underline the culturally invisible pathologies, such as obesity, heavy smoking, pathological innocence, pathological hope, square (nonsubjective) functioning, and overfunctioning. These forms of pathology are those present in the nonpatient family members. They are invisible because they are regarded as normal for the culture or in this family culture. The scapegoat is usually providing a counterbalance to these behaviors and is dedicated to undermining the indifference.

During the first interview, to provide more explicit models of family interaction, we ask about the relationship of the parents in the nuclear family to the grandparents. We sometimes find a current stress in the family, such as a grandparent who has recently gone to a nursing home or who had a mild heart attack, or we may find models in that first generation which are being recapitulated now.

We always read our own responses in the assessment. What is our anxiety level? Do we gain access to our own primary process as we talk with *this* family? Do we experience physical sensations: muscle tightness, beginning erection, depersonalization feelings, absence of anxiety? We listen for voice tone, changes in posture, changes in subject matter, facial set, and special metaphorical words.

The trial of labor is managed in several ways. First, there is the *battle for structure*. This is basically our demand that the family capitulate to the therapist's mode of operating. The second is the *battle for initiative*. We ask questions as a way to prime the family's pump and to orient family members to the kind of process that takes place in therapy. We take no responsibility for getting them to talk about themselves. If they stay impersonal and nonsubjective, we may complain about it or we may congratulate them, telling them that we've already seen one depressing family today and we're glad to see one that doesn't want to talk about problems. The third method of testing is a kind of biopsy of the family's response to ambiguity or increasing anxiety. For example, when we were talking with the divorced parents of a delinquent daughter, the father said, "My wife was the candy kid and I was the son-of-a-bitch." The therapist said, "Can you see it the other way around? You decided to be the son-of-a-bitch to ease the pain on both sides." That gave them another metaphor to visualize the problem. It changes the role of the son-of-a-bitch into the rescuer and, in a small way, upsets the balance of the family. Or, take the situation where the mother says that sonny boy is into drugs and possibly stealing. Father insists he's just a healthy boy. The therapist says, "Is it true that you, mother, had a delinquent brother? And you, father, wanted to be a delinquent but never had the courage to do it when you were a teenager?" A response by the mother and father that shows they are available to such input bodes well for future therapeutic change. A rejection of that interpretation hints that the family is not willing to increase their anxiety and, thus, is not a good candidate for psychotherapy. It also suggests a poor prognosis.

We work in various settings, our office, on the ward, in the school or at the social service agency. Our usual interaction pattern is the verbal interview in the office. Little effort is made to expand content after the initial history. The beginning stages of therapy may follow a pattern, but as we join the family, strategy drops out. We have a number of toys in our offices: doll house, clay, toy cars, teddy bears, Magic Markers and drawing paper, puzzles, gimmicks and checkers. We have some batacca bats and a fish aquarium. All of these objects have real and symbolic use.

The initiative for therapy must come from the family. One way to force this is to pull back and let the family ask questions, make statements or start a fight with the therapist. One may also tease, cajole and push the family, thus inducing confusion so that their initiative starts by an attempt to reorganize themselves. If the whole family does not show up, we are likely to send the subgroup home. Alternatively, we sit with them and complain for the hour how we can't do anything without the whole family. It is a therapeutic non-interview, if you will (Kramer, 1978).

Structured interaction tasks are not an important part of our work, which is not to say that we don't use them. A consistent task is to interdict metacommunicating outside the appointment. All marriages are distorted by a bilateral pseudo-psychotherapy process in which she thinks that this is just the man for her as soon as she gets his alcoholism straightened out, and he thinks that she is just the girl for him as soon

as he gets her over some of her compulsiveness. This effort to straighten out the partner may escalate. Therefore, we suggest they will get more if they do not talk about the interviews when they are not in the office.

Our verbal interview is designed to symbolically invade the family relationships using metaphor, teasing, humor, free association, fantasy, and confrontation to increase the confusion around the compromise character of the family's resolution of stress. The metaphors are utilized as challenges. "It's obvious you two could never get a divorce," or, "Was your marriage really precipitated by her mother?" or, "You act like you are your mother's mother and that would make you your own grandmother." When we use structured interaction tasks, it is actually a form of play with the family. We may have them practice family rituals just for fun instead of being controlled by them. We propose tasks, but they do them only if they are curious enough. A common one lately has been to get the spouses to take turns being in charge, either on a daily or weekly basis. The two spouses are like five-star generals. Neither has the right to order the one around. It is not important to us if they do the task. If they have not done it or if it has not worked well, we might say, "It's probably smart that you didn't try to change things too much. I forgot to warn you that things could get worse." Or, to the sexually deprived husband, "It's probably just as well that you stayed in charge, because if she ever discovered how powerful she is, she could turn out to be more than you could handle." Another favorite is to suggest to the impassed family that they change roles every Tuesday evening. If the family likes it, they may develop it and have fun with it in a way that becomes their own.[5]

GOAL-SETTING

The goals of family therapy are to establish the members' sense of belongingness and si-

---

[5]*Editors' Note.* Note that even though the tasks that might be suggested by Whitaker and Keith could be stated in virtually the same words as those a behaviorist might use (cf. Jacobson, Chapter 15), the *tone, optionality* and *goal* of the present authors would be quite different: The task would be viewed as optional, not required, for effective treatment; the tone would be quite casual, and the goal would be the family's enjoyment rather than a learning experience.

multaneously to provide the freedom to individuate. In our system of therapy, social adaptation is not a goal; we seek to increase the creativity (what we call craziness) of the family and of the individual members.

These goals are accomplished by the aggregate effect of the following: 1) We *increase the interpersonal stress*. We assume that all families can tolerate any increase in anxiety. The homeostatic power of the family is massive in comparison with the therapist's input.[6] This can be accomplished in several ways. One is to convert symptoms into systems problems, thereby increasing the interpersonal stress. For example, a young mother had a phobia about being dangerous to husband and daughter. She refused to describe the content. We said that if she was so selfish with her crazy thoughts we could not stand working with her. Another method is to expose another problem, like father's obesity or mother's tearfulness. In other words, the anxiety is not expanded in the same territory but is expanded horizontally. 2) The family's presence and increased power emerge from shared anxiety in the *development of a family nationalism*. The family members become more of who they are, a team with increased morale. 3) We push to *expand the family's relationships with the extended family*. The relationship to the extended family has a psychic introject of at least three generations and probably more. 4) We push to *expand the family's relationship to the culture and community members*. In this way, the family establishes an interface with the culture, accentuating their sense of belonging to the culture and simultaneously maintaining the freedom to move in and out of it. 5) We push for a *sense of the family boundaries* with joint understanding of and connection with family expectations. 6) An effort to *separate the generations* is critical. Although mother and father should be able to play at being children from time to time and the children should be able to play at being adults, there are real differences between the generations and a separate structure for each.

Especially dangerous are cross-generational triangles, because they disrupt the separation between the generations. When the child carries the delusion that he is mother's peer or when mother completely deserts her adult role and becomes a bonded partner with her son against her husband, it is more dangerous than the triangle between three children or between father, mother and her sister, or father, mother and his secretary. 7) Simultaneously with the clearer structure, *the family must learn how to play*. This goal sounds simple, but family groups oftentimes have great difficulty with it. To be more specific, families need to differentiate between playful sadism and real murder. They need to differentiate between sexual intercourse and flirting. Play is universal. It must be present to maintain health and facilitate growth (Winnicott, 1971). One manifestation of playfulness is the role availability in the family. All roles should be available to each person depending upon the situation and with the family's agreement. 8) We strive to develop a we-they union between the therapeutic team and the family with the *constant cycle of separation and rejoining*. In this way we model the we-ness of the children to the parents and model for the parents a relationship to their own two families of origin. 9) We want to *explode the myth of individuality*. We want the family to believe in themselves as a unit, but it is important that this belief be flavored with a strong sense of its absurdity. 10) *Each family member ought to be more of who he/she is*, with added access to him/herself.

The more specific ultimate goals involved in work with a family tend to evolve out of the process of the therapy. That is, they are often established without any verbal definition by the co-therapists, evolving out of their interaction with the family. Those goals which are established by the therapist nonverbally have an advantage because the usual intellectual thinking tends, in both the family and the therapy team, to divert, dilute and avoid change. Methods which bypass this intellectual game-playing are more effective. In the same way that parents need to maintain their roles, we assume that therapists will remain faithful to their role responsibilities, while at the same time using the "self" to the fullest possible effect.

---

[6]*Editors' Note.* While this is a position that is often assumed by family therapists, it does not follow that, therefore (sic), "families can tolerate any increase in anxiety." Moreover, there is sufficient empirical evidence (Gurman & Kniskern, 1978a) of the negative effects of family therapy to question this assumption.

The goals of treatment are evolved by the therapist and the family, both jointly and separately. Many are largely unconscious during therapy and can only be acknowledged in retrospect.[7] The family usually has goals which are quite different from those the therapists aspire to. In essence, our goal is to become more human in the context of the family. The therapist's early goals are usually covert but dominant. For example, he/she may merely try to help the patients stay in treatment, or he/she may elect to invade massively in hopes of accomplishing what is needed within the first few interviews. The piano teacher metaphor is useful in defining the family's ongoing expectations and interests. The pupil may come the first time just because his parents send him, or he may stay on for a brief time to learn a few techniques and then decide he does not want to know anything about piano. On the other hand, he may gradually change from being a reluctant victim of his mother's interest to becoming an enthusiastic student, and even go on to play Beethoven. This metaphor accurately describes the range of what is available in our style of family therapy. The differences in goals between therapists and family are often resolved in a mutual experience with learning one another's language as the therapist highlights the significant interpersonal events. In some way, with each family, we try to create a new culture or a new family, with us as grandparents. We work at developing a dream gestalt with the family. However, it is valuable for the family to know explicitly the personal agenda of the therapist. The most honest way of revealing the therapist's personal agenda is to admit we do family therapy as a way for us to aid our own growth. We do not operate altruistically out of any saintly inner wish to help the patients change in order to counterbalance the gargantuan pressures of the culture.

Usually the family's painful symptom is only a ticket of admission. Symptom relief is certainly valuable in itself or as a cultural goal, but we assume there is always a more serious distress. Then, relief of the symptom may prevent a more adequate handling of the hidden stress. For example, one patient came in for sexual impotence. His symptom disappeared when the therapist exposed a delusion that he would get the Nobel prize. The interpersonal life-style that generated the two symptoms was not modified, only diverted.

Our goal is to bring about change in the patient so that we can thereby change ourselves. Psychotherapy, like a courtship, demands some understanding of the investment the therapist has, the vulnerability he hopes to establish in himself and his respect for both the family's rights and his own rights. The goals of the therapist should be overt because it is a test of the teaming established between the family and the therapist. Any deliberate dishonesty tends to weaken that bond. The way we discuss goals depends upon the developmental age of the family. If we give the family members objective information at the beginning or end of the first interview, we often find later that they have a complete amnesia for it. We usually discuss goals when the family asks for them. We don't always respond in the frame of their question. Sometimes we define goals in a double-binding way or invent a koan or paradox. When one drug addict asked what Keith was trying to do, Keith told him that he was trying to teach him how to suffer. A rigid, stand-offish couple returned for three very boring interviews. Near the end of the third interview, the wife, a behavioral therapist, asked, "What are your goals? I don't know what you're up to." The therapist responded, "I'm not up to anything, I'm just trying to get through the third carbon copy of the first interview." The impression may be created that we refuse to talk straight about goals. This is not true. We do wait until the family asks, and respond according to the terms in which they ask. The terms, of course, have both verbal and nonverbal components. The nonverbal carry the greatest importance. As much as possible, our goals are established in metaphorical language, a language that incorporates more than one level of meaning and expands meaning rather than narrowing it. Thus, another goal is to reactivate metaphors in the family process, to stimulate the use of expanded meanings. The use of metaphorical language and visual or pictorial metaphors is most valuable because they can be left incomplete. Extended metaphors lose their cre-

---

[7] *Editors' Note.* While such a position may shock researchers, our view is that creative investigations of such phenomena, which we agree exist, would be enormously informative.

ative stimulus. The open gestalt or the nonverbal component in any metaphor makes it less easy for the family to memorize it and thus dismiss it, making it one more thing which they recognize but don't learn from. Change necessitates owning something as your own; an incomplete gestalt makes for learning rather than recognition only.

The changes that we look for come in small packages. As therapists we are frequently in danger of missing change. Change is seen in the way the husband walks at the end of the interview. It may show by a change in voice tone. The change may emerge as one talks about the trouble, whether they say "we" or "I."[8] For example, the two of us saw a family with a schizophrenic son. He was very aloof and difficult to work with. In one interview, we had a long arm wrestling match with him. At the end of the hour, when the young man was leaving the interview, he said good-bye to Whitaker and held out his hand. Keith wasn't involved in the good-bye and did not even notice it. When he left, Whitaker asked, "Did you see that?" He was talking about the *offered* hand and a new personal intensity in the man's eyes. Keith missed the whole scene.

Change is difficult to measure and can be looked at from several points of view. At the end of the eighth interview with a particular family, Keith complained that we were failing. The father said, "I don't think you are failing. I feel like things have changed a lot with us. I'd hate to be around when you think that you are being a success." Thus, there are some families that don't change at all in the therapy hour but may experience quite a different change outside. The reverse is also true. There are families that appear to be changing significantly in treatment, but little change occurs in the outside world. These are discouraging cases.

TREATMENT APPLICABILITY

The main countraindication to family therapy

is the absence of a family therapist. There is also a relative contraindication, the absence of a family, i.e., the absence of relatives. Our method of clinical practice is family therapy. *We do not simply do family therapy; we are family therapists.* Any psychotherapy venture ought to begin with a family interview. If the whole family is not available, then someone from the patient's world should be there for at least the first interview. The presenting problem is not what determines the suitability for family treatment. Suitability depends upon the extent to which they share our culture's implicit belief about how the world works. It works best with people who believe in families. It works less well with people who do not believe in the family.

Families Most Likely to Have a Therapeutic Experience with This Approach

These families are most likely to find this approach therapeutic:

1) Crazy families who are in for fun and/or involved in a dilemma which is multifaceted and multipersonal.
2) Therapists who would like a family therapy experience or families with psychological sophistication.
3) Nonsubjective families with psychological problems. Again, the system is not based upon intellectual understanding but rather upon an interactive process, metaphorical language and personal interaction.
4) Families in crisis.
5) Families with a serious scapegoat, for example, with a schizophrenic in the family (pre-, acute or chronic).
6) Families with young children seem to get more from working with us. We become parents to these new families.
7) Families with multiple level problems.
8) High-powered or VIP families.
9) Families who are disorganized by the culture, i.e., a family who has a probation officer, a social worker, or an alcoholic counselor overattached to them. Our effort is to increase the family's unity so that they can get rid of intruders.

---

[8]*Editors' Note.* We agree with Whitaker and Keith and would like to suggest that it may be empirical research into such subtle and "small" changes that will help to bridge the gap between researcher and clinician.

Families Who Are Immune to Infection by Family Therapy

The families for whom there is no "take" in experiential/symbolic therapy are idiosyncratic. We have no way of predicting a priori what families will and will not work well. The approach has developed in work with biologically intact families. It works better when all three generations are available. It works less well when members are not available by reason of death or distance or simply refuse to come. We assume this referral to be a family ploy. We do adapt our work to all sorts of situations, but the likelihood of a "take" is reduced. We work with extended families, social networks, divorcing couples with simultaneous affairs, divorced couples with a child in crisis, and lesbian and homosexual couples. Still, families who seem immune to infection by this method of family therapy are:

1) Those that are panicked by spontaneous feelings, e.g., post-divorce situations where wounds are still healing and are too tender for reexploration.
2) Those with long-standing pathology and no strong inducement to change.
3) Those in which the scapegoat is an adopted child.
4) While we often work with acutely psychotic schizophrenics outside the hospital and without drugs, we are less successful with manic psychotics who are new to us.

Deciding About Referrals

It is unusual for us to make a referral to someone else once we have started with a family. If the family members decide they don't care to see us, we counsel them to do their own referral. We have a substitute system; the use of co-therapists and consultants can abrogate the need for referral.

Case examples

1) A wealthy WASP family was at war about daughter's engagement to a black high school teacher. The therapist brought in a black co-therapist.
2) A pediatrician referred a family with a child who he thought was autistic. The therapist asked a child psychiatry fellow to work as co-therapist. After a therapeutic alliance was established with the family, they were referred for a more extensive assessment of the child's educational needs. The family continued in treatment.
3) Two male co-therapists worked with a family with a schizophrenic adolescent. The mother was put off by the uneven sex ratio. A woman was brought in as a consultant for three visits.

We refer for individual therapy when the family therapy experience is completed. When there is a question of neurological difficulty, we refer to a neurologist. In the case of a manic attack, we refer the patient for lithium. We do not want to supersede the family therapy. Two schizophrenics were in marital treatment. The wife was experiencing anxiety which was painful to her. She requested medication. The therapist told her that he did not believe in medication and would not give medication to her. However, he did not feel it appropriate for him to make a final decision about it and told her that, if she wanted medication, he could suggest another physician whom she might see. The family treatment continued; however, it lost some of its excitement for the therapist.

Situations in Which No Treatment Is Recommended

No treatment is recommended in certain instances:

1) When there has been a completed treatment case, the family has had a therapeutic experience and ended. When a new symptom emerges or an old one reemerges, we have the family come back for a single-visit consultation. If there is excitement in the whole family and they are handling the symptom well, then it is not useful to reactivate treatment. These situations are like fire drills. The family is testing its ability to respond to a crisis and checking out our availability.
2) Families who have had too much therapy, i.e., professional patients, are advised that

they should stop looking for treatment. They are to come in if a crisis arises.

3) Families who are seeing a good therapist and come to us out of a negative transference response. We send them back with the suggestion that we would be glad to act as consultants if the therapist so desired.

There are some situations where we are not likely to continue or to begin treatment, but it is not because treatment is not indicated. If the family is only willing to send a segment, that is the husband, one child, or husband and wife or husband, wife and one child only, then we suggest they find someone else. If the father is against psychotherapy, we would rather not be involved. The family members are free to do whatever they want with our refusal. We leave the opportunity open to return to family therapy at any time father may decide that he is willing. The same is true if there is not enough anxiety in the family to make psychotherapy worthwhile. Then it is our preference to decline the referral rather than trying to carry their part of the anxiety load.

THE STRUCTURE OF THE THERAPY PROCESS

It is critical to begin the treatment process with the whole family. In this way the therapy team gets permission from the whole system to change components of the system. If it is not possible in the beginning to have the whole group, we set it up so that the extended family comes in as soon as possible. Once they have been in and the intrapsychic projections of the different generations onto each other have been contaminated, modified and weakened, they can return whenever possible, but they are not necessary. It is best, however, if all those people who are living together join the interviews.

Our demand to have the whole family in is the beginning of the "battle for structure." It begins with the first phone call. It has to do with when we meet and who will be there. We never split a marital pair for the first interview, but we may accommodate by splitting the generations. If the parents are in a panic about impending divorce or father's newly discovered affair and they do not want to bring the children,

we tell them that it is all right the first time, but they must plan to bring the children for the second interview. An internist referred a policeman who was having severe work-related anxiety attacks. Neither the man nor his wife had had previous psychotherapy. He did not feel that he could talk about some of his feelings with his wife present. Keith set up the initial interview structure so that we would balance. There were 20 minutes with him alone, 20 minutes with her alone and 20 minutes with the couple. We followed this pattern for three interviews and then met conjointly thereafter. A second example with a different flavor involved a minor league VIP from Los Angeles. He was planning to move to our area with his daughter. He was divorced from his wife, who lived near our medical center. He was concerned about his daughter, who had had extensive psychological and medical evaluations in Los Angeles. The evaluation produced an indeterminant diagnosis somewhere between schizophrenic reaction and hysterical personality. Family therapy with himself and his daughter had been initiated and in his eyes it had been a failure. Father decided to move back closer to his ex-wife. He was referred to one of us. "Would I see his daughter?" Keith said, "I would be delighted to see her as long as you and your ex-wife come along." "Oh, but we wanted her to be seen individually in addition to the family treatment." "Sorry, I do not work that way." "Would you see me and her alone?" "Oh, no, I would need to have both you and mother in. And, by the way, both grandmothers would have to come for the first session." The family never called back. Keith set up this structure because of the father's attempt to prescribe the type of therapy necessary. They were not psychotherapeutic virgins and had already had a family therapy failure. Keith needed all the power possible on his side in the beginning. It is better to fail to start than to start and fail.

As the therapy goes on, we push to get the entire family at each meeting. We also suggest "consultation" visits by three or four generations, as well as related network people, including boyfriends, girlfriends, sexual partners, neighbors, or previous therapists. This effort is to help evolve a large system anxiety. We at times schedule conjoint play therapy with small children, or occasionally with subgroups of the family. We discover and rediscover that the power to change anything in the family, whether schizophrenia, divorce or internecine fighting, requires a voltage amplification in the suprasystem. Subgroup or individual therapy tends to develop massive covert paranoia among the people who are in and the people who are out and is much less functional than small changes arising in the large group. Our intent is to infiltrate the largest system possible and get permission for change. The permission can be overt, although it is usually implicit in any meeting of the larger group. We strive not to allow any favoritism, such as individual interviews with the family scapegoat, whether it's the black sheep or the white knight hero.

Combining treatments is not a favorite method, but, again, there is not a hard and fast rule against concurrent therapy. The chance of being ineffective is increased when several unconnected therapists are involved. Patients need all of their emotional energy available in one place for treatment to be effective. Sometimes we functionally divide our effort. In our work with anorexia nervosa, the pediatrician monitors the weight and physical effects, while the psychiatrists do family therapy. Occasionally, at referral one of the family is on psychotropic medication. Then we have another psychiatrist monitor the medication to avoid seeming like a magician. We use very little medication in our practice. While we rarely start medication, we do not take people off medications prescribed by another.

Family therapy is the best way to start any psychotherapy process. The family members need to be implicated in one another's living. Individualism without individuation, i.e., the absent-without-leave family member, is a common psychiatric illness in our culture. Therapeutic experiences are most valuable when they occur with significant others. By this process, the experiences are built into one's living rather than "in the head" insights.

If causation is circular, change is circular. Everybody in the family is altered by change at any level.[9] A cross-generational group carries the most power for change. Grandparents have amazing symbolic power and it is amplified when they remain separate from the treatment process. By bringing them into the interviews, the grandparent homeostatic power may be modified or adapted to catalyze change in the family system.

It is difficult to do process-focused family therapy without the children. They are more flexible, more honest and more affectively available than the parents. The therapist may use them as a lever to invade the family's boundary. With children, he can model for parents the methods and freedom to individuate and to reunite. The therapist moves in-and-out, the children soon learn to move in-and-out, thus defeating the parents' attempt at embedded consistency. When the children are not present, the sacred component of their role in the family is ritualized and keeps the system from changing.

Thus, the experiential quality of family therapy requires the children's presence. Frequently, change is ignited by the therapist's playing with the children and teasing by his parent-child fun. It tips the parents to be childlike and drop their prideful, adult status role. It is particularly useful to help father avoid the isolation that the culture dictates. Mother may get some sense that she doesn't have to endure battle fatigue but may fight for her personal individuation. Play with the kids includes taking them on our lap for cuddling, rubbing shoulders and backs or play fighting. Parents enjoy this physical contact personally. When the 11-year-old son's shoulders are massaged, mother often rolls her shoulders perceptibly. Children usually grow in the family therapy. We do not see situations where they are injured by their presence in the therapy. Usually, their anxiety about the family whole is somewhat alleviated. The children's dreams and nightmares are more distressing than any reality component.

Co-therapy

Co-therapy is a regular component of our work. Mostly, two therapists join together in a professional marriage for ongoing treatment; however, we use alternatives. A therapist may work alone, but use a colleague as consultant along the way. The consultant comes into interviews on call. We also get together as therapists to share case fragments and problems.

---

[9]*Editors' Note.* This is another view commonly held by family therapists. We know of no research evidence for such a belief (cf. Gurman and Kniskern, 1978b) and would certainly welcome data relevant to this fundamental clinical assumption.

There are a number of reasons for operating as a team.[10] 1) Teaming allows more creativity and variability in functioning. At root this gives more power to the co-therapy team. 2) Psychotherapy is anticultural and it is important to have a close colleague in order to not pay the price of being depersonalized. When two professionals are present in the name of therapeutic change, the spiritual power increases exponentially. When subjective perceptions are shared by two members, they are less easily disregarded. 3) The therapist's pathology intrudes less. This component may be less important if the therapist uses a structured method of working. In co-therapy each therapist may use him/herself and his/her subjectivity with a colleague there to counterbalance. 4) Co-therapy offers the freedom to think. While one therapist is working actively with the family, the second therapist may sit back, look at what is happening from a distance, think over what is said and arrive at some differing conceptions. 5) Co-therapy helps prevent the therapist from stealing one family member for a therapeutic helper. Either the black sheep or the white knight, when used in this way, distorts the process of family unity and further isolates the scapegoat of the family. 6) It is our belief that co-therapy reduces affect spilling outside the interview. There is less chance of the therapist's holding himself aloof during the interview and taking his affect out in a supervisory or curbstone consultation with another therapist, his spouse or some unrelated person. 7) Co-therapy decreases the sense of loss at the family's leave-taking. Protective withdrawal of the individual therapist from his next patient and the grieving which might distort the family's leave-taking are minimized. When the family ends, the therapists have each other. Thereby, the therapist augments his professional development, his increasing competence and his increasing enjoyment of family therapy. More simply, it is much easier for two therapists to avoid compromising their integrity or their goals because of the impending departure of the family. 8) Finally, it is possible in the co-therapy setting for one therapist and one patient to have an extended experience in a one-to-one relationship while the family is present but not feeling extruded. This may take place either in a single interview or over a period of interviews. Such special empathy and interaction between one member of a team and one member of the family will not distort the therapeutic process as it does when one therapist wears several hats.

There are obvious disadvantages in working as co-therapists. It costs the patients more, there are more scheduling problems with a whole family, it reduces each one's grandiosity, and interpersonal complications between the therapists can arise. We use marriage as a metaphor to guide our work as co-therapists. At the heart of a growthful marriage is the struggle between the two spouses to remain autonomous "I's" and at the same time to join in a dependent "we." This same struggle is at issue for both the family and the co-therapy teams.

We do most of our work in our offices. However, we do not exclude working in other settings by any means. The spatial arrangement in the therapy room is simple, yet it is a significant factor in the therapeutic process. The family who comes to our office for help is dependent and one-down. The therapeutic team should be physically grouped rather than invading the family's seating arrangement. The bilateral transference relationship between the team and the family develops a suprafamily, or a surrogate extended family. A subsequent extended-family conference occurs against the background of this transference and allows more fluidity in structure for the family itself. The flux of closeness and separation between the treatment team and the family is clearer when there are physically established boundaries. We preserve playing space in the middle of the family room for children or for adults since the process usually involves physical interactions, e.g., arm wrestling, seating changes or play therapy on the floor.

Ordinarily, our therapy is unlimited in time. Time-limited therapy is invoked when there are reality reasons: the family moving out of the state, not having insurance or being concerned about the financial aspects of treatment. Time-limited therapy is also useful for people who don't know whether they want psychotherapy, or are just interested in having the experience of being in a therapeutic state. For example, a

---

[10]*Editors' Note.* Included in the list that follows are several eminently researchable hypotheses.

psychiatric resident and his wife may want therapy with their baby so they can get as much as possible in the way of growth input, but they are not interested in extended probing.

We try to pick up any evidence of the family's desire to take on fuller responsibility for itself and for the therapy. If the therapy is working well, the therapeutic team says, "We better quit while we are ahead." If the therapy is not proceeding in a useful way, we suggest, "Why don't we give the whole thing up? Maybe it really isn't worth the stress."

Unlimited time allows the family's objectives to change as time goes along, just as a piano teacher may have one pupil who starts out with little enthusiasm but becomes intrigued and ends up five years later playing Beethoven. If the family is intent on expanding its flexibility and increasing its creativity, we see no reason to stop at the originally defined goal or goals. It seems to take a year for creativity to blossom and interest in Beethoven to bear fruit. In the reality of practice, there are many variations in time. The average family comes 10 to 15 times consecutively and then terminates for good. Some make several later follow-up visits. A large percentage of families comes in for a consultation or crisis intervention. These families may come to the clinic only one to three times and not return.

Sessions are usually offered once a week, although if only a minimum of anxiety is present or if the family is unusually rigid and with low anxiety tolerance, we may spread out to two or more weeks. In contrast, appointments might occur every day if anxiety is high.

In the early part of therapy, decisions about the therapeutic time and structure are made by the therapeutic team. It is the way that all psychotherapy begins. The family starts like a small infant, taking only limited responsibility for themselves. They require structure. We often repeat in our workshops and residency training that the therapist always has the right to make unilateral decisions. The nature of the unilateral decisions is variable from family to family. The freedom to make them decreases as one becomes closer to the family. At the beginning, they are made arbitrarily; later on in therapy they are often made more out of frustration.

Some critics fear we drive people away by being too structured or making too many demands early in treatment. This has not been our experience. We do not bribe people into therapy by agreeing to do whatever they want. We, in fact, challenge their motivation with the result that they push for therapy or go away if they are hesitant. Once we have managed to win this battle for control, however, we soften considerably. This same model applies to rearing children. If the children are in control, the flow of love between parent and child is much inhibited. And in the long run, both parent and child are cheated.

In the mid-phase, decisions about treatment are made by common agreement. Later in therapy, the decisions are usually made by the family alone. As the therapy becomes more a suprasystem, the family takes more and more responsibility for making their own out-of-therapy decisions and the therapist is given the opportunity to back out of being the parental figure in a parent-infant relationship. Finally, the family becomes better integrated in changing themselves so they do not need an outside person. The model for this process is once again the evolving parent-child relationship. It begins with infancy and goes to late adolescence, where the initiative is with the kids, who then bear responsibility for their own living.

ROLE OF THE THERAPIST

The therapist is like a coach or a surrogate grandparent. Both roles demand structure, discipline and creativity, as well as caring and personal availability. Balance between these components is established through experience. Our availability is different from the biological parent in that it does not involve the whole self of the therapist.

We are very active as therapists. We don't exclude being directive and may use silence as one unusual activity which is used to increase anxiety. The therapist overtly controls the first few sessions of family therapy. He is very active, both in infiltrating the family and exposing anxiety-laden territory, but usually without being directive. We expect to be part of the family's interaction. Although we do not forbid family members from talking to each other, we assume the main process to come from the family's interacting with the therapeutic team.

We always prefer to work as co-therapists. The therapeutic team is modeled after a marriage with children. The family is seen as a new baby who, with luck, grows to be a child, an adolescent, and finally leaves home. The two "parents" ordinarily assume the roles described in the small group literature as executive or educational director and the supportive or nurturant individual. These roles with the family can be stabilized, but, ordinarily, they move back and forth in a single interview or from the early part of therapy to the later part. The third therapist, the co-therapy "we" (or, from the other side, the paranoid "they"), functions as a decision-making discussion center.

The evolving role of the therapy team moves through several stages. In the early part of therapy, the parental co-therapy team is all-powerful, but it quickly defines itself as impotent, unable to push the whole family around. The co-therapists depend upon the family to lead the suprafamily. The therapeutic team declines all efforts to be regarded as magic or possessing supra-knowledge of how that family should conduct its life. We assume that each family culture has a style all its own and that our function is to help perfect it and give it more explicit and specific direction defined by its own function patterning. It is like teaching tennis to an advanced player. The entire game cannot be made over; rather the player's strong points are consolidated and emphasized and weak points corrected.

In the second interview, the family says, "What should we talk about?" The therapist replies, "I don't know. What do you want to change?" "Well, we told you last time." "I know, but that has probably altered since then. You carry the ball and we'll be glad to try to help."

In the mid-phase of therapy, the parental therapeutic team functions as a stress activator, a growth expander and a creativity stimulator. In this phase, when the family is secure, the therapist may say, "By the way, mother, when you spoke like that to your husband, you sounded like you were talking to your mother or your father. I wonder if you really want to let him get away with that." This implies that it is a joint arrangement between the two spouses. She is being infantile not only because

she wants to be, but also because he needs her to be infantile. The difference between the early and mid-phase is often best seen when the grandparents are brought into ongoing therapy. Two things commonly happen. First, the whole family reverts back to first interview behavior. It is like a sociable family reunion. The therapist asks questions. The second possibility is that the subsystem of the family that has been having interviews pushes ahead with their work, bringing the grandparents right into the middle phase therapy. In a subsequent interview, we hear reports that the older generation reports that they didn't think anything happened and it wasn't very useful. Too much was being made of too little is their frequent comment.

In the adolescent or late phase, the team has no function except to be there and to watch. The co-therapists provide a time and place for the family to get together. Of course, they are available. The therapists depend upon the family to carry all of the initiative and should not try to interfere even if they see they can contribute. In this later phase, the therapeutic team functions as a proud parent, watching the family yet mitigating its own role. This follows the patterning of the parent relationship to a late adolescent who is about ready to leave home. Parents who try to continue educating their children at this late stage are making a serious mistake. The adolescent's independent functioning should be more than respected; it should be revered. The therapeutic team needs to do this with a late-stage family. For example, mother says to father, "I think I may end up divorcing you." It is tempting for the therapist to say, "You've never done it all these 18 years. I don't see why you think you could do it now." Or, contrariwise, "It looks like you two are more loving. I cannot see why you talk about divorce." These are a contribution in the early or midphase of therapy, but are certainly not pertinent in the late phase.

We often use self-disclosure, sharing minutiae in a metaphorical manner, imposing upon ourselves the limits of our own role models. We use it in specific ways, usually sharing fragments or facets of our lives which we have worked over in our own therapy or through our living (Fellner, 1976). Going beyond the role model must be carefully monitored so that there is not a role reversal where the therapist becomes an organizing educator while the family is not allowed full opportunity for its own initiative. *Like humor, personal disclosure is used to increase the interpersonal focus, to shatter a gestalt which is becoming too set—never to diminish anxiety.*

Later in therapy, the therapist's participation can at times be increased, moving towards fragments of his fantasy as they occur during the interview, or bits of his personal history. As the family becomes more secure in handling his input, he can feel free to be increasingly nonrational, free associative, fantasy organized, confronting or paradoxical in any one of many different models. For example, "Dad, I don't think you have to worry about the family getting along so much better. It's not going to last anyway. They'll go back to isolating you and beating on mother by next week or at least the week after." Or, on another occasion, "Mother, I'm certainly glad I'm not married to you the way you take off after your husband. I think I would run for the hills if you were my wife." Or, to one of the kids, "Hey, you know the way your father looks at you when he tells you to either clean up your room or he's going to paddle your behind, I would be tempted to head for San Francisco and probably get on drugs just to get back at him." Noting physical responses to interactions can be extremely powerful. "The way you glared at me just then gave me a prickly feeling in the back of my neck."

Another method of self-disclosure which we use is interaction between the co-therapists. It may be in the form of a private joke or a comment about our outside life. We may share a childhood recollection with our co-therapist. Or we may ask if she thinks we are too judgmental about the mother. The therapist is sharing fragments of himself and not really asking for help. It is important to note that the therapist is not raising questions for the family to answer, but is making statements about his own set for which he can be fully responsive. He is not imputing to them anything that they have to face, reject, rebel against or become dependent about.

Therapists do not have a choice about joining the family. If the family continues to come to the clinic, they do so because they have given the therapist some role. We actively join the family. Our transference to them we assume to

be the anesthesia for their tolerating the anxiety precipitated later in the middle phase. Ongoing therapy demands both joining and distancing sequences. That is, the therapist must be able to leave the role by his own initiative and later reenter it. It's as though the co-therapists take turns jumping over Wynne et al.'s (1958) "rubber fence" into the family, holding hands with the partner and jumping back. They thus take turns being "in" and "out." They model the basic problem in family growth. The process of uniting and individuating is both a group stress and the fluctuating experience of individual members as well as family subsystems. The co-therapy team joins the family and in so doing forms a therapeutic suprafamily of which it is a subgroup.

The sequence of joining and distancing is important. It is a lot like being with children. A father can get furious with his kids one minute, then be loving the next. We take the same stance with families. If Keith gets angry, he does not hold onto it. If Keith is joking with the son about his flirtation with mother, he retains the freedom to empathize with father's sadness about being left out. A model is Don Juan, Carlos Castaneda's (1975) teacher. He describes a number of quasi-real, quasi-metaphorical situations where the teacher moves close and then away, and then disappears and suddenly reappears. This is a nice model for the family therapist. It is a difficult, advanced technique for the therapist to master. Less experienced therapists oftentimes do not have a sense of when they are in and when they can afford to withdraw. There is a difference in the way that we handle this. Whitaker can allow himself to be disinterested, suddenly become involved deeply with a family member, then just as suddenly change the topic or dissociate himself. Keith operates more cautiously. He is apt to lead gradually toward a confrontation, engage in the interaction, and then move back more slowly.

The therapist's role changes throughout therapy. In the beginning, the therapist is a kindergarten teacher/shepherd. Within the therapy he moves from being this dominant, all-giving parent of the infant to being the "as if" pal, an agemate of the young child, then to be the advisor and resource person of the older child, and eventually the retired parent of an adult. As the family becomes more independent, the therapist team can become more personal, more educational, and more outside the family as such. When a family moves toward termination, we respect it as a real initiative, not a symbolic one. We always stand ready to end with them. We do not "look" at reasons why the family wants to leave, but begin to help planning the termination as soon as it is mentioned.

TECHNIQUES OF MARITAL-FAMILY THERAPY

Earlier we noted that structuring in our therapy sessions is implicit. The first interview includes a systems history of the family. We actively attempt to learn about the family emotional system: Where are the stresses located, who has had symptoms, what are the individual character structures and what about past stress episodes? We try to expose the personality style of each individual, as well as the personality of the total family and its subgroups. We ask about grandparents from each family of origin. Where are they? How are they? What do they think about the situation? We propose an extended family interview. When can they come?

We follow a pattern in our first interview. The family is told that we will talk with each member singly to get a multiple view of what is going on with the family. We start with the member who is psychologically most distant, most often the father. After father, we go around to the different siblings, saving the mother for last. In most cases, the mother knows what is going on and is most available to be a symptom bearer. This style of interviewing may seem awkward and may go against the instincts of many therapists, but the interactions that develop around it and the messages that are sent result in a big therapeutic payoff.

If one or another of the family members interrupts the talking person, we politely ask him/her to wait his/her turn and reiterate that each will have a chance. If an argument breaks out which sounds like one that has been ongoing, we ask them to hold it, because we are not trying to cause trouble but to find out what is up with the family. While we get the history, we are continually restructuring what they say by deciding who talks, minimizing some information, and highlighting other areas.

Joining the Family

The family therapist must develop a basic empathy with the family. We hope his/her transference feelings will include an identification, a feeling of pain and a sense of the family's desperate efforts to self-heal.

We work hard to capture the family in the first interviews. If the therapist can develop a liaison with father, there is a good chance that the family will continue in therapy. If not, the chances are they will drop out. Additionally, the chance of losing the family is increased if the therapist gets overinvolved with the mother too soon. The overinvolvement can happen in several ways: 1) sexually-tinged seduction; 2) taking her on as the identified patient too soon, thus stealing her from the family; and 3) making her angry.[11]

Another way the therapist gains membership in the family is by the bilateral transference. We adopt some of their language, softer accent, or rhythm. The therapist's posture may be the same as that of someone in the family. We listen for their metaphorical set and attempt to make use of it.

Playing with the children is one important way to join the family. It need not be explicitly significant, but often is by surprise. We described earlier our techniques for this.

Specific Techniques

One of our standard early techniques is to precipitate in the family a taboo against the bilateral pseudo-therapy which develops in every marriage. We give the parents full credit for what they have accomplished in straightening each other out. We declare the end of that therapy, its failure, and demand they turn that therapeutic function over to us. They are to allow

---

[11]*Editors' Note.* Indeed, there is research evidence to support the necessity of early involvement of the father in family therapy (Gurman and Kniskern, 1978b). Whitaker and Keith's speculations about overinvolvement with the mother are certainly researchable.

no further crying on shoulders, no further talking about illness, symptoms, or their relationship except during the interview. Isolating the metacommunication to the interview setting induces a great reality to the home-edited interpersonal communication. It interrupts the parentification typical of the ordinary marriage. It undercuts the secondary gain they had accrued as each took a turn at being infantile to precipitate the parental (therapeutic) function in the spouse. The technique is most ably activated in the middle of the first interview. When father says, "You see, Mary, that's exactly what I was saying to you." The therapist may say, "Shut up! This is my project, I don't want you helping. You'll just make things worse and think of the joy of not having to listen to her whining anymore." This kind of specific interdiction is a modeling of what we hope will happen outside the interview.

Changes in the family structure many times result from the therapist's invading the family dynamic operation. We tend to emphasize non-educational, non-insightful patterns, such as paradoxical intention, the posing of dissonant models, teasing, deriding or reversing a family's statements, or presenting arguments which are ego-syntonic. For example, mother says, "I am unhappy with my husband." The therapist suggests that the next time she should get a younger man since she looks more energetic. Maybe she could pick a professional athlete who likes a lot of exercise. She could consider taking all this husband's money and going to San Francisco where life is very exciting and the possibility of happiness much greater.

We like to use personal confrontations, even presenting our own boredom. "Mrs. Zilch, the way you responded to your husband just then made me have the nicest feeling that I was not married to you. I don't know whether I would cringe and leave the house or move to counter-attack, but it certainly was upsetting to me and I'm just a visitor here." In like manner, if mother, for example, is talking about how weak she feels in the family, we tease her by presenting contrary evidence. She has raised five children who were born one year apart, her husband was absent during that time and it is a wonder that she is not flat on her back with battle fatigue or maybe psychotic.

Our intent with these techniques is to produce transcendent experiences, that is, to help the individual members or even the family as a whole to move above the pain and stress to savor the laughable situations the therapist verbalizes, or to indeed enjoy the experience of looking from a completely different frame. We hope to attain the kind of existential shift that Ehrenwald (1966) presents. In like manner, we confront patients on praxis, that is the accommodation he makes to her projection. For example, she wants a mother and looks up to him and he very obligingly agrees to play the mother game, even though they both agree it is a pseudo-mothering she gets.

With our emphasis on the power of the experience in the therapy hour itself, it is not surprising that homework is rarely used, except to interdict the generation flip as described previously. We try to end their pseudo-therapy work on each other. We also advise getting the extended family in and pressure until this is accomplished. We may suggest that each person visit his home of origin without the other so as to regress in the service of that family's ego. If the extended family cannot come in and a home visit is not possible, we suggest that the members of the marriage send empty audio cassettes to their families. The instructions are for the parent to dictate a tape describing their lives up until the kids were born.

These techniques are used gently and early in therapy to test out the family's tolerance. Later on, we push them more specifically. The techniques we consider most important follow.

1) *Symptoms are redefined as efforts for growth.* We then increase the pathology and implicate the whole family. The family seen is converted into an absurd one. Our effort is to depathologize human experience. The wife was complaining that her husband was trying to get rid of her. "He's never loved me, you know," she said. "He said once that he would cut me up. Another time he threatened me with a gun." The therapist replies, "How can you say he doesn't love you? Why else would he want to kill you?" Psychosis in one of the family members can be defined as an effort to be Christ-like: "I'll be a nobody so that you and father will be saved." Or the des-

peration felt by one member of the family can be redefined as a hopeful sign since it means the family cares enough. Just a mild degree of tongue-in-cheek quality must be included with this technical play so that the confrontation will not be too painful.

2) *Modeling fantasy alternatives to real life stress.* A woman who has attempted suicide can be pushed to a fantasy. "If you were going to murder your husband, how would you do it?" Or, "Suppose when you got suicidal you decided you were going to kill me. How would you do it? Would you use a gun or a knife or cyanide?" In a family with a schizophrenic son, the daughter's conversation with her father was understood by the therapist as a sexual pass. The family was embarrassed and perplexed by that. At the end of the hour, however, the father tenderly held his daughter and rocked her in his arms. Thus, teaching the use of fantasy permits expansion of the emotional life without the threat of real violence or real sexual acting-out.

3) *Separating interpersonal stress and intra-personal fantasy stress.* For example, the patient who has attempted suicide can be encouraged to talk with the group about whom her husband would marry if she killed herself, how soon he would marry, how long he would be sad, how long the children would be sad, who would get the insurance, how her mother-in-law would feel, what they would do with her personal belongings, etc. This conversion of intrapersonal fantasy stress to an interpersonal framework is valuable since it contaminates the fantasy. It allows the family a new freedom in communication among themselves since they discover that such frightening words do not mean the end of the world.

4) Technically, once the relationship is established and the supra-unit team is operational, the therapist can *add many practical bits of intervention which in one-to-one therapy would seem like inappropriate moves*, but in the context of the family are safe since the family will utilize what it wants and is perfectly competent in discarding what is not useful. For example, the husband whose wife is having headaches can be offhandedly of-

fered the possibility that if he should spank her, the headaches might go away. Or the wife who is "driven" up the wall by her children's nagging or dad's aloofness can casually be offered in the presence of the whole family the idea that she could run away to her mother's for a week and let the family make its own meals.

This brings us to the question of homework. We underplay it in our effort to bring all of the experience into the therapy. Keith favors positive feedback absurdity assignments like suggesting the couple take turns being in charge and change roles next Wednesday, or suggesting to the juvenile delinquent daughter that she and her mother change bedrooms. *Our most important homework assignment is to avoid discussing the interviews between sessions.*[12]

5) *Augmenting the despair of a family member* so the family will unite around him. This is usually most efficient when used with a scapegoat. For instance, we might say to a schizophrenic son, "If you give up and become a nobody and spend the rest of your life in a state hospital, do you really think mother and father will be happy with each other 20 years from now or will they still be at each other's throats as they are now and you will have given up your life for nothing?"

6) *Affective confrontation.* This is the kind of event that takes place vis-à-vis the parents, most often in defense of the children. It is the change in tone that occurs when the child in play therapy goes from knocking over a pile of blocks to throwing a block at a window pane. An eight-year-old boy and the therapist were mock fighting during a family interview. The parents viewed it as a distraction and continually interrupted, as though the

---

[12]*Editors' Note.* Note the enormous difference between this extra-therapy injunction and the explicit, systematic use of out-of-therapy time, via homework, in other approaches to family therapy (e.g., Jacobson, Chapter 15; Stanton, Chapter 10; Epstein and Bishop, Chapter 12). While not explicated here by Whitaker and Keith, we think they would agree that the main function of such an injunction is to attempt to preclude family interaction (e.g., at home) which may reduce the level of affect available for therapy sessions. In this way, diminishing somewhat the day-to-day family struggle makes it more available to be changed during the interview.

boy were the initiator, although it was clearly the therapist. After several minutes of the parents' complaining to the boy, the therapist got angry and told them to bug off. He said he was playing with their son and he did not want to be interrupted by them.

7) *Treating children like children and not like peers.* Younger children, at times, like to tease us or to fight us physically. We enjoy taking them on and always overpower them. We are willing to be supportive and understanding of teenagers but we also set strong limits with them. Despite our usual openness and acceptance, we can be very moralistic when chewing out a teenager for pushing us around.

Choice of Technique

Decisions to use a particular technique at a particular time are based on clinical experience. Each therapist, out of his own style, develops a set of opening game procedures. It is in the beginning that any therapy process is most structured and therapy is professional, not personal. However, mid-phase or late-phase participation on the part of the therapist should arise out of his creativity and his aliveness at the moment rather than out of preplanning or some set decision-making at an intellectual level. The best interventions to those ends are the therapist's free associations or fantasies. Paradoxical patterns that we use with great frequency usually result from frustration at simple relationship therapy, or a meta-product of the absurdity offered by the family. The dream of a magical cure, the conviction that all the pathology is in one person, the inability to conceptualize or even accept other options than the one they have decided upon—all indicate an absurd, reality-narrowing life-style. It is absurd to argue about absurdities. Our usual response is to be absurd ourselves, to play in such a way that we counterbalance the squares in the family. Many times we use disconfirmation of the whole situation or the family or the individuals as a way to avoid being co-opted and to disrupt their preset opinions. We repeatedly use non sequiturs to derail a train of rationalizations or excuse-making which feels pointless, empty or repetitive. We utilize silence as a deliberate effort to

stop the "blahs" or the pathology of reason and may move out of the situation physically as a way of expressing our inability to be part of it. One response to frustration is the impotence ploy, really a direct statement of the therapist's impotence. "I see no way we can be useful to you folks; your fight is so important to you and your capacity to blame each other is so well established that I see no way to help you get rid of it and it's very possible that this is the best life you can make for yourselves. We suggest you go ahead this way until something further develops or maybe this will become more enjoyable."

In reference to the family as a whole, our basic objective is to induce regression by way of confusion. Regression may be precipitated by two-level messages or three-level messages, e.g., a symbolic statement which is verbal but in contrast to a nonverbal message. The therapist says warmly, "Have you ever thought that killing yourself might make the family happy?" Many a double message includes a pseudo-disconfirmation, "If you were my wife, I would probably try to increase your interest in me by doubling your allowance." Similarly induced regression can be brought about by non sequitur statements, or statements which have only a very tangential and metaphorical relationship to the things that are going on in the family at the moment. These may come out of fantasies or errant thoughts that arrive in the therapist's head or may be the result of putting together signals given by the family which are in direct contrast or not related to the subject at hand. The same induced regression may be brought about by nonrational participation or even by quite irrational presentations, such as teasing, play or jokes. We feel no obligation to make sense and we enjoy our inconsistencies. One may pay attention to the story that mother is telling while at the same time rubbing father's neck or cuddling the baby. Similarly, the therapist may deliberately mishear a delinquent's cursing as his physical offer to play with the baby or as an expression of love for the mother. "Fuck you," may be translated into, "I love you." Similarly, the mother's request that junior stop watching so much TV may be interpreted to mean "I'm jealous of your intimate relationship with our TV set."

Dealing with Resistance

We have trouble with the concept of resistance. It implies that the therapist must do something about it. Perhaps it could be better thought of as differential motivation for change, or the absence of desperation. In family therapy, resistant, differential motivation or ambivalence about therapy is a problem for the whole system. One member of the family may express it for the rest of the family, but we assume that everyone shares in it. After several visits, the adolescent scapegoat says he thinks that the family therapy is a waste of time and that they ought to quit. Usually the kid is expressing the family's ambivalence. The family looks on to see how the adolescent is handled and then factions in the family begin to express their ambivalence. We don't simply regard the resistance as being individual; we always regard it as the family's conviction that their present solution is the best available. One way to induce desperation is to move to the negative side of the ambivalence and offer to end the therapy so that the family can reunite after they get rid of the therapist. Another move is to augment the differences and suggest that the family members cannot really get together as long as they are clearly fighting each other. One can devise a high level drama by getting the family to vote about how many would like to kill big brother. Or, a mother who wants to drop out of therapy because of father's infidelity can be confronted with other options. Divorce would be a possibility, staying home to nag him is a possibility, or she could get a boyfriend or tell his mother and the people around town that he is homosexual.

No one in a family system is untouched by a major therapeutic change in the system. These changes are usually nonvoluntary and are most often behavioral in the broadest sense. On the other hand, everyone in the family does not have to make a decision to change behaviors. We want everyone in the family to be at the interview, but everyone does not have to be a patient. In fact, when another patient emerges to replace the one identified by the family, it often produces a good outcome. Each family member is encouraged to change out of his/her own initiative. If someone wants individual therapy, we can provide it while the rest of the family watches. We defend everyone's right to remain the same. We defend each one's right to be who he/she is and not to change just because someone else wants him/her to. Early on we insist that each member give up trying to get something from the family. If the family as a whole fights against us, we usually give up and send the family off on its own, assuming that its winning may be as effective as intervention.

Technical Errors

What are the most common and most serious technical errors the therapist can make with this approach? An important part of our method is the use of our own affect and intuition. The method is regarded by some as dangerous and unteachable. It may be dangerous, but it is teachable. The teaching of it is difficult because it requires apprenticeship, as well as some interest in changing oneself and growing more in relating to one's own family. Psychotherapy is powerful and therefore dangerous. However, in our estimation it is important to teach people how to be effective, not just safe. Surgery is a dangerous business, but that is not to say that it should not be practiced.

Common technical errors occur on two levels. The first is a meta-level which has to do with being a therapist. Errors on the second level are more specific and have to do with doing therapy. Let us start with a list of the meta-errors:

1) It is an error to be co-opted by the family. The therapist enjoys seeing the family and is warm and friendly with them. He becomes so much a part of the family that he cannot help it change.
2) Another serious error is to be so professional or so inimicable to the family that one stays aloof from it, using only technical processes of communication training or interpretive work, both of which have little power to produce the kind of change we aim for. The therapist's anesthesia for his/her operating to bring about change is his own affective empathy with the family. This may be either a positive concern for the family members' pain or a negative response to them within himself, but in either case he is emotionally invested in them and that enables his partic-

ipation to be authentic. In truth, his own affect is anesthesia for doing whatever he feels right in doing. The game of playing at being concerned or playing at changing the family may be useful in sensitivity training groups or in gestalt groups that have to do with the early experience of a family or an individual, but is so distancing and so chilling that it weakens the affect and induces the family to reconstruct its rubber fence so that the therapist gets only as far in as they want him to and then they thrust him/her out again. Control of change is in the hands of the family and they won't be any closer to the therapist than he to them.

3) Another error is to make believe the therapist feels no stress and no inadequacy. For example, a white therapist treating a black family is playing a trick on himself. He cannot be consonant with that kind of family. He/she can try to be closer by having a black co-therapist. The same problem exists where there are strong religious differences or other cultural differences. The therapist is less adequate when he works with natives of other countries because the nonverbal behavior signals given in any one culture make good psychotherapy most effective to someone who belongs to that culture.

4) Family therapists develop methods for pulling the family out of its chosen anxiety-binding system. That is implicit in our way of working. We deliberately manipulate the family, so that the scapegoat cannot function in his usual way, or so that the family is forced into a different kind of behavior. Such tricks can explode the immediate setting and/or precipitate serious stresses outside. For example, in one family, the father, a physician, had recurrent manic attacks and was brought into family therapy, whereupon mother immediately flipped into an acute paranoid psychosis. The family wisely discontinued therapy and a serious failure was prevented.

5) Another problem develops when the therapist plays insight games. He assumes that the family is able to take intellectual input and convert it to a family change process. We don't believe that this can happen.

6) Another error occurs when the therapist makes believe that the family lives in his

value system and tries to treat the family as though they were from the same family that he grew up in. Good examples are when the therapist confuses psychological investigation with psychotherapy, or when a Protestant tries to treat a Catholic family while assuming they have the same emotional culture bond.

Next are specific problems in methods. The problem is not, however, that they are apt to do damage to families, but rather that they will just be ineffective.[13]

1) The therapist moves too fast for the family without reading their responses. It is possible to intervene in a way comparable to early interpretations in individual therapy.

2) Failure to treat intuition as intuition. The therapist has an idea which comes out of his own free associations and the family does not hear it or they reject it. The therapist needs to remember that his intuition is his own subjective perception. It may not correspond with the family's view of things. When they resist, it is best to back off very quickly.

3) Failure to know when the therapist is in with a family. The therapist may maintain a first interview posture too long. He dares not use his own affect and is afraid to withdraw from the family lest they view it as rejection.

4) Scapegoating someone else in the family. That is, the therapist may identify with the scapegoat and then scapegoat mother, father or the marriage. The scapegoat must become the whole family, all three generations of it.

5) Another mistake is to select an emotional or ego set and retain it. It is important to use a lot of variability in work with families. For example, the therapist is sociable when the

---

[13]*Editors' Note.* We ourselves have argued (Gurman and Kniskern, 1978a) that some deterioration can be transitory and necessary for long-term change in family therapy. Still, there is a good deal of evidence (Gurman and Kniskern, 1978a) of worsening in family therapy, at both the point of the termination of treatment and at follow-up. We are very dismayed to have heard a number of prominent family therapists assert publicly that because of the "homeostatic power" of families, it is virtually impossible for family therapy to do any lasting harm. We believe this is a naively self-serving and dangerously irresponsible stance which teachers of family therapy have a responsibility to counteract.

family arrives, as they talk about the weather or the road conditions, and then starts to gradually switch the content to symbolic by either going silent or by making a symbolic inference.

6) A final problem is the failure to recognize the utility of not treating someone. (See our earlier discussion of treatment applicability.)

Termination

The ending of family therapy is usually based on a lessening of stress. The family members gradually stop pushing each other, their living together becomes more enjoyable, and talking about life becomes quite empty. They spread out appointments or set up some preliminary subgroup appointments. Usually the therapist picks up symbolic symptoms of his diminishing affect for the interviews and raises the question of how much more is needed. The family is invited to return if it wants to. Individual therapy may be offered if requested. An extended family conference may also precipitate an ending point.

The disengagement of the therapist is a very limited problem in co-therapy, since the "parents" have each other and do not need to use the children. The children recognize a deeper involvement with their live-in parents than with the therapists. The therapist had begun to disengage from the family in the first interview and maintains his freedom to move in and out throughout the entire process. The initial contact is based on the therapist's concern for the family, but the therapist must turn away any effort to make inroads into his personal life or his decision-making. The therapist maintains his functional separation in the same way a parent does. With freedom to disengage and re-engage, the eventual termination is fairly simple. The therapist has shared those times when he is bored, the patients are experiencing less and less dependence on the therapist, the symptomatic relief has taken place, and the family members are more and more involved with their real living.

Usually, the therapist makes efforts to reinterpret symbolic signals the family gives about ending. Junior talks about the fact that football is going to begin, Mother talks about the fact that she almost forgot the appointment because she had a bridge game, Daddy complains that coming down here is making it more and more difficult for him to earn his full salary, or one of the family members starts talking about somebody else's problems. Any of these events symbolically indicates the family's decreasing interest in working on themselves; if a therapeutic experience has occurred, these can only be construed as evidence that the therapy is nearly ended.

There are other indications. One patient does not show or everyone is late. These symbolic expressions of the readiness for ending may also come from the therapist. He may forget the appointment time, double schedule another family at the same hour, fall asleep in the middle of the hour, discover himself being noncreative or educational with the family, thus indicating that they are in a stage of late adolescence and ready to leave home.

The wish to terminate by the family is never viewed as a symbolic wish. If they suggest stopping, we agree with them. Our rationale is that if we try to get them to metacommunicate about why they wish to quit and turn that into a therapeutic issue, we all become locked into a pseudo-therapeutic relationship. The model is the teenager who decides to leave home, but then keeps postponing it. At some point, the parent must decide that he has done what he could and, although the offspring is never a finished product, he has to let go so the kid can finish growing up on his own.

CURATIVE FACTORS IN SYMBOLIC-EXPERIENTIAL FAMILY THERAPY

It is assumed that, preliminary to a curative process, the family must develop a sense of its wholeness. "We are all in this together and something has gone wrong which has made the first baseman goof-up, or something has gone wrong that we're losing one baseball game after another, or something's gone wrong that the pitcher and catcher are fighting with each other." This offer of change is ordinarily set up so that change is induced and carried out on a covert implicit level and a general attack on the symptoms is minimal. Families that do not achieve a sense of the whole seldom stay in therapy.

We do not believe that insight is necessary to change, although it is a frequent by-product of change. Historical and genetic insight brings recognition and change may follow. The important thing is that insight not be overvalued, because recognition can easily occur without learning. Real learning is based upon experience plus evaluation. Learning most often takes place after change has occurred. We push for insight to recalibrate the family's self-image and the individuals' sense of themselves. When families are intellectually sophisticated, it is difficult to shift their intellectual system by interpretation or educational processes of a simple, direct nature. Interpretations are most valuable if they are metaphorical.

Interactional insight is most valued. At best it involves an interactional experience inside the therapy room. The most common interactional insight is the one which involves joint participation in the family complaint. For example, husband complains of the wife's sexual unavailability. We assume that she remains unavailable because he is impotent when she is too eager. These interactional insights break up the web of relationships in the family so that the individual can feel less inhibited by the system.

Interpretations are not essential. Sometimes history is important and must be taken into account. However, interpretation, insight or history can become an obstruction to therapeutic experience. It is our inclination to save these components of therapy for the later phase. For example, in work with autistic children, Keith avoids a child evaluation early in the treatment. His main emphasis is on developing a therapeutic alliance with the family as a whole. This gives the family a symbolic experience without reifying its distress. Later on, they can be referred for evaluation and a more specific educational process. We cite this as an example of the underlying family change focus we give priority in our work, regardless of the presenting problem.

We do not struggle to teach new skills in any didactic fashion. We may offer to expand the options they fix on. For example, the wife says, "I want a divorce." The therapist replies, "Where will you go? Will you go home to mother? Do you think you'll get your old room back? Do you think Fred will remarry or will he be too bitter about this first marriage?" In the later stages of therapy, the family may ask for certain educational bits and pieces and these are offered, but in an after-the-fact, casual manner. For example, if the family asks for help in understanding the psychodynamics that brought them into therapy, if they want to talk about their relationship to previous generations, if they want to discuss the relationship of the family to the community or alter their family boundaries, whether individual or group, the therapist can be explicit, supported by the affect that has been accumulated in the earlier part of therapy. He is free to express his opinion without dominating or subjecting the family to something extraneous and irrelevant. The family is by then capable of taking his educational input and insightful additions into the framework of their experience. They can freely modify the therapist's advice, discard it or utilize it, depending upon its value to them. In the early stage, however, such information would be taken symbolically and thus be highly dangerous.

The therapist's personality and psychological health yield the greatest rewards in treatment. Where the therapist is in his own personal development (personal adequacy and place in the life-cycle) intermeshes with the kind of helpfulness he can provide to the family. If the therapist does not get therapeutic input from his work, chances are the patients will not get much from therapy. The difference between the patient and therapist in this regard is that the patient brings his whole self into the experience while the therapist must restrict himself as a function. Another way of saying it is that, in effect, the dynamics of therapy are in the person of the therapist (Betz and Whitehorn, 1975).

The presence of two therapists offers not only the differential adequacy of the two individuals but also a separate experience with the quality of the co-therapy relationship. We think the co-therapy treatment model provides a very valuable meta-experience for the family. The intimacy achievable in the family during therapy may even be limited by the intimacy available between the co-therapists. Therapist factors which we value include personal adequacy, the ability to be caring, the ability to combine lovingness with toughness, the ability to combine craziness with structure, the willingness to let patients go and the ability to be inconsistent.

Two ideas which we use frequently cause trouble with some other therapists. The first is *craziness*; the other is *the importance of being inconsistent.* The word craziness sometimes implies immaturity and a symbiotic lock-in to another. The craziness that the therapist should have available is the craziness which is not symbiotically locked in to anything, but is available to him as another component of his personhood. It is not necessary to be immature in order to think nonrationally. It is not necessary to be immature in order to have irrelevant, free associative fantasy components. It is not necessary to be immature to talk wartzlot or schizophreneze. All of these are available to the healthy, free person who has broken with the culture bond, who has broken with his parental transference struggles, who is free to be infantile; as Rioch (1944) said many years ago, "Maturity is the capacity to be immature." That is, maturity is the capacity to function on a regressed level in the service of the therapeutic process, just as many patients regress in the service of the family ego or as neurotic patients regress in the service of the individual ego. A deliberate functional regression often takes place in us in relationship to the therapy setting. The patient family is forced to take over the function of being the "sane" component of this suprafamily "we." While the therapists enjoy the crazy component of the "we," they simultaneously give the patient (family) permission to stay crazy in the right time, in the right place, with the right people and to be unbound from his symbiotic bind to his mother's phobia about psychosis (Whitaker, 1978).

It is, of course, true that we are more mature in our functional relationship to patients than we are in the outside world of our own families and our work. It seems as though we have more of both our rational and irrational selves available when we have the security of the other therapist. We have the security of the co-therapy as a subculture: a "we" which gives us a sense of belonging while rebelling against the outside culture which wants us to be sane, rational, reasonable and altruistic.

In order to be an effective change agent, we believe therapists need to learn to be inconsistent and to live with their inconsistency. A model for this is the parent who must admit to and live with his inconsistency in parenting. The parent who perceives himself as consistent is either delusional or being consistent with his kids at the expense of being personal. The therapist's inconsistency helps to undermine the family's attempt to maintain a rigid pattern of living.

Techniques are important for the inexperienced therapist and for the early stages of all family therapy. Techniques, once developed, however, become mechanical and then should be discarded. It is important that techniques be incorporated into a game plan. It is like the young football quarterback who can throw long passes well. He is not as valuable as the quarterback who can develop a good game plan and get together a series of plays in order to make a touchdown. More important than explicit techniques are the meta-techniques such as timing, application of emphasis, how and when to apply pressure, when to back off or when to be cautious.

Techniques, once developed, become mechanical and then fade out. The objective of all techniques is to eliminate techniques, to get beyond technique in the same way that the experience of loving transcends the experience of sexual intercourse techniques.

In our frame of reference, psychotherapy does not occur without transference, but transference does not work unless it is bilateral. In family therapy, transference is more complicated by the number of subgroups and people present and the fluctuations in ego states which continually go on. We make little attempt to keep the field sterile, except in specific situations where the voltage has increased and there is some obvious therapeutic gain immanent. The transference between the therapists is also assumed to be apparent and a valid part of the interaction within the suprafamily.

Countertransference is dangerous in family therapy when it blocks the transference relationship, i.e., goes counter to the transference. One way to think of countertransference is as a consistent pattern of operating which has no built-in alternative. For example, Keith frequently got into fights with mothers in his early years of therapy. The fights were not harmful to the family, but oftentimes ended the treatment. He has learned now to sidestep these wars and save them for later. The result has been an increase in effectiveness and in satisfaction with his work. Countertransference is not seen as a major risk when it is exposed and made part of the ongoing process. Most of the affect available is transference affect in all directions. The transference that mother has toward her oldest son from her husband is just like the transference she has to her husband from her father, and the transference that the youngest daughter has to the female co-therapist from her mother. All of these are responded to and utilized as a valid part of the family therapy experience.

When Keith started working with families, he felt like a failure unless every family member showed change. A few years' experience has made it clear that every family member does not change overtly. The likelihood of a useful experience for the family is diminished when some members do not accept any change. Each member of the family ought to become involved with his own personhood and must bring to the therapeutic process his anxiety about himself, about the subgroups and about the family as a whole. We believe that men are hopeless because they are so fact- and time-oriented that it is almost impossible for them to be intimate or to think esthetically. Oftentimes father does not appear to change but the other family members lose their terror about him. They love him and regard his unavailability as his form of craziness.

Oftentimes the scapegoats appear beyond change. Sometimes by the time we get to them their character structure is very well established. The scapegoat may not appear to change, but he may take up less space in the family unconscious. It is not, therefore, uncommon for the scapegoat to still have symptoms when the therapy ends and the family has changed.[14]

The so-called healthy member of the family is usually pathological in the same sense that we psychotherapists are. He is preoccupied with doing good, helping others and may become a nonperson in the process.

The likelihood of the family problem being resolved is reduced when everyone does not change. We insist that even if the family member does not wish to become a patient, he still must attend all the therapy sessions. The family problem is not only a systems problem of its own, but it is augmented and reinforced by each family problem that the individual members carry.

The most powerful factor limiting or enhancing success is the pressure from the family as a whole. If the entire extended family is convinced that "something has to be done about us," psychotherapy is at a very good place. A difficult factor is the non-biological groups within the family, for example, the adopted child, the second marriage, the non-marriage combination, the triangulation with father's girlfriend or mother's boyfriend. Secondly, there is greater stress and less pressure for change if the individuals in therapy do not live together. The chance of working things out well is much reduced if there has been a good bit of previous treatment, either individual or, even worse, family treatment which has not been successful. Growing cynicism, lack of hope and a facility with psychological terminology are vectors which frustrate therapy.

Rigid, socialized paranoids are troublesome in family therapy; they have too much belief in individuals and individuality and frequently too much support from the community. Long-standing, well stabilized pathology decreases the possibility of much change. Psychosomatic families are frequently seen as difficult to work with in family therapy. In the psychosomatic area, there are two components. First is the attempt to translate the family search for help from the pediatrician or internist to the psychiatrist, and second is the therapist's demand that they switch from body language to psychological language. It is important not to force the leap with these families and to treat them either with administrative effort or metaphorical pressure.

Some other components that make change difficult include the family who is not very concerned, or where one or two are concerned and the others are on the opposite side and think things are fine. As noted above, symptoms present for many years have been adapted to by the

---

[14]*Editors' Note.* A provocative idea, indeed, but one which needs a good deal of empirical bolstering.

family and any attempt to get treatment will be a pseudo-effort. Success with families is greatly inhibited by the withdrawal of any family member from treatment. The more family members withdraw, the less chance there is of success. It usually behooves the therapist to give up if one or more members have decided to drop out. Even if these are the healthy members, it is many times true that, although the therapist may be tempted to let them go on with their lives since it's working well, the family then tends to change less by having lost its hero or heroine. The family without initiative is almost a family without potential for change. The therapist must face the fact that he usually cannot induce real change in such a family. If family members want to change, he may be able to stimulate them with his effort to help and the result may be useful, but without their initiative, little can be done.

In the final analysis, the most important family factor which relates to change or failure to change is desperation. When family members are desperate, they change; when they are not desperate, they remain the same. Some factors which help to move the project along are the self-interests of family members and the tolerance for ambiguity (love/hate, body/mind, the open gestalt).

Good/successful termination is like the adolescent's individuation. Sometimes it works out peacefully and gradually and other times the adolescent leaves in an angry rebellion. Most of our terminations with families tend to be abrupt. At a given interview we note that they are living in the here and now and suggest that they go off on their own. Some families take up our offer and do so, others resist and the termination occurs more slowly and on their terms. Like adolescents, some leave, promising to come home for Christmas, then cannot make it or they forget their promise, go off and live their lives.

A good termination is characterized by increasing here-and-now living, increasing here-and-now therapeutic process in the interview, the freedom to make family decisions without consultation with the therapist, the freedom of the family to correct the therapist and be therapeutic to him, the greater freedom of the family to be silly, comfortable, separate, close and quite physical with the therapeutic team.

Another kind of success occurs with the family which terminates early. We believe that the flight into health in family treatment is always useful. It means that the family has decided, whether on the basis of negative anger or positive success, that they will reorganize its lifestyle. The therapeutic experience, even if it is only one interview, contributes to the decision-making and may even be more useful than a longer period of psychotherapy. Learning to pick up this symbolic effort to withdraw from therapy or to recapture the family territory is very important in the training of any therapist.

A bad/unsuccessful termination is the one where the family stops unilaterally and goes to another therapist who takes them on within four weeks. A failed therapy followed by a rebound is the same as rebound marriage after divorce. The whole self is not available.

The dynamics of ending in family therapy are not well understood. The therapy process is certainly not like a bus ride out to the end of the terminal. We dispel the idea that we direct ourselves toward a nirvana-type endpoint. We attempt to add ten percent to the family's living. Such a partial success is seen in a family with four children where the parents are two months away from finalization of the divorce. The pediatrician asked for assistance from one of us because the 14-year-old son was depressed. There were three interviews with the whole family and it seemed like a useless cause. Two weeks after the last interview, the father called the pediatrician to apologize for being uncooperative. He was glad they had come because his kids were no longer isolating him. He was back in touch with them and said he had not realized before how much he missed them.

Families end their treatment in diverse ways. Usually, the typical rejection of the parent takes place in some form. One sign is the forgotten interview. The family may begin to reject the therapist's value system or, as children do in play therapy, refer to another family as a replacement.

EFFECTIVENESS OF THE APPROACH

There is very little objective evidence for the success of this model of family therapy. The goodwill of the community, the fact that most referrals come from previous patients, the statements of families who have apparently failed but are later seen in the community and report their gains from the therapy are all clinical evidences of success, but of very little help in research.

Probably the most solid data are the enjoyment of the psychotherapist in his personal ongoing change. It does not seem possible that the therapist himself could stay happy and fun-loving or creative if the feedback on the covert level were not successful. He/she would become bitter, withdrawn and suicidal if the therapy he/she did were not successful. Further evidence is the therapist's freedom to participate in the patient's change. The therapist's own change through the constructive/creative experiences of the family should be seen as evidence that the therapeutic process was useful for the family as well.[15]

Bandler and Grinder (1975) have explored some of the territory that we are interested in, that of describing and investigating the infrastructure of psychotherapy. Other important researchers who have added a great deal to our sense of psychotherapy are Scheflen (1967, 1973), Birdwhistell (1970) and Haley (1963, 1976). Minuchin et al.'s (1978) recent study of psychosomatic families, which shows somatic responses to family therapy interventions, is interesting and we would like to see much more of this. It would be of interest to see such studies expanded to include the therapist's response to the interview experience. Studies of co-therapy functioning would be very interesting. It would be interesting to discover how the team becomes the therapist, how the dynamics of the teaming are reflected in the marriage and vice versa. We definitely need more outcome studies with follow-up, and studies of therapy process.

We also wonder about the effects of children on family therapy and what is lacking when the children are not present.

THE TRAINING OF FAMILY THERAPISTS

Learning to be a family therapist occurs in three different stages: 1) learning *about* family therapy, which is probably best done in seminars and workshops; 2) learning to *do* family therapy, which requires the pressure of clinical experience; and 3) *being* a family therapist, which involves orienting one's clinical work around families, a reorientation in which the therapist comes to believe in families rather than individuals.

A first question has to do with who should do family therapy. It is important that the persons have a background of some powerful existential experience—some kind of zen-like explosion, a brief episode of craziness, individual therapy, or some other identity crisis or confrontation with himself. These might include therapy, an extended work experience outside of psychotherapy, perhaps military service. One characteristic of such experience is that the person loses the sense of his uniqueness while retaining fascination with his complexity (Fowles, 1977).

A background of clinical experience is useful, including that of frustrated physicians or battle fatigued social workers who have come to the point of giving up without going nonsubjective. These people usually have an experiential sense of systems and have learned to work through and within experience more than ideas. They are acquainted with their own impotence. We think that this method of family therapy is best practiced by professional therapists. The discipline of the therapist is not critical, but discipline is required.

There are, however, problems with professionally qualified people attempting to learn family therapy. Physicians with training in the specificity of functioning may have the most to unlearn and more ambivalence about the switch to working with a group. A problem in their value orientation, however, is counterbalanced by their sense of systems and the massive load of intensive clinical experience behind them. Persons with Ph.D. training sometimes seem

---

[15]*Editors' Note.* Indeed, it would be fascinating to investigate whether changes within the family therapist correlate strongly with changes within the family under treatment. What should be evaluated as therapist changes seems quite unclear, however. Moreover, we do not believe that an unsuccessful clinical practice would necessarily lead to a therapist's bitterness, etc. Therapists are also people and have the same defenses (denial, repression) available as do their patients to reduce anxiety. More concretely, we ourselves personally know sizeable numbers of therapists who continue to practice when it seems quite obvious that they generally achieve limited therapeutic success. Certainly, it makes sense that a therapist should enjoy his/her work, but we disagree strongly that such criteria offer "the most solid data" on which to base clinical effectiveness (see, e.g., Gurman and Kniskern, Chapter 20, this volume).

to have troubles switching to family therapy because of their lock into research.

Learning About Family Therapy

This is best initiated by reading and seminars, which introduce trainees to the new language that goes with family work, stimulate their thinking and help interest them in conceptualizing about families and family therapy.

Some clinical experience is necessary to learn about family therapy. It can be acquired in several ways, such as by watching an experienced family therapist work or by seeing families in a context, such as an inpatient psychiatry service, a medication clinic or social agency. These experiences provide a look into the back window of family therapy. There is no great demand for change in the families, but it is a way to learn about the family and how it works.

Learning To Do Family Therapy

We think that one learns to do family therapy best in an outpatient setting. This is the kind of training we try to provide our general psychiatry residents. A person who is capable of doing family therapy should be able to 1) take a family system history, 2) understand basic systems thinking and the ways in which it complements and is related to clinical work in mental health areas, 3) assess family structure and process, 4) provide crisis intervention for couples and families, 5) do long-term couples therapy, 6) organize and construct a family conference around a crisis in a family or an illness in a family, 7) know the potential use of family therapy in general psychiatric practice, as, for example, in doing medication checks or in seeing patients with psychosomatic illness, and 8) utilize consultation in the practice of psychotherapy.

Being a Family Therapist

This is a much more complicated process. One should recognize that marital therapy is a psychosocial process and family therapy is a biopsychosocial process and thus the voltage is

higher, the problems are more difficult and the pressures are much greater. Individual therapy is also biopsychosocial but operates in an intrapsychic framework dealing with introjects. The model that we believe in for learning family therapy utilizes co-therapy. The co-therapy team should be imbedded in a cuddle group of other co-therapy teams. Our ideal sequencing of clinical experiences in becoming a family therapist is as follows:

1) We like to think that the process of learning begins with a co-therapy team, where one member is the supervisor who is treating a marital couple. This opportunity is really a play at psychotherapy. The actual process is to supervise the bilateral pseudo-therapy between the husband and wife, who are already deeply transferred to each other.

2) The co-therapy team treats a couples group. Here the process moves from the husband and wife supporting each other to a later effort to offer themselves as patients. The couples group also must resolve the male vs. female subgroup and thereafter the emotional triangulation that challenges each couple.

3) The next stage in training to be a family therapist is for the co-therapy team to treat an individual, preferably an individual who is or has been in treatment with his family by another therapist. The patient could be someone who is residual from a family therapy success and wants to go on in his intrapsychic development. It may be a person who has been working through a divorce in the family and who is now on his own, or it might be an older adolescent who has individuated after family therapy and is living at a distance from his own family.

4) The final stage is co-therapy with a family. With this stage completed, it is possible for the trainee to go back through the whole process in several different patterns: (a) with a peer for co-therapist, (b) without a co-therapist but with a consultant who comes in on the second interview and is available from time to time to evaluate and help clarify the situation in therapy. Thus, the trainee should learn couples therapy first, individual therapy later, and family therapy last.

If the beginning family therapist does individual therapy too early, he becomes frightened of the symbolic transference experience and tends to play defensive games. He operates out of a watered-down individual therapy theory such as a half-hearted psychoanalysis. However, it is important for family therapists to learn to do individual therapy. This one-to-one way of working is deeply entrenched in our language and culture. People who do family therapy exclusively from the start may misunderstand the way relationships provide healing. Individual treatment also gives therapists new to psychotherapy a way to learn about therapeusis (mutual therapeutic neurosis). Lack of exposure to individual therapy may also run the risk of a therapist becoming oversystemsatized (systems-addicted).

Learning individual therapy should include individual therapy with children, using the model we described above. It is difficult to become a family therapist without an extended experience with children. Doing therapy with children teaches the therapist nonverbal methods as well as extensive work with the use of fantasy in communication. Therapy for the therapist is crucial. We think that one is not prepared to do psychotherapy until one has had the experience of being a patient. The family therapist should start his investment by having marital therapy and then family therapy with three generations. Where family therapy is not available, a useful substitution is to do a study of one's own family with a group of colleagues involved in the same project. After work with his/her own family, the therapist may decide to go into extensive intrapsychic therapy to increase his/her access to his/her own creativity.

The reason for family therapy for therapists and the study of one's own family is not only to get them individuated out of their families but also to help them develop more belongingness to their family. They need to gain a sense of the flexibility of the triangles in their own families. Jung (1961) said of people who leave their families that their development is arrested at the point where they depart. This developmental arrest is profoundly damaging to family therapists.

We would like to expand some of the ideas generated earlier in this section. First, we are dedicated to co-therapy as the primary model of training. We operate our co-therapy training as peers. We do not invite the resident or other trainee in as a co-therapist so that we can provide him with an experience. We invite him in because we need him. Some think that co-therapy should not be done except between equal and heterosexual peers. This is ideal, but rarely available. We think that any co-therapy pairing develops a model of pairing which has therapeutic value to the family.[16] Much of our co-therapy with trainees works out something like an older man's marriage to his young second wife. The less experienced member of the co-therapy team attaches him/herself to the more experienced. For example, when Keith works with Whitaker, Keith is much more likely to follow Whitaker's lead. On the other hand, Whitaker uses Keith's working time as a time to pull away from the family so that he may reenter at a very different point. The same pattern pertains when Keith works with residents. They are more likely to match something that he is up to or to take a tangent from it, while Keith finds himself dissociating while they're working and then coming in on a completely new tack from them. When the co-therapy team is made up of peers of the same generation and experience, functioning is always much more mixed and provides more competition and more freedom for each. It takes time to develop a co-therapy team so that the team members can work together and trust each other. One learns the most about co-therapy when working with another individual in different treatment settings.

The co-therapy method for training is especially useful when family therapists are advanced in their training. It matches the way that a surgeon learns to do surgery. The resident performs surgery with his professor. There is a strong tradition for this model in medicine which may have to do with why we prefer it. The method has much to do with an identification with the teacher. The Hippocratic Oath

---

[16]*Editors' Note.* Certainly, there are no empirical data to support such a position (Gurman and Kniskern, 1978b). Moreover, logic alone, with just a pinch of social learning theory added, should be sufficient to predict that to expect such a uniformly positive effect is quite unrealistic.

suggests that the professor and student will live together as father and son. It is very clear to us that our investment in a resident has to do with his learning and vice versa. Many trainees ask if they can see a family, do so, and then drift away. Others become more invested in the work and we naturally become more invested in them.

It is important to mix up methods of training so that the therapist does not end up programmed to a set pattern. It is useful to watch therapy from behind a one-way mirror and to be watched from behind a one-way mirror. It is useful to use videotape so that the therapist can look at his work after the fact. Keith recalls a day spent with Jill Metcoff watching Whitaker work from behind the mirror. She was interested in a process phenomenon that she called a microevent (Metcoff, in press). During these interviews, we did not even listen to the content but just watched the nonverbal behavior in relation to who spoke when. It was fascinating.

Something more needs to be said about the importance of using couples groups in training family therapists. It is a unique, valuable experience, especially when working with couples who may have been in therapy with the therapist previously. In the beginning, it is best if couples are selected who are not too disturbed. Co-therapy with a couples group allows the trainee and supervisor to take part with other couples, but simultaneously to operate in an administrative role and to lose themselves in or utilize personal involvement. The dynamics of the individuals supporting their spouses gradually weakens and the war goes on between the four males and the four females. Once the battle of the sexes has been worked through, triangles between husband One, his wife and wife Two, or wife One, husband One, and husband Two preoccupy the couples group. The therapist has the opportunity to live through the experience of these family dynamics.

Does a family therapist need to have full child therapy training? We do not think so. As noted above, the more that the therapist knows about children, the better. He can also learn about children from having his own, from working part-time in a child-related agency such as a school or other treatment facility. The important factor is that he learn how to relate to children, that he learn the importance of children and the special stresses that they generate and are exposed to in any multigenerational group.

SUMMARY

In this presentation of one method for helping families develop a quality change in their living pattern, we have not been able to fully describe the reciprocal effects of such efforts on a therapist as a person. Interaction obviously has an effect on each interactor. As a father in a family so accurately put it at the family's ending interview, "Overall, I've really enjoyed coming here . . . but something must happen to you guys in all this, too. I, mean, even if you just sat there, you would have to get something personal out of it."

Like becoming a parent in the nuclear family, the qualitative effects of becoming a family therapist are often dramatic. Treating families is both painful and deeply moving. Doing psychotherapy is change-inducing in its symbolic effect on the therapist. The power of the family, like the power of the infant, is seductive and threatening. The therapist and the conceptual framework that emanates from his work live between the pressure for constrictive narrowing toward more specific definition and allowing for openness, vulnerability which leads to growth and reparative experience. Next year we would not be able to write this chapter in quite the same way.

REFERENCES

Allen, F. *Psychotherapy with Children*. New York: Norton, 1942.

Angyal, A. *Foundations for a Science of Personality*. New York: The Commonwealth Fund, 1941.

Bandler, R. & Grinder, J. *The Structure of Magic*. Palo Alto, CA: Science & Behavior Books, 1975.

Benedict, R. *Patterns of Culture*. Boston: Houghton-Mifflin, 1934.

Betz, B. & Whitehorn, J. C. *Effective Psychotherapy with the Schizophrenic Patient*. New York: Aronson, 1975.

Birdwhistell, R. L. *Kinesis and Context: Essays on Body Motion Communication*. Philadelphia: University of Pennsylvania Press, 1970.

Castaneda, C. *Tales of Power*. New York: Simon & Schuster, 1975.

Ehrenwald, J. *Psychotherapy: Myth and Method: An Integrative Approach*. New York: Grune & Stratton, 1966.

Fellner, C. The Use of Teaching Stories in Conjoint Family Therapy. *Family Process*, 1976, *15*, 427-433.

Fowles, J. *Daniel Martin.* Boston: Little, Brown, 1977.

Grinker, R. R., Sr. Biomedical Education on a System. *Archives of General Psychiatry,* 1971, *24,* 291-297.

Haley, J. *Problem-solving Therapy.* San Francisco: Jossey-Bass, 1976.

Haley, J. *Strategies of Psychotherapy.* New York: Grune & Stratton, 1963.

Jung, C. G. *Memories, Dreams, Reflections.* A. Jaffe (ed.). New York: Pantheon, 1961.

Klein, M. *The Psychoanalysis of Children.* London: Hogarth, 1932.

Kramer, D. Personal communication, 1978.

Langer, S. *Philosophy in a New Key.* London: Oxford University Press, 1951.

Metcoff, J. Family Microevents: Critical Sequences. In F. Walsh (ed.), *Normal Family Processes: Implications for Clinical Practice.* New York: Guilford Press, 1980, in press.

Midelfort, C. F. Personal communication, 1976.

Minuchin, S. *Families and Family Therapy.* Cambridge, MA: Harvard University Press, 1974.

Minuchin, S., Rosman, B. & Baker, L. *Psychosomatic Families: Anorexia Nervosa in Context.* Cambridge, MA: Harvard University Press, 1978.

Rank, O. *Will Therapy.* New York: Knopf, 1936.

Rioch, M. Personal communication, 1944.

Rogers, C. R. *Client Centered Therapy: Its Current Practice Implications and Theory.* Boston: Houghton-Mifflin, 1951.

Scheflen, A. E. *A Psychotherapy of Schizophrenia: Direct Analysis.* Springfield, IL: Charles C. Thomas, 1967.

Scheflen, A. E. *Communicational Structure: Analysis of a Psychotherapy Transaction.* Bloomington, Indiana: Indiana University Press, 1973.

Slavson, S. R. *The Field of Group Psychotherapy.* New York: Schocken Books, 1971.

Sonne, J. *A Primer for Family Therapists.* Moorestown, NJ: The Thursday Press, 1973.

Whitaker, C. A. Co-therapy of Chronic Schizophrenia. In M. Berger (ed.), *Beyond the Double Bind: Communication and Family Systems, Theories and Techniques with Schizophrenics.* New York: Brunner/Mazel, 1978.

Whitaker, C. (ed.) *Psychotherapy of Chronic Schizophrenic Patients.* Boston: Little, Brown, 1958.

Whitaker, C. A. & Malone, T. P. *The Roots of Psychotherapy.* New York: Blakiston, 1953.

Winnicott, D. W. Hate in the Counter-transference. *International Journal of Psychoanalysis,* 1949, *30,* 69-74.

Winnicott, D. W. *Playing and Reality.* New York: Basic Books, 1971.

Wynne, L. C., Ryckoff, M., Day, J. & Hirsch, S. I. Pseudomutuality in the Family Relations of Schizophrenics. *Psychiatry,* 1958, *21,* 205-220.

EDITORS' REFERENCES

Gurman, A. S. & Kniskern, D. P. Deterioration in marital and family therapy: Empirical, clinical and conceptual issues. *Family Process,* 1978, *17,* 3-20. (a)

Gurman, A. S. & Kniskern, D. P. Research on marital and family therapy: Progress, perspective and prospect. In S. Garfield & A. Bergin (Eds.), *Handbook of Psychotherapy and Behavior Change.* Second edition. New York: Wiley, 1978. (b)

Neill, J. R. & Kniskern, D. P. *Selected writings of Carl Whitaker: The growth of a therapist.* New York: Guilford, 1981, in press.

CHAPTER 7

Family Systems Theory and Therapy

Michael E. Kerr, M.D.

The emphasis of this chapter is theory, both from the perspective of its historical development and the current state of knowledge. At Georgetown, therapy and technique have always been viewed as logical extensions of theory and have received, therefore, secondary emphasis in the training programs.

Homo sapiens are certainly fascinating and puzzling creatures, and they have two particularly interesting characteristics that are relevant to the field of family therapy. One is their *intense urge to offer and adhere to explanations for things they do not really understand.* There are many examples of this on a societal level, ranging from ancient beliefs that events on earth were caused by wars among the gods, to the more modern view that environmental pollutants are the cause of cancer. There is nothing wrong with such conjectures, but people do tend to make emotional commitments to these ideas, converting them into truths. Once these are regarded as truths, it becomes difficult to introduce new ideas. In the closer realm of psychotherapy, this kind of conversion to truth process is evident in the therapist's emotional commitment to his explanations for why people do the things they do.

The second interesting characteristic of this creature we call homo sapiens is a *tendency to intrude anxiously into emotionally charged problem situations.* This intrusion impulse could be called a "fix-it" mentality and leads either to an exaggeration of activities that have been creating the problem in the first place or perhaps to short-term solutions that are loaded with long-term complications. An example of the latter would be psychiatric hospitalization to relieve immediate family anxiety.

Beginning family therapists are all too eager to learn what one should say to a family or do to a family in therapy. In the Georgetown program we have tried to resist this kind of pressure from trainees and from within ourselves, keeping the main emphasis on theory and the therapist's ability to avoid simplistic concepts and solutions to human problems. If a therapist can be clear that he or she can never have more than a very small percentage of answers, best called reasonably accurate assumptions based on current knowledge, this attitude will do more

226

than anything else to help the problem family out of its own "fix-it" or "make-it-go-away" mentality into a more inquiring, contemplative mode.

The training takes a long time because these urges are deep in people's emotional makeup and are particularly pronounced when they are anxious. It takes a long time to recognize and gain some control over this process within oneself.

THE FAMILY MOVEMENT AT GEORGETOWN[1]

Contributions of Freud

Family systems theory and associated therapy can be considered a logical step in development following the work of Sigmund Freud. Prior to Freud, mental illness was considered a product of organic brain pathology for which treatments, few that there were, were medical. The courage and contributions of Freud cannot be overstated. Though trained as a neurologist and told repeatedly "the way it was," he was able to develop new formulations about the origins of mental illness. He introduced the new dimension of *functional illness*, the concept that mental illness could be the product of a disturbance in brain functioning rather than an organic or structural defect. Perhaps more importantly, Freud conceptualized this functional disturbance to be the product of a disturbed parent-child relationship during the patient's early years. *That emotional illness developed in relationship to others was a new paradigm.*

Freud also extended that theory to a method of therapy in which the problem could be improved or corrected in a therapeutic relationship with a therapist. Freud introduced the notion of transference, the patient relating to the analyst as he had to his parents, with the analyst's job being to interpret and help the patient resolve this transference. Freud gave conceptual structure to the therapeutic relationship and

gave birth to the profession of psychotherapy.

Freud's concepts were strictly individual in that they were based on the study of the individual and pertained to the individual, with the concept of the unconscious perhaps being the key concept in the theory. Despite later differences of various splinter groups from Freud, his two basic ideas—that emotional illness develops in relationship to others, and the therapeutic relationship as the universal treatment for emotional illness—remain the cornerstones of all individual theories.

Period Following Freud

In the 50 years following Freud, the focus remained on the patient, but with this new dimension that recognized the influence that one life could have on another. By the mid-1930s, psychoanalysis was achieving acceptance as a therapeutic method. World War II and the emotional problems encountered in the experience gave psychoanalytic concepts, as well as psychiatry as a medical specialty, an additional major boost. While psychoanalysis had an explanation for the total range of emotional problems, it was disappointing in its effectiveness as a treatment method for the more severe problems like schizophrenia. Many young psychiatrists after World War II began experimenting with variations in the psychoanalytic therapeutic method, seeking more effective treatments for schizophrenia. The study of the family was one of these new areas of interest. Murray Bowen was one such psychiatrist whose original background was psychoanalytic. He had considerable early experience with hospitalized patients and a special interest in psychoanalytic psychotherapy with schizophrenia.

In a sense, interest in the family was not new. Freud (1909) had published *Little Hans*, describing the treatment of a phobic boy through letter exchanges with the boy's father. Flugel's (1960) *Psychoanalytic Study of the Family* was published in 1921. The child guidance movement had involved itself with families through casework with the parents. Sociologists and anthropologists had been studying family before the family movement in psychiatry. Marriage counseling had begun its growth in the 1930s.

---

[1]Most of the ideas represented in this section reflect the perspective of Bowen and several other pioneers in the family movement. These views are drawn from their writings, exposure to their ideas at meetings, and personal discussions.

But it is the view of a number of the early family researchers coming out of psychoanalysis that these related activities had only an indirect role on the emergence of the family movement (including theory, research and therapy) and that much of the contributions of sociology and other fields were recognized in retrospect by people working within psychiatry.

Origins of Family Thinking

By the early 1950s, there were ever-increasing efforts to involve the family in the therapy of the patient. It had been recognized for some time that the success of the patient's therapy was in some way tied to the support and reactions of his or her family. Most had had the experience of "cured" patients leaving the hospital, returning to their families, and promptly regressing into renewed symptoms. Many of the early efforts with families were attempts to deal with this problem. It appears that the family movement in psychiatry started in the late 1940s and early 1950s period with several investigators working independently and all beginning with the clinical or theoretical notion that family was important. *This shifting focus from individual to family confronted these investigators with the dilemma of describing and conceptualizing a family relationship system.* Most of these early researchers operated with the basic assumptions of individual theory. They knew little of each other's research, describing that early period in retrospect as working underground. Bowen thinks that since psychoanalysis had, in fact, admonitions about a therapist seeing more than one member of a family, for fear of contaminating the transference, early family researchers were reluctant to talk openly about what they were doing. During this early period, family research with schizophrenia played a major role in starting the family movement, the development of family therapy, and the evolution of theory.

Bowen and the Menninger Period

Bowen's shift to family also began in the early 1950s while he was doing individual therapy with schizophrenic patients and various mem-

bers of their families. A program had been started at The Menninger Clinic, where Bowen trained and worked from 1946-54, to find better ways to involve the family in the patient's therapy and to improve outcome. Doing this work, he became interested in the intensity of the emotional attachments between patients and relatives. Gradually, he had done enough psychotherapy with parents to recover from what he called the "hate the parents syndrome" and began doing concurrent psychotherapy with the parents and the patient. This experience led to an initial working hypothesis in the 1951-52 period of the mother-patient symbiosis (Bowen, 1971). The hypothesis was as follows: The mother's incomplete self incorporated the self of the developing fetus and was emotionally unable to give up the child in later years. This *emotional stuck-togetherness*[2] was considered a primary phenomenon of almost biological proportions. Phenomena like maternal deprivation, hostility, rejection, and castration anxiety were considered *secondary manifestations* of this underlying intense attachment. The mother-patient symbiosis was viewed as a natural phenomenon for which no one is blamed. Bowen went on to hypothesize that *this intense symbiotic attachment is the basic process on which clinical schizophrenia is later superimposed.* In retrospect, Bowen believes that this focus at that time on the mother-child symbiosis, with the larger view of the family obscured, was related to his being fixed in individual thinking. In addition, symbiosis had already been described in the literature as an extension of individual theory and so was, in a sense, acceptable. Limentani's (1956) is one of several fascinating articles about symbiosis in schizophrenia that came out about that time. He presented detailed descriptions of the symbiotic attachments between mothers and their schizophrenic offspring and even suggested that a disturbance or upset in that relationship was the critical factor precipitating acute psychosis. But Limentani's *interpretations* of the phenomenon were strictly individually oriented psychoanalytic formulations and he saw maternal deprivation as *pri-*

---

[2]*Editors' Note.* This "emotional stuck-togetherness" has also often been referred to as the family's "undifferentiated family ego mass" (Bowen, 1978).

mary in the patient's disturbance. He apparently did not regard the symbiotic attachment itself and disturbance therein as primary.

The NIMH Project

In 1954, armed with the symbiosis hypothesis, Bowen moved from the Menninger Clinic to the National Institute of Mental Health (NIMH). At the NIMH he began a then unique project in which mothers and their schizophrenic offspring lived on a research inpatient unit for extended periods of time. When this project began, the focus was on the mother-patient relationship and the thinking that guided the research design was still based on individual theory. As evidence of this individual theory base in the early days of the project, each mother and each schizophrenic patient were still seen in individual psychotherapy and the research focused on their interlocking, individual psychopathologies.

But during the first six months or so, some rather dramatic and exciting changes occurred. Bowen's thinking about what he and his colleagues were observing underwent major shifts in conceptualization. The symbiotic mother-patient relationship was found to be much more intense than had been initially hypothesized. In the outpatient setting, the degree of emotional influence that mother and patient had on each other had not been fully appreciated, but in the day-to-day, live-in situation, the intensity of the process came into view. But the profound conceptual shift was in the discovery that *this mother-patient symbiosis was but a fragment of a larger family emotional system*. It became clear that fathers were equally involved in the process, either through active support of or passive withdrawal from the mother-patient interaction. The emotional process was seen to extend to the whole central family and beyond, even to staff and other relatives. It could no longer be viewed as just a mother-patient problem. Because of these observations and new conceptualizations, the structure of the project was then changed to include fathers and siblings as part of the live-in group. Concepts of individual psychopathology were being rapidly discarded as *the schizophrenia of the person came to be viewed as symptomatic of a process involving the entire family*.

As things progressed, Bowen and his group soon saw a need for some sort of therapy for the family. The shift to therapy for the family was not an easy one for Bowen, as evidenced in this quote from a later publication (Bowen, 1965b):

I had strong misgivings regarding family psychotherapy, still believing analysis of the transference was the road to emotional maturity. But when individual therapy was discontinued on the project, this total commitment to family opened new doors. It was a shaking experience for me, long-schooled in psychoanalysis, to become aware that psychoanalytic theory was not fact and psychoanalytic therapy was just another method (p. 95).

This pioneer NIMH group encountered more than minor difficulties in attempting to reorient itself away from individual concepts and think in terms of the family as a unit. Conventional psychiatric jargon was even dropped as an aid to this transition. The more Bowen observed and was surrounded by whole families on the unit, the easier it was to detach from the boundaries of individual theory and think towards family concepts. With each step in the detachment from individual theory, it became then easier to observe more family patterns, patterns previously obscured by the conceptual bias of the observer. Said in another way, people were initially seeing what they had been long trained to see, namely, individual psychopathology. To become observers of the family as a unit, they literally had to untrain themselves. This remains the major thrust of our family training program, namely, untraining people from individual concepts.

During that 1954-55 period, Bowen began to question many of the then accepted explanations of emotional illness. For example, if maternal deprivation was as important as most mental health professionals considered it to be, then what about the normal people who had seemingly experienced even more deprivation than those with emotional illness? What was the explanation for some of the children of so-called schizophrenogenic parents being normal? If psychiatric theory was on solid ground, why did the diagnostic nomenclature remain based on symptom description and not etiology?[3] Could conventional psychiatric theory account for what appeared to be the occurrence of emotional illness in animals? Why did some people survive traumatic events without problems, while for symptomatic people such events were frequently evoked as explanations for their disorders? These were but a few of the questions Bowen posed to himself and his colleagues, questions for which there are no answers, but had obvious value in pointing out the problems and inconsistencies of individual thinking.

The significant conceptual shifts were paralleled by equally significant shifts in therapy. The therapy that was developed on the NIMH project could best be called *family group therapy* (Bowen, 1971). The individual sessions with various family members were discontinued and the whole family was seen in therapy as a group. Bowen came to regard this type of family therapy as quite useful for relief of symptoms, but not really effective for resolving what he was perceiving as the important underlying emotional stuck-togetherness of the family.

During the NIMH project, in the 1955-56 period, important changes began occurring nationally as a family movement surfaced. The various family researchers across the country began to learn about each other and there were numerous visitors to the NIMH. Much surprise and fascination were expressed over Bowen's having hospitalized the whole family. The first family research papers presented at a national meeting were presented in March 1957 at a panel organized by John Spiegel at the American Orthopsychiatric Association meeting in Chicago. Bowen's was one of those papers in collaboration with several co-workers (Bowen, Dysinger, Brodey and Basmania, 1957). Two

months later, in the same city, Spurgeon English organized a similar family research panel for the American Psychiatric Association's annual meeting. The family movement was thus launched on a national level, beginning a period of what Bowen called a healthy, unstructured state of chaos. Bowen referred to it that way because he was predicting that as increasing numbers of people moved enthusiastically, if not evangelically, into therapy for the family, they would inevitably be confronted with the conceptual dilemmas inherent in trying to use individual concepts to understand family process.

Development of a Family Systems Theory

The thinking that ultimately became the basis for the main part of Bowen's family systems theory evolved rapidly between 1957 and 1963. Most of his early work focused on nuclear family process, specifically in nuclear families with a schizophrenic member. His early papers (e.g., Bowen, 1965a) reflect this focus in describing the main elements of what eventually were called the concepts of *nuclear family emotional process* and the *family projection process*.

From 1959 on, Bowen attempted to extend his theoretical orientation from a family concept of schizophrenia to a family theory that would encompass the full range of emotional illness. His NIMH research, coupled with a growing outpatient psychotherapy experience and with research in his own family, contributed to Bowen's comparing the intense patterns in schizophrenia with the less intense patterns in other problems, *this comparison becoming the basis for a new theory*. The difference between the psychoses and the neuroses came to be viewed as *quantitative* and not *qualitative*; in other words, the patterns of emotional interacting in neurotic level problems were seen to be quite similar to the patterns in schizophrenic level families, just less intense. This view contradicted most of the thinking of the time and soon evolved to placing all human functioning on a continuum, known as the *scale of differentiation*, a concept developed in the early 1960s.

The other concepts of the theory also had their roots in the 1950s. The concept of *triangles* was started in 1957, then referred to as the "inter-

---

[3]*Editors' Note.* Indeed, during the time period in question (1950s), the Diagnostic and Statistical Manual (DSM) of the American Psychiatric Association included very little descriptive information of the various psychiatric disorders. Moreover, while etiological biases were not explicit in DSM-I and DSM-II, it is clear that psychodynamic formulations exerted the predominant influence on the conceptualization of these disorders (Spitzer, 1980). It is only with the arrival of DSM-III in 1980 that (a) elaborate symptom description has been included and, as a corollary, (b) strenuous efforts have been made to avoid etiological implications (except, of course, for clearly physical disorders, e.g., organic brain syndromes).

dependent triad." The notion of a *multigenerational transmission process* was part of a 1955 hypothesis about the development of schizophrenia, but it was not clarified until the 1959 to 1962 period when more families were available for study. The sixth of the original concepts, *sibling position*, was poorly defined in the late 1950s and it was not until the publication of Toman's (1961) book, *Family Constellations*, that orderly structure was given to the idea.

By 1963, these six interlocking concepts were sufficiently defined by Bowen to call them *family systems theory.* Those ideas were published three years later (Bowen, 1966), with only extensions and refinements since that time. In 1975, two additional concepts were added to the theory, *emotional cutoff* and *societal regression* (Bowen, 1976). These eight concepts will be discussed in detail later in this chapter.

Early Developments in Therapeutic Method

Bowen's techniques of family therapy have changed considerably over the years (cf. Bowen, 1978). Increasing development of the theory, pressure of an ever-increasing clinical caseload, personal experiences with his own extended family (e.g., Anonymous, 1972; Bowen, 1974), and the opportunity to work with the same families over long periods of time have been important factors influencing Bowen's changes in emphasis and techniques.

During the 1954-59 period, when the NIMH project was active, Bowen was also doing some outpatient practice. At that time, he made a distinction in his own practice between family therapy, individual psychotherapy and psychoanalysis and had some patients in each category. He was calling it "family" only when two or more family members were seen together in sessions. The technical effort was to analyze the already existing emotional process between family members, keeping himself emotionally disengaged, or what he called "staying out of the transference." If only one person was seen, Bowen called it individual therapy. Bowen's retrospective reasoning for this individual-family dichotomy in the 1950s, a dichotomy he eventually discarded, was that he had neither dealt with his own emotional functioning sufficiently

at that point nor yet developed techniques to avoid transference when just one person was seen. So he called it "family" when the emotional process was largely contained among the family members and "individual" when this containment was not possible.

When a couple was seen together, Bowen's technique was to ask questions about the intrapsychic process of one spouse and then solicit the other partner's emotional reaction to what he/she had heard. He would then go back and forth between the spouses this way, insisting the family members talk directly to each other. If the presenting family problem was in a child, therapy sessions usually included both parents and the symptomatic child, a slight modification of the "whole family" therapy that was structured into the NIMH project. Bowen later considered this modification a slightly more effective therapeutic method than with the whole group, but still found that the child was never able to really separate emotionally from the parents, nor the parents from each other, as the result of such sessions. *Though symptoms often dramatically improved, the basic underlying emotional stuck-togetherness or fusion was not being altered.* Some of Bowen's awareness that symptoms were being reduced but basic fusions were remaining unaltered came from opportunities to see so-called "cured" families many years later, discovering that problems had resurfaced, though perhaps in a different form. A family, for example, where a conflictual marriage had been restored to ideal harmony through therapy, later produced a severely dysfunctional adolescent.[4]

The Georgetown Period

In 1959, Bowen left the NIMH and moved to the Department of Psychiatry at Georgetown

---

[4]*Editors' Note.* This view, of course, is reminiscent of the "symptom substitution" fears which psychoanalysis holds out for such symptom-focused therapies as behavior therapy. The existing empirical evidence on the matter (in the case of behavior therapy) shows that such outcomes are rare, and that symptom change, in fact, often facilitates change in untreated areas of patients' lives. Moreover, enormous conceptual and methodological difficulties are involved in testing the notion empirically (Bandura, 1969), not the least of which is that, if one posits such a phenomenon, one must specify in advance, i.e., *predict*, the nature of the symptom that will emerge.

University, the medical school where he has continued his family research and training programs until the present time. It was originally planned that the entire schizophrenia project would be moved to Georgetown, but a number of circumstances interfered with the realization of that goal. Bowen became and remained a part-time faculty member at Georgetown, continuing research activity and expanding training, particularly with psychiatric residents. The remainder of his time was spent in a busy private practice, giving him an ongoing volume exposure to less intense clinical problems, in addition to some additional continuing work with schizophrenic families.

About a year after the move to Georgetown and accompanying expansion of outpatient practice, a major change occurred in Bowen's technical approach to family therapy. When a family presented with a child-focused problem, Bowen stopped including the child in the therapy sessions and inserted himself as the third point in the triangle with the parents. A number of things influenced Bowen in this regard. One was the repeated observation that when parents and child were in a session together, a potential important emotional issue between the parents could be obscured by their focus on the child. This shift in focus could be initiated by the parents or the child. So it was often technically difficult to concentrate on an issue between the parents long enough to really work on it. A second problem encountered was that when the child was involved in the therapy, the parents often tended to sit back and wait for the therapy to change their child. By excluding the child, it put more pressure on the parents to *make a project out of themselves*. The assumption behind this approach was that the family was a system and that changes in the parents would ultimately be reflected in changes in the child, without needing to involve the child in direct therapy.

Another important development during this early 1960s period pertained to psychotherapy sessions with one person. Bowen was beginning to find it impossible to see a single person without automatically "seeing" the entire family like phantoms alongside. This growing perception of one person as a segment of the larger family

system had come to govern the way he thought about and responded to the individual. Psychoanalytic interpretations of behavior were giving way to seeing the *functional significance* of that behavior in relationship to the family system. No longer was the family seen as a collection of individuals, each operating out of his/her own unconscious conflicts. Now the functioning of each member was seen as integrally tied to that of every other member. Bowen now called all of his therapy "family therapy," even though a third of his practice hours were with one person. His rationale was that *a theoretical system that thinks in terms of family, with a therapeutic method that works toward improvement of the family system, is "family" regardless of the actual number of people in the sessions.* This view often placed Bowen in sharp contrast to others in the family field who regarded family as a new technique, still grounded in psychoanalytic theory. Bowen was proposing family thinking as a new theory of human behavior.

The next major turning point in method was perhaps the most interesting and exciting of all. In March 1967 Bowen made a presentation (Anonymous, 1972) about his own family to a national meeting of family researchers and therapists in Philadelphia. Bowen had spent over 12 years trying to apply systems theory to his own extended family and to find a way to be in the midst of his family without emotionally participating or fusing with it. Early on he had used psychoanalytic concepts to interpret the behavior of family members, which achieved little. Gradually, he began using the systems concepts that had evolved from family research, particularly the knowledge of interlocking triangles, to observe and objectify the process he was enmeshed in. Then, in 1966, on a visit home, he succeeded in relating to the family around emotional issues without getting caught in the process himself. It was an exhilarating experience that completely changed his thinking about what is, in fact, therapeutic.

Following that 1967 presentation, he began teaching the ideas he had developed about his own family to psychiatric residents and other mental health professionals associated with him at Georgetown. It began what Bowen later referred to as a new era in his professional orientation. Throughout his professional training and career, he had emphasized, as had all psychoanalysts, the importance of the therapist's resolving his own problems as an essential first step towards being effective in clinical work. Prior to 1960, Bowen believed this resolution could best be accomplished in the transference relationship of psychoanalytically-oriented psychotherapy. Between 1960 and 1967, that view changed and he recommended that psychiatric residents work out their problems in conjoint family therapy with their spouses. But in 1967, when the residents and other trainees became enthusiastically involved in trying to resolve some of the emotional attachment to their own families of origin, the emphasis shifted.

Much of Bowen's *coaching* of the residents' efforts in their families was done in a weekly group meeting. The residents would take turns describing recent trips home and what they were learning about the multigenerational process in their families, using Bowen's knowledge of family systems principles to help them gain objectivity. A resident might talk about his family once or twice a month or as little as every few months, but in the interim would have the opportunity to listen to and "go to school on" the others' efforts and experiences.

It is difficult to capture the excitement generated by the program during that period, but it was exemplified by the droves of mental health professionals attracted to Georgetown from that time on wanting to learn "how to" differentiate a self in one's own family.

Two important observations from that early experience with focus on extended family were that trainees who were motivated to seriously undertake an effort in their extended family and who were at least partially successful clearly made much more rapid progress toward becoming adept in clinical work than those who were not so motivated and, secondly, those who achieved some success with their families of origin also reported significant changes around issues in their nuclear families, even though such issues were never directly discussed. The replication of nuclear family patterns with those from family of origin, though "known" prior to the late 1960s period, became much more obvious to all involved. Focus on the extended

family came to be regarded as the "high road" for change, both for people in training and for a number of motivated people presenting for therapy for immediate life problems.

By the late 1960s, Bowen had assembled over ten faculty members who volunteered their time to the family programs. The early members of the group were several psychiatrists who had trained under Bowen during their residency, although the group soon expanded to include people from all the mental health disciplines. The development of a faculty permitted the initiation of a formal postgraduate program in family in 1969. This program attracted professionals largely from the local area, but a growing number of requests for training from interested mental health professionals outside of Washington prompted the beginning in 1975 of a special postgraduate program taught four times a year. These postgraduate programs, initially designed as two-year programs, were soon expanded to three and four years. This change grew out of the greater appreciation for how much successful clinical work depended on the trainees' doing a reasonable job in their own families and that that rarely occurred in just two years.[5] A full-time fellowship program for psychiatrists was inaugurated in 1975 and it is hoped that eventually full-time training can be made available to all the mental health disciplines.

Early 1976 is the most recent nodal point in the program. At that time Bowen and his faculty moved out of a few small offices in the Department of Psychiatry into a large off-campus space called The Family Center. These more spacious surroundings have been a catalyst for a marked increase in family training, research, and clinical activity.

While working at Georgetown, Bowen was also on the faculty of The Medical College of Virginia in Richmond. Traveling to Richmond several times a month, Bowen developed an extensive videotape library of his long-term work with several families in therapy. The vi-

---

[5]*Editors' Note.* Kerr echoes this view later in this chapter when he writes that "it is difficult for a family to grow beyond the level of differentiation of their therapist." It is our view that for no other "school" of family therapy is this a more important question for future research (Kniskern and Gurman, 1980).

deotape project now continues at Georgetown and is the basis for the development of a large number of teaching tapes.

FAMILY SYSTEMS THEORY

Individual vs. Systems Thinking

A key to understanding the difference between individual and systems thinking is knowing what is meant by *functioning position in a system*. Suppose you had a gifted intellect and a mechanical mind, but knew absolutely nothing about automobile engines. Now you are given a carburetor and told to study it and discuss it. You might then weigh it, note its color and shape, and do a few other things, all aimed at *describing* it. If you really knew nothing about engines, you could accomplish no more than description. Now suppose another equally gifted person, but equally ignorant about engines, was presented with an engine minus its carburetor and told to design a piece that would make the engine work. He would then study the engine and deduce what functions were missing. He could then design a piece of equipment to fulfill those functions. The piece may or may not look like a standard carburetor, but that would be immaterial. The important thing is that the piece be designed to fulfill the functions required of its position in the engine.

Individual theories are analogous to the man given the carburetor's situation in that they *describe* the individual, but have no way to conceptualize those aspects of the individual that are related to or dictated by their functioning position in a family system. Systems theory, on the other hand, is analogous to the situation of the man given the entire engine to study. Systems theory conceptualizes the relationship system and the functioning positions of the people who comprise the system. It does look at the individual, but in a completely different way than individual theory. For a therapist to say he switches back and forth between individual and systems theory in his practice is to betray the fact that that particular therapist has never gotten free of individual thinking. *Individual and systems thinking are two distinctly different ways of conceptualizing human behavior and attempts to mix them reflect a failure to appreciate their difference.*[6]

Individual thinking is probably best represented by Freud's psychoanalytic concepts. Although Freud believed that psychopathology was related to reactions to early life experiences with one's parents, when symptoms erupted, either in childhood or adult life, *the cause of the symptoms was sought for within the intrapsychic conflicts of the individual.*

From a systems perspective, Freud's concepts of psychopathology can be considered reasonably accurate descriptions of what can occur within an individual, but they cannot be considered to explain the cause of their occurrence. Systems thinking does not look for the cause within the individual. In contrast, systems theory conceptualizes the appearance of a symptom as reflecting an *acute and/or chronic disturbance in the balance of emotional forces in that individual's important relationship systems, most particularly the family system.* Which person becomes symptomatic is strongly dictated by his/her position of functioning in the relationship system; for example, the one upon whom the successful emotional functioning of others depends is generally the most vulnerable to dysfunction him/herself.

Symptoms as Failures in Adaptation

It may be a bit of hair-splitting, but when trying to gain a systems perspective, there is some value in trying to avoid thinking of disease states as pathological. When a system is stressed, the usual balance of forces is disturbed and the system is inclined towards a state of imbalance. To adjust to this, it appears that all biological systems have adaptive mechanisms that can be activated to cope with the increased stress on the system. However, if the stress is too great and sustained, or the basic reserve of the system

---

[6]*Editors' Note.* As the Duhls (Chapter 13) emphasize so strongly, most distinctions between individuals and systems are arbitrary and probably even artificial, in that, from the view of general systems theory (which is not equivalent to family systems theory), individual persons are *sub*systems of the family, and these subsystems themselves contain subsystems, e.g., levels of awareness, such as conscious and unconscious experience.

too low, then the stress-induced imbalance of forces can overload these adaptive mechanisms and symptoms emerge. *The type of symptom that develops is frequently a complication or exaggeration of the mechanism that has been used to preserve the system balance in the first place.* In this sense, symptoms reflect a failure of adaptation by the system and are exaggerations of normal processes. Thinking of symptoms as pathological can obscure this view of the underlying system forces.

Let us take as an example the symptoms representing failures in adaptation of the cardiovascular system as it progresses towards congestive heart failure. The initial mechanisms used by the cardiovascular system to adjust to a failing heart are the same ones used by all of us in the course of daily activities, namely, an increase in heart rate and the flow of adrenalin to make the heart beat stronger. As failure progresses and the basic imbalance of forces in the system increases, another adaptive mechanism comes into play, fluid retention. Some fluid retention can be a stimulus to a weakening heart to pump a little harder. But as the problem worsens and increasing amounts of fluid are retained, the system becomes congested and the person has difficulty breathing, the liver and abdomen swell with fluid, and the legs become swollen. It can be easily seen that these signs and symptoms of heart failure are merely exaggerations of mechanisms designed to preserve balance or equilibrium in a failing system.

Try considering alcoholism or schizophrenia in this frame of reference. Alcoholic or schizophrenic symptomatology that is seriously impairing a life course is an extreme. At the early stages of their development, both sets of symptoms were designed to adapt to an emotionally charged situation, but over time, the situation and mechanisms become exaggerated. To define them as pathological states is to fail to recognize the intensity of the problem in the larger system that created the need for these mechanisms in the first place and also the adaptive aspects of the behavior. This is not an argument for calling alcoholism and schizophrenia normal, but to emphasize that they are exaggerations of mechanisms present in all people, designed to adapt to a system problem.

Counterbalancing Life Forces in Nature

The idea of a balance of forces is central to systems thinking, whether it is a cell, a cardiovascular system, a person, a family, or an entire society that is under scrutiny. When this balance of forces is seriously disturbed, symptoms are not far behind.

Nature, of course, is one grand balance of forces and, as knowledge increases, the consistency of the principles defined from the study of human relationship systems with the principles that operate in other natural systems will become more obvious.

Bowen has defined two counterbalancing life forces from the study of the family—a force towards *individuality* and a force towards *togetherness* (Bowen, 1971). These forces will be discussed in the next section of this chapter, but to first gain some perspective on them, let us look at some interesting parallels in nature—living cells and social insects.

Living cells have the ability to suppress their reproductive potential or tendency to duplicate themselves, and become specialists. As specialists they can become part of a larger system of cells and perform certain functions required for the stability of the whole. As part of the liver, for example, they may produce special enzymes required for the storage of glucose in the liver. Kidney cells do not produce these enzymes, although they presumably have the potential to do so. The process of specialization is referred to as cellular differentiation. Interestingly, *cells only differentiate when they are organized into relationships with other cells.* This fact suggests that cellular differentiation is related to the forces cells exert on each other. No one has yet defined the nature of these forces between cells, but it seems clear that they exist. Cancer cells are cells that violate the rules of this federation of cells by returning to their reproductive mode. They appear selfish, individualistic, and unresponsive to the forces that normally dictate to them. An intriguing question is whether the cancer cell has gone haywire and overwhelmed the forces that act on it or is the organization of forces somehow disturbed, permitting the cancer cell to emerge? Obviously, no attempt will be made to tackle such a question here, but the example is raised to illustrate that there is likely a balance of forces among cells, one acting on the cells, dictating that they specialize and function in certain ways, and another that has the potential for more individualistic behavior.

Wilson (1975), the noted sociobiologist, in discussing some of his favorite study subjects, the social insects, talks about a struggle between forces in the social group that dictate the individual's functioning be subjugated to the whole and forces for individual independence. At first glance, the force for the individual independence seems nonexistent in the higher social insects. Each member of the group seems totally subjugated to the whole. Each organism becomes highly specialized, structurally and behaviorally, to perform certain functions in the group. But on close inspection, these qualities are balanced by some interesting qualities of independence. There is, for example, evidence of competitiveness and conflict between the colony queen and the other females over "rights" to egg laying. Bumblebee queens will control their daughters by aggression, attacking them whenever they attempt to lay eggs. When groups of female wasps are starting a colony together, they will contend for dominance and the egg laying rights that go with the top position. The losers then perform as workers, but once in a while they will try to sneak their own eggs into empty brood cells.

Countless other examples of the counterbalancing forces in nature could be presented, but it is hoped that these two brief examples highlight the fact that systems principles may be consistent throughout nature, from the human family system to the cell. That this is so is by no means established and the examples given are only suggestive.

Individuality and Togetherness Forces

Bowen (1971) has proposed that in human relationship systems there are two natural forces that act to counterbalance each other: a force towards individuality or autonomy and a force towards togetherness or fusion. The individuality force is rooted in an instinctual drive to be a self-contained, independent organism, an individual in one's own right. The togetherness force is rooted in an instinctual need for others,

a sense of being connected to the group or another person. In addition to the need for others, this togetherness force is also manifested in the emotional pressure people put on each other to guarantee the meeting of that need, the pressure people put on each other to think and act in certain ways.

The balance of these two forces in a relationship is never static. The forces are in constant motion, with each member of the relationship carefully monitoring the current status of the balance. A feeling of too much togetherness with its accompanying sense of loss of self will trigger efforts to recover some individuality. A feeling of too little togetherness will stimulate moves toward emotional closeness. If one person devotes increasing energy in an individual direction, he/she will experience both feelings within him/herself inclining him/her to restore the togetherness and pressure from the other partner to restore the togetherness.

These are natural, instinctual forces producing a fascinating homeostatic interplay and it is a mistake to consider one force positive and the other negative. These forces are a part of all people and all relationships. They can be accentuated in one direction or another by life experiences, but their roots are part of all living things. The fact that they are so automatic and operate largely outside of awareness indicates how deeply ingrained they are in the human organism.

Intellectual vs. Emotional Functioning

Man tends to focus on the ways in which he is different from other forms of life. Though Darwin's concepts of evolution have been accepted by many people on an intellectual level, emotional reactions to the ideas still remain. Many thinkers emphasize the cultural determinants of man's behavior, relegating biological determinants to a place of unimportance or, at best, to explain deviant behavior.

Systems theory has a concept aimed at bridging this dichotomy between the intellectually determined and emotionally determined aspects of human functioning and the concept is really very simple. It proposes that man has both a capacity for intellectually determined functioning, a product of his *intellectual system*, and emotionally determined functioning, a product of his *emotional system*. When these two systems can remain functionally separate and operate in harmony with each other, man has a *choice* between operating on an intellectual, objective basis, or on an emotional, subjective basis. Having a choice is a by-product of recognizing the difference between intellectual and emotional functioning within oneself. When these two systems are not functionally separate, man loses that choice and his behavior and thinking become more emotionally determined. The choice is lost as the perception of the difference between intellectual and emotional functioning disappears. Practically speaking, *the more anxious or emotionally intense a person gets, the greater the tendency for the fusion of these two systems.*

Bowen developed the idea of intellectual and emotional centers in the brain based largely on clinical observation. Calm people can think fairly clearly and objectively. However, these same people, placed in an emotionally charged situation, can begin to operate more based on emotional reactivity. Seemingly well thought-out principles are dropped in favor of expediency, retaining approval, placing blame on others, trying to dominate somebody and other such reactions. Bowen was observing what he called varying degrees of fusion of the intellectual and emotional centers or systems based on the level of anxiety of the person. Many people can sustain a certain number or intensity of emotional inputs without losing objectivity, but if the inputs are very intense or prolonged, the brain seems to lose its ability to preserve the separateness of its intellectual center. *The intellect then begins to function in the service of emotionality instead of as a counterbalancing force.*

Another man who has worked at the NIMH since about the time Bowen first arrived there is Paul MacLean. MacLean is a well-known brain researcher who, through the extensive comparison of the brains of reptiles, lower mammals, and higher mammals, including man, developed concepts about intellectual and emotional functioning that are similar to Bowen's (MacLean, 1978). MacLean's findings are that many parts of man's brain are identical to those of lower mammals and reptiles. What is unique

about man is the phenomenal development of the cerebral cortex, the most recent evolutionary development in his brain and the center for his abstract thinking processes. MacLean's view is that just because man has a large cerebral cortex, that is no reason to assume that the older areas of his brain, for example, the limbic system, no longer influence his behavior. MacLean has fascinating studies linking many human behaviors with areas of the brain man has in common with lower animals.

This concept of the intellectual and emotional systems is probably the most important and least understood concept in family systems theory. Many people react emotionally to hearing the idea as if what is being advocated is a race of non-feeling automatons. The key element in the concept is the *retention of choice* and not that one type of functioning is superior to another. Perhaps one of the main difficulties in accepting the concept is that so many mental health professionals operate based on the view that repression of emotion is an important cause of mental illness. Keeping the intellectual and emotional systems separate seems to be heard as advocating the very process therapists are trying to undo. "You are trying to make us all into obsessives," is a frequent comment.[7] Actually, obsessionalism is as much a product of the fusion of the intellectual and emotional systems as hysteria. People with a reasonable degree of separateness of intellectual and emotional functioning are at a midpoint between these two emotionally based extremes. The thinking of people at the midpoint would be freer, lacking the scatter of the hysteric and the rigidity of the obsessive.

Emotional Dominance and the Togetherness Orientation

People are not the same in terms of their ability to recognize when their ideas and actions are based on thinking and when they are based on emotionality. Nor are people the same in their ability to retain some choice over whether to follow their thinking or their feelings in a

---

[7]*Editors' Note.* Our experience, to the contrary, is that critics of the family systems model are more likely to object to what they see as a lack of attempts at *integration* of the intellectual and emotional systems in this model.

given situation. People whose functioning tends to be dominated by their emotions are referred to as having a low degree of *basic differentiation* between their intellectual and emotional systems. People who can maintain reasonable separateness of the intellectual and emotional systems in a variety of situations, particularly emotionally charged ones, are said to have a high degree of basic differentiation. All people fall somewhere between these two extremes in terms of what is average for them over the course of their lives. The ability to maintain separateness of the intellectual and emotional systems is not constant within a given person because that ability tends to be eroded by sustained anxiety and improved by calmness. These anxiety- or situation-related changes are referred to as *functional* shifts in differentiation. *The greater this fusion or lack of differentiation between the intellectual and emotional systems, the greater the influence of the togetherness life force on a person's functioning.* This togetherness influence is manifested in a variety of ways.

Perhaps the best measure of the degree of influence of the togetherness force is the degree to which a person's thinking, feeling, and actions are dependent on or influenced by the emotionality of other people. This vulnerability to emotional influencing from others is rooted in our affinity and *need for other people*—the need for some input or particular reaction from them in order to feel secure within ourselves. This need can be manifested in overt emotional dependence on others or in reactive withdrawal from others—an "I don't need you" posture. Closely tied to this need for others is *emotional reactivity to what the other person says and does.* Seeking approval and being dependent on pleasing the other and feeling obliged and comforted by conforming to what the other seems to want are part of this reactivity. The emotionally equivalent opposite of seeking approval, namely, courting disapproval and rebelling against the perceived wishes of the other, is also part of the togetherness influence. This emotional reactivity of people to each other is what produces the *emotional pressure people feel from each other to think and act in specified ways.* Exerting this kind of pressure on another and being vulnerable to it are, again, emotional equivalents. Being able to observe this emo-

tional meshwork or webbing that binds people together and dictates how they are to function is what it means to *think systems.* The intensity or stickiness of this emotional meshwork depends on the basic emotional reactiveness of the people who make up a given relationship system and the amount of stress they are under.

There are a number of other manifestations of *fusion* of the intellectual and emotional systems and a togetherness orientation. The greater the fusion, the more difficulty coping with or keeping emotions in balance. This can be reflected in an impaired ability to be aware of and express feelings or in an inability to control volcanic outbursts of emotions. The togetherness force is also reflected in *poorly defined boundaries between self and other.* An obligatory sense of responsibility for the emotional well-being of another person or the expectation that someone else is responsible for the emotional well-being of oneself is such a boundary problem. Fusion of intellectual and emotional functioning leads to *unrealistic assessments of oneself and others.* This could be the person who overvalues himself and blames others for his misfortunes or the person who undervalues himself and is an excessive self-blamer.

One of the most interesting aspects of fusion of the intellectual and emotional systems is what it does to thinking. Perhaps there should be two words for thinking, one that indicates thinking based on emotional influence, the subjective type, and one that indicates thinking that is kept separate from emotional influence, the objective type. If emotionality is pervasive in all aspects of someone's life, e.g., the schizophrenic, that person may never think on an objective level. He/she acts almost totally on feelings. On a less emotionally intense level are people with ideas and opinions, but whose ideas have so much emotional coloring that they are adhered to and expressed in dogmatic and authoritarian ways. This person's thinking is usually uneven in that he/she can be objective about certain areas of his/her life and totally emotionally biased about other areas. As the intellectual system gains still more separateness from emotional influence, it is freer to define principles and beliefs based on objective assessments of available knowledge. The development of well thought-out principles and beliefs is the core of the individuality force;

this is who I am, what I believe, where I stand. Individuality means the courage to stick by principles and stand alone if necessary while at the same time not pressuring others to change their beliefs and actions. Individuality is not to be confused with selfishness, the latter being a rather primitive type of individuality comprised mainly of emotional elements. Selfishness may define the boundaries of self, but fails to respect the boundaries of others.

Anxiety, by promoting more fusion of the intellectual and emotional systems, promotes an increase in the togetherness orientation. As anxiety increases, people with a high degree of differentiation, based on their well defined principles and beliefs and better emotional self-control, can counterbalance their emotionality and adapt well to the situation. In contrast, people with low differentiation quickly become prisoners of their emotional reactivity. But no person, regardless of his/her basic differentiation, is immune to being overwhelmed by emotion. It is a question of degrees of vulnerability. As the emotionality increases, all of us experience a greater need for emotional closeness to others or greater allergy to emotional closeness. There is more of a tendency to blame ourselves or others and to have problems permitting each other to be what we each are.

Fusion in Relationships

The degree of fusion of the intellectual and emotional systems within an individual parallels the degree to which that person fuses into or loses self in relationships. Fusion of intellectual and emotional functioning permits overriding of the togetherness force and it is that force that undermines a person's ability to maintain his/her individuality in relationships.

People with equivalent degrees of togetherness needs are attracted to each other in terms of forming potentially long-term relationships such as marriage. The more intense the togetherness orientation of the partners, the more strongly the relationship will be balanced towards togetherness or, said in another way, the more intense the relationship fusion.

Characteristically, each partner in a relationship fusion plays out the opposite side of many of the manifestations of togetherness that were described earlier. The end result often gives the appearance of one partner being more independent or differentiated than the other, when, in fact, both have equivalent needs for togetherness and equivalent capacities to be a self. It is common, for example, for one partner to function as the dependent one who feels vulnerable and frustrated in the need for relationship closeness. This spouse is frequently oriented to pleasing the other and compromises his/her views to gain approval and preserve harmony. He/she will often feel inadequate and not see himself/herself as capable of holding opinions or having thoughts of his/her own. The other spouse, in contrast, seems independent, cool, and unemotional. That spouse will, in fact, often experience less *felt* need for closeness and approval than his or her mate. That spouse may overvalue him/herself and criticize the seeming inadequacy of the other. This stronger-appearing spouse comes to hold the opinions in the relationship and is the decision-maker for the twosome. The important point to remember is that each of these mates has an equivalent emotional problem, but it is played out in mirror-opposite ways. This is what is meant by Bowen's original phrase, *emotional complementarity.*

The more the basic differentiation of the people in a relationship, the more their relationship is balanced towards individuality. It is less emotionally intense and the togetherness manifestations are not so prominent. For example, while the need for the other exists, that need is not so strong that it impairs independent functioning. There is less psychic energy tied up in concerns about whether each is paying enough attention to the other, being rejected by the other, being "understanding," etc. Consequently, more energy is available for non-relationship pursuits. Approval is somewhat important to both, but the self-image of each is not so dependent on what the other spouse says or thinks about him/her. Being fairly self-contained people and not so emotionally reactive to each other, they place fewer emotional demands on each other, keeping their expectations realistic. It is possible for one to be anxious about a problem, tell the other one about it and not have the other become so emotionally involved him/herself that he/she either has to cut off discussion or start preaching.

Relationship Fusion and Anxiety

Fusion into a relationship can provide both a relief from and a source of anxiety. It is an interesting paradox. The more intense the togetherness needs of the people who comprise a relationship, the more they will look to the relationship to meet those needs and to relieve anxiety. At the same time, the more intense the fusion, the greater the chance that the emotional pressures of the relationship will force them into compromised uncomfortable positions. This leaves people with the dilemma of needing closeness to relieve the anxiety of emotional isolation and needing distance to relieve the anxiety of relationship suffocation.

This need for and allergy to emotional closeness exist in all relationships to some degree. *It is an emotional phenomenon and so is more pronounced in the relationships of people with a low degree of differentiation of intellectual and emotional functioning.* As the fusion in relationships becomes progressively more intense, this closeness-distance dilemma becomes ever more difficult to equilibrate. At the extremes of emotional fusion, there are periods of time when this dilemma is so intense that there is *no solution that permits the intactness of the relationship and/or the relatively unimpaired functioning of each person.*

So the more intense the relationship fusion, the more unstable the basic balance of the relationship and the more chronic anxiety generated by the relationship. This basic fusion and basic level of chronic anxiety in a given relationship are important to recognize for understanding the adaptiveness of a relationship system to additional stresses. Relationships with a high degree of fusion generate so many problems of their own that they have less reserve to cope with additional increments of anxiety. When the system's ability to adapt is exceeded, then acute and/or chronic symptoms appear. The basic patterns of a relationship that were adaptive and functional at one level of stress on the system can be driven to their extremes and become dysfunctional at a higher level of stress. All relationships are vulnerable to some type of

dysfunction if the anxiety is sufficient in intensity and duration.

As an example of the way reasonably functional relationship patterns can become dysfunctional when driven to their extremes by anxiety, let us look again at the relationship described in the previous section. As anxiety increases, the activity of the togetherness force increases, disturbing the basic individuality-togetherness balance. People become more needy and at the same time increasingly anxious about the emotional neediness and demands of the other. The one functioning in the dependent-inadequate position becomes even more dependent and less confident. The one in the strong-overadequate position may become more authoritarian and critical, but at the same time begins to feel trapped by the greater neediness and dependency of his/her mate. Each develops more expectations of *the other* for change, hoping a change in the other will relieve his/her own anxiety. One or both partners may experience a feeling of erosion of individuality accompanied by increasing internal discomfort. The increasing tension may be expressed primarily in relationship disharmony and conflict, primarily in one of the two people or, typically, in a combination of both. The one most vulnerable to experiencing the most internal tension and disequilibrium is the one who has made the most compromises in his/her own functioning in an attempt to preserve relationship harmony. The "dependent" one can be most compromised, feeling increasing discomfort with a sense of loss of control over his/her own life, or the "strong" one can feel compromised by the increasing burden of the other's underfunctioning. Remember that the strong-weak or overadequate-inadequate positions may have relieved the internal anxiety of each and been functional up to a point, but driven to the extreme, the pattern becomes symptomatic. The process is driven by anxiety and *both* partners are at the mercy of it. At moderate levels of tension, it is still possible for one partner to feel little discomfort, while the other more compromised partner is quite uncomfortable. It is characteristic for this uncomfortable one to view the problem as primarily his or her own creation, "If only I were a better person," etc.

It is these emotional dilemmas, present always in tightly fused relationships and present periodically in better differentiated people subjected to increased chronic anxiety, from which the concepts of family systems theory logically follow.

The Interlocking Concepts of Family Systems Theory

1) Triangles

As mentioned in the preceding section, when tension increases, it may lead to relationship conflict and/or be felt as internal discomfort by one member of the relationship. When the latter is the case, relationship harmony has been preserved by one partner's absorbing the potential relationship problem. Which partner absorbs the anxiety is determined by the patterns of interaction of the twosome. The process operates automatically and enough out of the awareness of either partner that the non-absorber is often genuinely surprised to hear the other is uncomfortable or unhappy.

In any event, a predictable move that occurs in this kind of situation is that the more uncomfortable person "resolves" the relationship dilemma by moving towards relationship fusion with a third person. If successful in fusing with another person, the other member of the original twosome becomes an outsider to this new fusion or togetherness. The outsider can feel either relief or discomfort with this position. An example of a mother-father-child triangle may help explain these different reactions to an outside position.

If a mother directs her relationship interests towards one of her children, the father can feel the relief of not having to deal with his wife's anxiety about him and not having to confront potential emotional issues in their marital relationship. On the other hand, the mother's emotional overinvestment in the child may leave the father feeling rejected and uncomfortable. In this case, he will make moves to restore the marital togetherness, moves ranging from looking a little depressed to actually claiming he is being rejected. If tensions develop between mother and overinvested child, the mother may seek the father's help, through various overt and covert emotional cues, in dealing

with the child. Tension or conflict may then erupt between father and child, allowing mother the temporary comfort of an outside position. But the ever alert child may then reinvolve mother by claiming unfair treatment by the father, or the mother may reinvolve herself in reaction to what she perceives as the father's harsh tactics. At this point, mother may attack father and the child achieves the comfortable outside position. It is a constantly shifting emotional process that is fed by a multitude of verbal and nonverbal cues.

When the tension level is mild to moderate, it may be contained primarily in one central triangle, for example, father-mother-specific child. With increasing levels of tension, other people may be involved, creating adjoining or interlocking triangles. The father may involve another child by insisting he speak to his acting-up sibling. Conflict may then erupt between the two kids, leaving the original mother-father-child triangle relatively quiet. The tension can thus shift about through these interlocking triangles. The emotional forces are in constant motion, but increased anxiety in the system, as with the increased Brownian movement of heated molecules, will increase the activity of triangles.

Characteristically, then, in triangles, there are two insiders and one outsider. During periods of high tension, the outside position is preferred. When tensions are low, the outsider's gain, namely, relative freedom from the anxious twosome, is lost and the outsider begins to feel the discomfort of isolation. During periods of moderate tension, there are two comfortable sides of the triangle and one side in conflict and it is possible for people to occupy relatively fixed positions in this regard. The family, for example, may come to view *the* family problem as the conflictual relationship between the father and a particular child. Indeed, both the marriage and the mother's relationship with that child may be fairly harmonious. In fact, the family's overall anxiety has been chronically shifted into the father-child relationship based on the way the interlocking triangles operate. All family members have contributed equally to the process. Just as an individual cannot be understood out of the context of their important relationships, no relationship can be understood out of the context of the way it interlocks with other family relationships. The calm or harmony in one relationship can be maintained by the conflict in another relationship.

An interesting facet of triangles is seen in marriages that can maintain harmony best by excluding outsiders, versus marriages in which harmony depends on outside involvements. In the first case, one or both partners are so sensitive to signs of involvement away from the twosome that the presence of a third person can increase anxiety. In the second case, the marital relationship dilemma is "solved" by focus on a third person. There are, for example, marriages that are significantly disturbed by the birth of a child and those whose disturbance is calmed by the addition of a child.

The key to understanding triangles is recognizing that emotionality drives them. The greater the togetherness orientation of the people, the greater the potential anxiety and the greater the likelihood of triangling. A multitude of issues are bandied about in triangles, but the issues are *not* the driving force. The process is driven by the emotional reactiveness of people and the level of emotion that gets attached to a particular issue. Reduction of anxiety and emotional reactivity will reduce the activity of triangles, but the basic pathways remain intact for future use.

Triangles can reach outside the family system to involve work, social, and institutional systems. These systems, in turn, have triangles of their own that can reach out and involve families. To know triangles is to see the absurdity of asking people "why" they do what they do and the absurdity of assigning cause to any particular event in a system. Looking for cause obscures the view of the interdependence.

2) Nuclear family emotional process

The basic elements in the concept of nuclear family emotional process are logical extensions of the discussion of triangles. When acute or chronic tension builds in a marriage, people have four options in responding to it: They can distance from each other; they can get into conflict with each other; one can compromise his/her own functioning to preserve relationship harmony; or the couple can band together over a common concern, for example, a child. When any of these options is overused, it can lead to the categories of problems that families commonly seek help for, namely, marital conflict, impaired functioning of a spouse, or problems with a child.

Each one of these options or mechanisms is an attempt to preserve stability within the individual and/or the family system, but the stability of one person's functioning may be preserved at the expense of someone else's functioning. The more one mechanism is used to preserve equilibrium in a system, the less other mechanisms are required. Some families use predominantly one mechanism; others demonstrate a mixture. The greater the basic fusion of a nuclear family, the greater the chronic anxiety and potential instability it generates, and, therefore, the greater the requirement for these mechanisms. Regardless of the basic fusion, the greater the anxiety based on external stresses the family is experiencing, the greater the use of the mechanisms.

Emotional Distance. This term describes the distance that develops between people based on their emotional reactivity to each other. It is a compromise people make to reduce the anxiety or discomfort of too much closeness. Reasonably well differentiated people may choose to be distant from each other because they are busy with other pursuits. That *choice* is a different process than what is meant by emotional distance. Distance based on emotional reactiveness is an automatic process and usually goes beyond what people "want." The distance can range from the avoidance of certain subjects, subjects with an emotional charge, to not speaking to or even looking at each other for extended periods. The distance can be accomplished by physically avoiding each other or through internal mechanisms that insulate one from the other even though in each other's presence.

When spouses distance from each other, they may focus their togetherness needs elsewhere. A wife, for example, may get into psychotherapy and satisfy her fusion needs in a transference relationship. She might also turn to an affair. The husband might substitute an affair or seek approval and acceptance through career accomplishments. What people are avoiding with emotional distance is their own emotional reactivity to each other. The other person can seem like the problem, but the problem exists equally in both people.

Marital Conflict. Conflict in the marriage often provides an amazingly stable "solution" to the relationship dilemma of the need for emotional closeness on the one hand and the allergy to too much closeness on the other. Conflictual marriages are extremely intense relationships in which much of each spouse's emotional reactiveness is focused on the other spouse. Both partners are usually up to it, in that neither buckles under the intense pressure and attack. Each is exquisitely sensitive to giving in to the other, lest he/she be the loser. It is taken to the point of having to make a "federal case" out of one issue after another in order to maintain the stances they have taken. When they are apart, each is preoccupied with the "unfair" treatment he/she has received, each feeling his/her point of view has not been heard. Periods together are often characterized by protracted discussions and desires for explanations of why the other did or did not do such and such. Long periods of conflict in which distance is "justified" are usually followed by periods of brief, but equally intense, closeness. Then a remark, a look, or a change in tone of voice can set off another escalating and at times exhausting cycle of debate and conflict. Perhaps exhausting is the wrong word in that it may just seem that way to an outsider. In fact, each spouse seems willing and able to summon tremendous energy to participate in the conflictual drama. In most instances, disturbances in the balance of the relationship can be re-equilibrated by virtue of this energy and time each is willing to expend on the relationship. At points in their marriage when they are unsuccessful in restoring relationship equilibrium, they will seek therapy. Their goal in therapy is to bring the tensions back down to manageable levels and, to this end, they are willing to spend long hours with a therapist going over the minute details of their disagreements. A multitude of issues are introduced as "causes" of the disharmony and they are not only grateful for the therapist's interest in their issues, but welcome him warmly into their debates. But it is the emotional intensity that is all important, not the specific issues that get tied into it.

One couple the author treated provides some interesting insights into some of the basic elements of a conflictual marriage. The wife was the more overtly anxious of the twosome and most of her comments expressed dissatisfaction with her husband and his seeming unresponsiveness to her. She had a myriad of trigger words and remarks that produced a highly predictable defensive and angry outburst from her husband. In spite of the "hurtful" nature of some of his backlashes, she found his periodic emotional explosions somehow reassuring in that he had finally responded to her. He complained of her perpetual harassment and said she had been "hell-on-wheels" throughout the 37 years of their marriage. The therapist innocently suggested that the wife try to tone down her reactivity to her husband, a suggestion she did try to follow. The husband reported the following week that it had been one of the best of their married life, hardly any tension in the relationship. The wife, in contrast, said she had been unable to sleep, felt enormous tension within her muscles and was experiencing severe headaches. The next week they had returned to their conflictual pattern and her symptoms cleared up. Then, after about four months in therapy, a peculiar thing happened. The wife came in reporting she was getting the message about being truly less reactive and that a new calmness had settled over her. She was genuinely less preoccupied with what her husband said or did and had newfound energy for a small business of hers. Within another two weeks, the husband, feeling his wife no longer cared about him, initiated an affair that he did little to conceal. She immediately forgot her business interests, became preoccupied with his "disloyalty" and their confrontations resumed. He then quit the affair and they quit therapy.

Intense marital conflict can protect the children from parental overinvolvement in their lives. If each of these parents had focused his/her emotional energies on one of the children instead of on the spouse, it takes little imagination to realize the child would be headed for significant problems of his own. As it was, this couple's children were doing fairly well. That is not to say that intense marital conflict precludes overinvolvement with a child, because a family may require more than one mechanism to absorb, bind, or stabilize the anxiety experienced.

Spouse Dysfunction. Marital tensions can be reduced by one spouse giving in or compromising him/herself to go along with the other spouse. Pressure for this kind of solution can come from both partners, with the giving-in spouse not wanting decision-making responsibilities and the dominant spouse feeling he/she knows what is best anyway. It is unlikely that there is any marriage in which the expertise of the partners is the same in all areas and so the capacity of each to defer to the other's judgment in certain areas would be a sign of differentiation. But when the decision of who gives in to whom is based on subjective or emotional factors, there can be complications. An emotionally determined dominant-submissive or overfunctioning-underfunctioning pattern will remain reasonably functional for both partners as long as the stress on the system is within manageable levels. But if the system experiences a sustained increase in the level of anxiety, the overfunctioning-underfunctioning pattern is taken to extremes and gradually impairs the ability of one spouse to function. The impairment may manifest itself in physical illness, mental illness, or some type of social acting-out behavior. The spouse who is vulnerable to symptom development is the one who has made the most compromises of his/her own functioning over an extended period to preserve harmony in the system. The compromised one can be either the one who has tried to overfunction or the one who has been the underfunctioner. Said in another way, the symptomatic spouse is the one whose sense of self has been most eroded by the relationship system, either through overfunctioning or underfunctioning.

The more the basic differentiation of a person, the more realistic that person is in his/her expectations of him/herself and other people. When there is fusion of intellectual and emotional functioning, people are characteristically expecting too much or too little of themselves and others. In a marriage, unrealistic expectations can be reflected in one spouse feeling it is his/her responsibility to preserve harmony in

family relationships and preserve a sense of emotional well-being in other family members. This overresponsible feeling can range from mild and uncomplicated all the way to psychotic level distortions, such as a feeling that energy a person puts into his/her own life is a threat to the very existence of others. Another variant of overresponsibility is one spouse feeling he/she knows what is best for the other spouse and anxiously monitoring the functioning of the other to keep him/her on a certain track. This kind of anxious hovering can impair the other's ability to function. In each case, the overresponsible feeling in one spouse is complemented by an equally distorted expectation of the other spouse that the mate function in this overresponsible position. This, of course, is not a verbal contract, but is built into the patterns of people. The greater the undifferentiation of the people, the more automatic the process becomes.

It cannot be overemphasized that the above described patterns can remain quite functional. It is only when the system is acutely (weeks to months) or chronically (years) stressed beyond its ability to adapt that a functional arrangement progresses to the impairment of one person.

Nobody wants to impair the functioning of the other. Everybody loses something in the process. The impairment, rather, is a function of the anxiety in the system and the series of compromises people make in relationships to allay that anxiety. Such compromises are characteristically short-term "solutions" that generate even more difficult binds to be faced further down the road. As time passes, either through the lifetime of an individual or nuclear family or over the course of many generations, people can become progressively boxed in to certain positions that are more and more difficult to change.

When the impaired spouse develops some type of physical or mental illness, potential relationship tensions can be reduced by the caretaking, ministering, or feeling sorry for postures that family members take toward the "sick" person. The appearance of an illness, then, can reflect family anxiety, but, if it becomes chronic, can actually reduce family anxiety. In the latter case, the family system preserves stability by settling for a less than optimum level of functioning, family equilibrium depending on the presence of chronic symptoms. There are some striking examples of dramatic improvements in chronic physical or mental illness in a person after his/her spouse dies or after a divorce. Granted, there are probably an equal number of cases that get worse in such situations, but the improvements highlight that what we call disease or illness is actually a *symptom* of a more fundamental emotional disturbance in the individual, which, in turn, is symptomatic of a disturbance in the family relationship system.

Impairment of Children. The mechanisms of distance, conflict, and spouse dysfunction all describe processes in which the undifferentiation of the spouses is absorbed, played out, or contained, either in the marital relationship or within the functioning of one spouse. Potential fusion-generated problems and anxiety between spouses can be avoided, as was described in the section on triangles, by parental focus on one or more children. When this occurs, the most common pattern is the mother focusing much of her emotional energy on a particular child, with the father supporting it by being in sympathy with it or by distancing from it. Even though most of the activity may transpire between mother and child, the father is equally fused into the process.

This focused-on child, relative to his siblings, is the one whose emotional system becomes the most reactive and who grows up with the greatest fusion of his intellectual and emotional systems, a greater fusion often than that of his parents. This focused child is the most sensitive to disturbances in the balance of the family relationship system and, at points of significant tension, is vulnerable to the development of mental, physical, or social problems.

This fusion view of the underlying process in the etiology of mental disorders contrasts with the still widely accepted maternal deprivation hypothesis, a hypothesis accepted by parents as well as mental health professionals. Most parents, when faced with a problem in their child, will accentuate their activity and involvement with that child in an effort to fix the problem. When parents feel overwhelmed, they will seek out professional help, hoping the professional will be able to *do* something. From a systems perspective, this kind of often frenzied activity

is generated out of the intense fusion between parents and child and, while some of it may provide the illusion of change, such activity will complicate the problem in the long run.

Family systems theory describes such a totally different way of conceptualizing the maternal-child relationship that it has been considered important to make overinvolvement with a child a separate concept in the theory, the *family projection process.*

3) Family projection process

The concept of a family projection process describes the way the undifferentiation of the parents is transmitted to their children. The result of this transmission is that the capacity for differentiation in the children generally approximates closely that of their parents. Since the process does focus unevenly on the various children, it is possible for some children to grow up with slightly less capacity for differentiation than their parents, others with the same capacity, and still others with somewhat more ability to maintain differentiation in an emotional system.

The projection process is so much a part of the atmosphere of a family that much of it is not easily described. The transmission of undifferentiation from one generation to the next is, in a general way, related to what parents stand for and what they do. This is not to be confused with what parents say they stand for and what they say they do. There are more tangible aspects to the projection process that can be easily recognized and described. As an example, a mother who feels insecure about her abilities in interpersonal relationships may manifest this by focusing on any sign in the child that can be interpreted as a sign of a similar insecurity in the child. If the mother thinks she sees such a sign, it can quickly become a *fact* in her mind that the child is insecure. As a result, she increasingly relates to him as if he were insecure and the child is molded by the mother's anxious focus. The child begins acting more and more in a way that confirms the mother's original diagnosis. Once this process is established, both mother and child play equal roles in continuing it. The projection process, in other words, is a process in which parental emotionality defines what the child is like, a definition that originally may have little to do with the realities of the child, but that eventually does become a reality in the child. Such a process can permit the parents to stabilize their own functioning and relationship at the expense of the child. The areas of parental focus can include the emotional well-being of the child, his or her physical health, or behavioral traits; the particular area of focus is related to the parents' own experience in their original families.

The parents' thinking and behavior may be far more emotionally determined in relationship to one child than to the others. This focused-on child, in a sense, absorbs parental emotionality and, to the degree the child does this, the other children are protected. The parents worry less about the other children and respond to them more realistically. Parents view the one they worry about as needing that extra attention and worry because of the child's particular problems and needs. It is difficult for them to see that the focused child is mirroring a process in themselves.

The characteristics of the parent's overinvolvement with a child may range from overly positive to overly negative or conflictual. It may change from positive to negative at some point in the child's development, adolescence being a particularly likely time for this to occur. Regardless of the type of parental reaction, the child becomes programmed to evoke that kind of response from the parents and others, and the response is more important than whether it is positive or negative.

The most focused-on child may demonstrate behavior at either end of the continuum: the driven overachiever, the rebellious underachiever, the one who clings to others and is easily led, the rebel who leads an antiestablishment group, the loner or the groupie. Whatever the type of behavior or personality, the focused child is more of an emotional reactor and has less capacity for individuality than his siblings.

Clinical symptoms or problems can appear at any point during the child's growing up. The two critical variables that influence symptom development are the level of anxiety in the family system at a given point and the degree of undifferentiation in the child. The greater the anxiety and the greater the undifferentiation, the greater the likelihood of a symptom.

The classic family situation is demonstrated by the family in which one child's functioning is significantly impaired while the other children function on a good level. Not being repeatedly caught in an intense emotional triangle with the parents, the emotional systems of the "spared" siblings are less programmed for reactiveness and their intellectual systems are freer to engage the world around them. These siblings pick up more of the strengths of their parents and of important others in their environment. The greater the basic level of undifferentiation of the parents and the more the projection process is used to stabilize the system, the more likely it is that several children can be impaired.[8] When it is just primarily one child, several variables influence "selection" of the particular child: the firstborn, the first of a particular sex, one born at a time of family turmoil, one born with a defect, or the youngest child. It is important to keep in mind that it is not the particular trait of a child that *drives* the process. A trait plays a role in *attracting* the process, but the process itself is driven by parental emotional reactiveness.

4) Differentiation of self

The differentiation of self concept describes the fact that people are not the same in terms of the way they manage individuality and togetherness in their lives. People can be viewed as existing on a continuum, a continuum called the *scale of differentiation*, ranging from the lowest to the highest levels of differentiation of self. The highest levels of the scale are theoretical in that they are reserved for a capacity man may evolve to, but has not yet achieved. People at the lower end of the scale are people in whom the togetherness force dominates their thinking and activity. People towards the upper end of the scale are people in whom the individuality and togetherness forces approach an optimum mix or balance, a balance that permits

---

[8] *Editors' Note.* Here, and at numerous other places in this chapter (e.g., in the preceding paragraph), Kerr offers *specific* theoretical propositions of an "if-then" nature, regarding symptom formation, the impact of sibling position, the effects on the family of increased differentiation in one family member, the effects of the therapist's stance (e.g., de-triangulation), etc. Statements of this sort offer rich investigative possibilities.

the person to be a well-defined individual in his/her own right as well as an effective team player. Most people appear to fall somewhere in the midrange between these extremes. Family "teams" at the lower end of the scale are prone to get into difficulty because, to use a football metaphor, they lack individuals capable of making "the big play." They lack the calm leader or leaders who can step forward at critical times and define a direction based on principle. Lower-level families are constantly awash in a sea of emotionality. But individuals and families at any point on the scale are all dealing with the same basic life forces and it is a question of relative success or lack thereof in managing those forces that makes people different.

The scale of differentiation concept is not, at least at this point in its development, a tool or instrument that can be used to accurately categorize people. To date, the concept has been considered to be of mainly theoretical importance, defining one important way in which human beings are different. One of the reasons it is so difficult to place people at specific points on the scale is related to the difference between *basic* and *functional* levels of differentiation. This distinction will be discussed further in the next paragraph. The scale is not intended to be equated with psychiatric diagnoses. People high on the scale are not thereby considered normal psychiatrically nor people low on the scale abnormal. In fact, people anywhere on the scale can develop significant emotional, physical, or social acting-out symptoms provided they experience anxiety of sufficient intensity and duration. It is a fact that people higher on the scale are more adaptive to stress, in that they are less vulnerable to symptom development than people lower on the scale and have a better prognosis if they do get sick. But assigning any point on the scale as normal would be purely arbitrary and not especially useful.[9]

---

[9]*Editors' Note.* As Kerr implies, the differentiation of self scale is not a scale in the usual psychometric sense. Unfortunately, this "scale" often has been reified, even though family systems theorists or therapists have not offered empirical evidence for the scale's elaborate descriptions of the functioning of individuals at various levels of differentiation, or of its reliability or validity (Gurman, 1978). Thus, as one of us has argued elsewhere (Gurman, 1978), it is misleading to speak of "facts" in the context of this scale; a term such as "frequent clinical impression" would be more accurate.

Now, to the difference between basic and functional levels of differentiation: Earlier in the chapter, basic differentiation was described as being reflected in a person's *average* ability, examined over the course of his/her life, to keep intellectually and emotionally based functioning distinct, retaining choice about which system influences his/her activity in a given situation. Basic differentiation was said to be fixed at a certain level during the growing-up years, the specific level depending on the degree of emotional fusion the person had with his/her family of origin. After the level is set, changes in it are uncommon except through systematic efforts to make them. Basic level of differentiation is also described by the phrase *solid self.* Solid self refers to that part of the individual that is nonnegotiable under pressure from the relationship system: "This is who I am and what I believe, and this is the point beyond which I will not go." To the degree to which solid self exists within the individual, it permits him not to be totally at the mercy of emotional pressures from the group to think and act in certain ways. It is that part of the individual's functioning that is not dependent on the relationship system to support it.

Functional level of differentiation was described earlier as shifts in the degree of fusion between the intellectual and emotional systems that are based on shifts in the level of anxiety the person experiences. There is another way to describe functional level of differentiation and that is called *pseudoself.* Pseudoself can look like solid self, "This is who I am and what I believe," but the clue that it is not solid self is in the discrepancy between what a person says and what he/she actually does when under pressure from the relationship system. Pseudoself is negotiable. It is easily given up or changed under pressure. Acceptance by the group, for example, becomes more important than *living* by what one says he/she believes and risking rejection and isolation.

An example of pseudoself and functional level of differentiation would be a person whose life is floundering and who may be experiencing significant physical or emotional symptoms. Now, say that person gets into psychotherapy and, as a *result of a relationship fusion with the therapist,* begins to function better. This is a functional and not a basic change in differentiation in that it *depends* on the relationship fusion to sustain it. A certain amount of this is unavoidable and acceptable in psychotherapy, but, in our opinion, most therapeutic "change" involves a lot more of this than therapists would like to believe. Getting married or joining a cult can provide a similar fusion and functional pull-up. The gain is pseudoself.

The opposite situation can also occur where the person's functional level of differentiation is being impaired by a relationship fusion such as marriage. If that person gets a separation or divorce, he/she may experience a dramatic improvement in functioning, but there has been no change in basic differentiation or basic maturity. These functional shifts in differentiation become more pronounced and frequent in people as you move towards lower basic levels of differentiation. In the lower half of the scale, so much of a person's functioning depends on a borrowing of strength or self from others that significant ups and downs are inevitable. People are depending on the system for too much. At the upper end of the scale, people are more self-contained and consistent in their functioning.

One of the most interesting and useful teaching exercises that Bowen has devised to help highlight the differentiation concept is assigning trainees in the family therapy program the task of trying to define their important beliefs and thinking through where they came from. This is a written assignment that can be mind-bending and hits right at the heart of the differentiation concept. People quickly realize that they carry around a bunch of opinions and beliefs that they have "borrowed" from a hundred different places, their families, their friends, newspapers, books, experts, etc., but have never really thought through for themselves. The emotional commitment to these ideas can often be intense, despite being acquired haphazardly. How about the "knee-jerk" liberal or conservative as two beautiful examples of pseudoself? The liberals and conservatives who get hopelessly polarized are the ones who have arrived at their dogmatic positions based on emotionality. The liberals and conservatives who can deal with each other calmly, genuinely respecting each others' positions, are the ones who have arrived at their views based on a more intellectual, objective process. They are fairly realistic about the strengths and weaknesses of their positions and neither liberals nor conservatives see themselves as having *the truth*, just a point of view with some merit. They view their differences as healthy for the group as a whole. The ability to tolerate difference and gain from it is at the heart of a high level of differentiation of self.

At the lowest end of the scale, it is difficult for people to find the energy to assemble even a pseudoself. These are the *no-selves*. So much of life energy is tied up in emotional survival that they simply do not develop any kind of belief system. Feeling loved and approved of is so dominant in their functioning that no-selves simply go along with the crowd or withdraw into an isolated existence.

5) Multigenerational transmission process

The multigenerational concept describes the ebb and flow of emotional process through the generations. The concept expands the perception of the nuclear family as an emotional unit to the perception of the multigenerational family as an emotional unit. To think in these multigenerational terms is to be able to see serious physical, emotional or social dysfunction in this generation as an end product of an emotional problem that had been growing in the family for many generations. The mother of a schizophrenic child did not create the schizophrenia in the child. She is but one player in a long line of players down through the generations. Viewed in this broader focus, schizophrenia can be thought of not as a disease, but as an outcome of the way natural systems operate. Schizophrenia is a by-product of a long series of compromises the system has made, compromises that stabilized the whole at the expense of some of its parts.

The multigenerational concept is a logical extension of some of the ideas presented earlier, namely, that people who marry each other have equivalent levels of differentiation of self and that one important mechanism for stabilizing a marital fusion is projection of parental undifferentiation onto one or more children. Projection can result in one or more children growing up with a lower level of differentiation than their parents or siblings; they, in turn, marry people at their level of differentiation and repeat the process. Over the course of multiple generations, the contrasts between basic level of differentiation of various segments of the family can become greater and greater, with some segments of the family having a significantly lower level of differentiation than the original ancestors and other segments having a higher level than the original ancestors.

The rate of progression of the multigenerational process is quite variable, ranging from gradual to rapid. It may be slowed, for example, by the undifferentiation of a particular generation being played out in marital conflict as opposed to projection. If much of the undifferentiation is bound by projection for several successive generations, then, in a span of just three or four generations, people can go from a good level of functioning to marked impairment. The degree of *emotional cutoff* between the generations (the avoidance of emotion-laden areas between the generations) is another factor that can influence the process and is of such importance that it will be discussed as a separate concept. Favorable life circumstances can calm family anxiety and deintensify the projection in a given generation. By the time serious impairments in functioning are emerging, the projection process is usually very intense and the parents' degree of cutoff from the previous generations is marked.

Changes in the basic level of differentiation over multiple generations of a family are manifested in a variety of ways. Better differentiated people and families experience less chronic anxiety, have more emotional reserve and adaptiveness, require less use of stabilizing mechanisms such as projection, and experience fewer acute and chronic problems of all types—physical, emotional, social or marital. As the generational line and the individuals it produces progress towards increasing fusion, people and families experience more chronic anxiety, have less adaptability to stress, and experience more of the full range of human problems. These families can become increasingly infertile and progress towards extinction or may experience uncontrolled reproduction with increasing disorder and chaos. The problems may become progressively internalized, such as with schizophrenia, or progressively acted out, as with the social dysfunctions. Defined in this way, the schizophrenic can be thought of as an individual with such an intense fusion of the intellectual and emotional systems and such intense togetherness needs that it is virtually impossible for him/her to keep a relationship in balance. He gradually makes a series of internal compromises to the relationship dilemma that lead eventually to the clinical picture called schizophrenia.

Schizophrenia is only one type of outcome to increasing fusion in the family system. Intractable obesity, serious criminal behavior, the extremes of alcoholism, serious physical dysfunction early in life, and a host of other things are possibilities. In each instance, the emotional forces that drive these dysfunctions have their roots four, six, eight, maybe ten generations back in the family.

6) Emotional cutoff

The concept of emotional cutoff describes the way people commonly deal with unresolved fusion to their families of origin, namely, by insulating themselves or cutting themselves off emotionally from the parental family. This cutoff can be accomplished by physical distance, keeping contacts with family brief and infrequent and/or through internal mechanisms such as withdrawal and avoidance of emotionally charged areas while in the presence of the family.

The more intense the emotional fusion the person experienced while growing up, the greater the likelihood of a significant cutoff later on. In looking at a family over many generations, the lines of the family which experience increasing fusion will be the lines also experiencing greater and greater degrees of emotional cutoff between segments of family and family members. Not all lack of involvement between segments of family is related to emotional reactivity, but too little is often attributed to it.

Emotional cutoff is an interesting paradox in that it at one and the same time *reflects* a problem, *"solves"* a problem, and *creates* a problem. It reflects the problem of the underlying fusion between the generations. It "solves" a problem in that, by avoiding emotional contact, it reduces the anxiety of the moment. It creates a problem in that it isolates and alienates people from each other, people who could *benefit* from contact with each other if they could deal with each other better. Once cut off from each other, people are vulnerable to equally intense fusions into other relationship systems. People will sometimes say that *until* they "broke" contact with their extended families, their marriages were in constant turmoil, responding to the emotionality in their extended families. People must recognize, however, that they bear responsibility for half the problem and that running away is no more than a short-term solution.

The person with significant unresolved fusion or attachment to the parental family is as likely to describe his/her relationship with parents as "ideal" as to describe it as "horrible." It just depends on the way the fusion was played out, harmoniously or discordantly. Frequently, people will say there were problems in their relationship with parents while they were at home, but since being on their own or after the first child, all has been "worked out." This kind of statement *does not reflect a resolution of the fusion*, but just a toning down of the anxiety related to a variety of factors.

An example of emotional cutoff would be a person programmed for intense togetherness needs through an intense fusion with his/her parents, who in adolescence begins cutting off from parents and seeking new equally intense involvements outside the family, girlfriends, peer groups, etc. It is probably accurate that all adolescents do this to some degree, but the ones with the most intense fusions will do it most intensely. When the person leaves home, he/she then goes from relationship to relationship, seeking satisfaction of his/her needs, but cutting off from the relationship when the involvements get too intense. Another variation would be the person who can maintain the relationship through a lot of internal cutting-off mechanisms, but, with ever-increasing emotional distance in the marriage, he/she may cut off into an affair. Even an intense psychotherapy relationship can suffice. In the affair, the person can often satisfy his/her intense togetherness needs without a sense of losing self or being taken over by the partner. So the existence of the affair reflects a cutoff in the marriage which reflects a cutoff with the previous generation.

Recognition of the importance of emotional cutoff between the generations has become a cornerstone of family psychotherapy based on this version of family systems theory. The existence of or reestablishment of viable emotional contact between three or more generations of a family can be an important symptom-reducing influence. Some of the details of this process will be discussed in later sections, but it is not just a simple matter of going home for a visit. The intensity of the emotional forces that created the cutoffs must be understood and respected.

7) Sibling position

Bowen credits the publication of Toman's (1961) *Family Constellation* with the clarification of his own thinking about sibling positions in families. The fact that people born into the same sibling position in different families grow up with so many common personality characteristics is perhaps the best illustration of what is meant by *functioning position* in family systems. The emotional forces in the system dictate that individual members will function in certain ways. A child simply grows into the position, becoming increasingly molded by it as he or she gets older. The functional expectations of oldests, youngests, oldest sons, etc., are so built into the structure of families through the generations that they go far beyond the wishes or desires of any one person. They run far deeper than cultural values, as evidenced by the fact that a similar molding process can be observed in nonhuman primates, as the older offspring take over and help the parents with the younger ones.

Toman's ten profiles of different sibling positions are fascinating and amazingly accurate. They are worth reading in detail. The marriage of an oldest child to a youngest often beautifully highlights some of the contrasts in the positions. Regardless of whether the oldest is male or female, when married to a youngest he or she will be more comfortable taking responsibility, making the decisions, and taking action on various issues. The oldest also has a tendency to think he/she knows what is "right," what is "best," and to inflict that on the mate. It also appears that oldests tend to carry a lion's share of the guilt. The youngest, on the other hand, will be more inclined to let his/her oldest spouse assume the responsibility, make the decisions, and have the initiative. The youngest also tends to believe the oldest really does know what he/she is talking about. A marriage of two youngests has some interesting twists. Both are inclined to feel a little burdened by responsibility and having to make decisions. Neither is quick to take initiative and there can be a paralysis in the decision-making process. A marriage of two oldests, on the other hand, is more likely to be a head-knocking affair.

Sibling positions are, of course, only a part of what influences the characteristics of a marriage. There are advantages and disadvantages to all the positions. The toxicity of an oldest's sometimes overbearingness is no greater than the toxicity of a youngest's sometimes unwillingness to take action. In a marriage the two different orientations can complement each other and be a highly functional arrangement. But *the greater the basic emotional fusion in the marriage and/or the greater the level of existent anxiety, the more likely the patterns are to be exaggerated and dysfunctional.*

One of the most important modifying influences on sibling profiles is the degree to which the person has been involved in the family projection process. If an oldest, for example, is part of an intense triangle with the parents, he or she may grow up with either an intense exaggeration of the characteristics of an oldest or a profile more typical of a youngest. In the first case he may feel so intensely overresponsible that he consistently takes on commitments he cannot possibly meet and functions irresponsibly, failing to do what he feels others expect of him. In the second case, if the parents related to the oldest as weak and inadequate, the younger sibling may then grow up as the *functional* oldest in the family.

8) Societal emotional process

In retrospect, the extension of systems concepts towards a theory of societal emotional functioning seems a logical step. But from the author's observation of Bowen in the 1969-72 period, when much of his earlier thinking about society began to gel, it was then and remains an extremely difficult conceptual leap. When-

ever Bowen has spoken on this topic at conferences or even at small meetings of people supposedly knowledgeable about systems, much of the audience is quick to want to engage Bowen in an emotional debate and accuse him of being unduly pessimistic about society.

Basically, the concept of societal emotional process states that forces towards individuality and togetherness operate to counterbalance each other on a societal level in a manner similar to what exists in individual families. Increasing societal anxiety alters the functional balance of these forces by increasing the activity of the togetherness forces, gradually eroding functioning based on individuality and lowering society's functional level of differentiation. As the togetherness orientation progresses, there are ever-increasing complications or symptoms of the imbalance. The process continues until the complications or symptoms reach such a magnitude that the disturbance or discomfort they create forces the process to level off and move back towards a more differentiated level of functioning. When that turnaround occurs, the symptoms begin to decrease.

Bowen's initial observations about societal process grew, in part, from reviewing clinical cases of families with acting-out adolescents whom he had treated at different periods in his practice. He noticed changes during the 1960s in the way the courts and school systems dealt with these families. The changes were in the direction of the courts and schools dealing with the problems more and more like the families did. In an anxious family with an acting-out teenager, the teenager is making increasing demands for his rights. The parents are unsure of themselves and give in to the demands to relieve the anxiety of the moment, but creating a larger problem for the future. Parents get into pleading, coaxing, do-it-for-me postures with their kids, the opposite of a differentiated or well-defined self position. They are vulnerable to the child's pleas of being misunderstood and alternate between being overly sympathetic and overly harsh when the child makes yet another demand. The child becomes adept at sensing the parents' weaknesses and exploiting them. It is an anxiety-driven process, with the parents putting increasing pressure on the child to be different and the child making increasing demands on the parents. The acting-out symptoms become greater and greater. At this point, the author will leave it to the reader to decide whatever parallels exist on a societal level.

Presumably, within any group and for society as a whole, there is an optimum balance between the individuality and togetherness life forces. An ideal would seem to be each person being conscious of his/her own autonomy while at the same time being conscious of the overall team effort. In a calm social group, individuals insist on their rights as individuals, but at the same time have an interest in the total group. There is a tolerance for differences within the group and people are not putting emotional pressure on each other to conform in certain ways. As anxiety in the society increases, people sort of implode into subgroups. Concern for the whole is lost and the intensely fused subgroups begin to fight among each other. The we-they phenomenon becomes more prominent. Each subgroup insists on its rights and will attack the larger structure with its demands to the point of even destroying the larger structure. The irony is that to a great extent the existence of the subgroups depends on the existence of a larger structure. The analogy would be a cancer destroying the body even though the cancer depends on the body for its nourishment.

Bowen originally used the phrase "societal regression" to describe this anxiety-driven emotional process in society that interferes with society's ability to solve its problems. The rising rate of violence, rising divorce rate, instability of governments and a host of other parameters are symptoms of this ever-intensifying emotional process. Although society has experienced such periods before, Bowen believes this current period is unique. The overpopulation problem, depletion of natural resources, and a sense of no more frontiers to which to flee are creating a level of chronic, intense anxiety that is unique in the history of man.

FAMILY EVALUATION

When a family presents for help with a problem, there are two things that can be said with certainty. The first is that the level of anxiety is up in that family, and the second is that the high level of emotional reactivity that exists is undermining the ability of family members to define themselves in relationship to each other and in relationship to the issues that exist. The therapist's task is to stay objective and accurately assess what is occurring. Objectivity is what the family needs. The family members rarely need to be told what to do because somewhere within themselves they *know* what to do. It is just that they have had a hard time doing it. An emotional response to a situation is in some ways the easy way out. It frequently offers the promise of immediate relief despite the long-term consequences. To function as a self, particularly in a crisis, is to go against an emotional tide that threatens to leave one standing naked in the wind. For this reason, most of us have to be pushed close to the wall before the consequences of not being a self outweigh those of being a self. If the therapist cannot stand outside this emotional tide when evaluating the situation, the evaluation is doomed to perpetuate the problem rather than help it.

The mechanics of an evaluation, the kind of information collected, are determined by the theory. Symptoms reflect an anxiety-driven imbalance in the relationship system—an acute and/or chronic imbalance. Where the symptoms appear depends on the basic mechanisms the family uses to bind anxiety in the system. The intensity of the anxiety is related to the number and kind of anxiety-generating events that have occurred, to the basic differentiation of family members, and to the degree of emotional cutoff from support systems, particularly the extended family. The evaluation is designed to gather the information that will assess these areas.

There are so many facets to a family evaluation and so many ways it can be done that all that can be offered in this brief section is a general framework. The structure of the evaluation interview is broken down into five sections: 1) history of the presenting problem; 2) history of the nuclear family; 3) history of the husband's extended family system; 4) history of the wife's extended family system; and 5) conclusion.

History of Presenting Problem

This part of the evaluation focuses on what the symptoms are, who has them, when they emerged, and what has been the clinical course.

Remember that physical, emotional, and social acting-out symptoms are all considered to be manifestations of disturbances in family emotional process. Also recall that the symptomatic person reflects something about the way anxiety is managed in the family, namely, one spouse being significantly deselfed, projection to a child, or marital conflict. Exact dates of symptom development and exacerbations may be later correlated with other events, for example, a death in the extended system. The family members may be so preoccupied with the immediate problem that they have lost sight of the influence of other events.

History of the Nuclear Family

This part of the history begins with when the two parents met and comes up to the present time. Their ages when they met, what they were doing with their lives at that time, the nature of their courtship, the marriage, the period before the birth of the first child, the impact on the family of the births of the various children, and some assessment of the present functioning of each child are all important areas to ask about. Where the family has lived and when any moves occurred are important, particularly if moves have taken the family significantly closer to or away from the extended families. The health, educational, and vocational history of each parent is also collected in this part of the evaluation. No one piece of data alone means very much, but collectively they can give a picture of the nuclear family emotional system. A very brief or very long courtship, for example, is generally consistent with lower levels of differentiation of self in the partners. Serious symptoms following the birth of a child also reflect a lower level of functioning. A better differentiated family will have fewer and milder symptoms and generally more orderly lives. Marriages, births, and moves, for example, are not likely to create more than minor disturbances in the balance of the emotional system of a reasonably well differentiated family.

History of Husband's Extended Family

The husband's sibling position, some assessment of the emotional process in the families of each of his siblings, and an evaluation of the past and current functioning of his parents is a minimum for this part of the evaluation. Basic data on his parents' health, educational, occupational, and marital histories, as well as similar data on siblings, are important. The relative stability or instability of the husband's family of origin, past and present, is reflected in this data and gives some estimate of the basic differentiation of the family. Where people have lived and are currently living is also important. In addition to physical proximity of the extended family, an assessment of the quality of the husband's emotional contact with his family is critical, but usually not easy to evaluate. People are full of misleading statements about the emotional contact with their families and the therapist's ability to evaluate cutoff usually improves with experience. Exact dates about extended family events, deaths, divorces, etc., are important because they may correlate with events in the nuclear family.

History of Wife's Extended Family

This part of the evaluation is a repeat of what was done with the husband's family.

Conclusion

The goal of this final part of the evaluation is simply to get something defined that the family will be working on. If the therapist is maintaining his differentiation with the family, he will be asking questions that tap the objective, though likely somewhat submerged, self of the parents. What I try to do is to get the focus off the symptom and get the family members to define, in their own words, the emotional atmosphere of the family. The next step is to emphasize that *every* family member is *reacting to and contributing to* the tension and that blaming or hoping each other will change is not a very productive direction. The family knows this, but the knowledge keeps getting submerged in the automatic emotional responses to each other. It just takes one family member to bring him/herself and remain under a little better control, to follow his/her head and not his/her emotions, to set off a chain reaction of other family members beginning to do this, too.

FAMILY THERAPY

It is probably obvious after this long discussion of theory that, in my view, the way the therapist thinks about the problem is what determines calling it family vs. individual psychotherapy and not the number of people in the room for a session. A therapist who does "individual," "couples," "marital," and "family" therapy is thinking of family therapy as a technique and not as a theory. If the therapist is thinking "family" or thinking "systems" and that thinking is reflected in the kinds of questions he asks and types of actions he takes in a session, then it is legitimately called family psychotherapy. It can be done with one person or a whole group.[10]

Following this line of reasoning, the question of indications and contraindications for family therapy becomes meaningless. Systems thinking is a new theory and if that way of thinking makes sense to the therapist, then it is applicable in any situation, whether the family is in an acute crisis or dealing with a more long-term problem, or whether the presenting problem is severe obsessions and phobias in a young woman or an overt conflict between mother and son. The techniques of applying the theory in various therapy situations may vary, but the modifications are rather obvious once the theory is well understood by the therapist and *influential in the way he/she lives in his/her own life.*

The method and techniques of family therapy are logical extensions of the theory. Bowen has frequently made the point that innovations in technique grow out of new developments in theory and not the other way around. That is one of the reasons so much of this chapter is devoted to theory. What a therapist says and does in a session is determined by the way he/she thinks about the problem, whether it be an individual or a systems frame of reference. The success or lack of success of the therapy is mainly determined by the way the therapist thinks about the people he/she is dealing with. What he/she observes and asks questions about or what interpretations he/she makes are obviously related to his way of thinking. If a therapist ever hopes to change the way he/she does therapy, he/she must change the way he/she conceptualizes what transpires in front of him/her. Of course, so much of the way he/she thinks about the lives of others is related to the way he/she thinks about and lives his/her own life.

The theoretical base of systems theory can be reduced to two key variables: the *organization of the individual*, namely, his or her level of differentiation, and the degree of *anxiety in the emotional field* of which the individual is a part. As described earlier, a person with a high level of differentiation of self can function in a high anxiety emotional field and be at low risk for developing symptoms within himself *or* for doing and saying things that promote symptom development in others. People at increasingly lower levels of differentiation are at increasingly higher risk of developing symptoms or promoting them in others when the anxiety in the emotional field is high. When anxiety is low, all members of the system are at less risk of symptom development, regardless of their basic level of differentiation.

While the level of differentiation and the degree of anxiety in the emotional field are the two primary variables for understanding symptom development and progression, a third important set of variables to be considered is the mechanisms for dealing with or binding anxiety. There are mechanisms that each member of the family uses within him/herself and there are already described mechanisms that are part of the relationship system. The two sets of mechanisms are interrelated in ways that cannot be detailed here. The kind of anxiety-binding mechanisms used greatly influences both where a symptom develops in a family and the type of symptom that develops.

The therapeutic method is based on a recognition of the importance of the above-mentioned two primary variables. The method then is based on two assumptions: 1) that reduction

---

[10]*Editors' Note.* While Kerr is conceptually consistent on this important matter, it remains an empirically unaddressed question as to *when* the treatment of different family units (e.g., individual, couple, whole family) is maximally effective. Surely, identical outcomes cannot be expected regardless of who is in the room and/or regardless of the type of family problem at issue. Moreover, the impact of family systems theory and therapy on the family therapy field has been so pervasive and profound that sophisticated controlled empirical studies of its clinical outcomes, heretofore lacking (Gurman and Kniskern, 1978), must be given a position of high priority by its advocates.

of anxiety in the emotional field will improve the *functional* level of differentiation of self and reduce symptoms; and 2) that improvement in basic level of differentiation will increase the adaptability of the person to intense emotional fields. Reduction of anxiety and improvements in functional level of differentiation can be accomplished in a day or two, but more likely occur over a span of months. Improvement in basic level of differentiation is a long-term process that takes place in incremental steps over a period of years. With either of these two types of changes, the requirement for internal and relationship anxiety-binding mechanisms diminishes and the clinical symptoms, which are in part related to the exaggerated use of these mechanisms, improve. This is a fact regardless of the type of clinical problem that exists, for example, a sexual problem, psychosis, marital turmoil, physical illness, alcoholism, or an acting-out teenager. Each of these problems is a *symptom* of an underlying family emotional process, and the therapist's ability to keep that underlying process in focus is the essence of systems-based therapy.

As outlined in the section on history, the techniques of family therapy have undergone significant modifications over the years. Bowen and his colleagues found that family group therapy was useful in reducing family anxiety and improving functional levels of differentiation, but not particularly useful for facilitating basic changes in the underlying fusion of the emotional system. Seeing the parents and only the symptomatic child together seemed slightly better, but still far short of the mark. Throughout the history of changes in technique, the consistent goal has been designing a technique that would most likely permit the emergence of some increase in the level of differentiation of self in at least one family member. It is a kind of reverse domino theory, in that if one domino begins to stand up again, this will trigger off the process in the other dominos as well, regardless of whether the other dominos happen to be symptomatic or not. The therapist does not have to instill differentiation into the family. The force for differentiation is there, just submerged in the overriding togetherness. The therapist is trying to create an atmosphere in which differentiation can emerge; experience has proven that seeing the couple or whole family together can, at times, work *against* a family member's working towards a better level of self.

For many years, the therapist seeing just the two parents together was the mainstay of family therapy technique at Georgetown. A modification of that approach was multiple family therapy, in which the therapist worked with one couple at a time while several other couples had the opportunity to learn through observation. The time in the one-and-a-half- to two-hour session was divided equally between three or four families. This was not a group therapy session in that the therapist, in an effort to contain the emotional process within each individual family, structured the multiple family sessions in a way that did not encourage much interaction among the families. This is not to say that one family was not reacting emotionally at times to what was heard in the other families and getting triangled in to the other families' problems, but, by the therapist not focusing on this reactivity during the sessions, the emotional process *between* the families was toned down.

When seeing a couple together, the therapist has two basic goals. One is to *ask questions about the emotional process* that exists in the family and the second is to *stay detriangled* from that emotional process him/herself. It is a fact of triangles that, if one person, in this case the therapist, can relate to the emotional process between two other people, in this case the spouses, without taking sides (and this does not mean pretending not to take sides), the emotional process between the couple will *automatically* move towards some resolution. Not even any brilliant interpretations on the part of the therapist are required. Again, the differentiating force is there and will emerge in an atmosphere that permits it. On their own, the spouses can get so locked into what Bowen calls an "emotional two-step" that it becomes extremely difficult for either spouse to develop and sustain differentiation. A successful session is one in which one or both spouses have been able to *think* about the emotional process, describing it accurately, instead of just continuing to react emotionally to each other. It is another fact about emotional systems that, in the course of therapy, when one spouse begins to try to function with a better defined self, one hundred percent of the time the other spouse will react emotionally to the change and will try to undermine it.[11] The individuality-togetherness balance is simply constructed that way. When one moves towards individuality, the other will say and do things designed to preserve the togetherness. A togetherness-preserving move can range from the silent treatment to intense criticism, from threats to withdraw love to threats to have a heart attack or even commit suicide. In this differentiating process, in addition to the pressure from the other spouse and family, an incredible degree of pressure can develop within the one trying to be more of a self, a pressure that says, "give it up, it is not worth it." If the therapist has done a reasonable job of working on differentiation him/herself, he/she can recognize its emergence in a family and not get triangled in to the protests of the other spouse. If the therapist does get triangled in, he/she will focus on whatever doubts the differentiating spouse has about his/her effort and squash it. For this reason, it is difficult for a family to grow beyond the level of differentiation of its therapist. The therapist, motivated by his/her *own* anxiety about disturbances in the togetherness, can say and do things that will block a family member's effort towards differentiation. When this occurs, a well motivated family will either quit therapy or find a better therapist. Keep in mind that the person working towards a better level of differentiation is working *against* powerful emotional forces within him/herself that say, "If you do this, it will seriously threaten having your need for the other met, will threaten his/her acceptance and approval of you, and will leave you feeling you have not met your responsibility for his/her happiness and well-being." At the same time, the person making the effort is being told these things by other family members. It is never easy to sustain the effort and the family members will never support and encourage it, since they are too locked in themselves. But if one person can resist the pressure long enough, it will often dramatically subside and the whole family will

begin to function with a better level of differentiation. At this point, the symptoms will rapidly diminish. Over a long-term course of family therapy with a couple, characteristically one spouse will work on differentiation for a time, then the other will do it, and perhaps back and forth like that several times over a period of years.

A question that frequently arises about this differentiating process is what is the difference between differentiating from and reactively distancing from the other. This is a difficult question to answer, but in the first instance the change in self is not dependent on avoiding the other and, in fact, occurs very much *in relationship to* the other. With emotional distance, the change in self remains solvable, so to speak, when in relationship to the other.

Working just with a couple and focusing on the nuclear family relationships very definitely limits the potential for change. It can be slow and difficult to see things about one's own functioning and one's own lack of self when focusing primarily on relationships that you live in day in and day out. In the mid-1960s, with the new emphasis on differentiation of self in relationship to one's family of origin, it was as if a new plateau had been reached in terms of potential for change. With this shifting emphasis to extended family, some significant changes in the techniques of family therapy also occurred. One very tangible change was the appearance of blackboards in therapists' offices, used primarily as a visual aid to help people think in terms of multigenerational process. Another change was more and more sessions in which the spouses were seen separately and, at times, they were never seen together throughout the entire course of therapy. Another change came from the recognition that the success of an effort in the family of origin depended greatly on what people did on their own between sessions and so sessions were often spaced out to ten to 12 times a year.

An entire book could be written on the subject of differentiating a self in family of origin. Learning about what this process means comes from doing it and not having it explained. To work seriously at it requires the help of someone who has done a reasonable job him/herself.

The rationale for focus on the extended family is that the fusions that exist in our nuclear fam-

---

[11]*Editors' Note.* In addition to noting the homeostatic pessimism of this view, we also want to point out that there is not yet convincing evidence of such a universally contingent relationship. Since this issue is central to the conduct of family systems therapy, this clearly stated proposition deserves careful empirical study.

ilies are a reflection of each spouse's unresolved fusion with his/her family of origin. Any degree of success in differentiation of self in the original family will be predictably followed by a greater ability to be a self in one's nuclear family. In many ways, it is easier to work at differentiation in the extended family because you do not live in it and depend on it the way you do your nuclear family. It is a little easier, therefore, to make observations and get the space necessary to think through ways for dealing with it. There are no specific steps to follow other than the general one of being in better contact with parents, siblings, and the larger extended system. *The theory is the guide.* The main obstacle is one's own emotional reactiveness to the family, one's own subjective assessments of people. The blaming, the "mads," the overidealizations of some people, the guilts, the indifferences, etc., are the obstacles and they are within oneself. The success of your effort is not dependent on your family or what they do, although some families are obviously easier to deal with than others. The people who have the most difficult time are the ones who think they are objective when they are not. "My relationship with my parents is not good. I have changed, but they have not," is a subjective view of things. The best measure of change in self is the long-term effect it has on others that are important to you. If you "change" and your family does not, then either you have not changed as much as you think you have or you are using a lot of distance to deal with others. There are exceptions to this but they are not frequent. *A well differentiated person can maintain a self even with a schizophrenic and the schizophrenic will respond favorably to it.* So saying, "I can't deal with my parents because they're crazy," is a cop-out. Highly emotionally charged systems require more careful planning and progress may be more sluggish and this is where the objective "coach" becomes critically important. And no, not everyone will be successful in an effort with his/her extended family and there are a variety of different reasons for this, e.g., lack of ability of the person making the effort to really see the emotional process, the peculiar structure of the extended family, and the lack of objectivity and knowledge of the therapist.

The various techniques of therapy that have been described are applied based on the nature of the particular clinical situation. Therapy with the individual couple, which focuses on nuclear family relationships; multiple family therapy; work with individual family members, which focuses on family of origin, and various combinations of these—are all in frequent use and are effective techniques. A brief clinical example will highlight some of the basic principles involved in the process of family systems therapy.

CLINICAL EXAMPLE

The family to be discussed was chosen because the course of its therapy approached being ideal. Each spouse was able gradually to defocus the presenting problems and devote considerable energy to developing better emotional contact with and more objectivity about his/her original families. In the process, the presenting problems were significantly resolved.

Mr. and Mrs. W. sought therapy because of considerable tension in their marital relationship and a seeming deterioration over the past several years in the husband's physical and emotional functioning. The couple sought professional help on the wife's initiative. Mr. W., 48, was a retired military officer who was currently working in a civilian capacity for a government agency. He had moderate diabetes and hypertension and also some left-sided weakness, particularly in the leg. The weakness developed seven years earlier and resulted in a medical discharge from the armed services. The weakness was thought to be caused by an injury-related stroke. In addition to worrying about Mr. W.'s physical problems, Mrs. W. was concerned about her husband's seeming lack of initiative in regard to family and social responsibilities. "It's all on me and if I didn't push him, he would just vegetate," was her comment. Mrs. W., 46, was a nurse and had worked full-time for the past five years. The couple had been married 20 years and had a 16-year-old son who appeared to be functioning quite well. Although they had moved many times in the course of their marriage, based on the husband's military assignments, since his discharge seven years ago they had lived in the Washington area.

Mr. W. grew up in Massachusetts as the younger of two boys. His mother had died 15 years earlier of the complications of diabetes, but his father remained vigorous and healthy at age 84 and was living in Massachusetts. There were large maternal and paternal extended families in the New England area. Mrs. W. grew up in Oklahoma as the oldest of three children. Both of her parents were still living and in Oklahoma, but her father had been in a nursing home for two years with a diagnosis of senility. Like her husband, Mrs. W. also had a large extended family in the area where she grew up. Although both spouses came from big and fairly intact families, each was significantly cut off from the family of origin at the beginning of therapy. The frequent geographic moves, coupled with his wife's strong negative reaction to his family, had inclined Mr. W. to drift away from his family. Mrs. W. had more actively cut herself off from her family, not wanting to deal with the intensity of the emotional problems that existed there.

During the first year of therapy, the couple was seen conjointly twice a month. The early sessions were devoted to trying to help the spouses, through the therapist's questions, describe the nature of their emotional interaction. The goal was for them thoughtfully to reflect on it rather than act it out in the sessions. Mrs. W. described how uptight she got when her husband had difficulty walking or when he would be slow in doing things. Even though she sensed, at some level, that her husband seemed to function below his capabilities in a kind of stubborn defiance against her pushing, she would still keep at him about his not trying and nag at him to do better. *It was an anxiety-driven process in both spouses, going far beyond what either wanted for the relationship.* Mrs. W. felt threatened and panicked by her husband's poor functioning and Mr. W. simply felt paralyzed to act differently. He considered the problem to be his physical incapacities and his temper and criticized himself for periodically flying off the handle at his wife.

As the therapist during this early period, I was concerned with defining the problems in systems terms in my own thinking and also with monitoring emotional reactions to the couple. For example, in my "thinking-self," I believed that if the wife could deal with her own anxiety better and not focus so much on her husband, Mr. W. would likely function better. In my "feeling-self," I had a tendency to view the hus-

band as impaired and to side with the wife in her efforts to get him to try harder. Another of my emotional reactions was feeling angry at the wife for being such a nag. Fortunately for the family, I was usually able to operate based on my thinking-self in the sessions. If the therapist is able to maintain a systems orientation, being genuinely neutral about the family problem, it will be reflected as much in his attitude toward the family as it will be reflected in what he actually says. Objectivity and emotional detachment are reflected in the way the therapist sits, how often he talks, in the absence of preaching, in his tone of voice, and sense of humor. These more subtle things seem to be of most use to the family members in dealing with their own emotional reactivity. In one of the early sessions, I said to the husband, "You know that your wife wouldn't be on your back like this if she didn't love you, don't you?" If my comment had been motivated by over-seriousness about the situation, it could have made it more difficult for the husband to think clearly, and Mr. W. might have responded, "Yeah, I know I have let her down." But since my tone had a touch of humor in it and was said with a slight smile, the husband responded, "Yeah, the bitch!" When he said that he started laughing and soon Mrs. W. was laughing, too. My question and attitude had been successful in helping to defuse an intense issue. Later in the same session, I said to the wife, "Your husband knows that you know what is best for him—why have you been so inept at implementing it?" Again, how the remark is delivered is the key and it will be useful only when the therapist is operating outside the family emotional system. In this case, the wife chuckled at herself, but the husband took it seriously, saying, "What do you mean, she knows what's best?" Seeing my smile, Mr. W. started to laugh and soon everyone was laughing.

The therapist can try to force humor on a family and have it be counterproductive. It may be interpreted as sarcastic or as reflecting that the therapist does not understand the problem. There are times when the family itself, particularly one spouse, is using jokes to avoid looking at a problem. In this case, a more serious tone by the therapist is obviously in order. But, in general, an appropriately light attitude on the part of a therapist seems to be more helpful to the family's effort to control emotional reactiveness than any speech or explanation the therapist might deliver on that subject.

After about a year of therapy with this couple, resulting in a moderate reduction of anxiety, I introduced more formalized teaching of family systems ideas. Prior to that, I had talked about the difference between operating out of one's "head" versus operating based on emotionality, and also about the value of looking at the way Mr. and Mrs. W. mutually influenced each other's functioning, but nothing more elaborate than that in terms of concepts was said. It is important to remember that *whatever teaching is done is not heard by people when the level of emotional reactivity is high.* Anxious people will incorporate the therapist's ideas into their existing emotional biases, using those ideas as justification for existing positions. But with this couple, when anxiety had settled down and each was expressing a desire to try to accelerate progress, it was suggested that they read some articles about family systems theory and also take a course in systems theory sponsored by the Family Center. The course is intended for interested people who are not mental health professionals. The couple was also invited to attend some of the Family Center symposia relating to theory and therapy. Both of the spouses took these suggestions and seemed to benefit tremendously from the experiences. It appears that family systems theory is a body of knowledge that people often learn about more quickly in educational as opposed to therapeutic settings. *The therapist's main task is to help people recognize and deal with their lack of objectivity when applying the concepts to their own situations.*

There is one type of teaching that is particularly useful even early in therapy, and it was used productively with Mr. and Mrs. W. That teaching involves some discussion of multigenerational emotional process. This is a type of teaching that is best done through questions rather than through lecturing about it. It is usually difficult for families really to see that one generation's problems are related to the previous generation's problems, but placing a three or four generation diagram on the blackboard and asking questions about it can be a step toward helping the family gain that kind of perspective. I did this with the W.'s in about the fifth session after they began more formal instruction about family systems. The husband's insight from this discussion was realizing how much he had lost contact with his family in the last ten years. That awareness came simply from asking questions about who was who in his extended family and how much contact he currently had with each individual. After the husband's comment about being out of contact, I simply asked, "Do you have the motivation to recontact your family?" Mr. W. responded positively, which made it easier than it is with many people. In the case of Mrs. W., diagramming her extented system led to a discussion of how much the relationship between her parents paralleled her own marriage. Mrs. W. expressed a fear that her husband would wind up dysfunctional and perhaps institutionalized like her father. It was easier for Mrs. W. to see the influence of her mother's anxiety on how her father functioned than it was for her to see the role of her own anxiety in how her husband functioned, but putting the diagram on the board and discussing it seemed to help Mrs. W. clarify things she had to work on. I asked her if she would be able to spend time with her parents and not take sides in what went on between them. She said she did not think she could do that, that she simply got too emotionally involved. "Do you want to try?" was the next question. "Yes, particularly if you think it can help with our marriage," was her response. She went on to add that she wanted to improve the relationship with her parents apart from concerns about her marriage and that she thought her father was not as senile as he was made out to be. She thought that he had retreated from a volatile marriage that he simply could not deal with.

It is, obviously, not always this easy to steer people towards their families of origin. When it is, it suggests a good prognosis for therapy. With some families, the therapist is well advised to mention extended family casually, picking up the subject again farther down the road in therapy. It is essential to be tuned in to the intensity of the emotional process in the family and to be able to respect the problem people have in being able to see it and deal with it. Again, when the therapist recognizes the problem in him/herself, it is easier to respect it in others. The rule of thumb with extended family is, "easy does it." If the therapist keeps pushing someone towards the family who seems reluctant to engage it or who bluntly states that he/she does not feel capable of dealing with it right then, then the person is liable to go into his/her extended system and make a mess of the effort or look for a new therapist.

It was Mrs. W. who first tried to engage extended family issues. Recognizing the intensity of the emotional charge between her and her parents, I suggested she not concentrate there in the beginning. Instead, she was encouraged to try to contact the surviving spouse and children of her mother's deceased older sister. This older sister, Mrs. W.'s aunt, had cut off from the family after her marriage and died later of cancer at age 36. The story sounded as if this older sister was the one upon whom the projection process had focused most heavily. I thought that by Mrs. W.'s making contact with this cutoff segment of the family, it would put her in touch with emotional issues that were important in her mother's family, but were no longer discussed. Finding the uncle and cousins required considerable effort and ingenuity. In addition to trying to locate these people, she talked with her mother and her mother's other siblings and was amazed to learn how little they seemed to know about their sister's life. Interestingly, as Mrs. W. pursued this puzzle of her aunt, she found that she was beginning to think about her mother in different terms. She was thinking beyond just what her mother was like in relationship to herself and her father and seeing her mother as her grandparents' daughter. Somehow, this perception helped her towards being a little less reactive to the kind of person her mother was. Mrs. W. found her uncle, but he refused to talk to her. The reception from her missing cousins was altogether different. They were ecstatic over the contact; letters and pictures were exchanged and, eventually, personal visits were made. Making contact with these cousins was a tremendously emotional experience for Mrs. W. It was a kind of "roots" experience, although the personal gain went beyond just a sense of connecting with her past. One such gain was a firsthand observation about how families deal with emotional intensity,

namely, through cutoff, and the toll that can take on people, particularly her newfound cousins.

In addition to her efforts to connect with the missing segment of her family, during the second year of therapy, Mrs. W. made two trips home to Oklahoma. Those trips included contacts with other aunts, uncles, and cousins and some multigenerational research, but their main purpose was to try to spend time with her parents and not get emotionally embroiled in what went on between them. *Staying outside the emotional system of one's parents does not mean some defensive distancing posture* like, "I don't want to hear about that," or, "I'm not taking sides here." Such statements are usually a reflection of being *caught* in the emotional system while proclaiming not to be. Mrs. W. spent time with her father in the nursing home and was able to recognize that her views of her father as a senile man who had been a burden to her mother were more feeling than fact. She was able to relate to him in a much more relaxed fashion and he responded beautifully to the change in her attitude. He talked more to her in three days than he had to the rest of the family in a whole year! The family was amazed and explained it as his having an unusually good day.

In dealing with her mother, Mrs. W. made a mistake many people make when armed with newfound knowledge about emotional systems. She tried to explain to her mother how it worked. She said, "Mother, if you were not so anxious about Dad, he would probably do better." "What do you mean anxious? Dad's sick. How would you react?" was the reply. Attempts to explain to the family how relationship process works are usually ill-advised. Parents can be expected to react defensively to such statements and perhaps appropriately so. Explanations to the family by a family member are usually anxiety-motivated attempts to change what goes on in the family. It is essential to remember that *efforts in the extended family or with one's spouse and children, for that matter, are not intended to change others or other relationships. The effort is to gain enough knowledge about oneself and the system to be able to change oneself in relationship to others.* It is true that if Mrs. W. can change herself in relationship to her father and change herself in relationship with her mother, there is an excellent chance that a secondary spin-off will be gradual change in what goes on between her parents.

Later, Mrs. W. was able to listen to her mother talk about her father and begin to see that as a reflection of her mother's emotional reactiveness. She eventually got loose enough about the situation to make comments like, "Mother, I'd like to see you and Dad move into the nursing home together. Getting mad like you do keeps you young and vigorous." Mrs. W. was well beyond feeling critical of her mother at that point and they both had a good laugh out of the remark. As Mrs. W. spent more time with her father, although he said less about his marriage, she began to get a clearer picture of his emotional reactiveness to his wife. It became clear to her that they presented an equal problem for each other and that to blame either would miss the point. A spin-off of the humorous, defusing remarks by Mrs. W. was a more relaxed atmosphere that permitted more personal conversations with each of her parents.

About 18 months into therapy, I started seeing each spouse individually once a month. There were no more conjoint sessions. Most of the time, about two-thirds of each individual session, was devoted to discussion about extended family, and about a third of the time devoted to marital and other issues. Mr. W.'s effort with his extended family was somewhat different from his wife's. He began by writing lots of letters to his very large family, but, in the beginning, he did it as an assignment from the therapist. The responses from the family to his early efforts were minimal, and Mr. W. got angry at the family, underplaying his part in letting himself get so far out of contact in the first place. But gradually, over the next three or four years, he started making more trips home to Massachusetts by himself and became a very active participant in the family again. Mr. W. was not quite as good an observer of emotional process as his wife, but the intensity of his family contacts was every bit as strong as hers. His efforts moved him from a position of emotional isolation and retreat from an anxious wife to being a real plugged-in person again. The change in him was rather dramatic.

All of these efforts with their extended families did not produce immediate changes in their marriage. *Changing emotional reactiveness and operating as a little more of a self in relationship to people you live with is a long, very gradual process.* Mrs. W., for example, was aware of tensing up when she was on the way back from trips to see her extended family, a tensing she related to facing her husband again. Mr. W., in many ways, began to function better when she was gone. Not infrequently, Mrs. W. thought, "Wouldn't divorce be easier than this?" But she did not want a divorce and she knew the problem was emotional reactiveness, in her and in her husband. She had a growing perception of the process as a multigenerational one and was motivated to continue to try to change. A critical juncture for her came when she really began to see and develop conviction about the fact that her anxious focus on her husband accentuated the very things she wanted to prevent. At one level, she saw this early in therapy, but it was not useful to her. She did not have enough conviction about it then for it to be any kind of balance for her emotionality. Seeing the process operate in her parents and keeping a lot of focus on extended family contacts elevated the anxious focus idea from a level of vague awareness to a kind of principle. It became evident that what she wanted with her "head" and the direction her emotions inclined her towards when she was anxious could be 180 degrees in opposition to each other. Ever so gradually, she gained in her ability to watch her husband appearing withdrawn and depressed or to watch him limp when he walked and to contain her anxiety about it, instead of saying, "Why do you do that?" She began to question whether she really did, in fact, know what was best for him. That sounds simple, but it is never simple for anybody.

Within about three years of therapy, the level of chronic anxiety in the family had been significantly reduced. Mr. W.'s blood pressure was near normal on less medication and the diabetes was under complete control. His doctor was amazed. The couple was motivated to continue in therapy because both wanted to do more at trying to function with a better level of self. Several incidents occurred in the next two years in which the husband got into some difficulty in his own life, incidents that presented important challenges to the adaptiveness of both of them. The major occurrence was the husband's agency trying to retire him as medically disabled. This attempt had more to do with shifts in the organization than it did with Mr. W.'s functioning. The wife had tremendous emotional reactivity to this, based on a lot of things, some of which were financial concerns. The husband was initially floored by it, doubting his own abilities. Mrs. W. was again faced with a conflict between a principle that said, "If my husband takes charge of this, it will likely work better than if I get into it," and an emotional reaction that said, "I know the best way to handle this and I need to get involved and advise him." She was able to contain her reaction and ask no questions. Mr. W. told her only a few essentials and seemed to delight in his freedom to manage his own affairs. It eventually became obvious that he knew quite well how to handle himself; abilities and initiative were emerging in him that had not been seen for years.

Described here are but a few vignettes spanning five years of these people's lives. There is obviously much more to the story, but this case illustrates some of the important principles and techniques of systems-based family psychotherapy. It may sound paradoxical, but these two people, operating now as better contained selves, have more capacity to depend on each other and cooperate, particularly during crisis periods. They also have more of a capacity for sustained closeness than at any previous point in their relationship. They had a clinging kind of closeness early in their relationship, but their current closeness is based on more realistic expectations of themselves and of each other.

TRAINING

Georgetown's family training programs are designed on the premise that reduction of anxiety and promotion of better levels of differentiation in a clinical family are primarily dependent on the therapist's ability to manage his/her *own* anxiety and maintain his/her *own* differentiation when dealing with a clinical family. So, in addition to didactic sessions about theory and the techniques of therapy, much of the training program is focused on helping the trainee work on his/her own emotional functioning, particularly in his/her own family.

Selection of applicants for training is determined by a variety of factors. Based on what has already been discussed, obviously one of the most important factors influencing acceptance into the program is the mental health professional's motivation and ability to work on his/her own life, his/her own differentiation. A goal is to not have trainees come into the program thinking they are "normal" and it is the clinical families who have the problems. The average mental health professional, based on being human and based on his/her own conventional training, has a very strong tendency to focus on the "pathology" in the patient. From experience, the people who do least well in the training are the ones who have the hardest time seeing their own problems, their own emotional reactiveness. Such trainees will often say they see their emotional reactivity, but their actions speak otherwise. Few of us see very much of our own emotionality, but if people can start with at least some inkling about it, then they have something to work on. Once the project of studying one's own emotionality in a systems framework is underway, there is really no end to the process. It is something people can keep working at for a lifetime and still gain. The more one sees emotional reactiveness in oneself, the easier it is to be objective about it in others. It has probably been said thousands of times before, but the more anxious, judgmental, frustrated, angry, overly sympathetic, and omnipotent one feels about the problems of others, the more it says about the unresolved problems within oneself. Such unresolved problems are the major obstacles to doing effective therapy with the full range of clinical situations.

When there is recognition of the importance of the therapists' working on their own lives in order to make the theory a part of them, instead of something that is just intellectualized, the training, by necessity, becomes long-term. The better therapists will spend a minimum of three to four years in the formal training program and then structure some more informal long-term contact with people who have a good understanding of the theory. Like college, Georgetown's family training programs are no more than an introduction to something. People can lose much of whatever progress they do make if they do not continue to develop it. Systems thinking in reference to human emotional functioning is new and most people are either not aware of it or just aware of it as words. If trainees begin to grasp systems and then immerse themselves back into a setting that is thinking individual concepts, the trainees' ability to retain a systems orientation will be eroded without their ever knowing it. What most works against the trainees' retaining a systems orientation is their need for acceptance by the group they are involved with. They will begin to water down their systems ideas until they are acceptable to their colleagues. The point at which these ideas become acceptable to their individually-oriented colleagues is the point at which they become systems words attached onto a basic individual orientation. In other words, maintaining differentiation in the professional community is every bit as difficult as maintaining it in one's own family. The emotional forces are relentlessly pushing for agreement, for sameness, "If you are not like us, then we reject you." Such rejection can be subtle and not so subtle and, when one is not on one's own, extremely difficult to deal with.

One of the most important thrusts of the training, which is a little more in the background than the focus on one's own family, is helping the trainee towards seeing man's functioning as consistent with the rest of nature. Several years ago in the training program, a film about an ant colony was shown. The very first question was, "What does this have to do with family therapy?" There is no way to really answer that question for that person. Some trainees can sense the relevance and others cannot. Georgetown, obviously, has not integrated the principles of human emotional functioning with the principles of other natural systems. But our belief is that the more people can comfortably think about such an idea and work at understanding it, the more integration will gradually occur.

The actual structure of the training is rather simple. There is a weekly program for people who live in the Washington area and a four-times-a-year program for people living out of town. The teaching time is divided equally between didactic sessions, clinical supervision, and focus on the trainee's family of origin. Much of the clinical supervision is done by reviewing videotapes of the trainee's family therapy ses-

sions. In supervising these tapes, the faculty member is concerned not so much about what the therapist says to the family, as with how what he says reflects the trainee's degree of fusion into the emotional system of the clinical family. Experience has shown that if the trainee is beginning to develop a better level of differentiation in his/her own family, review of his/her clinical work will reflect more capacity for differentiation in that arena as well.

Part of the training involves watching the work of other well-known family therapists. The goal in watching these therapists is for the trainee to be able to see the person's techniques of therapy as a reflection of the way he/she conceptualizes the problem. It is not a question of the "right" theory or "right" technique, but rather that the therapist be clear on what he/she believes about human emotional functioning and see the relationship of that set of beliefs to what he/she says and does in therapy.

Current Directions

In spite of the useful gains in family therapy, Bowen has long believed that the major contribution of the family movement would be in theory more than therapy. This view has a major influence on the current directions of the Georgetown program.

Since the 1940s, Bowen has been strongly influenced by reading and lectures in aspects of evolution, biology, the balance of nature, and the natural sciences. He has considered it likely that the systems theory developed from the study of the family is patterned after systems principles in nature and that emotional illness comes from that part of man he shares with lower forms. Consequently, when developing the theory, concepts were chosen that were consistent with recognized science, especially biology and the natural sciences. Bowen tried to develop a theory that was consistent with man as related to all living matter and in harmony with man as a protoplasmic being—man being viewed as more related to lower forms than he is different from them.

This thinking about biology and the natural sciences has been the basis for considerable effort in recent years to integrate the principles of emotional systems with the other sciences.

Most meetings sponsored by the Family Center now include presentations by experts in sociobiology, genetics, cell biology, cancer research, physiology, biofeedback and a host of other areas. While clinical work, research into improving treatment methods, and training of family therapists will always be a major part of the Georgetown program, the years ahead will be marked by increasing efforts to link family systems with other sciences, believing that only that link can give the family a solid base for the future.

REFERENCES

Anonymous. On the differentiation of self. In: J. Framo (Ed.), *Family Interaction: A Dialogue Between Family Researchers and Family Therapists*. New York: Springer, 1972.

Bowen, M. Family psychotherapy with schizophrenia in the hospital and private practice. In: I. Boszormenyi-Nagy & J. Framo (Eds.), *Intensive Family Therapy*. New York: Harper & Row, 1965(a).

Bowen, M. Intrafamily dynamics in emotional illness. In: A. D'Agostino (Ed.), *Family, Church, and Community*. New York: P. J. Kennedy & Sons, 1965(b).

Bowen, M. The use of family theory in clinical practice. *Comprehensive Psychiatry*, 1966, 7, 345-374.

Bowen, M. Family therapy and family group therapy. In: H. Kaplan & B. Sadock (Eds.), *Comprehensive Group Psychotherapy*. Baltimore: Williams and Wilkins, 1971.

Bowen, M. Toward the differentiation of self in one's family of origin. In: F. Andres & J. Lorio (Eds.), *Georgetown Family Symposia*, Vol. 1 (1971-72). Washington, D.C.: Department of Psychiatry, Georgetown University Medical Center, 1974.

Bowen, M. Theory in the practice of psychotherapy. In: P. Guerin (Ed.), *Family Therapy*. New York: Gardner, 1976.

Bowen, M. *Family Therapy in Clinical Practice*. New York: Jason Aronson, 1978.

Bowen, M., Dysinger, R. H., Brodey, W. M. & Basmania, B. *Study and Treatment of Five Hospitalized Families Each with a Psychotic Member*. Paper presented at the American Orthopsychiatric Association, Chicago, March, 1957.

Flugel, J. C. *The Psychoanalytic Study of the Family*. London: Hogarth Press, 1960.

Freud, S. (1909), Analysis of a phobia in a five year old boy. *Standard Edition*, 10, 3-152.

Limentani, D. Symbiotic identification in schizophrenia. *Psychiatry*, 1956, 9, 231-236.

MacLean, P. A mind of three minds: Educating the triune brain. In: *Seventy-seventh Yearbook of the National Society for the Study of Education*. Chicago: University of Chicago Press, 1978.

Toman, W. *Family Constellation*. New York: Springer, 1961.

Wilson, E. (1975), *Sociobiology: The New Synthesis*. Cambridge, MA: Harvard University Press, 1975.

EDITORS' REFERENCES

Bandura, A. *Principles of Behavior Modification*. New York: Holt, Rinehart & Winston, 1969.

Gurman, A. S. Contemporary marital therapies: A critique and comparative analysis of psychoanalytic, behavioral and systems theory approaches. In: T. J. Paolino & B. S. McCrady (Eds.), *Marriage and Marital Therapy*. New York: Brunner/Mazel, 1978.

Gurman, A. S. & Kniskern, D. P. Research on marital and family therapy: Progress, perspective and prospect. In: S. L. Garfield & A. E. Bergin (Eds.), *Handbook of Psychotherapy and Behavior Change*. Second edition. New York: Wiley, 1978.

Kniskern, D. P. & Gurman, A. S. Family therapy research: Toward an integration with theory and practice. In: J. P. Vincent (Ed.), *Advances in Family Intervention, Assessment and Theory*. Vol. 2. Greenwich, Ct: JAI Press, 1980.

Spitzer, R. Introduction. *Diagnostic and Statistical Manual of Mental Disorders* (DSM-III). Washington, D.C.: American Psychiatric Association, 1980.

PART IV

Systems Theory

Approaches

CHAPTER 8

The Interactional View: Family Therapy Approaches of the Mental Research Institute

Arthur M. Bodin, Ph.D.

It would be misleading to refer simply to *"the family therapy approach of the Mental Research Institute,"* since a number of approaches have been developed by MRI staff members, who have often been mavericks with interdisciplinary or unconventional training and highly individualistic thinkers whose ideas cannot be compressed into a single approach under the monolithic label "MRI."[1] This independence also characterized Gregory Bateson. Bateson and members of his research projects, as well as the early MRI staff, are referred to as "The Palo Alto Group," a nickname which has incorrectly been assumed to be synonymous with MRI. These points will emerge in more precise perspective in the context of a history of MRI's first two decades only slightly modified from the one written by Lee-Merrow (1979).

---

[1]*Editors' Note.* Stanton (Chapter 10) provides a comprehensive overview of "strategic" approaches to family therapy. While Stanton also discusses the contributions of the MRI, a separate chapter on the MRI approaches is included in this *Handbook* because of the enormous and seminal influence that MRI staff members have had on the development of family therapy in the last two decades.

HISTORY OF THE MENTAL RESEARCH INSTITUTE

Prehistory

It has been said that MRI began before it came into existence, and in a way it did. In the early 1950s, Gregory Bateson, the eminent anthropologist, was awarded a grant to study communication, its different levels and channels, and how one message modified or was significant in understanding another. Together with Jay Haley, William Fry, and John Weakland, Bateson began a communication project at the Veterans Administration Hospital in Menlo Park, California. The group chose to study the "strange communications" which were going on at the hospital and the "nonsensical" language of schizophrenics. Haley (1968) has presented a thorough insider's view of this project.

In 1954 Don D. Jackson gave a lecture at the VA Hospital on "family homeostasis." Bateson was in the audience. That encounter was the beginning of a collaboration between Jackson and the Bateson project which would lead, five years later, to the formation of the Mental Research Institute.

Jackson acted as a consultant on the Bateson project because of his experience in treating schizophrenics and their families and his ideas about homeostasis, which dovetailed with the others' notions about feedback and cybernetic systems. From this project, the seminal double-bind theory of schizophrenia was developed. Its impact on the mental health community was extensive and still continues.

First Ten Years

In 1959, Jackson, with private financial backing, started MRI as a division of the Palo Alto Medical Research Foundation (PAMRF) in order to study schizophrenia and the family. The original staff consisted of Jackson, a secretary, and two people who had heard of the double-bind and family work: Virginia Satir and Jules Riskin. The Bateson project was awarded another grant that same year from the National Institute of Mental Health (NIMH) to study schizophrenics and their families. While this project was separate from MRI, it was also carried out through PAMRF.

As interest increased in conjoint family therapy, Satir received a grant in 1960 from the Hill Foundation of Minneapolis for a two-year family training project. She had not only been practicing but was by now informally teaching other therapists, often late in the evening. Then, in 1962, the NIMH awarded a sizable grant—its first ever for formal training in family therapy—to cover five more years of the training project. With these grants, MRI's training program was launched.

In 1961, Paul Watzlawick, an Austrian who had spent several years teaching psychology in San Salvador's National University, became intrigued by the work in Palo Alto. He soon began working, with the help of Janet Beavin, on a recorded anthology of verbal communication taken from tapes of conjoint family therapy sessions.

Also in the early 1960s, Haley, who along with Weakland had recently joined MRI, was experimenting with ways of measuring communica-

tions in families. He used a number of objective measurements, including a mechanical device which automatically recorded who spoke and after whom. Riskin was also working on quantifying family interactions. He began to develop a methodology for studying family interaction. This project was funded by NIMH and, eventually, with the help of Elaine Faunce, produced the Family Interaction Scales (FIS) (Riskin and Faunce, 1970).

One of the major technical aspects of these early works was the recording of all therapy and research interviews. Traditionally, an accounting of what took place in a therapy session had been based on notes and memory. The Bateson project and the MRI staff broke with this tradition—first audiotaping, then directly observing, then filming, and finally videotaping sessions. This practice created something totally new: family interactional data which could be studied directly.

By 1963, MRI was large enough to become an independent organization, with several psychiatrists, psychologists, and other professionals in the behavioral sciences who conceptualized the family as an interactional social system. Research expanded from the original focus on schizophrenia to examining how family interactions affected such diverse phenomena as ulcerative colitis in children, asthma, and preschool children's academic potential.

Family therapy training continued through 1966 under the direction of Satir. Her program evolved into a federally funded project, directed by Elaine Sorenson, to train nurses in communication skills. The Institute was also conducting special training programs at neighboring universities and hospitals; staff members were speaking to an increasingly wider variety of professional groups and conducting seminars and workshops.

MRI staff members were important contributors to the literature of interactional therapy and research. Haley (1962, 1963) was making seminal contributions to the family research and family therapy literature. Satir's first book was published (1967); Jackson was writing his significant theoretical papers on family rules and the marital quid pro quo (1965); and Watzlawick was writing about the pragmatics of communication (Watzlawick, Beavin and Jackson, 1967).

MRI, in conjunction with the Family Institute of New York (now known as the Ackerman Institute for Family Therapy), started the journal *Family Process* in 1962, with Haley as editor. *Family Process* (which incorporated in 1974) publishes papers devoted to family research and treatment.

During the 1960s, Weakland was studying Communist China films. While these were blatant instruments of political propaganda, he used them to explore and better understand the social patterns of Chinese families and larger social groups, and their relevance to political and international relations.

In 1967, the Brief Therapy Center (BTC) of MRI opened under the direction of Richard Fisch. The staff included Watzlawick and Weakland, as well as Arthur Bodin, who had come to MRI in 1965. BTC's original intention was to explore what could be achieved therapeutically in a brief time with a variety of specific problems. The duration of treatment was limited to ten sessions, with very active intervention and a primary focus on the main presenting problem. It was soon found that this approach was effective and that successful resolution of the presenting problem often led to changes in other problem areas as well.

Second Ten Years

January 1968 brought the untimely death of Jackson. With the loss of the charismatic director and the tightening of federal monies on research, some difficult years lay ahead. MRI's programs, however, were supported by grants from local, private foundations. Despite the declining research monies, the federal Administration on Aging awarded MRI and its new director, John Bell, a grant to work with families having older members. Hence, the Family Futures Center (FFC) was formed, growing in part out of the training program for nurses. FFC evolved into the Family Interaction Center, directed by Elaine Sorensen, and work continued for three years. This project led to Herr and Weakland's (1979) volume on counseling elders and their families.

Under the leadership of John E. Bell and Norma Davies, MRI developed a program to help patients hospitalized for physical illness to reenter their families. This project was carried out in conjunction with the Department of Physical Therapy at the Stanford University School of Medicine.

In the early 1970s, a research project began in which first-break schizophrenics were viewed as going through a developmental crisis instead of being "mentally ill." This concept was consistent with the family interaction theories developed at MRI. Funded by the NIMH, Soteria House, MRI's alternative community residential treatment center, opened in San Jose under the direction of Alma Menn. Loren Mosher of the NIMH's Center for the Study of Schizophrenia served as consultant. Eight years later, Soteria House still operates, along with Emanon House, a replication study in an adjoining county. The progress of residents of the houses is compared with a matched sample being treated at the county hospital psychiatric wards. This form of residential treatment (in which most of the patients do not receive any drugs) appears to be at least as effective as and definitely more cost-efficient than treatment in the traditional hospital environment for certain types of first-break schizophrenics.

In 1973, Bell resigned as the full-time director, and Riskin became MRI's third director, serving part-time.

About this time, Bodin became interested in working with police who were called to deal with families in crisis. Together, he and Diana Everstine created a demonstration project based on a 24-hour crisis intervention strategy. This project soon became established as the Emergency Treatment Center, funded by Santa Clara County. ETC, directed by Diana Everstine, offers 24-hour crisis intervention, especially geared towards victims of assault—rape, child abuse, family violence, incest, and child molestation.

Also during the 1970s, Riskin shifted his focus to the study of "healthy" families. Five years have now been spent on the "Non-labeled" Families Project, which has involved meeting with two "normal" families once a month over the course of two years, with follow-up interviews every six months during the subsequent two years. The interviews were taped, and they continue to be analyzed from both quantitative and qualitative perspectives.

In 1978, MRI started an outpatient psycho-therapy clinic under the direction of Davies. She and her colleagues are working to develop a pool of research data. Davies and her colleagues are launching a project to study the outcome of psychotherapy in terms of effectiveness, future problems, etc.

The MRI training programs consist largely of short-term workshops with offerings announced quarterly. In addition, off-site workshops and seminars are presented regularly, and MRI staff members criss-cross this continent and Europe, presenting their work to wider audiences. In 1978, Carlos Sluzki and Watzlawick began year-long externship training programs in family therapy, and intensive ones for Spanish-speaking visitors.

In MRI's second decade, work on dimensions of communication, family systems, and larger social systems was actively continued and expanded.

MRI is still characterized by a unique blend of research, clinical, and educational activities. The list of staff publications contains an ever-growing number of influential books and articles.

Twenty years of work were celebrated in August 1979 by the Fourth Don D. Jackson Memorial Conference, when six preeminent family therapists reflected on their enormously active field, one that 20 years earlier was the domain of but a handful of people.

At the close of MRI's 1979 Conference it was announced that Jules Riskin had asked to step down as Director of MRI and that Nicholas A. Cummings, then President of the American Psychological Association, was accepting the position. Under Dr. Cummings' leadership the institute expanded staff participation in forming institutional policy. During this period some new MRI directions were conceived, such as Soteria Alternatives for Education (SAFE), designed to ease the transition of schizophrenics back into the community.

Nick Cummings limited his directorship of MRI to one year, because of his major role on the U.S. Senate Finance Committee, which is overseeing clinical trials to test the efficacy of different forms of psychotherapy in preparation for the development of a national health insurance policy.

He is succeeded by Carlos E. Sluzki, an Argentine-born psychiatrist, psychoanalyst, and family therapist, who has been a Guggenheim Fellow and a Fellow of the Foundations Fund for Research in Psychiatry. A Research Associate of the Mental Research Institute since 1965, Carlos Sluzki has published widely, serves on five editorial boards and on the Board of Directors of the American Family Therapy Association. His appointment as Director of Mental Research Institute brought about a broadening of its training activities and an emphasis on intertwining the multiple threads of the interactional-systems paradigm by exploring the conceptual relationships among models developed at MRI and at other research and training centers.

In sum, during the first 20 years since the establishment of MRI, more than 30,000 medical and mental health professionals have participated in MRI courses. In that time, MRI sponsored 52 research projects, 21 books (many in foreign editions), more than 300 other publications, and five national conferences. These activities reflect MRI's pioneering work in research and training concerning the family, and communication, and in the development of family therapy, brief therapy, and emergency treatment. Many aspects of this work have been reviewed by Greenberg (1974, 1977) and by Wilder-Mott (1979). The developments stemming from MRI's diverse yet focused activities emerged within conceptual frameworks which will be the recurrent theme of much of the remainder of this chapter.

BACKGROUND OF THE APPROACH

Major Influences

Don Jackson often acknowledged his indebtedness to Harry Stack Sullivan for focusing on interpersonal aspects of etiology and psychotherapy. Jackson also acknowledged his indebtedness to Ludwig von Bertalanffy for elucidating general systems theory (Bertalanffy, 1950). With particular explicitness, Jackson (1968a) acknowledged the pivotal influence Gregory Bateson had upon him:

On a bleak January day in 1954, I gave the Frieda Fromm-Reichmann lecture at the Palo Alto Veterans Administration Hospital. In the audience was Gregory Bateson, and he approached me after the lecture. My topic was the question of family homeostasis, and Bateson felt the subject matter related to interests that he shared on a project with Jay Haley, John Weakland and William Fry.

From that moment on I became more closely related to the social sciences than to medical psychiatry. I have never regretted this decision (p. v).

It is intriguing to note that this same paragraph that so explicitly affirms the impact of Bateson on Jackson implicitly alludes to the impact of Freud, inasmuch as the reference to a transition from psychiatry to the social sciences almost precisely echoes a statement by Freud (1954) reminiscing about his transition from medicine to psychology.

Virginia Satir, through her training at the University of Chicago School of Social Work, was probably heavily influenced by the Chicago Psychoanalytic Institute. Her focus on ego psychology and, specifically, on the importance of self-concept and self-esteem derives from that psychoanalytic background, as does her emphasis on the corrective emotional experience.

Jules Riskin is similar to Virginia Satir in having been influenced by his early psychoanalytic training. He was influenced by Virginia Satir in his focus on self-esteem and by Jackson in his penchant for looking for patterns. Regarding the parallel development of his respect for psychoanalytic theory as well as for general systems theory, Jules Riskin has remarked, "I was juggling two models."

Haley and Weakland, both influenced by Bateson (with whom they had worked closely prior to joining MRI), also were impressed at some point by Frankl (1960), through his conceptualization of the "paradoxical intention," and by the endless ingenuity of Milton Erickson in the artful design and implementation of tailored paradoxical interventions. In addition, Weakland was probably influenced by his work with Margaret Mead, in which there was an emphasis on the selection of important problems, the recording of careful observations, and the progressive construction of theory. Beyond being impressed with anthropology in general and Bateson in particular, Weakland was impressed by firsthand data as the Bateson project

began looking at families and, as Bateson puts it, by his "absence of familiarity with the revealed wisdom."

Watzlawick, like Haley and Weakland, acknowledges the influence of Frankl and of Erickson. In addition, he was influenced by his background in languages and philosophy and his familiarity with the works of philosophers and mathematicians such as Wittgenstein, Whitehead and Russell, Bolzano, and Gödel, as well as by playwrights such as Albee and novelists such as Dostoevsky and Koestler. At one time a training analyst in Zurich, Watzlawick had become dissatisfied with Jungian training and with the length of treatment and the paucity of results.

The cybernetic model of Wiener (1947) influenced the work of the early MRI staff members, as a foundation for making their therapy behavioral in its attention to interaction patterns. For example, Jackson always wanted to deal with what was before him; sometimes he would translate this into therapeutic tactics, as in asking a couple to continue their argument but to discontinue the use of the past tense. This tactic eliminates the escalatory retrospective mutual blaming which, as Bodin (in preparation) has noted, metaphorically turns people stone cold in response to looking back by their loved ones, as in the story of Orpheus and Euridice from Greek mythology and in the story of Lot's wife from the Bible.

Certain ways of approaching science unified the MRI staff. One was the conviction that science progresses step-by-step and that an odd bunch of people struggling together might facilitate this process by simplifying an area through taking a view rather different from the prevailing one with all its assumptions. This early group of MRI staff members stumbled over things which they had not expected and which they would later notice had applications in other fields. Perhaps it was the mix of disciplines, including mavericks with cross-disciplinary training, that prevented unexpected observations from being ignored as spurious merely by virtue of their being surprising in the light of "established knowledge."

Forerunner Forms of Therapy

Though Jackson was trained as a psychoanalyst, the role of psychoanalysis in directly contributing to the development of family therapy at MRI was very modest. The interpersonal focus of Harry Stack Sullivan influenced Don Jackson, and the importance of corrective emotional experiences, ego psychology, and self-concept (as taught by Franz Alexander at the Chicago Psychoanalytic Institute) influenced both Satir and Jules Riskin. The "paradoxical intention" of Frankl (1960) influenced many of the MRI staff, and the "reductio ad absurdum" or "reenacting the psychosis" tactics of direct analysis, developed by Rosen (1953) interested Bateson, influenced Haley and Weakland, and had special impact on Watzlawick, who had worked directly with Rosen. The conceptual, framing, tactical, and linguistic aspects of hypnotherapy as developed by Milton Erickson influenced the MRI staff in general, particularly those associated with the Brief Therapy Center, and most of all Erickson's expositor, Haley (1963, 1973).

Although family therapy resembles group therapy in having more than two people present, neither psychoanalytic nor process-oriented group therapy has contributed much to the development of family therapy at MRI. The reason is not hard to discern. Therapy groups usually contain people who did not know each other before the therapy and who will go their separate ways after the therapy. They are what Beukenkamp (1971) called "fortunate strangers" in his book by that title. Families, on the other hand, are what sociologists term "traditioned groups." That is, families have a history of interaction and an expectation of future interaction and interdependence. Thus, the political power that is so passionately contested in family conflicts has only a pallid counterpart in ordinary therapy groups. What happens in such groups can be put aside at the close of each session; what happens in a family therapy session may have profoundly desirable or undesirable consequences in the car ride home and throughout the intervening time until the next session. In other words, the family is an *ongoing system* in which the principles of general systems theory operate more plainly and more powerfully than they do in ad hoc therapy groups.

Although behavior has been central in the development of family therapy at MRI, both as the focus of observation and as a prime target and indicator of change, the principles of behavior modification and of social learning theory have not figured prominently in the development of MRI's approach. This is probably due in large measure to the fact that the early MRI pioneers were trained in fields other than psychology. There are, however, additional reasons for the lack of influence from behavior modification, including the fact that some MRI interventions are indirect and even counter-intuitive to the extent that they would initially cause consternation for a strict behavior therapist. One example is the tactic described in Watzlawick, Weakland and Fisch (1974), in which pennies are handed calmly and without comment by a distraught parent to an obstreperous teenager, as a means of puzzling the young person and disrupting the usual interaction pattern rather than as a reinforcement. Nevertheless, there has been some attention paid by MRI staff to the family as a learning context. This was particularly evident in the original double-bind paper (Bateson, Jackson, Haley, and Weakland, 1956) and in Sluzki and Veron (1971) and Riskin and Faunce (1970).

In an informal conversation, Gerald Patterson of the Oregon Social Learning Center offered a definition of a family which is pregnant with possibilities for linking general systems theory with social learning theory, as well as with the communication concepts described by Watzlawick, Beavin and Jackson (1967). Patterson's comment was to the effect that "A family can be regarded as a social system whose members share *mutual* control over one another's social reinforcement schedules." In this single comment are encapsulated the concepts of the family as a *traditioned* group, the *circular causality* operating in the family as a system, and the possibilities of rule-governed reciprocal behavior in the realm of either reward or retaliation, characterized as *family rules* or the marital quid pro quo by Jackson (1965). Patterson's comment, taken with the dysfunctional communication patterns described by Watzlawick (1964) and by Watzlawick, Beavin, and Jackson (1967), suggests a possible linkage between these dysfunctional communication patterns and social learning theory, affording perhaps some of the least positive but most powerful shaping influences of behavior within families. Communication which flows freely because of an absence of such dysfunctional patterns will be more suiable for conveying positive feelings.

As suggested, for example, by the fact that Rosen's (1953) direct analysis focused on actions that could be seen and on actions that could be instigated, rather than on unobservable events in the past, a variety of therapeutic approaches served as lenses which focused the attention of MRI staff on interactional events which could be observed rather than merely reconstructed or inferred.

Types of Patients with Whom the Approach was Initially Developed

Schizophrenia was the initial nexus around which MRI staff members converged. Jackson, (1953) had already begun addressing the subject. Weakland had become interested in the fact that one could list in parallel the phenomena of schizophrenia and hypnosis. Bateson, Jackson, Haley, and Weakland (1956) then produced their seminal paper on the double-bind, based on communications analysis derived from the Theory of Logical Types (Whitehead and Russell, 1910-13). There were several dozen articles published by Jackson (e.g., 1960, 1964), Haley (e.g., 1959, 1960, 1965), and other MRI staff members on schizophrenia. MRI's first decade was characterized by a branching out from the focus on schizophrenic families to families with many other kinds of problems in the hope of finding patterns specific to particular problems: delinquents (Ferreira, 1960), school underachievers, patients suffering from anxiety neurosis (Fry, 1962), asthmatics (Weblin, 1962), borderline personalities (Jackson, 1959), and ulcerative colitis patients (Jackson and Yalom, 1966), as well as couples in conflict (Haley, 1963).

Early Theoretical Formulations and Therapy Techniques

Early theoretical and therapeutic developments at MRI were so often published in papers authored or co-authored by Jackson that an overview of MRI's first decade can be gleaned from an article by Greenberg (1977), subtitled "A Study and Examination of the work of Don D. Jackson." Major theoretical formulations described by Greenberg include: 1) *family homeostasis*; 2) *negative* and *positive feedback*, or, respectively, deviation-counteracting and deviation-amplifying processes among family members leading to improvement or worsening of dysfunction; 3) the *rule hypothesis* based on the idea that people in continuing relationships interact in increasingly patterned ways which can be discerned as *redundancies* from which may be inferred the "descriptive rules" governing the particular family system; 4) *descriptive and prescriptive rules*, indicating identified regularities and patterns which are stabilized by the imposition of sanctions in response to pattern disruption or deviation, or, at another level, rules about rules or "meta-rules"; 5) the development of a new or enlarged set of rules as a means of effecting change in relationships; 6) the *quid pro quo* as a conscious or unconscious family rule; 7) *punctuation* as a relativistic rescue device for couples in conflict because they have carved reality at different joints; and 8) *circular causality* (vs. lineal causality), or the negation (or potential enlargement) of the behavioral S-R paradigm.

The "double-bind" hypothesis was generated by researchers, several of whom later joined the staff of MRI after it was founded. Still standing as a particularly revolutionary, integrated, and seminal concept, the double-bind is most thoroughly reviewed by Sluzki and Ransom (1976). The redefinition of the therapeutic situation so as to focus on the transactions among related "significant others," rather than on their often pallid reflection through becoming aware of transference and countertransference phenomena, is best delineated in Jackson (1962), Jackson and Haley (1963), and Haley (1963). Communication concepts developed and applied at MRI have been summarized in Watzlawick (1964, 1976, 1978), Watzlawick, Beavin, and Jackson (1967), and Jackson (1968a, 1968b). The interested reader wishing to distill these communication concepts would probably do so most economically by reading Watzlawick, Beavin and Jackson (1967), and then Watzlawick (1978).

THE HEALTHY FAMILY

In "The Myth of Normality," Jackson (1967)

expressed his skepticism about the concept of the normal family as follows:

As a student of the family for many years, I think it is safe to say that there is no such thing as a normal family any more than there is a normal individual. There are parents who appear to live in extreme harmony together but have nervous children, and parents who get along miserably but whose children appear to be functioning well. When one hears the expression, "Gee, they're a normal family," the speaker is usually referring to some facet of family living and not to the total familial interaction, which is unknown to the casual observer. Such statements are usually made by persons who value conformity and see this family as one that lives up to all the ideals of the ladies' magazines, including the cardinal principle of "togetherness." Truly, such behavior has little to do with mental health. There are cultures and families within our own culture, in which the family structure is very different from what is commonly considered normal. Yet the individuals therein are creative and productive (p. 161).

Jackson asks, "What can replace the concept of normality?" and goes on to answer: "It is time to give up the false security borne of labeling what we are doing as 'right' or 'normal' instead of using the more accurate but less reassuring term 'conventional' " (p. 32).

Following Jackson's model of modesty about refraining from the use of the word normal with families, Riskin (1976) first reported on his work with non-therapized families. Though such terminology preserves ideological integrity and scientific modesty, it attracts little of the public attention that such important exploratory work deserves. Perhaps MRI's traditional appreciation of the importance of labeling will have to be consciously employed to reframe research with well-functioning families as this work becomes sufficiently advanced to emerge from the closet into the consulting room. Meanwhile, some preliminary comments may nevertheless be made about this area of family theory. Jackson's point of view was that there is no *one* model of health or normality in families or marriages, and that any attempt to declare such a standard would pose very sticky ethnopolitical problems which could best be averted by sticking to a statistical concept of normality approximated by the term "conventional."

Role Definition

Jackson was a man ahead of his time in attacking sex-role stereotypes before the feminist movement had given birth to the concept of "androgyny." Jackson viewed roles as a priori cultural abstractions and as essentially individual rather than interactional concepts. Thus, there has been little interest at MRI in the generalized notion of "roles," except perhaps as the sociological molds of marital expectations which may be broken when the actual redundancies or rules evolve.

Problem-solving

While it is tempting to slip into the assumption that a normal family solves its problems, the prevailing view at MRI is that *in a well-functioning family problems may persist but not paralyze*. Such families may attempt to work on their problems by discussions which may even become heated at times or what some people would call "good arguments." A good argument is defined as one which gets the matter settled and leaves the participants feeling closer together afterwards rather than farther apart. Problems will be solved in such families in any ways that work for smooth operation of the family, and these could include the invocation of reasonably stable rules or of meta-rules which allow for changes in rules without having to resort to symptom development.

The "Non-labeled" Families Project currently being conducted by Riskin seems to be confirming an idea mentioned by Satir (1967) that *scapegoating* is a behavior characteristic of dysfunctional families, inasmuch as Riskin's non-labeled families seem to display no scapegoating and no notion that someone must be blamed when something goes wrong (Riskin and McCorkle, 1979). Moreover, this project seems to be confirming a concept of problem formation developed in MRI's Brief Therapy Center (Weakland, Fisch, Watzlawick, and Bodin, 1974). This concept is that *problems* develop from *difficulties* as a result of persistence in expending effort on the very approaches which are proving unsuccessful in dealing with these difficulties. Examples fall into three major categories: denial; overemphasis; and well-intentioned efforts, usually in a direction supported by the culturally accepted version of common sense, though not supported by systematic study of the result of its application, as in the time honored, logical, and humane tradition of trying to cheer up a person who is depressed. Riskin's research is beginning to show that non-labeled families deal with their difficulties with sufficient foresight and skill so as to prevent them from developing into insoluble "Problems" with a capital "P." For example, a particularly major change, nest-leaving, does not have to be accomplished by running away in any of its three most common varieties: 1) in response to overt or covert messages from one or both parents that the child should leave; 2) in response to overprotection experienced as parental pressure for prolonged dependency; and 3) by default in the wake of nest abandonment by peripatetic parents frenetically pursuing either enlightenment or their lost youth through immersion in each new fad.

Family Changes

Family life-cycle considerations are set forth in some detail in Haley's chapter on "The Family Life Cycle" in *Uncommon Therapy* (1973). The family life-cycle characteristically has markers of two types: predictable and unpredictable. The predictable junctures, in turn, may be of two types: expected and unexpected. "Expected" is used here to denote lack of surprise rather than societal or extended family injunction. Events which typically occur with a timing which has been expected include marriage, birth of a child, a child starting school, a child leaving school, a child leaving home, a child getting married, becoming grandparents, and retirement. Death is an example of an indeterminant marker, the time of which can be either expected or unexpected, though in either case the fact that the event will occur is, of course, predictable. Divorce, on the other hand, is an event the occurrence of which cannot be predicted but the timing of which may or may not be expected, though in the overwhelming majority of instances it is expected by one spouse who initiates it and unexpected as well as unwelcomed by the other. Unpredictable and un-

expected life-cycle markers include major illnesses, serious accidents, and unusual failures or triumphs in the course of school or career. Such events would also include non-accidental misfortunes such as robbery, rape and murder. Unpredictable but expected events may also occur, such as a woman returning to work when the child(ren)'s age permits.

The importance of the dimensions of expectability and predictability is that both bear on the amount of preparation which is possible. The more prepared a person is for what happens, the better able to cope he or she would probably be. If an event is both unexpected *and* unpredictable, it is likely that the opportunity to prepare for coping will be minimal and the perception of unwarrantedness and injustice will be maximal. Data from Riskin and McCorkle's (1979) study of nontherapy families seem to show one family changing over time in the direction of *increased affective intensity, increasing freedom to interrupt, greater spontaneity, more talk about the community*, and *sharing more information without being asked*. There is evidence, however, that the changes may result in part from the impact of the study itself.

The Balance of Separateness and Togetherness

It is not simply a curious fact that Riskin has avoided asking detailed questions about affection and sexuality in his work with nontherapy families. Rather, his approach has been non-intrusive in the sense that it is designed to encourage discussion of various topics without any high pressure probing. Moreover, Riskin has tried to remain very sensitive to the families in his study by heeding cues they give regarding what they would be comfortable talking about or avoiding. The fact that he has not extensively probed the area of affection and sexuality suggests that he is responding to an implicit family rule that such matters are private or to the family's ability to state explicitly to the interviewer that these matters are private; however, in individual interviews greater ease has been shown over time. Nevertheless, where the marital relationship has seemed good, the atmosphere has been warm, and even where the marital relationship has seemed less good, the parent-child interaction has been warm. In the first instance, there seems to be a tacit message that sex is fun.

Family closeness seems connected with or, perhaps it would be more accurate to say, enabled by easy access to distance. Thus, people are allowed a lot of autonomy while also having a sense of family, of reciprocity, of mutuality, and of connectedness. Perhaps most important, the family members seem to sense and maintain a balance between autonomy and the bonds of their family, distance and closeness, separateness and togetherness. Refraining from unnecessary coercion may be an expression of love. Children are allowed to say "no" without parents getting upset or punishing them. Even such freedom, however, is comfortably limited by the parents when they feel it is necessary, as when one mother and father insisted on maintaining weekly visits for dinner by grandmother, refusing to allow the children *not* to participate at the Sunday dinner, and thereby teaching respect for elders and conveying a sense of family connectedness. This firm maintenance of a partially open door to the extended family is matched by openness to non-family members and the community at large as manifested by participation in school activities on the part of the children and by volunteer work (the unpaid feature is not viewed as salient) with community, school, and church organizations.

Rules and meta-rules get set early. These rules and meta-rules operate in healthy families so as to assure both stability and change. That is, they maintain a state of equilibrium despite and perhaps because of the continual conflicts arising in smoothly functioning families. In this connection, it may be useful to recall the Batesonian metaphor of a tightrope walker having to keep his pole in constant motion in order to maintain the stability of the whole system. Keeping a family system in balance requires monitoring of outside forces and coordination with them as they change. Thus, the rules and meta-rules in healthy families enable them to coordinate internal changes in concert with external or contextual changes. In some sense, it is the job of *parents* in non-labeled families and of *therapists* in labeled families to catalyze the coordinated functioning of rules and meta-rules so as to enable the family to function homeostatically though beset with internal conflicts and

external changes. It is Riskin's impression that such families acknowledge their problems, are able to comment on their family rules, and tend to conceptualize their problems and proposed solutions in non-extremist and hence non-escalatory terms (Riskin and McCorkle, 1979).

THE DYSFUNCTIONAL MARRIAGE OR FAMILY

Family Classification Systems: Informal and Formal

The most fundamental classification of families is a two-way division into functional and dysfunctional families. Such a division, however, is not as simple as it sounds, for it is mired in the same tautology that plagues attempts to define health as the absence of disease. Satir (1967) has provided some hints as to what she regards as dysfunctional, inasmuch as she lists her criteria for terminating treatment, and it may be inferred that families failing to meet these criteria would be regarded by her as dysfunctional. In this framework, dysfunctional families would *not* be able to:

1) complete transactions, check, ask;
2) interpret hostility;
3) see how others see them;
4) see how they see themselves;
5) tell one another how they manifest themselves;
6) tell one another their hopes, fears, and expectations of one another;
7) disagree;
8) make choices;
9) learn through practice;
10) free themselves from harmful effects of past models;
11) give a clear message, that is, be congruent in their behavior, with a minimum of difference between feelings and communication, and with a minimum of hidden messages;
12) be direct, using the first person in criticizing, evaluating, acknowledging observations, finding fault, reporting annoyance, and identifying being puzzled;
13) be delineated by using language which

clearly acknowledges the attributes of the speaker as distinguished from the attributes of the listener;

14) be clear by using direct questions to gain knowledge of others' directions or intentions in order to accomplish an outcome.

Within the category of dysfunctional families, the first subdivisions were drawn according to the name of the presenting complaint. By this semantic fiat we had "schizophrenic families," "psychosomatic families," and, more specifically, "asthmatic families," "ulcerative colitis families," as well as "delinquent families," just to give a few examples. Such a nomenclature labeled the whole family according to the main presenting complaint. Complexities arise when there are two or more important presenting complaints. Further difficulties arise because of violations of the implicit assumption that all families with a certain presenting complaint will display certain interactional patterns. In other words, the principles of *equifinality* (Bertalanffy, 1968) and *equipotentiality* introduce many exceptions to the foregoing implicit assumption. The principle of equifinality is that many different origins can lead to the same results, while the principle of equipotentiality states that the same origins can lead to many different results.

The occurrence of protection and scapegoating in pathological families has been studied by Watzlawick, Beavin, Sikorski and Mecia (1970). In 48 intact families with 129 children, each family member was required to write the main fault of the family member on his or her left. All were then asked to state to whom each item best applied. The families were of three diagnostic types: 10 delinquency, 19 ulcerative colitis, and 19 other (four psychosis, nine school underachieving, four cystic fibrosis, one marital problems, one nonspecific pathology). Across the three categories, identified patients were significantly less protected though more accurate in correctly attributing items written by others and in honestly acknowledging the item written by them. While specific patterns were found across the three diagnostic groups regarding the degree of self-blame, self-scapegoating, self-protection, scapegoating of others, and protection of others, perhaps the most salient finding

was the high accuracy of interpersonal perception existing in delinquent families in contrast to the low accuracy of interpersonal perception in the ulcerative colitis families. One might speculate that *inaccurate interpersonal perception is akin to the defense mechanism of denial, both being elevated in the psychosomatic families.*

A typology of dyads was devised by Sluzki and Beavin (1965) based on an operational definition of *symmetry* and *complementarity*, terms introduced by Bateson (1958) in 1936 when he described human interaction based on his anthropological observations of the Iatmul tribe of New Guinea. Essentially, what Bateson described were patterns of interaction characterized by people culturally labeled as assertive interacting with people culturally labeled as submissive, or assertive people interacting with other assertive people. He noted that the first type of interaction was characterized by a tendency for its participants to polarize each other, a process he termed *complementary schizmogenesis*; the second type of interaction was characterized by a tendency for its participants to remain even with one another, no matter how casual or intense the competition, a process he termed *symmetrical schizmogenesis*.

Watzlawick, Beavin, and Jackson (1967) later added the concepts of *meta-complementary* relationships and *meta-symmetrical* relationships to indicate, respectively, one person allowing or forcing the other to be in charge of him or her, and one person allowing or forcing the other to be equal to him or her. Lederer and Jackson (1968) introduced the concept of *parallel* relationships in which spouses alternate comfortably between symmetrical and complementary relationships as they adapt to changing situations. Nevertheless, none of these three additional terms was adopted for the seven-way classification scheme advanced by Sluzki and Beavin. Their scheme rests, first of all, on operationally defining "complementary" and "symmetrical." "Complementary" is defined by them to mean the reciprocal giving and taking of instructions, the reciprocal asking and answering of questions, the reciprocal asserting of and agreeing to statements, all of these reciprocal relationships being characterized by inequality stemming from the participants' occupying a one-up and a one-down position. "Symmetrical" is defined by them as mutual exchanging of referential statements, the mutual exchanging of agreements, and the mutual exchanging of instructions, all three of these instances being characterized by equality.

Sluzki and Beavin went on to devise a method for assigning speech scores, reflecting essentially the view of each speaker concerning how his or her interactional position is defined according to his or her last speech. The pairing of successive speech score assignments results in transaction scores, which comprise the typology of dyads devised by Sluzki and Beavin. This dyadic typology consists of seven configurations:

I. *Stable Symmetry* (The successive speeches of A and B each define the relationship as symmetrical.)
II. *Stable Complementarity* (The successive speeches of A and B concur in defining one of them as dominant and the other as submissive.)
III. *Symmetrical Competition toward One-Up* (The successive speeches of A and B conflict in that each claims the one-up position.)
IV. *Symmetrical Competition toward One-Down* (The successive speeches of A and B conflict in that each claims the one-down position.)
V. *Asymmetrical Competition toward One-Up and Symmetry* (The successive speeches of A and B conflict in that one claims the one-up position and the other claims a symmetrical position.)
VI. *Asymmetrical Competition toward One-Down and Symmetry* (The successive speeches of A and B conflict in that one claims the one-down position and the other claims a symmetrical position.)
VII. *Fluid* (The successive speeches of A and B are not predominantly of any of the other six configurations, but fluctuate.)

It should be noted that the "fluid" category of Sluzki and Beavin resembles the "parallel" category of Lederer and Jackson, except that the latter includes the concept of dyadic adaptation to changing circumstances.

The concept of stability and the other side of the coin, instability, both appear in the four-fold marital typology advanced in *The Mirages of Marriage* (Lederer and Jackson, 1968). These categories rest on three aspects of the marital relationship: *functionality* (suitability of behavior for achieving common goals while minimizing impasses and backlogs), *temporal compatibility* (being on acceptably similar wavelengths regarding short- and long-term goals), and *vector relations* (synchrony in being able to handle marital change by heading toward a collaborative relationship rather than a collision course). Though Lederer and Jackson suggest that attention be paid to these three areas, no specific method of assessing them is presented. The four-fold marital typology they advance is sketched in broad strokes to represent the spectrum of marriage rather than presented as a reliable classification scheme. They state that at a given moment a marriage "can be regarded as belonging *more or less* in one of the listed categories. The categories are arranged in order of desirability and functionality. The one at the top is the 'best,' and the one at the bottom is the 'worst' " (p. 153). Each category has two subcategories, based in turn on previous ideas by Jackson (1959b).

I. The Stable-Satisfactory Marriage
   1. Heavenly Twins
   2. The Collaborative Geniuses
II. The Unstable-Satisfactory Marriage
   1. The Spare-Time Battlers
   2. The Pawnbrokers
III. The Unstable-Unsatisfactory Marriage
   1. The Weary Wranglers
   2. The Psychosomatic Avoiders
IV. The Stable-Unsatisfactory Marriage
   1. The Gruesome Twosome
   2. The Paranoid Predators

Lederer and Jackson state that the Heavenly Twins appear to have been "born for each other," usually having acquired the same tastes and values from the same background. The Collaborative Geniuses, a category assumed rather than observed by Lederer and Jackson, do not come from extremely similar backgrounds but evolve a highly cooperative relationship around creative team endeavors in which they are engrossed, aided by above average similarity in tastes, values and background, plus an uncommon degree of flexibility. The Spare-Time Battlers oscillate between marital heaven and hell with most days spent feeling just plain "married." The husband is too busy and the wife substitutes covert sabotage for forthright complaints, which she had learned will be trivialized by her husband. Except in the bedroom they spend little time alone together. The Pawnbrokers are forever making unspoken adjustments to compensate for the lack of romantic emotional attachment. Lederer and Jackson (1968) summarized this pattern as follows:

Thus spouses of this type have themselves in hock to each other. They are willing to pay the required interest, and refuse to take themselves out of marital pawn because the payment they received from the pawnbroker seems to them to be a fair exchange for what they give (p. 138).

The Weary Wranglers have learned from years of preliminary bouts precisely how to cause each other the most exquisite pain. Their mutual involvement consists of extracting pleasure from the defeats of the other. They are locked in combat and tend to draw in third parties to form coalitions. Their conflicts tend to escalate and expressions of their anger damage both participants. The Psychosomatic Avoiders battle covertly rather than express anger directly. In addition to sarcasm, double-edged humor, and tangentialization, such nonverbal means may be employed as illness, alcoholism, and orgasmic difficulties. Psychosomatic Avoiders find open opposition harder than suffering in solitude. The Gruesome Twosome and the Paranoid Predators, as participants in Stable-Unsatisfactory marriages, are what Lederer and Jackson (1968) termed "the 'worst' of the lot." The authors continued their description as follows:

In a quiet, socially respectable manner the people in this group suffer more pain, hate more profoundly, and cause more discomfort to others than do the members of the other three groups. Yet the spouses appear to be unaware of their behavior. There is a deadly virulent glue of hate that is only visible to the keen eye of the behavioral scientist or the brilliant novelist.

The Gruesome Twosome partners grow old together, oblivious of the fact that they cannot live with or without each other. When they seek counseling or therapy, they do so "for the sake of the children." They are particularly prone to minimize their pain by intense investment in outside activities which place special demands on them, such as cults. Reciprocal avoidance of criticism is the rule, since each fears retaliation. The Paranoid Predators unite against the outside world, using their shared criticism of others as the cement to bond themselves. They are suspicious and disdainful of other individuals, though they may support extremist organizations to deny and distract from the desolation of their own relationship. Their desperate behavior is destructive, since it enables them to maintain their marriage at great cost to themselves, as well as to their children and to society.

To learn what differentiations might be made on the basis of Riskin's Family Interaction Scales, Riskin and Faunce (1970) studied families from various points on a continuum of functionality-dysfunctionality. The families studied were grouped according to a five-way classification developed on the basis of information about the family functioning, as well as about psychiatric problems, marital problems, school labeling, and police contacts. These five categories are as follows:

Group A. This group contains the multiproblem families. These families have three or more labeled problems, including neurotic and/or psychotic, and/or psychosomatic, and/or acting-out, and/or underachieving, and/or the "marriage," i.e., they are the most troubled families. . . . A typical group A family would have the following diagnoses: Parents have marital problems; father has been labeled as a schizoid personality; mother has been labeled as depressed; two children have been labeled as underachievers; and one child has an acting-out label, either from the school or the police.

Group B. This group contains families that have two or three labeled problems. These families are basically seen as "constricted" and usually have one labeled neurotic member plus a marital problem and/or an underachiever. . . . A typical group B family would have the following diagnoses: The parents are in therapy for a marital problem and one of the children has a neurotic-reaction label.

Group C. This group contains families that have child-labeled problems only, either acting-out (delinquency) or underachieving in one or more children, or both. . . . A typical group C family would have the following problems: One of the children has been picked up by the police for shoplifting or setting fires and another child has been labeled by the school as an underachiever.

Group D. This group contains families that were from the school sample and were originally part of group E. These families have no official labels of any kind, but all the interviewers agreed that there seemed to be significant problems in the family, either between the parents, or with the children, or between the parents and the children. . . .

Group E. This group contains families that have no labels and the interviewers all agreed that they were functioning well (pp. 113-114).

It is worth noting that no single system of classification has emerged as suitable for all situations from among the many proposed at MRI. Each, however, has been helpful to bear in mind while doing therapy, sometimes because of the implications for the direction of therapy, and occasionally because an awareness of these categories may be helpful to the family members, whether their insight into their own pattern is gained by comments from the therapist or by reading such works for the general public as Lederer and Jackson (1968) or Satir (1972).

The Development of Dysfunction

The double-bind theory advanced by Bateson, Jackson, Haley, and Weakland (1956) has proved particularly seminal in the evolution of family therapy, linking it to communication theory as well as to general systems theory. In that paper, the double-bind is defined as follows:

The necessary ingredients for a double-bind situation, as we see it, are:

1) *Two or more persons.* Of these, we designate one, for purposes of our definition, as the "victim." We do not assume that the double-bind is inflicted by the mother alone, but that it may be done either by mother alone or by some combination of mother, father, and/or siblings.[2]

2) *Repeated experience.* We assume that the double-bind is a recurrent theme in the experience of the victim. Our hypothesis does not invoke a single traumatic experience, but such repeated experiences that the double-bind structure comes to be an habitual expectation.

3) *A primary negative injunction.* This may have either of two forms: (a) "Do not do so and so, or I will punish you," or (b) "If you do not do so and so, I will punish you." Here we select a context of learning based on avoidance of punishment rather than a context of reward seeking. There is perhaps no formal reason for this selection. We assume that the punishment may be either the withdrawal of love or the expression of hate or anger—or most devastating—the kind of abandonment that results from the parent's expression of extreme helplessness.

4) *A secondary injunction conflicting with the first at a more abstract level, and like the first enforced by punishments or signals which threaten survival.* This secondary injunction is more difficult to describe than the primary for two reasons. First, the secondary injunction is commonly communicated to the child by nonverbal means. Posture, gesture, tone of voice, meaningful action, and the implications concealed in verbal comment may all be used to convey this more abstract message. Second, the secondary injunction may impinge upon any element of the primary prohibition. Verbalization of the secondary injunction may, therefore, include a wide variety of forms; for example, "Do not see this as punishment"; "Do not see me as the punishing agent"; "Do not submit to my prohibitions"; "Do not think of what you must not do"; "Do not question my love of which the primary prohibition is (or is not) an example"; and so on. Other examples become possible when the double-bind is inflicted not by one individual but by two. For example, one parent may negate at a more abstract level the injunctions of the other.

5) *A tertiary negative injunction prohibiting the victim from escaping from the field.* In a formal sense it is perhaps unnecessary to list this injunction as a separate item since the reinforcement at the other two levels involves a threat to survival, and if the double-binds are imposed during infancy, escape is naturally impossible. However, it seems that in some cases the escape from the field is made impossible by certain devices which are not purely negative, e.g., capricious promises of love, and the like.

6) Finally, *the complete set of ingredients is no longer necessary when the victim has learned to perceive his universe in double-bind patterns.* Almost any part of a double-bind sequence may then be sufficient to precipitate panic or rage. The pattern of conflicting injunctions may even be taken over by hallucinatory voices (pp. 253-254, emphasis added).

The four originators of the double-bind theory

---

[2]*Editors' Note.* As many others before us have pointed out, fathers as well as mothers can be major contributors to such a double-binding relationship. An emphasis on the mother's contribution, in our view, has arisen as the result of common patterns of child-rearing in Western cultures, in which the amount and intensity of mother-child interaction are often greater than of father-child interaction.

go on to hypothesize that its impact on any individual will be a breakdown in the capacity to discriminate between Logical Types whenever the double-bind situation occurs. They then state the general characteristics of such situations as follows:

1) When the individual is involved in an intense relationship; that is, a relationship in which he feels it is vitally important that he discriminate accurately what sort of message is being communicated so that he may respond appropriately.

2) And, the individual is caught in a situation in which the other person in the relationship is expressing two orders of message and one of these denies the other.

3) And, the individual is unable to comment on the messages being expressed to correct his discrimination of what order of message to respond to, i.e., he cannot make a meta-communicative statement (Bateson, Jackson, Haley, and Weakland, 1956, p. 254).

Its originators have written many additional articles on the double-bind and these are conveniently collected, along with various critiques, counter-arguments, comments, and conceptual expansions in Sluzki and Ransom (1976). This book also contains three contributions relating to the double-bind authored at least in part by other MRI staff members, although the original source must be consulted to locate "A Review of the Double Bind Theory" (Watzlawick, 1963). The contribution of the double-bind theory extends even beyond the merging of communication theory, general systems theory, family theory, and concepts of pathogenesis: *It stands as perhaps the most definitive landmark in the revolutionary shift from an individual to a systems focus in concepts of psychopathogenesis.*

The contributions of communication to the development of dysfunction and, for that matter, to the maintenance of good functioning and, even more broadly, to the whole spectrum of interactional influence as people deal with one another has been most rigorously organized in *Pragmatics of Human Communication* by Watzlawick, Beavin and Jackson (1967). This landmark presentation builds upon earlier work by Bateson, the Bateson projects, and the MRI group. These authors develop in considerable

detail a number of communicational contributions to pathogenesis. These include such concepts as the *denial of communication*, the *rejection of communication*, the *disqualification of communication*, and the role of symptoms as forms of communication, all these being examples of the axiom of "the impossibility of not communicating." In all, five such tentative axioms on the pragmatics of communication are postulated, each accompanied by some description of its own pathogenic derivatives. The five axioms are postulated as follows:

1) One cannot *not* communicate (p. 51).
2) Every communication has a content and a relationship aspect such that the latter classifies the former and is therefore a meta-communication (p. 54).
3) The nature of a relationship is contingent upon the punctuation of the communicational sequences between the communicants (p. 59).
4) Human beings communicate both digitally and analogically. Digital language has a highly complex and powerful logical syntax but lacks adequate semantics in the field of relationship, while analogic language possesses the semantics but has no adequate syntax for the unambiguous definition of the nature of the relationships (pp. 66-67).
5) All communicational interchanges are either symmetrical or complementary, depending on whether they are based on equality or difference (p. 70).

Dysfunction-producing derivatives of the second axiom, concerning the level structure of communication (its *content* and *relationship* aspects) include confusion of these levels, disagreement within either level, rejection of the definition of oneself or the other, disconfirmation or virtual ignoring of one of the interacting parties, and imperviousness to corrective feedback through ignoring or misinterpreting it and, at a second level, through failure to register that such feedback has not been received and comprehended and, hence, failure to repeat it.

Pathogenic derivatives of the third axiom, concerning the *punctuation* of the sequence of events, include discrepant punctuations (such as a husband and wife each claiming that the *other* originated the escalating sequence of criticisms) and self-fulfilling negativistic prophecies.

Dysfunction-generating derivatives of the fourth axiom, concerning *digital and analogic communication*, center around errors in translation between these two modes. Such errors include not being able to terminate an increasingly unpleasant interaction occurring at the analogic level (because analogic communication lacks specific ways of expressing the concept "not") and the emergence of hysterical symptoms as re-translations from the digital to the analogic mode.

Pathogenic potentialities of the fifth axiom, concerning symmetrical and complementary interaction, encompass several possibilities. These include *symmetrical escalation* (runaway competitiveness to remain on an at least equal footing with the partner), *rigid complementarity* (dissimilar but mutually confirming functions fixed by fiat or by unspoken rules such as mutually accepted cultural traditions), and *unresolved meta-complementary relationships* (relationships in which either partner allows or forces the other to be in charge *or* to be symmetrical, thus leading to confusion as to whether the ostensible complementarity *or* symmetry is discerned to consist at a deeper level of precisely its opposite. The initial impression or "official" version oscillates with a more penetrating vision of the relationship which may then remain mired in doubt for the participants as well as for any observers).

General systems theory, as well as communications theory, provides bases for the development of dysfunction, as further delineated in Watzlawick, Beavin and Jackson (1967). Any failure to give or receive feedback may initiate a runaway situation, as may any failure to follow regularly observed relationship rules or to be able to change the operation of such rules through recalibration of the feedback-triggering level of tolerance for deviation.

While relying to some extent on such communication and system concepts of pathogenesis, Satir (1967) links such concepts with additional ones, some of them intrapsychic, upon which she relies at least equally heavily. These include the following:

1) Inappropriate mate selection may be based on low self-esteem, which in turn may be based on such childhood deprivations as not having physical needs met, not having continuity in relationship, not having contexts which foster learning how to influence and predict the responses of others, not having contexts which permit accurate cognitive categorization and semantic structuring of the world, not having support for seeing oneself as a masterful and as a sexual person, and not having prolonged opportunity to observe the kinds of parental interaction which would serve as sex models for future interaction.

2) Difficulties may be caused by disagreements, not so much because of the fact of disagreement per se, but because of assumptions about the meaning of the discovery of differentness between partners and because of the feelings that these presumed implications arouse, such as dread of desertion and subsequent isolation stemming from an assumed inability to establish other significant relationships.

3) Many stresses can adversely affect modern families. These may stem from external sources, such as depersonalization meaninglessness, and mobility engendered by the Industrial Revolution. These may also stem from the questioning of previously accepted assumptions, values, and norms in the face of post-war and post-marital disillusionment, leaving child-rearing as the reason to live and as the reason to stay married, hence burdening the child with excessive power and responsibility in relation to the parents and their happiness. Unmet marital expectations, whether realistic or unrealistic, comprise disappointments with myriad deleterious consequences for the children.

4) Weak marital relationships threaten the child through affording insufficient evidence of strength to reassure the child that oedipal fantasies will not somehow slide toward reality, either literally or emotionally.

A framework has been evolved for conceptualizing *problem formation* in terms designed to provide a platform for specific and tailored interventions aimed at *problem resolution* in the course of the therapy, thinking, and teaching at MRI's Brief Therapy Center, spanning the 14 years from 1966 to the present. Contributions to problem formation have been conceptualized by Weakland, Fisch, Watzlawick, and Bodin (1974) as resulting from the exacerbation of an everyday life difficulty into a "Problem," with a capital "P," by the overemphasis or under-emphasis (exaggeration or denial) which so often characterize the attempted solutions by means of which people inadvertently prolong and elaborate their problems. Watzlawick, Weakland, and Fisch (1974) described a single, overarching principle of problem formation, namely the persistence of the participants in continuing to attempt a solution despite available evidence that it is precisely what is *not* working. This tendency to become mired in attempting *more of the same* already demonstrably unsuccessful solution is what converts the *solution* into the *problem* by creating a knot or tangle through the mishandling (inappropriate attempted solution) of what was previously a mere *difficulty*. Thus, an everyday life difficulty is capable of solution, though possibly only with the expenditure of considerable time, effort, money, or emotional pain. It is the mishandling of such a difficulty which transmutes it into a problem, perhaps paralyzing the participants until they avail themselves of outside help to enable them to break out of their stalemate. Three main types of mishandling are described:

1) Action is necessary but is not taken.
2) Action is taken when it should not be.
3) Action is taken at the wrong level (Watzlawick, Weakland, and Fisch, 1974, p. 39).

These three types of mishandling are detailed in the three chapters which follow their introduction in the book *Change*. The first such chapter has as its theme the idea that:

. . . [O]ne way of mishandling a problem is to behave as if it did not exist. For this form of denial, we have borrowed the term *terrible simplification*. Two consequences follow from it: (a) acknowledgment, let alone any attempted solution, of the problem is seen as a manifestation of madness or badness; and (b) the problem requiring change becomes greatly compounded by the "problems" created through its mishandling (p. 46).

The second chapter has as its theme the refusal to accept any proposed solution other than one based on a Utopian premise that things *should be* a certain way, thus precluding the more modest and attainable goals by insisting on the impossible and making a "federal case" out of the fact of its unattainability. This type of problem formation is self-evident except to those sharing the particular underlying Utopian premise. It is probably apparent, by now, that the denial and exaggeration of difficulties (underemphasis and overemphasis) are types of mishandling which, though apparently opposite, are alike in presenting *extremist* types of proposed solutions: ignoring the problem, on the one hand, or making of it a cause célèbre on the other.

The third type of mishandling is presented in a chapter titled simply, "Paradoxes," the theme of which is the unresolvability of various marital and parent-child paradoxes without the introduction of a *second-order change* which transcends the level containing the contradictions of the paradox. In other words, the usually unstated quid pro quo originally underlying the relationship may need revision, but the relationship contains no rules which allow its participants to acknowledge, agree upon, or adopt necessary revisions. Thus, commands to be spontaneous, demands to be dominated by the other, and demands that the other disobey all comprise examples of paradoxes requiring another level of analysis, perhaps stemming from outside intervention, to envision and effect the second-order change essential to resolving the problem promoted by the paradox. It should not be surprising that such situations may require paradoxical interventions which, themselves, go beyond traditional folk wisdom and, for this very reason, have for the most part evaded invention or acceptance. The development of psychotherapy, like so many other fields, has been delayed by acquiescence to the view that "common sense" is a sufficient basis for contradicting and rejecting proposed solutions which are counter-intuitive. However, it is this very characteristic of certain possible solutions which prevents them from being exhausted in unsuccessful attempts to resolve whatever problem is at hand.

Though there has been work on a variety of psychological and psychosomatic conditions at MRI, the factors determining "choice of symptom" have not been definitively established. Learning through modeling, inculcation of a script, and induction of resignation to the power of a self-fulfilling prophecy are mechanisms influencing such "choices." Modeling may also operate through the power of repulsion, that is, by stirring resolve to avoid its repetition. In a sense, example is a powerful form of long-term communication. Other influential forms of communication encouraging the emergence of particular symptoms include the focusing of attention on particular areas. While this may appear to occur contextually, that is, by the mere fact of a parent's occupation, closer examination of such situations reveals that more is going on. For example, *it is almost axiomatic among family therapists at MRI that the symptoms of children relate surprisingly often to the work of one or both parents.* Thus, when we learn that the parents are teachers, we are not surprised to hear that they have come in about a child who is having some form of school problem, either academic or behavioral. Similarly, we are not startled to learn that the child of a lawyer or of a policeman is having repeated difficulties with the law.

It is tempting to interpret such dovetailing of children's symptoms with their parents' careers as evidence that the symptom was somehow selected, either consciously or unconsciously, as the most pinpointed way of punishing their parents for whatever it is that the child is angry about and attributes to them. That there are other possible explanations is illustrated by a case described in a therapy outcome research symposium many years ago. Patients were asked whether therapy had helped them and, if so, how. One young woman told her psychologist that he had particularly helped her to abandon her hypochondriasis, not only because of the insight she had acquired in therapy regarding the fact that her father, a rather emotionally cold physician, paid little attention to her except when she seemed sick, but also because her therapist, a psychologist rather than a physician, had shown that he could not be counted on for rapt attention and endless interest in her physical complaints. This incident leads to a therapeutic application of the linkage between parental occupation and children's symptom. By intentionally displaying a different attitude toward the symptom than that displayed by the parent, the therapist affords an opportunity for extinc-

tion to occur as well as an opportunity for emotional re-education.

Aside from any hereditary predispositions ("diatheses") which may render some family members more vulnerable than others, the individuals may be subject to stress differentially. Such differences may be qualitative as well as quantitative, and may result from inequalities not only in stresses experienced within the family but also in stresses experienced outside the family and even in stresses experienced as conflicts between intrafamilial and extrafamilial demands. A particular member may be identified as the patient by his or her family because of such factors as availability (the only child available to serve as glue for the parents' fragmenting marriage), resemblance (consequent script enactment or prophecy fulfillment based on real or projected similarities to salient others such as when a divorced mother reacts to her custodial son as she would to her divorced husband), and scapegoating (using an expendable decoy to draw fire from an essential family member, such as an overwrought sole wage earner). Sometimes the situations are more complex, as with one couple who had a six-year-old depressed son, whose birth followed almost immediately upon the death of their firstborn, also a son. The couple had tried to have a baby for more than a dozen years without any success. Finally the wife had gotten pregnant. Their long-awaited son developed a brain tumor in his first year. The couple expended their entire savings on several neurosurgical operations, all of which proved futile. The second son, born while both parents were still depressed about the first son's death, was nevertheless looked upon consciously as a welcome replacement. When asked about how they had mourned the death of their first son and when asked to describe the funeral, they said they had never buried him but had had him cremated. The ashes were then put in an urn which was stored in a mausoleum. Every Sunday morning, right up through the time of that session, the parents would visit the mausoleum, take out the urn, rest it on some solid support in front of them, and sit and look at it and beyond it into the distance. The Sunday mornings of their six-year-old, too, were spent in this sad ritual, the continuation of which may have served as a repeated communication to him that he had never quite attained the status of sufficing to enable his parents to move beyond his deceased brother. Thus, it is possible to become a patient because of some pall cast over a person's life in the present by a family ghost from the past.

Though all family members will be affected by the symptomatology or patienthood of any family member, according to general systems theory, they may be affected in different degrees and even in different directions. Thus, there may be a continuum of individual psychopathology within a family, ranging from extremely disturbed to not disturbed at all, other than being upset about one or more of the other family members.

ASSESSMENT OF FAMILY SYSTEMS

In considering how family systems have been assessed at MRI, it is worth bearing in mind several preliminary points. One is that it is important to take note of whether the assessment is conducted in the context of research or in the context of therapy. Techniques imported from the former arena to the latter might easily result in the disenchantment of the family unless they had agreed to participate in a research project. Another preliminary point is that we are as interested in the well-functioning as in the malfunctioning aspects of the family system, particularly in research, since it is in the well-functioning features of families that we may find clues to how to get malfunctioning families back on a better track. Even in therapy we are very interested in how a particular family functions well or used to function well, since such knowledge may provide a foundation for building on strengths as a means of overcoming specific dysfunctions. Since much of the therapy at MRI is focused on symptom removal or at least amelioration, the focus on family strengths is not quite as intense in assessing families in the context of therapy as it would be in the context of research. Such a focus on strengths, however, in the therapy context is particularly valuable and applicable in the tactics of change. Still another preliminary consideration is the orientation of the person conducting the assessment, a point which becomes particularly pertinent in relation to the balance between individual and interactional factors. These are not necessarily simple to distinguish, since individual characteristics or personality features may develop largely through experiences in interacting with others.

System Assessment with Combined Focus on Individuals and their Interaction

MRI presents no monolithic view about the balance between individual and interactional factors in family assessment. Satir and Riskin, perhaps because of the impact on them of the Chicago Psychoanalytic Institute, retained a focus on the individual along with a focus on the family system. Haley, Weakland, Watzlawick and Fisch, on the other hand, adopted the position that the system in its current functioning embodies regularities, patterns and rules, affording information about what would constitute useful changes and how these might be instigated. I once heard Haley call into question the existence not only of personality but even of the individual. I was then stimulated to construct an informal scale to assess the relative emphasis on intrapsychic and interpersonal factors on the part of therapists at MRI and found Satir to have the greatest relative focus on the individual, Haley to have the greatest relative focus on the system, and Jackson in the most central position between the other staff members, an equal number of whom were to be found dispersed in each direction between the mid and most positions. The emphasis on interactional change rather than insight which has characterized the pioneering work at MRI has been put pithily and powerfully by Watzlawick and Weakland (1977):

If, on the other hand, he [the therapist] takes into account the marital interaction as described in the foregoing, he will attempt to discover *what* is going on here and now and not *why* the spouses' respective attitudes evolved in their individual pasts. He will identify their pattern of interaction as well as their attempted solutions (the more-of-the-same quality of their escalating behaviors) and he will then design the most appropriate and effective therapeutic intervention into the present functioning of this human system.

It is not too difficult to see that these two procedures will differ to the point of incompatibility and what may be the most appropriate and correct course of action for the one may be tabooed for the other. What is not equally apparent is that these incompatibilities are the direct result of the discordant and discontinuous nature of the two *epistemologies* underlying the two procedures and not—as is often and naïvely assumed—of a more or less correct view of the nature of the human *mind*. Or, to borrow Einstein's famous remark: It is the theory that determines what we can observe (p. xiv).

Despite doubts raised about the compatibility of intrapsychic and interactional points of view, their combined utility impresses the author for several reasons. Some people seem to change after appearing to obtain insight and, even if this is not due to bringing unconscious impulses under conscious control, it may be due to having provided them with the kind of ceremony that their epistemological socialization has prepared them to accept as the royal road to rational behavior. Moreover, even the most exclusively system-focused therapists at MRI place considerable emphasis on sizing up the individuals involved in the system in terms of who is most likely to change, what kind of approach is most likely to "click," and what sort of language system (usually the patient's own) is most likely to convey the therapist's thought in such a way as to have much appeal to the patient. This attention to particular individuals, so important in the process of framing requests or reframing existing perceptions, need not rest on inferences about intrapsychic processes remote from observable data. Thus, *even for the most staunchly system-oriented therapists, the study of individual styles is salient for designing interventions with precision and leverage.*[3]

Instruments and Observations

The evolving field of conjoint family assessment was reviewed by Bodin (1968), who defined a new category of assessment techniques appropriate to the concepts and methods of conjoint family therapy. This category was distin-

guished by evaluation of interaction patterns of whole and partial families as *systems* requiring simultaneous focus on two or more family members in terms of their interactions. The assessment situation was reconceptualized to emphasize interpersonal factors even more than intrapsychic factors, though in relation to them. The aim was defined as follows:

. . . to find out, not only how the individuals characteristically respond to certain kinds of stimuli, but also what kinds of stimuli these family members characteristically present to one another, and in response to what. Thus, the family members are viewed as participants in interaction sequences that cannot be understood in purely individual terms, because such event chains cannot occur in isolated individuals, except perhaps at an imaginary level. Though the fantasied relationships of family members may be interesting and important, their actual relationships are at least as important and cannot be investigated merely by attempts to integrate individual family members' fantasies into a coordinated picture of the crucial family facts.

One reason why this extrapolation is impossible is that a salient feature of many families is the range and intensity of disparities that bar any integrated picture based on simple summation or comparison of individual points of view. Another factor making such extrapolation a futile exercise is the emergent quality of unpredictable uniqueness in family interaction or, for that matter, in any interpersonal interaction. Indeed, this quality constitutes the defining characteristic of conjoint family therapy. It is extremely difficult to predict family interaction from results of individual testing, because the subject's responses are so largely determined by his relationship with the tester. The best results may therefore reflect the tester-subject relationship to an indeterminate degree, thus actually obscuring analysis of family interaction. It is better to obtain family interaction data in the first place.

Since the investigation of family interaction is still in the experimental stage, there is no widely accepted conceptual scheme suitable for family diagnosis in a formal sense. Normative data on family interaction are still woefully unavailable. Consequently, most family assessment is based on clinical experience and is descriptive of individual cases (p. 224).

---

[3]*Editors' Note.* This is a point worthy of a good deal of emphasis in light of the fact that, in our experience, when clinicians initially become exposed to MRI ideas, they often are mostly impressed by strategic therapists' technical wizardry and do not so readily appreciate the enormous sensitivity to individual differences that such therapists must have.

Research instruments for family assessment devised by MRI staff include an "unrevealed differences" technique (Bodin, 1965, 1969; Ferreira, 1963; Ferreira and Winter, 1965, 1966).

These modifications of the Strodtbeck Revealed Differences Technique (Strodtbeck, 1951) require the individuals to make independent commitments to particular points of view from a finite list and then to agree on a single alternative after each person's individual selection has been revealed to the total group. Relative dominance, flexibility, rigidity in preserving the closest possible approximations to individual preferences, and mutual "spoiling" tendencies reflected in group selection of alternatives not wanted by any individual members comprise some of the features of family functioning which can be observed directly or extracted from these unrevealed differences questionnaires.

The ability to guess which three-color flags had been drawn by which family members was utilized by Ferreira (1963) in his exploration of family myth and homeostasis. Lights and buzzers activated by push buttons were arranged by Haley to fit in three segregated partitions around a circular table for research described in his seminal article, "Family Experiments: A New Type of Experimentation" (Haley, 1962). This landmark article contains eight generalizations Haley made about the criteria for family system experimentation. These include such concepts as the need to study interaction by requiring family members to interact with one another rather than with the experimenter; the necessity for reliability in measurement; the need to assure freedom from contamination by factors such as intelligence, education, or manual dexterity; the importance of having family tasks which all members of the family can accomplish, regardless of their symptomatology; and the need to measure a family's typical functioning rather than its ability to shift under stress, unless that capacity to change is the quality being measured.

A structured family interview was described by Watzlawick (1966) and summarized by Bodin (1968) as follows:

. . . the MRI Structured Family Interview is administered, not by a tape recorder, but by an interviewer who observes parts of the proceedings from another room. The interview is designed to give the interviewer and any observers a wealth of clinically valuable impressions in a space of about an hour. Furthermore, it is designed to interest the family participants in the kinds of mutual exploration it demands, so as to begin engaging them in the tasks of therapy from the outset. Thus, this assessment procedure serves also as a catalyst in the initial stage of therapy and, in fact, is itself often felt to be therapeutic by all concerned. Clinicians who have both given and observed this interview find they can get more out of it when they are freed from the requirements of participation. For this reason, at least within the context of the training of family therapists at MRI, another clinician generally gives the Structured Family Interview while the therapist observes through the one-way mirror. The procedure ends with the interviewer introducing the therapist, who then has a brief discussion with the family about the interview. All five parts of the MRI Structured Family Interview have been vividly presented by Watzlawick (1966).

Numerous variations of the MRI Structured Family Interview have been tried over the past six years in the family therapy training courses at the Mental Research Institute. Some of these variations—introduced by Virginia Satir (1966)—are mentioned briefly below.

In the decision-making part of the interview ("Plan something together"), a series of overlapping stages has been used, with the following family members present at each of these junctures: (a) all, (b) all except father, (c) all except mother, (d) children only, (e) mother and daughter(s), (f) mother and son(s), (g) father and son(s), (h) father and daughter(s), and finally (i) husband and wife. This step-wise sequence permits comparison of all the foregoing combinations, a process akin to the disentangling of relationships that Virginia Satir alludes to as having the complexity of a "can of worms." At the cost of considerably lengthening the interview, this variation sometimes reveals striking contrasts as a function of (sub)group composition. For example, one family's members showed great animation and enthusiastic interaction at all steps except the final one, involving only the marital pair. Their sudden switch to a diametrically opposite emotional climate of interaction could scarcely be attributed to sheer fatigue, particularly in the light of their earlier discussion of how they got together; father described it as, "Just chance, it took months to recognize it; it just evolved," to which mother replied, "It was a *blind* [italics mine] date; it never would have happened except that I was . . . ready to get married." With these bits of information it is reasonable to surmise that the parents rely on their children to infuse an otherwise missing bit of joie de vivre.

Another variation is the addition of a final section on Similarity and Differentness. With the whole family together, father and mother are asked, in turn, "Which one of your children do you think is most like you?" and also, "Which one do you think is most like your wife (husband)?" Each child is then asked, "Which one of your parents do you think you are most like?" Next, each child is asked these stereotype-disrupting questions: "You said you were most like your mother (father). How are you like your father (mother)? How are you *unlike* your mother (father)?" Finally each mate is asked, "How are you like your spouse? How are you different from your spouse?" Even without detailed presentation, it is obvious that such questions provide a basis for summarizing data in an "identification matrix" with potential utility for both research and clinical application.

In one instance a delinquent daughter, whose younger sister had the same first name as her mother, made clear dis-identification with her mother by stating first that she was most like her father, and then that the way she was like her mother was that their little fingers were similar.

As with other conjoint testing procedures, a posttest period of mutual feedback is helpful. The interviewer can often extend his own understanding of the family—as well as theirs—by commenting on some of the interactions, telling them some of his impressions or inferences, and trying to fit these together with any different explanations offered by members of the family (pp. 229–230).

A more detailed analysis of the "Blame" section of the MRI Structured Family Interview has been described above (Watzlawick, Beavin, Sikorski, and Mecia, 1970) along with the method for studying symmetry and complementarity devised by Sluzki and Beavin (1965). Although the sample selection for the work on Family Interaction Scales by Riskin and Faunce (1970) has also been presented above, the major categories themselves were not described but are briefly defined as follows:[4]

1) *Clarity*: "Whether the family members speak clearly to each other."
2) *The topic continuity*: "Whether family members stay on the same topic with each other and how they shift topics."
3) *Commitment*: "Whether the family members take direct stands on issues and feelings with one another."
4) *Agreement and disagreement*: "Whether family members explicitly agree or disagree with one another."
5) *The affective intensity*: "Whether family members show variations in affect as they communicate with one another."
6) *The quality of relationship*: "Whether family members are friendly or attacking with one another."

A method of analysis of a family interview, somewhat informal though detailed, was described by Jackson, Riskin and Satir (1961). This analysis of the first five minutes of a family therapy interview was made from two viewpoints: 1) communication theory, concerned with the formal aspects of the interaction, and 2) the interacting dynamics of the spouses, emphasizing how the needs and defenses of each are affected by and affect the other. Satir (1967) offers guidelines for taking a family life chronology. Because of the detailed nature of the 22 pages of recommendations made by Satir, only her 52nd and final point will be presented here, along with her rough flow chart for the whole procedure:

52) The chronology listed here is really a general plan from which the therapist deviates, depending on responses he receives to questions.

(a) Via this plan, he introduces new concepts into the family's ideology, concepts to which he will return in later sessions.

(b) Via this plan, he can move quickly but safely into his role as therapist, find out what he needs to work on first, what can wait. He behaves like a dentist who asks the patient "Where is the pain?" and then proceeds to look where the patient points and explore further. He relies on the family to help him, but he never forgets that he is the leader of the therapy process (p. 134).

At MRI the assessment of family functioning has been separate from treatment only when it has been undertaken exclusively for the purposes of research. In the clinical context, assessment is both an early and a continuing part of the treatment, though its early emphasis is on sizing up the family system and its problems, while its later focus is on sizing up changes in the family system in response to attempted interventions.

Some of the assessment techniques described above have been used in family therapy, par-

---

[4]A detailed manual for the entire scoring procedure is available from Jules Riskin at MRI, as is a new, briefer and therefore more widely applicable form of the Family Interaction Scales.

TABLE 1
Main Flow of Family-Life Chronology
to Family as a Whole:

Therapist asks about the problem

TO MATES:

Asks about how they met, when they decided to marry, etc.

TO WIFE:	TO HUSBAND:
Asks how she saw her parents, her sibs, her family life.	Asks how he saw his parents, his sibs, his family life.
Brings chronology back to when she met her husband.	Brings chronology back to when he met his wife.
Asks about her expectations of marriage.	Asks about his expectations of marriage.

TO MATES:

Asks about early married life. Comments on influence of past.

TO MATES AS PARENTS:

Asks about their expectations of parenting. Comments on the influence of the past.

TO CHILD:

Asks about his views of his parents, how he sees them having fun, disagreeing, etc.

TO FAMILY AS A WHOLE:

Reassures family that it is safe to comment.

Stresses need for clear communication.

Gives closure, points to next meeting, gives hope.

From V. Satir, *Conjoint family therapy*. Palo Alto, CA: Science and Behavior Books, 1967, p. 135. Reprinted with permission.

ticularly the structured family interview and, perhaps most of all, the individual therapist's modification of the family life chronology. Home visits have been used to learn about families in research and training contexts, as well as in the context of therapy, where it has received its greatest use from the staff of MRI's affiliated Emergency Treatment Center, as described by Everstine, Bodin and Everstine (1977). Not only can a family's general life-style be sized up from "the grand tour" of all the rooms during the home visit, but also an opportunity is provided for the therapist to experience the serendipity of noticing and comprehending the meaning of details which would probably never have been mentioned in the course of office therapy.

Thus, an early morning home visit which included observing the family at breakfast elucidated the fact that the parents sat at opposite ends of the dinette table with all three children crowded on one side of the table, elbowing each other and complaining loudly, causing consternation and crossness on the part of both parents, who commented angrily that the day had started magnificently once again. I later asked why at least one child was not seated across from the other two rather than alongside them, and was informed that it was only because of my presence at this particular breakfast that the family had departed from its usual practice of watching television throughout breakfast, placing the set on the opposite side of the table!

On another occasion, I went to the home of an alcoholic woman in response to a telephone call from the police, who had been called there because she was suicidal. During the home visit I asked for a cup of coffee and caught a glimpse of a huge spice rack out of the corner of my eye while entering the kitchen behind the wife. I commented, "Wow, what a spice rack!" But the husband replied, "Look again, Doc; that's no spice rack. It's my pride and joy—my collection of airline liquor bottles, all in mint condition!" I was then able to use this new information by saying to the husband, whom I knew to be almost as pious as his wife, "You devil! You're supposed to be God-fearing people who know about the devil and temptation. And you put your pride and joy in the one room where your woman spends most of her time so she'll have to look at it all day long." The woman fell to her knees and literally grasped my knees, saying, "Thank God! Somebody sees at last!"

The main approaches to family assessment at MRI are through face-to-face interviews and concomitant behaviorial observation. In the brief therapy described by Weakland, Fisch, Watzlawick and Bodin (1974), the system is assessed largely in terms of its impasses, which reveal themselves as symptoms or problems. Two main questions comprise the backbone of the assessment process in this framework. The first is: "What do *you* see as the main problem or problems?" (This question may be asked of the family members individually, without the others present, a practice I frequently follow in order to gain one-to-one rapport and provide opportunities for vital but utterly private statements such as, "I'm *going* to get a divorce."; "Fix my husband so he doesn't kill himself, as he's tried to three times before!" However, in the context of MRI's Brief Therapy Center the family members or at least the parents are usually seen jointly throughout the assessment which goes on during the first session.) The responses to the therapist's request for each member's view of the main problem or problems can be of two basic types: clear or vague. Vague replies require clarification; they probably indicate a vague style of thinking and perhaps even some commitment to evasiveness or habit of keeping things undefined, in either case suggesting that the particular patient will not respond well to forthright requests to be more specific. Techniques for evoking more details have been evolved at the Brief Therapy Center but are not germane here.

The second main question developed at the Brief Therapy Center for assessing families (or for that matter, couples or even individuals) is designed to follow a satisfactory response to the first main question, and is usually presented about like this: "How have you been trying to deal with these problems so far?" Recalling what has already been stated about three main mismanagement styles which can convert ordinary life difficulties into "Problems," the reader can relate the response to this question and the direction the therapist must *not* take. Whatever it is that has been tried so far is precisely what is *not* working. In some few instances, the failure of the attempted solution has been due to inadequate resources, poor timing, less than optimal delivery; but more often, the failure is due simply to the fact that the appropriate remedy was overlooked precisely because it was counter-intuitive! Thus, something new is called

for rather than more of the same.

GOAL-SETTING

For the sake of continuity, the Brief Therapy Center goal-setting technique is presented next, necessitating only a slight postponement of our broader consideration of goal-setting. Once the problems and their unsuccessfully attempted solutions have been presented, it is tempting to assume that the goals can be inferred. While this is usually true, amounting to nothing more than the alleviation of any problems which the patients have agreed upon, *the goals of therapy do not invariably flow with such obvious ease from the mere statement of the problems*. For example, a husband and wife might disagree about the definition of the problems. Or, as a subtler example, a husband and wife might agree that their problem is that they receive too much criticism and argue too much; yet one may propose the solution (goal) of getting divorced while the other may propose the solution of improving the marriage. *The therapist, in such an instance, must take both proposed solutions into account in formulating some goal of his or her own*. If each spouse is willing to tell the other one his or her proposed solution, then the therapist can propose trying them in sequence, probably proposing that the first solution to be tried would be improving the marriage, on the basis that success might change the mind of the partner who is initially favoring separation.

Some goals have been propounded as useful for all family therapy cases, but just which goals are so regarded is a function of which staff members are asked and at what point in the evolution of family therapy at MRI. Thus, Satir (1967) emphasized maturation, functional communication, self-esteem, unlabeling the "identified patient," and handling the presence of differentness. Although she then explores what each individual wishes to accomplish through the therapy, Satir provides the following suggestion for the therapist to present his or her own orientation:

"As you know, we work with families here. And we have found that when one member has pain, all share this pain in some way. Our task is to work out ways in which everyone can get more pleasure from family life. Because I am sure that at one time this family had better times."

By speaking in general, the therapist prevents any specific member from feeling responsible for the unhappiness in the family.

Also, by accentuating the idea of pleasure as the goal of therapy, the therapist continues to decrease fear and increase hope.

Finally, by talking about "what we see" in families, the therapist uses his special knowledge about families in order to help family members to see themselves as not *especially* bad or hopeless (pp. 117-118).

In spoofing the more amorphous forms of family therapy, Fisch, Watzlawick, Weakland and Bodin (1973) stated:

There are better, less crude ways of firmly implanting in the minds of all concerned your own certainty that family therapy is a long-term, open-ended process of restructuring personalities and changing deep-rooted patterns of communication and of family homeostasis. It is usually best to deal with this question subtly. Announce in a matter-of-fact way, "I have Tuesday at 3:00 open now, so that will become our regular hour." One may then inquire about "parental models," the nature of their parents' marriage, how they were raised by their parents, etc., but perhaps the most effective way is to translate all marital or family complaints into forms of "communication difficulty." From long experience we can guarantee that with a minimum of effort you can thereby dispel any naive notions of rapid change—so that even if rapid change were somehow to occur in the course of treatment, the family would themselves realize that they must be doing the right thing for the wrong reason, i.e., that they were merely escaping into health. By no means should the therapist encourage any discussion about concrete goals of treatment, since the family would then know when to stop treatment (pp. 600-601).

Writing in a more serious vein, Weakland, Fisch, Watzlawick and Bodin (1974) state the first principle of their work as follows:

We are frankly symptom-oriented, in a broad sense. Patients or their family members come with certain complaints and accepting them for treatment involves a responsibility for relieving these complaints. Also, since deviant symptomatic behavior and its accompanying vicious circles of reaction and counter-reaction can themselves be so disruptive of symptom functioning, we believe that one should not

hasten to seek other and deeper roots of pathology. *The presenting problem offers in one package what the patient is ready to work on, a concentrated manifestation of whatever is wrong, and a concrete index of any progress made* (p. 147, emphasis added).

These early members of MRI's Brief Therapy Center did not specify any universally applicable treatment goal; they did specify that the goal was to resolve the problems, usually situational difficulties involving interaction between people, such as a family and their identified patient. They specified that such problem resolution entailed substituting behavior patterns which would interrupt the vicious, positive-feedback circles maintaining the dysfunctional behavior. They advocated accepting what the patient offers, and reversing whatever principles have been unsuccessfully applied to the resolution of the problem at hand (whether the usual "treatment" or the "common sense" of the patient, the patient's family, and friends). Such reversal is designed to disengage the unsuccessful problem resolution approaches which are regarded as precisely the force which has been maintaining the problem. These authors also advocate focusing on *what* is occurring in human interaction systems, *how* such functioning is maintained, and *how* it may be most effectively altered—avoiding the question, "Why?" That latter question is viewed as promoting a focus on highly inferential intermediate motivational states and voluntaristic conceptions of human behavior, thus distracting the therapist from close observation of concrete behaviors manifesting and maintaining the present problem.[5]

This approach also entails goals which are reasonably small, as well as clearly stated, since enabling the patient to experience a small but definite change in a problem which had seemed fixed is. easier than making progress in more grandiose leaps, and is nevertheless far-reaching, through encouraging additional self-in-

---

[5]*Editors' Note*. It would be quite inaccurate to assert that interactional or strategic views, such as those represented by MRI, avoid asking, "Why?" The MRI view does reflect a strong concern with the causes of psychological events and patterns, yet it proposes a view of causality which is quite different from traditional views of causality among psychotherapists. As is the case in behavior therapy, the use of abstract inference is obviously not necessary in order for an explanatory model to address the issue of causality.

duced changes by the patient in areas beyond the symptom presented. By the application of the principles under discussion, a concrete goal may be set early, though it is subject to revision or the addition of secondary goals.

In selecting a particular goal from all the possible goals for a given family or couple, a therapist may follow a few guidelines set forth by Watzlawick, Weakland and Fisch (1974). They recommend that the goal be *concretely definable* and reachable within the constraints of practicality. These guidelines are designed to steer the therapist away from accepting or devising vague or grandiose goals. Such goals allow therapy to drag on endlessly because of an absence of any criterion for discerning completion, since clarity or conclusiveness will be lacking. The goals selected within the above guidelines will follow further principles, such as pleasing the participants, making theoretical sense to the therapist, and being modest enough to minimize the possibility of evoking discouragement or refusal from one or more of the family members on the basis of difficulty or even impossibility. The most modest of all goals is the request for no change as *yet*, that is, the request that the family keep things as they are a little bit longer, but with the minor modification that more careful note be taken of how this is accomplished. This limiting case, located at the lower bound of possible change, is recognizable as "symptom prescription" which reframes the symptom as behavior occurring under some volitional control rather than through helplessness to halt unwilled drift.

Distinctions between intermediate or mediating goals on the one hand and ultimate goals on the other are handled differently in the contexts of MRI's Brief Therapy Center and the Emergency Treatment Center. In the first instance, a single goal is usually selected, though secondary ones may be added. These may be sequenced according to the therapist's judgment concerning which must be achieved first in order to facilitate the other goal or goals. The secondary goals, then, may have priority in terms of the time at which they are tackled, though not in terms of the overall importance attached to their accomplishment. When used in this way, secondary goals are to the primary goal what tactics are to the overall strategy. On the other hand, secondary goals may simply be desirable outcomes less central than the primary goal, like distant shores eventually reached by the ripples spreading from the attainment of the primary goal. In either case, the primary goal is selected with special attention to how it functions as a fulcrum in maintaining the problem. Similarly, the behavioral target of the primary goal is regarded as analogous to the keystone of an arch supporting itself by translated gravitational forces pressing in from both sides; just as the arch collapses following the removal of its keystone, *the problem may resolve if a sufficiently central symptom-maintaining pattern is disrupted.*

In the Emergency Treatment Center, on the other hand, it is not uncommon for multiple goals to be established in the first session or two of therapy. The sequencing of these goals within the context of ETC's 24-hour-a-day, seven-day-a-week, mobile emergency work is regarded as extremely critical, since escalation has often reached an intensity allowing little loss of time for effective interdiction to halt the rapid rush toward system "runaway," with explosive events which the participants believe themselves powerless to prevent. As in the work of the Brief Therapy Center (BTC), therapists in the Emergency Treatment Center (ETC) do not hesitate to select goals of treatment themselves, though they are guided by what different family members say. Like therapists in the BTC, those at ETC sometimes set treatment goals without discussing their formulations with all or perhaps any of the family members. Such a decision, along the lines of playing one's cards close to one's vest, is usually predicated on some evidence or intuition that one or more of the family members would prove oppositional, and wittingly or unwittingly sabotage the attainment of overt goals arrived at through open and explicit discussion.

Both centers have become very familiar with the deftness of extremely rational, somewhat obsessive-compulsive people (often males in high technology or other scientific fields), who can paralyze the process of change by parrying every therapeutic thrust with some principle of logic.

While feelings and thoughts are viewed as important, behavior is viewed as the bottom line in the family therapy of MRI. It is only through behavior that the affective and cognitive experiences and events are manifested. Attention is paid to nonverbal and verbal behavior, as well as to the "fit" or congruence between these two channels of expression. Thus, as aptly observed by Greenberg (1977):

> While Jackson and his associates, in creating a behavioral format, moved away from mentalistic constructs, they did not deny the existence of internal or intrapsychic mechanisms that influence, alter, and/or facilitate human functioning. In fact, they developed techniques such as "reframing" that were in part designed to affect cognition or "perception." Where they made a major shift was in arguing that one cannot know the perception of another, and that scientifically the best that could be accomplished was to characterize performance, depict behavior, and to operate upon the observable phenomena (p. 403).

Greenberg observes that interactional therapy as developed at MRI is a therapy focused on the modification of behavior without being "behavior modification" therapy. Thus, MRI therapy is behavioral therapy, though not the more widely known and more narrowly defined behavior therapy which derives its technical armamentarium from learning theory. About this relationship without a marriage, Greenberg notes that neither family therapy nor behavior therapy has integrated within its boundaries the fundamental components of the other.[6] He concluded, "The potential integration of classical behavioral approaches and the family interactional perspective represents only one direction along the new pathways that Jackson and his associates pioneered" (pp. 403-404).

TREATMENT APPLICABILITY

Family therapy developed at MRI from theoretical research and clinical work with a wide variety of families and couples. The emerging conceptualizations seem applicable not only to the full spectrum of family systems, but to other human systems as well. General principles have

been applied in families beyond those which contributed to their initial formulation, such as in counseling elders and their families (Herr and Weakland, 1979), as well as in consultation to other organizations, such as probation and police departments. The wide applicability of the principles developed at MRI stems partly from their foundation on applications of *general* systems theory and partly from their explicit insistence that treatment be *specific*, that is, tailored to the problems and participants at hand.

Though there are few families or couples for whom the approaches developed at MRI are inappropriate, their acceptance is relatively uncertain for those families unlikely to be attracted specifically to family therapy at MRI, such as families whose members are devotees of "touchie-feelie" therapies, encounter group experiences, and the almost endless parade of "boredom therapies" immortalized in *The Serial* (MacFadden, 1977), impaled in *Psychobabble* (Rosen, 1977), and described with balance in *The Encounter Game* (Maliver, 1973). Practicing psychotherapy in California, MRI staff members naturally see families, couples and individuals currently or previously immersed in such therapies, and the applicability of MRI principles has been seen with these families. They do not, however, comprise any specific demographic classification, except that whatever avant-garde therapies they have tried have not worked with them. The attraction of these families to such therapies may represent, in some instances, a form of the "Utopia Syndrome," described by Watzlawick (1973) as "extremism in the solving of human problems [which] seems to occur most frequently as a result of the belief that one has found the ultimate, all-embracing answer." The Utopia Syndrome takes three forms: the first involving self-blame for the inability to attain the unattainable, the second involving devotion to endless quest and hence the experiencing of fulfillment as a loss, and the third involving a morally self-righteous mission to encourage all to embrace whatever simplistic premise the true believer has accepted as the ultimate, all-embracing answer and, if need be, to silence dissenters.

Referrals to practitioners of other treatment modalities might be made when the family or

---

[6]*Editors' Note.* Prominent examples of such attempts at integrating behavioral and family interactional approaches can be found in Barton and Alexander (Chapter 11), Weiss (1979) and Birchler and Spinks (1980).

identified patient insists that only chemotherapy—or some other distinctly different form of therapy—will work. Even in such instances, however, some attempt at reframing might be made, such as pointing out that chemicals carry powerful signals not blockable by the conscious mind, and that other ways of generating such powerful signals are available, for example hypnotherapy. If this reasoning is accepted, the application of hypnotherapy is well within the scope of treatment either developed or polished at MRI (Haley, 1963; Watzlawick, 1978).

The question of when *no* treatment of any sort will be recommended is a particularly intriguing one since that amount of treatment is at the extreme limit of brief therapy, an area of intense development at MRI since 1966, when the Brief Therapy Center was founded. A recommendation of no treatment might be made for patients whose problem consists of making too much out of ordinary life difficulties, but such a recommendation would probably not be followed. In fact, it is precisely such patients who are most likely to be therapy addicts who must be weaned by such techniques as tapering off the sessions or, still better, by terminating without termination, as described by Weakland, Fisch, Watzlawick and Bodin (1974) in the following way:

That is, we say we think enough has been accomplished to terminate, but this is not certain; it can really be judged only by how actual life experience goes over a period of time. Therefore, we propose to halt treatment, but to keep any remainder of the ten sessions "in the bank," available to draw on if the patient should encounter some special difficulty later. Usually, the patient then departs more at ease and does not call upon us further (p. 162).

While this last instance does not qualify as an example of recommending no treatment of any sort, it comes close inasmuch as it does exemplify recommending no *further* treatment of any sort by the one means likely to bring this about with therapy addicts: having them remain in what might be termed "dormant therapy."

THE STRUCTURE OF THE THERAPY PROCESS

The most common setting for the application of family therapy as developed at MRI has been the office or clinic, but the setting has also included hospitals; residential alternative treatment centers; and, particularly in the context of the Emergency Treatment Center, any place in the community where the crisis occurs, such as the home, the school, the street, the emergency room, or even the local doughnut shop.

Treatment at MRI has been conjoint, concurrent, individual, marital, family, multigenerational (up to four), and sometimes involving the extended family network. Not all therapists at MRI use all these approaches, but most prize flexibility, and structure their therapy process in whatever way seems most appropriate for the problems and participants at hand. Such structuring may include a combination of individual plus family therapy, as when some individual is perceived as needing an opportunity to ventilate without triggering explosive reactions on the part of other family members. Another such instance would be one in which a marital partner uncertain about whether to continue the marriage wants to do some individual work on this conflict before deciding whether to invest in attempting to improve the marriage; such individual work by the ambivalent spouse might be accompanied by individual work on the part of the other spouse attempting to improve the situation through what amounts to family therapy in absentia, that is, therapy with an individual focused on affecting the marital or family system. The foregoing techniques, which I often use, emphasize working in parallel but not in tandem, that is, working with the same therapist so that there is some coordination without stultifying self-determination. Such concurrent phases may be interwoven with conjoint phases. Also, in the wake of a decision to divorce, I shift from a conjoint to a concurrent approach, that is, if both partners wish continued therapy, so that the format of the therapy reflects the format of the participants' lives, now following separate paths. Riskin and I both refer for individual therapy some teenagers at nest-leaving time who appear to need the most favorable circumstances for facilitating their individuation.

The number of therapists usually involved at MRI varies with the particular context and is sometimes an artifact of that context's training or research requirements. For example, the training context has involved a partner observing all sessions and acting as a peer-consultant, though not participating as a co-therapist. The Brief Therapy Center has typically involved at least three observers acting as peer consultants, free to telephone into the room with questions or advice for the therapist or the patient, or even to enter the room for similar purposes. Such transient transactions permit interventions by someone other than the therapist, a factor sometimes found advantageous when it has seemed important to preclude the possibility of an argument with the person who delivers the question or advice, and when it has seemed worthwhile to spare the therapist the onus of making a particularly painful or provocative remark. Thus, the Brief Therapy Center has capitalized on its format to develop techniques specifically suited to the personnel and physical plant available.

Fitting format to function has been a necessity from the inception of the Emergency Treatment Center. Preliminary "sizing up" of the situation by telephone is usually followed by a mobile response to the home or wherever else in the community the crisis has come to a head. Often the mobile response is made by a team of two, frequently one male and one female, not only because the male provides some safety for the female through at least the appearance of strength, while the female provides some safety for the male through evoking gentlemanly behavior on the part of the typical men present at the scene when ETC responds, but also because the presence of male and female co-therapists allows choice on the part of the individuals we see, increasing the chance that they will be able to relate well to at least one of the two therapists.

In the MRI clinic, on the other hand, therapy has typically been by a solo therapist, though junior staff members and those not yet licensed may be in supervision with some senior staff member. The advantages of co-therapists were explored by Haupt (1972) and include the availability of alternative models and of people from each gender who can either support or disagree so as to give a feeling of safety while eventually challenging sex-role stereotypes. The disadvantages go beyond mere lack of economy in terms of time and money, since few co-therapists have known each other long enough or worked together extensively enough to have developed mutually facilitative teamwork rather than merely keeping out of each other's hair. Such teamwork requires being on the same theoretical wavelength, as is exemplified by the multitherapist approach in the Brief Therapy Center, though usually only one at a time will be present in the therapy room. Co-therapy by therapists not sharing the same theoretical framework or activity level or tempo might be extremely disruptive, particularly if one of the therapists believed in specific planning and tailored tactics while the other believed in "being oneself," "flowing with the energy," and other platitudes of nonspecificity.

The spatial arrangement within the therapy room varies within the particular setting so that, for example, there is a low round coffee table in the room used by the Brief Therapy Center, and the chairs are all the same, namely, "director chairs" (one size fits all). This table strikes a note of informality, while permitting observation of hand-wringing, finger-picking, and foot restlessness, which would be hidden by higher tables that some people therefore prefer. In the home visits which constitute most first sessions for the Emergency Treatment Center, the structural aspect of the therapy room (house) is of vital importance, especially for the safety of the therapist or team. Precautions in approaching the house, sizing it up once inside, and using space so as to foster safety by discouraging violence are issues which have been addressed by Everstine, Bodin and Everstine (1977). Special consideration must be given to spatial factors such as not taking the "papa" chair without papa's permission and seating the others in low sink-in furniture such as couches (but far enough apart to avoid hitting, if tempers seem high), while seating oneself in a firm, higher chair with a straight back so as to facilitate agility in standing up quickly if need be. Potential hazards, such as being cut off from a direct escape route to the door, or sitting in the kitchen where all the knives are within arm's length, or leaving heavy ashtrays near someone fighting to maintain self-control of his or her temper (particularly when shattered glass is already all over the floor), must be noted and considered as a matter of second nature.

In the typical therapy office of MRI staff members, the desk is against the wall rather than dividing a space with the therapist sitting on one side and the patients on the other. The therapist, while sitting *at* the desk, is usually seated sidewise to it rather than *behind* the desk. Thus, the therapist is facing the patients. Most commonly there is a pair of chairs facing the therapist, symbolizing the marital pair, while other chairs in the room or a couch are different from the primary pair. The couple's pair of chairs, if closer to each other than to the therapist's chair, forms the base of a nonequilateral, isosceles triangle. If all three chairs can swivel and tilt, it is surprising how much family interaction gets expressed through utilization of these features. Family interaction may also be expressed through the selection of either of these two somewhat larger chairs by children who rush into the room ahead of their parents. In chaotic families lacking firm limits, such brashness by children goes unchallenged.

Like the room setup, the time structure of therapy at MRI varies with the context. In the externship training programs, the therapy tends to last most of the duration of the training, almost two-thirds of a year. In the Brief Therapy Center, there is a ten-session time limit, but the average treatment is closer to six or seven sessions. Brevity also typifies therapy in the MRI Clinic and in the Emergency Treatment Center, though therapy lasts considerably longer in some instances in each of these settings. In the externship context and the Brief Therapy Center, the sessions are held weekly. While this is not strictly the case in the MRI Clinic and in the private practices of MRI staff members, it tends to be true in the Emergency Treatment Center context only after the situation has calmed down somewhat. In any of the last three contexts it is common for sessions to occur more than once a week if some crisis imparts a sense of urgency, and it is common for the sessions to be spaced at intervals greater than one week as a means of acknowledging success and preparing for termination.

Decisions about therapy structure are made by the therapist in most instances, but by the family in such instances as when one person is out of town on business and the other or others want to have a session anyway, or in such circumstances as when parents tell their therapist that they wish to speak to him or her without the children being present. Sometimes the decisions are made jointly and with the emphasis on therapeutic considerations, while in other instances the decisions are made jointly, perhaps with an emphasis on some scheduled recreational event important to the patient; the therapist may do well to acknowledge the importance of the family's or individual members' having fun and the value of flexibility in recognizing that there is nothing sacred about the typical seven-day therapy interval.

THE ROLE OF THE THERAPIST

In family therapy as developed at MRI, the therapist controls the session to a very great degree. Therapist control may not be overt at all points, since the therapist may appear to be following the patient's lead in various directions. When this is the case, the therapist has probably decided to remain passive, perhaps because of having learned that it is as important to let many comments go by without responding to them, as it is to "pick up" on other comments. Perhaps Haley (1969) has most powerfully put forth the importance of the family therapist's need for technical mastery in his tongue-in-cheek guide for guaranteeing failure as a psychotherapist:

Step B: Refuse to treat the presenting problem directly. Offer some rationale, such as the idea that symptoms have "roots," to avoid treating the problem the patient is paying his money to recover from. In this way the odds increase that the patient will not recover, and future generations of therapists can remain ignorant of the specific skills needed to get people over their problems (p. 56).

MRI therapists tend to be active and directive, using a vast array of techniques, many developed at MRI, ranging from the faintest suggestion, such as appearing to hold the patient back by asking him or her not to change *yet*, to practically coercing change by making the continuation of therapy contingent upon acceptance of a *Devil's Pact*, i.e., by giving the therapist carte blanche, and agreeing in advance to do whatever is asked, a technique particularly useful with obsessive-compulsives and others whose incessant intellectualizations are forever postponing even the smallest concrete steps toward change. This was so for a man in his early thirties, still living at home, not even searching for a job because of his stated ambition to become a golf pro, about which he was doing virtually nothing. He was full of reasons why no other alternative would be good enough. What seemed fundamentally important was to break through his aversion for undertaking any practical task within his capabilities. He was therefore asked to accept a small but vital assignment, without knowing what it was, as a condition for continuation of therapy. The assignment consisted of his painting a room, a task even less complex than the electrical wiring skills he said he had acquired in the armed services. This was readily admitted by the therapist. It is worth bearing in mind that the particular task designed for assignment to the patient, though conceivably of some special symbolic importance, is usually less vital than the crucial component, namely the patient's agreement in advance to take a risk.

Another specific intervention technique used at MRI's Brief Therapy Center encourages *advertising instead of concealing*, that is, calling attention to a characteristic that one fears others may notice, since doing so eliminates the fear by settling the question on one's own terms. For example, a woman successfully treated in five sessions for marital problems involving her parents' reaction to her husband was about to summarize as part of the final session. The therapist, however, noticed for the first time that she had entered the room with a slight limp. He asked whether she had hurt herself and she replied that she had not but that she had been born with a congenital hip condition. At this point a colleague-observer on the Brief Therapy Center staff knocked on the door for permission to enter. Once in the room he addressed the young woman approximately as follows: "I, too, had not previously noticed your faint limp. Would you mind standing up and walking down the room and turning around for me so I can observe it more closely? (She complies.) Ah-h-h-h. *Now* I can barely make it out. You know—it has a kind of nice lilt to it—the way you move your hips (wobbling his right hand from side to side). I wonder whether you have considered the possibility of emphasizing such an attractive characteristic, not only for its aesthetic qualities but also for its tactical possibilities. For instance,

you have mentioned that you and your husband are often among the first to leave dinner parties; with a little teamwork your husband could work in a brief mention of 'my wife's hip acting up' as a graceful way of easing the two of you out of the situation without causing the host and hostess to lose face through feeling you weren't enjoying their company and hospitality."

Still another intervention technique often used in MRI's Brief Therapy Center is *symptom prescription*, often applied as a paradoxical preparation for change to occur in the future. For instance, if a woman in couples therapy has been complaining of orgasmic difficulty and of her husband's anxious inquiries about whether she has climaxed, the therapist might say something to her, with her husband present, about as follows: "What I'm about to ask of you may not seem to make a lot of sense, particularly since you are so eager to make progress with this problem. However, since the problem has persisted for several years, a little bit longer shouldn't be too much of a sacrifice, particularly if it paves the way for progress. (Therapist turns and talks to wife—ostensibly.) Since you are not having an orgasm anyway, I'm going to make a small request of you, namely, that you somehow manage to go on, at least during the coming week, not having an orgasm, but studying and mentally noting the process as you proceed. If, by some mischance, you should happen to feel even the faintest beginnings of what might be an orgasm at any time during the coming week, for goodness sake keep that entirely to yourself no matter how much your husband presses you for details. After all, it's your orgasm, not his!" Aside from relieving the woman of the anxiety to the husband's emotional pressure and demotivating the husband from continuing to subject her to his inquisitions, the woman has been encouraged to interpret the faintest tinglings as signs of success. This latter feature is akin to asking a man complaining of impotence whether he might be able to manage a 1% erection.

Yet another brief intervention technique entails the *harnessing of self-fulfilling prophecies*. More specifically, this technique comprises intentionally designing a prophecy tailored to fulfill itself with the people involved and their situation. To illustrate, a father complaining that his child *never* turns off the light when he leaves his room might be asked to get a still clearer picture of the existing situation so as to be able to have an accurate baseline when improvement is attempted, and in case the father has been forming a general impression rather than noticing specific exceptions to the boy's "irresponsibility." Such a father reported the next week that, to his astonishment, the boy was leaving his light on only 50% of the time rather than 100% of the time as the father had thought. Thus, the logging task, with its framing designed to loosen prematurely crystallized perceptions, served also as a self-fulfilling prophecy designed to get the father to notice behavior not contained within his overgeneralized conclusion. This kind of intervention is like the one that matchmakers used to employ in getting a particular young man and woman interested in each other by alerting each one separately to the alleged interest of the other through planting the thought independently in each by saying, "Have you noticed how Sarah [or David] has been eyeing you with that special look recently?"

Another intervention is *reframing of incomprehensible behavior* so as to begin the unlabeling process through normalizing its appearance. Such demystifying interpretations, as luck would have it, usually contain more than a grain of truth. Thus, parents may be distraught by the distracting actions of their schizophrenic teenager which intensify in synchrony with their involvement in discussing or arguing some point toward an overdue conclusion; the therapist may reframe the youngster's behavior by making some such comment as, "I notice, John, that you have nearly perfected a difficult skill, namely, the art of attracting attention to yourself by your ingenious and imaginative range of unusual behaviors, which only look 'crazy' on the surface level. Actually, you are to be complimented for your rare ability and superb timing and sensitivity in drawing attention away from your parents precisely when it looks as if they are in danger of becoming too heated as the discussion becomes an argument. It would not be accurate to describe what you're doing as 'crazy'; rather, it would be fairer to say that you have been acting 'crazy like a fox,' and so skillfully that your parents had not noticed the method in your 'madness.'"

Another intervention which, like the one just mentioned, does not depend upon the cooperation of the patients, is the *undermining of an existing suspicion by the planting of another and more desirable suspicion.* For example, parents who are sure their own son is always getting into mischief may be so inclined to be suspicious that they will readily accept a substitute suspicion. The therapist might plant this substitute suspicion by talking to the child in front of the parents about as follows: "This week, Sam, whatever else you do, would you make it a point to have some sport with your parents by performing some small good deed in secret so that they cannot possibly catch on to the fact that you have accomplished this."

One of the relatively few interventions that might be suitable for use in the first session would be a symptom prescription for a couple mutually complaining of too much criticism and not enough appreciation. The therapist could say, "What I'm about to ask you may sound nonsensical or even utterly wrong. However, it's not much to ask since you're both already able to do almost all of it as your reported typical behavior at home indicates. Specifically, I'd like you each to keep an accurate and detailed log of each instance in which the other behaves in a way that annoys you. I know this may seem like a lot of trouble, particularly since you're making mental notes of this kind of thing anyway, but I think it's going to be important for us to be certain of eliminating the danger you run of losing track here and there when you keep score mentally. Each night please leave your gripe log on your dresser where your mate is free to look at it if he or she insists on being a masochist. By the way, I'd also appreciate it if you would keep another list—for this one a 3×5 card should be more than enough—just on the off chance that by some quirk your mate does anything that happens to please you. This list is to be kept absolutely secret from your mate, though I would like to have a look at it if there's anything on it next week." Some couples laugh at all this but nothing is lost by their sophisticatedly sensing what is afoot. One not so observable feature of this intervention is that suspicion is planted in the mind of each partner that the continued lack of expressed appreciation during the coming week may, for the first time, be due to something other than sheer inattentiveness or orneriness, i.e., that it may be due merely to "doctor's orders," so that the attempt to earn appreciation may finally be worthwhile, not stultified by lack of prompt appreciation and encouragement.

An intervention suitable, for example, when parents have exhausted themselves being direct and nice is termed *benevolent sabotage*. The therapist should particularly consider this approach when he can practically see or hear the steam coming out of the parents' ears. The technique essentially consists of surprising the person whose behavior is so upsetting by reacting in a different and more frustrating way than usual, implicitly disclaiming any intention for the action by some only partially irrelevant and thoroughly plausible offhand remark. For example, a teenage daughter returning home at increasingly late and unpredictable hours usually keeps her parents awake and worrying. The therapist can comment to the parents that the typical reaction of a caring mother or father is to appear at the door when the youngster returns home, with an endless sermon or with a look of pained restraint and conspicuous eyeing of one's watch and throat-clearing coughs. The therapist can then say, "I don't know whether you're angry enough to do what I have in mind to ask of you." Sufficiently steamed parents reply, leaning forward to the edge of their chairs, "Try me!" The therapist then explains that the door is to be bolted and chained and that the bedroom lights, usually left on so the parents can intersperse some reading with their wakeful worrying, are to be left off so as to avoid signaling the protective watchfulness which, of course, has continued. The therapist goes on to suggest that when the key is heard jiggling in the lock no move be made to switch on the light, except when the jiggling has become frantic and, in fact, has begun to subside as discouragement sets in. (By now it should be obvious that this technique is best reserved for winter months and most effective in the colder climes.) Suddenly, then, the parents are to turn on the light and one of them is to don a robe and shuffle to the door slowly and with difficulty, opening its various latches, appearing then with hair thoroughly mussed and utterly bleary-eyed. At this point, it will not do to sermonize or cough while referring to a timepiece. Rather, the parent now mumbles, barely audibly but clearly apologeti-cally, "I'm sorry. I don't know how this could have happened. I guess I'm just not myself these days. I'll try not to let it happen again," thus planting the thought that it very well *could* happen again, and perhaps even the more sophisticated inference that the parental upset might stem to some degree from the teenager's handling of time. Of course, such a technique cannot be applied in the same manner with parents who do not have steam coming out of their ears but seem to be eagerly accumulating it, though perhaps with increasing pressure, following a high principle such as turning the other cheek. Such parents should not be asked to try benevolent sabotage, a term infinitely appealing to the former parents, but could be asked to engage their child by sacrificing themselves through suspending their usual approach for one which will demonstrate even more concern and care, namely, true benevolence.

Some Beginning Steps Toward an Intervention Typology. Some elements for an intervention typology are contained in a list prepared by this author for a Brief Therapy staff meeting about ten years ago. This list, designed to identify possibilities sometimes considered by therapists in their treatment planning within the Brief Therapy Center, reflects considerations of openness, coerciveness, and reciprocity:

1. *Context*
   A. *Setting*
      1. Within the sessions
      2. Between the sessions (homework)
   B. *Framing*
      1. Openness to other family members about giving of an assignment
         a. All family members know about the assignment
            i. All family members are present when the assignment is given
            ii. Absent members are to be told about the assignment
         b. Some family members do not know about the assignment
            i. Secrecy is unacknowledged: absent members or those not invited to this session simply do not learn of the assignment
            ii. Secrecy is acknowledged: if

knowledge of the assignment—or of its details—would nullify its effect, members for whom this would be true are asked to wait outside when the assignment is given

2. Openness about the reason(s) for the assignment
   a. Actual reason(s) are explained spontaneously
   b. Actual reason(s) are explained in response to inquiry
   c. Actual reason(s) are withheld, even in response to inquiry
   d. Some other plausible but tangential reason(s) are given

3. Degree of pressure
   a. Permission
      1. Direct
      2. Indirect
   b. Suggestion
      1. Direct
      2. Indirect
   c. Prescription
      1. No consent is sought
      2. Consent is sought after presentation of prescription
      3. Consent is sought before presentation of prescription
      4. Sanctions are specified if prescription is not fulfilled

II. *System Focus*
   A. *Individual assignment is given*
      1. Directly involving only oneself
      2. Directly involving others
   B. *Multiple assignment is given*
      1. Independent assignments, not interlocked by reciprocity
      2. Dependent assignments, interlocked by reciprocity
         a. Symmetrical exchange of behaviors: one mutual interaction loop
         b. Complementary exchange of behaviors: one mutual interaction loop
         c. Paired behavior exchanges: more than one mutual interaction loop, such as in negotiations in which each agrees to do something for the other, and the therapist also

makes or elicits stipulations that the fulfilling of each request is to be responded to by the requester

3. Sequencing
   a. Simultaneous
   b. Specifically sequenced
   c. Unspecified

III. *Substance*
   A. *Mode*
      1. Action (communicating differently, seeking a job, moving, dating, etc.)
      2. Thinking (noting certain events or characteristics of self or others)
      3. Dreaming ("You may have already made up your unconscious mind, and the decision may become clear to you from a dream you might have this week.")
   B. *Content*
      1. Plain English
         a. Stopping something old (direct suggestion)
         b. Trying something new (direct suggestion)
      2. "Reverse English"
         a. Continuing something old (symptom prescription)
         b. Not yet starting something new (indirect suggestion)
      3. Consolidating control over reduced symptom
         a. Reversing the change
         b. Re-reversing the change

Many other specific tactics have been devised at MRI's Brief Therapy Center and are described in Watzlawick, Weakland and Fisch (1974) and in Watzlawick (1978). While detailing these tactics for change is beyond the scope of this chapter, it is pertinent to observe here that the therapist's role includes being aware of the conceptual framework which calls for initiating "second-order change," usually in a counter-intuitive direction, one *inconsistent with the dictates of common sense.* In addition, fulfillment of the therapist's role requires a repertoire of techniques for instigating second-order changes. As Watzlawick (1978) has observed:

At the beginning of this book I mentioned that its

thesis is simple but its application is not. The crucial point remains its practical application—but not in the sense of the old joke: *There is no such thing as piano playing; I have myself tried it several times and nothing came of it.* (p. 160)

Patients talk to the therapist as well as to each other in couple therapy and to one another in family therapy, the particular balance of these kinds of interaction being controlled to a large extent by the therapist's operating within the MRI frame of reference. The degree and direction of self-disclosure and the degree to which the therapist joins or remains outside the family system tend also to be technical decisions under the control of the therapist. At MRI there are therapists who typically remain outside the family system, perhaps because they are more comfortable there or because they believe it gives them a clearer perspective, while others tend to join the family system at least partially, while remaining partially outside it, believing that one foot should feel the turbulence of the troubled family while the other should remain on terra firma. The therapist can avoid being dizzied or drowned in a swirling vortex by restricting his or her immersion in the family system to just "a toe in the water," particularly when presented with what appears to be a raging torrent.

The progress of therapy brings at least some changes in the therapist's role. Initially, the therapist must introduce the format of the therapy, gain rapport, gather enough information to define the problem, surmise what behaviors maintain the problem (by inquiry and observation), and learn enough of the participant's wishes to integrate them with the foregoing information so as to set treatment goals. In the mid-phase of therapy the activity of the therapist consists largely of conceiving and conducting specific behavioral interventions, particularly those designed to instigate second-order change. At the close of therapy, the stance of the therapist must still be tailored to the particular patients, possibly reminding them that the treatment was aimed at initiating some kind of breakthrough which they can continue to enlarge, or, particularly with more negativistic patients, by expressing pessimism about any progress in the future and even some skepticism about the likelihood that present progress will

remain. Termination with potential therapy addicts by stopping treatment while they still have at least one session "in the bank" has already been discussed. There is, of course, some consistency in the therapist's role across these stages of progress. The therapist guides the process at all times, first ascertaining what needs to be done, secondly advising on how to accomplish it, and finally acknowledging progress to some measured degree.

In the era at MRI which preceded the emphasis on the crucial importance of second-order change, a treasure trove of lore about the role and technique of the therapist was provided by Satir (1967). She emphasized such common sense factors as creating a setting with sufficient safety to allow patients to take risks; daring to ask questions and, in so doing, helping the patients to gain courage to follow suit; refusing to make assumptions beyond one's actual knowledge; realizing that people are grateful to be told how they affect others (at least in some instances); demonstrating the giving and getting of information in a non-judgmental manner; building the self-esteem of others; decreasing threat by setting the rules of interaction; interpreting anger as hurt; handling loaded material with care; re-educating the patients for maturity and responsibility; helping patients connect the influence of their past models on their present expectations and behavior; delineating roles and functions so as to reduce chaos; completing gaps in communication and interpreting messages; and, in sum, stimulating hope throughout the process and, eventually, recognizing by many signs of progress that it is time to terminate treatment.

TECHNIQUES OF MARITAL AND FAMILY THERAPY

Although the techniques of therapy with couples and families would appear to be the core of a chapter on the family therapy approach of MRI, other fundamental matters are of at least equal importance, such as the conceptual framework from which interventions are formulated. Suffice it to say that the patients are treated with enough dignity and warmth to foster formation of a therapeutic alliance when this seems feasible or desirable, though mobilizing the oppositional or negativistic tendencies of patients so inclined may be more beneficial in other instances (cf. Fisch, Weakland, and Segal, in preparation; Watzlawick, 1978; Watzlawick, Weakland, and Fisch, 1974).

Changes in structure or transactional patterns are the fundamental kinds of changes sought through instigating second-order changes. Such changes often require the therapist to transcend the patient's logical processes, which may be raising rational objections that serve as roadblocks to progress. Though "homework" is often used in therapy at MRI, it is not usually of a simple "practice makes perfect" or "you try that and he'll reward you" variety; it is more likely to be of a type which is not explained in advance to the patient and thus serves to stimulate the patient's interest in discovering something new about himself or herself either alone or in interaction with others.

Ideally, disengagement of the therapist is determined by the therapist, though in conjunction with progress being made by the patient and also, we would hope, being noted and enjoyed by the patient. When a therapist fails to acknowledge progress on the part of a patient, it communicates that the therapist is more interested when functioning is poor than when it is good. Thus, *failure to recognize and acknowledge progress is one of the most serious technical errors a therapist can make in operating within the MRI therapeutic approach.* This error, in turn, is most likely to occur when the therapist has overlooked the necessity of setting specific goals after having learned the participants' definition of the problems and their perceptions of how these problems have been addressed so far, that is, what kinds of coping attempts have proved unsuccessful. The absence of such solid baseline data makes it difficult or impossible to notice the changes needed in therapy, let alone to be able to bring them about.

Since so much emphasis has been placed on the importance of second-order change and the special role of paradox in paralyzing intellectual, logical rationalizations for preserving the status quo, it is perhaps necessary to devote some attention to the question as to when, if ever, a common sense, apparently rational intervention may be worth trying, perhaps even ahead of one

that dazzles and confuses onlookers and participants because of being counter-intuitive. In other words, we must not overlook the fact that some people relate well to authority and follow directions without having to be told twice, without either forgetting them or going overboard, and without resentment or sabotage. *It is when people appear oppositional either by their interaction style in the therapy sessions or through the interactional history they relate that we may have to resort to "reverse English" tactics.*[7] Such tactics are not designed to "throw the patient for a loop." Rather, they are designed to prevent the patient from "throwing himself for a loop" by persisting in the present patterns of dysfunctional interaction which lack self-correcting feedback loops. Thus, if we are referring to a feedback loop which maintains dysfunctional behavior, it might not be correct to say that we are interested in throwing the patient *for* a loop, but reasonable to say that we aim to throw a patient *from* a loop. This and other features of marital and family therapy techniques are detailed in Sluzki (1978).

CURATIVE FACTORS IN MARITAL AND FAMILY THERAPY

It would, perhaps, be more accurate to speak of helpful or beneficial factors than of curative factors in marital and family therapy, since the concept of cure presupposes the presence of disease. While such a concept makes sense metaphorically for families, it may be clearer to think in terms of dysfunction rather than "disease." The spectrum of methods designed to decrease family dysfunction is a broad one, including such traditional components as gaining rapport, creating a safe atmosphere for self-disclosure, instilling hope, fostering self-esteem, encouraging responsibility, providing feedback so that one can learn to see oneself as others see one and to manifest oneself more congruently

---

[7]*Editors' Note.* For a comprehensive and detailed discussion of these paradoxical interventions, see Stanton (Chapter 10). Also note Papp's (1980) position that ". . . paradox is neither always necessary nor desirable . . . [its use depends on] the degree of resistance to change in that part of the system that the symptom is regulating . . . if [the system] is responsive to direct interventions, there is no need to resort to the use of paradox" (p. 46).

in terms of expressing what one is actually feeling, and gradually gaining trust as others receive gently the direct communication of wishes the patient has finally risked expressing.

These are among the many factors espoused by Satir (1967). Such methods allow for the possible utility of both historical-genetic insight and interactional insight, the first being gained in the course of participation in providing the therapist with the "family life chronology," and the latter being gained in the course of receiving increasingly honest feedback as the tolerance for differentness improves, and along with it the trust that others will not punish those who risk openness. In Satir's approach there is considerable emphasis on the learning of new skills, particularly in the realm of clear, direct and specific communication, but also in the realm of becoming an accurate observer of the actions of others and of one's own feelings, and an expressive reporter of these observations at increasingly appropriate times. Such skills may be taught didactically, shaped by the expression of appreciation as their approximations occur naturalistically during treatment, or encouraged through modeling by the therapist. Thus, the therapist's personality and psychological health play an important part in conjoint family therapy as conceived by Satir.

Though Satir's approach includes such elements as reframing, the systematization of second-order change factors is most intensive in the context of MRI's Brief Therapy Center. As described by Weakland, Fisch, Watzlawick and Bodin (1974) and by Watzlawick, Weakland and Fisch (1974), the MRI Brief Therapy Center principles of problem resolution are applicable in the therapy of individuals as well as of couples and families. These principles include an emphasis on observable behavior in the present rather than on historical genetic factors, since intrapsychic insight is not regarded as the royal road to change, although it may follow as an epiphenomenon or ex post facto rationalization as a result of change instigated through any of a number of techniques for reframing or behavioral prescription. Within this framework, *interpretations are not offered in order to initiate insight, though they may be presented as part of a reframing or as a means of persuading a patient to carry out a symptom prescription.*

While the learning of new skills may be seen as important, they are not taught through didactic, shaping, or modeling means; rather, they are more likely to be discovered and appreciated by the patient as a result of the experience and feedback obtained in the course of carrying out a symptom prescription.

The therapist's personality and psychological health play a relatively small role in such an approach, except inasmuch as they may interfere with the disciplined focus required.[8] Naturally, extreme instances of uncaringness, lack of warmth, or tactlessness can ruin therapy of any kind, no matter how well conceived. It would also be fair to surmise that the therapist's personality makes some difference in the approach being described, in that it requires a combination of information-gathering and integrating skills, ability to interact in a way that appears free and easy while actually being highly controlled, and considerable restraint against such temptations as "picking up on" interesting but trivial tangents and seeking to appear smart by demonstrating accurate empathy where it might be preferable to keep the patient doing more of the work and the therapist appearing in a more "one-down" position.

Thus, knowing what *not* to say is as important as knowing what *to* say, particularly in a directive form of therapy, since techniques and tactics are of such importance in this approach. Importance is attached to the abandonment of the usual therapy assumptions, such as: "Problems have deep roots which took a long time to develop and will take a long time to change"; "these roots are unconscious and this fact necessitates looking beneath the surface of the patient's presenting problems, since these are only a superficial or surface manifestation of the underlying trouble"; "depth is directly related to duration of therapy"; and "chronicity necessitates long-term treatment." To take only the

---

[8]*Editors' Note.* While this position is conceptually consistent with other aspects of the MRI approach, and while the contribution of therapist factors to the outcome of MRI-type therapy has rarely been studied directly (cf. Barton and Alexander, Chapter 11), the weight of evidence from other technique-heavy therapies, such as behavior therapy (Wilson and Evans, 1977), is that therapist-patient relationship factors play a very central role in facilitating positive treatment outcomes.

last assumption, for example, its acceptance could become a negative or deleterious self-fulfilling prophecy, while its rejection could permit the intentional application of a positive or beneficial self-fulfilling prophecy, such as by saying to the identified patient or family, "You certainly have suffered greatly and patiently. I wonder whether this suffering has been enough for you to feel entitled to some self-pity or, better yet, relief?"

The parataxic distortions of transference and countertransference are neither greatly utilized nor regarded as risks in marital and family therapy at MRI, since the framework is not psychoanalytic and the actual family members are available for participation, so that transference is a less vital phenomenon than it would be in the absence of the actual "significant others." In their seminal paper on transference, Jackson and Haley (1963) stated:

The fact that psychoanalysis could not be conducted without an emphasis upon understanding does not mean that self-understanding is causal to change: paradoxical factors in this peculiar relationship appear equally important as a cause of change. . . . When one shifts from a focus on the individual to an interpersonal orientation, many problems in psychotherapy appear in a different light (pp. 370-371).

The question, "Must each family member change?" is a particularly interesting one in family therapy. It has a certain undecidability, since people have the power to disprove whichever position the therapist takes. Thus, there is a curious relationship between the concept of interactional linkage through joint system membership, on the one hand, and individual responsibility and free will, on the other. Few family therapists today would automatically accept the concept that a particular family cannot change if one of the members is unavailable to participate in the process, through being either geographically or emotionally remote and disengaged. It is true that the return of such a member to the family fold, once he or she sees that the family is changing without benefit of his or her input, may be followed by some desperate sabotage, such as the redefinition of symptom disappearance as a new form of pathology. In this regard, the patient's family mimics those therapists who ignore early signs that it is time

to terminate by discounting the disappearance of the presenting problem as a "flight into health," thus inadvertently revealing also their conviction that there is no technique within their repertoire which could have produced rapid yet genuine improvement.

The therapist's own attitude upon the termination of treatment will very probably determine "how well the stitches hold." With straightforward patients it is probably best to acknowledge their progress, making sure not to claim any credit for their achievement, lest some ornery impulse be stimulated which might undo the results. With worrisome patients, it may be in order to predict or prescribe a relapse followed by a re-recovery, a sequence which gives greater confidence in the trustworthiness of the outcome. With negativistic patients, some skepticism may be useful, and if the negativism takes the form of addiction to therapy, the technique of leaving one session "in the bank" is a useful one since the patient thinks long and hard before using up this final session.

EFFECTIVENESS OF THE APPROACH

Stringent criteria along the lines of goal attainment scaling were employed in evaluating the results of the first 97 cases seen within the context of MRI's Brief Therapy Center. It would have been desirable to have obtained two sets of cases: one in which the therapist's goals for behavior change had been met and the patient's problem completely resolved, and one in which neither of these conditions was present. No such neatness was to prevail, however, for there were cases in which the therapist's goal was reached or approached and much improvement was evident but without complete resolution of the presenting problem. There were also some cases in which the goal had not been formulated in sufficiently explicit and concrete terms to permit any check on its achievement with certainty. Finally, there were still other cases in which the planned changes occurred but did not bring relief or did not occur although relief came anyway. The data were finally reduced to three outcome criteria: 1) success (complete relief of the presenting complaint); 2) significant improvement (clear and considerable, but not complete, relief of the complaint); and 3) failure (little or no change). The first 97 cases involved an average of 6 sessions and resulted in 39 successes (40%), 31 significant improvements (32%), and 27 failures (28%). Weakland, Fisch, Watzlawick and Bodin (1974) concluded that, "These results appear generally comparable to those reported for various forms of longer-term treatment."[9] (In case any confusion has arisen in the mind of the reader concerning the relationship between MRI's brief therapy and family therapy approaches, suffice it to say that the Brief Therapy Center, while sometimes seeing individuals, sometimes couples, and sometimes families, has some conjoint or otherwise family-focused treatment in about 98% of its cases.)

While much anecdotal evidence exists from MRI trainees and staff conferences, this will not be cited as "evidence," since we take seriously the kinds of considerations raised by Meehl (1977) in his essay on "Why I Do Not Attend Case Conferences." There is, however, one additional source of hard data about the effectiveness of the MRI approach to family (and brief) therapy. It comes from the evaluation of the first two years of a contract under which the Emergency Treatment Center senior staff members provided all the psychotherapy services for a local police department. Goal attainment scaling was used to evaluate treatment outcome. Of 52 deputies seen in the first year, 32 were seen with their spouses; of 72 deputies who started therapy in the second year, 37 were seen with their spouses. Twenty-five additional collateral clients were seen over these two years. Visits averaged 8.5 per case during the first year and 6.9 during the second year. Primary objectives were met in 30 of the 34 cases closed in the first year and in 60 of the 76 cases closed in the second year. It should be noted, however, that this 82% success rate in meeting the principal objectives was attained over *all* cases completed

during the first two years; couple and family therapy cases were not analyzed separately but did comprise almost two-thirds of all cases.

There is no shortage of questions remaining to be answered by future empirical study. Questions of efficacy and limitations, indications and contra-indications abound for MRI therapies; all need research attention through systematic clinical trials.[10]

TRAINING OF MARITAL AND FAMILY THERAPISTS

In evaluating Satir's family therapy training program at MRI, I (Bodin, 1971) noted a number of questions about the focus of family therapy training. In discussing these with Haley, I became aware that such questions can be couched as dichotomous choices ("either/or") or as matters of relative emphasis ("both/and"). I presented these questions as follows:

A number of important training issues have been brought into focus, though not completely resolved, by the experience at MRI. Those remaining unresolved are questions of balance, involving optimizing the "mix" of several values so that integration may be appropriate to the particular course. Ideological issues include the balance between interpersonal and intrapsychic points of view, action, and insight-oriented interventions, the seminal viewpoint of one pioneer and an eclectic spectrum of views. Pedagogical issues include: the balance between theory and practice, studying and treating families, prestructuring and evolving the course with trainee participation in decisions, personal style, lecture and discussion, observation and doing, substantive feedback by video and audiotape, and unaided observer feedback; supervision by the teacher and outside consultation; task-centered teaching and supervision and trainee-centered teaching and supervision, with personal and perhaps therapeutic elements. Training needs include more knowledge of when to see which subgroups within a family, a new interactional vocabulary, earlier and more continuous teaching of family therapy, audio and videotape libraries, co-teachers, more knowledge on therapist selection of families, and balancing brief therapy of several families and extensive

---

[9]*Editors' Note*. In fact, this was not a controlled study, the patient population treated was quite heterogeneous, and the treatments not well specified, so that generalizations drawn from the study reflect these limitations. The outcome criteria used in the Weakland et al. study were symptom-focused and unidimensional and, therefore, not easily compared with the results of research on other forms of psychotherapy, which very often include multidimensional assessment of change, including nonsymptom-focused criteria.

[10]*Editors' Note*. In light of the high degree of emphasis within MRI family therapy approaches on achieving visible, concrete change, it is indeed striking that, to date, no well controlled empirical tests of the efficacy of these approaches have yet appeared.

therapy of one family (p. 127).

The question of whether a family therapist should learn individual therapy at all, and if so, whether this should precede, accompany, or follow the learning of family and marital therapy is an interesting and significant one. However, I have not heard of any empirical research on this question or, for that matter, any formal or informal curriculum experimentation to gain even a rough impression of the relative costs and gains of each of these three sequences of learning.[11] One might argue that there is an "experiment of nature" in California, inasmuch as there are literally thousands of graduate students preparing for licensure as Marriage, Family, and Child Counselors, often in programs with marriage counseling titles and receiving marital therapy training first, if not exclusively. Since the duration and content of such training are different from that of psychiatrists, psychologists, and licensed clinical social workers, it would be difficult if not impossible to make meaningful comparisons.

The question of whether previous personal therapy is important is as intriguing for family therapists as for individual therapists. The fact is that the overwhelming proportion of psychiatrists and clinical psychologists have had some form of individual or group psychotherapy, but I am unaware of data indicating what the proportion is of family therapists who have experienced family therapy. I may have come close to a "first" of some kind by asking my psychoanalyst in 1956 to see my girlfriend; the request was denied, but the Zeigarnick effect may have exerted some career development influence in the direction of family therapy. It would be going too far, however, to conclude from this that the absence of experiencing family therapy is important to the development of family therapists!

The question of whether paraprofessionals can do marital or family therapy as taught by the MRI approach is perhaps possible to answer, since Haley participated in the early development of this approach at the Philadelphia Child

Guidance Center and has, in fact, trained paraprofessionals to do family therapy. The specific focus on observable behavior rather than on high level inferences renders MRI's brief therapy approach particularly suited for bright paraprofessionals. The actual application is more complex than the conceptual formulation; however, some attempt has been made to teach paraprofessionals to make limited applications of these concepts, for example, in an MRI training series for Primary Care Associates (physician's assistants). The training was strictly didactic and aimed at such skills as interviewing and at recognition and clarification of behavioral and relationship aspects of complaints brought to physicians' offices. Thus, it did not permit us to draw conclusions about how well paraprofessionals can learn to do marital and family therapy according to MRI's approach.

The question of the usefulness of co-therapy as a training device has not arisen much at MRI. Difficulties with co-therapy have already been alluded to, so two advantages of its application in therapy will be mentioned here. Due to the diffusion of responsibility and dilution of pressure, co-therapy might provide a relatively comfortable mode of entry into the field. A rather different advantage may be that, in the linking of a junior therapist (trainee) with a senior therapist, the latter may utilize the reality of their discrepant experience levels by asking directly that the junior co-therapist observe much and say little. This technique has been advocated as a means of modeling clear role differentiation for chaotic families whose parents are unable to make specific requests and structure appropriate generational boundaries (MacGregor, Ritchie, Serrano, Schuster, McDonald and Goolishian, 1964).

What is an ideal program of training, especially in light of the therapeutic approach developed and represented by MRI? Family therapy training requires integration of theory and technique. Variety and flexibility characterized the early family therapy training offered by Virginia Satir and many other teachers in the early years of MRI. They used teaching aids and techniques, including audiotapes, videotapes, observation, specific structured techniques for assessment and therapy, information on the results of family research, interactional techniques

---

[11]*Editors' Note.* See Kniskern and Gurman's (1979) extensive discussion of the many issues in the training of family therapists which have not yet been addressed by research.

resting on the trainee group's examination of its own ongoing process, demonstrations, participation in simulated family interviews, receiving supervision, doing supervised supervision, and consultation with individually-assigned family therapists outside the formal structure of the course.

This early experience spanning the first decade of MRI's history evolved into briefer workshops on more specialized topics in response to the increasing sophistication of family therapists in the San Francisco Bay Area. In our current workshops and externships, while we encourage a certain amount of familiarity with pertinent literature, our main emphasis is on helping the trainees arrive at a conceptually clear framework for formulating specific interventions tailored to the problems and participants at hand. Opportunity to observe and give feedback and be observed and receive feedback is an essential part of the experience designed to help trainees integrate the theoretical and applied aspects of our externship programs. Some of this feedback is by videotape, using techniques among those described by Bodin (1977). The application of MRI principles is not as simple as it looks or as the conceptualization would imply. Fortunately, this difficulty and complexity afford some challenge, just as putting these principles into practice affords the dual satisfactions of engaging in a form of therapy which is frequently fun as well as effective.

REFERENCES

Bateson, G. *Naven* (2nd ed.). Stanford, CA: Stanford University Press, 1958.

Bateson, G., Jackson, D. D., Haley, J., & Weakland, J. Toward a theory of schizophrenia. *Behavioral Science*, 1956, *1*, 251-264.

Berger, M. M. (Ed.). *Beyond the Double Bind: Communication and Family Systems, Theories, and Techniques with Schizophrenics.* New York: Brunner/Mazel, 1978.

Bertalanffy, L. von. An outline of general systems theory. *British Journal of the Philosophy of Science*, 1950, *1*, 134-165.

Bertalanffy, L. von. *General Systems Theory.* New York: George Braziller, 1968.

Beukenkamp, C. *Fortunate Strangers.* North Hollywood, CA: Newcastle Publishing Co., 1971.

Bodin, A. M. *Family Interaction, Coalition, Disagreement, and Compromise in Problem, Normal, and Synthetic Family Triads.* Doctoral dissertation, State University of New York at Buffalo, 1965.

Bodin, A. M. Conjoint family assessment: An evolving field. In P. McReynolds (Ed.), *Advances in Psychological Assessment* (Vol. 1). Palo Alto, CA: Science & Behavior Books, 1968.

Bodin, A. M. Family interaction: A social-clinical study of synthetic, normal, and problem family triads. In W. D. Winter & A. J. Ferreira (Eds.), *Research in Family Interaction.* Palo Alto, CA: Science & Behavior Books, 1969.

Bodin, A. M. Family therapy training literature: A brief guide. *Family Process*, 1969, *8*, 272-279.

Bodin, A.M. Training in conjoint family therapy. In *Project summaries of experiments in mental health training.* Chevy Chase, MD: National Institute of Mental Health, U.S. Department of Health, Education and Welfare, 1971.

Bodin, A. Family violence. In D. Everstine & L. Everstine (Eds.) *Violent Interaction.* Book in preparation.

Bodin, A. M. Videotape applications in training family therapists. In P. Watzlawick & J. H. Weakland (Eds.), *The Interactional View.* New York: W. W. Norton & Co., 1977.

Everstine, D. S., Bodin, A. M., & Everstine, L. Emergency psychology: A mobile service for police crisis calls. *Family Process*, 1977, *16*, 281-292.

Ferreira, A.J. the "double bind" and delinquent behavior. *Archives of General Psychiatry*, 1960, *3*, 359-367.

Ferreira, A. J. Family myth and homeostasis. *Archives of General Psychiatry*, 1963, *9*, 457-463.

Ferreira, A. J., & Winter, W. D. Family interaction and decision-making. *Archives of General Psychiatry*, 1965, *13*, 214-223.

Ferreira, A. J., & Winter, W. D. Stability of interactional variables in family decision-making. *Archives of General Psychiatry*, 1966, *14*, 352-355.

Fisch, R., Watzlawick, P., Weakland, J. & Bodin, A. On Unbecoming Family Therapists. In A. Ferber, M. Mendelsohn & A. Napier (Eds.) *The Book of Family Therapy.* Boston: Houghton Mifflin, 1973.

Fisch, R., Weakland, J. & Segal, L. *The Tactics of Change.* Book in preparation.

Frankl, V. E. Paradoxical intention. *American Journal of Psychotherapy*, 1960, *14*, 520-535.

Freud, S. *The Origins of Psychoanalysis: Letters to William Fliess.* New York: Basic Books, 1954.

Fry, W. F., Jr. The marital context of an anxiety syndrome. *Family Process*, 1962, *1*, 245-252.

Greenberg, G.S. *Conjoint Family Therapy: An Entree to a New Behavior Therapy.* DSW Dissertation, Tulane University, New Orleans, 1974.

Greenberg, G. S. The family interactional perspective: A study and examination of the work of Don D. Jackson. *Family Process*, 1977, *16*, 385-412.

Greenberg, G. S. Problem focused brief family interactional psychotherapy. In L. R. Wolberg & M. L. Aronson (Eds.), *Group and Family Therapy 1980.* New York: Brunner/Mazel, 1980.

Haley, J. The family of the schizophrenic: A model system. *American Journal of Nervous & Mental Disorders*, 1959, *129*, 357-374.

Haley, J. Observation of the family of the schizophrenic. *American Journal of Orthopsychiatry*, 1960, *30*, 460-467.

Haley, J. Family experiments: A new type of experimentation. *Family Process*, 1962, *1*, 265-293.

Haley, J. Marriage therapy. *Archives of General Psychiatry*, 1963, *8*, 213-234. (a)

Haley, J. *Strategies of Psychotherapy.* New York: Grune & Stratton, 1963. (b)

Haley, J. The art of being schizophrenic. *Voices*, 1965, *1*,

133-142.

Haley, J. (Ed.). *Advanced Techniques of Hypnosis and Therapy: The Selected Papers of Milton H. Erickson, M.D.* New York: Grune & Stratton, 1967.

Haley, J. An interactional explanation of hypnosis. *The American Journal of Clinical Hypnosis,* 1958, *1*(2), 41-57. Reprinted in D. D. Jackson (Ed.), *Human Communication, Volume 2: Therapy, communication, and change.* Palo Alto, CA: Science & Behavior Books, 1968.

Haley, J. *The Power Tactics of Jesus Christ and Other Essays.* New York: Grossman Publishers, 1969.

Haley, J. *Uncommon Therapy: The Psychiatric Techniques of Milton H. Erickson, M.D., A Casebook of an Innovative Psychiatrist's Work in Short-term Therapy.* New York: W. W. Norton & Co., 1973.

Haupt, E. I., Jr. *A Male-Female Co-therapy Team as Model.* Doctoral dissertation, California School of Professional Psychology at San Francisco, 1972.

Herr, J. J., & Weakland, J. H. *Counseling Elders and their Families: Practical Techniques for Applied Gerontology.* New York: Springer, 1979.

Jackson, D. D. Psychotherapy for schizophrenia. *Scientific American,* 1953, *188,* 58-63.

Jackson, D. D. The managing of acting out in a borderline personality. In A. Burton (Ed.), *Case Studies in Counseling and Psychotherapy.* New York: Prentice-Hall, 1959. (a)

Jackson, D.D. Family interaction, family homeostasis, and some implications for conjoint family psychotherapy. In J. Masserman (Ed.), *Individual and Family Dynamics.* New York: Grune & Stratton, 1959. (b)

Jackson, D. D. *The Etiology of Schizophrenia.* New York: Basic Books, 1960.

Jackson, D. D. Interactional psychotherapy. In M. I. Stein (Ed.), *Contemporary Psychotherapies.* Glencoe, IL: The Free Press, 1962.

Jackson, D. D. *Myths of Madness.* New York: Macmillan, 1964.

Jackson, D. D. Family rules: The marital *quid pro quo.* *Archives of General Psychiatry,* 1965, *12,* 589-594.

Jackson, D. D. (Ed.). *Human Communication, Volume 1: Communication, Family, and Marriage.* Palo Alto, CA.: Science & Behavior Books, 1968. (a)

Jackson, D. D. (Ed.). *Human Communication, Volume 2: Therapy, Communication, and Change.* Palo Alto, CA: Science & Behavior Books, 1968. (b)

Jackson, D. D. The myth of normality. *Medical Opinion and Review,* 1967, *3*(5), 28-33. Also in P. Watzlawick & J. H. Weakland (Eds.), *The Interactional View.* New York: W. W. Norton & Co., 1977.

Jackson, D. D., & Haley, J. Transference revisited. *The Journal of Nervous and Mental Disease,* 1963, *137,* 363-371.

Jackson, D. D., Riskin, J., & Satir, V. M. A method of analysis of a family interview. *Archives of General Psychiatry,* 1961, *5,* 321-339.

Jackson, D. D., & Yalom, I. Family research on the problem of ulcerative colitis. *Archives of General Psychiatry,* 1966, *15,* 410-418.

Kuhn, T. S. *The Structure of Scientific Revolutions* (2nd ed.). Chicago, IL: The University of Chicago Press, 1970.

Lederer, W. J. & Jackson, D. D. *The Mirages of Marriage.* New York: W. W. Norton & Co., 1968.

Lee-Merrow, S. MRI started before it began: A history of MRI. *Newsletter of the Mental Research Institute,* June, 1979, 1, 3-4.

MacFadden, C. *The Serial.* New York: Knopf Publishing Co., 1977.

MacGregor, R., Ritchie, A., Serrano, A., Schuster, F., McDonald, E. & Goolishian, H. *Multiple Impact Therapy With Families.* New York: McGraw-Hill, 1964.

Maliver, B. L. *The Encounter Game.* New York: Stein and Day, 1973.

Meehl, P. E. *Psychodiagnosis: Selected Papers.* New York: W. W. Norton & Co., 1977.

Riskin, J. "Non-labelled" family interaction: Preliminary report on a prospective study. *Family Process,* 1976, *15,* 433-439.

Riskin, J., & Faunce, E. Family interaction scales I: Theoretical framework and method. *Archives of General Psychiatry,* 1970, *22,* 504-512.

Riskin, J., & Faunce, E. Family interaction scales III: Discussion of methodology and substantive findings. *Archives of General Psychiatry,* 1970, *22,* 528-538.

Riskin, J., & McCorkle, M. E. "Nontherapy" family research and change in families: A brief clinical research communication. *Family Process,* 1979, *18,* 161-162.

Rosen, J. N. *Direct Analysis.* New York: Grune & Stratton, 1953.

Rosen, R. D. *Psychobabble: Fast Talk and Quick Cure in the Era of Feeling.* New York: Atheneum, 1977.

Satir, V. *Conjoint Family Therapy: A Guide to Theory and Technique* (Rev. ed.). Palo Alto, CA: Science & Behavior Books, 1967.

Satir, V. *Peoplemaking.* Palo Alto, CA: Science & Behavior Books, 1972.

Sluzki, C.E. Marital therapy from a systems theory perspective. In T.J. Paolino & B.S. McCrady (Eds.), *Marriage and Marital Therapy: Psychoanalytic, Behavioral and Systems Theory Perspectives.* New York: Brunner/Mazel, 1978.

Sluzki, C. E., & Beavin, J. Symmetry and complementarity: An operational definition and a typology of dyads. *Acta Psiquiatrica y Psicologica de America Latina,* 1965, *11,* 321-330.

Sluzki, C. E., & Ransom, D. C. (Eds.). *Double Bind: The Foundation of the Communicational Approach to the Family.* New York: Grune & Stratton, 1976.

Sluzki, C.E., & Veron, E. The double bind as universal pathogenic situation. *Family Process,* 1971, *10*(4), 397-410.

Speer, D. C. Family systems: Morphostasis and morphogenesis, or "is homeostasis enough?" *Family Process,* 1970, *9,* 259-278.

Steinbock, L. *Nest-leaving: Family Systems of Runaway Adolescents.* Doctoral dissertation, California School of Professional Psychology at San Francisco, 1977.

Strodtbeck, F. L. Husband-wife interaction overt revealed differences. *American Sociological Review,* 1951, *16,* 468-473.

Vogel, E. F., & Bell, N. W. The emotionally disturbed child as the family scapegoat. In N. W. Bell & E. F. Vogel (Eds.), *A Modern Introduction to the Family.* Glencoe, IL: The Free Press, 1960.

Watzlawick, P. A review of the double bind theory. *Family Process,* 1963, *2,* 132-153.

Watzlawick, P. *An Anthology of Human Communication; Text and tape.* Palo Alto, CA: Science & Behavior Books, 1964.

Watzlawick, P. A structured family interview. *Family Process,* 1966, *5,* 256-271.

Watzlawick, P. *How Real is Real?* New York: Random House, 1976.

Watzlawick, P. The Utopia syndrome. *Swiss Review of World Affairs,* 1973, *22,* 19-22. Also in P. Watzlawick & J. H. Weakland (Eds.), *The Interactional View: Studies at the Mental Research Institute, Palo Alto, 1965-1974.* New York: W. W. Norton & Co., 1977.

Watzlawick, P. *The Language of Change: Elements of Therapeutic Communication.* New York: Basic Books, 1978.

Watzlawick, P., Beavin, J. H., & Jackson, D. D. *Pragmatics of Human Communication.* New York: W. W. Norton & Co., 1967.

Watzlawick, P., Beavin, J. H., Sikorski, L., & Mecia, B. Protection and scapegoating in pathological families. *Family Process*, 1970, *9*, 27-39.

Watzlawick, P., Weakland, J., & Fisch, R. *Change: Principles of Problem Formation and Problem Resolution.* New York: W. W. Norton & Co., 1974.

Watzlawick, P., & Weakland, J. H. *The Interactional View: Studies at the Mental Research Institute, Palo Alto, 1965-1974.* New York: W. W. Norton & Co., 1977.

Weakland, J. H., Fisch, R., Watzlawick, P., and Bodin, A. M. Brief therapy: Focused problem resolution. *Family Process*, 1974, *13*, 141-168.

Weblin, J. E. Psychogenesis and asthma: An Appraisal with a view to family research. *British Journal of Medical Psychology*, 1962, *36*, 211-225.

Whitehead, A. N. & Russell, B. *Principia Mathematica* (3 vols.) Cambridge, Eng.: Cambridge University Press, 1910-1913.

Wiener, N. Time, communication, and the nervous system. In R. W. Miner (Ed.), *Teleological mechanisms.* Annals of the New York Academy of Sciences, *50*, 1947.

Wilder-Mott, C. The Palo Alto group: Difficulties and directions of the interactional view for human communication research. *Human Communication Research*, 1979, *5*, 171-186.

EDITORS' REFERENCES

Birchler, G. R. & Spinks, S. Behavioral-systems marital and family therapy: Integration and clinical application. *American Journal of Family Therapy*, 1980, *8*, 6-28.

Kniskern, D. P. & Gurman, A. S. Research on training in marriage and family therapy: Status, issues and directions. *Journal of Marital and Family Therapy*, 1979, *5*, 83-94.

Papp, P. The Greek chorus and other techniques of paradoxical therapy. *Family Process*, 1980, *19*, 45-57.

Weiss, R. L. Strategic behavioral martial therapy. In J. P. Vincent (Ed.), *Advances in Family Intervention, Assessment and Theory.* Vol. 1. Greenwich, CT: JAI Press, 1979.

Wilson, G. T. & Evans, I. The patient-therapist relationship in behavior therapy. In A. S. Gurman & A. M. Razin (Eds.), *Effective Psychotherapy: A Handbook of Research.* New York: Pergamon, 1971.

CHAPTER 9

Structural Family Therapy

Harry J. Aponte, A.C.S.W.

and John M. VanDeusen, Ph.D.

HISTORICAL BACKGROUND

Families of the Slums (Minuchin, Montalvo, Guerney, Rosman and Schumer, 1967) marked the first attempt at a comprehensive exposition of a structural type of family therapy. It was the sixties. There was a social revolution in progress in the United States and family therapy was beginning to gain wide acceptance. Minuchin and his co-workers were at a juncture where these two forces met and led them, aided by a federal grant, to attempt an experiment in the application of the budding theory of family therapy to low socioeconomic families. Minuchin and his colleagues were working at the Wiltwyck School for Boys, an institution primarily serving black and Puerto Rican youngsters from New York City's ghettos. It was an institution for boys, but the staff made it a treatment for families.

The families they met at Wiltwyck were grappling with day-to-day survival, seeking real solutions to the real problems in their lives. They were poor. The urgency that poverty generates about obtaining the necessities of life inclines families to approach psychotherapy as a practical

means for solving problems that are causing them trouble. When they enter therapy, they look to see that what is being done has a tangible relationship to their problem and that results are perceptibly forthcoming from their efforts. Therapies that depend heavily on talking about rather than talking directly to problems, that are aimed towards understanding and insight rather than action, that seek the expression of feeling instead of the integration of feeling with behavior, that aim to change attitudes about life and not the conditions of life are too removed from the pressures of the everyday problems of poor people to be useful to them.

Minuchin and his co-workers developed a therapeutic approach that was founded on the immediacy of the present reality, was oriented to solving problems, and was above all contextual, referring to the social environment that is both a part of and the setting for an event. The structural orientation itself was shaped by the exigencies of the social conditions of these boys from Wiltwyck School.

There have been others over the years who have influenced the formation of structural family therapy. Haley (1976) was associated for several years with the Philadelphia Child Guidance Clinic, to which Minuchin and some of his coworkers migrated from Wiltwyck. Although Haley has been viewed more as a strategic therapist (see Stanton, Chapter 10) he contributed significantly to the development of both the theory and the technical repertoire of the structuralists. His problem-solving approach and strategic techniques are evident in structural family therapy. The ecological approach of Auerswald (1968), who had been at Wiltwyck, and the network therapy of Speck (Speck and Attneave, 1973), who worked for a brief time at the Child Guidance Clinic, also had their influence on those in the structural school, who began including systems outside the nuclear family in their work with families.

During the seventies and going into the eighties, some from the structural school maintained a focus on the poor and expanded the approach to increase the inclusion of the community in assessment and interventions with these families. During this same time, a number of the structural therapists became involved in the treatment of and research on the so-called psychosomatic family. Unlike most therapies which had their roots in the middle-class and were adapted to work with lower socioeconomic patients, structural family therapy was generated from work with the poor and subsequently expanded to other socioeconomic strata. It was a timely response with a practical perspective to a population and an era that generated a theory of therapy that had universal application.

BASIC STRUCTURAL CONCEPTS

The theoretical foundation of this model of family therapy rests on the belief that, "the whole and the parts can be properly explained only in terms of the *relations* that exist between the parts" (Lane, 1970). Its point of focus is the link that connects one part of the whole to another. Since all human social phenomena are considered expressions of these linkages, all human products, whether they be behavioral, linguistic, institutional or material, essentially communicate a social relation (Lane, 1970). Structuralism approaches all human phenomena with the intent of identifying the "codes" that

regulate the human relationship. This pursuit constitutes the structuralist method of observing and ordering human phenomena.

This method is built on the assumption that, "there is in man an innate, genetically transmitted and determined mechanism that acts as a structuring force" (Lane, 1970, p. 15). The nature of the human being and society are seen as bearing within them certain predetermined dynamics that strongly influence the directions and ranges of the rules that govern human relationships. According to Lane, the explanation of these rules lies in the realm of belief and value as represented in religion, philosophy and political ideology. The various approaches to psychology, with their implicit and not so implicit values about normality and abnormality, should also be added to this list.

If the codes that regulate human relationships are the form, the operational patterns of human relationships are the content or the manifestation of these codes. As stated by Piaget (1970, p. 69), "Structures are inseparable from performance." These structures that are manifested in society emanate from human reason and reflect the structure of the human mind. Piaget's psychology of individual intellectual development embodies such a structural perspective.

Structural family therapy represents a theoretical and methodological approach to therapy that is consistent with the thrust of general structuralist thinking. "Good" and "bad" functioning in structural family therapy is described in terms of social organization, mostly family structure. The psychological structure of the individual is viewed as interdependent with the person's social structure, and that social structure is treated as the medium through which the individual functions and expresses him/herself. The social system which is most often assumed to form the basis of the individual's socialization is the family, and therefore structural therapy has been implemented primarily through family interventions. The eco-structural approach to therapy, which is a part of this structural therapy movement in therapy, is an effort to include, along with the family, other social systems as contributors to the structure of human behavior, and to work through all these systems to achieve change.

The structure of the social system in relation to its functions provides the parameters by which the therapist will measure the family's adjustment. The *structure* refers to the regulating codes as manifested in the operational patterns through which people relate to one another in order to carry out functions. These *functions* are the modes of action by which the system fulfills its purpose and the *operations* are those functions actualized in specific activities. The members of the system structure their relationships in accordance with the requirements of each operation. The parenting function of discipline is carried out, for example, in operations as specific as a mother telling her daughter by what time to come home from a date.

The repertoire of structures that the family develops to carry out its ongoing functions through their recurring operations takes on a character as unique to each family as the personality structure is to the individual. The *dominant structures* are those upon which most of the family operations are based. These patterns may cut across many functions in a family. The *subordinate structures* are those which are less frequently called upon, yet which also serve to undergird the dominant structures. The woman who determines when her daughter is to return home from her dates may also make most of the major decisions dealing with the privileges and discipline of all her children. If her husband generally asks his wife's opinion before making even occasional decisions with the children, this relationship would form a structure subordinate to his wife's relationship with the children. The wife's structural pattern vis-à-vis the children may also be a dominant structure in the family which carries over into other functions of the family not having to do with the children.

A judgment about what is functional and dysfunctional in a social system such as a family rests upon an understanding of the family in its societal context. One needs to know what codes regulate that family's relationships in its social context. For example, the family model for psychoanalytic theory was derived from the Middle European, white, middle-class, Victorian family, with two parents, an authoritarian father and a nurturing, dependent wife/mother. Within this model, the poor, black, single-parent, urban family, headed by a strong, independent woman is an aberration. In the former model, the children are incubated in a dependent family posture through their early twenties, if not longer. In the latter family, the children are urged toward self-reliance at a relatively more rapid pace. The societal and ethnic context of each family dictates different requirements for survival and growth.

To know the regulating code of a social system, one must know the manifest patterns through which the system carries out its functions. To know what is not functional, one must know what is functional. The development of criteria for judging "good" and "bad" functioning is still at a rudimentary level. Nonetheless, there has been progress in identifying dimensions of structure that will assist in the classification of structural patterns. Structural family therapists have also identified some family patterns that appear to be associated reliably with certain clinical problems.

The structural dimensions of transactions most often identified in structural family therapy are *boundary, alignment* and *power* (or *force,* as preferred by some.) Each and every stroke of a transaction contains all three of these structural dimensions. In therapy, one or another of the dimensions of a transaction may have more significance to a therapist, depending on the issue being addressed.

Boundary

Minuchin (1974, p. 53) states, "The boundaries of a subsystem are the rules defining who participates, and how." These "rules" dictate who is in and who is out of an operation, and define the roles those who are in will have vis-à-vis each other and the world outside in carrying out that activity. The unit directly engaged in the operation may be one member of a family with all the others excluded, or any combination of family members plus persons outside the family. Furthermore, the various individuals or groupings carrying out the operation define their own and each other's roles with respect to the operations of a particular function. Parents, for example, have roles in relation to their children that they choose for themselves and that society will define, which will determine what tasks the parents themselves will do for the children, what they will share with others, and what they will hand over to others completely. The extent to which sex education of children should be a parental, school or shared task is an illustration of such an issue that is being actively debated in today's society.

Alignment

Aponte (1976a, p. 434) speaks of alignment as the "joining or opposition of one member of a system to another in carrying out an operation." This dimension includes, but is not limited to, the concepts of coalition and alliance. Haley (1976, p. 109) defines coalition as, "a process of joint action *against* a third person (in contrast to an "alliance" where two people might share a common interest not shared by the third person)." Within the boundaries of any family the members have patterns of working together or in mutual opposition about the many activities they must engage in as family members. Boundary statements would refer to how in a particular family the mother has the role of rulemaker. Alignment statements would indicate whether the father agrees or disagrees with his wife's disciplinary action towards the children.

Power

Also described as force, power has been defined as "the relative influence of each [family] member on the outcome of an activity" (Aponte, 1976a, p. 434). Power is not an absolute attribute. First, structurally, power is relative to the operation. The mother's influence on her adolescent children's behavior may be effective at home, but minimal in terms of their social conduct outside the home. Secondly, power is generated by the way family members actively and passively combine, enabling the intention of one or more of the members to prevail in determining the outcome of a transaction, e.g., the mother's authority depends upon the cooperation of her husband and the acquiescence of her children.

In any set of operations, boundary and alignment define the members of a family system as in or out (boundary), and for or against (alignment), but do not account for the motive energy that activates the system and carries it through an action. These structural dimensions depend on power for action and outcome. In terms of boundary, the parents, in our example, are the disciplinarians, with the mother the rulemaker and the father in a role supportive of hers. Alignment indicates on what disciplinary issues they agree and disagree with one another and with the children. Power informs about which of the parents will prevail if they disagree, and whether they can impose their discipline on the children even when they do agree.

THE WELL FUNCTIONING AND DYSFUNCTIONING FAMILY

From a structural perspective, functional and dysfunctional levels are determined by the adequacy of the fit of a system's structural organization to the requirements of an operation in a set of circumstances. The *structural organization* of families refers to relational patterns common to all families, colored by the personal idiosyncracies of each family with its traditions, culture and socioeconomic situation, and adapted to its functional requirements. The functions relate to all areas of human social activity which are in accord with the nature of the social unit and its point of development. The *circumstances* refer to the context, that is, the time and place and social parameters within which the family or family members are to operationalize the structure in carrying out a function. Dysfunctional structures are not specific to symptoms, since it is the appropriateness of the fit of a family and its subsystems to the requirements of the functions in given circumstances that determines the presence or absence of a problem. In a school avoidance situation, for example, to say that a youngster does not go to school because he and his mother are locked into a stable coalition against the father does not in itself explain why the boy is not going to school. One would need to understand not only the current structural patterns of these relationships, but also the functional purposes they serve for the family members in their family and social contexts.

Therapists may describe families by the labels of relational patterns and speak of the patterns themselves as dysfunctional in order to abbreviate communication. Neither individuals nor families are constituted by a single or a few structures. They are made of a myriad of structures, complexly interconnected. Nor do the structures themselves communicate whether they are functional or dysfunctional. When the therapist talks of an "enmeshed" family, he/she is describing a family in which enmeshment is a dominant pattern. The enmeshment the therapist is describing is not the enmeshment that a functional family must be capable of in order to experience moments of intimate affection or to meld in unity when facing an external crisis. It is the enmeshment that structurally supports the family's symptomatic behavior.[1]

With this understanding, one can then speak of dysfunctional structures in families and of the symptoms and types of problems that are often associated with some of these patterns. Dysfunctional family structures are best classified according to the structural dimension to which they are most closely related, whether that be boundary, alignment or power.

The concepts of *enmeshment* and *disengagement* reflect an emphasis on *boundary* (Minuchin, 1974). In describing a family along this axis, one is addressing questions of differentiation, permeability and rigidity of boundaries among and between individuals and subgroups in a family, and between the family with its subsystems and its social environment. At the enmeshment end of the continuum, the boundaries among some or all of the family members are relatively undifferentiated, permeable and fluid. These family members function as if they are part of each other.[2] At the disengaged end,

the family members behave as if they have little to do with one another because within their families their boundaries are so firmly delineated, impermeable, and rigid that the family members tend to go their own ways with little overt dependence on one another for their functioning. Another common dysfunctional structure related to boundary is the *violation of function boundaries*. This refers to the inappropriate intrusion of family members into functions that are the domain of other members. The parental child is a classic example: the child assumes responsibilities for his or her siblings that belong to the parent.

The terms *stable coalition, triangulation* and *detouring coalition* (Minuchin, Rosman and Baker, 1978) speak mostly to *alignment*. These are some of the more common types of dysfunctional coalitions described in structural family therapy literature. They are not mutually exclusive. A *stable coalition* is the joining together of family members against another so that the pattern becomes a dominant, inflexible characteristic of their relationship. In well functioning families members can shift alignments flexibly depending on the issue. The *detouring coalition* is a form of stable coalition distinguished by its intent to diffuse the stress between the members of a coalition by designating another party as the source of their problem and assuming an attacking or solicitous attitude toward that person. In *triangulation*, each of two opposing parties seeks to join with the same person against the other, with the third party finding it necessary, for whatever reasons, to cooperate now with one and now with another of these opposing parties. Some of these dysfunctional structures involve more than one category of structural dimension as a dominant characteristic, such as, for example, the *cross-generational* (boundary) *stable coalition* (alignment). It must still be understood, however, that regardless of which structural dimension dominates the structure, every other dimension of structure is necessarily involved at least in a subordinate role.

Problem structures relevant to *power* are defined in terms of who has the power in relation to whom and about what. The execution of power is clearly dependent upon who is actively or passively, willingly or unwillingly, accommodating to whose attempt to influence, and upon the area of functioning that is involved.

---

[1]*Editors' Note.* Here, we wish to underscore Aponte and VanDeusen's important point, above, that terms such as "enmeshment" are shorthand ways of efficiently communicating a large amount of information about a family. The danger in the use of such terms, however, is that they may become reified. Thus, therapists may (and, in our experience, often do) unwittingly endorse the nominalist fallacy, i.e., that because they have named something, they have explained it. "Enmeshment" is a hypothetical construct, an abstraction from direct observation. Thus, it is not "enmeshment", but rather "enmeshed" behavior, that supports symptomatic behavior.

[2]*Editors' Note.* Minuchin (1974, p. 55) addresses explicitly the developmental impact of such recurrent patterns: "Members of enmeshed subsystems or families may be handicapped in that the heightened sense of belonging requires a major yielding of autonomy. The lack of subsystem differentiation discourages autonomous exploration and mastery of problems."

For example, consider the asthmatic child whose mother fosters a dependency upon her that hinders him from playing with his friends, but who can stay up later than his mother wants to watch television, because by wheezing he can stop her from forcing him to bed. The mother has relatively more power than he about his being with friends, while he has the power about his bedtime. While defining the dimension of power according to whom and about what is not unique to this structural dimension, its relative nature needs to be emphasized because power is so often conceived of as absolute and as a characteristic of individuals rather than social interactions. The basic structural problem with power is the *lack of functional power in the system.* It is the generic problem for individuals or groups who are not able and/or allowed to exercise the force necessary to carry out functions appropriate to themselves in the system in which they are operating. A commonly cited example is that of *weak executive functioning,* in which parents do not have the leverage required to direct their children. Another is the *inhibition of developmental potential* in which the individual, because of family organization, cannot act in ways appropriate to his/her age within the family.

There is another structural problem worthy of mention which cuts across all three structural dimensions, *underorganization.* It refers to "a deficiency in the degree of constancy, differentiation, and flexibility of the structural organization of the family system" (Aponte, 1976a, p. 433). Underorganization describes how families who have a relatively limited repertoire of ways of organizing themselves to solve problems may be relatively rigid in how they employ the structures they have, and inconsistent in the use of those structures. While underorganization can be a problem for any family, it is most often identified with low income families because their social circumstances foster underorganization. Underorganization is most often associated with chronically unsupportive and disruptive social conditions that undermine the efforts of families to acquire the structural organization needed to cope with the multitude of developmental, interpersonal and social tasks that families face.

The ability of a family to function well depends on the degree to which the family structure is well defined, elaborated, flexible and cohesive. The family structure must be adequate to and harmonious with functions of its individual members, its subgroups and the social environment of which it is a part. Where its structure is not adequate, it has the capacity to generate new structure. Where it is not in harmony with the requirements of some of its members or its social environment, it has the ability to negotiate different relational structures that still meet the basic needs of the family and each of its members.

Structure is not essentially deterministic. It offers channels for functioning within a greater or lesser range of possibilities without necessarily determining choice. In that respect, the functioning of the system rests on having a range from which to select the structures that meet its needs. In a successfully functioning family, all members of that social complex have the ability, through their structural linkages, to cooperate with one another and to balance the respective demands of the family and each other.

ASSESSMENT AND GOAL-SETTING

Because structural family therapists do not use diagnostic interviews or diagnostic instruments, except for research purposes, the place of assessment in this therapy is often misunderstood or overlooked altogether. Structural therapy incorporates both assessment and goal-setting into the therapeutic process so that they become integral facets of therapeutic interventions.

The goals of therapy are to solve problems and change the underlying systemic structure. The structural family therapist sees the problem to be dealt with as sustained by the current structure of the family and its ecosystem. Therefore, whatever the history of the problem, the dynamics that maintain it are currently active in the structure of the system, manifesting themselves in the transactional sequences of the family. The structural therapist assumes that there is no better way to understand these sustaining structures than by seeing and experiencing them in action in the therapy session. Moreover, the therapist prefers to investigate what the family structures can and cannot do by intervening directly in the transactions of the family to bring about change in the structural patterns of their sequences.

Conceptually, the process of assessment can be broken down into identifying the *problem*, determining its *locus* in the ecosystem, and defining the system's *structures* that sustain the problem. Identifying the *problem* means looking for where in the operationalization of the structure the system fails to carry out its function. For the purposes of therapy, the problem is not the insecurity of a woman, but her avoidance of people; not the competitiveness of a couple, but their fighting over their son's loyalty.[3] Through the operations of the system the therapist expects to see the problem with its structure and to have a tangible context in which he or she can intervene.

Identifying the problem also involves seeing a problem in relation to the other problems to which it is structurally related (Aponte, 1974). Because of the nature of a system, problems do not appear in isolation. They do, however, have varying degrees of autonomy and dependence in relation to one another. A problem is autonomous to the extent that it stands free of other issues identified as problems. On the other hand, a problem can be dependent in two ways. First, the problem is linked with another in a mutually reinforcing relationship, even though each has its own relatively separate structural base. Secondly, one problem is dependent upon another as an effect is on its source. Still, even in the case where one problem derives from another, because of the nature of systems, the derivative problem and the source problem will themselves be mutually reinforcing.

An example of a problem that might stand, relatively speaking, on its own is the depression of a man who has been told he has a malignancy. The same problem would be linked with another if the man's attitude toward his illness were to compound his despair about a conflict-ridden marriage. His discouragement about his mar-

riage would also deepen his sense of hopelessness about his health. Furthermore, if an adolescent son of this marriage were to begin acting out in a delinquent manner because of what was happening between his parents, the youngster's problems would be a derivative of the parents' difficulties.[4] Knowing the other problems related to a central problem and their interdependence informs the therapist about what other problems must be solved to successfully deal with the central issue and about the order in which the interlocking problems must be approached, thereby helping to set the therapist's strategies.

The quest for the problem is by no means a narrow goal in itself since the structural underpinning is often highly complex, carrying with it satellite problems with their own sustaining structures. Moreover, the exploration of the problem is also a search for what family functions are being blocked by the symptom. The functions with which the problems interfere are often not immediately evident, but understanding the functions is essential to comprehending the full nature of the problem. It is not enough to know that the young man is acting out because of his parents' problem. It is necessary to know that his guilt about his parents and the splitting of his loyalty between them is preventing him from venturing out of his home and into the world of his peers without considerable guilt and emotional turmoil.

From an intervention perspective, the therapist also envisions the problem in terms of what is to be solved more than in terms of what is wrong. The therapist's vision is being "funneled through" the problem as it responds to the therapist's efforts to solve it. Focusing on *the problem in the process of change* is very different from merely exploring the pathological history and nature of the problem itself, or from trying

---

[3]*Editors' Note.* This is an enormously important point: that the therapist needs to be sensitive to and aware of the idiosyncratic experience of individual family members, i.e., needs to understand it, but that, for the purpose of inducing structural change, the therapist must focus not on the family members' private experience, but on their *behavior*. Perhaps this is, in part, what Minuchin had in mind when he said that "Family therapy requires sophisticated thinking to arrive at simple interventions" (Freeman, 1978, p. 6).

[4]*Editors' Note.* While the authors may appear to be speaking here about unidirectional causality ("because of what was happening between his parents"), this is not the case; indeed, such a position would be greatly at variance with the fundamental assumption in structural therapy of circular causality. Rather, in this illustration, the therapist may choose to *punctuate* a long string of interactions in this way for purposes of intervention; thus, "what was happening between his parents" *becomes* primary (not: *is* primary) by virtue of the therapist's plan and purpose for intervening into the sustaining structure of the son's acting-out.

to survey all the other psychological difficulties of the family in one's investigation. Treating the youngster primarily as someone who is to be continuously taking discrete steps in the therapy to separate from his family differs from working with him as a subject of the study of his dependency. In the first case, the therapist gives priority to the change intended by his/her intervention. In the second case, the therapist gives priority to what is to be understood in order to remove the blockages. In the former, the therapist assesses through the efforts to produce change, while in the latter through exploring his history of failure. In the former, the therapist is exploring the interference with change as change is being attempted, and in the latter, the therapist is studying the history of the interference as a prelude to change.

Primarily studying problems as problems moves from dysfunction to dysfunction and failure to failure. The process that is so directed stimulates regression, not growth. In contrast, an investigation which couches each probe, as far as possible, in a change-directed intervention, looks at a problem as something that is to be solved and encourages change. While some pathological facets of the problem may be neglected in the impetus toward change, some of the potential for change will be discovered, which would otherwise be lost. The family itself is more likely to be drawn up into the positive momentum of solving its problems.

The focus on the problem in structural family therapy distinguishes it from those therapies that are looking for some broadly defined growth in the individual or family. The emphasis on the problem in the process of change separates it from those that are geared toward insight and the understanding of the problem. The search for the structures underlying the problem differentiates this approach from those that are related essentially to symptom removal.

Determining the *locus* of the problem in people's lives is not so simple a task as it may appear because of the complexity of the ecosystem. It is a difficult task to pinpoint the systems among which the problem is shared. Not everyone in a family is involved in a problem in the same way. The locus of the problem concerns for whom the problem is an issue currently, not at its time of origin. In structural terms, the *primary locus* is the system or systems which is structurally engaged in the essential and habitual generation and maintenance of the problem. The *secondary locus* is the system or systems which form the habitual but not the essential environment of the problem. The *tertiary locus* is that part of the ecosystem in which the problem is being actualized but which does not contribute essentially or habitually to its generation or maintenance.

The *primary locus* is made up of those systems locked in a relationship that generates a problem for all or some of those systems. The system or systems with the problem, the *problem bearers*, are those in the primary locus that have been stymied in trying to carry out some necessary function and are therefore experiencing failure. Those through whose relationship the problem-bearing systems are being stressed are the *participant components* of the primary locus. Where the locus is depends on one's definition of the problem. The structural family therapist will define the problem in terms of both the problem bearers and the participant components. This means that the vision of the therapist will encompass the larger system or complex of systems to whose interaction the failure can be attributed rather than just the problem bearer. The actors in a play are the primary locus of the play.

The *secondary locus* refers to that structure of systems that supports generation and maintenance of the problem without being essential to the problem. The secondary locus is the active environment of the primary locus. The actions of the systems in the secondary locus may reinforce the problematic structure through an accommodation that supports the structure, but the problem would continue to exist whether these systems were present or not. These are the stagehands of the theater.

The *tertiary locus* is the passive environment of the problem, the part of the context in which the problem structures are set, but which is only incidental in its role in the problem. In the metaphor of the play, the individual members of the audience roughly approximate the relationship of the tertiary locus to the primary locus.

If in a family in which the marital couple is in chronic conflict the son were never or only occasionally to be swept up into the fighting, and were basically irrelevant to the fighting, that youngster would be part of the passive environment, or tertiary locus. If, on the other hand, he were often to take sides in the fights, heightening the level of conflict, but were incidental to the reasons for the arguments, he would be part of the active environment, the secondary locus. Finally, if the boy were to side with his mother habitually, and she counted on his support to be able to contradict the father, the boy would be part of the primary locus, essential to the parental power struggle. Because *the primary locus of the problem rests on the sustaining structure and not on the original generating structure to the problem*, the boy need not have been part of the beginnings of the parental discord to be now an essential part of the dysfunctional structure.

As the therapist assesses what and where the problem is, he/she will investigate the sustaining *structure* of the problem, that is, how these systems are organized currently that they generate and maintain the problem. Since the problem does not arise from the structure by itself, the therapist must determine the appropriateness and adequacy (fit) of the structures of the ecosystem to enable a system to carry out its functions in the necessary circumstances.

The therapist is looking for the connection of the relational structures among the family members and others in their social context to the problem. The therapist will conceptualize these relationships in terms of boundary, alignment and power. He/she will distinguish, as discussed earlier, between the dominant structures that sustain the problem and the subordinate structures that support the dominant structures but are secondary in sustaining the problem. The structures will have qualities which will require examination, including *richness-paucity, flexibility-rigidity* and *coherence-incoherence*. The richness spectrum describes the variety of structures the system has available to carry out its functions. Flexibility refers to the system's ability to shift its organization to achieve a goal and to create new structures for itself as required by circumstances. The coherence factor is the relative consistency and continuity of the system's identity and relationship to its ecosystem as its structure evolves and modifies through the change of circumstances and the passage of time.

The therapist's principal diagnostic tools are the observation and experience of the transactions among the members of the ecosystem connected with the problem as they act to solve the problem with the therapist. Moreover, within the session, the therapist is in a position to control for variables in the context of the transaction akin to a laboratory experiment. The therapist can influence who will be involved during the enactment of a problem sequence, around what issue the participants will interact, and how the sequencing will be organized in terms of boundary, alignment and power. The therapist's influence is proferred through his/her interventions in the sequences that make up the scene for the participants. The therapist's actions will be guided through the building of *hypotheses* about the problems and their solutions.

One can abstract several steps from the quasi experimental process that takes place in a session (Aponte, 1979):

1) *Problem*. The therapist determines the issues around which to explore and intervene in the session.
2) *Data*. The therapist draws together all data relevant to the issue as gathered from prior information and the in-session experience leading up to the moment when the therapist is to intervene.
3) *Hypotheses*. On the basis of the data, the therapist commits him/herself to hypotheses about the significance of the current transactional sequence to the nature of the problem, its locus and sustaining structure.
4) *Goals*. To the extent permitted by the hypotheses, the therapist determines immediate goals, in context of the tentative long-range goals of treatment, for the intervention that is to follow.
5) *Intervention*. The therapist simultaneously acts in light of all the above:
   (a) to affect a change in the patterns of the transactional sequences among the family members and/or between self and/or family members, and
   (b) to control for variables in the transaction so that the effects of the intervention can be assessed.
6) *Feedback*. On the basis of the reactions of the family members to the intervention, the

therapist restarts the cycle from the second step.

An example to illustrate a way of organizing information to build hypotheses and of testing the hypotheses must of necessity be a gross oversimplification because the determinants of the therapist's thinking and interventions are so very many. Consider a single-parent family with a mother, 26, and two daughters aged ten and four. The children had different fathers. The mother married neither man. The mother had lived with her own mother until two years before when she moved out on her own, except for a year when she lived with the father of the younger child. The family is on welfare. The problem the mother presents is that the ten-year-old is having difficulties in school, is inattentive in class and is neglectful of homework. The mother came at the school's recommendation. This information was gathered by the intake worker on the telephone.

On the basis of these data the therapist hypothesizes that the mother has had little opportunity to adequately define her own personality and her parental relationship on her children (boundary problems). It appears to the therapist that until two years ago she may have been trying to work out for herself her roles as a mate, mother and adult while functioning mostly as her mother's daughter. He tentatively assumes that her lack of a job and independent source of income also helps undermine her sense of identity within her social and family environment. The therapist further hypothesizes that her functions as a parent in relation to her children may be so ill defined that the children do not clearly sense their accountability to her as their mother. As a result, the family may well be poorly organized in carrying out many of its functions, being thereby underorganized. These considerations in turn imply to the therapist other difficulties related to a lack of personal maturity on the part of the children in their relationships with each other and others outside the family, including school. The situation for the older girl would have its own special difficulties if she had been raised primarily by her grandmother, which the therapist does not know. If that were so, she may well relate to her grandmother as to a mother, and to her

mother as to an older sister. The older girl might also feel that when she moved away from her grandmother's, she moved away from her "real" mother. The younger child would hardly remember the grandmother as a parent, but would not experience her mother as an authoritative figure if the mother herself were not clear about her executive role. The mother may look at the younger child more as her own than the older.

The therapist meets the family for the first session with these suppositions in mind. He greets them and invites them to sit down. The mother and older daughter do, but the younger daughter continues to explore the office. The therapist, in order to clearly set the contextual parameters for the session, restates to the mother the suggestion that all take a seat. She plaintively asks the four-year-old to sit, but is ignored as the youngster accelerates her level of activity. The mother looks at the therapist helplessly, appearing torn between pleasing the therapist and her daughter. All the while, the ten-year-old is sitting sullen, arms crossed, watching what is happening.

The therapist is expected to commit himself to act on the basis of his hypotheses. His intervention is to be therapeutic in intent, while also serving to test his hypotheses. The therapist formulates three basic hypotheses on the basis of the brief history and the family's transactions in the interview: The mother favors the four-year-old; the ten-year-old feels distant and resentful of her mother; the mother has poor control over the younger child. The goals will correspond accordingly. He will want the mother to equalize the treatment of the two girls, help the ten-year-old to feel accepted by her mother, and support the mother's assuming more effective control of the younger child.

The therapist considers three interventions: going over to the four-year-old to engage her himself, ignoring the four-year-old and talking to the mother and ten-year-old, and placing the expectation on the mother that she get the four-year-old to sit down. The first would follow the structure of the family, but would also allow the therapist a chance to separate the four-year-old from her mother in the session and perhaps establish some leverage for himself with the youngster. However, he risks temporarily alienating the ten-year-old and reinforcing the four-year-old's attention-getting behavior along with the mother's tolerance of it. With the second course of action, he would be deemphasizing the four-year-old and by addressing the mother and the older child, possibly linking them more closely together for the moment. Still, he would risk challenging the younger child to escalate her attention-getting behavior, if such it is, and would chance belittling the mother's directive to her to sit down, as well as his own expectation that she sit. The third possible action could magnify the authority of the mother by having her get the four-year-old to sit down as her sister is doing and would give the two girls an experience of seeing the younger of them being treated with the same kind of expectation as the ten-year-old. The disadvantage is that the four-year-old's behavior would become the center of the action and that the mother may be put into a position in which she will fail by losing a direct challenge to her younger daughter.

In the actual session, the therapist chose the third course of action. Another therapist might well have chosen the first or second or have determined on yet another. This therapist chose to commit himself to creating a context in which everyone was expected to sit down, and to an intervention that directed the mother to get her younger daughter to comply. The goals have just been enunciated along with the therapist's hypotheses. To test his hypotheses the therapist made his expectation known to the mother and observed her reaction and that of the children. Two possible extremes of consequent behavior could have resulted. The mother may have emphatically restated her request to the four-year-old who immediately sat. Or, the mother may have wistfully renewed her plea, with the child continuing to ignore her and the mother reacting with confusion and discouragement. The first consequence would have tended to disconfirm the hypothesis about the mother's lack of control, while not saying much about the other two hypotheses. The second consequence would have been a step in the direction of confirming the therapist's hypotheses about the mother's lack of control over the four-year-old and would have also left open the other two hypotheses. The second scenario actually occurred.

The processes of identifying the problem, *gathering data, formulating hypotheses, setting tentative goals and intervening accordingly are implicit in each and every action of the structural family therapist throughout treatment.* Assessment is inherent in every therapeutic intervention of the therapist, and just as one therapeutic intervention builds upon the last, the formulation of each hypothesis builds upon the previous one. As the therapy proceeds, so should the understanding of the therapist increase.

APPLICABILITY

There are enough techniques that are closely linked with structural family therapy that one could well present this approach strictly from an interventional standpoint. However, a view of structural family therapy that treats it principally as a body of techniques will miss the theoretical significance of this therapeutic orientation. The purpose of structural theory is to describe the organizational relationships of the parts to the whole in the social ecosystem. The theory allows for a broadly encompassing perspective on the personal and social problems of the family and its members.

Furthermore, structural family therapy is also widely applicable because of the breadth of techniques useable within its theoretical framework. Aside from certain technical interventions that are closely identified with this form of therapy, such as chorography and enactment, to be described later, there are those coming out of other forms of therapy that can be and are used within a structural framework, such as interventions developed by the schools of strategic therapy, network therapy and behavior modification (Liebman, Minuchin and Baker, 1974). The compatibility of the theory with a broad range of technique expands the applicability of structural therapy.[5]

From a practical standpoint, nevertheless, structural family therapy has been more widely

---

[5]*Editors' Note.* As we discuss elsewhere (Kniskern and Gurman, 1980a) in greater detail, a theory of family therapy that admits a wide choice of techniques as compatible with the theory makes it difficult on research grounds to both: (a) validate central aspects of that theory, and (b) identify the components of the treatment qua treatment that uniquely contribute to its efficacy.

applied with certain populations than with others. There has been research in and extensive use of structural therapy with the treatment of low-income families and with so-called psychosomatic families having children suffering from asthma, diabetes and anorexia nervosa. Structural family therapy has also been used as the therapeutic foundation for a variety of treatment settings. For example, at the Philadelphia Child Guidance Clinic in recent years the structural approach provided the therapeutic framework within which a family-oriented inpatient psychiatric hospital operated that admitted entire families along with individual children and that also included a therapeutic school and day hospital program (Goren, 1979). However, except for the major research study conducted with the families of adult drug addicts by Stanton and Todd (1979), structural family therapy has been applied and researched systematically for the most part with families presenting with child problems.

Because the formal development of the approach has taken place in centers dealing primarily with children, there is still much work to be done to demonstrate the degree to which it can be applied in adult-oriented contexts.[6] This is not to deny that structural family therapists have also been working with the adults in the families of the children they targeted. Moreover, structural therapy is also being used in a growing variety of clinical settings throughout the country to treat all kinds of patients, including adults.

The issue of its applicability with adults raises questions, for example, about concerns adults may also bring to therapy which are often more characterological and long-standing than the practical and situational problems associated with children, such as school avoidance, behavioral acting-out and somatization of stress. An adult may enter therapy because of concerns about his/her own sense of adequacy, identity and the like. The structural therapist will attempt to particularize such issues at some operational level in the individual's relationship to self, family or therapist, and indeed, probably with all three at various points of the therapy.

He/she will want to address the issue at an operational level in which the individual's personality problem is brought into play. With a long-standing, deep-rooted characterological issue, the therapist expects to have to confront many different aspects of the problem in a variety of contexts.

Because most of the research and writing in the structural field has been about children and their families, the work being done with adults is often being subsumed under the clinical discussions of the families of children. Therapy with adults and their families offers its own parameters, which requires more development of the application of the structural orientation to therapy with adults. A body of clinical studies and research of structural therapy with adults and their families would also allow better comparison with other family therapy approaches that have grown out of work with adults.

The structural approach to therapy has been applied to social networks and with institutions. The family-school interview (Aponte, 1976b), in which the family is brought together by the therapist with representatives of the child's school, for example, provides a model for expanding the scope of structural family therapy beyond the family. This is an area in which one expects further elaboration as structural therapy is used more for therapeutic intervention into the community to solve personal and family problems arising from the family's relations with the community.

Experience has not yet evinced psychological problems that would be outside the applicability of the structural approach. This does not confirm its universal applicability, but does suggest that the theoretical and technical frameworks of the approach are broad enough to lend themselves to being tested with the broadest range of problems in all clinical settings.

STRUCTURE OF THE THERAPY PROCESS

Structural family therapy is a naturalistic approach to therapy in the sense that the therapist views the ecosystem in which the problem exists as the field for assessment and intervention. Historically, this has meant mostly the nuclear family and occasionally the extended family. For some of the structuralists it has also come to

---

[6]*Editors' Note*. For an excellent illustration of an application to marital therapy, see Stanton (1981).

include parts of the community network (Aponte, 1980). It is not a form of therapy that has encouraged groupings of families for therapy unless the group forms a base for a natural network in the community. Parent, child and family groups in structurally oriented inpatient and day treatment programs have been brought together on the principle that the hospital is also a community of sorts. The therapist will interview anywhere as dictated by strategy and practicability, although most interviews that include only the family are conducted in the therapist's office where the therapist has the greatest freedom and leverage to intervene. Where the issue is primarily at the interface between the family and a segment of the community, the interview is often held where the two systems would naturally meet. Wherever the interview and whoever the non-family participants, the family is central to the process and is included as an active and co-equal participant in the session with the other interviewees.

Who to involve in the therapy has to do with who shares the problem, as well as what components of the ecosystem are resources for solving the problem. Bringing in a person, family or non-family, who does not share in the origins or maintenance of the problem but may be able to share in its solution, is important for an approach that focuses primarily on problem-solving. The determinations about what problem sharers or resources to include are ultimately made on the bases of what is strategically indicated and who is accessible. Strategy considers not only what has to be done with whom, but also the timing in the process. Therapy is an ecological balancing act in which the therapist has to take into consideration at every stage of treatment every resource in the ecosystem of the family as the therapist disrupts, maintains and creates new structures.

Joint, Concurrent and Sequential Process

The work with these systems can be in *joint*, *concurrent* or *sequential* processes. Having all those involved with the problem in the same room allows them *jointly* the opportunity to work on their relationships with mutual awareness, consent and effort. The structural therapist will usually start therapy with a joint session. If the therapist is to meet with subgroups this will happen later in that first session or in subsequent sessions. However the therapist arranges to work with subgroups of the system, more often than not, he/she will at least periodically reconvene the larger system in a joint session, which serves as the bench mark of the therapeutic process. Indeed, the joint session is more the rule than the exception in structural family therapy.

The *concurrent* processes are those interviews with different groupings of the family and its ecosystem that the therapist conducts separately during the same period of treatment. The therapist may have concurrent sessions with different groupings of a family because those in these groupings are not able during a particular period in treatment to negotiate directly with each other. These parallel efforts may have therapeutic goals specific to those in each separate process, but they are usually also intended to help both parties prepare to negotiate the issues together. An example may well be that of the married couple that was in such intense conflict that they could not sit together for any period of time to talk. They struggled with each other because while tenaciously holding fast to their respective viewpoints, each in his/her insecurity demanded total agreement from the partner. Concurrent sessions with each of the two and with them together were held. In the individual sessions they were each aided to feel secure in their respective points of view. In the joint sessions the therapist paradoxically asked each to work to understand the other's thinking without conceding any ground on his or her respective opinion, guaranteeing each an apparently safe haven from which to open his or her mind to the other.

Two other reasons for having concurrent interviews are that the discrete nature of issues themselves may require separate sessions for the parties, and also that the parties involved may have their own distinct goals to pursue that are strategically best dealt with separately. The assumption in each of these instances considered above is that, while the people and the issues may need to be addressed separately, they are also dealt with concurrently because in some way or another they feed into each other's treatment process. Although treated separately, they are linked together somehow in the total family's treatment. An example of discrete issues that call for separate but concurrent treatment processes would be in the case of parents who have been involving their daughter in their marital conflicts. They may agree to discuss the wife's inattention towards her husband alone with the therapist, while the daughter talks individually about her lack of social contacts outside of home. An illustration of distinct goals for different groupings dictating separate but parallel sessions would be in a case in which a single parent wants to clarify her thinking privately about how to organize her adolescent children about their chores before talking with them in the joint session, and where the youngsters want to work out some of their competitiveness with each other so that they can be mutually supportive when the parent finally decides the distribution of assignments. Whatever the reasons for the concurrent sessions, the therapist works with the separate groupings within the framework of the whole family's goals.

The *sequential* process with groupings of a family and its ecosystem has to do with phases in the treatment in which the therapist must resolve an issue with a part of the family before continuing with the whole or another part of the family on the same or another matter. Embarking on one phase of therapy may depend upon completing another. An illustration of a sequential process involved a couple who came for help because their daughter was highly anxious. The husband and wife were themselves in turmoil about whether they should separate, and were obviously using the girl as their battleground. The therapist asked that before their daughter became a part of the treatment they either separate or enter into marital counseling. The couple chose the latter course and their daughter did not join them in the treatment until they had their emotional fencing under control. After the parents resolved the marital issues through work as a couple and the daughter had gained some emotional distance from them, through a period of joint sessions, the youngster spent a period of time seeing the therapist alone because she needed to find some direction for her-

self. Regardless of the reason for the sequencing of the phases, the therapist as always conducts the work in any part of the treatment in the light of the treatment of the whole family.

Co-therapy

Co-therapy does not have a clearly defined niche within structural family therapy. The prevalence of its use among structuralists has varied during the course of the development of the structural approach. During its early period, when most of the work of structural therapists was focused on poor urban families, co-therapy was more the rule than the exception. In the context of working with those families, the therapists were often dealing with large multigenerational families that were often underorganized and were steeped in a variety of critical problems within the family and outside in their social environment. It was not uncommon in those days for more than two co-therapists to be involved simultaneously with a family. In recent years, as the concentration for many of the practitioners has moved toward working with middle-class families, the use of co-therapy has diminished considerably.

Another reason for the infrequency of co-therapy among structural family therapists is the inherent technical problems that co-therapy creates for this therapeutic approach. Within the ongoing transactional process, the structural goals are implicit in every intervention, with each intervention ideally building upon the previous one within a session, and similarly each session upon the last. The task of continuously testing hypotheses is also borne by those interventions, requiring the therapist to organize the sessions so as to permit evaluation of the premises of the interventions. The therapist is always attempting to influence the structural patterns of transactions within the session and controlling for variables to test hypotheses, while committing him/herself to explicitly formulated structural postures in the transactions. With these expectations of the therapist, the addition of a co-therapist puts significant demand for coordination on both therapists. With co-therapy it is technically impossible to maintain the same degree of control over the transactional process as can a single therapist. The difficulties of this kind of continuous, coordinated effort have not encouraged co-therapy among the structuralists.

However, the problems of a tight flying formation have not stopped co-therapy among the structural therapists, only inhibited its prevalence. When it is practiced, therapists commonly have it understood or have openly agreed that one of them will be the lead therapist with a particular case, allowing the other to follow the former's pace and direction. Another solution to the problem of coordination has been to predetermine which of the therapists will assume primary responsibility for which of the subsystems if the family is one which will require splitting of attention among different subsystems during joint or concurrent processes. Both solutions help settle ahead of time issues that must be dealt with in any co-therapy, but they also constrain spontaneity in the session. Co-therapy teams with long-standing experience have been the most successful. These are the therapist combinations that have negotiated their relationships through many difficulties, and have learned how to communicate and negotiate efficiently and honestly in and out of sessions. They understand one another's clinical thinking and range of skills. They are sensitive and responsive to each other as people. Their co-therapy is spontaneously coordinated and flexible.

Co-therapy is more often employed by structural therapists in interviews with large and complex families and also when representatives from their communities participate, simply because too much may be going on at once for the therapist to attend to alone. However, independence from one another and divergence of interests in relation to the problem are more critical factors than the mere size of the group. *The more adults, the less related they are, and the more conflicting their viewpoints, the more directions will the therapist be pulled and the greater his/her need for a co-therapist.* A couple that is truly near the point of divorce, with each party having vital, competing interests, may require co-therapists. Interviews with three-generational families, and with families and institutional representatives having conflicting positions may well require co-therapy. On the other hand, simply having a large family, such

as a mother with many children, does not necessarily indicate more than one therapist if in such an instance the mother has enough leverage to exercise good control over the children.

Paradoxically, the very small family may also require co-therapists. The classic example is of the single parent with an only child where the two have been alone for years and have no other relatives involved in their lives. Such a twosome may be so intertwined that the therapist may be in the position of dealing with a virtual single entity. The therapist may not be able to talk with one party without the other one being effectively included. This may be true whether the therapist is seeing them together in the same room or separately in concurrent sessions. A second therapist will allow for more relational alternatives and one therapist will protect the other from being swallowed up by the intensity of the twosome's enmeshment.

This leads into another rationale for adding co-therapists. This is the type of structural difficulty encountered by the therapist in the family at the extremes of the enmeshed-disengaged spectrum. For example, the psychotically enmeshed family whose members are fused at primitive levels of their personalities can provide a formidable barrier to the outsider, the therapist. If and when the therapist is able to intrude into the family's boundaries, the suction into the force field of the family's relational structure can be overwhelming. With the extremely disengaged family, the therapist faces the same problem as when dealing with a family with highly autonomous members who have divergent agendas. Finally, the underorganized family may also require more than one therapist because of the paucity, rigidity and disjointedness of its relational patterns, particularly if the family happens to be large and especially if it is also struggling with diverse community agencies.

Duration of Treatment

Any discussion about length of sessions and duration of treatment must take into account that most of the experience of structural family therapists has been with the families of children who were the professed target of treatment. The average number of treatment sessions in the outpatient department of the Philadelphia Child

Guidance Clinic when it was most structurally oriented was between six and ten sessions, equal to about one and a half to two and a half months of treatment, since most families were seen once per week. This includes families that broke off treatment after one or two sessions and some that were seen for over a year, although after 20 sessions, or about five months, the number of families that continue in treatment drops precipitiously. While these numbers are based on clinical work with a broad range of problems and families, the large majority of these families were also poor and black. In the psychosomatic research project reported in *Psychosomatic Families* (Minuchin et al., 1978), the average treatment time was about seven months. These were mostly white, middle-class families. In the Stanton and Todd (1979) research with adult heroin addicts, the average length of treatment was between four and a half and five months. Length of session has not been systematically reported, although it appears that the majority of structural family therapists see families for an hour at a time. Certainly, however, therapists who work with larger and more complex families and with families together with social organizations have longer sessions. Other special circumstances, such as initial interviews and crisis-inducing and alleviating interviews, also may require longer sessions.

The structure of the process of therapy in structural family therapy is flexible in terms of the number of therapists on a case, what family and non-family members participate in an interview and the location, length and frequency of interviews. The theory allows for flexibility of implementation while providing a cohesive framework.

ROLE OF THE THERAPIST

The therapist, in an active and personal manner, directs his/her own behavior and communications with the family so as to influence selected aspects of the family's transactions within or outside of the session. The therapist's task is to develop relational contexts that will allow, stimulate and provoke change in transactional patterns around issues that are associated with the problem. The structural goals determine his/her interventions. How the therapist carries out these actions is reflected in the kinds of personal involvement he/she engages in, and with whom.

The therapist can be involved with the family in essentially two ways, one that encourages interaction among the family members, which we call *facilitating engagement*, and the other that discourages intrafamilial interaction by promoting transactions directly between the family members and the therapist, which we call *centralizing engagement*.

The therapist can engage in a facilitating manner from inside the family transaction by participating in it, or from outside by not engaging directly in the transaction. When the therapist engages with the family in a way that facilitates interaction from inside the family transaction, he/she temporarily becomes an integral and active participant in the structure of the system. The therapist can talk to those he/she wants to include in a discussion and can exclude the others, can side with one person against another on an issue or can support one's influence over another. He/she can engage with the family on one issue instead of another. In other words, the therapist has the ability to influence from within the family's transactional sequences the boundaries, alignments and power of the family and the operations around which family members work their relational structures. The transactional sequences can be continuous, such as are those that take place among the persons present in a session, or they can be segmented, as when a party to a transaction is not in the session and transactions take place in episodes with part of the sequence in the session and part outside.

An example of a facilitating engagement by a therapist from inside a family transaction is taken from a session in which a father is struggling to establish his relationship with his teenage son. The boy has been in a stable coalition with his mother against the father for years. The father's aloofness from the family and the mother's need to lean on her son have drawn the boy into such a tight bond with his mother that he is having trouble coping with the independent tasks of mastering his school work and moving ahead with his own plans for college. In one session the therapist has asked to meet with the boy and his father without the mother to discuss the boy's choice of colleges. The youngster has only applied to one school, where he is not assured acceptance, and has refused to consider a less competitive school, which also happens to be his father's alma mater. The father is genuinely concerned about his son's approach to choosing a college and is trying to get the boy to explain his thinking to him. However, the son dismisses his father as incapable of understanding him the way his mother does. The father flounders in trying to defend himself and the therapist responds to the youngster that neither the therapist nor the father could understand since he has not explained himself clearly. The therapist joins the father in questioning the young man until he breaks down and emotionally tells his father how he sees himself as a failure in school and how he must enter what he considers the higher status college in order to bolster his image with his friends. The therapist acted to help the father get his son to open up to him by aligning himself with the father in the boy's eyes, enhancing the father's leverage in the discussion and supporting the father's parental status. The therapist did all of this as a full participant in the discussion, and not as an outside commentator.

The therapist can also engage with the family from outside the family transaction to encourage intrafamilial interaction. In this role, the therapist acts more like an observer, commentator, advisor or director. From the outside, the therapist may influence the sequences in the transaction without being a participant discussant. The therapist can intervene accordingly to encourage the family transaction to take place in the session or outside of the session.

Two segments from the session just cited with the father and son can serve as illustrations of how the therapist can facilitate family interaction from outside the family transaction. In a part of the same interview, earlier than the segment discussed, the father had insisted to his son that he knew why his son was applying to the more competitive college. The therapist asked the father not to talk for his son but to help him by expecting him to explain himself clearly to his father in the session. The father's approach of trying to speak for the son had had the effect of making the youngster feel shut out and talked down to by his father. The therapist's

request of the father was calculated to encourage an interaction between father and son in which the father would assume a more open and receptive attitude toward the son in the discussion. It was meant to align the father more with the son, to broaden the boundaries of the son's space in the discussion and thereby to assist the father to give his son the experience of having some leverage in presenting his argument to his father for his choice of colleges. The therapist was maneuvering from outside the father-son transactions to encourage a particular interaction within the interview. At the end of the session the therapist supported the father's taking a couple of days of work off to travel with his son to his college interview with the understanding that the point of their being together would be that they would talk with one another about the experience of the college interview for the youngster. The therapist was facilitating a transaction away from the session that would align them more closely.

Centralizing engagement describes the kind of involvement by the therapist with family members that draws them into a relationship with the therapist and not with one another as the primary medium through which the therapeutic activity takes place. In these circumstances the structure of the relationship between therapist and client becomes the principal structural concern of the therapist. This is not like the direct involvement the therapist has with the client in facilitating family engagement from outside the transaction, although even in that instance the therapist will assume responsibility for the structure of the transactions between family member and him/herself. In a facilitating type of engagement the intent and effect of the therapist's behavior are to further family interaction, while in a centralizing intervention it is to influence a sequence between the therapist and the family member that will have its own inherent structural goal.

This centralizing activity can take place with an entire family or with an individual, in or out of a family session. With the individual in a family session, the therapist centralizes the individual by excluding everyone else from his/her transactions with that person. He/she engages centrally with the entire family when the therapist exhorts or sympathizes or explains to the family as a group. Finally, the therapist may act as a "switchboard" in the family, engaging with one member at a time around an issue under discussion. In this instance the therapist who listens and responds to each member individually in the presence of the others acts as a conduit of information while being a barrier to direct interaction. This is not the same as the therapist who serves as a facilitating interpreter between family members by framing and reframing what two or more family members are trying to say to one another to ease and direct their communication in the session. The centralizing engagement in family therapy is distinguished from individual therapy essentially by virtue of the fact that, while the centralizing segment or interview has its own structural goal, it also fits as part of the overall strategy with the family.

When the therapist engages an individual in the presence of the family, either when acting as a switchboard or when simply focusing on a single person, the therapist is always conscious of talking to a person within the context of the family. This *centralization in context* calls for the therapist to organize the interaction with the individual in a way that will also communicate purposefully to the family and will give the individual the experience of being perceived by the family as he/she appears in the light of the conversation with the therapist. It is not unlike having the family observe the individual with the therapist from behind a one-way vision mirror. The family observes without being able to interfere, which forces a more receptive observation, since instant response is being inhibited. The individual is able to speak and behave with the protection of the relationship with the therapist and thereby communicates to the family the part of the self expressed in the relationship with the therapist. Paradoxically, centralization in context, while inhibiting family interaction, may make possible communications otherwise impossible among the family members.

The same father-son case described above can serve as an instance of centralizing engagement with a family member in an individual session. The therapist was having a series of individual interviews with the adolescent son concurrently with the family sessions. The youngster was having difficulty with his school work, but originally was denying the importance of school for himself and, therefore, of the poor grades he was receiving. The therapist was able to assist the boy to be more candid with the therapist and himself about what he was doing with his school work, which was to avoid it by inattention, daydreaming or other distractions. The youngster was helped to experiment with new approaches to his homework and to gauge their effect on his classroom performance. He began to assume control over his output. In these sessions the therapist assumed a supportive attitude toward the young man, but just as he sought to help the father give maneuverability to the son in their relationship, the therapist gave the youngster plenty of room to voice his attitude to the therapist about school and what he thought he wanted to do about his school work. These sessions were limited in number. They had goals specific to the youngster, as well as goals related to the family. As the young man assumed greater responsibility for his school performance, he became better prepared to share his plans about school with his father. Along with the help the youngster received, the centralized individual interviews also served to prime the pump for interaction between father and son in the family sessions.

When the therapist is engaging with an individual or with an entire family, is facilitating an intrafamilial transaction or centralizing the interaction and is operating from inside or outside a transaction, the therapist is working to assume structural postures in relation to the family and each of its members. Whatever the role the therapist assumes, he/she attempts to execute it within a transaction that is congruent with the structural goals of the treatment at any given point in the process. *The therapist is never in a structurally neutral position with respect to the persons being dealt with because the structural perspective underpins everything the therapist does.*

In structural family therapy the therapist is actively and continuously organizing his/her part of the relationship with the family to conform with the structural goals of each transaction. Much of this is done at a conscious level and much unconsciously, once the therapist has determined the goals. Understanding and being

committed to the goals will help to spontaneously shape the direction of the trained therapist's behavior so that he/she will be able to
respond in ways consistent with the structural
objectives even unconsciously.

The therapist's professional role is also a very
personal role. To understand, the therapist must
be sufficiently accessible to the family and its
members to be affected personally by their
transactions with him/her or among themselves.
The therapist's private personal reactions become the plate upon which the family leaves its
imprint for him/her to read and decipher. Moreover, the availability of his/her own personal reactions allows the therapist the means through
which to reach and touch the family in natural
responses. The relatively uninvolved, observing
part of the therapist that conceptualizes what
he/she is experiencing also helps to direct and
discipline the personal aspect of the therapist's
responses.

Ultimately, the therapist's structural goal is
to see the family transact differently without the
therapist's involvement. In the beginning of
therapy the therapist is likely to be more forceful
in structuring the contexts within which the family members will interact. The therapist will be
continuously testing the family's relational
changes and will diminish the level of force of
his/her intrusion into the family transactions according to the degree of autonomy the family
demonstrates in maintaining altered structural
patterns. The therapist eventually becomes peripheral to the family's new transactional patterns. At the point at which the family members
autonomously maintain the functional, restruc-
tured relational patterns having also resolved
the problems for which they asked for help, the
therapy is completed.[7]

---

[7]*Editors' Note.* In terms of judging therapeutic outcome, in
both clinical practice and research, this is the key factor that
differentiates structural family therapy from other influential
approaches, e.g., behavioral (Gordon and Davidson, Chapter 14; Jacobson, Chapter 15) and problem-centered (Epstein and Bishop, Chapter 12) which are also problem-
focused. For the latter such therapists, problem resolution
is a sufficient index of positive change, while for the structural therapist change in the identified problem without
concomitant change in the structure of relationship patterns
that underlie the problem is quite insufficient. The important distinction, then, involves assessing outcome on the
basis of second-order *vs.* first-order change.

TECHNIQUES OF STRUCTURAL FAMILY THERAPY

One needs to consider methods in relation to
what they are meant to accomplish. Some techniques are related to the *creation of the transaction* the therapist is to work with, some are
for the therapist to *join with the transaction*,
and others are basically to *restructure the transaction* (see Table 1).

In terms of *creating the transaction*, there are
three ways in which to do this: structuralization,
enactment inducement, and task-setting within
the family. *Structuralization* is the therapist's
purposeful organization of his/her part in the
sequences of a transaction with family members
to influence the pattern of their interaction.
Enactment inducement is the process through
which the therapist promotes in the session the
family members' transacting their habitual patterns of relating. *Task-setting within the family*
is the assignment by the therapist to the family
members to carry out among themselves an operation within prescribed transactional parameters.

Structuralization is at the core of the therapist's activity in the centralization role of a structural family therapist. The therapist, for example,
may intend that a woman in a family, who is
wont to assume an attitude of inferiority with
her husband, relate to the therapist from a position of status and power. The therapist conveys
to her an attitude of regard for her judgments
about her problem. He consistently defers to
her right to determine her own responses to the
difficulties she faces within her marriage. He
raises questions with her and expresses his personal opinion, but makes certain never to take
for granted her responses to him. He respects
the boundaries between them and her control
over her own thinking and actions within their
transactions. In effect, the therapist assumes a
specifically defined structural posture toward
the woman in order to influence her to assume
the corresponding complementary attitude toward him.

Structuralization is also at the base of the centralizing aspect of the transactions that occur
between therapist and family in the process of
negotiating the task or other assignment when
the therapist engages in a facilitating manner

TABLE 1
Major Techniques of Structural Family Therapy

I. Creation of
Transaction

Structuralization
Enactment Inducement
Task Setting within the family

II. Joining with the
Transaction

Tracking
Accommodation
Mimesis

III. Restructuring the
Transaction

a. System Recomposition:	b. Symptom Focusing:	c. Structural Modification:
Adding Systems	Exaggerating the Symptom	Disassembling (Emphasizing Differences)
Subtracting Systems	Deemphasizing the Symptom	(Developing Implicit Conflict)
	Moving to a New Symptom	(Blocking Transactional patterns)
	Relabeling the Symptom	Constructing
	Altering the Affect of the Symptom	Reinforcing Reorganizing

from outside a transaction. In other words, the therapist structuralizes his/her relationship with the family in the process of negotiating the task. In an illustration involving an outside facilitating engagement, the therapist may want to assign a task to the couple with the same self-demeaning wife referred to above. She is to deliberately provoke an argument daily with her intimidating husband which she is promptly to arrange to lose as she sees fit. The task is meant to provide her with some protection against her own anxiety and to begin to give her control over how she reacts toward her husband, while taking some of the urge to fight out of the husband who knows she plans to lose. In the process of assigning the task to the couple, the therapist structures his position in the transaction so as to remain tentative about the task until the wife were to insist firmly enough that it is her own decision to carry it out. The approach to the wife is intended to provoke her to take possession of the task from the therapist and of the losing from her husband. The therapist structuralizes his interactions with the woman to be congruent with the structure the task is intended to create in the relationship between her and her husband.

The therapist can help induce a family *enactment* from outside or from inside the transactions of an enactment. In either case, it is a facilitating intervention on the part of the therapist. Of course, the family will at times spontaneously enact its relational patterns in the session, but aside from those occasions the therapist will also need to be able to influence when and under what conditions the family will replicate these patterns in his/her presence. As an example of inducing an enactment from outside the transaction, one can take the couple already cited in an operation around which they habitually have conflict, the relatively higher expenditure of money for his needs over hers. The therapist requests that the spouses discuss with each other how much they spent for personal items in the last three months for each of them. The therapist chooses an issue which he has reason to believe is likely to spark the same kind of discussion they say they have at home. While such an enactment has obvious value as an assessment tool, it can be utilized therapeutically through the appropriate structuralization of the way the request is made of the couple, in the timing of the enactment itself in the therapy, and in the use the enactment will serve as a base for another intervention by the therapist.

The therapist can also induce the enactment of the transaction from inside the interaction. Experiencing the transaction from inside will provide the therapist with an intimate perspective of the family's relational patterns. However, to the extent that the therapist's involvement is primarily to restructure, his/her participation will distort the accuracy of the enactment as a replication of what happens outside the therapy. If, again with the same couple, the therapist were to join the wife against the husband by agreeing with her in the midst of their argument that he was being "unfair" to her, he would be joining the argument on the wife's side.

In task-setting within the family the therapist prescribes to the family members an activity to carry out among themselves in a more or less specified time frame within defined structural parameters. The task may be assigned to be carried out in the presence of the therapist or outside the session. While tasks may be used in many different ways, including as a technique for prescribing activities between an individual and the therapist, the reference here is only to its use as a technique to direct interactions among family members or with others in a person's ecosystem. It is distinguished from enactment by the prescription of the parameters. An example of task setting within the family has just been described under structuralization in which the timid wife was to provoke and lose an argument at home daily with her intimidating husband. The same task could just as well have been assigned for the session itself.

Structuralization, enactment and task-setting within the family are all ways of creating a transaction among the family members with or without the therapist as a part of the transaction. These interventions may also serve as joining techniques for the therapist with the family, and as restructuring techniques to accomplish the structural reorganization intended.

Joining with the transaction is relevant to all aspects of the therapist's work, whether the therapist is assuming a centralized or facilitating role, and whether the therapist is working from inside or outside a family transaction. Joining refers to relating personally for professional purposes. In analyzing this aspect of the professional relationship one is dissecting a human interaction so particularly that it may convey both a mechanical and a manipulative flavor. Indeed, in structural family therapy the pull to act artificially exists because of the constant demand to respond purposefully to the family to influence the reactions of its members. This raises an ethical question, which will not be dealt with here, about whether a therapist is

expected to "really" care when the therapist says, "I am concerned," and whether the therapist need "really" be angry when saying, "This offends me." From a technical standpoint, the problem with acting or responding artifically is that what the therapist is offering of self may not go deeply enough to release his/her full energies and conviction to effectively communicate the intended message.

How a therapist joins with a family both on personal and professional levels is as complex as the human relationship. Our position is that the therapist must give genuine personal interest, attention and responsiveness to the family. However, there are also technical skills that have been identified by Minuchin (1974) that can be called upon in the therapist's efforts to join with the family, among which are *tracking, accommodation* and *mimesis*.

Through *tracking* the therapist adopts symbols of the family's life through which to communicate to the family and around which to build relationships. The language, life themes, history, values of the family, all come to represent aspects of the family's identity. The family's relational structure is packaged within these symbols of what the family is. In other words, for the family each symbol is laden with associations about what the family is and how it functions. These symbols are usually found in the content of the family's communications. By grabbing hold of the symbols and using them to communicate with the family, the therapist joins the family in using an instrument of communication of the family members and influences the family's transactional patterns through them. The therapist "leads by following" (Minuchin, 1974, p. 127).

Tracking can be illustrated through another example from the couple with the self-demeaning wife in which the therapist strives from inside a family transaction to induce an enactment. This couple was of second generation southern European descent with strong traditional views from their parents' culture. The therapist wished to align with the wife in a discussion he was attempting to induce between her and her husband about the husband's disproportionate spending on his personal needs over hers. The therapist, recalling the husband's pride in "providing" for his family, chose to encourage the wife to talk with her husband by asking her in his presence to tell him where she felt he had provided for her well and where she felt he did not provide for her needs. The therapist hoped that he was using vocabulary that would usher the therapist into a sensitive area with some part of both the husband and wife accompanying him.

In *accommodation* the therapist joins by relating to the family in congruence with the family's transactional patterns. The therapist respects the rules that govern the relationships within the family, and demonstrates that respect through a general acceptance of the family's communication channels. By accepting the family's ways, the therapist tries to enter the family's supporting network and fortify thereby his/her basis from which to push for change in the family.

An illustration of accommodation with the same couple is drawn from early in the first session of treatment, when it became clear to the therapist that they conducted their relationship with the implicit understanding that the husband was the spokesperson for the family and the proclaimer of the family rules. The couple had been referred by the family physician because of the wife's recurring bouts of depression. The husband observed that these depressive times alternated with periods of peevishness. The wife concurred, although she minimized the peevishness. The therapist cautioned the husband that if his wife were to be "cured," they would need to go through a period of "digging out" all of her frustrations with the family. The husband agreed, expressing his support of anything that would help his wife. The therapist respected the family rules by getting the husband's approval to conduct the treatment in a way that would lead the wife to act against the established understanding that the wife was not to vent her frustrations toward her husband, especially in the presence of an outsider.

Through *mimesis* the therapist joins with the family by becoming like the family in manner or content of his/her communications. The therapist can become like the family or one of its members through adopting the manner of speaking, body language, tempo or other behavioral mode of communication of the family. The therapist can also join the family mimetically through the content of his/her communi-

cations by conveying personal experiences, traits or interests that are similar to those of the family. This latter effort becomes a form of self-disclosure that is done to help the family identify the therapist with itself. Like tracking and accommodation, this type of joining establishes a common base with the family from which the therapist can intervene in the family.

Continuing with the same couple as pictured in their first interview, while the therapist is talking with the husband about what needs to be done to help his wife, the therapist mirrors the husband's air of formality. The husband takes seriously his responsibility for the well-being of his family, and, in particular, his wife. The therapist hopes that the husband will also see in the therapist's formal air a communication of his own sense of responsibility and be prepared to trust the therapist.

Restructuring, the third category of technique, covers those that exist primarily to change the structure of the transactions of the family or other system involved in the problem. All these techniques are utilized to address two broad types of structural problems, stemming from system conflict and from structural insufficiency.

System conflict refers to those problems which arise out of competing needs of the components of a system or ecosystem. These problems are the products of counterdemands of functions within the individual and/or between people in which the conflict cannot be resolved to the satisfaction of the components of the conflict without a dysfunctional compromise by one or more of the components involved. Behind the manifestation of the conflict there is, by its very nature, a compelling quality to the symptomatic or problematic behavior since there are functional needs to be satisfied. The depressed father with an alienated wife leans too heavily on his adolescent son for emotional support and seeks closeness at a time when his son needs distance. The beleaguered ghetto school systematically protects itself from any significant involvement and communication with its students and their community, while they look to engage the school in their needs and interests.

Structural insufficiency refers to those problems that result from a lack of structural resources in the family or other social system to meet the functional demands of the system. With these problems, the individual or social entity is not able to carry out a function because it does not have the resources or structural organization to do what is required. This inability to function may result from the lack of opportunity in its *development* due to an absence of family and social supports or from a conflict situation in that ecosystem. The insufficiency may also derive from a lack of supports to the functioning of the family or its members from some part of its *current* familial-social ecosystem. For example, this insufficiency may be seen in a poor, ghetto family in which there is a single parent and a large number of children, with the mother lacking the social and family experience to prepare her for the complex management problems of raising a large brood alone. Such a mother may try to handle each child's needs individually, overextending herself, exhausting herself and ultimately not satisfying any of the children. The insufficiency of structure would exist both in the development of the mother's skills and in the lack of differentiated hierarchy and delegation within the sibling subsystem. Another illustration of insufficiency of structure would be in the chronic lack of employment opportunities for particular minority communities and the impact that such conditions have on the personality development of the youth in these communities.

The techniques that are designed to address problems from system conflict and structural insufficiency are not exclusive to one or the other of these categories of problems. However, they do tend to cluster. Those that deal with system conflict fall more along the lines of those that break down or reorganize structures, while the techniques that are more appropriate to structural insufficiency tend to come under building new structures or reinforcing existing structures. Under those that break down structure are techniques such as exaggerating symptoms, blocking transactional patterns and developing implicit conflicts. Under building new structures are techniques which help persons learn new ways of functioning or that add resources to a family by linking the family up to new systems. Obviously, in system conflict type situations there will be times when people need to learn new skills for dealing with issues

as a way of unlocking conflicting demands. In the same way, there will be structural insufficiency problems that require techniques that will break down old patterns in order to be able to begin building new ones.

The differences between problems of conflict and those of insufficiency suggest differences in technique, and also in how techniques are employed. With conflictual situations, for example, the therapist is more often called upon to apply techniques in a confrontative manner, while in circumstances of insufficient structure, a supportive approach is more likely to be used.

The three basic types of restructuring techniques for the treatment of both types of problems are *system recomposition, symptom focusing* and *structural modification*. *System recomposition* describes techniques that address structural change by adding to or taking away systems from those systems that are involved in the creation and/or maintenance of the problem. One can add systems at all levels of family organization. A mother and son may have problems because of the exclusiveness of their relationship. Adding a spouse and thereby a father to the household will enrich the family structure. Including older female siblings in the negotiations between a young adolescent daughter and her parents about appropriateness of dress can lend the younger girl some leverage in the discussion with her parents. Adding a church community to a lone mother's life can break down the woman's isolation. In subtracting systems, the removal of an in-law from the home of a newlywed couple may better enable them to resolve the normal conflicts of a new marriage. A temporary separation may force a marriage partner to face his or her own failures and to stop projecting them onto the other spouse.

Symptom focusing techniques approach change directly through the symptom. A number of techniques borrowed from strategic therapy fall within this category. The techniques in this category identified by Minuchin (1974) are *exaggerating the symptom, deemphasizing the symptom, moving to a new symptom* and *relabeling the symptom. Changing the symptom's affect* may also be included in this list.

The symptom or problematic behavior is viewed as an effect of the dysfunctional structure. The family members whose relationships contribute to the symptom and those who bear the symptom are all linked together in the symptom. The symptom itself may offer the most direct door to reaching all those involved in order to solve the problem or it may represent its greatest obstacle to a solution. In any case whatever strategies the therapist is following, he/she must decide what approach to take toward the symptom.

Every symptom serves to compensate for needs that cannot be otherwise satisfied adequately in the thinking of the person or persons involved. Most of the techniques in this listing that focus on the symptom suggest means through which a therapist can frustrate the function of the symptom, laying the groundwork for its removal.

Among the ways to work through the symptom is *exaggerating the symptom*, which is to increase the dimensions of the symptom beyond the point that it can any longer serve its compensating purpose. As an illustration, consider the man who would periodically withdraw into a corner of his living room feeling sorry for himself and appearing to the family to be dejected. Feeling inadequate, he was not able to reach out to his family to get their attention except through this maneuver. The therapist sympathized with his feeling of rejection and elicited from him that he felt this way much more often than he actually let on. The therapist prescribed in the presence of the family that the man not hide his suffering from his family and exhibit this behavior on a daily schedule, which approximated the frequency with which he had the impulse to withdraw into his corner. One effect of prescribing a scheduled increase in the symptom was that, since the family now knew to expect the behavior and that it was being produced to comply with the therapist, their anxiety about the withdrawals diminished considerably. For the man, himself, withdrawing on a frequent and fixed schedule not only denied him his family's former level of concern, but also made his action burdensome and unrewarding for him. He stopped the behavior and with the therapist's help began looking for other ways to satisfy his need for attention and increased status at home. This example also serves as an example of *prescribing the symptom*, which can be added to this list of techniques.

Opposite to exaggerating the symptom is *deemphasizing the symptom*. The deemphasis of the symptom draws away from the symptomatic behavior the investment of energy that gives it the impetus to succeed in its compensating function. Often coupled with this technique is *moving to a new symptom*, which is intended to attract the energy of the family and/or of the individual away from the original symptom and to a structurally related symptom around which the family is less rigidly organized. The focus on the new symptom not only debilitates the old one, but introduces the family to a new door that should eventually lead to the original problematic relationships. Going to the new symptom allows the therapist to work with an operation that has a supporting infrastructure, which has components in common with the structure of the original symptom, but which is different enough not to have invested in it the binding conflictual energy of the original symptomatic operation.

An example of the above is a prepubertal girl who developed an embarrassing skin rash. This youngster who had been overprotected by her mother was fearful of stepping out of her house, which was becoming more of a personal conflict for her as adolescence began to press upon her. The rash gave her mother an opportunity to be preoccupied with her daughter and a good reason to rationalize the girl's staying home. The therapist observed that the girl was slightly overweight and learned that she did little at home but watch television, which was an irritation to the mother, who wanted her to help with the housework. The therapist made an issue of the girl's weight and its implications for her health. He was able to draw the mother's attention to the issue of the weight by building on her excessive worry about the girl's health. This concern, along with the mother's suppressed irritation over the youngster's reluctance to assist her at home, allowed the therapist to focus the mother on the weight by having her supervise her daughter's diet and keep the girl active with a full schedule of household work. With the mother making rules about eating and housework, the house could no longer serve as a comfortable refuge for the girl, but more than that, the conflictual context between mother and daughter around these issues enabled them to begin negotiating the boundary and power structures between them. The therapist helped them to rework the rules governing these dimensions of their relationships in order to strengthen and redefine the personal and generational boundaries between mother and daughter. In these circumstances the therapist can deal with the rash without attending directly to it by working on the relational structures that support the rash as they appear in the negotiations around the weight and housework.

Relabeling the symptom follows the same principle as deemphasis and moving to another symptom. It redefines symptoms, and by giving a symptom another meaning to the family, it opens alternate structural pathways for family members to deal with one another around an issue. This technique requires that the new interpretation of the problematic behavior be one that indeed does carry with it structural underpinnings similar to those of the original problems, but that is significantly different enough to offer the family alternate relational pathways for working together on the structural issues common to the original problem and to its redefinition. A young man living in a dependent relationship with his parents at home explains that he suffers from depressions and cannot manage on his own. From the evidence of the young man's behavior the therapist feels free to tell him and his parents that he is not depressed, but that he is remaining home to prevent his parents from fighting. The therapist reassures the family that it is not necessary for the son to camouflage his actions under an artificial depression, and that if the parents want him to protect their marriage, they need only agree to have him at home for this purpose. By deciding on whether to accept his help, the parents decide on whether he is to remain in their home acting depressed and dependent. A close cousin to relabeling is *altering the affect of the symptom*, whereby the affective significance of the symptom is altered, modifying the meaning of the symptomatic behavior for everyone experiencing it.

All of these techniques, including other symptom-focused ones, such as are found in behavior modification, work to eradicate symptoms. In structural family therapy the techniques are used within the structural goals of the therapy,

thereby taking into full account the purposes of the symptoms, and the process of the therapy. More often than not, such techniques are carried out within a comprehensive process that not only removes symptoms, but also opens and firms up new structural channels for responding to the motivations that were sustaining the symptoms in the first place.[8]

The third category under restructuring techniques is *structural modification*. Techniques under structural modification are those that are aimed at the structural composition of the ecosystem that serves as the primary locus of the problem to be solved. These techniques can themselves be divided into those that *disassemble*, *construct*, *reinforce* and *reorganize* the structure. These are all techniques that are employed to directly affect the alignment, boundary and power structures within and among the systems. These techniques may be directed at any manifestation of the habitual relational dispositions of people toward one another in a family or other social system.

What technically distinguishes structural family therapy from other forms of therapy is this explicit concentration on modifying structure. From outside the transaction of a family the therapist can communicate suggestions, instructions, and directives that are intended to assist the family to modify the structures of its relationships. From within the transaction the therapist can say, emote and behave with the family members in ways that will accomplish that same end. The structural family therapist tries to intervene throughout treatment in a planful, coherent and continuous manner to modify the structural underpinning of the problem being worked on. All other techniques he/she uses in the treatment are employed within the framework of the structural goals.

There are many examples of what it means to attempt explicitly to modify the manifest representations of structural dimensions in social

---

[8]*Editors' Note.* In both conceptual and clinical terms, it is the structural therapist's emphasis on the *purposes* of symptoms that most clearly and significantly differentiates this model from other problem-centered family therapy approaches. The reader may want to refer again to *Editors' Note* 7 to consider the implications of this distinction regarding the meaning of symptoms for the assessment of treatment outcome.

relationships. One such generic intervention that deserves some mention only because it is so commonly used by structural family therapists at a nonverbal level is *chorography*. This intervention, which the therapist can implement from outside or inside the social grouping, treats the physical arrangement of the people in relation to one another while engaged in a transaction as a form of communication about the transaction. The therapist, from outside or inside the physical grouping, rearranges the grouping so that the reorganization will itself affect the meaning of what is being communicated about the relationships within the group.

An example of a therapist chorographically aligning with a dejected youngster from inside the family arrangement would be the therapist's going to sit with him when he noticed the boy situated alone outside the periphery of the family circle. An aligning intervention from outside the same family arrangement would be to ask a sibling to sit with the peripheral youngster to keep him company. The intervention can also be interpreted as drawing the youngster into the boundaries of the family grouping and as giving him greater power in that situation because of the attention and company he received. Although the intervention was first described in terms of alignment, it affects the other structural dimensions simultaneously since every transaction conveys aligning, boundary and power intentions.

As mentioned earlier, interventions that are aimed at explicitly modifying structure fall under four divisions—disassembly, construction, reinforcement, and reorganization. To *disassemble* a structural pattern is simply to break it down. To *construct* a structural pattern is to develop structures either new to the system or underdeveloped in the system. To *reinforce* structure is to act to help maintain what exists or to amplify its scope and/or strength. To *reorganize* relationships structurally is to rearrange patterns in a particular problem area along lines that are already accessible to the system, often in other areas of functioning.

Disassembling is a necessary part of all modifying of structure in the sense that to bring in the new, one often has to alter or do away with the old. A family may resist changing structure because the old pattern is a familiar entrenched habit, and/or because it represents its best solution to an existing problem. The obstacle represented by an entrenched habit may be seen in a family in which the learned pattern of behavior remains long after the original motivation for the behavior has been eradicated. The task of breaking down entrenched habits may be quite difficult, but may be more a question of discovering how to develop new structural alternatives than of blocking the old. On the contrary, the family is more likely to hold on tenaciously to old transactional patterns if they have been its only solution to an existing problem, particularly in a system conflict type situation. Knowing how to disrupt such a pattern may be a prerequisite to changing it.

The divisive techniques of emphasizing differences and developing implicit conflicts, which are described by Minuchin (1974) for disassembling transactional patterns, are most often used with structural patterns undergirding system conflict type problems. *Emphasizing differences* makes overt those distinctions between family members that have been kept hidden to maintain a lack of separation between them. *Developing implicit conflicts* not only draws out the differences, but also the suppressed reasons for mutual opposition. For example, to emphasize differences with a couple that claims absolute agreement in the discipline of their delinquent daughter, the therapist may engage each parent individually in the presence of the other to discuss how each would handle a particular issue over which the therapist suspects the parents secretly differ. If any differences between the parents come into the open with this intervention, the therapist can subsequently act to make overt the implicit conflicts between them by asking the parents to decide together which of their respective viewpoints should prevail in the discipline of their daughter.

Finally, *blocking transactional patterns* is another disassembling technique. The therapist acts from outside or inside the transaction to prevent the participants from following their accustomed pattern, without necessarily offering them an alternative channel. This technique may be used to intervene with any pattern, in situations of either insufficiency or conflict. Open conflict between family members is most likely to result from this intervention if the accustomed channel had served to suppress conflict within the family. In the same couple under discussion, if disagreement about their daughter were being avoided by the father's soft-pedaling his opinions whenever the mother became insistent about hers, the therapist could deny the father this outlet by reminding the wife each time it occurred that her husband's apparent agreement was only half-hearted.

Constructing patterns, the second category under modification of structure, is called for in situations of structural insufficiency or of entrenched habits of relating. Here one has people who for whatever reasons have not learned to do things differently. Within this category fall many of the instructional interventions, including techniques derived from learning theory. In structural family therapy these efforts at structural development are made mostly through experiential exercises. The therapist will work with instructional type techniques whenever he/she believes that the lack of structure is due to the absence of opportunity for development or to the blocking of possibilities on account of a conflictual situation. Along with acting to stimulate the development of the relevant structures, the therapist must address the circumstances contributing to the structural problem if they still exist.

A woman raising her children alone finds herself in too many struggles over control with her young son because she resorts too often to physical discipline. She may be using the methods she learned from her mother or she may have learned to resort to physical means to compensate for a sense of personal weakness. Whatever the reason for her not developing more of a range of disciplinary approaches, she may still need to learn how to deal more positively with her child through, for example, some basic behavioral techniques based on reinforcing behavior by reward. If her original inhibition to learning stemmed from a need to make up for a feeling of inadequacy, she will also require other therapeutic work aimed at her sense of incompetence.

Reinforcing patterns, the third category of structural modifiers, involves the therapist in helping to maintain existing structural patterns in a family, or to amplify them in order to handle a larger scope of operations and/or to manage the operations with greater effectiveness. Helping to maintain a structure may be done in the midst of creating other structural change, that is, to change one pattern without sacrificing another. Assisting a mother to hold on to her tenderness with her child as she develops new disciplinary firmness may on occasion be a prudent and necessary goal to accompany the change-producing effort. On the other hand, a therapist may work to amplify a pattern at the neglect of others to make the pattern that is supported the dominant pattern in an operation. When an overly aggressive husband attempts to be supportive to his wife, he tries to direct her, and she invariably feels controlled and resists his help. The therapist encourages the husband to listen to her, which he does comfortably in other circumstances, but this time to listen actively when she is troubled at the exclusion of all other supportive gestures. Reinforcing techniques are often employed in situations where there is inadequate structure in the family.

Reorganizing patterns the fourth of the structural modifiers, calls for techniques that are aimed at utilizing existing but blocked potential in families to alter structure. Reorganizing usually involves removing obstacles to existing alternate structures to make them accessible. This is not the building of new structures where they had been lacking. The obstacles are created by conflicting motivations that prevent a family from doing differently within defined areas of functioning what would be possible in other functions and circumstances. An illustration would be the family in which a man unwittingly controlled everyone in his family because he feared losing their personal loyalties, a trait not evident in his external relationships. The control produced resentment in his family, but also the dependency that kept them close to him. He was trying to guarantee positive alignments and their presence within the boundaries of his life by the exercise of power. A task in which he was absolutely not to direct them or request anything of them at first left him doing what he wanted by himself and feeling desperately alone. With time the task gave him the experience of personal self-sufficiency within the family and eventually it earned him a more willing responsiveness from his family. This set the basis for their renegotiating new relational structures.

Conclusion

This section on techniques touched upon three basic categories of techniques for joining with, creating, and restructuring transactions. It must be restated that the techniques of joining with and creating transactions are employed to create change, that in joining and restructuring the therapist works within spontaneous or therapist-created transactions, and that in restructuring and creating transactions the therapist acts in the context of joining the family. In practice, each category of technique is dependent upon the other two. The techniques described earlier are especially representative of structural family therapy. However, the list is not exhaustive, nor does it include all the techniques commonly borrowed by structuralists from other approaches, such as behavior modification and strategic therapy.

CURATIVE FACTORS

Change in structure produces change in functioning. This basic tenet of the rationale for change in structural family therapy rests on the premise that all functioning is the product of the structure of the system from which it springs. With this assumption the therapist labors to access the manifest structure of a system in order to change the regulating codes or mediating structure (Lane, 1970) as it relates to the operations that embody the problem.

Structural family therapy is built on the expectation that the therapist will intervene in transactions that are manifestations of the problem-bearing structure in such a way that the system will internalize the structural changes and operate differently as a result. The relevant transactions are actualized in certain operations that carry out the functions of the system related to the problem. The therapist targets those operations or other operations that are structurally connected. The operation must bring with it enough investment from the persons in the system or become so invested by means of a technical maneuver that an alteration in the structure

of the transactions in the operation will reverberate deeply in the problem's support structure. The technical interventions must be able to disrupt or supersede the existing structure and to offer alternative structures to carry out more fittingly the functions of the system that were being served by the problematic structures.

Structural change in treatment is induced by the maneuvers of therapists of all orientations. The structural family therapist may employ any or most of these technical means, but he/she will use any such technique within an ongoing transactional process in which the therapist participates continually in a structurally purposeful way. The therapist attempts to read the structure in family transactions and to adopt structural postures at least consistent with the structural aims of the therapy and at best calculated to actively induce the structural changes. The therapist is working from the belief that the impact of the therapy can be maximized by behavior on his/her part that continually reinforces the structural goals. Each operation around which the therapist and the persons in treatment engage presents another opportunity to affect the problem's supporting structures or other structural patterns connected with the targeted structures. Both the common relationship maintenance type intervention and the high intensity intervention, such as a task, are implemented within a relational process among the therapist and family members, which has its own structure that evolves in line with the goals of the therapy.

This approach serves as a framework for a broad range of therapeutic techniques, structural and otherwise, and therapy formats, including outpatient and inpatient care. In terms of particular schools of intervention, strategic techniques are compatible with the structural model and are frequently employed by most structural family therapists. These techniques, which are essentially therapist-initiated tactics (Haley, 1973), act to reorganize transactions between the therapist and the person being treated, or among the family members. Behavior modification is also not infrequently used, often within a family context, providing yet another kind of method by which to structure a transaction. Certainly, work is done within the structural approach to foster the learning of new skills in patients or families through generating new experiences in the context of family transactions. While history is commonly gathered in the process of negotiating relationships, its collection and interpretation are likely to be carried out as structural interventions. If medication were used as part of the therapy, wherever possible it would be prescribed and administered in ways that would further the structural goals of the treatment. Whatever the technique, it is used within a multidimensional effort to bring about structural change, which is seen as the essential therapeutic element.

The therapist's personality and family and life circumstances, with whatever strengths or problems they present, are at any moment what the therapist is and all that the therapist has to relate with in therapy. The personal problems both handicap and add new dimensions to the therapist's ranges of experience, awareness and response. Whatever he/she can do to increase self-awareness, accessibility to his/her own psyche and control of his/her personal response in therapy will enhance the effectiveness of his/her work. Nevertheless, structural family therapists are not commonly encouraged to enter into insight-generating personal therapy or into the exploration of their family networks because however useful these efforts may be in other respects, as mediums for training they draw the trainee into examining psychological phenomena from historical perspectives and into intervening from an interpretive standpoint. Training for self-awareness and self-directedness in the therapist in the context of doing therapy is all important to a therapist who has to be as personally active as the structurally-oriented therapist must be. However, just as the therapeutic approach seeks to intervene in the context of the family transacting the actual operations it wants changed, changes in the therapist are sought as an integral part of the training of the therapist to treat families.

In structural family therapy the therapist focuses on defined problems to solve. On the assumption that these problems emanate from the structures of their systemic base, he/she aims to change the structures along with eliminating the symptoms. Depending on the dominance of the structure and the breadth of functions it covers,

a change of structure in the process of solving problems can have far-reaching effects on the functioning and development of the system. The structurally-oriented therapist strives for the changes that are achievable and are agreed to implicitly or explicitly by the family and its members.

TRAINING

Structural family therapy is a therapeutic approach that pursues solutions to problems in their current social reality. Similarly, the training takes place through mediums that most closely represent the actual experience of a therapist transacting with the family. What follows in this section represents our views on the ideal approach to training structural family therapists.

The therapist must have theory, knowledge and skills. The theory is about structure in social systems, and the forms in which that structure operates in individuals, families and their social contexts, both from ecological and developmental perspectives. This means that the therapist must know something about individual psychological structure and development, family organization and the aspects of community that interface most proximately with individual and family functioning, and the relationships of all of these to one another. The knowledge is informational data about individuals, families and communities to which the theory can be related, as, for example, about people and families in various cultural and socioeconomic circumstances to form a baseline about effective functioning for these families in their social and cultural contexts. The skills the therapist must learn have to do with learning to see the structure of the whole in the structure of the current transaction and to act in the current transaction to affect the structure of the transaction and that of the system it represents.

To learn the theory, informational base and skills, the therapist will go through a training process that is mostly experiential and is closely related to actual tasks and circumstances in which the therapist must perform. In that respect the training parallels the therapy. There is a place in training for literature and lectures to communicate concepts and informational data. Nevertheless, this mode of teaching is not the most profitable for the practitioner who must develop not just ways of thinking, but skills for doing. Reading and lecturing do not precede practical training. They are given concurrently with and as a part of the experiential exercises.

For example, in the beginning phase of training, therapists need to learn about family development and organization. As part of that learning therapists can both observe and conduct "normal" interviews with client and nonclient families. In these sessions the interviewer engages the families in discussions of a broad range of their current interests, activities and functioning, with the family jointly and with individual members of the family separately. Along with a survey of current endeavors, the exploration takes an historical developmental perspective, as did Minuchin's (1974) interview with the Wagners in *Families and Family Therapy*. The task of the interviewer is to be concentrated on learning about family adaptive and coping patterns along with dysfunctional patterns in their historical and current contexts. With the client families the results of the "normal" interviews are compared with taped clinical sessions of the same families to contrast and correlate information obtained in each. The didactic teaching is integrated with the experiences of these exercises.

Clinical training in which trainees are to learn to see the structure of transactions, and to act to affect these structures take four basic forms: observing model interviews, role-playing, live supervision and supervision through videotape. At the very beginning of training, clinicians need models against which to judge their own performance. They learn from observing experienced and skillful therapists. Even if the modeling leads to "aping," that form of identification in the early stages of training gives way to internalization as the trainee masters the skills. This kind of observation is most useful when the model interview is also accompanied by an analysis of the thinking behind the senior therapist's activity, done in person by the therapist or through recorded commentary. Otherwise, an experienced therapist's performance can be more mystifying than illuminating to the trainee.

Role-playing is the next in the sequence of early training experiences, and is begun while the model interviews are still being presented.

Role-playing is one of the most effective mediums through which the trainee can capture the flavor of new and alien skills in clinical observing, doing and hypothesizing. It is an ideal practice situation because it does not involve a real family, but at the same time, if organized well, offers a real enough experience for the trainee role-playing therapist and for these role-playing family members. The role-playing therapist can practice with impunity to self and family, while the role-playing family can see what it is like to walk in the family's shoes. The circumstances of the session can be controlled and the process of the interview can be interrupted at any time for instant feedback and analysis from the trainer and role-playing therapist and family members.

One model of role-playing is to put together a simulated family, identifying family roles, but not the problem or dynamics of the family. The family walks in, with the role-playing therapist having no prior information. The simulated family and therapist create their characterizations and circumstances spontaneously. The effort to fill in the blanks extemporaneously facilitates a more personal and genuine projection into the role-playing by the participants, whose relational patterns form on the spot. It also provides a more reliable siuation from which to hypothesize because the artificiality of group preplanning is minimized. The trainer prevents the role-players from projecting themselves too deeply into the simulation by frequently cutting off interaction at junctures when the role-playing therapist is about to or should respond to the family. At those moments the trainer assists the trainee to recall observations of the preceding transactional sequences in detail and his/her personal reactions to them. The therapist is helped to hypothesize about the significance of the transaction in itself and in light of the earlier portions of the session, and to decide on the intervention. The trainer for the most part keeps the family players in their roles during those discussions and at longer intervals elicits from them their personal reactions to the therapist and his/her interventions. The role-playing is also an effective tool to assist trainees to see themselves as family members see them.

Once the trainee has some models about what is expected, and has had a chance to practice being a therapist, he/she can begin to accept families and to be supervised live. The assignment of families with live supervision starts later than, but overlaps with, the first two exercises. This part of the training actually begins early in the training. Depending on the structure and length of the training, it is well started by the end of the first quarter of training. Being coached live by a supervisor working from behind a one-way mirror is the most practical of the training experiences, as it is literally on-the-job training. The family is real and the clinical situation is real. The therapist has the opportunity to receive observations about the family and self from the supervisor, along with suggestions about what to do while in the midst of the therapy session. The response of the family to the therapist's interventions is not up for speculation. It is real and immediate, and the feedback loops between family, therapist and trainer can all build on one another to help develop the trainee's skills.

The trainee receives help on the spot from the supervisor to see, hypothesize and do. The constraint is that the trainee and supervisor must exploit the situation for training purposes within the primary concern of providing proper service to the family. This may sacrifice the trainee's learning needs in terms of the time allowed during the session for thinking through speculations and planning action. It may also inhibit the trainee's freedom of action, as the family's needs may dictate a kind of activity or intervention on the part of the therapist that has little to do with the areas of development the trainee may be concentrating on at the moment. Moreover, the trainer may even need to intervene personally in the session if the family's situation requires it. For the trainee this experience can be disconcerting and not always productive for learning, but if the eventuality is anticipated and the supervisor enters the session respectful of family and therapist, the intrusion can be instructive. Indeed, at times the trainer and the therapist-trainee may agree that the former should intrude on a session and handle an issue with the family directly to demonstrate how to do something while the occasion exists. Live supervision requires time after the session for debriefing in terms of what took place between therapist and family, and therapist and supervisor.

The need for the opportunity to analyze and speculate is best fulfilled by the opportunity to videotape one's own work with the trainer. Viewing videotapes affords the ideal opportunity to learn to observe and hypothesize, although not to act. It does not permit the therapist to execute an intervention that might in retrospect appear to have been appropriate at a particular moment in a session, and since those precise circumstances will never again be duplicated, only approximated, a speculative intervention cannot be tested. Live supervision provides the best opportunity for testing interventions. Videotape supervision is best for analyzing past transactions. Videotape supervision assumes that the trainee and the supervisor have a common theoretical language and experiential framework best gained through working together in live supervision. For this reason the videotape supervision begins after the beginning of live supervision, although it continues to overlap with live supervision for the duration of the training course. The trainee and trainer who have worked together through the earlier stages of experiential clinical training can eventually depend almost exclusively on videotape supervision. Because they have a common theoretical framework and shared clinical experiences, they can communicate quite effectively about clinical events through a video representation.

Much of the clinical training of structural family therapists is done in groups. Observing other trainees being supervised live or in discussion with their supervisors about their videotapes is also useful. The vicarious experience of seeing other therapists with other families allows exposure to a greater variety of families, other therapist approaches, and a variety of supervisory coaching of therapist performance. There is also the effect of the group process on the learning in which the group has the potential to be supportive, to reinforce certain learning and to offer a greater variety of channels through which ideas can be discussed and absorbed. This parallels some of the benefits of therapy within a family context, but as with the family, the group environment is not always the optimum circumstance for dealing with more uniquely personal issues. The option must exist for individual supervision.

In structural family therapy, self-development for the therapist is sought within the training for therapy as it relates to doing therapy. Personal treatment and "growth-inducing" experiences of whatever kind are incidental to the training program. Helping the trainee to know him/herself in the clinical context and to develop the fullest use of the self for therapy is an integral aspect of all the clinical training experiences from role-playing, through live supervision to videotape supervision. The training experience within the training group and what time is spent in individual supervision are also used in the effort to help the trainee develop the fullest use of the self as a therapist. Proper training requires that the trainer draw a profile of the trainee in terms of skills, limitations, difficulties and style. All of these are rooted in the person of the trainee, which should be understood as it relates to therapist performance. The trainer must not only plan systematically to increase the understanding and skills of each trainee, but also to utilize his/her person purposefully with the family.

Through all these experiences the therapist is learning how to join with people, how to create transactions and how to modify them. The therapist learns to do all this within a conceptual framework and with an informational data base geared to people functioning in their families and their ecosystems. Clinical training is particularly aimed at preparing the would-be therapist to see structure in current transactions, to hypothesize about them and to intervene actively and personally in the process of those transactions. Throughout the training effort, particularly in the experiential part of the training, there must also be a conscious effort to expand the vision of the therapist to include the self in transactions, to make accessible to the therapist the fullest potential of his/her person for use in the therapy and to tighten the therapist's discipline in the use of the self with others. The training intends to produce a therapist with an integration of theory and technique who can invest him/herself purposefully in a free and disciplined manner with families in therapy.

RESEARCH ON THE STRUCTURAL APPROACH

Like several other approaches to family therapy, the structural paradigm has been repeat-edly improved through research.[9] In the family sector, several descriptive and etiologic studies have been conducted. A second program of studies has concerned treatment outcome. There also have been some evaluations of structural therapy training programs for professional and allied personnel. Other applications of the structural tenets have been less scrutinized. Mental health epidemiology, service development and program evaluation remain nearly uncharted regions.

Here, we will summarize the results of the major studies on family functioning, family treatment and therapist training conducted by structural researchers. Twenty-five published reports, covering 20 separate studies, met minimal standards for inclusion in this review. Supplementary background material is provided for these studies, indicating how the research is conceptually and historically linked with evolving models of structural theory and practice.

This review consists of a summary of research studies, which is subdivided into separate sections on family functioning studies and treatment studies. The family studies subsection contains summaries of descriptive and etiological (causal) studies of family mental health. The subsection on treatment studies includes summaries of therapy outcome, process and training research.

Family Functioning Studies

The intent of the present section is to summarize the plans and findings of family studies conducted by structurally-based researchers. While descriptive and causal modes in family research are ideally synergistic, descriptive studies are generally more exploratory in scope, conducted in the early stages of a research program. In contrast, etiological studies incorporate more explicit theoretical models and venture tests of relevant hypotheses. Greater attention

---

[9]*Editors' Note.* Would that this were true! Indeed, with the obvious exception of behavioral approaches (e.g., Gordon and Davidson, Chapter 14; Jacobson, Chapter 15), this state of empirical affairs simply does not exist. As evidence of our assessment, we offer the research sections of many of the chapters in this *Handbook*, and some of our own contributions to the literature on family therapy research (e.g., Gurman and Kniskern 1978a; Chapter 20, this volume; Kniskern and Gurman, 1980b).

is given, in the causal studies, to subtle forms of interaction among variables and to long-term dynamics of family process. As shown in Table 2, structural researchers have initiated several lines of descriptive inquiry. In these studies, the characteristics of behavior that most typify families regarded as "dysfunctional," "symptomatic" or "clinical" have been sought out. Some investigators have gone a step further and assessed which characteristics differentiate these families from "functional" ones, by comparing the behaviors of samples drawn from clinical and control populations. Four types of clinical families have been described in studies appearing to date, including the *low socioeconomic family* (Minuchin et al., 1967), *psychosomatic family* (Minuchin et al., 1978), *alcoholic family* (Davis, Stern and VanDeusen, 1977), and *addict family* (Kaufman and Kaufman, 1979; Stanton et al., 1978; Zeigler-Driscoll, 1977, 1979). There have been fewer etiological studies; these, also discussed here, have each been linked with prior or concurrent descriptive studies with the same four family types.

The family studies have all incorporated a focus upon communicative behaviors within the family unit, a perspective that is highly congruent with the transactional tenets in structural theory. Unfortunately, no uniform system of variables has been used across the studies of various family types. This is a consequence of the youthful stage of inquiry, disparity of interests between investigators, and the current nonexistence of any schema that thoroughly translates the structural paradigm into operational form. In the absence of homogeneity among studies, consistent presentation and consolidation of findings are hindered. Variables will be reported as used by each study. Only those findings which bear importance, either by their statistical significance or their unexpected lack of significance, have been included.

Low socioeconomic families

The first formal inquiry into family characteristics from a structural perspective was made by Minuchin et al., 1967). The Wiltwyck School, site for the studies, is a residential treatment center for delinquent and runaway boys from the New York City area. The organization and

dynamics of the families of these boys were assessed through the use of supplementary methods. Behavioral data on family interaction was gathered via structured interaction tasks developed by the authors (Elbert, Rosman, Minuchin and Guerney, 1964). Ratings of member's transactional behaviors were made by independent observers. A projective measure, the Family Interaction Apperception Technique (FIAT), was also developed, to obtain corresponding projective data, rated from the content of members' stories about family functioning. Twelve patient families and 11 non-patient control families were tested prior to the onset of family therapy. Posttherapy assessments were also conducted with the patient group (without controls) to evaluate changes in family characteristics subsequent to intervention.

Analysis of pretreatment status on formal aspects of communication showed bimodal trends in the distribution of the data, indicating that patient families tended to exhibit one or two extremes of behavior. Mothers and children in patient families talked and were spoken to significantly either more or less than their control counterparts. Their statements were also less clear than those of the controls. Posttreatment assessments showed no changes in these patterns among patient families, despite clear shifts in other areas of behavior.

Three types of executive behavior, defined as *leadership, control*, and *guidance*, were studied. Leadership included activity directing task performance. Behavior control concerned statements regulating non-task behaviors of other family members, but focused on immediate control. Guidance statements, in contrast, regulated others' behaviors by pointing to inappropriate aspects of behavior and giving instruction as to more appropriate ways of behaving (Minuchin et al., 1967). Prior to treatment, patient and control mothers were not found to differ in their use of leadership or guidance statements. The appropriateness and effectiveness of these statements were generally lower in the patient families, however, before treatment. Patient mothers used significantly either more or less behavior control, yet their children were uniformly more disruptive in tasks than were control children. Older patient children actively resisted their mother's executive con-

TABLE 2
Summary of Structural Family Functioning Research

Study	Design	Presenting Problem	Measures	Instruments	Sample
Minuchin, Montalvo, Guerney, Rosman and Schumer (1967)	a. Descriptive, Controlled Comparison (Multi-Method)	Delinquency, Aggression, Behavioral Adjustment	Communication Patterns (rated) Executive Behaviors (rated) Affective Relations (rated)	Structured Interaction Tasks, Family Interaction Apperception Technique (Elbert, Rosman, Minuchin & Guerney, 1964)	12 Patient Families 11 Control Families
	b. Descriptive, Pre/Post-Tx Differences Uncontrolled	Delinquency, Aggression, Behavioral Adjustment	Communication Patterns (rated) Executive Behaviors (rated) Affective Relations (rated)	Speaking Process and Content Rating Scales adapted from those used in Structured Interaction Tasks, above.	12 Patient Families No Controls
Minuchin, Rosman and Baker (1978)	a. Descriptive, Controlled Comparison	Diabetes Mellitus, Anorexia Nervosa, Chronic Asthma	Enmeshment (rated) Rigidity (rated) Overprotectiveness (rated) Conflict (rated)	Structured Interaction Tasks	9 Psychosomatic Diabetic 7 Normal Diabetic 8 Behavioral Diabetic 11 Anorectic 10 Chronic Asthmatic
	b. Etiologic, Prospective, Experimental (Multi-Method) Controlled	Diabetes Mellitus (3 sub-types)	Communication (rated) Affective/Conflict (rated) Physiological Stress (FFA level changes)	Three-Stage Diagnostic Stress Interview	9 Psychosomatic Diabetic 7 Normal Diabetic 8 Behavioral Diabetic
Davis, Stern and VanDeusen (1977)	a. Descriptive, Controlled Comparison (Multi-method)	Alcoholism	Communication (rated) Enmeshment (rated)	Structured Interaction Tasks	17 Alcoholic Families 16 Control Families
Stanton, Todd, Steier, VanDeusen, Marder, Rosoff, Seaman, and Skibinski (1979)	a. Descriptive, Controlled Comparison (Multi-Method)	Heroin Addiction	Communication (rated, electronic) Executive Behaviors (rated) Affective Relations (rated) Interpersonal Perceptions (test)	Structured Interaction Tasks, L'Abate Family Assessment Battery	65 Addict Families 25 Control Families
	b. Descriptive, Pre/Post-Tx Differences Controlled	Heroin Addiction	Communication (rated, electronic) Executive Behaviors (rated) Affective Relations (rated) Interpersonal Perception (test)	Structured Interaction Tasks, L'Abate Family Assessment Battery	46 Addict Families 24 Control Families
Zeigler-Driscoll (1977; 1979)	Descriptive, Uncontrolled Comparison	Drug and Alcohol Addiction	Family Structure, Demographics	Clinical Data, Questionnaires	46 Addict Families 44 Alcoholic Families

trol. Patient mothers' leadership and guidance did not accord with their children's requests for governance, however; these mothers were less responsive to their children's requests than were control mothers. The control parents' directives were clearer and more firm. Control families were thus more cooperative and productive in task performance than the patient families. FIAT projective data paralleled these transactional trends, with more instances of inappropriate executive behaviors, vacillation between extremes of executive functioning, lack of effective impact in parental control, and higher amounts of sibling control of siblings in patient stories.

After treatment, patterns of executive behavior shifted in the patient families. Mothers used less behavior control than before, yet were more effective in their use of directives. The older children also increased their requests for leadership from mothers. FIAT stories mirrored these shifts, reflecting more effective and affectionate behavior from mothers, accompanied by less instances of aggression or control in the family.

Patterns of agreement and disagreement, as observed in the behavioral tasks, did not differentiate patient from control families before treatment, nor did they change in the patient group after treatment. However, pretreatment FIAT stories of patient family members did contain fewer reports of nurturance, and more accounts of aggression between family members, than controls' stories. More nurturance and less aggression appeared in patient stories after treatment.

While the concepts of enmeshment and disengagement were actually elaborated after these studies, these descriptive data tend to support those concepts. For instance, the clustering of patient mothers and children at poles of interaction, before treatment, suggests enmeshed vs. disengaged positions. During treatment, families were clinically rated as either enmeshed or disengaged by their therapists, and ratings on this dimension correlated significantly with the success at outcome: Enmeshed families succeeded quite often, while disengaged families did not evidence change. After treatment, among the enmeshed families, shifts were observed away from extreme transactional patterns, indicating a move to more functional boundaries between parent and child subsystems.

Psychosomatic families

An extensive and productive line of family inquiry was later initiated in a research collaboration on psychosomatic families between the Philadelphia Child Guidance Clinic (PCGC) and a sister institution, the Children's Hospital of Philadelphia (CHP). The focus of the partnership became centered, in the mid-1960s, upon the modeling of relationships between emotional arousal and episodes of ketoacidosis in children with diabetes mellitus. This condition usually entailed emergency hospitalization of the patient. Pediatricians had long noted that emotional precipitants (in the patient or other family members) often accompanied such episodes, while clear-cut medical explanations (e.g., omission of insulin injection) were rare. Over 200 such cases were studied at CHP, and results showed that the symptoms were correlated with certain aspects of family process. A cyclical relationship appeared to be operating, wherein family conflict would precipitate the eruption of ketoacidosis. The symptom would subside after medical treatment in the hospital, only to reemerge soon after the patient returned home. The cycle in some cases ran from week to week (Baker, Minuchin, Milman, Liebman, and Todd, 1975). On the basis of differences found in these sample studies, the PCGC/CHP investigators proposed a new taxonomic schema, reclassifying the various forms of diabetes mellitus and including a specific psychosomatic subtype (Baker and Barcai, 1970).

A second round of research with diabetics sought to determine the causal sequence precipitating ketoacidosis crises in the psychosomatic-type diabetic. Under controlled, prospective trials, psychological mechanisms were supported and physiological factors excluded (Baker, Minuchin, and Rosman, 1974). Two particular mechanisms, an excessive *turn-on* of emotional stress and subsequent impaired *turn-off*, seemed to distinguish the functioning of psychosomatic diabetics from their patient peers.

Continuing, the researchers developed a prospective design to observe and manipulate symptom behavior in conjunction with the child's involvement in stressful parental interaction. This study intended to verify the hypothesis that the symptom is brought to function as a regulator of the level of stress in interpersonal relationships between family members. To map relations between patterns of family conflict and symptom arousal, a three-stage stress interview was administered to three subtypes of diabetic patient: psychosomatic ($N = 11$), behavioral ($N = 7$) and normal ($N = 8$), and their parents. Transactions and conflict were scored on measures similar to those employed in Wiltwyck task ratings. Physiological measures were obtained on changes in free fatty acid (FFA) levels in blood samples, taken from family members at regular intervals during the stress interview.

Transactions between fathers and mothers in a baseline phase of the interview (with patients absent) showed the sole difference on transactional variables, across groups, to be on *level of conflict*. Normal spouses were most intense in mutual confrontation, while the psychosomatic couples exhibited a range of conflict avoidance maneuvers. The content of task discussions showed normal and behavioral groups as centering on marital and parenting issues, while psychosomatic parents expressed protective concerns for their child foremost.

In the second stage of the stress interview, a therapist pressed the conflict earlier expressed by the parents, while the patient observed from outside the room, behind a one-way mirror. Normal couples continued their conflicts at the previous level, while psychosomatic spouses became more direct and expressive than they had been in the first stage, rising to emotional levels approximating those of the normal group. In this phase, the psychosomatic patients manifested exaggerated FFA increases or *turn-on* behavior.

In stage three of the interviews, the patient joined the parents. Normal and behavioral spouses again continued as before. The behavior of the psychosomatic families again differed from the other groups. The parents *detoured* the conflict, drawing in the child either passively (as subject/target) or actively (as discussant). The

psychosomatic patient's behaviors in this segment complemented those of the parents. Children entered alliances, manifested increased stress discomfort, suppressed issues, etc. Far more protection was elicited and given between child and parent than in the other groups. The index patient's FFA levels continued to rise, while parents' levels fell (the "cross-over phenomenon"), mirroring the transactional patterns. Similar behaviors were also exhibited in a Wiltwyck-task. In both settings, the FFA levels of the psychosomatic patients remained elevated well after the end of the discussion. This residual effect can be described as an analogue to unresolved conflict in the psychosomatic families. On the basis of both physiological and transactional measures, the concept of the child's centrality in the regulation of familial stress was confirmed.

A descriptive component was also included in this research. Using Wiltwyck-type tasks, Minuchin et al. (1978) studied 30 psychosomatic families, including *anorectic* ($N = 11$), *diabetic* ($N = 9$) and *asthmatic* ($N = 10$) subgroups. The diabetic families were also compared to two patient-control groups, including *normal* diabetics ($N = 7$), and diabetics referred for *behavioral* problems but evidencing good medical control ($N = 8$). The tasks were scored by raters, using scales modified from those used in the Wiltwyck studies. Data were aggregated to permit analysis of *family, subsystem* and *individual* levels.

Formal characteristics of communication have not been reported to date. Executive functioning of the *behavioral* group in tasks was poorer than that in the *normal* families, but better than that of the psychosomatic families. The psychosomatic group displayed the highest asymmetry in executive roles, with one parent (mother or father) dominating task direction. Along with this authoritarian skew, their performance was least productive, and often marred by intrusions of inappropriate behaviors by family members. Posttreatment data on changes in executive behaviors are not reported.

Patterns of handling conflict were studied, and appear to differentiate psychosomatic families from the normal and behavioral groups. While normal families occasionally *denied* conflict in addressing the argument task, their accounts more often exhibited *clear statements of issues, consideration of a greater number of alternatives as solutions*, more *open agreement and disagreement* between members, and *more complete resolutions*, than did those of the psychosomatic families. The behavioral group's descriptions of family arguments were more *diffused*, and less resolved than those of normal families, but also more directly expressed than were those of psychosomatic families. Suppression and denial were prevalent in the psychosomatic group, e.g., in expressions of instant agreement. Their discussions tended to focus on the index patient (inappropriately), often centering on *overprotective* or *blaming* gestures by the parents. Psychosomatic families' discussions tended not to come to focus or closure.

Rating scales were developed to measure levels and categories of enmeshment-type behaviors exhibited in task discussions. Results indicated clearer subsystem boundaries and greater interpersonal differentiation in normal families, than in psychosomatic families. The psychosomatic group displayed poorest differentiation between parental and child subsystems. Their transactions also revealed more *mediating, go-between type statements* than did those of the other two groups.

In a subsequent phase of etiologic study, data were sought linking salient characteristics of family transaction with the manner of the child's involvement in conflict management. The PCGC/CHP researchers at first described the parents' influence on their child as psychosomatogenic, inferring a one-way causal linkage. Further analyses of the stress interview data revealed a more complex, two-directional process. In some families, the child actively initiated his/her involvement in parental conflict. Three variant forms of parent-child transaction were differentiated: *triangulation, parent-child coalition*, and *detouring*. In triangulation, each parent tried to ally with the patient against the other parent, resulting in a splitting of the spouse dyad. In parent-child coalition, a longer-term alliance remained between one parent and the child, accompanied by a dysfunctional, negative relationship between the more peripheral parent and the child. Detouring consisted of a unification of the parental dyad, through shared concern for their sick child. This concern could be expressed either in an attack against the child, e.g., that he/she is ruining their marriage, or, in a protective manner (Minuchin et al., 1978). With these findings, the unit of diagnosis has been shifted from the individual patient to the family transactional system. The etiological model has also been subsequently reiterated, from a linear to a nonlinear (systemic) one (Minuchin et al., 1975).

Further substantiation of the etiological concepts issuing from the diabetes studies came when structural family therapy was found to be effective in alleviating the medical crises (described below in the section on *Treatment Studies*). The PCGC/CHP researchers also expanded the research to test the applicability of structural constructs to other forms of psychosomatic illness. In family tasks and stress interviews, the model was found to be useful in predicting the patterns of family process in cases of anorexia nervosa, chronic asthma, psychogenic pain and other psychosomatic disorders (Minuchin et al., 1978). The investigators have interpreted the collective results of these studies as substantiation for the nonspecific, general validity of the structural theory for all psychosomatic families.

Alcoholic families

Davis et al. (1977) studied characteristics of interaction in 17 alcoholic families and 16 matched control families. In the alcoholic sample, the index person was the father, who was not in treatment at the time of the study. Wiltwyck-type tasks were used to observe and score several parameters of communication process and enmeshment variables. No posttreatment measures were taken.

The results showed that alcoholic fathers and mothers spoke to each other less, while the children talked to each other more, than did counterpart subsystems in the non-alcoholic families. Simultaneous speech was also analyzed, but no differences were found between groups on patterns of speech overlap. Alcoholic families took considerably longer to execute the tasks than did control families. The primary focus of the study, enmeshment variables, revealed some interesting qualities. Speaking patterns in alcoholic families indicated that the parental subsystem was disengaged from the child(ren). Fathers' extensive use of self-referential pronouns ("I") alluded to a further disengagement from the rest of the family. Patterns of enmeshment behavior were also rated directly from family members' statements in the tasks. Scores revealed that the absolute number of enmeshment statements expressed during tasks was identical for both groups (about 5% of all statements in each). Subcategories of enmeshment differed significantly, however. Control-family members chiefly used mind-reading, while alcoholic members favored "personal control" and "mediated response."

While these patterns of enmeshment *differ* from those observed in the Wiltwyck and psychosomatic studies, reasons for this are not clear. The differences could stem from aspects of the research design (e.g., in the alcoholic study, the index person is the father, rather than the child), or from true effects associated with symptoms or other family characteristics.

Addict Families

Addiction researchers have been seeking evidence of family correlates of drug abuse for some time. Their studies have, until recently, focused chiefly on aspects of childhood experience which might predispose individuals toward addictive personalities or behaviors. Departing from this tradition, a conceptual model elaborated by Stanton et al. (1978) views contemporary family transactional processes as central determinants of drug abuse. This model derives from the clinical impressions obtained by structural therapists and researchers in their work with families of heroin addicts. It has been subsequently supported by empirical data from diagnostic and treatment studies by Stanton et al. (1979).[10]

The first study reported by Stanton, Todd and colleagues compared transactional characteristics of 65 families with a heroin-addicted son, to those of 25 control, non-addict families. Wiltwyck-type interaction tasks were used, and speech process and content characteristics scored by raters and via electronic instrumentation. (An interpersonal-perception projective test, the L'Abate Family Assessment Battery [Golden, 1974] was also administered. Results on this in-

strument were not significant and will not be reported here.) A second study linked to the transactional one compared pre- and posttreatment status for 46 of the addict families and 24 of the control families.

In a pretreatment assessment, the electronic interaction measures indicated greater amounts of speaking in control families than in addict families. Within families, members' relative amounts of speaking differed significantly. The relative positions were similar in both addict and control groups, however. Mothers spoke most, followed respectively by the index patient, father and siblings. Other communication variables, including measures of simultaneous speech and speaking sequence, did not differentiate between groups.

Among the rater-scored communication measures, patterns of who-speaks-to-whom and who-follows-whom were found to be significantly more *rigid* in the addict families, than in the control group families. Assessments of longer-interval transactional trends showed addict family process to be more continuous, in that dyadic exchanges were maintained longer than in control families. The addict mothers were more often represented in these continuous episodes than any other members, while addict fathers were least successful in *interrupting* dyadic exchanges to enter discussions.

Re-assessments of communication characteristics after treatment showed significant effects on the electronic measures for *position* in the family and *treatment* condition. However, no simple trends were found in the therapy to explicate the meaning of these changes. Other electronic measures of speaking interaction again revealed no significant differences between groups. On the evidence of rated interaction measures, communicative competencies in addict families appear to have improved after therapy. Significant changes occurred in transactional characteristics of fathers and sons. There was an increased ability, in addict families, to successfully block intrusions into relational dyads. Mothers' centrality in these dyads decreased after treatment, while fathers participated more often than before.

In terms of *execution* of tasks, before treatment, addict family members were found to be highly disruptive of performance. Addict moth-

---

[10]Empirical studies by Kaufman and Kaufman (1979) and Zeigler-Driscoll (1977, 1979) have also described addict families in terms which support this conceptual model.

ers and sons tended to use *discontinuous, inappropriate* topic statements more often than controls. Task-oriented leadership was also weaker among addict families. After treatment, these executive patterns shifted and addict families became more openly expressive in task-appropriate ways. More requests for orientation, more willingness to give directives, and more explicit kinds of directives appeared in task statements.

Conflict measures indicated that addict families avoided open confrontation prior to treatment, exhibited as fewer negative coalitions, fewer opinions given, and less disagreement than in control families. After treatment, addict families showed increased expression of agreement and solidarity in tasks.

The findings on communication characteristics support the general notion of an active coalition between mothers and sons in addict families, while fathers appear disengaged. Posttreatment trends showed shifts in relationships between fathers, mothers and sons, with decreased amounts of mediation, protectiveness, etc. These changes collectively imply better boundary-maintenance between subsystems, yet better integration among functions, also.

Synthesis

Integration of findings on low socioeconomic, psychosomatic, alcoholic and addict families is hindered by differences in the sampling and recruitment methods used by the respective studies (see Table 3). The four studies also differed in terms of the index patient's sex, age, position in the family and status in treatment. Despite this lack of congruence in sampling, several patterns of family dysfunction do recur across the studies. These show most strongly in parameters of *instrumental* functioning. Patient families generally appear to be operating under transactional rules and boundaries which are much less productive than those in control families: taking longer to finish tasks; offering responses that are less complete and less clear; digressing more often from appropriate topics; offering fewer directives and initiatives; and sustaining more coalitions against closure of tasks. These trends are not manifest uniformly in every patient family, however. Dysfunctional behaviors

can lean toward either of two extremes. Communication may be dense or sparse, evenly distributed or skewed across family members; leadership may be authoritarian or anarchic, controlling or passive; affect may be blatantly protective or aggressive; conflict may be either openly waged or covert.

TABLE 3
Sampling Differences in Structural Family Functioning Research

| Study | Subject Demographic Status | | |
	Race	Socioeconomic Status	Parental Status
Minuchin et al. (1967)	black Puerto Rican	lower	single-parent
Minuchin et al. (1978)	white	middle, upper class	two-parent
Davis et al. (1977)	white	mixed	two-parent
Stanton et al. (1979)	white black	mixed	two-parent

Whatever the specific configuration of behaviors in a particular family, patient families as a whole are consistently less productive than controls in their task-related interpersonal processes. The findings collectively support the use of transactional measures in the assessment of family dysfunction. Simple measures of family process are readily interpretable as indices of functioning and provide clues of underlying structural characteristics (e.g., differentiation and integration among subsystems). That such indices are highly useful to the formulation of therapeutic strategy is demonstrated by the significant changes exhibited among patient families' posttreatment assessments in several studies. A particularly potent example of such changes comes from Stanton et al. (1979), who found the canonical correlation between pre-post shifts in patterns of drug abuse and shifts in family transactional behaviors to be .93 to .999. In practical terms, family transactions constituted the only dimension significantly related to changes in symptomatic behaviors.

External support or refutation of the results obtained by structural researchers has been sparse. Doane (1978), reviewing a large number of controlled comparison studies of family interaction, has independently verified several relevant findings. Doane found that disturbed families manifested more cross-generational coalitions, greater husband-wife conflict, more frequent spontaneous agreement (conflict-avoidance) among children, less acknowledgment of other members' statements, lower clarity of message content, and less productive task-completion. Where one parent was ascribed a symptomatic/pathologic status, several studies showed the importance of the other parent in either an exacerbating or a counteractive role. Perhaps her major finding was that secondary analysis showed *subsystem* behaviors to be more informative units of analysis than either whole family or individual measures.

Treatment Studies

The most popular mode of treatment studies, outcome studies, explores the many influences, in and out of therapy, that may account for changes on criterion and other factors. Aspects of therapeutic process may be studied relative to treatment outcome or independently. The immediate or extended effects and costs of specific techniques, strategies and stages in treatment can be isolated in process studies. A further, albeit indirect, means of measuring the utility of a treatment model is to assess its transferability. Training studies performed by structural researchers have thus looked at the impact of teaching programs on trainees' knowledge and skills.[11] Each of these modes of treatment research are represented in the following review. Outcome and process studies appear in the same format used earlier, i.e., in terms of the type of family treated. Training programs are discussed under a single heading. Table 4 summarizes the design aspects of the structural treatment studies.

Therapy with low socioeconomic families

"Conflict resolution family therapy," as the

structural prototype was called at the time, was first evaluated in the Wiltwyck studies by Minuchin et al. (1967). A global evaluation of therapy outcome was conducted with 11 families. Seven were judged by the therapist to be improved after a course of treatment lasting between six and 12 months. Four families were rated as unimproved. No negative rating category was used, making it impossible to assess deteriorating effects (although it is stated that several other families dropped out of the study before completing treatment). No control group was used in this study, comparing the therapy with conventional treatment at Wiltwyck. Given the authors' statement that regular treatment was effective in roughly 50 to 55% of cases, the family therapy appears to have been moderately superior.

It is important to note that the degree of improvement in these families is highly correlated (but not statistically, owing to the small sample size) with specific structural categories. Three of the four families regarded by clinicians as enmeshed improved after family therapy, as did another four described as having a peripheral father. None of the three families described as disengaged improved after treatment, and the authors admit to difficulties in keeping this type of family enlisted in therapy.[12]

The Wiltwyck project also obtained data relevant to questions of treatment process, which help to explicate reasons for differential success with enmeshed and disengaged families. A descriptive analysis was made of verbal behaviors in therapy, comparing trends in an early session (the sixth) with those in a later one (the twenty-eighth). Raters worked from a coding system similar to that used to rate the structured interaction tasks (reported in the *Family Studies* section, above). Twelve patient families were studied. Therapists' *amount of speaking* did not change over the course of therapy, but remained constant at 45% to 50% of total speech occurring

---

[11]*Editors' Note*. But they have not (as will soon be made evident) examined the impact of training on trainees' clinical effectiveness. Unfortunately, this is a common deficiency in the literature on family therapy training and education (Kniskern and Gurman, 1980c).

[12]*Editors' Note*. We would speculate that this interesting finding, which matches our own clinical experience, may often reflect different referral routes to family therapy: Disengaged families, compared to enmeshed families, more often enter treatment because of the concern of some agency (police, school) outside the family, while members of enmeshed families, being more sensitive to the state of other family members, are more likely to initiate treatment themselves.

TABLE 4

Summary of Structural Treatment Research

Study	Design	Presenting Problem	Treatment Length/Setting	Outcome Criteria (Measures)	Sample	Outcome Status[1]
OUTCOME STUDIES						
Minuchin, Montalvo, Guerney, Rosman and Schumer (1967)	Uncontrolled, Prospective, Single-Treatment	Delinquency, Aggression, Behavioral Adjustment	Long/Inpatient	Index Patient Functioning and Family Functioning (clinical ratings)	12 Patient: Family Therapy No Controls	Family Functioning: 7++, 5[b] (no record of attrition; no follow-up)
Minuchin, Baker, Rosman, Liebman, Milman and Todd (1975)	Uncontrolled, Prospective, Single-Treatment (Multi-Group)	Diabetes Mellitus, Anorexia Nervosa, Chronic Asthma	2-24 mos./IP and OP	Index Patient Symptom and Psychosocial Functioning (physiological and clinical ratings)	13 Diabetic: Family Therapy 23 Anorectic: Family Therapy 10 Asthmatic: Family Therapy No Controls	Combined Indexes: 10++, 3+ 20++, 2+, (3[a]) 10++ (follow-up 6 to 80 mos.)
Liebman, Honig and Berger (1976)	Uncontrolled, Prospective, Single-Treatment	Psychogenic Pain	5-11 mos./OP	Index Patient Symptom and Psychosocial Functioning (clinical rating)	10 Psychogenic: Family Therapy No Controls	Combined Indexes: 10++ (follow-up 8 to 25 mos.)
Berger, Honig and Liebman (1977)	Uncontrolled, Prospective, Single-Treatment	Psychogenic Abdominal Pain	Short to Medium/IP and OP	Index Patient Symptom and Psychosocial Functioning (clinical rating)	19 Psychogenic: Family Therapy No Controls	Combined Indexes: 17++, 2+ (follow-up 6 to 18 mos.)
Liebman, Minuchin, Baker and Rosman (1977)	Uncontrolled, Prospective, Single-Treatment	Intractible Asthma	5-22 mos./OP	Index Patient Symptom and Psychosocial Functioning (clinical rating)	14 Asthmatic: Family Therapy No Controls	Combined Indexes: 14++ (follow-up 12 to 48 mos.)
Minuchin, Rosman and Baker (1978)	Uncontrolled, Prospective, Single-Treatment	Anorexia Nervosa	2-24 mos./IP and OP	Index Patient Symptom and Psychosocial Functioning (physiological and clinical ratings)	53 Anorectic: Family Therapy No Controls	Combined Indexes: 43++, 2+, 3[0], 2−, (3[a]) (follow-up 1 to 84 mos.)
Rosenberg and Lindblad (1978)	Uncontrolled, Prospective, Single-Treatment	Elective Mutism	Mid-Long/OP	Index Patient Symptom and Psychosocial Functioning (clinical rating)	10 Elective Mute: Family Therapy No Controls	Combined Indexes: 9+, (1[a]) (follow-up 1 to 72 mos.)

TABLE 4 (Continued)

Study	Design	Presenting Problem	Treatment Length/Setting	Outcome Criteria (Measures)	Sample	Outcome Status[1]
Zeigler-Driscoll (1977; 1979)	Controlled, Prospective, Comparative-Tx	Drug and Alcohol Addiction	3-6 mos./IP and OP	Index Patient Symptom and Psychosocial Functioning (clinical rating)	49 Drug & Alcohol: 22 in Family Therapy 15 in Relative Groups 12 Controls (Patients)	Drug Use: $16++$, 21^{0} (12^{a}) ns $3++$, 7^{0} (3^{a}) ns (follow-up 1 to 6 mos.)
Stanton, Todd, Steier, VanDeusen, Marder, Rosoff, Seaman and Skibinski (1979)	Controlled, Prospective, Comparative-Tx	Heroin Addiction	3-6 mos./OP	Index Patient Symptom and Psychosocial Functioning (physiological and clinical ratings)	106 Heroin Addicts: 20 Paid-Family Therapy 23 Unpaid-Family Therapy 17 Paid-Family Placebo 46 Controls (Patients)	Drug Use: 61% drug-free days 51% drug-free days 28% drug-free days 30% drug-free days ($<.009$) Psychosocial: n.s. (follow-up 1 to 12 mos.)

Study	Design	Presenting Problem	Focus of Study	Criteria/Measures	Instruments	Sample	Results
PROCESS STUDIES							
Minuchin, Montalvo, Guerney, Rosman and Schumer (1967)	Descriptive, Uncontrolled, Prospective, Single-Treatment	Delinquency, Aggression, Behavioral Adjustment	Changes: Early vs. Late Stages in Therapy	Verbal Behaviors (ratings of communication process and content)	Family portions of 6th and 28th therapy sessions	12 Patients No Controls	Fathers' and Children's speaking doubled in later session. Executive Functions shifted
Rosman, Minuchin and Liebman (1975)	Uncontrolled, Prospective, Experimental, Single-Treatment	Anorexia Nervosa	Effects of First Therapy Interview (Family Lunch Session)	Index Patient Physiological Function (weight change)	Diagnostic/Therapeutic Interview	8 Anorectic No Controls	All 8 patients reversed from weight loss to gain after the session.
Stanton, Todd, Steier, VanDeusen, Marder, Rosoff, Seaman & Skibinski (1979)	a. Descriptive, Controlled Comparison	Heroin Addiction	Recruitment: Refusers vs. Engagers in Family Therapy	Index Patient Drug Use and Demographic Characteristics.	Intake Questionnaire and History Interview	145 Addict: 27 Refusers 65 Engagers 53 Controls	Refusers had better prognosis than Engagers, but not different from Controls.
	b. Controlled, Prospective, Comparative-Treatment	Heroin Addiction	Effects of Payment on Attendance in Family Therapy	Family Members' Attendance at Sessions	Attendance Records	64 Addict: 21 Paid FT 25 Unpaid FT 18 Paid-Cont.	Payment increased attendance in therapy significantly.

TABLE 4 (Continued)

Study	Design	Setting	Focus of Study	Criteria/Measures	Instruments	Sample	Results
TRAINING STUDIES							
Flomenhaft and Carter (1974)	Uncontrolled, Post Hoc Evaluation	MH/MR Centers. Professionals in practice	Effects of 20 week training program on practice	Changes in direct services to families; other improvements	Mailed Questionnaire (one year after termination of training)	53 Alumni No Controls	Significant increase in direct services to families.
Flomenhaft and Carter (1977)	Same as (1974)	Same as (1974)	Same as (1974)	Same as (1974)	Same as (1974)	152 Alumni No Controls	Increased direct services to families.
Betof (1977)	Uncontrolled, Post Hoc Evaluation	MR Centers: Professionals in practice	Effects of 40 week training program on motivation, practice	Agency and trainee motivation; trainee practice improvemts.	Mailed Questionnaire and Interview	68 Trainees No Controls 11 Agencies	Trainees from motivated agencies improved most
Kaplan, Rosman, Liebman and Honig (1977)	Controlled, Pre- vs. Post-Evaluation	Pediatric Hospital: First-Year Residents	Effects of one-year child psychiatry training program	Residents' participation in training; interviewing skills	Log of participation in training; Videotape ratings of physical exams	20 Trainees 5 Controls	Trainees' interview skills improved after program, in correlation with participation.

[1] + +Greatly improved, + Slightly improved, [0]No change, − = Slightly deteriorated, = Greatly deteriorated, a = attrition.

in the session. Among family members, mothers did not change amount of speaking (20%), but fathers' and young children's speaking nearly doubled, while older children spoke slightly less in the later session. Family members' speech was less often directed toward the therapist, and more toward each other, later in treatment (down from 80% to 60%). Analysis of *message content* revealed that a majority (70%) of all statements made by the therapist and family consisted of exchange of information or expressions of neutral feelings, reflecting a heavy emphasis (particularly on the therapist's part) on communication structure (e.g., clarity, specificity, address, etc.). Shifts in *executive functioning* during therapy included increases in mothers' control of older children, and in harmony between spouses. Negative aggressive statements and complaints about lack of role fulfillment decreased during therapy. These trends, especially the heavy emphasis on restructuring of basic communicational patterns, surprised the Wiltwyck researchers: "we did not anticipate the extent to which we would rely on . . . establishing and promulgating effective means and techniques of communication (in the interventions)" (Minuchin et al., 1967, p. 407). The stress placed on communicational patterns in the operative strategy of therapy led to the formulation of the basic structural tenets and techniques as described by Minuchin (1974), yet no studies have since been reported on any of the techniques emanating from this philosophy (with one exception, noted below).[13]

Psychosomatic families

Reports of treatment outcome in the psychosomatic area have been published continually since 1973. As summarized in the reports of Minuchin et al. (1978) and Minuchin et al. (1975), results of therapy with anorectic, asthmatic and diabetic cases have been very positive (see Table 4). Additional data on family therapy for psychogenic pain as the primary symptom are provided in Liebman, Honig and Berger (1976) and Berger, Honig and Liebman (1977).

These papers are tantamount to cumulative progress reports on continually growing samples. The psychosomatic studies have persisted without interruption at PCGC/CHP for over ten years. Repeated follow-up assessments of the cohorts participating have steadily transformed the data base to a longitudinal one.

Most psychosomatic patients improved greatly in both symptom and psychosocial behaviors after treatment. Re-hospitalizations were rare for all types of patients. Long-term follow-ups have shown little deterioration on either physiological or psychosocial criteria, even after several years. A small minority of cases are reported as requiring additional therapy for other family problems, such as parental marital difficulties. Unfortunately, control groups were not included in the psychosomatic studies. The authors indicate that their results with anorectic cases are superior to those achieved by other investigators with similar patients, using behavioral and analytic psychotherapies.

Crisis-induction is an important intervention in the structural armamentarium, used to escalate stress in a manner useful to further restructuring moves. The crisis induction technique is first described by Minuchin and Barcai (1969) in the case of a 12-year-old diabetic girl. Therapy sessions were held immediately after hospitalization for acidosis, at whatever time of day this occurred. Sessions focused on the parents' initiation and resolution of conflicts without involving the daughter. After several months of therapy, conducted whenever hospitalization occurred, the frequency of acidosis episodes was greatly reduced. In families with a very rigid transactional structure, the tactic in crisis-induction has been described as pitting the patient against the parents, to breach the usual ceiling of conflict in the family. Issues are then reframed, as the parents are aided in considering new alternatives and in effecting them with the patient. This crisis-induction technique is the only structural family therapy technique which has been subjected to formal inquiry.[14] Rosman, Minuchin and Liebman (1975) describe its use

---

[13]*Editors' Note.* It is interesting to note that this important finding is fully in accord with Jacobson's (1978) conclusion that the single most salient treatment component in behavioral marriage therapy is structured communication training.

[14]*Editors' Note.* This significant observation highlights our belief (Kniskern and Gurman, 1980b) that investigation of the most salient change-inducing components of structural family therapy deserves the highest empirical priority for structural family therapy researchers at this time.

in the Family Lunch Session (FLS) to initiate therapy with anorectic cases. The FLS is conducted a few days after hospitalization of the index patient. During the interview, lunch is ordered and later brought into the session (paradoxically, a stressful occasion for anorectic families). This permits enactment of problems around eating, and is thus useful to diagnosis and intervention. Three variant models have been used, dependent on the age of the patient and predominant transactional patterns of the family. One variant focuses on increasing the parents' executive effectiveness with the child; a second on increasing distance between parents and child; and a third on neutralizing family interactions with respect to eating.

Eight anorectic cases, hospitalized between three and 16 days, were measured on weight change over several days preceding and following the FLS. All members of this group had been steadily losing weight during the four days prior to the session. All reversed this trend significantly after the session and steadily gained weight over the following week. Each of the three variants used appeared to be equally effective. (Note: The authors caution that this session is an "opening move" in a larger treatment program, used to initiate change and not interpretable as "cure".)

The Family Lunch Session study presents a model design for research on the effectiveness of various techniques in the structural paradigm. It echoes, at reduced scale, the design of treatment outcome studies and is thus subject to the same criteria of sampling, measurement and control.

Addict families

Two major studies have assessed the efficacy of structural family therapy for the treatment of drug and alcohol addictions. Each study included two distinct experimental treatments and a conventional control treatment. In the first, Zeigler-Driscoll (1977, 1979) contrasted conjoint therapy of the addict and other family members with a parents' or spouses' group treatment modeled on structural precepts but not including the addict, and with an individual inpatient program. Detailed descriptions of the treatment are not provided, but the two experimental conditions appears to be similar in general protocol and strategy. In the second study, Stanton et al. (1979) compared a family therapy model incorporating structural and strategic approaches with a family placebo treatment condition and a conventional individual treatment for addiction.

The designs of both studies are quite sophisticated (Gurman and Kniskern, 1978). Zeigler-Driscoll (1979) reports that the Eagleville project suffered in implementation, however. Analyses showed that heterogeneity occurred within groups, on several demographic factors, as a consequence of difficulties met in recruiting and retaining subjects. Refusal and early attrition thus heavily undermined the representatives of samples in the Eagleville study. Stanton et al. (1979) report instances of similar problems early in their project as well, but developed structural interventions that minimized these in later recruitment (VanDeusen, Stanton, Scott, and Todd, 1980).

One aspect of the Stanton et al. (1979) study recently criticized (Wells and Dezen, 1978) is the "extraordinary efforts" that therapists put into enlisting families into therapy. While pointing out that treatment assignment occurred after this effort, so that it did not affect groups differently, Stanton and Todd (1980a) agree that enlistment was a key intervention, properly viewed as an active component of family therapy. Interventions, by design or by default, commence with the first contact between family and therapist. This occasion often precedes a formal initial interview, and can convey much information between parties which will affect future expectations and arrangements. VanDeusen et al. (1980) report that introductory discussions in a structural model, conducted with 92 heroin addicts, resulted in successful enlistment of 71% of the families selected into the family therapy study. This recruitment rate is two to four times above those reported by other family therapy programs directed at addicted populations. The average amount of time required to engage addicts' families in structural family therapy was between five and six hours (Stanton and Todd, 1980b). Home visits were necessary in about one-fourth of the cases. A cost analysis showed that the price of recruitment, including families engaged and those not engaged, averaged $60. per family, an amount which is more than offset by the reduction of medical, legal and other costs of drug dependency made possible by the therapy.

Taking into account the differences experienced in implementation, direct comparability of the results of the two addictions studies is questionable. In fact, outcome data obtained by one contrast strongly with those of the other. In assessments at one and two months after the termination of treatment, Zeigler-Driscoll (1977) found no differences in levels of abstinence and recidivism between experimental and control groups: Roughly 55% in each group had returned to active drug use. These groups continued to deteriorate; 40% were abstinent by the end of the sixth month—still, a higher rate of abstinence then achieved by most drug programs. Zeigler-Driscoll concludes that the main effect of the family therapy was to "reinforce the abstinence pattern learned in the Eagleville program, and also to improve the family's ability to cope when the index patient returns to drug use" (1977, pp. 185-186).

In contrast, the results reported by Stanton et al. (1979) recall those of the psychosomatic outcome studies. Symptom reduction was significantly affected by structural-strategic family therapy. The level of positive change attained after family therapy was more than double that achieved in the non-family treatment conditions. The effects of therapy persisted at follow-up intervals of six and 12 months after termination. Changes were minimal on the measure of the index patient's psychosocial functioning, however, and did not confirm the investigators' hypotheses of improvements in job or school status. This lack of improvement is puzzling and requires further study.

A payment condition was also tested by Stanton et al. (1979). The amount of payment was calculated at each family session on the basis of (a) attendance by family members, and (b) symptom control by the index patient during the previous week (assessed via urinalysis for traces of illicit drugs). This arrangement constituted an explicit behavior modification condition, aimed at both the patient and the family. It was rigorously controlled with a nested, two-factor design comparing family therapy with and without payment to the family control group (paid only).

This design allowed the investigators to isolate the effects of the payment condition from those of the therapy. Results showed that during the first six months after treatment the paid-therapy group was significantly better than the paid-placebo group on six of nine categories of drug use. Only one drug category (alcohol use) differentiated the paid from unpaid family therapy conditions, however, suggesting that payment had an only slightly positive effect over and above therapy. Attendance was more strongly related to the payment variable: Both paid groups (therapy and placebo) exhibited greater regularity of attendance than the unpaid-therapy group. Analyses of transactional data (described in the *Family Studies* section above) also showed effects for the payment variable: Patients in the paid condition exhibited more continuity in participation in tasks, fewer intrusive behaviors, less tension and less disagreement, after therapy, than did patients in the unpaid-therapy group. Payment thus seems less a direct intervention into symptomatic behavior than a supportive influence, promulgating conditions that are beneficial for the conduct of therapy.

Therapist training programs

Structural family therapy has been extensively taught at pre-professional, allied and continuing education levels. Many of the tenets used in the practice of therapy have been incorporated also into the training models, including an emphasis upon observation and active restructuring of behaviors through live supervision (Montalvo, 1973). Several training programs have been documented in evaluative reports of a research quality.

The effectiveness of a training program incorporating structural techniques was first demonstrated in the Institute of Family Counseling, conducted at the Philadelphia Child Guidance Clinic between 1969 and 1974. Persons who were indigenous to minority communities, with no previous professional education or experience, were developed into full-fledged family therapists in this program (Haley, 1972). Trainees were recruited and put through a two-year cycle of case-oriented "on-the-job" training. Intensive supervision was provided throughout the program via live and videotape review methods. Although no objective, detailed evaluation of the training has been reported, a brief follow-up conducted one year after the conclusion of training indicated that all graduates ($N = 26$) were employed in some capacity as mental health personnel. This could be interpreted as significant success, relative to the results of the other "paraprofessional" training projects conducted in the United States during the same decade (Ritzer, 1974). Despite this success, the wider impact of the program on community mental health services is not known, nor is the clinical effectiveness of the trainees.

Flomenhaft and Carter (1974, 1977) have reported on a multi-year program conducted by the Philadelphia Child Guidance Clinic to develop a statewide family therapy training network for Pennsylvania. The primary recipients of training were the professional personnel employed at county mental health/mental retardation centers, with emphasis upon rural areas in the state. The first phase of the program was administered on site, one day per week, for 20 weeks. Six to eight trainees, including line and supervisory staff, met in each training group. The training day was divided between a morning seminar and an afternoon practicum. Curriculum included structural family therapy and crisis family therapy (Langsley, Pittman, Machotka, and Flomenhaft, 1968) techniques. Live and videotape supervisory methods were used, and these skills were transferred to the supervisors in each agency. Each trainee was supervised in the entire course of treatment for at least two families. In a second phase of training, the faculty remained available to the centers for one day of case consultation per month. The graduate trainees were free to use this service and PCGC training materials as they wished. A third phase of the program focused on the development of selected graduates as local trainers for each county.

During the first two years of the statewide (ITFT) program, 35 centers were served, including 150 professionals from all of the mental health disciplines. The professional experience of trainees prior to the program ranged from zero to 20 years. All graduates continued into the second phase of training. Fourteen centers had implemented the third phase, their own training programs, by the end of the second year, with 30 staff training an additional 50 therapists. An outcome questionnaire mailed to alumni one year after the end of phase one training ($N = 53$) showed that direct service time devoted to working with families had risen ($p < .01$) from an average of 17.5% before training to 38.5% after training (Flomenhaft and Carter, 1974).

In a second report (Flomenhaft and Carter, 1977), by the end of the fourth year, 38 of 41 targeted centers had received training, with over 300 graduates. A one-year follow-up questionnaire ($N = 152$) showed that direct service time of alumni had decreased by 12.5% after training, but that the difference was taken up by new administrative and training duties—a move up the career ladder. Despite the reduction in absolute direct service, trainees' work with families increased by 26% after training. Fewer recommendations for hospitalizations were also reported among cases after training. Also, by the end of the fourth year, 64 local trainers were in place and had trained over 200 additional therapists. Despite this success, there is no report of any replication of the program in other areas.

Betof (1977) has described the effects of a 40-week in-service program conducted with staff in mental retardation services at public and private agencies in Philadelphia. Professionals ($N = 68$) from 11 agencies were trained in structural techniques via an on-site, seminar-practicum format similar to that used in the ITFT program. Trainees had had an average of six years' experience prior to the program. In a questionnaire mailed after the program, alumni indicated variable effects. The results were closely correlated with the quality of the relationship between the trainee and the motivation of his/her agency for the program. Betof concludes that successful delivery of a training program of this type requires a combination of trainee and agency motivation. In order for learning to be sustained and fully applied, the trainee must have a receptive institutional base. This may require that agency infrastructure and other contextual factors be considered in planning and implementing in-service programs, possibly through extended application of structural tenets.

Medical-psychiatric collaboration in the psychosomatic research on family functioning and treatment has provided a logical base for extension of training into the areas of medical residency and continuing education. In 1972, the award of a ten-year grant from NIMH permitted the testing of a pediatric liaison program between the Philadelphia Child Guidance Clinic and Children's Hospital of Philadelphia (Honig, Liebman, Malone, Koch, and Kaplan, 1976). The program provides pediatric residents with structural-type skills in working with children and parents. The goals are to integrate into pediatric practice skills in treating minor family problems, and in detecting and referring major problems. Senior pediatric staff take primary teaching roles, while child psychiatric faculty (family therapists) serve as consultants and supervisors. A seminar-practicum format is used, one day per week, focused upon normal development, clinical syndromes, and interviewing skills. Live and videotape supervision is used.

Kaplan, Rosman, Liebman and Honig (1977) have described the results obtained on several evaluative methods. A log, maintained by faculty, of each student's patterns of participation in training, was content-analyzed and results were correlated with ratings of students' interview performance. Pre- and posttraining interview performance correlated significantly with the log, indicating better performance in conjunction with more contact between student and teacher during the program. The rating of pre- and post-interview performance utilized a videotape analysis method similar to that seen earlier in studies of family functioning. First-year residents ($N = 20$) in the program were compared to controls who were in residence at other hospitals ($N = 5$). Raters scored seven variables of performance in a family interview, including: 1) chief complaint, 2) history-taking, 3) joining, 4) language, 5) relating to parent during the physical exam, 6) relating to child during the physical exam, and 7) closure. Tapes were scored by raters blind to the pre- vs. post- and experimental vs. control status. Results indicated changes in the predicted direction of improved performance after training, on all variables except chief complaint. These measures constitute the strongest evidence obtained to date for the effectiveness of structural training methods. While the sampling used in this case

may be questionable (control group residents scored lower than trainees on all categories, at both pre- and post- assessments, discounting the comparability of the two groups), the methodology is intrinsically stronger than the more pop-

Synthesis

Integration of findings from treatment outcome, process and training research studies is difficult, again as the result of differences in designs and methods used. Among the factors that may have an impact on results are heterogeneity in the protocol of administration and diversity of outcome measures. Therapy has been conducted in and out of the hospital, for short and long durations, with children and adults as primary patients, in the structural outcome studies. Change measures have varied between fine-grained and global scales, with absolute (e.g., number of cases) and relative (e.g., percentage of time) quantification.

If these differences are temporarily ignored for heuristic purposes, a tentative summary of the effectiveness of structural family therapy can be derived by aggregating the results of major reports.[15] Examining the clinical outcome studies discussed above, a total sample of 201 families treated in family therapy is obtained. As measured on indices of symptom and psychosocial change in the index patient, structural family therapy was described as effective with 73% of these cases, and ineffective for the remaining 27%. Effectiveness varied from study to study, however, ranging between 50% and 100%. Across these studies, therapy appears to have been deterioration-inducing in between 3% and 15% of the ineffective subsample.[16] Attrition was marginal.

Among these eight outcome studies, there is no consistent evidence in favor of short- vs. long-term, or inpatient vs. outpatient formats, or for therapist-family matching (e.g., ethnicity, sex).

---

[15]Gurman and Kniskern (1978) have described several cautions to be observed when making comparisons in the face of such design disparity.

[16]*Editors' Note*. Note that these data refer to percentages of the unsuccessful cases, *not* of the total sample of 201. These reported deterioration rates, then, are a bit lower then those that have thus far been reported for other family therapy approaches (Gurman and Kniskern, 1978b).

Highest success rates appear in the psychosomatic studies, and could be attributable to either or all of several factors, including symptom, index patient's age, family socioeconomic status, and race. Lower rates of success occurred in the treatment of low socioeconomic and addict families; interestingly, the authors in these studies reported difficulty in recruiting and retaining black families in treatment. Types and configurations of social stresses outside the family may affect psychosomatic, low socioeconomic and addict families differently, making some cases generally more difficult to treat than others. Whether this led to poorer outcome for the addict and low socioeconomic studies, or whether external stresses were directly addressed by the family therapy, are not clarified in the reports.

Other plausible sources of poorer success in outcome studies are the single-parent structure of low socioeconomic families; adult age of addict patients; therapist-family racial differences; and therapist level of experience. More comprehensive or artful sampling designs need to be adopted by future studies to address questions pertaining to the concomitants of high *vs.* low effectiveness. Even lacking such detailed data, however, the levels of overall effectiveness can still be compared with the results of other family therapies. Relative to other studies reported by Gurman and Kniskern (1978), structural family therapy appears to be at least as successful as any of the current schools.

Two process studies demonstrated the effectiveness of particular facets of structural technique. Engagement of the family at the outset of treatment (Stanton et al., 1979) is an important aspect of therapy, as is crisis-induction (Rosman et al., 1975). The results showed these techniques to be highly effective, and there is merit in conducting future studies of similar design to test other interventions within the structural armamentarium.

Finally, several training studies indicate that structural family therapy can be effectively taught to persons with widely different backgrounds in social, academic and clinical experience. They have also demonstrated that similar training curricula and methods can be utilized for most groups, at various levels of expertise. Particular emphasis is placed on live, participatory supervision of practice. The quality of evaluative methodology in the training area has generally been less rigorous than that used in family interaction and treatment studies. Thus, more is known about the transferability of training methods than is known about the impact of training on the conduct of therapeutic practice and treatment outcome.[17]

CONCLUSION

As we have seen, the structural theory takes into account the individual, family and social contexts and their interrelationships. Structural techniques are aimed at the internal organization of each and the linkage between them, their ecostructure. And the theory and technique of structural family therapy rest upon our understanding of the individual and the family in their social contexts. However, while the field of psychology has studied the individual, much more needs to be learned about the family itself and about the dependence of the functioning of the family and its members upon their ecostructure.

The cumulative research record on structural family therapy stands as a substantial body of studies, crossing several important lines of inquiry and offering considerable evidence in support of a number of the school's major tenets and techniques. As creditable as the research has been, these inquiries, along with the development of the theory and techniques, are still in the beginning stages of growth and need to be studied, applied, tested and expanded from diverse corners of the field. The clinical application and investigation of structural family therapy must be taken up by a broader variety of practitioners and researchers in the field. Furthermore, it cannot continue to evolve wholly from within the "laboratory" of the clinical setting. Its models for family functioning and dysfunctioning must be tested against family patterns in the varied contexts of daily life.

A solid foundation for structural family therapy has been established. Its maturation will depend on a broadening and a further articulation of the base of theory and the superstructure of technique.

---

[17]*Editors' Note.* For a detailed discussion of methodological and clinical issues involved in the transferability of psychotherapy treatment from the parent setting in which it originated to other clinical settings, see Klein and Gurman (1980).

REFERENCES

Aponte, H. J. Organizing treatment around the family's problems and their structural bases. *Psychiatric Quarterly*, 1974, *48*, 8-12.

Aponte, H. J. Underorganization in the poor family. In P. J. Guerin, (Ed.), *Family Therapy: Theory and Practice*. New York: Gardner, 1976. (a)

Aponte, H. J. The family-school interview. *Family Process*, 1976, *15*, 303-310. (b)

Aponte, H. J. Diagnosis in family therapy. In C. B. Germain (Ed.), *Social Work Practice*. New York: Columbia University Press, 1979.

Aponte, H. J. Family therapy and the community. In M. Gibbs, J. R. Lachenmeyer, & J. Sigel (Eds.), *Community Psychology: Theoretical and Empirical Approaches*. New York: Gardner Press, 1980.

Auerswald, E. H. 1968, Interdisciplinary vs. ecological approach, *Family Process*, 1968, *7*, 202-215.

Baker, L. & Barcai, A. Psychosomatic aspects of diabetes mellitus. In O. W. Hill (Ed.), *Modern Trends in Psychosomatic Medicine. Vol. 2*. London: Butterworths, 1970.

Baker, L., Minuchin, S., Milman, L., Liebman, R., & Todd, T. Psychosomatic aspects of juvenile diabetes mellitus: A progress report. In *Modern Problems in Pediatrics. Vol. 12*. Basel: Karger, 1975.

Baker, L., Minuchin, S., & Rosman, B. The use of beta-adrenergic blockade in the treatment of psychosomatic aspects of juvenile diabetes mellitus. In A. Snart (Ed.), *Advances in Beta-Adrenergic Blocking Therapy. Vol. 5*, Princeton: Excerpta Medica, 1974.

Berger, H., Honig, P. & Liebman, R. Recurrent abdominal pain: gaining control of the symptom, *American Journal of Disorders of Childhood*, 1977, *131*, 1340-1344.

Betof, N. *The effects of a forty-week family therapy training program on the organization and trainees*. Unpublished Dissertation, Temple University, 1977.

Davis, P., Stern, D., & VanDeusen, J. Enmeshment-disengagement in the alcoholic family. In F. Seixas (Ed.), *Alcoholism: Clinical and Experimental Research*. New York: Grune and Stratton, 1977.

Doane, J. Family interaction and communication deviance in disturbed and normal families: A review of research, *Family Process*, 1978, *17*, 357-376.

Elbert, S., Rosman, B., Minuchin, S., & Guerney, B. A method for the clinical study of family interaction. *American Journal of Orthopsychiatry*, 1964, *34*, 885-894.

Flomenhaft, K. & Carter, R. Family therapy training: A statewide program for mental health centers, *Hospital and Community Psychiatry*, 1974, *25*, 789-791.

Flomenhaft, K. & Carter, R. Family therapy training: Program and outcome, *Family Process*, 1977, *16*, 211-218.

Golden, R. *A validation study of the family assessment battery*. Unpublished Doctoral Dissertation, Georgia State University, 1974.

Goren, S. A systems approach to emotional disorders of children, *Nursing Clinics of North America*, 1979, *14*, 462-465.

Gurman, A. & Kniskern, D. Research on marital and family therapy: Progress, perspective and prospect. In S. Garfield & A. Bergin (Eds.), *Handbook of Psychotherapy and Behavior Change: An Empirical Analysis*. Second edition. New York: Wiley, 1978.

Haley, J. We became family therapists. In A. Ferber, M. Mendelsohn, & A. Napier (Eds.), *The Book of Family Therapy*. Boston: Houghton Mifflin, 1972.

Haley, J. *Uncommon Therapy*. New York: W. W. Norton & Co. 1973.

Haley, J. *Problem-Solving Therapy*. San Francisco: Jossey-Bass, 1976.

Honig, P., Liebman, R., Malone, C., Koch, C., & Kaplan, S. Pediatric-psychiatric liaison as a model for teaching pediatric residents. *Journal of Medical Education*, 1976, *51*, 929-934.

Kaplan, S., Rosman, B., Liebman, R., & Honig, P. The log as a behavioral measure in a program to train pediatric residents in child psychiatry, *Special Interest Group/Health Profession Education Bulletin*, 1977.

Kaufman, E. & Kaufman, P. From a psychodynamic orientation to a structural family therapy approach in the treatment of drug dependency. In E. Kaufman & P. Kaufman (Eds.), *The Family Therapy of Drug and Alcohol Abuse*. New York: Gardner, 1979.

Lane, M. *Introduction to Structuralism*. New York: Basic, 1970.

Langsley, D., Pittman, F., Machotka, P., & Flomenhaft, K. Family crisis therapy: Results and implications. *Family Process*, 1968, *7*, 145-158.

Liebman, R., Minuchin, S., & Baker, L., 1974. An integrated treatment program for Anorexia Nervosa. *American Journal of Psychiatry*, 1974, *131*, 432-436.

Liebman, R., Honig, P., & Berger, H. An integrated treatment program for psychogenic pain. *Family Process*, 1976, *15*, 397-405.

Minuchin, S. *Families and Family Therapy*. Cambridge, MA: Harvard University Press, 1974.

Minuchin, S., Baker, L., Rosman, B., Liebman, R., Milman, L., & Todd, T., A conceptual model of psychosomatic illness in children. *Archives of General Psychiatry*, 1975, *32*, 1031-1038.

Minuchin, S. & Barcai, A. Therapeutically induced family crisis. In J. Masserman (Ed.), *Science and Psychoanalysis. Vol. 14*, 1969.

Minuchin, S., Montalvo, B., Guerney, B., Rosman, B., & Schumer, F. *Families of the Slums*. New York: Basic Books, 1967.

Minuchin, S., Rosman, B., & Baker, L. *Psychosomatic Families*. Cambridge: Harvard University Press, 1978.

Montalvo, B. Aspects of live supervision. *Family Process*, 1973, *12*, 343-359.

Piaget, J. *Structuralism*. New York: Basic, 1970.

Ritzer, G. Indigenous non-professionals in community mental health: boon or boondoggle? In P. Roman & H. Trice (Eds.), *The Sociology of Psychotherapy*. New York: Jason Aronson, 1974.

Rosenberg, J.B. & Lindblad, M.B. Behavior therapy in a family context: Elective mutism. *Family Process*, 1978, *17*, 77-82.

Rosman, B., Minuchin, S., & Liebman, R. Family lunch session: An introduction to family therapy in anorexia nervosa. *American Journal of Orthopsychiatry*, 1975, *45*, 846-853.

Speck, R. & Attneave, C. *Family Networks*. New York: Vintage, 1973.

Stanton, M. D. & Todd, T. C. Structural family therapy with drug addicts. In E. Kaufman & P. Kaufman (Eds.), *The Family Therapy of Drug and Alcohol Abuse*. New York: Gardner Press, 1979.

Stanton, M. D. & Todd, T. A critique of the Wells and Dezen review of the results of nonbehavioral family therapy. *Family Process*, 1980, *19*, 169-176.

Stanton, M. D. & Todd, T. Engaging resistant families in treatment: II. Some principles gained in recruiting addict families. *Family Process*, 1981, *20*.

Stanton, M. D., Todd, T., Kirschner, S., Kleinman, J., Mowatt, D., Riley, P., Scott, S., & VanDeusen, J. Heroin addiction as a family phenomenon: A new conceptual model. *American Journal of Drug and Alcohol Abuse,* 1978, *5,* 125-150.

Stanton, M. D., Todd, T., Steier, F., VanDeusen, J., Marder, L., Rosoff, R., Seaman, S., & Skibinski, E. *Family Characteristics and Family Therapy of Heroin Addicts: Final Report, 1974-1978.* Philadelphia: Philadelphia Child Guidance Clinic, 1979.

VanDeusen, J., Stanton, M. D., Scott, S., & Todd, T. Engaging resistant families in treatment: I. Getting the drug addict to recruit his family members. *International Journal of the Addictions,* 1980, *15,* 7, in press.

Wells, R. & Dezen, A. The results of family therapy revisited: The nonbehavioral methods. *Family Process,* 1978, *17,* 251-274.

Zeigler-Driscoll, G. Family research study at Eagleville Hospital and Rehabilitation Center. *Family Process,* 1977, *16,* 175-190.

Zeigler-Driscoll, G. The similarities in families of drug dependents and alcoholics. In E. Kaufman & P. Kaufman (Eds.), *The Family Therapy of Drug and Alcohol Abuse.* New York: Gardner Press, 1979.

EDITORS' REFERENCES

Freeman, M. Brief therapy and crisis aid explored. *American Psychological Association Monitor,* September/October, 1978, 6-7.

Gurman, A. S. & Kniskern, D. P. Research on marital and family therapy: Progress, perspective and prospect. In: S. Garfield & A. Bergin (Eds.), *Handbook of Psychotherapy and Behavior Change.* Second edition. New York: Wiley, 1978. (a)

Gurman, A. S. & Kniskern, D. P. Deterioration in marital and family therapy: Empirical, conceptual and clinical issues. *Family Process,* 1978, *17,* 3-20. (b)

Jacobson, N. S. A review of the research on the effectiveness of marital therapy. In: T. J. Paolino & B. S. McCrady (Eds.), *Marriage and Marital Therapy.* New York: Brunner/Mazel, 1978.

Klein, M. H. & Gurman, A. S. Ritual and reality: Some clinical implications of experimental designs for behavior therapy of depression. In: L. Rehm (Ed.), *Behavior Therapy for Depression.* New York: Academic Press, 1980.

Kniskern, D. P. & Gurman, A. S. Future directions for family therapy research. In: D. A. Bagarozzi (Ed.), *New Perspectives in Family Therapy.* New York: Human Sciences Press, 1980. (a)

Kniskern, D. P. & Gurman, A. S. Advances and prospects for family therapy research. In: J. P. Vincent (Ed.), *Advances in Family Intervention, Assessment and Theory.* Vol. 2. Greenwich, CT: JAI Press, 1980. (b)

Kniskern, D. P. & Gurman, A. S. Research on training in marriage and family therapy: Status, issues and directions. In: I. Zwerling & M. Andolfi (Eds.), *Dimensions of Family Therapy.* New York: Guilford, 1980. (c)

Stanton, M. D. Marital therapy from a structural/strategic viewpoint. In: P. Sholevar (Ed.), *Marriage is a Family Affair,* New York: Spectrum, 1981.

CHAPTER 10

Strategic Approaches to Family Therapy

M. Duncan Stanton, Ph.D.[1]

Strategic approaches to family therapy fall under what Madanes and Haley (1977) have termed the "communication" therapies. Haley (1973b) has defined strategic therapy as that in which the clinician initiates what happens during treatment and designs a particular approach for each problem. Strategic therapists take responsibility for directly influencing people. They want at least to enhance temporarily their influence over the interpersonal system at hand in order to bring about beneficial change. In fact, they are not as concerned about family theory as they are with the theory and means for inducing change. Prominent figures subscribing to this approach are Milton Erickson, Jay Haley,

the Mental Research Institute (MRI) group[2] (including John Weakland, Paul Watzlawick, Richard Fisch, Arthur Bodin, and Carlos Sluzki), Gerald Zuk, Lynn Hoffman, Mara Palazzoli-Selvini and associates in Milan, Italy, and Richard Rabkin.[3]

This chapter will present an analysis of the commonalities and differences among the major strategic approaches represented by the above groups—starting with general principles which apply to most of them, followed by more detailed material about their particular contribu-

[1]The author would like to express appreciation to the following for their helpful comments on portions or all of an earlier version of this manuscript: Maurizio Andolfi, M.D., David Berenson, M.D., Jay Haley, M.A., Lynn Hoffman, M.S.W., Monica McGoldrick-Orfandis, M.S.W., Mara Palazzoli-Selvini, M.D., Thomas C. Todd, Ph.D., John H. Weakland, Ch. E., Gerald Weeks, Ph.D., Gerald Zuk, Ph.D.

[2]*Editors' Note.* The MRI perspective on family therapy is presented separately elsewhere in this *Handbook* because it is conceptually different enough from several of the strategic approaches discussed by Stanton, and because of the enormous historical importance of the contributions of the MRI staff (see, e.g., Gurman, 1981).

[3]Since the emphasis in this chapter is on family treatment, the work of Rabkin will not be covered. Although he does work with families, and thinks in terms of systems, his writings—particularly his book (Rabkin, 1977)—preponderantly deal with individuals. The reader is referred to this stimulating volume for a more complete understanding of his techniques.

tions. A number of more recent contributors to the field also will be covered in an effort to be as current as possible. While strategic therapy has often been associated with the use of "paradoxical" techniques, it should become clear from the material to follow that this is just one of its facets, and that its theory and operations encompass a broad spectrum of techniques and clientele. Finally, although there are a great many similarities between the strategic and structural approaches to family treatment, the latter is covered elsewhere in this volume (Aponte and VanDeusen, Chapter 9), and will not receive major emphasis; the reader is referred to several other publications (Stanton, 1980; 1981b; 1981c) for clarification of this interface.

BACKGROUND

Two figures stand out as most foundational in the development of strategic approaches to family therapy: Gregory Bateson and Milton Erickson. An anthropologist by training and early professional experience, Bateson participated with Norbert Weiner and others in a series of Macy Foundation conferences immediately after World War II. From these conferences sprang the field of cybernetics, incorporating a number of seminal ideas in systems and communication theory. In 1948 Bateson joined Jurgen Ruesch as a research associate at the Langley Porter Neuropsychiatric Institute in San Francisco, beginning what was to be a long association with the field of psychiatry. Four years later he launched a communications project of his own at the Palo Alto VA Hospital and was joined by Jay Haley, John Weakland and William Fry. At approximately the same time, Don D. Jackson was starting to work with schizophrenics and their families at the same hospital and was developing the concept of family homeostasis (Jackson, 1957). He joined the Bateson project as a consultant in 1954. From this collaboration came the important work which led to the double-bind theory of schizophrenia (Bateson, Jackson, Haley and Weakland, 1956). While the double-bind was originally associated with the early life experience of the schizophrenic, the Palo Alto group eventually determined that it also applied to *current* situations, i.e., schizo-

phrenic behavior was a response to a present situation existing in the family (Haley, 1972). These revelations, tied together with (a) communications and cybernetic systems theory and (b) studies (by Haley and Weakland) of Milton Erickson's hypnotic and therapeutic techniques, formed the basis for the therapeutic work which developed later, i.e., the strategic approach. Haley's (1963) influential book, *Strategies of Psychotherapy*, which deals with the maneuverings of therapist and patient during individual treatment, also stems from this period.

In 1959, Jackson formed the Mental Research Institute (MRI) and brought Virginia Satir aboard. They were joined by Haley in 1962. Subsequent to Jackson's death in 1968, several others have served as director of MRI, including John Elderkin Bell, Jules Riskin, Nicholas Cummings and the present director, Carlos Sluzki. The MRI strategic therapy work has primarily been carried on by Weakland, Paul Watzlawick, Richard Fisch, Arthur Bodin, and Sluzki.

The other major early figure in strategic therapy was Milton Erickson. His innovative and successful therapy techniques, especially hypnosis and paradoxical instruction, caught the attention of Haley and Weakland. They began to visit Erickson regularly—an association that continued for many years—in order to better learn the ingredients of his therapy. Erickson's influence on these two investigators, and on the field of strategic therapy as a whole, cannot be overestimated. In fact, Haley feels that almost all of the therapeutic ideas applied in this approach had their origins in his work in some form.[4]

In 1967 Haley left Palo Alto to join Salvador Minuchin and Braulio Montalvo at the Philadelphia Child Guidance Clinic. Minuchin and Montalvo had arrived there in 1965 from the Wiltwyck School for Boys in New York. These people worked with other staff to transform a traditional child guidance clinic into a family-oriented treatment center. They also collaborated in the development of what came to be known as "structural" family therapy and established a program to train poor and black people to treat families. In the early and mid-1970s, Haley rekindled his interest in the family ther-

---

[4] Jay Haley, personal communication, August 1978.

apy of youthful schizophrenics, or, as he calls them, "disturbed young people" (Haley, 1980). In 1976, he left for Washington, D.C. to join the faculty of the University of Maryland Medical School and establish his own family therapy institute in conjunction with his wife, Cloé Madanes.

Gerald Zuk was working with the mentally retarded in the late 1950s and became interested in the family reactions to such children. In 1961, he joined the staff of the Eastern Pennsylvania Psychiatric Institute (EPPI) in Philadelphia where he remains to this day. In 1964, he organized the first national meeting of experienced family therapists. He collaborated with the psychodynamically-oriented family therapists at EPPI, such as Ivan Boszormenyi-Nagy, David Rubinstein, and James Framo, but began to shift more toward a systems approach as time went on. Much of his early work was with schizophrenics. His writings (e.g., Zuk, 1966) on a triadic-based, go-between therapy emerged in the late 1960s.

In the mid-1960s Lynn Hoffman began an association with Haley toward a comparison of various approaches to family therapy. The fruit of their collaboration was the book *Techniques of Family Therapy* (Haley and Hoffman, 1967), an analysis of the techniques within five different family therapy approaches. Later she joined the staff of the Philadelphia Child Guidance Clinic and remained there until 1975, when she was appointed to the clinical faculty of Downstate Medical Center, leaving in 1977 to join the Nathan Ackerman Institute of Family Therapy. Hoffman's contribution has been less in the development of therapeutic techniques per se than in the elucidation of the components of the family therapies. Her ability to conceptualize and to distill the essence of an approach has made her a unique and valuable contributor to the field, and she remains one of its clearest thinkers. In recent years her interests have turned primarily toward the examination and teaching of strategic techniques.

Mara Palazzoli-Selvini had been working from a psychoanalytic perspective with anorexia nervosa cases in Italy in the 1960s, with particular interest in the mother-child dyad. Her studies began to expand to include the total familial context as it related to the symptom, and she even-

tually started treating whole families (1970, 1978). In 1967 she established the Institute for Family Study in Milan. She was influenced early on by the studies of Lyman Wynne and Margaret T. Singer (e.g., Singer and Wynne, 1966) on communication patterns within families with a schizophrenic member. Later figures of importance included Bateson, Haley, Watzlawick and others. In 1971 the Institute was reorganized to include its present four members—Luigi Boscolo, Gianfranco Cecchin, Giuliana Prata and Palazzoli-Selvini. The group began its work with families in schizophrenic transaction in 1972.

HEALTHY FAMILIES

Strategic therapists have devoted more of their writings to dysfunctional than to healthy families, but they are keenly aware of normal family developmental patterns; for example, Haley's (1973b) book gives considerable space to such comparisons. Concerning the healthy-dysfunctional family distinction, some strategic therapists have noted that healthy families are less preoccupied with themselves and their own motivations or problems, showing less interest in any kind of "search for insight." As Bateson (1978) puts it, "a great deal of growing up, of maturation in the normal environment, does not depend on insight at all" (p. 81). While some therapists might contend that insight may possibly be useful to less optimally adjusted people, Erickson has commented that, "If you look over the lives of happy, well-adjusted people, they have never bothered to analyze their childhood or their parental relationships. They haven't bothered and they aren't going to" (in Haley, 1973b, p. 246).

The one area in which normal vs. dysfunctional family differences are most clearly described by strategic therapists is in the family developmental life cycle. All families undergo normal transitional steps or stages over time, such as birth of the first child, children beginning school, children leaving home, death of a parent/spouse, etc. These are potential crisis points which, although sometimes difficult to get through, are usually weathered by most families without inordinate difficulty. Dysfunctional families, on the other hand, are identified by their inability to make such transitions (see below).

To paraphrase Haley (1976), in normal families the hierarchies and structures are usually in line with cultural practices. There is a tendency to organize which is natural to humans and animals and its particular form is both biologically and culturally dictated. The most elemental hierarchy involves the separate generations. In most societies, parents are expected to be in charge of their children and cross-generational coalitions, such as one parent-child dyad siding against another parent-child dyad, are not predominant. In many societies grandparents are higher in the hierarchy than parents. In healthy families there is little confusion about what the hierarchical organization should be, and there is general adherence to the socially-sanctioned hierarchical structure. In contrast, dysfunctional families usually display a confusion in hierarchy, with cross-generational coalitions being common.

DYSFUNCTIONAL FAMILIES

Symptoms

Strategic family therapists see symptoms as the resultants or concomitants of misguided attempts at changing an existing difficulty (Watzlawick, Weakland and Fisch, 1974). However, such symptoms usually succeed only in making things worse. For example, the case of the depressed person whose family frantically tries to cheer him up, only to make him more and more depressed, is prototypic. In such cases Watzlawick et al. (1974) note that the family is "unable to see (and the patient to say) that what their help amounts to is a demand that the patient have certain feelings (joy, optimism, etc.) and not others (sadness, pessimism, etc.). As a result, what for the patient might originally only have been a temporary sadness now becomes infused with feelings of failure, sadness and ingratitude toward those who love him so much and are trying so hard to help him" (p. 34). Thus the family's attempt to alleviate the problem only exacerbates it.

From the above, the strategic therapist regards individual problems as manifestations of disturbances in the family.[5] A symptom is regarded as a communicative act, with message qualities, which serves as a sort of contract between two or more members and has a function within the interpersonal network. It is a label for a sequence of behaviors within a social organization (Haley, 1976). A symptom usually appears when a person is "in an impossible situation and is trying to break out of it" (Haley, 1973b, p. 44). He is locked into a sequence or pattern with the rest of his family or significant others and cannot see a way to alter it through nonsymptomatic means.

The family is, then, an interpersonal system which is in many ways analogous to other cybernetic systems (Hoffman, 1971). It is of the nonlinear type (e.g., the relationship between A and B is cyclic rather than A *causing* B), with complex interlocking feedback mechanisms and patterns of behavior which repeat themselves in sequence. If one observes a given family long enough, such sequences can be observed and particular phases within a sequence can even be predicted before they recur. An example might be when parents and a child are driving in a car together. Spouse A is driving and Spouse B is in a hurry to get to their destination (and conveys this before the trip). A accelerates through a yellow light, B grabs a dashboard handle and criticizes A, who retorts and steps on the gas. B protests more loudly, A shouts back and the child, C, starts to cry. At this point the argument stops while B attends to C and A slows down. Thus C's behavior becomes one element in a feedback process or "loop" (Hoffman, 1971) which serves to restore homeostasis. Chances are that such a pattern had occurred before and will reappear in the future. All families show such patterns, albeit in more pleasant ways, too, such as in a round of joking or showing affection.

---

[5]*Editors' Note.* Note that regarding such problems as "manifestations of disturbances in the family" speaks to the *functions* of symptoms, while "seeing symptoms as the resultants . . . of . . . attempts at changing an existing difficulty" (see Stanton, above) speaks to the *consequences* that follow "symptomatic" behavior. The notion of symptoms as "functional" is often meant to imply that symptoms are purposive or goal-directed (though the "purpose" need not be in the conscious awareness of any family member), whereas "consequences" speak only to descriptive, i.e., non-inferential, aspects of a symptom. In this way, then, functions and consequences are not equivalent, and they need to be dealt with differently in treatment.

However, in the event that difficulties or symptoms occur in a family, one member may be labeled as the problem, even though his/her contribution is but one part of a total family process. If the family in this example were a "child-centered" one, the child might be seen as the problem for "crying too much." (In other families an adult could have been viewed as the problem-maker.) The child is then scapegoated and becomes the "identified patient" if brought to a facility for treatment. A more realistic assessment might portray the identified patient as the member expressing a disturbance existing in the entire family. His behavior may protect or stabilize the family. Nonetheless, this should not be misconstrued as a "poor, mistreated child" syndrome, because the child contributes to the process. If the pattern has occurred many times before, our lachrymose child might have erupted into crying as soon as the family entered the car, even though no feelings of animosity had existed between the parents at the outset of this particular trip.

Life-Cycle

Haley (1973b) and Erickson, in concert with Weakland, Fisch, Watzlawick and Bodin (1974), have stressed the importance of the family developmental process as a framework for explaining symptomatology. Dysfunctional families develop problems because they are not able to adjust to transitions which occur within the family life-cycle. They become "stuck" at a particular point. As examples, Haley (1973b) cites the difficulty that families of schizophrenic young people have in allowing them to leave home, while Stanton, Todd, Heard, Kirschner, Kleiman, Mowatt, Riley, Scott and Van Deusen (1978) note this, as well as a related pattern revolving around adolescence, in families of drug addicts. The "problem," then, is not the young person, but rather the way the family reacts, interacts and attempts to adapt to the crisis stage it has entered. The therapist would thus be well advised to talk of families (and also to design interventions) in developmental terms rather than to try to define a family typology or a family symptomatology (Haley, 1971a).

Triads and Hierarchies

Since the 1950s a number of family therapists have identified the triangle as the basic building block of any emotional (interpersonal) system (Madanes and Haley, 1977). When tension between members of a two-person system becomes high, a third person is brought into the picture. An "emotional system," e.g., a family, is composed of a "series of interlocking triangles" (Bowen, 1966). Haley (1971b, 1973a) and Zuk (1966, 1971) have stressed the importance of the triangle or triad for conceptualizing "psychological" problems and their treatment. Specifically, Haley notes that most child problems include a triangle consisting of an overinvolved parent-child dyad (a cross-generational coalition) and a peripheral parent. When a child displays symptoms, the therapist should assume that at least two adults are involved in the problem and that the child is both a participant and a communication vehicle between them. In single-parent families, a grandparent may be involved—a three generational problem. Conflicts can cut across several levels in the familial hierarchy. Haley typifies the psychotic family as one in which grandparents cross generational lines, parents are in conflict over a child, and a parental child saves the "problem" child from parents. Haley posits that "an individual is more disturbed in direct proportion to the number of malfunctioning hierarchies in which he is embedded" (1976, p. 117).

The strategic view of dysfunction can be summarized as follows: 1) "symptoms" can be viewed simply as particular types of behavior functioning as homeostatic mechanisms which regulate family transactions (Jackson, 1957, 1965); 2) problems in an identified patient cannot be considered apart from the *context* in which they occur and the *functions* which they serve; 3) an individual cannot be expected to change unless his family system changes (Haley, 1962); 4) "insight" per se is not a necessary prerequisite for change. Such a view is radically different from and discontinuous with individually- or intrapsychically-oriented cause-and-effect explanations of dysfunctional behavior. Taken together, these postulates form a new orientation to human dilemmas (Haley, 1969).

ASSESSMENT OF SYSTEM DYSFUNCTION

Diagnosis in strategic therapy is often done by making an intervention—a therapeutic act—and observing how the system responds to it. Particular attention is paid to the interactional *sequence* of behaviors. Thus the therapist fosters interaction among the members. For example, he may want to see if father and son can relate comfortably in the presence of mother, so he requests that the two males discuss some matter together. If mother interferes in this dialogue, the therapist has clarified a problem area. By further encouraging the father and son to interact and concurrently supporting mother, the rigidity of the system can be tested further—i.e. he can better determine how difficult it is for them to manage this exchange. This sort of diagnosis is different from the conventional kind, and is geared directly to the treatment effort. From this perspective, every therapeutic intervention has diagnostic value, while every diagnostic move has therapeutic potential. Further, the use of conventional diagnostic labels can actually hamper treatment, because they place the therapist in the position of confirming the family's belief that (a) the identified patient is the problem (rather than the relationships within the system), and (b) the identified patient or the symptom is immutable. "Buying into" the system and the family's view can crystalize a problem and make it chronic (Haley, 1976).

GOAL-SETTING

One goal shared by strategic therapists is that of changing the dysfunctional *sequence* of behaviors shown by families who develop problems. This is an implicit goal, however, and, while it might be stated to the family, strategic therapists more commonly use the family's overtly expressed goals or target complaints as rallying points for actually altering dysfunctional sequences.

First contact with the family is generally taken through several stages by the strategic therapist. Following a "social" stage (similar to "joining," as defined by Minuchin [1974], and an important and planned part of the session [Haley, 1980]), the therapist inquires about the problem and solicits information. In the next phase, the family members are asked to talk to each other, eventually leading to a stage where goals are set and desired changes clarified (see Haley's [1976] excellent chapter on the initial interview for further details of this process). Unlike most other family therapy approaches (Madanes and Haley, 1977), the immediate intent is to accept the problem as defined by the family, even if focus remains on the identified patient. Emphasizing the presenting problem maximizes the family's motivation for change and increases leverage toward that end. Strategic therapists are very wary of getting caught in overt power struggles. Thus, they will employ skill and maneuvering to get covert control, but do so in the service of the situation as defined by the family. They accept what the family offers, since that is what it is ready to work on. They may ask each member what is his/her minimal goal for treatment, i.e., what would indicate some success in therapy, and then use implicit or indirect ways of turning the family's investment to positive use (Weakland et al., 1974). Final responsibility for the decision about treatment goals rests with the therapist, since he is the agent of change. Further, the problem to be changed must be put in solvable form. It should be something that can be objectively agreed upon, e.g., counted, observed, or measured, so that one can assess if it has actually been influenced. Even if, for instance, a couple appears for treatment in which neither is seen as "the problem," i.e., there is no index or identified patient (IP), and/or the problem is presented in vague terms such as "we're too emotional," the therapist will try to identify the elements in the behavioral sequence preceding and following the problem—who does what, when? He will want specifically to pin down the sequential and cyclical components of the problem and identify potential behaviors for change. Once this information is gleaned, an additional option is to attempt to "reframe" the problem (see below) as a means for removing some of the emotionality surrounding it and opening the door to change. In any event, and no matter how they may verbally redefine a problem, strategic family therapists, as a group, are perhaps second only to behaviorally-oriented family therapists in their insistence on objectively defined goals.[6]

The focus which strategic therapists place on goals related to the symptom and/or the priorities set by the family is understandable when viewed within its historical context. The earlier strategic work dealt for the most part with particularly difficult families, usually those of schizophrenics. This was partly because the Palo Alto group was interested in schizophrenic communication and partly because cases which had been treated unsuccessfully by other modes were more likely to be referred. These families, in holding to their homeostatic patterns and in resisting treatment, were found to be extremely skillful at throwing a therapist off track. Often the only lifeline the therapist had during such maneuverings was to cling to the symptom, avoiding getting misled by side or "bogus" issues. If he stayed with the presenting problem, however, he could justify his moves as being in line with the goals of the family (Haley, 1980). Thus, he played on what may be the only source of leverage a therapist has to keep the therapeutic effort on its intended path. Such factors have influenced the work of the Palo Alto group since its beginnings.

One of the early precepts of family treatment was to "spread the problem" among the children in the family, often by noting that the siblings have problems, too. Haley (1976) has cautioned against this because he feels it only succeeds in making the parents feel worse. They may end up by increasing their attack upon the problem child because he has caused them to be put in a situation in which they are accused of being even more "awful" for fostering a *second* problem child.

Behaviorally-oriented therapists and others have questioned the notion of symptom substitution, i.e., the idea that if one symptom is removed, another will appear in its place and fulfill the same function. Haley agrees with the behaviorists on this, but has rephrased it. He sees the issue as one of symptom salience. People may come in with several problems, but choose to work on the most bothersome first (or they may have several but only mention one). If that problem is eliminated, they may request to deal with the second priority problem, etc., until all are attenuated or eliminated. At times, this process has given the appearance of symptom substitution.

Sometimes it is necessary to set intermediate goals en route to the primary goals. These usually are determined by the therapist and they may or may not be explicitly shared with the family.[7] Haley (1976), in particular, has emphasized the use of intermediate goals and the various stages required during the process. Such stages may involve several shifts. For example, it is sometimes better in a single-parent family to deal with the grandmother first and then the mother, before the child's problem can be confronted. In such a case the therapist might try reframing the problem or using a rationale to the mother such as, "We need to give you a chance to handle this problem with your kid, but first we need to see if Grandmother could help in a different way—one that doesn't drain her so much"; thus an attempt is made to justify the intermediate stage within a framework which "makes sense" and is acceptable to the participant(s). Further, the intermediate stage(s) which is (are) passed through may appear as abnormal or aberrant as the presenting stage; this may be required before a "normal" adaptation can be achieved. For instance, if a father and daughter are too involved with each other and the mother is peripheral, an intermediate step might be to try to get mother and daughter to spend an inordinate amount of time together, while partially excluding father, before finally shifting to a point where the involvement of each parent with the child is roughly equivalent. This is going from one problem stage to another problem stage before heading for a "normal" stage. In other words, the therapist may not be able to go directly from the problem at the outset to a "cure" arrangement at the end.

---

[6]*Editors' Note.* While strategic therapists undoubtedly do place as much emphasis on operationalizing treatment goals as do behavior therapists (e.g., Gordon and Davidson, Chapter 14; Jacobson, Chapter 15), this similarity should not lead to the false conclusion that these approaches are otherwise very much alike. Note two major differences: (a) As Stanton notes above, the strategic *therapist* has the final responsibility for determining treatment goals, while in behavior therapy the patient bears this responsibility (Jacobson, Chapter 15); (b) while behavioral marriage and family therapists give enormous attention to teaching skills to patients, this rarely occurs in strategic therapy (Gurman, 1978).

---

[7]*Editors' Note.* Again, a behavioral family therapist would be very unlikely to fail to disclose such goals.

The reader should not be misled into thinking that treatment quickly changes direction toward, say, problems of other members, such as between parents. For the most part, strategic therapists keep the focus on the identified patient and his problem. If other problems are presented, the tendency is to put off dealing with them until the presenting problem is handled—a sort of "one thing at a time" approach which has both pragmatic features and, as stated earlier, can also serve as a lifeline for the therapist if a family shows resistance by flooding the session with problems. Once the presenting problem has been satisfactorily dealt with, of course, a re-contracting can be undertaken to deal with additional problems.

TREATMENT APPLICABILITY

Since strategic therapists assume that treatment for any behavioral problem or dysfunction must in some ways be tailored to a given family, they believe that their approach is not limited to any particular symptoms. Of course, much of the earlier work was done with schizophrenics, but succeeding years have seen a plethora of problems dealt with by strategic family therapists. They have worked with cases ranging widely in age, ethnicity, socioeconomic status, and chronicity. The following is a sampler of some of the disorders which have been treated and written about from the strategic viewpoint: *adolescent problems* (Erickson, in Haley, 1973b; Haley, 1973b, 1976; Mandel, Weizmann, Millan, Greenhow and Speirs, 1975; Papp, 1980; Watzlawick, Beavin and Jackson, 1967; Watzlawick et al., 1974; Zuk, 1971, 1975); *aging* (Erickson, in Haley, 1973b; Haley, 1973b); *alcoholism* (Andolfi, 1980; Berenson, 1976a, 1976b, 1979, and in Stanton, this chapter; Erickson, in Haley, 1973b; Stanton, 1981b; Watzlawick et al., 1967; Weakland et al., 1974); *anorexia and eating disorders* (Erickson, in Haley, 1973b; Erickson and Rossi, 1979; Haley, 1980; Palazzoli-Selvini, 1970, 1978; Palazzoli-Selvini, Boscolo, Cecchin and Prata, 1974, 1977, 1980a, 1980b; Weakland et al., 1974); *anxiety* (Erickson, in Haley, 1973b; Weakland et al., 1974); *asthma* (Erickson, in Haley, 1973b; Erickson and Rossi, 1979); *behavior problems and delinquency* (Erickson, 1962; Erickson, in Haley, 1973b; Haley, 1973b, 1976, 1980; Hare-Mustin, 1976; Jesse and L'Abate, 1980; Stanton, 1980, 1981c; Watzlawick et al., 1974; Weakland, et al., 1974; Zuk, 1971, 1975); *childhood "emotional" problems* (Erikson, in Haley, 1973b; Garrigan and Bambrick, 1975, 1977a, 1979; Haley, 1973a, 1973b, 1976; Stanton 1980, 1981c; Weakland et al., 1974; Zuk, 1971); *crying* (Hare-Mustin, 1976); *depression* (Erickson, in Haley, 1973b; Hare-Mustin, 1976; Rohrbaugh, Tennen, Press, White, Raskin and Pickering, 1977; Watzlawick and Coyne, 1980; Watzlawick et al., 1974; Weakland et al., 1974; Zuk, 1975); *dizziness* (Rohrbaugh et al., 1977); *drug abuse and addiction* (Haley, 1980; Stanton, 1978, 1980; Stanton and Todd, 1979; Stanton, Todd and Associates, 1981; Zuk, 1971); *encopresis* (Palazzoli-Selvini et al., 1974); *enuresis* (Erickson, 1954; Erickson, in Haley, 1973b; Madanes, 1980); *fire-setting* (Madanes, 1980); *homosexuality* (Erickson, in Haley, 1973b); *hysterical blindness* (Erickson, in Haley, 1973b); *identity crises* (Weakland et al., 1974); *insomnia* (Erickson, in Haley, 1963; Erickson and Rossi, 1979); *leaving home* (Erickson, in Haley, 1973b; Haley, 1973b, 1980; Papp, 1980; Stanton and Todd, 1979; Stanton et al., 1978, 1981;, Zuk, 1971); *marital problems* (Erickson, in Haley, 1973b; Haley, 1963, 1973b, 1976; Rohrbaugh et al., 1977; Sluzki, 1978; Stanton, 1981b; Teismann, 1979; Watzlawick et al., 1967, 1974; Weakland et al., 1974; Zuk, 1971, 1975); *obesity* (Erickson, in Haley, 1963, 1973b); *obsessive-compulsive behavior* (Erickson, in Haley, 1973b; Hare-Mustin, 1976; Rohrbaugh et al., 1977); *obsessive thoughts* (Erickson, in Haley, 1973b; Solyom, Garza-Perez, Ledwidge and Solyom, 1972); *chronic pain* (Erickson, in Haley, 1973b; Erickson and Rossi, 1979; Watzlawick et al., 1967); *paranoia* (Jackson, 1963; Watzlawick et al., 1967); *phobias* (Erickson, in Haley, 1973b; Erickson and Rossi, 1979; Haley, 1973b, 1976; Rohrbaugh et al., 1977); *postpartum depression and psychosis* (Erickson in Haley, 1973b); *premature ejaculation* (Erickson, in Haley, 1973b); *public speaking anxiety* (Rohrbaugh et al., 1977; Watzlawick et al., 1974); *schizophrenia* (Andolfi, 1980; Andolfi, Menghi, Nicoló and Saccu, 1980; Erickson, in Haley, 1973b; Haley, 1963, 1971a, 1973b, 1980; Jackson, 1963; Palazzoli-Selvini et al., 1977, 1978a, 1978b, 1980a, 1980b; Watzlawick et al., 1967, 1974; Weakland, et al., 1974; Zuk, 1971, 1975); *school problems and truancy*

(Erickson, in Haley, 1973b; Garrigan and Bambrick, 1975, 1977a, 1979; Haley, 1976; Papp, 1980; Rohrbaugh, et al., 1977; Watzlawick et al., 1974; Zuk, 1971, 1975); *sexual problems* (Erickson, in Haley, 1973b; Rohrbaugh et al., 1977; Weakland et al., 1974); *sleep disturbances* (Erickson and Rossi, 1979; Hare-Mustin, 1976; Madanes, 1980; Rohrbaugh et al., 1977; Watzlawick et al., 1967, 1974); *stammering* (Watzlawick et al., 1974); *suicidal gestures* (Erickson, in Haley, 1973b; Papp, 1980; Watzlawick et al., 1974; Zuk, 1971, 1975); *excessive sweating* (Erickson and Rossi, 1979); *temper tantrums* (Erickson, 1962; Hare-Mustin, 1975, 1976; Papp, 1980); *thumb-sucking* (Erickson, in Haley, 1973b); *tinnitus* (Erickson and Rossi, 1979); *vomiting and stomach aches* (Erickson, in Haley, 1973b; Madanes, 1980; Stanton, 1980a); *work problems* (Erickson, in Haley, 1973b; Watzlawick et al., 1974; Weakland et al., 1974). In addition, Weakland (1977) has suggested that this approach to therapy has been unnecessarily overlooked in the treatment of physical illness and disease.

There are certain instances in which strategic therapists have expressed doubts about the appropriateness or timing of treatment. Erickson once turned away a man who had been treated unsuccessfully by a series of therapists because it became apparent that he simply wanted to add Erickson to his list of conquests. Zuk (1975) feels that the primary contraindication for family treatment is when a family has a fixed attitude that the therapist is serving as an agent of some other person or institution such that therapy has a disciplinary function. Haley sometimes recommends postponement of treatment to a more suitable point in the future, such as in a case discussed with the author in which he suggested that a drug addict's family return in six months because they were not willing to work to get the patient off methadone. It may be clear from these examples, however, that strategic therapists are less likely to reject particular *kinds* of problem families than they are to shun situations where the context of the situation permits little or no leverage.

STRUCTURE OF THE THERAPY PROCESS

Strategic family therapists assume responsibility for determining the structure of the therapy process. The usual procedure is to try to involve in treatment all systems of import to the problem, in addition to the immediate family. This could include grandparents, the school, work colleagues, etc. As a rule, it is not recommended to see a client alone in therapy because this requires that the therapist be able to estimate from talking to the individual what his situation is and what effect interventions will have on those not present; it is felt that the average therapist does not usually have this skill and, if he can avoid working at such a handicap, he should (Haley, 1976). However, this is not a hard and fast rule, and strategic therapists will see individuals, parents, or couples alone as the situation demands, provided they conceptualize the problem as involving at least two and usually three people (Madanes and Haley, 1977). In particular, Erickson, Rabkin and the MRI group may work only with the complainant, e.g., the wife or parents of the IP, since it is held that (a) this person (or persons) is concerned enough to do something different, and (b) effective intervention can be made through any member of the system (Weakland, 1976). Another alternative is to exclude the IP and work solely with the family (Watzlawick and Coyne, 1980).

Most strategic therapists do not engage in cotherapy as it is usually practiced, although they routinely work with one or more colleagues observing sessions from adjoining rooms; these colleagues may help out at times and even enter the room and take sides on an issue as a way of facilitating a change in the process (Weakland et al., 1974).[8] A variation on this approach is used by the Milan group: whereas they originally operated with a heterosexual team of cotherapists working in the room and being observed by a second, similar team (Palazzoli-Selvini et al., 1978b), as they gained more experience and competence they switched to having one therapist meeting with the family, with between one and three colleagues observing.[9] An extension of this idea is described by Papp (1980), in which a "consultation group" observes and com-

---

[8]*Editors' Note.* We speculate that one of the main reasons why strategic family therapists rarely do co-therapy is that very systematic and consistent control of the treatment process must be maintained during treatment sessions in this approach, and a second therapist's presence would run the "risk" of introducing uncertainty and a less "united front" into the treatment.

[9]Mara Palazzoli-Selvini, personal communication, June 1979.

municates to therapist and family much like a "Greek chorus," perhaps informing them of a "vote" taken by the group as to whether, for example, it is correct for a father or mother to change his or her behavior. In another variation, Todd and associates at the Harlem Valley Psychiatric Center in New York use a method in which co-therapists are observed by up to eight collaborators, the whole group even making home visits.[10]

Compared to many individual and family therapies, such as psychodynamic approaches, strategic therapists tend to follow a brief therapy model. Zuk (1976) notes that short-term therapies may work partly because that is the timeframe which the majority of families will accept—*they* limit the therapist to six months or less. Some strategic therapists limit treatment to 10 sessions as a standard procedure (e.g., Stanton, 1978; Palazzoli-Selvini et al., 1978a; Weakland et al., 1974). More commonly the number of sessions is contingent upon the problem, extending from one to up to 20-30 sessions with "severely disturbed" cases (Haley, 1980). Zuk (1976) has noted that the length of treatment is contingent on the kind of problem and the contract made with the family, and offers the following parameters: crisis-resolution, 1-6 sessions; short-term therapy, 10-15 sessions; middle-range therapy, 25-30 sessions; long-term therapy, 40 or more interviews. Zuk (1975) also doubts the value of family treatment which extends beyond 15 months.

For most strategic therapists, weekly spacing of early sessions is common, with less frequent meetings near termination. Erickson (in Haley, 1973b), Haley (1980) and Stanton and Todd (1979) advocate "posttreatment" follow-ups or "check-ups" to ensure that positive change continues—serving a kind of "inoculative" function. Again, the Milan group has their own variation. Partly because many of their families travel long distances for treatment, they tend to space their sessions from two weeks to several months apart, the average being one month. They rarely meet more than 10-12 times total and frequently limit therapy to 3-6 sessions. Palazzoli-Selvini et al. (1978b) note that monthly spacing is also appropriate because, following an accurate or

effective strategic directive or intervention, the family needs time for systemic change—a certain amount of time must pass while internal family change is taking place. In fact, the Milan group feels that a shorter interval between sessions can act in favor of family resistance, especially if the family calls to insist on an earlier session; they note that to give in to such requests "condemns the therapist to impotence" (p. 15), because the system changes which have been set in motion by the therapist have not had a chance to congeal. Finally, Todd[11] adds that it is not always easy to come up with dramatic, convincing paradoxical prescriptions for a family as often as every week and a longer interval makes the therapist's job easier without apparent loss in effectiveness.

ROLE OF THE THERAPIST

Decisions about therapy are the responsibility of the (strategic) therapist. This does not necessarily mean that a rigid format is adhered to. Decisions are made in response to what is occurring in and around treatment and to the behavior of the family. In addition, the therapist must have control of the case, including (a) primary decision-making over medications, (b) which family members are to be involved, and (c) the interface with other treating agencies (Haley, 1979, 1980; Stanton and Todd, 1979).

Frequently strategic therapists want the family members to interact together, at least for diagnostic purposes, but they wish to control when this occurs. This might include allowing particular members to interact freely, e.g., following a therapeutic directive, to see how the intervention "takes." There is some variability among therapists on this, but they generally try to avoid getting triangulated or distracted by family members. In addition, since the therapist is trying to alter dysfunctional repetitive sequences—to halt the family's "game without end" (Watzlawick et al., 1967)—he/she must take deliberate action to do this. Being thoughtful, reflective and sitting back and making interpretations merely allow the family to repeat the patterns it exercises outside of treatment; such

---

[10]Thomas Todd, personal communication, January 1979.

[11]Thomas Todd, personal communication, January 1979.

a nondirective approach does not help to bring about change.

Strategic therapists also differ in the extent to which they engage in "joining" families. The MRI group, tending to be more distant, probably devotes less effort to this than Erickson, the Milan group, Stanton or Todd. Self-disclosure for its own sake is avoided, except perhaps as a vehicle for either joining or shifting power (e.g., making the therapist appear less potent when members appear intimidated by him).

Considering the therapist's values, Zuk (1978) has emphasized their importance in the therapeutic process. He defines a continuity-discontinuity dichotomy which pervades family systems:

"Continuity" values are those that stress the goodness of human interconnectedness, caretaking and nurturance. They emphasize the wholeness and indivisibility of human experience, and stress the essential quality of people. "Discontinuity" values are those that stress the goodness of rationality, of orderliness and efficiency, of adherence to rules and regulations, of analytic procedures (Zuk 1978, p. 18).

Zuk notes that wives and children tend toward continuity values, while husbands and society (or neighborhoods) lean toward the discontinuity side. Conflicts among any of these subsystems are usually drawn along the line between the two types; an impasse is reached in which those advocating one value attempt to subjugate proponents of the other, leading to pathogenic relating. The therapist must beware of unknowingly embracing one kind of value or the other when making interventions, being able to synchronize his position with the direction and family structure he wishes to emerge.

The therapist's role may change somewhat during treatment, particularly regarding his interventions. A family in crisis requires more control than later on, when the tone may have changed to a more jovial one. Andolfi et al. (1980), in their work with families with a member showing schizophrenic patterns, tend to shift from a more paradoxically oppositional stance toward the whole family, initially, to one of making structural subsystem-oriented moves as treatment progresses, as does Stanton (1981b, 1981c).

There are certain roles which the therapist may assume in lieu of their absence in the larger society. Haley (1973b) notes that, in attempting to wean parents and children from each other, Erickson often presides at a kind of "initiation ceremony," thus establishing a ritual which, although common in many cultures, is lacking in America. Taking this further, Zuk describes how in recent years the therapist, much like a judge, priest or civic official, is often called upon to serve as a "celebrant." He officiates at or "celebrates" an event "that has been deemed important by the family, such as a death or a birth, a separation or reconciliation, a runaway or return from runaway of a family member, a hospitalization or release from hospitalization, a loss or recovery of a job. As celebrant the therapist confirms and signifies that the event did indeed occur" (1975, p. 13). Thus he seals and labels a change—gives it his stamp. His input serves as testimony to whether a change is important or not. He can use this role to expand a family's narrow definition of a problem, thus employing his influence in effecting beneficial change.

If treatment fails, strategic therapists believe the fault lies with the therapist rather than the "poor motivation" of the family. The fact that the family showed up is proof enough of their motivation, so if treatment falters the therapist did not do something right. Stanton and Todd (1981) have extended this logic to the process of getting families into treatment. They note that many of the most desperate families will allow the IP to be treated, but are resistant to being engaged themselves. Stanton and Todd assert that sitting and waiting for such families to come in under their own steam is a faulty treatment philosophy, and that strategic moves may be required to get them engaged.

On the other hand, if treatment succeeds, the therapist should be reluctant to overtly accept credit for it, even if he considers himself mainly or partly responsible for the change (Stanton, 1981a). This is an important point and one which the author has heard emphasized only by strategic and structural therapists. The idea is that the more the IP's *family* or *parents* feel responsible for helping him/her improve, the greater are the chances that the positive effects of treatment will *last*. If the family or parents feel overly indebted to the therapist, they will see themselves as less competent to cope effectively with new situations or future symptom-provoking events. On the other hand, a sense of accomplishment in having helped and corrected the original problem will prompt them to feel more confident in handling future difficulties. Thus it is tactically wise for the therapist to underscore to them the extent to which their own efforts, ideas, and commitment really "turned things around." If family members terminate a successful treatment feeling that they, rather than the therapist, were responsible for beneficial change, the chances for long-term success are increased.[12]

TREATMENT TECHNIQUES: GENERAL

Several techniques characteristic of strategic family therapy have been presented above. Since this chapter encompasses a number of variations or "schools" within the strategic approach, this section will deal with additional aspects of treatment which apply to most of the strategic family therapies.

Strategic therapists are generally quite pragmatic. They are concerned with techniques that *work*, no matter how illogical these might appear; minimally, this would mean that the symptom or presenting problem be eliminated or substantially reduced. They care less about "family dynamics" than about how their interventions can bring about beneficial change in the people involved, with due consideration for their individual personalities. Strategic therapists also tend to be symptom-focused. Their approach is essentially a behaviorally-oriented, "black box" one in which "insight" or "awareness" are not considered necessary or important for change to occur. Understanding one's motivation is of little value if one does not *do* something about one's problems. Perceptions and subjective "feelings" are seen more as dependent than independent variables, since they change with changes in interpersonal relationships. Because repetitive sequences in families

exist in the present and are seen as being maintained by the ongoing, current behavior of the family system, altering them requires intervention in the existent process rather than harking back to past events. However, the therapist does not necessarily want to make the family "aware" of the cycle by pointing it out to them, as this will usually engender more resistance.[13] Finally, *all aspects of the repetitive sequence may not have to be shifted, but only enough of them to cause the symptom to disappear* (Hoffman, 1976).

Just as the technique of psychodynamic therapy relies heavily upon interpretations, the main therapeutic tools of strategic therapy are tasks and directives. *This emphasis on directives is the cornerstone of the strategic approach.* Much of the discussion that takes place early in a session is aimed at providing information necessary for the therapist to arrive at a directive or task. Subsequent interaction might then center on either how to carry out the directive, or on actually performing the task in the session. Like Minuchin (1974), Haley (1976) notes that the best task is "one that uses the presenting problem to make a structural change in the family" (p. 77). Further, a task is usually designed to be carried out between sessions as a means of using time more fully and generalizing what transpires in the session to the world outside. Hoffman (1976) notes that if the problem behavior is a chronically pervasive one (e.g., a psychosomatic or communicational disorder) a more effective tack to take may be to focus on the *management* of the problem rather than the problem itself. This usually flushes out parental disagreement, so the task becomes one of getting the parents together so they can make the identified patient behave appropriately despite his "illness."

In addition to an emphasis on tasks and homework, strategic therapists attempt to unbalance

---

[12]*Editors' Note.* We think that these attempts to persuade families to attribute their success unilaterally to their own efforts often might be unpersuasive, when paradoxical interventions have been used, since very little behavioral skill-training or cognitive mastery occurs in strategic therapy. This stance is more often taken (appropriately) by behavior therapists.

[13]*Editors' Note.* While this is certainly a testable notion, it receives little indirect support from recent experimental studies of behavioral marriage (Jacobson, Chapter 15), family (Gordon and Davidson, Chapter 14), or sex (Heiman, LoPiccolo and LoPiccolo, Chapter 16) therapy. On the other hand, these data from behavioral studies have not come from clinical work with *very* homeostatic families, e.g., families of schizophrenics. Thus, therapists' attempts to increase families' awareness of their interactional patterns may produce different outcomes with different types of families.

a system by joining with one or more members on a conflictual point (what Zuk [1966] calls the "go-between" role). Strategic therapists also engage in fortifying generational boundaries, and in tactically supporting various members at certain times. All of these interventions could be considered examples of the kind of structural techniques described by Aponte and Van Deusen (Chapter 9), Minuchin (1974) and Stanton (1980; 1981c). Whether or not they acknowledge such moves as structural in nature, their therapeutic operations indicate that most strategic therapists are cognizant of structural issues; for instance, deciding which family member(s) should undertake a task and who should not be involved in it is, in and of itself, a structural decision.

It may be apparent that while strategic therapists are specific, behavioral or "digital" in their focus on the presenting problem, they conceptualize the problem in systems or "analogical" terms. Madanes and Haley (1977) clarify this distinction:

It is possible to describe human behavior as 'bits' of behavior; that is, one can describe it as events or acts which are countable. For example, the headaches of a man can be described as an event that can be counted as so many per day. This is a digital type of description which breaks down behavior into bits like a computer program.

Another way to describe human behavior is to say that any act has a meaning in a context of other acts. In that sense, any behavior is an analogy to other behavior. For example, when a woman is talking about her headaches to a therapist, she is talking about more than one kind of pain. That is, behavior is always a communication on many levels. The message 'I have a headache,' is a report on an internal state, but it may also be a way of declining sexual relations or of getting the husband to help with the children.

The behaviorists who classify a symptom as a 'bit' that can be counted as present or absent are thinking differently from therapists who consider a symptom to be a communication about a person's life situation and therefore an analogy about something else (pp. 90-91).

Strategic therapists tend to "go with" resistance demonstrated by family members, and avoid power struggles whenever possible—especially in initial sessions. They find that it is wisest to travel a path of least resistance, dealing with the problem as defined by the family. (The Milan group routinely minimizes such resistance by asking a third person to describe the interaction between two other members, so that the original two are not put in the position of having to defend their actions [Palazzoli-Selvini et al., 1980a]). If there is a family disagreement about what the problem is, the tendency is generally to emphasize the parental view of it. Should the parents disagree, a number of options are still open, such as: (a) siding with the parents, noting that their child has been able to finagle them into disagreeing with each other and thus get his own way through a "divide and conquer" strategy; (b) having parents alternate in the way the problem (as each defines it) is to be dealt with (Palazzoli-Selvini et al., 1978b); (c) noting that the *real* problem is one of disagreement between, for instance, "two people who care for each other and for their child"; or (d) some other way of relabeling which the therapist decides is appropriate and is least likely to engender resistance.

Much of what occurs in strategic therapy is to make explicit what has been implicit in a family's present interaction pattern(s) (Madanes, 1980).[14] For example, if it is found that a parent has been surreptitiously providing a drug-abusing child with drugs, a strategic therapist might attempt to negotiate a contract as to (a) how much drug use is allowed, (b) when, and (c) who should dole out the chemicals—just so long as it is aboveboard and agreed upon; this would essentially be a paradoxical move meant to stop the parent(s) from abetting their child's drug-taking.

Strategic therapists may make interpretations, but they are rarely done to bring about "understanding" as much as to shift views of reality—to "relabel." They are directed more at process than content. For example, in a situation in which there is antagonism between father and son, the therapist could state that since father had not practiced talking with his

---

[14]*Editors' Note.* Skynner (Chapter 2) notes that the power of the therapeutic paradox may lie in its potential to bridge the fantasy lives and the public lives of family members, i.e., to bring unconscious strivings into the awareness of individuals, and to interrupt two or more person collusions.

own father, he did not know how to pass this kind of behavior on to his son; he had had no model to learn from. In this case, the veracity of the interpretation is not as important as the change it is designed to bring about, i.e., it can be used as a means to facilitate father and son talking together by (a) removing blame from father, (b) giving him a non-accusatory reason for the difficulty he is having, (c) empathizing with him, and (d) indicating that the present problem is just a matter of practice—the implication being that change is possible and may not even be that hard to effect.

Paradoxical Intervention

No chapter dealing with strategic therapy would be complete without a discussion of the technique of paradoxical intervention. This technique has been described by a number of writers (e.g., Erickson, in Haley, 1967, 1973b; Frankl, 1960; Haley, 1963, 1976, 1980; L'Abate and Weeks, 1978; Madanes, 1980; Papp, 1980; Raskin and Klein, 1976, Rohrbaugh et al., 1977; Watzlawick et al., 1967, 1974; Weakland et al., 1974; Weeks and L'Abate, 1979), and recently reviewed by Soper and L'Abate (1977). It is hardly a new approach, as Foucault (1965) cites a case from the 18th century in which a physician used a paradoxical technique in treating a melancholic patient who imagined he had no head. Watzlawick et al. (1967) define paradox as a "contradiction that follows correct deduction from consistent premises" (p. 188). In a therapeutic context, Hare-Mustin (1976) has described paradoxical interventions as "those which appear absurd because they exhibit an apparently contradictory nature, such as requiring clients to do what in fact they have been doing, rather than requiring that they change, which is what everyone else is demanding" (p. 128). This has sometimes been called "prescribing the symptom."

The use of paradoxical intervention is partly based on the assumption that there is great resistance to change within a family and a therapist entering its context is put under considerable pressure to adopt its ways of interacting and communicating. Succumbing to this pull will render the therapist ineffective.[15] In addition, the family members resist the therapist's efforts to make them change. If, however, the therapist tells them to do what they are already doing, they are in a (therapeutic) bind. Should they follow his instructions and continue the prescribed behavior, they are doing his bidding and, therefore, giving him undue power; he gains control by making the symptom occur at his direction. If they resist the paradoxical instruction, and therefore the therapist, they are moving towards "improvement" (and in the long run also doing his bidding). The confusion which occurs as to how to resist leads to new patterns and perceptions and thus to change—at the very least it can help to achieve a certain amount of detachment from the disturbing behavior (Hare-Mustin, 1976). In this way, a directive which appears on the surface to be in opposition to the goals being sought actually serves to move toward them. It is often couched to the family in terms of "getting control" of the symptoms, e.g., "if you can turn this symptom on when you try, you will be able to control it, instead of it controlling you." The paradoxical directive can be given to the whole family or to certain members. For example, in a case seen by the author, a boy who got stomachaches when his parents left him alone was asked to try to get sick at a particular time, while the parents were instructed to go outside the house together for at least ten minutes at the same time.

Should a client improve too rapidly, or the therapist has other reasons to expect symptom recurrence, he might prescribe a relapse. This could also be justified as a means for the client's "maintaining control," but Erickson often introduced a nostalgic flavor to such a directive. He might say to the client, "I want you to go back and feel as badly as you did when you first came in with the problem, because I want you to see if there is anything from that time that you wish

---

[15]*Editors' Note.* An important caveat is Papp's (1979) point that, *"If motivation is high enough and resistance low enough* for a family to respond to direct interventions, such as logical explanations, suggestions or tasks, *there is no need to resort to a paradox"* (p. 11, emphasis added). We understand this warning as suggesting a greater chance of negative effects by using paradoxical interventions with well motivated families.

to recover and salvage" (Erickson, in Haley, 1973b, p. 31). Such moves take into account the benefits that usually accrue from symptoms and also serve to anticipate that improvement may increase apprehension about change; this danger is thus met paradoxically through "redefining any relapse that might occur as a step forward rather than backward" (Weakland et al., 1974, p. 160).

Drawing from the literature and their own experience, Rohrbaugh et al. (1977) have defined a useful classification of paradoxical interventions. They divide such strategics into three types: *prescribing, restraining* and *positioning*. They make these distinctions as follows:

Prescribing strategies have received the most attention in the literature. Here, the therapist encourages or instructs the patient to engage in the specific behavior that is to be eliminated. For example, he may instruct the patient to practice an obsessional thought, or to bring on an anxiety attack; he may encourage a rebellious adolescent to rebel, or an overinvolved mother to be more protective of her child. . . .

In using *restraining strategies*, the therapist attempts to discourage or even deny the possibility of change. For example, he may tell the patient to "go slow," or emphasize the dangers of improvement. In selected cases, he may even suggest that the situation is hopeless. Strategies of this type have been most clearly described by Jay Haley (1976) and by the Palo Alto group (Watzlawick et al., 1974; Weakland et al., 1974).

What we call *positioning* is also most clearly exemplified in the work of the Palo Alto group. Here, the therapist attempts to shift a problematic "position"—usually, an assertion that the patient is making about himself or his problem—by accepting and exaggerating that position. This intervention is used when the patient's position is assessed to be maintained by a complementary or opposite response by others. For example, when a patient's pessimism is reinforced or maintained by an optimistic or encouraging response from significant others, the therapist may "outdo" the patient's pessimism by defining the situation as even more dismal than he (the patient) had originally held it to be (pp. 5-6).

Haley (1976) has outlined eight stages in undertaking a paradoxical intervention: 1) a client-therapist relationship defined as one to bring about change, 2) a clearly defined problem, 3) clearly defined goal(s), 4) the therapist offers a plan, usually with rationale, 5) the therapist gracefully disqualifies the current authority on the problem, e.g., spouse or a parent, 6) a paradoxical directive is given, 7) the response is observed and the therapist continues to encourage the (usual) behavior—no "rebellious improvement" is allowed, 8) the therapist should avoid taking credit for any beneficial change that occurs, such as symptom elimination, and may even display puzzlement over the improvement. Haley (1963) has stated that the basic rule is "to encourage the symptom in such a way that the patient cannot continue to utilize it" (p. 55). As mentioned above, this can sometimes be done by making the cure more troublesome than the symptom itself, such as by prescribing an increase in the frequency or intensity with which the symptom is to occur.

Recently, several attempts have been made to provide alternative explanations of the ways in which paradox works. Andolfi et al. (1980) describe a sequential approach (discussed more fully below) based on the balance between the family and therapist in the extent to which they display either homeostatic or "transformational" (ability to change) tendencies. In short, the therapist, by advocating more homeostatic behavior than the family (e.g., denying the IP's "craziness," warning against "moving too fast," etc.), secures a position of greater power and control as the family moves toward transformation in its efforts to unseat him; they have to change in order to resist him.

Stanton (1981a) has proposed a mechanism of "compression" to explain paradox. Dysfunctional nuclear families and subsystems are seen as vacillating, in cyclic form, between an overly-close, "undifferentiated" or "fusion" state, through a disintegrating/expansive or "fission" state directed outward, to another fusion state with the family of origin. In other words, when the nuclear family implodes toward a point of near fusion, a counter-reaction occurs outward, away from fusion with the immediate family member(s) and toward a fusion state with the family of origin. This repetitive pattern of expansion and contraction is manifested by the behavioral sequences observed in families, and is especially obvious in families who are severely dysfunctional. The paradoxical intervention, by compressing either the nuclear family or the family of origin toward fusion, accelerates the process and causes an explosive counter-reaction. However, the therapist blocks the usual path of the reaction, diverting it in a new direction—one which requires different responses and an expanded repertoire. In this way, a pattern is broken and transformation has occurred. Stanton proposes that such a model can be applied not only to paradox and positive interpretation (discussed below), but also to other therapeutic devices and individually oriented therapies such as "flooding," crisis induction, certain aspects of "provocative" therapy (Farrelly and Brandsma, 1974), etc.; this latter point is based on the assumption that individuals interact and develop symptoms within an interpersonal, usually familial, system—whether the therapist recognizes this or not (Haley, 1971a).

Positive Interpretation

The tendency of people who treat families strategically is to ascribe positive motives to clients. This is primarily because blaming, criticism and negative terms tend to mobilize resistance, as family members muster their energies to disown the pejorative label. Such negative or depressive maneuvers by the family can render the therapist impotent. Consequently, the therapist might, for example, relabel "hostile" behavior as "concerned interest" (Weakland et al., 1974) or as a desire to "get the best care possible" for the IP. This approach has a paradoxical flavor, as the family finds that its efforts to fight are redefined (Haley, 1963). It is also a form of reframing (Soper and L'Abate, 1977). Another facet of this tack is that simply defining problems as interactional or familial stumbling blocks serves to have them viewed as *shared*, rather than loading the blame entirely on one or two members—this is a "we're all in this together" phenomenon (Weakland, 1976).

Certain strategic groups have taken positive interpretation beyond the application of a simple nonblaming stance or the avoidance of pejoratives alone, however. They have adopted the position that all symptoms are highly adaptive for the family, in a sense holding that "everything that everybody does is for good reason and is understandable." This notion devel-

oped somewhat independently within several quarters. Erickson and Haley, of course, had been implying this for some time in their emphasis on nonblaming, as had the MRI group, Minuchin, L'Abate (1975) and others. Boszormenyi-Nagy and Spark (1973), non-strategic therapists who eschew "techniques," have used positive interpretation indirectly for a number of years by noting to clients that their symptoms are adaptive for the family group across generations; members are thus, in a sense, fulfilling a script and are absolved of blame. Stanton and associates, although unaware at the time of the emphasis on such an approach by strategic therapists, found in working with addict families (who tend to be extremely defensive) that, for treatment to proceed, they needed to attribute noble motivations to even the most "destructive" behaviors shown by these families (cf: Stanton, (1977). They have termed these techniques *noble ascriptions* (Stanton and Todd, 1979; Stanton et al., 1981). While influenced by Boszormenyi-Nagy, their approach differs from his in that they took this tack with full cognizance of the effect desired.[16]

A group which has been particularly creative in applying what they term *positive connotation* has been that of Palazzoli-Selvini and associates in Milan. Positive connotation is one of their trademarks. They use it to gain access to the family system, generally preferring to positively address the homeostatic tendency of the family system rather than its individual members. For instance, they might praise an IP (or a family) for sacrificing herself/himself so that a sibling could grow up and leave home. Or, they might express appreciation to an offspring for acting as a grandfather in order to maintain heterosexual balance in a family which had become increasingly female dominated (Palazzoli-Selvini et al., 1978a). Palazzoli-Selvini et al. (1974) note that through positive connotation "we implicitly declare ourselves as allies of the family's striving for homeostasis, and we do this at the moment that the family feels it is most threatened. By thus strengthening the homeostatic tendency,

---

[16]*Editors' Note.* The more basic difference, though, is that Boszormenyi-Nagy does not use such noble ascriptions for their *effect*, but because he *really believes these ascriptions* (see Boszormenyi-Nagy and Ulrich, Chapter 5).

we gain influence over the ability to change that is inherent in every living system" (p. 441). In other words, total acceptance of the family system by the therapists enables them to be accepted in the family game—a necessary step toward changing the game through paradox (Palazzoli-Selvini et al., 1978a).

Among other things, what positive interpretation seems to do is to address, in a respectful way, the resistance and ambivalence which the family feels toward change. The therapist recognizes and acknowledges the functional and desirable aspects of the symptom. Todd[17] notes that families who have previously engaged in other forms of therapy often feel that the therapist who uses this approach is the first person they have met who really "understands" them and (what they perceive as) the magnitude of their struggle.

Oversights and Errors

Haley (1979) has discussed a number of concepts which handicap family therapists (e.g., repression, organicity, scapegoatism) and which can lead logically to failure. Haley notes that what are needed are theories that guide a therapist to success. This is an overriding and general concern which, of course, pertains to all therapies.

There are several areas in which strategic therapists can err if they are not careful. First, they have to avoid being too "pat" with directives, a danger which has been underscored, in particular, by Haley and the Milan and MRI groups. In other words, interventions, tasks and injunctions must be tailored to (and couched in terms of) a given family's values, sociocultural context, and distinctive "style," in addition to being tailored to the configuration (sequences, interactions) surrounding the problem itself; the therapist uses all these kinds of information in arriving at an intervention designed to have the desired effect, i.e., to bring about change in that particular family. Second, the therapist can become too mechanistic, overlooking affective cues given by the family and possibly appearing either too distant or insincere. Third, consid-

erable skill may be required to spot the essential elements in a family behavioral sequence (and the consequences of these), so care must be taken to avoid being misled by verbal content or by "red herring" behaviors. Fourth, awareness must be maintained of the sources of leverage or influence which exist for the family outside the therapeutic setting, a particular problem when only one member is seen in treatment. Fifth, a therapist can err by tending to prescribe the symptom without connecting it with the system, thus overlooking the need to redefine the symptom as it actually serves to regulate family behavior (Papp, 1980). Sixth, the therapist must give the paradoxical prescription with conviction and avoid smiling, laughing or appearing self-conscious, as this will cause the family to view him as insincere or sarcastic, rapidly leading to failure. Finally, once a therapist gives a prescription, he should beware of backing down in the face of an escalation in resistance or tension, for if he does he will lose the family's respect and will not be taken seriously in the future.

Several additional concerns need voicing specifically regarding the use (or abuse) of paradoxical techniques. Such strategies are "probably least applicable in situations of crisis or extreme instability" (Rohrbaugh et al., 1977, pp. 43-44) such as with acute decompensation, acute grief reactions, violence, attempted suicide, loss of employment, or unwanted pregnancy (Papp, 1980). Weeks and L'Abate (1979) caution that students learning to use paradoxical methods should first read several of the basic books on technique and study as many full-length cases as possible before attempting such work. They recommend that a student also have expert supervision, so that he/she does not make one intervention and then not know how to follow it up. Finally, they note that:

Paradoxical methods should only be used after the student has mastered basic clinical skills and developed clinical sensitivity. Even then, we suggest the beginner find a competent paradoxical supervisor.

Aside from the reasons mentioned above, a paradoxical therapist oftentimes finds himself pitted against a couple or family in a power struggle. Systems of behavior do not relinquish their pathology readily and will defeat the therapist to maintain this homeostatic system. Thus, without supervision the

---

[17]Thomas Todd, personal communication, January 1979.

therapist will feel isolated and begin doubting his working method. The consequences can be disasterous for treatment. Students who view paradox as some kind of magical answer eventually abuse it and risk the clients' welfare. Moreover, the use of paradoxical methods for their shock value and the power they promise raises the issue of senseless and unethical manipulation. Paradoxical techniques can be powerfully manipulative just as any other psychotherapeutic technique. They should always be used to enhance the client's growth—not the therapist's status (p. 74).

Termination

Strategic therapists prefer to keep therapy brief and to terminate as soon as possible following positive change in the presenting problem. This is particularly important as a means to avoid giving a mixed message. If a family has succeeded, and is feeling competent or even jovial, the therapist wants to release them soon. Unless a new contract is negotiated, he may move to recess within one to four more sessions. Otherwise, he conveys a message that their success is ephemeral, thereby negating it and undercutting whatever change has occurred. Instead of trying to solve all family problems, Haley (1980) recommends intense involvement and a rapid disengagement, rather than regular interviews over years.

TREATMENT TECHNIQUES: SPECIFIC

A number of strategic groups have developed or adopted particular techniques that are distinctly their own. Although these therapists' methods may overlap considerably, there are areas of divergence. Often such differences have arisen because they were working in unexplored areas and/or with specific kinds of problems which had not been dealt with successfully by other therapists. They were thus forced to innovate. This section is devoted to the contributions of several of these "schools" of strategic therapy. To the extent possible, they will be dealt with in rough chronological order, relative to when their work emerged, but in many cases this is a spurious distinction because their efforts proceeded concurrently. Erickson, Haley and the MRI group have clearly been the three most

potent forces in the development and proliferation of strategic family therapy, while the Milan group has more recently emerged as the fourth major contributor.

Milton Erickson

Although his approach might not be considered a "school," partly because his techniques are somewhat individualized, Erickson was the master of strategic therapy and the primary figure in the laying of groundwork for such approaches with families. For reasons of health and age he ceased treating people himself in the years before his death in 1980, but his techniques have been clearly presented in the literature (e.g., Erickson, 1954, 1962; Erickson and Rossi, 1979; Haley, 1967, 1973b).

Perhaps more than other contributors to strategic therapy Erickson would see individuals for treatment. This was partly due to his propensity for using hypnotic techniques—a field in which he had been a pioneer for many years. He also tended to think (or at least to write) in terms of unconscious processes more than most other strategic therapists. However, he carefully avoided "interpreting" people's behavior or translating "unconscious" communication into conscious form. Instead, he used metaphor and positive relabeling freely, as these are forms which patients are less liable to resist. He accepted their behavior, but in such a way that it could change (Haley, 1973b). He sometimes even reframed a symptom or defect as an asset, thus allowing the patient both to use it to advantage in some relevant social context and also to "gain control" of it.

In general, Erickson conceptualized his goals in terms of getting people unstuck and moving ahead in their natural life cycle. Therapy was designed to produce shifts or alternative patterns and also to introduce variety and richness into their lives (Haley, 1973b). Often he instructed a couple or family to go through the motions of a conflict but arranged that they do something differently, such as requesting that a couple have a fight out in a scenic country spot rather than at home. Normally Erickson adjusted his therapeutic style in accordance with the situation. Again, although he was often "accepting"—using indirect ways to influence a family—he might also be firm and *require* certain behavior from them. However, he frequently followed a sequence which he described in a vignette of his response to an accidental and painful fall by his son, Robert. Haley (1973b) discusses this typical example as follows:

[Erickson] first accepts completely the patient's position, in this case by saying "That hurts awful, Robert. That hurts terrible." Next he makes a statement that is the opposite of reassurance. He says, "And it will keep right on hurting." Many people might consider this a negative reinforcement, or a suggestion to continue in distress. To Erickson it is a way of getting together with the patient in a type of relationship that makes change possible, which is his goal. Once he has done this, he can offer a move for change by saying, "Maybe it will stop hurting in a little while, in just a minute or two."

Those who are concerned about "manipulating" people rather than behaving "straightforwardly and honestly" should read this description with some care. As Erickson points out, at no time was the boy given a false statement. It would be far less straightforward and honest to reassure the boy by telling him it didn't hurt, to try to minimize what had happened, or in other ways to dismiss the boy's experience of the situation (pp. 192-193).

Overall, it can be said that Erickson engaged in engineering people's responses to each other and to their environment, usually through subtle, indirect ways such that they were rarely aware of his intent. He worked smoothly and intuitively to get them to respond on *his* ground, but in such a manner that they were not always clear why change actually occurred.

Jay Haley

Most of the general material presented earlier applies to Jay Haley's therapy model. There are, however, certain principles and treatment situations to which he has given particular attention and emphasis, and some of these will be addressed briefly here.

Haley was one of the first to clarify the means by which conventional mental health institutions were not providing effective treatment. This arose from his early experience with schizophrenics, in which identified patients would improve in the hospital, return home, and suffer

rapid relapse. He noted that the hospital served to perpetuate a pattern which interfered with effective cure. If the identified patient improved while out of the hospital, a crisis occurred in the family, the person was rehospitalized and stabilized, and change could not come about (Haley, 1970, 1971a).

Over the years, Haley has worked with the families of severely disturbed young people and through trial and error has been developing a model for treating them. As he sees it, the problem revolves around the person's (a) leaving home, or being allowed to do so, and (b) becoming competent and individuated (Haley, 1973b; Hoffman, 1976). He notes that these parents often display a terror of separation. An important treatment principle is for the therapist to have maximum administrative control of the case, including medications, rehospitalization, etc. The general therapeutic strategy is to be fairly authoritarian and less exploratory, especially at the beginning of treatment, since this is usually a time of family crisis (Haley, 1976). He particularly wants to get the parents to hold together and be firm about their offspring's behavior—to weather a crisis together—so that the change will "take hold."

Haley warns therapists against dealing with the parents' relationship and marriage per se until improvement is brought about in the child, since "rushing to the marriage as a problem can make therapy more difficult later" (1976, p. 141). This is partly because such parents (usually) do not come to the therapist to work on their own relationship. They are aware of the existence of marriage counselors, and if they are not seeing one at present, it commonly means that they do not want to. Even if one of them states that their marriage is a problem, the other spouse may not agree and may be at least tacitly unwilling to go this route. Further, if change is brought about in the IP, it (a) frequently means that the parents had to work together in order for it to occur—thus possibly improving their relationship in the process, and (b) they will probably feel more optimistic (and brave) about tackling a second problem, such as their marriage.

In his recent book, *Leaving Home*, Haley (1980) has presented a clear and rather specific paradigm for the treatment of "disturbed" young people and their families. A synopsis by Haley of the approach appears in Stanton and Todd (1979, pp. 58-60) and is excerpted here, as follows:

There are certain assumptions that improve the chance of success with young adults who exhibit mad and bizarre behavior, or continually take illegal drugs, or who waste their lives and cause community concern. For therapy, it is best to assume that the problem is not the young person but a problem of a family and young person disengaging from one another (Haley, 1973b). Ordinarily, an offspring leaves home by succeeding in work or school and forming intimate relations outside the family. In some families, when a son or daughter begins to leave home, the family becomes unstable and in distress. If at that point the young person fails by becoming incapacitated, the family stabilizes as if the offspring has not left home. This can happen even if the young person is living away from home, as long as he or she regularly lets the family know that failure continues. It can also exist even if the family is angry at the offspring and appears to have rejected him. Family stability continues as long as the young person is involved with the family by behaving in some abnormal way.

A therapist should assume that, if the family organization does not change, the young person will continue to fail year after year, despite therapy efforts. The unit with the problem is not the young person, but at least two other people: These might be two parents, or a mother and boy friend or sibling, or a mother and grandmother. It is assumed that two adults in a family communicate with each other by way of the young person and they enter severe conflict if the young person is not available to be that communication vehicle. The therapy goal is to free the young adult from that triangle so that he or she lives like other normal young people and the family is stable without the problem child.

The therapy should occur in the following stages:

1) When the young person comes to community attention, the experts must organize themselves in such a way that one therapist takes responsibility for the case. It is better not to have a team or a number of separate therapists or modes of therapy. The one therapist must be in charge of whether the young person is to be in or out of an institution and what medication is to be given, and when. Only if the therapist is in charge of the case can he put the parents in charge within the family.

2) The therapist needs to gather the family for a first interview. If the young person is living separately, even with a wife, he should be brought together with the family of origin so that everyone significant to him is there. The goal is to move the young person to more independence, either alone or with a wife, but the first step to that end is to take him back to his family.

There should be no blame of the parents, but instead, the parents (or parent and grandmother, or whomever it might be) should be put in charge of solving the problem of the young person. They must be persuaded that they are really the best therapists for the problem offspring (despite past failures in trying to help him). It is assumed that the members of the family are in conflict and the problem offspring is expressing that. By requiring the family to take charge and set the rules for the young person, they are communicating about the young person, as usual, but in a positive way. Certain issues need to be clear:

(a) The focus should be on the problem person and his behavior, not on a discussion of family relations. If the offspring is an addict, the family should focus on what is to happen if he ever takes the drug again. If mad and misbehaving, what they will do if he acts bizarrely in the way that got him in the hospital before. If anorectic, how much weight she is to gain per day, and how that is to be accomplished.

(b) The past, and past causes of the problem, are ignored and not explored. The focus is on what to do now.

(c) The therapist should join the parents against the problem young person, even if this seems to be depriving him of individual choices and rights, and even if he seems too old to be made that dependent. After the person is behaving normally, his rights can be considered. It is assumed that the hierarchy of the family is in confusion. Should the therapist step down from his status as expert and join the problem young person against the parents, there will be worse confusion and the therapy will fail.

(d) Conflicts between the parents or other family members are ignored and minimized even if they bring them up, until the young person is back to normal. If the parents say they have problems and need help too, the therapist should say the first problem is the son, and their problems can be dealt with after the son is back to normal.

(e) Everyone should expect the problem person to become normal, with no suggestion that the goal is a handicapped person. Therefore, the young person should not be in a halfway house, a day hospital, kept on medication or on maintenance methadone. Normal work or school should be expected immediately, not later. Work should be self-supporting and real, not volunteer.

3) As the problem young person becomes normal (by achieving self-support, or successfully going to school, or by making close friends), the family will

become unstable. This is an important stage in the therapy and the reason for pushing the young person toward normality. The parents will threaten separation or divorce or one or both will be disturbed. At that point, a relapse of the young person is part of the usual pattern, since that will stabilize the family. If the therapist has sided with the parents earlier, they will lean upon him at this stage and the young adult will not need to relapse to save them. The therapist must either resolve the parental conflict, or move the problem young person out of it while it continues more directly. At that point, the young person can continue to be normal.

4) The therapy should be an intense involvement and a rapid disengagement, not regular interviews over years. As soon as positive change occurs, the therapist can begin to recess and plan termination. The task is not to resolve all family problems but the ones around the problem young person, unless the family wants to make a new contract for other problems.

The Mental Research Institute Brief Therapy Center

Since 1967, the MRI group has been developing a brief (ten-session), systematic, and pragmatically oriented therapy model for treating a multitude of problems (Watzlawick et al., 1974; Weakland et al., 1974). While they employ most of the general techniques discussed earlier, there are aspects of their innovative program which deserve special note. First, they view people as developing "problems" in two ways: Either they treat an ordinary difficulty as a problem, or they "treat an ordinary (or worse) difficulty as no problem at all—that is, by either overemphasis or underemphasis of difficulties in living" (Weakland et al., 1974, p. 148). The therapy approach that the MRI group uses is in some ways low-key, even if it is strategic. For instance, they feel that behavioral instructions which are carefully framed and made indirect, implicit or apparently insignificant are more effective; they tend, therefore, to *suggest* a change rather than order it. In this way, they differ from Haley, who may be more forceful in giving directives. They also tend to proceed in a step-by-step approach to eliminating a symptom, looking for minor, progressive changes rather than sweeping ones—they prefer to "think small" because in their experience it tends to

work better. Paradoxical instructions are a mainstay of the method and are considered the "most important single class of interventions" in their treatment (Weakland et al., 1974, p. 158).

Perhaps one of the more clinically useful contributions coming from this camp is a recent chapter on marital therapy by Sluzki (1978). He approaches the subject by providing a "how-to-do-it" manual. Starting with technique, he gives a rule and follows this with rationale and description. The presentation "consists of a series of 'naked' prescriptions about concrete, rather specific therapeutic interventions which can be carried out by the therapist whenever a member of a couple, or both members of it, display certain types of behaviors during the course of a session. Each prescription is separately formulated and conceptually grounded" (p. 368). Examples of such prescriptions are: (a) "If A and B concur in defining A as victim and B as victimizer, *then* find a way of reversing the roles/labels and state the reversal forcefully" (p. 377). (b) "If A and B describe a sequence of events that leads to conflict or to the emergence of symptoms, *then* search for the events or steps that precede what has been described as the first step in the sequence. If you cannot specify it, nonetheless state its existence. If it has been detected, and is accepted by A and B as possible, then repeat the cycle (i.e., search for a still previous step, or at least assert its existence)" (p. 378). (c) "If A has a symptom that fluctuates within the day or the week, *then* instruct A to select times in which the symptom improves to tell B that it is worse" (p. 381). Sluzki's approach here is an ingenious way of explicating the actual operations involved in treatment and coupling these with their applicable rationales. It is a method which would seem to make learning of these techniques much more rapid and, perhaps, enjoyable.

Gerald Zuk

The approach that Gerald Zuk takes to family treatment has been termed "go between" therapy (Zuk, 1966, 1971). This is less of a strategic "school" than it is the personal brand of therapy of a skilled, innovative, systems-oriented clinician who has been active in the field for many years. While Madanes and Haley (1977) categorize him as a strategic therapist, Zuk himself does not use this term. However, in addition to his emphasis on family systems and on dysfunctional sequences, Zuk is akin to other strategic therapists in his use of side-taking in therapy. Further, his interventions, and the order in which they are applied, often display the kind of planning and forethought exercised by other strategic therapists.

Zuk uses the term "pathogenic relating" to refer to a kind of process that goes on within a family (Zuk, 1971). It is identified by the therapist in an interview. The extent to which it exists is judged by the therapist from his observation of "tension-producing, malevolent, intimidating patterns of family members toward each other and the therapist" (Zuk, 1975, p. 15). Pathogenic relating is a destructive process and includes such interactions as the silencing of a member by the family, threats of physical violence, selective inattention, scapegoating, unfair or inappropriate labeling, myths or rituals of uncertain origin and accuracy, and shared family efforts at creating distraction (Zuk, 1971). The therapist decides the severity or level of pathogenic relating based on his experience.

The goal in go-between therapy is to shift the balance of pathogenic relating among family members so that new, more productive forms of interpersonal relating become possible (Zuk, 1966, 1971). The therapist wants to alter the kinds of "vicious, repetitive patterns" that occur in dysfunctional families. Although Zuk himself is not particularly symptom-focused, others who use this approach, such as Garrigan and Bambrick (1977b), stress the goal of symptom reduction.

A major initial goal in treatment is to get a commitment from the family to be treated on the therapist's terms. Usually, Zuk states to a family that he will need three or four sessions to make an "evaluation" of the problem in order to determine the best way to alleviate it. He tries to exact a contract from the family on this. The degree of resistance encountered in making this contract is used by the therapist as a prognostic sign. The engagement period is thus pivotal, setting the direction for the total therapeutic process.

Go-between treatment is a "clinical applica-tion of the concepts of coalition or alliance, mediation and side-taking" (Zuk, 1971, p. 14). In the go-between *process* the therapist takes and trades the roles of mediator, side-taker, and celebrant in family treatment. Alternatively, family members can conduct a kind of go-between process of their own as a means of resisting the therapist's interventions. There are four steps in the process: (a) identification of an issue by therapist or family member on which there are at least two sides or opponents; (b) intensification of conflict and movement by therapist or family member into a go-between role; (c) efforts by go-between and other principals to define and delimit their respective roles or positions; (d) reduction of the "conflict associated with a change in the positions of principals or with a redefinition of the conflict, or both" (Zuk, 1971, p. 47).

The go-between therapist begins treatment with the idea of first assessing what is "wrong" with the family, i.e., the nature of its pathogenic relating, and then to communicate this (tactfully, in most cases) to them. Since this may catalyze conflict, the family is not expected to accept this communication without testing; it is a kind of engagement process and is one of the "critical events" in go-between therapy. The therapist then moves into a go-between role. He selects an issue or issues to be struggled over or negotiated and he takes the mediator role. In the third step, the therapist switches from the role of go-between to that of side-taker and sides judiciously with one, then the other. He may make an open alliance with one member in order to disrupt the existent homeostatic balance. During this discussion, he sets limits or rules out certain behaviors, while evolving toward the point where he can introduce initiatives or alternatives which had not occurred to the principals in the conflict. Thus, he is constantly structuring and directing the treatment process.

The therapist must remain flexible and unpredictable in go-between therapy to avoid feeding into the pathogenic process or being sidetracked from his attempts to produce change. At times he can be active and intrusive, at others inactive and passive. He can take sides or refuse to do so, selectively supporting members holding either "continuity" or "discontinuity" values. Interpretations might be used for their content or validity or, following Haley (1963), as maneuvers to keep in a one-up position vis-à-vis the family. Sometimes informing a family of intent to terminate because of lack of progress can mobilize them to work harder to change. Behavioral assignments can also be used to allow generalization outside the treatment setting, although they are not accorded as much emphasis as that given by other strategic therapists.

The Milan Center for Family Studies

As stated earlier, the work of Mara Palazzoli-Selvini, Luigi Boscolo, Gianfranco Cecchin and Giuliana Prata in Milan has evolved into the fourth major force within the field of strategic family therapy (and other three being Erickson, Haley and the MRI group). Staff at their center have developed a kind of "long, brief" family therapy for treating such problems as anorexia, encopresis, and, in particular, families in schizophrenic transaction. Cases are seen by a single therapist and observed concomitantly by a team of from one to three colleagues or "supervisors."[18] Between three and 20 sessions are usually involved, although it is common to contract with a family for ten sessions. Normally they are spaced one month apart from each other. This interval was instituted because many of the families had to travel hundreds of miles for treatment, and also because it actually seemed to work better—a kind of "incubation" period between sessions proved more effective. The first session includes all members of an immediate family living together, as do most succeeding sessions. Sessions follow a more or less standard format including (a) information giving and discussions which allow observation (without comment) of the family's transactional style; (b) discussion of the session in a separate room by the therapists and colleagues; (c) rejoining the family by the therapists in order to make a brief comment and a (usually paradoxical) prescription; and (d) a post-session team discussion of the family's reaction to the comment or prescription, along with formulation and writing of a synopsis of the session.

More important than the simple mechanics of this approach, however, are at least two techniques which are the Milan group's trademarks. The first of these, positive connotation, has been discussed earlier. The second, and perhaps the most distinctive and creative feature of their approach, is their handling of paradoxical instruction. They have carried this technique to new heights. Rather than limiting themselves to directives pertaining primarily to the symptom or the identified patient, they try to give prescriptions which include *the whole family system*. For example, they might direct all members to continue the specific symptom-related behavior patterns they had already been exercising. Granting that the family may resist exhortations to do something different, i.e., to change, Palazzoli-Selvini and associates turn this resistance back on itself. They are in a sense asking that the family "remain the same." It is difficult to capture in the printed word the dramatic, even startling, directives they come up with. For example, they might instruct the children in a family to become parents to their parents. Another (related) approach could be for the therapists to publicly prescribe for themselves the task of doing their utmost to become, for a parent of the identified patient, the (grand)parents that had disappointed him in early life; but this time they will avoid the (grand) parents' mistakes. Or, the therapists might declare total impotence, having "no idea what to do." This is a way of attempting to force the family to do something, anything, different, in order to retain their adversaries (the therapists) and keep the game going. Such interventions are based on hypotheses about the function of a problem in a particular family and are made in order to test these hypotheses. The family's reaction then becomes the litmus whereby a given hypothesis is confirmed or not (Palazzoli-Selvini et al., 1980a). Often this is a trial and error process, as all interventions of this sort cannot be expected to be effective. Palazzoli-Selvini et al. (1974, 1978a) emphasize, in addition, that each family is different, so that the prescription will vary from case to case and must be appropriately tailored. They find it rarely

---

[18]Mara Palazzoli-Selvini, personal communication, June 1979.

helpful to try to transpose to later situations prescriptions which had been successful with earlier, perhaps similar, cases.[19]

A particular therapeutic tactic developed by the Milan group is the "family ritual" (Palazzoli-Selvini et al., 1977, 1978a, 1978b). This is a method of prescribing that family members *put into action* (rather than simply verbalize) an act or a series of acts designed to alter the rules of a "game" in which they had heretofore been engaged. The prescription includes a regular sequence of steps for the family to take, in which nearly every datail is spelled out by the therapists: time, place, number of repetitions, who is to say or do what, in what order, etc. It is not necessarily a paradoxical exercise, but frequently includes elements designed to alter family structure. As an example (Palazzoli-Selvini et al., 1974), the therapists saw a case in which an overinvolved, martyr-like mother and her emotionally distant, wealthy husband had concealed from their two-year old daughter the actual birth and continued ailing status of their seven month old brain-damaged son. The baby boy was kept in the hospital and mother visited him daily, while telling the daughter she was seeing someone else's child. The daughter developed anorectic symptoms soon after the baby's birth, and these had continued. The boy died and was buried after the fourth therapy session and the therapists decided to prescribe a ritual. They assigned to father the task of explaining to the daughter everything that had happened, including the birth of the baby, his illness, the reason why these facts had been kept from her, and that, while he was already buried, it was also important to bury the brother's clothes. The family carried out this burial of their "phantom" baby the next day, with father digging the hole, mother placing each item of clothing in the grave, daughter placing flowers, and father filling in the hole and planting a tree on the site. Thereafter, the child no longer refused to eat.

The ritualized prescription described above could be seen as having a number of specific effects. The secret was exploded, the girl treated as a member of the family in her own right, and the baby brother was no longer her competitor. The mother was decentralized and relieved of the responsibility both of "protecting" her daughter from this tragedy and of having to handle it by herself. The father was brought more prominently into the picture, as a supporter and interactor both with his wife and with his daughter. The whole family was doing something together toward a common goal. Thus, a pattern had been interrupted through the introduction of a "counter-game" which, once played, eclipsed the original game (Palazzoli-Selvini, 1978). New rules had been substituted, altering both the elements in the sequence and the family structure.

More recently, the Milan group has provided a sort of standardized format for ritualized prescription which is designed to block interference by each parent as the other parent interacts with the IP. It can be applied to nearly any symptom and normally includes all family members. It serves as an alternative to pointing out to parents how they interfere with each other (a tactic which rarely works), and functions to divert the family's attention away from the therapist's goals. It is usually dictated for a member to write down at the end of a session. The essential text (from Palazzoli-Selvini et al., 1978b) is as follows:

On even days of the week—Tuesdays, Thursdays, and Saturdays—beginning from tomorrow onwards until the date of the next session and fixing the time between X o'clock and Y o'clock (making sure that the whole family will be at home during this time) whatever Z does (name of patient, followed by a list of his symptomatic behavior) father will decide alone, at his absolute discretion, what to do with Z. Mother will have to behave as if she were not there. On odd days of the week—Mondays, Wednesdays and Fridays—at the same time, whatever Z may do, mother will have full power to decide what course of action to follow regarding Z. Father will have to behave as if he were not there. On Sundays everyone must behave spontaneously. Each parent, on the days assigned to him or her, must record in a diary any infringement by the partner of the prescription according to which he is expected to behave as if he were not there. (In some cases the job of recording

---

[19]*Editors' Note.* Of course, an inability to transpose such interventions would seem to make controlled group design research on the salient treatment components of such therapy nearly impossible. *Experimental* study of single cases could still provide support for the model.

the possible mistakes of one of the parents has been entrusted to a child acting as a recorder or to the patient himself, if he is fit for the task.) (p. 5)

This ritualized prescription appears to function at several levels (Palazzoli-Selvini et al., 1978b). First, the rules of the game are changed and an intervention introduced for reducing cross-parental interference without the therapists actually stating that this is their aim. Second, the competition between the parents to gain the therapists' approval is exploited, diverting the parents from the problem of their relationship to the ways in which each of them can achieve commendable results. Third, even if the prescription is not followed, the therapists gain valuable information about the family. This can provide clarification as to the nature and extent of the problem and can help in determining what subsequent interventions need to be made.

It is important to note that several conditions apply to the above ritualized prescription. To begin with, it is only used once and is but one part of the whole treatment process. Further, in order for it to work, the therapist must first form a relationship with the family; he/she must be important to them. Otherwise, the parents will not compete for the therapist's approval or confirmation and will not obey the directive. Therefore, such a prescription is not to be given during the first session, but at a later point in treatment.[20]

One aspect of treatment which the Milan group has found requires considerable attention is the relationship between themselves and the referring person. This is a feature of therapy which has not been given much coverage by family therapists. The Milan group has determined that a good portion of the first treatment session must be devoted to discussion with the family as to why they were referred, what the family's relationship has been to the referral source (i.e., the source's role in the family), and what the source expects of their therapeutic team. Sometimes they found that factions in the family were still aligned with the referring person and that the Milan team had been brought

into the picture to bolster a different, opposing family faction. Sometimes cases were sent to them out of spite—a sort of "OK, smarty pants, let's see what you can do with this one" idea—and the family was given a subtle message to try to "beat" them. In all such instances the referring person had been inducted into the family system. Such factors can introduce triangulations into the treatment process which alter the structure of the therapeutic system, requiring different strategies than with families who are not encumbered in this way. The Milan group has found that when they overlooked such variables the probability of success was considerably reduced; thus, compensatory interventions were required (Palazzoli-Selvini et al., 1980b).

In recent years variations on the techniques developed by the Milan group have been applied with diverse types of cases by a number of therapists in the United States. One of these is Thomas Todd. Two others are Peggy Papp and Olga Silverstein, who are doing "practitioner research" and a good deal of training at the Nathan Ackerman Institute in New York; like the Milan group and Weeks and L'Abate (1979) they often use written prescriptions and have also found it most helpful not only to give such a prescription in the session, but also to mail separate copies home to each family member afterward (Papp, 1980). Also at Ackerman, a team composed of Gillian Walker, Lynn Hoffman, Anita Morawetz, Joel Bergman and Peggy Penn has been expanding and experimenting with the Milan model with a limited number of families.

David Berenson

Berenson's approach to the family treatment of alcoholism is being classified here as a strategic approach perhaps for the first time. Although Berenson's work is heavily influenced by Bowen and Thomas Fogarty, and also somewhat by the structural camp, I consider it to be primarily strategic in its operations for several reasons. First it rests firmly on the use of directives. Second, it is a planned approach, in which several stages have been identified and frequently handled by fairly specific methods. Third, it does not depend on interpretations,

---

[20]Mara Palazzoli-Selvini, personal communication, June 1979.

except as these might be used to reframe. Fourth, Berenson (1976a) acknowledges the regular use of strategic techniques.

The material described here derives from Berenson's (1976a, 1976b, 1979) publications, and also from my personal interactions with him.[21] It is unique and valuable work and much of what will be presented has not been published. Emphasis will be on his approach to families in which drinking is the major presenting problem, rather than being incidental to another problem.

In general, Berenson is more concerned with *change* than with the elimination of drinking, per se. Aside from history-taking about alcohol use, he prefers to head for (substantial) changes in drunken behavior—a transformational shift or quantum leap—rather than taking a resolute stand in favor of total abstinence (a topic which, incidentally, has been the focus of considerable emotion in the alcoholism field). He considers it tactically unwise to take a "hard-line" on abstinence, even though this is usually his ultimate goal. At the start of treatment several rules apply: (a) A major effort must go into getting the family system calmed down (reducing the "emotionality" and increasing the distance among members); (b) the therapist must have no expectations that change will occur—rather than "hoping" he must be "hopeless"; (c) the therapist also wants the family to feel both helpless and hopeless—to "hit bottom"; (d) the therapist must not look for a *single* strategic intervention to turn the situation around; (e) paradoxical interventions should be avoided, at least at this stage.

Therapy is seen as having two phases. The first involves "management of an ongoing, serious drinking problem and setting up a context so that the alcoholic will stop drinking" (Berenson, 1976b, p. 33). This is an important point, because switching to deal with other, or "underlying," family or individual problems can postpone the achievement of sobriety. Berenson starts by working with the most motivated family member or members so as to obtain maximum leverage; usually this is the spouse of the drinker (often an "emotional pursuer"), but it might also include the alcoholic or, infrequently, a parent,

[21]David Berenson, personal communication, April 1976 and March 1980.

sibling or child. Commonly he meets with the spouse several times at the outset. He tells the spouse (henceforth referred to as "she") that while she cannot change her husband and make him stop drinking, she can definitely make sure he *keeps* drinking. He points out to her how hard it is for her to take a position because her husband undercuts each attempt. Berenson wants her to feel hopeless. Eventually, normally within the first session or two, he states "you are not going to like this, but . . ." and he offers her three choices, each one of which he expects will be unacceptable to her at first: 1) to continue the situation exactly as it has been, since "You've been living this way for ten years"; 2) to learn to accept the drinking—to stay with him and not do anything about it except be more detached and distant; often this is interpreted by the spouse as simply tolerating the drinking rather than true acceptance, and in such cases it leads to perpetuation of the drinking problem, thus, becoming, in fact, the first option; 3) if the spouse cannot accept either of these options, Berenson then offers the third option—that she separate or physically distance herself from her spouse; while the separation may be brief, Berenson tries to give the impression that this would be a permanent arrangement. He also makes it clear that eventually she is going to have to take one of these positions. If she starts to balk because of what she sees as the difficulties involved in these options, he states, "If I knew an easier way I would tell you," or "If there were an easier way you would have discovered it by this time." He also tells her that therapy may take anywhere from one month to five years. If she rejects all of this, he says, "Fine. You're still hoping. The problem will come up again and you have all the time in the world. Come back when there is no hope."

Should the spouse at least tentatively accept treatment, Berenson takes three steps toward helping the wife "detach." First, he wants to get her into a support group, usually Al-Anon or a wives or couples group or *est* training, since he feels that the therapist cannot do everything by himself; however, the wife's system of girlfriends may not be helpful, since they tend to oversympathize with her and disparage her husband. Second, he prepares her for an impending period of pain and depression, perhaps even noting that both partners may have suicidal thoughts as time goes on; he tells her she will probably have to "hit bottom." Third, he starts working toward the third option (above) of having her gain distance from her husband (since he knows that the second option of "accepting" the situation will, again, usually be misinterpreted, so that his drinking will be perpetuated). Often this will involve some sort of brief separation (e.g., a week away from home), with the idea of helping her to differentiate. He warns her that her husband may try to get her back by intensifying the symptom or conflict, usually be increasing his drinking.

At this point Berenson may involve the husband more, empathizing with him as to how isolated and alone he may feel. Concomitantly, he tries to get the wife to stick to a plan, so that her husband has a chance of getting sober; he notes that she should not expect her husband to improve, but if she is hopeless enough to realize that she cannot control him, he *might* be able to make a move for himself.

Eventually the therapist wants to cut the drinker off from all supports so that he will enroll in Alcoholics Anonymous or a couples group—"It's too bad you don't think you're an alcoholic, since AA is terrific and I've known people who've lied so as to get the advantage of going"; on occasion Berenson has even given the alcoholic instructions to sneak out of the house, go to an AA meeting and not tell his wife where he has been. However, he avoids giving the husband "advice." Also, he should not support the wife on any (hostile) moves she makes against her husband, but only on moves she makes for herself. Should the husband cease drinking and join AA, the therapist must be prepared for undercutting moves by the non-drinker, e.g., statements such as "I liked him better when he was drinking." He should try to maintain an unemotional tone in the sessions at this time, and increase distance between the spouses. Throughout this whole process, even if change starts to occur, the therapist should avoid hoping that "They're going to make it this time."

During treatment, Berenson recommends not making regularly scheduled appointments. He tells the clients to "Get back to me in a month or so." This treatment may extend across a period of some length, sometimes involving, for instance, 10-15 sessions over a year.

Once the family system is "dry," the therapist is faced with a different set of problems. It is usually advisable to have a hiatus or interruption at this time. The couple may have drifted into a kind of emotional divorce, or have a feeling of "walking on eggs" at home. They are encouraged to continue their AA or Al-Anon activities with the understanding that if this state continues after six or 12 months, family treatment will resume with a different goal.

The aim of the second phase of therapy is to decrease the emotional distance between the couple without a return either to drinking or to discussions centered on alcohol. The emphasis is on conjoint couple or family sessions. A direction frequently taken is to work on the severe sexual problems that are not uncommon in such marriages. Other approaches might include "fighting therapy," multiple couples groups, or work with the extended family if the nuclear family is beset by disruptions from relatives or in-laws.

Structural/Strategic Approaches

The case could probably be made that nearly all family therapies require a structural component in order to operate (whether acknowledged by the therapist or not). For instance, any therapeutic move which either fortifies an intergenerational boundary—such as supporting parents as a unit in relation to their offspring—or separates two overinvolved family members is a structural intervention. However, some therapists have more openly described their work as a combination, or at least a sequential application, of both structural and strategic principles. This is no accident, since Haley was instrumental in the development of structural family therapy. (In fact, while he does not use the term "structural" with great regularity, his concern with family hierarchy is tantamount to the same thing.) The two approaches discussed here use one tack or the other selectively, depending primarily on the level of resistance or the rigidity of the homeostasis shown by the family.

Andolfi and colleagues

One of the more complete and sophisticated conceptualizations of the process and use of paradoxical instruction has been proposed by a group at the Italian Society for Family Therapy in Rome, Italy. Under the leadership of Maurizio Andolfi, the group includes Paolo Menghi, Anna Nicoló and Carmine Saccu, and the model they have developed stems from their work with families of schizophrenics (Andolfi, 1980; Andolfi et al., 1980). The general procedure is to start with a strategic approach and conclude therapy in a more structural vein. The therapist addresses the interplay between the two major components of a therapeutic system, the family on one hand, and the therapist on the other. Within each component there is a balance between the tendency to espouse homeostasis ("remaining the same") and the ability or tendency to transform, i.e., to change. The therapist modulates the extent to which he advocates or pushes for homeostatic behavior by the family in accordance with (a) the homeostatic leanings of the family at the moment, and (b) the particular stage to which the therapy has progressed. This is a model of *relative contrasts*, set in stages, in which the therapist tries to stay one step ahead of the family and, until later stages, almost invariably pushes for more homeostasis than the family is comfortable with. In a sense he "one ups" them, and, in their resistance to his directions, they start to change in an opposite direction. An example may provide clarity.

The family enters treatment expecting the therapist to push for transformation—the "expectation" stage. They anticipate that the therapist will head toward altering the behavior of the IP in order to make him "less crazy." At this point they are mobilized to resist the therapist, conveying the double message that they want to be helped, but that this is impossible; their homeostatic investment is great. They may even try to provoke him by explaining how other therapists have failed to help in the past. In this way they attempt to make him deal directly with the IP and thus set him up for failure. However, the therapist does not fall into this trap. He views the IP as a door for the family, i.e., a person who regulates communication among members and also between the family and outsiders; the IP becomes their controller and his craziness affords him undue power. The therapist challenges this system by not accepting the IP as a door. He denies the craziness. He relabels the IP's symptomatic behavior as logical

and voluntary. (He knows that as soon as he sees the IP as crazy, he becomes part of the system and his effectiveness as a therapist is lost.) He asks, "Why are you coming to me? I only see people who are really crazy." This is the "battle" stage. The therapist, through such an assertion, becomes crazier than the IP, becoming available to the family on a different level. He denies the utility of therapy, thereby challenging the system, since *his* investment in the homeostasis appears greater than *theirs*. He becomes more rigid, allowing, by contrast, the family to become more flexible.

As the behavior of the IP improves in the sessions, therapy enters the "strategically unacknowledged improvement" stage. Andolfi notes that severely dysfunctional families cannot easily accept individuation or differentiation on the part of the IP, so they will deny this improvement. The task of the therapist is to "beat them to the punch" and deny the positive change before they do. He might assert that things are getting worse, looking at the IP and stating, "You look bad," or at the family and claiming, "Something bad must have happened." Alternatively, he might predict that things will get worse. Another approach is to tell them, "If you want my help, you must collaborate with me to keep things from changing," i.e., he prescribes no change. By labeling any improvement as dangerous, he anticipates the family's fear of change. The "don't change" message pushes the family backward toward homeostasis, thus allowing them actually *to* change. He becomes "ridiculous" in a family system made up of controllers—people who do not allow personal space, and who cling to a kind of interpersonal space which overlaps all (family) members. The therapist's ridiculous behavior puts him on a higher, more controlling level. By anticipating and prompting their homeostatic moves, he is in a position of telling them what to do. If, as is their normal tendency, they follow the homeostatic tendency, they allow him power and control. He becomes the controller of controllers, and the only way they can unseat him is by changing.

In the "restructuring" stage, the family begins to disagree with the therapist, stating that in reality things are improving. The therapist again challenges them, building up stress by repeatedly emphasizing that he does not believe the family has changed—or *should* change. He claims not to trust them, exhorting them to "show" him, cautioning them to "be careful," or claiming they are "crazy." The family members then can take delight in showing him that he is wrong; they can mobilize to work against him. By his actions, then, the therapist is establishing a new level of craziness. Futher, the transition from abnormality to normality cannot be accomplished without passing through this new "crazy" stage.

Toward the end of the restructuring stage, the IP will become less central. The family members will start to present as a group of *people* rather than a massively reactive system. At this point the therapist can shift to more conventional structural moves, such as creating boundaries and other forms of restructuring.

The final stage is that of the "therapeutic system schism." There is a balance between homeostatic and transformational tendencies, both within the family and between the family and therapist. The family members note that things have changed and that they are able to continue to progress. They assert that they can make it on their own. The therapist asks them to show him how they will do this. As he moves toward termination and disengagement, he warns them to "watch out" in the future.

Andolfi et al.'s system is a clear advance, serving as a therapeutic guide, in particular, with severely dysfunctional families. Although they are not presented here, schematic diagrams are used to illustrate the homeostatic/transformational balances, both of family and therapist, within the various stages. The model could probably use some refinement at points (for instance, is not the "restructuring" stage actually two separate stages?), but these may come in time. One of its strengths is its simplicity, but this is also perhaps its biggest flaw. For example, much of the humor of the therapists' personal style, and many of the therapeutic "micro-moves" involved are lost in the schematic presentation. Nonetheless, this model holds great promise for future application in the field.

Stanton's approach

Two somewhat different versions of a combined structural/strategic model have been applied by the author and colleagues. In work with families of drug addicts (Stanton and Todd, 1979; Stanton et al., 1981) the general thrust, such as emphasis on treatment goals and on symptom change, was primarily strategic, but many of the moment-to-moment or "micro moves" within sessions were of a more structural nature. Put differently, the broad strokes tended to be strategic and the brushwork, structural, with the single exception of the regular use throughout of positive interpretation.

More recently the author (e.g., Stanton, 1981b, 1981c) has adopted a general procedure, applicable to a broad spectrum of problems, in which treatment initially assumes a structural posture (joining, reinforcing boundaries, altering interactional patterns among members in accordance with a structural schema, etc.), and involves an ongoing process of testing, probing and checking out. Interventions which are more typically strategic are held in abeyance until or unless considerable (usually massive) resistance is encountered. Some families, such as those with an alcoholic or schizophrenic member, are not readily responsive to typically structural interventions. They counter the therapist's every move with monolithic attack or resistance, attempting to render him impotent and refuse him control. In fact, their sense of being threatened and their homeostatic tendency may be so obvious at the outset that the therapist may even skip the structural step. In any case, the therapist knows that when he encounters such heightened resistance he will probably have to shift quickly to some form of positive interpretation, praising the family and members and trying to reduce their resistance through ascribing the most noble of intentions to their actions (Stanton, 1981b, 1981c). Other strategic interventions may follow, such as a directive, which may or may not be of the paradoxical sort. Later, as treatment progresses, the therapist aims toward returning to a structural model, in much the same manner as Andolfi et al. (1980).

As an additional note, one strategic technique that the author commonly uses is that of *over-estimation*, which is similar to Rohrbaugh et al.'s (1977) "positioning." This is another kind of relative contrast. The idea is that the therapist, upon sensing that a client or family fears some effect or backlash as a consequent of making a change, overestimates the amount of time, effort or trouble to be expected. He agrees with them that their fear is justified, and then paradoxically estimates that it will be much worse than they anticipate. Obviously, this is a technique which (a) depends on the therapist's possessing a certain amount of credibility at the time; (b) is generally appropriate for people who are feeling stronger; and (c) may sometimes be incorrect for those presently in a state of depression or hopelessness, as it is liable to make them even more so. As an example of a case where overestimation seemed to fit, a single-parent mother expressed concern that her other adult children would give her considerable flack for throwing her "wastrel" son out of her home. The therapist responded by informing her that "Yes, it may be three or four years before they speak to you." Since she was feeling somewhat confident at the time, and also believed rather firmly (based upon past experience) that things would die down after six months, the (over)estimate of several years, by contrast, made her six-month period seem rather paltry. She went ahead and evicted him. In another case, the female member of a premarital couple was resisting taking action to change a vicious, draining cycle of battles and infidelities that she and her fiancé had experienced several times over the previous three months. She wondered whether the cycle might eventually just go away if she waited long enough. She was told, "Yes, you probably won't have to go through this more than ten or 15 times and it should all be over in two or three years." The prospect of suffering that many times over that long a period was enough to scare her into bravery, and she decided to take a chance on change.

CURATIVE FACTORS

Comparison with Psychodynamic Approaches

It should be understood that strategic therapists do not deny either the existence of individual psychodynamic events or the fact that past experience may play a role in the present in some way. What they decry is the emphasis on these events for efficiently bringing about change. The reasoning is as follows: We cannot change the past, because it no longer exists.

Patterns which may have existed in the past are also occurring now, in the present. Focusing on the past and on repression of prior events is not necessary and may in fact distract the therapist from his task of bringing about change in the present. Such methods have not, overall, demonstrated their efficacy and tend to be unnecessarily costly both in time and money.

There is no concern with historical or even intellectual "insight" into unconscious processes in strategic therapy. "Interpretations," when they are used, are not aimed at producing a "deeper awareness," but rather are used to reframe a situation. "Lifting repression" is not valued. If a person or family "can get over the problem without knowing how or why, that is satisfactory, since so much necessarily is outside awareness" (Madanes and Haley, 1977, p. 97). In fact, it is my experience that intellectual "insight," if it occurs at all, not infrequently lags about three months behind actual change, and thus is obviously not necessary for transformation in such cases.

This is not meant to imply that strategic therapists, like some behavioral therapists, deny the importance of unconscious processes or events which occur outside of awareness. Indeed, such cognizance is central in the work of Erickson, Haley, the MRI group and others. The therapist uses behaviors of which the client may be unaware as clues for designing his interventions, but he is not likely to point them out with hopes of either making them conscious or of bringing about "understanding." For instance, Haley (1973b) describes Erickson's theory of change as a complex one, based upon the interpersonal impact of the therapist *outside of the client's awareness*, in which (a) directives are provided that cause changes in behavior, and (b) emphasis is on communicating in metaphor.

Related to the above, the expression of feelings or emotions per se is not encouraged by strategic therapists, primarily because they have found that it is not particularly helpful. Haley engaged in such activity for years before finally abandoning it. In fact, emotional behavior can even retard progress by diverting attention from change, e.g., a wife who cries when her husband tries something different, giving a clear signal to keep things as they are or were. With the (misguided) encouragement of a therapist, a member can prevent family reorganization, avoid an issue, or disrupt a session at any time by becoming emotional (Haley, 1979). This is not to say that strategic therapists ignore emotions, but that they use them as signals or guides for therapy rather than as ends in themselves. Or, from another direction, they might encourage a member to display a different emotion at a given point in an interactional sequence, such as having a wife laugh rather than frown when her husband does something she doesn't like. However, *the important distinction is that an emotion may be encouraged because it is different, not because it is inherently desirable, cathartic, or "releasing."* Much as they use "interpretations" to reframe, strategic therapists can use "emotions" to alter the experiences of the members of the family. This and the aforementioned notions, then, require an entirely different perspective on what to do (or rather what *not* to do) about repression, the unconscious and past events.

Theory of Change

There is slight variation among strategic therapists as to what they emphasize as the important variables in bringing about change. However, all of them subscribe to the following tenets: (a) Therapeutic change comes about through the "interactional processes set off when a therapist intervenes actively and directively in particular ways in a family system" (Haley, 1971a, p. 7); (b) the therapist works to substitute new behavior patterns or sequences for the vicious, positive feedback circles already existing (Weakland et al., 1974), promoting flexibility by "shaking up the system"; (c) all elements in a sequence do not necessarily need to be altered, but only enough of them to cause change (Hoffman, 1976); (d) producing change does not require working with or initially bringing about change in all family members, if system change can be produced by seeing, for example, only one member—although it is perhaps more *efficient* to have access to them all, at least at the outset of therapy; (e) treatment is not considered successful if there has been no beneficial change in the presenting problem.[22]

Perhaps the primary dissenter to several of the above points is Zuk, who is less symptom-focused. He also prefers to define change as either an input into or an outcome of a process of *negotiation* "in which the therapist takes an active role in actually defining the change he wishes for the patient(s)" (Zuk, 1971, p. 10). Zuk views change as arising out of the various contests between therapist and family. The therapist serves not only as a "releaser" of change but also as a "fashioner" of it.

In its application to family treatment, systems theory has been very influential among strategic therapists. It permits the therapist to spot repetitive, sequential patterns in the family and to make predictions about their recurrence. However, Haley (1979) notes that it also has limitations vis-à-vis issues of change. In its homeostatic emphasis, it is a theory of stability and does not account for the transformation of a system. It also tends to ignore hierarchies, describing the various participants as equals. For these (and other) reasons Haley has shifted towards an emphasis on the aspects of change. He notes that "one can plan a therapy in which a crisis is induced, thereby forcing the whole system to reorganize. Or one can start small change and persistently push it until the change is so amplified that the system must change in order to adapt to it" (p. 41). In the former of these two tacks his approach is similar to that of Minuchin (1974; Minuchin, Rosman, and Baker, 1978), and in the latter, to that of the MRI group (Weakland et al., 1974).

Perhaps one of the most important contributions of the MRI group has been in their conceptualization of the levels and nature of change (Watzlawick et al., 1974). They have defined two kinds of change. *First-order* change is the allowable sort of moving about within an unchanging system in a way which makes no difference to the group or family. *Second-order* change is a shift which actually alters the system. An example might be of a family which appears for treatment of a son who is failing in school. As therapy progresses, the son's grades improve. However, at the same time, a sister's schoolwork deteriorates precipitously or another child develops a problem. Even though there appears to be change because the IP shows improvement, the family system is not really altered, since an offspring continues to be maintained as a problem; this is "isomorphic" change and

---

[22]*Editors' Note.* These central postulates, of course, are quite testable but, as yet, remain relatively untested.

is of the first-order kind. On the other hand, if the son starts to make academic strides (without manifesting new problems) and his siblings remain at their pre-treatment levels (or better), it is more likely that second-order change has occurred; the system itself and the son's position in it have changed, the implication being that the family no longer requires that he be dysfunctional. To be successful, therapy must bring about second-order change. The MRI people have held that paradoxical techniques, partly because they are often dramatic and unexpected, produce a reframing of the situation such that second-order change is made possible; the situation has been reframed and defined at a different level. Thus it can no longer be viewed the same, and the members within the (family) system are more open to something new or different, i.e., to a change.

The concept of *compression* noted earlier has also been proposed by Stanton (1982) as a curative factor. The therapist, by pushing a family toward a fusion state, causes a reaction away from this state. However, he blocks or diverts the usual path or pattern of return, stretching the family's repertoire toward other options and new learning, thus causing change.

As a final note, it should be clear that the notion of transference has little place in strategic therapy, especially as a process for inducing change. While transference may occur in treatment, the therapist wants to direct it as quickly as possible either back to its source (e.g., parents), or toward another support system such as friends, siblings or other relatives. The last thing a strategic therapist wants is for clients to be dependent upon him and therefore neglectful of more natural attachments. Instead, he is more liable to try to steer the client, when appropriate, toward development of or improvement in these other relationships.

Therapist Factors

In strategic therapy, developing hypotheses and checking feedback from interventions are all important, and therapist personality and "characteristics" are underplayed. The therapist must be personally involved, human (rather than distant and overly objective), and persuasive (Haley, 1979). He also must be active. How-ever, the notion of countertransference is not one that strategic therapists attend to. Rather, they orient toward the therapist's practicing new ways of handling a problem if he seems to be having difficulty in a particular situation. To the therapist who gets "stuck," they might say, "That way isn't working—it isn't helping. Try it a different way. For instance, ..." Given that people do differ, they would still assume that the therapist can be flexible enough to alter his approach, or else he/she should not be a therapist.

There is a creative aspect of strategic therapy which may be recognized by its proponents, but is not often written about. Devising tasks and directives which are "on target" requires a certain dipping into one's pool of innovative potential. For instance, in the case of ritual prescriptions, Palazzoli-Selvini (1978) states: "The 'invention' of a family ritual invariably calls for a great creative effort on the part of the therapist and often, if I may say so, for flashes of genius, if only because a ritual that has proved effective in one family is unlikely to prove equally effective in another" (p. 239). This requirement for creativity in strategic therapy (as well as, of course, other therapy approaches) will undoubtedly be around for a long time, since we are far from a technology which dictates every move in treatment. And, indeed, some might question whether such precise refinement, even if possible, would be desirable.

TREATMENT EFFECTIVENESS

Examination of the effectiveness of interventions (checking feedback, outcome, etc.) is an integral part of the strategic model. Perhaps only behaviorally-oriented family therapists have emphasized this aspect to the same degree. There are at least seven research studies investigating treatment outcome with strategically-oriented family therapy. The earliest of these was by Langsley and associates (Langsley, Fairbairn, and DeYoung, 1968; Langsley and Kaplan, 1968; Langsley, Machotka and Flomenhaft, 1971; Pittman, Flomenhaft, DeYoung, Kaplan and Langsley, 1966; Pittman, Langsley, Flomenhaft, DeYoung, Machotka and Kaplan, 1971). This group investigated family crisis therapy using many techniques similar to those of both the MRI Brief Therapy Center and, especially, of Haley (much of whose work also developed through working with families in crisis). These similarities include the following: (a) A planned, seven-step process was developed early in the project and applied to most subsequent cases; (b) emphasis was placed on the family life-cycle as a framework for identifying the critical elements in a crisis; (c) therapy was brief and problem-focused; (d) emphasis was on the present, rather than on past events; (e) symptoms were viewed as veiled communications and were explicated as such in family sessions; (f) slight, rather than sweeping, changes were the goal, in a manner similar to that of the MRI group; (g) there was considerable concern with family hierarchy and how to correct it if it was dysfunctional; (h) often, therapists refused to acknowledge a patient's pathology, choosing to reframe it; (i) sometimes therapists used symbolic conversation (a somewhat paradoxical move) by speaking to the patient in his own chosen language; (j) when a straightforward approach did not work, the therapists would take a more indirect or "manipulative" tack, such as encouraging a separation between a battling alcoholic and his/her spouse, knowing full well that this would drive the couple together in alliance against the therapists; (k) family members were never blamed, but rather the therapists regularly used positive interpretation—profusely supporting each family member's good intensions; (1) specific, usually firm, directives were given, including a variety of concrete tasks and homework, and involving any and all members, in much the same style of other strategic therapists.[23]

The design of the Langsley et al. project involved 300 cases admitted to a psychiatric emergency service in which a recommendation had been made to hospitalize. Half of the cases were then randomly assigned to family crisis therapy (without hospitalization), and the other half to standard inpatient treatment. Results from an 18-month follow-up showed that family crisis therapy, as an alternative to hospitalization, cut in half the number of days patients subsequently spent in the hospital compared to controls who were hospitalized according to standard procedures; the cost was also one-sixth as much. While the impressiveness of these outcome results is mitigated by a design which did not separate the hospitalization versus nonhospitalization variable from the contribution of family therapy versus other psychotherapies (Gurman and Kniskern, 1978), the difference in *cost-effectiveness* is striking even if the two groups had produced no differences in outcome.

In one of the best designed studies to date, Alexander and Parsons[24] (1973; Parsons and Alexander, 1973) compared a behaviorally-oriented, crisis-centered family therapy based on strategic techniques and systems theory (Haley, 1963, 1971b; Parsons, 1972; Watzlawick et al., 1967) with three other approaches to treating delinquency: a client-centered family approach, an eclectic-dynamic approach, and a no-treatment control group. Results for the systems treatment were markedly superior to the other groups—recidivism was cut in half. The remaining three treatment conditions did not differ significantly from each other. Equally important, a three-year follow-up (Klein et al., 1977) showed that the incidence of problems in siblings was significantly lower for the family systems treatment—a clear-cut case of secondary prevention.

The MRI group (Weakland et al., 1974) performed short-term follow-ups on 97 of their cases, involving a broad spectrum of problems or disorders, and found approximately three-quarters (72%) of them were either successful (40%) or significantly improved (32%). These results are somewhat higher than the gross improvement rates of 61-65% noted for non-family

---

[23]*Editors' Note.* We remain unconvinced that the Langsley group's therapy can be reasonably subsumed under the "strategic" rubric. It seems to us that crisis intervention principles and techniques aimed at (1) keeping the identified patient out of the hospital and (2) restoring the families' pre-crisis level of functioning were the most prominent aspects of the treatment. Moreover, paradoxical techniques, so central to the practice of strategic therapy, were given little emphasis. We do not think that the use of "specific, usually firm directives" and of "concrete tasks and homework" is sufficient to qualify a family therapy as "strategic."

---

[24]The Alexander and Parsons group originally started with a greater emphasis on behavioral techniques and shifted to a more strategic approach when the former proved inadequate. Parsons' (1972) manual for training therapists in this treatment is as clearly a strategically-oriented document as existed in the literature at that time. See Chapter 11 in this *Handbook.*

individual therapy (Bergin, 1971); and are more striking when one considers that no cases continued for more than 10 sessions. However, the lack of control or comparison groups greatly limits the conclusions which can be drawn, and it is difficult to accept without reservation their allusion that the success rate for schizophrenics was as high as for, say, work problems.

A structural / strategic approach to family therapy (described earlier) has been investigated with drug addicts in a methadone program by Stanton, Todd and associates (Stanton, 1978; Stanton and Todd, 1979; Stanton, Todd, Steier, Van Deusen, Marder, Rosoff, Seaman, and Skibinski, 1979; Stanton et al., 1978, 1981). The sample was composed of lower- and working-class males under age 36 and included an equal number of blacks and whites; all were in contact with two parents or parent surrogates (e.g., mother's boyfriend). Four treatment conditions were compared: paid family therapy, unpaid family therapy, paid family movie treatment, and non-family treatment (methadone and individual counseling). Random assignment was used. The three family treatments were brief, i.e., ten sessions. Family members in the paid group were reimbursed for attending sessions and could also earn additional money if their addicted family member was "clean" that week—an intervention which focused their attention on his drug-taking and reinforced them for putting pressure on him to abstain. Movie treatment required the members to come to the clinic as a family each week to view movies together. Some of the major clinical findings which emerged were: (a) a great deal of effort had to be expended to get families into treatment, but this was accomplished (including *both* parents or parent surrogates) with 71% of the cases; (b) the therapist had to have control over, or major input into, medication decisions in order for therapy to be successful; (c) a crisis in the family inevitably occurred approximately one month into treatment, as change started to take place; (d) urinalysis results were extremely important in allowing families to track ongoing progress; and (e) in cases with married addicts, the relationship with the family of origin had to be dealt with first, before focusing on the marriage, if treatment were to succeed. Follow-ups six months after treatment had terminated (Stanton et al., 1979) showed the following (statistically significant) results in terms of percentage of days free from various drugs ($N = 106$): (a) From the best to worst, the general order of outcomes was, respectively, paid family therapy, unpaid family therapy, family movie, and non-family; (b) payment seemed primarily to affect attendance, as the two paid groups (paid family therapy and movie) completed 50% more sessions than the unpaid group, while the payment contingency for clean urines did not significantly increase days free of any drugs for the movie group over the non-family group; (c) paid and unpaid family therapy did not differ significantly from each other on eight of the nine drug use variables, the exception being that paid had a better outcome for "all legal and illegal drugs excluding alcohol"; (d) paid family therapy produced better results than non-family on eight of nine variables, with no difference on alcohol use; (e) unpaid was better than non-family on five of the variables; (f) movie and non-family did not differ on any variables; (g) the rate of deaths during the first year posttreatment was several times higher (10% vs. 2%) for clients who were not involved in family therapy (movie, non-family) than for clients who were (paid and unpaid family therapy)—a difference which was statistically significant. No differences were found among groups as to percentage of days spent working or in school. On variables in which significant differences were found, the ratio of days free for paid family therapy was 1.2 to 4.0 times as great as for non-family (median ratio = 1.8); the ratios for unpaid vs. non-family ranged from 1.34 to 2.0 (median ratio = 1.65). For example, the mean percentages of days free of "all legal and illegal opiates" (including methadone) were: non-family—25%, movie—25%, unpaid family therapy—49%, paid family therapy—63%. For "all illegal drugs excluding marijuana" the means were: non-family—44%, movie—50%, unpaid family therapy—67%, paid family therapy—74%.

Another facet of the above research was an investigation of the relationship between therapy outcome (as measured by drug use of the IP) and pre- to posttreatment changes in family interactional patterns. Stanton et al. (1979) analyzed videotapes of family interactions obtained before and after treatment. The families were

videotaped while performing several tasks together, one of which involved decision-making
(planning a menu) and another which required
conflict resolution (discussing a recent argument). Raters scored the family interactions,
statement-by-statement, on 31 different content
and non-content variables. The extent to which
families shifted on these interaction variables
was correlated with the number of days during
the six-month posttreatment period in which the
IP was free of the aforementioned nine drug
variables (e.g., "illegal opiates," "all legal and
illegal drugs excluding alcohol," etc.). The conflict resolution task appeared to be the task most
sensitive to change, i.e., it was the best predictor of outcome, perhaps because of its nature
and because it was less structured, more free-
flowing and probably tapped patterns which occurred outside of the families' awareness. Results on this task indicated that successful cases
showed changes in some patterns which were
not shown by less successful cases on such measures as, for instance, expressing a "thought in
progress," giving directions to other family
members, "mindreading," and the extent to
which dyads were able to continue an interaction without being interrupted. Restricted entry
multiple regressions (up to ten interaction variables) produced multiple correlations which
were statistically significant at the .05 level for
seven of the nine drug categories (the remaining
two reaching the .10 level of significance). Values for the seven significant multiple correlations ranged from .56 to .84 (four being .75 or
higher). The two highest coefficients were for
legal (methadone) opiates (.82) and illegal opiates (.84). Perhaps even more striking was the
canonical correlation which emerged on the conflict resolution task. This measure correlated the
set of five non-composite, non-overlapping drug
variables (i.e., those which were singular, such
as "illegal opiates" or "marijuana" versus composite variables such as "all legal and illegal opiates") with pre-post changes in the set of
interaction variables. The resulting correlation
was .999 ($p < .0001$), indicating that the variance
in one set of variables could be accounted for
by the other set. Stanton et al. (1979) conclude
that (a) levels of drug-taking (or no drug-taking)
are related to certain ways in which the family
changes its interactional patterns, and (b) the

interrelationships are contrapuntal, with some
behaviors decreasing and others increasing in
concert with this cluster of outcome variables.
In other words, changes in the symptom are
related to changes in the family, as indicated by
its behavioral interactions. While the idea that
system change is necessary for symptom change
has been basic to family therapy for many years
(e.g., Bowen, 1966; Haley, 1962), this is perhaps
the first study to provide objective, experimental support for this notion.

Garrigan and Bambrick (1975, 1977a, 1979)
have embarked on a six-year research program
investigating outcomes of Zuk's go-between
therapy for families with a disturbed child or
adolescent. At this writing, the total number of
families involved has reached 70, 35 experi-
mentals and 35 controls, although the published
studies have smaller N's because data for later
cases have not been analyzed.[25] The first of this
series of studies (Garrigan and Bambrick, 1975)
did not use random assignment. The patients
were 18 white, middle-class boys, ages 11-15,
from intact families, who were enrolled in a
school for emotionally disturbed children and
adolescents. None had evidence of psychosis,
mental deficiency, hearing loss or language disorder. Half the group was involved in a short-
term family therapy program (six sessions). The
therapists were pre-doctoral counseling students. The nine matched controls went through
the normal school regimen, with parent participation in some cases, but without family therapy. Results of comparisons on pre- and
posttreatment measures showed the family therapy group to show more gains in the IP's perception of family adjustment, although teachers'
judgment of classroom behavior did not differ
significantly.

A second study (Garrigan and Bambrick,
1977a) was an extension of the first and was conducted in the same setting and with similar therapists and patients. However, the sample was
larger ($N = 28$), and older (age range 11-17),
girls were included, and random assignment to
treatment conditions was employed. Half of the
group was involved in brief family therapy (10-
15 sessions) and the other half (controls) had
parent group discussions and seminars made

---

[25]Andrew Bambrick, personal communication, August 1978.

available to them. All cases were involved in an ongoing process of educational and psychological treatment, and the family therapies were offered as an additional therapeutic element. One- to two-year follow-ups were obtained in 85% of the cases. The major findings were that the family therapy group showed significantly more improvement in the identified patient's symptoms in the classroom and home, plus perceived improvement in their parents' marital relationship.

In a third study (Garrigan and Bambrick, 1979), the same procedures, in the same setting, were followed as in the second study, except that all the 24 identified patients were oldest male siblings and one-third came from single-parent-mother families. Effectiveness of family therapy was not as pronounced in this third study, compared with the second; some classroom symptoms decreased, as did schizoid withdrawal. Overall results seemed to be affected by family structure, as less success was obtained with single-parent families. In fact, an interaction occurred in which mothers of intact families treated with family therapy perceived symptom reduction, while single-parent mothers perceived an increase in their sons' symptoms following treatment.

The research of Garrigan and Bambrick has, in at least the last two studies, involved very good experimental design and a number of valid, reliable measures. Unfortunately, these investigators have not reported the extent to which their controls actually engaged in parents' groups and seminars, so it is not clear whether these were "no-treatment" groups, "alternative treatment" groups, or a combination of the two. Nonetheless, Zuk (1976) feels they are among the most objective studies in the literature, partly due to replication of results with different samples, and partly because, although they tested his treatment model, they were not done by him or at his institution.[26]

Discussion and Conclusions

An overview of the above studies would indicate that, depending on the kind of patient

population, a strategic orientation to family therapy either shows (a) substantially better results, or (b) considerable promise, when compared with several other (standard) forms of treatment. This is especially true when issues of cost efficiency are considered. Further, the Alexander and Parsons study suggests the superiority of this approach over two other approaches to family treatment.

Another finding which stands out is that, even though seven is not a huge number of studies, investigators of strategic therapy have been more active than researchers on other family therapy approaches as far as performing controlled or comparative family therapy outcome research is concerned. In their review of family therapy outcome research, Gurman and Kniskern (1978) located 27 studies of family therapy which made comparisons either with control groups or with other forms of treatment (the Klein et al., 1977, study being counted with that of Alexander and Parsons', 1973, work). Inclusion of the Garrigan and Bambrick (1979) study, published after Gurman and Kniskern's review, brings the total to 28. Six of these 28 controlled or comparative studies investigated strategic family therapy. Considering the plethora of different family therapy subgroups and "schools" which presently exists, it appears that, relatively speaking, researchers on strategic family therapy have been appropriately industrious.

Perhaps of equal importance to the above, strategic studies have tended, on the whole, to utilize superior research designs in comparison with the average for studies of other family therapy approaches. Gurman and Kniskern (1978) have developed a scale of family therapy research design quality which includes four categories: poor, fair, good, very good. They applied this to 26 of the 27 aforementioned studies (one study being unscorable). Adding Garrigan and Bambrick (1979) to the pool results in a total of 27 comparative or controlled studies which earned ratings on the design quality scale. Of the six strategic studies, none were rated "poor" or "fair," three (50%) obtained ratings of "good" and three (50%) of "very good." This compares favorably with the following breakdown across categories for the 21 nonstrategic studies: poor—24%; fair—29%; good—33%; very good—14%. Assigning ordinal values of 1 through

---

[26]Gerald Zuk, personal communication, July 1978.

4, respectively, to the poor, fair, good and very good categories, a Mann-Whitney test can be calculated for comparing design quality between the strategic and nonstrategic studies. This was done by the author and the resulting value was significant at better than the .01 level.[27] Again, the conclusion to be drawn from this analysis is that strategically-oriented family therapy investigators have, on the average, applied higher standards of research design to their work than have investigators in the field as a whole.

The development of new techniques in strategic therapy has been occurring very rapidly in recent years. Numerous innovations have sprung forth, as this group has focused on new concepts and new populations. From a research standpoint, this is a mixed blessing, in that it is difficult to get a particular treatment paradigm to hold still so that it can be examined. Despite the relatively good track record in strategic outcome research cited above, there is certainly a need for more research which not only examines outcome per se, but also clarifies the crucial components of treatment technique.

Finally, researching the therapeutic process in strategic therapy is in some ways more complex and "tricky" than with other approaches. It is not uncommon for change to occur instantly and dramatically within a session, given the kind of therapeutic judo practiced by some strategic therapists such as Erickson and the Milan group. The researcher is faced with the task of catching and identifying these critical moments, and if he does not have videotape equipment, his task is doubly difficult—which is one reason why Haley and some others have devoted so much effort to explicating treatment process through videotape analysis. Then, too, most strategic therapists, especially the MRI and Milan groups, focus on extending their impact outside the session, to the home and the real world. Thus, the researcher who hopes to directly observe these kinds of phenomena is ambitious, indeed, and also sets himself up for reactivity effects if, while pursuing his data outside the treatment sessions, he becomes too intrusive into the family.

TRAINING

In addition to the usual fields of psychiatry, psychology, social work and nursing, I have seen competent strategic therapists emerge from such diverse (initial) backgrounds as the clergy, communications, community relations, vocational counseling, education, music, various paraprofessional fields and even a reformed pool hustler. What seems to be most important is the kind of thinking or prior therapeutic experience a trainee has had. Therapists accustomed to psychodynamic therapy or experiential groups have trouble with the strategic approach. In the former case this is because, in part, they are not used to thinking in terms of more than one person, and in the latter because such group experiences compete with the idea that it is the behavior within the *natural* group that must change, i.e., the therapist is trying to change repeating sequences involving people who are *habitually together* (Haley, 1976). Having considerable prior experience as an individual therapist is not necessarily harmful (although this is often the case), depending on the orientation of the experience. Some strategic therapists frequently work with an individual, but remain aware of the interaction among their interventions, the client, and those outside the therapy. The crucial difference is whether the therapist thinks and intervenes in response to an interactional and interpersonal model versus one which is individually anchored.

Haley (1976) has specified several criteria which, if met by trainees, are predictive of more rapid learning and better results in the training endeavor. First, trainees who have more experience in the real world (e.g., mature adults who are married and have children) are better equipped to perform a therapy that stresses problems in the real world. Second, besides a certain amount of intelligence, trainees who have skills in different kinds of social behavior—such as the facility to at times be authoritarian, playful, serious, flirtatious, helpless, etc.—can more easily adopt a wide range of therapeutic approaches. Finally, it is best that students, while in training, be cut off from other teachers of therapy so that they do not become pawns in the conflictual struggles between different schools, or end up either learning half of

---

[27]The appropriate Mann-Whitney U formula was used in this analysis in order to compensate for the size of the sample and the large number of ties. The obtained p value was .009.

what they need or becoming so eclectic that they believe "everything is so or nothing is so."

Neither previous personal therapy nor working as a co-therapist is considered important by most strategic therapists—the primary exception to the latter being the co-therapy team approach of Todd and associates.[28] Concerning a requirement of personal therapy, Haley (1976) feels that such a requisite is (a) demeaning to the trainee; (b) distracts him from the work at hand; (c) in its requirement for personal "insight," is antithetical to a therapeutic approach which deemphasizes insight; and (d) gives less recognition to the fact that a therapist grows with success in his work, and that the first task is to train him to solve problems he meets in therapy (e.g., if a therapist has trouble with an authority figure, such as a grandfather, he should be coached in specific ways for dealing with grandfathers, rather than steered toward an "understanding" of his personal authority-figure problem). As to co-therapy, strategic therapists prefer a live supervision paradigm with a one-way mirror in which a supervisor and possibly other students or colleagues can observe and make suggestions to the trainee during the actual course of treatment. Such a method is considered much more effective than co-therapy, both for correcting mistakes and for developing new skills.

Perhaps no other strategic therapist has devoted as much of his professional time, effort and writing to the training of therapists as has Haley. In particular, he has produced a number of highly instructive, narrated videotapes toward this end. Much of this emphasis developed from his concentrated collaboration with a group of colleagues at the Philadelphia Child Guidance Clinic, and has subsequently been extended by Madanes and himself at their Family Therapy Institute in Washington, D. C. His chapter on "Problems in Training Therapists" (in Haley, 1976) stands as the most comprehensive and specific model known to this author for training strategic therapists. Some of its major points are:

1) It is the supervisor's responsibility not only to protect the client(s) from a beginning therapist, but also to find a way to help the trainee

solve a problem or difficulty in treatment. This is analogous to the responsibility of the therapist to develop the means for helping the client(s) solve a problem.

2) Since reports by trainees of what happens in a session and the real events that occur are often disparate, supervision should be provided through direct observation—by either videotape or, preferably, live supervision. This also allows the supervisor to stop a failing intervention before it goes too far and to protect the client should the trainee do something untoward or unethical.

3) Strategic therapy is learned by *doing*. Reading about it, hearing lectures about it and discussing it are of peripheral importance when first learning. For the novice, practicing certain techniques beforehand is a form of doing and can be helpful. However, theory grows out of action and experience and should be presented later, when the trainee can fit what he is doing into a broader model of the field.

4) Since directives are a cornerstone of strategic therapy, a trainee must learn various ways of giving them, so that he can learn how to motivate someone to do what he is told. This includes practice in clarifying the directive, anticipating resistance to it, and determining whether it has been followed.

5) Therapy should be more oriented toward problems than toward methods, since a therapist's method will shift depending on the problem. Also, just as a therapist designs a therapy for a particular client, the supervisor should design a training program for a particular student.

Recognizing the quandary that students often face when selecting a program in which to train, Haley has provided them with guidelines for this in his training chapter. He lists a number of factors which are non-facilitive to learning strategic therapy, or for that matter most kinds of family therapy. Factors in a training program which should be viewed positively by the prospective trainee are as follows (pp. 190-191):

1) It is possible to observe therapists at work because there are one-way mirrors and they are used.

---

[28]Thomas Todd, personal communication, January 1979.

2) The student can be observed at work and given "live" supervision so that he can be guided while in the act of doing therapy.

3) Videotaping of sessions is easily and routinely done so that a student can go over the videotape with a supervisor at leisure.

4) It is assumed that the student needs to learn a variety of therapy techniques so that he can choose the one for a particular problem. The place should be one where whole families are interviewed as well as individuals.

5) The presenting problem is emphasized and taken seriously.

6) Outcome is emphasized so that case discussions are guided by the destination of therapy and not merely by the process of the journey.

An example of one strategic family therapy training program which has been examined closely is provided by Garrigan and Bambrick (1977b). They undertook a four-year project to train male and female counseling psychology doctoral students in a short-term, go-between therapy model. The results were generally positive (with no reported differences between the sexes). They estimate that 150 hours of training can enable such trainees to learn elements of the system and apply them effectively in the family treatment of emotionally disturbed children. However, they believe three years of intensive post-masters or doctorate training are necessary to function fully, independently and effectively as a family therapist.

There is one approach to strategic therapy on which the jury may still be out as far as training is concerned. This is the approach used by the Milan group and the related work of some others. While the techniques used by these therapists appear to be dramatically effective, Todd,[29] who has had considerable experience in training therapists in a number of different models (including both the structural and strategic), feels that it is very difficult for novice therapists to learn them. Perhaps because the approach requires so much of the creative genius noted earlier, beginning therapists—who are still mastering the basic moves of working with a family—are too bound by minutia to allow an innovative side to flourish. The level of theoretical integration

required may also be beyond the grasp of the parvenu. Whatever the factors involved, and whether or not these reservations are justified, it does seem that trainees working within the Milan group framework in its present form need very close supervision and a collaborating team of experienced therapists.

COMMENT

In closing, several additional points are worthy of mention. First, it is no secret that within the family therapy field there has been an ongoing struggle between two major camps—the psychoanalytically- or psychodynamically-oriented group and the communications (strategic, structural) groups. At this time, it seems fair to say that the communications groups hold the center of the stage and have been there since the death in 1971 of Nathan Ackerman, the most "creative and zealous" proponent of the psychoanalytic approach (Guerin, 1976). In the author's opinion, there are at least three major reasons for this development: (a) It coincides both with the growing popularity of systems thinking within the mental health fields in general and with the increasing unpopularity of psychoanalysis and other prolonged and expensive therapies; (b) the communications groups may have devoted greater effort to training therapists at all levels and have developed more teachable techniques and more and better training aids such as films and videotapes; (c) even though treatment outcome and efficacy data are not plentiful even among communications researchers, psychodynamically-oriented family therapists have shown an almost total lack of vigor in this respect, particularly in the child and adolescent area. As a result, their credibility, especially among younger professionals, has suffered.

Second, since the various strategic therapy schools hold many similar views on symptoms, change and treatment, and since most of them have observed each other's work, it is not surprising that considerable blurring has occurred among them, especially in their techniques. Sometimes they give different names to similar events. Sometimes they differ only in emphasis. The diversity that does exist can often be traced to the patient populations they were charged

---

[29]Thomas Todd, personal communication, May 1979.

with treating, or, of course, the context in which their work began. Examples of such seminal influences include the early interest in schizophrenia by Bateson et al. and its impact on the later MRI work, Haley's work with lower-income families in Philadelphia, the great distance that many of Selvini's families had to travel, which led to a need to work fast and space sessions further apart, Berenson's assignment to an alcoholism treatment unit in fulfillment of his Public Health Service commitment, Stanton's Vietnam experience in which drug abuse was so prevalent, etc. Thus, this diversity, where it exists, could be seen as arising from a number of singular and often fortuitous circumstances. Rather than viewing the field, then, as a somewhat like-minded but desultory collection of practitioners, it might be better described as a number of investigators and innovators who, working in tandem, toward similar ends, and within a new order of thinking, are attempting to flesh out the bones of a comprehensive and effective method for bringing about change in human problems.

Finally, it is apparent that strategic approaches to family therapy have been gathering a head of steam. In the past five years, especially, they have, as a group, perhaps broken the most *new* ground, particularly in the development of innovative treatment models. To quote Bloch (1977), strategically-oriented therapists have evolved powerful new techniques "that seem at times to be nothing short of miraculous in their ability to produce profound behavioral changes in patterns that seem unresponsive to other modes of intervention" (p. 2).[30] It does not seem presumptuous to look with excitement toward still more fulfillment of the promise inherent in the work which has emerged thus far.

REFERENCES

Alexander, J. F. & Parsons, B. V. Short-term behavioral intervention with delinquent families: Impact on family process and recidivism. *Journal of Abnormal Psychology*, 1973, *81*, 219-225.

Andolfi, M. Prescribing the families' own dysfunctional rules as a therapeutic strategy. *Journal of Marital and Family Therapy*, 1980, *6*, 29-36.

Andolfi, M., Menghi, P., Nicoló, A. & Saccu, C. Interaction in rigid systems: A model of intervention in families with a schizophrenic member. In: M. Andolfi & I. Zwerling (Eds.) *Dimensions of Family Therapy*. New York: Guilford Press, 1980.

Bateson, G., Jackson, D. D., Haley, J., & Weakland, J. Toward a theory of schizophrenia. *Behavioral Science*, 1956, *1*, 251-264.

Bateson, G. Discussion of ideas which handicap therapists. In: M. M. Berger (Ed.), *Beyond the Double Bind*. New York: Brunner/Mazel, 1978.

Berenson, D. A family approach to alcoholism. *Psychiatric Opinion*, 1976a, *13*, 33-38.

Berenson, D. Alcohol and the family system. In: P. J. Guerin (Ed.), *Family Therapy: Theory and Practice*. New York: Gardner Press, 1976b.

Berenson, D. The therapist's relationship with couples with an alcoholic member. In: E. Kaufman & P. Kaufmann (Eds.), *The Family Therapy of Drug and Alcohol Abuse*, New York: Gardner Press, 1979.

Bergin, A. E. The evaluation of therapeutic outcomes. In: A. E. Bergin & S. L. Garfield (Eds.), *Handbook of Psychotherapy and Behavior Change*. New York: John Wiley & Sons, 1971.

Bloch, D. A. Review of Rabkin's "Strategic Therapy." *Behavioral Science Book Service* (pamphlet), June 1977.

Boszormenyi-Nagy, I. & Spark, G. M. *Invisible Loyalties*. New York: Harper & Row, 1973.

Bowen, M. The use of family therapy in clinical practice. *Comprehensive Psychiatry*, 1966, 7, 345-374.

Erickson, M. H. Indirect hypnotic therapy of a bedwetting couple. *Journal of Clinical and Experimental Hypnosis*. 1954, *2*, 171-174.

Erickson, M. H. The identification of a secure reality. *Family Process*, 1962, *1*, 294-303.

Erickson, M. H. & Rossi, E. L. *Hypnotherapy: An Exploratory Casebook*. New York: Irvington, 1979.

Farrelly, F. & Brandsma, J. *Provocative Therapy*. Fort Collins, Colorado: Shields Publishing Co., 1974.

Foucault, M. *Madness and Civilization*. New York: Pantheon Books, 1965.

Frankl, V. Paradoxical intention. *American Journal of Psychotherapy*, 1960, *14*, 520-535.

Garrigan, J. J. & Bambrick, A. F. Short-term family therapy with emotionally disturbed children. *Journal of Marriage and Family Counseling*, 1975, *1*, 379-385.

Garrigan, J. J. & Bambrick, A. F. Family therapy for disturbed children: Some experimental results in special education. *Journal of Marriage and Family Counseling*, 1977a, *3*, 83-93.

Garrigan, J. J. & Bambrick, A. F. Introducing novice therapists to "go-between" techniques of family therapy. *Family Process*, 1977b, *16*, 237-246.

Garrigan, J. J. & Bambrick, A. F. New findings in research on go-between process. *International Journal of Family Therapy*, 1979, *1*, 76-85.

Guerin, P. J. Family therapy: The first 25 years. In: P. J. Guerin (Ed.), *Family Therapy: Theory and Practice*. New York: Gardner Press, 1976.

Gurman, A. S. & Kniskern, D. P. Research on marital and family therapy: Progress, perspective and prospect. In: S. L. Garfield & A. E. Bergin (Eds.), *Handbook of Psychotherapy and Behavior Change: An Empirical Analysis* (2nd edition). New York: John Wiley and Sons, 1978.

Haley, J. Whither family therapy. *Family Process*, 1962, *1*, 69-100.

---

[30]As a therapist, Donald Bloch has been more identified with psychodynamic than strategic approaches to family therapy, which makes this comment all the more notable.

Haley, J. *Strategies of Psychotherapy*. New York: Grune & Stratton, 1963.

Haley, J., Ed. *Advanced Techniques of Hypnosis and Therapy: Selected Papers of Milton H. Erickson*. New York: Grune & Stratton, 1967.

Haley, J. An editor's farewell. *Family Process*, 1969, *8*, 149-158.

Haley, J. Approaches to Family Therapy. *International Journal of Psychiatry*, 1970, *9*, 233-242.

Haley, J. A review of the family therapy field. In: J. Haley (Ed.), *Changing Families*. New York: Grune & Stratton, 1971a.

Haley, J. Family therapy: A radical change. In: J. Haley (Ed.), *Changing families*. New York: Grune & Stratton, 1971b.

Haley, J. We're in family therapy. In: A. Ferber, M. Mendelsohn & A. Napier, (Eds.), *The Book of Family Therapy*. New York: Science House, 1972, pp. 113-122.

Haley, J. Strategic therapy when a child is presented as the problem. *The Journal of the American Academy of Child Psychiatry*, 1973a, *12*, 641-659.

Haley, J. *Uncommon Therapy*. New York: W. W. Norton, 1973b.

Haley, J. *Problem Solving Therapy*. San Francisco: Jossey-Bass, 1976.

Haley, J. Ideas that handicap therapy with young people. *International Journal of Family Therapy*, 1979, *1*, 29-45.

Haley, J. *Leaving Home: The Therapy of Disturbed Young People*. New York: McGraw-Hill, 1980.

Haley, J. & Hoffman, L. *Techniques of Family Therapy*. New York: Basic Books, 1967.

Hare-Mustin, R. Treatment of temper tantrums by a paradoxical intervention. *Family Process*, 1975, *14*, 481-485.

Hare-Mustin, R. Paradoxical tasks in family therapy: Who can resist? *Psychotherapy: Theory, Research and Practice*, 1976, *13*, 128-130.

Hoffman, L. Deviation-amplifying processes in normal groups. In: J. Haley (Ed.), *Changing Families*. New York: Grune & Stratton, 1971.

Hoffman, L. Breaking the homeostatic cycle. In: P. Guerin (Ed.), *Family Therapy: Theory and Practice*. New York: Gardner Press, 1976.

Jackson, D. D. The question of family homeostasis. *Psychiatric Quarterly Supplement*, 1957, *31*, 79-90.

Jackson, D. D. A suggestion for the technical handling of paranoid patients. *Psychiatry*, 1963, *26*, 306-307.

Jackson, D. D. The study of the family. *Family Process*, 1965, *4*, 1-20.

Jesse, E. & L'Abate, L. The use of paradox with children in an inpatient treatment setting. *Family Process*, 1980, *19*, 59-64.

Klein, N. C., Alexander, J. F., & Parsons, B. V. Impact of family systems intervention on recidivism and sibling delinquency: A model of primary prevention and program evaluation. *Journal of Consulting and Clinical Psychology*, 1977, *45*, 469-474.

L'Abate, L. A positive approach to marital and family intervention. In: L. R. Wolberg & M. L. Aronson (Eds.), *Group Therapy: 1975*. New York: Stratton Intercontinental Medical Book Co., 1975.

L'Abate, L. & Weeks, G. A bibliography of paradoxical methods in psychotherapy of family systems. *Family Process*, 1978, *17*, 95-98.

Langsley, D. G., Fairbairn, R. H., & DeYoung, C. D. Adolescence and family crises. *Canadian Psychiatric Association Journal*, 1968, *13*, 125-133.

Langsley, D. G. & Kaplan, D. M. *The Treatment of Families in Crisis*. New York: Grune and Stratton, 1968.

Langsley, D. G., Machotka, P., & Flomenhaft, K. Avoiding mental hospital admission: A follow-up study. *American Journal of Psychiatry*, 1971, *127*, 1391-1394.

Madanes, C. Protection, paradox and pretending. *Family Process*, 1980, *19*, 73-85.

Madanes, C. & Haley, J. Dimensions of family therapy. *Journal of Nervous and Mental Disease*, 1977, *165*, 88-98.

Mandel, H. P., Weizmann, F., Millan, B., Greenhow, J., & Speirs, D. Reaching emotionally disturbed children: Judo principles in remedial education. *American Journal of Orthopsychiatry*, 1975, *45*, 867-874.

Minuchin, S. *Families and Family Therapy*. Cambridge, Mass.: Harvard Press, 1974.

Minuchin, S., Rosman, B., & Baker, L. *Psychosomatic Families: Anorexia Nervosa in Context*. Cambridge, Mass.: Harvard University Press, 1978.

Palazzoli-Selvini, M. The families of patients with anorexia nervosa. In: E. J. Anthony & C. Koupernik (Eds.), *The Child and His Family*, New York: John Wiley & Sons, 1970.

Palazzoli-Selvini, M. *Self-Starvation: From Individual to Family Therapy in the Treatment of Anorexia Nervosa*, New York: Jason Aronson, 1978.

Palazzoli-Selvini, M., Boscolo, L., Cecchin, G. F., & Prata, G. The treatment of children through brief therapy of their parents. *Family Process*, 1974, *13*, 429-442.

Palazzoli-Selvini, M., Boscolo, L., Cecchin, G. F., & Prata, G. Family rituals: A powerful tool in family therapy. *Family Process*, 1977, *16*, 445-453.

Palazzoli-Selvini, M., Boscolo, L., Cecchin, G., & Prata, G. *Paradox and Counterparadox: A New Model in the Therapy of the Family in Schizophrenic Transaction*. New York: Jason Aronson, 1978a.

Palazzoli-Selvini, M., Boscolo, L., Cecchin, G., & Prata, G. A ritualized prescription in family therapy: Odd days and even days. *Journal of Marriage and Family Counseling*, 1978b, *4*, 3-9.

Palazzoli-Selvini, M., Boscolo, L., Cecchin, G., & Prata, G. Hypothesizing—circularity—neutrality: Three guidelines for the conductor of the session. *Family Process*, 1980a, *19*, 3-12.

Palazzoli-Selvini, M., Boscolo, L., Cecchin, G., & Prata, G. The problem of the referring person. *Journal of Marital and Family Therapy*, 1980b, *6*, 3-9.

Papp, P. The Greek chorus and other techniques of paradoxical therapy. *Family Process*, 1980, *19*, 45-57.

Parsons, B. V. *Family Therapy Training Manual*. Unpublished paper, University of Utah, 1972.

Parsons, B. V. & Alexander, J. F. Short-term family intervention: A therapy outcome study. *Journal of Consulting and Clinical Psychology*, 1973, *41*, 195-201.

Pittman, F. S., Flomenhaft, K., DeYoung, C., Kaplan, D., & Langsley, D. G. Techniques of family crisis therapy. In: J. Masserman (Ed.), *Current Psychiatric Therapies*. New York: Grune & Stratton, 1966.

Pittman, F. S., Langsley, D. G., Flomenhaft, K., DeYoung, C., Machotka, P., & Kaplan, D. M. Therapy techniques of the family treatment unit. In: J. Haley (Ed.), *Changing Families*. New York: Grune & Stratton, 1971.

Rabkin, R. *Strategic Psychotherapy*. New York: Basic Books, 1977.

Raskin, D. E. & Klein, Z. E. Losing a symptom through keeping it: A review of paradoxical treatment techniques and rationale. *Archives of General Psychiatry*, 1976, *33*, 548-555.

Rohrbaugh, M., Tennen, H., Press, S., White, L., Raskin,

P., & Pickering, M. R. *Paradoxical Strategies in Psychotherapy.* Symposium presented at the meeting of the American Psychological Association, San Francisco, 1977.

Singer, M. T. & Wynne, L. Communication styles in parents of normals, neurotics and schizophrenics: Some findings using a new Rorschach scoring manual. In: I. Cohen (Ed.), *Family Structure, Dynamics and Therapy.* Washington, D.C.: Psychiatric Research Reports of the American Psychiatric Association (No. 20), 1966.

Sluzki, C. E. Marital therapy from a systems theory perspective. In: T. J. Paolino and B. S. McCrady (Eds.), *Marriage and Marital Therapy: Psychoanalytic, Behavioral and Systems Theory Perspectives.* New York: Brunner/Mazel, 1978.

Solyom, L., Garza-Perez, J., Ledwidge, B. L., & Solyom, C. Paradoxical intention in the treatment of obsessive thoughts: A pilot study. *Comprehensive Psychiatry,* 1972, *13,* 291-297.

Soper, P. H. & L'Abate, L. Paradox as a therapeutic technique: A review. *International Journal of Family Counseling,* 1977, *5,* 10-21.

Stanton, M. D. The addict as savior: Heroin death and the family. *Family Process,* 1977, *16,* 191-197.

Stanton, M. D. Some outcome results and aspects of structural family therapy with drug addicts. In: D. Smith, S. Anderson, M. Buxton, T. Chung, N. Gottlieb, & W. Harvey (Eds.), *A Multicultural View of Drug Abuse: Selected Proceedings of the National Drug Abuse Conference—1977.* Cambridge, Massachusetts: Schenkman Publishing Co., 1978.

Stanton, M.D. Family therapy: Systems approaches. In: G. P. Sholevar, R. M. Benson, & B. J. Blinder (Eds.), *Emotional Disorders in Children and Adolescents: Medical and Psychological Approaches to Treatment.* Jamaica, N.Y.: S. P. Medical and Scientific Books (division of Spectrum Publications), 1980.

Stanton, M. D. Who should get credit for change which occurs in therapy? In: A. S. Gurman (Ed.), *Questions and Answers in the Practice of Family Therapy.* New York: Brunner/Mazel, 1981a.

Stanton, M. D. Marital therapy from a structural/strategic viewpoint. In: G. P. Sholevar (Ed.), *Marriage Is a Family Affair: Textbook of Marriage and Marital Therapy.* Jamaica, N.Y.: S. P. Medical and Scientific Books (division of Spectrum Publications), 1981b.

Stanton, M. D. An integrated stuctural/strategic approach to famly therapy. *Journal of Marital and Family Therapy.* 1981c, in press.

Stanton, M. D. Fusion, compression, expansion and the workings of paradox: A theory of therapeutic and systemic change. Paper submitted for publication, 1982.

Stanton, M. D. & Todd, T. C. Structural family therapy with drug addicts. In: E. Kaufman & P. Kaufmann (Eds.), *The Family Therapy of Drug and Alcohol Abuse.* New York: Gardner Press, 1979.

Stanton, M. D. & Todd, T. C. Engaging "resistant" families in treatment: II. Principles and techniques in recruitment. *Family Process,* 1981.

Stanton, M. D., Todd, T. C., Heard, D. B., Kirschner, S., Kleiman, J. I., Mowatt, D. T., Riley, P., Scott, S. M., & Van Deusen, J. M. Heroin addiction as a family phenomenon: A new conceptual model. *American Journal of Drug and Alcohol Abuse,* 1978, *5,* 125-150.

Stanton, M. D., Todd, T. C., Steier, F., Van Deusen, J. M., Marder, L. R., Rosoff, R. J., Seaman, S. F., & Skibinski, E. *Family Characteristics and Family Therapy of Heroin Addicts: Final Report, 1974-1978.* Submitted to the National Institute on Drug Abuse (Grant No. R01 DA 01119) by the Philadelphia Child Guidance Clinic, 1979.

Stanton, M. D., Todd, T. C. & Associates. *The Family Therapy of Drug Addiction.* New York: Guilford Press, 1981.

Teisman, M. W. Jealousy: Systematic, problem-solving therapy with couples. *Family Process,* 1979, *18,* 151-160.

Watzlawick, P., Beavin, J. H., & Jackson, D. D. *Pragmatics of Human Communication,* New York: W. W. Norton, 1967.

Watzlawick, P. & Coyne, J. C. Depression following stroke: Brief, problem-focused treatment. *Family Process,* 1980, *19,* 13-18.

Watzlawick, P., Weakland, J., & Fisch, R. *Change: Principles of Problem Formation and Problem Resolution.* New York: W. W. Norton, 1974.

Weakland, J. H. Communication theory and clinical change. In: P. J. Guerin (Ed.), *Family Therapy: Theory and Practice.* New York: Gardner Press, 1976.

Weakland, J. H. "Family somatics": A neglected edge. *Family Process,* 16, 263-272.

Weakland, J., Fisch, R., Watzlawick, P., & Bodin, A. M. Brief therapy: Focused problem resolution. *Family Process,* 1974, *13,* 141-168.

Weeks, G. R. & L'Abate, L. A compilation of paradoxical methods. *American Journal of Family Therapy,* 1979, *7,* 61-76.

Zuk, G. H. The go-between process in family therapy. *Family Process,* 1966, *5,* 162-178.

Zuk, G. H. *Family Therapy: A Triadic-Based Approach.* New York: Behavioral Publications, 1971.

Zuk, G. H. *Process and Practice in Family Therapy.* Haverford, Pennsylvania: Psychiatry and Behavioral Science Books, 1975.

Zuk, G. H. Family therapy: Clinical hodgepodge or clinical science? *Journal of Marriage and Family Counseling,* 1976, *2,* 299-303.

Zuk, G. H. Value conflict in today's family. *Marriage and Family Living,* 1978, *60,* 18-20.

EDITORS' REFERENCES

Gurman, A.S. Contemporary marital therapy: A critique and comparative analysis of psychoanalytic, behavioral and systems theory approaches. In T.J. Paolino & B.S. McCrady (Eds.), *Marriage and Marital Therapy.* New York: Brunner/Mazel, 1978.

Gurman, A.S. Sources of influence in the family therapy field: Publishing patterns in three major journals. *Journal of Marriage and Family Therapy,* 1981, in press.

Papp, P. Paradoxical strategies and countertransference. *American Journal of Family Therapy,* 1979, *7,* 11-12.

CHAPTER 11

Functional Family Therapy

Cole Barton, Ph.D. and

James F. Alexander, Ph.D.

Functional family therapy represents an integration and extension of two major conceptual models of human behavior: systems theory and behaviorism. It is not, however, simply a juxtaposition of these models, nor does it represent an eclectic arbitrary selection of components from both. Instead, the integration of the two models generates new theoretical and clinical avenues that do not evolve from either one alone. Later sections will expand this concept, but one additional background influence should be considered.

This additional background influence merits discussion because the functional family model was not solely derived in a deductive fashion from theoretical constructs, nor was it solely derived inductively from solid empirical investigations. Rather, it also evolved from very real clinical experiences, sometimes painful ones. This is an important background influence since it has resulted in a simultaneous emphasis on scientific respectability *and* clinical relevance. The model has simultaneously pursued rigor and clinical application. The translation of this pursuit in the realms of clinical application, con-

ceptual development, and empirical scrutiny will be described in this chapter. The major emphasis is not placed on how to do this form of therapy; instead, the chapter will focus on why the therapy takes the form it does, and which elements are necessary to intervene successfully in families.

THE CLINICAL EVOLUTION OF THE FUNCTIONAL FAMILY THERAPY MODEL

Because the model evolved in response to clinical questions, it shall be introduced in the context of a real clinical case.

Twelve-year-old Paul had been seen by his therapist for three and a half months. Labeled (at different times) hyperactive and borderline schizophrenic, the therapeutic goals had included: 1) stopping Paul's impulsive and sometimes bizarre acting-out; and 2) providing Paul with more direct and appropriate verbal means for expressing his feelings and eliciting interaction from his environment (particularly parents, teachers and peers). Gradually Paul had experienced an extensive change in behavior. Whereas he had initially been almost nonverbal and often physically destructive in sessions, after three and a half months he had begun to share feelings with the therapist. He could play or work at a table for long periods of time, and together with the therapist he could behave appropriately in such situations as going to the movies, playing with other children, and other typical contexts for a 12-year-old boy.

Unfortunately, Paul was then abruptly removed from therapy by his parents and returned to the medication he had been taking at referral. The clinic chief had been called by the parents and informed the parents had adamantly refused to continue any form of contact between Paul and the clinic. According to the parents, Paul had told them "I hate you," his explanation being "Jim said I could say what I wanted to." Of course, Jim had never specifically indicated that Paul should say "I hate you" to his parents, but it was the case that Paul's behavior did reflect therapeutic progress in that Paul was verbalizing his momentary feeling rather than behaving in some bizarre way.

This change in Paul's behavior, seen as positive by the clinic staff, had produced a negative family reaction, which in a short time had completely reversed any therapeutic gain. For Jim, this experience represented the "last straw," since it was not unique in this particular case. Furthermore, a growing body of therapy outcome literature (Astin, 1961; Eysenck, 1961) was raising disturbingly critical questions about many forms of traditional one-to-one therapy.

Thus, Jim, like many other therapists, began searching for an alternative clinical framework which could explain the kinds of clinical situations that ended up like Paul's and provide vehicles for avoiding or changing them. For many clinicians, it is difficult to understand and resolve the whys of parents' seeming malevolence and lack of understanding. It is pessimistic and depressing to assume that parents are so selfish, uninformed, or malevolent as to be willing to allow their children to continue to suffer socially and psychologically. It is also difficult for clinicians to face doubts regarding the effectiveness of their traditional theories, their formal training, and the fact that they lack formal models to conceptually and clinically address these phenomena in a rational way. At the outset, then, the early impetus behind the functional family model consisted of clinical concerns of these sorts.

Fortunately, alternative models which formally considered these clinical concerns did emerge. Though pioneered by Bell (1962) over three decades ago, systems and communication theories received their major impetus from the seminal speculations of the Palo Alto group of the early 1960s (Haley, 1963; Satir, 1967; Watzlawick, Beavin, and Jackson, 1967). The formulations of this group, as well as later extensions of similar formulations into a wider range of clinical populations (e.g., Minuchin, Montalvo, Guerney, Rosman, and Schumer, 1967), provided a framework for understanding and modifying the apparently irrational forms of resistance, self-defeating cycles, and malevolence that characterize the relationships found in clinically referred families like Paul's. In particular, these systems and communication theorists hypothesized that individual behavior has meaning only when viewed in the context of the interpersonal relationships in which it is embedded.

These theorists also provided a relatively nomothetic model of relationships, which in turn posited some dimensions of the "volitional" roles of individual interactants in human relationships. The volitional role of interactants was characterized as one of creating and maintaining relationships with certain types of structure. These assumptions of volition by communications theorists offered an important complementary development to the research being performed on the behavioral basis of interpersonal behavior (e.g., Patterson, 1971). Learning theorists were, in fact, performing important research on the inherent dependencies or contingencies in forms of behaviors exchanged between members of families (Patterson and Reid, 1967; Stuart, 1971). As long as behavioral clinicians were willing to make value judgments, these behavioral data talked mostly to the appropriate or inappropriate, or appetitive or punishing, properties of human behavior as the sole criteria for evaluating relationships. This mechanistic and value-laden view of interaction between people suggested that the enterprise of conjoint change was solely one of helping family members acquire new behaviors, and creating an environmental context where they might be performed.[1] Unfortunately, as in most

---

[1]*Editors' Note.* Many behavior therapists would insist that their descriptive, pragmatic emphasis on the antecedents and consequences of behavior is value-free. Barton and Alexander's point here, in contrast, is that such an empirically oriented view *necessarily* assumes some very profound values.

behavioral models, the issue of relationship contingencies kept arising, as did the issue of what might be inherently reinforcing stimuli between family members. Practically speaking, it appeared that parents of adolescents had few tangible resources available to them to be sufficiently controlling influences on their children's behavior, and vice versa.

The more important issues seemed to be the contingency ones: Which family members determined the form of reinforcement and punishment, and who in families determined how they were to be distributed or allocated? Clinical experiences with resistant families and the reported data showed that the assumption that all family members were driven toward short-term positive reinforcement was untenable.[2] Rather, it appeared then (as it does now) that there were unexplored relationship determinants of human behavior. These problems required a more complete model to account for the role of relationships in determining behavior. Rather than assume interpersonal relationships are just one class of environmental settings in which behaviors are strengthened or extinguished, the assumption was made by communication theorists that behavior serves to define and create interpersonal relationships.[3] This seemed to offer a more promising set of links to understanding and changing people's subjective conceptual and affective states, as well as their behavior. Reappraisal of the meaning of behavior has been a critical starting point for understanding the basis of the functional family model.

CONCEPTUAL FOUNDATIONS OF THE FUNCTIONAL FAMILY MODEL

The conceptual foundations of any therapeutic model primarily involve that model's approach to deriving meaning from human behavior. Mental health professionals are reminded that in many instances they are using models for deriving meaning that have a relatively limited history of conceptual development. This developmental infancy is relevant because most traditional therapeutic approaches adhere to conceptual paradigms derived from traditional philosophical roots. A cursory review of the major personality models, the study of abnormal behavior, and the development of individually-oriented treatment strategies suggests that traditional approaches have the weight of the majority of formal Western thought behind them.

To grossly oversimplify these theories and models, it would appear that they are remarkably consistent with the conceptual dictums of Judaeo-Christian tradition. This tradition argues that individuals are largely responsible for their own behavior, which suggests that the critical locus of behavioral control and meaning lies within the individual, e.g., souls, psyches, or biology. It is also the case that both Judaeo-Christian traditions and traditional personality models have adopted a moral code or set of ethical classifications which place value on behavior. An individual is held responsible for behavior which is labeled by a cultural code as good or bad, or prosocial or antisocial. In a like manner, the traditional models of personality reflect these parallel classification schemes, when the normal-abnormal dichotomy is interchanged with good or bad.

The emphasis of traditional personality models on individual responsibility and the valence (i.e., good-bad) of human behavior results in a restrictive approach to meaning. Traditional personality models conceptualize the "intent," "end or purpose," "significance" and "expressive" meaning of behavior in individualistic terms. Individuals are the "cause" of behavior, and the meaning of the behavior can be derived only from understanding the individual. In

---

[2] *Editors' Note.* It is worth noting here, as discussed by Jacobson (Chapter 15), that behavioral *marriage* therapists recently have paid increasing attention to the long-range relationship consequences of positive and negative control, i.e., what they call the "bank account model" of behavioral exchange, and that this shift of emphasis from immediate behavioral consequences has shaped their intervention strategies perceptibly.

[3] *Editors' Note.* This was precisely one of the main points we have made in our critique of behavioral marriage therapy (Gurman and Knudson, 1978; Gurman, Knudson, and Kniskern, 1978). It is fascinating to us to see that some behaviorally-oriented family therapists, such as Barton and Alexander, now endorse this view as central to their treatment models, while others continue to deny steadfastly the relationship-defining function of overt behavior. For example, Jacobson and Margolin (1979) have taken the unambiguous position that "A behavioral exchange model does not accept the position that most target behaviors presented (by couples) can be best understood as metaphors serving a communicative and relationship defining function . . . Rather, behavior . . . is viewed literally rather than symbolically" (p. 151).

terms of clinical application, these assumptions about meaning have led to the individual's being the unit of treatment (e.g., one-to-one therapy), they have generated individually-oriented labeling or diagnostic schemes (e.g., objective or projective tests), and they have dictated the forms of traditional intervention (e.g., "talking cures"). The net effect of this paradigm development has been to minimize the role of both the natural and interpersonal environments as influences contributing to the meaning of behavior. Rather, individually-oriented therapists are placed in the role of being a nomothetic representative of culture. They are forced to evaluate the form of behavior as good or bad, and in their expert role presumably carry with them those criteria toward which clients' behavior should be changed. Individually-oriented therapists generalize from their examination of an individual client to reports or hypotheses about how the client behaves in other contexts, and make decisions about how the client's behavior typically influences others. These therapists must make a judgment as to whether the client's influence is culturally good or bad, or culturally adaptive or maladaptive.

Because the individualistic perspective represents the major historical approach to deriving meaning in clinical contexts, this discussion represents more than a thumbnail philosophical sketch. The problem of deriving meaning becomes particularly salient in any discussion of family therapy, given its status as one of the newest approaches to clinical intervention. In particular, the functional family model of intervention approaches issues associated with the *meaning* of behavior from a dramatically different perspective and utilizes different sources of data from traditional models. *For the functional family therapist the meaning of behavior is derived from appreciation and examination of relational contexts.* In adopting a relational perspective, the functional family model arrives at a different definition of meaning, this difference depending on whether or not the observer takes an individual or a relational phenomenon as a focus of interest. The functional family model proposes that the meaning of an individual's behavior is best derived from an examination of the relational process in which it is embedded, as well as the relational outcomes

that the behavior functionally elicits from others. The functional family model also implicitly legitimizes many forms of behavior which cultural traditions might mandate should be changed merely because they are "bad." The model makes the assumption that *all* behavior is adaptive in terms of its functional relationship properties; i.e., behavior is not inherently good or bad, or even normal or sick. Instead, behavior is a vehicle for both creating and deriving specific outcomes from interpersonal relationships.

The functional family model requires that the clinical practitioner adopt a relatively novel conceptual set and maintain a relatively unique set of assumptions about human behavior. This chapter will describe in greater detail how these fundamental assumptions have been incorporated into a functional family model of intervention. The chapter will describe how assessment is fundamentally an enterprise of deriving meaning by conceptually creating a relational context for behavior, and how the enterprise of assigning meaning to behavior requires understanding of this context by the therapist. This chapter will also describe how the functional family therapist intervenes or creates change by manipulation of the meaning of behavior within the interpersonal context of the family. The chapter will illustrate those supplementary and nontraditional aspects of the functional family conceptual model that lead therapists toward a framework which allows them to assign meaning to behavior. These conceptual aspects of the model will then be illustrated with data and clinical examples which relate the concepts to family life and intervention. A reappraisal of meaning for both therapists and, more importantly, family members will be portrayed as a necessary prerequisite for change.

THE MEANING OF BEHAVIOR IN THE FAMILY

One of the functional family model's first conceptual departures from traditional models is that of the characterization of behavior. In traditional individualistic models, a single behavior can be presumed to be meaningful in and of itself. A single behavior is taken as a "sign" (Meehl, 1965) of some internally mediated or generated event. For the classic personality theorist, the act of smoking can be taken in and of itself to represent the expression of some internal dynamic such as oral fixations. For the individually-oriented behaviorist, the act may reflect a presumed learning, wherein the smoker has actively or passively developed some associations between the act and internal consequences. In either of these instances, the individually-oriented practitioner assumes that the assessment and treatment of meaning of the behavior can be derived by generalizing from one reliably occurring discrete act of an individual. The individual model therefore presumes that the salient initial causes and consequences of the behavior reside within an individual, and that the behavior truly represents individually-oriented and derived purposiveness.

By contrast, the functional family model proposes that the acts of an individual are meaningless by themselves. Any individual's expressions of behavior must be conceptually integrated with the behavior of others into both "a *series* of actions directed to some end," at the same time that the individual is in "the state of being submitted to a continuing action or series of actions" (Urdang and Flexner, 1972).

The functional family model asserts that people simultaneously *create* an interpersonal environment and *respond to* that environment. In this sense, people direct their actions toward some end at the same time that their actions are being mediated by those of other people or other elements of the environment. People's behavior can be likened to a conditional probability phenomenon: A person can desire something from another person, but must behave in ways which are consistent with the likelihood of the other person's giving it to them. While people initiate forms of behavior, they do so in an environment which places constraints on its form. *The question of whether the person or the environment generates the form of behavior is meaningless, since both the person and the environment reciprocally create forms of behavior.* Kicking a stereo will not turn it on, but flipping an ON switch will, just as asking a boss for a raise might be more effective than demanding one.

The functional family model assumes that processes occur in circular and reciprocal ways, *and an occurrence of a relational context creates the meaning of any behavior, not an individual focus.* The important conceptual shift to recognize is that, for traditional individual models, the discrete occurrence of an individual behavior has typically derived or forced meaning from some cause-effect principle internal to the individual. By contrast, the functional family model has adopted a circular model of causes and effects identified by the interaction processes occurring between people which create relational contexts. The functional family therapist makes the assumption that behavior is relevant or assumes meaning only insofar as it is related to other behavior in an interpersonal field. This necessarily means that the functional family therapist must use a broader focus in looking at the temporal frame in which behavior occurs and also relate more than one person to the behavior. Interactive processes then become the major unit of analysis, and are useful only insofar as the functional family observer is able to identify the behavior of others and the sequential patterns or regularities in the ways that the behavior of others interacts with the behavior(s) of interest. This necessarily implies that, to generate meaning from behavior, the functional family therapist must be able to identify interactional regularities in behavior.

The Family as a Context for Interpersonal Process

The functional family model has targeted the nuclear family as the optimal context for evaluating important regularities in interpersonal behavior process. It is clear from sociological studies that the nuclear family is the interpersonal environment where children and adolescents spend their most contact time, and that members of the nuclear family are spending more time together than ever before (Risley, Clark, and Cataldo, 1976). It is, therefore, unsurprising that studies of family life have shown strong arguments for the family as an arena for identifying regularities in family process.

One well-researched approach to understanding and identifying meaningful regularities in behavioral processes is represented in behavioral studies of the family. Behaviorists have typically examined rates of overt behaviors in family settings. They have found that parents' and children's rates of prosocial and antisocial behavior are related (Patterson, 1976), and that these rates of sequential emission of behavior can be related to either parental consequences or antecedents (Patterson, 1974) of behavior. Similarly, children's behavior is positively correlated with that of adults, both in terms of antecedents (Patterson and Cobb, 1972) and consequences (Martin, 1967). Married partners also show patterns of behavior exchange related to both antecedents and consequences (Patterson, Weiss, and Hops, 1975; Weiss, Hops, and Patterson, 1973).

Other researchers have examined regularities in family processes of verbal exchange. They have identified significant familial correlations between structural properties of speech, such as talk time, silences, and interruptions (Haley, 1967; Murrell and Stachowiak, 1967; Stabeneau, Tupin, Werner, and Pollin, 1965). Researchers have also identified regularities between family members in certain forms of speech, such as "pleases and displeases" (Weiss, Hops, and Patterson, 1973), passive and active verbal expressions of dominance (Safilios-Rothschild, 1970), or defensiveness and supportiveness (Alexander, 1973).

The results from this body of research show that families do appear to have some regularities in family processes and, more importantly, that these processes distinguish between certain types of families. For example, it would appear that nondistressed families can be distinguished from families of schizophrenics by more equivalently distributed talk time, and by more direct and clear qualitative properties of speech (Mishler and Waxler, 1965). In a similar vein, Alexander (1973) has found that analyses of family processes distinguish adaptive adolescent families from those of juvenile delinquents. It was found that adaptive families have a more egalitarian distribution of talk time, and that the most pronounced relatedness or correlated communication (i.e., process) between members of adaptive families was "supportive" in nature. Supportive communications are those which promote the integrity of an interpersonal system, and are presumed to function to maintain a social system focus as an effective problem-solving unit (Alexander, 1973; Gibb, 1961). By contrast, families of delinquents were found to have a less egalitarian distribution of talk time, and these families reflected interpersonal processes or correlated interpersonal communications which were primarily "defensive" in nature. Defensive communications function as systems-disintegrating types of messages, because they preclude effective task focus and unit problem-solving.[4] From these data it is clear that a *process* evaluation of behavior suggests several critical features of delinquent behavior. First, delinquent behavior is related to a set of processes which are qualitatively different from processes of normal families. It is the case that in both delinquent and normal families regularities in behavior occur, but considerations of the characteristics of the defensive-supportive dependent variables argue that these processes are different for the different family types. Adaptive adolescent families engage in processes which promote interpersonal system integrity, while the families of delinquents engage in processes which can be ultimately system-disintegrating.

In evaluating families as a context, then, two useful conceptual characteristics of families and processes can be identified, or lead to clearer understanding of the meaning of behavior. First, regular patterns of exchange do occur in families. No matter what the form of their dependent variables, researchers have consistently identified ritualized patterns of exchange of behavior or messages among members of families. These strong and consistent demonstrations are compelling arguments for perceiving the family as a context in which the relatedness of family members is most evident. These data

---

[4]*Editors' Note.* In a personal communication to us (Barton, 1979), the senior author wrote that, "Defensiveness *isn't really* an internal event to reduce anxiety in the analytic sense. From Gibb (1961), it's more as though for most people, most of the time, defensive communications are defensiveness-producing, and their central characteristic is taking people out of the mainstream of group communication." This was written in response to our earlier correspondence with Barton and Alexander in which we raised the issue of whether defensive communications follow from *internal* events that are anxiety-reducing, i.e., whether defensive *inter*personal behavior is caused by *intra*personal defensive mechanisms, with such defensive behavior, of course, being negatively reinforcing. While we agree that defensive communications by one person may lead others to reciprocate such behavior, we believe that the intrapersonal function of defensive behavior should not be passed over in clinical work with families.

would also argue that the occurrence of certain forms of behavior is typically embedded within a process context or backdrop of similar forms of behavior; forms of behavior seem to occur with like forms of behavior.

This assertion illustrates yet another point, that while all types of families seem to show similar patternings or processes of exchange, the form of behavior embedded in these regularities is much different. This *form* is typically the focus of intervention for family therapists, though families often seem reluctant to change it (Barton and Alexander, 1976). Therapists oftentimes make the assumption that just as there are "ideal forms of mental health" for individuals, there are "ideal forms of process" for people to perform. This presumption reflects the idea that there is a skill which produces the "right" way for all people to communicate, and attainment of this skill is a sufficient condition for change.

This set of assumptions overlooks a critical functional family model consideration about the nature of process, that consideration being that characteristic processes lead to certain ends or purposes. While processes do occur lawfully in families, the discrete and momentary links between units of behavior in processes are less critical than what they *lead* to. To better understand the processes themselves, the functional family model considers the *function* of behavior processes in the family context.

Conceptual Characteristics of the Function of Behavior

To the functional family therapist, the most critical feature of behavior is the relationship outcome that it produces. It is presumed that behavior is embedded within regular patterns of interaction, and that these processes produce certain outcomes. It is the case, however, that different processes can produce similar outcomes. For example, certain forms of either verbal or physical exchange which are seductive may both lead to a couple being "close"; similarly, forms of either verbal or physical abuse may both lead to a couple being "distant." Conversely, *the notion of "ideal forms of process" is rejected by the functional family model as insufficient for understanding the meaning of behavior, since the "same" process form could produce two entirely different outcomes.* All too often observers make the assumption that behavior is "ideal," "healthy," or "appropriate" based on their subjective reaction to an observed process. An observer might decide that the most relevant dimension of an interaction might be its technical competence, or its "fair" form of reciprocity. Nonetheless, technical competence and its reciprocal exchange do not always imply the same things about relationship. In contrasting "idealized" exchanges, a couple can clearly, briefly, honestly, and actively listen to each other describe a need for more time together (closeness) or negotiate separate vacations (distance). While interpersonal processes are a focus of interest for the functional family model, the relational or functional outcome represents "the purpose for which (processes) exist" (Urdang and Flexner, 1972). The communality or consistency of behavior in relationships cannot be derived from the disparate forms of processes that family members perform, but must rather be inferred from the relatively consistent functions or outcomes that processes produce.

Because of the lengthy temporal span over which behavioral processes occur, people are often not aware of how they achieve their functions, given the inherent complexity of the processes through which they attain them. For example, if a seven-year-old child who is practiced in reading is given the words "cow-grass-ate-the-the" and told to integrate them into a sentence that has meaning, he or she will probably be able to generate, "The cow ate the grass." If, however, that same child is asked to articulate the process by which he or she attained the functional outcome of the meaningful sentence, he or she would probably be unable to do so. As a first principle, then, the functional family therapist would argue that *people do not have to be able to articulate a general rule or appreciation of the complexity of their behavior to attain functional outcomes.* People can predictably and reliably attain functional outcomes without any understanding of how or why they produce them.

Lack of awareness of functions can also lead people or observers to interpret their world in light of potentially misleading cause-effect models. A wife may report that she has internal "needs" which cause her to talk to her husband in certain ways: If the outcome of her talking to her husband is that he leaves the house for the evening, the functional family therapist would argue that the salient feature of her behavior is that of creating relational distance, which may or may not be consistent with the verbalized need. Similarly, people may ascribe external causes for the behavior: The husband of this same wife might argue that he wouldn't mind talking to his wife if she were "reasonable," but her "emotionality" or "hassling" causes him to leave. In either of these instances, the "causes" are less relevant than the relational function of interpersonal distance between the spouses. "Curing" the husband to be responsive to his wife's "need" by "curing" the "hassling" so the husband can be responsive to her need implicitly accepts the legitimacy of discrete causes and effects, rather than the relational or functional purposiveness toward which both husband's and wife's behavior is directed.

If sequences or processes characteristically lead to consistent types of relational outcomes, then the functional family therapist assumes that people, in essence, produce the most desirable relational outcomes they can at that point in time. The functional family model makes the assumption that "causes" may explain the form of a process, but the significance of these explanations pales in comparison to the critical issue of the purposiveness of the process. The functional family model asserts that if processes are conceptually punctuated at their ending,[5] the nature of the relational function will be evident. This purposeful outcome is evaluated as the true determinant or function for which behavior is performed.

Earlier it was discussed how families can be characterized as an arena in which different processes occur which discriminate between different types of families. The relatedness of behavior forms the links between members of a family, or their *relationships*. These relationships or processes produce functional outcomes which are various forms of *intimacy* or *distance*.

Table 1 illustrates behaviors which produce rather reliable outcomes along a continuum from intimacy to distance. In addition, there is a middle region which represents a *regulation* function. The *regulator* function elicits both intimacy and distance: Some people engage in processes which elicit both distance and intimacy, which serves as a powerful vehicle to maintain others at some sort of optimal relational range. For the functional family therapist to make use of this scheme, each behavior should be indexed by some arbitrary unit which represents frequency and/or intensity of the *functions produced* by family processes. The therapist should note the relative frequency of intimacy

---

[5]We recognize that we are suggesting an *arbitrary* punctuation point as the end of processes. Decisions about when a meaningful end point occurs depend, of course, on the observer's phenomena of interest. If an observer were studying aggression, a process might be ended at termination of a fight, however operationally defined. Functional family therapists typically define end points by some recognizable manifestation of interpersonal distance or intimacy. The assessment portions to follow describe clinical decision-making procedures about end-point punctuation in more detail.

TABLE 1

Behaviors That Typically Produce Functional Outcomes of Intimacy and Distance

DISTANCE OR "GO AWAY" BEHAVIOR	REGULATION	INTIMACY OR "COME HERE" BEHAVIOR
Reading	Being polite but reserved	Taking care of baby
Listening to loud music	Taking someone to a movie	Sex
Parent working two jobs		Asking for help
Teen goes to college	Raising a child in the middle years	Communicating feelings
Teen gets driver's license	Maintaining a relationship with children by attending their sports functions, music recitals, etc.	
Teen spends time with peers		
Sending kids to camp		
	Double-dating, or only going out with spouse with other friends	

and distance-producing behavior for each family member underneath the column representing his or her purposive *functions*. Dependent on the frequency distribution of these points, the therapist can identify which class of interpersonal *function* is created and maintained by a given family member's behavior.

Therapists must take the frequency distribution into account in two ways. First, therapists should consider the distribution to be a rough "reliability index." People emit a qualitatively disparate range of behavior. Therapists can only have confidence in the validity of their assumption that a person is a "distancer," for example, if it would appear that there are several behaviors that represent distance, and if the majority of a person's behavior represents distance. Second, therapists must have an appreciation of the "range" and "algebraic mean" of arbitrary values assigned to intimacy and distance. If a person characteristically represents four behaviors which are distancing and four which produce intimacy, then the distribution of the behaviors and their qualitatively different algebraic sum would argue that the person may be an interpersonal "regulator." The examples provided in the table are arbitrary, but represent functions characteristically produced by these types of people in family roles; e.g., "active" fathers, who belong to the Jaycees, a bowling league, are active in church volunteer activity, and work two jobs physically and stylistically promote interpersonal distance; young children often elicit involvement from others by behavior such as crying or requests which require nurturance; a parent teaching a child to pursue some independent activity produces a blend of intimacy and distance with the child (and the relative proximity to the o,o point on the axes represents the intensity or amount of a family member's behavior which leads to his or her classification). Again, these functions must be inferred from what is *produced* by interaction processes.

An appraisal of family life shows that, over the temporal course of marriage, childbirth, and child-rearing relationships, both the form of processes and their purposive outcomes differ greatly. Morton, Alexander, and Altman (1976) have characterized family members as elements of a social unit, linked by communication processes, with several developmental epochs which lead to either interpersonal intimacy or distance. These communication processes are the vehicle through which family members structure and maintain their relationships, as well as regulating the degree of intimacy or distance between them. Intimacy and distance are necessary correlates of any aspect of human interpersonal exchange (Altman and Taylor, 1973; Jourard, 1964; Malouf, 1974).

The creation of a nuclear family typically begins when two partners engage in communication or behavior exchange, reciprocate physical endearments, talk about personal preferences, and engage in other ritualized courting behavior. The exchange of these behaviors creates a reciprocal process which typically produces a movement towards interpersonal *intimacy* or "a close, familiar, and usually affectionate or loving, personal relationship" (Morton, Alexander, and Altman, 1976, p. 125).

The birth of the first (and subsequent) children usually brings about a plethora of changes in both processes and functional outcomes in the living unit of the family. First, the birth of an infant requires a major redistribution of interpersonal resources and reallocation of process time within the home. Parents are bound to nurture, protect and support the extraordinarily "needy" new member—which optimally functions to create intimacy between parents and child (see Table 1). In so doing, spouses must accommodate changes in the relationship between them. A spouse returning home from work, for example, may find that she does not have claims on her partner's time "to discuss how the day went," given his involvement in changing a soiled diaper and warming a bottle. This representative process serves to create intimacy between father and child, at the same time that it can produce distance between spouses during this developmental phase of the family. Parents are, therefore, confronted with the processes of accommodating fewer opportunities for their own intimacy (as a colicky baby interrupts a quiet evening in front of the fire), at the same time that an infant places demands on them for intimacy of its own (which in many cases proscribes husband-wife distance). When confronted with intimacy bids from both a child and a spouse, people typically find it necessary to establish boundaries on their willingness or ability to meet everyone's intimacy needs. In short, the integration of a new family member is typically an extremely demanding time for families. In the instance of a second child, the complexity increases as parents conventionally must contend with jealousy or sibling rivalry issues between their children as well as deal with yet another set of demands or compromises on their own relationship time as husband and wife.

Parents can expect to exercise a greater degree of autonomy than their children in terms of their relationship definition with them during stages of child development from toilet-training to the onset of adolescence. Parents can typically enjoy this somewhat luxurious degree of interpersonal control of interpersonal processes, since they are in the position of controlling most tangible as well as relational vehicles of interpersonal control, i.e., they can mediate distribution of toys and cookies as well as bedtimes and "how you talk to your parents." Parents can opt for going on a picnic as a family or hiring a babysitter while they go to dinner as a means of regulating familial intimacy. Depending on how involved with their less demanding children they choose to be, parents may also find it easier to exercise options around their bids for intimacy with their spouses ("Let's put the kids to bed early") or, conversely, use some involvement with the children as a vehicle to create distance ("We can't go out tonight—I couldn't get a sitter I trust"). The post-toilet-training years can be a time when parents are in a relational position of relative process autonomy and control, both of their children's and their own relational forms and degree of intimacy-distance.

The adolescent years are typically a more difficult relationship time for the nuclear family (Coles, Alexander, and Schiavo, 1974; Rice, 1975). The salience of the intrafamilial environment becomes less and less potent as the emerging adolescent becomes increasingly peer-oriented. Parents are confronted with the task of accommodating adolescents' culturally mandated bids for autonomy and independence (interpersonal distance) in order to prepare for their children's role as adaptive, independent adults. Parents can be understandably confused when their early child-rearing models of relationship definition or influence (in which they are perceived as benevolent dictators of child behavior) are rejected by the adolescent. Parents must learn to accommodate a more "adult-like" relationship structure with their children, as well as accept more interpersonal distance as their children begin to perform much of their intimate interpersonal exchange with peers. While adolescence represents a novel phenomenon in terms of major restructuring of a previously established set of relationships, it also portends a major structural change which has widespread impact on the familial unit.

The adaptive structural and relational aspects of adolescence should be characterized as a family "exiting" process. Most adolescents do, in fact, ultimately leave the nuclear family, in terms of relational, physical, and psychological distance. This change can be difficult not only because children and adolescents must restructure their relationships to accommodate this process, but also because this exiting has implications and impact on those who remain at home. Parents must acknowledge yet another change in their roles, as they relinquish the relational time and contact invested as parents and are confronted once again with a primary role as that of spouses. Given that spouses have had to negotiate and maintain a relationship for some 18 years, during which the allocation of relationship time and resources as parents to children has necessarily proscribed some distance between them, they face a series of structural and relationship reorientation issues as the remaining members of the family unit. It can be extremely difficult for parents left at home to redefine a relationship with each other when process bids for intimacy and validation that have been focused on the children must be refocused onto the spouse. This problem can be exacerbated insofar as the initial intimacy bids performed during "courting days" are compromised by diminished personal factors such as physical attractiveness or historical relational factors which have necessarily proscribed interpersonal distance between spouses. In this light, the remaining members of a family are confronted with yet another developmental phase which requires a new set of relationship formation and maintenance issues.

This discussion of differing family processes and functional outcomes therefore asserts the characteristic role of behavior as embedded in both processes which are interdependent (e.g., in the adolescent years parents and children typically "argue" more) and in processes which produce certain typical outcomes (e.g., adolescent distance). Seen in this way, the functional family therapist views family life as the arena in which people enact behavior which produces and maintains functional outcomes of interpersonal intimacy or distance.

This discussion of the Morton, Alexander, and Altman (1976) view of family life suggests that there are many differing epochs in the developmental history of families where the functional outcomes of family processes are necessarily much different. This is not to say that people have needs for these differing functions "wired in," or that people have an appreciation of these needs beforehand and operate instrumentally to obtain them. Instead, *the functional family model asserts that most people do not have adequate appreciation of the complexity and temporal span of processes. The lack of appreciation of the outcomes that these processes produce leads to a lack of understanding of the meaning of behavior.*

Summary: Family Interaction as a Vehicle for the Functional Family Model to Assign Meaning to Behavior

This portion of the chapter is designed to give the reader an appreciation of how the functional family model derives meaning from human behavior. For the most part, there are formal conceptual aspects of this enterprise which represent major departures from more traditional paradigms or models of human behavior. In general, the functional family model argues that behavior must be understood on a *post hoc* (or end result) basis. This end result or function is manifested by the interactive processes between family members. The purpose of a given behavior is inferred from the relational outcome it produces, and the form and occurrence of the behavior are governed by the process in which the behavior is embedded. Hence, functional family therapists must develop two parallel appreciations of behavior. Consistent with behavioral

principles, functional family therapists acknowledge that the given form of a behavior or the contingencies surrounding its occurrence are mediated by certain aspects of the interpersonal field. As a departure from the behavioral position, however, the functional family model posits that interactants bring volitional properties with them into the interactional setting.[6] While the *form* of distancing may be mediated by the interpersonal field (a teenager who doesn't have access to a car for leaving the house might sequester herself in her room), the *volition to distance* is related to some purposeful developmental aspects of adolescence.

The descriptions of nuclear family life are included to both exemplify the conceptual departures from individual models and highlight the importance of the family as an arena of human function. Families are the most important context in which the behavior of individuals can be understood, as the people in them are the most salient determinants of the processes and outcomes for an individual. Families are the most constant set of behavioral exchange in any one person's life, and our culture has proscribed a set of constraints (such as divorce laws and legal proscriptions of parent-spouse roles) that make this exchange even more potent. Finally, no one can escape the most basic and fundamental properties of our existence: Each person is the product of two other people.

The following portions of the chapter will extend the implications of the conceptual bases of the functional family model and translate them into clinical practices. The conceptual implications of the model will be clarified and amplified by example and application.

ASSESSMENT FORMULATIONS IN THE FUNCTIONAL FAMILY MODEL

Before considering how families are assessed, it is necessary to describe how the functional family model valences behavior, or the decision rules about what constitutes "problem" behav-

[6]*Editors' Note.* Indeed, we think the authors understate the magnitude of this difference from the behavioral position by referring to it as merely a "departure," when, in fact, it is a *radical challenge* of the sufficiency of traditional behavioral thinking about interpersonal behavior.

ior. Definitions of *symptoms* are worth considering because of the relatively different corollary implications they contain. To be most consistent with traditional diagnosis, a symptom would be defined as a manifestation of internal disorder or sickness. The disorder itself is presumably hidden inside the individual, and the outward manifestations are presumably wrong, sick, evil, or in error because they are representations of some disease process. A symptom behavior is isolated from a field of other behavior and is taken as wrong, sick, or in error in its own right.

By contrast, symptoms can be defined as a "sign" or "indicator" (Urdang and Flexner, 1972). The functional family therapist would say, "Symptoms are a sign or indication of inefficient but functional interpersonal processes." The functional family therapist makes the assumption that the original valencing of a given behavior as symptomatic is done by a person who has some sanctions, power, authority, or interpersonal whatever to do so (Framo, 1972). Most family therapy referrals are made by a parent, court, school system, mental health center, or other socially mandated institution of power which has the authority to identify and label a behavior as a problem (though this is not to suggest therapists might not create their own referrals in similar ways). Rather than accept these relatively value-laden and subjective criterion of abnormality as valid, the functional family therapist assumes that problem behavior may constitute an inefficient process adaptation serving a *legitimate function*. This is much different from accepting a problem or symptom as representing sickness. The functional family therapist looks for how this problem behavior is: 1) mediated by interpersonal processes with other family members; and 2) serving some interpersonal function (i.e., distance or intimacy).

This representation of symptomatic behavior is supported by some corollary assumptions or interpretations of behavior. Communication theorists (Haley, 1963; Watzlawick, Beavin, and Jackson, 1967; Watzlawick, Weakland, and Fisch, 1974) assert that behavior, as represented in the process of interpersonal exchange, is a statement about the properties of a relationship at the same time that it defines a relationship. Perceived in this way, behavior as communication is a vehicle of interpersonal control, e.g., a person may *ask* for something or might *demand* it. The outcomes for the person must be evaluated at both the process and functional levels. Being demanding might both produce a tangible reward and promote interpersonal intimacy, or demanding something that one is not likely to get could create disappointment as a vehicle for interpersonal distance. Behavior is presumed to occur in relation to its probability of being responded to in ways which create predictable processes and which typically create certain types of functional outcomes in relationships.

When investigating family processes, several researchers have documented how processes of exchange are topographically different vehicles of control, but appear to be reliable vehicles of control nonetheless. Patterson and Reid (1967) have shown that parents of normal children seem to emit positive reinforcement for desired behavior, and their children seem to respond to these. These prosocial children can be said to generate positive reinforcement from their parents by behaving in desired ways. Families of "acting-out" or disturbed children, on the other hand, seem to be characterized by a different strategy. Parents respond more to "problem" behavior, and their children seem to get what they want by making a situation so aversive their parents "give in" to escape the unpleasant situation. Thus, Patterson and Cobb (1972) have shown that both aggressive and normal children receive attention, but in different ways. The aggressive child elicits attention when aggressive, while the normal child seems to elicit attention by behaving in desirable ways. As discussed earlier, Alexander (1973) has shown that family members in delinquent families engage each other in defensive ways, while members in normal families engage each other in supportive ways.

These studies support a general argument that problematic family behavior is associated with certain forms of family process. Alexander (Alexander and Barton, 1976; Parsons and Alexander, 1973) has discussed this feature of differences in behavior within a matching-to-sample philosophy. This philosophy asserts that there is not necessarily a theoretically-derived ideal form of family process, but rather that remediating family problems might best be accomplished by helping disturbed families attain the same patterns of family interaction that are characteristic of nondistressed families.[7]

In this light, differences in family processes are not ascribed to sickness or faulty learning, but rather represent the rules for interpersonal exchange that family members perform to meet their interpersonal functions or payoffs. The Patterson and Cobb (1972) data perhaps illuminate this concept best by showing that the behavior of *both* aggressive and normal younger children elicits attention (i.e., interpersonal intimacy or contact), though the interpersonal rules in their family environments require different means of attaining this outcome. By contrast, it could be argued that delinquent adolescents act out to obtain interpersonal autonomy or distance by nature of their rebellious offenses (Nye, 1958) and by nature of the autonomy or distance they often negotiate in remedial programs (Emery and Marholin, 1977).

Further, the data would argue that problematic forms of behavior do not represent a simple lack of understanding regarding what constitutes acceptable behavior. Delinquent adolescents know what prosocial behavior is expected of them; at the same time they acknowledge pessimism about their ability to negotiate directly for what they want in their families (Cheek, 1966). Jurkovic and Prentice (1974) have shown that scores on a Moral Development Scale do not distinguish delinquents from their normal peers, while family communication does.

The functional family therapist therefore assumes that problem behavior is the only way that some interpersonal functions can be met. Some family interpersonal rules engender interpersonal processes which preclude overt and direct means of communication as a suitable means for obtaining some interpersonal outcomes or functions. These difficulties can arise

in several ways. Our culture and popularized psychology create many stereotypes or expectations which influence behavior, and in the interests of psychological parsimony these are typically represented as idealized personal traits (Shaver, 1975). One set of such idealized traits is that people should work toward sharing, openness, directness, love, and other behaviors that we might describe as psychological intimacy. Rarely does our popularized or even formal psychology deal with the equivalence of interpersonal distance as a legitimate function of behavior. These stereotypes can create relational difficulties in both process and functional domains. An example of a disruptive process that is all too typical in family life might be when the child becomes an adolescent. When children are younger, both parents' and children's processes have a stylistic representation ("Son, come here so I can tie your shoes"; "Mom, can I have a quarter for some candy?") that engenders a "parents in charge" relational process, which at the same time promotes an adaptive interpersonal intimacy: The troublesome issue can occur when the child seeks to assert more autonomy or distance as an adolescent. If this change in interpersonal process cannot be directly communicated and obtained ("Mother, please, I'd rather do it myself"), then running away might serve the same function. If parents cannot recognize the adaptive properties of this shift in their child's functional outcomes, changes in process (like challenging authority) can be bewildering and ascribed to the process alone, if not the person ("He knows everything since he's 14"; "We can't talk for five minutes without getting into an argument").

Similarly, there can be "shoulds" attached to functions as well. Private or autonomous people might get bludgeoned by their Esalened or EST'ed friends to be more open, caring, trusting, or intimate with others. Males do not typically get substantial social-emotional types of training in this culture, but are rather charged by their parents and culture to be task-oriented problem-solvers (O'Neill and Alexander, 1974). These males can be extraordinarily threatened by situations in which their task-oriented problem-solving attempts do not function to promote popularized or idealized forms of intimacy, but can, in essence, produce "distance." Their at-

---

[7]*Editors' Note.* We view this matching-to-sample philosophy as being inconsistent with Barton and Alexander's clear (and to us, appropriate) emphasis on the importance of the *meaning* of (overt) behavior in interpersonal contexts. That is, the "same," i.e., "matching," behavior can have different functions and meanings for different families. That is, it is not the case (as implied by the matching philosophy, but decried earlier by Barton and Alexander) that behavior is behavior is behavior (cf. Gurman and Knudson, 1978; Gurman et al., 1978). Thus, it is conceivable to us that a change in behavior *may*, in the literal sense, be meaningless.

tempts to be task-oriented or problem-solve out of a threatening situation (or to promote distance) predictably lead to increased bids for intimacy from those seeking it from them. This leads to an escalating disruptive process where task-oriented process leads to increased bids for intimacy, countered with more task-oriented process, and so on.

These two examples also implicitly indict value-laden interpretations of either processes or functions of behavior. The functional family therapist is trained to accept the legitimacy of interpersonal functions as outcomes of behavior. Given that these functions can be seen as purposive and adaptive maintainers of behavior, they are not viewed as targets of change, though the form of the behavior might be. The functional family model takes a more sympathetic view of disruptive processes than most traditional "criterion mental health" models. Processes are evaluated on criteria of efficiency, rather than on how "healthy" they are. It is assumed that processes are very purposive in nature and represent the best presently available means to attain interpersonal functions or outcomes. Stated more concretely, people with little overt interpersonal potency may have to be somewhat covert or coercive to achieve their ends because their interpersonal environment does not respond to their being otherwise. The acting-out child may be ignored when quietly engaged in creative play (Hawkins, Peterson, Schweid, and Bijou, 1966), or the independence-seeking adolescent may get messages that he/she is not "capable enough" when looking for a job. Acting-out or running away are, therefore, seen as inefficient, but nevertheless effective, means of achieving intimacy or distance, respectively.

Occasionally, people may overtly request a change in interpersonal functions. The most common clinical example occurs when a marital partner requests more "intimacy" or "closeness." As a general *caveat*, functional family therapists are advised to attend more to what people *do* than to what they *say* they want. In this example, the functional family model would assume that if a wife or husband actually wanted the functional outcome of closeness, he/she would have arrived at an interpersonal process to obtain it. This process may or may not be symptomatic. As a clinical issue (discussed in

subsequent sections of the chapter), people's requests for changes in functions are commonly inconsistent with objective evaluations of their behavior. In some instances, people achieve closeness that goes unrecognized. In other instances, spouses may verbalize that they want closeness, and yet their behavior reliably promotes distance. The functional family therapist is trained to deal with either of these situations. The functional family therapist must nonetheless assume that the course of observation of families in assessment and treatment will show what family members *really* want (opposed to what they might verbalize), as revealed by an objective evaluation of the functional outcomes that are reliably produced.[8]

In summary, the functional family therapist approaches symptoms with a different conceptual and value framework than traditional models. The meaning of symptoms is consistent with an end result interpretation of the interpersonal functions (intimacy or distance) that they produce. Processes are seen as the powerful constraints and maintainers of the particular forms that behavior takes, and symptoms are unique only insofar as they are inefficient or are indicted and labeled problematic by some type of powerful cultural mandate (Framo, 1972). The functional family therapist is trained to assume that interpersonal functions are extremely powerful, and will not be changed solely by external controls. Rather, given that these functions are so pervasive and potent, the therapist must identify how and what problem behaviors or processes lead to the particular functions of each family participant and change these procedures and the environmental response to them. In this

---

[8]*Editors' Note.* First, in our experience, people overtly request changes in interpersonal functions such as intimacy a great deal more often than "occasionally." More important, it may be clinically quite limiting to assume *as a rule*, as Barton and Alexander suggest, that people get the relationships they "really" want, or, in particular, that therapists can determine what patients "really" want based on their behavior alone. That is, when seeing couples who say they want to be "closer," but who have been unable to produce this outcome on their own, many therapists assume that the partner(s) are *ambivalent* about such an outcome (e.g., Sager, Chapter 3) and/or that they lack the interpersonal skills (e.g., Jacobson, Chapter 15) to achieve it. That is, the lack of concordance between a person's behavior and his/her stated desires might be considered usefully in terms of the forces both within and between people that are outside their current awareness *and* in terms of skills that need to be learned.

way, functions can remain as legitimate, but inefficient ways to attain them may be replaced with more efficient or less painful ones.

The Functional Family Conceptual Framework as Translated into an Assessment Scheme

Simply stated, functional family therapists must determine both the amount and kind of information contained in the family which will allow them to assign meaning to behavior. Making abstract concepts useful and translatable into family behavior change requires functional family therapists to structurally create and organize three separate but related conceptual levels (Barton and Alexander, 1977b). First, therapists are asked to evaluate and appraise a *relationship* level of family functioning, wherein the therapist examines the patterns and processes represented by the interdependencies of family behavior. Second, the functional family therapist must address the *functional* level, or evaluate how family processes lead to adaptive and legitimate relational functions for each family member. Finally, therapists are required to assess the *individual* elements of the family system, to identify what distinct behavioral, emotional, or cognitive change should be structured and maintained for each member in order to change particular unwanted behaviors. This prioritizing and inclusiveness reflect the model's assumption about the necessary information for effectively performing family therapy. Functional family therapists must understand how the behavior change of an *individual* must be created and maintained while embedded within the powerful processes of family *relationships*, and how these behavior or other changes will consistently meet each family member's outcomes or *functions*. The model posits that therapists working with families are most effectively guided when they develop an appreciation of what levels of analysis are crucial for assessing families and implementing change. Each step is a necessary but not sufficient condition for developing a complete picture of the family.

Relationships

Therapists begin assessment by organizing family members' representations of family life or overt behavior into relatively reliable or lawful sequences within the family. As a first principle, the therapist must collect or generate information which assumes meaning because it seems to portray relatively consistent processes. The therapist needs to be active in generating this information, since family members characteristically portray themselves and others in isolation.

Identifying reliable and meaningful sequences is not complete until therapists understand how everyone in the family is involved in the sequence. When information on behavioral sequences is difficult to obtain, therapists can assess the more "structural" properties of processes by finding out who agrees with whom cognitively or emotionally, who's "left out" of interactions, who initiates with whom, who is the "peacemaker," etc. Therapists can also evaluate the topographical components of a characteristic process or sequence by identifying meaningful contingencies or interdependencies which influence the form and intensity of family members' stylistic behavior, affect, or attitudes. The therapist can identify relevant discrepancies that mediate problematic sequences, such as dad's desire for son to "stand on his own two feet and be a man" while mom wishes to "keep her little boy," or son's arguing making dad feel "proud" while mom feels "sad and angry." The crucial features of an evaluation of interpersonal relationships are for the functional family therapist to be able to 1) identify in what ways everyone in the family is linked to each other; and 2) identify relative reliable or regular occurrences of sequences or processes to establish their ritual-like flavor.

Functions

Having established the ritual-like properties of family relationships, the therapist then asks the post hoc question of what *functional* payoffs are involved for each family member, or, "Where is everyone when the dust settles?" (Barton and Alexander, 1977a). For the functional family therapist, these functional payoffs or outcomes are conceptualized in interpersonal terms of intimacy, distance, or a "back and forth" blend of the two. For example, mom and daughter fight right after school—daughter leaves the house angry—mom begins to cry—when dad comes home at six, mom cries some more and tells dad he must "do something"—dad calls daughter's girlfriends and finally finds daughter at midnight at a girlfriend's house. A post hoc interpretation of this sequence suggests that fighting with mom served as an excuse for daughter to exert some developmental adolescent bids for autonomy or independence, creating some interpersonal distance. The fight also served as an excuse for mom to elicit some support from dad, a form of intimacy. For dad the crisis allowed him to initiate some contact or intimacy with his adolescent daughter. The functional family model asserts that these relational functional outcomes, which reflect characteristic developmental aspects of family life, are the critical maintenance factors in "problematic" families.

It is also the case that the functional family therapist accepts these *functional* payoffs as legitimate in their own right, while the behavioral processes which mediate them may be inefficient. The therapist also assumes that these functional outcomes or payoffs must be protected or maintained within the family. Some people's functional payoffs may need to be substituted in both target and form, e.g., a mom who is having her intimacy needs met by nurturing a 19-year-old son may need to be redirected towards "fitting" these needs to her husband. The husband may, in turn, need to accommodate her needs and his own by terminating his extramarital affair, if this affair has been a vehicle for him to obtain intimacy he could not get from his wife. The functional family therapist assumes that these interpersonal functions or payoffs are sufficiently powerful and regularized thematic properties of people's relationship styles that efforts to change behaviors that are inconsistent with these functions will be doomed to failure.[9] It is highly unlikely that

mom and daughter will be willing to relinquish a 4:00 fight ritual if that implies daughter will no longer be able to initiate bids for independence and autonomy or if mom can no longer initiate nurturance and support from her husband.

In this light, behavior change technologies become a problem of "fitting." Rather than make the assumption that it is necessary to change people for optimal family functioning, the therapist assesses how symptoms are embedded within relationships as a vehicle to create interpersonal functions as payoffs. The functional family therapist should "use his/her gut" in some ways to evaluate functions. A therapist should attempt to psychologically place him/herself in the role of a relational recipient of family members' behavior. The therapist can hopefully begin to evaluate what function (either distance or intimacy) is produced by engaging with family members. The therapist might then appreciate firsthand the relational purposiveness created by relationships within the family.

At a very molar level, experience with the functional family model has yielded a few stereotypic family roles which *relatively often* produce certain types of relational outcomes. Table 2 and the discussion below are used to illustrate how the functional family therapist might "type" family members' functions by symptomatic forms of behavior.

In Table 2, there is, again, a continuum from intimacy to distance. Table 2 is read and interpreted in the same ways as Table 1. These examples convey some typical complaints or symptoms of distressed families, and the typical interpersonal function these particular behaviors produce when embedded in distressed family processes. As with the typical family functions portrayed in Table 1, the functions of these behaviors must be inferred from what the behavior actually produces. On the one hand, for example, it would seem that abusive parents would probably produce distance with their children; yet data (Love and Kaswan, 1974) suggest that these children are often extremely dependent and clinging. In this instance, abuse would generate the actual intimacy obtained, rather than interpersonal distance.

It is also the case that the behavior of any one family member may serve different relational functions with two other members. For exam-

---

[9]*Editors' Note.* Later in this chapter, Barton and Alexander take the unambiguous position that these functions "are such powerful purposive outcomes of behavior and process that *therapeutic goals should not include changing them*" (emphasis added). We have already noted (Note 8) that couples and families often want to change such functions. In addition, it strikes us as inappropriately limiting to assume that a therapist's efforts to do so, when not explicitly requested by the family/couple, are "doomed to failure." Indeed, some models of family pathology, interaction and therapy are based, in effect, on the premise that to change the emotional functions of behavior within the family is the *primary* task of the therapist (see, e.g., Skynner, Chapter 2; Sager, Chapter 3; Whitaker and Keith, Chapter 6).

TABLE 2

Examples of Symptomatic Behaviors That Typically Produce Interpersonal Functions

DISTANCE	REGULATION	INTIMACY
Extramarital affairs	Psychosis	Mild depression
Obsessive-compulsive	Hysteria	Incompetence
"Castrating" people	Flirtatious manipulation	Leaving drugs around to "get caught"
Frigidity, impotence	"Material provider" who's insensitive to emotional needs	Suicide gesturing
Psychopathy		Nightmares
	Agitated depression	Psychosomaticizing
		Worrier, being solicitous
		Dependency

ple, mom's fight with daughter may promote distance between them, at the same time that the fights elicit support or intimacy from father to mom. In considering any one person's behavior, the functional family therapist must conceptualize the grid schema in terms of the other people relevant to the interaction sequence. Daughter's acting-out might engender support from mom at the same time that it makes dad feel helpless and angry, which contributes to his drinking. In this case, daughter's acting-out serves to elicit intimacy from mom at the same time that it elicits distance from dad.

The functional family therapist, therefore, uses a schema of this sort, mainly as a tool to help organize information which allows him/her to "type" the family system's functions. This typing helps the therapist identify the inherently complex array of functions served through ongoing family processes, and guides the therapist to an appreciation of what functions maintain each family member's behavior.

Individual assessment

Given that the functional family therapist has been able to organize behavior into processes which produce outcomes, it still behooves him/her to evaluate the stylistic strengths and weaknesses of family members. Before implementing treatment or behavioral intervention, therapists are cautioned to consider the possible constraints individual family members pose to implementing treatment.

For example, a typically distant and uninvolved father is probably not as good a candidate for monitoring a behavioral contract or contingency management schedule for the children as a mother who actively dotes on and frets about them; a retarded adolescent may find it easier to respond to an externally imposed contingency management program than to initiate responsibility through an elaborate and complex communication training ritual; the irresponsible or alcoholic parent is probably not the best candidate for following through with contingencies in a structured program, but his/her elusiveness or unwillingness to "take a stand" on an issue may make him or her an ideal candidate for negotiating between "more responsible" people. Alcoholics are often excellent negotiators, since the same process qualities which render them indecisive are useful in helping more straightforward people see both sides of an issue.

Summary of Assessment Procedures in the Functional Family Model

The functional family therapist is trained in ways which first allow him or her to conceptualize discrete bits of information in ways which help him/her recognize sequential or relational *processes* in family life. The therapist is then forced to identify the ways in which these processes lead to purposive *functions*, which are accepted as legitimate and are outside the domain of externally imposed change. Finally, those *individual* characteristics of family members are identified which serve as constraints or aids in initiating and maintaining family change.

Because of the inherent complexity involved in evaluating a family system, therapists are cautioned to plan before their first session how to garner the necessary assessment data. More importantly, they are cautioned to monitor the process of assessment itself. Typical omissions occur in punctuating a process sequence before every family member is involved, which makes it impossible to identify functions for each family member. For example, a therapist may be hard-pressed to come up with a good reason why mother and daughter ritualistically fight after school, when daughter leaves the house angry and mom sobs until 6:30, when dad comes home. The therapist may be able to recognize daughter's bids for autonomy or distance, but mom's behavior makes little sense until it is hypothesized that her tears elicit concern (intimacy) from a father who typically spends his evening behind a paper (distance). For reasons such as these, therapists are urged to consider their assessments after each session, to determine which assessment information seems consistent with previous hypotheses. Through this process, the therapist can begin to evaluate how missing information must be forthcoming, as well as evaluate his/her own performance in obtaining it. Given the conceptual basis of the model, therapists cannot reasonably proceed into the therapy enterprise until assessment is complete.

TREATMENT FORMULATIONS AND PROCEDURES

This section will describe ways in which the conceptual basis and assessment of family behavior are translated into change. The functional family model dichotomizes family intervention into *therapy* and *education*. We will elaborate on this distinction and how it is translated into what functional family therapists actually do with families.

Stated very briefly, therapy is that portion of intervention which sets the stage for, allows, or motivates family members to change. While the "tools" of change (such as communication training, behavioral contracting, contingency management, etc.) are relatively well-developed, the processes of intervention which get family members to use them are less well understood. While therapists, scholars, and researchers might know what changes family members *should* make, getting them to do this can be the most difficult part of the therapy enterprise (Barton and Alexander, 1976; 1977b).[10]

[10]*Editors' Note.* For an enormously different view within the behavioral field of how family members' compliance with the use of specific techniques may be achieved, see Jacobson (Chapter 15) and Jacobson and Margolin (1979).

Trait Attributions and Family Resistance

Family therapy practitioners have long known about the tendency of families to resist efforts to change. Communication theorists (Framo, 1972; Haley, 1963; Satir, 1967; Watzlawick, Beavin, and Jackson, 1967) have articulated resistance as an inevitable property of social systems, and have posited that therapists should expect it in a variety of forms. This level of abstraction and generalization serves as a useful caveat for the family therapist, but does not suggest directly how the family therapist should deal with resistance other than to expect it.

Clinical experiences with most disturbed families show that family members' initial comments are usually very punitive or blaming regarding the identified patient and other family members. Further, these punitive or pejorative comments are usually relatively nonspecific or generic attributions such as "he's lazy," "irresponsible," or "sick." Family process in which these blaming attributions are exchanged does little to promote change, insofar as they constitute a form of therapeutic resistance by preserving the status quo.

These forms of resistance are consistent with social psychological principles about attribution processes (Shaver, 1975). When people are in a state of arousal or dissonance, they have a tendency to make "person" attributions to explain their own behavior and that of others (Kelley, 1972). These data show that people do not typically opt for or report more elaborate "situational" attributions, such as "I told him to clean up his room in a very direct and authoritarian manner, and because he was reading a magazine he was interested in, he resented both my tone and the request, which made me feel rejected, and so I told him to do it in even more nasty ways." This potentially useful and information-laden message is typically reported as "He's lazy and worthless." The data on how aversive or inefficient communications are exchanged in processes of disturbed families (Alexander, 1973; Patterson and Reid, 1967) reflect how pejorative "person" attributions engender processes in which information-free and value-laden attributions are counterexchanged.

Another form of family resistance associated with attributions is family members' self-reported inability to overcome their feelings or behavior, as in "I can't help the way I feel (or behave)." These attributions are person attributions as well, but they also presuppose some popularized notions about "internal dynamics." Social psychologists (e.g., Kanouse and Hanson, 1972) argue that many people explain their feelings or behavior as driven by some internal process that they either do not understand or are helpless to control. In communication theory terms, this message of "I am exerting this control but won't take responsibility for it" is one of the most troublesome features of symptoms (Framo, 1972; Haley, 1963; Watzlawick, Beavin, and Jackson, 1967).

The data show that people make *active choices* in labeling their emotions (Nisbett and Valins, 1972) and in determining their behavior based on these chosen emotional states (Berkowitz and Turner, 1974). While people can often be in a generalized state of physiological arousal (increased heart rate, dry mouth, sweaty palms, muscular tension, quickened breathing), it is not possible to discriminate "emotion" on the basis of objective measures of these physiological reactions (Thompson, 1967). It appears that people actively search the environment for information as to how to label their arousal as an emotion (London and Nisbett, 1974); e.g., "I see a threatening situation, so I must be scared and should run," or "I see a situation in which I am being aggressed against, so I should be angry and aggress back." People's labeling of emotion and acting on it can be manipulated with false physiological data representing arousal (Barefoot and Straub, 1974) and differing environmental information (Brehm and Cohen, 1962), and manipulation of these can lead people to behave in different ways (Bem and McConnell, 1970).

Family resistance, therefore, consists of several components which bear important implications for the functional family therapist. First, it would appear that family members are naive about much of their behavioral and emotional experience, and certainly about interpersonal contingencies of same, due to their predilection to make "person" attributions. Second, people do not recognize their active participation in labeling their personal emotions or the cause of behavior, assuming that these are due to the meaning of their behavior in terms of process and functions. The average person is a lay "personality theorist," since this conceptual scheme is the one most commonly represented in our culture.

This inaccurate or incomplete information nonetheless dictates much of how people behave. These models constrain people into inaccurate understanding of their behavior, emotions, and thoughts, let alone those of others. These inaccuracies certainly contribute to inefficient family processes, wherein family members seek validation that is not forthcoming for their inaccurate or incomplete views of their world. People can develop little sense of mastery or control of their world if they do not perceive it in useful ways.

Reattribution and Motivation for Family Change

Functional family therapists make the assumption that *family members cannot change their behavior until they change their view of themselves and other family members.* When people are responding to certain sources of information or data, they seek behavioral or affective means to validate this information and promote cognitive consistency (Heider, 1958; Newcomb, 1963). The functional family therapist therefore makes the assumption that family members must have new sources of information to respond to, and must validate this information through different behavior and affective reactions.

At the same time that functional family therapists are seeking to generate new information for the family members, they are confronted with the task of generating the necessary objective information to assess the family: The therapist is evaluating relational processes or sequences, establishing functions, and evaluating individuals' strengths and weaknesses. A traditional assessment strategy which focuses on "the problem" (as presented by the family) will preclude the functional family therapist's attainment of both goals. Focusing on the problem typically generates well-rehearsed and practiced accusations, blaming, and other indices of value-laden personal trait attributions. In such situations, families are allowed to resist and even attempt to convince the therapist that their view of "the problem" is correct. These personalistic messages also make it difficult for the therapist to generate necessary information to complete relational process sequences, functions, and individual strengths (as well as individual weaknesses).

In contrast, *the functional family therapist's first task is to "confuse" the family members or lead them to question their view of the family and "the problem."* This confusion or reattribution is accomplished at process, style, and content levels of the functional family therapist's activity.

At the *process* level, the functional family therapist asks questions of everyone in the family. First of all, it is probably necessary for the therapist to talk to or at least monitor everyone to gather the information he/she needs; however, this procedure of including everyone is in itself a message to the family. Including everyone says that the therapist defines phenomena in relational terms, that everyone's opinions and information are legitimate, and that the therapist sees everyone as influencing what occurs in the family.

As a *stylistic* phenomenon, the functional family therapist is urged to ask questions or comment in ways that are nonjudgmental or nonblaming. This style does not elicit defensive reactions, and it also challenges or negates the value-laden judgments family members place on each other. A question like, "What did you do after this happened?", will elicit much less defensiveness and more information than, "So, how soon after beating your kid did you get drunk?"

One important aspect of the functional family therapist's *content* in family sessions is that of providing family members with information about the contingencies or interdependencies between them. The therapist elaborates supplemental information to the family about those things they don't acknowledge or report, but which influence them nonetheless. Given that people are typically person-oriented and very molar in their self-reports, the functional family therapist communicates the inherent complexity of interrelationships to them. A mother who reports, "I'm just always mad at him," leaves few options open for change. The therapist can generate those options with the more complete view of the situation, "When he doesn't respond to your questions, you get angry." This message

has several new components of information to the family: 1) To mother, the message says that her anger is her reaction to a relatively specific circumstance which she has the option to change or avoid; 2) to "him" the message suggests that he has some influence on mother via a specific behavior of not answering, which he has the option to escape or avoid, and further, that mother's anger is not all pervasive toward him but contingent on his behavior; and 3) the therapist's statement points out that mother's reaction is a process-mediated relational phenomenon, not a capricious event. Functional family therapists therefore practice more detailed reinterpretations of molar events to generate new information about both personal and relationship-oriented contingencies.

The most active and powerful vehicle for reattribution and change for the functional family therapist is that of relabeling. Relabeling is a form of message that both "revalences" behavior and describes functions to family members. In order to "revalence" behavior, functional family therapists are advised to consider the dialectic or antonym properties of any given phenomenon. For example, rigid or authoritarian fathers can be portrayed as active leaders; people who do not disclose their feelings can be relabeled as not withholding, but rather considerate of laying their problems on others; "disrespectful" teenagers can be portrayed as struggling with their autonomy. In order to revalence a phenomenon, therapists are urged to consider the "positive" antonym properties of any given "negative" family phenomenon and to seek to portray family members as "victims." This revalencing of roles, behavior, emotions, or other dimensions of family life reduces defensiveness in family members, while helping to create an alternative value or affect associated with the phenomenon. This revalencing may, in itself, change the type of affective associations people attach to events in family life.

The idea behind "revalencing" behavior is to change family members' affective and behavioral reactions to their conceptual representations of others. The model makes the assumption that the "problem" aspects of family interaction lie in how family members selectively attend to and perceive each other's behavior. These conceptual representations and their affective results largely constitute the "psychological problem." The goal of revalencing or relabeling is therefore not to represent the "truth" to family members, but rather to portray family members and their behavior in ways which will better fit family members' desired expectations. Family members are more willing to accept a view of the world which leaves them blameless and which suggests they are not cruel or malevolent to each other. In turn, family members are more likely to change their cognitive labels, affective reactions, and behavior toward one another if the therapist "paints a picture" which portrays family members in ways they would like to perceive each other. In a sense, relabeling may therefore represent a conceptual or affective substitution process. A mother who experiences guilt or perceives herself as a failure is presumably relieved to hear that her son's acting-out represents his "struggle for independence," rather than a "rejection" of her. Similarly, father and other family members presumably experience a different affective reaction to hearing that father "assumes major responsibility" in a family, than to hearing "he's so bossy, he won't let anybody else make a decision." The changes in affect that occur as corollaries to these relabels are the ingredients that make it likely that family members will respond favorably to relabels.

The most potent aspect of relabeling occurs when family members are sensitized to the functional properties or relational impact of each other's behavior and emotions. To relabel, the therapist must first complete an assessment that allows him or her to understand the function of processes exchanged between people. Suppose, for example, that the function of most of husband's behavior is to distance wife, at the same time that she reports she wants a "closer" marriage (intimacy). The problem is exacerbated by wife's complaints that husband is never home and does not "share" with her and she feels rejected. These complaints would suggest that, at some level, she feels the impact of husband's distance. The therapist's task is not only to "revalence" husband's distance as not being "evil," but to suggest that this function also serves wife's functional needs for intimacy. The functional family therapist might reinterpret the distancing behavior itself by portraying husband as a man who "needs to protect himself from

being overwhelmed by feelings," at the same time suggesting that his distance arises from "not wanting to disappoint his wife with his inadequate expression of feelings." In this light husband's behavior can be perceived or valenced in a benign way, and wife's feelings of being rejected can be reevaluated as being protected, connoting greater caring and intimacy. A child who "bugs" his parents can be portrayed as "not having the right skills to best initiate contact," or a smothering mother can be portrayed as "not wanting to feel left out."

These relabels also imply that interpersonal functions are in many ways under the control of the person making the complaint. The intimacy-seeking wife can let her husband know that he will not disappoint her. If she were to give him this message, his function of distance can be preserved well, since he will not have to deal with her feelings. Parents can regulate contact with their children if their children do not use aversive controls, which implies children guarantees as to how they can initiate contact with their parents as well. A smothering mother can be legitimately included if she does not behave in ways which drive others away. Effective relabeling revalences behavior, describes functions in benign ways which lead to increased and alternative understanding, and even implies that there are ways family members can change to more directly obtain what they want.[11]

Summary: The Therapy Process

The therapy process in the functional family model is admittedly very manipulative, and does not reflect "reality" or "truth." By the same token, there is little truth or reality contained in family life. People seem to create their own conceptual reality and emotions, which are often determinants of inefficient behavior. Family members attend to very narrow and discrete bits of family life, omitting many others. An unfortunate by-product of this person attribution view of the world is that it is associated many times with inefficient family processes and a lack

---

[11]*Editors' Note.* See Stanton (Chapter 10) for a discussion of other techniques of relabeling as used by strategic family therapists.

of appreciation for legitimate functions of behavior processes.

The functional family therapist's portrait of
the family is no more truthful or real than the
family's, but it suggests ways in which families
can operate more efficiently to meet their functions. The goal of functional family intervention
is not to "trick" people, but to give them an
alternative set of attributions, which will allow
the family to behave in more efficient ways and
engage in more effective processes to protect
interpersonal functions more directly.

In actuality, reattribution or relabeling is a
trial-and-error process. The functional family
therapist seeks to create a different conceptual
and affective climate in the family. Whether or
not family members will accept these attributions is related to the therapist's consistency in
presenting these messages and the degree to
which the relabels are a plausible alternative
conceptualization of the family members' representations of the data. People are most likely
to change their attributions when the data are
both externally validated and consistent with
internal experience (Kelley, 1972).

A recent study by Barton and Alexander
(1979) was designed to assess the role of relational attributions of family members in influencing family process. Adaptive and delinquent
families performed an interaction task with both
a competitive and cooperative attributional set.
It was found that delinquent family members
substantially reduced their rates of defensiveness when given the cooperative set; in fact,
their absolute amounts of defensiveness were
not different from those of adaptive families in
this experimental condition. These data are
taken as strong support for the assertion that
induction of an artificial but adaptive relationship set is associated with improvements in family process. The data also imply that this set
induction may well be a crucial component of
intervention with delinquent families.

Seen in this way, therapy in the model is
largely a function of complete relational assessment and creation of an alternate conceptual
reality for the family. *This reattribution process
is a fragile one*, however, and people do not
maintain attributions which are not supported
by data from their environment (Kelley, 1972).
Functional family therapists must, therefore,
ensure that family members will maintain their
more benign and alternative attributions with
structured behavior change.

Education from the Functional Family Perspective

The functional family therapist's goals for education are considerably more constrained than
the more generic goals of education as practiced
in academic settings. Ordinarily, most people
assume that education is valuable in and of itself,
and that people will best benefit from education
in their own personalized ways. By contrast, the
functional family therapist adapts both the type
and form of education imparted to families to
be consistent with: 1) the functional outcomes
of family members' behavior; and 2) the therapeutic reattributions that the functional family
therapist has created within the family. The
functional family therapist is constrained to fit
an educational strategy to the particular functional outcomes of family members' behavior
and to do so in a form which is consistent with
family members' new view of the family created
through therapy (Barton and Alexander, 1977a,
1977b).

As discussed briefly earlier in the chapter, the
functional family therapist makes the assumption that the relational outcomes or *functions* of
individuals in the family are legitimate. The
functional family therapist does not presume
that intimacy, distance, or regulator functions
are undesirable, and they are not a focus of
change. The functional family therapist does
assume that these functions are such powerful
purposive outcomes of behavior and process that
therapeutic goals should not include changing
them.[12]

As a cardinal caveat for beginning education,
then, the functional family therapist must ensure that the behavior change strategy or education to be performed with the family will be
consistent with producing the same interpersonal functions for each family member that he

---

[12]*Editors' Note.* Again, we feel compelled to note the extreme pessimism implicit in this view, as well as the existence of alternative family therapy models which propose
quite the opposite, i.e., that changing such functions is a
sine qua non of effective treatment.

or she is obtaining prior to treatment. Functional family therapists are cognizant of the functional outcomes for each family member as obtained through assessment, but they must also have an appreciation of how the particular educational strategy they utilize will serve these functions. At this level of concern, therapists must have some feel for how adaptive the form of the intervention will be for the family. For example, in the instance where an adolescent is performing symptomatic behavior to achieve interpersonal distance, the therapist would not want to utilize a unilaterally controlled educational change strategy which precludes distance, such as contingency management. Contingency management programs typically require active monitoring and dispensation of a reward by some person in authority, such as a parent (Allyon and Azrin, 1968). Hence, the behavior change paradigm can be said to create both closeness in the form of monitoring and a process wherein parents are implicitly in charge. This process form and outcome are probably not a good fit with the adolescent's goal of distance and autonomy. The independence-seeking adolescent would be expected to resent and not perform behavior inconsistent with his or her functional and stylistic process concerns. In contrast, behavioral contracting may be a more desirable procedure. Much of the reason for its demonstrated success (Alexander and Parsons, 1973; Parsons and Alexander, 1973; Stuart, 1971) may be its "fit" with adaptive processes which still guarantee autonomy, independence, or distance for the adolescent. As part of the process of negotiation inherent to contracting, adolescents engage in a process wherein they assume responsibility for what they want, and also are offered the capability to negotiate for the type and amount of interpersonal distance they desire. The fixed structure of contracting might, therefore, better serve the therapeutic-educational needs for an effective process, which can nonetheless promote interpersonal autonomy or distance for the adolescent.

In presenting the rationale for a particular educational strategy to the family, functional family therapists are reminded that people most typically respond to and determine their behavior by more discrete person or behavior attributions, rather than by higher order abstract concepts such as distance or intimacy. Given that therapists lay the groundwork for more benign and adaptive interpretations of family life in the *therapy* phase, they must ensure that the educational strategy will fit these reattributions or relabels as well. The functional family therapist must convey how the particular forms of behavior performed by each family member will symbolically represent his/her wants. Returning to the earlier example of behavioral contracting, a "smothering" father would probably not be willing to support a program in which his adolescent son gains distance, if this were the salient feature of the contract that was portrayed to him by the therapist. However, if the contract is portrayed to the concerned father as a procedure which will guarantee him an opportunity to sit down with his son and hear what he wants and how he plans to responsibly attain it, then he may feel that the contract guarantees him a type of contact or intimacy with his son. Similarly, the procedure will let the adolescent hear his father's concern, but act on it through negotiating how responsive to it he wants to be. The functional family therapist thus tailors the process of behavior change, in verbal presentations to the family, to fit the more benign attributions or relabels that have been presented to the family in the therapy phase of intervention.

These strategies implicitly include some limits on the concept of *change* in the family. *The functions of behavior are not changed through education, but the form of process that generates or controls these outcomes is changed.* Hence, the enterprise of education or overt behavior change is a substitution and matching-to-sample paradigm for the functional family therapist. It is assumed that inefficient or less adaptive processes occur in troubled families as both vehicles of control and sources of constraints for meeting functions, but that a functional family assessment will reveal the functions nonetheless. Changes in the form of one person's behavior alone will not be maintained, and will even be actively resisted, unless *everyone* changes the form of his/her behavior to create a process environment which creates and maintains new behavior for all family members. For this reason, everyone in the family must be made "uncertain" or "confused" about his/her thoughts, feelings, and behavior. They are then given a new reality which creates a more benevolent environment. It is then critical that education, by fitting both actual functions and the functional family therapist's new cognitive and affective environment, maintains the integrity of behavior or process change. Adopting the cognitive dissonance paradigm (Brehm and Cohen, 1962), the functional family model dictates that overt behavior change will provide the supports for this differing affective and cognitive orientation to the world. The "fit" issues ensure that functional family therapists are taking the path of least resistance, both in providing people what functions they reliably obtain and in determining what behavior, feelings, or thoughts other family members can perform that will symbolize enhanced quality of life.

Implicit interpersonal functions and processes in educational technology

Given that functional family therapists are aware of this complicated set of "fit" issues, they are trained to utilize a variety of overt behavior change technologies that promote overt behavior change. The therapist selects from a repertoire of specific, overt behavior change techniques and assigns responsibilities for execution of these technologies consistent with interpersonal processes and specific individual styles in the family. Most overt behavior change procedures are discussed in the research literature and primary sourcebooks (see Bandura, 1969; Graziano, 1975; Rimm and Masters, 1974; Wolpe, 1969) and will not be discussed in procedural detail here. Rather, a few examples are included to represent how these overt procedures can be utilized within a functional family relational framework. In each of the following examples, it is presupposed that the therapist has done sufficient *therapy* so that the family members are ready and willing to adopt *education* or a technology for new behavior.

Example 1. Affective Distress. A single-parent mother consistently complains of "anxiety" and ineffectiveness. Her adolescent son typically responds to this anxiety by attempting to problem-solve regarding the source of the anxiety, which does not work. Through assessment,

the functional family therapist has determined that mom's anxiety serves to elicit an intimacy-promoting process between mother and son. Son consistently tries to help, although the son complains of feeling inadequate because of his inability to solve mom's problems.

The technique of systematic desensitization has been shown to be an effective procedure for the management of anxiety (Wolpe, 1969). The procedure utilizes a relaxation ritual, which is paired with a hierarchy of anxiety-provoking situations generated and rank-ordered by the distressed individual. Adopting a classical conditioning paradigm, the subsequent, pairing of fear-evoking situations and relaxation is presumed to desensitize the distressed person to the situation.

In this instance, the functional family therapist trained the adolescent son in executing the procedure with his mother. This gave the son a structured vehicle to interact with his mother that is presumed to be effective, and helped alleviate his perceived inadequacy. At the same time, mom had to exert personal control of her anxiety to the point of describing it in rank-ordered situational terms, and could only present her anxious symptoms to son at scheduled times. The ritual itself created a more adaptive process wherein mom could express her feelings and son could deal with them in a structured way. This scheduled and structured process "by appointment" also ensured both son and mother a guaranteed time to attain some form of interpersonal intimacy.

Example 2. Inappropriate Child Behavior. Parents and teachers complained of "acting-out," aggressive behavior by a seven-year-old boy. The parents also explained that because their son is an only child, they enrolled him in swimming classes, programs at YMCA, and other activities so that he could "have some fun." The functional family therapist noted that parents and teachers had very little interpersonal contact with the boy and that his "acting-out" typically got him kicked out of programs and schools and back into the home. Mother's artwork and father's extra accounting contracts kept both parents occupied at home, until required to discipline their son. "Time-out" was previously ineffective in remediating the problems.

The therapist decided that the function of the boy's behavior was to elicit contact or intimacy from his parents, and that contingency management (Ayllon and Azrin, 1968) might create a more adaptive process for the boy to "make contact" with the parents. In the contingency management procedure, the basic format is to create a structure of desired behavior and create a rule for when it is rewarded. This posed some problems for the therapist, since the parents seemed to consistently distance their son through lack of involvement, and it was presumed they might not actively monitor or reward their son enough to make the procedure effective.

The functional family therapist handled this situation with the boy and parents by having a fixed time of three hours in the evening in which the program was in effect. Further, the parents alternated nights in managing the program. This structured set of limits guaranteed each parent that half of his/her time could be spent in solitary pursuits, while guaranteeing son more contact time than he had before. Also the son, through a description of desired behavior contained in the program, was given a more adaptive way to elicit contact from his parents, while they were guaranteed a vehicle to maintain interpersonal distance at other times.

Example 3. A "Physiological" Problem. A concerned couple presented concerns about an apparently encopretic four-year-old son. The boy had "made progress" and seemed toilet-trained, but the situation had deteriorated in recent months. At the onset of the new bouts of encopresis, the parents had reinstituted their "reward" program for toilet-training; when this failed, they had begun to try "punishment," which did not work either. The parents were beginning to suspect a biological basis for the problem, if not retarded development in their son.

The functional family therapist attempted to determine when the soiling episodes occurred, and found that they were reliably associated with occasions when the family was at an older son's athletic events, where the parents attended solely to the oldest son. The younger son would typically try to elicit money or someone to play with at these games, but since the parents didn't want to "spoil" him, these at-

tempts weren't successful. By contrast, the outcome of pant soiling was that both parents would strip the son and clean him, or, as their frustration increased, stand and direct him in cleaning up himself.

The parents were told that the function of their encopretic son's behavior seemed to be to elicit attention. As a first step, they were urged to actively play and talk with him during their older son's athletic events, and this reduced the encopretic episodes during these occasions. The parents were then urged to reinstitute the reward procedure for the behavioral toilet-training ritual (Allyon and Azrin, 1969), but, rather than having their son independently perform the procedure and get a tangible reward, they should substitute tangible reinforcement with social praise for successive approximations to the complete procedure. This procedure was presumed to both provide contact for the younger son, by structuring a process for closeness or contact as well as training, and reduce parental concern and confine their attention to the "problem" to a few minutes a day.

It was found that this procedure was effective in reducing soiling, but that the boy was announcing his intentions to go to the toilet at an increasing rate, presumably to mediate intimacy (contact). The parents then became concerned that this was not an optimal basis for interacting with their son. At this point, the functional family therapist suggested that parents could begin to substitute other desirable behavior training as a substitute for toilet-training. The parents were given a program to structure in some type of "new learning" each week, via the same social reward for successive approximations process. The parents were then able to fade (Sidman, 1960) their reinforcement of toilet-training and substitute this into processes of learning the alphabet and other preschool skills. Given that the function of contact was preserved for the son and that parents could structure a fixed time each day to interact with him, the family was able to maintain a similar process across a variety of situations, which reduced the parents' concerns about their son's development as well.

Example 4. Seemingly Irresolvable "People" Differences. Occasionally, problems can appear which seem more "psychological" or "perceptual" than affective or behavioral in nature. Therapists and family members can both feel helpless when it appears that people want contradictory things, usually represented as one person wanting distance and the other person wanting closeness. In these instances, the functional family therapist is forced to manipulate both overt behavior and the perception of what that behavior means or to assign a positive attribution to the behavior itself.

One woman complained that her husband never talked to her about his feelings. Conversely, the husband demonstrated in terms of his behavior and his self-reports that he found it very difficult and undesirable to discuss his feelings. In this instance, the husband was helped through communication training to share with his wife his difficulty in discussing his deepest feelings. Note, however, that he never had to share what those feelings were (thereby maintaining his distance). His wife was told that these expressions did, in fact, represent very high self-disclosure on his part, and the most intense closeness of which he was capable. In this light, the wife was able to perceive these reports as intimacy, if the husband, in turn, responded to her bids for feelings with "I am feeling so (angry/anxious/depressed) right now that I can't talk." The wife perceived these reports as intimate, at the same time that the husband, not having to discuss himself at length, preserved his distance. Given that both husband and wife had these perceptual guarantees for what they wanted, these perceptions were embedded in a ritual in which wife took responsibility for monitoring her husband or initiating conversation with him when she wanted to. Conversely, the husband was able to distance with a statement of his inability to discuss the situation further because of his "emotions."

Distance-intimacy regulators can pose problems because their conflicting bids for intimacy at some times and distance at others confuse family members. A family complained because sometimes "Dad wants to talk" and other times "he gets really mad if you try to." Dad was similarly confused, angry, and feeling helpless because his family didn't "meet his needs." The functional family therapist used a green flag on a toothpick, a red flag on a toothpick, and a blob of modeling clay to improve the situation. The blob of modeling clay was placed on the kitchen table: When dad came home, if he wanted to talk or was available to talk he placed the green flag in the blob of modeling clay; if he didn't want to or was unavailable, he put up the red flag. This procedure lent predictability to the family interaction and alerted family members to optimal times to interact with father. This process also legitimized the regulatory function of dad's stylistic behavior.

While this example deals with how the function of a regulator can be used to initiate processes, environmental props can be used to terminate them as well. A "hysterical" mother complained that she could not communicate her well-meaning intentions to her husband or adolescent daughters. The family reported that mom overwhelmed them with her affect, which made it difficult for them to either hear or respond to her. In this instance, the functional family therapist issued red "feedback" cards to the family members. The rules for card use were that mom had to stop talking when they were flashed at her, because mom was "overloading" family members. However, family members were told they were also required to give mom feedback about how to better get her message across. These cards, therefore, represented reciprocal control of process for both mom and family: Family members could seek clarification on mom's position or give her information to either "speed her up" or "slow her down"; mom could likewise determine how she chose to respond to the feedback. If mom's regulation was for more intimacy or contact, she could elicit more feedback and also present more information. If mom's regulation was for distance, she could report that she needed to go work on responding to the feedback by herself.

Education and "cure"

The above examples convey the functional family mentality of tailoring or fitting overt change to the functions and processes of family life. The examples certainly do not represent all the change strategies used in the functional family model, but rather convey the flavor of how functional family therapists are willing to entertain any legitimate vehicle for behavior change which is consistent with family function.

Functional family therapists occasionally need to be reminded that the majority of behavior change strategies presently utilized by mental health professionals were derived from individual models of behavior. This can create a tendency for clinicians to make assumptions that the behavior change strategies work because they remediate "faulty individuals" in the family. Functional family therapists are reminded that these behavior change strategies are utilized because they fit the particular strengths or weaknesses of individuals in the family, but that these procedures *must also* fit into an adaptive family process and the functions of each family member. Also, the technique per se is not "good"—it is only effective because of fit.

Returning to the examples may illustrate these considerations. First of all, in each example behavior change is embedded in a process of participation with other family members. None of the behavior change strategies is possible without the initiation, maintenance, and consequation of all family members. Second, in each example, the behavior change strategies also meet the functions for all family members. An appraisal of these critical features of behavior strongly argues that the locus of control for behavior change resides in the process of family relationships.

These same sources of influence on behavior need to be considered when intervention *does not* work. The example of the encopretic boy serves here, since the behavior of the boy led the parents to believe that there may be biological limits to their son's ability to change. However, the functional family therapist's source of assessment suggested that a very similar form of intervention would work if made consistent with family processes and functions.

Functional family therapists are urged to consider the enterprise of behavior change to be a process of "hypothesis-testing." Failed interventions can represent several sources of poor fit. At an individual level of analysis, it would probably not work to tell the encopretic boy to assume responsibility for his own behavior, given his developmental stage, nor to tell the hysterical mother to control her emotionality. Their tendencies, as represented by their behavioral histories and capabilities, would suggest that these have not worked in the past. Rare

indeed is the client appearing in therapy who has not been given corrective feedback or criticism from others on how to behave. Other people must be considered as well in the process of change, since changes in relationships are never a unilateral phenomenon. At the process level of consideration, the distancing husband must report certain things to his wife or her bids for intimacy will not be met; the family members in the examples using environmental props must respond to and utilize them in certain ways or they will exert no meaningful influence on behavior. If therapists have not built in these critical influences and counterinfluences in the process level of behavior change, the behavior change will probably not be maintained.

Finally, no matter how reasonable or appropriate behavior change seems to the therapist, and how overtly enthusiastic family members seem to be about change, therapists should predict that family intervention will fail if each person involved in a family process does not get his/her functions met. This is typically the area when behavior change procedures will break down. Functional family therapists are reminded at these times that family members do not operate at the level of articulating and directly responding to their functions. Hence, the therapist will probably have to assume responsibility for identifying which functions are not being met and how they can be. The functional family model makes the assumption that family change is accomplished only when the change is consistent with all three of these levels of analysis. When families resist, or a change effort does not work, it is because it does not fit one or more interdependent levels of behavior. Functional family therapists are urged to reassess the family and seek ways to make this fit more optimal, as a vehicle for assisting the family to change.

The inherent complexity of the therapy and education phases of intervention, as well as the ingenuity necessary for implementing new procedures, suggests that much of the success of the model is dependent on the conceptual skills or understanding of the therapist (Barton and Alexander, 1977a). In addition, functional family therapists must also be considered as "service delivery systems" in their own right. The execution of therapy and education is dependent on the skills of the therapist in many critical ways.

THE FUNCTIONAL FAMILY THERAPIST

Given therapists' mastery of the critical conceptual features of the model, they must verbally and stylistically package the important ingredients of therapy and education in a way which will maximize their impact on the family. All too often, it has been a professional practice for therapists' training to be related only to their mastery of a set of techniques, and the presumption has been made that therapists are fairly homogenous as a group so that these techniques will be sufficient to change clients (Kiesler, 1966). The functional family model asserts that the relationship that the functional family therapist forms with the family is as important for change as consideration of family members' relationships and forms of influence. Family members must fit behavior change into an ongoing network of individual qualities, relationships, and functions, and therapists must likewise fit themselves and their forms of influence into the family in adaptive ways.

Recent research has shown that, within the procedural boundaries of behavioral models of intervention, the types of relationship that therapists create with families are a substantial determinant of how quickly and durably families change, as well as whether or not they change at all (Alexander, Barton, Schiavo, and Parsons, 1976; Stuart and Lott, 1972). Family change seems related to the functional family therapist's ability to form an adaptive relationship with the family, in order to structure adaptive ways for the family to change.

Relationship Skills

The stylistic form of the relationship that the functional family therapist creates with a family is the best predictor of the success of the functional family model. The data (Alexander et al., 1976) suggest that families are willing to remain in therapy when the functional family therapist does certain types of relationship-building with the family, making it possible for the therapist to structure behavior change.

Relationship skills include: integrating affect and behavior; being nonblaming; demonstrating interpersonal warmth; alleviating tension with humor; and using oneself as information through self-disclosure. Rather than being personality "traits" by which therapists are selected, these skills comprise a stylistic repertoire in which functional family therapists are trained to promote optimal therapeutic relationships with family members.

The *integration of the affect and behavior realms* of family experience is stylistically represented when the therapist complements family members' reports of either realm with the other. For example, a mother who reports an affective reaction such as, "I'm just angry at him all the time," might be told, "So you get angry with him when he seems to tune you out," to complement her affective report with a behavior. Conversely, a dad who reports, "He's always goofing off," might be told, "When he's goofing off, you feel disappointed in him." The integration of both behavior and affect is necessary when family members portray global and nonspecific attributes, such as, "He's a rotten kid." The therapist would then identify both a more specific behavior and an affect associated with the generic label, as in, "You both feel frustrated when he doesn't act in ways you'd like him to, such as going to school."

The impact of integrating affect and behavior is to sensitize family members to those aspects of family life which they probably ignore, or at least to those contingencies they do not actively convey to each other. In addition to creating this new information for the family, these messages also portray the functional family therapist's increased understanding and sensitivity to what's "really going on." The relative specificity and contingency linking of these messages also begin to convey the relatedness of family members to each other.

Nonblaming and the integration of affect and behavior are in many ways key ingredients of the reattribution and relabeling therapeutic processes. While integration of affect and behavior is new information that is created for the family, nonblaming is more critical for the ways in which information is valenced (either "good or bad," "positively or negatively," etc.) by the family. *Nonblaming* is the stylistic way in which functional family therapists try to "sugar coat" or at least emphasize positive aspects of messages in the therapy session. Blaming can occur both as content and process phenomena. Content issues are easier to recognize, since family members will typically begin therapy with punitive and pejorative labels for each other and their behavior. The family's blaming content message of, "He's a rotten kid," can be reframed as nonblaming by changing the description itself, as in "because he seems difficult for you to understand. . . ." It can also be reframed as nonblaming through the integration of affect and behavior, e.g., "You're feeling angry because you don't know how to interpret what he's doing." The therapist's task when presented with blaming content by the family is to use adjectives and adverbs which seem less pejorative and which remove any one family member as at fault or responsible for family problems. This is most typically done by changing the form of descriptive words so that they no longer sound malevolent or negative.

Blaming can also occur as a process phenomenon, however, or at least result from processes themselves. A common example occurs when the family member who is portrayed by the family as having "the problem" is the sole focal point of discussion by the family and therapist. Parents may continuously provide the therapist with explanations, school reports, and detailed accounts of why their teenager is a problem, or therapists might perseverate in trying to generate information from a recalcitrant "I don't know" teenager, whereupon parents might say, "See how we feel?" In either of these two very typical examples, the implication of processes and talk time about one person are that the one person is maintained in the role as "the problem." Functional family therapists are therefore alerted to the notion that session talk time disproportionately directed to or provided about any one family member is typically an implicit indictment or blame of that person. Therapists are trained to not only choose nonblaming words carefully, but to also bear in mind that they should legitimize each family member through directing information to or about each as equivalently as possible.

Warmth and *humor* are two stylistic forms which implicitly revalence the typical affect associated with therapy sessions. Warmth and humor are presumed to be effective with distressed clients because they are atypical reactions to the typically ponderous affect associated with psychological distress (Beier, 1966). The interpersonal potencies of affect such as anxiety, anger, or depression are relatively ubiquitous, insofar as people usually accept these as legitimate emotions requiring some form of help or retribution. Since the functional family therapist seeks in a variety of ways to alter family members' perceptions of their behavior and emotions, a first step in confusing family members about their feelings and their impact is to not respond to them in typical ways. Family members do typically at outset report their symptoms in very serious ways, and have had sufficient cultural experience to recognize that reactions to these are very potent. The functional family therapist stylistically reduces the potency or influence potential of these emotions by responding to them differently from most people in the culture.

Family members often elicit distance from each other via anger, reciprocated in a chaotic process of arguing. The therapist can slow down this chaotic process and confuse family members about the potency of anger by responding to anger directed at him/her with either warmth or humor. A direct aggressive attack such as, "What makes you qualified to help us?", could be responded to with a smile and, "At this point, I'm not sure, but I sure hope I'll be able to find out soon, so we'll all feel better," or with "Gee, did somebody just turn up the temperature in here?" An anxiety attack represented as, "I'm getting so uptight I'm just feeling like I might explode," could be responded to in the form: "Gee, I'm really concerned with how upset you're getting. Let's talk about it some more so I can understand it better," or "Uh-oh, should we duck?"

While these examples represent replies to comments directed toward the therapist, they can be interjected to slow down disruptive processes between family members as well. In an accusatory or blaming argument between a husband and wife, a therapist might interject, "I'm really getting concerned about what you folks are unable to get through to each other," or, "Do you folks issue crash helmets?" Because warmth and humor are atypical styles of responding, they confuse family members and can create an atmosphere in which people can consider themselves more objectively than if they are "out of control." Warmth can be particularly effective in eliciting content from intimacy or closeness-seeking family members, since they can feel understood or supported. Similarly, humor might be more effective for distancing people who have difficulty dealing directly with the seriousness of emotions.

When people have difficulty expressing either emotions or behavior directly to each other, the therapist can take a Miles Standish or John Alden role and talk about content through *self-disclosure*. Self-disclosure can be effective in terms of both content and process phenomena. As a content issue, the functional family therapist can create information for family members who may be reluctant to give it themselves. Occasionally, there are people in families who appear unskilled in expressing their emotions or who appear afraid to do so. If the therapist finds it useful for these emotions to be expressed, he or she can assist the family in hearing each other through personalizing the experience, such as: "I've had the experience of not being heard, and it makes me get pretty frustrated. Can you all see how it might be like that for her?" In self-disclosing messages like these, the therapist can assume responsibility for creating new information, as well as modeling an expression of this type of information.

It seems to also be the case that, as a process phenomenon, self-disclosure engenders reciprocity of self-disclosure in recently acquainted people (Morton, 1976). Given that therapists and families are typically recent acquaintances, functional family therapists can establish a norm for the degree of intimacy that will be exchanged in sessions by generating content and processes which engender psychologically intimate processes. Self-disclosure can influence the relative amount and type of intimacy created in the session in both content and process ways.

In general, the relationship skills of functional family therapists are both statistically (Alexander et al., 1976) and conceptually interdependent. Relationship skills represent the stylistic components of accomplishing the therapy phase of intervention with the family. Integration of affect and behavior, nonblaming, warmth, and self-disclosure are all components of an effective reattribution, such as, "It really pains me to see you struggling so hard to make contact and being disappointed when you can't." The relationship skills are crucial components of the therapy phase of functional family intervention, since it is through the vehicles of this stylistic "packaging" that therapeutic content is fit to the family.

Structuring Skills

It is presumed that a therapist's relationship skills will influence the family in ways that prepare them for change, while the structuring skills of a therapist will be more important in helping families implement change technology. Structuring skills are more closely associated with the education phase of intervention, and are related more to a therapist's effectiveness in conveying change information to the family. In essence, they include elements of an effective didactic style, including directiveness, self-confidence, and clarity.

Directiveness refers to a therapist's ability to optimally control processes of the family, and so a family's responsiveness to these attempts is largely a measure of the functional family therapist's ability to be effectively directive. Directiveness includes process forms such as giving instructions, prompting family members to speak, and giving them corrective feedback or support for their efforts toward adaptive behavior change. In facilitating a change technology such as communication training, for example, family members often require assistance and direction with therapist assertions such as: "Okay now, mom and dad, try steps one through five in giving a message"; "Mom, you respond now to dad's message in a way to let him know you heard what he said"; "Mom, you didn't feed back to dad what he said about your impact on him"; "Mom, that's a much more complete message." Some degree of directiveness is necessary in providing family members with a structure for behavior change, and even more directiveness is typically required if the therapist is having the family rehearse the procedure in a session.

Frank (1961) has persuasively argued that much of a client's willingness to perform change procedures under direction of a therapist is related to the client's perception of the therapist as credible or as an expert helping agent. Therapists' stylistic *self-confidence* is therefore related to their ability to help clients. Functional family therapists need to portray mastery of themselves and of procedures they present to clients in order for them to be effective. Functional family therapists' preparation, experience, and rehearsal of change techniques can aid considerably in enhancing their self-confidence with families. Therapists who must look through notes before giving the next instruction, or who say, "Now let me see, do you do this first or that first, let me think," appear hesitant, or are not otherwise assertively expert in their directiveness can compromise their credibility with the family, as well as the confidence the family has in a procedure. Functional family therapists are also trained to anticipate the family members' feeling foolish or awkward when they begin performing structured procedures that are new to them. Therapists should be prepared for comments from family members such as, "Gee, I feel foolish talking like this"; "You mean, I have to give him a token whenever he does something I want?"; "Do I have to ignore him when he's acting up?" and the like. If therapy has been truly effective and the therapist can assume the family members are not resisting change as much as they are uncomfortable with the novelty of a new way of behaving, then the therapist's self-confidence can facilitate their execution of the procedure. Comments like, "It's just like learning to ride a bike; it'll seem awkward at first and then seem natural," or, "This is the best way to guarantee that everybody gets what he or she wants," reflect therapists' competence, confidence in themselves, and, probably most importantly for the family, confidence in the procedure. Self-confidence by a therapist can eliminate much of a family's sense of awkwardness, confusion, or lack of trust in novel ways of doing things.

Clarity is a critical feature of any aspect of a therapist's direct change efforts. Functional family therapists are trained in ways to ensure that family members can hear and understand the critical elements of change. Therapists who are vague and nonspecific, provide too much information, are too abstract, or do not portray a reasonable organizational sequence for clients to follow can create obstacles for family members wishing to change. Functional family therapists must be clear portrayers of information, in order to provide the family with specific descriptions of skills they are to execute, as well as an organizational structure in which they can retain the information.

Just as in the class of relationship skills, the structuring skills are statistically (Alexander et al., 1976) and conceptually interdependent. It is also the case that an effective instruction to the family about how they should change probably includes directiveness, self-confidence, and clarity: "To make sure he hears what you're saying, talk more slowly and look at him as you talk." Structuring skills are typically more important and relevant during the education phase of intervention, when the family has shown a willingness to change and the functional family therapist has established a visible relationship with the family.

Relationship and Structuring Skills in Perspective

While families do not present functional family therapists with a universal timetable for when to use either class of skills, it is typically the case that therapists' relationship skills will be most relevant at the outset of therapy. Relationship skills are, of course, necessary throughout the course of therapy with families, but they are *critical* at the outset. A therapist's ability to initiate relationship skills early in the process of treatment appears to be a determinant of whether or not families will stay in therapy (Alexander, Barton, Schiavo, and Parsons, 1976). Families have an internal resistance to change (Haley, 1963; Watzlawick, Weakland, and Fisch, 1974), and the most troublesome aspect of this resistance usually takes the form of resisting the therapist as the external agent of change.

Families are usually primed to inform the therapist as to who the "sick" or "bad" member of the family is, with the result that they can constrain the therapist from doing effective intervention. It is, therefore, necessary for therapists to perform effective relationship-building with the family before structuring skills will be effective. Rare, indeed, is the family that merely wants information about how to change. If functional family therapists attempt to portray structuring skills before the family has been motivated to change through therapy, the therapist's stylistic directiveness, self-confidence, and clarity are likely to be challenged, if not refuted entirely. Most families are better prepared with reasons why they cannot, will not, or should not change, since they bring in a well-rehearsed history of interpersonal difficulty. Further, they have integrated this history into a very pessimistic outlook, and probably feel as though they will have to give up or give something to change. Functional family therapists must fit themselves into this interpersonal system in order to understand it and create new understanding for the family via relational skills, which are the optimal stylistic vehicles around the families' sources of resistance.

Accuracy or truth is not the salient dimension of a therapist's relational content, since the therapist is seeking to create an alternative therapeutic reality for the family. Accuracy is probably more critical in the structuring phase, since the therapist must integrate techniques from the professional literature into the particular and idiosyncratic needs of the family. The functional family therapist's level of activity or performance of the skills is probably the most relevant of all. Therapists cannot allow themselves to passively respond to the conceptual, affective, and behavioral reality that families will try to create in sessions. For intervention to succeed, the therapist must utilize both relationship and structuring skills to actively move the family towards change.

Functional Family Therapists' Personal Assessment of their Impact on the Family

Therapists need to consistently evaluate and assess the impact they are having on the family, in the same way that they evaluate the impact family members have on each other. Further, just as therapists fit therapy and education to the family, they must also consider what stylistic packaging and forms of their own interpersonal styles will fit the family.

One of the most difficult tasks for the therapist is that of responding atypically to messages that the family presents. Family members will be well-practiced in eliciting certain kinds of emotions, advice, support, arguments, agreements, or distance or intimacy with their interpersonal styles. If therapists respond like "most people," they will have very little impact or at least do nothing to promote change (Beier, 1966). Through use of the relationship skills, therapists can begin to create the environment for change. The families' reactions to these skills are a good indicator of the progress of the therapy phase.

Therapists also assume some risks when they begin using the structuring skills to implement change. If family members challenge or otherwise resist, then therapists should *not* assume that the technology will not work, that families cannot or will not change, or that the therapist is incompetent. Functional family therapists are, rather, urged to monitor their own behavior and assessment to ensure that the myriad of issues involving "fit" have been resolved.

Therapists must, therefore, continually monitor the interpersonal processes of sessions to consider: 1) what impact their styles have on each member of the family; 2) whether or not therapists are able to control the direction, flow, and sequencing of processes; and 3) what forms of family members' behavior represent distancing or coming closer as a result of therapists' messages. Therapists must possess a relatively sophisticated set of conceptual skills to be effective with the functional family model. They must be monitoring a complex array of relational phenomena occurring independently of them, at the same time that they are monitoring themselves as affecting and reacting to the same phenomena (Barton and Alexander, 1977a).

Therapists' skills are truly a critical determinant of the effectiveness of the functional family model, and therapists are urged to consider out-of-session preparation, planning, and supervision to be critical for the mastery and performance of the model. Functional family therapists are urged to review an assessment checklist (Barton and Alexander, 1978) between sessions to determine their progress in understanding the family, and to get live observation and supervision whenever possible, or at least to carefully evaluate audiotapes of sessions with a partner to determine the therapeutic stylistic impact on the family. Finally, therapists are urged to plan in advance for their next sessions, in order to "hypothesis test" how to maximize the impact of their styles, how to complete assessment, and what procedures for change might best fit the family. These concerns have all been derived from compelling data which show that the skills of therapists are critical for effective implementation of the functional family model (Alexander, Barton, Parsons, and Schiavo, 1976).

TRAINING THE FUNCTIONAL FAMILY THERAPIST

Training of functional family therapists is guided by development of the conceptual bases of the model, and by an appreciation of trainees' skill levels. First, therapists must be trained to develop an "interaction set" about human behavior. Just as most people are trait theorists and think in cause-effect terms, to some degree so do most trainees when they first begin training in interpersonal models. Following the assessment guidelines portrayed in this chapter, trainees are shaped to create an inclusive focus on all family members, and to approach families with the idea that they must conceptually create links among all of them. Beginning functional family therapists often require substantial didactic instruction, viewing of viedotapes, and role-playing experiences to help them abandon cause-effect models (such as parents are the "cause" of "bad kids"), and to include the role of *all* family members in mediating behavior (e.g., not just concentrating on conflict resolution between mother and daughter, but also understanding when and how dad must be included in the situation). Conceptually, most errors by beginning functional family therapists are errors of omission. Trainees are given structured role-play vignettes and videotaped data samples for which they must posit a plausible mediating role for *every* family member.

Practically speaking, shaping of this conceptual set requires most beginning trainees to begin to assume a longer temporal span for interaction sequences, and to be able to meaningfully "punctuate" conceptual beginning and end points for these sequences. Trainees are reminded that interaction sequences are not "over" until *everyone's* mediating role has been identified, and until a plausible functional out-

come or payoff can be posited for each family member.

Some trainees experience difficulty with creating positive aspects of relabeling, and much of the personal feedback content to trainees centers around the therapeutically limiting properties of their particular values. Most trainees experience some type of "countertransference" difficulty with a particular type of family member which can led them to take sides, not be objective, find fault, or otherwise work against therapy. Trainees are therefore presented with role-play vignettes and characterizations of seemingly "noxious" people, and are instructed to come up with positive and adaptive descriptions of the particular person, role, or behavior. Similarly, trainees are shaped to relabel seemingly aversive processes. Conflict-phobic trainees and their clients both profit if the trainee can label an "argument" as "an effort to arrive at a mutually satisfactory resolution." Trainees are encouraged to develop this conceptual flexibility by training experiences which force them to label the positive, adaptive, or functional properties of behavior that they might find personally reprehensible.

Therapists' relationship skills are evaluated by both supervisors and peers in a group setting. As a group norm, trainees are told that any critical feedback on relationship skills or trainees' styles requires a pragmatic solution. For example, if a trainee is presented with the feedback that he appears "hostile," he must also receive feedback on how to remediate the style (such as, "Don't frown"), as well as why it might lead to trouble in therapy sessions ("An aggressive, authoritarian parent might really want to take you down a peg").

Trainees' educational skills are evaluated in terms of how well the therapist presents the procedure as a ritual, and the trainee is required to present a rationale as to how the technique will "fit" a particular family. In general, therapists are urged to pursue independently published resources for learning well-packaged change techniques: Functional family training is geared more toward "fitting" these procedures to the family. Again, beginning trainees occasionally have a problematic naïveté. They are reminded that procedures like behavioral contracting can't *force* change, but that the therapist must create a situation in which the family members will adopt the procedure to help them operate more efficiently.

Finally, trainees are encouraged to create a professional situation for themselves where they can supervise another practitioner of functional family therapy and receive supervision and feedback in return. Most professional settings isolate therapists from one another, due to demanding caseloads and service delivery priorities. Functional family therapy trainees are urged to create either a formal or informal supervision arrangement to enhance their growth in the model and to ameliorate their professional isolation. Family therapists are typically outnumbered in their clinical work, and the functional family model is sufficiently complex and demanding to require ongoing supervision by an objective third party. This format offers trainees support, as well as objective assessments and appraisals of clients and of trainee effectiveness.

EMPIRICAL SUPPORT FOR THE FUNCTIONAL FAMILY MODEL

As described in fuller detail elsewhere (Alexander and Barton, 1976), the functional family model of intervention has been subjected to a sequential series of studies to evaluate its conceptual bases (Alexander, 1973), intervention technology (Alexander and Parsons, 1973), a within-model as well as comparative study of intervention efficacy (Alexander and Parsons, 1973), and extent of family impact (Klein, Alexander, and Parsons 1977). As many of its basic assumptions have been subjected to scrutiny, the model has been developed and refined.

In general, the research has been performed with the families of status delinquents. Since the research has utilized process or nonreactive outcome measures, however, this population limitation probably does not substantially compromise the assertions of the model. As discussed briefly in the *process* section of this chapter, the literature would suggest that the content of family distress, or what families talk about (such as delinquency, schizophrenia, neuroses, religion, peers), is probably less relevant than the ubiquitous processes of family life, or ways in which families talk about relevant aspects of their lives (Mischler and Waxler, 1965; Morton,

1976). Since research of the functional family model has been largely guided by a focus on typical family processes, the assumption has been made that both the model and research would therefore generalize across a wider range of familial content phenomena.

This focus on family process as an index of family life also illustrates another set of assumptions which has guided the development of the model. Just as functional family therapist training has been guided by what the most effective functional family therapists do (Alexander, Barton, Schiavo, and Parsons, 1976), so, too, has the intervention model for distressed families been developed on the basis of what nondistressed families do (Alexander and Barton, 1976). This empirical strategy reflects a matching-to-sample philosophy (Parsons and Alexander, 1973), rather than an idealized notion about what families "ought to be." This strategy has several implications for the focus and findings that have guided research with the functional family model. First, there is little attention devoted to the role of person variables in families, or what the ideal family member should be. Rather, the model targets exchanges between people as being the critical dimension of behavior. "Normality" or "treatment goals" are empirically reflected by particular changes in a given family's process and reduction of a target problem, since the particular content of processes and the functions which they serve are largely idiosyncratic to a particular family. Nonetheless, consistent and reliable changes across groups of families in this research are compelling arguments for both the matching-to-sample philosophy and a focus on process dimensions of family behavior.

Study 1: Conceptual bases of a systems approach

Alexander (1973) compared 20 delinquent and 22 nondelinquent family triads performing two interaction tasks. The "goal of the . . . study with delinquent families was to develop potentially modifiable measures that would: 1) reflect directly the nature of relationships; 2) identify system processes that characterize delinquent behavior; and 3) demonstrate that these processes are not present in adaptive, nondelinquent families" (Alexander and Barton, 1976, p. 170). The study utilized defensive and supportive (Gibb, 1961) dependent measures of family members' speech to characterize family process.

It was found that delinquent families characteristically demonstrated higher rates of defensiveness between all six possible combinations of dyads (parents to each other and to child; child to each parent) and lower rates of supportiveness in child to father, child to mother dyads. The study also demonstrated that nondelinquent families reciprocated supportiveness, while delinquent families characteristically reciprocated defensiveness.

Study 2: Utilization of a Technology to Modify Systems Processes

Based on the first study which revealed interaction processes that distinguished between delinquent and nondelinquent families, it was necessary to demonstrate that these processes were modifiable through some form of intervention (Alexander and Barton, 1976). Forty delinquent families characterized by maladaptive processes were randomly assigned to either family therapy, family and individual therapy in combination, individual therapy, or a no-treatment control condition. All families were pre- and posttested on the same interaction tasks utilized in the comparative study of delinquent and nondelinquent families. During the intervention phase of the study, families in family treatment conditions received conjoint communication training and behavioral contracting training, the individual treatment condition consisted of an empathetic nondirective form of therapy, while no-treatment controls received only pre- and posttesting (Alexander and Parsons, 1973). It was found that all families receiving a family intervention improved their processes of verbal exchange as reflected by a ratio of supportiveness/defensiveness. Parents of delinquent youth who did not receive family intervention did not improve at all, while no-treatment condition family members seemed to deteriorate in their quality of exchange. The results of this study led to the conclusion that problematic family processes could be modified with a relatively short-term functional family intervention.

Study 3: The Comparative Efficacy of the Functional Family Model on Modifying Family Process and Symptoms

While it had been shown that family processes which characterize families of delinquents could be modified in ways which made them more closely approximate nondelinquent families, it remained to be seen whether or not modification of these processes had any demonstrable relationship to target symptoms. A fundamental assumption of communication (Haley, 1963; Watzlawick, Beavin, and Jackson, 1967) and the functional family (Barton and Alexander, 1976; Klein, Barton, and Alexander, in press; Malouf and Alexander, 1974) models is that symptoms represent inefficient processes to have legitimate functions met. If this were the case, then it was anticipated that the creation of more adaptive processes for the delinquent family should reduce the need for symptomatic behavior as an inefficient vehicle for behavioral control. Hence, a larger follow-up study (Parsons and Alexander, 1973) was undertaken to determine if modifications of delinquent family processes would result in reduced delinquency, as measured by reduced recidivism.

Second, the study included comparison treatment conditions (client-centered and psychodynamic-eclectic) which were presumed to represent more conventional one-to-one treatment models. It was assumed that skilled practitioners of these models would represent a vehicle for determining if the functional family model represented a treatment efficacy superior to more conventional individually-oriented models targeted toward "criterion mental health." The study also included a no-treatment control condition, to assess whether or not the functional family model was superior to no intervention of any kind. Delinquent families were randomly assigned (with the exception of the church-sponsored dynamic group) to one of the four treatment conditions.

Process measures were based on dimensions of equality of family speech as an index to adaptive system functioning, and it was found that families treated with the functional family model "showed the greatest equality of speech, the least silence, and the most frequent and lengthy interruptions" (Alexander and Barton, 1976, p.

TABLE 3
Summary of the Program of Research with the Functional Family Model

Research Question	Contrast or Comparison	Form of Intervention or Manipulation	Finding	Implication
Is family adaptability related to family interaction or process? (Alexander, 1973)	defensive and supportive communication; between delinquent and nondelinquent families	structured interaction task	Delinquent families reciprocate more defensiveness than nondelinquent families.	Juvenile delinquency is associated with maladaptive family process which tends to be system disintegrating; maladaptive family process is an important target of intervention.
Is family process related to the conceptual set of interactants? (Barton & Alexander, 1979)	defensive and supportive communication; between delinquent and nondelinquent families	structured interaction under both: a) competitive relational set b) cooperative relational set	Delinquent families more defensive than nondelinquent; delinquent families no more defensive than nondelinquent in cooperative set.	Relational conceptual set is an important mediation of family process; positive relational attribution should be included as an important component of family intervention.
Can maladaptive family processes be effectively modified with intervention? (Alexander & Parsons, 1973)	defensive and supportive communications pre- and post-intervention; delinquent families assigned to one of four groups: a) family intervention b) family intervention and individual intervention for delinquent c) individual intervention for delinquent d) no treatment	structured interaction task for all families pre- and post-; family intervention was functional family model, individual intervention was client-centered model	Family intervention most effective in modifying process, in direction of nondelinquent families; b) not superior to a); c) no change; d) some deterioration of family process.	Functional family model most effective in modifying delinquent family process toward criterion of adaptive family process.
Does modifying family process modify symptom presumed to be associated with it? Is functional family model the best form of intervention relative to other models? (Parsons & Alexander, 1973)	equality of family process; recidivism; delinquent families assigned to one of four groups: a) functional family model b) client-centered c) dynamic-eclectic d) no treatment	structured interaction task; follow-up to investigate recidivism; families received intervention with one of the family models	Functional family model most effective in modifying family process in direction of nondelinquent families; recidivism: a) 26% b) 46% c) 73% d) 50% (same as County baseline)	Modifying family process modifies symptomatic delinquent behavior; functional family model is comparatively the most efficient at modifying both.

TABLE 3 (Continued)				
Research Question	*Contrast or Comparison*	*Form of Intervention or Manipulation*	*Finding*	*Implication*
Does modification of family process and symptoms remain stable over time, and generalize to other family members? (Klein, Alexander, & Parsons, 1976)	long-term (2½-3 years) court contact by siblings of delinquents treated in Parsons & Alexander (1973) study; a) functional family model b) client-centered model c) dynamic-eclectic model d) no treatment	none: long-term follow-up of previously treated groups	Court contacts by siblings of treated delinquents a) 20% b) 59% c) 63% d) 40%	Modification of process in family system maintains over time, and helps families deal with subsequent developmental crises of adolescence.
Does the performance of the therapist influence the effectiveness of the functional family model? (Alexander, Barton, Schiavo, & Parsons, 1976)	Defensiveness of delinquent families treated with functional family intervention; comparisons between relationship and structuring skills of functional family therapists producing one of four family outcomes: a) poorest-no change in family, didn't return after first session b) family remained > 1 session, but no change c) positive change in family, but took considerable number of sessions d) best-positive change in families in 6-8 sessions	functional family therapy	d) and c) groups of functional family therapists best reduced maladaptive family processes; Relationship Skills a) lowest b) low c) high d) high Structuring Skills a) low b) medium c) medium d) high; relationship and structuring of functional family therapists jointly predict 60% of variance in family outcome.	Relationship and structuring skills are independent but necessary classes of skills for effective implementation of the functional family model; should be a focus of formal training in the model.

180). It was also shown that for long-term follow-up (3-15 months) families treated with the functional family model showed a substantial reduction in recidivism relative to the court system baserate (26% for functional family therapy, 50% baserate), while the client-centered and control groups were fundamentally the same as baserate (47% and 50%, respectively). Surprisingly, families in the dynamic-eclectic condition showed a 73% recidivism rate.

Because this study demonstrated a high degree of controls for methodological confounds (see Alexander and Barton, 1976; Parsons and Alexander, 1973, for more detailed discussion of methodological issues), the results are taken as very convincing support for the theoretically-derived form of intervention and the nature of symptoms, as well as the superiority of the family system as an arena for change.

Study 4. Modification of Family Process as a Long-Term Effect and Preventive Phenomenon

To evaluate the long-term effect of the functional family model, juvenile court records were searched from two-and-a-half to three years after the completion of the original follow-up study (Parsons and Alexander, 1973). This time, the records were searched for instances of contact by siblings of the families of delinquents in the original recidivism study. The idea was to determine if the modification of family process would remain stable over time and help families of delinquents maintain more adaptive processes to deal with subsequent developmental crises of adolescence (Coles, Alexander, and Schiavo, 1974; Morton, Alexander, and Altman, 1976). These sibling data essentially replicated the findings from the original recidivism study. The sibling referral rates for each group were: 1) no-treatment, 40%; 2) client-centered, 59%; 3) dynamic-eclectic, 63%; and 4) functional family group, 20%. The consistency of both the magnitude and rank-ordering of these data relative to those of the 1973 study is taken to document not only the time-based consistency and stability of the therapeutic benefits and superiority of the functional family model, but some apparent preventive aspects of family-focused intervention as well.

Summary of Research with the Functional Family Model of Intervention

Table 3 represents a summary of all the research to date targeted directly toward the development and evaluation of the functional family model of intervention. The table is provided to represent how the myriad assumptions embedded within the chapter have been supported by empirical data and is designed to convey the compelling and persuasive nature of support for the model. More detailed primary sources of these studies elaborate on their formal conceptual derivation as well as their heuristic implications. Despite the lack of detailed content provided about the research, the highlighted findings of these studies are the basis for the more detailed accounts of implementing the functional family model as represented in the chapter.

As stated elsewhere (Alexander and Barton, 1976), these studies reflect a commitment to programatic research leading to refinement and increased understanding of the functional family model. While many of the assertions about and development of the model were initially derived from clinical experience or untested conceptual models, the commitment remains to continue to identify and operationalize critical components of the model and to submit them to empirical testing. The research implemented to date is by no means exhaustive or conclusive.

The data also imply that the functional family model requires further development. While a 26% recidivism rate with the model has been consistently replicated, this same comparatively superior figure of 26% reflects room for improvement as well. More data are clearly necessary to better understand the complexity of family functioning, let alone the increased complexity when intervention with the family is a target concern. Unfortunately, the field of family intervention is presently lagging in its methodological capability to deal with its complex intuition about interaction models (Alexander and Barton, 1980). These concerns are those of the family intervention field as a whole, as well as those of functional family advocates, and hopefully increased attention to interpersonal models, the family, and the therapy process itself will ultimately allow the family intervention field to make inroads on that 26%.

DIRECTIONS FOR FUTURE RESEARCH

There are several pressing research questions posed by the functional family model. There is a class of developmental questions centered around parent-adolescent relationships. Longitudinal or cross-sectional studies would illuminate the degree to which changes in the qualitative nature of relationships is a salient determinant of family life. There are also a host of issues surrounding the specificity with which parents and their problem offspring create qualitatively inefficient interactions. Are problem families characterized by inefficient communication between *all* members, or just identified patients? The role of both conceptual set and therapists' skills requires substantial research. A series of component studies (including operationalized manipulation of conceptual set, therapists' relationship and structuring skills) would enhance our understanding of effective ingredients of family change. Further descriptive research should also be performed to enhance our understanding of why families operate the way they do. Is there a way to quantify or objectify dimensions like intimacy or distance, to understand how and why families behave as systems? These are larger questions that would facilitate development not only of the functional family model, but of others as well.

CONCLUSION

At the outset of this chapter, the case of Paul represented the disappointment, frustration, and hopelessness associated with the ineffectiveness of a limited treatment model. Associated with this sense of disappointment, frustration and hopelessness were a limited clinical scope, a limiting set of value judgments, a limiting set of assumptions, and a limiting technology. The major emotional aspects of Paul's case were associated with these limits for the clinician.

The functional family model has been developed mainly in response to clinical value judgments, changing assumptions, and placing technology in a different clinical perspective. This development has been a product of reacting against certain traditional limits, but at the same time the development of the model requires consistent reconsideration and modification of its own limits.

The family intervention field has not yet established a consistent set of limits, and this is probably due more to its infancy than to the dangerous assumption that they are not there. Scholars of theory development assert that one hallmark of substantial theory is that it contains limits against which it can be definitively tested (Hall and Lindzey, 1970; Shaw and Costanzo, 1970). It is presently difficult for the family intervention field to articulate these limits, due in no small part to our very real limits of articulating interpersonal phenomena in a relational conceptual scheme and language.

A careful reading of the family intervention literature consistently reveals how much of the intervention procedures, assessment, and clinical value judgments described are related to traditional individualistic phenomena. If the field is to progress substantially, both in terms of generating useful data and offering newer and more effective means of interpersonal intervention, the field must in some ways force itself to appraise the world differently than our individually-oriented culture and psychology. Part of the fruits of an interpersonal or interactional orientation is being clinically realized. The continued enhancement of the functional family and other family-oriented models nonetheless requires that the family field continue to identify and resolve the limits of our understanding of an interpersonal world.

REFERENCES

Alexander, J. F. Defensive and supportive communication in normal and deviant families. *Journal of Consulting and Clinical Psychology*, 1973, 40, 223-231.

Alexander, J. F., & Barton, C. Behavioral systems therapy for families. In: D. H. Olson (Ed.), *Treating Relationships*. Lake Mills, Iowa: Graphic, 1976.

Alexander, J. F., & Barton, C. Intervention with delinquents and their families: Clinical, methodological, and conceptual issues. In: J. P. Vincent (Ed.), *Advances in Family Intervention, Assessment, and Theory*. Greenwich, Conn.: Johnson Associates, Inc. (JAI) Press, 1980.

Alexander, J. F., Barton, C., Schiavo, R. S., & Parsons, B. V. Systems-behavioral intervention with families of delinquents: Therapist characteristics, family behavior, and outcome. *Journal of Consulting and Clinical Psychology*, 1976, *44*, 656-664.

Alexander, J. F., & Parsons, B. V. Short-term behavioral intervention with delinquent families: Impact on family process and recidivism. *Journal of Abnormal Psychology*, 1973, *31*, 219-225.

Allyon, T., & Azrin, N. H. *The Token Economy: A Motivational System for Therapy and Rehabilitation*. New York: Appleton, 1968.

Altman, I., & Taylor, D. A. *Social Penetration: The Development of Interpersonal Relationships*. New York: Holt, Rinehart, and Winston, 1973.

Astin, A. The functional autonomy of psychotherapy. *American Psychologist*, 1961, *16*, 75-78.

Bandura, A. *Principles of Behavior Modification*. New York: Holt, 1969.

Barefoot, J. C., & Straub, R. B. Opportunity for information search and the effect of false heart rate feedback. In: H. London & R. E. Nisbett (Eds.), *Thought and Feeling: Cognitive Alteration of Feeling States*. Chicago: Aldine, 1974.

Barton, C., & Alexander, J. F. *Therapist skills in systems-behavioral family intervention: How the hell do you get them to do it?* Paper presented at the Annual Meeting, American Orthopsychiatric Association, Atlanta, 1976.

Barton, C., & Alexander, J. F. Therapists' skills as determinants of effective systems-behavioral family therapy. *International Journal of Family Counseling*, 1977a, *11*, 1-15.

Barton, C., & Alexander, J. F. Treatment of families with a delinquent member. In: G. Harris (Ed.) *The Group Treatment of Human Problems: A Social Learning Approach*. New York: Grune & Stratton, 1977b.

Barton, C., & Alexander, J. F. *Functional Family Therapy Assessment Checklist*. Unpublished training manual, University of Utah, 1978.

Barton, C., & Alexander, J. F. *Delinquent and normal family interaction in competitive and cooperative conditions*. Paper presented at the Annual Meeting of the American Psychological Association, New York, 1979.

Beier, E. *The Silent Language of Psychotherapy*. Chicago: Aldine, 1966.

Bell, J. E. Recent advances in family group therapy. *Journal of Child Psychology and Psychiatry*, 1962, *3*, 1-15.

Bem, D. J., & McConnell, H. K. Testing the self-perception explanation of dissonance phenomena: On the salience of premanipulation attitudes. *Journal of Personality and Social Psychology*, 1970, *14*, 23-31.

Berkowitz, L., & Turner, C. Perceived anger level, instigating agent, and aggression. In: H. London & R. E. Nisbett (Eds.), *Thought and Feeling: Cognitive Alteration of Feeling States*. Chicago: Aldine, 1974.

Brehm, J. W., & Cohen, A. R. *Explorations in Cognitive Dissonance*. New York: Wiley, 1962.

Cheek, F. E. Family socialization techniques and deviant behavior. *Family Process*, 1966, *5*, 199-217.

Coles, J. L., Alexander, J. F., & Schiavo, R. S. *A developmental model of family systems: A social-psychological approach*. Paper presented at the Annual Convention of the National Council of Family Relations, St. Louis, 1974.

Emery, R. E., & Marholin, D. An applied behavior analysis of delinquency: The irrelevancy of relevant behavior. *American Psychologist*, 1977, *32*, 860-873.

Eysenck, H. J. The effects of psychotherapy. In: H. J. Eysenck (Ed.), *Handbook of Abnormal Psychology*. New York: Basic Books, 1961.

Framo, J. L. Symptoms from a family transactional viewpoint. In: C. J. Sager & H. S. Kaplan (Eds.), *Progress in Group and Family Therapy*. New York: Brunner/Mazel, 1972.

Frank, J. D. *Persuasion and Healing*. Baltimore: Johns Hopkins Press, 1961.

Gibb, J. R. Defensive communications. *Journal of Communication*, 1961, *3*, 141-148.

Graziano, A. M. (Ed.) *Behavior Therapy with Children: II*. Chicago: Aldine, 1975.

Haley, J. Speech sequences of normal and abnormal families with two children present. *Family Process*, 1967, *1*, 81-97.

Haley, J. *Strategies of Psychotherapy*. New York: Grune & Stratton, 1963.

Hall, C. S., & Lindzey, G. *Theories of Personality*. New York: Wiley, 1970.

Hawkins, R. P., Peterson, R. F., Schweid, E., & Bijou, S. W. Behavior therapy in the home: Amelioration of parent-child relations with the parent in a therapeutic role. *Journal of Experimental Child Psychology*, 1966, *4*, 99-107.

Heider, F. *The Psychology of Interpersonal Relations*. New York: Wiley, 1958.

Jourard, S. M. *The Transparent Self: Self-disclosure and Well-being*. Princeton, N.J.: Van Nostrand, 1964.

Jurkovic, G. J., & Prentice, N. M. Dimensions of moral interaction and moral judgment in delinquent families. *Journal of Consulting and Clinical Psychology*, 1974, *42*, 256-262.

Kanouse, D. E., & Hanson, L. R. Negativity in evaluations. In: E. E. Jones, D. E. Kanouse, H. H. Kelley, R. E. Nisbett, S. Valins, & B. Weiner (Eds.), *Attribution: Perceiving the Causes of Behavior*. Morristown, N.J.: General Learning Press, 1972.

Kelley, H. H. Attribution in social interaction. In: E. E. Jones, D. E. Kanouse, H. H. Kelley, R. E. Nisbett, S. Valins, & B. Weiner (Eds.), *Attribution: Perceiving the Causes of Behavior*. Morristown, N.J.: General Learning Press, 1972.

Kiesler, D. J. Some myths of psychotherapy research and the search for a paradigm. *Psychological Bulletin*, 1966, *65*, 110-136.

Klein, N. C., Alexander, J. F., & Parsons, B. V. Impact of family systems intervention on recidivism and sibling delinquency: A model of primary prevention and program evaluation. *Journal of Consulting and Clinical Psychology*, 1977, *45*, 469-474.

Klein, N. C., Barton, C., & Alexander, J. F. Intervention and evaluation in family settings. In: R. H. Price & P. Polister (Eds.), *Evaluation and Action in the Community Context*, in press.

London, H., & Nisbett, R. E. Elements of Schachter's cognitive theory of emotional states. In: H. London & R. E. Nisbett (Eds.), *Thought and Feeling: Cognitive Alteration of Feeling States*. Chicago: Aldine, 1974.

Love, L. R., & Kaswan, J. W. *Troubled Children: Their Families, Schools, and Treatment*. New York: Wiley, 1974.

Malouf, J. L. *Interpersonal distance and reciprocity as determinants of communication in new and established systems*. Unpublished doctoral dissertation, University of Utah, 1974.

Malouf, R. E., & Alexander, J. F. Family crisis intervention: A model and technique of training. In: R. E. Hardy & J. C. Cull (Ed.), *Therapeutic Needs of the Family*. Springfield, Ill.: Thomas, 1974.

Martin, B. Family interaction associated with child disturbance: Assessment and modification. *Psychotherapy: Theory, Research, and Practice*, 1967, *4*, 30-35.

Meehl, P. E. Seer over sign: The first good example. *Journal of Experimental Research in Personality*, 1965, *1*, 27-32.

Minuchin, S., Montalvo, B. G., Jr., Rosman, B. L., & Schumer, F. *Families of the Slums.* New York: Basic Books, Inc., 1967.

Mishler, E. G., & Waxler, N. E. Family interaction processes and schizophrenia: A review of current theories. *Merrill-Palmer Quarterly*, 1965, 2, 269-315.

Morton, T. L. *The effects of acquaintance and distance on intimacy and reciprocity.* Unpublished doctoral dissertation, University of Utah, 1976.

Morton, T. L., Alexander, J. F., & Altman, I. Communication and relationship definition. In: G. L. Miller (Ed.), *Explorations in Interpersonal Communication.* Beverly Hills: Sage, 1976.

Murrell, S. A., & Stachowiak, J. G. Consistency, rigidity, and power in the interaction patterns of clinic and non-clinic families. *Journal of Abnormal Psychology*, 1967, 72, 265-272.

Newcomb, T. M. Stabilities underlying changes in interpersonal attraction. *Journal of Abnormal and Social Psychology*, 1963, 66, 376-386.

Nisbett, R. E., & Valins, S. Perceiving the causes of one's own behavior. In: E. E. Jones, D. E. Kanouse, H. H. Kelley, R. E. Nisbett, S. Valins, & B. Weiner (Ed.), *Attribution: Perceiving the Causes of Behavior.* Morristown, N.J.: General Learning Press, 1972.

Nye, F. I. *Family Relationships and Delinquent Behavior.* New York: Wiley, 1958.

O'Neill, M., & Alexander, J. F. *Family interaction patterns as a function of task characteristics.* Unpublished manuscript, University of Utah, 1974.

Parsons, B. V., & Alexander, J. F. Short term family intervention: A therapy outcome study. *Journal of Consulting and Clinical Psychology*, 1973, 41, 195-201.

Patterson, G. R. A basis for identifying stimuli which control behavior in natural settings. *Child Development*, 1974, 45, 900-911.

Patterson, G. R. Behavioral intervention procedures in the classroom and in the home. In: A. E. Bergin & S. L. Garfield (Eds.), *Handbook of Psychotherapy and Behavior Change: An Empirical Analysis.* New York: John Wiley, 1971.

Patterson, G. R. The aggressive child: Victim and architect of a coercive system. In: E. J. Mash, L. A. Hamerlynck, & L. C. Handy (Eds.), *Behavior Modification and Families.* New York: Brunner/Mazel, 1976.

Patterson, G. R., & Cobb, J. A. Stimulus control for classes of noxious behaviors. In: J. F. Knutson (Ed.), *The Control of Aggression: Implications for Basic Research.* Chicago: Aldine, 1972.

Patterson, G. R., & Reid, J. B. Reciprocity and coercion: Two facets of social systems. In: C. Neuringer & J. Michael (Ed.), *Behavior Modification in Clinical Psychology.* New York: Appleton-Century-Crofts, 1967.

Patterson, G. R., Weiss, R. L., & Hops, H. Training of marital skills: Some problems and concepts. In: H. Leitenberg (Ed.), *Handbook of Operant Techniques.* Englewood Cliffs, N.J.: Prentice-Hall, Inc., 1975.

Rice, F. P. *The Adolescent: Development, Relationships, and Culture.* Boston: Allyn & Bacon, 1975.

Rimm, D. C., & Masters, J. C. *Behavior Therapy: Techniques and Empirical Findings.* New York: Academic Press, 1974.

Risley, T. R., Clark, H. B., & Cataldo, M. F. Behavior technology for the normal middle-class family. In: E. J. Mash, L. A. Hamerlynck, & L. C. Handy (Eds.), *Behavior Modification and Families.* New York: Brunner/Mazel, 1976.

Safilios-Rothschild, C. The study of family power structure: a review 1959-1966. *Journal of Marriage and the Family*, 1970, 32, 539-552.

Satir, V. *Conjoint Family Therapy.* Palo Alto: Science and Behavior Books, Inc., 1967.

Shaver, K. G. *An Introduction to Attribution Processes.* Cambridge, Mass.: Winthrop, 1975.

Shaw, M. E., & Costanzo, P. R. *Theories of Social Psychology.* New York: McGraw-Hill, 1970.

Sidman, M. *Tactics of Scientific Research: Evaluating Experimental Data in Psychology.* New York: Basic Books, 1960.

Stabeneau, J. R., Tupin, J., Werner, M. M., & Pollin, W. A comparative study of families of schizophrenics, delinquents, and normals. *Psychiatry*, 1965, 28, 45-59.

Stuart, R. B. Behavioral contracting within the families of delinquents. *Journal of Behavioral Therapy and Experimental Psychiatry*, 1971, 2, 1-11.

Stuart, R. B., & Lott, L. A. Behavioral contracting with delinquents: A cautionary note. *Journal of Behavior Therapy and Experimental Psychiatry*, 1972, 3, 161-169.

Thompson, R. F. *Foundations of Physiological Psychology.* New York: Harper and Row, 1967.

Urdang, L., & Flexner, S. B. (Ed.), *Random House College Dictionary.* New York: Random House, 1972.

Watzlawick, P., Beavin, J. H., & Jackson, D. D. *Pragmatics of Human Communication: A Study of Interactional Patterns, Pathologies, and Paradoxes.* New York: Norton, 1967.

Watzlawick, P., Weakland, J., & Fisch, R. *Change: Principles of Problem Formation and Problem Resolution.* New York: Norton, 1974.

Weiss, R. L., Hops, H., & Patterson, G. R. A framework for conceptualizing marital conflict, a technology for altering it, and some data for evaluating it. In: L. A. Hamerlynck, L. C. Handy, & E. J. Mash (Eds.), *Behavior Change: Methodology, Concepts, and Practice.* Champaign, Ill.: Research Press, 1973.

Wolpe, J. *The Practice of Behavior Therapy.* Oxford: Pergamon, 1969.

EDITORS' REFERENCES

Gurman, A. S. & Knudson, R. M. Behavioral marriage therapy: I. A psychodynamic-systems analysis and critique. *Family Process*, 1978, 17, 121-138.

Gurman, A. S., Knudson, R. M. & Kniskern, D. P. Behavioral marriage therapy: IV. Take two aspirin and call us in the morning. *Family Process*, 1978, 17, 165-180.

Jacobson, N. S. & Margolin, G. *Marital Therapy: Strategies Based on Social Learning and Behavior Exchange Principles.* New York: Brunner/Mazel, 1979.

CHAPTER 12

Problem-Centered Systems Therapy of the Family

Nathan B. Epstein, M.D.

and Duane S. Bishop, M.D.

Family therapy has become an increasingly popular mode of treatment over the last two decades (Epstein and Bishop, 1973; Group for the Advancement of Psychiatry, 1970; Gurman and Kniskern, 1978; Haley, 1971; Olson, 1970; Zuk, 1971). Its acceptance has not been limited to psychiatry and other mental health fields, for it is increasingly viewed as an important development by family medicine (Comley, 1973; Epstein and McAuley, 1978; McFarlane, Norman, and Spitzer, 1971; McFarlane, O'Connell, and Hay, 1971; Patriarche, 1974; Stanford, 1972), by pediatrics (Finkel, 1974; McClelland, Staples, Weisberg, and Bergin, 1973; Tomm, 1973), and by those working with the disabled (Bishop and Epstein, 1979). Training programs and study curricula in family therapy have grown tremendously in the last ten years (Bishop and Epstein, 1979; Liddle and Halpin, 1978). Reports of a significant amount of research have also appeared (DeWitt, 1978; Glick and Haley, 1971; Gurman and Kniskern, 1978; Guttman, Spector, Sigal, Rakoff, and Epstein, 1971; Olson, 1970; Santa-Barbara, Woodward, Levin, Streiner, Goodman, and Epstein, 1975; Wells, Dilkes,

and Trivelli, 1972; Woodward, Santa-Barbara, Levin, Epstein, and Streiner, 1977; Woodward, Santa-Barbara, Levin, Goodman, Streiner, and Epstein, 1975; Woodward, Santa-Barbara, Levin, Goodman, Streiner, Muzzin, and Epstein, 1974). Several authors have pointed to the need for clear descriptions of conceptual orientations and the specifics of the therapy process (Epstein and Bishop, 1973; Liddle and Halpin, 1978).

However, approaches to working with family problems are still basically limited to clinical judgment and intuition. Literature reviews expose the variety of theoretical models underlying clinical work in this area and there is no generally accepted framework within which to perform family assessment and treatment. This variety is no justification for an undisciplined approach and it is important for those treating families to be clear and consistent about the conceptual frameworks they use. We feel that professionals working with families require both 1) a model that forms the basis for their understanding of family functioning and 2) a model that guides their approach to treatment.

We have described two such models which,

in combination, can form the basis for family work. The McMaster Model of Family Functioning (Epstein, Bishop, and Levin, 1978) provides a conceptual framework for assessing and diagnosing family functioning. The Problem-Centered Systems Therapy of the Family model (Epstein and Bishop, in press) provides an operationalized guide to the assessment and treatment of families.

In what follows we will present some historical background, a brief introduction to the family functioning model and then focus on treatment. In the process, we will detail the clinical use of both the family functioning and treatment models. Finally, we will review research and training procedures which are based on these approaches.

BACKGROUND

The senior author was first trained as a general adult and child psychiatrist and then went on to receive training in psychoanalysis. In those days, workers in child psychiatry began to highlight the role of the mother in the behavior of the child and also, to a considerably lesser extent, to take some note of the effect of other family members on the identified patient. Work with children and their mothers, plus exposure to Drs. Nathan Ackerman and Abram Kardiner during psychoanalytic training, led the senior author to an awareness of the need for a total systems approach in order to understand and help patients. Earlier research experience with a multidisciplinary medical research group studying the application of hormones to human patients had already resulted in his becoming aware of the powerful forces wrought by biological agents on human behavior.

Dr. Kardiner, a pioneer in transcultural psychiatry and a brilliantly effective teacher, demonstrated the effect of culture, values, religion, economics, history, social patterns and practices, etc. on behavior. His major works (Kardiner, 1939; Kardiner, Linton, Du Bois, and West, 1945) remain classics in the field.

Ackerman at that time (1951-1955) was developing his ideas on working with the family group in psychotherapy (e.g., Ackerman, 1958)—a radical notion during that period for which he received much abuse from his more conservative analytic colleagues. Although Ackerman had not yet developed clear formulations of family theories or family therapy technique (cf. Ackerman, 1966), it seemed that he was moving towards a more effective way of understanding and treating patients by having the significant actors in the patient's life in the therapy situation at the same time, thereby easing the job of "teasing out" the family interactions which led to the behavior being treated.

Struck by the exciting potential and common sense inherent in this approach, Epstein began to experiment with methods of involving family members of patients in the course of therapy. Various approaches were used, such as seeing the mother together with the child patient in play therapy; having both parents in for occasional sessions either with or without the child or adolescent patient present; having the mothers participate in activity group therapy with children and seeing those mothers in a separate weekly group without the children; seeing two spouses together when only one of them was the presenting patient; and bringing in different members of the individual patient's family at various times during the course of that individual's analytic therapy. As time went on, the approach being used most frequently was that where all members were seen together for conjoint family therapy regardless of the presenting problem.

During these early years, the conceptual model and therapy approach used were intrapsychic psychoanalytic, somewhat modified to fit the new situations. The actual family interactional patterns postulated as responsible for the creation of the intrapsychic and behavioral pathology in the identified patient were being observed, stimulated, inferred and interpreted. The analytic concepts most frequently used in interpreting the behavior observed in family sessions were those of role projection, displacement, incorporation of part objects, oedipal strivings, sibling rivalry, denial, and affective repression. As described elsewhere (Epstein, 1963), this primarily analytic approach changed gradually to one with more focusing on the interactional aspects of the intrafamilial behavior. There was much stress on releasing the affect underlying the inferred important family interactions and the associated intrapsychic conflicts and fantasies. The primary objective remained that of easing the intrapsychic conflicts of the identified patient, which were inferred to result in the pathological symptoms and/or behavior for which treatment was undertaken. In the late fifties, research was started on "nonclinical" families. This was reported in the *Silent Majority* (Westley and Epstein, 1969). It was only then, when we found that the family as a "system" was more powerful than intrapsychic factors in determining the behavior of individual family members, that our therapy approach began to change to a systems-oriented approach. Since this occurred, around 1963-1964, our approach has been continually evolving. The early change from a primarily psychoanalytic-interactional mode to a systems mode, where the family system itself is looked at as the factor to be evaluated as responsible for the difficulty in the behavior being examined, was most difficult. Fifteen years of training and orientation had to be strongly modified and a new approach based on controversial research findings had to be developed. The tendency to slip automatically into a primarily psychoanalytic approach to therapy was great and occurred frequently. With careful self-monitoring and experience, this now happens very rarely and only when it is based upon a conscious decision for purposes of furthering understanding and therapeutic progress. As stated, our therapeutic approach has been continually modified as the results from our research, clinical work and teaching indicated the need for same.

A conceptual framework, The Family Categories Schema (Epstein, Rakoff, and Sigal, 1968), originally developed in the course of the study of 110 "nonclinical" families (Westley and Epstein, 1969) mentioned previously, formed the basis of thinking for the current model. The

model which follows is the result of the many significant revisions and developments of the original concepts since they were first generated.

THEORY: UNDERLYING CONCEPTS[1]

The McMaster Model of Family Functioning

The McMaster Model of Family Functioning has evolved over a period of 20 years. Ideas gained from reading the family literature have been incorporated into the model in various ways. The development of the model has involved the development of a concept, then testing of the concept in clinical work, in research, and in teaching. Problems discovered in these applications have led to reformulations of the model. These were then tested out, new problems appeared and further reformulations occurred. The result of this pattern of development has been that the model is pragmatic. Ideas that work have been kept. Ideas that did not work in therapy, could not be measured reliably, or could not be communicated in teaching were discarded or modified.

The model has been used extensively in a variety of psychiatric and family practice clinics (Comley, 1973; Epstein and Westley, 1959; Guttman et al., 1971; Guttman, Spector, Sigal, Epstein and Rakoff, 1972; Postner, Guttman, Sigal, Epstein, and Rakoff, 1971; Rakoff et al., 1967; Sigal, Rakoff, and Epstein, 1967; Westley and Epstein, 1960) and by therapists who treated families as part of a large family therapy outcome study (Guttman et al., 1971; Santa-Barbara et al., 1975; Woodward et al., 1974, 1975, 1977). The framework has also been used in a number of family therapy training programs and found to be readily teachable (Bishop and Epstein, 1979).

The McMaster Model does not cover all aspects of family functioning but identifies a number of dimensions which we have found important in dealing with clinically presenting families. A family can be evaluated on the effectiveness of its functioning with respect to each dimension. On each dimension, a family may range from most ineffective to most effective functioning.

Since the development of the model has been

[1]The development of these concepts, the research, and training programs were supported by a number of grants from the Firestone Foundation. Dr. Lawrence M. Baldwin, our senior research associate, made special contributions to this paper for which we are particularly grateful. Our patient families, our trainees, and special colleagues, Dr. Sol Levin, Dorothy Horn and Dr. J. Rubenstein, all provided special experiences, support and ideas necessary for the development of this paper. The special skills and contributions of Shawn McLaughlin, Virginia Sofios, Beth Vetter, Carolyn Barlow, Pam Morton, Dr. Ian Goodyer and Louis Vlok in the preparation of this manuscript are also gratefully acknowledged.

oriented towards its applicability in the clinical setting, theoretical elegance has not been a major concern. Ideas from a variety of sources have been incorporated when they were useful. Spiegel (1971) presents a theoretical elaboration of many ideas we use. Many others have discussed some of the same concepts, but we do not wish to dwell here on the similarities and differences in usage between ourselves and other writers in the field.

The model is based on a systems approach.

In this approach the family is seen as an "open system" consisting of systems within systems (individual, marital, dyad) and relating to other systems (extended family, schools, industry, religions). The unique aspect of the dynamic family group cannot be simply reduced to the characteristics of the individual or interactions between pairs of members. Rather, there are explicit and implicit rules, plus action by members, which govern and monitor each other's behavior. The significance for therapy is the fact that the therapist is not concerned with what it is in the family which produced pathology in the individual, but rather with the processes occurring within the family system which produce the behavior which is labeled pathology. Therapy on this basis is directed at changing the system and, thereby, the behavior of the individual. The concepts of communication theory, learning theory, and transaction approach are drawn on, although the infrastructure remains the systems model (Epstein and Bishop, 1973, p. 176).

The crucial assumptions of systems theory which underlie the model to be presented can be summarized as follows:

1) The parts of the family are interrelated.
2) One part of the family cannot be understood in isolation from the rest of the system.
3) Family functioning cannot be fully understood by simply understanding each of the parts.
4) A family's structure and organization are important factors determining the behavior of family members.
5) Transactional patterns of the family system shape the behavior of family members.

The systems approach to the family is one important feature of our model. Another feature we should note is that of values. Since cultural, ethical and other similar values play such an important role in influencing human behavior, they must be sensitively appreciated and handled with care by practicing clinicians. Our approach to families is rooted in the Judaeo-Christian value system which emphasizes the optimal development of each human being. Other systems may emphasize other values and may be equally valid. We try not to impose our values in conducting therapy, but recognize that we do make value judgments and believe that behavioral scientists working in the field should be prepared to state the value base underlying their approach (Epstein, 1958).

Before proceeding, it is important to emphasize our previously stated assumption that "the primary function of today's family unit appears to be that of a laboratory for the social, psychological, and biological development and maintenance of family members" (Epstein, Levin, and Bishop, 1976, p. 1411). In the course of fulfilling this role, families deal with a variety of other issues and problems. These we group into three areas: The basic task area, the developmental task area, and the hazardous task area.

The *basic task area* includes issues that are instrumental and fundamental in nature. Examples are the provision of food, money, transportation, and shelter. The *developmental task area* encompasses those family issues that arise as part of the natural processes of individual and family growth and development over time. We differentiate two sets: those associated with the *individual developmental stages* which each family member goes through (e.g., infancy, childhood, adolescence, middle and old age crises); and those associated with *family stages* (e.g., the beginning of the marriage, the first pregnancy, and the birth of the first child). Developmental concepts and family functioning have been referred to by a number of authors (Berman and Lief, 1975; Brody, 1974; Group for the Advancement of Psychiatry, 1970; Hadley, Jacob, Milliones, Caplan, and Spitz, 1974; Scherz, 1971; Solomon, 1973). The *hazardous task area* includes the crises that arise in association with critical experiences such as illness, accidents, loss of income, job changes and moves. There is a substantial literature dealing with these topics (Comley, 1973; Hill, 1965; Langsley and Kaplan, 1968; Minuchin and Barcai, 1969; Parad and Caplan, 1965; Rapoport, 1965). The task areas are important since, in our experience, clinical presentation is often associated with the family's being unable to deal effectively with some of the tasks and issues subsumed under these three domains.

To understand the family structure, organization, and transactional pattern dysfunctions associated with family difficulties, we focus on the following six dimensions: problem-solving, communication, roles, affective responsiveness, affective involvement, and behavior control. Some groups studying family functioning conceptualize much of family behavior as occurring within a single dimension such as communication (e.g., Bateson, Jackson, Haley, and Weakland, 1956; Watzlawick, Beavin, and Jackson, 1967; Weakland, Fisch, Watzlawick, and Bodin, 1974) or role behaviors (Parsons, 1951; Parsons and Bales, 1955; Spiegel, 1971). They seem to imply that these "single dimensions" subsume all aspects of family functioning. The McMaster model does not focus on any one dimension as the foundation for conceptualizing family behavior. We argue that many dimensions need to be assessed for a fuller understanding of such a complex entity as the family. Although we attempt to clearly define and delineate the dimensions, we recognize the potential overlap and/or possible interaction that may occur between them. Further clarification will undoubtedly result from our continuing research. The dimensions of family functioning will be discussed in more detail later and elaborated in the context of our treatment model.

PROBLEM-CENTERED SYSTEMS THERAPY OF THE FAMILY

This model grew out of research and clinical work in the Departments of Psychiatry at McGill and McMaster[2] Universities in Canada (Comley, 1973; Epstein and Westley, 1959; Guttman et al., 1971, 1972; Postner et al., 1971; Rakoff et al., 1967; Sigal et al., 1967; Westley and Epstein, 1960, 1969; Epstein, and McAuley, 1978; McFarlane, Norman, and Spitzer, 1971; McFarlane, O'Connell, and Hay, 1971; Finkel,

---

[2]The Family Studies portion of the Clinical Behavioural Sciences Program, McMaster University, Faculty of Health Sciences, Hamilton, Ontario.

1974; Bishop and Epstein, 1979). The senior author and a colleague had previously worked together at McGill but had not observed each other's work with families for some years. While reviewing videotapes of each doing family therapy, clear differences were observed with respect to the *minor* moves and interventions they both made. This was not the case for the *major* steps they followed. Surprisingly, these showed striking consistency. Both therapists followed the same sequence of major steps, which we labeled the "macro stages" of therapy.

The effect of this observation was to substantially alter our thinking about family treatment. Perhaps we had been focusing on the wrong level in trying to teach therapy skills. Many psychotherapists value highly the subtle interventions, strategies and interpretations—the "art" of therapy. However, our observation of these two advanced therapists demonstrated significant differences in these areas and, yet, a striking similarity at a more general level of conducting therapy. We began to think that the subtle interventions, etc., were simply the tools therapists use to build the therapy structure. Our work since then has reinforced the view that the major structural components or stages of therapy are the essential building blocks of treatment. An added benefit is that these macro stages can be clearly operationalized and they are, therefore, more easily followed by therapists of a wide range of abilities. This led us to further delineate and analyze the differences between the major and minor therapy moves and the utility of these concepts in the teaching and research of family therapy.

We use the term *macro stages* to define the major stages of treatment. They are the large sequential blocks of the treatment process such as assessment, contracting, treatment and closure. Each incorporates a number of substages, which will be discussed later. Therapists make use of a variety of strategies and interventions in the course of leading a family through these macro stages. Here, "strategy" refers to the options and courses of action that may be taken to successfully complete a macro stage.

We differentiate the macro stages and the strategies required to negotiate them from the *micro moves*, the specific intervention skills, such as those outlined by Cleghorn and Levin (1973) and by Tomm and Wright (1979). These micro moves are the numerous interventions made by a therapist while carrying out the macro stages and include, for example, techniques for labeling, focusing, and clarifying.

Neither the macro stages nor the micro moves should be confused with "style," which is based more on the personal qualities of the therapist. Different individuals can intervene (focus) in very different ways. The differences are style, the intervention (micro move) is focusing, and both are directed at negotiating a course of treatment, the major steps of which are the macro stages.

Returning to our earlier discussion, we would emphasize that the macro stages of therapy are the most important level of focus at this point in the development of research in family therapy. We are aware that intervention skills (the micro moves) are important and will touch on general strategies when we feel they are important for an adequate and efficient completion of a given stage. We refer readers to the works of Cleghorn and Levin (1973) and Tomm and Wright (1979) for a detailed discussion of the many execution skill possibilities. In our experience, therapists vary in both their repertoire and number of such skills and we have no clear empirical data to indicate specifically which ones are required to negotiate most effectively given stages of the model. We feel, rather, that the wider the range of skills available to therapists, the more effectively and efficiently they will carry out treatment. The macro stages are, therefore, the focus of what follows; we feel strongly that they play a major role in effective treatment and, therefore, require special emphasis.

We are interested in studying and delineating the basic family functioning and treatment concepts, which, if consistently applied, will allow therapists to be reasonably effective with the majority of their cases. These concepts should be readily teachable to non-experts, be transferable to different settings, and be applicable to a variety of clinical family problems.[3] The ability to operationally define these concepts facilitates research on therapy process and outcome, as it allows the therapeutic process to be broken down into simple, discrete components which can then be analyzed and measured.

We believe that the problem-centered model meets these objectives. We are also aware that it has been criticized as being too simplistic. Some comments are, therefore, in order. First, the model was developed with research needs in mind and, as noted above, this requires clear and precise description. Clarity of definition often leads to the erroneous opinion that substantive truth is missing or that the underlying concepts are too simplistic. At the same time, complexity, density, and even incomprehensibility are often equated with wisdom and truth. Second, we hypothesize that adherence to the steps and sequences defined in the model will yield effective results, and we have initiated studies to test that hypothesis. Third, we are obviously aware that expert therapists bring a wealth of experience and skill to their treatment, but we believe that this model provides an important basic framework, particularly when dealing with difficult and complex cases. While following the macro stages as outlined, expert therapists can use the full range of their skills to enrich the treatment with their advanced techniques. However, for beginning therapists, the model provides the basis for a structured treatment approach on which to develop more focal skills. By using this model, the beginning therapist will be reasonably effective in the treatment of uncomplicated family problems. From a cursory, initial reading, the model may seem "simple," but the complexity of its concepts and its many nuances are soon recognized when it is applied in actual treatment. Before starting a detailed description of the Problem-Centered Family Systems Therapy Model, there are a few important general issues that need to be addressed.

The focus of therapy is on the specific problems of the family. These include not only those problems presented by the family on coming to therapy, but also those identified during the assessment stage.

The model stresses the active collaboration of the family members with the therapist at each stage. The family must agree to and work for this collaboration throughout the therapy proc-

---

[3]*Editors' Note.* We agree that the disseminability of a therapeutic method is an important component of its cost-effectiveness (see Gurman and Kniskern, Chapter 20). We do not agree, however, that the teachability of a treatment method to non-experts is a necessary characteristic of a well formulated approach, viz., that reconstructive surgery cannot be taught to laymen does not make it any less valuable.

ess, or else there is no therapy. The therapeutic contract is based upon this total mutual commitment to work at the therapy. The therapist's ideal role function in this model is that of a catalyst, clarifier and facilitator. The family members should do, and actually do, most of the therapy work. They are involved openly and directly in identifying, clarifying and resolving the difficulties and problems of the family. The therapist carefully explains his actions to the family every step of the way and makes sure they clearly understand and agree to what he/she is doing. This open approach throws the responsibility for its own actions to the family and ensures that the family understands, accepts and is prepared for each step of the therapeutic process. This approach fosters a very positive collaborative response on the part of the family to the treatment (Hoehn-Saric, Frank, Imber, Nash, Stone, and Battle, 1964; Orne and Wender, 1968).[4]

The therapist's stance during therapy facilitates the achievement of such major objectives of therapy as family openness, clarity of communication and the development of active problem-solving abilities on the part of the family members. In the process, family members become aware of their strengths as well as their shortcomings and develop effective problem-solving methods which can be generalized for use in resolving future difficulties. They are trained to become their own family therapists and problem-solvers, thereby diminishing the need for the therapist.

This therapy model is tailored to a treatment encounter involving from six to 12 sessions stretched over a period of time, varying from weeks to months to years, depending on the issues of each case. Length of the individual sessions may also vary considerably. The early assessment sessions may be longer (sometimes up to two-and-a-half hours), depending upon the needs of the case, the setting and the stamina of family and therapist. The later task setting

treatment sessions may be as short as 15 to 20 minutes. Beginning therapists obviously will need more time to complete a satisfactory assessment. They should not feel daunted by this and should not feel under pressure to "begin treatment." Except in an emergency, families usually respond positively to such thorough assessment. They respect and feel reassured by the therapist's obvious desire to know and to understand thoroughly the family before offering a prescription for and/or beginning treatment. Beginners, and even advanced therapists in complicated cases, should not feel they have to include the number of assessment sessions in the six to 12 treatment sessions we advocate.

In the assessment and very early treatment sessions, the family may be seen weekly. If all goes well, the sessions may then be spread out to every two weeks, then to once a month and, in some cases, gradually increased to once every three to six months or so. During these intervals, the family works on its own. Families should be encouraged to contact the therapist during these interim periods. We have found that most rarely abuse this privilege.

Our stress on limiting the number of treatment sessions is due to a number of factors. Our experience has been that imposing such limits on therapy stimulates therapists and families to more active involvement in the therapeutic work and this facilitates change. They keep the objectives of therapy more clearly to the forefront of their work together. It has been our experience that when no limits are set, families and therapists often develop a mutually satisfying relationship which they are reluctant to relinquish. Such therapy can, and often does, drag on for long periods to the seemingly mutual enjoyment of all concerned, but usually without any demonstrable relationship between length of therapy and effectiveness of results. In family therapy, as in other forms of psychotherapy, there has been as yet no evidence that long-term therapy is more effective than time-limited treatment (Gurman and Kniskern, 1978).[5]

---

[4]*Editors' Note.* But note the effects, in terms of clinical outcomes, of systematic preparation of *families* for therapy, via, e.g., explication of treatment expectancies, have not yet been tested empirically. Moreover, while such a "collaborative response on the part of the family" *may* be thus fostered, we doubt that it would be as common as in individual psychotherapy, where interpersonal disagreement is, obviously, minimized.

---

[5]*Editors' Note.* While this is quite true, it is important to remember that almost all of the research literature we (Gurman and Kniskern, 1978) reviewed was concerned with brief courses of family therapy. Thus, the relative effects of long-term vs. brief family therapy has, in effect, never been tested directly in controlled research.

Frequently, holding the family members to a limited number of sessions communicates to them that the therapist is confident of their ability to work at effecting change. This approach tends to emphasize the strengths rather than the weaknesses of the family and often leads to a quick reduction of the doubt and anxious tension often experienced when they first come for treatment. Family comments on termination of treatment, such as, "the fact that you felt you could treat us in so few sessions was really a relief which helped us to regroup and get on with it," support this view.

We believe that, whenever it is felt that treatment should continue beyond 12 sessions, a reevaluation of the treatment situation should take place and, if possible, a consultation should be sought. Obviously, there are times when the therapy has been going well and requires more sessions because of the complexity of the issues being dealt with or the fact that important new problems have arisen which have to be resolved. In our experience, these situations are much rarer than the cases where the therapy has gotten off track and become bogged down for various reasons. This may be due to inexperience of the therapist, but even experienced and skillful therapists can get caught in a pathological family system. Putting a time limit on the number of sessions, with a request for consultation and discussion built into such limits, is a very useful mechanism for all concerned.

Our concern for the cost-effectiveness of treatment is an important factor involved in our advocacy of limiting the number of therapy sessions. Long-term multiple sessions are very expensive financially as well as an exorbitant use of limited skilled resources.

Lastly, it should be clear that even upon termination, the family members are encouraged to call upon the therapist at any time they may wish in the future. In our experience, this is rarely abused and is a very helpful way of maintaining contact over the years. This approach allows us to act as real "family doctors" for the families we work with.

The macro stages are *assessment, contracting, treatment* and *closure* (Table 1). Each stage contains a sequence of substages, the first of which is always *orientation*. A major problem in clinical work is that practitioners often take too much for granted and suppose that patients know what to expect and what we are doing. The effect of this is to dehumanize patients, not because we as professionals are unsympathetic, but because we unjustifiably assume a knowledge and understanding on the part of the patients about the way we work. From the moment the family members come in, we repeatedly orient them to what we are doing and seek their permission and agreement before proceeding from one step to another. This is done out of our respect for the families we work with and our belief in their right to know exactly what is going on at all times. Furthermore, we believe that therapy can be more effective when the families are fully aware of and in agreement with what is being done. We do not believe in conducting therapy when these conditions are not present.

The orientation to the assessment stage is quite detailed and sets the tone and direction of therapy. All later orientations are much briefer and are used to indicate a change in the focus and task. We do not use orientation to allow for an easier and later interpretation regarding the violation of explicit expectations or rules. However, the family's agreement with the summary at the end of each stage does allow us to confront later resistance by labeling the family agreement previously obtained up to that point.

After a general orientation, each substage needs to be approached systematically, with the therapist guiding the process. At the conclusion of each step, the therapist and family also need to review and reach agreement on what has been accomplished before moving on to the next stage. As we review each stage, the goals and methods for assessing achievement will be discussed.

Assessment Stage

The first major stage is assessment, consisting of four steps: 1) orientation; 2) data-gathering; 3) problem description; and 4) clarifying and agreeing on a problem list. During the assessment stage, we are concerned with orienting the family to the beginning of the treatment process, identifying and detailing the structure, organization and transactional patterns of the family, and carefully elucidating all the prob-

TABLE 1
Stages and Steps in Problem-Centered Systems
Therapy of the Family

Assessment
1. Orientation
2. Data-Gathering
3. Problem Descriptions
4. Clarification and Agreement
   on a Problem List

Contracting
1. Orientation
2. Outlining Options
3. Negotiating Expectations
4. Contract Signing

Treatment
1. Orientation
2. Clarifying Priorities
3. Setting Tasks
4. Task Evaluation

Closure
1. Orientation
2. Summary of Treatment
3. Long-Term Goals
4. Follow-up (Optional)

lems that currently exist. The current problems consist of the presenting problem, as well as those that are identified during the course of a careful and complete assessment. Before proceeding with "therapy," we believe that it is mandatory that we understand the family system and its problems and strengths as fully as possible. The diagnostic workup must be thorough and complete before the treatment is prescribed, much less embarked upon.[6]

The therapist should, therefore, take as many sessions as necessary to complete a full assessment. The number of assessment sessions required will vary with both the therapist's expertise and the nature of the family problems. Beginning therapists can be expected to take longer in the assessment stage, while advanced therapists may also take longer with more complex problems and families. Paradoxically, we find that extra time in the assessment stage often reduces the number of task-oriented treatment

sessions required. This is so because a thorough assessment results in careful delineation of the issues involved in the family. In addition, the inherent family strengths, as well as deficits, are elucidated. Such exposure often points to quick and obvious solutions to problems the family may have been unsuccessfully struggling with for some time, thereby cutting down the number of actual "therapy" sessions required.

If further time is needed to complete the assessment stage when a session comes to an end, we summarize our findings to that point and clarify that we require more information before a decision is reached regarding diagnosis and treatment. Assessment should, however, be active and we seldom space the sessions more than a week apart at this stage. On the other hand, most families appreciate that relatively longer-standing problems can wait for completion of the assessment.

When confronted with a family emergency or acute crisis, a different and much more active intervention is called for. Appropriately dealing with the immediate issues delays the full assessment in such cases, but, once the crisis has been settled, it is important to return to and complete the full assessment stage before proceeding on to other stages of the model.

When seeing a family for the first time, we prefer to have present all the family members living at home. We also include others living in the home and may subsequently include significant extended family and outsiders who are actively involved with the family. This allows us to obtain a full range of views, resulting in a clear, comprehensive assessment of the situation, an indication of potential allies and supports, and direct observation of parent-child and sibling interactions, and enables us to clarify the general future course of action for everyone. We either set a separate session for the parents or have knowledgeable children wait outside when assessing the parents' sexual relationship.

Again, there are some exceptions. In cases of significant emergency, we vigorously attempt to have everyone present but will not refuse a beginning initial assessment solely on the grounds of all members' not being present. Reasonable medical illness and the inability of an acutely psychotic individual to participate without major disruption are other exceptions.

When a significant member, such as a spouse

---

[6]*Editors' Note.* In what immediately follows in their discussion of assessment, Epstein and Bishop present, we believe, an extremely useful, broad guide to clinical family evaluation. While we believe that it is not possible for the family therapist to efficiently answer (for him/herself) all the assessment questions posed here, we do think that the areas to which these questions direct the therapist's observational skills are important in treatment planning for any method of family therapy.

or the identified patient, fails to show for an appointment, the situation obviates against open and collaborative assessment and must, therefore, be dealt with directly by confronting the difficulty before beginning. We also insist that members who are a focus of discussion attend, so that if issues involving them arise they will be present for discussion.

When no emergency exists and a significant member has not shown up, we will sometimes cancel the session, pointing out that it makes no sense to begin the process without the presence of such an important member. We let the family members know that should they really want our help it is their job to bring the absent member and that we would be glad to give them another appointment.

All exceptions require careful consideration. However, our experience is that the therapist's confidence, clarity, sensitive understanding and intervention usually result in the desired members' being present for the first assessment.

Orientation

We orient the family by clarifying what each member expects will happen during the session, why they think they are here, how they think the session was arranged, and what they hope will come out of it. This often provides useful information and helps to avoid later resistance.

Example:

T: I'd like to find out from each of you what you thought was going to take place here today? Okay, I'd also like to know why you think all the family is here? And, I'd like to know what you'd like to see come out of this session: What do you particularly want to see addressed or have an answer to?

We condense and feed back their ideas and then briefly outline our ideas, including why we understand the family is there, what we already know about them in general, what we plan to do, and what we hope to achieve. At this time, we obtain their permission to proceed. We also explain our rationale for seeing them as a family.

Example (After summarizing the family's understanding and expectations):

T: Fine, now I have your ideas, let me explain

mine. I asked you all to come in because I need to have a clear idea of how you function as a family. This gives me a much clearer understanding of the entire picture and so helps me to work out with you how things can be more helpful for John and all of you. I know you had concerns about John's getting upset and being hard to manage. That obviously affects all of you and not just John. Part of the reason it is important for me to meet with all of you and understand how you function is that I know that the way a family functions and operates strongly influences what happens to each family member. If that's not the case, then serious events affecting one individual member will also affect the family and the way it operates. So, for both of those reasons I need to have a clear picture of how you function as a family before deciding on possible treatments. I'm going to jump around a bit to find out about your family, and ask a number of questions in a range of areas. Some may seem quite unrelated to John's problem, but they're important for me to know about. I'll clarify as I go along to make sure that I have a correct impression of how you operate as a family. At this point, I don't know where we're going to go. At the end of this session, however, I will summarize where we seem to be at that point. Do you have any questions? . . . Is that okay, then? . . . Can we go ahead with my finding out more about your family?

Data-gathering: Presenting problem(s)

During this step, data is gathered about: 1) the presenting problem(s); 2) overall family functioning; 3) additional investigations; and 4) other problems.

The therapist begins by asking the family to describe the problem(s) which brought them to treatment. Sufficient time is spent in gathering data so that the therapist develops an accurate picture of the nature and history of each problem. In doing so, the therapist explores the factual details, the affective components of the problem, the historical perspective, the precipitating events, and who is mainly involved with the problem and how.

An example will help. John's teacher's calling about his problems, what he/she said, and mother's observation of his withdrawal and increased disobedience would be factual details. Mother's reaction of frustration and later helplessness, father's being furious at John and at mother for not disciplining him, and John's feeling guilty and sad would be affective components. Information that the problem began six months ago, got better for a short while and then deteriorated further shows historical components. Father's having changed his job about that time is an example of a precipitating event and John's just entering adolescence is a developmental issue.

In detailing the presenting problem, we also utilize appropriate dimensions of the McMaster model (Epstein et al., 1978). For example, in the above presenting problem, we would also explore how the family had attempted to solve the difficulty, how they communicated about it, and the behavior control issues (see below).

In doing such an exploration of the presenting problem, other issues may arise and be defined as difficulties. (In addition to the presentation of John "as a problem," this stage of evaluation might also uncover that mother feels father is not supporting her in dealing with any of the children, that father doesn't feel that she understands his situation, and that John recognizes conflict in Mom and Dad, tells no one, and takes off.)

We then feed back to the family our understanding of the presenting problem and make sure that everyone feels we have a clear picture about it. We do this for each problem by feeding back condensations of our understanding. Haley has also supported the need to obtain a clear picture of the presenting problem (Haley, 1976).

Example (After a detailed exploration of the presenting problem):
T: At this point I'd like to make sure that I'm seeing things correctly. We seem to agree that 1) John has been harder to manage, particularly for you, Mom. John, you and your sister both notice Mom and Dad disagreeing, but this upsets you more than your sister and you take off, which gets you into even more trouble. 2) You, Mother, feel your husband has not been supporting you—not just with John but also in dealing with the other children and 3) Dad, you've been down because

of changes at work and don't feel your wife is understanding of that. The effect is you feel you're failing not just in the work area but also as a husband and father. All of this has recently developed within the past six months and was not the case previously and dad's job change seems to be the biggest stress associated with it all. Do I have it right to that point?

Data-gathering: Overall family functioning

This next step moves from an assessment of the presenting problem to an exploration of overall family functioning. We first orient the family to this change in focus:

Example:
T: Okay, now I'd like to switch to some general ideas of how you operate as a family. Is that all right?

Using the McMaster Model, the family is assessed on the six dimensions of problem-solving, communication, roles, affective responsiveness, affective involvement, and behavior control. This assessment focuses on detailing strengths and difficulties in each dimension and allows us to determine aspects of overall family functioning that influence the emotional and/or physical health of family members.

This assessment is based on family member reports. However, the therapist confirms the impressions gained in this manner by observation of behavior in the session and by confronting and clarifying contradictions between stated information and observed behavior and between information offered by different family members. The therapist's impressions are condensed and fed back until the family agrees that an honest appreciation of the family's functioning in that area has been obtained. The therapist should be careful to gather firm evidence to support his/her hypotheses before putting them forward to the family as his/her opinion. If he/she has a strong hypothesis (clinical hunch) for which he/she can gather no confirmatory evidence, it should be presented to the family as just that, a hunch or an impression, and they should be asked for their opinion as to the validity of the impression. This approach prevents the therapist from taking off into flights of fantasy without evidence, yet allows him to test his clinical hunches while exercising his clinical intuition. It also engenders confidence and respect on the part of the family for the therapist's objectivity, impartiality and respect for data. Further, it reinforces the role of the family members as participants in the treatment process. If there is substantial disagreement but the therapist has sufficiently clear data to make an accurate judgment, the therapist makes a statement such as, "Okay, you (we) disagree in this area, so let's agree it is at least problematic in that regard and move on to another area I wish to explore."

The important point is that this stage focuses on assessing overall family functioning and helps to avoid developing formulations based only on data related to the presenting problem, data that by their nature are more likely to be negative. The assessment is approached tactfully, directly and honestly. We explain carefully what we are doing, and all issues are discussed openly. As we examine each dimension, we feed back to the family members our understanding of both their assets and shortcomings in that particular area. We emphasize strengths, since this is helpful and supportive, as well as being central to any therapeutic planning which may follow.

Given those general comments, we will now discuss the clinical use of each dimension of the McMaster Model in assessing the family's functioning. For each dimension, we will present a definition and discussion of the concepts included in the dimension, clinical exploration of the dimension, and evaluation of the family's functioning on each dimension. The dimensions are summarized in Table 2.

Problem-solving

Theory and Definitions. The problem-solving dimension is defined as a family's ability to resolve problems to a level that maintains effective family functioning. A family problem is seen as an issue that threatens the integrity and functional capacity of the family, the solution to which presents difficulty for the family. Not all "problems" are considered, since some families have continuing, unresolved difficulties that do not threaten their integrity and function.

Prior to the senior author's earlier research studies (Westley and Epstein, 1969), it had been postulated that families who were ineffective would have more problems than more effectively functioning families. However, the study showed that this was not the case. All families dealt with a similar range of difficulties, but effective families solved their problems, whereas ineffectively functioning families did not deal, and seemed incapable of dealing, with at least some of their problems.

Problems are subdivided conceptually into *instrumental* and *affective* types. Instrumental problems are the mechanical problems of everyday life, such as money management or deciding on a place to live. Affective problems are those related to feelings. Clinical experience has shown that families may have problems which are restricted only to the affective area, whereas instrumental problems are almost always coupled with problems in the affective sphere. It is possible, of course, to identify problems that present an overlap of the instrumental and affective components. Getting a child to school for the first time may require dealing with instrumental issues regarding transportation and affective issues of fear or overexcitement. While the dichotomy is not complete in all cases, we retain this line of thinking because of its clinical utility.

We postulate that families which have difficulty in resolving both instrumental and affective problems function least effectively; those with difficulties in resolving only affective problems are more effective; and families which resolve both types are most effective in their problem-solving functions. Effective families solve most problems rapidly, easily, and without extensive consideration, so that at times there can be some difficulty eliciting and detailing the problem-solving steps they go through. Families that present themselves at clinics, however, bring their presenting problem as an unresolved difficulty. It is useful and important, therefore, to analyze their attempts at solving the presenting and any other problems. As an aid to clarifying the stages in the process of problem-solving, our model includes a sequence of operationally defined steps.

The *problem identification* stage includes determination of who identifies the problem. Is there a pattern? Does it vary with the type of problem (affective or instrumental)? Investigation at this stage also requires a judgment as to

TABLE 2
Summary of Dimension Concepts

Dimensions	Key Concepts	Dimensions	Key Concepts
PROBLEM-SOLVING	—Two types of problems: Instrumental and Affective —Seven stages to the process: 1. Identification of the problem 2. Communication of the problem to the appropriate person(s) 3. Development of action alternatives 4. Decision of one alternative 5. Action 6. Monitoring the action 7. Evaluation of success *Postulated* —Most effective: When all seven stages are carried out —Least effective: When cannot identify problem (stop before stage 1)		and accountability built in —Least effective: When necessary family functions are not addressed and/or allocation and accountability not maintained.
		AFFECTIVE RESPONSIVE-NESS	—Two groupings: Welfare Emotions and Emergency Emotions *Postulated* —Most effective: When full range of responses are appropriate in amount and quality to stimulus —Least effective: When very narrow range (one to two affects only) and/or amount and quality is distorted, given the context.
COMMUNI-CATION	—Instrumental and Affective areas —Two independent dimensions: 1. Clear versus Masked 2. Direct versus Indirect —Above two dimensions yield four patterns of communication: 1. Clear and Direct 2. Clear and Indirect 3. Masked and Direct 4. Masked and Indirect *Postulated* —Most effective: Clear and Direct —Least effective: Masked and Indirect	AFFECTIVE INVOLVEMENT	—A range of involvement with six styles identified: 1. Absence of Involvement 2. Involvement Devoid of Feelings 3. Narcissistic Involvement 4. Empathic Involvement 5. Overinvolvement 6. Symbiotic Involvement *Postulated* —Most effective: Empathic Involvement —Least effective: Symbiotic and Absence of Involvement
ROLES	—Two family function types: Necessary and Other —Two areas of family functions: Instrumental and Affective —Necessary family function groupings: A. *Instrumental* 　1. Provision of Resources B. *Affective* 　1. Nurturance and Support 　2. Adult Sexual Gratification C. *Mixed* 　1. Life Skills Development 　2. Systems Maintenance and Management —Other family functions: Adaptive and Maladaptive —Role functioning is assessed by considering how the family allocates responsibilities and handles accountability for them. *Postulated* —Most effective: When all necessary family functions have clear allocation to reasonable individual(s)	BEHAVIOR CONTROL	—Applies to three situations: 1. Dangerous Situations 2. Meeting and Expressing psychobiological needs and drives (eating, drinking, sleeping, eliminating, sex and aggression) 3. Interpersonal socializing behavior inside and outside the family —Standard and latitude of acceptable behavior determined by four styles: 1. Rigid 2. Flexible 3. Laissez-faire 4. Chaotic —To maintain the style, various techniques are used and implemented under role functions (systems maintenance and management) *Postulated* —Most effective: Flexible behavior control —Least effective: Chaotic behavior control

whether the family correctly identifies the problem. Families frequently displace real problems onto areas involving less conflict, and these are then identified as problems.

The *communication of the problem* stage considers to whom the identified difficulty is communicated and whether that was an appropriate person. For example, do parents communicate to a child when parent-to-parent communication is more appropriate, or does one spouse take problems to a physician or clergyman instead of to his/her partner?

The *alternative action* stage considers the types of plans considered and how they vary with the nature of different problems.

The *decision on a suitable course of action* stage raises such questions as: Can the family come to a decision? Is real consideration given to alternatives, or do they bypass this stage and act in a predetermined manner? Investigation at this stage also considers whether those ultimately involved in the action are informed of the decision.

The *action* stage embodies consideration of the degree to which the family carries out the alternative decided upon. When a family has decided upon a suitable course of action, a range of possibilities exist: The family may not act at all, may act in only a limited way, or may carry out all aspects of the action. We obviously view the latter as the most effective of these possibilities.

Monitoring the action refers to whether or not the family has a built-in accountability mechanism to check on whether the decisions were, in fact, acted upon and carried out.

Evaluating the success of actions, the final stage, involves an evaluation by the family of their own problem-solving success. Does the family review what happened in an attempt to learn from the situation, and does it evaluate which mechanisms are proving the most successful? Is it able to recognize its inappropriate problem-solving behavior?

It is postulated that the more effective a family's functioning, the more steps of this process it can negotiate. Families with marked functioning difficulties may not even be able to identify the problem. It is further postulated that it may be only exceptional families that carry out all of these steps: There may not be many families that actually carefully evaluate the mechanisms used and the success achieved.

Clinical Exploration. To explore the family's problem-solving ability, we ask them to identify some problems that have come up for them as a family in the past two to three weeks. We often indicate that all families have problems, many of which they resolve, and that we are interested in both problems they have solved and those they have had difficulties with. When they have identified such a problem, we ask them to describe it in some detail. If it was largely instrumental in nature, we ask about their responses and reactions to facing a problem like that in order to explore the affective component of the problem. If all the problems that they encountered in the past two to three weeks were instrumental, we ask them to identify the last problem they can remember where people had trouble with their feelings, were upset or felt down. After identifying any given problem, we explore the family's attempts at resolving the problem, using the steps described above. As we explore the step, we feed back our understanding to the family members to make certain that we have correctly identified how they handled that stage. The following are examples of questions that might be used to examine each step.

The questions on *identification* might include: When that problem arose, what did you think was going on? Did you feel anything else was involved? Did you all see the problem the same way? (Here we would explore specific differences, as well as elaborating on the instrumental and affective components of a given problem.) Who first noticed the problem? Are you the one who usually notices such things? Who else notices problems like that?

Questions to get at *communication of the problem* to the appropriate resource would be: When you first noticed the problem, what happened? Who did you tell about it? Is that who you would usually tell? When did you tell them? Did any of the rest of you notice the problem but not tell anybody? What stopped you? Is that the way the rest of you see it?

To assess the *development of alternatives* step, we would ask: What did you think of doing about the problem at that point? Did you think of any other alternatives? Who thought of the plan? Did any other people have ideas? Did you share them?

Decisions and actions might be probed by: How did you decide what to do? Who decided?

How did you decide on that alternative? What did you expect might happen if you used your other alternatives?

We check out *monitoring the action* with questions such as: When you decided on your choice of action, did you follow through? Who did what? Do you usually check to see that things get done after you have decided? Who usually checks?

Questions on *evaluation of success of action* that we might ask are: How do you think you did with that problem? As a family do you ever discuss how you think you did in handling problems? Do you ever go over the problems and what happened?

And, finally, we ask *summary* and further general questions, such as: Is that the way you would generally handle problems such as this? What is similar to your usual pattern? What is different? Do problems such as that make it hard for you as a family to function well? What other areas do you feel create problems? With the last question other problems might be identified and we revert to questions about the steps noted above to explore the new problems.

In exploring problem-solving, we make sure that we detail and have a solid understanding of the family's handling of instrumental and affective difficulties. It should also be pointed out that the above questions are very useful in exploring the presenting problem. In addition to generally understanding the presenting problem, it is most helpful to know about the identification, communication of the problem, development of alternatives, and the other processes listed above.

Evaluation of Functioning. Generally, the fewer unresolved problems, the healthier the family. Also, the more problem-solving steps accomplished by a family in pursuing a solution for a problem, the healthier the family. If, from one problem to the next, a family differs widely in its ability to solve problems, the therapist must determine which problems are most central to the family's functioning in deciding on an evaluation rating. In making such a decision, difficulties with instrumental problems lead to a more negative rating than difficulties only with affective ones.

At the healthy end of the dimension we conceptualize a family with few, if any, unresolved problems. When family members encounter a new problem situation, they approach the problem systematically and evaluate the outcome of their attempt to solve the problem. As we move towards the disturbed end of the spectrum, the families' problem-solving behavior becomes less systematic (they accomplish few problem-solving steps), and they are more likely to deny or mislabel the problem. At the very disturbed end of the dimension, families consistently deny or mislabel problems, have long-standing unresolved problems, and these problems generate much conflict within the family system.

Communication

Theory and Definitions. We define communication as how information is exchanged within a family. The focus is on verbal exchange. We are fully aware that this definition is restricted. Nonverbal aspects of family communication are obviously important but are excluded here because of their potential for misinterpretation and the methodological difficulties of collecting and measuring such data for research purposes.

Communication is also subdivided into instrumental and affective areas. As in problem-solving, although there can be overlap between the two areas, some families exhibit marked difficulties with affective communication, while functioning very well with instrumental communication. However, the reverse is rarely, if ever, seen.

In addition, two other aspects of communication are also assessed: Is the communication clear or masked? Is it direct or indirect? The former focuses on the clarity with which the content of the information is exchanged. Is the message clear, or is it camouflaged, muddied, vague, and masked? The latter considers whether the message goes to the person for whom it is intended.

With these distinctions, then, there are four *styles of communication* which can be observed. The first style is *clear and direct* communication. An example of this for the affective communication of anger from a wife to her husband, Tom, an electrician, would be, "Tom, I'm angry at you because. . . ." The second style is *clear and indirect* communication. Here the message is clear, but for whom it is intended is not. Following on the previous example, this communication would be, "Electricians sure make me angry when. . . ," a message that might, or might not, be intended for Tom when given in his presence. The third style is *masked and direct* communication. Our example would be, "Tom, you look terrible today!" Here, the content is unclear but directed to the person for whom it is intended. The fourth style is *masked and indirect* communication. The example might be, "You know, men give me a pain!" directed to no one in particular. Here, the content of the message and for whom it is intended are both unclear.

It is postulated that the more masked and indirect the overall family communication pattern, the more ineffective the family's functioning; the more clear and direct the communication, the greater its effectiveness. It is further postulated that masked and/or indirect communication elicits responses of similar style.

Lederer and Jackson (1968) present a more detailed consideration of communication. We have found that added complexity in description is not always useful. However, our definition of communication does not exclude consideration of other aspects of communication, such as the content, the potential for multiple messages, and whether communication once sent is received, correctly interpreted and attended to by the receiver. At times, the clinical situation requires the investigation of these other aspects.

Clinical Exploration. In assessing communication, we observe communication patterns that occur during the assessment process. We purposefully stimulate discussion and interaction among members to produce observable behavior. We also observe how they handle information that we feed back to them.

We ask a number of questions to explore the extent and nature of communication in the family. Examples would be: Do people in this family talk much with each other? Who does most of the talking in the family? We will also ask individuals who they talk with and try to pin down the frequency, regularity and pattern: Do you feel you can tell things freely to others in the family or do you have to qualify or be guarded about what you say?

To assess the clarity-masked or direct/indirect aspect, we use questions such as: How did

he/she let you know that? How do you get the message? What was he/she getting at? What is he/she telling you? What did "X" say just now? What did you make of that? "X," is that what you are getting at? Can you tell how "X" feels about that? Does he/she let you know things that way all the time or just around feelings? Do members in the family let you know they have understood what you are trying to say? How do they do that? Do you feel that you can get your ideas across to others in the family? Do you feel that others understand you? What happens that they don't? What's the problem when you try to tell others about things? What's the problem when you try to tell others about your feelings?

Evaluation of Functioning. We are primarily interested in producing a rating of overall family communication. Other factors being equal, the following rules of thumb are useful:

1) The level of health/pathology in the parents' communication pattern should be weighed more heavily than the level of communication functioning in the children.

2) The lower the level of communication functioning in a single member or dyad, triad, etc., the lower the overall rating of the family.

3) The greater the number of family members at a low level of health/pathology in the communication area, the lower the overall rating of the family.

In evaluating communication, the therapist must consider both the clarity and the directness of the communication within the family.

1) *Clear versus masked communication*: Optimal clarity is achieved when the information transmitted is relevant, concise, and consistent with other communications. Communication is masked when a sequence of messages contains contradictory information (e.g., a message is given and then immediately contradicted), when contradictory messages are given at different levels (e.g., nonverbal message contradicts verbal message), and when the communication simply does not make sense because it is out of context, grammatical nonsense, vague, wooley, and/or clouded.

2) *Direct versus indirect*: For effective com-

munication, the message should be clearly directed, both verbally and nonverbally, to the intended receiver. Communication is indirect when it is either directed to an inappropriate person or directed towards no one in particular.

At the healthy end of the dimension, we conceptualize a family that communicates in a clear, concise and direct manner in both the instrumental and affective areas. As we move towards the pathology end of the dimension, communication becomes less clear and direct, and problems may arise in the affective area. At the very disturbed end of the dimension, we conceptualize a family in which communication is consistently masked and indirect in both the instrumental and affective areas.

Problems of distinguishing between affect being experienced and affect being communicated are discussed later, under the dimension of affective responsiveness.

Roles

Theory and Definitions. We define family roles as the recurrent patterns of behavior by which individuals fulfill family functions. Our model divides family functions into instrumental and affective areas, with all of the implications referred to previously. In addition, the functions are subdivided into two further spheres, *necessary family functions* and *other family functions.* Necessary family functions include those with which the family must be repeatedly concerned if it is to function well. These functions may be instrumental, affective, or a combination of the two. Other family functions are those that are not necessary for effective family functioning but arise, to a varying degree, in the life of every family. Consideration of each group of functions is important.

Necessary Family Functions. Our model identifies five groupings of necessary family functions (see Table 2).

A clearly instrumental role is the *provision of resources.* This refers to the accomplishment of such instrumental tasks as provision of food, clothing, shelter, and money. *Nurturance and support* is mainly an affective role. It consists of the affective tasks of providing family mem-

bers with support, care, reassurance, and comfort. *Sexual gratification of marital partners* refers to the sexual functioning of the partners with a special emphasis on their ability to initiate sex and respond to each other in a manner that is sexually gratifying. The focus is therefore on the affective result of their sexual relationship. A fourth role area we label *life skills development.* This includes functions having to do with the adults as well as the children. This encompasses those tasks necessary to help a child start and get through school, those needed to help an adult pursue a career or vocational interest, and those required to maintain or increase an individual's level of personal development. These tasks have both instrumental and affective aspects. Finally, there is *maintenance and management of family systems*, which involves such functions as leadership, decision-making, and the handling of family finances. It also includes the function of maintaining the family system of boundaries with respect to extended family, friends and neighbors. Maintenance of family standards is considered here as well. This includes such tasks as disciplinary action, monitoring, labeling, and identifying relevant behavior within the family.

Other Family Functions. Families may also develop their own unique functions. These can be adaptive or maladaptive. Consider for example, one family which received support payments for its foster child. These payments were saved and used to finance family vacations which would have otherwise been unaffordable. This illustrates an adaptive and unique function to which the foster child contributed.

A maladaptive and unique function is that of *scapegoating.* By definition, this is the development in the family of a functional process which involves a family member's becoming an active recipient of negative affect and/or negatively perceived attributes on a continuing basis. The scapegoating process serves the special purpose of providing a displacement mechanism, i.e., a means of avoiding conflicts in other more threatening areas. The scapegoat is active in drawing attention onto him/herself and is not simply a passive victim of other family members. Elaborate patterns can be seen where conflict occurs, for example, between the parents.

A child in the family responds to this parental conflict by evoking negative behavior from a sibling, which has the effect of drawing the conflict away from the parental dyad onto the parent-scapegoat child triad.

There are two other concepts involved in family roles: *role allocation* and *role accountability*.

Role allocation refers to the assignment of responsibilities for family functions. Such allocations may be appropriate or inappropriate, may be carried out implicitly or explicitly, may be autocratically or democratically assigned. The issue is whether the allocated responsibilities are appropriately spread and shared among the family members, or laden onto already overburdened members. For example, it would be an inappropriate allocation for a six-year-old to take on a major family leadership role.

Role accountability involves the process of monitoring of tasks that have been allocated. Well-defined accountability reinforces the person's commitment to doing a task and the effectiveness with which it is carried out.

How the family fulfills functions must be thoroughly understood in order to satisfactorily evaluate the family role dimensions. We postulate that the healthier families are those in which most, if not all, of the family functions are adequately fulfilled and the allocation and accountability processes are most clear.

Clinical Exploration. Following are examples of questions that can be used to evaluate the different areas of role functions:

Questions of *provision of resources* would include: Who brings in the money? Are there separate bank accounts? Is there a common checking account? The therapist might continue with variations on that theme. Who gets the groceries and makes sure about meals? Is it always the same person? Who buys the clothes for the family members? Who pays for the clothes? Who goes to purchase the clothes? There would be further variations on that theme. Do you have a car? How do you all get around?

Questions on *nurturance and support* would include the following types of questions directed to individual members: Who do you go to when you need someone to talk to? Who do you go to when things get to you or when you are upset? Is it helpful when you talk to them?

If there are small children, we ask which parent usually comforts the children. How do they handle it when a child gets upset? Just what do they do? Do the mother and father do similar or different things? How do the mother and father divide their availability to the children? Do they talk about supporting each other and making themselves available for comforting the children?

Questions on *adult sexual gratification* are completed with the parents alone unless the children are very young. When children are asked to leave, it is done with a statement such as, "I would like you to leave long enough for me to ask mom and dad some specific questions that have to do only with them. We will not be talking about you while you are out of the room and any plans that affect any of you will be made with you here. Is that okay?"

We would explore with single parents how they meet their sexual needs. With spouses, we would start with questions similar to the following (if initial findings indicate the need, complete and detailed sexual functioning assessments might be made): How do the two of you feel about the affectionate and sexual aspects of your relationship? Are you having any sexual difficulties? Do you both agree about that? Are you both satisfied about all aspects of your sexual life? Would you change any aspects of your sexual life if you could? How?

Who initiates sexual contacts? Has it always been that way? How has it varied? Has your sexual life always been as it is now? Was it better or worse before? How often do you have sexual relationships? Is it satisfactory to each of you? Do you feel that you satisfy your partner? Do you feel that you know what is most pleasurable and satisfying to your partner? Do you personally feel satisfied by your partner? How do each of you say "no" when you want to? Can you do that easily? How would either of you like to change sexually?

Examples of *life skills development* questions are: Who usually oversees what is happening with the children's education? Who usually helps the children with school work? Who usually deals with the school? How do you, as a family, handle the stages the children go through? Who usually gets involved with problems that children face growing up? Is it always that way?

Who's responsible for teaching manners? Who gets involved in sex education of the children? Who is responsible for dealing with the children about their ways of relating with people? Who discusses their vocational choices? Adults go through stages too; who helps and gets involved in those discussions? Who is involved in discussions about changes in jobs? How do you help each other develop and do your own thing?

Examples of *maintenance and management of the systems* are: Who is involved in major decisions? Who has the final say? Who's opinion is taken if you can't reach an agreement? Where does "the buck stop"? Does it stop? Have you decided on the ultimate size of your family? Who decided on the size of the family? Who keeps track of the health of family members? Who decides when you see the doctor? Who decides when you go outside the family for help on any issue?

Who handles the money? Who handles the monthly bills? Who gets involved in large purchases? Who's involved in house cleaning? Who's involved in activities outside the house? How are the repairs handled? How is the decision to paint or remodel the house taken? How efficiently and effectively are these things done? Who looks after the car? Do you share these tasks or is it the same person all the time? Who handles the discipline of the children? How do you do that?

Questions on *allocation* would include: How do you decide who does all the jobs? Do you talk about it? Is that just the way it developed? Would you like the decisions about who handles jobs handled differently? Do you feel that some people have too many jobs? Do any of you feel overburdened by your jobs? Do you think it is reasonable to expect people to do the jobs they do or do you think some people are doing jobs they are not cut out for? Are some people doing jobs they should not do? What is it about the jobs and the people that makes you think that?

Questions on *accountability* would include: How do you check that the job gets done? Who does that? What do you do if it is not done?

Idiosyncratic roles are more difficult to assess. The adaptive ones generally come up in the course of exploring role functions relating to the other dimensions of family functioning. Scapegoating is a problem that requires both some

exploration and observation. The therapist must consider scapegoating as a transactional process when discussion around conflictual areas leads to a shift of focus from the topic area onto a given individual. We may label the process and see if the family agrees with statements such as, "I hear what you're saying, but I would like to comment that each time we discuss —, the topic shifts and it is almost like it is easier to deal with "X" as a problem than it is to deal with —. Does that happen at home? Do you think that's a problem?" We also may explore the responses going on in the potential scapegoat. This is done by asking questions at times when a possible scapegoat acts in a way that is guaranteed to draw the attention onto him/herself. Questions used could include, "What were we talking about just now? What were you thinking about that? What's your reaction at times when that topic comes up? What do you feel like doing? Are you aware of jumping in at such times and changing the focus onto yourself?" In addition, we may openly challenge the scapegoated individual and enlist his/her agreement to change the pattern through the use of supportive and confronting statements such as, "I notice that you jump in each time we approach this area and begin to explore it. We've talked about that and you obviously find it uncomfortable. Is that right? I wonder if you could agree to hold back and let me explore the area. I know it's difficult, but I also think that we can explore it and deal with it and then you won't have to feel so uncomfortable."

Despite the above comments, we should point out that we do not spend a lot of time in detailing this transactional pattern, particularly if it is a major de-focusing process. We will note it to ourselves and proceed with the rest of the assessment. When the pattern does present, it is usually in association with the presenting problems. We keep all the problems in focus rather than allowing ourselves to be restricted to the scapegoating process.

Evaluation of Functioning. In evaluating a family's role functioning, the therapist must consider the following questions:

1) Are all the necessary functions being fulfilled?
2) Has the family reached a working consensus

regarding the allocation of roles? If consensus has not been reached, it is possible that one or more role functions will be poorly fulfilled.

3) Is the allocation of family members to roles appropriate? A family can err by expecting someone to fulfill a function which he is not capable of carrying out, or by overloading a particular individual with too many functions.

4) Has there been an appropriate allocation of authority (power) to go along with the allocation of a particuar function? For example, a family cannot ask an older child to babysit and then not provide him/her with the power to maintain reasonable control.

5) Is there a procedure within the family for making sure that the jobs are carried out?

6) Is there cooperation and collaboration within the family in the accomplishment of role functions?

7) Is there sufficient flexibility within the system to permit reallocation of roles when and as needed?

At the healthy end of the dimension, we conceptualize a family that fulfills all necessary functions. Such a family reaches a working consensus on the allocation of roles, collaborates and cooperates, allocates both authority and accountability to assure that the functions are completed, and has some room for flexibility and shifting of roles. As one moves towards the disturbed end of the dimension, we conceptualize families that accomplish the basic functions less and less effectively. At the most disturbed end of the dimension, one or more of the basic functions are not being fulfilled and there are major problems with allocation and accountability.

Affective responsiveness

Theory and Definitions. Affective responsiveness is defined as the ability of the family to respond to a range of stimuli with the appropriate quality and quantity of feelings. In terms of quality, we are concerned with two questions. First, do family members respond with the full spectrum of feelings experienced in human emotional life? Second, is the emotion experienced consonant with the stimulus in situational context? In the latter case, for example, to re-

spond to a family member's real sadness with rage is inappropriate. The quantity aspect focuses on the degree of response and is viewed as extending along a continuum from non- or underresponsiveness to reasonable or expected responsiveness, to overresponsiveness. This dimension then considers the pattern of the family's responses to affective stimuli but focuses more than any other dimension on the individual, as this is the locus of the response. For an effective affective family life, we expect to find the potential for the full range of affective experiences that are appropriate in quality and quantity of response.

It is important to distinguish this dimension from affective communication. Affective responsiveness refers to the experiencing of feelings while affective communication refers to how family members transmit to each other the emotions they are individually experiencing. It is important to note that if a person does not experience an emotional response, then he/she cannot communicate it. If evaluation of affective communication leads to the decision that there are major and significant disturbances, then affective responsiveness problems may or may not underlie this. If there is clear communication of a full range of appropriate emotion, then affective responsiveness is viewed as appropriate, while the reverse assumption cannot be made. The absence of affective communication does not necessarily indicate that no affect was experienced, and the fact that affect was experienced does not mean that it was necessarily communicated.

As an aid to assessment, the responses are divided into two classes: *welfare feelings* and *emergency feelings* (Rado, 1961). Welfare feelings or emotions are exemplified by responses such as love, tenderness, happiness, and joy; emergency feelings or emotions by fear, anger, sadness, disappointment, and depression. A family which can respond appropriately with love and tenderness, but never anger, sadness or joy, would be considered restricted and somewhat distorted. It is hypothesized that the children in such a family would develop affective constriction, which might strongly influence their personal development. The more effective the family, the wider the range and the more appropriate will be the family members' responses in terms of quantity and quality.

We are aware that there may be considerable cultural variation in what is the appropriate level of affective responsiveness and how affect is expressed. The therapist needs to be aware of the potential for misinterpretation in making evaluations on this dimension.

Clinical Exploration. The following questions elicit information regarding emotional responses: What was your response to that? What did that do to you inside? How did you feel then? Did you feel anything else? Or is that all you felt? What did you feel besides that? Do the rest of you feel that way at times like that? What is similar about your response? What is different? Do you ever sense that you do not experience feelings that you feel you should, or that you think others do? Are there any feelings that you experience more intensely than you feel is reasonable given the situation? Are you a family that responds with a lot of feelings? Is that all feelings, or does that occur with some more than others? Which feelings do you not respond to or express? Do any of you feel that you are a family that underresponds in terms of emotions? Which emotions do you feel that you underrespond with?

We then discuss with the family as a whole, and with each individual member, their experiences regarding the following emotions: love, kindness, affection, tenderness, anger, depression, sadness, hurt, fear and tension, and rage or hate. As we assess this with each individual, we would check whether he/she or the family feels that he/she under- or overresponds in that area.

While doing this assessment, it is possible to gain further information regarding affective communication by asking the rest of the family how the person lets them know that feeling. This assesses the communication of the affective response.

Evaluation of Functioning. Ratings are based on whether the affective response is appropriate to the situation and appropriate in intensity and duration in a particular stimulus situation. Given the wide variety of stimuli and potential emotional responses, evaluation must take into account the total scope of emotional responsiveness.

At the healthy end of the dimension, we ex-

pect the family to possess the capability of responding appropriately with the full range of emotions and with the appropriate intensity and duration. We rate families at the very disturbed end of the dimension who are extremely constricted in the range of emotions with which they respond and/or are consistently inappropriate in either quality or quantity of the response. Families rated as functioning at a fairly healthy level on this dimension may contain one or several members who may not be capable of responding emotionally with the full range of affect, but the affective responses of other family members fill the gaps in the emotional spectrum.

There may also be instances where families may occasionally respond with inappropriate affect and/or experience occasional episodes of under or over affective responsiveness yet, overall, may be rated as being in the healthy range of this dimension.

Affective involvement

Theory and Definitions. The dimension of affective involvement is defined as the degree to which the family as a whole shows interest in, and values the activities and interests of, individual family members. The focus is on how much, and in what way, family members show an interest and invest themselves in each other. Their degree of involvement proceeds through the following range:

Absence of involvement applies to those cases where family members show no interest or investment in each other. Their only involvement is in their shared instrumental functions. They appear much like a group of boarders.

Involvement devoid of feelings applies to families where there is some intellectual interest, but little investment, of the self or feelings in the relationships. This interest and investment are demonstrated only when demanded, and even then may be minimal.

Narcissistic involvement occurs when the investment in others is primarily egocentric and there is no feeling of the meaning a particular situation holds for others.

Empathic involvement, the most effective type, refers to an emotional investment in other family members in which each member cares deeply about the significant activities and involvements of the others. Family members can demonstrate a true affective concern for the interests of others in the family even though these interests may be peripheral to their own.

Overinvolvement is an overintrusive, overprotective, often overly warm type of involvement. The "Yiddish-Mama" syndrome is an example of this type of involvement; it is well meant but rather "heavy" and at times disconcerting and even troublesome.

Symbiotic involvement refers to those pathological states where the involvement is so intense that the boundaries between two or more individuals are blurred. This type of involvement is seen only in seriously disturbed relationships. In its most extreme state, the individuals involved respond as one, and there is marked difficulty in differentiating the boundaries between them. An example of this pattern is the schizophrenic parent-schizophrenic child dyad.

Empathic involvement is viewed as the most effective form of affective involvement, involvement devoid of feelings, narcissistic or overinvolvement less so, and lack of involvement or symbiotic involvement least effective.

Clinical Exploration. Questions such as the following can be used to clinically explore this dimension:

For Any Family Member. Who cares about what is important to you? Why do you think they care about it? Is there anything that bothers you about the way they show an interest? How do they let you know they are concerned for you? Do they ever show too much interest? When "X" talks about that, what effect does it have on you? What were you thinking (or feeling) while they were talking about their interests?

What activities, interests, or areas are important to you individually or personally? How does the rest of your family respond to these? Are they interested? Are they too interested? Do you feel they are interested because it is important to you or for their own sake? Do you feel that other members of the family go their own way and do not care or notice what happens to you? Do you feel that you relate like a group of boarders? Are others in the family really interested in what you do or do they just minimally respond?

For Parent-Child Dyads. We would ask children questions like: Who bugs you most in the family? Do you feel people in the family are overprotective or overinvolved in your life? How do they do that? How do you handle it? How do you get them to stop it? If a child responds in a way that indicates problems, we would then ask the parents how they see it and what they think is going on. We also explore this area with the siblings.

We would go on to ask the parents question such as: How do you relate to the various children? Do you listen? Do you find it difficult? Does the child make it easy or difficult to relate to him/her? Do you feel your relationship with the child is close enough? If there are difficulties, we have the parents spell out how they see them and what steps they have taken to try to overcome them. We also ask the children concerned for their views of the situation.

Evaluation of Functioning. In rating the family in this dimension, the therapist must consider whether there is an appropriate amount of interest and concern shown among family members, whether the family members are overly engrossed in each other, or whether their involvement is restricted to sharing physical/instrumental surroundings and functions. We are interested in the nature of their involvement, how much they give of themselves and invest in understanding and being supportive of the interest of other members. We also evaluate whether they are interested primarily for their own sake or for the sake of others.

Rating of family health on this dimension requires that the different styles of affective involvement be looked at along a dimension. The least effective involvement is presented at either pole with lack of involvement and symbiotic involvement. Slightly more effective, but still problematic, are involvement devoid of feelings at one end and overinvolvement at the other. Narcissistic involvement denotes an evaluation of effectiveness between empathic, the most healthy involvement and either overinvolvement or involvement devoid of feelings.

Behavior control

Theory and Definitions. The behavior control dimension is defined as the pattern a family adopts for handling behavior in three types of situations:

First, there are *physically dangerous situations* where the family will have to monitor and control the behavior of its members, such as a child's running out on the road, playing with matches, or moving into dangerous surroundings, or, in the case of adults, preventing reckless driving or suicide attempts. Second, we consider *situations which involve meeting and expressing psychobiological needs or drives* such as eating, sleeping, eliminating, sex and aggression. And, finally, there are *situations involving interpersonal socializing behavior* both among family members and with people outside the family. This inside/outside distinction is stressed because patterns of acceptable behavior in each area may differ.

It is important to consider the behavior of *all* family members in each type of situation. In the course of assessing the appropriateness of the rules and standards of the family, the age and status of the individuals concerned must be considered. Families develop their own standards of acceptable behavior, as well as the degrees of latitude which they will permit in relation to these standards. The nature of these standards and the amount of latitude for acceptable behavior determine the four *styles of behavioral control*: rigid, flexible, laissez-faire and chaotic.

Rigid behavior control designates those families where the standards are very constricted and little latitude is allowed for negotiation and change. No allowance is made for any situation.

Flexible behavior control involves reasonable standards and degrees of flexibility, given the context. The standards and latitudes are adaptive to given situations.

Laissez-faire behavior control refers to those families in which standards do not really exist and extreme latitude is permitted. In these families, almost anything goes.

Chaotic behavior control is found in families when there is not a consistent style. This may be because the parents have different behavior control styles or because styles are subject to repeated changes. For example, one family was seen in which the mother consistently maintained a totally laissez-faire stance and believed that, "I really feel that anything the children want to do, they should be allowed to." The father felt that a flexible style was most reasonable and attempted to adopt that stance. The couple had never resolved this basic difference. Since the father had been allocated the role of disciplinarian, the result was a chaotic style where at one moment he would follow his own wishes and be flexible and, at another, give in and take a laissez-faire stance consistent with his wife's style. This would be followed by his becoming furious and rigid. This random shift in styles on the part of the disciplinarian father created a chaotic style for the family.

We view flexible behavior control as the most effective style. In decreasing order of effectiveness through to pathological, the styles are rigid, then laissez-faire and, finally, chaotic.

To maintain their style of behavior control, family members use a number of techniques to enforce acceptable behavior. The application of these techniques is a closely related issue considered under the systems maintenance and management function of the roles dimension.

Clinical Exploration. This dimension is explored with statements and questions such as the following: All families have rules. They also have ways of handling behavior in certain situations. In which areas are the rules most important in your family? What other areas would similar rules apply in? Are the rules clear and how do you handle dangerous situations? Can you give me an example of such a situation and the rules you have for it? Is that the same for everyone or does it vary from person to person? If so, how?

Do you expect everyone in the family to eat together? Do you have rules for table manners, going to bed, dressing, bathing, things like that? Are they consistent in each area or do they vary? How fixed are those rules? Do you make allowances for special situations? Are the rules the same for everyone?

Are the rules clear about how you relate to

each other? Can you give me an example? Do you allow hitting or yelling at each other? Do the rules vary from time to time? Is the rule the same for everyone? How much freedom are you allowed? Can you discuss the rules?

Do you know what's expected of you in terms of behaving with people outside of the family? Is that the same as behaving with each other inside the family or different?

Are there any particular rules that anyone in the family feels are really unfair? Mom and dad, do you agree on all the rules? Which ones do you differ on and how? Do you kids know that mom and dad agree, or do you feel that they disagree? If they do, how?

Tell me about how you enforce the rules? Is it always that way? Does it vary depending on who is doing the enforcing? Who does the enforcing? Do you know what to expect if you break a rule? Is it consistent or can you get away with it sometimes? Who's toughest in terms of punishment and consequences? Do they stick to being tough or do they give in later? Mom and dad, do you ever feel that the other one doesn't back you up?

Evaluation of Functioning. To determine an evaluation rating for behavior control, the therapist must decide if there is a sufficiently stable pattern of interaction among family members to identify family rules and the consequences for infraction of these rules. If there is not a sufficiently stable pattern, the two most likely styles are laissez-faire or chaotic.

A number of other concepts are used in making the evaluation. Are the rules clear and understood by all family members? Has the family reached a consensus regarding these family rules and consequences for infractions? Are the standards of behavior appropriate for the age (maturity) of each member of the family within each of the areas described? The standards of behavior could be either too high or too low. The standards could be appropriate in one area (or situation) but not in others. Is there an appropriate amount of rigidity/flexibility in the enforcement of rules? Ideally, there should be sufficient flexibility within the family system to permit modification of the rules when special circumstances arise. A family can err by being either too rigid or too flexible (e.g., in physically

dangerous situations for young children, relatively little flexibility would be expected). Are the consequences for infraction of the rules clear, understood, appropriate and flexible? Are the consequences applied in a consistent (predictable) manner?

At the healthy end of the dimension, we conceptualize a family that has clearly defined standards of behavior which are appropriate to each specific family member. While a family is consistent in its enforcement of its standards, there is sufficient flexibility in the system to permit exceptions to the standards. As we move towards the disturbed end of the dimension, standards become less clear and/or appropriate, or become increasingly rigid and authoritarian. At the very disturbed end of the dimension, family standards are completely absent, chaotic, or totally inappropriate.

Summary

The McMaster model provides a useful conceptual framework for understanding the functioning of clinically presenting families and for assessing their effectiveness on each dimension. We cannot overemphasize the need to do such a careful exploration as part of the assessment process. Assessment of families on each of these dimensions is clinically useful in two ways. First, it allows the therapist to assess areas of strength in contrast to the more negative picture gained by only looking at the presenting problem. These areas of strength can be utilized in the therapy. Second, exploration of these dimensions often turns up significant family problems other than those identified when only the presenting problem is considered. The fuller assessment allows the therapist to be more aware of problems that will be operative during the course of treatment.

The next step of data gathering is to consider the need for additional investigations.

Data-gathering: Additional investigations

Use of the "systems approach" in family therapy extends the factors considered in the assessment and diagnostic process. As the Group for Advancement of Psychiatry (1970) pointed out, the family's behavior can be influenced by factors at numerous levels, such as: the physical universe, the biological systems involved, the intrapsychic status of the individuals concerned, small groups, in this instance, the family, the extended social system and the values existing at that time and place. The diagnostic workup, therefore, comprises, in addition to what has previously been described, the necessary individual psychological and biological studies as well as those studies of the family's broader social system such as the extended family, school, place of work, patterns of social recreation, etc. Such additional investigations are basic to comprehensive work. Failure to make this point explicit has often led to the erroneous impression that a systems approach does not involve data obtained from such investigations.

The data gathered in the family workup to this point determines the further specific investigations to be carried out. They might include any or all of the following procedures. In the case of children, these procedures include developmental history, pediatric examinations including all necessary laboratory and x-ray studies, biopsychosocial assessment of child, intelligence and other psychological investigations. For the adults, there could be psychosocial history and formulation, psychiatric examination, medical history and physical examination, all the necessary laboratory and radiological studies, and psychological assessments as appropriate.

Data-gathering: Other problems

Finally, in concluding the data-gathering step, we ask if there are any other significant problems or difficulties that we have not touched upon. If there are, these are explored in appropriate detail.

Problem description

The purpose of this step is to develop a list of problems. First, the family members are asked to indicate the problems they would identify now that a detailed assessment has been completed. The therapist then adds any additional difficulties he has noted. The list should highlight the major issues but be comprehensive.

Problem clarification

The final step in the assessment process is to obtain partial or complete agreement regarding problems listed by the family and/or therapist in the problem description step. The family usually agrees to the list if the therapist has been active in clarifying and obtaining agreement during evaluation of the presenting problem and dimensions of family functioning and in the feedback of the results of other investigations.

Two types of disagreement can arise. First, family members may disagree among themselves, in which case the therapist can attempt to negotiate a resolution, reopen the area for further exploration and clarification, or obtain a temporary "agreement to disagree." If the problem differences are relatively minor, the therapeutic process can go on and, usually, the differences will resolve themselves in the course of the work. An example of this type of situation might be where one parent may feel the child is lazy and performing very badly at school, while the other parent feels the child is showing behavior normally appropriate for his/her age. This usually resolves itself as the work goes on and the family members become more collaborative and understanding of each other. However, if the differences regarding the child's behavior extend more deeply into basic and wider disagreements as to values related to child-rearing and goals for the children, these could lead to an impasse further along in the therapy process.

The second type of disagreement that can occur is between the family and the therapist regarding the problems added to the list by the latter. Here again, if the therapist considers the differences relatively minor in importance as far as the central therapeutic issues are concerned, he may decide to come to an "agree to disagree" solution for the moment and return to them later in the therapy process. If the therapy has gone well, these disagreements usually disolve almost automatically in the course of dealing with the more important issues and rarely have to be dealt with again. An example of this type of disagreement is that of a family where the father drinks moderately heavily and there is disagreement between the family and therapist on the degree of this drinking and its effect on the family. If this is not the central issue and the problem drinking is not too severe, the therapy can go on if the therapist shelves the disagreement. When the therapy goes well, the question of the father's drinking invariably comes up and is usually resolved by the family without any disagreement and with the father's participation. Rarely do the initial differences of opinion of this type have to be formally brought forward.

If the case were one in which the father's alcoholism was severe and a marked factor in the family problems such as violence, disruption, personal difficulties, etc., disagreement between the family and the therapist on the presence and importance of this issue would be basic and would preclude the continuation of the therapy process beyond this point. Were the therapist to "agree to disagree" in this case, he would merely be colluding with the existing pathological family system and this would obviate any successful therapy. The disagreement would have to be resolved at this point by the family's accepting the problem as is or they would have to withdraw from the therapy process at this time with the option of resuming the procedure should they change their mind.

At times, in cases of basic disagreement, the areas may be reexplored or the family may be asked to think about them for some time at home and return later for more discussion. With continued disagreement, the family might be offered the possibility of consultation with another therapist rather than termination at that point.

The assessment stage ends when mutual agreement is reached on a problem list. We cannot emphasize strongly enough the importance of basing such a listing on a full, thorough and comprehensive history before embarking on therapeutic interventions. Treatment should not begin without a full knowledge of the problems and strengths existing in the family.[7]

Contracting Stage

The second macro stage is contracting. Its goal is to prepare a written contract that delineates the mutual expectations, goals and commitments regarding therapy. The steps in this stage are: 1) orientation; 2) outlining options; 3) negotiating expectations; and 4) contract signing.

Orientation

The first step is to orient the family to the tasks in this stage and obtain their agreement to proceed.

Example

T: If those are the problems, let's move on to discuss what you might or might not do about them. Is that okay with you?

Options

We then outline the treatment options that are open to the family, which will vary according to the situation.

Example

T: You have a number of options. You may choose to not do anything about the problems we've listed and make no changes. I'm sure you will hope that things will improve somehow, but they may also stay the same or get worse as a consequence of that choice. The second option is to try and work on changing the difficulties on your own now that we've clarified them. Third, you may decide that you want a different kind of treatment not involving all of you. The difficulty there is that you've all agreed that family issues have a part to play so that option would be a bit like trying to balance the books with only half the figures. But it is an option you have. A fourth option is that we agree to work together and deal with the problems as a family. Which option seems best to you?

For each option, it is the therapist's responsibility to clarify what his function, if any, might be (some of the options would require no input from the therapist), and to explore the possible consequences of each alternative. Obviously, if somebody is significantly depressed and suicidal, the options and consequences are quite different than if the problem is minor in nature.

If the family chooses treatment, we then proceed to the next step. If any of the other options

---

[7]*Editors' Note.* Of course, one can never have a "full" knowledge of a family. Moreover, like most family therapists, we find it difficult to think of "assessment" and "treatment" stages of psychotherapy as being as non-overlapping as Epstein and Bishop urge that they be.

FIGURE 1

A Sample Family Treatment Contract

TREATMENT CONTRACT

Family: ____Smith____   Date: ____11/27/78____

Problems	Family Expectations and Goal
1. John's behavior at home and school.	1. No negative reports from school and positive reports at home.
2. Father not supporting mother with children.	2. Mother will report that father and she satisfactorily share dealing with children.
3. Father does not feel wife understands his situation.	3. Father reports he feels involved and that his wife and he can comfortably discuss his work problems.

THERAPIST EXPECTATIONS

1. All family members will attend.

2. The family will call in advance if unable to attend.

3. The family will work hard.

SIGNATURES

FAMILY _____

_____

_____

THERAPIST _____

---

are chosen, they are handled appropriately.

Negotiating expectations

Family members are asked to negotiate among themselves what they will want from each other (i.e., how they want each to change) if they are to feel they have been successful in treatment. The family is given the major responsibility for defining their expectations, while the therapist's responsibility is in clarifying and helping each family member to express his/her expectations in concrete behavioral terms to allow for clearly identifying and assessing progress.

The therapist monitors the process so that unrealistic goals such as wishing "to never again fight" are moderated into more reasonable statements like, "To be able to disagree and get angry but resolve the problem without a physical fight." Examples of expectations are shown in Figure 1, a sample treatment contract.

The therapist may make suggestions that might be included in their negotiations and also indicates his own expectations, including the commitment that all of the family will attend each session. The family is also given the approximate number of sessions that are anticipated with the proviso that this can easily be changed should the situation call for it.

We insist that all members of the family be present for the data-gathering and contracting stages. As a general rule, we prefer that all members participate in the total treatment process. Obviously, this is not always possible for various reasons, such as illness and absolutely necessary absences of some members and so on. There are also some situations where it is clinically advisable to see only some of the members and to exclude others. This would include sessions when the focus is on the sexual life of the parental couple. The therapeutic values and ethics and the therapist's judgment must be relied upon at other times when a decision is to be made regarding exclusion of some of the members. It is our experience that, except when the parental sexual relationship is being discussed, the need to exclude members occurs very rarely. Despite the concern of some, it is rare that members of the family (at whatever age) are hurt significantly by exposure to the family therapy process.[8]

There are many reasons for including all members in the therapy. Since the basic aim of the therapy is to modify the total system of the family, all the members are involved whether they like it or not. Even members not directly involved may be extremely helpful to the therapy process in the informal roles of co-therapists or auxiliary therapists. (Indeed, this is one of the basic strengths of family therapy. It trains family members to be therapists and more effective problem-solvers within their own family.) The presence and participation of all members allow the therapist to better evaluate the change processes in the system as a whole.

Contract signing

We then establish a written contract (see Figure 1) that lists the problems and specifies for each what has been agreed to as a satisfactory outcome. In addition, the negotiated conditions of treatment are included. The contract is signed by the therapist and the family members. It is emphasized that most of the work will be done by the family, but at the same time it is made clear that we, too, will work hard. We do not tolerate a dilatory approach, either by ourselves or by our patients!

Treatment Stage

The third macro stage is treatment, consisting of four steps: 1) orientation; 2) clarifying priorities; 3) setting tasks; and 4) task evaluation.

---

[8]*Editors' Note.* Indeed, we have shown (Gurman and Kniskern, 1978a) that such negative effects are not at all rare, but appear in approximately 5-10% of family therapy cases. In fact, Epstein and Bishop themselves seem to recognize implicitly that *some* aspects of family therapy may be at least very disconcerting, if not harmful, to some family members, e.g., their position earlier in this chapter about the advisability of excluding children from discussions of their parents' sexual relationships.

Orientation

Again, the first step is to orient the family to the new stage and to obtain their permission to proceed. We do this with a statement such as, "Well, now that we have agreed to work together, how would you like to begin?"

Clarification of priorities

This step involves ordering the problem list according to the family's priorities. We establish which problems they wish to tackle first, second, and so on, in order. Though we prefer to follow the order established by the family, we would have the therapist actively intervene to change the priority list if the family ignored urgent problems demanding immediate action (anorexia, suicide potential, severe alcoholism, etc.). Allowing the family to set the priority list reinforces the general emphasis of our approach, i.e., giving as much of the responsibility for the therapeutic work as possible to the family. We repeatedly make it clear that we do not consider the family to be passive partners in the therapeutic process.

Setting tasks

Taking their first priority, the therapist asks the family to negotiate and set a task, which if carried out during the next week would represent a move in the direction of meeting their expectations. This negotiation includes identifying individual responsibilities with regard to the task. If the family is unable to do this, the therapist suggests a task and checks to see if it is agreeable to the family.

In negotiating and assigning tasks, the following general principles need to be considered:

1) The task should have maximum potential for success.
2) The task should be reasonable with regard to age, sex and sociocultural variables.
3) Tasks should be oriented primarily toward increasing positive behaviors rather than decreasing negative ones. Families often ask someone to stop a behavior rather than asking him/her to do something. We prefer to

request positive actions.[9]

4) A task should be behavioral and concrete enough so that it can be clearly understood and easily evaluated.

5) A task should be meaningful and important to everyone involved.

6) Family members should feel that they can accomplish the task and they should individually commit themselves to carry out their part.

7) Emotionally-oriented tasks should emphasize positive, not negative, feelings. Fighting, arguing and open display of hostility should be strongly discouraged.

8) Tasks should fit reasonably into the family's schedule and activities.

9) Overloading should be avoided. A maximum of two tasks per session is usually reasonable.

10) Assignments to family members should be balanced so that the major responsibility for completing a task does not reside with just one or two members.

11) Vindictiveness and digging up the past should be avoided, with the focus placed on constructive dealings with current situations.

These principles are made explicit to the family in the form of instructions or suggestions when necessary. For example, if one spouse indicates he/she wants the other to "stop nagging" (violation of principle 3), we would respond with a statement such as, "I'm sure you do, and can understand that, but it's harder to ask someone to stop doing something than to start to do something. So what would you like him/her to do in the next week that would give you the sense that he/she is trying and that would begin to help in solving the problem?"

Examples

Using our previous case of John and his fam-

ily, we can indicate an example of negotiated tasks that follow the above principles.

A 16-year-old son agrees to come in by an agreed upon time; the father agrees to take the son to a ballgame later in the week if he does well, and to deal with the son if he is late; the mother agrees to back the father and send the son to him as well as agreeing to spend more time with the 15-year-old daughter, who agrees to keep her room tidy.

Examples of other family tasks are the following:

Father will take mother out once; mother agrees to go even if she doesn't want to; the older son agrees to babysit and younger brother agrees to behave.

A couple agrees to set aside 15 minutes after supper to talk about "good things," and the children agree to clear the table and do the dishes.

Once tasks have been assigned, it is important and valuable to designate a family member to monitor and report on performance at the next therapy session. Designating a monitor increases the involvement of the family, increases expectations regarding their sense of responsibility and accountability, and raises individual self-esteem. The role of the monitor may be rotated among members or may vary with the tasks (e.g., one member reports on one task and someone else on another). The role of the monitor should be given to members who are most objective, not actively involved in the area being dealt with, and most likely to keep the family at the task. We have not experienced any particular difficulties with this role.[10]

Task evaluation

During this step we assess whether or not the

---

[9]*Editors' Note.* Though not stated here, this guideline is in keeping with the relative strength and advantages of "positive control" (e.g., reinforcement) of behavior over "negative control" (e.g., punishment) addressed by behavior therapists (cf. Jacobson, Chapter 15; Gordon and Davidson, Chapter 14). Moreover, guidelines number 1, 4, 6, 7, 8, 10 and 11 have clear parallels in behavioral intervention methods (cf. Jacobson, Chapter 15).

[10]*Editors' Note.* This idea of using a member of the family as a monitor of other members' behavior regarding therapeutic "tasks" is certainly not a common one. For example, Whitaker and Keith (Chapter 6) would argue that such an approach would reinforce the pseudo-therapy game which the family has been playing all along. Moreover, while some family therapists might instruct a family member to monitor the behavior of another member, or even of a dyad, their purpose in doing so would be to *increase* the "monitor's" involvement by manipulating the family structure, e.g., dad might be instructed to check on son's room cleaning *not* to record its frequency, but to begin to get him more involved with the children.

task was accomplished. Information is obtained from the monitor and other appropriate family members as necessary. If the task was accomplished, we provide positive reinforcement, highlighting the positive aspects of the family's performance, including what particular individuals did which made things go so well.

Example

T: Well, how did the tasks go? . . . Okay, so —— got done but —— didn't. Is that right? We'll come back to the difficult one in a minute, but first what made the other go so well? Can you tell me what each of you did to help that go well? What did others do that made it easier for you to do your part?

*   *   *   *   *

That's very good and I'm sure you're pleased. Okay, let's return to the area you had difficulty with. (We would then explore with questions such as: What was the problem? Did nothing get done or did you do part of it? Were you aware of thinking about it? What could others do that would make it possible? Do you think it's possible to do it? Do you agree that if the task were carried out it would make things better?)

If there is a major block, the therapist should cycle back to the original assessment discussions and clarify that there was agreement regarding the problem and then renegotiate a related task. Perhaps the task was too difficult for this stage of treatment and the family and therapist should generate a simpler task having to do with the same problem. In general, after checking on the successfully accomplished tasks, the family and therapist then move on to negotiate the next task.

If all goes well, the process of task-setting and evaluation continues, at times negotiating new priorities, at times recontracting, until all contract expectations have been fulfilled.

If a family fails to complete its task and/or demonstrates no improvement over a period of three successive sessions, we share our feelings with the family that there is need for serious stocktaking. We indicate that, perhaps without being aware of it or without informing the ther-

apist, they have changed their chosen option from the stated one of family therapy to the option of no treatment. We then give them an opportunity to formalize the change if so desired. If the family members insist they still want family treatment, we point to the fact that they do not seem to be working at their tasks and that perhaps there is something wrong with the treatment process or the therapist's handling of the case, and a consultation is therefore indicated. Should the family reject the suggestion for consultation, we then recommend termination of therapy, since we have adequate evidence of failure and there is no point in denying it while continuing to spin our wheels in a charade of the treatment process.

Acute situational disturbances in previously well functioning families do well with this approach. However, at this stage of our studies we can make no definitive statements about which therapist skills, family problems or degrees of dimension ineffectiveness are most predictive of success or failure in our treatment approach. Hopefully, we will be able to gather accurate answers as our research continues into the future. At present, we have only soft clinical impressions as partial answers to the questions. We feel problem severity is as yet an unreliable predictor of outcome in any given case.[11] We are continually surprised by positive outcomes in cases that at intake appeared hopeless.

We feel that the success of outcome in most cases directly reflects the degree of rigor and thoroughness that the therapist maintains in family sessions. This includes following the principle of keeping the family actively involved in working with the therapist at each step of all the stages. The therapist must learn to function as a thorough assessor, evaluator and diagnostician, clarifier, investigator, catalyst, facilitator and, at times, a confronter. He must be prepared to give the major responsibility for the treatment to the family while he remains intensely involved in the treatment process. He must not need to feel so omnipotent that he cannot delegate the responsibility for working on its own problems to the family and cannot

---

[11]*Editors' Note.* Gurman and Kniskern's (1978b) review of family therapy outcome research confirms Epstein and Bishop's impression.

terminate therapy when there is ample evidence the family is not working adequately to resolve its problems. The family should be aware at all times that the therapist expects full commitment to change. We do not believe in "seducing" the family into a state of positive motivation. Families can always return for another trial of therapy at some future time should their motivation to change increase. We have had many positive experiences terminating some families on this basis and then having them return spontaneously at a later time ready to work hard at change they are more prepared to handle. There is no ill will generated in such terminations and they are left with the assurance that they can contact us any time they change their mind. This is further evidence that we respect their opinions, values, goals and objectives while, at the same time, making it clear we respect our craft to the point of not wanting to participate in "sham" therapy or merely going through the motions of a therapeutic process which continues interminably without evidence of successful change. We believe that by developing these skills and approach, therapists can look forward to quite successful outcomes.

Closure Stage

The final stage is closure, consisting of four steps: 1) orientation, 2) summary of treatment; 3) long-term goals; and 4) follow-up (optional).

Orientation

As an orientation to treatment termination, we point out that the family expectations, as set forth in the contract, have been met and that perhaps we should stop now.

If the family wants more therapy, we are willing to explore the issues or problems they wish to deal with and consider continuing. Although treatment might occasionally continue, most of the time families should be encouraged to resolve the new issues they want to work on by themselves. They should be encouraged to get in touch with the therapist any time they so desire. At such a time, the therapist could decide whether to see them again for another session or not, depending on the situation.

Summary of treatment

The family members are asked to summarize what has happened during treatment and what they have learned. We then confirm or elaborate on their perceptions, adding any points that may have been overlooked.

Long-term goals

At this point, we ask the family to discuss and set some long-term goals. We also ask them to identify how they will recognize if things are going well or badly, and what they will do if the latter occurs. We then ask them to identify those issues which they anticipate might either come up or become problematic in the future. The family is reinforced regarding their ability to cope with such problems, while at the same time the option of returning to obtain help is clarified.

Follow-up

Therapy ends at this point, although an optional follow-up appointment may be arranged. When a follow-up is arranged, it is scheduled far enough into the future to allow the family a full opportunity to deal with issues as they arise. It is also stressed that the follow-up visit is for monitoring and is not a treatment session.

RESEARCH ON THE McMASTER MODEL OF FAMILY FUNCTIONING AND THE PROBLEM-CENTERED SYSTEMS THERAPY OF THE FAMILY

There have been three major research projects in the course of the development of the McMaster family therapy model. The first of these is reported in The Silent Majority (Westley and Epstein, 1969). This was an interdisciplinary study combining psychiatric and sociological approaches to studying the organization of nonclinical families. The second project was conducted while the senior author was at the Jewish General Hospital in Montreal. This project investigated the relationship between therapeutic process in family therapy situations and therapeutic outcome. The project is reported in a series of papers (Guttman et al., 1972; Guttman et al., 1971; Postner et al., 1971;

Rakoff, et al., 1967; Epstein et al., 1968). The third project was a study carried out while the senior author was at McMaster University in Hamilton, Ontario. It investigated the relationship between a series of therapist and therapy variables and a set of outcome measures for families seen in family therapy at Chedoke-McMaster Child and Family Centre. This project is reported in another series of papers (Santa-Barbara et al., 1975, 1977; Woodward et al., 1974; Woodward et al., 1975; Woodward et al., 1977).

Silent Majority

The families studied in this project were a nonrandom sample of the English Protestant population of Montreal. Freshmen at McGill University were screened on a series of psychological inventories. From this screening about 100 students were selected for further study who covered the spectrum of emotional health (with the extremes overweighted). The families of the selected students were also asked to become involved in the research. Each member of the participating families filled out an extensive sociological questionnaire, had psychiatric and sociological interviews and completed Thematic Apperception Tests. The aim of the research was to identify factors in the families that predicted the emotional health of the students. There were a number of interesting findings. A positive relationship between the parents was found to be associated with good emotional health in the children. A balance of division of labor in the family, along with a sharing of some roles by the parents, was another positive factor. Power structure in the families was also predictive, with the pattern of the parents discussing decisions but the father being considered the boss being the pattern most often associated with emotionally healthy children. (Note that this was the case in Montreal 20 years ago. Other patterns may now be related to emotional health.) Another positive factor was the parents' acceptance of parental roles. In general, this study provided strong support for the idea that the way in which the family functioned as a system was an important factor in determining the emotional health of individual family members.

The Montreal Project[12]

The therapy process project established a set of communication variables coded from transcripts of 20-minute segments of therapy sessions. The therapy sessions coded were sampled at six-week intervals from families in ongoing conjoint therapy. One major finding of this project was that it was extremely difficult to achieve satisfactory reliability (inter-coder) on affective communication among family members (Guttman et al., 1971). Therapists' communications were less problematic. In the end, three categories of family speech were used: expression of welfare emotions; expression of emergency emotions; and emotionally neutral expression. Two categories of therapist speech were used: interpretative statements, and statements aimed at inducing speech from family members. The outcome measures were derived from the Family Category Schema (Epstein et al., 1968). (The Family Category Schema later evolved into the McMaster Model of Family Functioning.) Families were rated on the schema categories after each session. Judges then rated families on change with respect to the schema categories. There were some differences between families that improved and those that did not. However, findings were qualified by questions of reliability, differential dropout rates, and heterogeneity of the sample (Postner et al., 1971). The general evaluation of the project by the researchers was that using communication measures to investigate the course of family therapy resulted in little added insight and greatly increased complexity. While this study required a great expenditure of time and effort, there was no corresponding gain in predictive power. This approach lacked both effectiveness and efficiency. This led us to seriously question the ability of process variable studies to significantly contribute to a clinically useful understanding of family therapy. The next major research project therefore investigated how a number of therapist and family characteristics were related to therapeutic outcome assessed by the therapist, by the families, by outside observers, by recidivism and school record criteria.

---

[12]*Editors' Note.* See Pinsof (Chapter 19) for a fuller discussion of the Montreal Project.

The McMaster Family Therapy
Outcome Study

Two hundred and seventy-nine families were studied. All contained a child between the age of six and 16 who was perceived by the family as having behavioral and/or academic problems. The families entered treatment in the standard fashion for the Chedoke-McMaster Child and Family Centre. This meant (among other things) that they were assigned to therapists who varied in discipline, in training, and in experience with family therapy. The McMaster Model formed the basis of family assessment, and the treatment approach was an earlier and less detailed form of the problem-centered approach presented in this chapter. Two measures of outcome were provided at the termination of treatment by the therapist: perception of change in the family over the course of therapy, and an estimation of prognosis. Six months after termination, independent evaluators, not associated with the research team, collected three other outcome measures from the families: a recidivism measure, a measure of satisfaction with the therapy, and a measure of how the families then felt about the original presenting problems. In addition, the evaluations rated the families on individualized Goal Attainment Scales (For a detailed description of this use of Goal Attainment Scaling see Woodward et al., 1978.) In addition to these six outcome measures, background information on both the therapist and the families was also collected.

The results of this project were encouraging in some ways and discouraging in others. On the positive side, of the six outcome measures, one showed positive effects of therapy from 45% of the families, one for 58%, one for 64%, one for 70%, and the other two for 79% (Woodward et al., 1977). The family therapy procedures we used were clearly effective. However, when the results are examined in more detail, problems appeared. One major finding was that the outcome measures were not strongly interrelated. Family measures intercorrelated at moderate levels, as did therapist measures. However, family measures were only distantly related to therapist measures (Santa-Barbara et al., 1977).[13]

The conclusion to be drawn from this set of results is that there is not a simple direct way to conceptualize and measure outcome. Given that the notion of outcome was somewhat ambiguous, it is not surprising that outcome measures were related to therapist and family characteristics as they related to a summary outcome measure. Therapists with intermediate levels of expertise had lower success rates than either advanced or student therapists (Woodward et al., 1977). Single-parent families with a young (six- to 12-year-old) child did better than intact families with a 12- to 16-year-old child (Woodward et al., 1977). Families with parents employed did better than those in which the parents were unemployed (Woodward et al., 1977). Families in which the identified parent had had previous therapy did less well than those for whom this was the first experience of psychotherapy (Woodward et al., 1977).

The results from this project, while demonstrating the general efficacy of this method of family therapy, left many questions unresolved. There were some ways in which the design of the research was not ideal. The major problems were the variation in therapists and, thus, in the way in which they conducted therapy; the nonrandom selection of families; the lack of a control group; and, finally, the lack of fully satisfactory outcome measures. The last is a reflection of the current state of the field; the search for objective, multiple, relevant, quantifiable and generally acceptable outcome measures still goes on.[14]

It was the issue of variations among therapists which became the focus of our current research program. We decided to describe more clearly and fully what the therapist was doing while conducting family therapy. The McMaster Model of Family Functioning and the Problem-Centered Systems Therapy of the Family are the descriptions that we have developed. We have also developed instruments to assess various aspects of these models and have become in-

---

[13]*Editors' Note.* As we have discussed elsewhere (Gurman and Kniskern, 1978b; Chapter 20), there is very little good a priori reason to expect outcome measures that tap different

---

vantage points to show high levels of association, especially as the criterion becomes less objective and countable. When *different measures* are combined with *multiple rating sources*, even less association should be expected.

[14]*Editors' Note.* Elsewhere (Gurman and Kniskern, 1978b) we detail several reasons why we believe that the search for a battery of family therapy outcome criteria that are universally acceptable is likely to fail, at least in the near future.

volved in training therapists in the conduct of therapy according to these models. There are two general lines of research underway or planned. One line seeks to check out the model of family functioning; the other, through investigating training, seeks to check out the treatment model (which, of course, incorporates the family functioning model).

Research on the McMaster Model of Family Functioning

In designing research to test the model of family functioning, we have constructed assessment instruments to be answered by both families and therapists. In part, this reflected our belief that the family's, as well as the therapist's, perceptions need to be considered when describing a family. In part, having two instruments will provide a useful tool for identifying incongruence of perceptions, which, as we have argued in previous sections, is often a source of problems.

The two instruments are designed to tap the six dimensions of the family functioning model. One, the Family Assessment Device, contains a series of statements reflecting the family functioning model's characterization of families. All family members (over age 12) will be given the instrument, and for each statement, each person will rate the extent to which it describes the family. An individual's responses will be scored to provide his or her perception of the functioning of the family on the six dimensions of the model. Individual ratings of family functioning will be combined to arrive at a family's rating of its own functioning.

The other instrument, the Clinical Rating Scale, is filled out by the therapist after assessing family functioning according to the model. The therapist rates family functioning on each of the six dimensions, using a seven-point scale, where 1 is extreme malfunctioning and 7 is extremely good functioning. Anchor descriptions are provided for most ineffective (1), normal nonclinical (5) and most effective (7) functioning.

Both instruments are ready to be tested to establish their reliability and validity. Once this process has been completed, they will be used in a series of studies. We plan to conduct several large-scale epidemiological studies investigating the variability of the different aspects of family

functioning. We hope to investigate the relationship of family functioning to psychiatric illness. We also plan to look at the effects of acute and chronic physical illness on family functioning and, we hope, if all goes well, to launch a new generation of outcome studies.

TRAINING OF FAMILY THERAPISTS

We have a major interest in looking at and altering health care delivery systems. Family therapy training offers a vehicle to both broaden the perspective of the delivery base and upgrade health care professionals' understanding of systems generally. In both ways, family therapy training offers considerable potential in health care delivery system changes.

In addition, family therapy training offers a treatment modality that reinforces the central function of the family as a unit for the social, psychological, and biological development and maintenance of the individual family members. Acceptance of this goal, plus an understanding of the systems functioning of the family unit allows for important interventions in primary, secondary, and tertiary prevention.

As part of our interest in health care delivery systems, we are concerned about cost-effectiveness and efficiency. This has led us to outcome evaluation which is consistent with our philosophy of evaluating what we do.

The ultimate test of training is outcome evaluation. We are concerned about the effectiveness of training and we seek to assess the specific skills acquired by those we train. This focus allows for testing therapist skill against outcome, the ultimate test of both training effectiveness and the underlying treatment model.

Who is Trained?

We are primarily concerned with training health care professionals dealing with both physical and emotional problems. We are particularly interested in people who are members of the health care teams and institutions that provide such services. It is only in this way that the changes in health care system itself will come about. We are not particularly interested in training people in independent private practice, since this does not afford a major impact on the health care delivery system, and this population does not have the same potential for the development of support groups that may maintain family work.

Training is best given to support professional development, and we spend time in clarifying that the family treatment training fits with the individual needs, clinical needs, and institutional needs of the person being trained. Individuals vary in the degree of skill they wish to acquire in the family area. They may see some minimal training as a necessary part of their major training program (master of social work, master of health sciences, or psychiatry residents) or they may seek intense and in-depth training in this modality. Clinical needs also vary considerably. It seems pointless to train people in family work who will never be directly dealing with families and where those skills would not be beneficial to their particular clinical setting. We find it important to have the trainee's institution support the training with an indication that this particular modality of training makes sense in terms of overall institutional planning. Thus, we look for commitment from the institution for support of this modality.

We have fostered aspects of inter-institutional support by targeting specific trainee groups. As part of the development of the Clinical Behavioral Sciences Program at McMaster University, we provided training to health care professionals in a wide region. Within the family therapy modality, we purposefully targeted certain agencies and geographic regions. We then preferentially trained groups of people from those areas. After a period of some two years, cadres and groups were formed within regions and agencies. These groups could then carry on their own supportive supervision and training. An additional outcome of this approach was that of introducing members from those communities to each other and providing them with an ongoing inter-institutional relationship.

In general, our training has involved the mixing of people from many disciplines, including nursing, occupational therapy, social work, psychology, psychiatry, family medicine, pediatrics, and the clergy. Mixing disciplines in groups has worked well when the entering skill level of the trainees was homogeneous and when there was a reasonable appreciation of the con-text of practice. There were problems in mixing family practice residents in with other groups who did not fully understand the nature of family practice and where the time taken in making such a translation took away from the overall teaching effectiveness. This does not mean that it cannot be done, but there are potential problems.

Basic interviewing skills are seen as a prerequisit to training. We have had experience in working with health care professionals and paraprofessionals who had no formalized training and no basic skills in standard interviewing. Here family therapy training had to be halted while these basic skills were taught.

Training and Evaluation of Training

We purposefully focus initial teaching efforts on the use of the Problem-Centered Systems Therapy Model, and incorporate into it the McMaster Model of Family Functioning. Our experience is that both those who are new to the field and those who are trying to understand a new model require some in-depth immersion in one approach before they can begin to incorporate other models. It is hard to teach by comparison if the two models to be compared are not already well understood. Exposing beginners to multiple models creates conceptual confusion. We are also concerned that the teaching should itself implicitly demonstrate rigor and the serious consideration of issues. Presentation of multiple models early on in training tends to obviate against this and can lead trainees to infer "a bit of this and a bit of that" as the expected. After trainees have obtained a clear understanding of the model and are fluid in the use of its approaches, exposure and consideration of other models are actively encouraged.

In developing our training and training evaluation approaches, we have borrowed from Cleghorn and Levin's (1973) classification of family therapy skills into conceptual, perceptual and executive categories. The conceptual skills are largely cognitive and include an understanding of family functioning and an understanding of the definitions and concepts incorporated within the model. Perceptual skills include the ability to perceive data, to accurately identify family and treatment behaviors, and to integrate them within the conceptual models. Executive skills include the ability to execute and carry out treatment. This classification has considerable utility. The three skilled groups each require different training and evaluation methods, as will be demonstrated in the following section.

In our training programs, we begin generally with conceptual skills. We subsequently add in perceptual skill training and lastly executive skills. The following briefly touches on some of the methods we use to both teach and evaluate each grouping.

Conceptual skills

We have taught conceptual skills using a variety of approaches, depending on the needs of the trainers and the overall program. The approaches have included the use of a semi-programmed text, reading material, tutorials for integration and resolution of issues and seminars to explore the concepts in depth. These have been used singly and in combination. Instruments to evaluate these skills have been easiest to develop. Sets of questions matched for difficulty, the concepts covered, and the format (multiple choice, true and false, etc.) were developed in pairs. The instruments were then used for pre- and posttesting with a crossover design. We could show that the intruments were equal in their assessment ability both as a pre- and posttest, and that they could demonstrate significant change. Using such devices, we have demonstrated that there was significant skill acquisition as the result of training, and that longer programs led to greater skill acquisition than one-day workshops.

Perceptual skills

The design for perceptual skill training has involved the use of videotapes, role-playing, and in very specific situations movies, novels, and plays. This material provides the perceptual data which the students are asked to assess in terms of the model. Early in training the focus is on general assessment, while later training focuses on the question of whether or not there are sufficient data to make a judgment, and if there are, perceptual judgments regarding the relative effectiveness or ineffectiveness based on the concepts of the McMaster Model. During

this training, conceptual skills are reinforced and further developed. At this stage, trainers act as therapists in role-playing. This allows the focus of attention to be on family data, rather than be distorted by the treatment approach and/or the beginning therapist's lack of executive skills.

We have used a number of different methods to evaluate perceptual skill acquisition. In general, this has involved presenting trainees with perceptual data in the form of transcripts, written descriptions of families and videotape segments. They are then asked to answer questions and/or rate family functioning. Using these methods, we have again been able to use pre- and posttraining evaluations to demonstrate significant change.

Our experience with perceptual skill assessment has raised two important issues. When our techniques and instruments ask students to make judgments and evaluate family functioning, two skills are really being assessed. The first skill involves a decision about whether there are sufficient data, not enough data, or no data on which to make a judgment. As stated earlier, we feel this is crucial and that the therapist should only act when there are sufficient and clear data. The second skill is assessed when there are sufficient data and the trainees are evaluated on their ability to make judgments about the relative effectiveness or ineffectiveness of the family's functioning in that particular area. In our experience, students vary in the difficulty they have in one or both of these skill areas, and this requires careful and specific attention during training.

The other important issue arises due to the fact that, in assessing perceptual discrimination ability, the very nature of the task leads the subjects to feel that they are being tricked (i.e., they are asked to make judgments that are open to some interpretation.) Of even more concern is our experience that the better the subjects' skills in the perceptual area, the more subtleties they use as cues, and the more they can diverge in opinion compared to criteria groups or among themselves. This means that a high degree of perceptual discrimination skill has a negative effect during assessment and that the better subjects see greater possibilities and feel the criteria group responses are not valid, while those who don't have the skill can seldom even argue the issue.

Executive skills

Generally, we have broken executive skill training into two phases. The last of these phases involves intensive case supervision and is therefore very costly in terms of resources and time. For that reason, we begin with a more general experience and use this to develop skills and screen candidates for further training.

In the first phase of executive skill training, we focus on (a) continued conceptual and perceptual skill development condensing in the form of clear formulations; (b) details of the treatment model and perceptual skills associated with this; and (c) role-playing experiences to provide a beginning experience in use of the treatment model. The role-playing provides an experience of both "giving and receiving" and allows for stopping, starting and recycling, as well as setting limited objectives which decrease beginning therapist's anxiety. The latter involves the role-play therapist's designating ahead that he/she will only assess one dimension of the family functioning and stop.

To evaluate these skills, we use multiple choice instruments regarding concepts of the treatment model, transcript assessments, write-ups of videotapes and subjective evaluations based on trainee, trainee group and trainer assessments.

The second phase of executive skill training involves small group case supervision based on live, video or audiotape presentations.

We do not use co-therapists in treatment, but at times will have an early beginner sit in on sessions to observe and later discuss the experience. This affords a better sense of affective issues and a more intense experience. However, with our interest in more effective health care delivery, we find no justification for co-therapy except for this type of training experience.[15]

Evaluation of executive skills during the second phase is similar to the first.

---

[15]*Editors' Note.* Moreover, existing research shows little evidence of the superiority of co-therapy (Gurman and Kniskern, 1978b).

Summary

There are a number of other important issues that require comment. In the process of doing our training, we have developed a number of educational support packages, including videotapes, written material, etc. This allows us to put together consistent yet different modules that support instruction for varying groups.

Our emphasis on evaluating what we do has been carried over to our family therapy training. Studies to date indicate that as trainers we form impressions that may be incorrect if they are subjected to study. However, evaluation also clarifies and sharpens training approaches.

The use of pre-course evaluations allows us to place students in groups and levels that are commensurate with their competency, to give trainees and trainers feedback regarding areas of individual strengths and shortcomings on entry and indirectly to familiarize trainees with the skill development expectancies for that particular level of training. The use of pre- and post-training evaluation results allows us to evaluate both individual and group progress or deterioration and thereby give more objective feedback to both trainees and trainers, and hopefully, in the near future, to be able to indicate what type of trainee will do best in our training programs. Our experience with the objective measures has shown that they closely relate to the subjective ratings of trainers. Where there have been discrepancies, the identification and follow-up on that have been most fruitful and important in identifying either specific trainee or training problems.

We also collect data regarding the trainees, the impact of training on their work situation, and evaluations of the training formats, techniques and trainers. In these areas we have developed generic data forms to which we add specific and specialized data for a given program.

The advantage of our data collection is that we collect a subset of consistent data on all trainees and can now begin to assess the variables associated with successful training both within and across various programs. Evaluation of several such programs is currently under way and in preparation for publication.

Our models of family functioning and treatment lend themselves to effective teaching and the evaluation of skill acquisition. The evaluations of training that we have conducted so far are promising, but demonstrating the relationships between therapists' skill, adherence to the treatment model, family functioning, and outcome is our long-term goal.

REFERENCES

Ackerman, N. W. *The Psychodynamics of Family Life*. New York: Basic Books, 1958.

Ackerman, N. W. *Treating the Troubled Family*. New York: Basic Books, 1966.

Bateson, D., Jackson, D. D., Haley, J. & Weakland, J. Towards a theory of schizophrenia. *Behavioral Science*, 1956, *1*, 251-264.

Berman, E. M. & Lief, H. I. Marital therapy from a psychiatric perspective: An overview. *American Journal of Psychiatry*, 1975, *132*, 583-592.

Bishop, D. S. & Epstein, N. B. *Research on teaching methods*. Paper presented at the International Forum for Trainers and Family Therapists, Tavistock Clinic, London, England, July 1979.

Bishop, D. S. & Epstein, N. B. Family problems and disabilities. In: D. S. Bishop (Ed.) *Behavioral Problems and the Disabled*. Baltimore: Williams & Wilkins, in press.

Brody, E. M. Aging and family personality: A developmental view. *Family Process*, 1974, *13*, 23-37.

Cleghorn, J. & Levin, S. Training family therapists by setting learning objectives. *American Journal of Orthopsychiatry*, 1973, *43*, 439-446.

Comley, A. Family therapy and the family physician. *Canadian Family Physician*, 1973, 78-81.

Dewey, J. & Bentley, A. F. *Knowing and the Known*. Boston: Beacon Press, 1949.

DeWitt, K. N. The effectiveness of family therapy: A review of outcome research. *Archives of General Psychiatry*, 1978, *35*, 549-561.

Epstein, N. B. Concepts of normality or evaluation of emotional health. *Behavioral Science*, 1958, *3*, 335-343.

Epstein, N. B. Pratiques nouvelles dans le traitement de l'enfant et de la famille. *Service Social*, 1963, *12* (1 & 2), 159-164.

Epstein, N. B. & Bishop, D. S. State of the art—1973. *Canadian Psychiatric Association Journal*, 1973, *18*, 175-183.

Epstein, N. B. & Bishop, D. S. Problem-centered systems family therapy. *Journal of Marital and Family Therapy*, in press.

Epstein, N. B., Bishop, D. S. & Levin, S. The McMaster model of family functioning. *Journal of Marriage and Family Counseling*, 1978, *4*, 19-31.

Epstein, N. B., Levin, S. & Bishop, D. S. The family as a social unit. *Canadian Family Physician*, 1976, *22*, 1411-1413.

Epstein, N. B. & McAuley, R. G. A family systems approach to patients' emotional problems in family practice. In: J. H. Medalie (Ed.), *Family Medicine: Principles and Applications*. Baltimore: Williams and Wilkins, 1978.

Epstein, N. B., Rakoff, V., & Sigal, J. J. *The family category schema*. Unpublished manuscript, Jewish General Hospital, Department of Psychiatry, Montreal, Revised 1968.

Epstein, N. B. & Westley, W. A. Patterns of intra-familial communication. *Psychiatric Research Reports 11*, American Psychiatric Association, 1959, 1-9.

Finkel, K. Personal communication. 1974.

Glick, I. D. & Haley, J. *Family Therapy and Research: An Annotated Bibliography of Articles and Books Published 1950-1970*. New York: Grune & Stratton, 1971.

Group for the Advancement of Psychiatry. *The Field of Family Therapy*. Report 78, 1970, *Volume 7*.

Gurman, A. S. & Kniskern, D. P. Research on marital and family therapy: Progress, perspective and prospect. In: S. L. Garfield & A. E. Bergin (Eds.), *Handbook of Psychotherapy and Behavior Change: An Empirical Analysis* (2nd ed.), New York: Wiley, 1978.

Guttman, H. A., Spector, R. M., Sigal, J. J., Epstein, N. B. & Rakoff, V. Coding of affective expressions in conjoint family therapy. *American Journal of Psychotherapy*, 1972, *26*, 185-194.

Guttman, H. A., Spector, R. M., Sigal, J. J., Rakoff, V. & Epstein, N. B. Reliability of coding affective communication in family therapy sessions: Problems of measurement and interpretation. *Journal of Consulting and Clinical Psychology*, 1971, *37*, 397-402.

Hadley, T. R., Jacob, T., Milliones, J., Caplan, J. & Spitz, D. The relationship between family developmental crisis and the appearance of symptoms in a family member. *Family Process*, 1974, *13*, 207-214.

Haley, J. A review of the family therapy field. In: J. Haley (Ed.), *Changing Families: A Family Therapy Reader*. New York: Grune & Stratton, 1971.

Haley, J. *Problem-Solving Therapy*. San Francisco: Jossey-Bass, 1976.

Hill, R. Generic features of families under stress. In: H. N. Parad (Ed.), *Crisis Intervention: Selected Readings*. New York: Family Services Association of America, 1965.

Hoehn-Saric, R., Frank, J. D., Imber, S. D., Nash, E. H., Stone, A. R. & Battle, C. C. Systematic preparation of patients for psychotherapy. I. Effects on therapy behavior and outcome. *Journal of Psychiatric Research*, 1964, *2*, 267-281.

Kardiner, A. *The Individual and his Society*. New York: Columbia University Press, 1939.

Kardiner, A., Linton, R., DuBois, C. & West, J. *The Psychological Frontiers of Society*. New York: Columbia University Press, 1945.

Langsley, D. G. & Kaplan, D. M. *The Treatment of Families in Crisis*. New York: Grune & Stratton, 1968.

Lederer, W. J. & Jackson, D. *The Mirages of Marriage*. New York: W. W. Norton & Co., 1968.

Liddle, H. A. & Halpin, R. J. Family therapy training and supervision literature: A comparative review. *Journal of Marriage and Family Counseling*, 1978, *4*, 77-98.

McClelland, C. Q., Staples, W. I., Weisberg, I. & Bergin, M. E. The practitioner's role in behavioral pediatrics. *Journal of Pediatrics*, 1973, *82*, 325-331.

McFarlane, A. H., Norman, G. R. & Spitzer, W. O. Family medicine: The dilemma of defining the discipline. *Canadian Medical Association Journal*, 1971, *105*, 397-401.

McFarlane, A. H., O'Connell, B. & Hay, J. Demand for care model: Its use in program planning for primary physician education. *Journal of Medical Education*, 1971, *46*, 436-442.

Minuchin, S. & Barcai, A. Therapeutically induced family crisis. In: J. H. Masserman (Ed.), *Science and Psychoanalysis, Vol. XIV, Childhood and Adolescence*. New York: Grune & Stratton, 1969.

Olson, D. H. Marital and family therapy: Integrative review and critique. *Journal of Marriage and the Family*, 1970, *32*, 501-538.

Orne, M. T. & Wender, P. H. Anticipatory socialization for psychotherapy: Method and rationale. *American Journal of Psychiatry*, 1968, *124*, 88-98.

Parad, H. J. & Caplan, G. A framework for studying families in crisis. In: H. J. Parad (Ed.), *Crisis Intervention: Selected Readings*. New York: Family Services Association of America, 1965.

Parsons, T. *The Social System*. Glencoe, Illinois: Free Press, 1951.

Parsons, T. & Bales, R. F. *Family Socialization and Interaction Process*. Glencoe, Illinois: Free Press, 1955.

Patriarche, M. E. Finding time for couseling. *Canadian Family Physician*, 1974, *20*, 91-93.

Postner, R. S., Guttman, H. A., Sigal, J. J., Epstein, N. B. & Rakoff, V. Process and outcome in conjoint family therapy. *Family Process*, 1971, *10*, 451-473.

Rado, S. Towards the construction of an organized foundation for clinical psychiatry. *Comprehensive Psychiatry*, 1961, *2*, 65-73.

Rakoff, V., Sigal, J. J., Spector, R., & Guttman, H. A. *Communication in families*. Paper based on investigation aided by grants from Foundations Fund for Research in Psychiatry, Laidlaw Foundation, 1967.

Rapoport, L. The state of crisis: Some theoretical considerations. In: H. J. Parad (Ed.), *Crisis Intervention: Selected Readings*. New York: Family Services Association of America, 1965.

Ritterman, M. K. Paradigmatic classification of family therapy theories. *Family Process*, 1977, *16*, 29-48.

Santa-Barbara, J., Woodward, C. A., Levin, S., Streiner, D., Goodman, J. & Epstein, N. B. *The relationship between therapists' characteristics and outcome variables in family therapy*. Paper presented at the Canadian Psychiatric Association, Banff, Alberta, September, 1975.

Santa-Barbara, J., Woodward, C. A., Levin, S., Streiner, D., Goodman, J. T. & Epstein, N. B. Interrelationships among outcome measures in the McMaster Family Therapy Outcome Study. *Goal Attainment Review*, 1977, *3*, 47-58.

Scherz, F. H. Maturational crises and parent-child interaction. *Social Casework*, 1971, *52*, 362-369.

Sigal, J. J., Rakoff, V. & Epstein, N. B. Indicators of therapeutic outcome in conjoint family therapy. *Family Process*, 1967, *6*, 215-226.

Solomon, M. A. A developmental, conceptual premise for family therapy. *Family Process*, 1973, *12*, 179-188.

Spiegel, J. *Transactions*. New York: Science House, 1971.

Stanford, B. J. Counseling—A prime area for family doctors. *American Family Physician*, 1972, *5*, 183-185.

Tomm, K. M. A family approach to emotional problems of children. *Canadian Family Physician*, 1973, *19*, 51-54.

Tomm, K. M. & Wright, L. M. Training in family therapy: Perceptual, conceptual, and executive skills. *Family Process*, 1979, *18*, 227-250.

Watzlawick, P., Beavin, J. H. & Jackson, D. D. *Pragmatics of Human Communication*. New York: W. W. Norton & Company, 1967.

Weakland, J., Fisch, R., Watzlawick, P. & Bodin, A. M. Brief therapy: Focused problem resolution. *Family Process*, 1974, *13*, 141-168.

Wells, R. A., Dilkes, T. C. and Trivelli, N. The results of family therapy: A critical review of the literature. *Family Process*, 1972, *11*, 89-107.

Westley, W. A. & Epstein, N. B. Report on the psychosocial organization of the family and mental health. In: D. Willner (Ed.), *Decisions, Values and Groups (Vol. 1)*. New York: Pergamon, 1960.

Westley, W. A. & Epstein, N. B. *The Silent Majority*. San Francisco: Jossey-Bass, 1969.

Woodward, C. A., Santa-Barbara, J., Levin, S., & Epstein, N. B. The role of goal attainment scaling in evaluating family therapy outcome, *American Journal of Orthopsychiatry*, 1978, *48*, 464-476.

Woodward, C. A., Santa-Barbara, J., Levin, S., Epstein, N. B. & Streiner, D. *The McMaster family therapy outcome study III: Client and treatment characteristics significantly contributing to clinical outcomes*. Paper presented at the 54th Annual Meeting of the American Orthopsychiatric Association. New York City, April 1977.

Woodward, C. A., Santa-Barbara, J., Levin, S., Goodman, J., Streiner, D. & Epstein, N. B. *Client and therapist characteristics related to family therapy outcome: Closure and follow-up evaluation*. Paper presented at the Society for Psychotherapy Research, Boston, June 1975.

Woodward, C. A., Santa-Barbara, J., Levin, S., Goodman, J., Streiner, D., Muzzin, L. & Epstein, N. B. *Outcome research in family therapy: On the growing edginess of family therapists*. Paper presented at the Nathan W. Ackerman Memorial Conference, Margarita Island, February 1974.

Zuk, G. H. Family therapy during 1964-1970. *Psychotherapy: Theory, Research and Practice*, 1971, *8*, 90-97.

EDITORS' REFERENCES

Gurman, A. S. & Kniskern, D. P. Deterioration in marital and family therapy: Empirical, conceptual and clinical issues. *Family Process*, 1978, *17*, 3-20. (a)

Gurman, A. S. & Kniskern, D. P. Research on marital and family therapy: Progress, perspective and prospect. In: S. Garfield & A. Bergin (Eds.), *Handbook of Psychotherapy and Behavior Change*. Second edition. New York: Wiley, 1978. (b)

CHAPTER 13

Integrative Family Therapy

Bunny S. Duhl, M.Ed. and

Frederick J. Duhl, M.D.

I found that I could think of each bit of culture structurally; I could see it as in accordance with a consistent set of rules or formulations. Equally, I could see each bit as "pragmatic," either as satisfying the needs of individuals or as contributing to the integration of society. Again, I could see each bit ethologically, as an expression of emotion.

—Gregory Bateson (1972a)

A STORY OF FAMILY THERAPY

Phoebe's almost five-year-old build was lithe and slight. Her look of wide-eyed awe rippled into delight as she reached for the large grey rabbit puppet's head sticking out of Bunny's coat as Fred and Bunny entered her house.

"What's his name?" she demanded.

The coat was no sooner off than the puppet was on Bunny's arm, "talking" to Phoebe.

"My name is Wabbit, what's yours?" he answered, making his name up on the spot.

As Phoebe responded, she and Wabbit were in dialogue, oblivious to her family and Fred.

Phoebe's mother, Sally, had called us several weeks before. Phoebe, at four years and nine months old, had had continuous nightmares since age three, and was now having severe social problems in school. She would not let her mother pick her up or comfort her. Her parents were sure it was related to mother's hospitalization for six weeks with a postpartum infection, following the Caesarian birth of Rebecca two years earlier.

The previous week, Sally had taken Phoebe to a child psychologist, who recommended two years of weekly child therapy for Phoebe. Since she had a background which led her to think in family systems terms, Sally felt caught, as did her husband, who was a teacher. Their child needed help and the help offered prescribed was long-term individual child therapy. This prescription did not fit their phenomenology of the problem, and it increased their sense of having harmed their child.

When she called, we suggested that she and her husband Ted come in to discuss what options for help were possible. When they came in for two hours, the four of us decided to see what else we would all learn if we (Bunny and Fred) came to their home to see them with Phoebe and Rebecca. In the meantime, we heard their story of Sally's hospitalization, and recommended that they bring this up again with Phoebe several times, before we came to their home.

We made a home visit with all of them there. In this very fortuitous and not necessarily usual circumstance, that was all that was needed for:

1) mother and Phoebe to connect;
2) Phoebe's nightmares to disappear;
3) Phoebe to be able to make friends, drop the use of babytalk and her tantrums, and enjoy herself at school;
4) Phoebe to begin to feel good about herself and trust her mother's love for her;
5) both parents to feel good about themselves and be even more effective parents with Phoebe and Becca; and
6) everyone in the family to participate in and learn from a non-mystifying process which would give them some tools for the future.

HOW DO WE THINK ABOUT SUCH STORIES?

Taking into account the preparedness of the parents for our help, it is worth asking how these outcomes happened to occur so easily. We would describe the outcomes as new or renewed integrations, internal to the individuals (no nightmares), between members of the family in different subsystems (mother-Phoebe, father-mother), and between the members and external systems and individuals (Phoebe-friends, Phoebe-school).

We call the style of therapy that we do integrative family therapy. We look simultaneously and organismically at *all the levels of systems* that define behavior and attitudes to arrive at an integration. We consider: 1) the developmental levels; 2) the processes expectable and available in family members, individually and in their family life-cycle; and 3) system patterns and transactions the family exhibits. We feel that the moves for change that we make in this type of therapy must be congruent with individual developmental levels as well as the

stage in the family's life-cycle.[1] We assess and differentiate the degree of automatic behavior or fixed pattern repetition in relation to the degree of distress or pain. In that assessment, we are asking how much investment there seems to be in this family in keeping a maladaptive system pattern going and how much the pain stimulates a push and motivation to have such patterns shift. Obviously, the more the urge to change is present, the more overt cooperation there is and the easier the therapist's task.

In looking at the *juxtaposition* of events in a family's life, we rule out linear causality. However, since development is seen as having a linear time quality, we assess the impact of events on children based on their developmental level and cognitive/emotional "equipment" at the time events took place.

THE STORY AS PHOEBE COULD UNDERSTAND IT AT THREE

Phoebe at three had no possible means of comprehending the meaning of mother's disappearance, which seemed interminable to her. Although father stopped working and became "mother" for six weeks, and although mother sent her audiotapes and notes from the hospital, Phoebe, at three, could not give "correct" meaning to these symbolic substitutes for mother. As in too many hospitals, she was considered to be too young to see mother. In conjunction with mother's leaving, Becca had appeared on the scene, interrupting whatever ongoing private-time pattern Phoebe may have already had with her father. Thus, her whole, as yet narrowly defined, world view was abruptly shaken.

Mother's emergency, following her coming home with Becca, resulted in her being rushed back to the hospital while Phoebe was sleeping. Six weeks of not seeing or being held by mother totally interrupted the pattern of basic trust and connection previously developed. Although cognitively bright, Phoebe could not compre-

---

[1]*Editors' Note.* A recent publication by the Boston Family Institute (1979), co-directed by the Duhls, notes that the therapists and theorists whose work has most influenced and been found to be in harmony with integrative family therapy include Satir, Piaget, Bateson, Erickson, Minuchin and Auerswald.

hend this disruption as temporary and benign in intent, nor did she have language for her internal world of feelings. In addition, at three, she could not give language to her concerns, nor could she understand mother's taped voice-from-the-black-box as assurances of love for and connection with her. Mother had sent three tapes from the hospital, the first a month after she had been hospitalized.

THE STORY FROM THE VANTAGE POINT OF THE FAMILY'S DEVELOPMENT

As we look closer, we will see that this one event contained multitudinous interrelated impacts, which we needed to respect even as we chose the focus of our intervention.

If we look at the family's life-cycle, we learn that Phoebe's family was in its early stages of parenting when this disruption occurred. Ted's ability and willingness to drop work and take over in the mothering role were most unusual at that time in this culture. However, this sudden switch for him was not without the price of mixed concern, caring and resentment. Although a bright, warm and nurturing man, his usual patterns and expectations were severely disrupted by Sally's bout with near-death. In addition, their early parenting patterns had settled in around one child. Here he was the trail blazer, and alone, parenting two children, one of whom was a helpless newborn, and the other a perplexed three-year-old. According to Ted, Sally's mother, who had come to "help out," proved to be more of a stressful energy drain than a source of comfort and help to Ted.

And for Sally, the impact of fighting for her life, while knowing that Phoebe and her newborn baby and Ted needed her, created a circular stress cycle. She was at once grateful for, resentful of, and guilty in relation to Ted's mothering role.

Their stage of marriage and parenting had not yet developed the attitude of acceptance of positive role mutuality and interdependence that this experience was in the process of teaching them. As it always happens with such an event, both Ted and Sally's pain had an element of "why me?" mixed with caring for and reaching out towards each other.

It was our assumption when we first saw them that Phoebe, at three, conversely felt "It's me.

Mommy left because I was bad and I'm mad at her for leaving. If she knows I'm mad at her she won't like me." At three, one is the center of the universe, which revolves around one's very omnipotent/helpless self.

And Becca as newborn—one can only guess what she experienced.

THE "STUCK" PATTERN

Thus, when we went to their home, we already knew the specific events and circumstances by which the parents gave meaning to the present. We also knew that Sally and Ted had worked exceedingly hard and long to debrief and sort out their myriad diverse feelings and attitudes with each other after Sally came home. However, Phoebe had avoided Sally and would not let Sally comfort her or pick her up. Sally experienced a wide range of feelings and thoughts—from altruistic tolerance and understanding and the self-instruction, "Don't push—let her go at her own pace," to total rejection, and loss, anger and helplessness. While Phoebe would easily go to and from Ted, a fixed pattern had emerged between Sally and Phoebe.

In some unspoken way, over time, each felt stuck and expected the other to somehow break the pattern. This expectation was not expressed in an embittered and resentful manner by mother, as happens in some families. Rather, one sensed a yearning in Sally for a way to connect with her child so that both of them would feel relaxed and in contact with each other.

SOME THOUGHTS ABOUT INTIMACY, FLEXIBILITY, AUTOMATICITY AND AMBIANCE

There are those families who blame another or themselves in such a way as to render movement difficult, with tremendous loss of face for the one who moves first. Their core images are of fixed distances. Those families often fear replacing power games with meaningful connections because they have never been there before and do not know the processes for closer relationships. Their movements and conversations are automatic, stylized, routined, and familiar. These are non-intimate families.

And there are those families whose members

are pleading for connection, where missed moments, almosts, and not quites are the rule, and the stuckness is in the emptyness or dryness in their well of imagination. Their core image is one of closer, relaxed contact and freer movement. The experience is one of rigidly held distance. Once a little seed water is poured into the well, it begins to draw forth the family's own resources, which begin to fill the well again. These families are "once-intimate." The steps needed for each of these two families, despite the apparent similarity of circumstances, will then be different, depending on their core images, their push to have the images actualized, and the capabilities and resources available to draw upon.

In our talk with Ted and Sally, it became clear that they were of the second type of family. We felt that we had at least two allies with us as we entered their home a week later, given their own good communication level and the obvious caring for each other and their children. Their overt pain experienced in relation to the helplessness they felt in helping Phoebe and the strong desire to reestablish a close connection were the push for help. We had already given them the task of talking about the events two years ago with Phoebe, in as natural a manner as they could create, to see how much they themselves could do before we visited the family at home. After all, *therapists should only walk in where parents fear to tread—and even then with respect for the parents.*[2]

THIS STORY AS AN EXAMPLE OF INTEGRATIVE FAMILY THERAPY

Our work with this family, while not typical of all our work, certainly contains enough of the elements to exemplify aspects of how we help families. It allows us to present the cognitive maps that we use to travel the road of our work.

MAPS OF INTEGRATIVE FAMILY THERAPY

The "maps" are a series of connected, inter-

related frameworks that allow us to keep our fingers on the pulse of the system as well as of the individuals, and not lose sight of the individuals for the system nor the system for the individual.

We consider our collection a gazeteer, a collection of overlapping maps, each highlighting one aspect of the simultaneous events of the person/system/context. It is not unlike an atlas that contains the information about the yearly rainfall, the resources, the roads, the population density, the towns, of North America, all of which are hard to put on one sheet. Thus the atlas provides many maps of the same area in the same book. *It is our belief that all therapists have their own gazeteers and, in therapy, leaf through them in an individualistic fashion.* When others ask us about our ways of doing therapy, they often try to fit *our ways* into *their* maps. But then, we do the same.

WHAT'S IN A NAME?

It is of interest that in the last year or so people have asked us what type of therapy we do while others, without asking, have given titles to our work. The labels, coming from those who obviously have their own maps, reflect the wide variety of approaches to family therapy, as well as the need to find some order in this burgeoning field. Keeping the story of Phoebe in mind, it may be worthwhile noting what others have said of our work.

Some have called our approach "experiential family therapy" referring to our use of *nonverbal modes of communication* such as spatialization and sculpture (Duhl, Kantor, and Duhl, 1973), or role-playing and role reversal techniques, or puppets, as in this case. Yet we cannot define ourselves by any particular tool or methodology. We tend to use whatever tool will do the job with respect.

Others choose to define us as "experiential" out of our concern for the individuals within family systems and our direct work within families with *felt meanings*, similar to Gendlin's approach (1973 a,b). With Phoebe and her parents, this concern was certainly a central focus and we do use ourselves in the experience. Yet it is not sufficient.

Still others have called our type of family therapy behavioral or structural (Minuchin, 1974),

---

[2]*Editors' Note.* Despite the differences in language, it is interesting to compare this view of the Duhls with Skynner's (Chapter 2) notion of the therapist's efforts to identify and bring to consciousness the "missing emotions" of disturbed and distressed families.

referring to the fact that we *highlight behaviors, are goal-oriented, assign tasks and homework,* as ways of *helping family members realign, gather new information,* and *expand their range of roles and capabilities in solving their problems.* In this story of Phoebe, the parents were assigned the task of talking with Phoebe about the events around Becca's birth and mother's rehospitalization, between the office and home visits. They also undertook the task of listening to the old audiotapes to help review that earlier episode with new awareness.

Some have called our approach cognitive, since a central theme we attend to is that of *information-processing styles and stages of individual family members* (Duhl and Duhl, 1975). To us, it was vital that we had an awareness of what Phoebe was able to comprehend at three and at five and of the difference in the "logic" that guided her understanding. Utilizing such concepts allowed us to work with her rapidly in her own language of impact (Duhl, F., 1969), such as fantasy and metaphors.

Only recently, the label Gestalt family therapy was offered to us, for we attend to the *core images of past, present and future, which govern individual behavior within families and other systems* (Duhl, B., 1977). This certainly could be seen when we inquired into the images of each parent as to how they would see themselves, as individuals and as a family, if Phoebe were "fine." Wabbit also pursued with Phoebe her images of friendship, caretaking and fright.

And lastly (though who can be sure?), we have been called existentialist or humanistic family therapists, since we attend to the *pain and vulnerabilities* in people's lives, and often *share ourselves* in our therapy, where empathically appropriate, or merely share that we have been touched. The story of Phoebe and her family is filled with vulnerability and pain and mastery, in all members. We respect the pain as we inquire about the defenses used to shield each person from it. When we share stories with Phoebe and her parents about our own children's reaction to a parent's hospitalization, we are acknowledging our own painful experiences and mastery as we validate theirs.

It seems that we fit so many definitions and utilize many maps. How then do we "label" ourselves?

For us, the "title" which best fits our work at this time is *integrative family therapy* (Duhl and Duhl, 1979). One could say that we avoid definition by choosing such an inclusive label. But perhaps that is just the point. The label fits not any specific techniques, but how we think and approach our work.

The same phenomena can be described and explained from a variety of points of view or systems levels. *What we see as the challenge is to integrate in our work the awareness of the simultaneous existence of these levels.* We recognize that the family has its sub- and supra-systems in operation at the same time. The individual as a subsystem with its physical and intrapsychic systems is also existing simultaneous along with the culture and society.

We feel it is important to view the world in systems terms through a zoom or meta lens (Duhl, F., 1969), knowing there are multitudinous simultaneously existing "systems" only differentiated and distinguished by our way of comprehending, conceptualizing, focusing and describing. One is always choosing which units/threads are to be considered "in" the system and which are "not in," knowing full well that these are all arbitrary and momentary choices. There also is a choice as to which aspects shall be foreground for our focus and which background. Which system level is attended to? Which interaction, action or reaction catches the eye?

Thus, at this time, integrative family therapy represents our "Knot in the handkerchief" (Bateson, 1972), our connected series of maps by which we work with systems and the individuals who inhabit and comprise them.

A DIGRESSION ABOUT DICHOTOMIES

The emergence of systems thinking and the field of family therapy in the past 20 years or so takes place in the historical context of a world grown smaller and linked by technology, communication and interlocking economic systems. Yet much of the thinking about systems remains polarized. Today the dialectic pendulum swing of ideas poses a potential orthodoxy of thinking in family systems terms as antithetical to the orthodoxy and exclusivity of thinking in individual system terms. It is inconceivable to us to delimit our thinking by either orthodoxy or framework.

The East/West, the whole/parts dichotomies, the irrational/rational, right brain/left brain splits, the content/processes dichotomies—all are similar to the dilemma of wave/particle/quantum physics. The field of physics, which today touches on the mystic, still searches for a unified field theory, to join wave and quantum theory together.

Conceptualizers in family therapy search for a unified field theory, in the same search for comprehensive comprehension. Our integrative family therapy approach is our small attempt in this search, one which integrates the awareness that people live in all levels of system simultaneously. The key concepts in our thinking are *"and"* and *"all,"* which allow for both differentiation and connection.

In our approach, it is important never to lose the person in the system, nor to lose sight of the smaller and larger systems in which each person exists. After all, it is the individuals in family systems who change their system by changing actions, attitudes, behaviors, thoughts, feelings.

It is hard to kiss a system.

It is important for therapists to know which systems level is most useful, appropriate and/or available for intervention at a particular moment. The therapist always makes a decision as to which system level should be addressed, using one of the many maps toward the goal of unblocking painful or self-defeating automatic behaviors and enhancing individuation and connection in the people seeking help. Many times the decision is based on the therapist's own limitations, interests or special skill. We believe it is important for him/her to make a conscious choice—but with respect for the needs of the systems and individuals who seek help. Such an expectation on our part requires many maps, many skills and many techniques integrated in the mind of the therapist. We strive toward that goal in ourselves and our students. We have found over the last six years that an integrative weaving form of therapy—a way to use the atlas—may be taught along with the maps that comprise the atlas (Duhl and Duhl, 1979).

Now, in presenting our maps, our organizing principles, we will start with our values and assumptions, for indeed each therapist's approach is value-based and, additionally, implies concepts about how human beings change, learn and grow.

VALUES AND ASSUMPTIONS

1) *Life is sacred.* For each of us it is a limited resource of about 75 years more or less. In addition, individuals are more than the sum of experience, environment and genes as we know them. There is something else that defines life, call it spirit or soul or whatever. We respect its rarity and presence and the uniqueness with which it appears in each of us. On the other hand, we do not respect or accept violence as worthy of explanation or excuse. It has no place in families or life.

2) *Every person, couple or family has a story.* Stories are the personal felt experiences of each person's reality as framed by a personal world view. When people tell their stories, it grounds them in their own reality, and alerts the therapist to each one's *language of impact*, each one's *vulnerabilities and defenses* (Duhl, B., 1976, 1978a), *core images* (Duhl, 1978b), *learning styles* (Duhl and Duhl, 1975), *modes of representation* (Bandler and Grinder, 1975), *cognitive stages* (Piaget, 1952), and often to their automatic patterns. In addition to their stories, people are often caught in the ways they have learned to learn, in their automatic patterns. They are doing the best they can with what they have. Yet they do not generate new sentences (Chomsky, 1965) or new behaviors in some, many, or any contexts.

3) *People have a basic right and need to information* about themselves and to the tools or processes with which they can guide their own behavior and solve their own problems. They need to be able to write their own prescriptions for their life. If people do not own their own life and problem-solving skills, there will never be *enough* therapists. There are not enough now as it is, which may mean that, *if the solution is the problem* (Watzlawick et al., 1974), we should put energy not into training more therapists, but into developing everyone's personal and family competence through education.[3]

---

[3]*Editors' Note.* See L'Abate (Chapter 17) for a comprehensive discussion of such preventive educational methods with families. Also note here an important distinction in the rationale for the promulgation of such educational experiences: The Duhls are arguing that family educational models are

4) *Therapists are people first*, with both personal and professional stories that shape their reality, world views, definitions of and approaches to change, growth and discomfort, distress or jeopardy. Some of these stories are called theories and are told in the second and third person.

5) *Reality is relative.* There is no one reality, as Watzlawick points out in *How Real is Real?* (1977). Therefore, it behooves therapists to be humble *and* respectful in their interventions, which often arise solely out of their own version of reality.

6) *There must be a match, a fit, on some level, between the therapist's reality and world view and the patients'*, or else the therapist will totally manipulate the patients, or the patients will leave. The old concept of a therapeutic alliance is still useful, for systems only change with an inside and an outside ally working together.

7) *Therapists cannot want more for clients or patients than patients want for themselves.* If they do, therapists will be fighting with them for them, and no one has an ally.

SOME THOUGHTS ABOUT THERAPY FOR PEOPLE IN SYSTEMS

What follows from these values and principles are parameters for our approach to therapy:

1) It behooves the therapist to listen and get to know the patients from their own point of view: their stories, their language of impact, learning styles, vulnerabilities and defenses.

2) It is important never to lose the person in/for the system, nor to forget the power of the system on the person, nor the impact of a person upon a system.

3) It is important to understand the individual people who make up the marital or family system and their individual developmental processes, as well as those of the family system as a whole. Like actors, few people like to be known only by their roles. They want

the roles to be known as shaped by them.

4) Our view of the family system is one of a mystical nontangible essence—a hologram—a reflected metaphor in space and time, which can be changed though it cannot be touched. One can only touch individuals who play the system roles or parts.

5) Systems do not experience, no matter how glibly, or anthropomorphically we describe them; individuals experience.

6) People also impact with their behavior. There is no way to understand an individual without knowing his or her impact on others. The form and manner of communications, of inquiry, of connection are important functions of the individual. While we are aware of the individual, we do not want to celebrate his or her narcissism as the essence of therapy.

7) More people know more about power games in marriage and family than they do about intimacy. Unfortunately, this may also be true of therapists.

THE VISIT

Phoebe met us at the door and immediately wanted to show Bunny and Wabbit her room upstairs. They willingly followed her. Meanwhile, Fred met with Becca, Sally and Ted downstairs as he began to be charmed by Becca's two-year-old self.

Bunny had picked up the puppet and a Chinese magic wand as props when leaving home, not exactly sure how she would use them. However, once there, Wabbit made it perfectly clear to Bunny that he was the senior therapist with this child and that she could not possibly do the job without him. Wabbit showed that he could ask silly questions which grown-ups are not allowed to ask. He could also test boundaries for dead-centered serious or teasable subjects. In so doing, he could playfully check Phoebe's barometer of self-esteem, discovering in nonthreatening ways where it was high, medium, or low. He instructed Bunny to sit back since he could make mistakes, tell fantasies, and be accepted in ways Bunny's adult self could never be. And so Bunny sat back, on the rug, while Wabbit carried forth.

In this conversation between puppet and

important *not* because of the lack of severity of problems experienced by "normal" families, but because there are not enough well trained family therapists to meet the need for professional services.

child, while the focus was on Phoebe as an individual, there was always the awareness that the goal was to facilitate an unblocked caring connection between the parents and the child.[4] The dialogue is shown below.

As Phoebe told Wabbit of her dream, he asked over again every step of the way, how he could help her, be with her, protect her. As he validated her scared aloneness, Wabbit learned via metaphor what Phoebe's images were of being cared for, and being loved. With the exactitude of her five-year-old imagery, she spelled it out to him through her dream and, then, what *should have happened.*

Wabbit was also able to share times when he had had nightmares and wished others would do something. He told of times in the lives of the children with whom he lived when they had been sad, mad, or glad. They felt as she did. For instance, he shared that in his (and the therapists') house the little girl had been sad and mad when her mother went to the hospital to have a baby.

This was a move to provide a comparative event so that Phoebe could identify with the child and feel validated. Phoebe said nothing but stared wide-eyed at Wabbit. Uncomfortable and stiff, she changed the subject, but not the process, and said she would read Wabbit a story. At about that moment, Ted came in the room and sat on the rug near the bed. Phoebe began joking with Wabbit and then decided she needed

---

[4]*Editors' Note.* Again, despite language differences, note the similarity of this *core* treatment goal and Boszormenyi-Nagy and Ulrich's (Chapter 5) emphasis on existential reciprocity.

DIALOGUE BETWEEN PHOEBE AND WABBIT

Dialogue	*Commentary*
PHOEBE: I wuv you Wabbit. I have a Wabbit, too, but it's not as soft. (*Now showing her special toys and presenting her achievements with pride*). I can spell my name.	*Baby talk always protects against being too direct. P. connects around the rabbit.* *She is capable, big, and competent and not helpless at all. A typical five-year-old comment.*
WABBIT: Oh you can't do that!	*The therapist is testing the boundaries—what is truly important and what is "surface."*
PHOEBE: (*Huffily*) Yes I can! I'm not kidding!	*Her competency is at stake. The therapist backs off from challenging a core image.*
WABBIT: Golly. I can't spell. Would you show me how?	*W. being less capable than P. gives the girl an edge over W. and reopens the opportunity to show her skills and accomplishments.*
PHOEBE: (*Does so by teaching Wabbit how to spell Phoebe*) I can read, too. (*Takes picture book. Sits on floor near B. and W.*)	*P. having shown her competence, now risks the closeness, first in space, then in words.*
PHOEBE: I love you, Wabbit. Will you be my friend?	*No baby talk. Remembering P.'s problems in school, therapist responds to P.'s reaching out with validation and connection, and tries to get information about her core images. What do friends do? How do friends act? P. is offered the opportunity to control through self-prescription.*
WABBIT: I'd love to be your friend, but I don't know how. What must I do?	
PHOEBE: Just play with me.	*Play is child's work—and the learning arena.*

WABBIT: OK. I can do that. And friends take care of each other. What must I do to take care of you? (*W.'s paw touches her hand.*)

W. introduces caring as a possible function of friendship as he inquires about core image.

PHOEBE: I'll take care of *you*, Wabbit.

P. echoes her issues in the family that she will take care of herself. Staying in control, she establishes the relationship.

WABBIT: Of course you will. And I need to know how to take care of you, too.

The therapist, validating P.'s position, adds on the reciprocal process so that P can maintain her control as well as reveal her helplessness.

PHOEBE: Well, when I get scared . . . When I have nightmares . . . Well, if the house catches on fire, you will help me jump into a bathtub filled with water, so we won't get burned—or maybe into a lake. Or maybe we'll need more water—so maybe into the ocean. . . .

The therapist asks what the family has not asked, i.e., What do you need? The door opens to the risky area of vulnerability through fantasy.

WABBIT: Well, I can help you and me into a bathtub and maybe a lake—but I'll need your help with an ocean, 'cause I can't swim.

Therapist accepts and plays with the fantasy, respecting it as metaphor and using it to reinforce the concept that even competent caretakers, like parents, can be vulnerable.

PHOEBE: There'll be a big island—Wabbit (*petting it and head very close*). I won't let you drown.

P. flows back and forth between parent and child positions, helper and helped, as part of mastery.

WABBIT: Good. You know, I used to get scared at night, too.

W. offers more opportunity to model the process of revealing vulnerabilities and mastering them with someone who cares.

PHOEBE: You got scared? Oh Wabbit, what did you get scared of?

Will you really tell me your secrets? Can I get information from someone who is supposed to be "strong" (therapist)? Can we share vulnerabilities and be close? Here again is the model for the reconnection of the parents and Phoebe around shared information and vulnerabilities.

WABBIT: I once dreamed a nightmare about being all alone. It scared me a lot then. But then I woke up and told Racky Raccoon about it, and she held me and I wasn't alone anymore.
   Now I'm older and I can be your friend and protect you.

The story models how the child can connect while being scared. This story is part true since it is derived from the therapist's own childhood. Sharing the child in the adult offers children a way of seeing "growing up" as not losing the child, but adding on the adult competencies. W. becomes protective.

PHOEBE: (*Moving very close*) I have scary dreams, too. (*She pets Wabbit, looking at the puppet's face, and is serious and sad.*)

The trust is cemented here. P. is in almost a trance-like state—that state when the eye is on the inner world and it is safe to be with the listener. She is relieved to tell about her dreams to the puppet—her equal in size and vulnerability.

to show daddy and Wabbit how she could read again. As both admired her reading, Ted said quietly, with an amused shrug, that he wasn't sure if it was memorization or not. Wabbit continued to focus on Phoebe and included Ted as audience to Phoebe.

Shortly afterwards, Fred, Sally and Becca came into Phoebe's room and everyone was on the rug. Phoebe was proud of Becca and showed her off to us, too. Becca held her own at two, counting up to 30 (!) with delight and smiles.

Phoebe asked to put Wabbit in her bed for a nap, and he agreed to go, so, as Bunny watched Phoebe tuck Wabbit in, all the rest tiptoed downstairs to the kitchen for coffee, milk and cookies. Downstairs, Bunny shared with Fred and the parents what happened.

Fred also offered that Becca's precocity was partially a product of her relationship with Phoebe, who taught her younger sister what she learned in school. When all family members and therapists had been together in Phoebe's room, there had been no competition on either child's part for adult attention. Indeed, Phoebe had seemed pleased to share her room and the limelight with her younger sister. The observed process was testament to loving parenting.

SOME VARIATIONS ON THE THEME

When Phoebe came down, she had with her grandma's Christmas present, an as yet unworn nurse's uniform and kit. She put on the uniform. After Fred told her that he was a doctor she allowed him to help her put together the stethescope. He told her nurses and doctors took care of people, and that sometimes nurses and doctors needed others to take care of them. Picking up on one of the "symptom" themes, he asked Phoebe who took care of her. She answered, "I take care of myself."

Fred responded that it sounded as if Phoebe had some very special ideas about how she wanted to be taken care of and that she might need to tell others how they could do that job. "After all," he said, "God helps those who help themselves." At that point, Phoebe took Fred into the livingroom to show him a wooden Buddha the family possessed.

Meanwhile, in the kitchen, Bunny sipped coffee and continued to fill Ted and Sally in on the upstairs events, watching Becca's interactions with each of them as the child demonstrated her capacity for several glasses of apple juice.

Fred and Phoebe returned shortly hand-in-hand and Fred said that he and Phoebe had been discussing being mad, sad, bad and glad, and that Phoebe hadn't known that grown-ups sometimes have those very feelings too.

ON THE USE OF MAGIC

As Fred talked, Bunny took the Chinese magic wand out of her purse. She knew that Phoebe would have to hear grown-ups talk in a way that Phoebe could understand—in short sentences with simple concepts. The black Chinese magic wand had a string and bead at one end which can be pulled down. The string recedes into the wand as the wand is tipped slightly and the weight inside pulls the string up. Those who watch the bead on the string do not see the wand tipping ever so slightly.

So, as Fred shared how he'd told Phoebe that he, too, had a little girl who had been mad when her mommy went to the hospital, Bunny pulled the string out of the wand. Then, Bunny told Phoebe that this magic string and bead would go up and disappear when the answer was "yes" and would stay down if the answer was "no." Bunny asked the first question:

"Was Phoebe mad when Mommy went to the hospital?"

The string disappeared. "Yes."

"Was Phoebe sad when Mommy went to the hospital?" Again, the string disappeared. "Yes."

Sally joined in: "Was Mommy sad to leave Phoebe?" The string disappeared. "Yes."

"Did Mommy know Phoebe was mad and sad?" Sally asked. The string disappeared.

Sally continued: "Was Mommy mad at Phoebe?" The string stayed down. The answer was "No!"

At this point, Phoebe's wide eyes stared at Sally. As she looked up, she asked, "You weren't mad at me?"

"Oh no, honey. Not you. I just felt so sad to leave you!"

Ted chimed in, "And was Daddy mad at Mommy for leaving?" The string said, "Yes."

"And Sad, too?" asked Ted. The string went up again. Phoebe stared at Daddy.

Fred joined in, "Did Phoebe know that people can be mad and sad at the same time?"

The string stayed down. "No."

Mother then spoke about the hospital experience again, and reminded Phoebe that she had sent home audiotapes to her, and that Phoebe had sent Mommy drawing-letters which Mommy still had. Sally asked Phoebe if she'd like to hear the tapes sometime. Phoebe nodded yes. Her eyes were moist.

"Mommy," she said quietly and directly, "I'm very tired. You can pick me up." Sally's eyes matched Phoebe's as she gently gathered in and rocked her almost five-year-old. We were all very quiet. There are special moments to be respected.

After a while, we asked each one, "What did you find out?"

Each responded briefly about the newly shared awareness of the difficult time each had two years ago. In checking out and locking in the new information through summarizing, it was clear that we had achieved the beginning of what we set out to do. The family was connecting and in touch. It was time to leave. Knowing when to stop is an important thing to learn when you do therapy.

Phoebe got down from Sally's arms only long enough to retrieve Wabbit from her bed and return him to Bunny, asking when he could come and visit again. Then, giving both Fred and Bunny good-bye hugs, she reached out to be picked up by Sally again, her body relaxed and molding itself to her mother's form.

We suggested, before leaving, that the family listen to the audiotapes and look at Phoebe's pictures.

THE FOLLOW-UPS

A few days later, when we spoke to mother, she related that in the evening of the day of our visit, they had turned on the first audiotape she had sent Phoebe from the hospital, which included a lullaby. Phoebe had listened to it all with a five-year-old's rapt attention, and said to mother, "You really *did* care about me!" She went to sleep easily that night and has had no nightmares since that time. She also asked to hear the lullaby on the tape every night since then.

Six weeks later, mother called us to tell us that Phoebe's baby talk had dropped away both at school and at home, and she allowed herself

to be taken care of in a manner appropriate to a five-year-old.

Not surprisingly, Phoebe had tested her parents and her teachers several times with old behavior in those six weeks. Just prior to her fifth birthday, the child had had a horrendous week in school when, by some Jungian synchrony, her favorite teacher returned after a five-week absence during which she had been hospitalized. Phoebe had not acknowledged to her teacher that she had missed her. However, just before her birthday, Phoebe declared to mother, "You won't be here for my birthday. You'll be sick in the hospital."

Mother's answer, gently, "No I won't. I'll be here with you," brought forth an incredulous look and intense hugs and kisses from Phoebe.

Mother stated that Phoebe felt very self-satisfied now that she was "known," that she and Ted felt free to be parents in the ways that they had imagined, and that felt right to them.

WHAT WAS NEEDED

In this very human situation, this family, with its caring and genuine interest in each other, needed minimum though pointed intervention to allow it to right its course again.

As we make sense of it, the child needed the gaps in information filled in about the critical time when she was three. She needed the validation of knowing that feeling mad, sad and bad was: 1) okay; 2) not unique to her; 3) felt by mom and dad too; 4) not a cause for punishment; 5) not the cause of mother's illness or leaving. She needed to know that feeling mad would not destroy anyone nor would she be destroyed by feeling sad. She needed to hear her mother and father own their own experiences and feelings and to have them hear hers in her language and on her terms.

Her parents needed to acknowledge Phoebe's statements of her fears, meanings and feelings which they had never heard directly. They also needed to be assured that despite the child's symptoms, they had not permanently scarred her and that processes existed which could enable the family to change from fixed automatic patterns to freer, more flowing ones. Mother needed to be able to hold and comfort her child.

All three needed to be able to exchange, externalize and be validated for feelings in an atmosphere of acceptance and safety. From outside, they needed to hear a statement that they had coped as best they could, given the incredibly difficult situation in which everyone's resources were stretched far beyond ordinary limits. Permission to do something different was necessary, along with the processes for opening up a blocked conduit, processes which would present a novel way to make the covert overt.

AND WHAT WAS PROVIDED

These needs, we felt, were met in the two meetings. Tasks were set out for them—to review the story again, to listen to mother's audiotapes and look at Phoebe's pictures to mother at her hospitalization time so as to provide an integration of information. They were told that one review would not do the trick, that they could expect themselves and Phoebe to need review and rehearsal of new behaviors before the new information would lead to new patterns that were adaptive and connecting.

The parents thus were aware it would take time to go over the new information with Phoebe in many forms for her to believe it consistently. And they would need time and practice to react with acceptance rather than avoidance. With a framework, a model and encouragement, Sally and Ted, not the therapists, could own the task of reconnecting with Phoebe, and they could take pride in their own parenting.

Thus, in two sessions of two hours each, the family was well on its way to helping the individuals catch up with each one's life-cycle stage in a synchronous and harmonious manner. Each person's partitioned past and present were again continuous, and they all had a model for information-sharing processes to extend into their future. Perhaps most important, there were no heroes and no victims. There were no roles, only real people with real events, feelings and attitudes. As each could own pain, hurt and vulnerability without blame, so could each own his/her self-esteem, while being connected meaningfully in the family system.

SOME THOUGHTS ABOUT THERAPY AS AN ARENA FOR NOVELTY, CREATIVITY AND SUCCESS

The purpose of therapy is for our learning as well as the patients'. More specifically, each couple or family arouses in us an interest in them as unique individuals and unique groupings, similar to, but always different from, any others we have known. We take both their similarities and their uniqueness seriously. The similarities guide, rather than dictate to us, what to expect and what to do. The differences, their unique qualities, invite our exploration so that we may learn something new, and know yet another way of experiencing the world. Given our search for novelty, we have a hard time being bored with the couples and families we see. Somehow, we turn each situation, no matter how familiar, into a creative challenge of dialogue and exploration.

The business of working with people is a strange one, for in this field, while we are always using what is already known and "proven," we are still learning by doing and by exploring. Trusting that we will be successful with those in front of us, in our ability to connect as human-to-human, we work in such a way that, should this family or couple not turn out to fit into our "success" column, at least we will have caused no harm. Perhaps we have cooled off some automatic behavior or planted an image so that their lives can in time become different. Sometimes someone else can help them grow and change more effectively based on our attempts.

GOALS AND THE THERAPIST

Sometimes therapy has been terminated without all the goals having been attained. Sometimes, we have felt that we "failed," only to find out later that our clients have used their learnings to reorder their lives away from us.

We do try to get information at the end of each session as to what they learned and thus stay in touch with the immediate effects of therapy on them.

We are wary of being "expert" and knowing all the answers, for we see our descriptions of family systems as metaphors for what actually is—individual human beings who see, hear, feel and experience. When we begin to work with a couple or family, we cannot predict outcome with 100% surety; the variables are too complex, and many are as yet unknown. Our ultimate goal in any therapy we do is to have those individuals and families we work with reflect back, through their behavior, feelings and statements, images of their heightened sense of competence, well-being and self-esteem. Behaviorally, they should show an increased ability to exercise optional behaviors in place of the automatic repetitive ones, so as to move them towards the next stage in their development as individuals or in their family life-cycle. Goals, therefore, include the increasing ability to be differentiated yet connected to important others—to be contained in one's own skin and able to reach out and touch another.

The goals we actually agree upon with our patients are conjointly defined in 1) specific behavioral terms that can be seen by all, as well as 2) self-reports about new ways of making sense of previously apparently disconnected phenomena.

Though our goals are behavioral, we are not behavioristic. We keep our persons in the room while our therapists are working. In a world of mechanistic alienation and disconnection, created for us by the technologies and theories of our parents and grandparents, we feel strongly that technique is not enough, and humanistic concern is not enough. As psychiatirst Peter Martin (1975) has said, "Technique is what you do till the therapist comes." And a therapist, for us, is a person whose intelligence is guided by his/her heart. There is a motto over a French hospital that states: "Cure sometimes; Help often; Comfort always."

THE PROBLEM AND THE PEOPLE: THE SYSTEMS/INDIVIDUAL DICHOTOMY—AND SHARED AND UNSHARED IMAGES

When we do therapy, we work with people, not just with problems. There is no problem unless a person or persons define an event or pattern of behavior as a problem by comparing it (often covertly) with an expected image of what should be. The image may be idiosyncratic or consensual. In either situation, it resides in one or more minds where it is available for comparison with the experienced reality. Thus, a child is a problem, or has a problem, when his behavior does not fit the image of his teachers, his parents, or other adults.

The discrepancy or non-fit between the expected image and the behavior or event is not sufficient to fully define the problem. What is also necessary for the definition are the images and the behaviors toward attempted solutions and the resources available in the persons in the involved social system.

The assessment of the problem depends on assessing the stress, the discrepancy between image and experience, imaged solution and actuality, deviancy and resource. It involves as well the fit between therapists and people seeking help. We cannot see a problem in a social system without reference to the ways in which individuals, their minds and their behaviors fit or do not fit with each other.

ASSESSING THE PROBLEM, AND THE SYSTEM

With integrative family therapy, it is important to assess the condition of the people and the problem as one offers help (Duhl, 1978a). Families come now with problems "in the relationship," which are experienced as "uncomfortable", as well as those in which one or more people are in jeopardy,[5] as with an anorectic or suicidal adolescent.

Some families, despite a marked degree of jeopardy, reach out for new information easily, while others are blameful, angry and hesitant to try anything but more of the old patterns they know. In our assessment, we take this into consideration, along with the type of crises or situation, the sense of distress, the context, and the resources available in and out of the family at the moment. These comprise the ingredients of the condition or the "event-shape," as Auerswald (1977) has called it.

These assessment ingredients can be conceptualized along seven concurrent, interrelating continuua that define the 1) situation and precipitating event; 2) degree of distress as observed or reported; 3) system characteristics in terms of automaticity or flexibility; 4) access to information; 5) phase in individual and family developmental cycles; 6) pattern of relating; and 7) ambiance.

Before we discuss the resources available within as well as external to the family system, we will clarify the above continuua.

[5]The concept of a continuum ranging from "discomfort to jeopardy" was stimulated by listening to Dr. John Howells discuss Vector Therapy and patients at risk, May, 1978. Other continuua followed naturally. See Howells (1975).

Table 1

Continua for System Assessment in Integrative Family Therapy

A.		Living		Surviving		Dying
1.	Type of Situation (specific precipitating event)	Intimacy; Closeness	Normal (Expected) Crises	Unexpected Crises	Accidents; Illness	Depression; Suicide; Psychosis
2.	Felt and/or Assessed Experience	Discomfort	Distress	Pain		Jeopardy; Life-Threatening
3.	System Characteristics (Novelty/ Automaticity)	Novelty is a high priority	Flexibility; Novelty is usually present.	Novelty Balanced with continuity		Automatic behavior; Rituals; No novelty.
4.	Information Access and Boundaries	Active inquiry; Search for information; Open boundaries	Responsive but passive search for information; Open to most information	Passive Search; Lacks information, open to selective, non-threatening information.		Blocked to new information; Closed boundaries; No search
5.	Flow or Pattern of Relating	Fluid; Available to all; Willing to connect most times	Limited Relating; Part-time connection	Intermittent relating and availability	Jagged presence; Sudden intensities	Blocked; Unwilling and inaccessible
6.	Ambiance	Safe, Open, Caring Attentive; Decentered; Humor present		Blame & anger attenuated by apologies; Some caring; A bit hurtful		Dangerous, Blameful, Angry, Inattentive, Ego-Centered

B.	Family Development										
		Courtship	Early Marriage	Preschool Children	School Children	Adolescents	Grown Children	Midlife; Parents Dying	Retirement	Peer Losses	Old Age; Losses
		One plus One	Couple	Expansion	Stability	Numbers Shrink	Couple Again	Orphans	Moving Possible	Wisdom Possible	Senility; Loneliness

The continua, which are presented in Table 1, are not meant to be rigid scales for assessment. Rather, they are interrelated constructs developed, like the footpaths that cross Harvard Common, out of a practical need to get from one place to another. If one thinks of them as such pathways on our cognitive maps, then one can scan for the intersections and locate a family quickly.

Thus one can define the family's distress, as well as make an assessment of its coping skills, resources and the degree of automatic patterned behaviors present. What we also assess is the capacity to perceive new information, imagine new solutions and act with novelty so as to permit change. The degree of distress is often directly related to this capacity for flexibility, the resources available and the type of situation being coped with.

This first set of continua facilitate the assessment of the system as a whole and generate the initial therapeutic stance. For the therapist, the key ones are those numbered 1 and 2 which deal with the situation (living-surviving-dying) and the felt and assessed experience (discomfort-distress-jeopardy).

The Type of Situation and Assessment of Experience

When we listen to the family's story, we are assessing its type of situation and experience. We ask ourselves: "Are there persons in danger of hurting themselves or others?" If so, the therapist must take actions to prevent it. In doing so, he/she may be seen as "acting *on*" the family, rather than "acting *with*" the family at that moment in time.

Thus a suburban family of four, with an adolescent in school trouble, a father who binge drinks and beats his wife, a depressed and placating mother, and a young daughter who is detached, is in severe jeopardy and requires an approach with interventions which first throw a net of safety over the entire family by stopping ongoing dangerous processes immediately. Only then can such a family slowly learn new behaviors which both respect boundaries and connect across them.

Families in "pain" on our continuum are those whose inner and outer resources are stretched only to have yet one more crisis, such as severe illness in a member, hit them. These families need very structured guidelines for coping, as well as techniques to help them to include and connect all members, some of whom may well be immobilized. In order to prevent more crises from developing, resources must be found to provide some margin. One might get a homemaker to come in while undertaking therapy, or help obtain rehabilitation funds for a member of the family so as to increase the financial resources.

Families in "distress" on our *assessment of the experience* continuua include those who perhaps usually manage their lives with a fair degree of success and problem-solving skills, who find themselves in an otherwise run-of-the-mill life or developmental crisis for which they are ill-prepared.

We recently saw one family with three children who were all having various types of problems in a school to which they had just moved. While there were issues within the family system, they were secondary. The main interface of disturbance was the school/child interface and not the family process. The family needed coaching in how to intervene in a larger system which could easily blame and scapegoat it for the child's difficulties in the same way it blamed and scapegoated the child that did not fit its image. The stance used was more of a coaching one in which we worked *with* them rather than *on* them. The main interventions were to teach them "how to."

Then, there are those couples and families who never resolve conflict, or may never have had an argument. Such types, when a crisis hits, often "locate" at the "distressed" point on that continuum. Needing conflict resolution skills, they also must have permission to risk anger before they can feel less distressed. We provide the permission and teach the skills.[6]

Or, there are those couples who are not distressed but rather "uncomfortable" with each other. Yet they do little about it. One day one decides to take an unexpected action and leave the marriage. On that day we find both to be "in distress" or one is "in jeopardy" and feeling suicidal, while the other is guilty and yet relieved.

Finally, there are those families and couples who are uncomfortable in their lack of meaningful communication, but are not in great distress or jeopardy. They are often basically well-meaning people, who like each other and imagine a smoother, closer relationship. They manage to stop conversations before they start, or, in their tendency to dance with different rhythms, manage to step on each other's toes regularly. They may like each other, but have reservations about their future together.

In both the "distressed" and "uncomfortable" families, approaches which cool off the power games and demonstrate the processes of curiosity and intimacy are the appropriate ones. Clearly such interventions can and will only fit those couples and family members who wish to go beyond the psychopolitics of power in close relationships to intimacy.

Novelty/Automaticity

When we look at the characteristics of the system, we assess the system's ability to utilize novelty as opposed to continuing automatic patterns.[7] While all families and individuals have

---

[6]*Editors' Note.* For detailed discussions of some of the major methods of teaching conflict resolution skills, see Jacobson (Chapter 15) and Gordon and Davidson (Chapter 14).

[7]*Editors' Note.* Somewhat more concretely, the family's ability to utilize novelty may be assessed by, e.g., what Minuchin (1974) calls "experimental probes" (p. 90), the purpose of which is to "locate areas of possible flexibility and change" (p. 91) and to highlight "parts of the family structure that have been submerged" (p. 91).

and need automatic patterns, those that lead to stagnancy or self-destructiveness are the basis for both seeking help and negating it. The presence of novelty, on the other hand, with its tendency to make the familiar strange and thus lead to new options, is a strength, a major resource in families. The more that families have the ability to generate or welcome novelty or disorder as an element in the process of change (Shands, 1969), the easier is the therapist's task.

Access to New Information

A parallel map to novelty deals with the access to new information. When a system has appropriately open boundaries and the ability to actively inquire and search for information, life tasks, as well as the therapeutic tasks, are also easier. Some families lack information and do not know the processes of searching. They have not learned to learn well (Bateson, 1972b). Others may know how but lack the energy, the drive, the active search, out of earlier disappointments. Such families need to learn either how to search or how to become successful again in their inquiry. When families are blocked off or closed to new information, we know either they have learned to have no hope for the future, or old painful history has frozen them, and/or there is a secret that is being hidden. Therapy demands an active stance to open the family to new information. If there is also jeopardy, as in child abuse, one may have to take strong action to protect family members endangered by the closure to information.

Flow of Relating

The flow of relating deals with the dance within the family. It is tied in with the issues of information access and novelty, as well as the ambiance of the family. Yet it can be best thought of as the *rhythm of the family* when we assess the way in which information is exchanged. There are families that have an even pacing, some that explode and then are silent, and some in which there are arguments followed by quiet spaces for tenderness. Clearly, the more varied and orchestrated the rhythms, the more open and fluid the relating, the more avail-

able the family is for therapeutic influence.

When relating is limited as to person or time, there are limits on new options and change. When relating is intermittent, there is no time for new processes to take hold. If it is jagged, no one does anything but fight off new ideas.

Such an assessment is often made without one being fully aware. Instead, one feels comfortable or uncomfortable with the family without being sure about the stimulus for it.

Ambiance

Bateson (1972a) describes the feel of a culture as important for the anthropologist. Families, too, have such a quality for the therapist. It is not unlike the odors of the strange house we enter which are there and yet not in the foreground. In this continuum we attempt to describe the feel or ambiance of a family along the dimensions of safety, caring for others, and de-centered rather than egocentric attitudes. Families that are blameful, despairing and/or inattentive to others are more difficult to help. Blamefree families are quick to use help.

Family Development

The developmental stages of a family and of the individuals in each culture define expected behavior for the family members, as well as the appropriate tasks to be mastered. These are the expected crises of development. The child going off to school, the reduction of the family to couple size after children grow and go, and retirement are predictable events for the family, as menarche and adolescence are for the individual. The inability of a family or individual to master a developmental stage with self-esteem can be a problem for either or both. Such crises should always be explored as possible precipitating events in family distress.

THE SYSTEM RESOURCES

Along with the system assessment we have outlined, it is necessary for a more thorough look at system resources to reveal which resources provide for or limit the options for a family and its members. The therapist is better as orchestrator of resources than as the single resource for the family.

The Use of the Maps

In outlining the following maps of systems resources, we find they can serve as guidelines in *hand-tailoring interventions* and aid in fitting the approach to the condition in which families find themselves. We are aware that some families can be located at points on one or more of the maps for a brief period, while others seem to have been there for a lifetime. Grouping the locations presents us with images of the family, which in turn guide us in our expectations about and interventions for change.

1) Family Forms

In the increasing variety of family structures that exist, none is good or bad in itself. Yet the form of structure may delimit options for change. An extended family living in one town can provide alternative adult and child connections, as well as varied models of interactions and behavior. Yet extended families often have more rigid rules for belonging and for acceptable behavior than smaller family units.

The split-parent family may offer the children more time and attention with each parent through the defined visits than a two-parent household does with its usual routine. It is important to assess the resources available and needed within the family structure that exists, as well as the impact of present, absent, or distant friends and relatives on family and the individual. Single parents, for example, may have a wide friend network which is supportive despite the loss of a spouse.

"Normal" families still have different resources based on the numbers of children, the age range, etc.

2) Geography

Type of community defines the varieties of experience available, as well as access to institutions, agencies, schools, hospitals, etc., which fit the needs of the family at a reasonable cost of time and money. For example, a child in a suburban public school into which he just moved could not get the attention he needed from the teacher who could not see his behavior as reactive, but provocative. A parochial school principal nearby who had training in family therapy and educational assessment and could take him into her school was a resource of geography.

3) Economic

Money can buy a life-style, time, a pair of hands, access to better care or education and friends, and even therapy. It also provides for stability in living arrangements. When a family that experienced two deaths in two weeks was able to take a family trip overseas on the spur of the moment because it had money, it was able to place a new and shared life experience between its members and death. The shock and grief were dealt with more effectively. Kirsch (in press) indicates that widows who get more insurance money master their grief more competently.

4) Social

Is time spent with members of the family in recreation as well as work? Do they spend time talking each day? All work and no play makes a family dull, with little novelty. What is the availability of friend networks and support systems?

5) Educational

The parental level of education often defines options for the family. The expectations of parents for their children's education may play a part in conflicts and problems within the family and the schools the children attend.

6) Religious

The degree of involvement and the type of religion may offer a resource for caring, support and mastery, or negatively, for guilt and automatic behavior, and a sense of failure.

7) Political

The political view of the family defines the way it seeks help and from whom. Whether therapy is a right or to be paid for, whether welfare is acceptable or not—these are often beliefs based on political ideology.

8) Time

How time is allocated and spent is a major factor in therapy. If no time is provided to undertake the tasks suggested by the therapist except the time spent in the therapist's office, the chances for change are minimal. If time is not appropriated to spend on relationships at home, no amount of therapy will do the job.

It is important that clients understand that time is the only truly limited resource we have; after all, most of us have about 27,394 days to spend. It is spent inexorably. Our only choice is what to spend it on.

9) Energy

What emotional and physical energy is available to invest in change? A father may spend time with his son, but if no energy is invested, the message of rejection is also communicated. Physical illness always decreases the energy available for relationships and does so without malice.

10) Space

The way intimate or family space is provided by dwellings often defines what will happen. Scheflen's studies (1974) showed that low-income families never gathered to eat together when the kitchen was too small. They only sat around the TV set that was constantly on in the livingroom. The arrangement determined the relationships. Thus, it is important to find out: Who sleeps where? Who shares what rooms? What doors are missing? How are the rooms utilized in the house? A home visit is invaluable even in well-to-do families.

As we locate each of these resources we see how each one frames an aspect of the context in which lives are lived, and each helps define the strengths of the family system which therapists are asked to help change.[8]

---

[8]Issues of time, space and energy are discussed from a different and yet important family systems perspective in Kantor and Lehr (1975).

The Individual Attributes

As therapists begin to talk to people, they share their stories, their world views, their hurts and angers. While listening, each therapist is fitting the information he/she has into whatever maps are being used as guides. We have a series of maps of individual attributes which also help "account for" some of the system interactions. After presenting these, we shall explore the application of this series of system and individual maps to Phoebe and her family, and show how this integration of system and individual attributes and properties guides us to *interventions for the system that also fit each individual.*[9]

It is important to remember that, even when maps are detailed and overlaid, the map is *not* the territory. Each is a schematic symbolization for organizing felt or observed experiences and, like all maps, changes over time.

The particular individual attributes that attract our attention are those of: 1) vulnerabilities, defenses and images; 2) learning styles; 3) cognitive stages; 4) self-knowledge stages; 5) communication skills; and 6) physical health. While each of these aspects of self is interwoven with others, it is still possible to tease them apart.

Before presenting our outline of the individual and system maps in Phoebe's family, let us discuss these individual attributes we consider important.

1) Vulnerabilities, defenses and core images

A basic premise on which we work is that family systems are glued together by the strength of the vulnerabilities and defenses of each member as they are woven into patterned interactions.

In the early stages of individual development,

---

[9]*Editors' Note.* Recall here the Duhls' earlier emphasis on addressing "all levels of systems that define behavior"—the fundamental attitude of integrative family therapy. In our view, most of the major family therapy approaches that have been strongly influenced by general systems theory, cybernetics, and the like (e.g., Stanton, Chapter 10; Bodin, Chapter 8; Barton and Alexander, Chapter 11; Aponte and Van Deusen, Chapter 9) have too often deemphasized organismic factors that influence family process, i.e., variables *within* individual family members (Gurman, 1978).

core vulnerabilities emerge in the context of family relationships in which events are given meaning by the child not being offered or able to understand important information. In fact, most vulnerabilities arise out of such a *deprivation of information* or the inability to sort or integrate important information about significant others and oneself (Duhl, B., 1976, 1977). As such, the development of vulnerabilities relates to the absence of the communication processes noted below.

To protect onself when vulnerable, specific behavioral patterns, which we call defenses, develop. These defensive behaviors become automatic, and their presence indicates that a vulnerability has been touched. As such, *idiosyncratic defense patterns may be seen as signals*, which one may use in developing options for new and novel behaviors.

In one couple that came for therapy, the husband was attacked by his wife for not having any feelings. He came from a family that protected the children by not giving information. Though he was close to his grandmother, he was not told of her death when he was six. Rather, he was told that his grandmother was off on a long trip to her native Russia. He never heard of her again and never knew she had died in a local hospital until he was grown up. He became particularly vulnerable to not being told direct information. While growing up, he retreated to his room to learn science and shut out his parents from any information about himself or his feelings. His wife's indirectness often led to his withdrawal to his work.

These core vulnerabilities give shape to one's core images, which become one's "assumptive world views" (Parkes, 1971) even as a child. The defenses one develops early to protect oneself from letting these worst things or patterns happen again paradoxically can help provoke their recurrence. Early stages of development, thus, are the ones in which the young persons begin to build coping mechanisms for survival. These core vulnerabilities and early defense patterns comprise some of the core self-images, with the particular idiosyncratic meanings and styles of thinking about self we each develop over time.

Core images delimit the range of behaviors by which we relate and define ourselves as individuals, regardless of context, as well as in interactions with others. (How one experiences one's body heavier or thinner is not totally related to others.) Held in the repository of the mind like movie archives, they are enactments of actual past experiences or rebuttals of them, plotted and rehearsed through unperformed scripts, or snapshots symbolizing holographic multidimensional meanings, relationships and forms. Core images embody exceedingly positive and/or painfully negative experiences and fantasies of how self and others ought to be. Triggered by events and associations in the present context, they are often revealed when someone is simply and openly asked, "What is the worst (or best) thing that could happen or ever happened to you?"

These images of how the world is and should be and how one is in the world get projected into the future in a *feedforward* pattern (Richards, 1968). Our core images of "what will happen to us if" or "when" often are the basis for the script in which we run through an automatic set of actions and reactions. Rehearsal in this fashion does not stimulate new information or different alternatives. Rather, this rehearsal becomes a predictor of how we will act in those situations. In this way, our vulnerabilities and defenses and our core images begin to define not only who we are in relation to our inner selves, but who we are in relation to those around us.

The Patterns in Adolescence. The early years are years of trial and error, and if there are no sudden shifts in the larger systems around one, or in one's own body, these core images and beliefs tend to be fixed as on a tether within a fairly predictable range of possible self/system views. As children grow into their teens and adulthood, sudden drastic changes in the larger systems with which they are in contact can foster a redefinition of meanings and vulnerabilities. Adolescence often offers the opportunity to redo one's vulnerabilities through new learnings and experiences. The mastery of adolescence depends on the skills learned earlier to obtain information and connection, as well as on the new individuals who provide new ways or models for doing so. Teachers, friends, relatives offer the opportunities for change. One's ability to change, cope, or to defend at these moments of redefinition and crisis often depends on the individual's learning style, the capacity for novelty or diversification, and the degree of decentered (Piaget, 1952) or multicentric world views already available. As one therapist put it, it is the capacity to "cover your ass and pick up your options" that counts.

And yet, the tenacity of the vulnerabilities and defenses often guides persons into marrying familiar patterns and thus often makes happen their own worst core images. Such couples are usually aware of each other's defenses and rarely aware of the vulnerabilities that are being defended. In families, the defenses and vulnerability-response patterns tend to trigger others in a cybernetic feedback loop. Each defense hits another vulnerability with painful accuracy, and the loop becomes part of the family's negative automatic behaviors. In this automaticity, there is continued deprivation of information and little or no search for new information, thus guaranteeing the preservation of unrelenting maladaptive patterns of behavior.

Changing the Automatic Patterns. The defenses people use—old ones, out of awareness, brought into play in current situations—are individual attempts to "solve the problem," and, as we know, they rarely do. Indeed, they become part of the problem or the problem itself.

Just as *deprivation of information* in its widest sense is the key aspect of rendering people vulnerable (Duhl, B., 1976, 1978a), so *information integration* is a key factor (though not the only one) in an individual's ability to change his automatic behavior to more congruent and integrated ways. Individuals, who by an accident of history become part of a family, are not only shaped by the family, but can shape the family in turn, through their ability to stop their own automatic process and introduce novelty. One of the real pleasures in doing therapy came from watching a 41-year-old child and mother of two consciously and effectively change a fixed automatic pattern of which she was once a part in her family of origin by asking new and caring questions of her mother. The information generated allowed her to know her mother's vulnerability and bypass the defense. With that, the usual power games between them began to drop away.

The impact of various patterns of vulnerability and defenses within one family is not necessarily equal among members, given normal neurophysiological development. Young children, being less developmentally equipped and less differentiated, tend to become vulnerable to a wider range of events without the protective defensive devices. Older family members have usually developed a "thick skin" of socially useful defenses, along with an Achilles' heel.[10]

There are many ways of describing the same phenomena. If we look at the rules of relationship, power and control, distance regulation and intimacy in a family, we can see that they can also be described in terms of vulnerabilities and defenses.

We prefer this particular mode of reaching into systems because it works pragmatically, grounding people in the world as lived, connecting their internal core images and meanings with external experiences, integrating their past, present and projected future. In the five years we have used it, we have found that most people grasp and use this concept easily with or without the specific words of "vulnerabilities" or "defenses."

If one wants to see individual attributes and system processes in one gestalt, this viewpoint provides it most effectively. With this concept as part of the therapist's map, he or she can quickly capture, as in a flash picture, the circularity, the quasi-simultaneous, the ricochet-like release of automatic behaviors in a family, as one person's defense triggers another's vulnerability, or vice versa. The family pattern presents itself in an instant and there are options for interventions available.

2) Learning styles

Closely interwoven with vulnerabilities, defenses and core images are individual learning styles (Duhl and Duhl, 1975). Basically and briefly, we are referring to the different ways people have of processing information—taking it in, sorting it, storing it, connecting it, and putting it out in words and behavior. It is our contention that certain aspects of these styles

---

[10]And isn't it of interest that Achilles' mother, while protecting her son by dipping him in the river Styx, still set up his vulnerability?

are inborn and may be described as temperament (Thomas and Chess, 1977), while others seem to be influenced by the early contexts, such as the family or school in which each one "learns to learn" (Bateson, 1972b).

In many families, the individual differences in learning styles are the issue between members. Those who take in their information visually find themselves at odds with those who expect them to "listen and learn." Those who take in "one thing at a time," mull it over slowly in a reflective stance, and then respond, find they have irritated others who race from one thought to another, pulling in ideas from as many directions as an octopus has arms.

Briefly put, learning style includes the intrinsic differences of kinesthetic, visual, and aural representation which Bandler and Grinder describe (1975), the modes, intensities and rhythms of intake and output, and the digital or analogic modes of association which recently have been referred to in the literature as "left brain" or "right brain" thinking (Buzan, 1976; de Bono, 1970; Ornstein, 1972).

These differences in learning styles in a family may lead to the development of particular vulnerabilities and defenses, as well as personal boundaries. Nearsighted children who did not get glasses until age seven or later may well develop patterns to cope with the absence of distant information. When friends wave to them from across the street, they do not see them. They only take in information at close hand. They cannot see their parents' affect on their faces until they are close. This changes the way they relate and makes them vulnerable to sudden information. They may also move in on people to see them better and thus break the personal boundaries of others quite often, leading to conflict for reasons they cannot comprehend. Such conflicts are often given explanations or meanings other than nearsightedness.

In families where learning styles do not cause such conflict, the differences may be experienced as resources for the family, e.g., "He's so good with his hands" or "She's so thorough!" When there is the belief that there is only one learning style that is "right," people tend to label themselves and others, rather than to search for bridges between styles. Too often, it is the difference that is labeled and not the style that is known. Our task in therapy is often to build respect for the unique differences.

3) Cognitive stages

Conflicts in families may also arise through adults not recognizing the cognitive developmental stage of a child. Those parents who talk and treat their very young children as if they could think like adults set up expectations that the child cannot easily meet. Similarly, precociously bright or tall children may be treated as being more adult than they experience themselves to be, and dread that they may be discovered to be feeling and thinking like a child.

Yet, Piaget (1952) has pointed out the natural developmental sequence by which the child is able to comprehend the world and through which each every child grows, though not always at the same rate as others. In many ways, these concepts tie in with learning styles which also deal with comprehension, though as yet not developmentally. It is worth noting that Piaget and others (Flavell, 1963, 1977; Inhelder 1958) have stated that cognitive development may not take place evenly from the sensory-motor to the preoperational to the concrete operational to the formal operational, in all categories and arenas of experience. The caricature of the physicist who can evolve masterful logical theories of science but cannot predict nor comprehend his wife's behavior is the extreme representation of this uneven development.

In our work with family members of all ages, we keep the cognitive stages in mind as we listen to the type of language, the generalizations made, as well as the type of logical reasoning. We do not assume all adults use logical and sequential generalizations, though we are quite sure almost all five-year-olds do not.

The cognitive stage, as well as the learning style, the language used, and the experiences of each individual, defines the *language of impact* that determines the best way for the therapist to communicate new ideas. Helping family members to learn each other's language of impact facilitates the communication of connection.

Egocentered and decentered thinking. Connection is also influenced by whether one is, as

Piaget calls it, egocentered or decentered. "Egocentered" describes the way a person thinks who sees himself as the center of the perceived world with but a single view. It is a natural position for the child of two to six or seven years who is in the preoperational period. The child assumes himself to be both target and cause of significant events.

After seven or eight the child becomes more "decentered" and increases his/her ability to sit in another person's chair and see the world from that vantage point in addition to one's own. Much as we might wish the young to be different, children are not born with the cognitive structure to be socially empathic and decentered at an early age (Loevinger, 1976). Such abilities, in a context supportive of those behaviors, begin developing after age eight but do not usually reach fruition until the end of adolescence or later (Shantz, 1975). Moreover, not all people reach a decentered stage, no matter how old they become. Some adults in a family cannot decentrate—or in another language, differentiate—so as to see themselves and others as separate individuals. When they cannot reverse roles easily with others whom they care about, when they cannot "walk in that person's shoes," it is clear that any intervention based on an expectation of multicentricity or true empathy will fail. Usually such people have not had other adults validate their viewpoints when they were children—thus lacking the social context to facilitate decentration. It takes two to discover one. Only when children are truly heard for their pain, do they hear others, then or later.

4) Self-knowledge stages

Parallel to the ability to know others is the ability to know and describe oneself. The concept that we have found useful in tracking the individual attributes that contribute to system transactions is that of Alschuler et al.'s (1975) self-knowledge stages. This structural developmental theory delineates how people express their awareness of their internal world and their experiences. Essentially, a four-stage hierarchical sequence has been described.

People at the *elemental stage* tend to limit their descriptions to discrete singular events, to simple thoughts, gross emotions, conversation content, observable actions, with little or no causal connections made between events or elements, except with the word *and*. Like Phoebe, they used the words mad, bad, sad, and glad, happy to describe their internal experience. "I was mad at mother *and* ate my lunch."

Those at the *situational stage* are capable of describing events and their internal responses to them in detail and often in sequences. They assign causality to link them, using "so" and "because." The descriptions reveal very complex thoughts and internal responses, but there is no grouping or categorization of them. "Because I was unable to find the milk, I got mad at my mother when I ate my lunch."

The *internal pattern stage* refers to that next level in which people can group together events and reactions as connected, repetitive patterns within themselves, yet they do not know what to do with that awareness, except note it. "Whenever I eat at my mother's house, I get a tight stomach and realize I'm mad at my mother."

Those at the *internal process stage* have arrived at that stage of development where they can self-prescribe and verbalize what to do for themselves when they are experiencing a particular internal pattern with its concomitant emotions. "Whenever I go to my mother's, I know I'll get angry at her. So I don't eat there and don't get sick."

In our version, we have added two states, the *external pattern* between the situational and the internal pattern stages, and the *external process* stage preceding internal process stage. These additions have come out of the authors' awareness that one first gives language to internal experiences through a comparison from the outside to inside. One needs a concept, a metaphor from outside oneself first, just as early scientists could describe the heart as a pump because they had already seen both the pump and the heart (Gordon, 1972).

In the *external pattern stage*, the person describes others' patterns quite well, but not one's own. Similarly, in the *external process*, any others' ways of prescribing behavior to modify personal patterns is easily noted, although the person cannot do so for himself. (Many therapists may find themselves in these latter two stages!)

The stages as we use them, are: 1) elemental; 2) situational; 3) pattern: (a) external, (b) internal; 4) process: (a) external, (b) internal.

While the authors of the original self-knowledge theory have a validated method of testing for the stage of self-knowledge, which describes the presentation of self, the method is too complex for a clinical interview. What we do use is the framework to help us assess the ability of members of the family to use and reveal knowledge about themselves. If our therapeutic intervention depends on the individuals' owning their own behavior and experience, then approximating the level of self-knowledge helps us know how our interventions can best be phrased to have impact. One does not help a child of five change by asking him to consider the golden rule. Nor does it help to expect such a child to understand his pattern of behavior; one might do better to behaviorly reinforce the behavior patterns with any appropriate reward other than an M & M.[11]

5) Communication skills and stances

In the process of system and individual assessment, where family members, especially parents, have skills of communication, we find there is the ambiance of safety in a family, a sense of closeness and individuation, and the facilitation of information exchange and integration. They also, by communicating information with respect for the learning style and the cognitive stage of the child, decrease the possibility of vulnerabilities developing out of a deprivation of information about significant events.

We look for eight specific communication processes, all of which are interrelated and yet can be differentiated and defined as follows (Duhl, B., 1976, 1977; Duhl, F., 1976):

[11]*Editors' Note.* The Duhls are making two very important points here. First, behavior change strategies must be matched to a patient's (here, a child's) developmental (here, cognitive) level. Second, they are implicitly aware of the relative inefficacy of using what behavior therapists call "arbitrary reinforcement," rather than "natural reinforcement." For example, if a parent's goal is to increase a young child's frequency of independent play behavior, it would probably not be optimal to reinforce such behavior by arbitrary reinforcers such as candy. More potent reinforcers (what the Duhls call "appropriate reward") might be found in arranging rewarding consequences which follow naturally from such play, e.g., mastery of new motor skills.

(a) Validation. The process by which one person acknowledges with respect or affirms that which the other has communicated about what he or she has perceived, experienced, thought, or felt exists in the communicator's mind. It also denotes the verbal or behavioral recognition of one or another's self-perception and self-components as being equivalent to, though different from, one's own. It is a process of empathy at times, and of respect always.

If a man tells his wife that his job is driving him crazy and she responds, "How can you say that? It's such an important job," that is invalidation. If she says, "Your job really gets to you," that is validation.

(b) Ownership. The act of being responsible for one's own perceptions, feelings, thoughts, and deeds, all of which originate inside oneself though in response to an external stimulus.

To say, "You make me angry," is not a statement of ownership. Ownership exists when you say, "When you don't act as I wish, I become angry." After all, if someone does not act as you wish, you could laugh.

(c) Differentiation. The process of distinguishing between, or separating, one item from another. It is used also in the biological sense of increasing specialization or specificity. Every child thinks in all-or-nothing terms at first. Only with age and the aid of other more differentiated persons does he or she think with specificity. Such specificity includes time as well as persons, so that one distinguishes then from now, and the present from the past and the future.

In communication, specificity is important. "You are nice," is unspecific. "I like your way of smiling when I talk" is more differentiated and specific. "I get angry when you withdraw" is more specific than "I hate you."

(d) Process. An awareness of the sequence over time that leads from one point to another. Events take place as part of a process. To place an event or experience within a process provides information and disperses the mystery.

In other words, the sense of process is the awareness that all life is developmental and dynamic rather than static. It includes the awareness that, although the past is in the present (today is the sum of all our yesterdays), the present is *not* the past. It includes the understanding that there are often missteps or sidesteps in getting to there from here, and that change is evolutionary, in context and over time.

When someone explains his own behavior in a family by stating, "That's the way I am," he denies any sense of process. As therapists, always searching for process, we tend to ask *how* the behavior was initiated, at what moment, after what event, and in what context. Such a clarification of sequence reinstates the sense of process.

When we discuss the concept of process, we also consider that skills, too, are learned through a process, including knowing how to be intimate, how to negotiate, and how to fight. We always inquire as to whether such learning takes place or fails to take place in the families we assess.

(e) Context. A recognition of the setting in which processes take place. Like many parts of the environment, a context is itself seen as a process or the "sum" of all processes when examined. The same behavior means different things to us in different contexts. Nudity or anger in public may mean something different from nudity or anger in the bedroom.

Context implies the physical as well as the situational and dynamic aspects of one's surroundings, and includes the ability to differentiate and give "appropriate" meaning to each step in a process that becomes context. For example, when one has a party, the physical context remains the same throughout, but the situational and dynamic context changes as soon as the first guest arrives. In the *process* of more guests arriving, the situational or dynamic context keeps changing. The ability to include context in the communication dissolves blame or all-or-nothing thinking and presents a multicentric or decentered view of the world.

(f) Humor. Difficult to define, rare to find, and crucial to learning and knowing. It is linked to a capacity to have distance and yet to understand. With humor, children and clients comfortably grow. Without it, life and therapy are boring.

Humor is the saving grace. When one has

distance, one is able to be observer to the situation that one is in. Also, if someone has humor, he is able to comment on the situation he is in in such a way as to illuminate and capture it. Such humorous commentary tickles our nerves of paradox and novelty, touches our de-centering cells, and reminds us not to take ourselves so seriously. In some way, such humor points up that seeming opposites are the same, or that supposed identicals are opposites. This is not the sarcasm and attacking wit that disconnect, which some inaccurately call humor. This kind of humor connects people through recognition of the absurdity of this chaotic world.

(g) Inquiry. By this we mean the caring curiosity that makes someone else feel special. It is the process that allows for new information without blame or defensiveness. Lost often after courtship becomes marriage, it is essential to connection, novelty, new options and long-term caring relationships.

When it is missing, having one spouse role-play a "reporter" who is a stranger interviewing the other spouse about him/herself is a way of re-introducing inquiry to a couple who had been sounding like two tape recorders talking to each other.

When inquiry is present, "stuck places" become the beginnings for new explorations. Inquiry should not be the exclusive property of therapists, who should make it their task to help others rediscover it and use it themselves.

(h) Safety. If these communications skills have provided adequate respect, information and overview, they provide for a sense of safety and trust. Safety is the feeling experienced when you know that one's boundaries will be respected, that you are regarded by others with caring, and that you have sufficient information about an event or person to predict possible futures.

Feeling safe with someone, you can risk revealing the aspects of yourself with which you are uncomfortable so as to examine them with him or her. It is essential for therapy, but even more so for a family to grow, individuate and stay connected in ways appropriate to the culture and the ages of the members. Too little is written about safety as a prerequisite for change, for risk and for growth. All novelty and no continuity is not safe, nor is all continuity and no novelty. The essence of good therapy is the capacity of the therapist to provide for safety by his or her own skills in communicating the validation, ownership, differentiation, process and context with humor and inquiry to help the patients change.

Much of what we did with Phoebe and her family was based on their feeling of safety with us.

THE FAMILY STORY REVISITED AND ANALYZED

Looking once more at Phoebe and her family and consciously applying the set of maps we have laid out, let us examine the way we were guided by them in our assessment and interventions.

The System Assessment

In our assessment of the system, which began with the first interview with Phoebe's parents, we found:

1) Type of Situation: Unexpected crisis, prolonged response
   (Precipitating Events): Mother's elongated hospitalization
2) Assessment of Experience: Distress
3) System Characteristics: Flexible behaviors, except in one area; novelty usual
4) Information Accessing: Active inquiry and search for information
5) Flow/Pattern of Relating: Open, available, willing
6) Ambiance: Caring, searching, poignant, safe with humor
7) Phase in Family Life-Cycle: Early childhood, preschool

System resources

1. Family Form and Structure: Nuclear family, two parenting adults available, well connected
   System/subsystems bonding (from their descriptions).

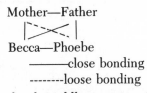

```
Mother—Father
  |  >  <  |
Becca—Phoebe
———————close bonding
-------loose bonding
```

2. Geographical: Middle-, upper-middle-class bedroom community, good schools
3. Economic: Good, sufficient, stable income, well budgeted
4. Social: Good friend networks, good recreational time together
5. Educational Level: Parents—professional; expectations for children—probably college
6. Religious: No longer active, not important; mixed religious backgrounds
7. Political (towards getting help): Positive and available
8. Time: Available for therapeutic work, high priority
9. Space: Adequate plus, for each
10. Energy: Physical, okay; emotional, strained, but can be invested

Individual Attributes

As Sally and Ted told their story, we made mental notes of their individual attributes and core self-images, in relation to this issue. We noted their resources as well as their assessment of their children. These are shown in Table 2.

If we look at the matrix of information here, at the system properties and resources, the individual attributes and particularly at the vulnerabilities, defenses and core images of individuals, we can integrate both individual and system data in our choice of system interventions that will be congruent with each member.

ATTEMPTED SOLUTIONS AS THE PROBLEM

But let us look first at the brief therapy "formula" that the Mental Research Institute (Watzlawick et al., 1974) described first:

The attempted solution is the problem. How does it fit here?

The attempted solutions were: 1) Audiotapes from the hospital, when Phoebe was three, did not and could not transmit the full message of mother's caring and connection. The first au-

TABLE 2			
Individual Attributes and Core Self-Images			
Individual Attributes	Mother: Sally, 33	Father: Ted, 36	Phoebe, 4¾	Becca, 22 mos.
Defenses: (usually seen before vulner-abilities)	denial of loss no discussion with Phoebe avoid issue with Phoebe don't upset Phoebe connect with Ted quiet self-blame	avoid discussion with Phoebe some annoyance with Sally connect with Sally quiet self-blame	avoid mother avoid issue "independence" self-blame, owns total responsibility and distances	?
Vulnera-bilities:	upset, hurt by experi-ence and loss, being hit from the "blind side." feels ineffective with Phoebe feels helpless feels rejected, pain disconnected from Phoebe—cannot fully be a mother to her	disconnection from Phoebe in one area helplessness, pain of loss	disconnection loss without informa-tion guilty	?
Core Self-Image (In relation to *this* issue)	I've tried *so* hard, yet I've failed with Phoebe	I've done the best I could and I don't know how to help them	I made mommy sick I can take care of my-self Mommy is angry at me—doesn't care about me	?
Symptoms/ Signals	sadness, depression anxiousness about this issue	sadness	Nightmares, babytalk at school, Tantrums in school Refuses parents' com-forting	?
Resources	Has continued to reach out to Phoebe and has connected in other ways Strong coupling Forgiveness, no blame for others	Same as Mother	Connected with each other Connected with father and mother through games, tasks, out-ings and intellectual pursuits Bright, verbal, outgo-ing	Connected to all, moves freely
	Humor			
Learning Styles:	hearing, mulling time, doing humor	doing, hearing, fast sorting humor	seeing and doing fantasy/magic	imitations
Cognitive Stage	cross-generalizes	cross-generalizes	specific, concrete; guesses	
Self-knowledge Stage	internal process	internal process	elemental, some situ-ational aspects	elemental
Ego-centered/ decentered	decentered	decentered	egocentered	egocentered

TABLE 2 *(Continued)*			
Individual Attributes	Mother: Sally, 33	Father: Ted, 36	Phoebe, 4¾	
State of Health (Physical)	good	good	good	good
Communication skills: (as Resources) Validation Ownership Differentiation Sense of Process Sense of Context Sense of Humor Sense of Inquiry	yes) yes) yes) most of) the time yes)) yes)) yes) on other issues	yes) yes) yes) most of) the time yes)) yes)) yes) on other issues	some too much not very much mythology not defined some—concrete on other issues	?
Imaged Solution:	Phoebe symptom free; all members able to move freely towards and away from each other; parents, mother particularly, able to comfort their child.		?	?

diotape from mother was made only after one month in the hospital, since mother was so critically ill in a life-death battle. It could only allow Phoebe to hear mother's disembodied voice and did not fit Phoebe's way of taking in information at age three. The tapes were put aside as not useful.

2) In the wish to protect Phoebe and themselves from reliving the pain of their helplessness in relation to her, the parents did not talk about this excruciating loss to Phoebe beyond one month after mother came home. Phoebe did not have the cognitive "equipment" to integrate the experience of mother's loss and reentry within one month.

The avoidance of continuing specific information-sharing between parents and child and the exchanging of the feelings and meanings around that information, arising from each one's defenses of their vulnerabilities, became rigidified into a pattern of fixed distance between mother and daughter, and somewhat between father and daughter.

The avoidance of the real information allowed Phoebe's child mind to make sense of her world as best she could, i.e., that it was her fault that Mother went away, that Mother was sick, and that now, she had to take care of herself, be perfect in school, and yet get caring through babytalk.

The avoidance of the real information, as well as the avoidance of connecting around the range of meanings and feelings attached then, was the problem.

Thus, to do "more of the same" would be ridiculous; to spend time in individual child therapy with the "sick" child out of her family context would be more of the same. It would continue the process of leaving out the important, willing and available participants in a life drama, by avoiding the sharing of their perceptions of that same event. The goals of the interventions had to include a process for this information to be shared by the original cast of players.

What, then, was our strategy? If we now analyze what we learned and what we did within the framework of the problem-solving/goal-directed paradigm we use in teaching at the Boston Family Institute, it would look like this:

Goals

1) For parents, particularly mother, to reconnect with their child.
2) For Phoebe to be free of symptoms of nightmares and "misbehavior" in school.
3) For Phoebe to feel good about herself.
4) For parents to regain their competency in parenting Phoebe and, in so doing, regain their self-esteem.
5) To provide new options and patterns for new interactions, to "generate new sentences."

Hypotheses

1) If we touch the untouchable, and open up the blocked channels where information and the meanings given that information have been jammed for two years, the same information which formed a dam can be made into a bridge. (Log jams take expertise, fancy footwork and sometimes dynamite to break them up. Bridges take steadiness, a theory about stress, and time to build.)

Assumptions about the Family, Based on Assessment Material

1) This is an extended, unexpected crisis in a distressed family, which is open, flexible, and searching for new information and help. The ambiance on the part of the parents is warm, caring, concerned, and filled with forgiving sadness. The parents are basically very competent, learners and doers, who want to help themselves and their child in her distress. They use humor easily, own their own experience, understand process, and exhibit a form of differentiation and self-observation. Their image of themselves is basically one of being innovative except on this issue, where they draw a blank. Their image of Phoebe is of a child who is bright, yet self-blaming and fixed around one issue, who blocks any appropriate emotional caretaking of her on their part.

The parents revealed a high degree of decenteredness, a formal operational cognitive level, and an internal process self-knowledge stage. These parental assets, combined with the verbal brightness of their child, whose caring, teaching connection with her sister showed an early step in decentration, made us hopeful of a quick response. The bonding between father and daughter, and in many areas between mother and daughter, indicated that they had many resources to draw on.

Assumptions About Ourselves with this Family

We will need to intervene in a setting and manner:

1) That is genuine, caring and safe for all.
2) That allows for communication in the language of the least developed person, without belittling others, and that attends to other person-specific characteristics.
3) That puts new options, processes and tools into the family's hands.

Interventions and Rationale

To achieve goals:

1) Have parents reopen subject of mother's hospitalization. Give them permission and license to do so. Reinforce their own earlier correct attempted solution whose timing was out of phase with a three-year-old's cognitive stage, in which she could not comprehend mother's disappearance in other than a total way.
2) Make a home visit. See this family in the environment that is most comfortable, safe, and familiar for the most distressed party, Phoebe. In so doing, there is no labeling of her as the problem. To do otherwise would only reinforce her "solution," i.e., "It's my fault that mommy left, that mommy was sick."
3) Bring something appropriate to her language of impact and cognitive stage. Children can take in information at the level of play and fantasy, in imagistic right-brain metaphors, far more easily than left-brain logical sequences.
4) Bring a puppet and magic wand since:
   —Fuzzy animal puppets allow for another or many voices, who can say the unsayable, and increase the therapist's range manifold.

—Puppets can be used to make the strange familiar and the familiar strange, to introduce safety, learning and innovation.

—Magic is where the world is at to a five-year-old. Much of the reasoning is magical. Fight magic with magic.

—Use of puppets and wands allows for comparison statements, options, and alternative images, and increases experiences so that she has an "N of 2."

Evaluation: Outcome

As the reader is already aware, our interventions were "successful." They accomplished the mutual goals of the family and ourselves. More than three years have passed since this family was seen, and Phoebe has had no return of symptoms. The parents and Phoebe have been able to maintain their open dialogue and transactions. In actuality, it was the family members who were successful, in that they were available and receptive to what we had to offer and acted upon it. Thus, the match of their individual qualities and receptivity with our offerings and ourselves was a positive one, and made it possible to put this case story in our "success" tally.

A WORD ABOUT METHODS, TECHNIQUES AND TOOLS FOR THERAPISTS AND FAMILIES

The methods and techniques we employed here do not fit any formula, although they fit an integration of values, meta-maps and submaps. For us, we feel free to choose a particular technique or methodology as one chooses a tool from a tool box—that is, the appropriate one for the specific job—in order to achieve the goal of a changed system interaction in a manner that fits all participants, goals, and processes.

All therapists need to learn and/or derive a variety of techniques and skills that communicate, illuminate and foster change. We encourage ourselves and our students to continue to invent new tools and new techniques to fit the need. But most important is that we encourage families to do the same.

In our approach to the introduction of novelty and new options, an act of creativity in a family

is of high value. It not only increases the family's options, but it increases its competence in being able to change itself. Often, once we have helped produce apparently magical change in families, we teach them how to do the magic tricks themselves.

A METALOG OR SOME THOUGHTS ON CHANGE

There is no process of therapy that does not have a theory of change to support and explain it. It is our belief that *in order for change to take place, that which is automatic and familiar behavior, maintained by a set image, must be made strange.*

In order to do this, therapists and change agents introduce novelty in some form or fashion. They change the timing, the focus, the players, the language, the size or quantity of the unit of interest, the intensity and tone of speech, the logic or the pacing of the behavior, and introduce new images and metaphors. All of these moves have the result of interrupting automatic behaviors by making the familiar strange[12] and are overt or covert forms of reframing experience.

Once automatic behaviors are interrupted, there is the potential for generating new sentences, new behaviors and new images. This allows the person or persons to have more than one experience around the same issue or, as we put it, an "N of 2." Thus the experiencer has a new "meta-position" of actor in and observer of two experiences, one old and one new. In the comparison, a cognitive dissonance exists.

When the new experiences, behaviors or images are repeated, that which was strange begins to become familiar and a new pattern emerges; the new image, sentence or behavior gradually becomes automatic but in a more adaptive fashion. The process of integration of the new pattern often follows that pattern of relearning a familiar action in a new form, such as serving

---

[12]Gordon's work (1961) in synectics has offered us these concepts: When the familiar is made strange, that is novelty. When the strange is made familiar, that is learning. The connection of this with Piaget's concepts of accommodation and assimilation is discussed by Jimenez (1976) and Duhl, B. S. (1978b).

a tennis ball differently or driving a stickshift car after many years of using an automatic shift.

With Phoebe, the novelty that led to the changes may have been one or more items that we introduced. It may well have been the permission that the puppet/person gave her to talk about herself in ways that did not have to fit anyone else's world view. The novelty may have been her learning that other children could also be mad, sad, and bad with their parents and still be loved. Or it may have been the process by which the mother, father and Phoebe were free to own their own range of internal experience in a shared way with the help of the magic wand. The closeness interestingly enough took place as they shared individually with an "oracle" in each other's presence but not directly with each other.

Each allowed the validation of his or her internal state without losing face and in the language of impact and metaphor of the least developed or differentiated family member. And it is a transmuting of the way that one perceives the world or of the metaphors for it that fosters the *"second order change"* which Watzlawick, Weakland and Fisch (1974) describe. As they point out, second order change is change of the system as a whole, rather than shifts within a system that do not change the system, which they term *first order change.*

In integrative family therapy, we are interested not only in second order change taking place, but in the way that individual minds provide the mechanisms for such change. In our concept of therapy, we always need to understand and communicate with those individual minds as they begin to change their system. The integration of previously unknown information into new core images and of patterns of behavior for the individuals in a system leads to a process with multiple goals. Not only is the system freed from automatic behavior and therefore changed, but there is individual integration which changes the individual (sub)systems with a sense of increased self-esteem and competence so they can survive in other systems as well.

We do not trust that any move which frees a family system necessarily leaves people prepared to continue to respect each other and with skills in communicating so as to feel safely connected. In our view, we need to be sure such respect and connection are present so as to prevent the creation of future situations in which people can be in jeopardy or distress.

For us, intervention without education, information-integration, and preparation for the future is akin to the surgeon who performs a coronary bypass without also educating the patient in system self-care for prevention of future heart trouble. Intervention without education may look like second order change in which the shape of a family is changed but, like some plastic, it may return to a version of the original shape with enough heat and stress.

There are developmental changes in all systems, individual (sub)systems, and the body. The mystery of the change in which a single celled blastomere becomes a complex human being in context with others who have also evolved is still available for our awe and respect. Our job as therapists is to provide a previously fixed system with optional modes for change and stability.

With some families, it is much like turning over a turtle that is upside down in the road so that it can walk again. With others, one may not only have to do that but also clear the road of debris so the turtle can walk.

The mysteries of a child's growth, of an adult's complexity, of the process of dying are still to be wondered about. The best bits of therapy are often accidents of history pounced upon with respect, wonder and regard for the novelty that has occurred and been given the opportunity to be integrated by making it familiar.

There is a need to be humble about our work, even when it goes well. In this paper we have described our way of thinking at the present time. Some of this will change as we uncover more information and grow older. The paradigm may well shift out from under us all.

In the search for certainty in this field, however, we must beware of the rigidification of thinking—that anyone knows for sure how systems work and change, or how people exist and grow—for we may well be so sure that we become as fixed in our thinking as the families who seek our help. There is so much yet to know. As Bateson (1972a) has said in this regard:

. . . I think we might do something to hasten matters, and I have suggested two ways in which this might be done. One is to train scientists to look among the older sciences for wild analogies to their own material, so that their wild hunches about their own problems will land them among the strict formulations. The second method is to train them to tie knots in their handkerchiefs whenever they leave some matter unformulated—to be willing to leave the matter so for years, but still leave a warning sign in the very terminology they use, such that these terms will forever stand, not as fences hiding the unknown from future investigators, but rather as signposts which read: "Unexplored Beyond This Point" (p. 87).

REFERENCES

Alschuler, A., Evans, J., Tamashiro, R. & Weinstein, G. *Self-Knowledge Education Project*. Final Report to U.S. Office of Education, Grant No. OEG-0-70-2174; OEG-900-75-7166. December 1975.

Auerswald, E. H. *Perceptions* videotape, *The Person in the Therapist*, interview, F. Duhl, Boston: Boston Family Institute, 1977.

Bandler, R. & Grinder, J. *The Structure of Magic*. Palo Alto: Science and Behavior Books, 1975.

Bateson, G. Experiments in thinking about observed ethmological material. In: *Steps Towards an Ecology of Mind*. New York: Ballentine Books, 1972a.

Bateson, G. Social planning and the concept of deutero-learning. In: *Steps Towards an Ecology of Mind*. New York: Ballentine Books, 1972b.

Buzan, T. *Use Both Sides of Your Brain*. New York: E. P. Dutton & Co., 1976.

Chomsky, N. *Aspects of the Theory of Syntax*. Cambridge, Mass.: M.I.T. Press, 1965.

de Bono, E. *Lateral Thinking*. New York: Harper Colophon Books, 1970.

Duhl, B. S. *The vulnerability contract: A tool for turning alienation into connection in individuals, couples and families*. Paper presented at the First International Family Encounter, Mexico City, November 1976.

Duhl, B. S. *Towards a theory of intimacy*. Paper presented at the Boston Family Institute, December 1977.

Duhl, B. S. *Interventions in intimacy*. Paper presented at the Boston Family Institute, May 1978(a).

Duhl, B. S. *Piaget, The Boston Family Institute, and metaphor*. Unpublished paper, May 1978(b).

Duhl, B. S. and Duhl, F. J. *Cognitive styles and marital process*. Presented at the American Psychiatric Association Annual Meeting, Anaheim, California, May 1975.

Duhl, F. J. Intervention, Therapy and Change. In: W. Gray, F. J. Duhl, and N. D. Rizzo (Eds.), *General Systems Theory and Psychiatry*. Boston: Little, Brown, 1969.

Duhl, F. J. Changing sex roles—Concepts, values, and tasks. *Social Casework*, 1976, 57, 87-92.

Duhl, F. J. & Duhl, B. S. Structured spontaneity: The thoughtful art of training in integrative family therapy at BFI. *Journal of Marriage and Family Therapy*, 1979, 5, 59-76.

Duhl, F. S., Kantor, D., & Duhl, B. S. Learning, space and action in family therapy: A primer of sculpture. In: D. Bloch (Ed.) *Techniques of Family Psychotherapy*. New York: Grune & Statton, 1973.

Flavell, J. H. *The Developmental Psychology of Jean Piaget*. Princeton, New Jersey: Van Nostrand Co., 1963.

Flavell, J. H. *Cognitive Development*. Englewood Cliffs, NJ: Prentice-Hall, 1977.

Gendlin, E. T. Experiential psychotherapy. In: R. Corsini (Ed.), *Current Psychotherapies*. Itasca, Ill.: F. E. Peacock, 1973a.

Gendlin, E. T. Experiential phenomenology. In: M. Nathanson (Ed.), *Phenomenology in the Social Sciences*. Evanston: Northwestern Universities Press, 1973b.

Gordon, W. J. J. Synectics, *The Development of Creative Capacity*. New York: Harper & Row, 1961.

Gordon, W. J. J., & Poze, T. *The Metaphorical Way of Learning and Knowing*. Cambridge, Mass.: Porpoise Books, 1966.

Gordon, W. J. J. On being explicit about the creative process. *Journal of Creative Behavior*. 1972, 6, 295-300.

Howells, John G. *Principles of Family Psychiatry*. New York: Brunner/Mazel, 1975.

Inhelder, B., & Piaget, J. *The Growth of Logical Thinking from Childhood to Adolescence*. New York: Basic Books, 1958.

Kantor, D., & Lehr, W. *Inside the Family*. San Francisco: Jossey-Bass, 1975.

Kirsch, C. *The Survivor's Handbook*. New York: Doubleday, 1981, in press.

Jimenez, J. Synectics: A technique for creative learning. *The Science Teacher*, 1975, 42, 33-36.

Jimenez, J. Piaget and synectics. In: C. Modgil and S. Modgil (Eds.) *Piagetian Research Abstracts*, Atlantic Highlands, NJ: Humanities Press, Inc., 1976, 4, 102-119.

Loevinger, T. *Ego Development*. San Francisco: Jossey-Bass, 1976.

Martin, P. Comment made at American Psychiatric Association Meeting, Anaheim, CA, 1975.

Minuchin, S. *Families and Family Therapy*. Cambridge, Mass.: Harvard University Press, 1974.

Ornstein, R. E. *The Psychology of Consciousness*. San Francisco: W. H. Freeman, 1972.

Parkes, C. M. Psycho-social transition. *Social Science and Medicine* (Oxford), 1971, 5, 101-115.

Piaget, J. *The Origins of Intelligence in Children*. New York: International Universities Press, 1952.

Piaget, J. In: H. E. Gruber and J. J. Voneche (Eds.), *The Essential Piaget*. New York: Basic Books, 1977.

Richards, I. A. The secret of "feed forward." *Saturday Review*, February 3, 1968.

Scheflen, A. Personal Communication, 1974.

Shands, H. C. Coping with novelty, *Archives of General Psychiatry*, 1969, 20, 64-70.

Shantz, C. U. *The Development of Social Cognition*. Chicago: University of Chicago Press, 1975.

Thomas, A., & Chess, S. *Temperament and Development*. New York: Brunner/Mazel, 1977.

Watzlawick, P. *How Real is Real?* New York: Vintage Books, 1977.

Watzlawick, P., Weakland, J., & Fisch, R. *Change—Principles of Problem Formation and Problem Resolution*. New York: W. W. Norton, 1974.

EDITORS' REFERENCES

Boston Family Institute. *Tenth anniversary series* (brochure). Brookline, MA, 1979.

Gurman, A. S. Contemporary marital therapies: A critique and comparative analysis of psychoanalytic, behavioral and systems theory approaches. In: T. J. Paolino & B. S. McCrady (Eds.), *Marriage and Marital Therapy*. New York: Brunner/Mazel, 1978.

Minuchin, S. *Families and Family Therapy*. Cambridge, MA: Harvard University Press, 1974.

PART V

Behavioral

Approaches

CHAPTER 14

Behavioral Parent Training[1]

Steven B. Gordon, Ph.D.

and Nancy Davidson, Ph.D.

In the past 15 years, the literature on behavioral parent training has burgeoned from a few single-case studies to a massive body of literature reporting the successful treatment of thousands of children with a wide variety of problems.[2] No longer viewed solely as an experimental technology, this mode of treatment has become an increasingly effective, accepted, and popular intervention. In an extensive review, Graziano (1977) concludes "parent behavior training, as a child psychotherapy approach, is a highly promising area that might prove to be one of

[1]Acknowledgment is given to Larry Siegel for his helpful suggestions in the preparation of this chapter.

[2]*Editors' Note.* Behavioral parent training (BPT) certainly has not evolved in the mainstream of family therapy and, indeed, we think there are a number of family therapists who do not consider BPT to be a method of family therapy at all. Our view is that such a position derives both from a very narrow definition of what constitutes family therapy and from a good deal of ignorance about the premises and practices of BPT. Moreover, it is our experience that large numbers of family therapists, while owing primary allegiance to some other approach to treatment, selectively include parent training interventions in their work. For all these reasons, BPT deserves a prominent place within the family therapies.

the most important developments in the child mental health field (p. 287)." Beginning in the late 1950s, behavior modification with children had its first impact with children diagnosed autistic, schizohrenic and mentally retarded (Gardner, 1971; Lovaas, Freitag, Gold, and Kassorla, 1965). Once behavior therapy was demonstrated to be effective, it was then applied to children exhibiting a wider variety of problems, such as school phobia, hyperactivity and enuresis (Graziano, 1975). As behavior therapists began to consider the questions of efficient delivery of services and the maintenance and generalization of behavior change, increased attention was focused on training the child's parents to be the agents of change (Berkowitz and Graziano, 1972; Johnson and Katz, 1973; O'Dell, 1974; Tavormina, 1974).

A variety of factors, both practical and theoretical, was responsible for this increased emphasis on behavioral parent training. One factor was the tremendous manpower shortage existing in each of the helping professions (Albee, 1959; Arnhoff, Rubinstein, Shriver, and Jones, 1969). There are simply too few professionals for too many cases. Another contributing factor has been the increasing disillusionment with traditional one-to-one child psychotherapy. Several compelling arguments have been put forth which question the efficacy of psychodynamic child-focused treatment. First, traditional therapy sessions take place in an essentially artificial situation and may be too brief, infrequent, and removed from the child's other life experiences to have a significant impact (Graziano, 1971). Second, the therapist rarely has an opportunity to observe the specific problem behaviors of the child (e.g., tantrums, fighting) or the parent-child interactions in the natural environment. Instead, there is a dependence on unreliable retrospective reports of the parents, as to the definition of the problem and the description of the child's behavior (Hawkins, Peterson, Schweid, and Bijou, 1966). Third, the therapist rarely makes useful suggestions to the parents as to how they might cope with the demands of a disturbing child. The emphasis on intrapsychic dynamics and the lack of information about the child's environment at home may result in suggestions that confuse the parents and contribute little to their child-rearing abilities (Patterson, McNeal, Hawkins, and Phelps, 1967; Russo, 1964). Finally, evaluation of the effectiveness of treatment is difficult due to the absence of objective measures of behavior change (Hawkins et al., 1966). Studies which have attempted to assess the effectiveness of traditional therapy Levitt, 1957, 1963) have led to the conclusion that "little evidence exists to support the belief that 'traditional' child psychotherapy techniques are more successful than no formal treatment in ameliorating childhood behavioral disturbances" (Cone and Sloop, 1974, p. 286). These well recognized deficiencies of the traditional model of child psychotherapy have contributed to its widespread disenchantment.

The resultant search for useful alternatives has fostered the development of behavioral parent training. This approach is based upon an empirical methodology and specific principles drawn from the field of social learning theory. Extensive research with laboratory animals has demonstrated unequivocally that a wide range of behavior is functionally related to environmental events. The application of the principles and procedures of this body of knowledge to the behavior of children suggests that many child behaviors are shaped and maintained by events in the natural environment and, therefore, can best be changed by the modification of these environmental contingencies. This has led to the conclusion that parents possess an extraordinary potential for generating behavioral change due to the fact that they are often the ones with greatest control over the significant elements in the child's natural environment. The behavioral approach has therefore emphasized the development of a technology for training parents in the effective use of social learning principles (e.g., reinforcement, modeling, punishment, etc.) to control or modify child behavior. The behavior of the parents is identified as the focus of professional intervention, rather than that of the child, who has heretofore been designated as the patient.

The traditional dyadic, professional-child model has been replaced by a triadic model in which the professional functions as a "consultant" to the parents who serve as the primary behavior change agents for their own children (Tharp and Wetzel, 1969). In this model, the individual in direct interventive contact with the problem child is not the professional specialist, but the parent. The task of the consultant is to help parents redesign their responses to the child's behavior in such a way as to strengthen prosocial behaviors and weaken or eliminate maladaptive behaviors.

There are several cogent lines of reasoning which support the contention that parental behavior should be the focus of intervention in dealing with problem children. As mentioned above, the primary attraction of this approach is that it utilizes the most powerful behavior change agents in the child's environment. In addition, parents constitute a continuous treatment resource with the ability to work conveniently in the home where the problem exists (Johnson and Katz, 1973). This approach also has obvious implications for preventive mental health. The general techniques which parents learn can be used with children other than those in need of immediate treatment. Their continued application to new behavior difficulties which may arise after training is completed may contribute to the prevention of additional childhood disorders. Finally, as mentioned earlier, the number of children with behavior problems is so large that the demand for services can only be met by involving the parents in the treatment of their children (Hawkins, 1972).

While the principles of learning offer a sound empirical base for the idea that parents should be trained in child behavior management, they also provide a basis for a technology which is highly adaptable to such training. The basic principles of social learning are relatively simple and there can be learned and applied by comparatively unsophisticated and uneducated persons (Bernal, Williams, Miller, and Reagor, 1972). The simplicity of this therapy also makes it applicable to the training of many persons at once (Gordon, Lerner, and Keefe, 1979) in a short training period (Wiltz and Patterson, 1974) with a minimum of professional staff (Rose, 1974; Wahler and Erickson, 1969). In addition, Gelfand and Hartmann (1968) point out that many of the problem behaviors for which children are referred are rather well defined and, therefore, highly responsive to contingency management techniques.

The theoretical and practical arguments in support of the development of behavioral parent training have been presented in greater length and detail in several previous reviews (Cone and Sloop, 1974; Graziano, 1977; O'Dell, 1974) and are, therefore, only briefly summarized here. The remainder of this chapter is devoted to a description and critical analysis of the underpinnings, assessment, client characteristics, and the technology associated with training parents in behavioral child management.[3]

BEHAVIORAL MODELS OF THE DYSFUNCTIONAL FAMILY

There are several behavioral models of the dysfunctional family which seem to vary along a narrowness-breadth continuum with regard to the hypothesized controlling variables. Since the behavioral model adhered to by the therapist has direct implications for family assessment

and treatment, this section reviews the *dyadic model*, the *broad-based model*, and the *social systems model* of dysfunctional families. An overview, the assessment and treatment and, finally, the strengths and limitations of each model are presented.

Dyadic model

Overview

Typically, the initial request for treatment is made by one or more adults who are upset by disturbing behaviors emitted by the child or by the child's failure to engage in age-appropriate behaviors. It is a rare situation when the request for psychological intervention emanates from the child. Further support for the child's lack of power is evident when the request for treatment is translated to mean "treat the child." A feature common to a systems and behavioral approach is the expansion and redefinition of the problem to include other persons within the child's social environment, i.e., parents, siblings, teachers, etc.

The dyadic model reframes the child's problems to that of a problem in the nature of the child's interactions with another person, e.g., parent. The dyadic model assumes that some type of faulty interaction between the child and parent is at the root of the difficulty. Patterson and Reid (1970) have posited the concepts of reciprocity and coercion to account for the development and maintenance of parent-child interactions. Reciprocity describes the process by which there is an equity in the exchange of positive and negative interactions between family members. Thus, a parent who emits a high rate of negatives toward a child is likely to get the same in return from that child. This appears to hold true for the exchange of positives as well. A parent who praises a child for picking toys off the floor is in turn reinforced by the child's compliance. The use of positive reinforcement is, therefore, not unidirectional. The concept of coercion as an attempt to influence behavior is characterized by punishment (i.e., the presentation or removal of a stimulus contingent upon a response which has the effect of *decreasing* the probability of the occurrence of that response) and negative reinforcement (i.e., the

---

[3]Although behavior therapy has been applied to adolescents as well as children, the focus of this chapter is with behavioral training for parents of preadolescents. This does not imply that the procedures and methodology described here are of no applicability to an older population.

removal of a stimulus contingent upon a response which has the effect of *increasing* the likelihood of the occurrence of the response). A parent who yells or spanks the child when the child misbehaves is attempting to use punishment to stop the child from performing some undesired behavior. The cessation of the undesired behavior may serve to negatively reinforce the parent for yelling, which in turn increases the likelihood that the parent will use this method of social influence in the future. As with reciprocity, coercion is also bidirectional. A child nagging a parent for money in order to go to the movies is positively reinforced for nagging when the money is forthcoming, whereas the parent is negatively reinforced for "giving in" by the cessation of nagging and the ensuing peace and quiet.

Assessment and treatment

The dyadic model suggests that assessment be directed toward gathering data regarding the nature of the interactions between the child and other family members. In reality, assessment is geared specifically toward parent-child interactions. The procedures used to gather this information consist of the behavioral interview, behavioral checklists, and analogue and naturalistic observations. The purpose of this assessment is to identify lawful relationships that exist within the social interactions between parent and child. By performing a functional analysis, i.e., the identification of the problem behaviors as well as their antecedents and consequences, the therapist is able to implement treatment interventions. Typically, treatment involves some form of systematic parent training in which the parent(s) is (are) trained to pinpoint problem behaviors, observe and record their occurrence, and finally, to systematically intervene using social learning principles to bring about mutually reinforcing interactions (Clark-Hall, 1978). Given the reciprocal nature of the parent-child interaction, theoretically one should also be able to effect change by training the child to be the initiator of the behavior change process. To date there are few studies directed at training children to be better contingency managers of parent behaviors.

Strengths and limitations

The advantages of the dyadic model are that the data base is somewhat circumscribed, less complicated, and that treatment very often is educational in nature. Systematic parent training (Miller, 1975) consists of clearly spelled out procedures and can be implemented with parents on an individual (Wiltz and Gordon, 1974) or group (Gordon et al., 1979) basis. The limitations of this model of the dysfunctional family become evident when parents are observed to drop out of treatment, "resist" or sabotage treatment efforts, or simply do not respond positively. Attention to factors which may interfere with direct parent training requires an expansion of the dyadic model.

Broad-Based Model

Overview

The broad-based model of the dysfunctional family suggests the influence of factors beyond the dyadic overt interactions between parent and child. Although the principles/concepts of modeling, reciprocity and coercion are relevant, a data base restricted to the topography of the parent-child interactions is felt to be insufficient to account for the development and maintenance of prosocial as well as deviant behavior. A case example illustrates this point.

A single parent being seen for behavioral parent training complained that her seven-year-old son was sorely disruptive, noncompliant, and causing her to be at her "wit's end." After a thorough behavioral assessment, it was mutually decided to begin a program of parent training whereby the mother would learn to make clear requests and provide consistent and contingent consequences. Although the mother was highly motivated and intelligent, difficulties were immediately detected when a home observation revealed that she was unable to set limits and follow through with a pre-arranged punishment for oppositional behavior. Feedback, modeling, and coaching by the therapist produced inconsistent and ephemeral results.

Earlier interviews revealed that the mother had a profoundly retarded child residing in an institution. It was hypothesized that this factor was somehow contributing to the mother's inconsistent parenting with her son. Confirmation of this hypothesis was obtained through a series of sessions devoted to cognitive behavior therapy (Mahoney, 1974). These sessions revealed that as she began to set firm limits for the child's oppositional behavior, she would have an image of her daughter in the institution. This image aroused feelings of guilt and sorrow as well as the accompanying self-statement, "I must be totally accepting and loving to make up for what I did to my daughter." The importance of private events via self-statements, fantasies, and images as determinants of overt behavior has been demonstrated clinically (Lazarus, 1971) and empirically (Mahoney, 1974; Meichenbaum, 1977). Three sessions of cognitive restructuring (Goldfried and Davison, 1976) led to an amelioration of this interference factors resulting in successful parent training.

Several issues are worth noting. First, many times these intrapersonal interference factors (Miller, 1975) became evident only *after* parent training has begun. Second, even when these potential factors are identified during the initial stages of behavioral assessment, the "readiness" of the client may preclude direct intervention. The empirical basis for the assessment and treatment of intrapersonal interference factors as they relate to deviant child behavior is not well established.

Finally, it is important to be aware that, in some cases, clinical issues may be identified which go beyond the initial therapeutic contract of behavioral parent training.[4] For example, demanding, critical parents may apply similar unrealistic standards, combined with negative evaluations, toward themselves as well. Although the goals of parent training may be reached without attending to parents' personal difficulties, the question for the therapist are, first, whether to acknowledge the existence of these problems and, second, whether to renegotiate the initial treatment contract. For a provider of mental health services, it seems clear that there is an obligation to identify, in general terms, the existence of other personal difficulties. The renegotiation of the treatment contract will depend on the parents' desire for help as well as the range of the parent trainer's clinical

---

[4]*Editors' Note*. And, indeed, the immediately following discussion welcomely also goes beyond issues that are usually addressed in parent training workshops or in the professional literature on BPT.

skills. If a parent demonstrates a high degree of anxiety and is interested in pursuing treatment, the parent trainer may feel it is in the client's best interest to initiate a referral to another therapist.

Assessment and treatment

A broad-based model of the dysfunctional family necessitates attending to the identical data suggested by the dyadic model, but, in addition, factors which may potentially interfere with behavioral parent training, such as the psychological well-being of each parent and the nature of the marital relationship, are also in need of assessment by means of clinical interviews and questionnaires. *When data identify the existence of family problems in addition to that of the child, treatment is directed at those factors which may preclude direct parent training.* In certain situations, successful treatment of these other family difficulties may obviate the need for any further treatment.

Strengths and limitations

The major advantage of the broad-based model of the dysfunctional family is that each family is subject to a behavioral assessment which examines a wide variety of interactions occurring within the family system. These interactions are not limited to the overt motor behaviors occurring between parents and children. Rather, causal relationships may exist between private events, i.e., self-statements, irrational beliefs, etc., and overt parenting behaviors. Finally, interactions between the mother and father may influence the child's problematic behaviors. Therapeutic interventions based on this model allow for an appropriate matching of treatment to client, which takes into account the motivational factors operating within each family system. Unfortunately, the absence of solid empirical foundation suggests that treatment efficacy is influenced by both art and science. Other limitations are the variety of skills required by a therapist (e.g., child management, marital therapy, sex therapy, and individual therapy), as well as a potential increase in the overall length of treatment.

Social Systems Model

Many nonbehavioral family therapists conceptualize deviant child behavior as representative of conflict elsewhere in the family, usually the marital relationship (Framo, 1975). Unfortunately, many proponents of this concept have exaggerated its pervasiveness and act as if the roots of all child problems can be traced to the interactions between the parents.[5] Such extreme pronouncements have contributed, in part, to behavior therapy's failure to evaluate this component of the family system. More recently, behaviorally-oriented researchers are beginning to critically investigate this hypothesis, e.g., Oltmanns, Broderick, and O'Leary (1977) found less marital satisfaction in families in which a child was referred to a psychology clinic than in nonreferred families. Clinical experience indicates that deviant child behavior occurs in families with *and* without marital discord. The simple presence of marital discord in these families may or may not be causally related to the child's problems. To complicate matters further, cause and effect are not often readily apparent. For example, a strained marital relationship may contribute to the development and/or maintenance of deviant child behavior, or the problems of the child may contribute to the development and/or maintenance of marital problems.

Overview

The social systems model of the dysfunctional family, like the broad-based model, suggests a focus beyond simple dyadic interactions. This, of course, is not a new concept. Nonbehavioral family therapists (e.g., Haley, 1976) have long argued that therapeutic interventions must deal with the entire social system in order to effect and maintain behavioral change. Whether one considers factors internal to the home or school setting, it seems logical that a model of assessment and therapy which focuses on a limited aspect of that system to the exclusion of potentially relevant factors may be incapable of initiating behavior change and/or dealing with the various types of generalization problems. Wahler, Berland, Coe, and Leske (1976) proposed a social systems approach as an expanded model which views behavior as "determined by subsystems which always form the components of other systems" (p. 4). Three subsystems are suggested: first, the various behaviors within the child's repertoire; second, the interacting behaviors of the child's primary group (e.g., mother, father, siblings); and third, the interacting factors of the community system (e.g., school, juvenile courts, etc.). Each level is viewed as a subsystem forming components of other systems of greater complexity. It is the addition of the last system which differentiates the social systems from the broad-based model. At this level of systems analysis, the assessment must consider the covariations that exist between larger groups, such as the family and school or the school and the police.

Assessment and treatment

The social systems model has direct clinical implications for behavioral assessment and therapy. A search for covariations among responses may suggest indirect modification procedures.

Through a school consultation, a behavioral parent group for parents of preschool handicapped children was being conducted. Although participation in the parent group was voluntary, there was near perfect attendance. As is not uncommon, the mother who rarely attended was the one parent of most concern to the teachers. The teachers believed that this mother neglected her child and, at times, may have physically abused him. She was nonresponsive to the teacher's requests for private meetings, as well as invitations to visit the parent group. It was hypothesized that this mother was avoiding contact with the school due to a past learning history of punishing interactions with social institutions (i.e., school, welfare, etc.). An indirect modification procedure was implemented whereby daily notes would be sent home with her son. Each note would be one hundred percent positive, indicating some new skill that her son performed or some pleasant event occurring in the classroom. After a few weeks the mother began sending similar positively oriented notes back to the teacher. Although she never became a consistent and regular participant in the parent group, over the year

---

[5]*Editors' Note*. While the pervasiveness of this phenomenon *may* be exaggerated in the field, there unfortunately exist few data on the basis of which to make such a determination.

she did begin to have private meetings with the teacher, who in turn imparted the behavioral principles utilized in the group.

Strengths and limitations

Although there is an obvious, intuitive, common sense appeal to the social systems model, questions need to be raised on both theoretical and practical grounds. How far does a clinician go in assessing the influence of various systems upon one another? It appears that one could have an infinite regression of contributing systems. Finally, on a practical level, how many variables can be influenced which will result in a favorable cost-benefit analysis? These and other questions, which are not yet formulated, point out the nascent stage of development of the social systems model.

BEHAVIORAL ASSESSMENT IN PARENT TRAINING

One of the more difficult tasks facing the clinician is the assessment associated with parent training. The initial questions to be considered are: Is behavioral parent training indicated and, if so, is this type of treatment sufficient or will it be used in conjunction with other treatments (e.g., marital therapy, anxiety management, etc.). If other treatments are felt to be necessary, then what sequence will produce the most favorable outcome? Should marital therapy, if indicated, precede behavioral parent training or vice versa? Is it possible for various treatments to occur concurrently? Answers to these and other questions are critical for the establishment of a scientifically based model of assessment and therapy. The varied approaches, characterized by clinical impressions and clinical experience, indicate that behavioral assessment is currently a mixture of art and science. This section presents a guiding framework for the clinician in the assessment of behavioral parent training.

Keefe, Kopel, and Gordon (1978) describe a comprehensive five-stage model of behavioral assessment consisting of 1) problem identification, 2) measurement and functional analysis, 3) matching treatment to client, 4) assessment of ongoing therapy, and 5) evaluation of therapy.

This five-stage model has been successfully applied to a wide variety of clinical problems, i.e., marital discord, sexual dysfunction and deviation, social-interpersonal anxiety, childhood conduct disorders, etc.

Problem Identification

The initial task is to engage in problem identification, which consists of pinpointing presenting problems, determining response characteristics, obtaining a history of the problem, identifying probable controlling variables, and selecting tentative targets for modification. Typically, this stage begins with the therapist conducting a behavioral clinical interview with the child's primary caretakers. Although the child's parents, foster parents, group home leaders, or even an older sibling may function as caretakers, it has been our experience that the initial interview is best conducted with both parents in the child's absence. The child's presence often has an inhibiting effect on information-gathering due to the child's attention-getting behaviors and/or the parents' reluctance to discuss matters they consider "private" but which may have a direct bearing on the nature of treatment. In addition, during the first meeting, the parents generally present the child in the worst possible light by highlighting the child's problems and negative actions. The child's presence during this type of meeting serves to reinforce the frequently encountered initial reluctance to participate in therapy. It has been suggested that the presence of the child during the initial interview is justified as it allows the therapist to observe the nature of the interaction between the parents and child. Due to the combined factors that the representativeness of this setting is highly limited and that other procedures are potentially more useful in collecting data regarding parent-child interactions, there seems to be little justification for subjecting the child to this format.

During the initial stages of the clinical interview, it often becomes quite evident that parents have difficulty pinpointing the child's problems. Typically, presenting complaints are stated by using trait labels as both descriptors and causes of behavior. Parents often describe their children as hyperactive, shy, willful, aggressive, negative, and the like. When questioned as to the reasons that a child hits, the answer is often, in effect, "because he is aggressive." The parents' problems are capable of being observed and measured.

THERAPIST: You've indicated that Eric is hostile. Could you tell me more about that?
PARENT: I can't control him. He always gives me backtalk. Whenever I ask him to do something, a royal battle follows.
THERAPIST: So when you ask him to do something, he fails to follow your instructions?
PARENT: Yes, and if he does what I ask him to do, it is always with a lot of complaining.

The process of specifying behavioral referents continues in this fashion until all the problems are pinpointed.

Through the interview the clinician attempts to identify the response characteristics of the pinpointed problems. These response characteristics are considered with regards to the frequency, intensity, duration, and social context of the targeted behaviors. The obtained information is not necessarily viewed as an accurate representation of reality, but rather as an interaction between the child's actual behavior and the parents' perceptions of the problem. For example, it is not uncommon for a parent to report that a child tantrums "all day long." However, when given the task of actually counting the occurrence of the behavior, the collected data often reveal varying degrees of discrepancy between reported and actual behavior. Problem identification is further enhanced by obtaining a brief history of the child's development and significant life experiences. Although a behavioral approach is somewhat ahistorical, clinical behavior therapy requires developmental information so as to distinguish between skill deficits and motivational factors, as well as to obtain valuable prognostic information. This orientation is also useful in that it allows the clinician to assess the parents' attribution as to the factors which caused the problem. An awareness of the parents' perception of causal factors aids the therapist in developing a personalized treatment strategy.

A well established tenet of behaviorism is that behavior is a function of the environment, more specifically the social environment. This view requires the gathering of information regarding possible response-response relationships that exist between the child's problematic behaviors and the responses by the social environment, i.e., parents, teachers, peers, etc. One appraoch we have found useful in establishing behavioral referents, identifying responses characteristics, and determining controlling variables is to ask the parents to describe a typical day for their family from the time the first person arises to the time everyone retires. This single question yields a rich source of useful information. An example follows:

THERAPIST: Could you describe for me a typical day? I'd like you to be as specific as possible.
PARENT: The little one (age four) is up really early, about six in the morning. I usually hear him banging on our door.
THERAPIST: He bangs on your door?
PARENT: Oh yes, I didn't mention that we have to lock our bedroom door. We started doing this about three months ago because he would crawl into our bed otherwise and it was just too early.
THERAPIST: That must have been annoying. What do you do while he is banging on the door?
PARENT: I try to ignore him but it seems that the more I ignore him the worse it gets.
THERAPIST: What do you do then?
PARENT: I usually go out and take him downstairs with me so that he doesn't bother the other kids, or when I am totally exhausted I bring him into bed with us.

The "typical day" interview proceeds in this fashion, identifying problems that may exist during morning (getting up, dressing, eating, and leaving for school), afternoon (returning home from school, chores, homework, leisure time, dinner, sibling/peer relationships), and evening (chores, homework, leisure time, bedtime) activities. In addition to highlighting problem areas, this procedure often demonstrates parental differences with regards to values and expectations.

Problem identification is further enhanced by the administration of behaviorally-oriented checklists and questionnaires, such as the Louisville Behavior Checklist (Miller, 1979) or the Walker Problem Behavior Identification Checklist (Walker, 1976). The information gathered from these sources is useful in providing the therapist with information that may have been omitted or overlooked in the interview. These instruments also have the advantage of providing a referent group for purposes of comparison, so as to better assess the severity of the problem.

A fair amount of clinical experience and, more recently, empirical evidence (Oltmanns et al. 1977) suggests that the quality of the marital relationship plays a role in the initiation and maintenance of deviant child behavior. Therefore, an adequate assessment for behavioral parent training requires an assessment of the marital relationship. This is accomplished through the use of the interview supplemented by a marital adjustment questionnaire (e.g., Locke and Wallace, 1959).[6] The presence of severe marital problems in addition to deviant child behavior may preclude behavioral parent training as the initial form of treatment.

The final step during problem identification is to select tentative target behaviors for modification. This selection process is rarely made explicit and therefore appears to be highly unreliable. It is not certain that a behavioral assessment of the same family performed by two different behaviorally-oriented therapists would result in an identical selection of target behaviors for treatment. Among the factors which may influence the selection process are the therapist's knowledge of childhood development and psychopathology, the therapist's clinical experience, the parents' perception of the severity of the problem, and the parents' level of motivation to participate in the training program.

Measurement and Functional Analysis

The second stage in the behavioral assessment process is the measurement and functional analysis of the problem(s). All too often naive behavior therapists and experienced nonbehavioral therapists adopt a behavioral approach with parents but fail to incorporate this vital stage into the assessment and treatment of the case. Often, the result is a less than satisfactory outcome, with the therapist attributing the failure to the inadequacies of the behavioral approach rather than to the fact that the approach was inappropriately applied. The measurement and functional analysis of child problem behaviors should not be confined to those cases that are designated as research. Instead, this stage of behavioral assessment must be applied to *every* clinical case involved with parent training. This is, in fact, the very essence of a clinical behavioral approach—the utilization of a scientifically based methodology applied to real life human problems.

One of the most frequently cited reasons by parents for their inadequacies in dealing with children is their own level of inconsistent responding, often characterized by an overreliance on negative forms of interaction. Miller (1975) cogently points out that parents should receive basic discrimination training to recognize both the occurrence and nonoccurrence of the child's praisable, ignorable, and punishable behavior. At the same time, they need to be able to discriminate aspects of their own behavior directed toward their children which consist of positive attention, negative attention, and no attention. Systematic parent training consists of training parents to make an appropriate "match" between the child's behavior and their own behavior (e.g., praisable child behavior followed by positive adult attention). One method of maximizing the likelihood that such an appropriate match will occur, as well as maximizing a more consistent manner of responding, is to directly train parents to observe and measure children's behavior and probable controlling variables. These controlling variables often turn out to be responses within parents' own behavioral repertoire.

The measurement and functional analysis that occur in behavioral parent training may be performed by therapists as well as by parents themselves. These procedures are often used during the problem identification stage when the interview and questionnaires fail to provide clear understanding as to the nature of the problem.

---

[6]*Editors' Note*. As we note in the Chapter in this *Handbook* on sex therapy (Heiman, LoPiccolo and LoPiccolo, Chapter 16), we are surprised to find behavior therapists using such self-report inventories since they furnish no data of direct usefulness in the functional analysis of problem behavior.

Much has been written with regard to naturalistic observations of children and the reader is encouraged to become familiar with the issues associated with this procedure (Johnson and Bolstad, 1973).

For purposes of parent training, a variety of measurement procedures appears to be the most useful. Parents are often instructed to perform a functional analysis or "three-term contingency" consisting of observing and recording those events that set the stage for the problem behavior (antecedents), a description of the actions that the child performs (behavior), and finally, those events that immediately follow the child's responses (consequences). Table 1 illustrates the results of this procedure. These parents of two boys, ages six and three, were concerned about what they labeled "extreme jealousy" by their six-year-old when he was not the center of attention. The use of this procedure for one week contributed toward the parents' gaining "behavioral insight" as to the way in which they were contributing to the problem. Their willingness and desire to learn more effective ways of interacting with their children underline the fact that the distinction between assessment and therapy is often not clear and that in many cases they are one and the same. A variety of other measurement procedures that parents can use has been outlined by Hall (1971). These are direct measurement of a permanent product (e.g., number of tantrums per day), time sampling (e.g., percent of five-minute intervals in which a child was playing appropriately with toys at the end of each interval), and duration record (the length of time it takes a child to complete homework). One of the more difficult tasks for the parent trainer is to guide the parents in developing an appropriate match between the target behavior in question and the most suitable and practical measurement procedure.

Matching Treatment to Client

An ancient myth exists about a most hospitable innkeeper who provided food and rest for weary travelers. Unfortunately, in spite of the various shapes and sizes of the different travelers, the innkeeper had only one size bed. In order to best accommodate the many travelers, the hospitable innkeeper would stretch the short travelers on a rack and cut off the legs of the tall travelers so that the bed might be a better fit. Unfortunately, behavioral parent training, with its systematic structured approach, runs the risk of being used in much the same way as the host in the ancient Procrustean myth applied his trade. Behavioral parent training must be viewed in a flexible fashion so that the treatment can be designed to "fit" the parents rather than the parents being made to "fit" the treatment. This stage of behavioral assessment often turns out to be pivotal with regard to maximizing the likelihood of a successful outcome.

There are at least four factors to be considered prior to a decision for parent training. *First, it is important to assess the degree to which environmental control is even possible.* A single parent of limited resources with three "professional monsters" may simply not be in a position to adequately alter the social environment. The intense pressure felt by a parent in such a situation may contribute to a "hidden agenda" whereby the goal of treatment is to fail in order to justify the removal of the children from the home.

Second, interpersonal problems between the parents may preclude their working together in a collaborative set. Miller (1975) states:

The parents' lack of agreement or cooperation with each other in parent training may indicate the presence of more general negative or ambivalent attitudes about each other which interfere with their response to treatment. Such parents may show intense conflicts about any joint decision involving the family life, and brief parent counseling often can do no more than provide temporary control over the parents' attempts to negate each other's work in the parent training. Thus the problems that occur in the intervention programs can only be successfully dealt with when the therapist is able to improve the parents' daily communication with each other (p. 98).

A cautionary note is in order there. On several occasions we have observed parents whose marriage is characterized by extreme dislike for each other who have, nevertheless, been able to put aside their differences in order that they may work together in a constructive fashion to help their child. Thus, we must be careful to avoid

TABLE 1

Results of a Mother's Three-Term Contingency
Data Collection Procedure for One Week

Name: Benny, six years old
Date of Observation: 8/3/75–8/10/75

Setting Events: Mother, father, two children sitting in family room watching T.V. after Dinner.
Father reading newspaper.

What Happens Before	Behavior	What Happens After
8/3		
6:50 P.M.: Entire family watching T.V., Marty sat next to me.	Benny said, "I was going to sit there," sucking thumb.	Lou began to sternly reprimand Benny. I made room for him and he sat next to me.
8/4		
11:30 A.M.: Benny was showing his grandmother some new tricks he learned in gym; Marty began to imitate the tricks.	Benny pushed Marty, sucked thumb, frowned.	I asked Marty to sit down and wait until Benny was finished.
8/6		
7:30 P.M.: Lou and the boys were playing basketball and he let Marty go first.	Benny frowned and ran into the house.	Lou followed Benny into the house and tried to explain that he had to share.
8/8		
4:30 P.M.: Benny came in from playing a game with Marty.	Benny threw a book at me and sucked his thumb.	I hit him several times and sent him to his room. I went up to him 15 minutes later and we talked things out.
8/8		
8:00 P.M.: I asked Benny and Marty a question and Marty answered first.	Benny hit Marty.	I tried to talk to both of them for five minutes.

developing hard and fast rules which serve to stifle clinical creativity.

Third, since parents are people, they, too, are subject to all the various forms of dysfunctional behavior that might possibly occur. *Intrapersonal interference factors* (Miller, 1975) *such as depression and anxiety may severely limit parents' ability to benefit from behavioral parent training*. When behavioral assessment points to this, then other forms of intervention (e.g., cognitive restructuring, systematic desensitization) may need to occur prior to or in conjunction with the parent training.

Finally, the resources and motivation of the child may suggest different forms of intervention. Self-control procedures with the child (Graziano, 1975) in conjunction with parent training may be the most effective combination of all. The concept of matching treatment to client is the essence of doing effective therapy, whether it be behavioral parent training, play therapy, or nonbehavioral family therapy.

Assessment of Ongoing Therapy and
Evaluation of Therapy

Continuous and ongoing assessment is a vital component of behavioral parent training. In reality, a false dichotomy is created when assessment and treatment are considered as two separate processes. Rather, assessment not only continues throughout the training process but assessment, whether performed by the professional or the parent, may be corrective in and of itself. The methods of assessment that were used during the initial phases of parent training (i.e., verbal interview, observations and record-keeping by parents and therapist, and the readministration of behavioral checklists) are in continuous use to varying degrees.

The purposes of this approach are threefold: First, the data are used to determine whether or not the techniques are being applied correctly; second, with the determination of the correctness of the procedure, the emphasis is upon its effectiveness, namely, whether or not the desired results are being obtained; and finally, if the techniques are being correctly applied and the outcome is less than desired, the data then provide for a feedback loop between outcome and decision-making by leading to the selection of a different set of procedures. Obviously, by adopting this model of behavioral assessment the usually thorny problem of evaluating treatment is greatly facilitated. The clinician is in an excellent position to address the issue of the effectiveness of the training program. Finally, through periodic reevaluations after termination, the behavioral parent trainer is knowledgeable as to the maintenance of treatment effects, as well as the development of new problems should they arise.

APPLICABILITY OF BEHAVIORAL PARENT TRAINING

There have been very few attempts to systematically evaluate the effects of child and parent characteristics upon treatment outcome. Our knowledge of the influence of client characteristics has also been hindered by the fact that in most parent training studies: 1) The children involved were boys, 2) mothers, and not fathers, were the primary recipients of training, and 3) a large portion of the children were treated for behavioral excesses which were maladaptive or disturbing, rather than for behavioral deficits (Graziano, 1977). There is, however, no explicit rationale for the predominance of these client characteristics. It is most likely a reflection of the types of children referred for treatment and the fact that mothers are usually more available and willing to participate in treatment than fathers.

Child Characteristics

The most obvious and important child characteristic is the behavior of the child which the parents wish to modify. The data in this area strongly suggest that parent training in behavioral strategies has been successfully applied to almost every class of overt child behavior (Graziano, 1977; O'Dell, 1974). Graziano (1977) has categorized these child behavior problems into six broad areas: 1) problems involving somatic systems, 2) problems grouped in complex "syndromes," 3) negativistic, noncompliant, oppositional and aggressive behavior, 4) children's fears, 5) language and speech disorders, and 6) common behavior problems in the home.

A wide range of problems involving somatic systems has been successfully modified by parents. These have included seizures. (Zlutnick, 1972), eating problems (Bernal, 1973), thumb-sucking (Tahmisian and McReynolds, 1971), self-injurious behavior (Graziano, 1974), encopresis (Edelman, 1971), nocturnal enuresis (Paschalis, Kimmel, and Kimmel, 1972), chronic constipation (Lal and Lindsley, 1968), toilet training (Foxx and Azrin, 1973), and asthma (Neisworth and Moore, 1972). A promising new area of intervention with somatic problems is parent modification of childhood obesity (Gillick, 1974; Grace, 1975). Although these somatic disturbances are more serious in nature than perhaps some other forms of childhood problems, they do appear to offer the advantage of working with a highly motivated set of parents. Our clinical experience suggests that, as a group, these parents are eager to achieve quick and effective resolution of the problem.

Recently, parents of a seven-year-old girl were referred by her pediatrician because of infected sores over the better part of her body due to allergies and "compulsive" scratching. A behavioral assessment revealed both parents to be highly preoccupied with their own lives, leaving little time for involvement with their daughter. Although the mother was not overly negative, neither was she very positive. The father, on the other hand, was extremely sarcastic and would, on occasion, resort to hitting as a means of discipline. A pattern emerged whereby a tremendous amount of parental attention (albeit negative) was made contingent on scratching behavior and any verbalization about the "itch." Behavioral parent training consisted of pinpointing, recordkeeping by both parents and child, basic discrimination training, and a token system. Within six weeks of intervention, scratching episodes were reduced from a baseline average of 11 per day to one every other day. Reports from the pediatrician indicated the infection had been totally eliminated. Although the child still had numerous allergies, she no longer resorted to the "compulsive" scratching. Most importantly, the family members began to respond differently to one another. Their relationship was now characterized by more frequent positive interactions with very few instances of yelling, screaming, and hitting. A one-year follow-up found these gains to be maintained.

This case study serves to illustrate the way in which an apparent physical problem is under environmental control and the manner in which parents are involved in behavioral parent training. A more complete review of behavioral treatment of somatic problems in children can be found in Siegel and Richards (1978).

The problems grouped in complex "syndromes" involve children labeled brain-damaged, retarded, schizophrenic, autistic, and psychotic. The parents of these children often require extensive training to help them deal with a wide variety of behavioral deficits and/or excesses. In most cases, parent training is offered as an adjunct to institutional or day care treatment in a specialized program. Training parents of retarded children to use behavior modification techniques to teach their children new skills has been a very successful intervention (Mash and Terdal, 1973). Rose (1974) demonstrated that these parents should be trained in groups, by trainers who themselves had relatively little training. A comparison of the effectiveness of behavioral training and reflective group counseling for parents of retarded chil-

dren showed that, while both groups manifested improvement on a variety of outcome measures, behavioral training was far more effective (Tavormina, 1975).

Home programming by parents is accepted as an essential part of treatment with autistic and psychotic children, whether the child lives at home and receives day care treatment, or is in a residential program, but will eventually be returned to the home. Because many of these treatment programs rely heavily on behavior modification techniques, there have been many reports of attempts to involve these parents in behavioral training (e.g., Allen and Harris, 1966; Dunlap, Egel, Killion, Kogel, Mills & Schreibman, 1978; Wolf, Risley, Johnson, Harris & Allen, 1967). Two reports (Graziano, 1974; Lovaas, Koegel, Simmons, & Long, 1973) indicate that autistic children whose parents have been trained in behavioral skills maintained their gains when released from structured programs, whereas those whose parents had not been trained regressed. Dunlap et al. (1978) are in the process of comparing parent training with no direct clinic treatment for the child, with direct clinic treatment without parent training. They report that pilot data "provide compelling evidence that parent training is a plausible form of the treatment as compared to direct clinic intervention." Nordquist and Wahler (1973) reported a single case in which a four-year-old autistic child was successfully treated at home by his parents, who received training in their clinic.

While these reports are encouraging, they are far from conclusive. Training usually requires a tremendous effort on the part of the parents and the trainers, very often with little change in a practical sense. Dubey and Kauffman (1977) developed a year-long training program involving an extensive series of home and school visits. Despite intensive efforts, some autistic children showed very limited progress. Browning (1971) found that after three years of 24-hour daily programming by a professional staff, all five treated autistic children showed disappointing results. Graziano (1974) has concluded, from this and other studies, that training parents to work with their autistic children "promises limited effectiveness for maximum effort." Clearly, behavioral parent training for parents of these children is not a panacea, but it does seem that every parent of such a child should be given the opportunity to benefit from this approach.

Negativistic, noncompliant, oppositional, and aggressive behaviors constitute the class of behavior which has drawn the most attention and effort from behavioral parent trainers. Most of the children included in this category exhibit multiple severe problems and cause a great deal of disruption in the home, school, and community. Initially, parents received intensive individual training to help them cope with these children, but there are now an increasing number of group training programs available to this population. Parents have been trained to successfully deal with a wide range of disturbing behaviors, such as screaming, fighting, bossing, destroying property, (Hawkins et al., 1966; O'Leary, O'Leary, and Becker, 1967; Wahler, 1969; Zeilberger, 1968) hyperactivity, (Johnson and Brown, 1969), and physical and verbal abuse (Bernal, et al., 1972). Patterson and his colleagues have consistently reported some of the best results in training parents to deal with severely aggressive boys (Patterson, Reid, Jones, and Conger, 1975).

In a recent review, Forehand (1977) concluded that noncompliance is the primary problem in most of these cases, and certainly constitutes one of the most commonly reported child problems. Forehand defines noncompliance as any instance in which a child fails to *initiate* compliance within five seconds of the termination of a parental command (Forehand, Peed, and Roberts, 1975). This definition applies to commands which require the performance of a desirable response or the inhibition of a negative behavior. Forehand and his colleagues have reported a series of studies on the effectiveness of time-out (Gardner, Forehand, and Roberts, 1976; Hobbs and Forehand, 1975; Hobbs, Forehand, and Murray, 1978; Scarboro and Forehand, 1975), and negative attention and ignoring strategies (Forehand, Roberts, Doleys, Hobbs, and Resick, 1976) with noncompliant children. All these techniques were found to increase compliance to maternal commands. However, it should be noted that Forehand's subjects were not all clinically referred problem children and even those who were are not described as having problems as severe as those reported by Patterson (1974). In summary, the literature in this area is encouraging, but it seems to indicate that parents of children with severe multiple conduct problems require more intensive individually tailored training, while less severe problems of noncompliance can be treated by the teaching of a few relatively simple techniques.

There are only a few reports in the literature which describe training parents to treat children's fears and phobias. In a review of behavioral treatment of school phobia, Hersen (1971) mentions several reports in which parents were trained to assist in their child's treatment. Kennedy (1965) reported treatment of 50 school phobic children by instructing the parents in appropriate responses to the phobic behavior. Tahmisian and McReynolds (1971) taught parents to use a shaping procedure with their school phobic daughter. In two cases, parents were trained to use in vivo desensitization. Tasto (1969) used this method to treat a four-year-old's fear of sudden loud noises, and Bentler (1962) used a modified procedure to help a mother treat her aquaphobic son. The simplicity and efficiency of the aforementioned reports on training parents to treat children's fears and phobias make it difficult to understand why there is so little work being done in this area. Perhaps it is merely a reflection of the overall dearth of clinical investigations regarding childhood fears and phobias. In a recent review, Graziano (1979) found only 40 behavioral case studies of childhood fears published over a 54-year period. These studies involved a total of 130 children, with 112 being school phobic. Since 1960, there has averaged less than one published case study per year. Although parents have been trained to reduce their children's fears, it has clearly been an area which has not received a great deal of attention.

Reports of parent participation in the treatment of language and speech disorders are limited to a few single-case studies involving autistic children (Hewett, 1965; Miller and Sloane, 1976; Risley and Wolf, 1966), and elective mutism (Nolan and Pence, 1970; Wulbert, Nyman, Snow, and Owen, 1973). While the treatment of elective mutism was effective, training parents to assist in language acquisition with autistic children yielded less significant results. Graziano (1977) has suggested that this may be due to the complexity of this type of language problem and the fact that the requisite skills are also complex and not well-known.

The most comprehensive program reported in the literature designed to train parents to deal with common behavior problems in the home is the Responsive Parenting Program developed by Clark-Hall (1978). This program focuses on training parents of "normal" children who are interested in learning better child management techniques. The emphasis is on preventive as well as remedial parent training. The results of this training, as measured by parent reports of their home behavior change projects and the Walker Behavior Checklist, are quite positive (Hall, Grinstead, Collier, and Hall, 1978). However, the program's directors concede the need for validation of these parental reports by other methods and are currently conducting this research. Four participants in a slightly more extensive but similar course reported successfully completing home programs to modify the wearing of an orthodontic device, bedroom cleaning, persistent whining and shouting, and the duration of time spent dressing in the morning (Hall, Axelrod, Tyler, Grief, Jones & Robertson, 1972). While the contribution that this type of program can make to the prevention of more serious child behavior problems is not established, it seems likely that it might increase parents' confidence and satisfaction in their parental role and reduce the level of conflict between parent and child.

In almost all of the reports mentioned thus far, the target behavior was the only child characteristic systematically studied in relation to treatment outcome. Other child characteristics have received relatively little attention. Patterson (1974) reported no differences in treatment outcome data as a function of the number of siblings, ordinal rank of the problem child, or the age of the child. Dubey and Kaufman (1977) reported no effect of age or sex on outcome. One rather provocative finding was made by Arnold, Levine, and Patterson (1975) in their study of aggressive boys. Their finding of no differences between nonreferred siblings and problem children in their rates of deviant behavior raised the question of the appropriateness of solely treating the referred child in

parent applied intervention programs. *Another similar issue involved in assessment for parent training is the question of whether the referred child is actually exhibiting deviant behavior which warrants change, or whether the problem is primarily due to a false perception on the part of the parent.* Several studies comparing referred and nonreferred children have shown considerable overlap in the amount of deviant behavior between the two groups (Delfini, Bernal, and Rosen, 1976; Lobitz and Johnson, 1975). Lobitz and Johnson (1975) found parent attitudes to be better predictors of referral for psychological treatment than child misbehavior. This has important implications for both the focus of treatment and the measures of outcome. Unfortunately, due to the lack of established norms for either child behavior or parent attitude questionnaires, research and treatment in the area of behavioral parent training are exceedingly difficult.

Parent Characteristics

As mentioned previously, in almost all reports, mothers are the primary recipients of parent training, with fathers being involved in only a few cases.[7] This fact has drawn very little attention until quite recently, and to date, only one study has specifically focused on the relative effects of including or omitting fathers from training. Martin (1977) found improvement in mother-child problems was the same whether or not fathers were included. However, this finding is limited by the fact that all fathers in the study expressed a willingness to participate in training, a condition rarely found in clinical populations. Graziano (1977) has suggested that parent trainers may be overlooking crucial factors by not examining father-child interactions, comparing skill levels of fathers with those of mothers, and not routinely utilizing these "other" parents. Very often, fathers are not directly involved in behavioral parent training because of

---

[7]*Editors' Note.* In addition to the empirical evidence in support of the central role of the father in family therapy (Gurman and Kniskern, 1978a), involving only the mother also runs the risk of unwittingly reinforcing the stereotyped gender role of the mother as *the* nurturant parent who carries the major responsibility for insuring family harmony (Gurman and Klein, 1980).

their own refusal to view themselves as having a problem they are incapable of solving themselves and/or the realities of a work schedule which conflicts with the parent trainers' availability. Admittedly, the former is a more serious threat to a successful outcome.

In one case of a four-year-old oppositional child, the mother and father were seen for the initial session, but the father's schedule prevented him from attending all future meetings. At the father's suggestion, behavioral parent training was implemented for the mother, with all sessions recorded on audiotape to which the father would listen while driving in his car to and from his office. Weekly telephone calls to the therapist allowed for clarification of the concepts, techniques, and homework assignments.

This case illustrates that when a parent is committed to effect a change and willing to work on learning new parenting skills, it may be possible for behavioral parent training to be successful even when the father is not physically present during the clinical sessions. Although the chances for obtaining success are greatly reduced when the father refuses all help, our experience has indicated that it is not as hopeless as we first thought. In a few select cases where the father refused treatment, beginning intervention with the mother led to improved child behavior, not as great perhaps as it would have been if the father were involved, but enough so that the situation became "tolerable."

At some point, the behavioral parent trainer must make a decision of whether or not to provide treatment to families where a father refuses to be involved. Some of the factors that will enter into this decision are the severity of the child's behavior, the resources of the mother, the interference of the father, the number of cases waiting for treatment, the policies of the agency or clinic, and the personal beliefs of the parent trainer. As yet, there are few, if any, empirical investigations which offer sound guidelines.

A few studies have reported data on parent characteristics in relation to treatment. Salzinger, Feldman and Portnoy (1970) reported that parents with a higher level of formal education and superior reading ability were more successful in a group program which emphasized verbal learning of operant principles. Rinn, Ver-

non, and Wise (1975) found that low-income parents (less than $5,000 per year) attended fewer classes and were less successful than middle-income parents ($5,000 to $20,000 per year) in a large lecture class. Patterson (1974) found a slight correlation between poor treatment outcome and lower social class in a program with considerable individual behavioral training. He reported a nonsignificant trend for father-absent families to show less progress. On the other hand, Rose (1974) and Mira (1970) found no differences in outcome related to social class or educational level. Rose also reported that foster parents did as well as natural parents. O'Dell (1974) has suggested that investigators who tend to minimize verbal learning and emphasize "direct" training through modeling, coaching, and behavioral rehearsal are more successful with parents from lower socioeconomic and educational backgrounds.

Research in child psychopathology has often focused on the relationship between child deviance and parental adjustment. The two parental adjustment factors most often suggested as relating to child deviance are marital discord and parent psychopathology. Although experience has led several authors (Bernal, 1973; Ferber, Keeley, and Shemberg 1974; Patterson, 1974) to advise that parents with serious marital problems do not do well in parent training programs and should therefore be screened out, there is only one study which has directly investigated this problem.

Reisinger, Frangia, and Hoffman (1976) found mothers with reported marital difficulties notably less able to demonstrate generalization of toddler management skills in the home over a 12-month follow-up than were their counterparts who had not reported marital distress. They attributed the outcome differences to lack of parental support for the mother's interventions, frequent arguments between spouses, and extramarital relationships which decreased the spouses' investment in the program. This suggests that *marital discord may have to be reduced prior to or simultaneously with behavioral parent training*. Finally, while there are no supportive research data available, it is common practice to exclude parents who have severe emotional disturbances (Patterson, 1965; Wiltz, 1969).

O'Dell (1978) has recently discussed the advisability of doing a broad-based assessment of each individual family, which would include the following: socioeconomic level, education level, intelligence, spouse absent, family size, family isolation, parental personality and emotional problems, child-rearing philosophy, conceptualization and labeling of child problems, and type of child problem. He points out there are currently few data to guide such assessments as applied to behavioral parent training. The fact that therapists increasingly cite problems in these areas points out the need for future research, which will help to establish clinical guidelines.

Finally, although there are no data to support the practice, it is commonly believed that behavioral parent training is more effective when all family members and/or child caretakers who control contingencies in the child's environment are trained to carry out the intervention. A consistent approach across all caretakers is believed to make behavior change more rapid and generalizable. A recent report demonstrated that even siblings can be trained to function as behavior change agents for their disturbed brothers and sisters (Colletti and Harris, 1977; Lavigueur, 1976).

STRUCTURE OF BEHAVIORAL PARENT TRAINING

Walder, Cohen, Breiter, Daston, Hirsch, and Leibowitz (1969) described three structural approaches to training parents. These are 1) consultation with individual pairs of parents in the therapist's office; 2) the establishment of a controlled learning environment in the clinic or home; and 3) educational group meetings. A brief overview of some of the programs and settings in which these approaches have been used is presented so as to clarify their unique advantages and disadvantages.

Individual consultation is often done without the therapist ever directly interacting with the child. Typically, parents describe the problem to the therapist, who then helps the parents develop a specific behavioral program for changing the problem behavior. This is a common procedure, particularly when the problem involves a single, well-defined behavior, such as thumbsucking (Ross, 1975), asthma (Neisworth and Moore, 1972), or school phobia (Tahmisian and McReynolds, 1971). Mira (1970), in a summary of a large number of cases, reported that parents seen individually required an average of only two hours of training for each successful case. Individual consultation is, of course, the most economical in terms of the therapist's own schedule; however, it does have the disadvantages of requiring the parent trainer to inefficiently repeat the presentation of concepts and techniques with each new case.

While this type of limited consultation is successful in many cases, it is usually not sufficient for the treatment of more complex sets of behavior problems, such as the "brat behaviors" reported by Bernal, Duryee, Pruett and Burns (1968) or the oppositional behaviors reported by Wahler (1969). These cases often require a complete restructuring of the parental reponses to the child. The reshaping of parental behavior may be greatly facilitated by the use of a controlled learning environment either in the home or the clinic. Such a controlled learning environment often consists of a comfortable room equipped with age-appropriate toys and/or common, everyday household items, such as a television, record player, or a kitchen table complete with dishes and utensils. At times, a controlled learning environment may be equipped with one-way mirrors which allow the therapist to observe the parent-child interaction or for the parent to observe demonstrations of the therapist interacting with the child. Depending upon available resources, a "bug in the ear" permits the therapist to communicate with the parent while the interactions are ongoing. A controlled learning environment often produces rapid behavioral change and is especially suited for those parents requiring "hands-on" demonstrations. Its use is somewhat limited in that it often requires an extra expenditure of therapists' time as well as the availability of appropriate space.

Educational groups are usually composed of three to ten sets of parents and one or more therapists. Material is presented primarily by didactic instruction and discussion. The group setting can be used to facilitate parents' exposure to a wider range of target behaviors and intervention strategies. Rose (1969) points out that the group is a source of exchange of ideas for potential reinforcers and other treatment plans. It also allows for numerous opportunities for modeling and behavioral rehearsal. Another obvious advantage of groups is their efficiency in terms of staff time. Both Rinn et al. (1975) and Rose (1969) have reported that even in small groups the staff time investment per changed behavior was substantially less than individual treatment.

Rose (1974) and Lehrer, Gordon and Leiblum (1973) have trained parents in small group settings. Rose's group members attended between seven and ten 90-minute meetings, which included didactic instruction and discussions, with modeling and role-playing by both parents and trainers.

In Lehrer et al.'s program, parents attended ten two-hour sessions in which the first hour was didactic instruction attended by parents from ten different families and the second hour was devoted to small group discussion with two or three sets of parents and one trainer. Hall et al. (1972) describe a "responsive teaching" course offered for three hours of college credit. The class met for a three-hour session each week for 16 weeks. Lectures, films, quizzes, and discussion groups of about ten parents led by a graduate student leader were used to present the course material. Rinn et al. (1975) reported a successful evaluation of a training program in which over 1,100 parents attended five weekly, two-hour sessions at a community mental health center. Groups ranged in size from 16 to 90 with a mean of 41.

Some investigators have combined two or all three of these training approaches. Wahler, Winkel, Peterson, and Morrison (1965) combined the educational group, individual consultation and the controlled learning environment in a 16-week training program. Patterson, Cobb, and Ray (1972) also combined these three approaches. In a group, parents were taught the general principles of operant theory and the provided individual assistance and supervised training in specific interventions.

In addition to the selection of one of the basic formats discussed above, the therapist must consider such variables as: the size of the group, number of trainers, length, number and spacing of sessions, amount of material presented in each session, and, in some cases, the relative amount of time allocated to didactic instruction, direct training, and/or individual consultation. In what appears to be the most comprehensive and well-organized behavioral group training program for parents, the Responsive Parenting program provides some clinical guidelines (Clark-Hall, 1978). Parents meet for ten weekly, two-hour group sessions. In a large group format, didactic information is presented via brief lecture by the program director for no more than 20 to 30 minutes. Parents then break up into small groups of four to six with a group leader, where they develop a personalized home behavior change project. Weekly homework assignments involve recordkeeping, as well as actually implementing the various techniques presented through lectures and role-playing. The structure of large and small groups, combined with numerous parent trainers, is both efficient and highly effective (Gordon et al., 1979; Hall et al., 1978).

The choice of format is obviously a complex one and unfortunately there has been no systematic research on structural variables in behavioral training programs. Therefore, therapists are usually influenced by their personal preference as well as that of the parents, the availability of physical resources (video equipment, one-way mirrors, "bug in the ear," etc.), the number of parents available for treatment at any one time, the clinician's assessment of the needs of the client, and administrative policies of the agency sponsoring the parent training program.

CONTENT OF BEHAVIORAL PARENT TRAINING

Training programs in child management differ widely in their content, ranging from those which emphasize teaching parents the general theory and concepts of operant behavior to those which focus on specific techniques designed to modify specific target behaviors. Many programs have adopted an approach which combines the teaching of general principles with training in specific skills. While there is a substantial amount of research supporting the efficacy of specific skills training (O'Dell, 1978), the data on the value of teaching general behavioral principles are less consistent.

There is little doubt that parents can acquire a conceptual knowledge of behavioral principles (O'Dell, Flynn, and Benlolo, 1977; Patterson, Cobb, and Ray, 1972). The controversy centers around the question of whether or not this knowledge contributes to their ability to change their child's behavior. Glogower and Sloop (1976) found four mothers who were taught a combination of general principles and specific skills performed better on several outcome measures than four mothers trained only in specific skills. Patterson (1975) reported a modest but significant improvement in problem child behavior achieved by parents who had merely read a general programmed text. On the other hand, Matefy, Solanch and Humphrey (1975) concluded that their training of a single mother in general principles had little effect on her behavior. This conclusion was supported by a recent study comparing three groups of parent attending a skills oriented child behavior modification workshop. (O'Dell et al., 1977). Parents were randomly assigned to one of three conditions consisting of six hours of pretraining in general behavioral principles, six hours of placebo pretraining, and no pretraining. Although all three groups derived benefit from the specific skills oriented workshop, there was no evidence of any superior performance on any of the outcome measures by any of the groups. The authors speculated that the theoretical pretraining may make parents more likely to analyze problems and less likely to use their skills. Although this study considered a wide range of variables, it does not eliminate the need for further research on the teaching of general behavioral principles. In addition to the need for replication, future studies should include measures of generalization to new behaviors and to the behavior of siblings over longer periods of follow-up.

Since different programs demonstrate a great deal of variance in material taught to parents, it is difficult to present the content of a typical program. However, the following is an attempt to summarize the basic core content presented in many of these programs. After a brief and simple introduction to social learning theory, parents first learn to *pinpoint behaviors*, that is, to define them in specific behavioral terms which require a minimal amount of subjective judgment and are objectively measureable. They are often asked to select one or two behaviors which they wish to modify and are assisted in pinpointing these behaviors. They are then taught to analyze the effects of *antecedents* and *consequences* on the target behavior. Next, they learn techniques for monitoring behavior, such as counting the frequency or duration of the behavior or using time or event sampling procedures. They are instructed in the importance of obtaining *baseline data* on all behaviors before beginning any intervention. Once parents have collected baseline data, they are taught how to *graph* and the way in which to use the graphs in helping them assess their progress. It should be noted that, while almost all parent trainers report teaching some form of recordkeeping, there is no consistency across programs as to the importance placed on the actual recordkeeping practices of the parents. While some programs have required record sheets for admission to training sessions (Patterson et al., 1975), others have found it difficult to get parents to comply and have chosen to proceed with training in intervention strategies without records from parents.

The actual training in behavioral intervention often begins with instruction on how to state and enforce rules and the importance of being consistent. The selection of the specific behavioral techniques to be included in any given parent training program should depend upon the level of sophistication of the parents, the time available for training, the age of the target children, and the types of behavior to be changed. Most programs include techniques for both accelerating desirable behaviors and decelerating undesirable behaviors, to be used in conjunction with each other.

Training in the use of positive reinforcement usually focuses on increasing the frequency and the range of reinforcers, especially social reinforcers, used by parents. This may involve helping parents identify potential reinforcers (Rinn et al., 1975) or demonstrating for them the positive effect of consistent, contingent reinforcement. In many cases, parents report acheiving successful results by simply increasing their use of praise (Dubey & Kauffman, 1977). In a careful study of two mothers instructed to count their episodes of attention to appropriate child behavior in their homes, Herbert and Baer (1972) reported the percentage of maternal attention given following appropriate child behavior increased, as did the child's appropriate behavior. On the other hand, instructions to count attention to inappropriate behavior and to decrease it did not produce change in either the mother's attention or the child's behavior. It is interesting to note that the positive results in this study were obtained despite inaccurate parent self-recording. In a later study, the same group of researchers (Herbert, Pinkston, Hayden, Sajwaj, Pinkston, Cordua, and Jackson, 1973) reported adverse effects of differential parental attention in four out of six children studied. Child deviant behavior was found to increase in response to differential attention procedures. In their analysis of these results, the authors suggested several factors which may have contributed to the negative outcome, including: 1) the presence or absence of competing activities; 2) decreases in absolute levels of maternal attention; and 3) the possibility that maternal attention was percieved as punishing, or that maternal ignoring served as a discriminative stimulus for the child to increase severe deviant behavior.

Although these results were based on a small sample and many other trainers report successful use of training in differential attention (Wahler, 1969), it may be necessary in some cases to consider the child's behavioral repetoire, the mother's value as a reinforcer and the child's prior history of reinforcement in order to maximize the effectiveness of this procedure. A more elaborate program designed to increase social reinforcement of desirable activities involves first training mothers to describe and attend to these behaviors and then requiring that, during training sessions, mothers use four rewards per minute with at least two of the four being praise or physical contact (Forehand and King, 1977). Parents may also be instructed to identify and selectively reinforce behaviors which are incompatible with an undesirable target behavior and at the same time to reinforce the child for gradual decreases in the frequency of the target behavior (Leitenberg, Burchard, Burchard, Fuller, and Lysaght, 1977). In addition to teaching parents techniques to increase the frequency of desirable behaviors which already exist in their child's repetoire, training often

includes methods for developing new behaviors. These include shaping, modeling, giving instructions, and prompting.

While training parents in the use of reinforcement emphasizes parental consequences to child behaviors, several investigators have also examined the effects of instructing parents to change antecedent events. These studies focused on the relationship of the number of parental commands to child compliance and noncompliance. Research has shown that mothers of clinic referred children issued significantly more commands than mothers of nonclinic children (Forehand, King, Peed, and Yoder 1975; Lobitz and Johnson, 1975). This lead to the hypothesis that compliance would decrease when the number of commands increased. This was partially supported by a study in which mothers were asked to give 12 commands to their children and compliance to the first six commands was compared to compliance to the second six (Forehand and Scarboro, 1975). This comparison indicated significantly less compliance to the latter commands, but this difference occurred only during the first 30 seconds after the command was given. Increasing the number of commands appears to affect the latency of complaint responding, but not its probability. Two other studies also failed to find a decrease in compliance when commands increased (Johnson and Lobitz, 1974; Zegiob and Forehand, 1978). It is important to note the results of these studies do not resolve the question of the effect of decreasing commands on child compliance and, unfortunately, this has not been directly investigated. Despite the lack of empirical support, Forehand and King (1977) trained parents to eliminate commands, basing this practice on the convincing argument that command behavior is incompatible with the use of reinforcement. It seems likely that while a reduction in the number of commands may not directly increase child compliance, it may facilitate attending to positive behavior and issuing reinforcers, and thereby contribute to an increase in compliance.

The techniques described above share at least two features. First, they are all designed to increase prosocial behaviors, and second, they make use of social interventions which have the advantage of causing minimal disruption to the ongoing system due to their natural availability.

The content of most behavioral parent training programs usually begins with these types of interventions. At this point, programs begin to differ depending upon whether the focus remains on acceleration techniques or on a "naturalness" dimension. An emphasis on acceleration techniques results in teaching the use of token systems, whereby an emphasis on "naturalness" results in teaching simple punishment procedures. Although there is no empirical evidence, we advocate the guideline of minimal disruption to the prevailing system. This leads to the teaching of techniques to decelerate behavior as the next content area.

The most commonly taught behavior deceleration technique is *time-out* from positive reinforcement. Time-out usually consists of removing of the opportunity to gain reinforcement (Spitalnik and Drabman, 1976), isolating the child in an area devoid of reinforcing persons and objects (Resick, Forehand and McWhorter, 1976), withdrawing stimulus materials (Barton, Guess, Garcia, and Baer, 1970), or ignoring the child (Sachs, 1973). While these procedures have been shown to be effective with a variety of child problems (Forehand and MacDonough, 1975), the exact parameters of the technique which contribute to its success have rarely been studied in clinical settings. However, Forehand and his colleagues have conducted a series of analog studies examining the effects of several parameters of this procedure (Forehand, 1977). They have found time-out to be equally effective whether the mother leaves the room or simply removes all sources of reinforcement and ignores the child. However, the latter procedure required significantly more administrations and is therefore less efficient (Scarboro and Forehand, 1975). Another important parameter is duration of the time-out period. A comparison of three different durations, ten seconds, one minute, or four minutes of time-out showed that the four-minute time-out duration was the most effective in suppressing noncompliant behavior (Hobbs et al., 1978). In addition, children in the four-minute group remained at a significantly lower level than the other two groups during a return to baseline period. Several clinical studies have suggested that the effectiveness of short time-outs (one or five minutes) will be diminished if a longer time-out (15 or 30 minutes) has

previously been employed (Kendall, Nay, and Jeffers, 1976; White, Nielsen, and Johnson, 1972). There is also some evidence that increasing the duration of time-out to more than five minutes does not increase its effectiveness (Kendall, Nay, and Jeffers, 1976; Pendergrass, 1971).

Contingent release from time-out has also been identified as an important parameter. A comparison of contingent release (15 seconds of quiet required prior to the termination of the time-out procedure) and noncontingent release (subjects yoked to those in the contingent release group in terms of length of time-out) found less disruption occurred during time-out and less noncompliance to maternal commands occurred outside of time-out for the contingent release group (Hobbs and Forehand, 1975). Although duration and contingent release have been shown to effect the modification of child noncompliance, the addition of a verbalized reason for the punishment, such as, "You were told not to hit your brother and you did, so I am going to put you in time-out," did not facilitate its effectiveness for children between the ages of three-and-a-half to six-and-a half (Gardner et al., 1976). Two other parameters, high ratio schedules of punishment and time-out imposed in an impoverished natural environment, have been shown to diminish the efficacy of time-out (Hobbs and Forehand, 1977).

In teaching time-out to parents, many trainers emphasize the importance of giving a warning to the child before time-out is administered. It is thought that the pairing of the warning with the punishment will eventually make the warning a sufficiently strong stimulus to control the behavior. There is no empirical support for this, however, and others argue that it is more important that time-out be administered immediately after the undesirable behavior is imitated. Guidelines for the use of time-out are presented in Table 2, based on the combined factors of empirical evidence and clinical experience.

Deceleration techniques have not been limited to time-out. Forehand's group has also performed laboratory investigations of several other techniques commonly used to reduce noncompliance. In one study, the contingent use of negative attention (verbal reprimand) decreased noncompliance, whereas the simple repetition of a command did not effect child behavior (Fo-

TABLE 2

General and Specific Guidelines for the
Administration of the Time-out (TO)
Procedure

General Guidelines for Parent Trainer
1. Meet with parents to plan, rehearse, and review each of the steps in the TO sequence in
   advance, with the child present whenever possible. Use written material, audiotapes, or videotapes, if available.
2. Select a suitable place in the home for TO (dull,
   boring, yet well-lighted and well-ventilated).
3. Determine an optimal time for TO duration
   (two to four minutes for preschoolers and five
   minutes for children ages six through 12).
4. Plan consequences for refusal to go to TO, and
   for destroying property while in TO.
5. Integrate the TO procedure into existing interventions.

Specific Guidelines for Parents
1. Explain entire procedure to the child.
2. Role-play TO with the child prior to first real
   application.
3. Make clear requests to initiate an activity (e.g.,
   Gary, please put your toys away) or terminate
   an activity (e.g., Jennifer, please stop running
   through the house).
4. Try to remain as calm as possible.
5. Be consistent.

rehand et al., 1976). A second experiment
within the study compared negative attention,
isolation (mother takes toys and leaves the
room), ignoring (mother remains in the room
but withdraws all attention), and a combination
of all three techniques used alternately. Results
indicated that each of the four procedures significantly reduced noncompliance from baseline
levels; however, the negative attention group
maintained a lower level of noncompliance than
the ignoring group during a return to baseline
period, whereas the combination condition was
the only procedure that maintained noncompliance at the treatment level. It should be noted
that, in contrast to the results of this experiment,
two studies with clinical populations reported
that ignoring noncompliant behavior was not an
effective treatment procedure (Green, Budd,
Johnson, Lang, Pinkston & Rudd, 1976; Wahler
et al., 1965).

Perhaps the most unnatural, yet highly effective, technique is the use of a *token system*. It
is the most unnatural because it involves adding
elements (i.e., tokens, contracts, reward menus,

etc.) that are not present in the family's natural
environment *and* requires building in a plan for
its eventual removal. Some parent training programs have reported successfully teaching parents fairly complex and sophisticated methods
of achieving behavior change using token reinforcement (Christophersen, Arnold, Hill, and
Quilitch, 1972) and contingency contracting
(Patterson, 1974). Home point systems were
administered by sets of highly motivated and
cooperative parents, each with more than one
child exhibiting a variety of deviant behaviors.
The programs allowed for points to be earned
contingent on the performance of desirable behaviors and lost for undesirable behaviors.
While these programs are highly effective, especially when the parents are motivated, several
important points must be considered before using this procedure. *The token system for each
parent should be designed by the therapist and
administered by the parents under close supervision.*

The process of designing a good program may
require several weeks of trial and error, with
consistent parental cooperation in both using
the program and maintaining accurate records.
Common problems that parents have in admin-
istering token systems are failing to give tokens
immediately, "forgetting" to provide back-up
reinforcers, adding extra behaviors to the program too quickly, becoming overwhelmed by
the demands of maintaining the system, and,
perhaps most importantly, viewing the token
system as a substitute for personal involvement
with the child. It may be necessary for the therapist to invest a substantial amount of time in
direct contact with the parents in order to minimize these potential problems. Christophersen
et al. (1972) also pointed out that parents tend
to discontinue the program when contact with
the therapist is terminated. However, in their
study, parents reported satisfaction with their
children's behavior after the token system was
removed. Token systems, when used, should be
kept relatively simple. For example, a star chart
for a single behavior can be a very effective technique, especially as a means of establishing a
new behavior in a child's repertoire. With older
children, parents often need to learn the art of
negotiation, a process that may be facilitated by
seeing the parent and child together.

In summary, there are a few generally accepted guidelines related to the content of training which are based on theoretical considerations rather than empirical research. The first is that programs *begin by teaching parents positive reinforcement and other, nonpunitive techniques*. Parents, encouraged to change behavior without the use of punishment, are often surprised by their success. Many families referred for problems with deviant child behavior rely totally on coersive controls and, if punishment techniques were to be included in the early sessions of training, they would be less likely to attempt change without them. *Parents are also encouraged to use natural consequences as much as possible in disciplining their children*. The use of natural consequences minimizes the need to change family routines and increases the likelihood that parents will maintain new child management programs. The Responsive Parenting outline illustrates the sequence and range of concepts/techniques used in behavioral parent training (see Table 3).

Finally, behavioral parent trainers must be aware that *parents are often confused and/or unrealistic about the expectations they have for their children's behavior*. This is especially true of parents with physically or mentally handicapped children. Since many require help setting realistic goals, *parent trainers must be prepared to deal with basic issues of child development*.

TABLE 3

Responsive Parenting Outline

Session I:	Learning to define and measure behavior—the first two steps in teaching behaviors
Session II:	Graphing behavior—a roadmap for teaching behaviors
Session III:	Using consequences to change behavior—step three in teaching behaviors
Session IV:	How to apply reinforcement to behavior—step three in teaching behaviors
Session V:	Using good teaching procedures with your child—step three in teaching behaviors
Session VI:	Responsive punishment: How to decrease undesired behaviors—step three in teaching behaviors
Session VII:	What to do regarding specific behaviors
Session VIII:	How to maintain your responsive parent image

METHODS OF BEHAVIORAL PARENT TRAINING

In the previous section a variety of techniques were presented which have been shown to be effective in modifying child behavior. However, the modification of child behavior by these techniques represents only one aspect in this model of treatment. The methods for helping parents acquire the ability to put these techniques to use in their homes are as important as the techniques themselves. These methods can be divided into two categories—*verbal methods* and *performance methods* (direct demonstration and manipulation of behavior).

Most training programs include some form of verbal or written transmission of information to the parents. This may be in the form of instructions, lectures, discussions, texts, or handouts. Behavioral parent trainers often use books as instructional aides to teach social learning theory to parents (Ferber et al., 1974; Lehrer et al., 1973; Patterson et al., 1972). Three of the most popular texts are Patterson's (1971) *Families: Applications of Social Learning to Family Life*, Patterson and Guillion's (1968) *Living with Children*, and Becker's (1971) *Parents are Teachers*. Arkell, Kubo and Meunier (1976) assessed the grade readability levels of several behavior modification books for parents. The results indicated the books ranged from a sixth grade to a college reading level. The authors suggest that behavioral parent trainers choose written material commensurate with parents' last grade obtained in school.

Several authors have also developed paper and pencil assessments which can be administered before and after training to assess parents' acquisition of social learning principles (Becker, 1975; Patterson et al., 1975). O'Dell, Tarler-Benlolo and Flynn (1979) have developed a general instrument to assess knowledge of behavioral principles. Most studies report that parents show significant improvement on such measures after reading the texts (O'Dell, Tarler-Benlolo, and Flynn, 1979; Patterson et al., 1972). While the question of whether or not parents are able to translate their knowledge of general principles into new behaviors at home remains largely unanswered, there has been some recent evidence showing that parents can acquire new behavior skills from verbal training methods.

McMahon and Forehand (1978) gave parents a brochure which described the procedures of differential attention and time-out by presenting a short rationale for each technique, along with step-by-step instructions for their implementation to correct children's inappropriate meal-time behaviors. They reported the behavior of both parents and children changed significantly in the desired direction and that these changes were maintained at a six-week follow-up. A parent advice package for improving child behavior on family shopping trips was also used successfully by parents without professional intervention (Clark, Greene, Macrae, McNees, Davis, and Risley, 1977).

Butler (1976) reported that the text *Toilet Training in Less Than a Day* (Azrin and Foxx, 1974) combined with written presentations, phone calls, lectures, and a question-and-answer period enabled 77% of the parents to successfully train their child after only three one-hour classes. Another study (Matson and Ollendeck, 1977), using the same text, suggested most parents may require at least some supervision in order to successfully carry out its procedures. Green et al. (1976) also found simply providing parents with specific written instructions on differential attention and time-out was not sufficient to assure behavior change in all cases. The data from these and other studies (Eyberg and Johnson, 1974; Johnson and Green, in press) suggest the most reasonable approach is to *first provide parents with written materials, supervise them in their use, and then provide performance training for those who have not achieved the desired behavior change*.

While the idea of self-administered, packaged behavior change programs is certainly attractive due to its cost-efficiency, the potential of this approach may be limited to simple discrete behavior problems. Materials need to be developed which give precise behavioral descriptions of the desired parental responses to very specific child behaviors. The success of parents in using materials must then be studied in relation to such variables as education, intellectual level, or reading ability.

The finding that parents often have difficulty translating verbal knowledge into behavior has lead to an increased emphasis on demonstration and direct modification of parent behavior.

These performance training methods include: *modeling, prompting, shaping,* and *behavioral rehearsal*. Modeling of appropriate responding to deviant and prosocial child behavior has been done both by professionals in the home (Patterson and Brodsky, 1966) and a "demonstration mother" in a clinic setting (Mash, Lazere, Terdal, and Garner, 1973). Modeling, of course, can be more efficiently presented by means of videotapes (Davidson and Siegel, 1977), films (O'Dell, Mahoney, Horton, and Turner, 1979), or audiotapes (Patterson and Forgatch, 1975). One of the authors (NPD) developed a series of seven videotapes which present general behavioral principles as well as demonstrations of a variety of techniques, performed by real parents in home settings. These were shown to parents who were then given assistance in carrying out home behavior change projects. Videotapes, audiotapes and films can also be used to present vignettes of problem situations to which the parents can then practice responding. An increasing number of demonstration materials has become commercially available in the last few years. They include: *Time Out: A Way to Help Children Behave Better* (Hanson, 1969), a film; *The Family Living Series* (Patterson and Forgatch, 1975), a series of audiotapes; and *Who Did What to Whom* (Mager, 1972), a film.

Another frequently used training procedure involves placing the parent and child in an analog situation, observing or videotaping their behavior, and then cueing or prompting them when they perform desirable or undesirable behavior. Hawkins et al. (1966) used three gestural signals to cue a mother to perform appropriate responses while interacting with her son at home. Wahler (1969) went into the client's home and verbally corrected inappropriate parent behaviors and gave social approval when the parent followed his instruction correctly. Johnson and Brown (1969) trained a child's mother and grandmother to shape the child's play behavior by cueing the adults with a light. They first used the light to signal when reinforcement was to be given and later used it to indicate when they had rewarded the child appropriately or when they had missed an opportunity to reward her. Bernal et al. (1972) developed a training program for parents of young antisocial children designed to give parents step-by-step instructions in how to respond socially to specific child behaviors. Various signals such as a buzzer and lights as well as a walkie-talkie were used to help parents follow the instructions. A similar program is used by Forehand (1977) to train mothers of noncompliant children. The mother is observed with her child; the therapist then discusses the interaction with her and uses modeling, role-playing, and practice periods with the child. The mother is given instructions and feedback either by means of an audio transmitter or signal cards. Such an intensive training approach is very costly, but direct behavioral feedback produces behavior change quickly and may be necessary for parents who have trouble translating verbal instructions into behavior.

The decision as to which training method, or combination of methods, will be effective in any given clinical situation is a complex one. This decision will ultimately depend, at least in part, on clinical judgment. However, in recent years, investigators have focused attention on the evaluation of the relative effectiveness and efficiency of the various training approaches. Gardner (1972) compared a group of institutional attendants who received training in behavior modification concepts via a series of lectures, with a similar group trained in specific behavior modification skills by means of demonstration and rehearsal. The fact that the content of training was confounded with the method of training precluded a comparison of the methods above. However, the study did suggest that role-playing was more effective in teaching principles of behavior modification, and there was little generalization from one to the other.

Nay (1975) compared four instructional techniques used to train 77 mothers in time-out procedures. He found written presentation, lecture, videotaped modeling, and modeling with role-playing were all superior to no treatment, but there were no significant differences between the methods on a questionnaire assessing knowledge of time-out. Assessment of mothers' ability to apply time-out to a child in simulated situations presented on audiotape showed modeling coupled with role-playing to be superior to either written presentation or lecture, but not to modeling alone. The validity of this study has been questioned (O'Dell, 1978) due to several methodological problems, such as the audio analog, unequal time in training, variation in the content of the presentations, and the relatively high educational level of the parents.

In a similar study, parents were trained in the use of time-out via written presentation, lecture, videotape modeling, or role-playing (Flanagan, Adams, and Forehand, 1979). The three outcome measures (questionnaire, audiotape, analog and home observations) each yielded different results. All groups were superior to no treatment on the questionnaire, role-playing was superior to lecture on the audiotape analog, and modeling was superior to written presentation on the home observation measure. There are no clear reasons for the differences in outcome on the different measures.

Siegel and Davidson (1978) studied the relative efficiency of training via a series of videotape programs as compared to training via lecture and discussions. The content of the lectures and videotapes was identical and both groups were given additional help with home behavior change projects. The results showed the treatment groups to be more effective than the no treatment control, but that neither of the treatment groups was superior to the other on the outcome measures. The value of the videotape programs was, however, evidenced in a substantial savings in therapist time; almost one-half as much time was spent with the videotape group as with the lecture and discussion group.

O'Dell and his colleagues have performed a series of studies comparing a number of instructional techniques for teaching time-out (O'Dell et al., 1979; O'Dell, Krug, Patterson, Faustman, and O'Quinn, 1978). Parents were randomly assigned to one of the following training groups; written materials plus individual check-out; filmed modeling; filmed modeling plus individual check-out; brief live modeling plus rehearsal; live modeling plus rehearsal; and live modeling plus rehearsal by a therapist who was specially trained. "Check-out" refers to seven minutes of brief rehearsal with a check of parents' understanding of the material. The first study, which assessed parents' acquisition of skills in the clinic immediately after training, suggested that a film plus brief check was superior to all other methods, followed by modeling alone. The written manuals and live modeling with rehearsal were significantly less effective than the film plus check-out, and equally effective to one another. The second study, which assessed parent skills in the home one week following training, yielded significantly different results. This study involved three training groups: written material, filmed modeling, and live modeling with rehearsal by a therapist. All parents were given the manual to take home. The home assessment, using a child actor to present problem behaviors, showed almost no difference among the three groups. O'Dell (1978) offers the possible explanation that, with unlimited time to read the manual at home, previously learned materials tend to be forgotten and the manual becomes the most recent source of remembered information.

In conclusion, research on the relative efficacy of the various training methods is inconclusive. However, it does seem to suggest that, in many cases, *modeling is particularly effective, even in comparison to more extensive interventions like behavioral rehearsal with feedback or cueing.* The fact that modeling is also potentially one of the most cost-effective methods of training clearly justifies further research in this area. Given the state of the art at this time, the most efficacious approach to training may be the method used by Patterson et al. (1975), which is based upon the individual response of the parent. Their program provides parents with progressively more direct intervention until success is achieved. They begin with verbal methods such as texts, verbal rehearsal, and sometimes audiotape modeling, then continue treatment by means of frequent phone contacts. They report that only one-fifth of the parents require additional training. Those who do receive home visits with live modeling and behavioral rehearsal.

This description of verbal and performance methods used in various studies provides a thorough, but not complete, account of the methods used in behavioral parent training. Every therapist is faced with the problem of trying to motivate the unmotivated. These are parents who force the behavioral parent trainer to the analyst's couch by refusing to follow through on homework assignments, attending sessions on an irregular basis, and dropping out of treatment.

The question of *why* these parents are unmotivated has rarely been addressed by behavioral parent trainers. The development of a singular theory which enhances predictability and control is unlikely due to the wide range of potential interference factors. Rather, the behavioral parent trainer attempts to focus on current factors which are hypothetically maintaining less than perfect compliance with the treatment regimen. The various methods used here are based more on clinical experience and intuition than on empirical research. Perhaps the first method is to make use of *parent counseling*.

Miller (1975) states:

Parent counseling can be an important aspect of *any* intervention, and is actually being utilized anytime the therapist, judging that the family's progress is slowed or interrupted, attempts to improve that parents' commitment or involvement regarding the treatment (p. 93).

Parent counseling consists of, first, recognizing and identifying the nature of those factors interfering with behavioral parent training and, second, resolving those factors. These factors may be as simple as situational problems involving scheduling difficulties or as complex as inadequate parental responsiveness characterized by parents' contradictory message, "Help me but don't expect me to change" (Miller, 1975). Just as these interference factors can be simple or complex, the methods used to reduce or eliminate them can also be simple or complex.

Parent counseling often requires the parent trainer to make a therapeutic "shift" to deal with various personal issues of the parent(s). These issues are quite varied, ranging from family "crises" to chronic feelings of never really wanting to be a parent and resenting the child for being the cause of their predicament. The effective parent trainer needs to be familiar with a variety of behavioral strategies (e.g., cognitive restructuring, assertion training, systematic desensitization, communication skills training, etc.) to adequately resolve the complexity of problems presented.

In addition to parent counseling, we have experienced varying degrees of success in motivating parents through the use of contracting, refundable deposits, telephone contact, feedback of results, social reinforcement and self-disclosure. Contracting involves a clearly spelled out agreement, verbal or written, between the parent trainer and the parent, indicating the length of treatment, the responsibilities of the parents, the responsibilities of the parent trainer, the goals for treatment, and the methods used to achieve these goals. A more stringent form of contracting, to be used cautiously, involves the use of some consequence, i.e., money, contingent on the performance of some aspect of treatment. Eyberg and Johnson (1974) made a refundable deposit contingent on attendance and completing homework assignments. Parents subjected to these contingencies showed superior performance. To assess consumer satisfaction, a questionnaire administered at the end of treatment indicated that parents felt positive about its use. Gordon et al. (1979) found similar results in a Responsive Parenting Group. Clearly, such an extreme measure should be used judiciously. There are obviously parents who are highly motivated for whom such an approach would be inappropriate. On the other hand, for those parents who present a very different picture, it may be "just what the doctor ordered."

Another method we have found particularly useful is frequent telephone contact between face-to-face sessions. These contacts allow for checking the understanding of information presented, determining the degree of implementation of homework assignments, and collecting of data assessing the results of treatment. In addition, these prearranged telephone contacts convey the very significant and powerful message that the parent trainer is a concerned professional who will be reaching out to the parents to maximize the likelihood for success.[8]

In most cases, reinforcement for the parents' efforts comes in the form of improved child behavior. Unfortunately, the attainment of this goal is too delayed to sustain persistent effort and the parent trainer must utilize other, more short-term reinforcers. One that we have found particularly useful is feedback of the data. The data collected from the parents via telephone are graphed by the parent trainer for purposes

of feedback to the parents. This visual picture of improvement serves to reinforce the parents for their hard work.

A second type of short-term reinforcement is the social reinforcement provided by the therapist. Support, warmth, and encouragement play a vital role in motivating the unmotivated. Finally, the degree to which there is some perceived similarity between parent(s) and trainer is likely to result in greater compliance with treatment. Thus, an appropriate amount of therapist self-disclosure regarding parenting serves to create an alliance between parent(s) and trainer. The strength of this alliance is in all likelihood positively related to outcome. Such self-disclosure should be done judiciously, as the possibility exists that additional information about the therapist may serve to add distance between the therapist and parent. It would, of course, be unwise for a parent trainer counseling physically abusive parents to disclose that hitting children has *never* been part of his/her parenting repertoire. However, it is probably not stretching the truth to reveal that he/she has *felt* like hitting his/her children. The point here is that some aspect of shared experiences exists and that the discussion of these experiences can contribute to a beneficial therapeutic outcome. The tentative nature of this section indicates the lack of a sound empirical foundation for many of these methods. Behavioral parent trainers must currently rely on their own clinical skills and educated guesses as to what might work for very unmotivated client families.

EFFECTIVENESS OF BEHAVIORAL PARENT TRAINING

The issue of evaluating the effectiveness of parent training in behavior modification as a treatment for child behavior problems is extremely complex due to the wide range of variability among different parent training programs in terms of parent characteristics, content of material presented, training methods, and targeted child behaviors. In addition, the empirical nature of behavior therapy has provided us with an enormous amount of data from a variety of outcome measures. These data can be summarized according to four major criteria for validating a psychotherapeutic approach: 1) The

[8]*Editors' Note*. Indeed, the issue at hand, i.e., what should constitute the relative contributions of patient and therapist initiative-taking and motivation for change, is quite controversial in the field, as a reading of many of the chapters in this volume (cf., especially, Whitaker and Keith, Chapter 6) reveals.

client's distressing problems have changed significantly in the desired direction; 2) new problems have not been created; 3) the improved behaviors have generalized and become stable outside the treatment setting; and 4) the improved behaviors are maintained over a substantial time period (Paul, 1969).

The outcome measures used by parent trainers in assessing child behavior change can be grouped into three major categories: parent opinion obtained through parent-completed questionnaires; parent-recorded frequency of child behavior problems; and frequency of child behavior problems measured by independent observers. In a recent review of 24 studies, Atkeson and Forehand (1978) attempted to determine the amount of agreement among these different measures. They found observation data collected by independent observers agreed with those obtained by parent-recorded data in 78% of the studies, and with those obtained by parent questionnaire data in 74% of the studies. Results obtained by parent-recorded data agreed with those obtained through parent questionnaires in 93% of the studies. Considering 13 studies in which all three outcome measures were utilized, 69% had agreement across all three. In four studies in which independent observer data disagreed with parent-collected data, the trend was *always* for the independent observer data to be negative and the parent-reported data to be positive. In general, the results indicated that all outcome measures yielded positive results in the majority of studies, but that parent reports on both questionnaires and frequency counts are associated with more positive outcome results than data collected by independent observers. The authors point out that this finding raises questions as to which outcome measure should be the primary criterion for determining therapy effectiveness. This issue was first raised by Gordon (1975), who pointed out that the more easily biased measures (namely, parent-collected data) cannot be weighed equally with the independent observer data to arrive at an overall evaluation of outcome.[9] Atkeson and Forehand

(1978) suggest the continued use of multiple outcome measures, but recommend that the determination of which measure to employ to evaluate therapy outcome should depend upon the presenting problem.[10] In cases where a child is obviously deviant, the outcome measures should focus on the child's behavior. If the problem is more one of the parent's perception of the child as deviant, then parent questionnaires are the appropriate outcome measures. Unfortunately, there are, as yet, no well established norms for use in differentiating or identifying these two problems.

Overall, there is a sufficient body of evidence to indicate that behavioral parent training meets the first criterion for validation as a psychotherapeutic approach. There are literally hundreds of reports of its successful use with a wide variety of problem children. In particular, this approach is most effective in producing desired behavior change in children with discrete problems. Perhaps due to its focus on specific target behaviors to the relative neglect of "underlying" causes, behavior therapy was suspected of causing "symptom substitution." Fortunately, this straw man argument is no longer considered very potent.[11] In fact, in many cases there is actually a measureable decrease in rated problems across all behavior categories (Gordon et al., 1979). This is not to say that there have never been any reports of negative effects attributed to this approach. As discussed in a previous section, Herbert et al. (1973) reported an increase in deviant behavior after parents were trained in the use of differential attention. A family systems view would suggest that behavior change in parent or child affects other relationships in the family. The few studies which have addressed this question in relation to behavioral parent training reported a significant increase in family cohesion (Karoly and Rosenthal, 1977) and significant reductions

---

[9]*Editors' Note.* Still, it is interesting to note the paradox that while behavioral researchers see parents' ratings as quite "biased" at the end of treatment, parental views are not viewed as "biased" at the beginning of treatment or during treatment.

---

[10]*Editors' Note.* In addition to the content or topography of a given behavior targeted for change, we also suggest that the subsystem(s) within the family should receive differential outcome assessment under different treatment conditions (see Gurman and Kniskern, Chapter 20).

[11]*Editors' Note.* In addition, as Barton and Alexander (Chapter 11) emphasize, symptoms serve important interpersonal functions; hence, a treatment that fails to properly address these functions could be predicted to at least show high rates of relapse, if not "symptom substitution."

in rates of deviant behavior for siblings of the target child (Arnold et al., 1975). Given the known positive correlation between deviant child behavior and marital difficulties, it is surprising that there have been no attempts to assess the effect of behavioral parent training on marital adjustment.[12] In conclusion, negative effects due to treatment appear to be rare in terms of the immediate behavior of the target child, but the question of more pervasive problems produced in the family system remains far from answered.[13]

Until recently, the assessment of generalization of treatment effect has been largely neglected. After an extensive review of the research on generalization, Forehand and Atkeson (1977) concluded that rigorous assessment methods have not been utilized and results from various studies have been contradictory. Basically, three types of generalization must be evaluated: setting generalization from the clinic to home and school, behavioral generalization to behaviors not targeted in treatment, and sibling generalization to behaviors of the siblings of the targeted child. The most critical and the most heavily investigated area involves generalization from the training setting to the home. While several researchers have reported successful generalization of both parent and child behavior change to the home (Forehand, Sturgis, McMahon, Aguar, Green, Wells, and Breiner, 1979; Humphreys, Forehand, Green, McMahon, and Roberts, 1977; Reisinger and Ora, 1977), other studies have failed to detect transfer of treatment effects (Embry, Kelly, Jackson, and Baer, 1979; Wulbert, Barach, Perry, Straughan, Sulzbacher, Turner, and Wiltz, 1974). Several attempts to increase generalization by maximizing the similarity of stimulus conditions in the two setting provided disappointing results (Mindell and Budd, 1977; Nidiffer, O'Dell, and Pritchard, 1978). However, in some cases, the generalization of parent skills to the home setting was accomplished by specifically instructing

parents to do so (Mindell and Budd, 1977; Peed, Roberts, and Forehand, 1977). Other procedures associated with increased setting generalization are parental homework assignments involving self-recording (Budd, Pinkston and Green, 1973), daily practice of techniques with the child (Forehand and King, 1977), and written instructions (Johnson and Green, in press). Several variables which have not been systematically studied but which seem to enhance generalization are: 1) middle- and upper-class parents versus lower-class parents, 2) discrete behavior problems versus complex problems, and 3) individual training using performance methods as opposed to group classes.

While all children with behavior problems in the home do not exhibit deviant behavior at school, many do (Johnson, Bolstad, and Lobitz, 1976). This has lead to the question of whether improvements in child behavior at home resulting from behavioral parent training generalize to school behavior, or whether they may, in fact, result in a contrast phenomena in which school behavior becomes more deviant. The data on this question are inconclusive, but suggest that improvements in child behavior do not generalize to the school, and in some cases there is a slight increase in school behavior problems following home improvements (Johnson et al., 1976; Wahler, 1975). Several studies found improvements in school behavior of children only when contingencies for school behavior were changed either directly by the teachers at school (Wahler, 1969; Wulbert, Nyman, Snow, and Owen, 1973), or by incorporation of school behaviors into home-based contingency management programs (Bailey, Wolf, and Phillips, 1970).

The literature on the ability of parents to generalize their skills to modify disruptive behaviors which were not the focus of treatment is very sparse and less than encouraging. After a series of studies in which nontargeted deviant behaviors failed to show significant decreases, Patterson (1974) concluded that there is only minimum support for the occurrence of such generalization. The only strategy which has been specifically studied as a method for increasing the generalization of parent skills has been training parents in general behavioral principles, as opposed to training in specific skills to modify specific behaviors. The controversy

---

[12]*Editors' Note.* We agree and think this should be a high priority area for research. Certainly, the issue of *intra*family generalization of treatment effects is of both theoretical and practical importance.

[13]*Editors' Note.* On the other hand, a strikingly high percentage of studies in the area *do* show evidence of some deterioration during parent training (Gurman and Kniskern, 1978b).

over these two approaches has been presented in a previous section of this chapter. In the three studies where these approaches were systematically compared, two investigators (Glogower and Sloop, 1976; Koegel, Glahn, and Nieminen, 1978) reported the superiority of the general training, while the other (O'Dell et al., 1978) found no differences. Wahler (1975) has suggested that child behaviors are organized into functional clusters such that treatment of one behavior may affect other behaviors in the same cluster without any changes in parental responses to these nontargeted behaviors. The mechanism whereby this occurs has not been identified, but Wahler proposes that the identification of clusters may make it possible to indirectly treat behaviors that are difficult to change.

The final area of generalization to consider is sibling generalization. The transfer of treatment effects from the target child's behavior to the behavior of siblings becomes an important issue in light of the fact that Arnold, Levine, and Patterson (1975) found no significant differences in rates of deviant behavior between siblings and identified problem children. Despite this, very few investigators have adequately evaluated changes in sibling behavior in response to behavioral parent training. Recently, Laviguer, Peterson, Sheese, and Peterson (1973) found sibling behavior changed in the desired direction. Siblings can show a significant reduction in rates of deviant behavior even when they are not involved in the treatment program, and this reduction is not significantly less than that found in siblings who are included in the intervention (Arnold et al., 1975). At least in some cases, parents are able to generalize the behavioral skills learned in parent training to the behavior of children other than the targeted child (Humphreys et al., 1977)

In conclusion, there is an obvious need for researchers and clinicians to take a much more careful look at the generalization of treatment effects in the above three areas before any definitive statements can be made. Overall, the literature leads to the conclusion that the transfer of treatment effects must be programmed rather than expected (Stokes and Baer, 1977). The identification of specific training methods which facilitate generalization is just beginning.

In addition, it must be assumed that many nontraining variables such as family structure and individual characteristics of family members affect the generalization of parent training results and are therefore worthy of investigation.

The question of whether or not therapeutic changes are maintained after treatment has always been a major problem for all types of therapy. In the case of behavioral parent training, the data on this are encouraging but incomplete. The evidence is fairly strong for the maintenance of change in highly discrete behaviors (e.g., enuresis) where problems of definition and observation of outcome are minimized. A factor which may contribute to the long-term success with many of these behaviors is the fact that once the parents carry out a brief intervention program, the persistence of change in the child no longer depends upon parental behavior change. In contrast, most cases of complex deviant behavior syndromes require parents to make significant and long-lasting changes in their interactions with their children. Recently, Patterson and Fleischman (1979) reviewed the results of eight major research projects studying parent training as a treatment tactic for these "out-of-control" youngsters. They found that several social learning-based family intervention programs demonstrated successful treatment, with gains being maintained at follow-up periods of up to 18 months (Patterson and Fleischman, 1979; Wahler, Leske, and Rogers, 1976). They noted that similar programs which have failed to produce change at termination and follow-up (e.g., Eyberg & Johnson, 1974; Ferber et al., 1974; Johnson and Christensen, 1975) have all involved time limited treatment (maximum of 12 weeks) and graduate student therapists, whereas the successful programs offered open-ended treatment by experienced parent trainers. They also summarized four studies which compared behavioral parent training to waiting list controls (Martin, 1977), child guidance clinic treatment (Christophersen, Barnard, Ford, and Wolf, 1976), juvenile court services (Christophersen, 1976), and client-centered and eclectic treatment (Alexander and Parsons, 1973).[14] In all cases the

---

[14]*Editors' Note*. This is misleading since the behavioral treatment studied by Alexander and Parsons is *not* accurately characterized as behavioral parent training (cf. Stanton, Chapter 10, and Barton and Alexander, Chapter 11).

social learning approaches were superior at six-, 12- or 18-month follow-up.

A major procedure used to increase the maintenance of treatment effects has been the provision of "booster shots" (Patterson, 1974) or "refresher courses" (Wahler, 1975) during the post-termination follow-up period. Patterson (1974) reported that half the families in his sample required additional treatment because they began to return to old behavior patterns during the first six months following termination. To date, there have not been any investigations comparing parents who receive additional training to those who do not. Another technique which has been used to increase the persistence of treatment gains has been the training of parents to verbally support one another's use of their newly learned child management skills (Kelly, Embry, and Baer, 1977). A common belief is that newly acquired parent behaviors will be maintained if they are reinforced in the natural environment.

The scientific rigor applied to evaluating the effectiveness of behavioral parent training has surpassed that for evaluating other therapies. Nevertheless, one area which has not received a great deal of attention is the rate at which parents drop out of treatment. Failure to consider attrition can lead to overestimates of therapeutic success. In perhaps the most comprehensive evaluation of behavioral parent training, Patterson (1974) provides data which indicate the successful treatment of 27 conduct disorder boys. This study allows for a rare examination of attrition. A total of 35 families were referred for treatment. Of these, eight dropped out after baseline data were collected but before treatment began. An additional six families terminated before treatment was completed. This results in a surprisingly high dropout rate of 40%! This figure is much greater than what we have experienced in clinical practice. Obviously, more research is needed to identify parents predisposed to prematurely terminating therapy. In a critique of Patterson's work, Kent (1976) pointed out that those children whose parents did not drop out where significantly less deviant than those children whose parents did drop out.

In the overall evaluation of behavioral parent training as a psychotherapeutic approach, we can conclude that it is an effective intervention for discrete, well specified behavior problems. In cases of more complex deviant behavior syndromes, the research is encouraging but not conclusive. Several parent training programs have reported that some of these very difficult families have met the criteria for success at one-year follow-up. On the other hand, Patterson's group (Patterson and Fleischman, 1979) has found that "Many of them require over 100 hours of treatment, and even then are a dubious success" (p. 172). Wahler et al. (1976) reported lower-class, father-absent ghetto families of children who steal and are truant may simply not show persistent follow-up effects. This underscores the importance of further research aimed at identifying client characteristics which predict success or failure with this treatment approach. Additional areas of major concern are the need for data over longer follow-up periods and the identification of those changes in family interactions during treatment which are related to long-term success.

TRAINING ISSUES

Just as behavioral parent training must focus on various characteristics of parents in need of training, attention must also be directed toward the persons actually training parents. The proper training of mental health professionals has been and continues to be a source of great debate. For a period of time, the issue of training in behavior therapy was also a topic of controversy. The controversy centered on the appropriateness of credentialing an individual to practice a certain form of therapy, in this case behavior therapy. Those in favor of some form of certification argued that as behavior therapy increases in popularity many therapists, improperly trained, will begin using the approach with their clients. The certificate would be viewed as a means of insuring quality control, and thereby protecting the consumer. Those who argued against certification pointed to the increased bureaucracy and suggested this type of control belongs to the professional organization (e.g., American Psychological Association for psychologists) to which the individual belongs. The issue with regards to behavior therapy appears to have been settled in favor of the latter position. Perhaps it is no mere coincidence that the nature of behavior therapy training is being discussed with greater frequency (e.g., Wisocki, 1978).

Training behavioral parent trainers is best viewed as within the mainstream of training in the more general area of behavior therapy. Most obvious is the need for the individual to be well grounded in learning theory and general experimental psychology. In addition to the areas of child psychology and psychopathology, the person specializing in behavioral parent training must be competent in the area of applied behavior analysis (Baer, Wolf, and Risley, 1968) and those interpersonal skills which distinguish the effective from the ineffective therapist. Among these skills and qualities are self-confidence, energy and warmth. In addition, the degree to which the parent trainer is able to create positive expectations is likely to contribute to parent behavior change.[15]

An approach to training behavioral parent trainers which incorporates modeling, shaping, feedback, and rehearsal has been used extensively by one of us (SBG). Predoctoral clinical psychology interns at the College of Medicine and Dentistry of New Jersey—Rutgers Medical School were given an opportunity to lead behavioral parent groups by first serving as an apprentice to the group leader. The apprentice was able to observe the manner in which the more experienced parent trainer led the large group, plus was responsible for helping a smaller group of parents actually apply the newly acquired behavioral skills. After participating in one such group, the intern assumed responsibility for independently leading the next group while meeting with the supervisor on a weekly basis. Feedback from the nearly dozen or so interns who have participated in this model of training over a five-year program has been very favorable. Currently, consideration is being given to certifying clinicians to serve as Program Directors in Responsive Parenting (Clark-Hall, M., personal communication).

Behavioral parent trainers have come from

the disciplines of psychology, social work, psychiatric nursing, psychiatry, and counseling. Recently, we have seen a shift toward the inclusion of nonprofessionals in the role as parent trainer. This development has the potential for addressing some important manpower issues, but with it comes the risk of potential iatrogenic failures. Quality control is the issue at hand regardless of the apparent qualifications of the parent trainer.

FUTURE DIRECTIONS

Very often, the concluding section of a behavior therapy chapter makes reference to the field being in transition from childhood to adolescence. This is meant to indicate that the foundations of the treatment approach have been established, but a great deal of uncertainty lies ahead. To continue with this metaphor, behavioral parent training has moved beyond adolescence and is clearly into early adulthood. This is not meant to imply that refinement is unnecessary or that all the significant questions have been answered (or asked for that matter), but rather, compared to other areas of application within behavior therapy, behavioral parent training represents perhaps our most advanced stage of development.

Several writers have cogently outlined numerous issues that must be addressed for behavioral parent training to become a more widely accepted and valid form of treatment (for more detail see Graziano, 1977; O'Dell, 1974, 1978). Among these issues are parent characteristics associated with successful delivery of services, social validation, behavioral norms, and mass distribution. Typically, parent trainers often exclude parents who are psychotic (Wiltz, 1969) and have poor marriages (Bernal, 1973). To conclude that behavioral parent training cannot be used with these types of parents implies that it is best suited for the more functional members of society. We are clearly at a stage where these cautionary notes should not become dogma. In our clinical practice we continue to be amazed at the large numbers of parents with dysfunctional relationships who are still able to derive benefit from parent training.

Further research is needed to best match the type of training program with parent character-

---

[15]*Editors' Note.* As the research of Alexander and his colleagues has shown (see Barton and Alexander, Chapter 11), the salience of these therapist interpersonal skills obtains in the practice of behavioral family therapy as much it does in nonbehavioral treatment (cf. Gurman and Kniskern, 1978a)

istics. Less reliance on verbal instruction and a greater emphasis on modeling and behavioral rehearsal may be needed with less intelligent parents. Parents with marital discord may be better served through individual consultations than by participating in a group. These and other decisions will continue to be made on the basis of clinical judgment until that time when sound research is able to provide more scientifically based guidelines.

The majority of behavioral parent training has been conducted within clinical, as opposed to educational, settings. Thus, most parents are offered this type of treatment at some point after they have entered a formal mental health system. Very often, the rationale for recommending behavioral parent training may have to do less with the efficacy of the model than with the composition of the staff, length of waiting list, availability for other more time-consuming therapies, etc. A cost-benefit analysis suggests that short-term behavioral parent training be made available for the majority of child cases seen within a clinical setting. A structure could be established in which a new parent group begins each month for approximately eight to ten weeks. Such a program, staffed by no more than two clinicians trained in this approach, has the potential for enabling a large portion of cases to exit the mental health system, as no further services would be necessary. For those families that fail to derive any benefit or are in need of other more time-consuming forms of treatment, an appropriate disposition could be made. Data on parent, child, and therapist characteristics would be collected so as to identify those variables which predict responsiveness to treatment. Such a research program would have the advantages of matching specific treatments to specific patients, as well as providing services to large numbers of parents with minimal wait.

Recently, increased attention has been focused on the so-called "softer" side of behavior therapy, i.e., subjective feelings of satisfaction with the treatment by the client and/or those purchasing such treatment. Perhaps this is a reflection of the increased national consciousness of consumerism. Behavioral parent trainers may be delighted with data that indicate an increase in compliance from 20% to 50%, or a decrease in tantrums from ten to five times a day, but a concern with social validation directs the assessment to consumer satisfaction as well as to more objective data. An emphasis on the parents' feelings about treatment may possibly result in some modifications in parent training, e.g., less reliance on operant jargon, alternatives to time-out, etc. Consumer satisfaction ratings may also be useful in evaluating unique and at times controversial elements.

An area in need of additional research is the establishment of behavioral norms for both parents and children. Very often parents (and therapists) have unrealistic expectations regarding the goals for treatment. Failure to establish clear goals often results in the "changing goal" phenomenon in which the parent initially states a goal, but with the attainment of the goal expresses dissatisfaction and proceeds to "up the ante." This is best illustrated by a mother who indicates that a successful outcome would be attained when her child is able to increase compliance from 20% to 40%. With the attainment of 40%, however, she expresses that she is not really pleased but instead requires 60%. This frustrating cycle is minimized with knowledge of behavioral norms. Knowing that nonreferred children between the ages of four and six comply to 60% of parental requests allows the clinician to better inform the parent as to the establishment of realistic goals.

Behavioral norms, although helpful, will still not answer the question of "when does a difference make a difference?" The objective data regarding behavioral frequencies will need to be combined with subjective data regarding parental perceptions, attitudes, etc. It is still a mystery as to why one child with a behavioral pattern is referred by parents whereas another child with the similar pattern is not referred. This is an area in need of basic research akin to that within developmental psychology.

The progression in the development of child behavior therapy has been from the most disturbed children (autistic, retarded, schizophrenic) to the lesser disturbed children (enuretics, oppositional) to nondisturbed, normal children. It is, therefore, not surprising to consider that behavioral parent training is also developing in similar fashion. The first attempts to train parents to be behavior therapists occurred within clinical settings. More recently, large-scale parent training are being conducted within educational settings, very often prior to a referral to a mental health clinic. The growth of nonprescription therapies in which parents use written materials, i.e., pamphlets, books, etc., has been well documented (Rosen, 1976). Such materials for parents have been developed, ranging from general social learning primers on child management to workbooks for specific problems such as fighting. The most obvious risk in the development of such materials is the failure to establish an empirical basis to justify widespread dissemination. The dissemination of the concepts and techniques of behavioral parent training need not be restricted to the printed form. Developing technology allows for this vital information to be transmitted to multitudes of parents through audiotapes and videotapes.

The potential for widespread distribution of information related to behavioral parent training raises the issue of preventive mental health. Normal everyday problems of childhood can be successfully dealt with by parents before they develop into more negative, coercive types of behavioral patterns. Ultimately, behavioral parent training needs to be made an elective part of the school curriculum. The educational system, being society's last formal link with every future parent, provides the correct soil for the growth of parenthood. Although there is still a need for more research, the clinical demands of dysfunctional families require behavioral parent training now. We cannot afford the luxury of waiting for more data before providing this form of treatment, nor should we apologize or assume a defensive posture when recommending parents for training in the application of behavior therapy.

REFERENCES

Albee, G.W. *Mental Health Manpower Trends*. New York: Basic Books, 1959.

Alexander, A.B., Chai, H., Creer, T.L., Miklich, D.R., Renne, C.M., & Cardoso, R.R. The elimination of chronic cough by response suppression shaping. *Journal of Behavior Therapy and Experimental Psychiatry*, 1973, *4*, 75–80.

Alexander, J.R. & Parsons, B.U. Short-term behavioral intervention with delinquent families: Impact on family process and recidivism. *Journal of Abnormal Psychology*, 1973, *81*, 219–225.

Allen, D., & Harris, F. Elimination of a child's excessive scratching by training the mother in reinforcement procedures. *Behavior Research and Therapy*, 1966, *4*, 79–84.

Arkell, R.N., Kubo, H.R., & Meunier, C.P. Readability and parental behavior modification literature. *Behavior Therapy*, 1976, *7*, 265–266.

Arnoff, F.N., Rubinstein, E.A., Shriver, B.M. & Jones, D.R. The mental health fields: An overview of manpower growth and development. In: F.M. Arnoff, E.A. Rubinstein, & J.C. Speisman (Eds.) *Manpower for Mental Health*. Chicago: Aldine, 1969.

Arnold, J.E., Levine, A.G. & Patterson, G.R. Changes in sibling behavior following family intervention. *Journal of Consulting and Clinical Psychology*, 1975, *43*, 683–688.

Atkeson, B.M. & Forehand, R. Parent Behavioral Training for Problem Children: An examination of studies using multiple outcome measures. *Journal of Abnormal Child Psychology*, 1978, *6*, 449–460.

Ayllon, T., Smith, D., & Rogers, M. Behavioral management of school phobia. *Journal of Behavior Therapy & Experimental Psychiatry*, 1970, *1*, 125–138.

Azrin, N.H. & Foxx, R.M. *Toilet Training in Less Than a Day*. New York: Simon and Schuster, 1974.

Baer, D.M., Wolf, M.M., & Risley, T.R. Some current dimensions of applied behavior analysis. *Journal of Applied Behavior Analysis*, 1968, *1*, 91–97.

Bailey, J.S., Wolf, M.M., & Phillips, E.L. Home-based reinforcement and the modification of predelinquents' classroom behavior. *Journal of Applied Behavior Analysis*, 1970, *3*, 223–233.

Barrett, B. Behavior modification in the home: Parents adapt laboratory-developed tactics to bowel-train a 5.5 year old. *Psychotherapy: Theory, Research and Practice*, 1969, *6*, 172–176.

Barton, E.S., Guess, D., Garcia, E. & Baer, D.M. Improvements of retardates' mealtime behaviors by timeout procedures using multiple baseline techniques. *Journal of Applied Behavior Analysis*, 1970, *3*, 77–84.

Becker, W.C. *Parents are teachers: A Child Management Program*. Champaign, Ill.: Research Press, 1971.

Becker, W.C. *Review Tests for Parents are Teachers: A Child Management Program*. Champaign, Ill.: Research Press Company, 1975.

Bentler, P.M. An infant's phobia treated with reciprocal inhibition therapy. *Journal of Child Psychology and Psychiatry*, 1962, *3*, 185–189.

Berkowitz, B.P., & Graziano, A.M. Training parents as behavior therapists: A review. *Behavior Research and Therapy*, 1972, *10*, 297–317.

Bernal, M.E. Behavioral feedback in the modification of brat behaviors. *Journal of Nervous and Mental Disorders*, 1969, *148*, 375–385.

Bernal, M.E., Duryee, J.S., Pruett, H.L., & Burns, B.J. Behavior modification and the brat syndrome. *Journal of Consulting & Clinical Psychology*, 1968, *32*, 447–455.

Bernal, M.E. *Preliminary report of a preventive intervention project*. Paper presented at the Rocky Mountain Psychological Association, Las Vegas, May, 1973.

Bernal, M.E., Williams, D.E., Miller, W.H., & Reagor, P.A. The use of videotape feedback and operant learning principles in training parents in management of deviant children. In R.D. Rubin, H. Festerheim, J.D. Henderson, & L.P. Ullmann (Eds.), *Advances in Behavior Therapy*. New York: Academic Press, 1972.

Browning, R.M. Treatment effects of a total behavior modification program with five autistic children. *Behavior*

Research and Therapy, 1971, *9*, 319–327.

Budd, K., Inkston, E.M., & Green, D.R. *An analysis of two parent-training packages for remediation of child aggression in laboratory and home settings*. Paper presented at the 81st Annual Convention of the American Psychological Association, Montreal, August, 1973.

Butler, J.F. The toilet training success of parents after reading *Toilet Training in Less Than a Day*. *Behavior Therapy*, 1976, *7*, 185–191.

Christophersen, E.R., Arnold, C.M., Hill, D.W., & Quilitch, H.R. The home point system: Token reinforcement procedures for application by parents of children with behavior problems. *Journal of Applied Behavior Analysis*, 1972, *5*, 485–497.

Christophersen, E.R., Barnard, J., Ford, D., & Wolf, M. The family training program: Improving Parent/Child interaction patterns. In L.A. Hamerlynck, L.C. Handy, & E.J. Mash (Eds). *Behavioral Modification and Families*. New York: Brunner/Mazel, 1976.

Christophersen, E.R. *Outcome for parent training in families of delinquent children*. Paper presented at the meeting of the Association for the Advancement of Behavior Therapy, New York, 1976.

Clark, H.B., Greene, B.F., Macrae, J.W., McNees, M.P., Davis, J.L., & Risley, T.R. A Parent Advice Package for Family Shopping Trips: Development and Evaluation. *Journal of Applied Behavior Analysis*, 1977, *10*, 605–624.

Clark-Hall, M. *Responsive Parent Program*. Lawrence: H & H Enterprises, 1978.

Colletti, G., & Harris, S.L. Behavior modification in the home: Siblings as behavior modifiers. *Journal of Abnormal Child Psychology*, 1977, *5*, 21–30.

Cone, J.D., & Sloop, E.W. Parents as agents of change. In: W.W. Spradlin & A. Jacobs (Eds.) *The Group as Agent of Change*. New York: Behavioral Publications, 1974.

Conway, J.B., & Bucher, B.D. Transfer and maintenance of behavior change in children: A review and suggestions. In: E.J. Mash, L.C. Handy, & L.A. Hamerlynck (Eds.) *Behavior Modification and Families*. New York: Brunner/Mazel, 1976, 119–159.

Conger, J.C. The treatment of encopresis by the management of social consequences. *Behavior Therpay*, 1970, *1*, 386–390.

Davidson, N.P., & Siegel, L.J. Positive Oriented Parenting Video Tape, University of Missouri-Columbia, 1977.

DeLeon, G., & Mandell, W. A comparison of conditioning and psychotherapy in the treatment of functional enuresis. *Journal of Clinical Psychology*, 1966, *22*, 326–330.

DeLeon, G., & Sacks, S. Conditioning functional enuresis: A four-year follow-up. *Journal of Consulting and Clinical Psychology*, 1972, *39*, 299–300.

Delfini, L.F., Bernal, M.E., & Rosen, P.M. Comparison of deviant and normal boys in home settings. In: E.J. Mash, L.A. Hamerlynck, & L.C. Handy (Eds.), *Behavioral Modification and Families*. New York: Brunner/Mazel, 1976.

Dubey, D.R., & Kaufman, D.F. *Teaching behavior management skills to parents: The group approach*. Paper presented at the 85th Annual Convention of the American Psychological Association, San Francisco, August, 1977.

Dunlap, G., Egel, A., Killion, J., Koegel, R., Mills, J., & Schreibman, L. *Parent training versus clinic treatment: Impact on family and child*. Paper presented at the meeting of the Association for the Advancement of Behavior Therapy, Chicago, November, 1978.

Eastman, A.M., & Ingersoll, B.D. *The effectiveness of an innovative parent training program: Exercises in successful parenting*. Paper presented at the meeting of the Association for the Advancement of Behavior Therapy, Chicago, November, 1978.

Edelman, R.I. Operant conditioning treatment of encopresis. *Journal of Behavior Therapy & Experimental Psychiatry*, 1971, *2*, 71–73.

Embry, L.H., Kelly, M.L., Jackson, E., & Baer, D.M. *Group Parent Training: An analysis of generalization from classroom to home*. Research Brief: Kansas Research Institute, 1979.

Eyberg, S.M., & Johnson, S.M. Multiple assessment of behavior modification with families: Effects of contingency contracting and order of treated problems. *Journal of Consulting and Clinical Psychology*, 1974, *42*, 594–606.

Ferber, H., Keeley, S.M., & Shemberg, K.M. Training parents in behavior modification: Outcome of and problems encountered in a program after Patterson's work. *Behavior Therapy*, 1974, *5*, 415–419.

Flanagan, S., Adams, H.E., & Forehand, R. A comparison of four instructional techniques for teaching partents the use of Time Out. *Behavior Therapy*, 1979, *10*, 94–102.

Forehand, R. Child noncompliance to parental requests: Behavioral Analysis and treatment. In: M. Hersen, R.M. Eisler & P.M. Miller (Eds.) *Progress in Behavior Modification*. New York: Academic Press, 1977.

Forehand, R., & Atkeson, B.M. Generality of treatment effects with parents as therapists: A review of assessment and implementation procedures. *Behavior Therapy*, 1977, *8*, 575–593.

Forehand, R., & King, H.E. Noncompliant children: Effects of parent training on behavior and attitude change. *Behavior Modification*, 1977, *1*, 93–108.

Forehand, R., & MacDonough, T.S. Response contingent time out: An examination of outcome data. *European Journal of Behavioural Analysis and Modification*, 1975, *1*, 109–115.

Forehand, R., Peed, S., & Roberts, M. *Coding manual for scoring mother-child interactions*. Unpublished manuscript, University of Georgia, 1975.

Forehand, R., King, H.E., Peed, S., & Yoder, P. Mother-child interactions: Comparisons of a noncompliant clinic group and a non-clinic group. *Behaviour Research and Therapy*, 1975, *13*, 79–84.

Forehand, R., Roberts, M.W., Doleys, D.M., Hobbs, S.A., & Resick, P.A. An examination of disciplinary procedures with children. *Journal of Experimental Child Psychology*, 1976, *21*, 109–120.

Forehand, R., & Scarboro, ME. An analysis of children's oppositional behavior. *Journal of Abnormal Child Psychology*, 1975, *3*, 27–31.

Forehand, R., Sturgis, E.T., McMahon, R.J., Aguar, D., Green, K., Wells, K.C., Breiner, J. Parent behavioral training to modify child noncompliance: treatment generalization across time and from home to school. *Behavior Modification*, 1979, *3*, 3–25.

Foxx, R.M., & Azrin, N.H. Dry pants: A rapid method of toilet training children. *Behaviour Research and Therapy*, 1973, *11*, 435–442.

Framo, J.L. Personal reflections of a family therapist. *Journal of Marriage and Family Counseling*, 1975, *1*, 15–28.

Gardner, H.L., Forehand, R., & Roberts, M. Timeout with children: Effects of an explanation and brief parent training on child and parent behaviors. *Journal of Abnormal Child Psychology*, 1976, *4*, 277–288.

Gardner, J.M. Teaching behavior modification to nonprofessionals. *Journal of Applied Behavior Analysis*, 1972, *5*, 517–521.

Gardner, J.M. Behavior modification in mental retardation: A review of research and analysis of trends. In: R.D. Rubin, H. Fensterheim, A.A. Lazarus, & C.M. Franks, (Eds.) *Advances in Behavior Therapy*. New York: Academic Press, 1971.

Gardner, W.I. Behavior therapy treatment approach to a psychogenic seizure case: *Journal of Consulting Psychology*, 1967, 3, 209–212.

Gelfand, D.M., & Hartmann, D.P. Behavior with children: A review and evaluation of research methodology. *Psychological Bulletin*, 1968, 69, 204–215.

Gillick, S. *Training mothers as therapists in treatment of childhood obesity*. Unpublished doctoral dissertation, State University of New York at Buffalo, 1974.

Glogower, F., & Sloop, E.W. Two strategies of group training of parents as effective behavior modifiers. *Behavior Therpay*, 1976, 7, 177–184.

Goldfried, M.R., & Davison, G.C. *Clinical Behavior Therapy*. New York: Holt, Rinehart, & Winston, 1976.

Gordon, S.B. Multiple assessment of behavior modification with families. *Journal of Consulting and Clinical Psychology*, 1975, 43, 917.

Gordon, S.B., Lerner, L.L., & Keefe, F.J. Responsive Parenting: An approach to training parents of problem children. *American Journal of Community Psychology*, 1979, 7, 45–56.

Grace, D. *Self-monitoring in the modification of obesity in children*. Unpublished doctoral dissertation, State University of New York at Buffalo, 1975.

Graziano, A.M. (Ed.) *Behavior Therapy with Children*. Chicago: Aldine, 1971.

Graziano, A.M. *Child Without Tomorrow*. New York: Pergamon, 1974.

Graziano, A.M. *Behavior Therapy with Children*. Chicago: Aldine, 1975.

Graziano, A.M. Parents as Behavior Therapists. In: M. Hersen, R.M. Eisler, & P.M. Miller (eds.) *Progress in Behavior Modification*. New York: Academic Press, 1977.

Graziano, A.M., & DeGiovanni, I.S. The clinical significance of childhood phobias: a note on the proportion of child-clinical referals for the treatment of children's fears. *Behavior Research & Therapy*, 1979, 17, 161–162.

Graziano, A.M., DeGiovanni, I.S. & Garcia, K.A. Behavioral treatment of children's fears: A review. Psychological Bulletin, 1979, 86, 804–830.

Green, D.R., Budd, K., Johnson, M., Lang, S., Pinkston, E., & Rudd, S. Training parents to modify problem child behaviors. In E.J. Mash, L.C. Handy, & L.A. Hamerlynck (Eds.) *Behavioral Modification Approaches to Parenting*. New York: Brunner/Mazel, 1976.

Haley, J. *Problem Solving Therapy*. San Francisco: Jossey-Bass, 1976.

Hall, R.V. *Managing Behavior*. Lawrence, Ks.: H & H Enterprises, 1971.

Hall, R.V., Axelrod, S., Tyler, L., Grief, E., Jones, F.C., & Robertson, R. Modification of behavior problems in the home with a parent as observer and experimenter. *Journal of Applied Behavior Analysis*, 1972, 5, 53–64.

Hall, M.C., Grinstead, J., Collier, H., & Hall, R.V. *Responsive Parenting: A preventative program which incorporates parents training parents*. Paper presented at the meeting of the Association for the Advancement of Behavior Therapy, Chicago, Ill., December, 1978.

Hanson, R. *Time Out: A Way to Help Children Behave Better*. Detroit, Mi.: Informatics. 1969.

Hawkins, R.P. It's time we taught the young how to be good parents (and don't we wish we'd started a long time ago?) *Psychology Today*, 1972, 6, 28.

Hawkins, R.P., Peterson, R.F., Schweid, E., & Bijou, S.W. Behavior therapy in the home: Amelioration of problem parent-child relations with a parent in the therapeutic role. *Journal of Experimental Child Psychology*, 1966, 4, 99–107.

Herbert, E.W., & Baer, D.M. Training parents as behavior modifiers: Self-recording contingent attention. *Journal of Applied Behavior Analysis*, 1972, 5, 139–149.

Herbert, E. W., Pinkston, E.M., Hayden, M.L., Sajwaj, T.E., Pinkston, S., Cordua, G., & Jackson, D. Adverse effects of differential parental attention. *Journal of Applied Behavior Analysis*, 1973, 6, 15–30.

Hersen, M. Treatment of a compulsive and phobic disorder through a total behavior therapy program: A case study. *Psychotherapy: Theory, Research and Practice*, 1968, 5, 220–225.

Hersen, M. Behavior modification approach to a school phobia case, *Journal of Clinical Psychology*, 1970, 26, 128–132.

Hersen, M. The behavioral treatment of school phobia. *Journal of Nervous and Mental Disease*, 1971, 153, 99–107.

Hewett, F.M. Teaching speech to autistic children through operant conditioning. *American Journal of Orthopsychiatry*, 1965, 35, 927–936.

Hirsch, I., & Walder, L. *Training mothers in groups as reinforcement therapists for their own children*. Paper presented at the 77th Annual Convention of the American Psychological Association, 1969.

Hobbs, S.A., & Forehand, R. Effects of differential release from time-out on children's deviant behavior. *Journal of Behavior Therapy and Experimental Psychiatry*, 1975, 6, 256–257.

Hobbs, S.A. & Forehand, R. Important parameters in the use of timeout with children: a reexamination. *Journal of Behaviour Therapy and Experimental Psychiatry*, 1977, 8, 365–370.

Hobbs, S.A., Forehand, R., & Murray, R.G. Effects of various durations of timeout on the non-compliant behavior of children. *Behavior Therapy*, 1978, 9, 652–656.

Humphreys, L., Forehand, R., Green, K., McMahon, R., & Roberts, M. *Generality of treatment effects resulting from a parent-training program to modify child non-compliance*. Paper presented at the meeting of the Association for the Advancement of Behavior Therapy, Atlanta, December, 1977.

Johnson, C.A., & Katz, C. Using parents as charge agents for their children: A review. *Journal of Child Psychology and Psychiatry*, 1973, 14, 131–200.

Johnson, M.R. & Green, D.R. The effectiveness and durability of written instructions on parental modification of undesirable behavior in children. *Journal of Applied Behavior Analysis*, in press.

Johnson, S.M., & Bolstad, O.D. Methodological issues in naturalistic observations: Some problems and solutions for field research. In: L.A. Hamerlynck, L.C. Handy, and E.J. Mash (Eds.) *Behavior Change: Methodology, Concepts and Practice*. Champaign, Ill.: Research Press, 1973.

Johnson, S.M., Bolstad, O.D., & Lobitz, G. K. Generalization and contrast phenomena in behavior modification with children. In: E.J. Mash, L.A. Hamerlynck, & L.C. Handy (Eds.), *Behavior Modification and Families*. New York: Brunner/Mazel, 1976.

Johnson, S.M. & Brown, R.A. Producing behavior change in parents of disturbed children. *Journal of Child Psychology and Psychiatry*, 1969, 10, 107–121.

Johnson, S.M. & Christensen, A. Multiple criteria follow-up of behavior modification with families. *Journal of*

Abnormal Child Psychology, 1975, *3*, 135–154.

Johnson, S.M., & Lobitz, G.K. Parental manipulation of child behavior in home observations. *Journal of Applied Behavior Analysis*, 1974, *7*, 23–31.

Karoly, P., & Rosenthal, M. Training Parents in behavior modification: Effects on perceptions of family interaction and deviant behavior. *Behavior Therapy*, 1977, *8*, 406–410.

Keefe, F.J., Kopel, S.A., & Gordon, S.B. *A Practical Guide to Behavioral Assessment*. New York: Springer, 1978.

Kelly, M.L., Embry, L.H., & Baer, D.M. *Training parents in child management skills and mutual support for maintenance*. Paper presented at the meeting of the Association for the Advancement of Behavior Therapy, Atlanta, December, 1977.

Kendall, P.C., Nay, W.R., & Jeffers, J. Timeout duration and contrast effects: A systematic evaluation of a successive treatment design. *Behavior Therapy*, 1976, *7*, 609–615.

Kennedy, W.A. School phobia: Rapid treatment of fifty cases. *Journal of Abnormal and Social Psychology*, 1965, *70*, 285–289.

Kent, R. A methodological critique of "Interventions for Boys with Conduct Problems". *Journal of Consulting and Clinical Psychology*, 1976, *44*, 297–302.

Koegel, R.L., Glahn, T.J., & Nieminen, G.S. Generalization of Parent-training results. *Journal of Applied Behavior Analysis*, 1978, *11*, 95–109.

Lal, H., & Lindsley, O.R. Therapy of chronic constipation in a young child by rearranging social contingencies. *Behavior and Therapy*, 1968, *6*, 484–485.

Lasser, B.R. Teaching mothers of mongoloid children to use behavior modification procedures, *Dissertation Abstracts*, 1970, *30*, 5239A–5340A.

Lavigueur, H. The use of siblings as an adjunct to the behavioral treatment of children in the home with parents as therapists. *Behavior Therapy*, 1976, *7*, 602–613.

Lavigueur, H., Peterson, R.F., Sheese, J.G., & Peterson, L.W. Behavioral treatment in the home: Effects on an untreated sibling and long-term follow-up. *Behavior Therapy*, 1973, *4*, 431–441.

Lazarus, A.A. *Behavior Therapy and Beyond*, New York: McGraw-Hill, 1971.

Lehrer, P.M., Gordon, S.B., & Leiblum, S. *Parent groups in behavior modification: Training or therapy*. Paper presented at the 81st Annual Convention of the American Psychological Association, Montreal, August, 1973.

Leitenberg, H., Burchard, J.D., Burchard, S.N., Fuller, E. J., & Lysaght, T.V., Using positive reinforcement to suppress behavior: Some experimental comparisons with sibling conflict. *Behavior Therapy*, 1977, *8*, 168–182.

Levitt, E.E. The results of psychotherapy with children: An evaluation. *Journal of Consulting Psychology*, 1957, *21*, 189–196.

Levitt, E.E. Psychotherapy with children: A further evaluation. *Behaviour Research and Therapy*, 1963, *1*, 45–51.

Lobitz, G.K., & Johnson, S.M. Normal versus deviant children: A multimethod comparison. *Journal of Abnormal Child Psychology*, 1975, *3*, 353–374.

Locke, H.J., & Wallace, K.M. Short marital-adjustment and prediction tests: Their reliability and validity. *Journal of Marriage and Family Living*, 1959, *21*, 251–255.

Lovaas, O.I., Freitag, G., Gold, V.J., & Kassorla, I.C. Recording apparatus and procedure for observation of behaviors of children in free play settings. *Journal of Experimental Child Psychology*, 1965, *2*, 108–120.

Lovaas, I.I., Koegel, R., Simmons, J.Q., & Long, J.S. Some

generalizations and follow-up measures on autistic children in behavior therapy. *Journal of Applied Behavior Analysis*, 1973, *6*, 131–166.

Madsen, C.H. Positive reinforcement in toilet training of a normal child: A case report. In: L.P. Ullmann & L. Krasner (Eds.) *Case Studies in Behavior Modification*, New York: Holt, 1965.

Mager, R.F. *Who Did What To Whom?* Champaign, Il.: Research Press, 1972.

Mahoney, M.J. *Cognition and Behavior Modification*. Cambridge: Ballinger, 1974.

Martin, B. Brief family intervention: effectiveness and the importance of including father. *Journal of Consulting and Clinical Psychology*, 1977, *45*, 1002–1010.

Mash, E.J., Lazere, R., Terdal, L., & Garner, A. Modification of mother-child interactions: A modeling approach for groups. *Child Study Journal* 1973, *3*, 131–143.

Mash, E.J., & Terdal, L. Modification of mother-child interactions: Playing with children. *Mental Retardation*, 1973, *11*, 44–49.

Matefy, R.E., Solanch, L., & Humphrey, E. Behavior modification in the home with students as co-therapists. *American Journal of Psychotherapy*, 1975. *29*, 212–223.

Matson, J.L., & Ollendeck, T.H. Issues in toilet training in normal children. *Behavior Therapy*, 1977, *8*, 549–553.

McMahon, R.J., & Forehand, R. Nonprescription behavior Therapy: Effectiveness of a brochure in teaching mothers to correct their children's inappropriate mealtime behavior. *Behavior Therapy*, 1978, *9*, 814–820.

Meichenbaum, D.H. *Cognition and Behavior Modification: An Integrative Approach*. New York: Plenum, 1977.

Miller, L. *Louisville Behavior Checklist*. Western Psychological Services, Los Angeles, 1979.

Miller, S.J., & Sloane, H.N. The generalization effects of parent training across stimulus settings. *Journal of Applied Behavior Analysis*, 1976, *9*, 355–370.

Miller, W.H. *Systematic Parent Training*. Champaign, Ill.: Research Press, 1975.

Mindell, C., & Budd, K.S. *Issues in the generalization of parent training across settings*. Paper presented at the 85th Annual Convention of the American Psychological Association, San Francisco, September, 1977.

Mira, M. Results of a behavior modification training program for parents and teachers. *Behaviour Research and Therapy*, 1970, *8*, 309–11.

Nay, W.R. A systematic comparison of instructional techniques for parents. *Behavior Therapy*, 1975, *6*, 14–21.

Neisworth, J.T., & Moore, F. Operant treatment of asthmatic responding with the parent as therapist. *Behavior Therapy*, 1972, *3*, 95–99.

Nidiffer, F.D., O'Dell, S.L., & Pritchard, D.A. *Minimizing setting discrimination as a strategy for increasing setting generalization of parent training*. Paper presented at the meeting of the Association for the Advancement of Behavior Therapy, Chicago, November, 1978.

Nolan, D.J., & Pence, C. Operant conditioning principles in the treatment of selectively mute child. *Journal of Consulting and Clinical Psychology*, 1970, *35*, 265–268.

Nordquist, V.M., & Wahler, R.G. Naturalistic treatment of an autistic child. *Journal of Applied Behavior Analysis*, 1973, *6*, 79–87.

O'Dell, S. Training parents in behavior modification: A review. *Psychological Bulletin*, 1974, *81*, 418–433.

O'Dell, S.L. *A comparison and evaluation of methods for producing behavior change in parents*. Paper presented at the Association for the Advancement of Behavior Therapy, Chicago, November, 1978.

O'Dell, S.L., Flynn, J.M., & Benlolo, L. A comparison of

parent training techniques in child behavior modification. *Journal of Behavior Therapy and Experimental Psychiatry*, 1977, *8*, 261–268.

O'Dell, S.L., Krug, W.W., Patterson, J., Faustman, W., & O'Quinn, J.A. *A comparison of alternate methods for teaching time-out skills to parents*. Unpublished manuscript, University of Mississippi, 1978.

O'Dell, S.L., Mahoney, N., Horton, W., & Turner, P. Media-assisted parent training: Alternative models. *Behavior Therapy*, 1979, *10*, 103–110.

O'Dell, S.L., Tarler-Benlolo, L., & Flynn, J.M. An instrument to measure knowledge of behavioral principles as applied to children. *Journal of Behavior Therapy and Experimental Psychiatry*, 1979, *10*, 29–34.

O'Leary, K.D., O'Leary, S., & Becker, W.C. Modification of a deviant sibling interaction pattern in the home. *Behaviour Research and Therapy*, 1967, *5*, 113–120.

Oltmanns, T.F., Broderick, J.E., & O'Leary, K.D. Marital adjustment and the efficacy of behavior therapy with children. *Journal of Consulting and Clinical Psychology*, 1977, *45*, 724–729.

Paschalis, A.P., Kimmel, H.D., & Kimmel, E. Further study of diurnal instrumental conditioning in the treatment of enuresis nocturna. *Journal of Behavior Therapy and Experimental Psychiatry*, 1972, *3*, 253–256.

Patterson, G.R. A learning theory approach to the treatment of the school phobia child. In L.P. Ullmann & I. Krasner, (Eds.) *Case Studies in Behavior Modification*. New York: Holt, 1965.

Patterson, G.R. *Families: Applications of Social Learning to Family Life*. Champaign, Ill.: Research Press, 1971.

Patterson, G.R. Interventions for boys with conduct problems: Multiple settings, treatments, and criteria. *Journal of Consulting and Clinical Psychology*, 1974, *42*, 471–481.

Patterson, G.R. *Professional Guide for Families and Living with Children*. Champaign, Ill.: Research Press, 1975.

Patterson, G.R. & Brodsky, G. A behaviour modification programme for a child with multiple problem behaviours. *Journal of Child Psychology and Psychiatry*, 1966, *7*, 277–95.

Patterson, G.R., Cobb, J.A.., & Ray, R.S. A social engineering technology for retraining the families of aggressive boys. In: H.E. Adams & I.P. Unikel (Eds.), *Issues and Trends in Behavior Therapy*. Springfield, Ill.: Charles C Thomas, 1972.

Patterson, G.R., & Fleischman, M.J. Maintenance of treatment effects: Some considerations concerning family systems and follow-up data. *Behavior Therapy*, 1979, *10*, 168–185.

Patterson, G.R., & Forgatch, M.S. *Family Living Series*. Champaign, Ill.: Research Press, 1975.

Patterson, G.R., & Guillion, M.E. *Living with Children: New Methods for Parents and Teachers*. Champaign, Ill.: Research Press, 1968.

Patterson, G.R., McNeal, N., Hawkins, N., & Phelps, R. Reprogramming the social environment. *Journal of Child Psychology and Psychiatry*, 1967, *8*, 181–195.

Patterson, G.R., & Reid, J. Reciprocity and coercion: Two facets of social systems. In: Neuringer, C., & Michael, J. (Eds.) *Behavior Modification in Clinical Psychology*, New York: Appleton-Century-Crofts, 1970.

Patterson, G.R., Reid, J.B., Jones, R.R., & Conger, R.E. A social learning approach to family intervention. *Families with Aggressive Children*. Eugene, Oregon: Castalia Publishing Company, 1975.

Paul, G.L. Behavior modification research: Design and tactics. In: C.M. Franks (Ed.) *Behavior Therapy: Appraisal and Status*. New York: McGraw-Hill, 1969.

Peed, S., Roberts, M., & Forehand, R. Evaluation of the effectiveness of a standardized parent training program in altering the interaction of mothers and their noncompliant children. *Behavior Modification*, 1977, *1*, 323–350.

Peine, H.A. The elimination of a child's self injurious behavior at home and school. *School Application of Learning Theory*, 1972, *4*, 12–16.

Pendergrass, V.E. Effects of length of timeout from positive reinforcement and schedule of application in suppression of aggressive behavior, *Psychological Record*, 1971, *21*, 75–80.

Pumroy, D.K., & Pumroy, S. S. Systematic observation and reinforcement technique in toilet training. *Psychological Reports*, 1965, *16*, 467–471.

Reisinger, J.J., Frangia, G.W., Hoffman, E. H. Toddler Management training: Generalization and marital status. *Journal of Behavior Therapy and Experimental Psychiatry*. 1976, 7, 335–340.

Reisinger, J.J. & Ora, J.P. Parent-child clinic and home interaction during toddler management training. *Behavior Therapy*, 1977, *8*, 771–786.

Resick, P.A., Forehand, R., & McWhorter, A. The effect of parent treatment with one child on an untreated sibling. *Behavior Therapy*, 1976, *7*, 544–548.

Rinn, R.C., Vernon, J.C. & Wise, M.J. Training parents of behavior-disordered children in groups: A three year's program evaluation. *Behavior Therapy*, 1975, *6*, 378–387.

Risley, T.R. The effects and side effects of punishing the autistic behaviors of a deviant child. *Journal of Applied Behavior Analysis*, 1968, *1*, 21–34.

Risley, T.R., & Wolf, M.M. Experimental manipulation of autistic behaviors and generalization in to the home. In R. Ulrich, T. Stachnick, & J. Mabry (Eds.) *Control of Human Behavior*. Glenview, Ill.: Scott, Foresman, 1966.

Rose, S.D. A behavioural approach to the group treatment of parents. *Social Work*, 1969, *14*, 12–29.

Rose, S.D. Training parents in groups as behavior modifiers of their mentally retarded children. *Journal of Behavior Therapy and Experimental Psychiatry*, 1974, *5*, 135–140.

Rosen, G.M. The development and use of nonprescription therapies. *American Psychologist*, 1976, *31*, 139–141.

Ross, J.A. Parents modify thumbsucking: A case study. *Journal of Behaviour Therapy and Experimental Psychiatry* 1975, *6*, 248–249.

Russo, S. Adaptations in behavioral therapy with children. *Behaviour Research and Therapy*, 1964, *2*, 43–47.

Sachs, D.A. The efficacy of time-out procedures in a variety of behavior problems. *Journal of Behaviour Therapy and Experimental Psychiatry*. 1973, *4*, 237–242.

Sacks, S., & DeLeon, G. Conditioning two types of enuretics. *Behaviour Research and Therapy*, 1973, *11*, 653–659.

Salzinger, K., Feldman, R.S., & Portnoy, S. Training parents of brain-injured children in the use of operant conditioning procedures. *Behavior Therapy*, 1970, *1*, 14–32.

Scarboro, M.E., & Forehand, R. Effects of two types of response-contingent time-out on compliance and oppositional behavior of children. *Journal of Experimental Child Psychology*, 1975, *19*, 252–264.

Siegel, L.J., & Davidson, N.P. *Partially automated training in child behavior management: Problems and promises*. Paper presented at the meeting of the Association for the Advancement of Behavior Therapy, Chicago, November, 1978.

Siegel, L.J. & Richards, C.S. Behavioral intervention with somatic disorders in children. In: D. Marholin (Ed.), *Child Behavior Therapy*. New York: Gardner Press, 1978.

Spitalnik, R. & Drabman, R. A classroom time out procedure for retarded children. *Journal of Behavior Therapy and Experimental Psychiatry*. 1976, 7, 17–21.

Stokes, T., & Baer, D. An implicit technology of generalization. *Journal of Applied Behavior Analysis*, 1977, 10, 349–367.

Tahmisian, J. A. & McReynolds, W. T. Use of parents as behavioral engineers in the treatment of a school-phobia girl. *Journal of Consulting and Clinical Psychology*, 1971, 18, 225–228.

Tasto, D.L. Systematic desensitization, muscle relaxation and visual imagery in the counter conditioning of a four-year old phobic child. *Behaviour Research and Therapy*, 1969, 7, 409–411.

Tavormina, J.B. Basic models of parent counseling: A review. *Psychological Bulletin*, 1974, 81, 827, 835.

Tavormina, J.B. Relative effectiveness of behavioral and reflective group counseling with parents of mentally retarded children. *Journal of Consulting and Clinical Psychology*, 1975, 43, 22–31.

Tharp, R.G. & Wetzel, R.J. *Behavior Modification in the Natural Environment*. New York: Academic Press, 1969.

Wahler, R.G. Some structural aspects of deviant child behavior. *Journal of Applied Behavior Analysis*, 1975, 8, 27–42.

Wahler, R.G. Oppositional children: A quest for parental reinforcement control. *Journal of Applied Behavior Analysis*, 1969, 2, 159–170.

Wahler, R. G., Berland, R. M., Coe, T.D., & Leske, G. *Social systems analysis: Implementing an alternative behavioral model*. Paper presented at a conference Ecological Perspectives in Behavior Analysis, Lawrence, Kansas, 1976.

Wahler, R.G., & Erickson, M. Child behavior therapy: A community program in Appalachia. *Behaviour Research and Therapy*, 1969, 7, 71–78.

Wahler, R.G., Leske, G., & Rogers, E.S. *The insular family: A deviance support system for oppositional children*. Paper presented at the Banff Conference on Behavior Modification, Banff, 1976.

Wahler, R.G., Winkel, G.H., Peterson, R.E. & Morrison, D.C. Mothers as behavior therapists for their own children. *Behaviour Research and Therapy*, 1965, 3, 113–24.

Walder, L.O., Cohen, S.E., Breiter, D.E., Daston, P.G., Hirsch I.S., & Leibowitz, J.M. Teaching behavioral principles to parents of disturbed children. In B.G. Guerney (Ed), *Psychotherapeutic Agents: New Roles for Nonprofessionals, Parents and Teachers*, New York: Holt, 1969.

Walker, H. *Walker Problem Behavior Identification Checklist*. Western Psychological Services. Los Angeles, 1976.

Webster, C.D., McPherson, H., Sloman, L., Evans, M.A., & Kuchar, E. Communicating with an autistic boy by gestures. *Journal of Autism and Childhood Schizophrenia*, 1973, 4, 337–346.

White, G.D., Nielsen, G., & Johnson, S.M. Timeout duration and the suppression of deviant behavior in children. *Journal of Applied Behavioral Analysis*, 1972, 5, 111–120.

Williams, C.D. The elimination of tantrum behaviors by

extinction Procedures. *Journal of Abnormal and Social Psychology*, 1959, 59, 269–270.

Wiltz, N.A. Modification of behaviors through parent participation in a group technique. (Doctoral dissertation, University of Oregon) Ann Arbor, Mich.: University Microfilms, 1969, No. 70–9482.

Wiltz, N.A., & Gordon, S.B. Parental Modification of a child's behavior in an experimental residence. *Journal of Behavior Therapy and Experimental Psychiatry*, 1974, 5, 107–109.

Wiltz, N.A. & Patterson, G.R. An evaluation of parent training procedures designed to alter inappropriate aggressive behavior in boys. *Behavior Therapy*, 1974, 5, 215–221.

Wisocki, P.A., & Sedney, M.A. Toward the development of behavioral clinicians. *Journal of Behavior Therapy and Experimental Psychiatry*, 1978, 9, 141–147.

Wolf, M.M., Risley, T., Johnson, M., Harris, R., & Allen, E. Application of operant conditioning procedures to the behavior problems of an autistic child: A follow-up and extension. *Behavior Research and Therapy*, 1967, 5, 103–111.

Wulbert, M., Barach, R., Perry, M., Straughan, J., Sulzbacher, S., Turner, K., & Wiltz, N. The Generalization of newly acquired behaviors by parents and child across three different settings: A study of an autistic child. *Journal of Abnormal Child Psychology*, 1974, 2, 87–98.

Wulbert, M., Nyman, B.A., Snow, D., & Owen, Y. The efficacy of stimulus fading and contingency management in the treatment of elective mutism: A case study. *Journal of Applied Behavior Analysis*, 1973, 6, 434–441.

Young, G.C., & Morgan, R.T.T. Overlearning in the conditioning treatment of enuresis. *Behaviour Research and Therapy*, 1972, 10, 147–151.

Zegiob, L.E., & Forehand, R. Parent-child interactions: Observer effects and social class differences. *Behavior Therapy*, 1978, 9, 118–123.

Zeilberger, J., Sampen, S.E., & Sloane, H.N. Modification of a child's problem behaviors in the home with the mother as therapist. *Journal of Applied Behavior Analysis*, 1968, 1, 47–53.

Zlutnick, S. *The control of seizures by the modification of pre-seizure behavior: The punishment of behavioral chain components*. Unpublished doctoral dissertation, University of Utah, 1972.

EDITORS' REFERENCES

Gurman, A.S. & Klein, M.H. Women and behavioral marriage and family therapy: An unconscious male bias? *Women: Counseling, Therapy and Mental Health Services*, 1980, in press.

Gurman, A.S. & Kniskern, D.P. Research on marital and family therapy: Progress, perspective and prospect. In: S. Garfield & A. Bergin (Eds.), *Handbook of Psychotherapy and Behavior Change* (Second edition). New York: Wiley, 1978.(a)

Gurman, A.S. & Kniskern, D.P. Deterioration in marital and family therapy: Empirical, clinical and conceptual issues. *Family Process*, 1978, 17, 3–20.(b)

CHAPTER 15

Behavioral Marital Therapy

Neil S. Jacobson, Ph.D.

Behavioral marital therapy represents an amalgamation of many forces that have influenced the development of psychotherapy and behavior change procedures over the past 15 years. Its birth in the late 1960s represented a leap of faith, reflecting unbounded optimism that one could apply reinforcement principles to almost any clinical problem. In 1969, when Richard Stuart presented the first published data applying behavior therapy to marital problems (cf. also Liberman, 1970), behavior therapy had survived its first full decade with a devoted band of enthusiastic adherents. A clearly detectable movement was underway to extend the applications to new domains of human misery and suffering.

The most obvious influence in the early development of behavioral marital therapy was the operant conditioning approach used to modify the behavior of children (Patterson, 1974). As behavior modifiers began to train parents to modify the behavior of their children, they also collected data on the exchange of reinforcement and punishment among family members. Interest began to shift from the behavior of the in-

dividual deviant family member (usually a child) to the interaction patterns of family members, including the marital dyad itself (Patterson and Hops, 1972; Patterson and Reid, 1970). Initial attempts to modify the behavior of distressed couples essentially transferred the operant principles used to modify children's behavior to the problems manifested by couples in distress.

This extrapolation from children to adults had certain limitations. A purely operant approach requires that the behavioral change agent maintain control over the delivery of reinforcers and punishers. In the treatment of children, this control was easily provided, either by an institutional setting or through consultation with intermediaries, usually the parents. The therapist possessed no such control when treating married couples. Instead, the therapist had to induce couples to collaborate in producing an environment which was supportive of desirable relationship behavior. This required that the couple learn to negotiate with one another. Hence, the purely operant approach first suggested by Stuart (1969) was augumented by programs designed to teach couples communication

556

and problem-solving skills (Patterson and Hops, 1972; Jacobson and Weiss, 1978). In a marital dyad, behavior exchanges are continuous, and the behavior of each member serves as both antecedent and consequence for the behavior of the partner. As a result, any attempt to establish functional relationships between behavior and the environment by applying a unidirectional cause-effect model was unsatisfactory. Thus, early investigators read and borrowed from theorists who had attempted to grapple with the complexities of understanding ongoing systems of two or more individuals (Homans, 1962; Steinglass, 1978; Thibaut and Kelley, 1959).

In this chapter, an attempt will be made to introduce the basic principles of behavioral marital therapy (BMT). In the initial section, a theoretical model of relationships and relationship distress will be presented. Then assessment techniques will be discussed. The third section will detail the major elements of a behavioral approach to treating couples. Finally, the outcome research evaluating the effectiveness of behavioral marital therapy will be presented.

Although this overview will not concentrate on research, documentation will be cited whenever it is available, and in some cases important studies will be described. What distinguishes BMT from other approaches to treating couples is its single-minded commitment to empirical investigation as the optimal road to development. Despite its brief history, a substantial body of research investigations has already been completed, helping to establish effective clinical procedures, firmer theoretical foundations, and assessment techniques of demonstrated utility.[1]

_____

[1]_Editors' Note_. As the reader begins this chapter, he/she should be aware that elsewhere Jacobson (in collaboration with Robert Weiss) and the editors of this _Handbook_ (in collaboration with Roger Knudson) have published a very spirited debate about behavioral marriage therapy (BMT) (Gurman and Kniskern, 1978; Gurman and Knudson, 1978; Gurman, Knudson, and Kniskern, 1978; Jacobson and Weiss, 1978), in which the editors were quite critical of a number of basic assumptions of BMT. We certainly did not intend to continue our "debate" in our Editorial Notes to Jacobson's chapter, since Jacobson's lack of an opportunity to respond to our comments would constitute a very unfair editorial one-upmanship. Nonetheless, we still have many concerns about BMT, so that the frequency of our Notes in this chapter exceeds that of all the other chapters in this _Handbook_. Still, we hope we have succeeded in our attempt to temper our comments so that our editorial style is consistent throughout this _Handbook_.

SUCCESSFUL AND UNSUCCESSFUL MARITAL RELATIONSHIPS FROM A SOCIAL LEARNING PERSPECTIVE

The theoretical underpinnings of behavior therapy as a strategy for treating couples have been labeled _behavior exchange theory_ (e.g., Jacobson and Margolin, 1979; Rappaport and Harrell, 1972). The model described in this chapter will be referred to as a _social learning_ model. The preference for this latter label is based on its identification with recent trends toward broadening the definition of behavior therapy (Bandura, 1973; Mahoney, 1974). _Social learning theory_ includes in its theoretical formulations not only principles of learning derived from the laboratories of experimental psychology, but also theoretical contributions from social, developmental and cognitive psychology. While the influence of the environment is still emphasized, social learning theory also attends to the role played by private events (thoughts, images, and feelings) in the regulation and control of behavior. Social learning theory also attempts to describe the pervasive effects of social influence on the development of behavior in human beings.

Although early applications of social learning theory to marriage paid little direct attention to describing the successful marriage, there have been a great many contributions to delineating the characteristics of distressed relationships (Gottman, Markman, and Notarius, 1977; Jacobson and Margolin, 1979; Patterson and Reid, 1970; Weiss, 1978). Most of the behavioral descriptions of healthy marriages are by extrapolation and inference from knowledge of distressed relationships. However, in recent years investigators have begun to delineate the characteristics and determinants of successful marriages directly (Jacobson, Waldron, and Moore, in press; Markman, 1979; Wills, Weiss, and Patterson, 1974).

In some respects, it is inconsistent with the principles of social learning theory to define _a_ successful marriage. This is because it is believed that each partner brings into a relationship his/her own unique reinforcement history, and his/her own goals for a long-term relationship. The social learning model adopts a largely idiographic stance toward each couple's attempt to form and maintain a mutually satisfying relationship. Just as they are many routes to marital distress, similarly there are many paths to marital satisfaction, and any general attempt to describe *the* successful marriage must take into account the wide divergence of standards and goals on which couples may base their union.

Two criteria which at first glance seem to provide a solution to this dilemma are those of *stability* and *satisfaction*. Once stability is used as the definition of success, then a model must simply locate the best predictors of longevity, and one has an instant formula for marital success. Unfortunately, many marriages which maintain themselves until death do they part are characterized by a very low rate of mutually exchanged benefits, and/or a high rate of mutually exchanged punishment; success, when defined in terms of satisfaction on the part of both partners, is not the only determinant of longevity, and often not even an important determinant (Hicks and Platt, 1970). Conversely, a relationship can be relatively brief yet still be successful in the sense that for some period of time it provided each partner with largely positive outcomes. On the other hand, ignoring stability completely and basing one's determination of marital success solely on its reinforcement value for the participants does not seem quite satisfactory. A relationship can be extremely gratifying to both partners during its initial stages, only to crumble when they must traverse their initial major conflict or make their first major joint decision. It would be problematic to describe a relationship as successful, however euphoric its beginnings, if the participants were unable to make any of the necessary transitions toward sustained intimacy.

The social learning theorist is, in other words, faced with a dilemma: Despite the obvious advantages provided by a general model of the successful marriage, the framework implies that there are numerous paths to success. The solution to this dilemma has been to emphasize the skills which couples need to sustain a satisfying relationship over a long period of time, regardless of the content of their exchanges and their standards for success. Every relationship is satisfying to the degree that couples provide one another with benefits, and it is also true that the benefits must be high relative to the costs

inherent in being in the relationship (Thibaut and Kelley, 1959). Although the maintenance of a high reward/cost ratio was not always a criterion for marital satisfaction (Lederer and Jackson, 1968), we have embraced it in the 20th century. Thus, it can be stated initially that, however couples may define the benefits they seek in a long-term relationship, whatever they are they must be plentiful, although couples vary widely in terms of their standards for a sufficiently high reward/cost ratio.[2]

It is also posited, within the present framework, that costs are incurred whenever a couple attempts to sustain a long-term relationship. This is because there are certain reinforcers that are more easily attained alone. The costs of being in a particular relationship will vary directly with the benefits denied to a particular person as a result of entering into a state of relatedness. People whose reinforcers hinge primarily on the benefits which one can only receive from a relationship will experience the commitment to such a relationship as less costly than those who receive a substantial proportion of their daily reinforcement from activities that are incompatible with an intimate relationship.[3]

Thus, any coupled individual has a minimum reward/cost ratio which determines the degree of satisfaction in a relationship. Thibaut and Kelley (1959) refer to this minimum standard as the *comparison level*. *A social learning model posits that the rate of reinforcers received from*

---

[2]*Editors' Note.* As will be seen, the "benefits" of which Jacobson speaks are based overwhelmingly on *overt* interactions and behavior. Elsewhere (Gurman and Knudson, 1978; Gurman et al., 1978) we have argued, consistent with most psychoanalytically-oriented models of marriage and of marital therapy, that these "benefits" may also (and do frequently) occur and accrue at unconscious and preconscious levels of experience. We will illustrate such phenomena in some of our Notes which follow.

[3]*Editors' Note.* As an example of the view we expressed in the preceding Note, we want to point out that such "daily reinforcement" may also be *negative reinforcement* (remember that negative reinforcement, like positive, always *increases* the probability of a behavior, but through the *removal* (via avoidance or escape) of an aversive stimulus, rather than (in the case of positive reinforcement) through the addition of a stimulus). For example, some couples in which both partners find intimacy anxiety-arousing (aversive) may be continuously reinforced by avoidance of emotional self-disclosure. That is, successful and repeated avoidance of this source of anxiety will tend to increase the chances of non-intimate behavior (thus, negative reinforcement).

the partner determines not only the degree of subjective satisfaction but also the rate of rewards directed in return toward the partner. This principle, that *over time* rewards given and received within a marital relationship are highly correlated, is termed *reciprocity*, and by now numerous investigations have supported the lawfulness of this phenomenon in couples (Birchler, 1973; Gottman, Notarius, Markman, Bank, Yoppi, and Rubin, 1976; Gottman et al., 1977; Jacobson, Waldron, and Moore, in press; Patterson and Reid, 1970; Robinson and Price, 1980; Wills et al., 1974). Thus, if we somehow had access to knowledge regarding the important reinforcers for a particular couple, we could predict with a substantial degree of accuracy how often one spouse would receive them on the basis of how often that same partner was provided with them.

The analysis becomes further complicated by a need to evelute the characteristics of the environment external to the couple's exchanges. This need follows from the observation that the persistence of a relationship depends to a large degree on the attractiveness of this environment, that is, the availability of comparable or superior reward/cost ratios if the person in question were not engaged in the current relationship. Cognitive mechanisms are extremely important here, since partners must estimate and appraise their alternatives to arrive at a comparison level for alternative relationships (Thibaut and Kelley, 1959). These estimates may be either veridical or distorted, but in any case they are determinants of the longevity of a marital dyad.[4]

To summarize, an individual enters into a relationship with a learning history as well as a constitution which predisposes him/her to find certain partner-initiated behaviors reinforcing.

---

[4]*Editors' Note.* Note that the "comparison level" for a given individual need not be based solely on his/her evaluation of the reward/cost ratio offered by the partner, or other potential partners. It may also be significantly mediated by his/her (often implicit) estimation of his/her own personal worth (e.g., "I don't deserve any better"). In addition, comparison levels may also be influenced by a person's image of an idealized partner, or by one's vicarious experience of the marital relationships of other people. While such observations would probably not be discounted by behavioral marital therapists, we see little evidence of their attempts to deal directly with such self-assessments in therapy.

Dependent on the history, the relationship will also be somewhat costly. The reinforcement history and predilections for certain reinforcers are not static, fixed entities, but are constantly being modified by experiences in the relationship. Couples have both internal and external criteria by which to evaluate their current relationship, and perhaps the former should be equated with the criterion for "happiness" and the latter with "stability." It should be clear by now that the social learning model depends on an interaction between the stimulus value of behaviors received by each spouse and the way these stimuli are interpreted by the receiver. Attributions, appraisals, and other mediational processes can fundamentally alter the impact of spouse's behavior.

Since both satisfaction and persistence depend on maintaining a high level of rewards relative to costs, success will depend upon a couple's coping successfully with numerous obstacles to the maximization of this ratio. During the course of a relationship, couples are faced with factors which threaten either to deplete the current rate of rewarding exchange or to add to the incurred costs. Maintaining a high ratio is not much of a problem for couples during the early stages of a relationship, particularly given a large degree of initial attraction. Reinforcing value is at its peak, fueled by the novelty inherent in the exchanges and shared activities. Couples ensure during these periods that the contacts are as positive as possible. None of the costs inherent in a long-term commitment has been realized as yet. However, as the spouses spend more and more time together, interacting in a greater variety of situations, the costs begin to manifest themselves. For one thing, spouses experience each other in new roles, not all of which are as inherently rewarding as the carefree activities characteristic of courtship. Moreover, as interdependence grows, the costs of being committed to someone become more prominent. Commitment entails that each spouse accommodate to the other. Inevitably, some of the indulgences of independence must be foregone.

It is only a matter of time before a couple is in conflict over some issue. *Social learning models have suggested that a critical skill in determining a successful marriage is skill in con-*

flict resolution (Jacobson, 1977d, 1977c, 1979b; Jacobson and Margolin, 1979). Spouses who are not excessively alarmed or surprised by the occurrence of conflict will speak openly and directly to one another about conflict issues *when* the conflict occurs, and will establish this precedent early in their married life. When they do talk to each other about conflict, they will keep the issue in perspective and focus specifically on the behaviors that are of concern to them. They will attempt to understand the partner's point of view and listen carefully to what is being said. Spouses who respond less adaptively to initial areas of conflict are bound to experience significant difficulties in maintaining a viable union.

One of the tragedies of the socialization process is that, while people are trained in numerous survival skills as a concomitant to becoming a mature adult, people receive little training in the skills necessary to sustain a viable relationship. One of the myths of our culture, so eloquently described by Lederer and Jackson (1968), is that relationship skills are unnecessary because love will conquer all. Couples in our society have been unprepared to handle conflict. Many experience it as a contradiction to the basis for their union. To acknowledge imperfections in the partner is viewed as being tantamount to a denial of love. Thus, many partners avoid discussing problems in their relationship, hoping that time will magically attenuate them. Unfortunately, time usually exacerbates rather than attenuates conflict. Other couples rightly choose to discuss their conflict areas, but do so in a way that simply adds to the discord. Such spouses attempt to coerce, threaten, intimidate, or humiliate their partner into behaving differently. Given their lack of preparedness and their stereotyped, idealized expectations, spouses feel cheated by their partner's undesirable behavior, and any precedent for constructive resolution of problems is drowned in a cacophony of accusation, blame, and fury.[5]

In short, many couples enter marriage without anticipating either the inevitability of con-

flict or the necessity for behavior change in a long-term relationship. Even in the most gratifying of marriages, spouses occasionally want either increases or decreases in certain aspects of the partner's behavior. Couples need behavior change skills in order to maintain successful relationships. It is not the existence of conflict per se that separates the successful and unsuccessful relationship, but the collective response to conflict.

But problem-solving or conflict resolution skills comprise only a portion of the skills that couples need in order to be successful. Communication skill level, however it is defined, differentiates between satisfied and dissatisfied couples more powerfully than any other class of relationship behavior (Jacobson, Waldron, and Moore, in press; Markman, 1979). Communication serves so many functions in a marriage that any attempt at delineation is bound to be too exclusive; writers of numerous theoretical persuasions have speculated on a number of these functions (Ables and Brandsma, 1977; Guerney, 1977; Haley, 1963; Jacobson and Margolin, 1979; Satir, 1967; Weiss, 1978; Weiss and Birchler, 1978). Similarly, the increased interest in sex therapy which followed publication of Masters and Johnson's (1970) classic book has contributed to a recognition that sexual gratification and the continued growth and development of sexual interaction can be extremely important to long-term success in a marriage. More will be said of this below. Finally, there exists a variety of skills which couples must master in order to survive, although these skills seldom provide the basis for marital satisfaction; nor do couples marry in order to engage in these *instrumental behaviors* (cf. Weiss and Birchler, 1978). Nevertheless, many couples have failed to endure the consequences of inadequate financial management, household and domestic deficiencies, or conflicts over personal living habits.

Thus, the social learning model places heavy emphasis on the skills necessary for enactment of relationship roles and functions. However, it is obvious that a couple can combine exemplary skills to no avail if neither has any reinforcement value for the other. People marry because of both the actual and perceived potential for the provision of benefits and rewards. During court-

---

[5]*Editors' Note*. We agree with Jacobson's observations here, but would point out that, as Sager (Chapter 3) makes clear, this "cheating" usually operates in both directions and, more important, may derive from unconscious inconsistencies of expectations of one's spouse, within each partner.

ship, partners experience one another in a limited but often substantial number of situations, and they each sample the other's ability to provide them with benefits. The commitment to cohabitation and/or marriage always involves both an appraisal of the adequacy of current outcomes and a forecast, albeit often implicit, regarding the continuance and expansion of such outcomes into new domains. Since it is considerably more difficult to maintain a high rate of rewards during marriage than during courtship, successful marriages require more than an initially high rate of reciprocal reinforcement. *Successful couples adapt effectively to the requirements of day-to-day intimacy. In particular, they expand their reinforcement power by frequently acquiring new domains for positive exchange.* Spouses who depend on a limited quality and variety of reinforcers are bound to suffer the ill effects of satiation. As a result, over time their interaction becomes depleted of its prior reinforcement value. Successful couples cope with this inevitable reinforcement erosion by varying their shared activities, developing new common interests, expanding their sexual repertoires, and developing their communication to the point where they continue to interest one another.

Successful marriages also have rules, as many previous theorists have noted (Haley, 1963; Jacobson and Margolin, 1979; Weiss, 1978). Since functioning in an intimate relationship requires a complex division of roles, responsibilities, and obligations, the system can function smoothly only if there is considerable consensus between the partners regarding which behaviors are appropriate and inappropriate in particular situations. If spouses habitually operate according to discrepant versions of a marriage contract, or if the contract includes excessive lacunae which necessitate ad hoc decisions, discord will follow. Thus, two requirements exist: one, that relationship behavior is at least somewhat under the stimulus control of rules (Weiss, 1978); two, that there is some consensus as to the content of these rules.

The rules which govern relationship behavior are not always explicit, although they are usually identifiable through the careful interviewing of a couple (Sager, 1976). Moreover, they exist not only for instrumental tasks but for potentially conflict-inducing situations, such as how sexual activity is initiated, how leisure activities are to be planned, and when or by whose initiation physical affection is appropriate. The rules are comprehensive and flexible rather than narrow and rigid (cf. Jacobson and Margolin, 1979).

To summarize this section, a number of factors have been identified which determine the long-term success of a marital relationship. All of them emphasize the capacity for adaptability, flexibility, and change. Couples must be capable of evolving together and coping with the multitude of challenges and external forces which life imposes on them. Social learning theory views these coping competencies as learnable. It will be apparent to the reader that the above model pays little attention to the learning history of either spouse prior to their initial meeting. Obviously, the learning history plays a fundamental role in determining each partner's preferences for certain reinforcers and the standards each person presents as criteria for a satisfying relationship. It is also quite obvious that the success of a relationship requires a certain basic compatibility in reinforcement preferences and expectancies regarding marriage. *But, notwithstanding the partners' learning history, the development, maintenance and enduring success of the relationship depend primarily on the characteristics of the partners' exchanges and the environmental forces to which they are subjected, rather than any preordained historically shaped personality characteristics.*[6] Individual differences are important, to be sure, but their role is most important in bringing individuals together and providing for initial attraction. What happens subsequently can be best predicted by the events which occur in the social environment produced by their state of relatedness, and by the exogenous factors which sometimes facilitate and at other times impede their growth as a couple.

---

[6]*Editors' Note.* Jacobson's presentation here of the influence of "historically shaped personality characteristics" is somewhat overstated. As one of us (Gurman, 1978) has emphasized elsewhere, these characteristics themselves preordain nothing in intimate relationships. Rather, a co-participant is required in order to make these characteristics manifest. That is, "personality" must be activated in interaction with others; it does not exist "within" people, rather it requires an appropriate "environment" to blossom.

Reference has already been made to the role of the environment in shaping marital partners toward greater distance or increased intimacy. In addition to providing alternatives to the current relationship, the sociocultural milieu surrounding the couple can produce changes in the important reinforcers for one or both partners. These changes can be concordant or discordant, so that couples might either continue to develop and evolve together, or their experiences outside the home can create distance and conflict. One common contemporary example of the latter is the impact of the women's movement on marriage. The movement has changed the standards against which many women measure the adequacy of their marriage. These women have begun to demand more egalitarian relationships, which involve changes in the division of labor in regard to instrumental and noninstrumental tasks. Many marriages have not survived this escalation in demands. It is hardly surprising that partners change at different rates and in discordant directions. Given the omnipresent impact of the environment on behavior and the constant accommodation to social and cultural developments, it is testimony to couples' coping capacities that so many do remain together.

A Behavioral Analysis of Marital Distress

The social learning model predicts that, despite heterogeneity in the antecedents of relationship distress, there are certain rather predictable, general distinctions between the exchanges of distressed and nondistressed couples. Research in our laboratories (Jacobson, Waldron, and Moore, in press) has begun to confirm our hypotheses regarding these differences. A brief summary of the distinctions follows.

First, whether the terms "reward" and "punishment" are defined by observers or by the spouses themselves, distressed couples engage in fewer rewarding exchanges and more punishing exchanges than nondistressed couples. These differences are apparent both in their direct verbal communication (Birchler, Weiss, and Vincent, 1975; Gottman, Markman, and Notarius, 1977; Gottman, Notarius, Markman,

Bank, Yoppi, and Rubin, 1976; Klier and Rothberg, 1977; Vincent, Weiss, and Birchler, 1975; Wills, Weiss, and Patterson, 1974) and in the exchange of reinforcers other than verbal communication (Jacobson, Waldron, and Moore, in press; Robinson and Price, 1980; Wills, Weiss, and Patterson, 1974).

Second, there is some evidence that the juxtaposition or patterning of exchanges may differ in distressed and nondistressed couples. Distressed spouses are more likely than nondistressed spouses to reciprocate the partner's use of punishment (cf. Jacobson, 1979a). It appears that many of these spouses are extremely sensitive to the partner's use of punishment (Jacobson et al., in press). Some authors have suggested that distressed couples are generally more reactive to immediate stimuli delivered by the partner, whether the impact of those stimuli as positive or negative (Jacobson and Margolin, 1979; Jacobson and Martin, 1976; Weiss, 1978). It has been suggested by Gottman et al. (1976) that nondistressed couples operate according to a "bank account" model of exchange, where rewards and punishers are deposited into a relationship account, and positive behavior is sustained without a need for quid pro quo exchanges. That is, the primary distinction between distressed and nondistressed marriages is the relatively high ratio of positive deposits to negative withdrawals found in nondistressed marriages. There is no immediate contingency linking these positive exchanges, and, in fact, it is the very absence of a contingent linkage in the context of frequent positive exchange that characterizes nondistressed couples, according to this model.

Another way of describing this distinction between distressed and nondistressed couples is in terms of short-term versus long-term contingencies; that is, unhappy couples respond to immediate stimuli while satisfied couples are less likely to react to such stimuli alone and respond instead to the reservoir of accumulated rewards. Currently, the evidence favors a qualification of this hypothesis. Although the tendency to respond to immediately preceding negative behavior is stronger in distressed couples, the distinction may not hold for positive behavior. Distressed couples are no more likely to reciprocate positive behavior than are nondistressed couples, and in fact may be even less likely to do so (Gottman et al., 1977; Jacobson, 1979a; Jacobson, Waldron, and Moore, in press; Robinson and Price, 1980). Perhaps, in regard to positive behavior, other factors counteract the tendency for distressed couples to be sensitive to immediate stimuli. For example, there is some evidence that distressed couples "selectively" notice and attend to negative behavior (Robinson and Price, 1980). To the extent that this is true, this selective attention may negate whatever tendency distressed couples might have to respond to positive behavior.

There is also some evidence that marital distress is associated with different topographical classes of rewards and punishers (Jacobson et al., in press). Whereas direct communication seems to be salient for both types of couples, nondistressed couples provide reinforcement through positive communication. Positive communication, even when it does occur, does not appear to be as reinforcing to distressed couples. The reverse is true for negative communication. Distressed couples control the behavior of one another through the presentation of negative communication and the withholding of positive communication. Such stimuli do not appear to be as compelling for nondistressed couples, when they do occur. Participation in shared activities provides an important reinforcing function for nondistressed couples, whereas such activities, even when they do occur, are not generally reinforcing for distressed couples. Overall, the results of preliminary research support the contention of behavior exchange theory that unhappy couples tend to produce behavior change and compliance through aversive control tactics, that is, by strategically presenting punishment and withholding rewards.

The *social learning* model of relationship success emphasizes the factors which are currently maintaining desirable and undesirable behavior, whether these factors involve the partner's behavior, the impact of the social environment, or person variables. Yet it is also a developmental model which attempts to link current conflict to antecedents in the couple's relationship history. In designing a marital therapy treatment plan, this elucidation of antecedents is thought

to greatly expand the ability of the therapist to aid his/her clients. The process of assessment attempts to uncover variables of both current and historical relevance. The topic of assessment will be addressed in the following section.

BEHAVIORAL ASSESSMENT OF MARITAL DISCORD

In keeping with the emphasis in behavior therapy on the multidimensional assessment of verbal, physiological, and behavioral variables (cf. Goldfried and Sprafkin, 1974), the assessment of marital dysfunction includes a variety of procedures designed to evaluate both the strengths and weaknesses of a relationship in terms of the partners' interactional behavior, the numerous and variegated ways that rewards and punishments are exchanged in the natural environment, and the spouses' subjective appraisals and feelings about the relationship. In addition, the social learning model offers a set of hypotheses regarding the possible antecedent events and skill deficiencies which may be responsible for the current dysfunctional interaction. Thus, a number of skill areas are evaluated for their possible contributions to current distress: the ability of the spouses to discuss relationship problems; their current reinforcement value for one another; their skill in pinpointing the relevant reinforcers in their relationship; their general competencies in the areas of communication, sex, child-rearing, financial management; their strategies for utilizing their leisure time in an effective and personally satisfying manner; and the distribution of roles and decision-making responsibilities. Behavioral assessment is characterized by a number of features which distinguish it from other approaches to assessment.

First, behavioral assessment is primarily concerned with identifying the current behavioral excesses and deficits that have produced the current dissatisfaction in the relationship, and the variables that are responsible for their occurrence. These goals are based on the conviction that the common denominator in all distressed relationships is the relative absence of rewarding behaviors and/or plethora of punishing behaviors. Whatever the basis for the current level of behavior exchange, the ultimate goal of therapy is to provide for behavior changes that will subsequently increase the satisfaction level in both partners. This requires a careful delineation of all problem areas and their controlling influences. Of course, often the target areas include cognitions as well as overt interactional behavior. Either one or both spouses may impose attributions onto the other person's behavior with the result that its impact becomes considerably less positive or more negative than its stimulus value warrants.

Second, and following logically from the previous point, a behavioral assessment aspires toward the direct measurement of behavior in lieu of a focus on personality dynamics and the labeling of clients according to hypothesized underlying constructs. A behavioral analysis emphasizes description and the elucidation of functional relationships between behavior and its environmental covariates.

Third, the treatment plan which is ultimately adopted is directly related to the results of the initial assessment. This correspondence has little direct counterpart in more traditional forms of individual psychotherapy, where the treatment approach depends upon the technical predilections of the therapist rather than a systematic assessment procedure.[7]

Fourth, behavioral assessment is continuous, occurring throughout treatment rather than simply terminating at the conclusion of the pretreatment phase. After a treatment plan has been formulated, the continued assessment provides both therapist and client with feedback regarding the progress toward early detection and modification of inefficacious treatment plans.

With this background providing a unifying

perspective, let us now examine the various strategies for collecting treatment-relevant information.

Interview

Compared to other approaches, the behavioral assessment of marital disorders deemphasizes therapist-client interaction as a source of information (Jacobson and Margolin, 1979). Much of the information required is more efficiently obtained either through written questionnaires or through the direct observation of the couple's interaction. However, there are certain types of information that are not easily obtainable from other sources and are accessible through the interview format. For example, a developmental history of the relationship, which is important in determining the historical antecedents of the current distress, is best obtained through the interview. In addition, the interview is often a useful device for obtaining details regarding behavioral sequences characterizing the relationship, along with the antecedents and consequences of those sequences. Finally, the initial interview serves important therapeutic as well as assessment functions (Jacobson and Margolin, 1979). These will be discussed in greater detail below.

Self-report Measures

At the University of Washington, we typically employ three different types of assessment questionnaires: an inventory yielding a global rating of marital satisfaction (Locke and Wallace, 1959; Spanier, 1976); the Areas-of-Changes Questionnaire (A-C) (Weiss et al., 1973), which asks couples to indicate which of 34 partner behaviors they would like to see changed, as well as how much change is desired and the direction of the change (more-less); and the Marital Status Inventory (MSI) (Weiss and Cerreto, 1975), a set of true-false questions which indicates the steps toward separation and divorce already undertaken by both spouses.

Both the Locke-Wallace Marital Adjustment Test (MAT) (Locke and Wallace, 1959) and the Dyadic Adjustment Scale (DAS) (Spanier, 1976)

---

[7]*Editors' Note.* Again, while we are hardly champions of the psychoanalytic movement (cf. Gurman, 1978), we think Jacobson's portrayal of assessment methods in "traditional" psychotherapies is inaccurate. In our view, even the most rigorous and comprehensive of behavioral assessments pale in comparison to the searching assessment period for determining an individual's suitability for psychoanalysis. Moreover, we disagree with Jacobson's observation in the next paragraph that, in "traditional" psychotherapy, assessment ends shortly after treatment begins. Behavior therapists are not unique in doing continuous assessment, though they certainly are more formalized about it than most other therapists.

provide well validated indices of marital satisfaction. Both are of limited value in a behavioral analysis because they do not yield specific information regarding the problem areas in the relationship. However, they do provide a reliable measure of global subjective satisfaction.

The A-C correlates highly with the MAT and is significantly more useful in pinpointing the behaviors which trouble each spouse. The MSI allows the assessor to acquire much necessary information without placing spouses in an embarrassing situation. Often couples are reluctant to admit to the extent of their movement toward separation. The *MSI* provides them with a less stressful way of responding by requiring only that they answer "true" or "false" on a series of items.

Spouse Observation

Weiss, Patterson and their associates developed an instrument to aid couples in their collection of observational data in the home. The Spouse Observation Checklist (Patterson, 1976; Weiss et al., 1973) consists of about 400 spouse behaviors grouped into 12 topographical categories: companionship, affection, consideration, communication, sex, coupling, child care, household responsibilities, financial management, work (school) activities, personal habits, self and spouse independence. The task is for couples to check each item that occurs during a given 24-hour period. The instructions can be varied so that spouses are instructed either to record all behaviors that occur or to limit their recordings to those behaviors that have "pleasing" or "displeasing" impacts on them. In addition, each spouse is instructed to give the relationship a daily rating on a scale of 1-7, based on overall satisfaction.

The SOC can serve a variety of assessment functions. First, it provides the therapist with daily frequencies of relevant behavior. Second, by correlating behavioral frequencies with daily satisfaction, it is possible to uncover the behaviors which seem to be most important to the satisfaction of each spouse. The SOC also provides a way to monitor the ongoing progress of therapy, since, by continuing the daily recordings during the treatment period, the therapist

can observe relevant changes in areas targeted for intervention.[8]

Direct Observation of Problem-Solving and Communication

Since behavioral marital therapy places such a great emphasis on skills in conflict resolution and communication, direct observation of spouses' interaction is an important part of the assessment process. For the clinician, this observation is relatively informal, but nevertheless essential to the overall evaluation. For the clinical researcher, this means training observers to reliably code spouses' interactional behavior into relevant categories.

The codes are then tallied to produce a profile of the couple's problem-solving ability, based on either the rate at which certain behaviors occur (reflections, verbal reinforcement, putdowns, etc.), or the sequence in which behaviors occur (e.g., the probability of the wife complaining given that the husband has just complained). Whatever the resources of the assessor might be, the important point is that she/he aspires towards an unbiased, representative sample of the clients' interactional behavior.

Through the combined contributions of interviewing, self-report questionnaires, spouse observation, and observations of couple interaction, the relevant questions can be answered, and a treatment plan formulated. By the time a pretreatment assessment has been completed, the therapist/assessor should have answered at least the following questions:

A. *Strengths and skills of the relationship*
   What are the major strengths of this relationship?

---

[8]*Editors' Note.* We suspect that, in using such correlational data, there is a danger of unwittingly reinforcing a couple's point-for-point exchange orientation. Such an orientation, of course, is quite inconsistent with Gottman's "bank account" model of successful marriages, described earlier by Jacobson. We wonder, then, how does (can) a behavioral marriage therapist teach what we may call "bank account skills"? Within this economic metaphor, it is interesting to note that short-term financial investments with low risk usually yield small gains, while long-term high risk investments have the potential for very large payoffs (as well as, perhaps, for bankruptcy!).

Specifically, what resources do these spouses have that explain their current level of commitment to the relationship?

What is each spouse's current capacity to reinforce the other?

What behaviors on the part of each spouse are highly valued by the other?

What shared activities does the couple currently engage in?

What common interests do they share?

What are the couple's competencies and skills in meeting the essential tasks of a relationship: problem-solving, provision of support and understanding, ability to provide social reinforcement effectively, sexual capabilities, child-rearing and parenting skills, ability to manage finances, household responsibilities, interpersonal skills regarding interaction with people outside the relationship?

B. *Presenting Problems*

What are the major complaints, and how do these complaints translate into explicitly behavioral terms?

What behaviors occur too frequently or at inappropriate times from the standpoint of each spouse?

Under what conditions do these behaviors occur?

What are the reinforcers that are maintaining these behaviors?

What behaviors occur at less than the desired frequency or fail to occur at appropriate times from the standpoint of each spouse?

Under what conditions would each spouse like to see these behaviors occur?

What are the consequences of these behaviors currently, when they occur?

How did the current problems develop over time?

How are current lines of decision-making authority drawn?

Is there a consensus on who makes important decisions in regard to various areas of the relationship?

What kinds of decisions are made collectively as opposed to unilaterally?

C. *Sex and affection*

Are the spouses physically attracted to one another?

Is either currently dissatisfied with rate, quality, or diversity of sex life together?

If sex is currently a problem, was there a time when it was mutually satisfying?

What are the sexual behaviors that seem to be associated with current dissatisfaction?

Are either or both partners dissatisfied with the amount or quality of nonsexual physical affection?

Are either or both partners currently engaged in an extramarital sexual relationship?

If so, is the uninvolved partner aware of the affair?

What is the couple's history regarding extramarital affairs?

D. *Future prospects*

Are the partners seeking therapy to improve their relationship, to separate, or to decide whether the relationship is worth working on?

What are each spouse's reasons for continuing the relationship despite current problems?

What steps has each spouse taken in the direction of divorce?

E. *Assessment of social environment*

What are each person's alternatives to the present relationship?

How attractive are these alternatives to each person?

Is the environment (parents, relatives, friends, work associates, children) supportive of either continuance or dissolution of present relationship?

Are any of the children suffering from psychological problems of their own?

What would the probable consequences of relationship dissolution be for the children?

F. *Individual functioning of each spouse*

Does either spouse exhibit any severe emotional or behavioral problems?

Does either spouse present a psychiatric history of his/her own? Specify.

Have they been in therapy before, either alone or together? What kind of therapy? Outcome?

What is each spouse's past experience with intimate relationships?

How is the present relationship different?

A vast amount of information is required in a thorough pretreatment assessment, considering that each of the above questions is, in reality, a summary question requiring a great deal of specific information. In our clinic, we typically devote three weeks to the pretreatment assessment.[9] During this time there are three therapist contacts: (a) an initial conjoint interview focusing on a developmental history; (b) sessions where one interviewer meets separately with each spouse; and (c) a session devoted solely to the assessment of communication and problem-solving. Concurrent with this series of interviews, the clients are completing the SOC nightly at home. In addition, clients complete a variety of questionnaires regarding the relationship, as well as questionnaires designed to assess their individual competencies and vulnerabilities.

At the conclusion of this pretreatment assessment period, the couple meets with the therapist(s) to receive their treatment recommendations. During this meeting the findings from the evaluation are summarized, and the therapist(s) either offer marital therapy along with a description of the treatment program, or explain why marital therapy is contraindicated and suggest alternatives to the couple. With this information, it is left for the couple to decide, on the basis of the information received, whether or not to adhere to the therapist's recommendations. In most cases, adherence means committing oneself to a time-limited (between eight and 12 weekly 90-minute sessions), structured treatment program with specific goals designed to improve the relationship in accordance with the couple's verbally-stated desires. To reiterate, assessment is not over once that commitment is made, but its scope changes as the subsequent assessment data serve primarily to provide feedback regarding progress, and help decide on modification of the treatment plan when such changes seem desirable. The treatment options provided by a social learning perspective are described in the paragraphs below.

---

[9]*Editors' Note.* As Jacobson will emphasize later in this chapter, this assessment format is *not* used in crisis situations.

THE EARLY STAGES OF BEHAVIORAL MARITAL THERAPY: INDUCING POSITIVE EXPECTANCIES AND THE CREATION OF A COLLABORATIVE SET

Successful marital therapy is predicated on the spouses' willingness to work collaboratively to improve their relationship. Unfortunately, couples seldom enter therapy in a collaborative spirit (cf. Haley, 1976). On the contrary, it is more typical for each spouse to expect the therapist to demand that the partner change, without anticipating any mutuality in this change process. Thus, collaboration cannot be assumed, but must be fostered and shaped by the early contacts with the therapist. In addition, the early phases of therapy are dedicated to the creation of positive outcome expectancies in both partners. It must be remembered that discord is usually at its peak when couples finally seek professional assistance; there is often a great deal of confusion, anxiety, and hopelessness connected with the request for help.

To the extent that the therapist can produce an expectation on the part of each spouse that the treatment program can help the relationship, there will be some immediate therapeutic benefits in the amelioration of anxiety and hopelessness per se. Moreover, positive expectancies can mediate a positive outcome by enhancing the degree of behavioral commitment, that is, the willingness to respond appropriately to the therapist's directives and persevere in the face of hard times during the course of therapy.

Even the pretreatment assessment phase of BMT is designed to create positive expectancies and build a collaborative set. In part, positive expectancies may be a serendipitous consequence of the thorough assessment procedures charcterizing BMT. The therapist(s) contribute to the process by initially outlining the entire assessment process for the partners, explaining to them the rationale for each procedure. Clients benefit both from an informed understanding of why they are being asked to engage in various activities and from the imposition of an initial trial period between their initial contact with the therapist and the time when they must commit themselves to therapy. The former information alleviates much of the confusion and uncertainty regarding the content of therapy.

The period of information-gathering, devoid of any commitment to therapy, allows the couple time to become comfortable with the therapist; couples are seldom firmly committed to marital therapy when they first make contact, and when their tentativeness is supported at least for the duration of the pretreatment assessment period, clients are less likely to experience the first few contacts as aversive.

The entire assessment period encourages spouses to identify and acknowledge the strengths of the relationship as well as the current problems. Since distressed couples tend to focus exclusively on their problems and often ignore positive elements in their relationship (e.g., Robinson and Price, 1980), the inducement to become reacquainted with both past and present benefits can serve to enhance spouses' commitment to the relationship and foster collaboration during therapy.

For example, our initial interview devotes little attention to the presenting problems and instead concentrates on the early history of the relationship (Jacobson and Margolin, 1979). Spouses are asked to describe in detail how they met. They are also asked to reflect on what characteristics of the partner made him/her attractive during this initial encounter. Details regarding the courtship experiences are elicited. In this way, by encouraging spouses to relive the happier times, the therapist helps them to view their current problems in proper perspective.

Other assessment tasks are designed to facilitate a focus on increasing the positive aspects of the relationship, rather than eliminating the negatives. Such an emphasis is justified on several grounds. First, pleasing and displeasing relationship behaviors have been shown to be independent of one another (Margolin and Weiss, 1978; Wills et al., 1974); therefore, simply eliminating aversive behaviors is unlikely, in and of itself, to produce an increase in positive behaviors (cf. Weiss, 1978). Second, there is some evidence that negative behaviors decrease naturally as therapy progresses without explicit focus; on the other hand, positive behaviors do not increase unless there is a specific emphasis on such an increase in therapy (Margolin and Weiss, 1978). Third, and most relevant to the present discussion, such an emphasis is more conducive to a constructive, collaborative set.

The therapist's first direct attempt to build a collaborative set occurs at the conclusion of the pretreatment assessment phase. By presenting an analysis of the relationship in social learning terms, the therapist introduces a focus which implies reciprocal causality and mutual responsibility for the current problems. The description of their problems in a language which resists the attributing of blame to either partner, delivered as an objective and expert opinion, can enlarge each spouse's perspective and lead to a consideration of other views, facilitating their acceptance of mutual responsibility for maintaining the current distressed state. Although each spouse may enter therapy with an investment in viewing himself/herself as an innocent victim of the other's oppression, and is therefore unlikely to yield to a verbal exhortatin, no matter how convincing, from the therapist, the broader perspective offered by the therapist usually fosters an awareness of alternatives and constitutes the first step toward acceptance of mutual responsibility. To the extent that an improved relationship is highly valued by the couple, collaborative behavior in therapy will be proportional to each spouse's acceptance of responsibility for creating and maintaining their current level of discord.

The second major strategy for enhancing spouses' collaborative behavior involves obtaining their commitment to following the therapist's instructions, and then instructing them to collaborate. Although this strategy may seem excessively glib, it is extremely effective. Once couples have signed a written therapy contract committing themselves to following the therapist's instructions, most couples will act accordingly. There are a wide variety of behaviors which follow from a collaborative set, all of which add to the probability of a positive outcome. Instead of awaiting the emergence of such a set, the therapist can request the appropriate behaviors regardless of cognitive set. If couples do engage in these behaviors, the relationship is likely to improve, and collaboration will follow from these initial positive changes.

Finally, and most importantly, treatment sessions are graded so that, in the early stages, the requirements are less demanding and require minimal collaboration. These strategies, described in the next section, are low risk and have a high probability of success. Initial improvements resulting from such strategies will usually enhance collaboration and thereby prepare spouses for the more demanding phases of therapy where success requires collaboration.

Let us conclude this section by reaffirming the importance of maintaining positive expectancies and a collaborative set throughout therapy. On the one hand, the partners must be confident that their sustained efforts at improving the relationship will meet with success; at the same time, they must not be lulled into a belief that the relationship will improve without their hard work. The couple must also be prepared for a jagged rather than a linear trend toward a happier relationship. When progress is interrupted by a return to pretreatment patterns of interaction, an unprepared couple may become defeatist. However, by reminding couples of the ever-present possibility of "relapses," and by occasionally predicting them, the therapist minimizes the likelihood of a catastropic reaction to such a development. Let us now lend substance to these recommendations by describing the treatment strategies which form the technology of BMT.

Behavior Exchange Procedures

In the most generic sense of the term, behavior exchange in marital therapy refers to any procedure that directly helps spouses gain an increased frequency of desired behaviors from one another. Although there are many procedural variations among strategies of behavior exchange, two basic steps are common to all of them. First, behaviors described as desirable by one or both spouses are pinpointed. Second, there is some attempt to increase the frequency of these behaviors. In short, behavior exchange is a structured way for spouses to increase the benefits that they provide for one another.

Examples of behavior exchange procedures abound in the literature (e.g., Jacobson and Margolin, 1979; Margolin, Christensen, and Weiss, 1975; O'Leary and Turkewitz, 1978; Stuart, 1976). A fairly typical example involves having each spouse list three behaviors in which he/she would like the other person to engage more often. For example, one wife requested three changes in the husband's behavior, all of

which were designed to relieve her of excessive domestic responsibilities: "1) He would cook once a week; 2) he would assume full responsibility for the children on Sundays; 3) he would vacuum all of the carpeting once a week." The wife agreed to three requests from the husband: "1) She would help me choose clothes whenever I go shopping for them; 2) she would give me back rubs at night if I ask for them; 3) she will initiate sexual activity when she wants it."[10]

Behavior exchange procedures are derived from a reinforcement model of marital exchange. These interventions capitalize on whatever reinforcement potential exists in the relationship. In directly instructing couples to systematically increase the rate of beneficial exchange, the therapist can immediately enhance each spouse's satisfaction without a great deal of costs accruing to either. The apparently simple and straightforward act of increasing positive behaviors can often be a powerful therapeutic intervention because distressed couples, by the time they enter therapy, are often greatly underutilizing their current repertoire of reinforcers. In some instances, each spouse is withholding positive behaviors as a strategy for minimizing the costs of a relationship which has been overrun with conflict. A characteristic stalemate often presents itself, where couples lack an equitable, systematic, face-saving way of reversing the destructive cycle of diminishing rewards. The numerous strategies for inducing an increase in positive behaviors provide a face-saving way of utilizing the resources already existing in their repertoires. Since couples often retain a great deal of reinforcement potential for one another despite the small number of positive exchanges, behavior exchange procedures provide a less intensive, relatively nondemanding basis for immediate improvement in the relationship, and set the stage for whatever intensive work is later necessary to overcome deficits in various relationship skills.

The induction of positive exchanges is fre-

___

[10]*Editors' Note.* Here, we will simply raise the issue, to be elaborated on in a later Note, of the role of BM therapist regarding the choice of treatment goals. As the above examples of marital exchanges suggest, and Jacobson later makes explicit, it is not the place of either spouse *or* of the BM therapist to question or challenge either spouse's behavior change objectives.

quently accompanied by training in techniques for recognizing and effectively providing reinforcement at critical times. Just as parents involved in a behavior therapy program are often taught to conduct a functional analysis of the factors which control their children's behavior, distressed spouses can become sensitized to the contingencies which govern both their partner's and their own emission of positive behavior. Many strategies designed to increase the frequency of positive behavior also help partners relearn how to maximize their reinforcing impact on one another.

Behavior exchanges are ideally suited for the early stages of therapy, since they are both nondemanding and likely to generate positive changes which can serve as a foundation upon which other changes can be erected. However, several factors need to be considered when formulating intervention strategies in the early stages. First, since couples are unlikely to have adopted a collaborative posture this early, the intervention strategies must not pressure either partner into concessions on fundamental areas of disagreement. The behavior changes should be discrete, easily delivered, and exchangeable without the need for either extensive negotiation or new skill development on the part of either spouse. Second, since one of the purposes of behavior exchange procedures is to foster subsequent collaboration, the procedures during these early stages of therapy should not assume or depend on collaboration. The inducement of positive exchanges despite the virtual absence of collaboration challenges the ingenuity of even the seasoned marital therapist. Third, the focus must be on increasing positive rather than decreasing negative behavior (Weiss, 1978; Weiss, Birchler, & Vincent, 1974). Usually, the high frequency or high intensity negative behaviors are major reasons for seeking therapy, and their elimination can only coincide with the intensive collaborative effort in the later stages of therapy. A reduction in negative behaviors at this stage would require aversive control tactics (punishment or negative reinforcement), tactics which should not be encouraged even temporarily in couples already replete with high rates of negative exchanges.

Taking the above point into consideration, an important distinction can be made between two sets of behavior exchange strategies. One is characterized by one spouse asking the other to increase the frequency, intensity or duration of particular reinforcing behaviors. The other occurs when each partner decides how to please the other more effectively. The distinction is that, in this latter case, the decision as to which behaviors are increased resides with the giver rather than the receiver.

This latter strategy is exemplified by an early intervention described by Jacobson and Margolin (1979). During a three-to-four week baseline period, each spouse has been tracking the daily frequency of numerous spouse behaviors, based on the Spouse Observation Checklist. Concurrently, each has been rating each day on a 1-7 scale for overall relationship satisfaction. By correlating behavioral frequencies with daily satisfaction ratings, it is possible to pinpoint those behaviors which seem to be the most important determinants of daily satisfaction, i.e., the "reinforcers" in the relationship (Jacobson et al., in press; Wills et al., 1974). In therapy, spouses are instructed to form hypotheses regarding which behaviors on their part are most reinforcing to the partner. Then they are each given the assignment of testing their hypotheses by systematically increasing the behaviors which they have identified and observing the effects on the partner's daily satisfaction rating. The goal is to increase the partner's daily satisfaction rating. Each spouse is to conduct the experiment privately, without consultation with the partner, except to scan the partner's checklist each evening to observe the effects of the experiment.

This intervention, if implemented skillfully, almost always leads to a "spike" in the frequency of positive behavior for both spouses. The assignment is presented to the couple as a challenge; each spouse wants to demonstrate his/her capability in "pleasing" the other. To emphasize the challenge, the therapist can supplement the instructions with a proviso such as the following:

We find in our work with couples that they often lose touch with how to make each other happy. They think they know what the other person wants, but it turns out that they are wrong. Let's see if you can do it.

The very absence of collaboration can be harnessed by a skillful therapist. In spite of themselves, as each spouse competes with the other to demonstrate to the therapist that he/she knows more about his/her spouse than the spouse does about him/her, they both deliver high frequencies of positive behavior and often return to therapy the following week visibly happier. In the process, they begin to pay attention to the impact of their behavior on one another and adopt a less passive role toward their problems. They often rediscover their power to effect changes in the relationship, and hopelessness may have begun a course toward extinction. Since the giver has decided what behaviors to increase, and the receiver has not had to ask for them, they are both more likely to attribute the changes to the other's active effort and initiative. Couples enter therapy with an expectation that they should not have to specify their needs to one another. Although a behavioral approach is diametrically opposed to this point of view and eventually attacks it directly, couples are not easily persuaded until positive changes have already occurred.

There are many ways to vary the basic task of focusing spouses on pinpointing and increasing their delivery of positive behavior. Weiss and his associates (Weiss and Birchler, 1978; Weiss et al., 1973) ask couples to have "love days," where, for a given day, one spouse attempts to double his/her output of "pleasing" behaviors. Similarly, Stuart (1976) has couples alternate "caring days," where one spouse devotes the day to demonstrating his/her caring for the other in as many ways as possible. These methods differ from the strategies described above only in their focus on specific days as those targeted for change.

In addition to positive changes initiated by the giver, many persons derive benefit from learning to ask for changes in behavior from the partner. Spouses may be unaccustomed to asking for change from the partner, and, as was mentioned above, assume that they should not have to ask for change, that the other should somehow *intuit* what they want and provide it forthwith. Yet the direct communication of each person's desires is an important skill in maintaining a satisfying relationship. Other spouses do ask for changes in their partners, but the requests are so global or nebulous that it is un-

clear what is being requested. Behavior exchange requires that spouses learn to request change *directly* by *pinpointing* the precise behaviors that they wish to see occurring more often; thus, "I want to feel closer to you" might become, "I want you to tell me what you're feeling." "I want you to be more aware of my needs" may translate into, "Ask me what is wrong when you see that I'm upset." At times, requests as sublime as "Be more tuned in to the relationship" refer to mundane desires such as "Help me with the dishes after dinner." Not always, certainly, but often, negative feelings can be directly tied to rewards that are being withheld.

In therapy, spouses practice asking for those behaviors that they want more often from one another. If possible, the requests are simple and straightforward; it is up to the receiver to decide whether the requests are granted. If the request requires extensive negotiation, it probably touches on some central relationship issues and is better reserved for later stages of therapy.

Various exercises are available to structure these exchanges. Weiss and Birchler (1978) have suggested that couples conduct a "cost-benefit analysis," in which each spouse rates the amount of benefit that would be obtained by the delivery of particular behaviors, and the giver rates the "costs" to himself inherent in providing the particular behavior. It is hoped that exchanges can be arranged which reflect a balance between benefits and costs. At other times, couples might prefer to focus on a particular area, such as parenting, and each requests specific behaviors from the other to improve their interaction regarding child-rearing decisions. These procedures tend to work best when each has the opportunity to refuse requests that are too costly. The exercise involves a high level of demand for compromise, and few spouses refuse all requests. By minimizing the costs, yet inducing some concessions and change agreements, collaboration is more easily maintained.

When spouses are simultaneously agreeing to change their behavior in response to requests from the other, the changes can either be contingent on one another or independent of one another. The former constitutes a *contingency contract* (Weiss et al., 1974) since each partner's change is contingent upon the other person's change. Compliance is cross-linked between partners. Consider the following quid pro quo between Jerry and Melinda:

A. Jerry agrees to wash the dishes nightly.
B. Melinda agrees to straighten the house prior to bedtime each night. This includes removing all clothing from the floor and piling up papers and reading material on coffee table.

If Jerry has washed the dishes on a given night, Melinda must comply with her end of the contract. Similarly, following each night that she has straightened the house as promised, Jerry must wash the dishes after dinner. If, however, Jerry fails to wash the dishes by 10:00 p.m. on a given night, Melinda is obligated to refrain from straightening the house. She is to resume her task as soon as Jerry has once again washed the dishes. Similarly, if Melinda goes to bed without straightening the house, Jerry is free of his obligation to wash the dishes on the following evening. His obligation to the dishes is postponed until the evening following Melinda's resumption of her contractual responsibilities.

The quid pro quo contract is one way of creating an environment which is supportive of behavior change. If we can assume that people usually behave in accordance with the principle of maximizing rewards and minimizing costs, then at any given time behavior in a relationship reflects the most positive outcomes that either can currently receive. It is naive to expect them to change their behavior in a way which would decrease their overall reward/cost ratio. Therefore, if change is to be given a reasonable chance, the reinforcement contingencies must be altered in such a way as to render the overall environment more reinforcing, given the new behavior, than was the case for the old behavior. Since Jerry found dishwashing to be punishing, he would agree to wash the dishes only at great cost, unless dishwashing produced compensating rewards which more than assuaged these costs. If Melinda's improved house-straightening is more rewarding to Jerry than dishwashing is costly, dishwashing may be maintained under the above contract.

The principle embodied in the contingency contract is that behavior will only change if the environment reinforces the change, and indeed, if the reinforcing impact exceeds that provided for the status quo. The therapist must attend to this necessity for a supportive environment, whether or not the contingency contract is his modus operandi.

The contract between Jerry and Melinda reflects some innovations added to the original formats for quid pro quo contracting. First, rather than one partner's behavior being contingent on the other's, there is a *circular contingency* specified. Each partner's behavior is functionally related to the other's, according to a specified contingency. This reciprocal causality is more reflective of natural contingencies governing marital behavior than a unilateral contingency would be.[11] Besides the enhanced realism embodied in the circular contingency, two potential liabilities of contingency contracting are finessed: The "who goes first" problem is avoided, and one act of noncompliance is minimally disruptive to the long-term integrity of the agreement. An optimal quid pro quo contract should contain as many of the following characteristics as possible: (a) The exchange should be equally costly (and beneficial) *for both* spouses; (b) the exact nature of the contingency should be specified, that is, when, where, and how much of the behavior must occur in order to produce the partner's "reinforcer"; (c) the contingency should include a specification of how the exchange becomes reinstated in the event of a transgression by either partner.

The alternative to specifying a contingency between each spouse's agreement is to simply have both partners agree independently, without the inclusion of an explicit contingency. Thus, Jerry and Melinda would each agree to the same behaviors, but in the absence of a cross-linking between them. This type of agreement was once thought to be unsuitable (Stuart, 1969; Weiss et al., 1974) because the creation of a supportive environment was left to chance.

---

[11]*Editors' Note.* We think that the behavioral marriage therapy emphasis on environmental contingencies is exaggerated. For example, it seems to us that a good deal of "marital behavior" is controlled by each spouse's *self-administered* contingencies, e.g., "I will do this for him/her (unasked) because it pleases me to see him/her happy." Such an analysis, of course, fits comfortably into a functional analysis of behavior, but clarifies that contingencies exist within, as well as between, people.

But these concerns may have been unwarranted (Jacobson, 1978c). First, the mere specification of a contingent relationship by no means ensures its actualization; couples may or may not adhere to the fine print of the contractual specifications. Even assuming their good intentions does not guarantee an effective implementation of the specified contingency, since the instructions are often complex and somewhat ambiguous. More importantly, in the process of implementing behavior exchanges, quid pro quos operate implicitly, and the advantages of additional specifications in a contract are questionable.

A final consideration in choosing between noncontingent (or implicitly contingent) and contingent exchanges is the potential liability of a contingency contract. Some spouses may devalue changes demanded by a contingency contract (Jacobson, 1978c), because they appear to be motivated by the contingency rather than by the "spontaneous desire" to behave differently. In the absence of direct evidence that attributions qualify the reinforcing impact of behavior change in marital therapy, one must appeal to research in social psychology (cf. Jacobson, 1978c) which is highly supportive of the present speculations. At our present state of knowledge, contingency contracting is only justified in the event that its inclusion clearly enhances the efficacy of marital therapy. This remains an empirical question.

Notice that these cautions do not apply to the notion of a written contract, but simply to the contingency contract. Regardless of whether a contingency is specified, written change agreements are highly desirable. First, written agreements obviate the necessity of relying on memory when attempting to recall the specifics of the exchange. Second, written agreements place behavior under stimulus control; especially if posted at highly visible locations, they act as cues, reminding spouses that they have agreed to change their behavior. Third, commitment in writing may have symbolic value for couples, enhancing their motivation to comply. The public commitment to behavior change can provide powerful insurance against inertia and may arouse sufficient cognitive dissonance to impel behavior change in the desired direction.

Thus far, the discussion has focused exclusively on behavior changes by one spouse, desired by the other. But behavior exchanges may also reflect *couple* deficits rather than behavioral deficits in one spouse (Jacobson and Margolin, 1979).[12] Mutual agreements to increase the rate of shared activities, the planning of leisure time activities, and the acquisition of new hobbies or common interests can be beneficial to many couples who are deficient in any of these areas.

In closing this section on behavior exchange procedures, the issue of compliance with therapist directives must be addressed (see Jacobson and Margolin, 1979, for a detailed discussion of this issue). Couples tend to be much more compliant with homework assignments when the task is explicitly made synonymous with therapy than when the link between these tasks and their in-session use is unclear or unspecified. When the treatment sessions center around the tasks engaged in at home, and when an incomplete assignment robs the therapy session of its agenda, noncompliance is rare. Once the therapist has invested the homework with this much importance, a spouse who does not comply is tacitly admitting that she/he is not interested in therapy. Few spouses are willing to be implicated or blamed for interfering with the progress of therapy. Thus, the skill and ingenuity of the therapist should be directed at consistently and persistently defining the therapy session itself as obtaining its raison d'être from the completion of assignments. Successful behavioral marital therapy is instigative and its fundamental business is the instigation of change in the natural environment (cf. Kanfer and Phillips, 1970). The sessions themselves, especially when the emphasis is on behavior exchange, are largely brainstorming sessions which plan strategies for enhancing the relationship in the natural environment. The therapist who can produce an ambiance of this nature will produce compliance.

Communication and Problem-solving Training

From its inception, behavioral marital therapy has emphasized direct training in communication skills. Behavior therapy is far from unique in this regard since an emphasis on com-

---

[12]*Editors' Note*. Of course, there is a third relevant domain which Jacobson does not address, ie., behavior changes desired not by the partner but by oneself.

munication training has characterized psychoanalytic (Ables and Brandsma, 1977), systems theory (Satir, 1967), and Rogerian approaches (Guerney, 1977) to marital and family therapy. However, behavioral communication training is unique in a number of respects. First, it utilizes a systematic method of training adapted from other skill training paradigms in behavior therapy (Jacobson, 1977b). Second, the communication training tends to be change-oriented rather than expression-oriented. That is, whereas most approaches to communication training focus on communication per se, i.e., the expression and reception of feelings, behavior therapy teaches couples how to communicate *in order to facilitate the resolution of conflicts*. This is not to say that training in feeling expression is not important to behavior therapists; on the contrary, many prominent writers in the field regularly include modules to help couples communicate support and understanding to one another (e.g., Weiss, 1978; Weiss and Birchler, 1978). The point is that problem-solving receives great emphasis in behavior therapy; couples are taught strategies for resolving conflicts with the hope that these skills will help them cope with future conflict. Third, the specific skills that are taught include behavior change principles deemphasized by other approaches to communication training, such as pinpointing, shaping, and providing for the effective use of social reinforcement.

Regardless of the content of the treatment program, behaviorists have relied upon a systematic method of communication training based on the concept of reinforced practice. The training method can be divided into three basic components: *instructions, feedback,* and *behavioral rehearsal*.

Instructions

Any skill training program has a content, and the training involves an attempt to impart that content to the clients. Behavioral communication training is no exception. This content can be presented to the couple verbally or by modeling the desired behavior. By modeling, we refer to the role-played demonstration of the desired behavior by the therapist. Modeling is widely used for a number of reasons: It is an

efficient way to demonstrate complex interactional skills; it provides the spouses with a face-saving way to change their behavior; by imitating an esteemed role model, it allows the therapist to demonstrate in a compelling manner the facilitative effects of the new skills (Eisler and Hersen, 1973). With the therapist assuming the role of one spouse and role-playing with that spouse's partner, the interaction sequence usually proceeds more desirably, and it becomes clear that there are benefits to be derived from the adoption of these new behaviors.

If modeling is used to impart communication skills, the therapist must guard against mere imitation by the spouses. For the new behaviors to be useful in new situations, couples must learn the general principle behind the new behavior. Various strategies can be utilized to ensure that spouses are not just mindlessly imitating, but also are actively processing information and learning the "rules." For example, discussion can be encouraged after the modeling demonstration, where spouses are asked to pinpoint these aspects of the modeled behavior responsible for the enhanced interaction sequence.

Behavior rehearsal

The dictum "practice makes perfect" is directly applicable to behavioral communication training. The rehearsal of those new behaviors modeled by the therapist is thought to be an essential component of the treatment program. As couples rehearse the new behaviors, they gradually achieve mastery of the new skills. Although the therapist may prompt these new behaviors and reinforce their occurrence, ultimately the spouses must actively demonstrate their ability to enact them. Behavior rehearsal provides feedback to the therapist regarding the spouses' competencies, indicating the extent to which they are assimilating the didactic material.

Feedback

This is the final step in the training sequence. Spouses' practice attempts are followed by feedback from the therapist. Both desirable and undesirable aspects of their performance are underscored. The feedback can either be molecular, focusing on specific "behavioral units," or it can be molar, focusing on a sequence of behavioral units and the relationships between them. In contrast to the type of feedback which might occur in a nonbehavioral treatment context, behavioral feedback tends to be descriptive rather than interpretive, and tends to focus on the functional, as opposed to the content, characteristics of behavior. Thus, the therapist will point out the behavior ("You just interrupted her") and emphasize its impact. Feedback can be provided either verbally or through the use of tapes. Videotaped or audiotaped feedback appears often to be more powerful than simple verbal feedback; this is both an asset and a liability (cf. Alkire and Brunse, 1974). Spouses can benefit greatly from viewing themselves from the perspective of an observer, but the feedback can at times be devastating. Couples should be prepared for the impact of videotaped feedback, and the therapist must provide support so that the feedback can be used constructively.

The entire training sequence can be thought of as a shaping process. Usually, the therapist's instructions are imperfectly adopted at first. With continued feedback, which includes reinforcement for all increments in desired communication, performance should gradually be refined and perfected. It appears that this shaping process, which includes both practice and performance-based feedback, in addition to the instructional content of the program, is necessary in order for couples to acquire new complex communication skills (Jacobson and Anderson, 1980). Although communication training depends on the instigation of new behaviors in the natural environment through the use of homework assignments, instigation is only part of the story.

Herein lies the essential distinction between skill training and behavior exchange procedures. Whereas the latter are content-oriented, focusing on behavior change and, hence, instigative almost by definition, skill training is fundamentally concerned with the *process* of interaction and only secondarily concerned with the content of the behaviors serving as the focal point of discussion. However, problem-solving training has the virtue of effectively producing behavior change despite the process orientation. The relationship problems which serve as the raw material for problem-solving training tend to be those which are not easily amenable to behavior exchange procedures. Some of these problems require negotiation because the recipient of the complaint will not agree to the request for change; others are refractory to simple behavior exchange because a statement of the problem does not immediately suggest a behavioral solution. An example of the latter would be one partner's complaint that "I am unhappy with your behavior toward me when we are at parties together." Clearly, before behavior change can become a real possibility with a problem such as this, the referents of this spouse's unhappiness must be pinpointed and, in all probability, a series of possible solutions will need to be considered.

Problem-solving training is a very promising approach to teaching couples how to negotiate the solutions to problems in their relationship (Jacobson, 1977a, 1977b, 1977c, 1978a; Jacobson and Anderson, 1980; Jacobson and Margolin, 1979). It is often necessary because distressed couples tend to exacerbate rather than resolve their conflicts by discussing them. Conflict resolution can be circumvented by a number of communicative tactics prevalent in the repertoires of distressed couples. A common obstacle is the absence of a clear definition: The problem can be stated in abstract terms (e.g., "You seem to always want to humilate me"), or the definition may be so global and all-encompassing that it communicates no specific information to the partner ("Our relationship is the pits"). The problem may be "heard" in a way discrepant with the intent of the presenter; this can result either from the presenter's expressive deficit or from the receiver's deficiencies in receiving or accurately interpreting communication from the partner. Since negotiations between dissatisfied partners are often viewed as battles to be won rather than mutual problems to be solved, there is a tendency for the receiver to be inattentive and listen to only portions of the speaker's remarks. Complaints which actually refer to very specific issues become accentuated and interpreted as total attacks. Actions are interpreted as reflecting malevolent intentions. Before much time has transpired, the spouses have alluded to every problem in their relationship, and they have created an overwhelming task which terminates with an exacerbation of discord.

Another common pattern, not mutually exclusive of the above, consists of emphasizing insight rather than behavior change. Couples often assume that if they can successfully trace a present conflict to its historical roots, the problem will magically disappear.[13] If insight is to be pursued as a goal in and of itself, then it should not be treated as a substitute for behavior change. Only future-directed, solution-focused discussions lead to change, although discussions of the past may be interesting, enlightening, and even enjoyable.

The most appropriate label for what is lacking in a distressed couple's problem-solving efforts is *collaboration*. Typically, each partner defends a position, and an implicit scoring system seems to be tabulating points. In competitive struggles befitting a "Wide World of Sports" production, there is a winner and a loser, but no relationship change.

The key to counteracting these behaviors is the establishment of a collaborative set (Jacobson, 1977c, 1977b). Behaviorists have been criticized (Gurman and Knudson, 1978; Gurman, Knudson, and Kniskern, 1978) for the practice of discouraging angry interchanges during problem-solving negotiations, implying that our goal is to remove passion from marital interaction.[14] *On the contrary, the behavior therapist's goal is not to eliminate anger and its concomitants from marriage, but simply to help couples discriminate between arguing and problem-solving.* As previous sections of this chapter have indicated, therapy is usually structured in such a way as to postpone problem-solving training until a collaborative set has been firmly established, usually by positive changes that have

already occurred. Problem-solving training is sufficiently charged that the maintenance of a collaborative set is a struggle. The therapist attempts to increase spouses' awareness of their own behavior in this regard. When they stray from collaborating during a therapy session, the response is often to send them to a different part of the room designated as the "fight corner." Thus, spatial manipulations are used to sharpen the distinction between collaboration and non-collaboration. Similar procedures are practiced by couples at home; they are encouraged to use different parts of the home for fighting and for problem-solving.

Problem-solving training is highly structured and controlled by a series of guidelines, which are specified elsewhere (Jacobson and Margolin, 1979), and will be described below. The structure and the guidelines provide cues for the acquisition of new behavior. By initially constraining spouses' behavior within this structure, the therapist minimizes the likelihood that destructive pretherapy interaction will intrude upon the problem-solving process.

The program teaches that a problem-solving session has two distinct phases: a phase for problem definition and one for problem solution. During the definition phase, the goal is to arrive at a clear, specific statement of the problem. Suggested solutions are not allowed during this phase. Then, once the couple agrees that the problem has been defined, the discussion enters a solution phase, during which the effort is directed toward resolution of the problem.

The use of two distinct phases facilitates the separation of tasks which, when intertwined, disrupt and confuse the problem-solving process. By devoting a brief period of time solely to the careful description of the problem, without a premature attempt at resolution, communication tends to be sharpened. When effort can be concentrated on arriving at a mutual understanding of what the problem is, a major impediment to effective problem resolution has been circumvented: Because descriptive information is vague and ambiguous, spouses often operate with discrepant assumptions about the nature of the problem.

In order to foster a solution-focused discussion of behavior change options, the solution phase is guided by the directive not to return

---

[13]*Editors' Note.* Indeed, we think it is Jacobson's expectations that are "magical," not the expectations of therapists who emphasize the role of historical insight. First, we know of *no* psychodynamically-oriented marriage therapists who emphasize insight "rather than" behavior change. Indeed, "insight" without behavior change is generally useless. The purpose of insight is *not* to "trace a conflict to its historical roots" with the assumption that problems will quickly disappear. As Yalom (1975) has put it, "it is the reconstitution of the past, not simply the excavation of the past, that is crucial" (p. 28). That is, historical insight is useful to the extent to which it helps to elucidate the present.

[14]*Editors' Note.* Not surprisingly, we think this statement misrepresents our position. See the original papers to which Jacobson refers plus our more recent article on these issues (Knudson, Gurman, and Kniskern, 1980).

to definitional issues. This rule counteracts spouses' tendencies to focus unproductively on speculations regarding the origins, implications, and ramifications of a problem, to the exclusion of possible solutions.[15] Irrespective of definitional concerns, the goal of the problem-solving session is to arrive at a decision which will eliminate the problem and improve the relationship.

In our training program at the University of Washington, we recommend a set of guidelines, which can be parceled into three sets: general guidelines for problem-solving etiquette; guidelines for defining problems; guidelines for solving problems.

General guidelines

First, *discuss only one problem at a time*. Couples are instructed to limit a given problem-solving discussion to a focus on one problem. Although all relationship problems may seem to be connected, the task is to discuss one issue. It is much easier to resolve one problem then to attempt two simultaneously. Attempts to interrelate multiple concerns in a single session limits the possibility of reaching any agreements, so complex and incoherent has the task become.

Second, *paraphrase*. Each spouse is encouraged to begin his/her response to the other's remark by summarizing what the other has said. Then the speaker indicates whether or not the summary was accurate. If not, the statement is repeated. Although such a directive might appear somewhat mechanical, the summary statement serves a number of important functions in a problem-solving discussion. The directive ensures that each person carefully listens to the other's remarks and immediately protects the couple from protracted miscommunication. In addition, interruptions are far less likely to occur. Finally, the summary statement increases the chances of each partner adopting the other person's perspective.

Third, *avoid making inferences about the other person's motivation, attitudes, or feelings*.[16] Problem-solving is often hindered by *mind-reading*. A particularly pernicious form of mind-reading involves the inference of malevolent intentions from undesirable behavior. The proper focus of problem-solving is on upsetting or undesirable behavior, not speculative, unverifiable excursions into the other's head. The latter interferes with a collaborative set, since the partner often feels obliged to defend his intentions rather than accommodate to the other's complaint.

Fourth, *avoid verbal abuse and other aversive exchanges*. When collaboration is constrained by cathartic attempts at revenge, humiliation, and other forms of punishment, effective problem-solving is precluded.

Guidelines for defining problems

First, when stating a problem, always begin with something positive. Usually, the positive beginning includes an expression of appreciation for some other positive behavior or, better yet, some mention of certain aspects of the problem under discussion which are already "pleasing" to the spouse who is stating the problem. For example, instead of restricting the opening remark to, "You don't help me clean up after dinner," one might say, "I appreciate the way you've been helping me around the house lately. Don't think I haven't noticed. My only remaining gripe is that you don't help me clean up after dinner." To reinforce the notion that problems describe unwanted behavior rather than bad people, the person whose behavior is being criticized should be reminded that he/she is being criticized for one aspect of his/her behavior, not for being a failure as a spouse. Distressed spouses are particularly guilty of selectively tracking those behaviors which displease them, and ignoring or not reinforcing the pleasing behaviors that already occur. The opening positive remark increases the likelihood that the prob-

---

[15]*Editors' Note*. Of course, it is sometimes the case that exploration of the origins of a problem (historically) provides a vehicle for self-disclosure which itself can form the basis for empathy from the partner. At such times, it is not uncommon, in our experience, that spouses become a great deal closer, more expressive and collaborative, *without* any formally negotiated behavior changes.

[16]*Editors' Note*. On the other hand, "mind-reading," in the sense of having an intuitive understanding (based on prior experience) of what one's spouse is feeling or thinking, *can* be extremely helpful if it is not used as a weapon against one's spouse. Note also Sager's (Chapter 3) point that very often it is the spouse who provides the therapist with the most accurate understanding of his/her mate's way of experiencing the world.

lem will be received in the spirit of collaboration.

Second, when defining problems, *be specific*. Problems should be defined in precise, behavioral terms. "You don't want to sleep with me anymore" is more aptly defined by a specific behavioral deficit, for example, "Most of the time I initiate sex." Problem definitions which are vague and not anchored in the person's overt behavior leave room for doubt as to the specific actions that are upsetting. *Pinpointing*, a skill which is also emphasized as part of the behavior exchange intervention, continues to be emphasized in problem-solving training. Vague problem formulations are frowned upon, not only because they hinder communication efficiency, but also because they tend to inhibit collaboration. Defining a problem by describing the partner in terms of derogatory adjectives (e.g., "lazy"), personality trait labels (e.g., "neurotic"), and overgeneralizations (e.g., "you never treat me with respect."), tend to produce defensive behavior in the partner, whereas a circumscribed comment on one's behavior is usually easier to accept.

Third, in stating a problem, *feeling expressions* are encouraged. The spouse who is pinpointing a problem is taught to include in his/her description an indication of the experiential impact of the problem. Instead of simply stating, for example, "The problem is that you make weekend plans without consulting me," one spouse was urged to include the feelings that were engendered by the behavior: "I feel rejected and unloved when you make plans without consulting me in advance." Partners tend to be more sympathetic to complaints when the negative impact is made explicit.

Fourth, *both partners are to acknowledge their role in perpetuating the problem*. This guideline is designed to intercept the tendency to try to justify one's behavior instead of simply accepting the other's formulation as a reflection of "the way she/he sees it." Admitting to one's role implies that the receiver simply admits to the occurrence or lack thereof of the behavior in question. It does not imply an acceptance of responsibility for changing. Furthermore, most relationship problems contain contributions by both members; by admitting to being "part of the problem," the complainer increases the like-lihood that the transgressor will become "part of the solution." The receiver's reaction to the initial problem formulation has important implications for the remaining discussion. When partners are truly collaborating and adhering to the present guidelines, the problem definition phase will remain uncontaminated by attempts to deny the validity of a complaint. The issue is irrelevant to a problem definition, since, when a behavior is upsetting to one spouse, it is *a priori* valid. This does not necessarily imply that by "accepting" the complainer's formulation the receiver is committed to behavior change. The solution phase determines the actions to be taken. What is important is the purity of the definitional exchange, and the necessity of not challenging the legitimacy of *any* problem, as long as one person is upset by a deficit or excess in the other's behavior.[17]

Fifth, *problem definitions should be brief*. Ideally, the formulation stage will be limited to two exchanges. The first involves a statement of the problem by one partner followed by a paraphrase, culminating in a mutual understanding of the nature of the problem. Then, the definition is broadened by each person's acknowledgment that the problem is an interactional one. Spouses are then ready to move into the solution phase of problem-solving. The brevity of the definition phase constitutes an attempt to avoid the "verbal masturbation" that often occurs in partners' fixation on unnecessary explorations of the past. Extensive elaborations of the problem, including attributions of blame, tracing the problem's implications or its historical origins, are not avoided in principle, but they are eshewed as a *problem-solving* strategy. This practice is part of the general attempt to

---

[17]*Editors' Note*. As noted in Editors' Note 10, the obvious implication here is that it is never the proper role of the behavioral marital therapist to challenge, question or redirect any clearly stated patient goal. While we agree that personal bias, countertransference and the like have the potential to lead therapists to question their patients' goals insensitively, we think a pure consumer-oriented, hands-off approach is at least as pernicious. For example, as Gurman and Klein (1980) and Gurman (1979) have made clear, unquestioning acceptance by the therapist of overt patient behavior change goals runs enormous risks of implicitly reinforcing stereotyped views of women and their roles in marriage, e.g., the husband who objects to his wife's planned return to finish her college education and "requests" an increase of "house cleaning behavior" in its place.

isolate change-oriented discussions and separate them from other types of discussion which tend not to produce change agreements.

"What is to be done?": Guidelines for reaching agreement

First, once couples have defined a problem, the remaining discussion should be solution-focused. To ensure a solution-focus, spouses are taught to generate solutions through the *brainstorming* technique (D'Zurilla and Goldfried, 1971; Goldfried and Davison, 1976). Couples brainstorm by generating as many proposed solutions as possible, without regard to their quality. The idea is to be imaginative and not censor solutions because, when considered privately, they seem silly or unworkable. To emphasize the lack of concern with quality, the therapist models and prompts a quota of patently absurd, humorous proposals within the overall list. In addition to inducing a structure which facilitates the maintenance of a solution focus, brainstorming disinhibits couples from their tendency to withhold proposals. Brainstorming is particularly useful when the couple is "stuck" at the solution phase. Brainstorming often liberates spouses and enhances their production of creative suggestions. By its inclusion of "funny" and "absurd" solutions, it also adds levity to the problem-solving endeavor. It is important that the partners not evaluate the solutions as they are being generated. Once the list is complete, and the absurd suggestions eliminated, then the advantages and disadvantages of each proposal can be evaluated.

Second, behavior change should be based on mutuality and compromise. This guideline summarizes a number of behaviors which couples are taught, all designed to produce an equitable change agreement following from a collaborative set. For example, each final solution is to involve some change on the part of each spouse. The complainer is urged to ask, "How can I help you do something about this problem?" Moreover, spouses are taught to moderate their demands, to recognize that in the long run the relationship will benefit more if change does not excessively burden either party.

Third, final agreements should be in writing, and they should be very specific. Any agreed-upon behavior change needs to be described in terms of frequency, duration, and the conditions under which the new behaviors are to occur. The agreement should also provide for cues which remind spouses of what they have agreed to.

Summary and conclusions regarding problem-solving training

Problem-solving training has been, in our experience, a very powerful treatment strategy for a wide variety of distressed couples. Systematic research into the efficacy of behavioral marital therapy seems to support our intuition (Jacobson and Margolin, 1979). Its power seems to stem from two primary sources. First, it focuses simultaneously on *process* and *content*. Couples solve presenting problems as they acquire problem-solving skills, and at the same time they acquire skills which lead to more reinforcing interaction and allow them to solve their own problems more effectively in the future.

Second, problem-solving training epitomizes the reinforcing power of collaboration. In the process of mastering the art of solving relationship problems, spouses learn that they will be much happier working together on their relationship than dealing with their conflicts as adversaries. The key to successful training lies in inducing couples to behave as a team so that the advantages of collaboration have an opportunity to present themselves. Every guideline in the manual is designed to circumvent the typical subversive strategies which couples use when they approach conflict resolution as adversaries. Reluctance to adopt specific guidelines defines the refusal to collaborate; any spouse who knowingly adopts the former stance must accept responsibility for the latter.

The therapist should notice that the rules and guidelines are interdependent, such that the adoption of one facilitates performance on another. For example, when spouses obey the directive to refrain from problem-solving at the time some undesirable behavior occurs, the conflict often disappears. Couples report that if they postpone the discussion to the next scheduled problem-solving session, by the time the session occurs the problem seems trivial. The conflicts created by unproductive verbal exchanges can be considerably more destructive than the persistence of the problem which served as the impetus for the discussion. Thus, deferring the discussion to a prearranged problem-solving session diffuses it and often eliminates the need for the discussion; at the very least, it transfers the discussion from a situation likely to produce a negative outcome to one where the potential for a favorable settlement is much greater.

Perhaps the most difficult response class to modify in a problem-solving session is the tendency of spouses to defend themselves and their transgressions. The most common instance is the accused spouse's attempt to deny the legitimacy of the other's complaint, deny responsibility for the action or inaction on which he/she is being called to task, or enumerate circumstances which render the behavior beyond his/her control. The guidelines for problem definitions attempt to circumvent this tactic by designating the function of this phase as one of simply pinpointing the target behavior. The legitimacy is *assumed*, since one partner is upset, and there is no need for evaluation. The spirit of collaboration obviates an evaluative focus. This does not mean that the receiver of a complaint agrees with the problem, nor does acceptance of a problem definition obligate one to change. The solution phase will determine what is to be done about the problem. The point is that the destructive debate centering around the justifiability of the proposed problem is deflected. This is likely to frustrate spouses, but their opportunity to evaluate the problem will occur during the solution phase, when they consider the pros and cons of various strategies for solving the problem. The advantage of deferring this type of discussion until the solution phase is that, by this time, if all the guidelines have been followed, the response of the receiver of the complaint is likely to be mellowed. She/he has not been attacked, the complaint has been contained to a specific pinpointed set of behaviors, and the mutuality of problem-solving has remained intact.

Another fringe benefit of problem-solving training is that it forces spouses to confront their *real* goal in discussing relationship problems. If they cannot, will not, or do not observe the guidelines, they are tacitly endorsing the combative, adversary type of interaction. Angry ex-

changes occur in all relationships, and perhaps they are functional, but they do not lead to behavior change.

The important discrimination couples must master is the difference between fighting and problem-solving. It is not incumbent upon them to stop fighting, but simply to separate fighting from problem-solving. If spouses are fighting rather than problem-solving, they should be taught to acknowledge what they are doing, relabel the session as an argument, and reschedule the problem-solving session.

Finally, problem-solving training follows smoothly from the less intensive focus on increasing positive behavior which occurs earlier in therapy. Often, our treatment program begins with general instructions to identify and increase pleasing behavior, followed by a more specific focus on exchanging specific behaviors, and concluding with problem-solving to deal with major problems. Spouses' success in prior, less demanding stages fosters greater collaboration in subsequent phases. Occasionally, the major presenting problems can be resolved without problem-solving training. In these instances, therapy can terminate, or, given an ambitious couple, problem-solving skills can be taught for preventative purposes.

At its best, problem-solving training is preventative as well as ameliorative. But in order for it to serve a preventative function, the therapist must ensure that couples are actually learning skills that can be applied in the natural environment, independently of the therapist (Jacobson, 1977b; Jacobson and Margolin, 1979). Generalization must be sufficiently programmed so that spouses continue to enact their newly acquired behaviors outside the therapist's office. A number of tactics can facilitate the process of generalization. First, termination should be gradual rather than abrupt. Rather than suddenly moving from weekly sessions to a cessation of therapist contact, sessions should be *faded*. As partners move from weekly to biweekly and then to monthly sessions, they are presented with the opportunity to gradually assume control over their own marriage again. Second, the therapist should become less *active* and *directive* as therapy progresses. If the clients are actually acquiring new skills rather than simply responding to cues provided by the therapist, they should exhibit an increased ability to deal effectively with relationship problems even in the absence of direct guidance from the therapist. Third, the content of the change agreements or solutions should come from the couple. Fourth, the training must be structured so as to insure spouses' active involvement in the learning process. For example, spouses can be asked to critique the therapist's simulated problem-solving behavior, with the therapist role-playing either positive or negative problem-solving behaviors. In a performance-based treatment program, the therapist must ensure that the spouses are capable of functioning on their own so that the maintenance of treatment-derived gains will be possible even after termination (Jacobson, 1977b).

GENERAL CONSIDERATIONS

In this section, some general considerations in the practice of behavioral marital therapy will be discussed. Much of what is discussed could be abstracted from the descriptions of "behavior exchange" and "problem-solving" procedures in the previous sections. But, as will be emphasized, BMT is a highly idiographic approach which eludes any attempt at reduction into one or two basic intervention strategies.

Definitional Issues

Is behavioral marital therapy a set of techniques, the application of certain theoretical principles, or the application of a methodological style? All three definitions have been used at one time or another by various writers (cf. Jacobson and Margolin, 1979). In practice, BMT is distinguished most by a style of intervention which transcends the specific techniques utilized for a given case. The critical component of this method is the engagement in a *functional analysis* of the spouses' presenting complaints. During the assessment phase, the therapist attempts to uncover the environmental antecedents of the current relationship problems, along with the reinforcement contingencies currently maintaining the dysfunctional interaction. The analysis includes an assessment of the cognitive mediators of current marital interaction, such

as each spouse's appraisals of the current relationships, his/her attributions regarding the causes of his/her own and the partner's behavior, and his/her overall perceptions of the relationship. From this functional analysis, a set of hypotheses is generated regarding the important causes of the current problems, and an intervention strategy is planned to produce a more desirable relationship. The functional analysis continues into the intervention phase in order to evaluate the effects of treatment. In the event that treatment is unsuccessful, hypotheses are reformulated and the treatment plan is modified. Both the conceptualization of marital behavior as being a function of antecedent and consequent stimuli in the environment and the ongoing evaluation of the effort to create a more favorable environment for positive marital behavior are included in a functional analysis.

Positive tracking

Throughout therapy there is an emphasis on spouses' strengths and the attempt to supplement and maximize those strengths. The focus on positive behavior is designed to maneuver partners into altering the tendency to selectively track negative behavior. The negative bias often serves to exacerbate an objectively distressed relationship by preventing partners from viewing their problems as simply part of a total configuration which includes both positive and negative behavior. As spouses surrender their negative bias and begin to focus constructively on increasing the amount and quality of reinforcing exchanges, they derive benefit from their new world view; collaboration becomes easier because the situation seems less hopeless.

Positive control

A key observation on the part of the behavioral marital therapist is that distressed couples often rely on faulty behavior change operations in attempting to produce desirable behavior in one another (Jacobson and Margolin, 1979; Weiss, 1978). These strategies typically involve the use of punishment and negative reinforcement (Jacobson, Waldron, and Moore, in press). For example, verbal threats, demands, and other forms of coercion are used; more passive means of aversive control include a withholding of rewards through withdrawal. These aversive strategies are appealing in the short run because they are compelling and often produce short-term changes. The costs accrue gradually, as aversive exchanges become the predominant mode of control. Therapy is often predicated on the desirability of reversing this pattern by providing partners with more effective ways of inducing desirable behavior in one another. Positive control refers to the use of mutually rewarding exchanges to maintain positive relationship behavior. Both behavior exchange procedures and problem-solving training exemplify the use of positive control strategies.

Reciprocity

Research conducted in the laboratories of behavioral marital researchers has repeatedly demonstrated that successful relationships are characterized by a certain lawfulness which has been defined as reciprocity (Gottman et al., 1977; Gottman et al., 1976; Jacobson, Waldron, and Moore, in press; Wills et al., 1974). Therapy attempts to persuade spouses that their distress reflects a *mutual* withholding of benefits which can be modified only by each spouse's careful, systematic attention to increasing his/her delivery of rewarding behaviors. Often much cognitive restructuring is necessary before partners accept the premise that *reciprocity* is operating in their marriage, and that each spouse is responsible both for the current level and the ultimate amelioration of discord.

Conceptualization of relationship skills

As previous sections of this chapter have emphasized, the behavior therapist sees the successful relationship as requiring the mastery of numerous skills. The skill orientation leads to a therapeutic emphasis on prevention, since the goals of therapy are not merely to remediate the current situation, but also to teach the skills which couples will need in order to successfully cope with conflicts subsequent to the termination of therapy. The role of the therapist resembles that of a teacher. The generalization and maintenance of changes are programmed into the treatment program rather than being left to chance.

Differences between Behavior Therapy and other Approaches to Marital Therapy

Recent books on marital therapy document the numerous procedural similarities between behavior therapy and other approaches based on other theoretical frameworks (e.g., Ables and Brandsma, 1977; Guerney, 1977; Haley, 1976; Sager, 1976). However, several fundamental distinctions are identifiable. First, BMT is unique in its preoccupation with systematic, multidimensional assessment of relationship dysfunction. Second, BMT has a relatively optimistic regard for spouses' capacity for commitment to change. Third, BMT emphasizes the significance of overt behavior as the therapist's primary focus. Fourth, BMT advocates highly structured, specific procedures for changing behavior, based in large part on principles derived from the laboratories of general psychology. Fifth, whereas the importance of private events is recognized, behavior therapy, more than any other approach, views spouses as primarily sensitive to environmental contingencies. Of these five basic distinctions, only the second has not been addressed; since this distinction may be the most subtle and philosophically the most significant, it will receive further attention.

One of the trademarks of marital and family therapy has been the assumption that family systems resist change. Both psychodynamic (e.g., Meissner, 1978) and systems theoretical perspectives (e.g., Haley, 1963) describe an investment on the part of couples in the status quo, despite their obvious suffering.[18] It follows from this belief that couples will rebel against most direct, straightforward attempts on the part of the therapist to change their behavior. Jacobson and Margolin (1979) have pointed out the circularity in this conception of resistance. Typically, resistance is invoked only after treatment strategies have proven unsuccessful (e.g., Ables and Brandsma, 1977). This post hoc inference is then used to explain the behavior from which the inference was drawn. Why do couples

---

[18]*Editors' Note.* Actually, Jacobson is mentioning only one "half" of the change-resistance to change process from a systems perspective, i.e., homeostasis. The other half, or dimension, is the push toward growth, or heterostasis. See Wertheim (1973) for a discussion of the clinical implications of the meanings of each.

resist change? Because of resistance![19] How do we know that resistance is operating? Because the couple has not responded to the therapist's change induction techniques. This position is not disconfirmable and, therefore, is unacceptable both logically and scientifically. What is of greater concern than the intellectual shortcomings of this position is its implications for the practice of marital and family therapy. As Jacobson and Margolin (1979) argue, "Resistance to change seems to function . . . as a way of rationalizing unsuccessful treatment. The presumption that couples will resist change has the potentiality of a self-fulfilling prophesy. If therapists expect couples to resist their change efforts, their in-session behavior will be significantly affected, and they are likely to generate resistance" (p. 45). In its extreme form, the concept implies that couples must be tricked into changing, against their real wishes (Haley, 1976)! Thus, a therapeutic stance is fostered which depends on strategies which are indirect, ill-defined, and based on covert manipulation.

Behavior therapy begins with a different premise, namely that most couples seeking therapy are capable of a rational, collaborative effort to improve their relationship. This does not imply that couples embrace the prospect of behavior change without ambivalence, but ambivalence about change and the difficulties that couples experience in altering their relationship behavior are not viewed as stemming from an opposition to the *goals* of therapy. Rather, obstacles to change reflect the costly nature of the change process itself. Change is both difficult and risky for couples in conflict. It is the therapist's task to remind couples of the potential long-term benefits of an improved relationship so that they can be considered along with the short-term costs. The failure to comply with the therapist's instructions, or other signs of "resistance," is interpreted as evidence that the short-term costs rather than the long-term benefits remain dominant.

Critiques of Behavioral Marital Therapy

Behavior therapy has become recognized as one of three major theoretical models in marital therapy (Gurman and Knudson, 1978; Paolino and McCrady, 1978). Yet, at the present time, it has remained on the periphery of the marital and family therapy movement, as reflected by the near absence of behaviorists from the editorial boards of most professional journals specializing in marital and family therapy, as well as the relative lack of behaviorists' participation in organizations such as the American Association for Marriage and Family Therapy. In the view of this author, BMT is still widely misunderstood by marital and family therapists. A recent debate appearing in *Family Process* between critics of behavior therapy (Gurman and Knudson, 1978; Gurman and Kniskern, 1978b; Gurman, Knudson, and Kniskern, 1978) and its defenders (Jacobson and Weiss, 1978) identifies a number of fundamental criticisms which have been levied at BMT.[20] These criticisms are, I believe, representative of the concerns generally voiced by advocates of alternative theoretical perspectives. Let us examine each of these major concerns, along with a summary of the response and clarification offered by Jacobson and Weiss (1978).

Criticism 1: BMT is predicated on the assumption that couples entering therapy are capable of collaborating in a reciprocal, step-by-step effort to improve their relationship.

It is true, as this chapter has indicated, that a collaborative set is a necessary precursor to the success of BMT. *However, couples seldom enter therapy prepared to work collaboratively; on the contrary, the induction of a collaborative set per se is an important goal in the early stages of BMT* (Jacobson, 1977b). Thus, rather than assuming that partners can collaborate, as the criticism implies, the behavioral approach systematically attempts to facilitate the adoption of such a set.

Criticism 2: BMT focuses exclusively on the modification of the frequency of overt behavior.

It is true that the early papers describing BMT

---

[19]*Editors' Note*. Patients may resist change *not* "because of resistance" (resistance is not a thing or a force), but because of the *anxiety* aroused by the prospect of change. Resisting change, then (at least at times), is motivated by a desire to avoid pain (in behavioral terms, resistance to change is negatively reinforcing, i.e., such behavior functions to avoid an aversive stimulus, thereby *increasing* the probability of such behavior).

[20]*Editors' Note*. A summary of this debate and a more elaborated discussion of our views of BMT more recently appeared in Knudson, Gurman and Kniskern (1980).

dealt primarily with the modification of overt behavior (Eisler and Hersen, 1973; Rappaport and Harrell, 1972; Liberman, 1970; Stuart, 1969). *However, in concert with the recent cognitive trend in behavior therapy* (Mahoney, 1974; Meichenbaum, 1977), *behavioral marriage therapists have begun to emphasize the importance of cognitive events in the analysis and treatment of couples in distress* (Jacobson, 1978b, 1978c; Jacobson and Margolin, 1979; Margolin, Christensen, and Weiss, 1975; Margolin and Weiss, 1978; O'Leary and Turkewitz, 1978; Weiss and Birchler, 1978).[21]

Criticism 3: BMT assumes an unwarranted homogeneity across couples in regard to what is reinforcing and punishing, what is good and bad communication.

Our critics are accurate to the extent that problem-solving training is based on a standardized set of guidelines which are applied to all couples receiving such training. *However, the essence of a behavioral analysis involves an attempt to define empirically what is reinforcing and punishing for each particular couple, without any preconceptions regarding universal reinforcing and punishing marital behaviors.* In particular, recent investigations have attempted to pinpoint both the generally important rewards and punishers in distressed and nondistressed couples, and the variability across couples in their preferences for certain classes of behavior (Jacobson, Waldron, and Moore, in press). Recent modifications in the Spouse Observation Checklist (Weiss, 1978) reflect this tendency to avoid any a priori assumptions about the valence of specific behaviors.

Criticism 4: BMT aspires to the creation of couples devoid of passion and affective exchange.

Perhaps the terminology used by behavior therapists and the emphasis on constructive

problem-solving have lead to the misconception that we wish to eliminate all conflict from marriage. By now it has hopefully become apparent to the reader that such a goal would not only be undesirable to a behavior therapist, but also totally unrealistic. *Conflict is an inevitable concomitant of intimacy, and rather than eliminate it, our goal is to expand spouses' options by helping them learn to contain conflict, if and when they wish to do so!* What concerns the behavior therapist is not the existence of anger and hostility in marriage but the habitual lack of control exhibited by distressed couples and their inability to separate anger from constructive attempts to solve relationship problems.

Criticism 5: BMT preaches that the therapist is a technician, and deemphasizes the importance of relationship skills on the part of the therapist.

Jacobson and Margolin (1979) have recently asserted that the most frequent impediment to successful BMT is not the unskillful application of behavioral technology, but rather relationship skill deficits on the part of therapists attempting to implement the technology. Indeed, no approach to marital therapy has attempted to specify the skills necessary to produce therapeutic change as much as behavior therapists have in recent years. Nevertheless, our critics cannot be blamed for their perception, since this literature is very recent and was largely unpublished at the time of their critique. Technology has been the focus in BMT until very recently, but the criticism is no longer appropriate.

In presenting a summary of our reply to the criticisms levied against BMT by Gurman and his associates, I do not mean to imply that the critique was misguided or gratuitous. As they clarified in their rejoinder (Gurman et al., 1978), they are favorably disposed toward BMT, and their critique was aimed at logical, theoretical, and clinical misgivings regarding the practice of behavior therapy in its *pure* form. On the basis of the literature that they reviewed and their assessment of the potential for simplistic extrapolation from that literature on the part of practitioners, their arguments are understandable. Efforts such as theirs can only enhance and broaden the thinking and behavior of both behavioral and nonbehavioral therapists.

---

[21]*Editors' Note*. We are still (cf. Gurman and Knudson, 1978; Gurman et al., 1978; Knudson et al., 1980) quite unconvinced of this. Nowhere in Jacobson's chapter, e.g., do we see any evidence of the importance of the BM therapist challenging and correcting his/her patient's faulty assumptions or perceptions of his/her behavior or that of his/her mate, as would occur often if BMT had truly begun to incorporate cognitive therapy methods (e.g., Beck, Rush, Emery, and Shaw, 1979).

Contraindications

Marital therapy is not always indicated. Although it appears that a substantial majority of couples seeking therapy can benefit from a conjoint treatment program, not all couples are suited for marital therapy, nor will all couples opt for such a treatment program, even when, from the therapist's perspective, the couple could benefit substantially from such a regimen.

First, marital therapy is not indicated, as the primary treatment, when the marital problems are *primarily* a consequence of a severe psychological or medical disturbance on the part of one spouse. Marital therapy can play an ancillary role in such instances, but an individually-based treatment focusing on the dysfunctional individual will be the primary treatment. This phenomenon is exemplified by, but not exclusive to, many distressed couples where one member is schizophrenic. At times the assessment issues here are very complex and subtle. For example, clinical depression can be a response on the part of one spouse to a distressed marriage, or it can be functionally related to factors extraneous to the relationship. Marital distress may be observed in both instances, but in one case marital therapy will serve as *the* primary treatment modality, whereas in the other case it will play a subordinate role (cf. Jacobson and Margolin, 1979; Weiss and Birchler, 1978).

Second, it is my view that when the primary precipitant of marital distress is one spouse's involvement in an extramarital sexual relationship, conjoint marital therapy may be futile. This does not mean than an extramarital affair is a "red flag" which should necessarily contradict a treatment plan based on conjoint marital therapy. A substantial proportion of such relationships can be helped by a focus on increasing the quality of the marital relationship for both spouses. It is obvious that many extramarital affairs are themselves precipitated by marital discord. But behavior exchange theory, with its emphasis on the environment outside the relationship, as well as the stimuli exchanged by the spouses within the relationship, predicts that even in a relatively satisfying relationship, a very attractive alternative to the marriage, such as a desirable new partner, can produce

distress. The author's clinical experience confirms the existence of such situations. It seems as if some people turn to the novelty of a new relationship despite a satisfactory marriage, since the novelty of courtship experiences can be very appealing given the reinforcement erosion that inevitably accompanies a long-term marital relationship. In such cases, marital therapy is hard-pressed to improve the situation, although the situation will often reverse itself without therapy, as the novel reinforcers provided by a new partner lose their potency.[22]

Third, marital therapy is not indicated when one or both spouses do not want it, preferring instead to end the relationship. Although this may appear obvious, it is important to mention because therapists can easily shape their clients into accepting a treatment regimen designed to improve their relationship, despite extreme ambivalence on the part of the clients regarding the optimal path. The mandate of a marital therapist is to serve the interests of the clients, not to protect or foster the institution of marriage. If, at the conclusion of a pretreatment assessment, the clients decide that separation rather than marital therapy is the optimal path, some assistance from the therapist may still be indicated, but such assistance will take a very different form than that prescribed in this chapter. Divorce counseling is beyond the scope of this chapter, but it bears little resemblance to marital therapy in either its goals or tactics (cf. Jacobson and Margolin, 1979; Johnson, 1977).

Fourth, in addition to the above examples where marital therapy may be contraindicated, there are also times when, even though marital therapy is indicated, it assumes a form very different from the general procedures outlined in this chapter. In fact, behavioral marital therapy

---

[22]*Editors' Note.* First, in our experience, extramarital affairs are among the most common precipitants of (overt) marital distress. Second, and more important, many marital therapists find that a marital therapy that aims to increase understanding (insight) of the causes of or antecedents to the affair(s) is very often anything but "futile." The key difference between this view and Jacobson's lies in his overriding efforts to *improve* the marriage (i.e., produce behavior change by changing cost/benefit ratios), while, for other therapists, increased understanding of the forces leading to affairs is an acceptable treatment goal, at least during the early stages of treatment.

is a highly idiographic approach to marital therapy, and the general procedures are little more than guidelines. One example of a clinical situation where the general format presented in this chapter requires extensive modification is the crisis situation. Occasionally, a couple enters therapy in acute crisis, and the thorough pretreatment assessment must be discarded in favor of an immediate, directive intervention. When there are immediate risks of physical harm to one or both spouses, or when the day-to-day functioning is so severely impaired that immediate action must be taken, a crisis intervention approach is preferred. The therapist might tell each spouse what to do for the next week; these instructions might be formalized into a written contract. They may involve hospitalization of one spouse, a trial separation, a commitment to abstain from alcohol, or any set of instructions which seems necessary to modify the high level of stress. Later, when the crisis has been eased, other more typical intervention strategies can be utilized.

These crisis situations are extremely rare. Most couples are severely distressed when they first contact a mental health professional, but the situation is seldom so desperate that immediate intervention is essential. Most couples stand to benefit much more from a carefully planned intervention based on a careful evaluation and assessment.

Finally, in those cases where marital therapy is indicated, are there instances when behavioral marital therapy is contraindicated? The model presented in this chapter attempts to encompass the gamut of marital problems, and thus does not delimit itself. Theoretically, there is no marital problem which simultaneously indicates the need for marital therapy and contraindicates the use of a behavioral approach. However, in practice, some couples will find a behavioral framework for viewing their problems unacceptable. The tactics outlined in this chapter may appear mechanical, excessively contrived, and the like. Such couples may simply find this approach incompatible with their view of the world, and will prefer an approach which makes more intuitive sense. Happily, although most spouses do not subscribe to a behavioristic, or even a cognitively behavioristic view of the world, the efficiency and effective-

ness of the procedures are usually sufficient to overcome initial reticence based on philosophical differences. However, now and then, we find a couple who believe that the cure is worse than the disease.

EFFECTIVENESS OF BEHAVIORAL MARITAL THERAPY

At the time of this writing, only six controlled outcome investigations of the effectiveness of BMT have been published. Four of these investigations involved a clinical investigation of BMT with distressed couples, while the other two were analog studies. Given the short history of controlled research, the conclusions that can be drawn are extremely limited. To emphasize just how limited the research into marital therapy is, it should be noted that the few controlled studies investigating BMT constitute the most substantial body of such experiments in the entire field of marital therapy (Jacobson, 1978b). This research has been examined in detail both by the author (Jacobson, 1978b, 1979; Jacobson and Margolin, 1979; Jacobson and Martin, 1976) and by others (Greer and D'Zurilla, 1975; Gurman and Kniskern, 1978a). Thus, the summary here will be brief.

Of the four controlled outcome studies which included both distressed populations and a comprehensive treatment program, one (Tsoi-Hoshmand, 1976) shall not be considered since it failed to meet minimal methodological prerequisites for establishing internal validity. The remaining three investigations investigated the effectiveness of a BMT treatment package which included both communication training and behavior exchange components (Jacobson, 1977a, 1978a; Liberman et al., 1976). Thus, none of them allows for a parceling out of the procedures which are contributing to the effectiveness of the treatment package. However, two of the studies included comparison treatments which, at the very least, controlled for placebo effects (Jacobson, 1978a; Liberman et al., 1976).

Jacobson's studies were both strongly supportive of the effectiveness of BMT. In both, BMT was significantly more effective than waiting-list control groups; in the second study, BMT was more effective than a very credible placebo control group (Jacobson, 1978a). The improvements occurred on both observational measures of reinforcing and punishing communication and on self-report measures of marital satisfaction. The improved relationships endured through the collection of six-month and one-year follow-up data. Liberman et al.'s study found BMT conducted in a group setting to be significantly more effective than an insight-oriented couples group on objective measures of marital communication; however, the groups did not differ in the subjective ratings of marital satisfaction subsequent to treatment. Couples in both groups improved significantly. The findings proved to be persistent through a one-year follow-up.

In a study reported by O'Leary and Turkewitz (1978), behavioral exchange procedures were compared to a group receiving a combination of behavioral and nonbehavioral communication training. Compared to a control group, both groups improved significantly on self-report measures but not on behavioral measures. Although there were no overall differences in effectiveness between the two treatment groups, young couples responded more positively to behavior exchange procedures, whereas older couples responded more favorably to communication training.

Thus, the published investigations generally support the effectiveness of BMT, although discrepancies between the findings of behavioral and self-report measures render the findings in the Liberman et al. and O'Leary and Turkewitz studies inconclusive. Other investigations have examined more discrete behavior change procedures in an attempt to ferret out the active change agents in BMT. For example, Margolin and Weiss (1978) compared two forms of behavioral communication training to a nondirective treatment condition. All treatments were brief and highly structured. On both observer-coded and spouse-coded measures of positive behavior, behavior conditions tended to be more effective than the nondirective treatment condition. Overall, a behavioral group which included a cognitive restructuring component was more effective than a behavioral group without cognitive restructuring. All three treatments were equally effective in reducing the incidence of negative behavior. The study provides tentative support for the importance of cognitive

restructuring in BMT. Jacobson (1979b) evaluated the effectiveness of problem-solving training used in isolation with severely distressed couples in a series of single-subject experimental designs. As measured by spouse records of positive and negative behavior in the home, problem-solving training lead to substantial improvements, maintained at six-month and one-year in four of the six couples. In an analog study, Jacobson and Anderson (1978) studied the effects of videotape feedback and behavior rehearsal on the acquisition of problem-solving skills in couples. Problem-solving skills were acquired only in those groups where couples received both feedback and the opportunity to rehearse.

Finally, in another analog study, Harrell and Guerney (1976) found BMT groups to be effective (compared to a control group) in improving communication, but not in enhancing subjective reports of marital satisfaction.

In conclusion, these early investigations of BMT must be considered promising. In particular, problem-solving training appears to be a powerful treatment approach. In all studies which included a problem-solving component, BMT was more effective than comparison control groups. In one study, problem-solving training was effective even when used alone to treat very distressed couples. There is some evidence that behavior rehearsal, combined with feedback and instructions, is essential to the effectiveness of a problem-solving training program. However, definitive evidence regarding the effectiveness of BMT awaits the outcome of future research. In particular, the inconsistencies in outcome depending on whether behavioral or self-report measures are used may be eliminated by the continued development and refinement of the methods for measuring marital satisfaction.

TRAINING MARITAL THERAPISTS

Marital therapy involves two basic sets of skills: skills in the effective presentation of a technology, and clinical skills which are required by any practicing marital therapist, whatever his/her theoretical orientation.

The training model practiced by the author is based on the assumption that both sets of skills can be learned. Marital therapy is viewed as a set of skills which can be acquired through the combination of practice, supervised feedback, and modeling.

When graduate students first begin to treat couples, they typically work in opposite-sexed co-therapy teams. Co-therapy is extremely useful for training purposes, since the beginning therapist is provided with peer support as well as supervision from a mentor. Although there is no evidence that co-therapy is a superior modality from the standpoint of treatment efficacy, it probably enhances the effectiveness of beginning therapists, by allowing the co-therapists to divide the various responsibilities and duties. Students usually meet on their own to prepare the upcoming therapy session, subsequent to the meeting with the supervisor. Typically, one student will assume responsibility for presenting didactic material on a particular week, while the other remains less active but focuses his/her attention on clinical concerns, such as whether or not the spouses seem to be comprehending the instructions. As these roles switch from week to week, each student experiences all aspects of the therapy process, but the task is less overwhelming.

Part of the problem in training therapists concerns our collective ignorance regarding the skills which comprise good therapy. The focus in our training program is on a number of clinical skills which seem to play a role in successful marital therapy. Some of the more prominent areas of focus are as follows:

1) *Clarity of presentation*: training students to speak in short, unambiguous sentences, which are geared to the level of verbal sophistication of the spouses.
2) *Structuring*: this refers to a whole set of behaviors designed to aid the therapist in structuring and maintaining control of therapy sessions. Structuring skills include setting an agenda at the beginning of a session, maintaining a focus on the agenda, etc.
3) *Use of humor*
4) *Confrontation skills*
5) *Provision of support and understanding*
6) *Strategies for enhancing credibility*
7) *Social reinforcement skills*
8) *Strategies for inducing compliance*

9) *Responsiveness to nonverbal cues*

The above does not comprise an exhaustive list, although it does represent areas which consume an inordinate amount of supervision time. Some of them seem to be more teachable than others: Structuring and clarity skills can be shaped, for example; on the other hand, it is exceedingly difficult to teach the humorless therapist to be funny.

In preparation for a marital therapy case, students complete relevant readings. The supervisor plays an active and directive role during the first few cases, but as the levels of skill and experience increase, the supervisor provides increasingly less structure. The supervision is intensive, involving both live observation and taped feedback.

The strategies utilized for training marital therapists are no different than those utilized for training therapists to treat individual clients. Rather than being guided by an underlying philosophy regarding the optimal strategies for training marital therapists, the training program is based on a loose set of untested assumptions, such as the already stated belief that being a good therapist means possessing a set of skills which can be learned. Anecdotally, it is obvious that students improve over time, some more than others. This seems to provide some vindication for our training methods, although the obvious factor that confounds this interpretation is experience: Perhaps students develop their skills independently of supervision, simply from the feedback they receive from their own experiences with clients. It is clearly an area that we know very little about; training programs for therapists are not nearly as sophisticated or empirically based as treatment programs for couples. The question of how to impart the skills of a good therapist remains virtually uninvestigated.

CONCLUSION

This chapter provided an overview of behavioral marital therapy. I have attempted to convey its essential features from the standpoint of theory, assessment, and practice. Since behavior therapy has been used in treating couples only in the last ten years, it is still an evolving approach. As a subarea of behavior therapy, its development has adhered to the tradition of progress through controlled research, a fact which has been predictably underemphasized in a clinically oriented chapter. Research will continue to shape its development, and hopefully will produce an approach which will become increasingly broad in its applicability and generally more effective.

REFERENCES

Ables, B. S., & Brandsma, J. M. *Therapy for Couples*. San Francisco: Jossey-Bass, 1977.

Alkire, A. A., & Brunse, A. J. Impact and possible causality from videotape feedback in marital therapy. *Journal of Consulting and Clinical Psychology*, 1974, *42*, 203-210.

Bandura, A. *Social Learning Theory*. Englewood Cliffs, NJ: Prentice-Hall, 1974.

Birchler, G. R. Differential patterns of instrumental affiliative behavior as a function of degree of marital distress and level of intimacy. (Doctoral dissertation, University of Oregan, 1972). *Dissertation Abstracts International*, 1973, *33*, 14499B-4500B. (University Microfilms No. 73-7865, 102.)

Birchler, G. R., Weiss, R. L., & Vincent, J. P. A multimethod analysis of social reinforcement exchange between maritally distressed and nondistressed spouse and stranger dyads. *Journal of Personality and Social Psychology*, 1975, *31*, 349-360.

D'Zurilla, T. J., & Goldfried, M. R. Problem-solving and behavior modification. *Journal of Abnormal Psychology*, 1971, *78*, 107-126.

Eisler, R. M., & Hersen, M. Behavioral techniques in family-oriented crisis intervention. *Archives of General Psychiatry*, 1973, *28*, 111-115.

Goldfried, M. R., & Davison, G. C. *Clinical Behavior Therapy*. New York: Holt, Rinehart, & Winston, 1976.

Goldfried, M. R., & Sprafkin, J. N. *Behavioral Personality Assessment*. Morristown, NJ: General Learning Press, 1974.

Gottman, J., Markman, H., & Notarius, C. The topography of marital conflict: A sequential analysis of verbal and nonverbal behavior. *Journal of Marriage and the Family*, 1977, *39*, 461-477.

Gottman, J., Notarius, C., Markman, H., Bank, S., Yoppi, B., & Rubin, M. E. Behavior exchange theory and marital decision making. *Journal of Personality and Social Psychology*, 1976, *34*, 14-23.

Greer, S. E., & D'Zurilla, T. Behavioral approaches to marital discord and conflict. *Journal of Marriage and Family Counseling*, 1975, *1*, 299-315.

Guerney, B. *Relationship Enhancement*. San Francisco: Jossey-Bass, 1977.

Gurman, A. S., & Kniskern, D. P. Research on marital and family therapy: Progress, perspective, and prospect. In: S. L. Garfield & A. E. Bergin (Eds.), *Handbook of Psychotherapy and Behavior Change: An Empirical Analysis* (second edition). New York: Wiley, 1978. (a)

Gurman, A. S., & Kniskern, D. P. Behavioral marriage therapy: II. Empirical perspective. *Family Process*, 1978, *17*, 129-148. (b)

Gurman, A. S., & Knudson, R. M. Behavioral marriage

therapy: I. A psychodynamic-systems analysis and critique. *Family Process*, 1978, *17*, 121-138.

Gurman, A. S., Knudson, R. M., & Kniskern, D. P. Behavioral marriage therapy: IV. Take two aspirin and call us in the morning. *Family Process*, 1978, *17*, 165-180.

Haley, J. *Strategies of Psychotherapy*. New York: Grune & Stratton, 1963.

Haley, J. *Problem-Solving Therapy*. San Francisco: Jossey-Bass, 1976.

Harrell, J., & Guerney, B. Training married couples in conflict negotiation skills. In D. H. L. Olson (Ed.), *Treating Relationships*. Lake Mills, IA: Graphic Press, 1976.

Hicks, M. W., & Platt, M. Marital happiness and stability: A review of the research in the sixties. *Journal of Marriage and the Family*, 1970, *32*, 553-574.

Homans, G. C. *Social Behavior: Its Elementary Forms*. New York: Harcourt Brace, 1961.

Jacobson, N. S. Problem solving and contingency contracting in the treatment of marital discord. *Journal of Consulting and Clinical Psychology*, 1977, *45*, 92-100. (a)

Jacobson, N. S. Training couples to solve their marital problems: A behavioral approach to relationship discord. Part I: Problem-solving skills. *International Journal of Family Counseling*, 1977, *5*, (1), 22-31. (b)

Jacobson, N. S. Training couples to solve their marital problems: A behavioral approach to relationship discord. Part II: Intervention strategies. *International Journal of Family Counseling*, 1977, *5*, (2), 20-28. (c)

Jacobson, N. S. Specific and nonspecific factors in the effectiveness of a behavioral approach to the treatment of marital discord. *Journal of Consulting and Clinical Psychology*, 1978, *46*, 442-452. (a)

Jacobson, N. S. Contingency contracting with couples: Redundancy and caution. *Behavior Therapy*, 1978, *9*, 426-427. (b)

Jacobson, N. S. A stimulus control model of change in behavioral marital therapy: Implications for contingency contracting. *Journal of Marriage and Family Counseling*, 1978, *4*, 29-35. (c)

Jacobson, N. S. Behavioral treatments for marital discord: A critical appraisal. In: M. Hersen, R. M. Eisler, & P. M. Miller (Eds.), *Progress in Behavior Modification* (Vol. 7). New York: Academic Press, 1979. (a)

Jacobson, N.S. Increasing positive behavior in severely distressed marital relationships: The effects of problem-solving training. *Behavior Therapy*, 1979, *10*, 311-326.(b)

Jacobson, N. S., & Anderson, E. The effects of behavior rehearsal and feedback on the acquisition of problem-solving skills in distressed and nondistressed couples. *Behaviour Research and Therapy*, 1980, *18*, 25-36.

Jacobson, N. S., & Margolin, G. *Marital Therapy: Strategies Based on Social Learning and Behavior Exchange Principles*. New York: Brunner/Mazel, 1979.

Jacobson, N. S., & Martin, B. Behavioral marriage therapy: Current status *Psychological Bulletin*, 1976, *83*, 540-566.

Jacobson, N. S., Waldron, H., & Moore, D. Toward a behavioral profile of marital distress. *Journal of Consulting and Clinical Psychology*, in press.

Jacobson, N. S., & Weiss, R. L. Behavioral marriage therapy: III. "The contents of Gurman et al. may be hazardous to our health." *Family Process*, 1978, *17*, 149-164.

Johnson, S. *First Person Singular: Living the Good Life Alone*. Philadelphia: Lippincott, 1977.

Kanfer, F. H., & Phillips, J. S. *Learning Foundations of Behavior Therapy*. New York: John Wiley & Sons, 1970.

Klier, J. L., & Rothberg, M. *Characteristics of conflict res-*

olution in couples. Paper presented at the annual meeting of the Association for the Advancement of Behavior Therapy, Atlanta, December, 1977.

Lederer, W. J., & Jackson, D. D. *The Mirages of Marriage*. New York: Norton, 1968.

Liberman, R. P. Behavioral approaches to family and couple therapy. *American Journal of Orthopsychiatry*, 1970, *40*, 106–118.

Liberman, R. P., Levine, J., Wheeler, E., Sanders, N., & Wallace, C. Experimental evaluation of marital group therapy: Behavioral vs interaction-insight formats. *Acta Psychiatrica Scandinavia*, 1976, Supplement.

Locke, H. J., & Wallace, K. M. Short-term marital adjustment and prediction tests: Their reliability and validity. *Journal of Marriage and Family Living*, 1959, *21*, 251-255.

Mahoney, M. J. *Cognition and Behavior Modification*. Cambridge, MA: Ballinger, 1974.

Margolin, G. A multilevel approach to the assessment of communication positiveness in distressed marital couples. *International Journal of Family Counseling*, 1978, *6*, 81-89.

Margolin, G., Christensen, A., & Weiss, R. L. Contracts, cognition, and change: A behavioral approach to marriage therapy. *The Counseling Psychologist*, 1975, *5*, 15-26.

Margolin, G., & Weiss, R. L. A comparative evaluation of therapeutic components associated with behavioral marital treatment. *Journal of Consulting and Clinical Psychology*, 1978, *46*, 1476-1486.

Markman, H. J. Application of a behavioral model of marriage in predicting relationship satisfaction of couples planning marriage. *Journal of Consulting and Clinical Psychology*, 1979, *47*, 743–749.

Masters, W. H., & Johnson, V. E. *Human Sexual Inadequacy*. Boston, MA: Little-Brown, 1970.

McFall, R. M., & Twentyman, C. T. Four experiments on the relative contributions of rehearsal, modeling, and coaching to assertion training. *Journal of Abnormal Psychology*, 1973, *81*, 199-218.

Meichenbaum, D. H. *Cognitive Behavior Modification*. New York: Plenum, 1977.

Meissner, W. J. The conceptualization of marriage and marital disorders from a psychoanalytic perspective. In: T. J. Paolino, Jr., & B. S. McCrady (Eds.), *Marriage and Marital Therapy: Psychoanalytic, Behavioral, and Systems Theory Perspectives*. New York: Brunner/Mazel, 1978.

O'Leary, K. D., & Turkewitz, H. The treatment of marital disorders from a behavioral perspective. In: T. J. Paolino, Jr., & B. S. McCrady (Eds.), *Marriage and Marital Therapy: Psychoanalytic, Behavioral, and Systems Theory Perspectives*. New York: Brunner/Mazel, 1978.

Paolino, T. J., Jr., & McCrady, B. S. *Marriage and Marital Therapy: Psychoanalytic, Behavioral, and Systems Theory Perspectives*. New York: Brunner/Mazel, 1978.

Patterson, G. R. Interventions for boys with conduct problems: Multiple settings, treatments, and criteria. *Journal of Consulting and Clinical Psychology*, 1974, *42*, 471-481.

Patterson, G. R. Some procedures for assessing changes in marital interaction patterns. *Oregon Research Institute Bulletin*, 1976, *16*(7).

Patterson, G. R., & Hops, H. Coercion, a game for two: Intervention techniques for marital conflict. In R. E. Ulrich & P. Mounjoy (Eds.), *The Experimental Analysis of Social Behavior*. New York: Appleton, 1972.

Patterson, G. R., & Reid, J. B. Reciprocity and coercion:

Two facets of social systems. In: C. Neuringer & J. L. Michael (Eds.), *Behavior Modification in Clinical Psychology*. New York: Appleton, 1970.

Rappaport, A. F., & Harrell, J. A behavioral-exchange model for marital counseling. *Family Coordinator*, 1972, *21*, 203-213.

Robinson, E. A., & Price, M. G. Pleasurable behavior in marital interaction: An observational study. *Journal of Consulting and Clinical Psychology*, 1980, *48*, 117–118.

Sager, C. *Marriage Contracts and Couple Therapy*. New York: Brunner/Mazel, 1976.

Satir, V. *Conjoint Family Therapy*. Palo Alto, CA: Science & Behavior Books, 1967.

Spanier, G. B. Measuring dyadic adjustment: New scales for assessing the quality of marriage and similar dyads. *Journal of Marriage and the Family*, 1976, *38*, 15-28.

Steinglass, P. Conceptualization of marriage from a systems theory perspective. In: T. J. Paolino, Jr., & B. S. McCrady (Eds.), *Marriage and Marital Therapy: Psychoanalytic, Behavioral, and Systems Theory Perspective*. New York: Brunner/Mazel, 1978.

Stuart, R. B. Operant-interpersonal treatment for marital discord. *Journal of Consulting and Clinical Psychology*, 1969, *33*, 675-682.

Stuart, R. B. Operant interpersonal treatment for marital discord. In D. H. L. Olson (Ed.), *Treating Relationships*. Lake Mills, IA: Graphic Press, 1976.

Thibaut, J. W., & Kelley, H. H. *The Social Psychology of Groups*. New York: Wiley, 1959.

Tsoi-Hoshmand, L. Marital therapy: An integrative behavioral-learning mode. *Journal of Marriage and Family Counseling*, 1976, *2*, 179-191.

Vincent, J. P., Weiss, R. L., & Birchler, G. R. A behavioral analysis of problem-solving in distressed and nondistressed married and stranger dyads. *Behavior Therapy*, 1975, *6*, 475-487.

Weiss, R. L. The conceptualization of marriage and marriage disorders from a behavioral perspective. In: T. J. Paolino, Jr., & B. S. McCrady (Eds.), *Marriage and Marital Therapy: Psychoanalytic, Behavioral, and Systems Theory Perspectives*. New York: Brunner/Mazel, 1978.

Weiss, R. L., & Birchler, G. R. Adults with marital dysfunction. In: M. Hersen & A. S. Bellack (Eds.), *Behavior Therapy in the Psychiatric Setting*. Baltimore: Williams & Wilkins Co., 1978.

Weiss, R. L., Birchler, G. R., & Vincent, J. P. Contractual models for negotiation training in marital dyads. *Journal of Marriage and the Family*, 1974, *36*, 321-331.

Weiss, R. L., & Cerreto, M. *Marital status inventory*. Unpublished manuscript, University of Oregon, 1975.

Weiss, R. L., Hops, H., & Patterson, G. R. A framework for conceptualizing marital conflict, technology for altering it, some data for evaluating it. In: L. A. Hamerlynck, L. C. Handy, & E. J. Mash (Eds.) *Behavior change: Methodology, Concepts, and Practice*. Champaign, IL: Research Press, 1973.

Wills, T. A., Weiss, R. L., & Patterson, G. R. A behavioral analysis of the determinants of marital satisfaction. *Journal of Consulting and Clinical Psychology*, 1974, *42*, 802-811.

EDITORS' REFERENCES

Beck, A. T., Rush, A. J., Emery, G. & Shaw, B. *Cognitive Therapy of Depression*. New York: Guilford, 1979.

Gurman, A. S. Contemporary marital therapies: A critique

and comparative analysis of psychoanalytic, behavioral and systems theory approaches. In: T. J. Paolino & B. S. McCracy (Eds.), *Marriage and Marital Therapy*. New York: Brunner/Mazel, 1978.

Gurman, A. S. *Women's issues and behavioral marriage and family therapy*. Paper presented at the Association for the Advancement of Behavior Therapy, San Francisco, December, 1979.

Gurman, A. S. & Klein, M. H. Marital and family conflicts. In: A. Brodsky & R. Hare-Mustin (Eds.), *Women and Psychotherapy: An Assessment of Research and Practice*.

New York: Guilford Press, 1980.

Knudson, R. M., Gurman, A. S. & Kniskern, D. P. Behavioral marriage therapy: A treatment in transition. In: C. M. Franks & G. T. Wilson (Eds.), *Annual review of Behavior Therapy*. Vol. 7, 1979. New York: Brunner/Mazel, 1980.

Yalom, I. *Theory and Practice of Group Psychotherapy*. New York: Grune & Stratton, 1974.

Wertheim, E. Family unit therapy and the science and typology of family systems. *Family Process*, 1973, 12, 361-376.

CHAPTER 16

The Treatment of
Sexual Dysfunction

Julia R. Heiman, Ph.D., Leslie LoPiccolo, M.S.

and Joseph LoPiccolo, Ph.D. [1,2]

This chapter will review the history and current status of treatment focused on problems of sexual functioning in heterosexual couples. This type of treatment, once a secondary component of marital therapy, individual psychotherapy, and sex education, has come to be a more or less independent type of treatment, popularly referred to as "sex therapy."

HISTORICAL OVERVIEW

Until relatively recently, the mainstream of American psychiatry and psychology held to a basically psychodynamic and psychoanalytic view concerning the etiology and treatment of sexual dysfunctions. While behavioral psychotherapy techniques and other nondynamic approaches had been reported in the literature as early as the 1950s, these initial reports did not have a significant effect on prevailing therapeutic practice. It was only the publication of Masters and Johnson's *Human Sexual Inadequacy* in 1970 which changed the field. Masters and Johnson's report of a basically behavioral treatment paradigm was couched in nonbehavioral and, indeed, atheoretical language, causing some anguish among behavior therapists who felt, rightly or wrongly, that "their" techniques had been appropriated by Masters and Johnson.[3] It remains an undisputed fact, however, that the publication of *Human Sexual Inadequacy* marked a major turning point in the history of our conceptualization of sexual dysfunction. What follows is a brief synopsis of this history.

The Traditional Psychoanalytic Approach

The traditional analytic approach to sexual

[1]Contributions to this chapter were equally shared, with authorship decided by a coin toss.

[2]Preparation of this chapter was supported in part by a grant from the National Institute of Mental Health, U.S. Public Health Service.

[3]*Editors' Note.* While we recognize that Heiman et al.'s view of sex therapy is multitheoretical, as the reader will see, we have chosen to place it here in the section on behavioral approaches because of their frequent use of behavioral treatment strategies and techniques.

dysfunction is well known (e.g., Blum, 1949) and will not be presented in any detail here. Within analytic theory, failure to accomplish the childhood developmental tasks associated with the resolution of the oedipal complex has remained the major etiological factor in sexual dysfunctions (Fenichel, 1945; Freud, 1905; Rosen, 1977).

The analytic approach to the treatment of all presenting problems, including sexual dysfunction, follows logically from this formulation. Treatment consists of reenacting the oedipal situation in the transference relationship with the analyst, and thus finishing in a healthy way the developmental tasks which were not accomplished in childhood.

Critiques of analytic theory, especially in regard to sexuality, have been numerous. At a theoretical level, analytic theory was, of course, developed at a period when knowledge of the basic physiology of sexual response was non-existent. Thus, a number of Freud's inspired insights into the nature of sexuality—for example, his distinction between clitoral and vaginal orgasm—have since become unsupportable in the light of advances in our biological knowledge. There have been attempts to incorporate such new data into analytic theory, such as Bergler and Kroger's *Kinsey's Myth of Female Sexuality* (1954) and Sherfey's *The Nature and Evolution of Female Sexuality* (1973), but such attempts have done little to further the development of new and effective treatment techniques.

It is at the level of this question of therapeutic effectiveness that the analytic approach to sexual dysfunction is most vulnerable. In the few empirical studies that have been conducted, analytic therapy simply does not work very well for sexual problems (Lorand, 1939; Moore, 1961), and even its most ardent supporters admit that the length of time required for a successful analysis is simply prohibitive (Bergler, 1951).[4]

Common Sense Remedies for Sexual Dysfunction

Partially as a result of the failure of analytic

therapy to provide effective and practical treatments for sexual dysfunction, clinicians working with patients with sexual concerns in the past developed a wide variety of essentially folk medicine remedies. While some of these procedures are somewhat effective and have been incorporated into behavioral treatment programs, the majority of the techniques are of little demonstrable value beyond placebo effects.

For premature ejaculation, one commonly advocated folk remedy is advising the patient to think distracting, anti-erotic thoughts during intercourse. Another approach involves having the patient wear a condom or use a topical anesthetic cream to cut down on penile sensitivity. Still another procedure is to have the patient masturbate immediately before engaging in sexual relations with his partner. The use of alcohol or sympathetic blocking agents (e.g., phenothiazines) to delay ejaculation has also been widely recommended. While all of these procedures have some effectiveness in delaying ejaculation, they also reduce the sexual encounter to a joyless, non-pleasurable, performance-oriented experience for the man.

For erectile failure, folk remedies have been even less successful than for premature ejaculation. Approaches have included suggesting that the male patient have an affair with a more exciting sexual partner; the use of alcohol as an antianxiety agent; and the use of various penile appliances such as a rubber band around the base of the penis. Another remedy for impotence has been the administration of testosterone. In general, research tends to indicate that if the male has normal endogenous plasma testosterone levels, administration of exogenous testosterone has only a placebo effect (Jarvik and Brecher, 1977).

Folk medicine and common sense approaches to female sexual dysfunctions have a similarly poor record of effectiveness. For female orgasmic dysfunction, the most common advice has been for the woman to meet her husband's needs, to fake orgasm, and not to be concerned about her own lack of response.

The record for treatment of vaginismus is similarly bleak. The common treatments of vaginismus have been hymenectomy or surgical enlargement of the vaginal opening. Both of these procedures are generally ineffective, as

---

[4] *Editors' Note*. Of course, psychoanalysis was never designed to treat sexual dysfunctions per se, so that the time dimension is questionable as an index of success.

they do nothing to reduce the involuntary contraction of the vaginal musculature which characterizes vaginismus.

Behavioral Approaches to Sexual Dysfunction

"Behavioral approaches" refer to a type of therapy in which the therapist actively and directly educates the patient about sexual physiology and sexual techniques, restructures maladaptive behavior patterns and cognitions regarding sexuality, and uses anxiety-reduction and skill-training techniques to improve the patient's functioning. The history of the application of behavioral techniques to sexual dysfunction is a long one which much predates the rise of formal behavior therapy. In the late 18th century, a British physician, Sir John Hunter (cited in Comfort, 1965) described a treatment program for erectile failure which is very similar to the program described by Wolpe (1958) and by Masters and Johnson (1970). At the turn of the century, hypnotherapists such as Schrenk-Notzing (1895) used direct sex education and instruction in sexual techniques to successfully treat sexual dysfunction.

A major breakthrough in our conceptualization of sexual dysfunction occurred with the application of systematic desensitization to sexual problems. Salter (1949) and Wolpe (1958) conceptualized sexual dysfunctions as conditioned anxiety responses to the sexual situation. Engaging in a graduated hierarchy of sexual behaviors while forbidding the goal of orgasm or erection, sometimes coupled with muscle relaxation, proved quite effective in many cases.

Another behavioral technique used in this period was assertive training (Lazarus, 1965; Salter, 1949; Wolpe, 1958). In this approach, socially and sexually inhibited patients were given modeling and behavior rehearsal training to increase their communication skills.

Cognitive variables have not gone unaddressed in the literature. Although Ellis' (1962) rational-emotive therapy (RET) is not usually conceptualized as behavioral, RET techniques for sexual dysfunction do include skill training, education, and anxiety reduction through restructuring irrational cognitions about the catastrophic nature of sexual dysfunction.

Other Directive Approaches

Before the rise of direct "sex therapy" with the publication of *Human Sexual Inadequacy* in 1970, there were two therapists who had described very effective quasi-behavioral treatment techniques for sexual dysfunction. For treatment of premature ejaculation, Semans (1956) described his technique of repeated pauses during penile stimulation as nearly 100% effective. Hastings (1963) described simple retraining programs designed to instruct couples in effective sexual techniques, such as concurrent clitoral manipulation for coitally inorgasmic women.

Sex Therapy[5]

Following the publication of Masters and Johnson's *Human Sexual Inadequacy* in 1970, a number of other accounts of behavioral or quasi-behavioral approaches to treatment of sexual dysfunction have appeared (e.g., Hartman and Fithian, 1972; Kaplan, 1974; Lobitz and LoPiccolo, 1972; LoPiccolo and Lobitz, 1972). These accounts all differ greatly in the degree to which behavioral terminology is used and in the theoretical framework that is presented. However, if differences in language are ignored, all of these reports seem to describe fairly similar treatment procedures (LoPiccolo, 1977b). While there are unique elements in various programs, the *reduction of performance anxiety* (often through implicit counterconditioning and cognitive behavioral strategies), *sex education, skill training in communication and sexual technique, and attitude change procedures remain elements common to both "behavior therapy" and "sex therapy"* approaches to sexual dysfunction. "Sex therapy," as currently practiced, thus can be conceptualized as a type of cognitive-behavior therapy applied to couples with sexual problems.

---

[5]*Editors' Note.* In this book, the major contrasting views to those of Heiman et al. are the non-psychoanalytic systems theory models, in which sexual dysfunction is seen as, in effect, "just another symptom," for which specialized treatment techniques are not needed.

HEALTHY, WELL-FUNCTIONING SEXUAL RELATIONSHIPS

The process of defining a healthy, well-functioning sexual relationship is infused with sociocultural values of the person or group doing the labeling. Not only do cultural values shift across time, but the definition of a good sexual relationship may shift depending upon a person's sex, marital status, level of commitment to the sexual partner, length of relationship, and a host of other variables that carry meaning in present-day Western societies. It is not surprising, then, that satisfactory sexual functioning is rarely discussed except in terms of an *absence* of sexual dysfunction. A sexual problem still seems easier to precisely identify than does sexual happiness. This section attempts, briefly, to make explicit some of the components currently valued in a well-functioning sexual relationship. These components have been derived from explicit and implicit statements made by therapists and researchers in the area of sexual dysfunction.

In order to make these components explicit, a frame of reference must be acknowledged when evaluating any particular sexual relationship. This frame of reference can be divided into three parts: (a) the inter- or intrapersonal focus (individual/couple); (b) the interpreter or observer who evaluates (detached observer/target couple); and (c) the level of evaluation (surface/deep).

For instance, a female partner may claim to be very dissatisfied with the frequency of orgasm she experiences with her husband. Her husband is not dissatisfied with the sexual interactions and may not feel there is a sexual problem except for her personal dissatisfaction. In discussion with an outside person, a different picture might emerge—that the sexual relationship is in trouble because of the wife's perceived lack of involvement and caring on the part of the husband, the surface symptom of which is her lack of orgasm.

A central point of reference in acknowledging the functioning of a sexual relationship is the couple's self-report of the level of sexual satisfaction. Usually a couple's report of satisfaction is based on what can be identified as two global factors. One is the degree of overall enjoyment from the spouses' current sexual interactions;

the other is the extent to which their expectations of what a sexual relationship should be matches the current actuality. For most couples in an ongoing relationship, a satisfying sexual relationship must include shared pleasure and incorporate some common match of expectations (see Nowinski, 1979 for an elaboration on this point).

These global factors (degree of pleasure and expectations) can be broken down into components. The following list examines first the more specific and surface factors, those qualities which individuals within a relationship often identify as important to their sexual functioning. A second list contains more general and pervasive factors, those that reflect the supporting emotional involvement that seems to be necessary to the maintenance or growth of a couple's sexual relationship. One should keep in mind that these lists are not prescriptions for perfect sexual relationships. Nor must all of these factors be present for every couple. They are presented because, to a greater or lesser extent, they seem related to sexual satisfaction. Lists presented are drawn from clinical literature, our own therapy contacts, and what little research there is that has addressed the question. Couples in long-term, committed relationships (usually married) are the usual reference point, although many of the variables are relevant to a wide variety of relationship styles.

Specific to Adequate Sexual Functioning

1) *Pleasure from Sexual Activities.* Both people are able to enjoy the sexual activities they participate in with each other. While total agreement that foreplay, oral sex, intercourse or other contacts are equally enjoyable for each person is not necessary, there should be a positive correlation between partners on their general level of individual pleasure. It is important that a person not feel extremely anxious, physically or psychologically uncomfortable in sexual situations, or that there is a strong discrepancy between their current and ideal levels of pleasure. Being interested in the pleasure of one's partner for the partner's sake also contributes to sexual satisfaction (Ellis, 1971; Kaplan, 1974; LoPiccolo and Steger, 1974; Masters and Johnson, 1970)

2) *Frequency*. Most important is some general agreement between people regarding how often they each desire various types of sexual contact. Although statistical definitions of normal frequencies do exist, a better guide is the individual couple, for whom satisfaction depends more on their agreement with one another than on an external norm. Exactly what types of activities are highly preferred can vary as long as each person is somewhat flexible in any given sexual interaction. Some amount of "nonsexual" (i.e., not aimed at sexual arousal) physical contact seems to be important for maintaining feelings of closeness and intimacy (Kaplan, 1974; LoPiccolo, 1977b).

3) *Variety*. A number of therapists have mentioned variety of sexual expression as important to sexual satisfaction (i.e., Annon, 1974; LoPiccolo, 1977b). Having a range of sexual activities that is broader than the foreplay-plus-intercourse formula seems to decrease the pressure as to when and how often to have sex. Those couples who are satisfied with less variety are more likely to be in closer agreement as to the frequency with which they want sex.

4) *Arousal and Orgasms*. While most people have periods of difficulty in the areas of arousal (erections, lubrication) and orgasm (premature, retarded ejaculation for males; primary and secondary inorgasmia for females), most satisfied sexual relationships are functional most of the time. Therapists have defined "functional" with a variety of different percentages that include 50% of coital contacts, erections long enough for the female to experience orgasm 50% of the time (Masters and Johnson, 1970), or simply a categorized percentage (LoPiccolo, 1977b). For our purposes here, the adequate presence of arousal and presence or timing of orgasm are relative to the judgment of the individuals within a particular couple.

5) *Sexual Self-awareness and Acceptance*. This includes being aware of the levels of one's own sexual interest, pleasure, and preferences and accepting them rather than comparing oneself to others or to some impossible standard. Also important is an acceptance of the physical component of sex, including body-image. Included in a positive body-image is the feeling that one's body is worthy of appreciation, and the feeling that one's genitals and physical responses are part of one's self and not the product or possession of the partner (Barbach, 1975; Heiman, LoPiccolo, and LoPiccolo, 1976). Without some basic self-acceptance, a variety of problems can result, including the avoidance of sex, denial of sexual desire, lack of arousal, and orgasmic difficulty.[6]

6) *Acknowledgment and Acceptance of Partner's Sexuality*. Sexual relationships usually consist of differences in desires, frequencies, activities, attitudes, and pleasures. Thus, a certain degree of acceptance of differences in physical and emotional sexual needs is to be expected if the couple is to find sex satisfying. An essential component of acceptance is awareness of the partner's preferences; without this awareness, people will mind-read, stereotype, and otherwise assume desires and dissatisfactions that actually do not exist in their partner.

General Relationship Factors

1) *Flexibility*. Flexibility is relevant for a thriving sexual relationship in several ways. A very important function of flexibility has to do with solving problems which are part of any relationship, the sexual relationship included. The willingness to try to make changes or to adapt to changing circumstances usually is more successful if it is shared by both partners. A flexible-rigid partner combination also can work, of course, but it can often tend to plant seeds for later resentments on the part of the person who is bending more.

Sex-role flexibility is important to the extent

---

[6]*Editors' Note*. The implication here, with which we agree, is that interactional or relationship problems may arise from, or at least be influenced by, psychological difficulties *within* people as well as between them. While this notion is hardly novel to psychodynamically-oriented therapists (e.g., Sager, Chapter 3), it represents a view not often expressed (at least publicly) by behaviorally-oriented clinicians (cf. Jacobson, Chapter 15). In this context, then, we consider Heiman et al.'s theoretical persuasion to be "depth-behavioral." As the reader will see at many points in this chapter, Heiman et al. emphasize that effective sex therapy must be sensitive to the inferred *functions*, *purposes* and *meanings* of sexual difficulties, as well as to their antecedents and consequences.

that it permits each partner equal chance to express and receive affection. Each couple seems to require a somewhat different sex-role arrangement. In sexual interaction, the traditional roles assigned are for men to be initiators, aggressors, producers of sexual pleasure, with women being passive, receptive, sensual vehicles. This configuration puts heavy burdens and restrictions on both sexes. The more successful arrangement in terms of sexual satisfaction seems to be a relationship in which either person feels free to initiate sex (regardless of who usually does do it), refuse sex without wounding the other person, be the more active or the more receptive partner at different times, or suggest new activities.

Sometimes flexibility in sex roles extends beyond the sexual interaction itself; sometimes it does not. More important than total androgyny seems to be a sense of equality based on feeling mutually important and valued by one another. This serves as a basis for sharing and trust which can enhance the relationship.

2) *Openness: Receptive and Expressive*. Perhaps as a backlash against a history of emotional reserve between the sexes, the value of open sexual communication has become a central focus of therapeutic recommendations for building a good sexual relationship (Kaplan, 1974; LoPiccolo and Lobitz, 1973; LoPiccolo and Miller, 1975; Masters and Johnson, 1970). Communication in a sexual interaction has two components: receptive and expressive sexual communication.

On the receptive side is the willingness to listen to or take notice of a partner's responses and respond in either words or action. This is often difficult to do nondefensively if the message is negative, for example, if one person does not enjoy a certain kind of sexual touch from the partner. Receptive openness refers to partner awareness, acceptance, and responsiveness to suggestions for change. Part of the receptive attitude does depend on the way in which the message is given and/or perceived. The same content is more easily understood if the metamessage is not one of critical accusation, but instead, one of personal preference.

Expressiveness focuses on the other side of the interaction, letting the partner verbally or nonverbally know likes, dislikes, and general feelings. This is certainly important within a sexual experience, since the same kind of caresses may not always feel good, and the partner needs to be able to communicate this. Negative feedback seems harder for most couples than positive feedback, though both, in varying amounts, seem to be necessary if the sexual interactions are to remain mutually enjoyable. Also, most couples desire some expression of affection outside of, and not merely as a preliminary to, the sexual exchange itself. This may be physical or nonphysical, but it needs to be clearly interpreted as affection by both individuals.

3) *Active Intimacy and Involvement*. Most individuals in a relationship feel happier when they experience closeness and feel in some way special to their partners. Some relationships retain a sense of involvement with a lot of heated arguments inasmuch as this style serves to bond the couple in some kind of intensity. Characteristics of active intimacy with regard to sex vary among couples but include feeling equally valued in the relationship, showing care and concern in ways that matter to the other person, communicating a desire to feel close, and trying to be tuned in to a partner's reactions.

This description indeed has a "young" relationship or honeymoon flavor. Yet, at times, especially as relationships go through major changes and crises, intimacy has to be reestablished. Usually a reawakening of intimacy leads to, or from, increased sexual intensity in a relationship.

4) *Trust and Commitment*. Feelings of trust and commitment can influence the degree of vulnerability a person is willing to share with another. Since sex is often an area surrounded with vulnerabilities, some level of trust is important to feeling spontaneous, uninhibited, and even aroused and orgasmic. Anxiety about anything can interfere with sexual arousal and pleasure, as Kaplan (1974) has repeatedly noted. The types of anxieties related to trust include worries around being evaluated negatively, being compared to others, being rejected, or being forced to do something undesirable. Discovery that a partner has had a sexual affair outside of the relationship bears on the issue of trust and com-

mitment, but the effect on sexual interaction depends on the couple. Following an affair, the sexual relationship can be revived or actually improve if both people are still committed to one another. Often, however, affairs do not help closeness, intimacy, and trust in the primary relationship and can result in a dissolution of the relationship.

5) *Love*. It seems that love, in all the ways that people choose to define it, is not necessary for everyone in order to have a good sexual relationship. People who are miserable, have marriages that are disintegrating, and have never been really satisfied with their sex life will still say they love each other. Other people have a difficult time having sex with someone they love. And yet love for some people makes the difference between a good and bad sexual experience and between a temporary and enduring sexual relationship. The word love carries so many cultural meanings (e.g., intimacy, caring, flexibility, openness) that it needs to be acknowledged. It is one possibly vital ingredient for some couples to have a lastingly good sexual relationship.

6) *Erotic Attraction*. Feeling sexually attractive or sexually desirous of the other person may seem too obvious an ingredient. However, without it sex may be physically and emotionally unsatisfying, frequency may decrease drastically, and the result may be obligatory sex, sexual disinterest, or an active aversion to sexual activity.

7) *Freedom, Autonomy, Responsibility*. While not usually explicit, good sexual relationships seem to grant some freedom and autonomy to each partner. This means that one person's body does not "belong" to the other; one's body and sexuality are one's own possession that may be given. Thus, each person has a right not to want always to initiate or accept physical closeness, arousal or orgasm. Participating in sex does not mean one person has the right to expect orgasms or arousal from his or her partner.

Several comments about the preceding lists seem in order. One is to reiterate that the above factors are gleaned from clinical and research reports on the attributes of satisfying sexual re-

lationships but have not been systematically researched. Rigorous study of these components would indeed be valuable and it is hoped that this review will provide such an impetus. Second, because the factors were substantially derived from therapeutic contexts, it is possible that many of the variables that are apparently important to a well-functioning sexual relationship are as much related to making it easier for a therapist to help spouses make positive changes in their sexual relationship. Thirdly, not all sexually functional and satisfied couples need to fulfill all of the categories; strength and satisfaction in some are probably sufficient. Related to this, the above lists presume relatively healthy people who are not severely impaired physically or psychologically. Ideals of sexual satisfaction for impaired populations may be different. Ideals may also change with age, although the basic framework should remain the same.

Finally, this description is inseparable from current (therapeutic) cultural views of what a good sexual relationship should contain. Openness, intimacy, and pleasure are values that are completely irrelevant in less westernized cultures (Mead, 1949). One suspects that, as the nature of the sociocultural roles of the sexes changes, so will the nature of long-term relationships and the definition of good sex within them.

IDENTIFYING DYSFUNCTIONAL SEXUAL RELATIONSHIPS

As Szasz (1960) has repeatedly pointed out, accepting any person into therapy validates the idea that a problem exists. Consequently, while social values can remain implicit in the descriptive factors thought to contribute to adequate sexual functioning, the classification of sexual dysfunctions forces explicit statements about what sexual behaviors are valued.

The impact of the historical period and the individual investigator's beliefs has been dramatic in the sexual area. Clitoral stimulation was considered immature by Freud (1905) and normal and desirable by Masters and Johnson (1970). Premature ejaculation was considered biologically "superior" in the 1940s (Kinsey, Pomeroy, and Martin, 1948), and a dysfunction in the 1970s (Kaplan, 1977; Masters and Johnson, 1970).

Classification of Sexual Dysfunctions

Problems with classification have been mentioned by LoPiccolo and Hogan (1979) with a cautionary note for investigators to clearly state the purposes of their classification systems (i.e., for understanding, research specificity, prediction, and recommendation for appropriate treatment). Unfortunately, at the present time in sex therapy, classification formats have been used for a variety of purposes, with a resultant confusion of categories and limitations in understanding the various disorders. Among clinicians, the tendency has been to modify certain categories and create new ones. Thus, while Masters and Johnson (1970) dealt primarily with physical symptoms (erections, lubrication, and orgasm), Kaplan (1974, 1977) added the category of "sexual desire disorder"—a more psychological concept.

With the preceding reservations in mind, the following classification system is presented from two points of emphasis: first, a broad consideration for general clinical utility, and second, specific remarks on the relation between classification and research. Problematic aspects of the system will be mentioned in the hope that future revisions will better meet therapeutic and research needs.

From a clinical perspective, the most comprehensive classification system is Kaplan's (1974, 1977) which has been somewhat modified for the *American Psychiatric Association's Diagnostic and Statistical Manual of Mental Disorders* (DSM III) (Spitzer, Sheeny, and Endicott, 1977). Kaplan divides sexual response into three phases. The first phase is *sexual desire*, which includes too little (hypoactive) and too much (hyperactive) desire. Phase two is *sexual excitement*, consisting of female *general sexual dysfunction* (lack of sexual arousal, vasocongestion), and male *erectile dysfunction* (erections insufficient for intercourse). The third phase is *orgasm*, which includes *premature ejaculation* (no control over ejaculation reflex and ejaculating too quickly) and *retarded ejaculation* (inhibition of the ejaculation reflex) in males and *orgastic dysfunction* (inhibition of orgasm) in females.

Additionally, Kaplan subdivides dysfunctions along a temporal dimension (primary/secondary) and a situational dimension (absolute/situational). "Primary" refers to a dysfunction that has always been present, while "secondary" means that at one time the person was functional. "Absolute" dysfunctions cross all sexual situations and "situational" dysfunctions are specific to certain conditions or settings, but not others.

Although *vaginismus* (involuntary contraction of vaginal introitus muscles) and *dyspareunia* (painful intercourse) do not fit into the above classification system, for our purposes we can consider these special cases of inhibition in the excitement phase.

This classification scheme is one that many clinicians are likely to use with some modifications and it does not negate, but rather expands, the earlier Masters and Johnson (1970) diagnostic categories. Nevertheless, it is difficult to use productively, other than as a rudimentary beginning, in the understanding of sexual dysfunction. Knowing a couple has erectile or orgasmic problems is important, but as all clinicians are aware, in terms of therapeutic strategy it is only a first step. The task remains to find a more multidimensional classification system which retains some simplicity of structure. The multidimensional emphasis would help direct attention to relevant differentiating characteristics within dysfunctions, such as level of marital satisfaction, quality of communication, health, partner's sexual functioning, quality and quantity of past nonsexual and sexual relationships with the opposite sex, and other variables that clinically hold promise of suggesting differential treatment. Specifying subtypes of erectile failure, premature ejaculation, and situational orgasmic dysfunction has been attempted (Ansari, 1975; Cooper, 1968a, 1969a, 1970; Masters and Johnson, 1970) in terms of etiology and symptoms. This type of approach on a larger conceptual scale is still needed and will require research to explore relevant variables to include in differentiating subtypes. The problem of very broad categories is especially troublesome in outcome research. Lumping together all types of secondary inorgasmic women in a particular study, for example, may make the outcome statistics pertinent only to that individual investigator's particular sample.

In sum, Kaplan's classification system forms an initial typology of sexual dysfunctions. Although she has a psychosomatic view of sexual dysfunctions, the emphasis in the classification is on physical symptoms. Informally, then, it is left to clinicians to identify and classify intrapsychic and interpersonal factors that influence the development and maintenance of a couple's particular dysfunction. A more formally shared system which classified such factors would be useful. However, incorporating physical, intrapsychic, and interpersonal factors may be too cumbersome a task to form a practical typology. Eventually, a decision has to be made about the most valid and meaningful organizing factors. Currently, that factor is the physical system and it is not really satisfactory. In other theoretical camps, intrapsychic and interpersonal diagnostic systems (Leary, 1957; McLemore and Benjamin, 1979) have been proposed, the latter of which has undergone some clinical scrutiny and statistical refinement. These possibilities, or new ones, need future exploration for sex therapy and research.

Etiological Factors

Etiological factors also have tended to remain outside of sexual dysfunction typology. It is almost impossible to clearly identify etiological factors that result in sexual dysfunctions. The tendency in current thinking is to use an etiological model which integrates a large number of potentially interacting factors into a multi-causal model (Kaplan, 1974). Systems theory has also been explored in which relationship factors have been identified with dysfunctional patterns (e.g., Sager and Kaplan, 1972).

One of the problems in integrating etiological factors into a useful classification system is that etiology is generally still at the level of clinical speculation. No information exists which presently compares clinical and nonclinical populations. Symptoms arise usually within a context of other current, historical, personality, and relationship factors. The following discussion is presented to point out the complexity within each category and the difficulty of determining the type of symptom that is likely to appear for any given individual.

One should bear in mind that most of the etiological factors can also operate as maintenance factors of sexual dysfunction. Physical, psychological, and relationship variables interact in a way that sustains the dysfunctional sexual interaction. The therapist's task is to analyze which variables seem to contribute to the stability of the dysfunction and to examine the extent to which the sexual problem serves a useful purpose to the relationship (i.e., maintaining an equilibrium, masking more central relationship issues). This analysis is useful in estimating the effect of different foci of intervention and alerts the therapist to potential reverberations of the effect of specific changes on the couple's total relationship. Often, however, the maintaining factors are complex and not readily visible, in which case the therapist makes an intervention on one level, for instance a marital issue, and simply observes the effect on another level, such as the sexual interactions.

Physical factors can interfere with sexual response. Any illness which might result in pain, fatigue, or poor nourishment can interfere with arousal and enjoyment of sex (Kaplan, 1974; Masters and Johnson, 1970). Aging tends to slow down the sexual arousal cycle for men and can make lubrication more difficult for women (Masters and Johnson, 1970). Any problems with the nervous system, such as multiple sclerosis, or spinal cord injury, or any diseases affecting penile vascular supply (local thrombosis, diabetes) can influence the sexual response cycle. Anatomical factors can play a role as in genital abnormalities or episiotomy scars leading to dyspareunia (Kaplan, 1974; Wagner and Ebbehoj, 1978). A wide variety of drugs can also interfere with sexual desire or responsiveness; anticholinergic medication can lead to erection problems, while antiandrenergic medication contributes to ejaculatory problems (Kaplan, 1977, 1979). Alcohol and barbiturates tend to lower sexual arousability and eventually lower sex drive (Kaplan, 1974; Wilson, 1977; Wilson and Lawson, 1978).

Psychological factors believed to be important to the etiology and maintenance of sexual arousal include guilt (Kaufman, 1967; Masters and Johnson, 1970), low self-esteem (Barbach, 1975; LoPiccolo, 1977b), lack of trust (Fisher, 1973; Kaplan, 1974), anger or hostility (Cooper, 1968b; Kaplan, 1974), unrealistic or irrational expectations (Ellis, 1971), negative attitudes toward sex, past experience or religious upbringing (Masters and Johnson, 1970), and depression (Kaplan, 1974). The most often cited psychological factor in sexual dysfunction is anxiety; Kaplan (1974) places it in a central role; Masters and Johnson (1970) specify it as usually in the form of "performance anxiety" (worrying about sexual functioning); Wolpe (1969) claims a physiological connection is created such that anxiety conditioned to sexual situations inhibits response.

There has been support for (Cooper, 1969b) and against (Hoon, Wincze and Hoon, 1977) the role of anxiety in actually inhibiting sexual response, but generally it is agreed that anxiety, especially fear of sexual performance, inhibits physical response in a number of cases.

Relationship factors can be strongly influential in the development and continuation of sexual dysfunctions, but again, the role of causative factors needs further research. Early primary relationships (parental, peer) have been cited as important for later primary (mate, spouse) relationships. Parental influences, with regard to sex and affection (Kaplan, 1974; Masters and Johnson, 1970; Terman, 1938), quality of premarital sexual experiences (Kinsey, Pomeroy, Gebhard, and Martin, 1953; Masters and Johnson, 1970), and past history of sexual trauma (Kaplan, 1974; Masters and Johnson, 1970) have been implicated as factors that can be correlated with later sexual dysfunction. General dissatisfaction with a marriage and lack of trust and love have been suggested as etiological factors in orgasmic problems in women (Fisher, 1973; McGovern, Stewart, and LoPiccolo, 1975). Sometimes the relationship problem is merely an educational one in which one or both partners lack the general knowledge to provide or request adequate stimulation, a situation reported in cases of orgasmic dysfunction (Kaplan, 1974; LoPiccolo, 1977a). Purely educational problems seem to be less and less frequent, perhaps due to information provided by the popular press (LoPiccolo, 1977b).

What is lacking from etiological classification, particularly in the relationship factors, is a scheme for examining patterns among categories that would alert clinicians to focus on certain target areas. When, for instance, is it better to focus on the intrapsychic components of a dysfunction rather than the function of the sexual difficulty within the relationship? How is the clinician to know when sexual and marital issues can be dealt with separately, rather than attempting to cure the relationship difficulties before or along with the sexual ones?

Currently, therapists seem to deal with these questions on an intuitive level, making clinical judgments based on experience. A somewhat more systematic approach that we have used involves: (a) an analysis of possible ways that intrapsychic and relationship factors may be interfering with sexual functioning, and (b) embarking on a course of sex therapy, while remaining alert to intrapsychic or relationship factors that may hinder or halt the change process. The latter strategy essentially uses sex therapy as an assessment of the degree of enmeshment of sexual and nonsexual relationship factors.[7]

It is also unclear why certain people seem to be especially vulnerable to sexual dysfunction though others are not. Kaplan (1974) has suggested "individual response-specificity," a term borrowed from psychosomatics to refer to a tendency to respond to a variety of stresses in a particular physical response pattern (see Sternbach, 1966). More cognitive-behavioral approaches suggest a differential learning history (Ellis, 1971; LoPiccolo, 1977a; Masters and Johnson, 1970). What does seem to be critical is a careful analysis of the current sexual relationship. The safest assumption is that there are qualities of the relationship, and each person's role in it, that are contributing to the dysfunction. As alluded to earlier, *a dysfunction can be serving purposes very useful to the structure of the relationship and the psychological needs of each individual*. Neglecting to notice this functional character of the sexual problem may result

---

[7]*Editors' Note.* That is, initial sex therapy interventions may be of diagnostic as well as therapeutic use. Indeed, such a view is consistent with a number of other models of family therapy intervention, e.g., structural (Aponte and Van Deusen, Chapter 9) and strategic (Stanton, Chapter 10). The crucial issue here is that therapist flexibility in the use and purpose of even the most structured or directive interventions can reap genuine benefits to patients even when highly focal target complaints (e.g., premature ejaculation), for which "effective" techniques are presumably known, are presented by the patient.

in "resistance" or sabotage of therapeutic progress[8] (Kaplan, 1974; Sager and Kaplan, 1972).

ASSESSMENT OF SEXUAL DYSFUNCTION

The aim of assessment procedures is generally threefold: to produce a diagnosis or description of the problem; to clarify etiology of the problem; and to suggest an appropriate treatment regimen for the problem. Unfortunately, assessment procedures for sexual dysfunction fall short of all three goals in varying degrees. While this failure is more or less true of other psychotherapeutic endeavors, the field of sexual dysfunction has an obvious and unique handicap. Both social stigma and personal embarrassment (of both patients and therapists) make the gathering of truthful and complete data about a couple's sexual relationship inordinately difficult.[9]

Current Strategies for Assessment

Attempts to assess sexual dysfunction generally fall into three categories, which differ in their method of data collection.

1) Direct observations of sexual behavior, videotaping of sexual behavior, and "sexological" exams

One obvious approach to assessment of sexual dysfunction is to simply observe the patient couple during their sexual relationship, either by having the therapist present (Hartman and Fithian, 1972) or by videotaping the patient couple (Serber, 1974).

---

[8]*Editors' Note.* This view, that sexual dysfunctions can be *functional* for relationships, is one that is consistent with many models of treating relationships discussed in this book, yet, as noted earlier, is certainly a refreshingly deviant view among behaviorally-oriented clinicians. Therapists need to keep clear the distinction between the *functions* of behavior and the *consequences* of behavior. Since the term "functions" implies intentionality (at whatever level of consciousness) such notions generally fall outside the purview of behavior therapists (Knudson, Gurman, and Kniskern, 1980).

[9]*Editors' Note.* Could this be why some marital and family therapists deal with sex only as a metaphor? Also, as noted in Editors' Note 5, many family therapists believe that repetitive patterns of behavior are of greater diagnostic use than any particular symptomatic complaint.

Another variety of direct observation technique is the "sexological exam" (Hartman and Fithian, 1972). In this procedure, the therapist stimulates the breast and genitals of the opposite sex patient, for the purpose of assessing and demonstrating physiological responsiveness.

While such procedures may seem to offer the advantage of direct, non-distorted recording of actual sexual behavior, there are a number of issues which rather convincingly argue against their use. It seems unlikely that most couples with a sexual dysfunction will be unaffected by being observed, videotaped, or stimulated by their therapist. Thus, the behavior elicited in these situations may have little generalizability to the target stimulus situation—the partners interacting alone in the privacy of their own bedroom. Similarly, such assessment procedures would probably simply be unacceptable to the majority of dysfunctional couples seeking treatment. Finally, the ethical problems in patient-therapist sexual contact and the possibility for exploitation of the patient are obvious (LoPiccolo, 1977b).

2) Sex history interviews

A major element in many sexual treatment programs is the sex history interview (e.g., Kaplan, 1974; LoPiccolo and Heiman, 1978; Masters and Johnson, 1970). The format of such an interview is usually that of an extended (up to 8 hours) face-to-face semi-structured interview, conducted separately with each patient, by a therapist of the same sex.

The utility of such extensive history-taking has not been empirically demonstrated, and is open to question in terms of the most efficient use of therapeutic time. Certainly, many of the questions asked in the more extensive interviews have minimal clinical utility, as treatment procedures remain the same regardless of the varying nature of the patient's answer.

Information gathered during history-taking can be useful, however, in building rapport and in enabling the clinician to establish initial working hypotheses about the etiology and maintenance of the sexual problem in a particular case. This information is useful in deciding what therapy interventions will be tried and in alerting the clinician to areas which may be problematic in therapy. In this way, the clinician may be able to circumvent or minimize client resistance or defensiveness to particular therapeutic procedures.

3) Paper and pencil self-report inventories

There have been relatively few attempts to develop valid psychometric inventories with content specific to sexual dysfunction, with only a few symptom-specific sexual dysfunction inventories available in the literature (i.e., Derogatis, 1976; El-Senoussi, 1964). These instruments tend to be developed on logical (as opposed to empirical) grounds. That is, these inventories have either not been demonstrated to be empirically useful, or, as in one case, have actually been shown to be invalid (Beutler et al., 1975). Two very useful pencil inventories are the Sexual Arousal Inventory (Hoon, Hoon, and Wincze, 1976) and the Sexual Interaction Inventory (LoPiccolo and Steger, 1974). The Sexual Arousal Inventory is specific to females. The Sexual Interaction Inventory attempts to describe a couple's sexual relationship in terms of frequency and enjoyment of specific sexual activities. Both instruments are statistically sophisticated and provide guidelines for treatment, in that they identify arousal deficits and problem behaviors for therapeutic focus.[10]

Two new paper and pencil measures that are currently being evaluated are the Personal History Questionnaire (PHQ-A) (Heiman, 1978a) and the Predictors (P) Questionnaire (Nowinski, 1978). The first attempts to parallel the value of a sexual history interview and consists of questions on past and current emotional relationships, as well as demographics, health, and sexuality. The latter "P" Questionnaire, based on a social learning theory model, contains 15 scales suspected to be relevant for differentiating successful from nonsuccessful cases. These scales tap such dimensions as: partner trust, erotic interest, physical attraction to partner, romantic interest, expectancy for improvement, depth of involvement, and expectancy for injury.

There are two obvious problems with all such self-report paper and pencil inventories. First, they are highly reactive, in that asking couples in great detail about their sexual relationship undoubtedly has some behavior change effects. Secondly, such inventories are extremely susceptible to social desirability, defensiveness, and simple falsification by the respondent (Jemail, 1977).

The Need for Multidimensional Assessment

None of the strategies discussed above really offers an adequate assessment scheme for sexual dysfunction. Sexual dysfunction does not exist in a vacuum, but is related to a large number of historical, behavioral, personal, relationship, and physiological factors. An evaluation of each of the following factors needs to be conducted for an adequate assessment of a sexually dysfunctional patient couple.

1) *History*. Notwithstanding the reservations noted above, an examination of the sexual history of the patient is needed to best plan for successful treatment. A woman with a history of terrifying incestual sexual molestation as a child, for example, needs different therapy than an inorgasmic woman with an unremarkable sexual history.

2) *Current Behavior*. An understanding of the actual sexual behavior a couple engages in is obviously crucial. If the therapist does not know just what the patients *do* sexually, it is impossible to plan a therapeutic course of prescribed "homework" sexual assignments.

3) *Attitudinal and Cognitive Factors*. How do the patients think about their sexual dysfunction? Do they have negative attitudes toward sex, or religious beliefs which must be considered? Attitude change and cognitive restructuring are major elements in treatment, so careful assessment is crucial.

4) *Psychodynamic and Intrapsychic Defenses*. Although treatment of sexual dysfunction is basically a cognitive behavior therapy type of procedure, the role of intrapsychic defenses cannot be ignored in many cases. In occasional erectile

---

[10]*Editors' Note*. Recently D'Agostino, McCoy and Lacerda (1976) have raised some thought-provoking questions about the normative implications of the list of basic sexual activities included in the SII.

failure cases, for example, the client may be struggling with the issue of an unacceptable and, therefore, consciously denied homosexual orientation. The therapist should acknowledge that patients *do* have intrapsychic defense mechanisms for dealing with conflicts. Failure to acknowledge and work with these anxiety defenses often leads to therapeutic failure.

5) *Interpersonal Systems*. The importance of considering the role of the sexual dysfunction in the couple's broader emotional relationship cannot be overemphasized. For some couples, the dysfunction plays a very functional role in the maintenance of their emotional relationship and life-style. A dysfunction may be a means of avoiding intimacy, of expressing hostility, of maintaining control in the relationship, or of retaliating for other grievances in the relationship. A failure to assess such factors typically leads to treatment failures.

6) *Psychiatric Status*. At the present time, there is only very sparse evidence that the behavioral treatments for sexual dysfunctions are applicable to patients with a significant degree of overt psychopathology. However, some current work with psychotic inpatients looks very promising (Lobitz, 1979). Certainly, the effect of depression on inhibiting sexual drive and expression is well-known, and assessment for depression should be included in multidimensional assessment.

7) *Biological Factors*. Despite the fact that the majority of sexually dysfunctional patients are organically intact, it is becoming clear that there are a large number of biological processes which can be implicated in sexual dysfunction.

A complete evaluation of the patient's biological status requires consideration of a number of parameters not included in routine physical examinations. Obviously, complete and thorough pelvic examinations by a consultant urologist or gynecologist are indicated. Beyond this, tests for thyroid function, endocrine status (especially testosterone), and glucose tolerance should probably be routine, especially in low sex drive and erectile failure cases. An examination for neuropathy and peripheral vascular function may also be indicated, with penile pulse and blood pressure especially important

in erectile failure cases. In differentiating organic from psychogenic erectile failure, measurement by penile plethysmograph of nocturnal erection during REM sleep has been found to be a valid and highly useful measure (Karacan, 1978). Similarly, vaginal plethysmography shows great promise in the diagnosis of female arousal deficits (Heiman, 1978b).

THE CONDUCT OF TREATMENT

Establishing Goals

Assessment is a particularly crucial issue since behavioral treatment of sexual problems tends to be relatively brief when compared to more traditional forms of psychotherapy. Careful assessment is necessary to delineate problem areas and therapeutic goals for treatment.

The process by which clients and therapists establish goals for treatment serves several purposes aside from helping to insure an efficient use of therapy time. Goals also provide clients with a way of conceptualizing their problems and the therapy process. Often individuals enter therapy feeling confused, out of control, or totally out of touch with events and emotions which have contributed to their problems. Or they may have an understanding of events which is not facilitative of therapeutic change, such as "he doesn't get erections as his way of punishing me." The process of setting goals for therapy may help clients to conceptualize problems in new, more constructive ways. For example, operationalizing therapy goals in terms of acquiring new skills and attitudes encourages the clients to evaluate their past and present experiences from a learning theory standpoint. Often a change in the way individuals perceive themselves and their problems allows for a renewal of feelings of control over situations that may have seemed overwhelming in the past. A decrease in feelings of guilt, self-doubt, or anger may be the consequence of such a change in perspective, and a greater involvement in therapy is likely to be facilitated.

Another related function of goal-setting is to help the client make sense of the therapy process. Since sex therapy tends to be relatively brief (usually anywhere from five to 20 sessions), having to spend a great deal of time dealing with client resistance or defensiveness can interfere with achieving the optimum amount of treatment gain. Involving the clients in the process of goal-setting helps them to feel active and in control of important elements of their therapy. In a sense, the client and therapist, through the process of goal-setting, learn to share a common viewpoint and language for change. This facilitates a sense of rapport between client and therapist and makes the process of therapy more meaningful for the client. Having helped establish the goals of therapy, the client is in a better position to understand and accept the steps the therapist recommends as necessary to achieving those goals. In this way, a certain amount of resistance to therapy is circumvented.

Establishing goals for therapy is also valuable in that it models an approach to problem-solving which the clients can continue to use once therapy is over. The selection and operationalization of appropriate, realistic, short-term and long-term goals are skills which can be refined in therapy. Learning to implement a program for change that results in achievement of desired goals is a valuable skill to take from therapy.

Lastly, the establishment of therapy goals provides outcome criteria against which therapeutic changes can be measured. One advantage of using therapy goals as outcome criteria in addition to, or in place of, standardized measures is the ability to uniquely individualize criteria on the basis of particular cases (Bergin, 1978). Often, outcome measures do not accurately reflect the focus of therapy or indicate the degree of importance the client attaches to the goals which have and have not been achieved.

Although most sex therapy attempts to individualize therapy goals based on the needs of a particular individual or couple, certain goals may be applicable in all cases. These goals usually reflect the values of the clinician, in that they define what the therapist believes is important to good sexual functioning and a fulfilling sexual relationship. The components of a well-functioning sexual relationship mentioned earlier, such as flexibility, openness, intimacy, adequate arousal, and pleasure, are such goals. They can apply to almost all cases, regardless of the particular problem or sexual dysfunction that exists.

In addition, there are goals which reflect the needs of particular cases. Often these goals will reflect desired changes in other, nonsexual areas of the couple's relationship, or in the individuals themselves.

In general, sex therapy attempts to achieve greater concordance between the way sexual behaviors, attitudes, and experiences are for a couple or individual and the way they would like them to be. Areas such as actual frequency of various sexual behaviors and desired frequency of those behaviors are dealt with. The same is true for levels of pleasure and arousal, including orgasm. Increasing perceptual accuracy in terms of knowing each other's sexual preferences and improved communication are often major foci of therapy. Therapy also attempts to lessen inhibitions (i.e., those feelings which prevent full participation or enjoyment), anxiety, and feelings of pain or psychological discomfort. Expanding the range of sexual experiences a couple enjoys, increasing sexual knowledge and enhancing sexual pleasure are also focused on in therapy.

Goals that are established early in therapy need not remain static, but should be responsive to changes that take place in the therapeutic process. Goals need to be periodically reevaluated by client and therapist, since the focus of therapy may shift as some goals are achieved, amended, or assume less importance.

We are currently using a "goals sheet" for establishing goals at the beginning of therapy and as an outcome measure. Prior to therapy, clients are asked to list their goals and to rate each on the degree of importance it has for them currently. After therapy, the clients are again given the same list of goals and asked to rate current importance and the amount of progress they feel was made toward each goal. In this way, changes in importance of each goal to the specific client can be assessed and a more accurate measure of client perception of progress in therapy achieved.

Whatever the therapy goals are for a particular case, they should reflect the input of both the therapist and the clients. Typically, goals in the sexual area will cover a wide range of intervention, including behavior change, attitudes, and cognitive restructuring, as well as changes in physiological response. It is usually helpful to operationalize goals and to strive to be as specific as possible about what would be considered a desired outcome of therapy. At times, however, the therapist may have goals which he or she chooses not to make explicit to the client. For example, the therapist may have a lessening of defensiveness in one client as an unexpressed goal for therapy. The therapist may choose to work on this indirectly at first, as the issue may be too threatening to the client in the initial phases of therapy to address directly. As much as possible, however, goals should be made explicit since this is clearly facilitative of therapeutic progress.

Variations in the Structure of Therapy

Sex therapy is a complex, multifaceted psychotherapy procedure which shares certain commonalities with other forms of psychotherapy. However, variations in terms of treatment format or modalities have been used in sex therapy. Formats include individual therapy, conjoint or couple therapy, group therapy, co-therapy, self-help programs, and therapy that involves minimal contact with a therapist.

Clinicians vary on the degree of importance they ascribe to individual versus conjoint therapy. The model of therapy presented by Masters and Johnson (1970) emphasizes the need to deal with the couple as a unit. Mutual responsibility for the quality of a sexual relationship is a basic tenet of most sex therapy (LoPiccolo, 1977a). Sex therapy, therefore, tends to focus on couple interactions and systems dynamics which are maintaining problematic sexual patterns.

There is some empirical evidence which supports the view that conjoint therapy may be more effective than individual therapy (Cooper, 1969c; Gurman and Kniskern, 1978; Prochaska and Marzilli, 1973). However, techniques such as orgasmic reconditioning, masturbation therapy, cognitive restructuring and systematic desensitization have been effective in the treatment of individuals (Barbach, 1974; Ellis, 1971; Husted, 1972; Kockott, Dittmar, and Nusselt, 1975). It has been suggested that the issue of conjoint versus individual therapy is complex and may depend on such variables as the specific problem involved, the quality of the couple's relationship, and the type of treatment format employed (Hogan, 1978).

The group therapy format has been used successfully with individuals and couples for sexual enhancement (LoPiccolo and Miller, 1975), treatment of erectile failure (Lazarus, 1961, 1968), primary orgasmic dysfunction (Barbach, 1974; Schneidman and McGuire, 1976), and premature ejaculation (Kaplan et al., 1974).

Group therapy offers certain advantages not found in individual or conjoint therapy, such as positive social reinforcement. Problems with this format are maintenance of therapy changes once the group is disbanded and generalization of changes made in the group to outside relationships (McGovern, Kirkpatrick, and LoPiccolo, 1976; Schneidman and McGuire, 1976). However, there is clearly a demand for therapy formats which meet the needs of individuals without partners.

The necessity for dual sex co-therapy teams in the treatment of sexual problems is a matter of controversy. In *Human Sexual Inadequacy* (1970), Masters and Johnson state their belief that dual sex therapy teams are essential to the process of conjoint sexual therapy. This belief is based on the premise that, "no man will ever fully understand woman's sexual function or dysfunction," and vice versa. Each therapist, then, functions as an interpreter and representative of the same-sex client. In addition, dual sex cotherapists can serve as role models for each client as well as modeling positive patterns for interacting with the opposite sex.

Other advantages of the use of co-therapists are the opportunity to utilize one therapist as an observer of the therapy process, the opportunity for discussion and utilization of two sources of input on a case, and as a means to circumvent and deal with transference issues. The potential dangers of transference and countertransference in the process of sex therapy have been emphasized by Masters and Johnson (1970). These issues, such as attraction or strong emotional reactions between client and therapist, are believed to be minimized by the use of dual sex co-therapy teams.

An obvious disadvantage of co-therapy is the increased expense in terms of therapist time and the cost to the client. Private practice clinicians frequently do not have co-therapists available, and the effectiveness of this format over an individual therapist has not been empirically demonstrated (Mathews et al., 1976; Schmidt, 1977). There is also some evidence that co-therapy, where there is conflict between the therapists, may be more harmful than beneficial to the clients (Gurman and Kniskern, 1978). What clearly needs to be done is to correlate treatment results with therapy mode (dual or single therapist), type of dysfunction, and sex of therapist.

Self-help procedures have been utilized in the treatment of premature ejaculation (Lowe and Mikulas, 1975; Zeiss and Zeiss, 1977), mixed dysfunctions (Mathews et al., 1976), and orgasmic dysfunction (Heiman, LoPiccolo, and LoPiccolo, 1976). Programs involving minimal therapist contact for problems which respond to limited therapeutic intervention need to be evaluated further.

Variations in therapy structure also occur in regard to number of sessions, the interval between sessions, and whether in conjoint therapy the individuals are ever seen alone. While sex therapy is generally time-limited, there is no evidence to suggest that there is an optimum number of sessions. Two factors which influence the duration of therapy are the type of dysfunction and client participation in or resistance to therapy.

It is generally agreed that in cases without organic problems, premature ejaculation, vaginismus, and primary inorgasmic dysfuntion are usually easy to treat in short-term formats. Cases of ejaculatory incompetence, erectile failure, and secondary inorgasmic dysfunction, on the other hand, are usually more difficult and may occasionally require more extensive therapy. Too little work has been done with low sexual desire to know the optimal format for such cases, although Kaplan (1979) has recently proposed a promising-looking format.

Treatment Applicability

Initially, because of its behavioral orientation and relatively brief duration, sex therapy was considered to be appropriate primarily for cases of sexual dysfunction caused by lack of information or poor technique. Cases that involved individual psychopathology or marital disturbance were often referred elsewhere for therapy. More recently, the range of cases which are considered appropriate for sex therapy has broadened, as both intrapsychic and interpersonal factors have been implicated in the etiology and maintenance of sexual problems (Kaplan, 1974; Masters and Johnson, 1970).

In addition, research has been done to assess differential effectiveness with various patient groups. This research, as well as clinical experience, has shown that sex therapy which includes a combination of psychodynamic and behavioral approaches can often be effective even in cases involving severe marital dysfunction, intrapsychic dynamics, and organic impairment.

The question, then, of which cases are inappropriate for sex therapy has become more complex. Cases involving lack of information, poor technique, and poor communication in the sexual area are clearly appropriate for sexual therapy. In addition, therapy has also been done with sex offenders who wished to improve their heterosexual functioning (Annon, 1976) and with increasing numbers of physically disabled individuals (Cole, Chilgren, and Rosenberg, 1973). Sex therapy often serves a diagnostic function in cases where the extent of organic involvement in the sexual problem is in doubt. There is also evidence that sex therapy can be beneficial even in cases where there is an identified organic component to the sexual problem (Renshaw, 1975).

The probability of treatment effectiveness is one possible criterion that can be utilized in deciding treatment appropriateness. For example, cases of premature ejaculation are clearly appropriate for standard sex therapy, while cases of primary impotence (males who have never experienced an erection) might be deemed as inappropriate, given their relatively poor success rate in therapy. However, the success rate for treatment of sexual dysfunctions by most other forms of therapy is generally poorer than that achieved through sex therapy. Therefore, sex therapy may still be the most appropriate form of treatment, even for those dysfunctions where effectiveness has been limited.

Although there is little research correlating sex therapy outcome with client or therapist characteristics, it is generally agreed that certain client characteristics are probably not uniquely facilitative of sex therapy, but rather are helpful in any therapeutic context. Such characteristics are a lack of defensiveness and rigidity, a certain capacity for insight, motivation for change, a relatively good relationship between partners when both participate in therapy, and a life-style which is conducive to making and maintaining the desired changes.

Therapy, of course, attempts to deal with issues such as defensiveness, denial, and ambivalence toward change. The presence of such issues and the presence of marital distress, organic or other psychological problems, in addition to sexual problems, do not necessarily contraindicate sex therapy. Rather, careful assessment of the extent, duration, and severity of such issues or problems must be done to determine the degree of interference each is likely to pose to therapeutic progress. We agree with Lobitz and Lobitz (1978) who suggest assessing the following factors when deciding a couple's appropriateness for sex therapy:

1) The possible presence of organic pathology that might affect a person's sexual performance.
2) The degree of psychopathology in one or both partners.
3) Each partner's motivation for treatment, including commitment to the relationship and willingness to participate in treatment.
4) Relationship factors, including the level of intimacy or hostility between the partners.

In order to assess these factors, a complete physical and medical evaluation should be done. Certain psychometric tests can be administered to assess psychological functioning. A clinical interview and measures of sexual behaviors, such as the Sexual Interaction Inventory (LoPiccolo and Steger, 1974), should also be used in evaluating couples and individuals for therapy. Measures which assess the couple's relationship, such as the Locke-Wallace Marital Inventory (Kimmel and van der Veen, 1974) and the "P" Questionnaire (Nowinski, 1978), are useful.[11]

---

[11]*Editors' Note.* While the Locke-Wallace Inventory is useful in research contexts, e.g., for reliably discriminating between "distressed" and "nondistressed" couples, we are surprised that Heiman et al. find it useful for *clinical* assessment since the information it provides is so global as to be virtually useless for treatment planning, especially in a generally behavioral treatment, where behavioral specificity is so important.

As mentioned earlier, the presence of a physiological basis for a particular sexual problem does not necessarily mean sex therapy is not appropriate. New techniques in psychophysiological measurements, such as monitoring nocturnal penile tumescence in males with erectile problems (Karacan, 1978), will help clarify the role therapy can play in such cases. Where there is no possibility of restoring adequate functioning, therapy may be even more crucial as a forum for exploring alternative means for expressing closeness and sharing pleasure.

The degree of psychopathology in one or both partners has certain implications for therapy. If the condition is likely to interfere with daily functioning or the ability of the clients to actively engage in therapy (for example, carry out specific behavioral assignments), the possibility of treatment gain is reduced. Severe depression, chronic alcoholism or drug use, or acute psychoses are conditions which are often incompatible with attempting sex therapy. Sex therapy has been employed successfully in cases of moderate or mild depression, often in conjunction with administration of antidepressant medication. Likewise, a psychosis which is being controlled by medication need not contraindicate sex therapy.

The issue of motivation is an important one to assess in making decisions about the appropriateness of therapy. Sex therapy usually requires relatively active participation on the part of the client. It is crucial that clients have a willingness to try new experiences and to tolerate feelings of anxiety or discomfort during the process of therapy. Each individual's motivations for treatment should be explored. At times, it is evident that one partner is an unwilling client who is only seeking therapy because of pressure or threats by the other partner. Therapy is sometimes sought to assuage feelings of guilt in an individual who plans to terminate the relationship once therapy is over. Such motivations are likely to work against the aims of therapy and should be brought out in the open where they can be discussed with the aid of the therapist.

The appropriateness of sex therapy when one person in a couple relationship is actively engaged in an outside sexual relationship is also questionable. Often, individuals are asked to discontinue such outside relationships for the duration of therapy. In this way, the focus can be on the pattern of interactions between the two people involved in therapy. There are no data available on the influence of such outside sexual relationships on the outcome of sex therapy, however. In general, some commitment on the part of both partners to their relationship is beneficial for therapy. This commitment need not be defined as marriage, but rather a strong desire to work on the sexual problems and a willingness to invest time and energy in changing. Partners who are not married but are living together and feel a sense of commitment to each other would, therefore, be appropriate for sex therapy.

Cases of extreme hostility or resentfulness between partners, as well as a desire to leave the relationship on the part of one partner, should usually be referred for marital or divorce therapy. In addition, referral for other forms of therapy, such as individual therapy, group therapy, or an open-ended, less structured form of therapy which can include attention to sexual problems, should be made according to the needs of particular cases. Individual therapy may be indicated in those cases where unresolved or conflictual issues for one partner interfere with his or her ability to work out current problems with the other partner. In other cases, the presence of complicating factors, such as depression or psychopathology, argues for a flexible open-ended treatment format that can be modified to meet the broader needs of the clients. Likewise, group therapy, rather than individual couple therapy, might be the treatment of choice for couples where the chance for group support and exchange of information would be beneficial for attitudinal and behavioral change.

Recently, research into the effectiveness of self-help procedures in the area of sexual problems has shown some promising results (Lowe and Mikulas, 1975). In light of these data, sex therapy consisting of expensive weekly sessions with a therapist may not be needed for relatively easy-to-treat problems that respond well to a self-help format. Future research is clearly needed in the area to help delineate which individuals with what types of problems are most likely to achieve good results in sex therapy.

The Role of the Therapist

In sex therapy, as in behavior therapy, the therapist takes an active role in the therapy process. This role begins when the therapist actively engages with the client in the process of history-taking. Rather than be a passive recipient of information, the therapist uses this time to build rapport, to correct misinformation, and to begin to conceptualize the etiology and dynamics of the case. This conceptualization is shared with the clients during the process of goal-setting, which, as previously discussed, involves both clients and therapist.

As therapy progresses, the therapist interacts with the clients in a variety of roles. One of the basic roles the therapist plays is directing the course of therapy. Although the process of goal-setting involves both the clients and therapist, the therapist initially assumes responsibility for determining the content of the therapy hour in order to help the clients achieve their goals. As treatment progresses, an increasing amount of responsibility is turned over to the clients.

The therapist also serves as an information-giver and teacher. Through the use of films, books, anatomical models, or general educational remarks, the therapist attempts to correct misinformation and to educate the clients in the anatomy and physiology of sexual response, and in the effective use of sexual techniques. The therapist also teaches the clients effective communication skills and encourages sharing between the partners.

The educational role that the therapist plays contributes to the client's perception of the therapist as an authority who is knowledgeable and competent. The role of therapist as an authority is crucial in the initial phases of therapy for two reasons. First, it is important for the clients to feel that they can trust the therapist, since the therapist plays such an active role, at least initially, in directing the course of therapy. Second, the therapist can use this role to help the client try new experiences which would be beneficial to therapy progress. For example, trying self-stimulation might be more acceptable to a client if he or she can see it as something *the therapist* is asking the client to try, rather than taking responsibility for this him/herself. Being able to use the therapist's role in this way is often important early on in therapy, particularly in cases where the client is out of touch with his or her body, or where sexual desire or feelings are denied. As therapy proceeds, the therapist is gradually able to step out of this role as the clients begin to accept more responsibility for their own sexuality.

Another major role the therapist plays is that of facilitator of change. As part of this, the therapist functions as an interpreter and role model for the clients. In order to facilitate change, the therapist uses a variety of techniques which will be discussed in the following section. The therapist also acts as an interpreter at times, in an attempt to improve communication between the clients. In this way, the therapist models empathy and clarification skills and encourages the clients to talk to each other. At times, when communication breaks down or is destructive rather than constructive (as in the case of extreme hostility), the therapist may engage each client individually in dialogue. The major focus in sex therapy, however, is on the relationship between the partners, and so the therapist will generally aim to reestablish communication between the partners.

Another way the therapist acts as an interpreter is by presenting his or her own conceptualizations and perceptions to the clients. In this way, the therapist acts as a source of external input which can provide impetus for change.

The role of the therapist as a model for the clients is particularly important in sex therapy in that the majority of treatment interventions are aimed at behavioral or attitudinal change. Providing role models for both clients in couple therapy and the ability to model a relationship are two advantages to using a dual sex co-therapy team as mentioned previously. However, even in cases with a single therapist, utilizing modeling effects to facilitate change can be a powerful and effective tool. Ideally, the therapist serves as a model of an effective, competent, and likeable person who has a positive and joyful appreciation of sexuality.[12] *Selective* self-disclosure on the part of the therapist about his or her

own life experiences and feelings and attitudes about sex can be a powerful technique in effecting change in the clients. In addition, in the relationship with the client of the opposite sex, the therapist models more effective ways for the partners to interact. If the therapist is someone whom the clients trust and respect, the impact of modeling can be profound.

Lastly, the very fact that the therapist plays so many roles in therapy and that these roles change over the course of time enables the therapist to serve as a model of role flexibility. In order for individuals in a relationship to grow and change over time while maintaining a meaningful connection, they must be comfortable with some degree of role flexibility. The ability to change a relationship is an important element in insuring that treatment gains will be maintained, and that the couple will be able to cope with new problems as they may arise.

Techniques of Sex Therapy

Although the specific therapy content varies session by session, there is an overall structure that is generally followed by sex therapists. The following description is a composite of basic components, a subset of which have been applied by a variety of clinicians (Cooper, 1969a, b, c, 1970; Ellis, 1962; Hastings, 1963, Kaplan, 1974; Lazarus, 1965; LoPiccolo, 1977a; LoPiccolo and Lobitz, 1962; Masters and Johnson, 1970; Salter, 1949; Wolpe, 1958).

From the client's perspective, therapy structure begins, via homework assignments, with an initial period of sensual exploration, or sensate focus. This is an attempt to reintroduce positive elements into the couple's physical interaction, to defocus the emphasis on genital pleasure, and to begin to build a more satisfying, less performance-oriented, sexual interaction. Gradually, the partners are asked to include more genital stimulation in their sensate focus exercises. By the end of therapy, there is emphasis placed on using whatever components of sexual stimulation are mutually agreed on as pleasurable. In the context of various specifically behavioral assignments, clients develop sexual and nonsexual communication with each other.

From the therapist's perspective, the structure of therapy progresses from a very directive

---

[12]*Editors' Note.* This is an extremely important point. The use of cotherapy in the treatment of sexual dysfunctions has become so ritualized because of the impact of Masters and Johnson's (1970) approach that the assumption of the *routine* need for two therapists is rarely challenged.

therapeutic role to more of a consulting role. This process is followed in order to have the clients leave therapy feeling more in charge of and responsible for the pattern in which sex fits into their lives and more able to cope with future problems on their own.

To examine the techniques and tactics in more detail, they can be divided into three phases. The first phase might be termed *preliminary connection and conceptualization techniques*, consisting of a history-taking session and an establishment of some basic ground rules or norms for the course of therapy. History-taking is used, or not used, to a different extent by different therapy centers. Its potential power needs to be acknowledged, as it is usually the first in-depth contact between client and therapist. It also can be a unique occasion for the client to share otherwise extremely private, often hidden, or never revealed sexual background. The purpose of the sex history is to get a better understanding of the individual (and couple's) history of general health, relationships, and sex. The taking of a sex history also helps the therapist to conceptualize the problem and share that perspective with the client. The outcomes of the history session include: (a) cathartic feelings for some clients at having shared their backgrounds with, and being accepted by, the therapist, and (b) a sense of alliance between clients and therapist because of (a) and because of joint acknowledgment of the problem and its conceptualization.

Also, in this initial therapy phase, guidelines are provided. For instance, it is explained that the clients will have most of the responsibility for making the effort to change via the homework assignments.[13] Furthermore, most of the focus will be on the present and immediate future, though some time may be needed to air problems and see patterns from the past. Mention is also made of the temptation, but futility, of trying to establish blame for past and current problems, as blame hinders rather than facilitates desire to change.

The second phase of therapy might be labeled *change-focused techniques*. This phase begins as soon as the history-taking, problem concep-

tualization, and goal-setting have been accomplished. Since these techniques have been elaborated elsewhere (Kaplan, 1974; LoPiccolo, 1977a; LoPiccolo and Hogan, 1979; Masters and Johnson, 1970), we will review the major intervention categories and cite examples from each.

1) *Insight*. While not always a change tool, insight is useful in sex therapy, especially in instances where a "countercharge" pattern occurs. Thus, if a man complaining of erectile problems comes to therapy with a wife who is critical of his lovemaking, simply describing the cyclical pattern (her criticism, his sexual dysfunction, her feelings of rejection, her criticism) can be a useful first step.

2) *Anxiety Reduction*. A troubled sexual relationship is often surrounded with anxiety, even though anxiety itself may not be the "cause" of the dysfunction. A technique that is often used to decrease anxiety is desensitization. The structure of the sex therapy itself, beginning with low anxiety exercises and gradually adding in more anxiety-laden exercises, is an implicit desensitization hierarchy (see Dengrove, 1971; Laughren and Kass, 1975; and LoPiccolo and Hogan, 1979 for further discussion). Desensitization also may be used in addition to the general therapy structure, when anxiety seems to be particularly central to a couple's dysfunction. Thus, imagination and in vivo exercises are sometimes recommended for individuals who have phobic reactions to nudity, genitals, semen, or activities such as manual and oral stimulation or intercourse. The dilation procedure, using progressively larger vaginal dilators (or fingers) in cases of vaginismus, is a clear example of an in vivo desensitization procedure.

Implosion and guided imagery are two other techniques that have been used to reduce anxiety in sexual dysfunctions. Both techniques are used far less frequently than desensitization. Implosion, an attempt to produce maximum anxiety by having the client imagine a scene, tends not to be used for general sexual changes (except for Frankel, 1970), but rather for isolated problems within the course of sex therapy. For instance, problems connected with intrapsychic (rather than interpersonal) patterns, such as obsessive aversions, can sometimes be treated

---

[13]*Editors' Note*. Note the similarity of the view taken here with what Whitaker (Whitaker and Keith, Chapter 6) calls the "battle for structure" and the "battle for initiative."

with implosion. Guided imagery, having the client cognitively rehearse an entire scene, can be useful in both identifying and treating a person's "anxiety points." It tends to be used in conjunction with hypnosis (Dittborn, 1957; Hussain, 1964; Leckie, 1964).

3) *Sexual Enhancement.* While anxiety can maintain sexual dysfunctions, simply removing anxiety is not usually sufficient for change to occur. A variety of other techniques, such as education, skill training, cognitive therapy, or sensory awareness, is important for enhancing the quality of a couple's sexual relationship. Sexual information on anatomy, physiology, and current sexual norms can be helpful to correct a couple's misconceptions about what is required for a good sexual relationship. Further positive attitude change is encouraged through the use of bibliotherapy (Barbach, 1975; Heiman, LoPiccolo, and LoPiccolo, 1976), rational-emotive therapy (Ellis, 1971), and therapist self-disclosure (Lobitz et al., 1974). Permission to use and develop sexual fantasies has been recommended for getting clients accustomed to thinking about sex, replacing distracting thoughts, and increasing sexual arousal (Kaplan, 1974; LoPiccolo, 1977a). Sensory awareness exercises can be useful for connecting the cognitive and physical experiences of sex and for relaxation (Heiman et al., 1976).

Sexual and social skill development plays an important role in the building of a more satisfying sexual relationship. The most frequent foci of skill training are: the initiation and refusal of sexual activity, self-stimulation, partner stimulation, the squeeze or pause techniques for premature ejaculation, communication during sex, and communication of sexual and nonsexual feelings. Methods for improving these areas include behavioral rehearsal, bibliotherapy, modeling via slides, films and videotapes, and feedback from therapists and the sexual partner.

4) *General Relationship Enhancement.* While sex can remain an isolated problem, often the overall relationship also needs to change. Generally, therapeutic intervention is aimed at helping clients to express feelings to each other, to demonstrate caring and affection, to establish a sense of equal involvement in the relationship,

to problem solve, and to reach conflict resolution. Specific relationship problems can range from division of household chores to partners feeling unloved. The techniques to deal with relationship problems include intervention from systems, psychodynamic, and cognitive-behavioral approaches. These include reconceptualization, communication exercises, role-playing in new or reversed relationship roles, self-monitoring, monitored expression of small ways of caring, homework practice, showing tapes of client interactions to the clients themselves, and using the therapy hour to elucidate constructive and destructive communication patterns.

5) *Physical-Medical Techniques.* There are a few medical techniques that seem to be variously effective in treating certain sexual problems. For sexual disinterest that is connected with depression, antidepressive medication will usually be necessary before sex therapy can begin. There seems to be no consistency regarding the use of other drugs, although some improvement has been noted with a limited use of alcohol and tranquilizers. Alcohol can also be a source of problems in cases where a person is or has been alcoholic. Generally, most therapists do not recommend the use of alcohol or drugs except in very special circumstances.

For male erectile problems, surgery is sometimes recommended. Adequate diagnosis is necessary, including plethysmographic monitoring of nocturnal penile erections, a neuroendocrinological evaluation and psychotherapy (Karacan, 1978; Renshaw, 1975). One surgical procedure involves the implant of a penile prosthesis which makes the penis rigid enough for intercourse. Prostheses (Small-Carrion or Bradley-Scott devices) do not improve arousal and ejaculation ability, however, and are, thus, considered a last resort. There are no adequate outcome studies on these devices, but there have been many complications reported (Renshaw, 1975). An alternative, promising but similarly with poor outcome data, is a recent procedure of reestablishing penile blood flow through transplant of the inferior epigastric artery (Britt, Kemmerer, and Robinson, 1971; Gaskell, 1971). Further studies are being done on a surgical procedure for men with primary erectile failure. This procedure involves surgical repair of abnormal venous outflow from the corpora cavernosa of the penis (Wagner and Ebbehoj, 1978).

For females, there are two questionable procedures for improving orgasm ability. One is the clitoral circumcision or freeing of clitoral shaft and hood adhesions. The other is vaginal reconstruction surgery (Burt and Burt, 1975). The former makes physiological sense, but most nonorgasmic women do not seem to have these problems. The latter, because it includes cutting the pubococcygeal muscle to displace the vagina, calls into serious question future problems of pelvic support.

A physical training procedure that does seem to be useful for treating female orgasmic problems is the use of Kegel exercises (Kegel, 1952). Women are taught to voluntarily contract the pubococcygeal musculature surrounding the vaginal area, which seems to enhance orgasmic ability (Kline-Graber and Graber, 1975).

The above five categories of change techniques are used in different proportions according to therapist and dysfunction. It is obvious that the techniques are multifaceted and, in fact, individual techniques can be seen as a combination of changing behavior, cognitions, systems, personal dynamics, sexual and nonsexual relationships.

Specific Sex Therapy Techniques and their Applicability

There are a few techniques that are commonly used in the treatment of most sexual dysfunctions. Sensate focus, initiation and refusal, and feedback are examples of the most commonly used techniques to help set up a new sexual pattern of sexual interaction. *Sensate focus* exercises consist of initially nongenital sensual massage in which different kinds of touching are explored. While Masters and Johnson's (1970) introduction of this technique was focused on the "give to get" principle, current use of sensate focus is more diffuse. The goal is to create a comfortable, anxiety-free atmosphere for physical contact, with one person providing stimulation that is pleasing to give and is pleasing for the other person to receive. The tone of sensate focus "sessions" is one of discovery, rediscovery, or exploration, with an attempt to make each person aware of the other's needs and the changes in those needs from encounter to encounter. Feedback is a natural part of sensate focus, since verbal or nonverbal communication is necessary in order for the interaction to be satisfying. Clients are asked to develop ways of providing positive, as well as negative, feedback. This process is important for setting up the expectation that one person is not supposed to know or be responsible for the other person's physical response, though each person can be integral to the other's general enjoyment of the physical contact.

Initiation and refusal of sexual contact are common issues to individuals with a dysfunctional sexual pattern. Often initiations are surrounded with tension, guilt, anxiety, or dread and they have come to be ambiguous, annoying, or ill-timed. Therapeutic time is spent having the couple discuss good and poor ways to initiate and refuse a sexual exchange. This information is used during the couple's assignments at home. Gradually, through the initiation and refusal, feedback and sensate focus experiences, a basic sexual communication framework is developed.

Simultaneously, certain techniques are usually added that are designed for particular dysfunctions. For men with *premature ejaculation*, the squeeze (Masters and Johnson, 1970) or pause (Semans, 1956) is typically used. These procedures are designed to teach ejaculatory control by increasing awareness of the feelings that immediately procede ejaculation. Some therapists have men begin practicing these techniques in masturbation; other therapists begin directly with partner stimulation. In either case, the male is stimulated to a level of high arousal, just preceding the point at which he feels orgasm is about to occur. At that point, either the squeeze is applied or a pause period begins and continues until the pre-ejaculatory feelings subside. Stimulation begins again until another pause or squeeze is necessary. The goal is to teach the male to tolerate a considerable amount of stimulation, eventually with fewer pauses or squeezes, prior to orgasm. There is a tendency to prefer the pause technique since it allows a couple to continue other forms of physical contact while pausing and also decreases a temporary genital focus. However, for some couples, the squeeze can result in a more rapid reduction in the urge to ejaculate. However, a client should be cautioned to release the squeeze immediately should he begin to ejaculate as a result of squeezing too late. Otherwise, there is a possibility of retrograde ejaculation, which can cause bladder, prostate, or seminal vesicle irritation. It is useful to teach clients either method and allow them to choose the most satisfactory for them. In either case, there is an attempt to encourage men to enjoy the stimulation rather than avoid it, and to not worry about an occasional "too late" squeeze or pause, since that will help increase the awareness of the pre-ejaculatory signs.

Following the learning of the squeeze or pause techniques, the couple learns to apply one of the procedures to intercourse. Initially, this involves vaginal containment without movement. Gradually, slow pelvic thrusting can occur. Finally, unrestrained intercourse is possible. The need to use the squeeze or pause diminishes, although clients are told that it is expected that they will occasionally require the pause or squeeze to slow down the arousal buildup (Lobitz et al., 1974).

In cases of *erectile failure*, treatment is focused on eliminating performance demands and anxiety and on providing adequate sexual stimulation. Techniques to deal with erectile problems vary a great deal, depending on the particular clients, their history, their expectations, and the quality of their general marital relationship. A few of the more common approaches to erectile dysfunction include: (a) sexual communication issues including feedback and discussions of expectations; (b) increasing the variety and length of foreplay activities; (c) involving the female partner by acknowledging her implicit and explicit demands on her partner's performance; (d) desensitization of the male's anxiety about sex in general, or intercourse in particular; (e) anxiety reduction for the couple, with a focus on sexual contacts; (f) paradoxical instructions in which the male is expected not to become aroused; (g) the teasing technique (Masters and Johnson, 1970), which involves stopping stimulation once an erection has occurred; and (h) beginning intercourse with the female pushing the male's flaccid penis into her vagina.

Generally, erection problems have a cyclical position in the couple's interaction. The woman's "demands" may be the result of her own sexual frustration and feelings of rejection. The man's anxiety may be a combination of sexual conflict, self-doubt about his sexuality, and fear of failure to please his partner. Thus, the important features of therapy include interrupting whatever cycle has been developed, separating erections from feelings of love, affection, and even arousal, demonstrating that erections are possible, and elucidating and confronting clients' mutual expectations about successful sexual contact.

Ejaculatory incompetence treatment combines elements of the premature ejaculation and erectile failure programs. The woman is instructed in ways to provide a great deal of physical stimulation in a nondemanding manner. The male is instructed to explore avenues of psychological arousal while also learning various ways to trigger orgasmic response.

Primary inorgasmic or preorgasmic dysfunction in women has been successfully treated in a variety of ways. One method is through directed masturbation training followed by partner-training (LoPiccolo and Lobitz, 1972). In masturbation training, the woman is taught to examine and know the parts of her genitalia, become more comfortable with her genitals and more accepting of her body, explore her genitals for tactile quality and then for pleasure, use erotic materials and fantasy, use orgasm "triggers," and, if necessary, use a vibrator. The woman then teaches her partner what kinds of stimulation are pleasurable for her in a variety of sexual activities, including intercourse. It is expected that additional clitoral stimulation is necessary during intercourse. Throughout the program, the woman is instructed to do Kegel (1952) exercises, which are thought to increase orgasmic potential, and the couple is instructed to engage in a variety of mutually pleasurable, nondemanding, initially nongenital sexual experiences together. Some techniques of arousal disinhibition are also part of this program, including role-play of orgasm, in which the woman acts out an exaggerated imagined orgasm. Doing this with her partner can reduce some fears and embarrassment and, after several tries, the exercise becomes more amusing and less anxiety-ridden.

The relationship between the partners is of

vital importance in her orgasmic potential with her partner. The man's feelings about her masturbating (if she is on a masturbation program) and her increasing ability to become aroused must be carefully taken into consideration. He may feel left out, unimportant, or frightened that she may become uncontrollably sexual and demanding. It is, therefore, very important to integrate the woman's progress into the overall sexual relationship and, thus, pay attention to opening the couple's communication about sex and affection.

Some therapists do not use masturbation training (Masters and Johnson, 1970), but instead work exclusively on the couple's sexual interaction. In this situation, a gradual progression from less sexual to more sexual activities is combined with decreasing the woman's anxiety and expanding the couple's comfort and knowledge of different forms of sexual stimulation and communication. There have been no comparative studies of the relative effectiveness of including masturbation, and both approaches are reported to be quite effective. Some women are so intensely conflicted over masturbation that it is not a viable therapeutic choice. Nevertheless, the concepts of masturbation (the woman's knowledge of acceptance and responsibility for her own sexuality) are probably important ingredients to incorporate into the couple-only therapy format.

Secondary inorgasmic dysfunction is a broad category for which there is no major treatment structure. In some cases, a directed masturbation approach, along the lines of the primary inorgasmic treatment, is recommended. This is recommended for women who are orgasmic in only one restricted masturbatory pattern (i.e., through thigh pressure), which makes transfer to partner stimulation difficult. A modified primary program may be indicated for women who are very phobic towards their genitals, who are uncomfortable about the physical side of sex in general, or whose lack of orgasm is being maintained by the (sometimes unspoken) expectation that the woman's orgasm is her partner's responsibility.

For women who are orgasmic alone, but not with their partner, relationship issues around the topics of communication, conflict resolution, power, and control are commonly dealt with.

Some educational and attitudinal change can be helpful so that the woman is assured of adequate sexual stimulation. Often, the more general features of sex therapy—spending time exploring non-intercourse sensual stimulation and exploring meaningful forms of sexual feedback including initiation and refusal—are the major therapeutic strategies for encompassing the educational, attitudinal, and relationship issues surrounding sex.

A small group of women in sex therapy report being orgasmic only outside of their primary relationship. This situation permits the therapist to explore the factors that make orgasm possible for a particular client. The next step is to see if the client couple's interactions can be modified so as to make orgasm and enjoyment more likely.

For those couples who are orgasmic in different ways, but not during coitus, therapeutic caution is in order. Some therapists refuse to treat this category as a dysfunction since most women do not experience orgasm in coitus. Other therapists treat this group as sexual enhancement rather than sexual dysfunction. In either case, it is important to evaluate whether: the woman is receiving adequate clitoral stimulation before and during intercourse, the couple enjoys sexual contact, and what coital orgasms mean (i.e., being "normal," being adequate, intimacy, cooperation).

Sometimes, delaying the male's ejaculation via the pause or squeeze techniques can be a useful adjunct to secondary (and primary) orgasmic problems. The couple's sexual interaction needs to be dealt with as a whole, such that the woman's feeling of inhibition, performance anxiety, or unwillingness to take responsibility in the sexual relationship is complemented by the man's support, respect, cooperation, and decreased investment in viewing her orgasm as proof of his sexual adequacy.

In cases of *vaginismus*, the major addition to the general therapy program is the use of graduated dilators, introduced either at a gynecologist's office or with the couple at home. Using dilators or, alternatively, the woman's or husband's fingers, enables the woman to control the act of intromission while learning to tolerate vaginal intromission. While this procedure is easy and direct, there are often therapeutic issues to deal with in the couple's sexual interaction. This has to do with the fact that the sexual pattern had previously focused on her pain and anxiety and his frustration, anger, and sometimes guilt. Taking away the dysfunctional pain often does not take away the surrounding sexual interaction pattern.

Low sexual desire is an increasingly frequent category of dysfunction for which therapists are currently developing strategies and sorting out appropriate subtypes. L. LoPiccolo (1980), for instance, has mentioned that many of the therapeutic strategies for low sexual desire are not unique to this dysfunction. She suggests that the client-therapist relationship, couple relationship, ambivalence toward therapeutic change, and maintenance problems may be particularly highlighted in cases where sexual desire is a complaint. From examining cases presenting with complaints of sexual disinterest, among other issues, there was a presence of: marital problems (whether or not the couple initially acknowledged the relationship as an area of dissatisfaction), negative attitudes toward female genitals, sexual dysfunction, and prior or current complaints of depression (L. LoPiccolo, 1980). Zilbergeld and Rinkleib (1980) have pointed out that the meaning of sex to both partners must be explored. Whether clients see sex as a way to decrease distance, to perform perfectly, to solve problems, to release tension, to get attention, or whatever the "function" might be—will have an impact on each person's desire for sex. Likewise, the feelings surrounding sexual contact vary. Thus, Zilbergeld and Rinkleib (1980) suggest helping clients to reevaluate their assumptions about the personal gains and losses that they experience through sexual contact, as well as learning to broaden or delimit sexual from nonsexual cues. Transitions from sexual to nonsexual situations, exploring personally arousing situations, and relabeling internal feelings of excitement have been used with some success on a few cases (Zilbergeld and Rinkleib, 1980).

Resistance and Countertransference

There are innumerable occasions in which client resistance can become an issue in sex therapy. Two of the more common areas have to do with client-client and client-therapist types of resistance. Therapists need to explore resistance from the vantage point of assessing how frightening and chaos-inducing it may be for the clients to let their problems go. Thus, therapists should evaluate and sometimes point out the functional quality of the dysfunction. It can also be useful to confront, directly or paradoxically, the client's flight from a better sexual relationship.

Client-therapist resistance is probably most often seen in the dynamics surrounding sex-role and authority issues. Male clients, for instance, may resist intervention from a female therapist since that relationship structure is reminiscent of his current marital situation or his feelings about women in general. In couples therapy, differential motivation on the part of the clients can create a struggle between one client and the therapist. Client-therapist resistance issues seem to be interwoven with a variety of factors and there are no predetermined solutions for dealing with resistance other than attempting to explore it in ways that minimize defensiveness or countertransference problems on the part of client and therapist.[14] Letting clients express their feelings, acknowledging their right to such feelings, and exploring possible ways that the client-therapist relationship might be improved to both client and therapist satisfaction are general aspects of dealing with these forms of resistance.

Certain kinds of resistances can be dealt with by a penalty deposit system such as that mentioned by LoPiccolo (1977a). In this way, homework exercises are "contracted" and lack of participation can result in a financial loss. This type of procedure seems to be a "booster" to keep people going through the course of therapy. It still allows for deeper forms of resistance to continue and does not prevent patient sabotage of an assignment (such as doing an assignment in a way that is destructive to progress).

Client-therapist resistance problems are not necessarily the most frequent or the most serious interferences with therapeutic progress. There are several particularly common or especially dangerous pitfalls that can threaten the client-therapist relationship and, thus, therapy in general. One such pitfall is the creation of a

---

[14]*Editors' Note.* For an excellent and more extensive discussion of resistance problems in sex therapy, see Munjack and Oziel (1978).

permanent alliance with one person in a client couple. This situation can cripple the therapist's effectiveness by sustaining a wedge between clients, creating a two-against-one battle, and blinding the therapist to viable, couple-shared compromises. A second, related difficulty can occur when the therapist experiences serious feelings of *countertransference* towards one of both members of the couple. Differences in personality style or value systems, as well as lack of change on the part of the clients, can result in countertransference problems.[15] The outcome can be a stalemate and perhaps even a reversal of therapeutic gains. A third common error in this same vein is therapist vulnerability to *being manipulated* by one of the clients. Manipulation can vary in its effect on the therapist. For example, clients can convince the therapist that change is impossible or that one partner is the cause of the problem. The result is that, as much as the therapist joins into the problem, he/she interferes with a solution.

In the above situations, therapists must be on guard. Alliances, countertransference, and manipulation situations, if noticed early, can be used therapeutically to point out client relationship themes that are powerful and, thus, difficult to change. Nonetheless, they are experiences to work on directly with the couple. Sometimes, however, certain client-therapist relationships do not work and an alternative needs to be recommended.

Another pitfall that is very common, especially in dealing with couples, is that of *value conflicts* between therapist and client, most frequently seen in terms of social-political ideologies. This issue is complex, since one of the therapist's roles is to challenge generalizations and unrealistic expectations and to individualize sexual happiness to the couple's own preferences. Thus, a therapist is asked to confront a variety of assumptions clients make. However, there is often a vague territory between confrontation of values and suggesting a superior set of standards. The therapist's major task is to attempt to get clients to challenge their own values, and consciously evaluate them to see if they are an active choice. Also, it is important for the therapist to continually point out the consequences, positive and negative, of making a particular value choice.

A final area that is a very problematic aspect of sex therapy has to do with sex between client and therapist. While some sex therapists claim the validity of this approach, our view is that there are more dangers than advantages to this practice. The dangers include the unavoidable coercion of clients because of their vulnerable position in therapy, problems surrounding eventual rejection or termination of the relationship, and the questionable value of an "in-house" cure that may not generalize to outside problems. Legal difficulties are also a consideration. Alternatives beyond therapist-client sex exist, even for people without partners, although this group of people has been somewhat neglected in sex therapy. Depending on the sexual problems involved, group therapy focused on social interaction styles and problems and rational-emotional therapy can be viable alternatives.

Termination

The final phase of therapy is the termination phase. For some therapy centers, the length of therapy is fixed so that clients and therapist aim for this point and do not have to face typical difficulties of termination. During any termination phase, it is useful to attempt to decrease therapist involvement as much as possible so that the partners eventually make up their own homework assignments and prepare for the posttherapy period. Therapists help clients form goals for the maintenance period, specifying expected trouble areas, changes that need to be maintained, changes still desired, and the role of each person in furthering the sexual relationship. This period is, therefore, a good time to review, from both client and therapist perspectives, what changes have occurred in the course of therapy.

If not predetermined, sex therapy ideally ends with a joint decision between therapist and client that either the client's goals have been achieved or the sexual relationship seems to have progressed satisfactorily regardless of the goals originally stated. Often the marital or sexual relationship is not perfect for the couple but there is a sense that either no more change is

---

[15]*Editors' Note*. Some additional factors in the therapist's countertransference in sex therapy are discussed by Dickes and Strauss (1979).

likely to occur, at least for a while, or further change is not dependent on weekly therapy. In other instances, the partners may decide that they are no longer interested in remaining together or that they want to focus on their nonsexual relationship. Depending on the current therapist's expertise and interest, as well as the client's expressed needs, therapy can continue with a new emphasis or an appropriate referral can be offered to the clients.

FACTORS INFLUENCING THERAPEUTIC CHANGE

Evaluating the curative factors in sex therapy is still almost exclusively a task grounded in clinical experience and speculation rather than research results. Currently, there are no published factorial studies of treated and nontreated clients, and virtually no research has been aimed at a search for active ingredients of the therapeutic process. Nevertheless, in the light of clinical experience, some speculations worthy of further research have emerged. Using the categories developed in the preceding section, we can examine factors which do and do not seem to be important for change in sex therapy.

First, the role of insight in producing therapeutic change varies in importance. Some clients benefit tremendously from "seeing" their own problematic patterns; other clients simply use insight as an excuse not to change. For example, in the latter category, it is not unusual to have a client use past familial history as a reason to be unable to show nonsexual physical affection to his or her partner. On the other hand, insight into historical features of experience can provide a good therapeutic start for clients who feel that the problems they experience are their own fault. Seeing that one's past can be the explanation for the current problem is, for some clients, a relief from feeling intrinsically weak or incapable.[16] Interactional insight, in the sense of understanding how patterns of destructive interactions have developed, can provide a similar conceptual framework for the problem. Pointing out destructive interactions during the course of therapy can be useful as long as the clients (rather than the therapist) can eventually learn to identify the pattern and learn ways to divert the interaction into a more constructive direction. This process is a difficult one.

In sum, while insight seems beneficial for some clients, it does not appear to be critical for change. Furthermore, no clear signs are available from which to predict *which* clients will benefit from insight.

Regarding the curative value of various techniques, these factors are difficult to evaluate since therapy usually consists of a combined technique approach. Two techniques do seem to be fairly robust: They are the "squeeze" or "pause" for premature ejaculation, and the dilation procedure for vaginismic women. Additionally, the general therapeutic techniques of anxiety reduction are clearly beneficial for the large number of clients whose sexual dysfunction is bound up with tension and anxiety. Simultaneously, helping clients to find ways to enjoy sexual and nonsexual activities can have a renewing effect on the relationship and give clients a sense that things can change. And for those clients who need practice in skills training, techniques to expand communication and sexual interaction patterns are valuable.

Certain client characteristics can help the process and outcome of therapy. Cooper's (1969c, 1970) research has shown a number of variables to correlate significantly with treatment outcome. Important for male dysfunctions (erectile failure, retarded ejaculation, and retrograde ejaculation) were: satisfactory premarital coitus, male marital happiness, love for the wife, short duration of the sexual problem, strong sex drive, past intermittent sexual functioning in coitus, normal personality in each spouse, motivation for therapy, and wife's cooperation in therapy (Cooper, 1969c). For coitally inorgasmic women, Cooper (1970) found that positive prognostic indicators included: premarital coitus and orgasm, short duration of dysfunction, love for the husband, strong sex drive, normal personality, positive attitudes toward sex, positive attitudes toward partner's genitals, positive attitudes toward sexual techniques and experimentation, and emotional arousal in coitus. Not surpris-

---

[16]*Editors' Note*. In addition, provision of some historical insight can have general strategic value, in that it may help to enhance the patient-therapist relationship (specifically, the working alliance). At a still broader level, the implication of Heiman et al.'s view is that the provision of historical (as well as interactional) insight need not be antithetical to sound behaviorally-oriented practice and, in fact, may facilitate it.

ingly, these lists suggest that good outcome is associated with overall greater sexual health, marital happiness or involvement, and good personal and relationship functioning.

Our own clinical impression is that client personality styles may affect the process of sex therapy more than the specific outcome. For instance, with clients who feel that others are trying to control them, a helpful therapeutic relationship is one which is flexible in the presentation of change-focused techniques (i.e., gives the client a sense of choosing among alternatives for change). Regarding relationship variables, rather than self-reported marital happiness per se (which may reflect social desirability, defensiveness, or denial rather than marital satisfaction), the degree to which the couple shares the commitment to change the relationship seems most crucial. Included with the commitment change are whether each person feels he/she has something to gain from making changes and whether at least some of their goals are held in common. However, at the moment, the best way in which to assess shared commitment to change is to begin therapy.

Many clients with certain sexual problems can make significant changes without the partner's involvement in the therapy process. This is most likely to occur in cases of premature ejaculation or primary inorgasmic dysfunction. Usually, however, greater therapeutic gains occur when both partners are involved in the change process. Partner-assisted gains take many forms, including mutual support, encouragement, patience, and willingness to try difficult or awkward solutions. Believing that the other person can change and does want to make the sexual relationship better (even if it cannot live up to all expectations) is also important to motivation. A certain amount of therapeutic time can be devoted to helping clients to notice small but effortful changes that each partner is making.

In terms of the therapist's input to change, characteristics that seem to be important have to do with ability to understand existing patterns and, where possible, to translate that understanding into a change program. *Such characteristics include perceptiveness, empathy, flexibility, ability to analyze and synthesize patterns, openness as opposed to defensiveness, and*

ability to work with client value systems. None of these factors is specific to the sexual area. Whether it is useful for the therapist to be in a sexual relationship, married, or even sexually experienced, remains a question. Such personal experience probably helps in many cases, and may interfere in others. Personal experience probably is less critical than the therapist's ability to facilitate a positive (change-inducing) therapeutic relationship with the clients.

Regarding the therapist-client relationship, there is some indication that common trust, respect, and sense of involvement may be very important. These qualities may have special meaning to sexual problems since sex is typically a private and vulnerable area. Trust facilitates openness, while respect and involvement permit the challenging of values and the confrontation of issues. Such features help therapy to move, even with discouragements and setbacks, because there is a shared acknowledgment that the goals are worthwhile and deserve the effort made toward attaining them. Without mutual trust and respect, clients may hesitate to tell the therapist how they really feel. A lack of therapist involvement may communicate hopelessness to the clients, and a lack of client involvement signals the therapist to possible questionable motivation, simple disinterest, or differential goals between clients or between clients and therapist. A more psychoanalytic view might try to summarize these issues as components of transference and countertransference. In either case, the field is still left with the task of finding specific client-therapist characteristics, and combinations of those characteristics, which facilitate change.

A successful termination of therapy is one that has resolved a number, but not necessarily all, of the sexual issues. Resolution may not mean complete change of sexual patterns, but it usually means some increase in satisfaction, pleasure and, in some cases, frequency, *coupled with* greater acceptance of self and individual differences within the relationship. A few client couples reach this point but decide that, for other reasons, their relationship is not viable. Such an outcome is not, in and of itself, an unsuccessful one. The unsuccessful termination is characterized by the same or increased dissatisfaction with sex, polarized feelings about the other person's sexuality, feelings of discouragement, a pessimistic outlook on the future of sex within the commitment of the relationship, or a sense of failure.

From this summary, it is clear that while little research has tried to identify curative factors in sex therapy, the topic is a potentially rich one. The still private and value-laden nature of sexuality in this culture is likely to influence the client-therapist interaction in special ways. It will be interesting to see the extent to which future research shows predictors of therapeutic success to be similar for sexual and nonsexual problems.

EFFECTIVENESS OF SEX THERAPY

The ten years since the publication of *Human Sexual Inadequacy* by William Masters and Virginia Johnson have seen a tremendous growth of professional interest in the topic of sexual dysfunction. Numerous other books on treatment of sexual dysfunction have appeared in print in the ensuing years, and there are now at least two professional journals (*Journal of Sex and Marital Therapy, Journal of Sex Education, Counseling, and Therapy*) focused primarily on this new "sex therapy." This explosion of interest has occurred primarily at the clinical level. Hogan (1978), in a recent literature review, has noted that most of this new literature consists of case studies, uncontrolled or poorly controlled "demonstrations" of therapeutic effects, or badly confounded (and, therefore, uninterpretable) clinical studies. Much of this literature is further weakened by failure to clearly specify the characteristics of the patients, in terms of personality, relationship, or biological correlates of dysfunction. Similarly, little attention is paid to therapist characteristics associated with good or poor outcome. It is rare that therapeutic interventions are described with sufficient clarity and detail to make it possible for others to replicate procedures. The treatment interventions reported are generally broad spectrum, multifaceted combinations of a variety of procedures, with no attempt to differentiate the "active ingredients" and the "inert fillers" in the total package. In reporting the results of such treatment, formal psychometric assessment of patient functioning at a variety of levels pre- and posttherapy is rare. More commonly, the clinician's unsubstantiated global judgment of "success" or failure is simply reported. Longterm follow-up data are generally not obtained. Finally, *the most influential clinical literature in the field has been generated by a very small number of therapists, which creates at least the possibility that it is the charismatic personality or style of these therapists, rather than the techniques themselves, which accounts for the reported success of these new sex therapies*.

Because of these shortcomings, there is relatively little that can be said with any certainty about the effects of sex therapy in a brief review. For a comprehensive review of methodological issues in sex therapy research, the reader should consult J. LoPiccolo (in press). Similarly, a comprehensive review of outcome studies appears in Hogan (1978).

Within these limitations, some conclusions about treatment effectiveness, in terms of diagnosis, treatment techniques, and therapy modality will tentatively be offered here. It should be kept in mind that there are few, if any, rigorous, methodologically elegant empirical studies to support these conclusions. Unless otherwise noted, support for these conclusions is provided in Hogan (1978), LoPiccolo and Hogan (1979), Masters and Johnson (1970), and Kaplan (1974).

A. Effectiveness of sex therapy for the various diagnostic categories of sexual dysfunction.

1) *Premature Ejaculation*. Virtually all the clinical literature reports success rates of 90-95% or over for increasing latency to ejaculation, using the pause (Semans, 1956) or squeeze procedures (Masters and Johnson, 1970).

2) *Retarded Ejaculation or Ejaculatory Incompetence*. As this disorder is relatively uncommon, there is very little outcome literature available. Reported success rates seem to range from 50-82%, but all reported samples are too small to draw any firm conclusions.

3) *Erectile Failure*. Reported success rates for this disorder vary strongly according to whether the diagnosis is primary (never has had erectile functioning) or secondary (previously had adequate erectile functioning). For primary erectile

failure, samples are small, but success rates seem to average 40-60%. For secondary erectile failure, the prognosis is better, with success rates averaging 60-80%.

4) *Female Primary Orgasmic Dysfunction.* This dysfunction refers to the woman who has never experienced an orgasm in any form of sexual stimulation. If success is defined as reaching orgasm in either solo or partner genital manipulation, success rates are uniformly high, averaging 85-95% (Heiman, LoPiccolo, and LoPiccolo, 1976; Kohlenberg, 1974; LoPiccolo and Lobitz, 1972). In terms of reaching orgasm in coitus, success rates are lower, averaging 30-50%.

5) *Secondary Orgasmic Dysfunction.* This diagnosis is used to refer to different behavioral patterns by different sex therapists. "Secondary orgasmic dysfunction" is variously used to describe the woman who is seldom orgasmic, orgasmic only in solo masturbation, previously orgasmic but not currently so, orgasmic only with a partner other than the male with whom she is in treatment, able to have orgasm with partner via manual or oral manipulation but not in coitus, and so forth. With so many behavioral patterns subsumed under one diagnostic label, the label itself and the question of treatment outcome become almost meaningless. If one accepts a definition of success as involving an ability to regularly experience orgasm during some form of heterosexual activity, success rates seem to average 70-80%. If one requires regular *coital* orgasm as a success criterion, rates are lower, averaging 30-50% in current literature.

6) *Vaginismus.* Vaginismus, involving involuntary spastic contraction of the vaginal musculature, is similar to premature ejaculation in terms of being very successfully treated. Using some variation of a physical dilation program, success rates of 90-95% or over are usual (Fuchs et al., 1973).

7) *Low Sex Drive.* This disorder refers to those individuals with a very low level of interest in sexual activity, and is the focus of much recent interest (Kaplan, 1977, 1979; L. LoPiccolo, 1980). Outcome statistics are virtually non-existent at this point. Our clinical impression is that such cases can respond well during therapy, with higher levels of interest and behavior apparently developing, but often relapse after termination.

B. Treatment Techniques

If the literature on outcome by diagnostic category is weak, the literature on differential effectiveness of various treatment techniques is even more so. The few actual comparative studies in the literature have typically been so poorly designed and badly confounded as to make any conclusions highly suspect (Hogan, 1978). It is clear, as noted above, that the pause and/or squeeze retraining procedure is the treatment of choice for premature ejaculation, as is the case for dilation procedures for vaginismus. Beyond these two statements, there is a large volume of clinical literature reporting many different techniques to be effective, as was reviewed in the preceding section on treatment techniques. As the large variety of techniques reported makes clear, sex therapy is a multifaceted package involving many different procedures. At this point, it is entirely unclear what the active elements of the package are and what techniques are best applied to each sort of client (Hogan, 1978; J. LoPiccolo, in press).

C. Therapy Modalities

Again, there is little evidence to support differential effectiveness of various modalities of therapy. Clinical evidence indicates apparently equal success with individual and conjoint therapy; with one and with two therapists; with individual couple therapy and group therapy of several couples; with group therapy of women only; and with guided-self-help "bibliotherapy." Details and references for these clinical observation are available in LoPiccolo and Hogan (1979), but, again, it should be noted that much of this "evidence" is anecdotal rather than experimental.

D. Research Questions

The preceding discussion should make it clear

that questions outnumber answers in regard to the effectiveness of sex therapy. A detailed discussion of important potential research questions is available in J. LoPiccolo (in press). To briefly summarize here, the following sorts of research are badly needed:

1) What treatments are best for the currently treatment-resistant dysfunctions—primary erectile failure and low sex drive being two prominent examples.
2) Studies of differential effectiveness of various dysfunctions.
3) Studies of patient and therapist characteristics correlated with success or failure of treatment.
4) Studies which identify the "active ingredients" and "inert fillers" in multifaceted treatment packages such as Masters and Johnson's (1970).
5) Studies of the effects of sex therapy upon other areas of patient functioning, such as marital happiness, psychiatric status, etc.
6) Studies aimed at the development of more objective diagnostic and treatment outcome measures.
7) Studies of the "resistant" patient couple.
8) Studies of the long-term effects of sex therapy.
9) Studies of the role of biological/physiological factors in treatment of sexual dysfunction.

THE TRAINING OF SEX THERAPISTS

In this chapter, a model of sex therapy as a complex, multifaceted psychotherapy procedure involving elements of couple therapy, cognitive therapy, insight-oriented therapy, and behavioral therapy has been presented. However, in reading much of the popular literature (and some of the professional literature), one receives a distinctively different impression. Sex therapy is often presented as an educational program not requiring any psychotherapeutic skills on the part of the practitioner, or even as a simple physical training procedure. These two views about the nature of sex therapy lead to considerable disagreement about the training and skills required to do effective sex therapy.

There are at least two schools of thought on this issue of the training needed to do sex ther-

apy. On the one hand, the established mental health professionals tend to argue that sex therapy is a set of specialized procedures for use only by trained psychotherapists. On the other hand, a number of the "new sex therapists" argue that sex therapy is a separate new profession.

The point of view held by many, if not most, psychologists and psychiatrists is that sex therapy is a subspecialty of psychotherapy. It logically follows, then, that only those persons who are qualified by training and experience to do psychotherapy should be doing sex therapy. This viewpoint stresses that sexual dysfunction does not exist in a vacuum, but that it often is related to problems in the couple's emotional relationship, such as poor communication, hostility and competitiveness, or sex-role problems. Furthermore, even in those cases in which the sexual dysfunction is not related to relationship problems, the couple's emotional relationship is often damaged by the sexual problem and the feelings of guilt, inadequacy, and frustration that usually accompany sexual dysfunction. Therefore, it is stressed that training in psychotherapy (especially marital or family systems therapy) is required to deal with these problems. Finally, this viewpoint notes that sex therapy itself is a stressful procedure, and that psychotherapeutic expertise is required to deal with the patient's emotional reactions to the sex therapy process.

While the logic of this argument is certainly compelling, the new sex therapists point out that it is not based on any empirical research data. No one has conducted a study of effectiveness of sex therapy procedures when used by trained psychotherapists as opposed to lay persons trained only in sex therapy procedures.

Certainly those "sex therapists" who are not psychotherapists claim results every bit as good as those obtained by psychologists and psychiatrists (Hartman and Fithian, 1972). Indeed, even a written educational program without *any* contact with a sex therapist has been shown to be remarkably effective for premature ejaculation (Lowe and Mikulas, 1975). In this vein, a number of self-help books for sexual dysfunction (e.g., Heiman et al., 1976; McCarthy, Ryan, and Johnson, 1975) have recently appeared on the market. While formal research on their effectiveness is lacking, the authors all have numerous clinical examples to support the likely effectiveness of this "therapy without a therapist."

Even while acknowledging the truth of these counterarguments, it might be pointed out that those people who seek out a sex therapist may be more severely dysfunctional (or in a more troubled relationship) than those people who attend an educational program or choose only to read a self-help book. It may well be that the professional psychotherapists are correct in their assertion that their patients need their psychotherapy skills. It may also be true, however, that not all couples suffering from a sexual dysfunction need the services of a psychotherapist. For couples who have a loving and strong emotional relationship, but who are simply unskilled and naive sexually, education rather than therapy may be the treatment of choice.

The question may ultimately be reduced, then, to one of the nature of the patients seeking sex therapy. Most clinics that specialize in sexual dysfunction report that there has been a change in the characteristics of their patient applicants over the last few years. Some years ago, most couples seeking therapy were basically very naive about sex; an education and training approach was usually quite successful. Recently, fewer and fewer such cases appear. The current greater cultural acceptance of sexuality and the widespread availability of good information about sexual physiology and technique have apparently resulted in a lower incidence of sexual dysfunction caused by naiveté and ignorance. Current cases more commonly involve deep-seated negative attitudes about sexuality, relationship problems, or other factors not responsive to a sex therapy program which only includes education and behavioral retraining exercises.

Within the model of sex therapy presented in this chapter, the ideal training program might include the following elements:

1) Sex therapy training, being viewed as a subspecialty, would follow formal academic work and supervised clinical experience in both general outpatient psychotherapy and in marital therapy.

2) Didactic training in the area of human sexuality, including psychology and physiology of sexual behavior, patterns of sexual behavior, etiology and treatment of dysfunctions, would be provided. This formal course work would include surveys of the available empirical research literature on each topic, as well as the clinical and descriptive literature.

3) Supervised experience is crucial. In our own training setting, our trainees first observe experienced clinicians actually conducting therapy. Trainees then begin to conduct initial evaluation sessions, at first with a staff member as co-interviewer, and then alone. In these sessions, the trainee is not under pressure to produce therapeutic change, but merely learns to elicit information from patients and to be supportive. These sessions are videotaped for supervision of the trainee. After some experience conducting intake evaluation sessions, the trainee begins actual therapy with patient couples. We have had trainees begin alone, with another trainee as co-therapist, and with a staff member as a co-therapist. We no longer have trainees see their first cases with a staff member as co-therapist, as this inequality of status and experience seemed to inhibit trainees from taking a fully active role in the conduct of the therapy. Therapists do not have fixed roles within the sessions but are encouraged to interact with both partners and to take an active part in the therapeutic hour. All cases are videotaped, and supervision is conducted by the trainee viewing the tapes with a staff member.

4) Attitudinal-experiential training also is valuable. Our training program now includes an experiential component, stressing role-play of various common clinical problems and situations. Much of this role-play is focused on insuring that the therapist feels comfortable in dealing with the whole topic of sexuality. Viewing of explicit sexual films is also useful as a device for producing discussion and introspection about how one's own attitudes and preferred sexual patterns influence the therapy process. Our trainees are also encouraged to experience, at home with their sexual partners if they have one, the various behavioral procedures that they will be assigning to their patients. This increases the credibility of the therapist when instructing the client in new techniques. Experiential exercises and role-play are also vehicles for increasing therapist awareness about experiences they may not have encountered directly.

While there could certainly be additions or deletions from this program, the ideal is simply making intensive and specialized training in sex therapy available to professionals. Unfortunately, the actual situation in professional training schools is about as far from this ideal as it is possible to be. While most medical schools now have a general, broad content course in human sexuality as an elective part of the curriculum, opportunities for training and supervised experience in sex therapy are almost nonexistent. Similarly, most clinical psychology and psychiatry residency programs simply do not provide such training. Those institutions that do have such opportunities for their students generally do so out of fortuitous circumstances rather than by design, e.g., someone on the faculty happens to have a research interest in sex therapy.

Apparently, there is at least some legislative awareness of this lack of training in human sexuality in most professional schools and continuing education programs. Two laws recently passed in California (Assembly Bill 4178 and 4179), signed into law by the governor in September of 1976 require, as of January 1, 1978, evidence of training in human sexuality as a condition for licensure (or renewal of licensure) as a physician, psychologist, social worker, or marriage, family, and child counselor. If other states follow this model, professional schools and professional associations will be forced by law to do what they should have been doing in any case.[17]

A Final Comment

In discussing the current status of treatment for sexual dysfunctions, we have focused on what appear to be two different levels: research data and clinical experience. Further rapprochement between these two estranged areas of knowledge is important for several reasons. First, presenting either research or clinical impression alone gives an incomplete picture of the therapeutic process and the ingredients for therapeutic change. Second, isolating therapy from research makes it more difficult to see how one might be able to influence the other. Third, some form of objective and subjective analysis is necessary in order to acknowledge, and organize, the complexity of sexual interactions in the process of change. It is, thus, assumed that both researchers and clinicians will be responsible for developing a more complete understanding of the process of sex therapy as it influences, or fails to influence, patterns of sexual functioning.

---

[17]*Editors' Note.* While we agree that such legislation is a step in the right direction, we are concerned that a number of professionals who receive such training may delude themselves (or worse, others) into believing they have thus become qualified sex therapists. First, in our view, most mental health professionals who seek continuing education credits do so only because they are required to do so and infrequently seek to "learn for learning's sake." Second, the content of the human sexuality courses usually offered to meet these continuing education requirements typically emphasizes the anatomy and physiology of sexual behavior, with little attention paid to treatment methods.

REFERENCES

Annon, J. *The Behavioral Treatment of Sexual Problems, Volume II, Intensive Therapy.* Honolulu, Hawaii: Kapiolani Health Services, 1976.

Ansari, J. M. A. A study of 65 impotent males. *British Journal of Psychiatry,* 1975, *127,* 37-41.

Barbach, L. G. Group treatment of preorgasmic women. *Journal of Sex and Marital Therapy,* 1974, *1,* 139-145.

Barbach, L. *For Yourself: The Fulfillment of Female Sexuality.* New York: Doubleday, 1975.

Bergin, A. E. The evaluation of therapeutic outcomes. In: A. E. Bergin & S. L. Garfield (Eds.), *Handbook of Psychotherapy and Behavior Change.* New York: Wiley, 1971.

Bergler, E. *Neurotic Counterfeit-sex.* New York: Grune and Stratton, 1951.

Bergler, E. & Kroger, W. *Kinsey's Myth of Female Sexuality: The Medical Facts.* New York: Grune and Stratton, 1954.

Beutler, L., Karacan, I., Anch, A., Salis, P., Scott, F., & Williams, R. MMPI and MIT discriminators of biogenic and psychogenic impotence. *Journal of Consulting and Clinical Psychology,* 1975, *43* (6), 899-903.

Blum, S. A study of the psychoanalytic theory of psychosexual development. *Genetic Psychology Monographs,* 1949, *39,* 3-99.

Britt, D. B., Kemmerer, W. T., & Robinson, J. R. Penile blood flow determination by mercury strain gauge plethysmography. *Investigative Urology.* 1971, *8,* 673-677.

Burt, J. E., and Burt, J. C. *The Surgery of Love.* New York: Carlton Press, 1975.

Cole, T. M., Chilgren, R., & Rosenberg, P. A new programme of sex education and counseling for spinal cord injured adults and health care professionals. *Paraplegia,* 1973, *11,* 111-124.

Comfort, A. *The Anxiety Makers.* Camden, New Jersey: T. Nelson and Sons, 1965.

Cooper, A. J. A factual study of male potency disorders. *British Journal of Psychiatry,* 1968, *114,* 719-731. (a)

Cooper, A. M. Hostility and male potency disorders. *Comprehensive Psychiatry,* 1968, *9,* 621-626. (b)

Cooper, A. J. "Neurosis" and disorders of sexual potency in the male. *Journal of Psychosomatic Research,* 1968, *12,* 141-144. (c)

Cooper, A. J. Clinical and therapeutic studies in premature ejaculation. *Comprehensive Psychiatry*, 1969, *10*, 285-295. (a)

Cooper, A. J. A clinical study of "coital anxiety" in male potency disorders. *Journal of Psychosomatic Research*, 1969, *13*, 143-147. (b)

Cooper, A. J. Disorders of sexual potency in the male: A clinical and statistical study of some factors related to short-term prognosis. *British Journal of Psychiatry*, 1969, *115*, 709-719. (c)

Cooper, A. J. Frigidity, treatment and short-term prognosis. *Journal of Psychosomatic Research*, 1970, *14*, 133-147.

Dengrove, E. Behavior therapy of impotence. *Journal of Sex Research*, 1971, *7*, 177-183.

Derogatis, L. R. Psychological assessment of sexual disorders. In: J. Meyer (Ed.), *Clinical Management of Sexual Disorders*. Baltimore: Williams and Wilkins, 1976.

Dittborn, J. Hypnotherapy of sexual impotence. *International Journal of Clinical and Experimental Hypnosis*, 1957, *5*, 181-192.

Ellis, A. *Reason and Emotion in Psychotherapy*. New York: Lyle Stuart, 1962.

Ellis, A. Rational-emotive treatment of impotence, frigidity, and other sexual problems. *Professional Psychology*, 1971, *2*, 346-349.

El-Senoussi, A. *The Male Impotence Test*. Los Angeles, California: Western Psychological Services, 1964.

Fenichel, O. *The Psychoanalytic Theory of Neurosis*, New York: Norton, 1945.

Fisher, S. *The Female Orgasm*. New York: Basic Books, 1973.

Frankel, A. S. Treatment of multisymptomatic phobia by a self-directed, self-reinforced technique. *Journal of Abnormal Psychology*, 1970, *76*, 496-499.

Freud, S. *Three Essays on the Theory of Female Sexuality*. New York: Avon, 1962. First published in 1905.

Fuchs, K., Hoch, Z., Paldi, E., Abramovici, H., Brandes, J. M., Timor-Tritsch, I., & Kleinhaus, M. Hypno-desensitization therapy of vaginismus: Part I. "In Vitro" method. Part II. "In Vivo" method. *International Journal of Clinical and Experimental Hypnosis*, 1973, *21*, 144-156.

Gaskell, P. The importance of penile blood pressure in cases of impotence. *Journal of the Canadian Medical Association*, 1971, *20*, 1047-1051.

Gurman, A. S. & Kniskern, D. P. Research on marital and family therapy: Progress, perspective and prospect. In: S. Garfield & A. Bergin (Eds.), *Handbook of Psychotherapy and Behavior Change*. Second edition. New York: Wiley, 1978.

Hartman, W. E., & Fithian, M. A. *Treatment of Sexual Dysfunction*, Long Beach, California: Center for Marital and Sexual Studies, 1972.

Hastings, D. W. *Impotence and Frigidity*. Boston: Little, Brown, and Company, 1963.

Heiman, J., LoPiccolo, L., & LoPiccolo, J. *Becoming Orgasmic: A Sexual Growth Program for Women*. Englewood Cliffs, New Jersey: Prentice-Hall, 1976.

Heiman, J. *The Personal History Questionnaire-A*. Department of Psychiatry and Behavioral Science, State University of New York at Stony Brook, 1978. (a)

Heiman, J. Uses of psychophysiology in the assessment and treatment of sexual dysfunction. In: J. LoPiccolo & L. LoPiccolo (Eds.), *Handbook of Sex Therapy*, New York: Plenum, 1978. (b)

Hogan, D. R. The effectiveness of sex therapy: A review of the literature. In: J. LoPiccolo & L. LoPiccolo (Eds.), *Handbook of Sex Therapy*. New York: Plenum Press, 1978.

Hoon, E. F., Hoon, P. W., & Wincze, J. The SAI: An inventory for the measurement of female sexual arousal. *Archives of Sexual Behavior*, 1976, *5*, 208-215.

Hoon, P. W., Wincze, J. P., & Hoon, E. F. A test of reciprocal inhibition: Are anxiety and sexual arousal in women mutually inhibitory. *Journal of Abnormal Psychology*, 1977, *86*, 65-74.

Hussain, A. Behavior therapy using hypnosis. In: J. Wolpe, A. Salter, & L. Reyna (Eds.), *The Conditioning Therapies. The Challenge in Psychotherapy*. New York: Holt, Rinehart, & Winston, 1964.

Husted, J. R. Effect of method of systematic desensitization and presence of sexual communication in the treatment of sexual anxiety by counterconditioning. *Proceedings of the 80th Annual Convention of the American Psychological Association*, Honolulu, Hawaii, 1972, *7*, 325-326.

Jarvik, M. E., and Brecher, E. M. Drugs and sex: Inhibition and enhancement effects. In: J. Money & H. Musaph (Eds.), *Handbook of Sexology*, New York: Elsevier-North Holland, 1977.

Jemail, J. A. *Response bias in assessment of marital and sexual adjustment*. Unpublished Ph.D. thesis, State University of New York at Stony Brook, 1977.

Kaplan, H. *The New Sex Therapy*. New York: Brunner/Mazel, 1974.

Kaplan, H. S. Hypoactive sexual desire. *Journal of Sex and Marital Therapy*, 1977, *3* (1), 3-9.

Kaplan, H. S. *Disorders of Sexual Desire and Other New Concepts and Techniques in Sex Therapy*. New York: Brunner/Mazel, 1979.

Kaplan, H. S., Kohl, R. N., Pomeroy, W. B. Offit, A. K., & Hogan, B. Group treatment of premature ejaculation. *Archives of Sexual Behavior*, 1974, *3*, 433-452.

Karacan, I. Advances in the psychophysiological evaluation of male erectile impotence. In: J. LoPiccolo & L. LoPiccolo (Eds.), *Handbook of Sex Therapy*, New York: Plenum Press, 1978.

Kaufman, J. Organic and psychological factors in the genesis of impotence and premature ejaculation. In: C. W. Wahl (Ed.), *Sexual Problems: Diagnosis and Treatment in Medical Practice*. New York: Free Press, 1967.

Kegel, A. H. Sexual function of the pubococcygeus muscle. *Western Journal of Obstetrics and Gynecology*, 1952, *60*, 521-524.

Kennedy, B. J. Effect of massive doses of sex hormones on libido. *Medical Aspects of Human Sexuality*, 1973, *7* (3), 67-80.

Kimmel, D., & van der Veen, F. Factors of marital adjustment in Locke's Marital Adjustment Test. *Journal of Marriage and the Family*, 1974, *2*, 57-63.

Kinsey, A. C., Pomeroy, W. B., & Martin, C. E. *Sexual Behavior in the Human Male*. Philadelphia: W. B. Saunders, 1948.

Kinsey, A. C., Pomeroy, W. B., Martin, C. E., & Gebhard, P. H. *Sexual Behavior in the Human Female*. Philadelphia: W. B. Saunders, 1953.

Kirkpatrick, C., McGovern, K., & LoPiccolo, J. Treatment of sexual dysfunction. In: G. Harris (Ed.), *The Group Treatment of Human Problems: A Social Learning Approach*. New York: Grune and Stratton, 1977.

Kline-Graber, G., & Graber, B. *Woman's Orgasm*. New York: Bobbs-Merrill, 1975.

Kling, A., Kedenberg, D., & Kedenberg, N. *An ethological-endocrine study in a patient group*. Paper presented at the American Psychiatric Association meeting, Honolulu, Hawaii, 1973.

Kockott, G., Dittmar, F., & Nusselt, L. Systematic desensitization of erectile impotence: A controlled study. *Archives of Sexual Behavior*, 1975, *4*, 493-500.

Kohlenberg, R. J. Directed masturbation and the treatment of primary orgasmic dysfunction. *Archives of Sexual Behavior*, 1974, *3*, 349-356.

Kolodny, R. C., Masters, W. H., Hendryx, J., & Toro, G. Plasma testosterone and semen analysis in male homosexuals. *New England Journal of Medicine*, 1971, *285*, 1170-1174.

Kraemer, H. C., Becker, H. B., Brodie, H. K. H., Doering, C. H., Moos, R. H., & Hamburg, D. A. Orgasmic frequency and plasma testosterone levels in normal human males. *Archives of Sexual Behavior*, 1976, *5*, 125-132.

Kraft, T. Desensitization and the treatment of sexual disorders. *Journal of Sex Research*, 1969, *5*, 130-134.

Kraft, T., & Al-Issa, I. The use of methohexitone sodium in the systematic desensitization of premature ejaculation. *British Journal of Psychiatry*, 1968, *114*, 351-352. (Abstract)

Laughren, T. P., & Kass, D. J. Desensitization of sexual dysfunction: The present status. In: A. S. Gurman & D. G. Rice (Eds.), *Couples in Conflict: New Directions in Marital Therapy*. New York: Aronson, 1975.

Lazarus, A. A. Group therapy in phobic disorders by systematic desensitization. *Journal of Abnormal and Social Psychology*, 1961, *63*, 504-510.

Lazarus, A. A. The treatment of a sexually inadequate man. In: L. P. Ullmann & L. Krasner (Eds.), *Case Studies in Behavior Modification*. New York: Holt, Rinehart, & Winston, 1965.

Lazarus, A. A. Behavior therapy in groups. In: G. M. Gazda (Ed.), *Basic Approaches to Group Psychotherapy and Group Counseling*. Springfield, Illinois: Charles C Thomas, 1968.

Leary, T. *Interpersonal Diagnosis of Personality: A Functional Theory and Methodology for Personality Evaluation*. New York: Ronald Press, 1957.

Leckie, F. H. Hypnotherapy in gynecological disorders. *International Journal of Clinical and Experimental Hypnosis*, 1964, *12*, 121-146.

Lobitz, W. C. Personal communication, 1979.

Lobitz, W. C., & Lobitz, G. K. Clinical assessment in the treatment of sexual dysfunctions. In: J. LoPiccolo & L. LoPiccolo (Eds.), *Handbook of Sex Therapy*. New York: Plenum Press, 1978.

Lobitz, W. C., & LoPiccolo, J. New methods in the behavioral treatment of sexual dysfunction. *Journal of Behavior Therapy and Experimental Psychiatry*, 1972, *3*, 265-271.

Lobitz, W. C., LoPiccolo, J., Lobitz, G., & Brockway, J. A closer look at simplistic behavior therapy for sexual dysfunction: Two case studies. In: H. J. Eysenck (Ed.), *Case Studies in Behavior Therapy*. London: Routledge and Kegan Paul, 1974.

LoPiccolo, J. Direct treatment of sexual dysfunction in the couple. In J. Money and H. Musaph (Eds.), *Handbook of Sexology*. New York: Elsevier/North Holland, 1977. (a)

LoPiccolo, J. From psychotherapy to sex therapy. *Society*, 1977, *14* (5), 60-68. (b)

LoPiccolo, J. Direct treatment of sexual dysfunction. In: J. LoPiccolo & L. LoPiccolo (Eds.), *Handbook of Sex Therapy*. New York: Plenum, 1978.

LoPiccolo, J. Methodological issues in research and treatment of sexual dysfunction. In R. Green & J. Winer (Eds.), *Methodological Issues in Sex Research*. Washington, D. C.: U.S. Government Printing Office, in press.

LoPiccolo, J., & Hogan, D. Multidimensional behavioral treatment of sexual dysfunction. In: O. Pomerleau and J. P. Brady (Eds.), *Behavioral Medicine: Theory and Practice*. Baltimore: Williams and Wilkins, 1979.

LoPiccolo, J., & Lobitz, W. C. The role of masturbation in the treatment of orgasmic dysfunction. *Archives of Sexual Behavior*, 1972, *2*, 163-172.

LoPiccolo, J. & Lobitz, W. C. Behavior therapy of sexual dysfunction. In: L. A. Hamerlynck, L. C. Handy, & E. J. Mash (Eds.), *Behavior Change: Methodology, Concepts, and Practice*. Champaign, Ill., Research Press, 1973.

LoPiccolo, J., & Miller, V. A program for enhancing the sexual relationship for normal couples. *Couseling Psychologist*, 1975, *5*, 41-46.

LoPiccolo, J., & Steger, J. C. The Sexual Interaction Inventory: A new instrument for assessment of sexual dysfunction. *Archives of Sexual Behavior*, 1974, *3*, 585-595.

LoPiccolo, L. Low sexual desire. In: S. Lieblum & L. Pervin (Eds.), *Principles and Practice of Sex Therapy*, New York: Guilford Press, 1980.

LoPiccolo, L., & Heiman, J. Sexual assessment and history interview. In: L. LoPiccolo & J. LoPiccolo (Eds.), *Handbook of Sex Therapy*, New York: Plenum Press, 1978.

Lorand, S. Contribution to the problem of vaginal orgasm. *International Journal of Psychoanalysis*, 1939, *20*, 432-438.

Lowe, J. C., & Mikulas, W. L. Use of written material in learning self-control of premature ejaculation. *Psychological Reports*, 1975, *37*, 295-298.

Masters. W. H., & Johnson, V. E. *Human Sexual Inadequacy*, Boston: Little, Brown, 1970.

Mathews, A., Bancroft, J., Whitehead, A., Hackman, A., Julier, D., Bancroft, J., Gath, D., & Shaw, P. The behavioral treatment of sexual inadequacy: A comparative study. *Behavior Research and Therapy*, 1976, *14*, 427-436.

McCarthy, B. W., Ryan, M., & Johnson, F. A. *Sexual Awareness: A Practical Approach*. San Francisco: Boyd & Fraser, 1975.

McGovern, K. B., Kirkpatrick, C. C., & LoPiccolo, J. A behavioral group treatment program for sexually dysfunctional couples. *Journal of Marriage and Family Counseling*, 1976, *2*, 397-404.

McGovern, K., Stewart, R., & LoPiccolo, J. Secondary orgasmic dysfunction I: Analysis and strategies for treatment. *Archives of Sexual Behavior*, 1975, *4*, 265-275.

McLemore, C. W., & Benjamin, L. S. Whatever happened to interpersonal diagnosis? A psychosocial alternative to DSM-III. *American Psychologist*, 1979, *34*, 17-34.

Mead, M. *Male and Female*. New York: William Morrow, 1949.

Moore, Burness E. Frigidity in Women. *American Psychoanalytic Association Journal*, 9, 1961, 571-584.

Nowinski, J. *"P" Questionnaire*. Department of Psychiatry and Behavioral Science, State University of New York at Stony Brook, 1978.

Nowinski, J. *Factors affecting sexual conduct in non-dysfunctional couples*. Paper presented at Eastern Association of Sex Therapists, Philadelphia, Pennsylvania, 1979.

Prochaska, J. O., & Marzilli, R. Modifications of the Masters and Johnson approach to sexual problems. *Psychotherapy: Theory Research and Practice*, 1973, *10*, 294-296.

Renshaw, D. C. Impotence in diabetics. *Diseases of the Nervous System*, 1975, *36*, 369-371.

Rosen, I. The psychoanalytic approach to individual therapy. In J. Money & H. Musaph (Eds.), *Handbook of Sexology*,

New York: Elsevier-North Holland, 1977.

Sager, C. J., & Kaplan, H. S. (Eds.), *Progress in Group and Family Therapy*. New York: Brunner/Mazel, 1972.

Salter, A. *Conditioned Reflex Therapy*. New York: Creative Age Press, 1949.

Schmidt, G. *The outcome of different versions of partner-therapy of sexual dysfunctions: Results of a controlled study*. Paper presented at the Third Annual Meeting, International Academy of Sex Research, Bloomington, Indiana, 1977.

Schneidman, B., & McGuire, L. Group therapy for non-orgasmic women: Two age levels. *Archives of Sexual Behavior*, 1976, 5, 239-247.

Schrenck-Notzing, A. von. *The Use of Hypnosis in Psychopathea Sexualis, with Special Reference to Contrary Sexual Interest*. New York: Julian Press, 1956. First published in 1895.

Semans, J. H. Premature ejaculation: A new approach. *Southern Medical Journal*, 1956, 49, 353-357.

Serber, M. Videotape feedback in the treatment of couples with sexual dysfunction. *Archives of Sexual Behavior*, 1974, 3, 377-380.

Sherfey, M. J. *The Nature and Evolution of Human Sexuality*. New York: Vintage, 1973.

Spitzer, R. L., Sheeny, M., & Endicott, J. DSM-III: Guiding principles. In: V. M. Rakoff, H. C. Stancer, & H. B. Kedward (Eds.), *Psychiatric Diagnosis*. New York: Brunner/Mazel, 1977.

Sternbach, R. A. *Principles of Psychophysiology*. New York: Academic Press, 1966.

Szasz, T. The myth of mental illness. *American Psychologist*, 1960, 15, 113-118.

Terman, L. M. *Psychological Factors in Marital Happiness*. New York: McGraw-Hill, 1938.

Wagner, G., & Ebbehoj, J. *Erectile dysfunction caused by abnormal outflow from the corpus cavernosum*. Paper presented at the Third International Congress of Medical Sexology, Rome, Italy, 1978.

Wilson, G. T. Alcohol and human sexual behavior. *Behaviour Research and Therapy*, 1977, 15, 239-252.

Wilson, G. T., & Lawson, D. M. Expectancies, alcohol, and sexual arousal in women. *Journal of Abnormal Psychology*, 1978, 86, 358-367.

Wolpe, J. *Psychotherapy by Reciprocal Inhibition*. Stanford: Stanford University Press, 1958.

Wolpe, J. *The Practice of Behavior Therapy*. New York: Pergamon Press, 1969.

Zeiss, R. A., & Zeiss, A. M. *Prolong Your Pleasure*. New York: Simon & Schuster, 1977.

Zilbergeld, B., & Rinkleib, C. E. Desire discrepancies and arousal problems in sex therapy. In S. Leiblum & L. Pervin (Eds.), *Principles and Practice of Sex Therapy*. New York: Guilford Press, 1980.

EDITORS' REFERENCES

D'Agostino, P. A., McCoy, N. & Lacerda, S. A critique of the item content and format of the Sexual Interaction Inventory. *Family Therapy*, 1976, 3, 217-228.

Dickes, R. & Strauss, D. Countertransference as a factor in premature termination of apparently successful cases. *Journal of Sex and Marital Therapy*, 1979, 5, 22-27.

Knudson, R. M., Gurman, A. S. & Kniskern, D. P. Behavioral marriage therapy: A treatment in transition. In: C. M. Franks & G. T. Wilson (Eds.), *Annual Review of Behavior Therapy*. Vol. 7: 1979. New York: Brunner/Mazel, 1980.

Munjack, D. J. & Oziel, L. J. Resistance in the behavioral treatment of sexual dysfunctions. *Journal of Sex and Marital Therapy*, 1978, 4, 122-138.

PART VI

Special Areas and Issues:

Enrichment and Divorce

CHAPTER 17

Skill Training Programs
for Couples and Families

Luciano L'Abate, Ph.D.

The purpose of this chapter is to include and survey programs of intervention with marriages and families that do not fall within the topic of "therapeutic" interventions or "therapy" as understood and discussed in other chapters of this *Handbook*. The last decade has seen the upsurge of new methods of intervention which seem to possess the same characteristics, i.e., (a) time-limited contracts; (b) specific topics already agreed upon by clients; (c) application to couples and families who would not be defined as "clinical" but who, however, are aware of their need for some form of intervention that would not be therapy and which would not, therefore, define them as "sick" or as "emotionally impaired," even though there is still a need for (d) a form of specific skill training that is not necessarily oriented toward changing the basic structure of the couple or the family. Consequently, (e) the goals of these skill training programs are education- or enrichment-oriented rather than therapeutic.

How do these intervention strategies apply to clinical couples and families? To the extent that any form of therapy possesses some degree

of teaching, most of these methods are "quasi-therapeutic." Most of them deal preventively with nonclinical populations, and often screen out unsuitable dysfunctional or problem couples or families. Thus, skill-training programs as a *whole* have propaedeutic, prophylactic, and par-atherapeutic functions that justify inclusion in this *Handbook* but which, however, distinguish them also from most therapeutic methods reviewed in other chapters. Some of these methods have been developed to deal with parents (e.g., Parent Effectiveness, Gordon, 1970) rather than with whole families. Others were created specifically to train spouses in marital conflict resolution as mates rather than as parents (e.g., Fair Fighting, Bach and Goldberg, 1974). I shall limit myself to summarizing their major historical and procedural characteristics, their outcome and evidence of effectiveness when it exists. For a more extended treatment of these methods, the reader is referred to more detailed sources such as Birchler (1979), Gurman and Kniskern (1977), L'Abate (1977b), Jacobson (1978), Luber (1978), and Weiss (1978). As different and disparate as these programs may be, most of them share a common core of teaching couples and families to assert more personal responsibility in communicating, negotiating, problem-solving, and decision-making over conflictual issues.

Historical Antecedents

There are several trends in the evolution of skill-training programs that, together, have been tantamount to a "movement" (Note No. 1). Among these we need to consider, first, the *human potential movement*, with emphasis on (a) direct confrontation; (b) role-playing and psychodramatic techniques; (c) Gestalt therapy and related emphasis on direct awareness and nonverbal behavior; (d) sensitivity training, marathon, and group approaches, with an increasing deemphasis of accepted traditional "mental health practices," and a critical view of the "medical model" of illness as well as of human relations. These are seen humanistically in a positive rather than a negative light, emphasizing assets and strengths rather than liabilities and weaknesses, as a traditional mental health medical approach would have it. Second, parallel with the human potential movement, we have seen a definite increase in *self-help* groups (e.g., AA, Gamblers Anonymous, Neurotics Anonymous, Parents Without Partners), again with a relative rejection of credentials and credentialism. Part and parcel of these self-help movements have been the growth of paraprofessionalism and the use of individuals with interpersonal rather than professional competencies. A third historical trend has been the growth of *consumerism* and a push toward brief and cost-effective treatments with an emphasis on accountability for effective outcomes. The growth of alternative modes of treatment has allowed consumers a much wider choice than was possible heretofore. A fourth, but by no means minor trend, has been the enormous growth of *behavior therapy* and behavioral technology, emphasizing among other things self-control strategies and gradual, linear, step-by-step approaches that have developed into the programmed interpersonal relations movement (Brown and L'Abate, 1969; L'Abate, 1972; L'Abate, 1974). Part of this technology relies on audiotapes (as in encounter

tapes) and teaching machines, as precursors of programmed interpersonal relationship and skill-training programs.

A fifth and relatively minor trend has been the rediscovered emphasis on *games and play behavior*, the importance of playlike and playful behavior and the interaction of the playful with the therapeutic as found in play therapy with children (L'Abate, 1979). Furthermore, L'Abate has argued (Note No. 2) that a sixth historical trend, *family life education*, though moribund, may have evolved into skill-training and enrichment programs that hopefully have had and will continue to have much greater impact on family life than family life education.

SKILL-TRAINING, THERAPY, AND PREVENTION

The relatively structured nature of skill-training programs stands in contrast with the relatively unstructured nature of therapy, a form of treatment that is relatively open as to topics to be discussed, usually related to the family's symptomatology in terms of an "identified patient" or an "identifiable symptom or syndrome" (e.g., alcohol, idiosyncratic behavior, etc.).[1] A clearer differentiation between skill-training and therapy could be obtained if we consider three different levels of prevention: *Primary prevention* consists of large-scale screening and/or intervention with "normal" or functional couples and families. This is the level where most skill-training programs are relevant and relatively successful, as we shall see. *Secondary prevention* deals with the identification of relationships at risk, e.g., troubled marriages at risk for divorce or underachieving children at risk for juvenile delinquency or other problems (L'Abate and L'Abate, 1977). This is a borderline area where some, yet to be specified, skill-training programs may overlap with therapeutic approaches. *Tertiary prevention* does, indeed, im-

---

[1]*Editors' Note.* Of course, the degree of structure characteristic of the various family therapies discussed in this volume varies widely. At the extremes, e.g., compare Whitaker and Keith (Chapter 6) and Jacobson (Chapter 15). It is also worth noting that, in general, family therapists do a good deal more structuring than most individual therapists.

ply intervention with very disturbed couples and marriages that are beyond skill-training and who need a very specific tailor-made approach that can only be found in therapy. Some of these couples and families, carefully selected and supervised, may benefit by additional skill-training. However, it is also clear (L'Abate and Weeks, 1976; L'Abate, 1977b) that *skill-training programs cannot and will not apply to very chaotic couples and families, couples and families in crisis* (death, suicide, separation, abandonment), *uncooperative couples and families, and couples and families in which the symptomatology is such that only professional therapy may be relevant* (i.e., psychotic, paranoid, and psychosomatic syndromes).[2]

Therapists as a whole have little interest or involvement in preventive activities (Kessler and Albee, 1977; Klein and Goldston, 1977). It is important to consider, therefore, that one of the major functions of skill-training programs is preventive, because of their general orientation toward a large number of functional and semi-functional couples and families who still need "help" in specific areas of functioning. Their number is far greater than the number of dysfunctional couples and families. Their needs are just as real. Prevention, therefore, at least in the opinion of this writer (Notes No. 3) and Mace (Note No. 4), is just as important and in many ways more important than treatment. Yet, the fact still remains that, as stated above, therapists as a whole have no inherent commitment nor investment in preventive activities. This statement holds true for the private as well as public sectors of the mental health enterprise. If and when prevention is mandated and made part of the activities of community mental health clinics and other public mental health agencies, hospitals, etc., it will be through federal requirements rather than through the efforts of mental health personnel per se. They are not going to volunteer. After all, even in this *Handbook*, how many chapters are dedicated to treatment and how many pages are devoted to prevention?[3]

What better target of preventive efforts can there be than couples and families, if we accept prevention as an approach "directed toward reducing the incidence of a highly predictable undesirable consequence" (Note No. 4) and can safely predict that the chances of any couple making it these days are 50-50? It is clear that the amelioration of marriages in general could be a highly desirable preventive activity, as the Maces have repeatedly pointed out (Mace and Mace, 1975, 1976; Note No. 4). As far as families are concerned, the same argument can be made; i.e., most families, even the functional ones, in our experience could profit maximally by learning experiences which may enhance their awareness of each other, their collective problem-solving abilities, and their decision-making and communication patterns.

If psychopathology or dysfunctionality in relationships is viewed as deficiencies in social competence (Phillips, 1968) or social skills (Phillips, 1978), then it would follow from these models that training in specific interpersonal skills should be the most appropriate form of intervention! A sharp definitional differentiation between "therapy" and "skill-training" is a complex matter. Skill programs *generally* are more structured than therapy but not always (cf. behavioral marital and family therapy). But degree of structure alone seems an insufficient criterion. Likewise, the time-limited nature of skill programs *generally* offers a distinction, but even less often than does the degree of structure (i.e., a good deal of family-marital therapy is time-limited, as are therapies conducted according to various theoretical models). In addition to these two points, the following definitional-descriptive considerations seem necessary: (a) "Therapy" seems to stress patient factors that may *prevent* patients/families from learning directly structured "skills"[4]; (b) "therapy" seems

---

[2]*Editors' Note.* This is an extremely important qualification of the likely applicability limits of most of these skill training programs. Ford, Bashford and DeWitt (1979) offer data that support the notion that pre-intervention levels of relationship functioning are positively related to good outcomes in communication training for marital enrichment.

[3]*Editors' Note.* In fact, several of the contributors to this volume either explicitly (e.g., Boszormenyi-Nagy and Ulrich, Sager, Jacobson) or implicitly (Kerr, Skynner, Barton and Alexander) view their *therapy* models as offering preventive functions.

[4]*Editors' Note.* For further elaboration of clinical strategies relevant to this distinction, see Barton and Alexander (Chapter 11) in this volume.

to *not* make an assumption implicit in, but common to, skill programs, i.e., that skills that are as yet unlearned are unlearned, to an important extent, because of previously unavailable, naturalistic life conditions or experiences; (c) "therapy" may be to skills programs as teaching learning disabled children is to "normal" classroom education; (d) "therapy" models generally seem to stress the ambivalence that its recipients have about change more than skills approaches; (e) skills programs emphasize therapist- or leader-generated agendas for sessions, while "therapy" usually involves therapist interventions that are more immediately responsive to felt patient needs of the moment.

SKILL-TRAINING PROGRAMS

Skill-training programs can be classified according to a family life-cycle sequence: (a) premarital or neo-marital training; (b) marital; (c) parenthood; (d) total family; and (e) divorce mediation. A review of programs not considered here can be found in Mace (Note No. 5).

Pre- or Neo-marital Programs

Most pre- and neo-marital projects reported in the literature have not as yet achieved the status of programs. Consequently, this section is limited to citing a few published projects in this area, which is still wide open to programs of skill-training. Of the four projects reviewed, one (Schlein, 1971) dealt with dating couples without long-range follow-up. A report by Van Zoost (1973) dealt with premarital couples, also without follow-up, while the third, by Microys and Bader (Note No. 6) followed up couples from pre- to post-married adjustment. The fourth (Raush, Barry, Hertel, and Swain, 1974) dealt with newlywed couples. These studies suggest that most beneficial changes as a result of premarital intervention would take place after rather than before marriage. On a premarital basis it is difficult if not impossible to predict during the first months of marriage how the level of intimacy achieved after the honeymoon is going to affect each couple. Most pre- and neo-marital programs are similar in their emphasis on conflict-resolution, negotiation, and decision-making skills. However, even though these programs may be similar, the level of awareness in pre- and neo-marital couples is extremely different. Hence, it is important to intervene within a few months of marriage.

Marital Programs

Most of the program to be reviewed in this section have several common characteristics: (a) emphasis on open and direct exchange of feelings without emotional put-downs, blackmails or briberies; (b) assumption of personal responsibility for whatever is said (and done) in the marriage; (c) clarification and differentiation of feelings as being different from thoughts and actions, i.e., what we feel is one thing, how we negotiate and translate these feelings into mutually acceptable courses of action is another; (d) availability of the many options open to most of us, some more constructive than others. Each couple needs to find alternatives through trial and error, finally selecting which option is more constructive for its marriage.

Among the major programs to be considered in this section are: (a) the Minnesota Couples Communication Program (MCCP); (b) the Association of Couples for Marriage Enrichment (ACME); (c) Marriage Encounter; (d) Conjugal Relationships Enhancement (CRE); (e) Structured Enrichment Programs (SEP); and (f) a review of other miscellaneous projects.

MCCP[5]

This is the most widely and probably most thoroughly researched program in communication training (Miller, Nunnally, and Wackman, undated, 1975) and is also one of the oldest existing communication training programs. It is conceptually based on, and within the framework of, humanistic and competence training for awareness of rules and of metacommunication in the couple. It stresses disclosure, receptivity, and the teaching of skills. Another concept which is basic to this program is the building of mutual esteem for couples, and the develop-

---

[5]*Editors' Note.* The Minnesota Couples Communication Program (MCCP) is now formally referred to as the Couples Communication Program (CCP).

ment of a symmetrical relationship for an egalitarian marital working relationship. The major skills emphasized are *awareness*, which enables partners to understand their rules of interaction, and *communication skills* which allow them to change past rules and interaction patterns.

The goals of this program are to increase each couple's ability to reflect on, and accurately predict, its own dyadic processes by defining each member's private self-awareness and heightening each partner's awareness of his/her own contribution to the interaction. It helps couples explore hidden and not so hidden rules of their relationship, particularly regarding rules for conflict resolution and patterns of maintaining self- and other's esteem, as well as increasing each couple's capacity for clear, direct, open metacommunication, especially communication regarding the relationship.

Six major dimensions underline the Minnesota model: (a) an educational-developmental orientation which focuses on equipping couples rather than repairing them; (b) a focus on the system and the marital relationship is considered as the basic system; (c) a skill orientation to heighten oneself, the other, and the situation and the system's awareness; (d) presentation of a conceptual framework to eliminate some of the mystery surrounding relationships by helping couples systematically understand predictable properties of relationships; (e) to serve as advance organizers for learning specific skills and to provide a common base from which couples can amplify their awareness; (f) volunteers participate by choice, assuming that the learning is more effective when it is voluntary.

Groups are limited to five to seven couples which meet with one or two certified instructors for three-hour sessions one night a week for four weeks. A *Couple Workbook* and the textbook *Alive and Aware* (Miller, Nunnally, and Wackman, 1975) are used. In the first session there is a definition of the awareness wheel, which has five sections: acting, sensing, thinking, wanting, and feeling. Couples are taught six skills for verbally expressing their awareness: (a) speaking for self; (b) making sense statements; (c) making interpretative statements; (d) making feeling statements; (e) making intentional statements; and (f) making action statements. In the second session, focus shifts to

learning how to exchange important communication accurately with one partner through a shared meaning framework, which consists of checking out, stating intention and asking for acknowledgment, acknowledging the sender's message, confirming and clarifying. In session three, couples are taught the major styles of the Hill Interaction Matrix, which consists of incongruous ways of communicating and learning more efficient ways to communicate. The fourth and final session is a rehearsal of techniques learned in previous sessions.

A good deal of research has been done to support this program. Most of the studies support the conclusion that the program improves communicative skills. In fact, MCCP has been extremely fertile in producing a variety of evaluative studies, so many, in fact, that only their major characteristics and those of major interest will be reviewed here. Most of these programs follow a pre- and posttest design with occasional follow-ups. One unpublished study (Note No. 7) followed up couples who had participated in a variety of MCCP programs anywhere in the U.S. ranging from five years to six months previously. Measures used were self-report of (a) one's own communicative behavior; (b) styles of conflict resolution for both self and spouse; and (c) satisfaction with the communication experience. Eighty percent of the respondents reported improvements in their own and spouses' general communication and use of "positive" styles of conflict resolution, and reported overwhelming satisfaction with the training and various elements of the program.

Aside from this survey, most studies (Gurman and Kniskern, 1977) were designed to assess the immediate impact of MCCP. They used random assignment of couples to control vs. treatment conditions, thus providing an internally valid test of the immediate impact of the program.

As far as *sample* size is concerned, in most studies sample sizes are rather small, ranging from 30 couples at most to five or six in both experimental and control conditions. The modal size in most studies ranges between 15 and 20 couples. Samples are usually drawn from university populations and, therefore, are usually better educated than the general population. Most of these couples are also young, even though there is a tendency for more recent studies to use older couples. Most of these participants report themselves and their marriages to be functional and nondistressed.

Most *measures* have been of the self-report kind, even though at least three studies also used observational techniques to assess couple interaction. Most studies include measures of marital adjustment, interpersonal communication, as well as more tangential measures of acceptance of self and partner, self-esteem, marital satisfaction, sex-role stereotyping, and self-disclosure.

As far as *outcome* is concerned, most studies show significantly more improvement in experimental groups than in control groups, in the area specifically emphasized by MCCP, i.e., communication skills. Most studies also show some degree of positive transfer in other areas that are not specifically related or linked to communication outcomes, e.g., greater acceptance of self and partner, increased self-esteem, and lower sex-role stereotyping in comparison with controls. Most results do show that *not all* couples learn well all of the skills taught, just that *most* couples do (Note No. 8). The wide range of studies from various geographical regions, differences in the nature of the samples and, more importantly, use of different instructors show that most outcomes can be reliably attributed to the program itself rather than to the effectiveness of individual instructors or the already existing functionality of the sample.

ACME (Association of Couples for Marriage Enrichment)

In the last few years there has been an increasing number of programs designed to "enrich" marriage relationships. They have focused for the most part on assisting couples in enhancing communication skills, broadening and deepening emotional and/or sexual lives, and reinforcing and fostering existing marital strengths (Gurman and Kniskern, 1977). The programs, usually conducted through either a single weekend retreat or through six to eight weekly two-hour sessions, vary in their degree of structure, in their process techniques, in the type of leadership provided, in the degree of involvement permitted for participants, and in the range of topics covered.

In 1961, the Maces (1975) started with weekend retreats for Quakers. Otto (1976), with his pioneering work "The Family Resource Development Program," first initiated enrichment techniques in the United States. The first training program for leader couples was started by Antoinette and Leon Smith in 1966 (Otto, 1976) through the United Methodist Church. The Catholic Marriage Encounter Movement, developed in 1956 in Spain by Father Gabriel Calvo (Bosco, 1973; Calvo, 1975), was brought to the United States by Father Frank Heinan and James and Arthur Whelan in 1967. Thus, the first sources of enrichment programs were nonprofessional and religious in nature (L'Abate, 1977b).

ACME is a national organization composed of married couples with the primary goal of developing and maintaining effective support systems for Marriage Enrichment. It was founded through the charismatic efforts of David and Vera Mace (1975, 1976). The organization has stated its purposes as follows:

1) To encourage and help member couples to seek growth and enrichment in their own marriages.
2) To organize activities through which member couples can help each other in their quest for marital growth and enrichment.
3) To promote and support effective community services designed to foster successful marriages.
4) To seek to improve the public image of marriage as a relationship capable of fostering both personal growth and mutual fulfillment (Hopkins, Hopkins, Mace, and Mace, 1978).

The Maces cite two obstacles in our society which block attempts of couples toward their achievement of a happier and more fulfilling marriage. The first obstacle is the myth of naturalism, which has asserted that success in marriage should come almost effortlessly to the normal adult, and that anyone who has difficulties in this area is thereby identified as an inadequate person. The second obstacle is the intermarital taboo which states that "Marriage is very private, very personal. Whatever you do, don't ever talk to anyone else about what goes on inside your marriage." Because of these two restraining factors, the married partners are often prevented from seeking or receiving help until they are in a state of desperation (Mace and Mace, 1976).

The Maces attempted to halt this trend by the establishment of preventive programs through ACME. The weekend retreat is one type of program offered by ACME. In the retreat, a couple serves as participating facilitators rather than as leaders. The weekend contains no structured agenda, but instead deals with topics that participants bring up. These retreats, however, are seen as one-shot experiences which are only the beginning of improvement in a couple's relationship. Additional Marriage Enrichment supports are provided by local chapters through various programs and services.

Programs offered through ACME are designed for couples with fairly functioning marriages who desire additional growth. The main idea behind the programs is that in each marital dyad there exists inherent capacity for mutual fulfillment and development. The ACME Handbook (Hopkins, Hopkins, Mace, and Mace, 1978) makes the case for marital enrichment on the basis of social pathology and the increase in divorces and deterioration in family life, which still goes back to the nature of the marital relationship. After reviewing the history, rationale and future prospects of the marriage enrichment movement (also reviewed in L'Abate, 1977b), they focus on the three major models of enrichment: (a) weekend retreats, (b) growth groups, and (c) couples communication courses.

ACME is organized in chapters within each state, with each state then relating to national headquarters. Membership is open only to couples or couples preparing for marriage who affirm their support of the four purposes of ACME. The basic responsibility for each group of couples at the local level (support group) is given to a "contact" couple that may be responsible for a chapter or one area of a chapter. Once a support group is formed, it is up to it to define itself (as open or closed to additional couples) and to determine the frequency, extent, and nature of its meetings. Topics discussed in these meetings may include "intimacy," communication, friendships, the life-cycle, etc.

The basic entry in ACME is usually through a retreat or workshop. Methods are noncon-frontational, that is, people speak only if and when they want to speak, no one is pressured into speaking. However, one speaks only for oneself and in experiential rather than intellectual terms. "Concerns" rather than "problems" are raised in the present rather than past or future. The ACME Handbook contains specific instructions for reaching out to other couples in the community, as well as a general public relations principle and how ACME is to present itself to the public. A directory of national marriage enrichment organizations is contained in the Appendix of the Handbook, as well as standards for selection, training, and certification of leader couples (couples who can lead accepted retreats and/or basic or advanced workshops in the name of ACME). A selected annotated bibliography on marriage enrichment is provided at the end. A bimonthly newsletter keeps couples in touch with the national headquarters and with ACME developments throughout the U.S., Canada, and the world.

Marriage Encounter

Marriage Encounter is a program designed usually for weekend retreats, and is usually under the auspices of the Catholic church or other religious organizations (Bosco, 1973; Calvo, 1975; Demarest, 1977). There are as many marriage encounters as there are major Catholic, Protestant, and Jewish organizations. It is estimated that up to half a million couples have participated in encounter weekends, with the number increasing at the rate of perhaps 100,000 a year (Otto, 1975). The marriage encounter movement had its beginning in Spain under the sponsorship of Father Calvo, who essentially started with one couple and used them then to work with other couples on weekends. In the last decade, the marriage encounter movement has spread far and beyond Spain. In the United States, it has set up its own organization and publishing house. Its growth also produced some conflicts, which ended in two separate groups, the National Marriage Encounter, an ecumenical organization, and Worldwide Marriage Encounter, a more tightly-structured Catholicized group.

Most marriage encounter weekends are structured in the same way. Ten to 25 couples meet together from Friday night to Sunday afternoon at some suitable retreat house, regardless of age and socioeconomic background. Under the leadership of two or three previously experienced couples and a priest or a clergyman, they are encouraged to explore the meaning of their lives and of their marriages.

Four general themes are focused on during this weekend: the "I" theme, the "We," the "We-God," and the "We-God-World" themes. Leader couples give short talks throughout the weekend dealing with their own experience in going through the process. The general line of the structure is going from inspiration and information to personal reflection and to couple dialogue. It should be clarified that, in contrast to ACME, most of the dialogue occurs between the mates and there is no group interaction, which is such an important part of ACME. During the first session on Friday night, questions are put to couples for reflection and dialogue revolves around the couples' reasons for coming and positive aspects of their relationship. From the discussion of the marriage, there is a presentation on the status of marriage in the world today and the meaning of spiritual marriage and spiritual divorce. Couples are given various exercises and assignments that will encourage their dialogue with each other. The final session of the weekend involves drawing up a game plan for future commitment to each other, to the family, and to the world. It may or may not include a renewing of marriage vows in a group ceremony. After the weekend is over, couples are urged to join various follow-up programs that are available to give support to the couples and to commit themselves to daily practice of ten and ten: ten minutes of writing and ten minutes of couple dialogue. From these couples, some are recruited to become leader couples for other group retreats.

Doherty, McCabe, and Ryder (1978) acknowledge that marriage encounter responds to the need of many couples for greater marital closeness. Yet, they see some dangers involved in this process: (a) Perceived benefits may be temporary and illusory, i.e., results seem similar to a religious conversion experience and may not be lasting; (b) marriage encounter encourages a denial of differences and of separateness by holding up unity as the single definitive goal for all married couples; (c) stressing the dialogue technique may lead to a kind of ritual dependency. Furthermore, an unequal commitment to this technique could lead to guilt and resentment and might be a divisive element in a marriage relationship; (d) marriage encounter has been known to divide families and friends. Couples can become so caught up in their "born again" experience that they become fanatical and alienate their relatives and friends.[6]

Among the few studies on the effects and outcomes of marriage encounter is a dissertation by Newhaus (1977), who found that couples after encounter weekends showed significantly increased scores on the modified form of the Barrett-Lennard Relationship Inventory. Huber (Note No. 9) examined the effects of the dialogue technique in terms of the dimensions of loving and caring in Shostrom's Caring Relationship Inventory. The experimental group consisted of 77 married couples participating in one of three marriage encounter weekends. The control group was made out of 31 couples who were on a waiting list for the weekend. The pretest was completed on Friday night before the regular activities started, and the posttest on Sunday evening after completion of the weekend. Follow-up tests were given six weeks later. Huber found significant changes in the experimental group between pre-, and post-, and follow-up testing on scales measuring affection, eros, and empathy. No changes were found in the control group. Loomis (1977) studied the effects of time distribution (massed vs. space groups) on encounter group learning, finding that there were more significant positive changes for the twice-weekly group than for marathon groups on three measures: Personal Orientation Inventory, Rotter's Locus of Self-Control, and Shapiro's Adjective Checklist.

In conclusion, despite the paucity of outcome studies, it seems that the marriage encounter is the type of structural intervention that could be of considerable value in improving marriages. Basically, it tends to teach couples how to share feelings and to communicate on a deeper level than that to which they have been accustomed in the past. It is hoped that this self-

---

[6]*Editors' Note.* Another worthwhile critique of Marriage Encounter has been offered recently by De Young (1979).

disclosure could lead to increased competence in the tasks of marriage that seem to be discounted the most, namely, the sharing of pain and hurt and the fear of being hurt (L'Abate, 1977a). Couples who share religious values may be the ones who would be more turned on by this technique than couples who do not have a religious attitude or affiliation.

Conjugal Relationship Enhancement

Guerney (1977) developed a group format for his multi-purpose relationship modification programs, with at least three couples per group, in which two co-leaders aid spouses in replacing vicious communication cycles with more direct and open cycles. This process involves separating the communicating process into distinct components or "modes." Participants are systematically taught each mode: (a) to express feelings and thoughts clearly; (b) to emphasize and accept the expressions of another; (c) to facilitate and criticize their own communication skills from moment to moment; and (d) to discuss the constructive resolution of conflicts. Relationship enhancement draws from Rogers' approach (Rogers, 1951) in terms of unconditional acceptance and respect for feelings of others, as well as from social learning theory, especially in terms of modeling and power.

Originally, enhancement originated from helping parents and children. In terms of its successful application to parents, it generalized to other populations, including the marital dyad. On the basis of the success with what he called "filial therapy," Guerney (1977) made his first attempts at marital relationship enhancement in which spouses with troubled relationships were successfully taught to use therapeutic communication skills with each other. Classification of appropriate and inappropriate responses to allow coding of verbal sequences in terms of functional characteristics was done according to 19 basic subdivisions.

Thus, there are many points of contact between relationship enhancement and Rogers' (1951) basic philosophy of life. It has been expanded to include more relevant viewpoints, such as an analysis of ineffective ways of communicating, an emphasis on more appropriate constructive communication, and the use of par-

aprofessional personnel to develop the program. Guerney estimates that it takes about 80 hours to train a graduate student to learn this method at a professionally satisfactory level.

A great deal of research has been done by Guerney and his students to establish an empirical basis for this mode of intervention. The first comprehensive research in Conjugal Relationship Enhancement was conducted by Collins (1971). Collins hypothesized that through a six-month Relationship Enhancement Program couples would improve their communication as measured by the Primary Communication Inventory and the Marital Communication Inventory. He also hypothesized an improvement in overall marital adjustment as measured by the Marital Adjustment Test and the Conjugal Life Questionnaire, all measures developed by Guerney and his associates (Guerney, 1977). Collins recruited a wide range of subjects by contacting the Pennsylvania State University married students and faculty, local newspapers, lawyers, and clergy. The typical couple in the program was 30 years old and had two children. The pretest scores indicated that most couples were not as happy together as the average married couple, yet not as distressed as the typical clinical couple. Collins randomly assigned 21 couples to no-treatment control and 24 couples to an experimental treatment group. The experimental group was further subdivided into four relationship enhancement groups, each containing three couples and two co-leaders, for sessions of one-and-one-half hours each week over a six-month period. All couples were tested in a pre- and posttest in a manner previously mentioned. They also completed 30-minute homework assignments each week assigned from a manual developed by Guerney and his co-workers. Collins found a high correlation between communication and marital adjustment variables. The Marital Communication Inventory evidenced a significant improvement for the experimental group and a significant difference between experimental and control groups. Similarly, a significant improvement was indicated on the Marital Adjustment Test.

In one of the largest studies to support relationship enhancement, Norton (1971) studied 151 couples and found evidence of a significant relationship between empathic ability and marital adjustment. Rappaport (1971) designed a two-month extensive conjugal relationship enhancement program using 20 couples, who indicated significant improvement in their marriages during the enhancement process.

Harrell and Guerney (1976), in what they called a behavioral negotiation exchange program, used a traditional problem-solving process which was broken down into nine stages: (a) listen carefully, (b) locate the relationship issues, (c) identify one's own contribution to the issue, (d) identify alternative solutions, (e) evaluate alternative solutions, (f) make an exchange, (g) determine conditions of exchange, (h) implement a behavioral exchange contract, and (i) renegotiate the behavioral exchange contract. The skills to deal with each of the steps are outlined in this program. Ely, Guerney, and Stover (1973) obtained significant changes on feelings, experiences and responsiveness, communication skills, and acceptance and trust in 12 experimental couples, with no significant changes in 21 control couples.

Wieman (1973) compared CRE with Reciprocal Reinforcement Therapy, using 12 couples in each treatment and control group. Both treatments showed significant changes on a variety of outcome measures maintained at 10-week follow-up. D'Augelli, Deyss, Guerney, Hershenberg, and Sborofsky (1974) used measures of empathy and self-exploration with 34 experimental and 34 dating but not engaged couples. Significant changes on both measures were found.

In conclusion, Relationship Enhancement is a clearly structured program that has important benefits based on an educational model. In addition to the eclectic humanistic orientation, there is a strong educational flavor that offers a great deal of potential for larger applications from a preventive viewpoint.

Gurman and Kniskern (1977), reviewing the outcome literature of MCCP and CRE studies, observed that outcome criteria fall into three general categories: (a) overall marital satisfaction and adjustment, (b) relationship skills, and (c) individual personality variables such as self-actualization and self-esteem. In each of these categories, 60% of the investigations report positive change. These reviewers, however, noted several important methodological deficiencies common to these investigations. Eighty-four percent of the criterion measures used are based on participants' self-reports, with 58% of the studies using participants' reports as the sole criteria for change and the other 26% relying primarily on such data. While 40% of the studies observe change by objective instruments, only 16% of all measures used involve nonparticipant evaluation. Eighty-one percent of the objective behavioral measures demonstrate change, as opposed to only 57% of the self-report measures. However, self-report measures outnumbered behavioral objective measures by a ratio of five to one. The reviewers concluded that available information on outcomes should be cautiously studied. They recommended six specific issues which needed to be addressed: (a) durability of the enrichment-induced change; (b) generalizability of enrichment-induced change; (c) range of potential participants; (d) placement of enrichment programs within the developmental framework; (e) demonstration of change through nonparticipant rating sources; and (f) elucidation of salient change-inducing components in the programs.

Structured Marriage Enrichment Programs

L'Abate (1975, 1977b) developed a didactic, structured approach in his Marriage Enrichment Programs for Couples. The method has been designed with the goal of providing the most effective, humane, and inexpensive technique to couples so that they may achieve greater self-differentiation and a higher quality of family life (L'Abate, 1976). In this approach, Marriage Enrichment Programs are constructed for specific purposes and/or situations. They combine both affective and cognitive aspects of living.

Programs are arranged for both clinical and nonclinical couples in pre-planned and structured sequences. Each program is composed of three to six lessons, with each lesson containing five to six exercises. Each program is administered to one participating couple by the leader person or the leader couple through a general procedure which involves several steps. In the first step, the participating couple is interviewed so that rapport may be established, an explanation and description of the enrichment program may be given, and suitability for enrichment may be determined. A clear contract is usually reached. The second procedure involves an evaluation of the couple through rating sheets and tests. These include a Family Information Sheet, a Marital Questionnaire, a Semantic Differential Sheet, and the Azrin Marital Happiness Scale (L'Abate, Note No. 3). In the third step, the spouses are allowed to choose which type of enrichment program best suits their needs out of three presented to them. They are then given a series of six weekly enrichment lessons. The same instruments previously used are given to the couple once the six lessons are completed. The last step is a follow-up session where the couple's reaction to enrichment is asked for and recorded, the leader's feedback to the couple is given in a positive fashion, and various possibilities for the future are considered.

Enrichment Programs were designed to deal with three major areas of potential conflict: (a) premarital, (b) sexual, and (c) marital. In the first area, there are four programs on (1) confronting change, (2) problem-solving in courtship and marriage, (3) premarital problem-solving; and (4) cohabitation. In the second area there are two programs dealing with (1) clarification of sexual attitudes, and (2) sexual fulfillment for couples. In the third area, there are six programs designed to aid couples in dealing with: (1) assertiveness, (2) equality, (3) reciprocity, (4) negotiation, (5) conflict resolution, and (6) working-through.

Table 1 compares these five programs along five major dimensions: (a) degree of structure, (b) group composition, (c) major theoretical emphasis, (d) teaching modalities, and (e) length. Except for the degree of structure, most programs vary a great deal, to the point that the only overlap occurs between ACME and Encounter in following weekend retreats. They also vary as far as theoretical emphasis and teaching modalities. Most encounter retreats do not encourage the amount of inter-couple communication encouraged by ACME, with a much greater degree of didactic presentations in Encounter retreats than in ACME groups. *The major differentiating factor among many of*

Table 1

Comparison of Various Marital Skill Training and Enrichment Programs

Program	Degree of Structure*	Group Composition	Theoretical Emphasis	Teaching Modality	Length
Minnesota Couples Communication Program	Medium	Groups of 6-8 couples	Humanistic	Experiential Role-Playing	Four 3-hour sessions
Association of Couples for Marital Enrichment	Low	Groups of couples (no size limit)	Practical	Rational-personal	Weekend retreats
Encounter	Low	Large groups of couples (up to 18 to 20)	Religious-mystical	Didactic Experiential Individualistic	Weekend retreats
Conjugal Relationship Enhancement	Medium	Small groups (3-5 couples)	Rogerian, social learning theories	Rehearsal Modeling Role-playing	24 hours in various formats
Structured Marital Enrichment Programs	High	One couple	Eclectic	Role-playing Variety of techniques	6 weekly 1-hour sessions

* Relative to other marital programs in this Table.

these skill-training programs is whether they emphasize sharing of emotions and feelings or whether they are dealing with actions or negotiations. Thus, one way of differentiating among skill-training programs would be to distinguish according to how much emphasis each program gives to the underlying feelings and how much emphasis is given to actions and to negotiations of actions. Thus far, studies on the outcome of Marriage Enrichment Programs have reported positive results for couples completing them (L'Abate, 1977b; Note No. 3).

Screening for skill-training

Little or no reference is given to screening in the various skill-training programs reviewed, outside of clearly obvious couples and families who need therapy rather than skill-training. The Maces (1976) as well as Guerney (1977) do refer to some screening criteria using a pre-program interview to screen out couples who are too upset or troubled for skill-training (L'Abate and Weeks, 1976).

Miscellaneous related programs

It is difficult to select from the various models available which project will achieve the coveted status of programs, as those reviewed previously. Among these are: (a) Fair Fight Training (FFT); (b) Pairing Enrichment; (c) Assertiveness Training; (d) Communication Training; (e) Problem-Solving; and (f) Divorce Mediation.

Fair Fight Training. This procedure to deal with anger and aggression in marriage was developed by Bach and associates (Bach and Wyden, 1969; Bach and Bernhard, 1971; Bach and Goldberg, 1974) on the assumption that fighting even between mature intimate partners is inevitable. In fact, in some ways it is necessary. Consequently, fair fighting is a set of rules and procedures developed to help couples to fight creatively. There are four ways of expressing aggression constructively to produce intimate relationships. These ways are: (a) fair fighting, (b) fighting over trivia, (c) ritual fighting, (d) fighting against nice crazy-makers and hidden aggressors.

Fair fighting, the first of these four ways, is also fighting for a change in a relationship. It has received the most emphasis in Bach's constructive aggression project. It focuses on using impact aggression constructively so that valuable information and impact for change become part of the aggression that comes out of hostile feelings. The second, fighting over trivia, is essentially also known as fighting for fun. This type of fighting is acceptable as long as neither one of the partners is hurt by the other and topics are kept current rather than reflecting past issues. Ritual fighting, the third way of creative aggression, is another method of expressing irrational hostility in a constructive way. It is an adult life game in which basic rules are designed to promote dramatic display and communication of irrationally hostile feelings and thoughts. In ritual fighting, all fair fighting rules are suspended since no fighting is done seriously. The fourth type, fighting against nice crazy-makers and hidden aggressors, is in relationship to people who are passive in the way they show their aggression. Hidden aggression is identified as unconscious automatic style of masking hostility. The hidden aggressor is unaware of the real intention of his/her own behavior and disguises his/her hostility behind the noblest and most loving intentions.

There is no question that Bach's fair fighting is probably one of the most complete and encompassing contributions in the area of anger in marriage that anyone has contributed thus far. Taboos against anger and expression of hostilities are such that a great deal of this contribution is relevant to demystifying the whole area of anger and hostility. From a conceptual viewpoint, however, the labeling of anger and feelings as irrational and tying them to behavior are aspects of fair fighting that conceptually need to be clarified. This approach deals with the superficial expression of anger and fails to meet underlying causes ("that determine anger") (L'Abate, 1977a). The level of sophistication in differentiating most modes of aggression and anger is clearly a definite contribution that no one can take away from this approach.

The Pairing Enrichment Program (PEP). Travis and Travis (1975a, 1975b, 1976a, 1976b) are the designers of a structured, couple-oriented program based on the principles of self-actualization and interpersonal growth. It consists of five sessions: (a) *Being Aware*—this session enables the couple to gain awareness and acceptance of feelings; (b) *Being Authentic*—this session teaches the couple how to genuinely share in a relationship; (c) *Being Free*—this session involves an openness for experiencing each other; (d) *Being Secure*—this session helps the spouses to support and appreciate each other's individuality; and (e) *The Beginning*—this final session tries to encourage ways for the spouses to keep their partnership moving in the direction they want it to grow. PEP is an action-oriented experience in communication which involves a blend of couple and limited group discussions, fantasy experiences, educational films, exploring feelings and attitudes, experiencing sensory awareness, communication exercises, intimate encounter exercises and PEP leader-modeling, role-playing, and discussions.

Assertiveness Training. Alberti and Emmons (1974) are the early pioneers of assertiveness training to teach people skills to override their learning inhibitions against behaving assertively and to get rid of the anxiety that they may be experiencing in their interpersonal relationships. Assertiveness training is squarely based on behavioral approaches and found its historical antecedent in Salter's early work on conditioned reflex therapy, Wolpe's reciprocal inhibitions, and Lazarus' emphasis on learning role-play techniques to train people to become more assertive about themselves. Alberti and Emmons (1974) defined assertiveness as behavior which enables a person to act in his/her best interests and to stand up for him/herself without undue anxiety and to express his/her rights without destroying the rights of others. They categorized interpersonal behavior as either non-assertive, assertive, or aggressive. Non-assertive behaviors essentially are denying of the self, are inhibited and anxious, and allow others to take responsibility for the self. This position brings about guilt or anger and a failure to achieve one's desired goals. Aggressive behaviors are self-enhancing at the expense of others and essentially achieve goals by hurting others. Assertive behavior is self-enhancing without, however, denying the rights of others and without depreciating or denying the selves of others. Assertive behavior, more specifically, is deter-

mined by the ability to say no, the ability to ask for favors, to make requests, the ability to express positive and negative feelings, and the ability to initiate, continue, and terminate a general conversation.

Eisler and his co-workers (Eisler, Hersen, and Agras, 1973; Eisler, Miller, Hersen, and Alford, 1974) were the first to report an empirical investigation on the effects of assertiveness training on marital interaction using videotape feedback and focused instruction. Three couples were assigned to each of four experimental conditions: videotape; feedback alone; irrelevant feedback, videotaped feedback and focused instruction; and focused instruction alone. The results of these assignments indicated that videotape feedback in the absence of instructions effected a slight increase in nonverbal interactions of the married couple. Focused instructions led to marked changes in the target behavior of looking. A combination of videotape feedback and focused instructions was not significantly more effective than instructions alone. Eisler et al. found that assertive behavior, learned during role-play situations, generalized to real-life marital interaction. Additionally, they determined that if the role-play situation simulated relevant marital problems, the wives (who did not participate in the role-playing) would also become more assertive, even though they were not directly involved in the training. Other studies training one spouse (usually the wife rather than the husband) in assertiveness training indicated a generalization of assertive behavior for both spouses.

Studies by Shoemaker and Paulson (1974, quoted in Lehman-Olson, 1976) and by Blau (1978) support the general conclusion that training one spouse to be more assertive can increase the assertive behavior of the other spouse. Blau also found that there was a positive relationship between level of assertiveness and marital happiness.

Other contributors to the area of assertiveness training are Fensterheim and Baer (1975) and Baer (1976), who devote themselves most specifically to the application of assertiveness training to the marital dyad using reinforcement principles. Lehman-Olson (1976) was able to interpret assertiveness training principles into the framework of other theoretical positions, in addition to the reinforcement principles of learning theory adopted by most assertiveness training representatives. She feels that assertiveness training and family therapy are compatible concepts because most forms of intervention are directed toward allowing people to feel and to act as important as they think they are.

Epstein and Jackson (1978) compared assertion-related communication training, interaction insight training, and no treatment, with 15 couples randomly assigned to each treatment and control group. Outcome was measured by changes in marital verbal interaction and spouses' ratings of each other on Barrett-Lennard Relationship Inventory. Treatment lasted five one-and-a-half hour group sessions for three weeks led by the same male and female co-trainers, who were not aware of the major hypotheses of the study. Communication training produced a significant increase in assertive requests, compared to insight treatment and no treatment. Both treatments reduced disagreements significantly. Communication training produced a greater decrease in attacks and a greater increase in spouse-rated empathy than the control condition, while insight training and no treatment did not differ on those variables. As a whole, communication training led to more extensive changes in spouses' verbal behavior and perceptions of marital communication than insight training.

Epstein, Delgiovanni and Jayne-Lazarus (1978) compared 20 couples receiving assertion training with ten couples receiving minimal nonassertion-related treatment. Changes were measured on behavioral and self-report on a pre- and posttest design following the two-hour workshops for individual couples run by eight pairs of male-female co-leaders. Trained couples showed a significant increase in verbal assertion and a significant decrease in verbal aggression relative to controls. Significant increases in self-reported clarity by self and spouse and positive interaction by spouse were also reported by experimental couples. The major issue that needs to be unraveled in assertion training, according to these authors, is whether modeling or role-playing or both are the significant components of assertion training. In conclusion, the benefits of using assertiveness training in conjoint marital interventions needs further empirical investigation. So far, most of the studies do indicate that training one spouse in assertiveness training allows the other spouse to do likewise.

Communication Training. Gottman, Markman, Notarius and Gonso (1976) considered an empirical program using a "talk-table" to record intended and actual impact of messages sent and received. They wanted couples, rather than outside observers who might misjudge established dyadic communication behaviors, to code their own behaviors. After speaking, the first partner codes the intended impact of his/her own message. Before responding, the listener codes the actual impact of the message. The program consists of skills relating to (a) listening and validation, (b) leveling, (c) editing, (d) negotiating agreements, and (e) hidden agendas. Gottman et al.'s program, in contrast to the previous programs, is to be used for couples at their own pace. However, the material seems to appeal to highly motivated, relatively high-educated couples, even though the language used is simple and concrete and the material easily learned. It is very doubtful whether couples will use this program on their own without intervention of outside helpers. There is no evidence about the use of this manual and of its impact on couples, since most of their data are based on couples who worked with them.

Garland (1978) designed a communication program for ten couples per group, with an even number of couples necessary. In the first session, role-playing and exercises deal with the fact that one cannot help communicating, with the difference between verbal and nonverbal communication, and with guidelines for communication. Session two focuses on teaching listening skills, attending, and paraphrasing with role-playing exercises about this skill. Session three deals with negotiation of skills by pinpointing a question, staying with the pinpointed issue, deferring the question, labeling behavior, determining whether the question is one of fact or opinion. Sidetracking issues, such as mind-reading, refusal to discuss, bringing up past issues, and name-calling, are also discussed. Session four consists of an exploration of differences in concepts relating to facts and opinions and, finally, negotiation leading toward settling of arguments.

Garland's program seems designed primarily

for young couples in a structured setting. It is not designed for distressed couples. Skills and concepts are similar to those presented in the previous programs, and there is a great deal of overlap between some of these programs, even though some of the steps and sequences and emphasis may be different. For a theoretical review of this area, the interested reader should consult Raush, Greif and Nugent (1979).

Problem Solving. This approach, even though related to behavioral technologies like assertiveness training and behavioral management, has qualities and attributes of its own that need to be discussed separately (Klein and Hill, 1979). The basic contribution on problem-solving and interpersonal relationships can be found in D'Zurilla and Goldfried (1971), which is an extensive review of cognitive problem-solving in behavior modification literature. The problem is a specific situation in which a person must respond in order to function effectively where no effective response alternative is immediately available. Problem-solving is a process that makes available a variety of effective response alternatives and increases the probability of selecting the most efficient of these alternatives. The steps of problem-solving are fairly general: (a) definition of the problem; (b) formulation, that is, all available aspects of the problematic situation are defined in clear operational terms and classified in a consistent fashion; (c) generation of alternatives, which is essentially a form of brainstorming that deals with the various alternatives available to the couple; (d) alternative estimations of cost and rewards for each alternative in terms of the outcome; (e) implementation, whereby the chosen solution is implemented and staged; and (f) verification, where there is a cost/reward analysis of decision-making and the choice of whether to stick with the original decision, improve the original decision, or switch to a better alternative.

Among the various programs that are related to problem-solving solutions, that of Blechman, Olson, Schornagel, Halsdorf and Turner (1976) incorporates a good deal of the behavioral terminology and technology (Blechman and Olson, 1976). It is a board game designed for eventual independent use by clients. Although targeted for use in multigenerational families, it could be feasibly applied to childless couples. It follows another classification of problem-solving according to Aldous, Condon, Hill, Straus and Talman (1971), i.e.: (a) identification and definition of the issue; (b) collection of information relevant to the issue; (c) innovation of action alternatives; (d) choice of course of action; and (e) evaluation of consequences specified as: 1) pinpointing problems in observable, quantifiable terms; 2) tracking problem based on frequency; 3) selection of pleasing replacement behavior; 4) selection of reward; and 5) tracking frequency of pleasing and displeasing behaviors.

Another approach to problem-solving, given by Kieren, Henton and Marotz (1975), is specifically designed to deal with marriages. Their program instruction deals with finances, sex, in-law problems, parenting, and morale. It is an excellent sourcebook for a development of a structured intervention program to teach problem-solving skills to couples.

Spivack, Platt, and Shure (1976) offer a systematic review of problem-solving and the presentation of the problem-solving techniques which they have applied to a variety of situations and interpersonal relationships dealing with problem children, hospitalized patients, adolescents, or parent/child relationships, etc. They were the first ones to distinguish interpersonal problem-solving from impersonal problem-solving. People need to possess: (a) an awareness of the problem; (b) an ability to generate a variety of alternative solutions, to consider them all as options; (c) the ability to spell out step by step the means to the solution, including (d) the ability to delay gratification, (e) foresight, and (f) familiarity with possible obstacles. Using a procedure called means/ends problem-solving, Spivack et al. demonstrated that the ability to generate means/ends was differentiated significantly between normal controls and various impaired or disturbed patients. In fact, differentiation on this variable was the most significant determinant of social adjustment. Generation of alternative solutions was also clearly related to intellectual functioning (in addition to psychiatric disturbance). As of this date, there has not been a specific marital problem-solving technique derived from this approach. However, the feasibility of application of this approach to intervention with couples is high, especially in terms of the experiential nature of this program, in comparison or in contrast to the behavioral problem-solving emphasized by D'Zurilla and Goldfried (1971).

The third approach to problem-solving, specific to couples, has been presented by Carkhuff (1973a, 1973b). The progression of steps in this problem-solving program is similar to those listed above. Its simple presentation is such that it can be successfully implemented by paraprofessionals under the supervision of a more experienced professional. Pierce (1973) used Carkhuff's (1973a, 1973b) systematic helping skills for partners in distressed marriages. While the MCC program is purposefully designed for nonclinical couples, this program apparently is applicable to partners from distressed marriages, and is based on Carkhuff's method of training interpersonal skills, integrating both cognitive and behavioral approaches. Pierce used four groups, including a time control group, two treatment control groups of eight couples each, and a fourth experimental group of five couples seeking marital counseling for acknowledged poor communication as a major problem in their marriage. The procedure involved two-hour sessions once a week for several months for a total of 25 hours. The couples were trained in empathy, positive regard, and immediacy, as well as the initiative dimensions of genuineness and confrontation. The primary focus was development of empathy. In the first stage, pre-helping skills of attending, observing, and listening were presented and practiced in role-playing situations. The second stage was responding to feelings. The third stage was responding to feeling and meaning. In the fourth stage the helper learned to go beyond what the helpee had expressed and to understand what the helpee was really saying about himself/herself. Appropriate behavior was modeled by the trainer and media feedback was given by the trainer to the couples. Fifteen-minute interviews were conducted pre- and posttraining in which one spouse was designated the helper and the other the helpee; the roles were then reversed. Ratings were made on their communication patterns. Results showed that trained couples increased significantly in the critical response and initiative dimensions of communication. Depth of self-exploration also increased significantly as a result of increasing personal skills, which confirmed the hypothesis that increased communication skills should lead to increased self-exploration in the marital partner. The comparison of the training group with the treatment and time control group indicated a significant difference from the mean level of communication, confirming the hypothesis that training is more efficient than insight therapy in increasing interpersonal skill.

The last program for problem-solving with couples has been developed by Kessler (Note No. 10) to deal directly with couples in conflict and teach them more constructive ways of achieving conflict resolution. She outlines four major stages with minor substages within each of the stages:

A. Setting the Stage
   1) Establish rules.
   2) Set tone.
   3) Obtain commitment.
   4) Foreshadow any problems.
B. Define Issues
   1) Check out assumptions.
   2) Find facts relevant to the issue.
   3) Determine which are real issues and separate real issues from phony issues.
C. Process Issues
   1) Manage emotional climate.
   2) Encourage empathy.
   3) Maintain equality.
D. Resolve the issue, encouraging creative alternatives by expanding the boundaries of choices.

This program, in many ways, takes from the mediation model reviewed further on.

Parental Programs

The proliferation of child-rearing and child management approaches is such that any coverage here is necessarily incomplete. Nevertheless, among these approaches I can identify briefly a few major types of parental programs: (a) Adlerian, (b) behavioral, and (c) humanistic. I will discuss effectiveness training (Gordon, 1977), a widely practiced program, in greater detail.

Adlerian

Adlerian programs (Dreikurs and Soltz, 1967) focus on (a) the family constellation and birth order effects; (b) negative payoffs (i.e., power, attention, revenge, and helplessness); and (c) feelings attendant to negative payoffs; (d) positive payoffs (logical consequences, positive attention, substitutes for revenge, substitutes for helplessness, and positive alternatives); (e) rules of communication (impulsive acting, MYOB, responsibility and perfectionism); (f) family conferences and having fun together through agreed-upon rules of conduct and clear allocation of responsibilities.

Behavioral

Among the most successful behavioral programs one needs to mention Patterson and Gullion's (1963) program based on a programmed introduction of simple behavioral and social learning principles (Patterson, 1971) that parents can learn on their own. The reader is referred to Mash et al. (1974a, 1974b), Stedman, Patton and Walton (1973) and Gordon and Davidson (Chapter 14, this volume) for reviews of behavioral approaches to parent-child relationships.

Humanistic

Among the major humanistic parent training programs are filial therapy and parent-adolescent relationship development (PARD), originated by Guerney and his co-workers (1977). Basic aspects of these programs have been already described under Conjugal Relationship Enhancement. Applications of these basics to the parent-child and parent-teenage relationships are more specific. Clearly, the most successful of all parental skill-training programs is Gordon's (1977) parent effectiveness training (PET) which requires a section in its own right.

Effectiveness training

Parent effectiveness training (Gordon, 1977), which originated in work with the parents of problem children, has been modified and extended for use with a variety of potentially conflictful relationships, e.g., teacher-student, management-employer. Rooted in Rogerian tradition, with an emphasis on the power of unconditional positive regard and active listening, effectiveness training has become extremely popular and now involves a complex hierarchy of franchises and training methods.

Basic Premises. This method is tagged as "everybody-wins," in contrast to the win-lose aspect of other authoritarian or permissive methods. Both partners have to win rather than one winning at the expense of the other. Winning means clarifying what individuals (parent, child, mate, teacher, etc.) can and cannot accept in themselves and in the behavior of the other. Acceptance is equated with feeling "good" about oneself, while non-acceptance is equated with feeling "bad" about oneself. False acceptance is a gray area between acceptance and non-acceptance, in which one may act outwardly in an accepting manner, but inside one may be really unaccepting. Thus, two of the major obstacles to effective relationships are inconsistency, i.e., vacillating and contradicting one's words with deeds, and incongruity, feeling one thing and saying another. What is negotiated in parent-child relationships is power. In the authoritarian model, the parent has all the power and the child none. In the permissive model, the child is given most of the power and the parent gives it up. In the effectiveness model, nobody loses; power is negotiated and therefore shared by both the parent and the child.

Another basic premise of this method is the clear separation between personality and performance. Parents and children may love each other but do not need to accept certain behaviors in themselves or in each other, i.e., "I love you but that does not mean I accept your behavior." Unconditional acceptance is directed toward the individual. Conditional non-acceptance is directed toward the specific behavior that is problematic to the pair.

Basic Procedures. Acceptance is demonstrated through verbal and nonverbal means, such as non-intervention or avoidance of confrontation, passive listening, or methods which fail to "draw a line" where a line needs to be drawn. Win-lose methods of drawing lines are: (a) ordering, directing, commanding; (b) warning, admonishing, threatening; (c) exhorting, moralizing, preaching; (d) advising, giving solutions or suggestions; (e) lecturing, teaching, giving logical arguments; (f) judging, criticizing, disagreeing, blaming; (g) praising, agreeing; (h) name-calling, ridiculing, shaming; (i) interpreting, analyzing, diagnosing; (j) reasoning, sympathizing, consoling, supporting; (k) probing, questioning, interrogating; (l) withdrawing, distracting, humoring, diverting. These are the "typical 12" win-lose methods that fail to resolve an issue but which guarantee that the same issue, in some other garb perhaps, will appear again. Since there is no resolution, the business is not finished.

The most constructive no-lose gambit is to "open the door" and allow the other to say more. Such a goal is achieved through the use of "door-openers" that essentially are directed toward the goal of greater self-disclosure on the part of each member ("Tell me more"). Once the door is opened, it must be kept open for further and more detailed discussion and negotiation. The door is kept open through *active listening*, the basic principle on which most of parental effectiveness training rests.

The two major ingredients of active listening are: (a) paying attention, and (b) letting the partner know that one has heard what the other has said. Thus, active listening means checking back and rephrasing what one has heard in order to communicate that he/she has been heard and to give to the other the chance of affirming or clarifying what he/she meant to communicate. To use active listening, each person must want to hear what the other has to say, and want to be helpful to the other by accepting his/her feelings, whatever the feelings may be. Wanting to help is based on trusting the other and realizing that most feelings are transitory and changeable, and that one does not have or need to have the same or similar feelings as the other. Trust is related to ownership of the problem—whose feelings are whose and who owns the problem? Acceptance is directed toward clarification of ownership of specific feelings related to specific problematic behaviors. No solution is needed or forthcoming. At this point feelings are clarified first. Common errors in active listening at this juncture are: (a) manipulating the child through "guidance"; (b) opening the door and then slamming it shut; (c) parroting what the child has said instead of rephrasing it to clarify it; and (d) listening without empathy.

Confrontation of issues between parents and children most often takes place ineffectively through: (a) giving quick solutions that bypass feelings, as in the ways outlined previously; or (b) putting the child down, directly or indirectly,

by withdrawing or by criticizing. Effective confrontation takes place when "you-messages" give place to "I-messages" that deal with how one feels or is feeling in regard to the issue at hand. Especially after the pair has slowly fallen into the "You-trap" of entrenched *projective identification*, the use of "I-messages" is a difficult one to adopt. Thus, the clear switch from an ineffective to effective communication finds its basic solution in the substitution of I-messages for you-messages. This switch is at the very core of effectiveness or ineffectiveness.[7]

Once I-messages are exchanged about how each person feels about a particular issue and after these feelings have been received and basic sharing and exchange have taken place at the feeling level, can parents and children start looking for possible solutions and changes in their interaction and in their environment, by simplifying, limiting, expanding, or substituting less satisfactory activities for more satisfactory ones.

Negotiation of conflict needs to be done in terms of the relationship. "It" owns the problem, so that solutions need to be made in terms: "How can *we* solve it?" The inevitable power struggle that takes place between parents and children is dealt with after recognizing that neither authoritarianism (Model I) or permissiveness (Model II) is effective in problem-solving and decision-making. Model III, the effective no-lose method, requires finding a solution to conflict with which both parties can "feel good." It means recognizing the ineffectiveness of all the methods already outlined at the outset and confronting each issue from the viewpoint that both parties must be satisfied with the outcome. Creative no-lose solution does not mean compromise. It means finding a completely new solution that unites rather than separates the pair. Negotiation takes place along the same steps involved in the problem-solving process:

1) Identify and define the conflictual issue.
2) Generate possible alternative solutions.

---

[7]*Editors' Note.* Of course, merely instructing a (cooperative) patient to use "I-messages" rather than "you-messages" may produce a change in verbal behavior without a concomitant increase of individuation.

3) Evaluate alternative solutions in terms of payoffs and costs.
4) Decide on the best solution that is acceptable to both partners *equally*.
5) Work out a plan that will allow implementation of the solution.
6) Implement the solution.
7) Follow-up to evaluate the solution and make whatever adjustments are necessary to make it better.

What about if and when one party fails to or is unwilling to subscribe to this method? This is probably the most crucial of all questions pertaining to effectiveness. Supposedly, even if and when one party alone uses this method, if he/she uses it consistently, eventually it may help turn around the other party to negotiate according to a no-lose position.

Evaluation. The claims of success as measured by thousands of testimonials ("It works!") and the popularity of the movement need to be critically evaluated against: (a) contrasting theoretical positions; (b) evidence gathered by investigators outside the PET movement. It clearly differs from Adlerian or from behavioral methods of interaction. It is communication at its best. In fact, one of the major criticisms comes from another source, whose orientation, from an effectiveness viewpoint could be considered as representative of authoritarianism (Dobson, 1978). PET succeeds if a parent overtly or covertly wants to define the relationship with a child as egalitarian. However, if either parent or child allows one-upmanship over the other, then it is clear that effectiveness will not result. The anti-authority bias of PET is seen as being contradictory with the teaching of biblical scriptures, where the leadership and authority of the parents, especially the father, are sanctified (Dobson, 1978). While effectiveness assumes equality between parents and children, a traditional, biblical orientation toward this relationship would be based on the child "obeying" the parent. The issue of authority, of course, is relevant to the extent that responsibility is also accepted. If one party wants authority without responsibility, the other party will very likely object to this coercive discrepancy and demand that a more consistent and congruent arrangement be made that will include *both* parties on an *equal* footing as individuals—the no-lose approach.

Mitchell and McManus (1977) compared three groups of women (parents and nonparents): one group (N = 13) who received standard PET training, a second group (N = 13) who read *Parent Effectiveness Training,* and a third (N = 15) who did neither. They found that both parents and nonparents receiving PET expressed significantly fewer authoritarian attitudes on a posttest using the Parental Attitudes Research Inventory (PARI), while the book-reading parents showed a comparably significant change. Parents receiving PET showed significantly greater changes than nonparents receiving PET. Nonparents receiving PET did not change significantly more than parents who only read the PET book. Unfortunately, change in this study was evaluated only through the use of pre- and post-questionnaires. No evaluation was made of how these women behaved in relevant relationships. Finally, Rimm and Markle (1977) evaluated the literature concerning the effects of PET training on parents and their children. Most of this research was considered inadequate by a variety of methodological criteria, raising serious questions about it as a preventive intervention strategy. They concluded that: "We feel strongly that Effectiveness Training should make a systematic program of research and evaluation an essential part of their organization" (p. 108).

Gordon's (1977) own review of research findings indicated that parents showed: (a) an increase in trust, self-esteem, and confidence in themselves in their parental roles; (b) increased trust and acceptance of their children; (c) increased understanding of their children's behavior; (d) improvement in democratic attitudes and decrease in authoritarian attitudes and practices; (e) reduction in number of problems with their children and reduction in anxiety. A whole range of changes was reported in their children.[8]

In conclusion, parental effectiveness training stresses premises and procedures that can im-

---

[8]*Editors' Note.* In this generally positive context, we remind the reader of the results of a study of PET's outcomes by Knight (1975), who found no significant positive treatment effects, and even some deterioration, in a clinical sample of enuretic children and their families.

prove communication, problem-solving, and decision-making between parents and children. Its major assumption that they can and should behave as adults in confronting and negotiating issues indicates that its major target area would be preventive, i.e., with functional and mildly dysfunctional parents.

Parental training programs, even more than the marital, slide over into the therapeutic arena. Gordon (1970, 1977), as well as Adlerian and behavioral trainers, frequently characterizes parents being trained as being essentially dysfunctional. In fact, one could conclude that this very area shows strong overlap between educational and therapeutic models. Where does one end and the other begin? This line blurs to the point that eventually it is hoped mental health programs will be able to use a sieves approach (L'Abate, No. 11) that considers costs and effectiveness to the point that rehabilitation and treatment would follow at least four sieves: (a) self-help groups gathered according to a specific symptom or trouble (i.e., alcohol, gambling, incest, etc.); (b) structured skill-training programs as described in this chapter; (c) therapy as described in the rest of this *Handbook*; and (d) environmental manipulation and even hospitalization.

Family Programs

Most of the literature in this area has been reviewed by L'Abate (1977b). Two major promising developments are: (a) family clusters, and (b) family enrichment programs.

Family clusters

This method has been developed by Pringle (Note No. 12) and Sawin (1977), who are responsible for most of its rationale, theory, training, and basic format. Essentially, a family cluster is a leader-led group of four or five complete family units who contract to meet together periodically over an extended period of time for shared educational experiences relating to their problems, concerns, hopes, joys, questions, beliefs of living in relationships with the family. The cluster is meant to provide mutual support and skill-training to facilitate living within families, allowing a celebration of family life and beliefs together. Leaders are trained in a minimum of 30 hours of workshops, as well as in live demonstration sessions with families.

The objectives of family clusters are: (a) to provide an intergenerational group of families who want to share their values and insights; (b) to provide a group setting in which families can grow in support and mutuality; (c) to provide an opportunity for families to model aspects of their family systems for each other; and (d) to provide perspective for parents to observe their children in relationship to other children and children to do likewise.

Most clusters meet for a supper between 6:00 and 8:30 p.m., with each family bringing its own meal. Times of singing, games, and family sharing are included and the evening ends with families often celebrating their being together. Most educational experiences are chosen so that the youngest and the oldest may participate at their own level of experience and maturity. Content units of study in clusters may be communication patterns in the family, family stories and identity, values and beliefs, death, poverty, conflict resolution, freedom/responsibility, power, etc.

Family Enrichment

More recent and systematic attempts at improving poorly functioning family units have suggested a viable model for planned change or programmed, structured intervention. This method is the enrichment model of planned change. Recently, Otto (1975) surveyed marriage and family enrichment programs in the United States and Canada. He restricted his definitions of enrichment programs to their appropriateness for "fairly well functioning" couples or families who wish to make this functioning even better. According to Otto, existing programs can be arranged along a continuum of structured or planned change, with the Roman Catholic Marriage Encounter Program at the maximum structure pole and "sensitivity" or "encounter" sessions at the unstructured end. The results of his survey indicated that marriage enrichment programs are abundant. Otto (1975) concluded that there is a need for emphasis on *family* enrichment programs and for work in the area of sexual relations, as well as for more research on the effectiveness of marriage and family enrichment programs.

Implicit in the great degree of specificity and variety surrounding the enrichment model is a great concern for developing the most effective, humane, and least costly change strategies and for facilitating their application by professionals and paraprofessionals. Since interventions are planned and in written format, direct and systematic replication, as well as gradual and systematic modification of the techniques based on these empirical findings, is possible. In this manner, intervention can continually evolve and develop, and practitioners can easily communicate with one another about strategies, tactics, and techniques (L'Abate, 1976, 1977b).

Aiding family members to achieve a higher quality of family life and greater self-differentiation through planned change intervention and testing through empirical research should yield results that are synergistic. To achieve these goals, I have developed a systematic approach to intervention composed of programmed, preplanned structured enrichment programs.

The purpose of this section is to illustrate how intervention is related to the foregoing assumptions in at least three ways: (a) To increase differentiation in couples and families, intervention itself needs to be differentiated into structured and unstructured approaches; (b) an unstructured approach to traditional therapy derived from the theory with couples and families has been considered elsewhere (L'Abate, 1973a, 1975). A combination of both structured and unstructured approaches was summarized by L'Abate (1977b); (c) a structured approach in itself contains specific programs that are derived from theory and test it directly, as will be shown in the following pages.

Structured Intervention: Enrichment. The enrichment model (L'Abate, 1974, 1977b) has its empirical and technological underpinnings in the field of programmed instruction. Its theoretical base can be found in general information-processing systems, communication theory, and transactional psychology. It consists of written programs. Programs are prearranged with detailed instructions that an individual specifically trained for this work reads to the family. Each program consists of three to six sessions

or "lessons." Each lesson contains five to six exercises in which the family actively participates. Instructions range from simple questions concerning personal and occupational identity or parent-child relations to exercises to allow family members to talk to each other and to express themselves verbally and nonverbally, dealing with topics and problems not usually considered during the routine of daily living. A large library of programs has been developed (L'Abate and Collaborators, 1975a, 1975b) to cover a variety of areas relevant to marriage and the family.

The first manual (L'Abate, 1975a) deals with programs from a structural viewpoint (simple-complex; cognitive-affective; general-specific). The selection of a program for a particular family is based on structural qualities characteristic of a specific family. Some of the more common determinants are as follows: A lower educational level may indicate a simple program, while a family with highly educated parents may be better suited to a complex program. If family members have trouble with verbal expression, a cognitive program that instructs them in verbal expression may be selected. On the other hand, a family that does not express feelings may benefit from an affective program to aid in learning natural and comfortable nonverbal expression. The general-specific structure refers to the fact that some programs are oriented to general, overall enrichment along cognitive or affective lines, while others are problem-oriented, such as programs for families with adopted children or with a mentally retarded or physically handicapped family member.

There are 26 different programs with a total of 139 lessons, arranged along structural lines. Five simple introductory programs are an affective-general program, a cognitive-general program, financial management, democratic living, and behavioral principles. Five intermediary-general programs cover differentiation, extreme reactions, assertiveness, value clarification, helpfulness (L'Abate and Collaborators, 1975a), and negotiation in the family. Advanced-affective programs are introductory, intermediary, advanced, and two experiential-cognitive programs. The advanced-cognitive programs, based on the approaches of prominent family theorists, cover: "practical" matters, interrelational, dysfunctional, organizational, and transactional approaches (L'Abate and Collaborators, 1975a). Finally, there are six special purpose programs, i.e., single parents, adopted children, drug-oriented youngsters, physically handicapped and mentally retarded children, and families of alcoholics. Some of the latter programs can be used with groups of parents.

The second manual (L'Abate, 1976) contains enrichment programs from a developmental viewpoint, dealing with various phases of the family life-cycle. The manual includes premarital, sexual, marital, parental, and geriatric enrichment programs. Selection from this manual can be based on the specific developmental stage presented by a couple or family. Although the majority of the programs are suited to couples and parents, the manual also contains programs geared toward adolescents and various groups of adults, regardless of formal matrimonial or familial bonds: adolescent sexual awareness, the meaning of adolescence, separating teenagers from their parents, and communication between parents and adolescents. In this manual, major emphasis is given to the man-woman relationship (as reviewed in the previous section on marital programs), since this relationship is basic to the development and well-being of the offspring and of the family as a whole. Following this developmental logic, a program for expectant parents has been developed that can be presented to one couple or a group of expectant parents.

Developmental programs that can be presented to groups as well are: (a) clarification of sexual attitudes for use with groups of teachers, parents, or families with adolescents; (b) parental assertiveness; (c) parental effectiveness; (d) programs for divorcees and widows; (e) the single parent; (f) three-generation families, and (g) death. One of the tasks for the future is an extension of the pre-planned enrichment technique from couples and families to groups composed of diverse, unrelated people who may come together for the purpose of enrichment to improve the quality of their lives.

A typical process of involvement follows these steps. First, the couple or family is interviewed about the relevance of enrichment, to establish rapport, to explain the enrichment model and the choices of programs available, and to reach a clear contract. A written consent form is used. Second, the couple or family is evaluated with rating sheets and tests developed for the purposes of pre- and posttest evaluation, as it will be described shortly. Third, at the first enrichment meeting, the couple or family is informed of the programs that seem most suitable in terms of structural, developmental, and systematic considerations. Fourth, after a series of six enrichment seminars, usually once a week, the couple or family is reevaluated with the same instruments administered before enrichment. Fifth, a follow-up session is then scheduled at which the couple's or family's reactions to the enrichment are asked for and recorded, the enricher's feedback to the couple or family is given in a positive fashion and various possibilities for the future are either considered or in some cases recommended (no further intervention, more enrichment, professional help, referral sources, etc.).

The potential applicability of enrichment programs to preventive and facilitative family intervention is great. The model combines many advantages: (a) working with the individual members together as a family to change dysfunctional patterns in the system; (b) teaching and practice of interpersonal skills designed to minimize destructive conflict and maximize the pleasure of family living; (c) tackling specific relationship problems of all group members; (d) leaving the family with skills for continuing the enrichment of family life on their own; and (e) utilizing a structured approach where effectiveness can be more easily assessed and improved with repeated use than with relatively unstructured approaches like therapy. These programs can be used by family therapists and counselors, by other professionals desiring to work with families, and by less highly trained para- or subprofessional personnel under supervision of more experienced professionals (L'Abate, 1973b). The model is as flexible as the number of available programs and the creativity of practitioners in developing new programs.

The process of enrichment is not wedded to any particular setting and can take place in a private office, a clinic, or in the home of the family. It can serve at least two different functions in addition to the enrichment of families: (a) training of paraprofessional and professional personnel; and (b) serving as a research tool.

Training. The function of enrichment serves two goals in training. First, the student can learn theory by applying it instead of going the usual route from theory to practice. In essence, various programs are a translation of theory into direct application and serve as operational definitions of a particular theoretical viewpoint. Second, the student is able to gain a great deal of practical experience in working with families until he or she reaches a level of expertise sufficient to develop creative new programs. Since expertise is found in the specific program presented to the family, the student is free to learn the process of enrichment in real-life settings. Under supervision, the enricher can help families while continuously coming to better understand them and to develop greater proficiency in the method. Instead of going from books to practice or from individual to family therapy, the student starts practicing role-playing roles with peers in mock families (First Step), enriching normal, nonclinical families (Second Step), enriching clinical families (Third Step), and going on to work with families in unstructured situations (Fourth Step), using enrichment programs on the side to help the process of change (L'Abate 1977b).

Research. The direct operational translations of any theory or approach into an enrichment program and the standardized, pre-planned nature of each program allow direct testing of the methods, as well as of the theoretical basis, of each program, i.e., experiential versus practical, transactional versus behavioral, etc. An additional research advantage of the enrichment model lies in its applicability to essentially "normal" families who can serve as control or contrast groups for clinical families. For instance, it is possible to use clinical vs. nonclinical groups compared on enrichment vs. no enrichment (L'Abate, 1977b; Note No. 3).

Evidence of Effectiveness. Structured tests, combined with the structured nature of enrichment programs, facilitate research efforts. Assessment tools developed concurrently with enrichment assure a self-corrective process in refining an internally cohesive model. Validity and reliability of these new instruments and their theoretical underpinnings have been examined in a variety of studies, as yet unpublished (L'Abate, 1977b; Note No. 3).

The effects of enrichment programs with 55 families divided into clinical and nonclinical, with and without enrichment (control group), were evaluated. The change scores on pre- to posttests, consisting of a family evaluation battery described elsewhere (L'Abate, 1977b), indicated statistically significant improvements in the experimental groups of families, especially the nonclinical families. These results supported the use of enrichment programs for families at a preventive level. Additional studies have been concerned with testing the limits of the enrichment model, where failures in enrichment with both families and couples were reviewed to specify the conditions under which enrichment is *not* feasible and other methods of intervention, like therapy, may be more appropriate (L'Abate and Weeks, 1976).

Wildman (1977) compared both therapy and enrichment with two groups of clinical undergraduate couples, one group of nonclinical couples (enrichment only) and a control group of nonclinical couples. His preliminary results, using the same type of evaluation described by L'Abate (1977b), indicate that (a) at pretest, couples chosen to receive six sessions of therapy from professionals with an average of 12 years experience described themselves as being more disturbed than those couples chosen to receive six sessions of enrichment; (b) on post-intervention bases, both groups show significant improvement in their description of their marital relationship, with the therapy couples reaching the same level as the level reached by enrichment couples; (c) nonclinical couples receiving enrichment describe themselves at baseline as being significantly less disturbed or more satisfied than clinical couples, either in therapy or enrichment, yet their satisfaction scores improved even more significantly after enrichment; (d) a control group of nonclinical couples evaluated and reevaluated after a similar time span as therapy or enrichment (six weeks) but with no intervention showed no change in their scores on posttest.

Discussion. On the basis of these very preliminary results, it appears that the enrichment model may serve as an alternative technological tool to improve the quality of life in couples and families. Additional studies to verify the theoretical bases and strengthen the empirical results seem imperative. Further research to specify the range and limits of application of the model is also necessary. Finally, the appropriateness of combined structured enrichment programs with unstructured "therapy" approaches should be considered and investigated to widen the range of couples and families that can be reached through the use of professionals and intermediate level professionals (L'Abate, 1977b). Feasible models of overlap between these two approaches are: (a) *parallel*, use of both approaches, side by side; (b) *serial time*, use of one approach after the other; and (c) *collateral*, where the programs are used by the couple or families on their own at home with discussion of their homework activities in the professional's office.

Structured, planned change, such as the enrichment model presented here, has significant implications for current issues in mental health delivery. First, the related effects on manpower and cost are great (L'Abate, 1969, 1973b). Programmed change allows for greater utilization of intermediate-level professionals and paraprofessionals, resulting in decreased cost, both in terms of time and expense. Additionally, professionals can utilize the programs to increase their skills as change agents and, thus, facilitate their overall effectiveness. The increased availability of man-hours and an increase in successful, positive change efforts could greatly increase the reachable population and expand the number of available settings for change and improvement.

Besides cost-effectiveness, a second major area of concern in mental health delivery is accountability in the services provided. The structured nature of enrichment should facilitate efforts in accountability, since structure permits explicit agreements between couples or families and their enrichers on procedures, time, cost, and goals.

To summarize, in addition to a clear research function, the major social significance of the enrichment model lies in its (a) propaedeutic, (b) prophylactic, and (c) paratherapeutic functions. Therapy, because of financial, economic, and cognitive considerations, is limited to special families and special cases. Even if therapy were available to all families, any form of rehabilitation based only on one model is bound to fail and to succeed only with a percentage of the target population it claims to help. If it can be demonstrated that family enrichment programs can be useful to lower-class families in the hands of paraprofessional workers under the supervision of professionals (L'Abate, 1973a, 1973b), the cost of prevention and intervention can be cut drastically.

The Long-Range Effects of Enrichment. An important but often overlooked question regarding enrichment involves the extent to which the effects of enrichment endure over time. In hopes of providing some answers in this important area, Carter and I (Note No. 13) are conducting long-range follow-ups on couples and families who received enrichment over the past four years. Thus far, 12 of 15 couples or families responding described themselves as being "satisfied" or "very satisfied" with the enrichment experience, presumably indicating that it had some long-term beneficial impact on their marital or familial relationships. Three couples and families reported being less satisfied with enrichment and criticized various specific procedures.

Nontraditional Families: An Extension of Enrichment: Most of the programs heretofore considered deal mostly with traditionally married couples and/or intact families. What about nontraditional families? Little if anything can be found in the skill-training program literature. However, I have (1977b) reported on using enrichment programs with: (a) cohabiting couples; (b) single-parent families; and (c) one homosexual couple. The whole area of lower socioeconomic (deprived!) couples and families, who "should" be in greater need of interpersonal skill-training than middle and upper SES couples and families, remains wide open for experimental application and intervention.

Divorce Mediation

There is at least one special structured program dealing with divorce mediation, which was developed by Coogler (1978) to assist divorcing couples in working out the divorce settlement along the issues of child support, custody, alimony and division of property according to a time-limited framework and a contractual agreement that would banish or eliminate any kind of blame or emotional behavior on the part of the splitting couple. Coogler started this program on the basis of the failure on the part of many mental health professionals to intervene in an area that has usually been left to the legal profession. As a lawyer himself, Coogler felt very strongly about the need to develop an alternative that would take many of these issues out of the hands of a lawyer and put them in the hands of a properly trained professional. This model is based to some extent on the model of arbitration promulgated by the American Arbitration Association.

When couples agree to enter mediation, they sign a legal document which binds them to work out a settlement which is mutually agreeable in mediation. If they are not able to reach such an agreement through the mediation process, they are legally bound to go on to arbitration. This contract essentially means that neither one of the parties is allowed to go to a lawyer unless they both agree to stop mediation, forfeit their $400 deposit for the mediation sessions, and then go and see a lawyer. If they are able to work out an agreement in the first session at $40 per session, the remaining prepaid fees are returned. Under marital mediation, in rules which are given to them in written format and which they have to follow, issues are clearly defined and limited to those which must be resolved for settlement. Procedural methods are followed for collecting information. On the basis of information relating to budgets, tax forms, property, income and so forth, the couple is helped to come to a rational division of marital property, maintenance for the dependent spouse, if any, child support for dependent children, and custody and visitation rights. Marital mediation rules provide guidelines on how to resolve these four issues. Coogler and his center have also been involved in the training of divorce mediators who meet and develop specific skills, including those involving financial and legal matters, relevant to the process of divorce. Eventually this could become a definite subspecialty in the field of marital intervention with its own specific training. Mediation seems a valid and useful option for couples pursuing divorce settlement. As the concept and method are taking some time to be widely accepted, mediation may also have to wait some years. However, it is an important step to consider for alleviating the pain—physical, emotional, and financial—that many couples have to undergo during the process of divorce.

EVALUATION OF THE ENRICHMENT MOVEMENT

Smiith, Shoffner, and Scott (1979), in a review of the marriage and family enrichment movement, expressed some major concerns about it as a new professional area: (a) It is touted as a cure-all; (b) there is questionable training of leaders; (c) the expectations of participants are higher than programs can deliver; (d) there are beliefs that couples and families will be "totally enriched" and/or "closed"; (e) a major assumption is that enrichment may become one of life's "peak" experiences; (f) it cannot prevent major social ills; and (g) no direct and/or hard evidence is as yet available to claim any preventive benefit.

These authors summarized four characteristics of a professional area: (a) a differentiating set of assumptions and propositions; (b) a pool of trained personnel; (c) a stable societal agency to support its professional personnel; and (d) a recognized need and request for their services. The first two were viewed as "the weakest parts of the enrichment movement," especially in view of the claimed assumption of working with couples and families that would not fall under the rubric of "therapy" and/or "counseling":

Enrichment has yet to be defined adequately; the outcomes of enrichment have yet to be rigidly measured; and the underlying assumptions have yet to be stated. It is recommended that a set of differentiating assumptions and propositions be developed as the next step in building the professional area of marriage and family enrichment (Smith, Shoffner, and Scott, 1979, p. 92).

IMPLICATIONS

The studies reviewed in this chapter show that skill-training programs are capable of producing beneficial changes in a wide range of couples and families, from those who want to enhance already adequate adjustment to the more seriously disturbed. Even so, professionals working with these methods must be constantly alert to the possibility that this training may be ineffective with some couples and families. In other words, we must be sensitive to the possibility that skill-training may have limits, and we have an ethical obligation to determine what those limits may be (L'Abate and Weeks, 1976). Some early, uncontrolled investigation of this issue suggests that resistance to treatment may be one indication that skill-training is inappropriate for a couple or family. If a family is trying to defeat the helper, whether this resistance is open or deeper or more subtle, it appears that then therapy may give the professional helper the flexibility he needs to effectively counter the family members' attempts to defeat him/her and themselves (L'Abate, Note No. 11).

Even if skill-training were found to have serious limitations with some client groups, this finding would not automatically remove it from the arsenal of those professionals who work with such clients. Skill-training can be combined (by what "rules"?) with other approaches (L'Abate, 1977b). For example, a family's resistance to change could first be overcome through the use of unstructured therapy.[9] Then, skill-training could be used to teach the family members skills and coping mechanisms which are lacking. Other sequences which have been utilized successfully in the Georgia State University Family Study Center include using a series of enrichment sessions prior to therapy in order to accustom the family to the therapeutic process (L'Abate, 1977b). Also, skill-training may be offered at any point during the course of therapy to give the couple or family additional opportunities to work on problem areas. Skill-training may also be used in combination with techniques other than therapy. Homework assignments can be added to this process (L'Abate, 1977b). There seems to be no reason why feedback obtained from tape recordings, or many other techniques which might be developed in the future, could not be added to skill-training to enhance its effects. While skill-training programs vary in degrees of structure, their use can be characterized by flexibility, and they can be applied and changed creatively by workers in this field.

Skill-training can also serve an important role in the training of mental health professionals. Students wishing to become proficient in marital or family therapy can begin the learning process by learning various skill learning programs. Then, as they become accustomed to the special complexities which arise in dealing with families, they can move on to less structured therapeutic interventions. This additional step cuts down on the size of the gap between books and practice; this is a gap which has proven too wide for many aspiring family therapists! Skill-training can also be used to help professionals learn new techniques like family therapy.

One of the most exciting aspects of skill-training programs, in the author's opinion, is their relevance for research. Because of their relatively structured nature, the effectiveness of specific programs can be researched, and they can be systematically improved on the basis of the feedback obtained from evaluation. As soon as the most effective programs representing different approaches have been obtained, these programs may then be compared against each other in an effort to answer some basic theoretical issues. For example, the most effective Adlerian program could be compared against the most effective communication and information-processing program to determine which approach is most useful with which types of problems. In the past, such direct comparisons among theories have been confounded by the possibility that one approach may have been more skillfully administered than the other.

Training for Prevention

Future training programs are going to need identification and delineation of preventive versus therapeutic skills as well as attitudes, personality, and *Weltanschauung* that make an individual dedicate him/herself to preventive rather than therapeutic activities. What makes a

---

[9]*Editors' Note.* Again, see Barton and Alexander (Chapter 11) for some specific intervention strategies to accomplish such a shift and openness to structured skill-training interventions.

professional and a paraprofessional? What is the difference between a therapist and a professional interested in preventive work with functional couples? What is the difference between marriage and family therapists? What makes them choose one professional path over the other? It is unfortunate, indeed, that this needs to be stated as an either-or issue. Yet, the reality of therapy does indicate that a whole new profession of "preventers" rather than therapists needs to be built from the ground up. These individuals would have different skills, different perspectives, and different goals from therapists. Programs reviewed here do indicate that substantive, skill-directed programs would need *full-time* individuals who would become part and parcel of any community mental health program, especially *if* their employment were to become a *requirement* for federal and state funding, and *if* their salaries were to be comparable to those of therapists. Once these conditions were to obtain, it would not be difficult to train a special corps of preventers. As this chapter has attempted to show, the technology of marital and familial prevention is just as complex, varied, and exciting as the varieties of therapies reviewed between these covers. The day for the prevention of family and marriage dysfunction is here.

Gordon (1977) has some cogent thoughts about prevention and training for prevention, where his PET program is paradigmatic of learning and teaching effective rules of communication, problem-solving, and shared decision-making according to a "training-before-trouble" model that could become part and parcel of any training program for prevention. His experience, shared by other preventers (Note No. 4), is that most mental health practitioners avoid becoming involved in what they perceive as "second-class" or irrelevant activities from the viewpoint of treatment.

Relevant to issues of training in skill-training are the recent findings of Durlak's (1979) survey of 42 studies comparing the effectiveness of professional and paraprofessional helpers. Consistently, most studies indicated that:

Paraprofessionals achieve clinical outcomes equal to or significantly better than those obtained by professionals. . . . Moreover, professional mental health education, training, and experience do not appear to be necessary prerequisites for an effective helping person. . . . Future studies need to define, isolate, and evaluate the primary treatment ingredients of paraprofessional helping programs in an attempt to determine the nature of the paraprofessional's therapeutic influence.

Durlak's findings are supported by Wildman's (1977) study cited earlier. Wildman found comparable outcomes for equally matched couples treated therapeutically by professionals with an average of 12 years' experience and couples treated through enrichment by graduate students with one or two years of graduate training and individual clinical experience.[10]

CONCLUSION

Skill-oriented programs have shown themselves to be wide in scope and deep in content. Their potential for use with functional and semifunctional couples and families is almost assured—what else is there?[11] Their potential as additional, paratherapeutic modalities to supplement and complement therapies with dysfunctional couples and families needs to be explored completely. The issue will not be one of supplanting therapies—therapists need not be threatened—but one of supplementing them. If for every "clinical" or "dysfunctional" couple and family there are three to four other couples and families in need of help, then these programs could be in the front line to help prevent further individual, marital, and familial breakdowns. These programs and the issues that they

---

[10]*Editors' Note.* We think this conclusion requires an important qualification. While the limits of paraprofessional intervention have essentially never been put to an empirical test in family work, our prediction is that paraprofessionals' effectiveness is likely to be quite circumscribed and limited to a much smaller range of clinical situations than are interventions by professional therapists. Existing evidence in nonfamily treatment clearly supports the logic of this prediction (Gurman and Razin, 1977), and more research on this issue is greatly needed.

[11]*Editors' Note.* Indeed, some of the most influential of family therapists (e.g., Carl Whitaker and Lyman Wynne) for several years now have been experimenting with and exploring the limits of family *therapy* for "well families." Moreover, it is our impression that increasing numbers of "well" couples are seeking psychotherapeutic experiences to enhance their growth rather than to remediate dysfunction.

raise present a challenge to therapists of all persuasions; i.e., how much should therapists be involved in prevention? Should prevention become the privileged territory of one profession, i.e., family life education, or should it be open to all of those interested and qualified? These programs offer the hope of substantive contribution to prevention. Is this area destined to be a stepchild of therapy or will it develop its own independence, functionally separate and with little input from therapists?

We have seen how skill-training programs grew out of the very positive desire to improve ourselves, our marriages, and our families. They provide a broad range of approaches which have attracted public attention and even enthusiasm. In short, they have all the earmarks of a fad. Fortunately, skill-training programs have linked themselves to evaluation. Their limits are being tested and the processes of refinement and standardization have begun. As evaluation moves forward, so will skill-training. Evaluation can save skill-training programs from the demise which is the inevitable end of most fads. The major promise for this methodology, in its selective applicability to both clinical and nonclinical couples and families, is prevention. Current mental health practices lack or fail to possess clearly preventive measures. Skill-training is first and foremost a preventive intervention. That is where the major issues in mental health lie.

REFERENCE NOTES

1. L'Abate, L. Historical antecedents of family enrichment programs. Paper presented at a meeting of the proposed Georgia Association of Marriage and Family Counseling, Georgia State University, April 15, 1972.
2. L'Abate, L. Family life education, skill-training programs, and family enrichment. Paper delivered at a colloquium in the Department of Family Studies, University of Kentucky, Lexington, Kentucky, March 1, 1979.
3. L'Abate, L. *Enrichment: Skill building for family life*. Monograph submitted for publication.
4. Mace, D. Report on seminar workshop on preventive training for creative family relationships. Winston-Salem, North Carolina, P. O. Box 5182.
5. Mace, D. Preventive training for creative family relationships: Some experimental programs in North America. Paper prepared for a Workshop on Prevention at the Groves Conference on Marriage and the Family, Washington, D.C., April 27-30, 1978.
6. Microys, G., & Bader, E. Do pre-marriage programs really help? Department of Family and Community Medicine, University of Toronto, Ontario, Canada, December, 1977 (mimeograph).
7. Zimmerman, A., & Bailey, J. The Minnesota Couples Communication Program: An evaluation of the training and post-training communication behavior of its participants. Unpublished report, University of Minnesota, 1977.
8. Miller, S. Personal communication, February 15, 1979
9. Huber, W. Marriage encounter evaluated by CRI. Research and Developments, San Diego, California, 1977.
10. Kessler, S. *Creative conflict resolution and mediation: A leader's guide*. Atlanta: National Insitute for Professional Training, 1978.
11. L'Abate, L. A sequential (sieves) approach to intervention. Atlanta, Georgia, Georgia State University, unpublished manuscript.
12. Pringle, B. M. The family cluster: A way to augment the nuclear group. Unpublished paper, Southern Methodist University, Dallas, Texas, May 24, 1973.
13. Carter, D., & L'Abate, L. A long-range follow-up of enrichment programs. Atlanta, Georgia, Georgia State University (research in progress)

REFERENCES

Alberti, R. E., & Emmons, M. L. *Your Perfect Right: A Guide to Assertive Behavior*. San Luis Obispo, CA: Impact, 1974.

Aldous, J., Condon, T. B., Hill, R., Straus, M., & Talman, I. *Family Problem Solving: A Symposium on Theoretical, Methodological and Substantive Concerns*. Hinsdale, IL: Dryden Press, 1971.

Bach, G., & Bernhard, Y. *Aggression Laboratory: The Fair Fighting Training Manual*. Los Angeles: Kendal Hunt Publishing Co., 1971.

Bach, G., & Goldberg, H. *Creative Aggression*. New York: Doubleday & Co., 1974.

Bach, G., & Wyden, T. *The Intimate Enemy: How to Fight Fair in Love and Marriage*. New York: William Morrow & Co., 1969.

Baer, J. *How to be an Assertive, Not Aggressive Woman in Life, Love, and on the Job*. New York: Signet, 1976.

Birchler, G. R. Communication skills in married couples. In: A. S. Bela & M. Hertson (Eds.), *Research and Practice in Social Skill Training*. New York: Plenum Press, in press.

Blau, J. *Changes in assertiveness and marital satisfaction after participation in an assertiveness training group*. Temple University, Order No. 7812186, 1978.

Blechman, E. A., & Olson, D. H. L. The family contract game: Description and effectiveness. In: D. H. L. Olson (Ed.), *Treating Relationships*. Lake Mills, IA: Graphic Publishing Co., 1976. Pp. 133-149.

Blechman, E. A., Olson, D. H. L., Schornagel, C. Y., Halsdorf, M., & Turner, A. J. The family contract game: Technique and case study. *Journal of Consulting and Clinical Psychology*, 1976, 44, 449-455.

Bosco, A. *Marriage Encounter: Rediscovery of Love*. St. Meinrad, IN: Abbey Press, 1973.

Brown, E. C., & L'Abate, L. An appraisal of teaching machines and programmed instruction. In: C. M. Franks (Ed.), *Behavior Therapy: Appraisal and Status*. New York: McGraw-Hill, 1969. Pp. 396-414.

Calvo, Father Gabriel. *Marriage Encounter*. St. Paul, MN: Marriage Encounter, Inc., 1975.

Carkhuff, R. R. *The Art of Helping*. Amherst, MA: Human

Resource Development Press, 1973. (a)

Carkhuff, R. R. *The Art of Problem Solving*. Amherst, MA: Human Resource Development Press, 1973. (b)

Collins, J. D. *The effects of the conjugal relationship modification method on marital communication and adjustment*. Ph.D. Dissertation, Pennsylvania State University, 1971.

Coogler, R. J. *Structured Mediation in Divorce Settlements: A Handbook for Divorce Mediators*. Lexington, MA: Lexington Books, 1978.

D'Augelli, A. R., Deyss, D. S., Guerney, B. G. Jr., Hershenberg, B., & Sborofsky, S. L. Interpersonal skill training for dating couples: An evaluation of an educational mental health service. *Journal of Counseling Psychology*, 1974, 21, 385-389.

Demarest, D. *Marriage Encounter: A Guide to Sharing*. St. Paul, MN: Carrillion Books, 1977.

Doherty, W. J., McCabe, P., & Ryder, R. G. Marriage encounter: A critical appraisal. *Journal of Marriage and Family Counseling*, 1978, 4, 99-106.

Dobson, J. *The Strong-Willed Child: Birth through Adolescence*. Wheaton, IL: Tyndale House Publishers, 1978.

Dreikurs, R., & Soltz, V. *Children: The Challenge*. Chicago: Alfred Adler Institute, 1967.

Durlak, J. H. Comparative effectiveness of paraprofessional and professional helpers. *Psychological Bulletin*, 1979, 66, 80-92.

D'Zurilla, T. J., & Goldfried, M. R. Problem solving and behavior modification. *Journal of Abnormal Psychology*, 1971, 78, 107-126.

Eisler, R. M., Hersen, M. & Agras, W. S. Effects of videotape and instructional feedback on nonverbal marital interaction: An analog study. *Behavior Therapy*, 1973, 4, 551-558.

Eisler, R. M., Miller, P. M., Hersen, M. & Alford, H. Effects of assertive training on marital interaction. *Archives of General Psychiatry*, 1974, 30, 643-649.

Ely, A. L., Guerney, B. G. Jr., & Stover, L. Efficacy of the training phase of conjugal therapy. *Psychotherapy: Theory, Research and Practice*, 1973, 10, 201-207.

Epstein, N., & Jackson, E. An outcome study of short-term communication training with married couples. *Journal of Consulting and Clinical Psychology*, 1978, 46, 207-212.

Epstein, N., Delgiovanni, I. S., & Jayne-Lazarus, C. Assertion training for couples. *Journal of Behavior Therapy and Experimental Psychiatry*, 1978, 9, 149-155.

Fensterheim, H., & Baer, J. *Don't Say Yes When You Want to Say No*. New York: Dell Publishers, 1975.

Garland, D. R. *Couples Communication and Negotiation Skills*. New York: Family Service Association of America, 1978.

Gordon, T. *Parent Effectiveness Training*. New York: Peter H. Wyden, 1970.

Gordon, T. *PET in Action: Inside PET Families, New Problems, Insights, and Solutions*. New York: Wyden Books, 1976.

Gordon, T. Parent effectiveness training: A preventive program and its delivery system. In: G. W. Albee & J. M. Joffe (Eds.), *Primary Prevention of Psychopathology*. Hanover, NH: University Press of New England, 1977. Pp. 175-186.

Gottman, J., Markman, H., Notarius, C., & Gonso, J. *The Couple's Guide to Communication*. Champaign, IL: Research Press, 1976.

Guerney, B. G. Jr. *Relationship Enhancement*. San Francisco: Jossey-Bass, 1977.

Gurman, A. S., & Kniskern, D. P. Enriching research on marital enrichment programs. *Journal of Marriage and Family Counseling*, 1977, 3, 3-10.

Gurman, A. S., & Kniskern, D. P. Research on marital and family therapy: Progress, perspective and prospect. In: S. L. Garfield & A. E. Bergin (Eds.), *Handbook of Psychotherapy and Behavior Change: An Empirical Analysis*. New York: Wiley, 1978.

Harrell, J., & Guerney, B. G. Jr. Training married couples in conflict negotiation skills. In: D. H. L. Olson (Ed.), *Treating Relationships*. Lake Mills, IA: Graphic Publishing, 1976.

Heisler, R. N., Miller, P. M., Hersen, M., & Alford, H. The effects of assertiveness training on marital interaction. *Archives of General Psychiatry*, 1974, 30, 643-649.

Hopkins, L., Hopkins, P., Mace, D., & Mace, V. *Toward Better Marriages: The Handbook of the Association of Couples for Marriage Enrichment (ACME)*. Winston-Salem, NC: ACME, 1978.

Jacobson, N. S. A review of the research on the effectiveness of marital therapy. In: T. J. Paolino & B. S. McCrady (Eds.), *Marriage and Marital Therapy: Psychoanalytic, Behavioral and Systems Theory Perspectives*. New York: Brunner/Mazel, 1978.

Kessler, M., & Albee, G. W. An overview of the literature on primary prevention. In: G. W. Albee & J. M. Joffe (Eds.), *Primary Prevention of Psychopathology, Vol. I: The Issues*. Hanover, NH: University Press of New England, 1977.

Kieren, D., Henton, J., & Marotz, R. *Her and His: The Problem Solving Approach to Marriage*. Hinsdale, IL: Dryden Press, 1975.

Klein, D. C., & Goldston, S. E. *Primary Prevention: An Idea whose Time Has Come*. Superintendent of Documents, U.S. Government Printing Office, Washington, D. C., 20602, 1977.

Klein, D. M., & Hill, R. Determinants of family problem solving effectiveness. In: W. R. Burr, R. Hill, F. I. Nye, & I. L. Reiss (Eds.), *Contemporary Theories about the Family: Research-Based Theories. Vol. I*. New York: Free Press, 1979.

L'Abate, L. Aggression and construction in children's monitored play therapy. *Journal of Counseling and Psychotherapy*, 1979, 1, 2, 137–158.

L'Abate, L. Intimacy is sharing hurt feelings: A reply to David Mace. *Journal of Marriage and Family Counseling*, 1977, 3, 13-16. (a)

L'Abate, L. *Enrichment: Structured Interventions with Couples, Families and Groups*. Washington, D.C.: University Press of America, 1977. (b)

L'Abate, L. *Understanding and Helping the Individual in the Family*. New York: Grune & Stratton, 1976.

L'Abate, L. A positive approach to marital and familial intervention. In: L. R. Wolberg & M. L. Aronson (Eds.), *Group Therapy 1975: An Overview*. New York: Stratton Intercontinental Medical Book Corp, 1975.

L'Abate, L. Family enrichment programs. *Journal of Family Counseling*, 1974, 2, 32-38.

L'Abate, L. Psychodynamic interventions: A personal statement. In: R. H. Woody & J. D. Woody (Eds.), *Sexual, Marital and Family Relations*. Springfield, IL: Charles C Thomas, 1973. Pp. 122-180. (a)

L'Abate, L. The laboratory method in clinical child psychology: Three applications. *Journal of Clinical Child Psychology*, 1973, 2, 8-10. (b)

L'Abate, L. The continuum of rehabilitation and laboratory evaluation: Behavior modification and psychotherapy. In: C. M. Franks (Ed.), *Behavior Therapy: Appraisal and Status*. New York: McGraw-Hill, 1969. Pp. 676-484.

L'Abate, L., & collaborators. *A Manual: Family Enrichment Programs*. Atlanta, GA: Social Research Laboratories, 1975. (a)

L'Abate, L., & collaborators. *Manual: Enrichment Programs for the Family Life Cycle*. Atlanta, GA: Social Research Laboratories, 1975. (b)

L'Abate, L., & L'Abate, B. *How to Avoid Divorce*. Atlanta, GA: John Knox Press, 1977.

L'Abate, L., & O'Callaghan, J. B. Implications of the enrichment model for research and training. *The Family Coordinator*, 1977, *26*, 61-64.

L'Abate, L., & Smith, D. K. The laboratory evaluation and enrichment of families. In: L. L'Abate, *Enrichment: Structured Interventions with Couples, Families, and Groups*. Washington, D.C.: University Press of America, 1977.

L'Abate, L., & Weeks, G. Testing the limits of enrichment: When enrichment fails. *Journal of Family Counseling*, 1976, *4*, 70-76.

Lehman-Olson, D. Assertiveness training: Theoretical and clinical implications. In: D. H. L. Olson (Ed.), *Treating Relationships*. Lake Mills, IA: Graphic Publishing, 1976. Pp. 93-116.

Loomis, T. P. Skin conductance and the effects of time distribution on encounter group learning: Marathons vs. spaced groups. *Dissertation Abstracts International*, 1977, 37, 4993.

Luber, R. F. Teaching models in marital therapy: A review and research issue. *Behavior Modification*, 1978, *2*, 77-91.

Mace, D., & Mace, V. Marriage enrichment: A preventive group approach for couples. In: D. H. L. Olson (Ed.), *Treating Relationships*. Lake Mills, IS: Graphic Publishing, 1976. Pp. 321-336.

Mace, D. We call it ACME. *Small Group Behavior*, 1975, *6*, 31-44.

Mash, E. J., Hamerlynck, L. A., & Handy, L. C. (Eds.). *Behavior Modification and Families*. New York: Brunner/Mazel, 1974. (a)

Mash, E. J., Handy, L. C., & Hamerlynck, L. A. *Behavior Modification Approaches to Parenting*. New York: Brunner/Mazel, 1974. (b)

Miller, S. (Ed.). *Marriages and Families: Enrichment through Communication*. Beverly Hills: Sage Publications, 1975.

Miller, S., Nunnally, E. W., & Wackman, D. D. *Alive and Aware: Improving Communication in Relationships*. Minneapolis: Interpersonal Communications Program, 1975.

Miller, S., Nunnally, E. W., & Wackman, D. D. *Minnesota Couples Communication Program: An Instructor Manual*. Minneapolis: Interpersonal Communications Program, undated.

Mitchell, J., & McManus, D. L. Effect of PET on authoritarian attitudes toward child-rearing in parents and non-parents. *Psychological Reports*, 1977, *41*, 215-218.

Newhaus, R. H. A study of the effects of the marriage encounter experience of being on personal interaction of married couples. *Dissertation Abstracts International*, 1977, 37, 6793.

Norton, W. K. Jr. *Empathic ability and adjustment in marriage*. Doctoral dissertation, The Florida State University, 1971.

Otto, H. A. (Ed.). *Marriage and Family Enrichment: New Perspectives and Programs*. Nashville: Abingdon, 1976.

Otto, H. A. Marriage and family enrichment programs in North America. *The Family Coordinator*, 1975, *24*, 137-142.

Patterson, C. R. *Families: Applications of Social Learning to Family Life*. Champaign, IL: Research Press, 1971.

Patterson, C. R., & Gullion, M. E. *Living with Children: New Methods for Parents and Teachers*. Champaign, IL: Research Press, 1963.

Phillips, E. L. *The Social Skills Basis of Psychopathology: Alternatives to Abnormal Psychology and Psychiatry*. New York: Grune & Stratton, 1978.

Phillips, L. *Human Adaptation and its Failures*. New York: Academic Press, 1968.

Pierce, R. N. Training in interpersonal communication skills with partners of deteriorating marriages. *The Family Coordinator*, 1973, *22*, 223-337.

Rappaport, A. F. *The effects of an intensive conjugal relationship modification program*. Doctoral dissertation, The Pennsylvania State University, 1971.

Raush, H. L., Barry, W. A., Hertel, R. K., & Swain, M. A. *Communication, Conflict and Marriage*. San Francisco: Jossey-Bass, 1974.

Raush, H. L., Greif, A. C., & Nugent, J. Communication in couples and families. In: W. R. Burr, R. Hill, F. I. Nye, & I. L. Reiss (Eds.), *Contemporary Theories about the Family: Research-Based Theories. Vol. I*. New York: Free Press, 1979. Pp. 468-489.

Rimm, R. C., & Markle, A. Parent effectiveness training: A review. *Psychological Reports*, 1977, *41*, 59-109.

Rogers, C. R. *Client-Centered Therapy*. Boston: Houghton-Mifflin, 1951.

Sawin, M. *Family Enrichment with Family Clusters*. Valley Forge, PA: Judson Press, 1979.

Schlein, S. P. *Training dating couples in empathic and open communication: An experimental evaluation of a potential mental health program*. Ph.D. dissertation, Pennsylvania State University, 1971.

Smith, R. M., Shoffner, S. M., & Scott, J. P. Marriage and family enrichment: A new professional area. *The Family Coordinator*, 1979, *28*, 87-93.

Spivack, G., Platt, J., & Shure, M. *Problem Solving Approach to Adjustment*. San Francisco: Jossey-Bass, 1976.

Stedman, J. M., Patton, W. F., & Walton, K. F. (Eds.). *Clinical Studies in Behavior Therapy with Children, Adolescents and their Families*. Springfield, IL: Charles C Thomas, 1973.

Travis, R. P., & Travis, P. Y. Self-actualization in marital enrichment. *Journal of Marriage and Family Counseling*, 1976, 2, 73-80. (a)

Travis, R. P., & Travis, P. Y. A note on changes in the caring relationship following a marriage enrichment program and some preliminary findings. *Journal of Marriage and Family Counseling*, 1976, 2, 81-83. (b)

Travis, P., & Travis, R. The pairing enrichment program: Actualizing the marriage. *The Family Coordinator*, 1975, *24*, 161-165. (a)

Travis, P., & Travis, R. Marital health and marriage enrichment. *Alabama Journal of Medical Sciences*, 1975, *12*, 172-176. (b)

Van Zoost, B. Premarital communication skills education with university students. *The Family Coordinator*, 1973, 22, 187-191.

Wieman, K. J. *Conjugal relationship modification and reciprocal reinforcement: A comparison of treatments for marital discord*. Doctoral dissertation, The Pennsylvania State University, 1973.

Weiss, R. L. The conceptualization of marriage from a behavioral perspective. In: T. J. Paolino & B. S. McCrady (Eds.), *Marriage and Marital Therapy: Psychoanalytic, Behavioral, and Systems Theory Perspectives*. New York: Brunner/Mazel, 1978. Pp. 165-239.

Wildman, R. W. Structured vs. unstructured marital interventions. In: L. L'Abate, *Enrichment: Structured Interventions with Couples, Families, and Groups.* Washington, D. C.: University Press of America, 1977. Pp. 154-183.

Wright, L., & L'Abate, L. Four approaches to family facilitation: Some issues and implications. *The Family Coordinator*, 1977, *26,* 176-181.

EDITORS' REFERENCES

De Young, A.J. Marriage encounter: A critical examination. *Journal of Marital and Family Therapy*, 1979, *5,* 27-34.

Ford, J.D., Bashford, M.B., & DeWitt, K.N. *Prediction of outcome in behavioral-communication approaches to marital enrichment.* Unpublished paper, University of Delaware, 1979.

Gurman, A.S. & Kniskern, D.P. Marriage therapy and/or family therapy: What's in a name? *American Association for Marriage and Family and Therapy Newsletter*, 1979, *10*(3), 1, 5-8.

Gurman, A.S., Razin, A.M. *Effective Psychotherapy: A Handbook of Research.* New York: Pergamon, 1977.

Knight, N.A. The effects of changes in family interpersonal relationships on the behavior of enuretic children and their parents. Doctoral dissertation, University of Hawaii, 1974. (*Dissertation Abstracts International*, 1975, *36,* 783A.)

CHAPTER 18

Divorce and
Divorce Therapy

Florence W. Kaslow, Ph.D.

Traditionally, marriage vows contained a pledge of mutual commitment to stay wed "through sickness and in health" and promises about loving, honoring, protecting and cherishing. Marriage was entered into seriously and was to last as long as the partners lived; it was expected that when problems and misfortunes arose, which inevitably would happen, the couple would deal with and triumph over them. People settled into "making marriage work" and accepted, sometimes stoically, that they could not always have their own way and they would not always be happy. This attitude was reinforced by their own parents and by most churches, and reflected a widely held societal expectation.

In the United States, one might romantically speak of falling in love and getting married to the mate of one's own choice, rather than of entering into a marriage arranged by parents or marriage brokers, as was customary in some other countries. The covenant was considered an eternal bond and each partner was destined to make the most of it. With no viable alternatives, most couples settled into the routine of monogamous marriage, work, bearing and rearing children, and some family and or couple social activity. Some became involved in community affairs, sports, politics and cultural events, but marriage and the family were considered essential components of normalcy and the good life in adulthood. As recently as the 1960s, to remain unmarried beyond a certain age—often set at around 25 years, made a woman a "spinster" or "old maid," terms connoting that no man wanted her. For a man to be single past 30 years of age meant that perhaps he was "strange," overly finicky, or still "tied to mama's apron strings." And to be divorced made one something of a social outcast.

In the last decade, the scenario has changed radically. Marriage no longer is considered to be so permanent—"till death do us part" has been replaced with "till death of the marriage parts us." This chapter will look at the contemporary scene regarding divorce and divorce therapy by reviewing selectively the main contributions to the literature and to the practice of divorce therapy. I have attempted to critique and synthesize the literature from my perspective as a teacher, therapist, and supervisor engaged in working with couples and families going through the marital dissolution process. In this way, I am responding to Kressel and Deutsch's well taken point (1977, p. 414) that "no systematic, critical review of the literature exists" and that one is clearly needed.

The following topical areas will be covered in this chapter: 1) divorce statistics; 2) factors leading to divorce; 3) stages of the divorce process; 4) the impact of divorce on children—a look at custody and visitation arrangements, support payments, object loss, and loyalty conflicts; 5) intervention strategies, including contact with other professionals and efficacy as documented in the research literature; 6) the aftermath of divorce; 7) research on divorce therapy; 8) training of the divorce therapist; 9) a diaclectic summation.

Most of the relevant literature about divorce has been written for the layperson (e.g., Fisher, 1974; Hyatt, 1977; Johnson, 1977; Krantzler, 1974) rather than for professional therapists, and most of these publications have appeared in the 1970s. The numerous articles in professional journals discussing "stage theories" of the divorce process have also appeared largely in the past decade (e.g., Bohannan, 1973; Froiland and Hozman, 1977; Kessler, 1975; Wiseman, 1975). This chapter will build upon and go beyond Salts' (1979) comparative analysis of the major models of the divorce process. Stage theory will then be interwoven with Vines' (1979) theoretical framework for analyzing marital conflict in the context of adult development.

My approach to therapy is a "diaclectic" one—culling out from divergent approaches what seem to be the most efficacious strategies and melding these into a new synthesis—a dialectical and eclectic formulation. The "diaclectic model" reflects my professional roots in analytic, humanistic-existential and structural theories and techniques.

DIVORCE STATISTICS: THE MAGNITUDE OF THE SITUATION

According to The National Center for Health Statistics (1976, 1977a), in 1976, 2,133,000 marriages were entered into and 1,077,000 divorces were granted. Given that two adults are parties in each divorce action and that each couple had, at that time, an average of 1.08 children, over three million individuals were involved in and affected by the dissolution of marriages in 1976.[1]

While the number of divorces accelerated from 1963 to 1968 at an average annual rate of 5% per year, and while from 1968 to 1976 the average rate of increase jumped to 8%, the annual marriage rate began decreasing in 1972. In 1970, 6.9% of ever-married individuals in the 25-54-year age bracket were either separated or divorced; by 1975 the figure had climbed to 10.1%. Other trends noted by demographers in the late 1970s are that the age of first marriage increased by approximately 10½ months during the decade from 1966-1976, that is, for females from 20.6 to 21.3 years and for males from 22.8 to 23.8 years. Further, the median duration of marriages which terminate in divorce declined from 7.5 years in 1963 to 7.0 years in 1967 and 6.5 years in 1975 (U.S. Bureau of Census, 1976, 1977). In addition to the trends of later marriages, shorter duration of those that end in divorce, and a higher percentage terminating in legal dissolution, there is evidence that there is a higher than average probability that children of divorced parents will have their own marriages terminate in separation or divorce (Pope and Mueller, 1976). Thus, those interested in "the family" as a viable and valuable institution for child-bearing and child-rearing, gratification of affective needs of all members of the family unit, object constancy and mutuality, fun and companionship, continuity and security, a base from which to explore one's own unique identity and interests, and as a safe launching pad for future generations must be concerned about the reasons for and implications of these trends.

Although I do not equate divorce with dysfunction, it does appear that the decision to divorce is an attempt to extricate oneself from a trying, conflicted or unsatisfying relationship. It may well be a flight toward health—a seeking to escape from a living arrangement that has ceased to be tolerable and fulfilling.

---

[1]*Editors' Note.* In addition, 40% of the children born in the 1970s spent part of their childhood in single-parent homes, approximately 17% of children currently live in single-parent homes, and about 18 million children are living with step-parents (Martin, 1979).

FACTORS LEADING TO DIVORCE

The prince and princess meet and fall in love—totally, passionately, unequivocally; they get married, promising to love, honor and cherish—'til death do us part. So sayeth our fairytales, our folklore, and our childhood dreams. The scenario often ends there, with a fade-out, deftly implying or overtly stating, "and they lived happily ever after." Unfortunately, too rarely have the prince and princess incorporated the essence of what "living happily ever after" is about—both that it is an impossible dream and that happiness does not just happen magically as falling in love may have (or had the illusion of). Rather, it is something that must be built out of caring, consideration, communication, concern, playfulness, spontaneity, disagreements resolved and many more complex ingredients. If they were fortunate enough to have each come from families of origin where their parents were reasonably well matched and generally content with each other, then they are likely to have solid role models to emulate and to have internalized ways of living that balance the I, Thou and We needs and desires. To have lived during their childhood and adolescence in a home where reciprocity, mutuality, individuality and closeness all played a part is to have been lucky and to be a "good marital risk," as those who come from healthy families have the highest likelihood of creating successful marriages.

But, all too few people come from healthy families; many come from midrange or dysfunctional ones (Lewis, Beavers, Gossett and Phillips, 1976)[2] and their emotional heritage may include child abuse, chaos, continual unresolved tension and conflict, rigidity, role stereotyping, an alcoholic parent, and/or an erratic or mentally ill parent. As has been depicted so well in the literature on the world of abnormal rearing (WAR) (Kempe and Helfer, 1972), children who are abused are also usually deprived of sufficient and consistent nurturing, are and feel rejected and undeserving, and do not store up a sufficient reservoir of emotional supplies to be able to give to another on a sustained and rich basis. In their

quest for love, affection and affirmation, and in their desperation to leave a turmoil-ridden home, they often marry young, finding and clinging to someone who is likely to come from a similarly tumultuous and emotionally inadequate family. Like any other prince and princess under the spell of love and desire, they appear, at least briefly, beautiful and wonderful to one another. They, too, promise to take care of one another, to assuage all the old hurts and unfulfilled longings, to belong to one another and to protect each other from the harsh external world. Most enter marriage young and hopeful, truly wanting something better than their parents had; also, if they are in their teens, which is often the case with those who were abused, they are in a rebellious period in terms of lifecycle development (Vines, 1979) and are determined to fashion something very different for themselves.

Although those who have been abused might seem an extreme example, they are prototypical of many who grow up in dysfunctional homes that lack harmony, families that stifle growth and individuality and do not know how to play and live together at a level of satisfaction that makes life interesting and meaningful. Marriage then frequently represents an escape from an intolerable situation rather than a joyous going into a new phase of development.

As Markowitz and Kadis (1972) point out, many couples who run into severe marital discord are reexperiencing and reenacting in the present the "spouses' residual characterological problems originating in early familial experience" (p. 463). In the time-limited (ten weeks) couples groups they co-led, the majority of their patients (five couples in each group) perceived one parent as much stronger and more involved than the other; usually the constellation described was of a strong mother and a weak or absent father. Most of their patients entered marriage needing or wanting to perpetuate the dependence, resulting from an "unweaned state," onto their new partner. Many engaged in egosplitting, resulting usually from seeing the mother as all good and as supplying unlimited gratification, and the father as all bad, absent and ineffective and, therefore, as not there to provide the essential discipline and limitation of satisfaction which represents the reality prin-

---

[2]*Editors' Note.* For a fuller description of the differences among these family categories, see Skynner (Chapter 2).

ciple. Thus, their growth proceeded primarily by seeking instant gratification (pleasure principle) through impulsive acting-out untempered by development of good reality-testing and the ability to sometimes delay satisfaction in favor of pursuing long-range goals. Upon entering marriage, the fantasy is that their beloved will magically fulfill all of their grandiose expectations and complete missing parts of themselves. This is heightened by promises made during the intensive dating or premarital living together period that they will be everything the other needs and wants, that their love will conquer all, and that they will caress away all the old hurts and build a glorious life together.

Unfortunately, such guarantees and high expectations are difficult, if not impossible, to deliver. The romance of such rainbow-hued dreams can be retained and rooted solidly in a sounder understanding of what each really brings to and expects from the union if the couple seeks high quality premarital counseling—complete with physical examinations so that they become more fully aware of each other's biological and psychological family history, value and belief systems, goals in marriage, and attitudes about having and caring for children (Trainer, 1979).[3] Involvement of both sets of parents in one or two conjoint premarital sessions with the young couple enables them to learn more about the family they are marrying into and gives the parents a chance to make a commitment to support, yet not interfere with, the young couple.

Another way to explore one another's aspirations, intentions and areas of concern is to work together on creating a formal marriage contract either prior to the wedding or anytime thereafter. I encourage the partners to write part of their own wedding ceremony to personalize their vows. Sager (1976) addresses contracting as a dynamic and ongoing process and describes how it can facilitate both the marital relationship and, if entered into, their marital therapy.[4]

But most couples neither seek premarital counseling nor evolve their own unique contracts. They enter wedlock much more haphazardly, with a combination of stated, conscious longings and demands and unconscious needs and desires. Since the level of expectation and promise is extremely high, each partner is usually unable to fulfill the other's deeply felt desire for a spouse who is simultaneiously and/or sequentially several or all of the following: a nurturing parent, a sensuous lover, a dependent child, an erudite friend, a fun-loving companion, a stern prodder who sometimes insists he/she does resented chores, a partner in rebellion against parents and other authority figures, a good listener, an ego-booster, a rescuer or a sparring partner. Inevitably, disappointment over unkept promises and (sometimes insatiable) unmet needs leads to disillusionment, frustration and anger.

Some partners intuitively know how to tune into each other's annoyance, perhaps because they came from healthy families in which they had learned to be empathic as well as self-actualizing. When such is the situation, they deal with the disappointment which ensues when their idealized version of marriage fails to materialize, can laugh about their misconceptions, and can begin to appreciate what they really have to offer each other. They are then free to build a wholesome, durable relationship that can handle stress, accept that anger is a part of intimacy, and share rather than repress a wide spectrum of feelings.

A second group of couples, who did not acquire as sound a foundation of interpersonal relationship skills in their families of origin, have the love, determination and flexibility to enter into a thoughtful and sensitive type of give-and-take relationship and communication, leading to mutual trust and respect and toward a viable process for handling hurt, upset and irritation. These first two groups of couples are those who tend not to seek therapy; however, increasingly they are found in marriage enrichment groups (L'Abate, 1974, Chapter 17, this volume; Mace and Mace, 1977).

It is a third group that is of concern here—those who cannot alter their fallacious expectations to be more congruent with the reality of who and what they and their spouse are. Their sense of

---

[3]*Editors' Note.* Given the idealization and perceptual blinders that characterize most couples in this stage of their relationship, we think that conservative expectations of the power of premarital counseling are appropriate. Nonetheless, empirical research in this domain is almost non-existent and is certainly called for (Gurman and Kniskern, 1977).

[4]*Editors' Note.* Also see Sager (Chapter 3) in this volume.

again being short-changed exacerbates the earlier feelings of deprivation, depression and rage. They often cannot forgive their mate for promising so much, yet delivering so little. And so, rather than living happily ever after, the prince and princess are transformed into an irate, quarrelsome duo, or one becomes combative while the other retreats into silence, or they develop a generalized pattern of avoidance by going their separate ways physically and distancing emotionally. *The seeds for marital dissolution may be sown quite early in the history of the couple.*

Operating on the assumption that someone who is relatively "healthy" emotionally tends to attract and be attracted by someone else who functions quite well, has an optimistic life view, and is capable of making a commitment to a primary love relationship, leads us to note that often individuals who fall into categories broadly labeled personality disorders, severe neurosis, and psychosis also tend to select partners with similar or reciprocal dysfunctional patterns. (Eisenstein, 1956; Rubenstein and Timmins, 1978).[5]

A similar theme appears in Napier (1978). He discusses "the rejection-intrusion pattern" as a central dynamic rooted in each individual's respective family of origin. The pattern, common to marital breakdown, is characterized by one partner seeking "closeness and reassurance while the other desires separateness and independence. . . . One partner is seen as having been rejected or abandoned as a child, while the other was intruded upon or engulfed by the parents. The polarized pattern which later develops in marriage serves the purposes of identity definition, intimacy regulation and defense against covert anxieties" (p. 5).

These are just a few of the pathological interactions that may surface. Others that have been identified are sadomasochism, dominance-submission, and ambitiousness-lethargy. The discontent may be experienced almost from the outset of the marriage and the battleground may be such familiar turf as earning and handling money, in-laws, sex, where to live, whether to have children and, if so, how many, or dual-career conflicts.

In other marriages, the newlyweds are reasonably content until their freedom is reduced when the first child is born and their relatively carefree ways are interrupted by having a "little tyrant" in the home who demands constant attention. They may not be willing to assume parental roles or may not have a sufficient emotional reservoir to be nurturing, without feeling depleted by and resentful of the baby. Often, one parent may even view the infant as a rival for the spouse's attention. At times, this reaction is justified as one parent becomes symbiotically enmeshed with the baby, crossing generational boundaries (Minuchin, 1974) and transferring the libidinal attachment from parent to child. The neglected spouse may sulk quietly, balk openly, or seek comfort in an extramarital affair. As he or she withdraws from the action, the parent-child bonding becomes even tighter. Such enmeshment may become the forerunner of schizophrenia (Bateson, Jackson, Haley and Weakland, 1956). This strain taxes the tenuous ties of the marriage, yet may also serve to create an undifferentiated family ego mass (Bowen, 1978) which can be experienced as a smothering veil.

There are numerous other exigencies that place stress on the marital pair. For example, if a child is born with a mental or physical handicap, the parents may resort to self-castigation, guilt or blaming of the other as they seek an explanation for this misfortune (Abrams and Kaslow, 1976). The afflicted child is a constant reminder that their lovemaking did not produce a perfect child. Death of a child, birth of more children than the couple can handle, loss of a job, a job offer out of town for one partner while the other has a fine job or strong family ties and does not care to relocate are just a few of the unanticipated reality problems that contribute to severe marital tension. When they are combined with intrapsychic difficulties, the prospect of the marriage's survival decreases.

Many couples stay together for long periods of time despite a ubiquitous cloud of discontent, rationalizing that "no marriage is all that great," or that "it's better for the children to grow up in an intact family." One or both may sublimate in work, sports, hobbies, or volunteer activities. But eventually, the children grow up and move out and the couple is confronted with thoughts of "is this all there is?" "I do not have all that

---

[5]*Editors' Note.* Of course, the diagnostic categories into which spouses fall is far less informative for clinical practice than is the interplay of the partners' defensive structures.

many years left and I'm entitled to something for me." "I no longer care to live in this intolerable hell." "I've sacrificed long enough and now it is my turn to do my thing."

Some spouses grow in very different directions and eventually have too little left in common to appeal to one another. One may have blossomed and achieved a great deal while the other has virtually stagnated. Sometimes, one partner meets another person and becomes emotionally and sexually involved in an affair. This can either serve as a catalyst to heat up the marital war (Napier and Whitaker, 1978), so that the battle is waged with renewed vigor and some of what is learned in the affair is brought back to the marriage to enliven it, or propel the couple into therapy as a way of enlisting a neutral third party to help them improve their troubled relationship. Conversely, the affair may trigger the demise of the marriage. One partner may decide he/she will not, under any circumstances, remain in the marriage; he/she is eager for a divorce and wants to quickly remarry, or at least move in with his/her lover. Or the "spurned" partner may be unwilling to tolerate sharing his/her spouse with a lover and, in delivering an ultimatum, sever the marital bond.

One additional intriguing idea about psychodynamic factors which precipitate divorce bears mentioning. In ordinary conversation, in nightclub acts, and even in therapists' offices, in-laws are fair game for criticism and derision. They are often portrayed as interfering people and described as the enemy. Lager (1977) presents a markedly different perspective growing out of his analytic practice with individual patients who become depressed and/or seriously contemplate divorce following the death of an in-law parent. His thesis is that in those cases when there has been a strong devotion to the lost in-law parent, the distraught person was drawn to his/her eventual spouse partially because either or both potential in-law parents represented a "second chance family." The individual, at some level, sensed that this person could provide much that was missing in his/her own parent(s) or in the quality of his relationship with them. Thus, the marriage was, in effect, a package deal.[6] If, during the course of the marriage, the

in-law parent became the sought-after parent substitute, this served a solidifying function. The in-law parent's death triggers a great sense of abandonment and much grief which serve as precipitants of the depression. Following the loss of a critical element in the package, the marriage no longer appears viable and divorce is sought.

Sociological explanations of the rising divorce rate approach this phenomenon using different vocabulary but illuminate similar causative factors. Goetting (1978) presents five interrelated components in the social structure of the United States which are contributing factors: 1) the doctrine of individualism; 2) the trend toward equality of the sexes; 3) the trend toward acceptance of divorce; 4) growing systemness, and 5) affluence. Not only can the upper-middle and upper classes better afford divorce, but, as Nye and Berardo (1973) point out, so can the lower classes, since some costs are picked up by society in the form of Aid to Dependent Children and Food Stamps.[7] Also, with the increasing availability of low cost legal services for lower income people, the financial cost of divorce is no longer quite so prohibitive.

In concluding this section, it seems important to underscore the perspective that each individual brings to marriage his/her unique set of needs, expectations, goals and capacities, that these are multidetermined and deep-seated, and that they may not blend happily. During the course of marriage, people continue to develop and change and may grow in ways that are no longer complementary or parallel. They then may seek to dissolve their union.

STAGES OF THE DIVORCE PROCESS

In the past decade, several models of stages in the divorce precocess have been developed. These range from Weiss' (1976) two-stage progression of 1) transition and 2) recovery, through Bohannan's (1973) theory of a six-station process and Kessler's (1975) elaborate seven-stage model. Salts (1979) has offered a comparative analysis

---

[6]*Editors' Note.* Or, as Carl Whitaker has put it, "one of the biggest myths about marriage is to say, 'I didn't marry your family.' "

[7]*Editors' Note.* This growing awareness of the impact of public policy on the family, including marriage and divorce, has recently led to the publication of a special issue of the *Journal of Marriage and the Family* (1979) devoted entirely to this subject.

of these and several other models and suggested what "counseling direction" is indicated at each stage. A different approach is being utilized here. Initially, several of the models selected as most salient are discussed. In so doing, I draw on my own clinical observations to elaborate, extend or disagree with these conceptualizations. Then I integrate, elaborate and refine stage theory into a more comprehensive one with clearer clinical implications. Intervention strategies are dealt with later and interwoven with stage theory.

Of the models selected for discussion, Bohannan's (1973) is the earliest in published time sequence and one of the most clearly delineated. He captures the complexity of divorce as a traumatic personal experience and as a social phenomenon of increasing magnitude. He highlights that, on both the individual and societal levels, the customary way of dealing with trauma is to attempt to deny it, and then, if it does not disappear, to allow it into consciousness slowly so that it is more manageable. He indicates that his six "stations" may occur in varying sequences and at different intensities, but that inevitably each is experienced before, during or after separation. The pain and confusion felt by the individual are heightened because our society is ill equipped to handle it. Few guidelines or ceremonies are available to facilitate each transitional marker event and its accompanying emotions.

Bohannan's first station, *emotional divorce*, begins when the spouses become increasingly aware of feeling discontented and dissatisfied; they realize the marriage is deteriorating and the level of trust plummets. They focus more on the negative than the positive aspects of their relationship and may become hypercritical. One spouse may indicate that, if matters do not improve, he/she will leave. If the spouses can at this point air their grievances with one another and each take responsibility for changing some of their most irritating behaviors or modifying their expectations, then it is possible that the disenchantment can be reversed. Or, if therapy is sought at this point, both may be receptive and committed to making things better. But if this does not occur and the emotional divorce becomes more pervasive, the partners experience the grief that accompanies loss of a (former) love object. In continuing to live together, they

experience daily rejection, the knowledge of not being desired or cherished, and frequently a diminution of sexual and other sharing activities occurs. Not all couples cease sleeping together and/or having a sexual relationship. Some continue engaging in sexual activities despite their avowed dislike of one another—either out of habit and a disbelief that they are really about to "break up," or because they still "turn each other on" sexually and do not care to do without physical satisfaction despite the fact that in most other areas they find it difficult to tolerate one another. And, of course, sometimes one may use his/her sexuality as a way of trying to overcome the distance and reactivate the love.

Bohannan's second station is *legal divorce*. Divorce law in some states still reflects a tradition several centuries old in which the state expresses its interest in the institution of marriage through its adversarial procedures. One party is considered innocent and the other guilty; that is, one is at fault. The state assumes responsibility for punishing the guilty party and seeing that the injured, innocent person is awarded some settlement as compensation. Two people cannot, as they originally did when they decided to marry, merely agree to a divorce and set their own date for the event. Instead, each must be represented by his/her respective legal counsel whose role it is to advocate for his/her best interest. Often the legal action becomes quite embittered and escalates the marital war. Finances, custody, and/or jealousy over a new love object the spouse has become attracted to are major battlegrounds. But one must file for divorce on "grounds" acceptable within their state of residence and prepare a bill of particulars. To prove adultery may mean hiring a detective. This indeed makes the legal divorce phase a trying time.

Since Bohannan originally wrote his article, one major and significant change has occurred. Numerous states have enacted "no-fault" divorce laws. Often the proviso is that there be a designated waiting period from the time of the original declaration of intent to divorce until the final action. Some states mandate counseling during this time.[8] If, at the end of the cooling

---

[8]*Editors' Note.* Unfortunately, in most states, the required counseling is perfunctory and often little more than ritualistic. In fact, it seems doubtful to us whether, in most cases, it is possible to mandate a meaningful psychotherapy.

off period, the spouses still want to dissolve their marriage, the court is likely to consent. No fault is ascribed to either party. Where community property laws have been enacted along with no fault laws, everything material is split evenly. In states without community property laws, decisions still have to be made on who gets what. And custody remains a burning issue. The advent of the feminist movement and the press for equality has also had its impact on decisions in divorce cases. Men are more frequently petitioning the court to be the custodial parent or at least to be awarded joint or co-custody (cf. the *Family Advocate*, 1978, which devoted an entire issue to this topic). When the father is awarded primary custody and the mother is earning a substantial income, she may be asked to make support payments to her ex-husband. If she is granted custody and is working, her ex-husband may be told to contribute much less than formerly since she and the children are less dependent on his financial support. It is, therefore, not uncommon now for a woman's attorney to advise her to stop working during the process of legal divorce, so that she no lonnger shows an income, and to do so on the grounds that the divorce action has been so upsetting to her and the children that she has been unable to concentrate on her job while trying to stabilize matters at home. Such tactics are geared to playing on the judge's sympathies. Ironically, it is precisely at this juncture that many women need to find a job or remain in an existing position, as the structure and adult companionship of the workaday world help them maintain some semblance of continuity in their lives, and work represents an area of adequate functioning which contributes to maintaining some self-esteem. Thus, to quit work might make legal sense, but could be psychologically injurious and the manipulative tactics may be contrary to one's ethical precepts. This type of conflict arises in many spheres of the divorce process. Collaboration between divorce therapist and matrimonial lawyer can be useful in exploring the deception recommended and its broader implications.

Bohannon states that since the practice of divorce law is one of the "messiest" and "dirtiest" (1973, p. 181), it is low in the hierarchy of specializations in legal practice. Fees are less than in other areas of law, time in court for a divorce hearing—after much investigation and preparation—is brief, and after the divorce is concluded, the client may continue to call about nonpayment of support checks, conflict over child visitation and numerous other grievances. Judges who sit in divorce court have full dockets and often feel frustrated by their lack of adequate time to devote to each case.

There have been some important professional changes in the past few years relevant to these issues. The Mental Health and Family Law Divisions of the American Bar Association (ABA) and of some state Bar Associations have been giving increasing attention to humanizing divorce laws and divorce and custody proceedings. The Family Law Division of ABA began publishing the *Family Advocate* in 1978; its editorial policy is to collaborate with professionals from many disciplines who are interested in the family. In some states, there are groups of matrimonial lawyers engaged in sharing their common concerns, refining their practice and upgrading their image. Some law firms now have one or several attorneys who prefer domestic relations cases and become expert in this arena of law.

Areen's (1978) casebook details several divorce cases from the vantage point of different attorneys and illuminates some of the legal intricacies with which mental health professionals might wish to become conversant. She cogently discusses traditional fault grounds and defenses, no fault divorce, alternative dissolution procedures, and the divorce procedure per se. The ethical problems facing divorce lawyers are highlighted, evidentiary problems are presented and there is an informative discussion on providing the poor with access to divorce.

Bohannon's third station is the *economic divorce*, which he views as distinct from the legal divorce. This deals with division of property, the settlement at the time the legal divorce is finalized, alimony and child support payments. What is permissible and required varies from state to state. For example, some jurisdictions have community property laws while others do not; some require alimony payments to the ex-wife for as long as she lives; other states have done away completely with provisions for alimony. Bohannon indicates that, although "in most states the property settlement is not recorded in the public records of divorce, so precise information is lacking, in most settlements the wife receives from one-third to one-half of the property" (1973, p. 482). Unless the amount is quite large, the two lawyers usually negotiate for or with their clients and the settlement details do not surface in the courtroom.

Many other extenuating circumstances can be subsumed under the rubric of "the economic divorce." If the husband is already involved in a serious love affair and is eager for a rapid divorce, he may be willing to offer a generous settlement to assuage his guilt, buy his way out quickly, and continue to fulfill his commitment to his prior family. Conversely, if the wife is eager to be free of her husband because her new lover is waiting in the wings for her and finances will not pose a major problem when she remarries, she may settle for a smaller amount than she might get by biding her time. Other factors include 1) the veracity of one's income tax return and what might come to light in a legal battle, 2) how much a wife feels entitled to for the years she invested as a homemaker, and/or as the major family income producer while her husband completed school, or because she "sacrificed" her education or career in deference to his pursuits. Each is concerned with dividing the bounty in relation to past financial and emotional inputs, their current life-style, and desires to live as well as possible in the future. Some women want all they can possible get; others prefer nothing as that gives them more autonomy and freedom and helps close the door on the relationship.

Coparental divorce and the problem of custody constitute Bohannan's fourth station. He uses the term "coparental" to designate that although the adults are divorcing one another, neither is getting divorced from their parental relationship to the child. Since the marital failure shatters the kinship circle of the child, this is an unsettling period at best and a debilitating one at worst.

Although, in the early centuries of this country's history, children were considered property of the father and remained with him in the event of a divorce, there was a radical shift in the early 20th century when the doctrine of the "tender years" was espoused. That is, it was felt that a child belonged with his/her mother at least until age seven unless she was unfit because of severe mental illness or moral turpitude. As recently at 1973 (Areen, 1978, p. 536), an analysis of judicial decrees revealed that "although in theory, a father has an equal right . . . to the custody of his children, in well over 90% of the cases adjudicated, the mother is awarded custody." This may also be attributable to the fact that the courts were influenced by the thinking of developmental and ego psychologists who stressed the importance of nurturance and object constancy (Fairbairn, 1952) and it was generally agreed that mothers were better able to provide this than fathers, who were in all likelihood out of the home more hours each day earning a living.

Once custody is granted to one parent, it is rare that the decree will be changed. It requires a new hearing and custody will only be transferred to the other parent if it can be proven that the original custodial parent has been seriously delinquent in his/her parental role.

The doctrines of "the best interest of the child" and the "least detrimental alternative" standard have come into prominence in recent years (Goldstein, Freud and Solnit, 1973) and have influenced thinking in judicial as well as mental health circles. What constitutes "the best interest," however, is highly controversial. Freud, Solnit and Goldstein take the stance that consistency and object constancy are of paramount import and that if visits by the noncustodial parent are anxiety-producing or in other ways detrimental to the child, then the custodial parent should be able to end the visitations, thereby dispensing with the periodic disruption. They see the custodial parent's authority to make such a decision as superseding even the court's perogative in this area; for most family therapists, such a position is too extreme and rarely warranted.

Boszormenyi-Nagy and Spark (1973) intepret the "best interest of the child" in a totally different way. For them, the invisible loyalties inherent in relationships with one's biological parents, no matter who they are or what they have done, have a continuing existential reality and are inviolate.[9] Therefore, by extrapolation, regardless of the circumstances, the child of divorced parents should have ongoing access to

_____

[9]*Editors' Note.* See Boszormenyi-Nagy and Ulrich (Chapter 5) in this volume for an explication of this view.

both parents. My view is that where one parent is to have primary custody, a critical factor in determining which one it should be, assuming that both parents want it and are capable, is which parent is better able to share the child(ren) with the noncustodial parent and to facilitate visitation and phone contact, rather than to impede these.

When the wife is the custodial parent and support payments are a factor, money may be used as leverage, with the woman refusing to allow the father to see the children unless he sends the support checks and comes through with additional amounts when requested. Conversely, some fathers try to buy their children's love with material goods. They may withhold support payments to aggravate their ex-wife, use payments as bargaining power to force her to act in a certain way with the children or to obtain longer or more frequent visitation. Thus, the economic divorce is frequently quite entwined with the custody issue. The combination is fraught with manipulative strategies through which emotional issues get played out and in which lawyers and therapists are apt to get embroiled. The ideals of equity and fairness may be espoused but are more the exception than the rule.

As indicated earlier, more couples have been filing for joint custody in the 1970s. This arrangement, also called co-custody, coparenting and split custody, provides the parents with equal access to the children and takes a variety of forms. The children can spend half a week with each parent or alternate weeks or months. Sometimes the children have a home with each parent and rotate back and forth. In other split families, the parents take turns moving in and out of the family homestead so that the children are not constantly being shuffled around. The smooth functioning of any of these arrangements is contingent upon several factors, e.g., 1) commitment to the idea that both parents are vital to the child; 2) willingness to live in the same geographic area so that the children can attend one school; 3) willingness not to relocate; 4) reasonable flexibility and ability to cooperate with the former mate; 5) ability if they remarry to integrate their children into the subsequent marriage; and 6) willingness not to pry into matters in the other household that are not of direct concern to them. It takes great maturity and lack of residual rancor for co-custody to be a satisfactory arrangement.

Noncustodial fathers frequently report that the overpowering sense of aloneness that accompanies the loss of their spouse and usually of their home and many of their couple friends is made almost unbearable when it also entails forfeiting daily contact with their children. Perhaps co-custody at times also serves the "best interest of the father" in permitting him to retain an active role in his children's lives and the "best interest of the mother," who does not have to carry almost total parental responsibility alone.

Another knotty issue regarding custody decisions merits mention. Occasionally, when a marriage is dissolved, one partner is homosexual. Courts have been struggling with what constitutes "the best interest of the child" when a mother seeks custody and she is living with her homosexual lover. If the non-homosexual father also wants custody, and if he has or is planning to marry another woman, the court must decide if the sexual behavior of a parent should be the prime consideration, and whether a child has the right to two opposite-sex parents. Some key questions are: If seemingly heterosexual couples raise homosexual offspring, might a child not become heterosexual living with homosexual parents? Should being homosexual preclude one's right to raise one's children? The rights issue must be balanced against concepts of child psychology and analytic theory that, for optimal development and resolution of the oedipal conflict and other maturational tasks, a child should have two opposite-sex parents comfortable in their sexual identity who serve as sex-role models.

No matter what the custody arrangements, it takes a long while before everyone accepts and adjusts to the new situation and can juggle the various allegiances and expectations. This is likely to be a process fraught with many unnerving moments and disturbing uncertainties for all.

Bohannan's fifth station is *the community divorce and the problem of loneliness*. As the marriage dissolves, friends of the couple gravitate toward one or the other. To the extent that the pair lived in a social world peopled only by other couples, they no longer fit. Although close friends may include one or the other for a while, there is a tendency to feel like an extra, an unmatched person in a field of dyads. Friends may be willing to arrange dates, but have few single friends. Also, singles and marrieds tend to talk about different topics, frequent different places and move in different orbits. Thus, the newly single-again individual usually has a transitional phase of feeling isolated and of not belonging anywhere until he/she begins to make contact with other single, divorced or widowed people and slowly to build a new social support system and network of friends (Fisher, 1974; Johnson, 1977; Krantzler, 1974).

Perhaps because professional mental health agencies and churches were not quick to offer services to the spiraling numbers of newly divorced people during evenings and weekends when they could attend meetings, self-help groups emerged. Most communities now have some type of Parents Without Partners organization, a Women in Transition group, and apartment complexes that house the new singles (Hunt, 1966) and resemble an adult version of coed college dormitories.

Bohannan's sixth station is *psychic divorce*, when the problem of autonomy must be confronted and mastered. To him this means "the separation of self from the personality and influence of the ex-spouse" (1973, p. 488). He considers this the most difficult divorce because it entails "learning to live without somebody to lean on" (p. 488). Conversely, it also means one is in charge, much more completely, of one's own thoughts and behaviors and must take full responsibility for what occurs. He/she no longer has a partner to scapegoat or complain to or about.

The final resolution occurs after the individual has come to a reasonable understanding of why he/she married, what factors led to the choice of the specific mate, what unresolved intrapsychic difficulties contributed to the marital strife, and what combination of factors led to the divorce. One this hpapens, there can be some equanimity in acceptance of one's current status.

In 1975, Wiseman delineated five stages of emotional crisis in the divorce process: 1) denial; 2) loss and depression; 3) anger and ambivalence; 4) reorientation of life-style and identity; and 5) acceptance and a new level of functioning.

Wiseman's stages approximate those elucidated by Kübler-Ross (1969) in relation to dying and death. What seemed missing in this formulation was the "bargaining," a phenomenon I have observed in about-to-separate patients as the one being rejected pleads for one more chance and promises to change.

Two years later, Froiland and Hozman (1977) adapted Kübler-Ross' stages (1969) in the grieving process to divorce and included bargaining. Their interventions are related to the phases she originally postulated: 1) denial, 2) anger, 3) bargaining, 4) depression, and 5) acceptance. They utilize the standard loss model as the key to understanding the reactions of preadolescent children to their parents' divorce and this served as the theoretical underpinning for their counseling of such children.

Wiseman's (1975) formulation dovetails with that elaborated by Johnson (1977). Johnson presents anecdotal case material to illustrate how individuals move through the states, experiencing all the turmoil which accompanies separation, until they reach the realization that being a single adult can be exciting, interesting and challenging and can become a worthwhile lifestyle. This is contingent upon not dwelling in the past, not ruminating about "if only I had done thus and such" or spending his/her time full of self-pity and recriminations. He depicts the post-divorce period as a time of freedom to be oneself, to choose one's activities and friends, and to create a world of one's own design. He calls this a time of "autonomous adulthood" and delineates a "job description for the single adult" (Johnson, 1977). This includes a list of skills and attributes for autonomous adulthood, what the learning priorities might be, how to break out of one's personal prison, and ways to go about acquiring the requisite skills and attributes to be a self-actualizing single-again adult. Johnson's autonomous adulthood is analogous to Wiseman's (1975) stage of reorientation of lifestyle and identity and his acceptance and new level of functioning. It is also similar to Bohannan's (1973) psychic divorce and Froiland and Hozman's acceptance.

Kessler (1975) utilizes a somewhat different set of stage labels. She identifies seven stages in the continuum from recognition of the marital discord through separation and divorce: 1) disillusionment, 2) erosion, 3) detachment, 4) physical separation, 5) mourning, 6) second adolescence, and 7) hard work.

Kessler's conceptualization begins at an earlier point than any of the other stage theories, as she addresses the dawning awareness of the emotional conflict and tension, what we see as the uncertainty and *disillusionment* about the continued viability and vitality of the relationship, the gnawing doubts about whether they still love one another and want to continue spending their lives together. As this occurs, more of the annoyance with the disappointment in the mate and the relationship begin to surface—to reach consciousness and then be suppressed either out of fear of what voicing these concerns may bring or because of an inability to communicate feelings and needs. However, it is critical to the survival of the marriage, if it is to be a satisfying one, that the festering discontent be aired and resolved. If this does not occur, then the couple moves into the erosion stage and the disharmony becomes more apparent.

In overt and/or covert, verbal and/or nonverbal ways, the dissatisfaction is manifested. It may take the form of critical remarks or of refusal to do what the other requests, or it may be symbolized through avoidance in the form of withdrawal. The male may become impotent or the female non-orgasmic as the emotional hostility gets converted into its psychological correlate, mirroring the withholding and diminution of caring. Some couples remain stuck in this stage of *erosion* for many years—preserving an uneasy and unsatisfactory status quo, with perhaps brief interludes that are less unpleasant and a continuing vague hope that "somehow things will get better." They cling together for a variety of reasons, such as: 1) They dislike the idea of divorce; 2) they do not want to accept that their judgment was poor and they picked the wrong partner, or 3) that initially they were a fine combination but now want something very different in a relationship; 4) they are mortified by the sense of being a failure in a major area of life that divorce signifies to them; 5) they do not want to hurt, disappoint or embarrass their parents or suffer from their disapproval; 6) they feel an obligation to their children to remain a physically intact family and also do not want to face the prospect of either raising the children alone or not being involved in the children's lives on an ongoing basis; 7) the prospect of loneliness, of having to do everything for oneself and of having to adjust to a very different lifestyle is frightening; 8) it may be totally untenable if their religious conviction is that divorce is a sin; 9) they worry about not enough money to go around; and 10) it means finally giving up the "live happily ever after dreams" alluded to earlier.

Ultimately, one partner may feel increasing *detachment* and boredom. Once either mate's commitment to the marriage is substantially decreased over a prolonged period, it is extremely difficult for the other to rekindle any sparks, do anything right or sustain his/her own belief that the union is still a happy one. The spouses' energies may be diverted into work, volunteer activities or sports. As indicated before, one may become symbiotically enmeshed with a child as the primary love object in place of the spouse; the mate is thereby increasingly extruded from the affective life of his/her family and colludes by turning the focus of his/her attention elsewhere. Other patterns which occur are somatization into functional ailments, withdrawal of libidinal cathexes as one becomes depressed, or involvement by one or both in an extramarital affair or a swingers' group. Much of the above process entails engagement with a third person (child or lover), or a third force, such as work. This mechanism of triangulation (Bowen, 1978) is an effort to re-equilibrate a shaky dyadic relationship.

Finally, the situation becomes unbearable and this is when the *physical separation* occurs (Kessler, 1975). All the schemata address this phenomenon in some form; it is one of the most decisive steps in formalizing the schism, providing it is not done only as a threat to intimidate the other into a desired action. Until the past decade, the husband usually moved out, because he most wanted to end the marriage or was already involved in a new relationship and was eager to have his own "bachelor" pad without children running about, or because the expectation was widely held that this was the gentlemanly thing to do. With the advent of the Women's Liberation Movement, some women are moving out; they prefer living in a smaller and more attractive, manageable apartment, or they may no longer care to be a housewife-mother and have decided to leave their husband with the home and children. In situations where the wife wants the separation and the husband refuses to leave, she can choose to either remain in the same household or take full responsibility for implementing her decision by being the partner to depart—an ultimately assertive, autonomous and non-manipulative action. This may be psychologically sound and freeing, but the legal consequences of being charged with "desertion" must be weighed, as must implications regarding custody.

Mourning, Kessler's fifth stage, has been elaborated upon earlier. Suffice it to say here that the sense of loss can be overwhelming as one loses any or all of the following: a spouse, a sex partner, a helpmate, a friend, possibly one's children, in-laws, some of the shared friends who take sides, a home, possessions and a way of life. No matter how tense and odious the situation may have become, it was familiar and there are memories of a better time. In the event that one partner was astonished at the announcement that the other was leaving—a reaction that is hard to believe, as inevitably clues have abounded—or that he/she bitterly fought the breakup as he/she still cherishes the spouse, the overwhelming sense of abandonment is compounded by the rejection.

The death of a spouse is, in many ways, easier to mourn, particularly if the living partner is not plagued with guilt about having been a causative factor. There is a finality in death which is conducive to working through the gief. But death of a marriage, when each realizes its demise was contributed to by both and sought by at least one, is quite another matter. If, in addition, one remains in communication with the ex-spouse around children (who may long to help reunite their family), around finances or a family business venture, or through friends, then the fantasy of it "being the way it used to be" remains alive and the pain of the loss is periodically reactivated. Recovery hinges on mourning the end of the marriage and the many losses entailed so that one can stop living in the past and have his/her energies and thoughts sufficiently freed up to live in the present with some degree of optimism.

Second adolescence, Kessler's sixth stage, is the period in which one feels rejuvenated and comes alive. It is a time of exploring one's needs and interests, of reentering the larger world and expanding one's horizons, of making new friends and reevaluating old ones. Many recently divorced people frantically immerse themselves in the "swinging singles scene" as they seek to prove to themselves that they are attractive and worthwhile. They desperately need to validate their sexuality and may have a series of quick, superficial physical relationships, experimenting sexually with different partners to test how well they perform and to sample the previously taboo smorgasbord of potential partners. Others miss the closeness of being married and want to replace the missing person as quickly as possible. Hyatt (1977) dubs this the "making up for lost time" period when one attempts to leave behind the previous numbness. Eventually, for most, the frenetic pace and surface level pattern lose their appeal and, as self-esteem improves, they become more selective. Johnson (1977) offers many useful suggestions on how to get back into social circulation and discusses concerns surrounding intimacy. Patients to whom I have recommended his book have found it quite helpful.

Hard work is the mainstay of Kessler's seventh stage. This is when one integrates all that has occurred, expresses his/her new identity and values in decisions and behaviors and takes full responsibility for the direction of his/her life. It is now that one has recovered from the psychic trauma, again likes him/herself, perhaps better than before, and feels capable of coping with the present and future. Johnson (1977) sees this as the time when it is possible to form a reasonably long-lasting relationship and make a commitment to it.

Following Erikson (1968), I believe that individuals will cope with experiences of separation and divorce and the numerous accompanying tasks in much the same way that they have coped with other stresses and crises throughout their life-cycle. If they are reasonably levelheaded and self-confident, they will evidence some of the "craziness" which much of the literature indicates is normal for six months to a year in the divorcing population, but will remain functional, will not seriously consider suicide and will be determined to not be destroyed or become overly pessimistic. Those whose general pattern is to somaticize, play helpless, feel hopeless and become desperate are likely to react in these ways in this stage as well.

Each of the stage theories described approaches the process differently, yet there is a tendency to fail to differentiate feelings, behaviors and requisite tasks to be accomplished. In an effort to clarify these domains, Table 1 presents a diaclectic model of stages in the divorce process.

The stages of divorce do not occur in an invariant sequence. Rather, the process is like a roller coaster with alternating highs and lows and periodically a regressive pull back into the relationship to "give it one more try." Many couples do reconcile after a period of separation, sometimes successfully; for others the "one more chance" verifies the impossiblity of continuing. Others vacillate and return to an earlier stage in the process and get fixated there—lingering in anger, self-pity, or despair. Those in this latter group are the ones who never recover, the embittered divorced whose lives are filled with complaints and loneliness, who stay rooted in the past unable to create a meaningful present. They continue to battle in the courts over custody or money, try to force friends and relatives to take their side and see the ex-spouse as an "all bad" deserter. Often, they convey to their children an excessive obligation to make up for the perceived wrongdoing of the parent who left.

The "healthier" divorced individuals who recuperate and live productive and fulfilling lives seem to need approximately two years from the time the separation first occurs until the psychic divorce is complete. The grief work and the adjustment to a new way of life progress slowly. Each person can only proceed at his/her own rhythm according to the music of his/her internal drum beat.

Johnson and Alevizos (1978) recently conducted a cross-sectional study on divorce adjustment. The study sample contained 180 women, and 106 men; 189 were under 35 years of age, and 97 were older than 35. At the time of the testing, only 31 individuals (11.5% of sample) were not dating. There were an equal number of parent and nonparent individuals in the

study. They utilized two instruments in conducting the analysis—the Divorce Survey's Personal Adjustment Scale (PAS) and the Profile of Mood States. All subjects were mailed these instruments within a battery of tests. Reliability estimates for the PAS were high, although the scale correlated poorly with other standard measures of adjustment.

In their preliminary report, Johnson and Alevizos (1978) state that converging evidence from different facets of the study point to several conclusions: (a) The more time since separation, the better the adjustment; (b) re-coupled individuals have higher levels of adjustment, while ratings among daters and nondaters showed no differences; (c) numerous factors which appear to be closely linked to adjustment can be tentatively lumped into a category called disengagement; and (d) enjoyment and comfort in dating and satisfaction with sexual activity contribute positively to adjustment. They found a powerful and significant relationship ($r = .56$, $p < .001$) between disengagement and adjustment on the PAS. Additional positive correlations revealed better adjustment as individuals were less indecisive about divorce ($r = .73$, $p < .001$), had a more neutral attitude toward their ex-spouse, had fewer thoughts of reconciliation ($r = .78$, $p < .001$), had less contact with their ex-spouse ($r = .29$, $p < .001$), felt less pessimistic regarding the future ($r = .55$, $p < .001$), indulged in more satisfactory sex with greater frequency ($r = .27$, $p < .001$), had fewer feelings of guilt and failure ($r = .43$, $p < .001$), developed a positive attitude toward being self-sufficient ($r = .28$, $p < .001$), and were able to remarry.

Their preliminary findings lend support to the importance of disengagement and autonomous functioning in post-divorce adjustment and indicate the potential significance of this for the divorce therapist. Since my clinical observations have led to similar conclusions, this research validation of experiential knowledge is most welcome.

Vines (1979) incorporates relevant knowledge about adult development into an understanding of marital conflict. He assesses contradictory views, such as the view that unfolding is an unqualified index of pathology versus the view that unfolding is an unqualified index of health, and

TABLE 1
Diaclectic Model of Stages in the Divorce
Process

Divorce Stage		Feelings	Requisite Actions and Tasks
Pre-divorce Deliberation Period	I	Disillusionment Dissatisfaction Alienation	Confronting partner Quarreling Seeking therapy Denial
	II	Dread Anguish Ambivalence Shock Emptiness Chaos Inadequacy Low self esteem	Withdrawal (physical and emotional) Pretending all is okay Attempting to win back affection
During-divorce: Litigation Period	III	Depressed Detached Angry Hopelessness Self pity	Bargaining Screaming Threatening Attempting suicide Mourning
	IV	Confusion Fury Sadness Loneliness Relief	Separating physically Filing for legal divorce Considering economic arrangements Considering custody arrangements Grieving and mourning Telling relatives and friends
Post-divorce: Re-equilibration.	V	Optimism Resignation Excitement Curiosity Regret	Finalizing divorce Begin reaching out to new friends Undertaking new activities Stabilizing new life style and daily routine for children
	VI	Acceptance Self confidence Energetic Self worth Wholeness Exhilaration Independence Autonomy	Resynthesis of identity Completing psychic divorce Seeking new love object and making a commitment to some permanency Becoming comfortable with new life-style and friends Helping children accept finality of parents' divorce and their continuing relationship with both parents

indicates that it is neither in all cases. He also shows that sometimes unfolding is a function of changes in the correlation between the individual life-cycle and the marital life-cycle and that they may not proceed at the same pace. Further, he links adult unfolding to stages of moral development (Kohlberg, 1964) pointing out that partners at different levels of moral development will experience a good deal of marital discord as they conflict over values, goals and how to achieve these. Next, he analyzes unfolding as a function of the seasons of a person's life, building on the ideas of Levinson, Darrow, Klein, and Levinson and McKee (1978). Vines states "getting married is a marker event, and the decision to marry and the character of the marital relationship will be highly colored by the developmental tasks which are current at the time." (1978, p. 8). For example, if a man marries when he is 18 or 19 years of age, at the beginning of the early adult transition period, he is usually in the throes of separating from his parents and crystallizing his adult identity. Although he is striving to be self-sufficient and adult, he is not yet prepared for adulthood and is likely to form a relationship with someone on whom he can be dependent to replace the protective-caring-controlling parent(s) he is giving up. He may, therefore, transfer the incomplete struggle with his parents onto his spouse, so that he simultaneously wants to be nurtured yet rebels against her dominance.

Thus, it is important to understand where in the individual life-cycle a person was at the time when he/she selected his/her mate. Vines (1979) provides pertinent material on factors in selection at each stage. What a person seeks in a love relationship and what kind of intimate ties he/she is able to establish are continuing concerns in adult life. To be capable of intimacy one must have achieved "some degree of sexual freedom and some integration of sexuality and affection. If he is to form an enduring, mutually valued marriage, he must become capable of fidelity and commitment" (Vines, 1979, p. 9). Clearly, many individuals who seek to end their marriages may want something very different in their individual life-cycle than their marriage provides, since it may have become stagnant and dull, or their partner may no longer fulfill their current needs or share their changed val-

ues. To understand the dynamic quality of the individual life-cycle (Vaillant, 1977) enables one to comprehend more fully why so many people ultimately seek recourse to divorce—their marriage has ceased contributing to their adult unfolding and they are unable to successfully renegoiate the marital contract.

Within the adult developmental context of the work by Vaillant (1977), Levinson et al. (1978), and Vines (1979), it is easier to understand the late divorce phenomena discussed by Deckert and Langelier (1978). They studied the causes and impact of ending 20-year or longer marriages among 427 residents of Quebec, Canada. The experimental group consisted of 229 late divorced individuals; 198 long-term marrieds made up the control group. Mean age of subjects was 50.09 years. Among their most significant findings were that:

1) Late divorce occurs more often in traditional than in companionship type marriages.
2) Divorce was rated higher than any other major life event in terms of causing stress by both divorced and married subjects.
3) Late divorced females reported a significantly greater increase in independence and self-confidence than the late divorced males did.
4) The most frequently reported "real" causes of divorce were "multiple" and/or adultery, with 75% of divorced respondents reporting long-term marital unhappiness.
5) The decision to divorce was made over a period of two years or more by the majority of subjects.
6) Half of the subjects delayed the decision to divorce because of the ages of the children.
7) Many experience relief as well as stress as they become free of old sets of values, worries and unsatisfying interactional patterns.

Much of the literature on divorce bears a "gloom and doom" overcast and reflects a pervasive view that divorce is wrong, that someone who wants to terminate a marriage is sick or irresponsible, and that the high divorce rate reflects an immoral and selfish society. At the other extreme, there is the work of Krantzler (1974) and, in some respects, Johnson (1977), who portray a romantic and glamorous version of divorce. No doubt the reality covers the entire spectrum, with some people finding everything associated with divorce traumatic and horrendous and others turning it into a liberating growth experience.

THE IMPACT OF DIVORCE ON THE CHILDREN

Many couples are quite concerned about the effect of their conflicts and quarrels on the children and attempt to shield them as much as possible. Those who have less ego strength and ability to be concerned about the well-being of others draw the children into the fray, expecting them to take sides and perhaps even to protect them from an irate spouse's wrath. Children are sometimes used as the glue to keep the marriage together, so that a child might serve as a tearful go-between to plead with the parent who is desirous of leaving to stay because the family cannot survive without him or her. At a less conscious level, a child may become disruptive or manifest any one of a number of alarming behaviors or symptoms whenever the parents begin to argue. In this way he/she diverts their attention from the marital strife, deflects it onto him/herself and temporarily unites the parents as they discipline or minister to his/her needs. This is a skillful maneuver that may work for many years.

But when everything fails and the separation becomes a reality, it undoubtedly has a strong impact on the children, and conversely, their welfare influences the alternatives open to their parents. In his comprehensive review of the relevant research conducted by developmental psychologists on the effects of divorce on children's personality development, Lamb (1977) attempted to distill criteria to evaluate the potential consequences of divorce, in order to permit judicious decisions regarding custody. He identified as the major considerations age and sex of the child, the relative willingness and ability of the parents to care for the child, and the nature of the parent-child relationships. He emphasized the factor of father absence, and conceptualized the effects of divorce in terms of the following major social implications:

1) The absence of a male adult whose role sons can learn to perform through imitation and daughters can learn to complement through interaction.

2) The absence of a major socializing agent or disciplinary figure.

3) The loss of family income. The decline in income results because of both the withdrawal of a major breadwinner and the cost of maintaining two households rather than one, and usually entails substantial social stress or reorganization.

4) The loss of emotional support for the wife/mother. This combines with the loss of economic security (point 3) to depress the socioeconomic condition of the family and threaten its stability.

5) Social isolation, engendered not only by disapproval of divorce but also by the social exclusion inevitable in a social system in which families and couples are often treated as elemental units.

Despite the above frequent effects of father absence, still the prevalent pattern after divorce, Lamb found little support for the widely held assumption that divorce is necessarily harmful or that custody should always be awarded to the mother. His evaluation of the research evidence to date led him to conclude that children of divorced parents are more at risk for psychological damage than are children of intact families. I would add the proviso that this is only true if the intact family is functioning reasonably well together and not merely residing in the same house but riddled with discord. His second conclusion is that there are no *universal* effects of divorce" because there are no sequelae that can be identified as the inevitable consequences of divorce and family dissolution" (p. 171). Certainly, we see cases in which divorce marks the cessation of daily warfare. The ensuing more peaceful climate and, eventually, the calmer, more satisfied attitude of the divorced parents may produce positive personality and behavioral changes in the children.

Jacobson (1978) conducted a study of 51 children from 30 families in which she measured child adjustment following parental separation using the Louisville Behavior Checklist. Time and activity lost with each parent were identified by an instrument designed by Jacobson. She found a wide range of change in the amount of time and activity spent with each parent after separation—sometimes in the direction of loss; other times in the direction of gain. Her data revealed a statistically significant negative correlation between time lost with the father and the child's current adjustment, i.e., the more time lost with him, the higher the maladjustment. This trend was stronger for children aged seven to 13 than for those three to six. No significant association was found between time spent with the mother and child adjustment. Her work, like Lamb's, magnifies the importance of continuing father-presence in the lives of his children, especially during the crucial first year following parental separation.

In one of the best designed studies to date, Hetherington, Cox and Cox (1977) sampled 36 white, middle-class boys and 36 white middle-class girls and their divorced parents, all from families where custody had been awarded to the mother. An equal number of intact families comprised the comparison group. They had a child of the same sex, age and birth order attending the same nursery school as a child from the divorced family. An attempt was also made to match parents on the variables of age, education and length of marriage. The final study population was 24 family units in each sample.

Measurement techniques included interviews, structured diary records kept by the parents, observations of the parents and child interacting in the laboratory and at home, behavior checklists and parent ratings of the child's behavior, and a battery of personality scales on the parents. Observations of the child were conducted in nursery schools; teacher ratings of the child's behavior and measures of the child's sex-role typing, cognitive performance and social development were obtained. The parents and children were administered these measures at two months, one year, and two years following divorce.

Many of the findings of this study concern the reactions of the ex-spouses and are congruent with what has been discussed earlier. Of concern here are the findings regarding effect on the children. They found that when the ex-husband remarried, the first wife, even if she had already remarried, became angry in all cases and felt competitive or jealous in most. Often at this juncture old battles over finances, custody or visitation were waged anew: "The new wives seemed to exacerbate these feelings by entering a particularly hostile, competitive relationship with the ex-wife in which criticism of the children and the wife's child-rearing often were used as the combative focus (Hetherington et al., 1977, p. 18).

The interaction patterns between divorced parents and their children differed significantly from those in intact families on most variables assessed in the interview and on many of the parallel measures in the structured interaction situation. The differences were greatest during the first year. A process of restabilization seemed to occur by the end of the second year, particularly in mother-child relationships. Although many stresses were still evident in divorced parent interactions with their children at the end of two years, almost one-quarter of the fathers and one-half of the mothers reported that these relationships were better than they were during the marriage, when parental conflict and tension had had detrimental effects.

Hetherington et al. found that, at two months, about one-quarter of the divorced fathers, in their eagerness to maximize visitation rights and maintain contact, had more face-to-face contact with their children than they had before the divorce. However, fathers became markedly less available to their children and ex-spouse over the course of a two-year period.

They also found that divorced parents make fewer maturity demands of their children, communicate less well with them, tend to be less affectionate, and show marked inconsistency in discipline and lack of control over their children in comparison to parents in intact families. Poor parenting is most apparent when divorced mothers are interacting with their sons: "Divorced mothers exhibited fewer positive behaviors such as positive sanctions and affiliation, and more negative behaviors such as negative commands, negative sanctions, and opposition to requests of the child, with sons than with daughters . . . . The adverse effects of divorce are more severe and enduring for boys than for girls" (p. 20).

Poor parenting appeared most marked, particularly with mothers, one year after divorce; this seemed to be the highpoint of stress in parent-child relations. But by two years post-divorce, mothers were found to be demanding more independent and mature behavior of their children, communicating better, being more rational, nurturant and consistent, and better able to control their children. A similar pattern occurred for divorced fathers in terms of maturity demands, communication and consistency, but they gradually become less affectionate and more detached from their children.

Hetherington et al. underscore the finding that high use of negative commands was positively related to precipitating aggression in boys but not in girls. Although reasoning and explanation were not found to be clearly superior to issuing commands in gaining short-term compliance, in the long-range development of self-control, in inhibition of aggression, and in prosocial behavior in boys, they were more effective.

One year following divorce was found to be the peak of maximum negative behaviors for children; further, such behaviors were more sustained in boys than in girls. During the second year, marked recovery occurred and divorced mothers and children made constructive adaptations. Nonetheless, high rates of negative exchanges between mothers and their sons were apparent throughout the study. Divorced mothers of boys were found to be not only more likely than other parents to trigger noxious behavior, but also less able to control or terminate this behavior once it began.

Hetherington et al. (1977, p. 34) concluded that "There are many inadequate parents and children with problems in intact families. *Our study and previous research show that a conflict-ridden intact family is more deleterious to family members than a stable home situation in which parents are divorced. Divorce is often a positive solution to destructive family functioning*" (emphasis added).

Numerous intervention strategies have been proposed for helping children cope with their parents' divorce, their own reactions to it and its meaning for them. Cantor (1977) reports that the majority of the over a million children under 18 years of age who are annually involved in family breakups receive no professional assistance in coping with the crisis. Since many of the problems divorce causes for the child are manifested in school, often in the form of acting-out behavior, she recommends the establishment of situation/transition groups within the schools, led by school mental health personnel, to provide rapid crisis intervention and ongoing support in order to prevent the development of psychopathology. Her recommendation is predicated on a successful experience founding and leading such a group in an upper-middle-class elementary school in a New Jersey suburb. I believe the idea has merit, given that all children attend school and logistical difficulties would be minimal. In addition, sensitive school personnel see children daily and can spot changes in behavior and demeanor rapidly. Privacy and confidentiality, however, may be hard to maintain in a school-based peer group and parents may fear that their personal affairs will become too public. Also, the aspects of the family's life that find their way into the child's anecdotal record must be handled with great discretion.

Gardner (1976) draws an important distinction between two types of problems experienced by children whose parents divorce. First, there are the difficulties which result as a response to a psychiatric disturbance in a parent. Since these tend to become internalized, they may require in-depth psychiatric treatment. Second are the problems that eventuate from "misguidance, inexperience and naiveté" on the part of the divorcing parents. Gardner focuses on the second type of problem. He attests that not all children of divorcing parents need therapy and explodes many of the myths about children's reactions to divorce. Although his book is written from a psychoanalytic perspective, he has developed many alternative approaches for helping troubled children in the form of innovative uses of word association techniques, storytelling and dramatic procedures, etc.

Gardner finds the most frequent childhood reactions to parental divorce to be denial, grief and depression; fears of abandonment; blame and feelings of guilt about having caused the separation; immaturity or psuedo-maturity; and anger. In his comprehensive work, he discusses the etiology, development and treatment of children's pathological behavior. Along with his psychodynamic formulations, he also considers the impact of social, cultural, legal and interpersonal factors.

Like Hetherington et al. (1977), Gardner posits that divorce can have a constructive effect on children who derive the benefits of seeing emotions expressed authentically and of having to cope with loss and separation and seeing parents do so effectively. These children become determined to work diligently in later years to make their own marriages happy. He recommends individual psychotherapy as the treatment of choice when disturbed reactions persist for a prolonged period of time or if they are especially severe.

Likewise, Kelly and Wallerstein (1977) see individual psychotherapy of the child to be valuable and developed a preventive intervention model to be used at community mental health centers. In their study of 131 children from 60 families, they found that, contrary to the assumption that preschool and latency-age children have the most severe reaction to divorce, it was the adolescents who were hardest hit.

The time and expense involved for parents to bring children to a private therapist's office or to a clinic, even if one is reasonably accessible, often interfere with continuous treatment. Some parents are so engulfed in their own pain and turmoil and so busy trying to perform the daily chores necessary to keep going, that they may be somewhat oblivious to their children's suffering. Even if they realize it and try to assuage the hurts, they may be unable to muster the energy or funds to get the child to the therapist; it simply constitutes one more unwanted demand.

Kessler and Bostwick (1977) work with children, ages 10-17, whose parents are undergoing or have experienced divorce. They have created a workshop model, for which they present a well developed rationale and clearly describe the dynamics and format. During the first three hours of their workshops, they help the ten participants in the group define their special needs and problem areas. The second three hours focus on teaching specific communication skills designed to help the young people master these problems. The entire workshop occurs on one day; it begins with a brief orientation for the parents, who then leave. The young people, seated in a circle, are then asked to: 1) "Choose two adjectives that best describe you; 2) name the emotion that you find the hardest to express;

and 3) tell what you hope to gain from this workshop." They then explore the common issues which emerge, such as difficulty in expressing or controlling anger, trouble relating to stepparents, bewilderment about why their parents had to divorce. Next, they proceed with a sentence completion exercise to further relax the participants and foster more group cohesiveness. This is followed by assertiveness training in which the youngsters are taught to differentiate between non-assertion, assertiveness and aggressiveness and between "I" and "you" statements. They highlight an empathic model of assertion consisting of three parts: 1) empathy—what the other person is feeling; 2) content—what the speaker is feeling; and 3) action—what the speaker wants to have happen. These are illustrated by drawing upon what the children are struggling with in their own lives. After an informal lunch, a film showing several vignettes that are common in divorcing families is used to stimulate discussion of their reactions to the scenario and what appropriate assertive responses might be. The day concludes with asking the children to create their own vignettes, selecting situations that any of them might have to deal with.

Kessler and Bostwick's model seems to touch the critical divorce-related issues in the young person's life and to provide the context in which discussion of bewildering private feelings is permitted and encouraged, without fear of disloyalty or of upsetting one's parents. Finally, it normalizes each person's dilemma as it is shared by the other youngsters present and, therefore, no longer looms as one's solitary burden.

In this section, some current individual and group approaches to helping children comprehend, accept and live comfortably with the fact of their parents' divorce have been reviewed. Family therapy as a strategy will be dealt with later in relation to the adults and their children as a unit. However, Feir's (1979) thesis on "The Effect of Divorce on a Child's Concept of Family Image" warrants mention as she presents some provocative new formulations, the implications of which seem to be that family therapy constitutes the treatment of choice when divorce is imminent or has occurred. Feir elucidates the concept of family image as one variable affected by divorce which has possible long-range impact on children when they enter marriage and parenthood. She conceptualizes positive family image as a "triadic relationship composed of two generational levels—a parent generation and a child generation. Within this triadic context, two participants, the parents, have a special relationship (their marriage) and genital fulfillment, while one participant, the child, does not. In contrast, a negative family image contains several cross-generational dyads which are latently incestuous." Before the parents separate, "the triadic nature of the family breaks down into dyads across generational lines which jeopardize a child's sexual identification, oedipal resolution, psychosocial development, and loyal affiliations to both parents. Conceptually, the child is left with a family image deficit which (s)he brings to his/her own marital experience in adulthood. It is presumed that the prognosis for marriage is poor as the child of divorce was unable to learn about intimacy, the specialness of the marital relationship and the interrelatedness of marital and parental roles based on the experience with his/her family of origin." I find this a pessimistic overgeneralization; much depends on the age of the child at the time of separation, how much of the family image was already internalized, and the structure of the family fragments after divorce. Although conclusive evidence to support Feir's premise is lacking, one research study does point to the presence of some amount of intergenerational transmission of marital instability (Pope and Mueller, 1976).

Although the marital relationship may no longer exist, the parental relationship is an existential reality that will never end. Parents who can work together on behalf of their children minimize the opportunity for dyadic alignments across the generations (Feir, 1979). The child's heterosexual sense of reality will not be jeopardized when he is raised through a parental dyad rather than by each parent individually. What will be missing, however, is the specialness of a marital relationship for the child to orient him/herself to and incorporate into his/her personality. The remarriage of either parent may rectify the deficit, as well as provide another triadic context of a different order for the child, if the other natural parent does not interfere.

INTERVENTION STRATEGIES IN DIVORCE THERAPY

Somewhere in the voluminous literature on divorce which has mushroomed in the last decade, every known therapeutic approach has been adapted to working with individuals and couples in every stage of the divorce process. I have selected for review here those strategies which seem representative of this broad spectrum.[10]

Pre-divorce Period

When spouses begin to experience a fairly pervasive sense of discontent or disillusionment with their marriage, one or both are likely to suggest or insist that they seek professional help. Whitaker and Miller (1969) point out that

Psychotherapeutic intervention on one side or another in a marriage when divorce is being considered may serve to destroy the possibility of reconciliation. Despite the therapist's efforts to remain neutral, he inevitably finds himself thrust into the role of catalyst, judge or alternate mate (p. 57).

They recommend that both partners, and often children and other family members, be included in the therapy as a way of averting an outcome that might ultimately prove deleterious to all. Although they have found involving other family members to be a "powerfully helpful device" (p. 61), they are uncertain why. They hypothesize that it may be because 1) it represents symbolic proof that the therapist believes the marriage may dissolve and this is serious business (in which they all have a stake), and/or 2) it symbolizes their respect for the *fact* of the marriage.

---

[10]*Editors' Note.* In our view, the existence of such a "broad spectrum" of treatment approaches about divorce problems reflects the undeniable fact that there have been developed essentially no intervention strategies or treatment techniques that are *specific* to the emotional, behavioral and interpersonal difficulties caused by separation and divorce. On the other hand, as Kaslow makes clear, there are rather predictable stages in the divorce process, with similarly predictable emotional tasks to be addressed by the patient. Knowledge of such normative patterns in the divorce process is crucial for a therapist working with such patients, regardless of the particular treatment operations he/she chooses.

They caution against seeing one spouse alone originally and aligning with that partner, as the other spouse immediately feels outnumbered and threatened by the coalition. When he/she enters treatment later, therapist and original patient already have a therapeutic alliance going and the spouse is an outsider. Some patients skillfully triangulate the therapist into the relationship just as they have done with a child or a lover (Rubenstein and Timmins, 1978), again making the spouse feel insignificant, extruded and/or angry. They indicate further that where one partner is in prolonged individual psychotherapy, this "therapeutic marriage" to the doctor is what makes it tolerable to sustain a horribly empty marriage. The danger is, of course, that terminating the therapy means a double catastrophe, as both marriages will come to a sharp halt. Also, the therapist is not really available to the patient as an auxiliary or alternative spouse-lover.

In seeing both partners together, the diagnosis shifts from identifying one as a sick mate to establishing the existence of a marital problem (Whitaker and Miller, 1969). This is a very different entry point and the therapy unfolds accordingly; that is, both consider their role in causing and perpetuating the problems and what each can do to hasten improvement. By way of illustration, Whitaker and Miller cite one case of a married couple who had not consummated their marriage. The husband was still deeply entangled with his mother and had acknowledged past homosexual episodes. Although he could have been diagnosed as presenting deep-seated pathology, the therapist chose to serve as a catalyst and build upon their feelings of love and desire by being reassuring and encouraging. He threw the weight of his therapeutic power on the side of the part of the spouses that was healthy and wanted to express their love sexually so that the marriage could flourish. In six weeks, they overcame their inhibitions and were delighted with each other—and the therapist!

Whitaker and Miller caution against permitting the spouse who is eager to break up the marriage to turn the unwanted mate over to the therapist with a message to the effect that, "now that she's in good hands and I know you will take care of her, I can leave." If the therapist gets caught in the trap, he/she may well have to continue filling in as a substitute for the departing spouse for a prolonged period of time.

To summarize regarding the issue of whether individual therapy for one or both spouses or conjoint marital therapy constitutes the treatment of choice when a couple is contemplating divorce, we again turn to Whitaker and Miller (1969, p. 61), since they capture the core issue.

Where the marital tie is weak and divorce threatens, intervention with one of the pair seems routinely to be disruptive. We are impressed that moving unilaterally into a marriage relationship, taking one of the two as the patient and referring or ignoring the mate, is very often a tactical blunder.

Kagan and Zaks (1972) recommend multi-couple therapy for marriages in crisis, as do Markowitz and Kadis (1972). Kaslow and Lieberman (1980) believe that it is the preferred mode of intervention when: 1) A couple need more forceful input than one therapist can provide and the other group members can function as auxiliary therapists, and 2) the sense of belonging and the support a group can provide seem imperative. Although each of these author pairs presents variations on the couples group therapy format, size of group, rules governing attendance, and duration of the group's existence, all concur that participants gain a great deal of insight into the causes of their conflicts, and that these are often rooted in unfinished business with their family of origin that is transformed into unrealistic expectations of the spouse. They acquire greater understanding of their own personality patterns and needs, heightened sensitivity to their spouse and children, a more realistic picture of how others perceive them and how they tend to interact, and ways to dilute the intensity of the demands on the marriage by opening it up so each can cultivate other friends and enrich his/her life by not having to do everything together—thus, permitting each some space and ultimately the freedom to choose to become close again. Kaslow and Lieberman (1980) recommend intergenerational sessions with parents as an adjunct to the group therapy when involving the family of origin directly in therapy appears essential for working through the unfinished issues from the past. If, either despite or because of the therapy group, they opt for a divorce, it is likely that the decision is made more rationally and for sounder reasons and that future important relationships will be better selected.

The Divorce Period

Once the spouses have decided to separate and have begun to move into the tumultuous middle period of divorce, it is important that the therapist help them deal with their sense of failure, anger and other explosive and debilitating feelings. But this is only part of the therapeutic task. It is imperative to help them utilize the experience as constructively as possible for themselves and for everyone else who is involved, so that they are proud of their actions and do as little damage as possible.

Therefore, the therapist may want to maintain a list of attorneys who are concerned about clients' psychological well-being and not just "getting the best possible deal," no matter how "dirty" they may have to fight. If requested to, the therapist can recommend from this list several lawyers they have found to be fair and ethical. Whether or not the therapist suggests attorneys, he/she may want to have some contact with the ones chosen, since the therapist is in the unique position of being concerned about the emotional growth and integrity of all members of the family, while each lawyer only represents one party's interests. I have found that many lawyers are responsive to such input and that, in collaborating in this way, we minimize the escalation of the hatred and the desire to retaliate for hurts suffered by demanding everything or trying to give nothing, drawing children into testifying to a parent's adultery, and other psychologically injurious practices. Fisher (1974) takes a similar stance and discusses the referrals from therapist to attorney and vice versa, areas of cooperation, and ground rules for living during litigation.

A relatively new approach called *structured mediation in divorce settlement* has come to the fore in the past five years. Coogler (1978) began developing the structured mediation model in 1974; in 1975 he founded the Family Mediation Association (FMA) and within a month mediated his first divorce settlement. By mid-1977, over 100 couples had utilized the services of Coogler and his colleagues. Speeches by the mediators and word of mouth reports from recipients of the services served to generate interest throughout the United States and in some foreign countries. The stated goals of the FMA are to improve the quality of family life by offering cooperative methods of conflict resolution to those who are divorcing. They now also offer professional training, certification for competence in using their methods, and consultation for establishing mediation service.

Mediated divorce settlement is geared to resolving the following type of issues: property division; terminating dependency upon the relationship; and continuing the ongoing business initiated by the partnership, for example, responsibility for the children. The partners must follow the specified procedure and agree on a value system, something most have been unable to do during the marriage. But, in order to utilize the services of the mediator, they must agree to follow the "Marital Mediation Rules." This entails establishing a mutually acceptable value system and an orderly procedural process for reaching settlement.

The mediator is a trained, neutral third party, who does not decide controversial issues. Rather, he stresses that his role is to help the two parties responsibly make their own decisions and be committed to honoring them. Coogler (1978) notes the following as advantages of structured mediation: 1) The issues to be decided are clearly defined; 2) the issues are limited to those whose resolution is needed for reaching settlement; 3) procedural methods are established for collecting and examining factual information; 4) all options for settlement of each issue are systematically examined; 5) options are selected within socially acceptable guidelines; 6) consequences likely to follow selection of each option are examined; 7) uninterrupted time for working toward resolution is regularly allocated; and 8) impasses are promptly resolved by arbitration.

This approach is being used to negotiate written settlement agreements for those intending a legal separation, for those who want a binding civil contract that will later become part of the divorce decree, and for those who want to revise an existing divorce decree. The population divorce mediators are best able to serve are between 28 and 45 years of age, married for six to 15 years, have an annual income of $18,000-$30,000, one to three children, some college education and often advanced degrees, possess property, have some savings, and own insurance. The mediator can work with both partners simultaneously; he is not subject to the restriction that an attorney is, i.e., that he/she advocate solely the interest of his client.

Thus, it appears the structured mediation model is a viable alternative to the traditional legal-adversary model. The more the spouses can resolve their conflicts and arrive at a mutually acceptable settlement through negotiation and compromise in a calm and just atmosphere, the better chance they have of achieving a psychic divorce and handling their children well, with ongoing respect for each other's input as parents.

Kressel, Deutsch, Jaffe, Tuchman and Watson (1977) became interested in the structured mediation model of Coogler and his associates and decided to test it. They did an in-depth analysis of nine complex divorce cases, each mediated according to Coogler's innovative procedures. All were couples seen at the Family Mediation Center in Atlanta, Georgia. Their research report is based on two primary data sources: 1) audiotapes of each couple's mediated sessions, and 2) extended, separate interviews conducted by the researchers, three to 12 months after completion of the mediation and finalization of the divorce.

The obstacles to effective mediation which became apparent were: high levels of internal conflict (emotional ambivalence and perhaps volatility), 2) scarcity of divisible resources, 3) naive negotiators, and 4) discrepancy in relative power—the wife frequently being "ignorant" (p. 11) about financial documents and arrangements. Kressel et al. concluded that, in order for one to be competent to handle the strategic problems in divorce mediation, he/she should: 1) take a pre-mediation course in divorce negotiations covering money management and tax law, as well as psychology of the divorcing process; 2) learn an "advocacy" model of mediation in order to be able to deal with and compensate for the unequal power balance between the parties; and 3) learn how to deal with the emotional issues that surface, perhaps also recommending

individual or couples group therapy sessions.

In a later exploratory study, Kressel, Jaffe, Tuchman, Watson and Deutsch (1979) again utilized the analysis of the audiotapes of the nine completed mediation cases and post-divorce interviews with both of the former marital partners. This time, they also did an analysis of couples, drawn from a similar population, but who used lawyers in the traditional adversary divorce model, to provide a comparative perspective.

They found that a high level of pre-negotiation conflict and non-mutuality of the decision to divorce were negatively related to attitudes towards mediation and behavior during negotiations. They evolved a typology based on three primary dimensions: degree of ambivalence; frequency and openness of communication; and level and overtness of conflict. Further, they identified four distinctive patterns of divorce decision-making. Couples exhibiting the *enmeshed* and *autistic* patterns of divorce were the most difficult for mediators to work with and had the poorest post-divorce adjustment; couples exhibiting the *direct* and *disengaged* conflict patterns fared better, both in mediation and in the post-divorce period. They mention the potential importance of the intercouple differences for the divorce mediation process and post-divorce adjustment.

It is encouraging to find therapist-researchers like Kressel et al. testing out and building upon the work of others like Coogler. Such well thought-out clinical research can certainly serve as a stimulus to others and can provide a more solid knowledge foundation for our therapeutic interventions.

Another study conducted by Kressel and Deutsch (1977) was an excellent in-depth survey of the views of 21 highly experienced divorce therapists regarding their criteria for a constructive divorce, impediments to achieving same, and strategies and tactics of divorce therapy. Their "primary criteria of a successful divorce were the successful completion of the process of psychic separation and the protection of the welfare of minor children."

Analysis of the survey data led to identification of three types of therapeutic strategies: "*Reflexive interventions* by which the therapist orients himself to the marital problems and attempts to gain the trust and confidence of the partners; *contextual interventions* by which he tries to promote a climate conducive to decision-making; and *substantive interventions* intended to produce resolution in terms the therapist has come to believe are inevitable or necessary" (Kressel and Deutsch, 1977, p. 413, emphasis added).

They found that the modal case was in weekly treatment for two years, included both spouses individually and/or conjointly at least part of the time, and included contact with others, such as children and attorneys. The criteria for a constructive divorce which were compiled from the survey were: 1) civility and cooperation in attitude and behavior to one another when contact is necessary around coparenting, but with minimal continued involvement in other ways so that psychological closure can occur; 2) arrangements which minimize psychic injury to the children; and (3) absence of strong, persistent feelings of failure and self-disparagement.

In concluding, they call for extended discussion by therapists of the kind of training that should be developed to best equip therapists to intervene once the decision to divorce is made. They point to some amalgam of the kind and content of training usually received by therapists, lawyers, negotiators and accountants (to handle the financial side of the settlement).

Johnson (1977) hails a combined rational-emotive and cognitive behavioral model for treating divorcing and divorced individuals and maintains a present and future time perspective. Modifying irrational thought and behavior patterns and gaining control of one's feelings and actions are primary foci. He mainly utilizes ideas predicated on Ellis' rational-emotive therapy (1962).

Fisher (1974) favors "active crisis intervention to assist with the situational demands of the divorcing process combined with an ego supportive approach," and also recommends intensive long-term psychotherapy when the crisis is over and the marriage is legally terminated. She stresses the process nature of the therapy and that its emphasis and the techniques utilized at any given time must be attuned to where in the phase of the divorce process the patient is. She sees developing insight into and understanding of the personal and marital conflicts and reor-

ganization of the personality structure as long-range goals of divorce therapy. This is geared to enabling the patient to acquire enough strength to make sound decisions and to deal effectively with problems consequent to the dissolution of the marriage. In addition, Fisher advocates counseling-education (CE) groups for the divorced because she has found that "they meet the needs of a large number of those who divorce whose maladjustment is a reaction to the life situation in which they find themselves." Group members are a tremendous help to one another in being supportive and in sharing their own experiences; these interchanges help them reflect about what they are feeling and doing and how they arrived at their current place. Members may be more able to confront one another than a therapist can since they are aware that each has undergone a similar painful experience. In these CE groups, Fisher has seen many divorced persons motivated to "grow away from self-involved egocentricity toward responsible independence" (p. 135). These groups fulfill the need for the divorced to congregate with others who share their life circumstances at this point in time and also provide the opportunity for developing new friendships. Since her groups are time-limited, they are task-oriented and structured. They seek at the educational level to reduce confusion, increase rational performance and problem-solving abilities and redefine roles that will be ego-syntonic. In the warm atmosphere which it is possible to create when an ongoing group is comprised of only eight to ten persons, group members define the problems they want to solve, the skills they would like to master, and the topics they would like to discuss. Individuals wanting therapy which delves into personal issues in greater depth can combine individual therapy sessions with their participation in the counseling-education group so that they can concurrently work on personality change and interpersonal relationship issues.

Transactional analysis is the preferred theoretical framework and treatment approach for some mental health professionals working with the population we are discussing. McKinney (1974) discusses TA with couples who tend to triangulate their relationship in a game guaranteed to aggravate their partner, arouse feelings of jealousy and possessiveness and activate the roles of persecutor, rescuer and victim. She entitles the game "Look Ma! She (He) Likes Me!" and states that it is usually played by a married couple and a "friend." The game may be played at various levels of intensity. The first degree is mild flirtation in a social group; the second is an extramarital affair designed to "persecute" the mate; the third is the threat of divorce. This latter is contrived to bring about a reconciliation, which McKinney calls a "reassurance payoff." In family therapy terms, this is comparable to using the affair to heat up a cold marital relationship and make it more enticing. The therapist sketches out the spouses' transactions so they become aware of their interplay and the payoffs being sought. He/she also attempts to improve the embattled relationship by teaching them to ask each other for what they want directly, to stay in the here and now and to refuse to accept "confessions" about "there and then."

Post-divorce

Morris and Prescott (1976) also use TA concepts in facilitating patient's adjustment to divorce. For post-partnership conflict resolution, they have found the TA concepts of "ego states," "strokes," "life-positions" and ways to structure time to be especially meaningful. They found TA provides group members with a "rational framework for self-understanding and a basis for constructive behavioral change" (p. 66), as they utilize it to clarify the dynamics of the past relationship. They indicate that group members reported that once they understood the basic TA concepts, they were capable of assuming more responsibility for their own thoughts and behaviors—a goal of all of the therapeutic approaches that have been discussed.

Consideration for fathers is much more professionally fashionable now than it was in the past when often the father was the forgotten or neglected person in the family unit. Dreyfus (1979), who counsels divorced fathers, states that each phase of the process is characterized by its own unique set of issues indigenous to the divorced father. In his utilization of an alternating pattern of confrontation and support in therapy, supplemented by homework assignments, he sounds very much like Johnson

(1977). However, he augments all of this with recommending participation in some kind of men's group—social, political, athletic or therapeutic. He believes this is one aspect of the male's recovery, since typically he has been heavily dependent on women to meet his emotional needs and has few male friends. In being single again, he will need male companions—to talk to, to go places with, and to explore his feelings and ideas. Dreyfus discusses many of the losses (described earlier herein) that the man suffers when he leaves his family and looks at how the therapist can help him restructure his life and fill these gaps.

Leader (1973) and Goldman and Coane (1977) press for family therapy after divorce. Leader emphasizes that "it is essential to include the separated member and thereby move beyond the symbol of finality, trauma and the old wounds to an examination of present ties" (p. 13). This may be a frightening prospect for all and is likely to meet with great resistance when proposed. The therapist's firm, persuasive, warm yet authoritative stance conveys the importance of the inclusion; it sometimes is sufficient. I have found that some patients are adamant and will sooner terminate treatment than agree to have the ex-spouse attend. Therefore, I urge, but do not insist, that everyone come, but believe it is the patient's decision. We cannot help patients become self-determining by insisting they follow our instructions. If they do not all choose to come initially, I find that in the not too distant future, when the original patients trust us and have come to have confidence in our skill, the idea can be broached again and generally meets with a response of at least, "Okay, let's try it." Or the excluded member becomes curious and decides to attend in order to have his/her say.

Goldman and Coane (1977) have devised a useful four-part model for intervention in the post-divorce family, which facilitates accomplishing some of the goals we have described. They see the first task as redefining the family as existentially including all members, even those no longer living together. Second, generation boundaries are firmed up in order to reduce the parentification process. This is consistent with Feir's view (1979) on the importance of maintaining a positive family image based on relationships with two opposite sex adults. Third, they hold that the family needs to replay the history of the marriage to correct distortions and offer a chance to mourn the loss of the intact family. Fourth, the therapist helps facilitate the psychic divorce.

In 1974, the Conciliation Court of the Los Angeles County Superior Court established a post-divorce counseling service for families returning to court for post-divorce litigation regarding custody and/or visitation dilemmas (Elkin, 1977). The counselors consider the by-products of post-divorce anger with everyone involved and attempt to work out a written amicable agreement. If this can be done, it is signed by the referring judge. This makes it a court order. A copy is placed in the divorce file and a letter is sent to the lawyer. Their experience to date has been that 50% of the families referred by the bench have reached amicable visitation agreements.

If the psychic divorce is reasonably complete, family therapy which includes the ex-spouse may be valuable for a few sessions to work out remaining problem areas regarding custody, visitation and/or coparenting. However, it usually should not continue for long lest the children's fantasies about reuniting the family be reactivated or the ex-spouse's closure on the relationship hampered by too frequent and intense contact.

Granvold and Welch (1977) utilize a treatment seminar format when intervening with those experiencing post-divorce adjustment problems. Since they see post-divorce restabilization as inherently involving emotive accommodation, cognitive restructuring, and behavior change, they employ a cognitive-behavioral treatment approach. Weekly seminars are led by co-leaders for seven weeks, three hours per session. Each week they deal with a different predetermined topic, using various techniques such as group discussion, problem-solving, modeling and role reversal. Topics include many already covered in this chapter, such as the emotional impact of separation/divorce and sexual adjustment as a single adult. To enhance the benefits of their short-term, problem-specific methodology, they give homework assignments, and the following week members report

back to the group. Their approach in group is similar to that used by Ellis (1962) and by Johnson (1977) in their work with individuals.

This overview reveals that numerous therapists have adapted their own theoretical perspective and preferred treatment methodology to divorce therapy. As the reveiw of the research literature shows in the next section, few studies of divorce therapy outcomes have been conducted to date. The art and science of divorce therapy are still very young.

Ceremonies and Rituals

Marriage begins officially with a ceremony, usually a religious one and always one that is in keeping with the requirements of civil law. Earlier, I stated that I encourage about-to-be married partners to participate in writing their marriage vows so that the ceremony encapsulates the unique commitment each has made to their union. Customarily and universally, in addition to the clergyperson or justice of the peace and the marrying pair, friends and relatives attend the event and the vows are spoken in the sight of a group of people, adding solemnity to the occasion and serving as a communal recognition of the married status of the couple. Their attendance also symbolically is indicative of their approval of and their willingness to welcome the pair as a couple into their midst. Everyone present celebrates together after the formal ritual is conducted and it is generally a joyous occasion.

Divorce, which is an equally serious event, is customarily a lonely time. The day the final decree is granted, each partner may go alone to court—accompanied only by his/her own attorney. Hearings are usually brief and brusk. The individuals come away empty-handed and unloved.

It is recommended that this marker event and the transition and readjustment that accompany it be eased by some form of ceremony and that it be attended by close friends and relatives who comprise the person's support network. My patients have taught me how necessary this is by spontaneously bringing me ceremonies they had their clergyperson write for them, by calling me on the day of the hearing for support or congratulations, or by bringing a bottle of champagne to drink in the therapy hour. This seems to facilitate the closure and to help deal with the question, "Is this all there is after years of marriage?" Therefore, when treating those who are divorcing, I suggest that they think about what kind of ceremony they want to mark the termination of their relationship. The idea is by no means original; neither is its usage widespread.

In the Jewish tradition, a religious person had to have a religious divorce. Although divorce was not frowned upon as in other religions, it was and still is perceived as a serious step. In Judaism, divorce is a recognition of the "failure" of one's love and represents a potential opportunity for a second chance—if one examines his/herself and realistically reevaluates his/her goals and prepares for the stresses likely to occur in the next several years. Like the marriage contract (*ketubah*), the divorce decree (*get*) is a primarily legal document in Orthodox tradition. In Conservative and Reform Judaism, if a "get" is sought, it is likely to signify an expression of one's faith in the future and in one's capacity to grow and meet the challenges of life. It is a simple paper, terminating the marriage, which states that it is a document of freedom and a letter of release. "It is a religious document and those who seek it find a source of strength in their faith in God" (Maller, 1978, p. 194). It also represents bona fide written consent from the Jewish community through the rabbi.

A therapist or clergyperson can help a person write his/her own "get" as a way of gaining awareness into what went wrong in the marriage and formulating his/her goals for the future. Persons can also be encouraged to verbalize their expectations about what is likely to happen in the next two years, the difficult time period, as a way of fending off anxiety and becoming able to cope with what is anticipated.

Having something in writing helps to concretize the finality of the marital relationship and may serve to allay fantasies of reuniting. Recently, a divorcing patient told the author that she had insisted on obtaining a copy of the affidavit presented at the hearing. It was a detailed chronicle of the marriage and what went wrong;

for her, having it and rereading it clarified the reality base of the decision to divorce, was evidence of what she had really experienced and reminded her of what she wanted to avoid in a remarriage.

Another patient gave me a copy of the following ceremony her priest had written for her (Anonymous, 1978).

PRIEST: Dearly beloved, we have gathered together here in the presence of God and before this company to acknowledge the dissolution of the bond of holy matrimony between P. and K. The bond of marriage was established by God at creation and is therefore not to be entered into, or not to be dissolved unadvisedly or lightly, but reverently, deliberately and in the love of God.

P., having been married in the Church, and having received the statement of divorce from the State, comes asking God and this company to recognize the dissolution of the bond of holy matrimony and asking God for forgiveness that she may live under God's grace and wiith honor in the eyes of people. We, her friends, gather in love to support her.

Have you reverently concluded that in the best interests of K. and you, this bond of marriage should be dissolved?

P: I have.

PRIEST: Have you acted toward K. with love and understanding, to the best of your ability?

P: I have.

PRIEST: After having considered the solemnity of your vows, do you wish to ask God to recognize the dissolution of the bond of holy matrimony between you and K?

P: I do.

PRAYER: for P. and for K., for forgiveness, for the future.

PRIEST TO CONGREGATION: Will you do all in your power to support and uphold her in this new way of life?

CONGREGATION: We will.

PRIEST: Will you, P., do all in your power to live with love for God and for all people so that you can be free to make a new beginning, in your life, with hope and confidence?

P: I will, with God's help.

The ceremony concluded with the Lord's Prayer and a blessing by the priest.

Turning from the religious to the therapeutic literature, Bach (1974) describes a ceremony he has devised for his patients. It is a therapy group ritual called the "unwedding," the goal of which is to ease the pain of separation and to attempt to provide some lasting lessons through the recapitulation of the history of the marital rift. He believes that, from this retrospective learning, the individual can transform a stressful situation into a creative divorce which helps to heal the psychic wounds.

In brief, the unwedding usually occurs toward the end of either a 13-week constructive-aggression lab course or an extended weekend marathon. Each couple selects the time for their own ceremony, when they both feel ready to let go of their crumbling relationship. They select their "unbridal party"—a group of participants similar to the original bridal party but with the prefix un- attached for each. The man spends some time prior to the ceremony with the other men, discussing the faded dreams and then looking to the future; the woman does the same things with her "unbridesmaids." Each faces what it will mean to no longer closely share his/her life with the other or to be able to be interdependent. The couple and the therapist plan the ceremony together, carefully choosing place and decor. During the ceremony, the couple joins hands and the minister ties something around the clasp. They pledge to liberate each other and promise to relinquish the dreams they had for the marriage. They vow to free themselves from bitterness, not to harbor anger or to contaminate future relationships with residual enmity against their former spouse. After the "I do's" are said, the minister concludes with:

In the presence of your understanding and compassionate friends, seeing that you are indeed earnest in your intention to liberate one another, I pronouce you unmarried (Bach, 1974, p. 317).

He unties their clasp, the rings are returned, and sometimes, the unbride's flowers are given to the minister symbolically to bury with the dead marriage.

Then the newly liberated woman is taken to a separate spot by the other men, congratulated, toasted, given presents and flattered. She is made to feel desirable and wonderful—quite a different aftermath than when one leaves the austere courtroom alone. The ex-husband is accorded similar treatment by the other women, in a different place, and so he too has his shattered ego boosted and gets a sense of his attractiveness and appeal. Thus, the "unwedding" ceremony and all that goes with it truly mark an ending and a beginning shared with friends. Those who have participated in this rite of passage indicate that the use of the group ritual helped them to define themselves and requisite future behavior and that they derived much support from the group context.

These ceremonies and rituals seem to merit consideration by therapists. They can be tailored as needed to the season of life that the person or ex-couple is in and therapist alone or in collaboration with a clergyperson can help the clients arrange for an appropriate ceremony which should serve to add closure to the legal and emotional divorce.[11]

THE AFTERMATH OF DIVORCE

This aftermath comprises the sixth stage and beyond of the post-divorce period. It is the time when the individual's search for self and the emergence of a clearer sense of a new identity begin to coalesce. This is when one realizes the importance of treating oneself well and begins to feel worthy of the effort. Although former friends and even children may label this selfishness, it is a key factor in launching oneself on a trajectory of coming alive and being vital.

The effort to fulfill one's potential may take many forms. Rice (1978) focuses on the return

[11]*Editors' Note.* While we see the merits in such divorce rituals and ceremonies as Kaslow has described, we must confess our pessimism about the range of couples for whom such experiences would be applicable, i.e., personally acceptable. For example, we would suspect that people who would be most open to such ceremonies, and likely to profit from them, would be those with enormous ego strength, social skill, and abundant alternative social support networks, in sum, those very people who might *need* such ceremonies least! In any case, empirical study of the characteristics of people most responsive to such experiences, and of the potency of such experiences themselves, would be very enlightening.

of the divorced woman to school. Her decision to do so may rest on her need to obtain additional education or training to support herself and her children. Given the complex and often conflicting demands of her role as mother, working woman and school girl, Rice suggests that colleges and adult education programs make part-time study more readily accessible, respond to the counseling needs of this large population of older female students, and help society provide funding for such students if they require financial assistance. Surveys of numbers of separated and divorced women returning for higher education indicate that they comprise roughly 15% of the female students in continuing education programs (Astin, 1976).

In addition to the reason Rice posits as to why women return to school, I have observed several others. They decide to pursue career goals that had been abandoned years earlier for marriage and/or child-rearing, or in deference to their husband's educational or job requirements or his negation of their aspirations. Some, who were not achievement-oriented earlier, feel a new surge of desire to enter the workaday world and are eager to acquire the education that earlier held little appeal for them. Another group craves the intellectual stimulation afforded by the classroom and yearns for the challenge of the academic environment. For many, campus signifies expansion of their horizons and a place to meet new and perhaps more dynamic people.

Another avenue for being and becoming for the divorced is the world of work. For the woman, it can mean the heady stimulus of entering or reentering this part of the mainstream of society. This may necessitate such a variety of changes as sharpening her work skills, maintaining a more regular schedule, perhaps losing weight, changing her hairdo and buying new clothes in order to look attractive and fit in at the office, laboratory or classroom, and adapting to the adult interpersonal environment with co-workers. If children are not involved, being unmarried, for both male and female, may open up the possibility of numerous jobs that previously may have been out of the question, e.g., those necessitating relocation or involving traveling or working evenings and weekends.

The third arena in which one's revitalized being is expressed is the social dimension. This may include the singles bar or singles apartment scene. It may mean joining a church-based group for older singles and divorced individuals or becoming active in Parents Without Partners. Those who like music may join a community choral group or orchestra; thespians may gravitate to the local repertory company or community musical theatre group. The athletes may seek out a ski club or enter the doubles-for-singles tennis games. The possibilities are infinite and ingenuity is the key. A sense of humor and a recognition of the absurdity of many situations also help.

RESEARCH ON DIVORCE THERAPY

In the foregoing sections I reviewed several research studies on the effects of divorce on children, on therapist's views of the divorce process and on various aspects of structured mediation of divorce settlements. In 1978, the few studies reported in the literature on divorce therapy as a subspecialty area of clinical practice were summarized by Gurman and Kniskern, who pointed out that "the fact of divorce does not serve as a useful criterion of the effectiveness of marital therapy without taking into account the goals tailored to a given couple's needs. Conciliation is not equivalent to reconciliation nor does divorce necessarily constitute evidence of ineffective therapy" (1978, p. 881). In the little empirical research which they found, four sub-areas had received attention: structured separation with counseling, reconciliation (court) counseling, post-divorce counseling, and the effects of different marital therapies on post-divorce adjustment.

Toomim's work (1972) described a humanistically-oriented program of "structured separation with counseling," in which married couples in therapy met conjointly and individually with their therapist during a three-month period in which they lived apart and made no permanent financial, property, or child custody arrangements. When the predetermined time period ended, the couple chose whether to live together permanently, live together on a time-limited trial basis, finalize their separation, or select a second period of structured separation. In a one-year follow-up of 18 couples she had seen in her private practice, Toomim found six couples had reinstated their marriage and 12 were divorced. Twenty-three of the 24 divorcees believed they had "gained equilibrium as single people by the end of the time they agreed to finalize their separation" (p. 310).

A "transient structured distance" (TSD) strategy was employed by Greene, Lee and Lustig (1973). It differs from Toomim's (1972) approach in that the marital partners do not live apart; rather, one spouse becomes a "boarder" in his/her own house. TSD is used to aid clarification of the marital relationship (29%) or to assess readiness for separation or divorce (16%). Data do not indicate its impact on the other 55%. Divorce occurred in 44% of 73 TSD arrangements, compared to Toomim's (1972) 66%. In a follow-up several years later, 23% of the couples were "incompatible" but together, and 33% were noticeably improved or "re-equilibrated" following a situational marital crisis.

Gurman and Kniskern (1978) reported that the effects of various conciliation court counseling formats on couples' reconciliation have been examined in three well-designed controlled studies. Graham (1968) found brief conjoint counseling to be superior to a combination of brief conjoint and individual counseling on the reconciliation criterion. No differences were found on other criteria (positive references to spouse, dominance and affiliation scores). Hickman and Baldwin (1971) found more change in attitudes toward spouse and a higher frequency of reconciliation in couples who underwent eight hours of communication and problem-centered counseling than in those who received audiotape-based communication training. Counseling outcomes surpassed those of controls on both criteria. The effectiveness of group meetings using encounter-tapes was compared with brief problem-centered counseling by Matanovich (1970). Counseling outcomes were not superior to controls on either change measure (reconciliation, dominance and affiliation), while the encounter-tape intervention surpassed counseling on the reconciliation criterion.

In a study of post-divorce counseling, the effects of a single two-hour problem-solving conjoint counseling session were compared with standard litigation processes for couples contesting visitation provisions. Margolin (1973) randomly assigned 150 such couples to these two interventions and served as the counselor for the 75 counseled couples. The mother had been granted legal custody of the child(ren) in all cases. Seventy-three of the 75 counseled couples reached a visitation plan agreement, while only one control couple independently formulated a plan prior to their court appearance (p <.001). Only nine of the counseled couples returned to Superior Court because of visitation quarrels in a four-month follow-up, compared to 59 of the 75 control couples (p <.001). Counseled couples reported greater satisfaction than controls on such issues as quality of the fathers' visits and effects of their decision on the children.

In addition to the studies reviewed by Gurman and Kniskern (1978), Polizoti (1976) examined the efficacy of direct decision therapy for decreasing indecision and irrational ideas and increasing self-acceptance in divorced women. The two major findings of this study were: 1) Direct decision therapy is effective in helping people to change fixed situations, and 2) a lower level of irrationality is associated with a more stable level of self-acceptance. Individuals exposed to the treatment were more self-directed than other-directed and their level of self-acceptance was self-defined rather than being highly contingent upon the social setting.

Johnson and Alevizos (1978) conducted a study of 40 women and 12 men, each separated from his/her spouse for less than two years, who had volunteered as subjects in a clinical outcome study of adjustment to separation. They completed a number of adjustment inventories prior to treatment and were randomly divided into four groups. Group 1 subjects (a) received eight weekly group therapy sessions, (b) read a behavioral self-help book on separation adjustment, and (c) completed daily self-observation of social contact forms. Subjects in Group 2 did (b) and (c) only. Group 3 did (c) only, and Group 4 served as waiting list controls, receiving no treatment until the end of eight weeks. At that time, all subjects again completed the adjustment inventories. They found that the separated adults in treatment groups were able to adjust more successfully to their separations than were control subjects who received no therapy. Subjects receiving group therapy reported the most significant changes and were the most satisfied with treatment.

Kressel, Lopez-Morillas, Weinglass and

Deutsch (1978) compared the views of expert groups of lawyers, psychotherapists and clergy on the divorcing process and the role of the professional in assisting the divorcing. They found greater variation in opinions among lawyers than among either clergy or therapists. The six distinctive lawyer orientations toward lawyer-client relationship identified are 1) the undertaker, who handles the thankless, messy business for an upset client, is cynical about human nature and does not believe a constructive outcome is possible; 2) the mechanic who takes a pragmatic, technically oriented stance, is less disparaging of the client than the undertaker but is also concerned only with legal issues; 3) the mediator, who leans toward mediated compromise and rational problem-solving; 4) the social worker, who is concerned about the client's overall welfare and adjustment; 5) the therapist, who accepts the fact of the stress and turbulence and tries to work with the emotional aspects of divorce; and 6) the moral agent, who rejects neutrality and proclaims what he/she considers right or wrong, thus becoming a pseudo-guardian or protector. These findings are related to my earlier discussion about therapists' having a knowledge of the lawyers who practice divorce in their community and being able to make appropriately matched referrals based on what the patient needs and wants.

Among their other key findings (Kressel et al., 1978) were that the three groups of professionals all discussed four major strategies of intervention: 1) establishing a working alliance; 2) diagnosis and information-gathering; 3) improving the emotional climate; and 4) assisting in decision-making and planning. Obstacles to effective intervention occur in all of these areas, both as a function of the practical and emotional complexity of the issues and as a result of structural problems inherent in the third-party role.

Obviously, there is still a paucity of research regarding divorce and divorce therapy. To date, no studies exist which examine the outcomes of divorce therapy when it is the modality in which the family unit is treated. Couples group therapy appears to have measureable positive value, but this has not been compared to the benefit derived from other treatment modalities. Nor does there exist research which addresses the comparative efficacy of different treatment techniques (e.g., cognitive restructuring, use of TA

scripts) within the same treatment format. Obviously, questions of these sorts must be addressed empirically if clinical research is to have an impact on divorce counselors and therapists.

TRAINING OF THE DIVORCE THERAPIST

Marriage counseling began in this country in 1932, and in 1942 the first national organization of those engaged in marriage counseling was formed.[12] It was called the American Association of Marriage Counselors (AAMC) and was the forerunner of the current American Association for Marriage and Family Therapy (AAMFT) (Kaslow, 1977). Many marital therapists found that patients who came ostensibly seeking help with repairing their troubled relationships were really seeking assistance in terminating the marriage. When others called overtly requesting therapy for depression following separation or divorce, marital therapists added divorce therapy to their repertoire of services. Initially, they groped on a trial-and-error basis in attempting to discern what kinds of interventions proved most fruitful. As indicated earlier, articles and books on the psychodynamics of divorce and divorce therapy did not begin to appear in the literature until the early 1970s when clinicians began reporting upon their observations in the form of conceptual schema of the divorce process and what they had found to be viable treatment interventions. The *Journal of Divorce*, the first journal to be devoted to this topical area, was begun in 1977.

The little formal training that has occurred has taken place in graduate or medical school programs or in postgraduate private institutes under the rubric of courses in marital or couples therapy or occasionally in a family therapy curriculum (Kaslow, 1977; *Journal of Marital and Family Therapy*, 1979). In the last five years, conference programs occasionally have symposia in divorce therapy and workshops bearing this title are now being given around the country. In the eight states that currently certify or license marital and family therapists, divorce therapy is usually written into the law as one aspect of this specialization.

---

[12]*Editors' Note.* For a comprehensive history of marriage counseling and related professional developments, see Broderick and Schrader (Chapter 1).

At a minimum, one needs a thorough knowledge of growth and development of the individual; concepts of union, separation and intimacy; communications and systems theory; dyadic relationships; power and conflict; family theory and therapy; loss, grief and mourning; and stages of the divorce process and accompanying feelings. Intervention skills should include individual, marital and family therapy, plus crisis intervention and breadth of familiarity with a variety of techniques from different schools of therapeutic thought to incorporate judiciously in accordance with the needs of the patients.[13] Ideally, from this writer's perspective, one's training should include personal therapy and having worked through issues of failure, rejection, loneliness and loss so as to better understand and empathize with the patients' pain and torment and be able to help them move through it with some dignity, integrity and optimism for what can be created on the other side of the mountain.

A DIACLECTIC SUMMARY

I have attempted a kaleidoscopic review of the literature on divorce and divorce therapy, interlacing the observations and research findings of others with formulations gleaned from my clinical experience. Although the material was divided into a number of different sections for the purpose of ordering it in some meaningful way, the goal was to integrate ideas and data from sociology, law, religion, and therapeutic practice.

What has emerged is a multidimensional, multi-tiered mural. There are no simple prescriptions for ensuring a happy and lasting marriage; neither are there simple formulas for easing the anguish and bewilderment which accompany divorce. Nonetheless, the outlook for the future is reasonably optimistic based on: 1) a realization that the spiraling divorce rate has made many young people delay the age for getting married and led them to think in terms of choosing wisely so as not to become a divorce statistic; 2) the trend to reform of divorce laws in the direction of no-fault which signifies a more enlightened societal sense of reality and thereby reduces some of the stigma associated with marital dissolution and being the guilty or injured party; and 3) the experimentation with many ways of aiding parents and their children to cope with the turmoil and turbulence of divorce.

REFERENCES

Abrams, J.C. & Kaslow, F.W. Learning disabilities and family dynamics. *Journal of Clinical Child Psychology*, 1976, 5, 35-40.

Anonymous. *A divorce ceremony*. Personal communication, 1978.

Areen, J. *Family Law: Cases and Materials*. New York: Foundation Press, 1978.

Astin, H.S. (Ed.) *Some Action of Her Own*. Lexington, Massachusetts: Heath, 1976.

Bach, G.R. Creative exits: Fight therapy for divorcees. In: V. Frank & V. Burtle (Eds.), *Women in Therapy: New Psychotherapies for a Changing Society*. New York: Brunner-Mazel, 1974.

Bateson, G., Jackson, D.D., Haley, J. & Weakland, J. Towards a theory of schizophrenia. *Behavioral Science*, 1956, 1, 251-264.

Bohannan, P. The six stations of divorce. In: Lasswell, M.E. & Lasswell, T.E. (Eds.), *Love, Marriage and Family: A Developmental Approach*. Illinois: Scott, Foresman and Company, 1973.

Boszormenyi-Nagy, I. & Spark, G. *Invisible Loyalties: Reciprocity in Intergenerational Family Therapy*. New York: Harper and Row, 1973.

Bowen, M. *Family Therapy in Clinical Practice*. New York: Jason Aronson, 1978.

Cantor, D.W. School-based groups for children of divorce. *Journal of Divorce*, 1977, 1, 183-187.

Coogler, O.J. *Structured Mediation in Divorce Settlement*. Lexington, Massachusetts: Lexington Books, 1978.

Deckert, P. and Langelier, R. The late divorce phenomenon: The causes and impact of ending 20 year old or longer marriages. *Journal of Divorce*, 1978, 1, 381-390.

Dreyfus, E.A. Counseling the divorced father. *Journal of Marital and Family Therapy*, 1979, 5, 77-86.

Eisenstein, V.W. (Ed.) *Neurotic Interaction in Marriage*. New York: Basic Books, 1956.

Elkin, M. Post divorce counseling in a conciliation court. *Journal of Divorce*, 1977, 1, 55-65.

Ellis, A. *Reason and Emotion in Psychotherapy*. New York: Lyle Stuart, 1962.

Erikson, E.H. *Identity: Youth and Crises*. New York: W.W. Norton, 1968.

Fairbairn, R. *Object Relations Theory of Personality*. New York: Basic Books, 1952.

Family Advocate. *Joint Custody: What Does it Mean? How Does it Work?* Chicago: American Bar Association Section of Family Law, Summer 1978.

Feir, E. *The Effect of Divorce on a Child's Concept of Family Image*. Unpublished Masters Thesis, Hahnemann Medical College, 1979.

---

[13]*Editors' Note.* Again, Kaslow's discussion seems to reflect the fact that there is little that is unique to divorce therapy training, as there is little that is strategically or technically unique to divorce therapy itself. Nonetheless, specialized knowledge of the common patterns in the divorce process does seem central to effective clinical work in this area.

Fisher, E.O. *Divorce: The New Freedom*. New York: Harper and Row, 1974.

Froiland, D.J. & Hozman, T.L. Counseling for constructive divorce. *Personnel and Guidance Journal*, 1977, 55, 525-529.

Gardner, R.A. *Psychotherapy with Children of Divorce*. New York: Jason Aronson, 1976.

Goetting, A. *Some Societal Level Explanations of the Rising Divorce Rate*. Mimeo, 1978, Western Kentucky University.

Goldman, J. & Coane, J. Family therapy after the divorce: Developing a strategy. *Family Process*, 1977, 16, 357-362.

Goldstein, J., Freud, A. & Solnit, A. *Beyond the Best Interests of the Child*, New York: Free Press, 1973.

Graham, J.A. The effect of the use of counselor positive responses to positive perceptions of mate in marriage counseling. *Dissertation Abstracts International*, 1968, 28, 3504A.

Granvold, D.K. & Welch, G.J. Intervention postdivorce adjustment problems: The treatment seminar. *Journal of Divorce*, 1977, 1, 81-91.

Greene, B.L., Lee, R.R., & Lustig, N. Transient structured distance as a maneuver in marital therapy. *Family Coordinator*, 1973, 22, 15-22.

Gurman, A.S. & Kniskern, D.P. Research on marital and family therapy: Progress, perspective and prospect. In: S.L. Garfield & A.E. Bergin (Eds.), *Handbook of Psychotherapy and Behavior Change: An Empirical Analysis*, 2nd Edition, New York: Wiley, 1978.

Hetherington, E.M., Cox, M., & Cox, R. The aftermath of divorce. In: J.H. Stevens, Jr. & M. Matthews (Eds.), *Mother-Child, Father-Child Relations*. Washington, D.C.: NAEYC, 1977.

Hickman, M.E. & Baldwin, B.A. Use of programmed instruction to improve communication in marriage. *Family Coordinator*, 1971, 20, 121-125.

Hight, E.S. A contractual, working separation: A step between resumption and/or divorce. *Journal of Divorce*, 1977, 1, 21-30.

Hozman, T.L. and Froiland, D.J. Families in divorce: A proposed model for counseling the children. *Family Coordinator*, 1976, 25, 271-276.

Hunt, M. *The World of the Formerly Married*. New York: McGraw-Hill, 1966.

Hyatt, I.R. *Before You Marry Again*. New York: Random House, 1977.

Jacobson, D.S. The impact of marital separation/divorce on children: Parent child separation and child adjustment. *Journal of Divorce*, 1978, 1, 341-360.

Johnson, S.M. *First Person Singular: Living the Good Life Alone*. Philadelphia: Lippincott, 1977.

Johnson, S.M. & Alevizos, P.N. *Divorce Adjustment: Clinical and Survey Research* (Preliminary Report). University of Oregon, 1978.

Journal of Marital and Family Therapy. Special issue: Training in Marital and Family Therapy, July, 1979 (Vol. 5, #2).

Kagan, E. & Zaks, M.S. Couple multicouple therapy for marriages in crisis. *Psychotherapy: Theory, Research and Practice*, 1972, 9, 332-336.

Kaslow, F.W. *Supervision, Consultation and Staff Training in the Helping Professions*. San Francisco: Jossey-Bass, 1977.

Kaslow, F.W. & Lieberman, E.J. Couples group therapy: Rationale, dynamics and process. In: P. Sholevar (Ed.), *A Handbook of Marriage, Marital Therapy and Divorce*. New York: Spectrum, 1980.

Kelly, J.B. & Wallerstein, J. Brief interventions with children in divorcing families. *American Journal of Orthopsychiatry*, 1977, 47, 23-29.

Kempe, H.C. & Helfer, R.E. *Helping the Battered Child and His Family*. Philadelphia: Lippincott, 1972.

Kessler, S. *The American Way of Divorce: Prescription for Change*. Chicago: Nelson-Hall, 1975.

Kessler, S. & Bostwick. S. Beyond divorce: Coping skills for children. *Journal of Clinical Child Psychology*, 1977, 6, 38-41.

Kohlberg, L. Development of moral character and moral ideology. In: M.L. Hoffman (Ed.), *Review of Child Development Research*. Vol. 1. New York: Russell Sage Foundation, 1964.

Krantzler, M. *Creative Divorce*. New York: M. Evans, 1974.

Kressel, K. and Deutsch, M. Divorce therapy: An in-depth survey of therapists' views. *Family Process*, 1977, 16, 413-443.

Kressel, K., Deutsch, M., Jaffe, N., Tuckman, B., & Watson, C. Mediated negotiations in divorce and labor disputes. *Conciliation Courts Review*, 1977, 15, 9-12.

Kressel, K., Jaffe, N., Tuchman, B., Watson, C., & Deutsch, M. *An Exploratory Study of Patterns of Divorce: Their Impact on Settlement Negotiations, the Role of a Mediator, and Post Divorce Adjustment*. Unpublished paper, Rutgers University, 1979.

Kressel, K., Lopez-Morillas, M., Weinglass, J. & Deutsch, M. Professional intervention in divorce: A summary of the views of lawyers, psychotherapists and clergy. *Journal of Divorce*, 1978, 2, 119-155.

Kübler-Ross, E. *On Death and Dying*. New York: Macmillan, 1969.

L'Abate, L. *Enrichment: Structured Interventions with Couples, Families and Groups*. Washington, D.C.: University Press of America, 1974.

Lager, E. Parents-in-law: Failure and divorce in a second chance family. *Journal of Marriage and Family Counseling*, 1977, 3, 19-24.

Lamb, M.E. The effects of divorce on children's personality development. *Journal of Divorce*, 1977, 1, 163-174.

Leader, A.L. Family therapy for divorced fathers and others out of home. *Social Casework*, 1973, 54, 13-19.

Levinson, D.J., with Darrow, C.N., Klein, E.B., Levinson, M.H. & McKee, B. *The Season's of a Man's Life*. New York: Knopf, 1978.

Lewis, J.M., Beavers, W.R., Gossett, J.T. & Phillips, V.A. *No Single Thread: Psychological Health in Family Systems*. New York: Brunner/Mazel, 1976.

Mace, D. and Mace, V. *How to Have a Happy Marriage*. Nashville: Abingdon, 1977.

Maller, A.S. A religious perspective on divorce. *Journal of Jewish Communal Service*, 1978, 55, 192-194.

Margolin, F.M. *An Approach to Resolution of Visitation Disputes Post-Divorce: Short Term Counseling*. Unpublished doctoral dissertation, 1973, United States International University.

Markowitz, M. and Kadis, A. Short term analytic treatment of married couples in a group by a therapist couple. In: C.J. Sager & H.S. Kaplan (Eds.), *Progress in Group and Family Therapy*, New York: Brunner/Mazel, 1972.

Matanovich, J.P. The effects of short-term group counseling upon positive perceptions of mate in marital counseling. *Dissertation Abstracts International*, 1970, 31, 2688A.

McKinney, S. Look, ma! She (he) likes me!. *Transactional Analysis Journal*, 1974, 4, 26-28.

Minuchin, S. *Families and Family Therapy*. Cambridge, Mass: Harvard University Press, 1974.

Morris, J.D. & Prescott, M.R. Adjustment to divorce

through transactional analysis. *Journal of Family Counseling*, 1976, *4*, 66-69.

Napier, A.Y., with Whitaker, C.A. *The Family Crucible.* New York: Harper and Row, 1978.

Napier, A.Y. The rejection-intrusion pattern: A central family dynamic. *Journal of Marriage and Family Counseling*, 1978, *4*, 5-12.

National Center for Health Statistics. *Births, Marriages, Divorces* (Monthly vital statistics report). Washington, D.C.: U.S. Government Printing Office, March 4, 1976, *24*, (12) and March 8, 1977[a], *25*, (12).

National Center for Health Statistics, *Final Divorce Statistics, 1975* (Monthly vital statistics report). Washington, D.C.: U.S. Government Printing Office, May 19, 1977[b], *26*, (2), Supplement 2.

Nye, F.I. & Berardo, F.M. *The Family: Its Structure and Interaction.* New York: Macmillan, 1973.

Polizoti, L.F. *The Efficacy of Direct Decision Therapy for Decreasing Indecision and Irrational Ideas and Increasing Self Acceptance in Divorced Women.* Unpublished doctoral dissertation, United States International University, 1976.

Pope, H. & Mueller, C.W. The intergenerational transmission of marital instability: Comparisons by race and sex. *Journal of Social Issues*, 1976, *32*, 49-66.

Rice, J.K. Divorce and a return to school. *Journal of Divorce*, 1978, *1*, 247-258.

Rubenstein, D. and Timmins, J.F. Depressive diadic and triadic relationships. *Journal of Marriage and Family Counseling.* 1978, *4*, 13-24.

Sager, C.J. *Marriage Contracts and Couple Therapy: Hidden Forces in Intimate Relationships.* New York: Brunner/Mazel, 1976.

Salts, C.J. Divorce process: Integration of theory. *Journal of Divorce*, 1979, *2*, 233-240.

Toomim, M.K. Structured separation with counseling: A therapeutic approach for couples in conflict. *Family Process*, 1972, *12*, 299-310.

Trainer, J. Pre-marital counseling and examination. *Journal of Marital and Family Therapy*, 1979, *5*, 61-78.

U.S. Bureau of the Census. Marital status and living arrangements, March 1975 and March 1976, *Current Population Reports* (Series P. 20—Nos. 287 and 306). Washington, D.C.: U.S. Government Printing Office, 1976 and 1977.

Vaillant, G. *Adaptation to Life.* Boston: Little-Brown, 1977.

Vines, N. Adult unfolding and marital conflict. *Journal of Marital and Family Therapy*, 1979, *5*, 5-14.

Weiss, R. *Marital Separation.* New York: Basic Books, 1976.

Whitaker, C.A. & Miller, M.H. A re-evaluation of "psychiatric help" when divorce impends. *American Journal of Psychiatry*, 1969, *126*, 57-64.

Weisman, R.S. Crisis theory and the process of divorce. *Social Casework*, 1975, *56*, 205-212.

EDITORS' REFERENCES

Gurman, A.S. & Kniskern, D.P. Enriching research on marital enrichment programs. *Journal of Marriage and Family Counseling*, 1977, *3*, 3-11

Journal of Marriage and the Family. Special issue: Family Policy, 1979, *41*, 447-664.

Martin, P.A. Dynamics of family interactions. *Journal of Continuing Education in Psychiatry*, 1979, *40*, 23-36.

PART VII

Research on
Family Therapy

CHAPTER 19

Family Therapy
Process Research

William M. Pinsof, Ph.D.

The family therapy field is characterized by a plethora of theories about the nature and relative effectiveness of different techniques and by a dearth of research testing these clinical theories. A considerable amount of research has been devoted to assessing the outcome of family therapy (Gurman and Kniskern, 1978; Wells, Dilkes and Trivelli, 1972; Wells and Dezen, 1978), but little has been devoted to systematically describing and evaluating the process of family therapy or attempting to relate process to outcome.

Within the field of individual psychotherapy research, a number of comparative studies have failed to find significant outcome differences between different treatment approaches (Glass and Smith, 1976; Luborsky, Singer and Luborsky, 1975). In most of these studies, treatment differences have been specified only in terms of what Orlinsky and Howard (1978) call "normative task definitions." With regard to this approach they comment:

It is not enough, in our opinion, that "everyone knows" the difference between behavior therapy and psychotherapy (Sloane et al., 1975) or between client-centered, rational-emotive and systematic desensitization therapies (Diloreto, 1971); it is essential to provide detailed specifications and observations of the actual processes (p.310).

Without such "specifications and observations," one falls prey to "the danger of assuming that there is a close correspondence between professed orientation and actual behavior (Orlinsky and Howard, 1978, p. 290).

In their review of family therapy outcome research, Gurman and Kniskern (1978) struggled with a similar problem. In reviewing studies dealing with the outcome of behavioral family therapy, they noted the apparent superiority of the behavioral approach in five out of six comparative studies. However, they commented that in several of the most well-designed comparative studies, the purely behavioral nature of the behavioral therapies was questionable. In fact, one of the most successful behavioral therapies (Alexander and Barton, 1976) apparently involved "many of the same type of treatment strategies common to 'nonbehavioral' family therapies" (Gurman and Kniskern, 1978, p. 864).

Outcome research can evaluate the effectiveness of a therapy, but it cannot operationalize and/or reliably describe the events that make up that therapy. Similarly, outcome research alone cannot test clinical theories about the nature and relative effects of different techniques and treatment strategies. These latter tasks fall within the domain of process research.[1] To test the accumulating mass of clinical theory within the family therapy field, to get beyond "normative task definitions" and to resolve the problem of "professed orientation," researchers must attend to the actual events that occur in the process of family therapy. Failure to do so can only hinder the field's efforts to answer the foremost question in the field of psychotherapy research, the specificity question—"What are the specific effects of specific interventions by specified therapists upon specific symptoms or patient types?" (Bergin, 1971, p. 245).

This chapter is intended to fulfill a number of tasks. The first is to review the relatively small amount (compared to outcome research) of extant family therapy process research. The second task is to identify and explore a number of critical methodological issues and problems that must be dealt with in family therapy process research. A third, primarily substantive purpose, involves the identification of a variety of clinical hypotheses that could be tested by process researchers. Overall, this chapter represents an attempt to "map" the terrain of family therapy process in order to facilitate its subsequent exploration and development.

In his book on individual psychotherapy process research, Kiesler (1973) defines process research as "any research investigation that, totally or in part, contains as its data some direct or indirect measurement of patient, therapist, or dyadic (patient-therapist interaction) behavior

in the therapy interview" (p. 2). Substituting "family" for "patient" in this definition yields the definition of process research that will be used in this chapter. This definition excludes certain types of research that other researchers (e.g., Orlinsky and Howard, 1978) have defined as part of the psychotherapeutic process. Essentially, it confines the focus of this review to research dealing with any aspect of the behavior/experience of the therapist(s) and/or family members during the family therapy interview. Research dealing with the structure of the therapy (fees, schedules, members present, etc.) or characteristics of the participants (age, gender, experience, personality characteristics, family behavior/experience patterns, etc.) does not fall within the limits of this definition or the purview of this chapter. Gurman and Kniskern (1978) have reviewed some of the research dealing with these aspects of family therapy.

For the purposes of this review, family therapy consists of any form of psychotherapy (or counseling) that is explicitly designed to modify family systems. This definition covers such variants of family therapy as marital therapy (Gurman, 1973; Paolino and McCrady, 1978) and the treatment of a family through one family or system member (Bowen, 1978).

FAMILY THERAPY PROCESS RESEARCH: A REVIEW

If the field of family therapy outcome research is still in its infancy (Gurman and Kniskern, 1978), the field of family therapy process research has just been born. As with most neonatal fields in the social sciences, it suffers from a variety of conceptual and methodological shortcomings. Few researchers have done more than a single study. Instruments (coding systems or questionnaires) are generally quite new and have not been used outside of the research group in which they were developed. Replication of research has not occurred and it seems that frequently one researcher or research group is not aware of the work of another.[2]

---

[1] *Editors' Note.* This distinction is true only if the treatment under investigation involves a single component, e.g., thought-stopping for obsessive ruminations, the use of a single paradoxical injunction with a family, etc. Clearly, testing the "relative effects of different techniques and treatment strategies" is one of the foremost purposes of controlled outcome research in psychotherapy. The major limitation of such outcome research for an understanding of the process of treatment is that in psychotherapy research in general, including family therapy research, implementation checks are a rarity. That is, it is uncommon to find an outcome study in which documentation of the occurrence of intended therapist interventions, and of the non-occurrence of unintended interventions, is provided.

[2] In their review of family interaction research, Riskin and Faunce (1972) characterized the literature with which they were dealing in similar terms. In fact, many of the criticisms they leveled at the field of family interaction research (pp. 369-371) apply as well to the closely related field of family therapy process research.

In reviewing the work in a field, it is customary to begin by delineating various adequacy criteria on which to evaluate the research to be reviewed (e.g., Gurman and Kniskern, 1978; Wells et al., 1972). Unfortunately, the small amount and diversity of the family therapy process research that has been done to date make the delineation of such criteria inappropriate and unnecessary. The field is still too young to be reviewed in that manner. This section will be primarily descriptive. Critical evaluation of the various strategies and tactics that have been used to study the process of family therapy will be a major focus of the following section on process research methodology.

The dearth of family therapy process research and the developmental primitiveness of the field can be accounted for on the basis of at least three related factors. The first and most critical factor is the difficulty of the task. In attempting to research the process of family therapy, the researcher confronts all of the problems inherent in the analysis of social interaction and interpersonal communication. In addition, family therapy is an extremely complex form of social interaction, particularly in relationship to other types of interaction that have been studied more extensively, such as stranger or ad hoc group interaction (Bales, 1950), parent-child interaction (Lewis and Rosenblum, 1974), family or marital interaction (Jacob, 1975; Riskin and Faunce, 1972) and the process of individual psychotherapy (Duncan and Fiske, 1977; Kiesler, 1973). This increased complexity makes family therapy process a particularly challenging and difficult area to research. Many of the specific complexities involved in researching this area are discussed in the methodology section below.

The second factor is the lack of adequate microtherapy theory in the family therapy field. Most of the clinical theory in the field occurs at a relatively high level of abstraction or generality that might be called strategic (as opposed to tactical) or macro. Duncan and Fiske (1977) commented: "In developing an area of inquiry, it is of central importance to establish in the first instance a set of low level constructs that can be tied directly and explicitly to the data" (p. 10). Unfortunately, strategic theory in the family therapy field does not provide such a set of constructs, making the journey from theory to data (or operational measure) exceedingly long and arduous. The intervening territory is theoretically unmapped. The efforts of Cleghorn and Levin (1973) and Tomm and Wright (1979) to develop instructional objectives for family therapy training represents initial attempts to develop "a set of low level constructs" or an "hypothesis map" that can function as a guide to family therapy process research.

The third and last factor to be discussed is the problem that psychotherapy researchers in general, and process researchers in particular, have been individually-oriented and have ignored, until very recently (Garfield and Bergin, 1978), family therapy as both a treatment modality and theoretical orientation. This scientific isolation has retarded the speed with which the knowledge and skills offered by the field of psychotherapy research have infused the family therapy field. Simultaneously, it has permitted general psychotherapy researchers to remain enmeshed within a predominantly individual psychotherapy research paradigm.

Basic Access Strategies

The history of the field of psychotherapy research has been characterized by two different research strategies for gaining access to the "reality" of the psychotherapeutic process. The first strategy relies on the use of self-report measures or instruments filled out by the participants (therapist and/or patients). This approach targets the experiential or phenomenological reality of the psychotherapeutic process.

Most of the research on the process of family therapy has used a different access strategy based on direct observation measures. This approach targets the intersubjective or observational reality of the family therapy process. It involves the application of coding systems (rating scales) by trained coders to transcripts or tapes (video or audio) of the family therapy session.

Frequently, choice of access strategy within the field of psychotherapy research has emerged as an either/or—self-report versus direct observation. By and large, family therapy researchers have not avoided this false dichotomy. Recently, a number of psychotherapy researchers have argued for the logical alternative of a multiple, complementary access strategy employing both self-report and direct observation measures (Gottman and Markman, 1978; Orlinsky and Howard, 1975, 1978). Clearly, a multiple access strategy offers the broadest and most complete approach to the description and analysis of the process of family therapy.

However, because most of the existing family therapy process research has used one or the other approach, the research using each approach will be reviewed separately. For the sake of brevity and consistency, this review will focus almost exclusively on statistically significant results. Despite its emphasis on substantive results, this research review will also focus on various methodological aspects of the systems and studies that produced the results. This will facilitate evaluation of the results and set the stage for the methodological section of this chapter. Many of the methodological features touched upon in the substantive review will be explored and evaluated in greater detail in the methodology section.

Self-report Studies

Self-report research on the process of family therapy has emerged out of three distict research programs.

Hollis. Coming out of a social work tradition, Hollis (1967a, 1967b, 1968a, 1968b) developed an individual therapy coding schema for classifying "various components of the casework process" (1967b, p. 489). Her schema is applied to the therapist's detailed, written case record (process notes). It is designed to tap a number of different dimensions of the content of the communications that take place between client and worker. The first and primary dimension is the *means* by which the treatment step or procedure would normally be expected to produce its effect (sustainment, direct influence, etc.); the two other dimensions deal with the *subject matter* (other people, client actions, etc.) of the reported communication and the *objectives of change* in the client's understanding that the worker's intervention is intended to produce (of others, of the effect of his own behavior, etc.). The major clause of each line of the worker's case record is rated on a coding sheet with as many of the categories from each dimension (or scale) as are applicable.

Despite the fact that Hollis' system was designed to study individual casework or therapy, Hollis' studies with the system (1968a, 1968b) are labeled "marital counseling" studies. Two of the three studies examined interviews in which the caseworker saw exclusively one client who was seeking help with marital problems. In the first such study, Hollis (1968a) profiled the casework process in the first five interviews of 15 cases. She found that the emphasis was on "description-ventilation and on reflection concerning the here-and-now, rather than on the study of general personality dynamics and causation in terms of early development" (1968a, p. 43). In her second individual interview study, Hollis (1968b) compared the initial sessions of 19 continuing cases (15 from her profile study, 1968a) and 15 discontinuing cases. The data failed to support any of her four specific predictions. However, an unexpected difference emerged: Discontinuing clients were lower in description-ventilation. In her third and last reported study, Hollis (1968b) compared initial conjoint and individual marital counseling sessions. She found the workers in the conjoint interviews to be more reflective and less sustaining (supportive).

The small number of significant and largely unpredicted findings from Hollis' studies is not encouraging. Another problem with the procedure used in these studies is their total reliance on the therapist's relatively unstructured case record or process notes. Although the reliability of Hollis' coding schema was adequate, she failed to investigate the reliability or accuracy of the therapist's record—the raw data to which the schema was applied.[3] These problems question the ability of her procedure, schema and findings to shed light on the process of family therapy.

Shapiro. Shapiro (Shapiro, 1974; Shapiro and Budman, 1973) examined factors related to termination and continuation in family (N = 66) and individual (N = 183) therapy. Patients were randomly assigned to treatments and the therapists in both modalities were child psy-

---

[3] *Editors' Note.* Moreover, we know of little evidence that would suggest that therapists' "process notes" are accurately reflective of actual in-therapy events.

chiatry trainees. The relevant process findings from this project were reported by Shapiro and Budman (1973), who used a structured, post-therapy telephone interview to collect their self-report data. They found that 21 of the 30 statements from the family therapy terminators involved negative evaluations of their family therapists' behavior: "The major finding was that 13 out of 21 statements remarked on the therapist's lack of activity. . . . Few statements reflected concern about the therapist's lack of empathy and interest" (p. 60). The individual therapy terminators also complained about their therapists' lack of activity, but more significantly, and in contrast to the family therapy terminators, they complained with even greater unanimity about their therapists' lack of concern and interest. Over two-thirds of the continuers in family therapy made positive comments about their therapists, "and all of these specified approval of the therapist for being 'active' " (1973, p. 63).

The sole process variable that clearly and consistently differentiated family therapy continuers and terminators in Shapiro's study was the therapists' activity level. Of course, what Shapiro was really evaluating was the clients' or family members' retrospective reports about their therapists' activity level. Shapiro did not validate these reports. Nevertheless, his research indicates that the client's perception of the therapist's activity is clearly related to termination and continuation in family therapy.

Rice et al. A common practice in family therapy involves the use of two co-therapists to treat a single client system. Until recently, hardly any research has focused on the process of co-therapy. To remedy this deficit, Rice and his colleagues (Rice, Fey and Kepecs, 1972; Rice, Gurman and Razin, 1974; Rice, Razin and Gurman, 1976) conducted a number of studies examining co-therapist "style." These studies have relied on the Self-Description of Therapist's Behavior questionnaire (Rice et al., 1972), which consists of 23 self-descriptive statements (Talkative, Passive, etc.) on which the therapist rates his behavior on a five-point ordinal scale (1 = never; 5 = always). The instrument targets the therapist's sense of his style in general—that picture of you which a panel of observing therapists would get from watching you work, over time, with a variety of cases" (p. 155).

Rice et al. (1972) factor analyzed the questionnaire responses from 25 experienced (E) and 25 inexperienced (IE) therapists who had treated 48 married couples in co-therapy and found six orthogonal factors that were thought to reflect six distinct therapist orientations or styles: Blank Screen, Paternal, Transactional, Authoritarian, Maternal, and Idiosyncratic. Rank order correlation of the mean scores of E and IE groups on the six factors revealed different rank orderings and self-descriptions for the two groups. E therapists described themselves as highest on Idiosyncratic and lowest on Maternal, whereas IE therapists showed exactly the opposite pattern.

As a group, the E therapists showed greater variability in their factor scores than the IE therapists. This lack of stylistic homogeneity was interpreted as reflecting "a more 'differentiated' therapy style for the E therapists" (1972, p. 156). In terms of co-therapist preferences, E therapists preferred co-therapists who rated themselves higher on Blank Screen and lower on Transactional than the co-therapists preferred by IE therapists. "The implication is that experienced therapists as a group prefer a more 'restrained' co-therapist, whereas inexperienced therapists prefer someone who will more actively join in the task with them" (p. 158).

Following up this research, Rice, Gurman and Razin (1974) explored the relationship between gender, style and theoretical orientation in a sample of 86 therapists (47 males and 39 females), some of whom had participated in the previous study (1972). Rice et al. (1972) were unable to study gender effects because there were only six females in their 50-therapist sample. In contrast to the six factors that emerged from that study's predominantly male sample, Rice et al.'s (1974) factor analysis on their sexually balanced sample revealed eight orthogonal factors that each accounted for at least 10% of the total factor variance. The eight factors and the corresponding six factors from the 1972 study (in parentheses) were Low Activity Level (Blank Screen), Directed Focus (Transactional), Cognitive/Goal Emphasis (Authoritarian), Traditional (Paternal), Rigid/Mechanical, Feeling

Responsiveness, Judgmental (Idiosyncratic), and Supportive (Maternal).

Rice et al. (1974) interpreted the factor correspondence or overlap from the two studies (1972; 1974) as support for the cross-sample reliability of their questionnaire. The two new factors in the 1974 study were seen as deriving from the increased number of female therapists in the sample (Rigid/Mechanical) and the increased influence of phenomenological therapies (Gestalt, etc.,) in the five years between the two studies (Feeling Responsiveness).

Gender differences emerged on two factors. On Rigid/Mechanical, the females described their behavior as more varying and less anonymous and on Judgmental they characterized themselves as more evaluative than males. Partitioning the subjects in terms of experience, E-IE differences emerged on three factors: Traditional (E>IE); Rigid/Mechanical (IE>E); and Feeling Responsiveness (E>IE). As a group, E therapists described themselves as more interested in history, patient, interpretive, varying in their behavior and self-disclosing than IE therapists.

Lastly, Rice et al. (1974) partitioned their subjects into three orientation categories—Analytic, Phenomenological and Rational-Behavioral. Rational-Behavioral therapists (20% of the sample) reported the highest activity level (Low Activity Level) and degree of cognitive, goal-directed, theory-based behavior (Cognitive/Goal Emphasis). The Phenomenological therapists (35% of the sample) described themselves as more emotionally oriented (Feeling Responsiveness), more varied in their behavior and less anonymous (Rigid/Mechanical) than the Analytic therapists (45% of the sample). The strongest orientation findings emerged on Traditional. All three groups differed, with the Analytic therapists the highest and the Rational-Behavioral ones the lowest. Not surprisingly, Traditional was defined in classical psychoanalytic terms: historically-oriented, patient and interpretive.

This second study (1974), in contrast to the first (1972), did not focus explicitly on co-therapist or family therapist behavior, targeting instead "general therapist" behavior. However, to evaluate the validity or accuracy of their questionnaire data, Rice et al. (1974) nested a critical methodological study within their larger one.

This study and the data it generated pertained specifically to co-therapy. Asking therapists in their sample who had worked as co-therapists with each other to describe their partner's in-therapy behavior on the Self-Description of Therapist's Behavior questionnaire, Rice et al. (1974) correlated the self and other descriptions of five co-therapy pairs (ten therapists) who varied in terms of intrapair reported style similarity. They found "a highly significant relationship between the self-report of a therapist's behavior and the independent description of that therapist's behavior by someone who had worked with him/her in co-therapy" (p. 419). Supporting the validity of the questionnaire data, this finding suggests that these data can be generalized to actual therapist behavior, at least as perceived by a co-therapist.

More recently, Rice, Razin and Gurman (1976) selected 24 co-therapist pairs from their 1974 study and assigned them to one of four groups on the basis of co-therapist marital relationship (married-M *vs.* not married to each other = NM) and experience level (E *vs.* IE). Each group contained six co-therapy pairs. The basic datum in this study was each group's score on the eight style factors identified in Rice et al.'s 1974 study. Two main effect findings emerged. M and NM co-therapists only differed on Traditional (M—more historically-oriented, patient and interpretive) and E and IE only differed on Feeling Responsiveness (E more casual and spontaneous). In general, this analysis revealed few differences between co-therapist groups.

However, evaluating within-pair correlations in different types of co-therapy dyads, Rice et al. (1976) found that across all eight factors the E-M dyads were more alike than any of the others. In a separate ANOVA based on difference scores, Rice et al. (1976) also found that M co-therapists described themselves as more alike than the NM co-therapists on Low Activity Level and Feeling Responsiveness. These two findings clearly indicate that married (M) co-therapists characterize themselves as more similar to each other than nonmarried (NM) co-therapists. As such, they may represent a "united front." Rice et al. (1976, p. 60) identified the critical validity question raised by this finding—under what conditions does such a "united front" facilitate change?

Rice et al.'s three studies suffer two problems. The first, a minor problem, is that due to overlapping samples (subjects) they cannot be considered independent tests of the validity and reliability of their instrument. The second problem has two aspects. The first concerns the instrument—the questionnaire is not context or modality specific, asking about the therapist's behavior in general. The second aspect concerns the studies—only the data from the first study (1972) appeared to be clearly linked to co-therapist behavior in marital therapy. Without greater context (co-therapy) or modality specificity (family therapy) it is very difficult to determine the extent to which Rice at al.'s data pertain specifically to co- and family therapist behavior.

Despite these problems, Rice et al.'s research presents convincing evidence that the Self-Description of Therapist's Behavior questionnaire generates reliable, accurate and valid data. The instrument was able to delineate eight factors that discriminated therapist groups on the basis of experience (1972; 1974; 1976), gender (1974), theoretical orientation (1974), and co-therapist marital status (1976). Additionally, Rice et al.'s (1974) evaluation of the accuracy of their self-report data suggests that their findings pertain not only to therapist self-descriptions, but to therapist behavior as perceived by a co-therapist. This finding and the methodological study from which it derived represent the first attempt within the area of family therapy process research to evaluate the "behavioral validity" or accuracy of self-report data. Additionally, Rice et al.'s research represents the first and most extensive investigation of co-therapist behavior to date.

Self-Report Research Summary. Clearly, there has been very little self-report research on the process of family therapy. Hollis' procedure and the studies in which it was tested yielded few significant results. The ability of those that did emerge to shed light on the family therapy process was questionable. The first clear and valid self-report result was Shapiro's perceived activity level finding. Rice et al.'s research undoubtedly represents the most thorough and well developed self-report research program in the field. Their development and evaluation of the *Self-Description of Therapist's Behavior* questionnaire provide the field of family therapy process research with a valuable and useful self-report instrument. Unfortunately, lack of specificity restricts the extent to which Rice et al.'s substantive findings can be generalized to family therapist behavior. Hopefully, in the future more attention (in the form of theory, instruments and studies) will be devoted to the systematic description and analysis of the phenomenological reality of the family therapy process.[4]

Direct observation measures: Family therapist behavior

Most observational research on the process of family therapy has involved the use of separate coding systems to describe and analyze the behavior of the therapist and family members. Generally, the systems that have been used to study the therapist have been more complex and differentiated. The majority of the coding systems have focused primarily on verbal as opposed to paralinguistic, kinesic or proxemic behavior. This increased complexity and verbal emphasis probably derive from the fact that most family therapy process theory has focused primarily on the verbal behavior of the therapist. Eight coding systems have been used to study family therapist behavior.

The Montreal Group. Most of the research coming out of the Jewish General Hospital research group in Montreal has involved the use of a two-category coding system derived from Dollard and Auld's (1959) individual therapy coding system. After identifying the person or group to whom the therapist has directed his intervention, a trained coder rates the intervention as either a *Drive* (D) or *Interpretation* (I) statement. The ratings are based on the rater's perception of the intention of the therapist's statement. Drive statements stimulate

---

[4] A fourth self-report research program has begun to emerge out of Orlinsky and Howard's (1975, 1978) individual therapy research. O'Mahoney (1978) has developed and just begun to test a variant of Orlinsky and Howard's Therapy Session Report (TSR) that is designed to study conjoint marital therapy from the perspective of each marital partner—The Marital Therapy Session Report (MTSR).

interaction, obtain information and/or provide support, whereas Interpretation statements are intended to clarify motivation, enlarge understanding about the family, label unconscious motives and/or suggest alternative behaviors (Postner, Guttman, Sigal, Epstein, and Rakoff, 1971).

This binary coding system has been used in three studies. The first and earliest study investigated both the process and outcome of family therapy on a sample of 11 families in treatment with nine relatively junior therapists (Postner et al., 1971). Actually, the original sample consisted of 20 families and was reduced to the final 11 by terminations or dropouts prior to the 18th session. In terms of process changes independent of outcome, Postner et al. found that the variation in the therapists' overall level of participation (proportion of all participants' acts performed by the therapist) was significantly greater across different families than across different sessions from the same family.[5] The therapists spoke most frequently to the most talkative parent in the session and, in contrast to expectation, "seldom spoke to more than one family member at a time" (p. 460). Additionally, the therapists' D/I ratio decreased over the course of therapy.

Based on an Overall Improvement criterion (derived from scores on three distinct outcome measures) Postner et al. partitioned their families into good (five) and poor (four) outcome groups.[6] They found that the therapists' D/I level in the second session was one of the only variables that was correlated (positively) with the overall outcome measure. Postner et al. theorized that

Under low Drive conditions, Interpretations may stir up a great deal of anxiety with which the family can only cope by fleeing therapy. It may be that without

the appropriate level of Drive, a solid positive therapeutic alliance is not established (1971, p. 466)

The only noncontent difference that emerged was that the therapists of the good outcome families talked more to fathers, whereas the therapists of the poor outcome families talked more to mothers.

Postner et al. concluded that "in the light of the large number of variables examined, there are few measureable differences between the Good and Poor Outcome families" (1971, p. 467). In attempting to account for such meager findings, Postner et al. (1971) mentioned the small size of the final sample and the heterogeneity of their families. Despite its shortcomings, this study was the first attempt to relate the process and outcome of family therapy. As such, it broke new ground in the family therapy field.

The second and third studies with the two-category system dealt with the stability of family therapist verbal behavior within and between two different situations. Sigal, Guttman, Chagoya and Lasry (1973) and Sigal, Lasry, Guttman, Chagoya and Pilon (1977) compared the interventions of family therapists in "real" therapy and in a simulated condition called the Situational Test of Family Therapists' Style (STFTS). In this latter condition, the therapists responded to a simulated family on videotape. In the earlier study (1973), Sigal et al. compared early and late real therapy session behavior with therapist responses to the STFTS. In terms of their two content categories, the only finding that emerged was a correlation between Drive in the early real therapy session and in response to the STFTS. The only noncontent findings were correlations between the early and late real therapy sessions for average number and length of speeches.

Cross-validating, extending and refining the earlier study, Sigal et al. (1977) sampled the behavior of 19 family therapy trainees at three points in both conditions. They found significant and positive correlations between Drive for all three real therapy samples but not for the three STFTS samples. Interpretation scores revealed the opposite picture: stable (positively correlated) in response to the STFTS, but not in real therapy. However, and more critically, no cor-

---

[5] Unfortunately, Postner et al.'s conclusion "that differences between a therapist's output for different families are much greater than differences between the therapist's output for several sessions of a family's therapy" (1971, p. 463) is either based on data they did not present or is unwarranted in light of their design and data analysis. Increased variability across families could be a function of the fact that nine different therapists worked with different families. Their failure to control this "therapist variable" invalidates their conclusion.

[6] The absence of two of the 11 families in the final process-outcome analysis was not explained by Postner et al.

relations emerged between Drive or Interpretation in real therapy and in response to the STFTS. Although stable within each condition, noncontent features of the therapists' verbal behavior were similarly unstable (uncorrelated) between conditions.

One of the problems that may have accounted for the Montreal group's failure to find significant content (D and I) results in the above-mentioned studies was their use of a "gross" or simple coding system. Dividing the entire content spectrum of therapist verbal behavior into just two categories required each category to cover widely divergent types of interventions. The two category system may not have been sensitive or differentiated enough to pick up significant findings.

Chagoya, Presser, and Sigal (1974) attempted to deal with this problem by developing the Montreal group's second system—The Family Therapists' Intervention Scale-I (FTIS-I). In contrast to the two category system, this nominal scale has 26 distinct code categories and provides a much more molecular and fine-grained analysis of family therapist verbal behavior. Fifteen of the FTIS-I categories deal with what the therapist says, and 11 deal with how he says it. Although not stated explicitly, it appears that an intervention can be coded simultaneously with as many of the code categories as are applicable.

Two studies have been reported that used the FTIS-I. In a primarily descriptive study, Presser, Sigal, Mayerovitch and Chagoya (1974) compared and contrasted the behavior of four experienced family therapists with different therapeutic orientations. Their analysis was based on the therapists' responses to the STFTS. The following four FTIS-I categories were used by all four therapists in over 50% of their interventions: Clarification, Refers to Interaction, Refers to Self without Including his Affect, and Refers to Here and Now. The following four categories "distinguished" among the therapists: Explanation, Refers to Future, Refers to Current Behavior and Refers to Nonverbal.[7]

Using a three-category, theoretical classification schema developed by Beels and Ferber (1969, 1972), Presser et al. (1974) characterized one of their therapists as a Conductor (dominant, controlling, charismatic, initiating), another as a Reactor-System Purist (reactive/adaptive, psychoanalytic, theoretically complex). They did not classify the fourth therapist, who had the lowest number of interventions —seven (as opposed to 23, 19 and 16 for the others). Fifty-two percent of the Conductor's STFTS responses involved Gives Instructions and 57% involved Refers to Future. Fifty-eight percent of the Reactor-System Purist's STFTS responses involved Asks Questions and 53% used Gives Instructions. In contrast to the other types, the Reactor-System Purist never used Explanation. The Reactor-Analyst had the highest scores on Explanation (41%), Refers to Non-Verbal (50%) and Refers to Current Behavior (75%). Every one of his interventions involved either Clarification or Explanation. These results fit Beels and Ferber's descriptions of their therapist classifications surprisingly well. Presser et al.'s preliminary findings with the FTIS-I suggested that the scale could be used to differentiate distinctive family therapist intervention styles, at least in response to the STFTS.

In the most recent FTIS-I study, Sigal, Presser, Woodward, Santa-Barbara, Epstein and Levin (1979) examined the relationship between the responses of 23 family therapy trainees to the STFTS and the outcome of therapy for the 59 families they had treated. Outcome was based on independent ratings of the families' satisfaction with treatment, the status of the presenting problem six months after termination, recidivism and the families' goal attainment scale scores. The therapists' responses to the STFTS were coded with the FTIS-I. However, a second coding system—the FTIS-II—was constructed when visual inspection of the data from the FTIS-I revealed that it did not discriminate different degrees of competence among the therapists used in the study" (Sigal et al., 1979, p. 3). These subjective judgments of competence (super expert, expert, intermediate and novice) were made by one of the authors (Presser) after listening to the therapists' STFTS responses. The FTIS-II, developed by Presser

---

[7] These conclusions derived from the therapists' frequency profiles on the FTIS-I. Presser et al. did not use comparative statistics.

and Sigal, appears [8] to consist of five distinct categories that identify whether the therapist's intervention refers to 1) the family as a whole; 2) alliances within the family; 3) the family's use of the therapist; 4) an individual's feelings, thought or actions; or 5) unscorable. Choice of these categories was determined by the authors' preferred orientation, which they described as "interactional dynamic." According to Sigal et al. (1979), "inspection of the distribution of the total number of responses codable by FTIS-II revealed cutting points that corresponded to our subjective ratings of the therapists' competence" (p. 4). Competence ratings for their data analysis were based on these FTIS-II cutting points.

Statistical analyses revealed no differences between any combination of the four levels of rated competence, the five FTIS-II categories and any of the four outcome criteria. However, "two significant differences were found. . . when ratings of satisfaction and symptom status were added together" (p. 4): Super experts obtained better outcome results than the novices, and super experts plus experts obtained better results than intermediates plus novices. In a recent personal communication, Sigal noted that when they grouped the upper and lower levels of therapists' competence, and the upper and lower outcome ratings in order to increase sample size and the reliability of results, they found differences on family satisfaction and symptom status separately. These findings suggest that the FTIS-II, when applied to STFTS responses, generates data that are related to family therapy outcome on certain dependent variables.

Overall, the process findings from the Montreal group have been mixed. In terms of validity, the D-I results were not encouraging. The FTIS-I findings have been inconsistent. In Presser et al.'s (1974) descriptive study, the FTIS-I appeared to distinguish therapist styles in response to the STFTS. In the other FTIS-I study, Sigal et al. (1979) reported that the family therapists' scale scores did not appear to be related to rated competence. The strongest results from this group derived from their third coding system. FTIS-II findings are just beginning to emerge and are encouraging, particularly in terms of predictive validity. A consistent bright spot in the Montreal group's research has been the high reliability coefficients that have been reported for their three process instruments: D-I, .74 (Guttman, Spector, Sigal, Epstein and Rakoff, 1972; Postner et al., 1971); FTIS-I, .90 (Mayerovitch, 1972); and FTIS-II, .87 (Sigal et al., 1979).

A major problem with the Montreal group's research, particularly in terms of the FTIS-I and FTIS-II findings, concerns the extent to which their results shed light on the process of family therapy. All of the results from these two instruments have relied completely on therapist responses to the STFTS, a form of process data that does not appear to be related to real therapy therapist behavior (Sigal et al., 1973, 1977). Thus, based on the available research, it is impossible to determine the extent to which the results can be generalized to the actual, in-therapy verbal behavior of family therapists. It is hoped that, in future studies, these instruments will not only be applied to STFTS data (which may be critical in terms of predicting outcome), but also directly to real therapy therapist behavior.

The McMaster-Northwestern Group. The first family therapist coding system developed by Pinsof (1979a), the Family Therapist Behavior Scale (FTBS), is a nominal scale that differentiates 19 specific types of verbal interventions. The scale was developed to identify "clinically relevant verbal behavior of a particular group of therapists practicing short-term problem-oriented family therapy" (1979a, p. 4). This type of family therapy, based on the "McMaster Model of Family Functioning" (Epstein, Bishop and Levin, 1978), was developed by Nathan Epstein and his colleagues at McMaster University (Epstein and Bishop, 1973). Along with the FTIS-I (Chagoya et al., 1974), the FTBS represents one of the first coding systems designed explicitly to study family therapists' verbal behavior. Both systems were developed independently at approximately the same time (1973-1975).

In contrast to the FTIS-I, the 19 FTBS categories are mutually exclusive. A therapist's statement (the FTBS scoring unit) can be coded

---

[8] The FTIS-II categories were not formally presented by Sigal et al. (1979) and it appears that a coding manual has not been developed to date.

with only one category. Each category deals with a specific therapeutic function. The 19 FTBS categories were derived theoretically and empirically.

Initially, they grew out of an attempt to operationalize the executive skills identified by Cleghorn and Levin (1973). Subsequently, they were modified on the basis of feedback during pilot testing. In order to be included in the final FTBS, a code category had to be reliable and had to be able to differentiate expert and novice family therapists in either an aggregate or sequential analysis (Pinsof, 1979a, p. 5).

Pinsof (1979a) assessed the validity of the FTBS by testing its ability to discriminate predicted differences in therapist verbal behaviors under two extreme conditions. Because there were different and non-equivalent therapists in each condition, Pinsof referred to them as "condition-groups" (1979a, p. 6). In the trainee condition-group, eight beginning family therapists at McMaster conducted initial family therapy interviews. In the supervisor condition-group, eight advanced family therapists at McMaster conducted initial "supervisory" family therapy interviews.[9] In this interview format, a common supervisory procedure at McMaster, the advanced therapist, a supervisor, "observed the first 20 minutes of one of his/her supervisee's initial family therapy interviews. After 20 minutes, the advanced therapist was sent into and took over the rest of the interview" (Pinsof, 1979a, p. 6). This extreme condition-group design presented the FTBS with a minimal test of its validity. If the scale could not discriminate significant, predicted differences in the verbal behavior of two such extreme condition-groups, its validity would be suspect.

Sampling 15 minutes from each therapist's videotape, Pinsof found support for over 40% of his research hypotheses. Differences in the predicted direction emerged on seven of the 16 variables with research hypotheses. In addition to being more active (Activity Level) and using a wider range of interventions (Intervention Range), the therapists in the supervisor condition-group were more interpretive (Function

Relationship-FR), maintained a greater explicit topic focus (Refocus-R), dealt more with behaviors that occurred in the here-and-now (Behavior-Now-BN and Sequence-Now-SN) and focused more on sequences of behavior (Sequence-Now-SN). In contrast, the therapists in the trainee condition-group focused proportionately more on the "isolated" or non-relational opinions and thoughts of the family members (Individual Cognition-Option-IOC) (Pinsof, 1979a, p. 16). There were no negative (unpredicted) findings. The reliability of the FTBS in this study, based on Cohen's k (Cohen, 1960), was .50. This k score, a conservative measure of the scale's interrater reliability, differed from chance at less than the .001 level of significance.

The findings supported the general hypothesis that the verbal behavior of the supervisor condition-group therapists would be more sophisticated and complex than the verbal behavior of the trainee therapists. Pinsof speculated that the behaviors tapped by three of the codes that discriminated the condition-groups, Refocus (R), Functional Relationship (FR) and Sequence-Now(SN),

may involve a common cognitive skill called "sequential thinking." This skill involves the examination of events-in-time in order to formulate hypotheses about the function, meaning or importance of specific events. Additionally, the Sequence-Now (SN) and Behavior-Now (BN) differences may reflect the use of an attentional skill that involves the conscious or preconscious tracking of events as they occur in the interview (1979a, pp. 17-18).

Pinsof cautioned that the findings from this study apply only to the verbal behavior of short-term problem-oriented family therapists during initial interviews. Additionally, the differences between the condition-groups cannot be tied solely to therapist experience or expertise differences, because the beginning and advanced therapists performed under different conditions. Pinsof concluded, "In the last analysis, the findings from this study can only be tied with assurance to the 'total package' of situational, experience and expertise differences embodied in the extreme condition-group design" (1979a, p. 17).

Based on his experience with the FTBS, Pinsof (1979b) developed another, more complex

---

[9] A number of the therapists in this study, particularly the more junior ones, were also subjects in Sigal et al.'s (1979) process-outcome study.

coding system called The Family Therapist Coding System (FTCS). The FTCS resolves a number of methodological problems and substantive limitations that afflicted the FTBS. Whereas the FTBS was designed to study the verbal behavior of one kind of family therapist, the FTCS was explicitly designed to "identify and differentiate the verbal behaviors of family therapists from a variety of theoretical orientations" (Pinsof, 1979b, p. 7). The FTBS consisted of one nominal scale, whereas the FTCS consists of nine nominal scales, each one containing a number of distinct categories and, in certain cases, subcategories. A therapist's intervention is coded on each scale. Each of the FTCS scales codes a distinct aspect of the therapist's intervention (Topic, Intervention, Temporal Oreintation, To Whom, Interpersonal Structure, System Membership, Route, Grammatical Form and Event Relationship). However,

the information derived from each scale can be used most meaningfully in the context of the information from the other scales. The scales constitute a system. They function synergistically; their combined information exceeds the sum of the information derived from the scales individually. This characteristic of the FTCS does not preclude the individual use of certain scales to test specific hypotheses (Pinsof, 1979b, p. 7).

The FTCS is the most complex therapist coding system in the field of psychotherapy research, as well as the field of family therapy research. It specifies more aspects of a therapist's verbal behavior than any other system. The breadth and specificity of the FTCS derive from the fact that it was designed "to permit clinically meaningful reconstruction of most therapist interventions from the total code data (nine codes)" (1979b, p.8). Pinsof referred to this characteristic of the FTCS as "reconstructivity." Operationalizing the synergistic quality of the FTCS, reconstructivity permits identification of a clinically meaningful "gestalt" from nine individual bits of data. This "whole" is intended to give clinicians and researchers a more distinct "picture" of the therapist's verbal behavior or of a particular intervention. This characteristic of the FTCS, along with other methodological features, is discussed in greater

detail in the section on methodological issues.[10]

The FTCS Coding Manual (Pinsof, 1979b) has just been finished after a series of revisions. Currently, in the first systematic evaluation of the validity and reliability of the FTCS, the 16 tapes from Pinsof's earlier study (1979a) with the FTBS, are being reanalyzed with the new system. Additionally, Tucker and Pinsof (1979) are using the FTCS to evaluate changes in the verbal behavior of family therapy trainees after one year of training at the Center for Family Studies, Northwestern University Medical School. The research and training potential of the FTCS has just begun to be explored.[11]

To date, the results of this research program have been generally positive. The first system, the FTBS, was able to discriminate significant, predicted differences in the verbal behavior of family therapists in two extreme condition-groups. The reliability of the FTBS was adequate. In an effort to resolve a number of the limitations of and problems with the FTBS, Pinsof developed the FTCS. This latter system, far more complex and extensive than anything that has been developed in the field to date, has a number of unique methodological features. However, the validity and reliability of the FTCS have not been tested yet. Currently, re-

---

[10] The following example, from the FTCS Coding Manual, illustrates the reconstructive ability of the FTCS. "For instance, 'Are you feeling angry at your wife right now?,' would be coded with all nine FTCS scales as NE/ST/N/HF/DC/MNF/D/QC/IS. From these codes one can "reconstruct" that *the therapist directly* (D = Direct from Route Scale) *asked* (QC = Question-Closed from the GRAMMATICAL FORM Scale) *the husband* (HF = Husband-Father from the TO WHOM Scale) *if he was feeling negative emotion* (NE = Negative Emotion from the TOPIC Scale) *toward his wife* (DC = Dyadic from the INTERPERSONAL STRUCTURE Scale and MNF = Nuclear Family – Marital from the SYSTEM MEMBERSHIP Scale) *in the current interview* (N = Now from the TEMPORAL ORIENTATION Scale). These code data also reveal that the *primary function of the intervention* was the *identification* (ST = Status from the Identification Subscale of the INTERVENTION Scale) *of the negative, experienced* (rather than communicated) *interpersonal emotion, and that the therapist dealt with only one event* (IS = Isolate from the EVENT RELATIONSHIP Scale)" (Pinsof, 1979b, p. 8).

[11] At least one aspect of the training potential of the FTCS involves teaching family therapists to use "specific interventions in the contexts in which they have been shown (through research with the FTCS) to be appropriate or effective" (Pinsof, 1979b, p. 9).

search is underway to evaluate both of these aspects of the FTCS.

The University of Utah Group. The sixth family therapist coding system to be discussed has been developed as part of an extensive family therapy research program under the direction of James Alexander at the University of Utah (Alexander and Barton, 1976; Alexander and Parsons, 1973). The coding system consists of eight five-point ordinal scales that were designed to rate the following verbal and nonverbal aspects of family therapist behavior: Affect-behavior integration; Humor; Warmth; Directiveness; Self-confidence; Self-disclosure; Blaming; and Clarity (Alexander, Barton, Schiavo and Parsons, 1976).

This eight-scale system has only been used in one study to date. In that study (Alexander et al., 1976), the scale ratings were based on direct observations of 21 family therapy trainees during training sessions. These training sessions, which lasted for ten weeks, involved role-playing, group interaction and "interviews." Alexander et al. did not specify the scoring unit for their scales or the amount of data (summarizing unit) that was sampled. In terms of reliability, "independent ratings by the project intern and supervisor demonstrated an overall effective percentage agreement of 75%" (Alexander et al., 1976, p. 9).

Alexander et al. (1976) examined the relationship between therapist characteristics (pretherapy scores on the eight scales), family behavior in therapy (as measured on a two-category system discussed below) and outcome with 21 families that were randomly assigned to 21 family therapy trainees. The family therapy orientation of the program and of the training that the therapists received was primarily behavioral.[12] The ratings of the therapists' behavior were made before the commencement of therapy and "constituted an a priori assessment of process characteristics, a form of 'prediction' of how therapists would behave in therapy" (Alexander et al., 1976, p. 8). The ratings were done by the training supervisor.

Therapist scores on the Blaming, Self-disclosure and Clarity scales did not correlate with outcome. However, scores on each of the other five scale correlated positively with outcome. Additionally, these five scales grouped themselves into two highly intercorrelated blocks that appeared to tap two distinct dimensions. Alexander et al. believed that the first block, consisting of the Affect-behavior integration, Warmth and Humor scales, tapped what they called a "relationship" dimension, whereas the second, consisting of the Directiveness and Self-confidence scales, targeted what they called a "structuring" dimension. Together the relationship and structuring block scores (mean of the composite scale scores) accounted for almost 60% of the outcome variance. Individually, the relationship and structuring blocks accounted respectively for 45% and 36% of the outcome variance. When the intercorrelated effects of the relationship block were parceled out, the structuring block, however, accounted for only 15% of the variance in outcome. These relationship versus structuring findings were particularly surprising in light of the allegedly behavioral orientation of Alexander's approach to family therapy.

The initial findings with Alexander et al.'s (1976) eight scales support the predictive validity of five of them. The three relationship scales seemed to have the greatest predictive power. The strength of this particular finding is increased by the fact that it was totally unexpected by the experimenters. However, Alexander et al. commented that "the methodological constraints in the present design do not allow for direct causal interpretations of the impact of therapist behaviors on changes in family interaction and outcome" (1976, p. 19). One of the major constraints was that the therapists' behaviors were not measured in therapy, but, rather, pretherapy in a variety of more or less analogous situations. The extent to which such "analogue" behavior reflects actual in-therapy

---

[12] *Editors' Note.* Indeed, Alexander et al.'s treatment has been "claimed" by more than one "school" of family therapy. For example, behavior therapists (e.g., Gordon and Davidson, Chapter 14) refer to it as based on operant principles, while some strategic family therapists (e.g., Stanton, Chapter 10) use the Alexander et al. findings as support for the power of strategic interventions. A reading of Alexander and colleagues' own representation of their therapeutic methods (Barton and Alexander, Chapter 11) reveals that both strategic *and* behavioral views have strongly influenced their clinical work.

behavior was not investigated by Alexander et al.

A number of problems with this study involve the use and nature of the eight scales. In reporting this study, Alexander et al. failed to specify their therapist behavior sampling procedure, as well as the exact nature of their scales (scale points and definitions). Additionally, their use of ordinal (as opposed to nominal) scales raises several problems that will be discussed in detail in the methodology section below. Basically, ordinal scales make it difficult to pinpoint what actually is being coded; they are also more subject to coder bias. This latter point is particularly critical in this study, because the single coder had supervised the therapists' training and was, therefore, quite familiar with most of the subjects. Alexander et al.'s scales require testing on real therapy therapist behavior in a study without some of the methodological constraints that limited this one.

The Brigham Young University Group. Coming out of an Adlerian tradition (Ansbacher and Ansbacher, 1956; Dreikurs, 1959), Allred (Allred and Kersey, 1977) has developed a system for analyzing the in-therapy verbal behavior of counselors and clients in family and marriage counseling—The Allred Interaction Analysis for Counselors (AIAC). This nominal scale consists of ten mutually exclusive code categories that deal with various aspects of counselor or client behavior (function, nature, or judged obstructiveness versus constructiveness). The first seven categories (Educates; Gathers Information; Interprets/Confronts; Seeks Alternatives/Recommends; Supports; Equivocates; Detaches/Aggresses) target the therapist's behavior, whereas the eighth (Works) and ninth (Resists) target the behavior of the client(s). The tenth category (Confusion or Silence) characterizes the interaction between the participants. Allred defines the first five (therapist) and the eighth (client) categories as "Functional"; the sixth and seventh (therapist) as well as the ninth categories are defined as "Obstructive." The counseling interaction is rated every three seconds (scoring unit).

Allred and Kersey presented the results of several unpublished AIAC studies. Based on the results of three studies, the AIAC is reliable.

The mean interrater reliability score was .90. Several studies have investigated the concurrent validity of the AIAC. Tripp (1955) found no relationship between the AIAC and MMPI scores of naive counselors.[13] Sanders (1974) explored the relationship between the AIAC and the Strong Vocational Interest Blank (SVIB) with a group of 35 naive counselors, each of whom counseled three previously "coached" parents presenting parent-child problems (Allred and Kersey, 1977). The Writing Scale was the only SVIB scale with scores that were correlated with male counselors' AIAC scores. Allred and Kersey (1977) did not interpret or discuss this finding. For the female counselors, Sanders (1974) found negative correlations between their AIAC scores and their scores on the Registered and Public Health Nurse Scales of the SVIB, and concluded "those who were most like nurses in interest were relatively low in therapeutic skills according to the AIAC" (Allred and Kersey, 1977, p. 21). Observing 96 "student nurses as they each counseled two previously coached patients" (Allred and Kersey, 1977, p. 20), Watson (1975) found a positive relationship between the nurses' scores on the AIAC and their scores on Truax's (Truax and Carkhuff, 1967) Accurate Empathy Scale.[14] In a factorial analysis, Kersey (1976) found that "categories 6, 7, and 9 had high factorial validity in their groupings (.77 and .87), but was unable to get strong groupings of categories 1 through 5 plus 8" (Allred and Kersey, 1977, pp. 21-22).

Allred et al. have only formally assessed the concurrent (as opposed to the predictive, discriminant, etc.) validity of the AIAC and the results have not been impressive. Tripp (1975) found no AIAC-MMPI relationship and Sanders' (1974) findings with the AIAC and the SVIB were few and of limited import or generalizability. Watson's (1975) AIAC-AE findings are of dubious value in light of the growing body of

---

[13] The experimental context in which the AIAC data were collected in this study (counseling one versus two "real" versus "coached" parents) was not specified by Allred and Kersey (1977).

[14] The AIAC scores that were used in Sanders (1974) and Watson's (1975) studies were referred to respectively as "the functional/obstructive ratio" and the "constructive/ unconstructive ratio." Only the latter ratio was operationally defined: "categories 1 through 5 plus 8 divided by categories 6, 7, and 9"

literature impugning the validity of the AE Scale (Garfield and Bergin, 1971; Mitchell, Bozarth and Krauft, 1977; Pinsof, 1976; Rappoport and Chinsky, 1972). Before substantive issues are addressed with the AIAC, more work needs to be done to determine the nature and relevance of whatever variables the scale and its categories are measuring.

The Cardiff Group. Emilia Dowling (1979) and her colleagues at the Family Institute in Cardiff, Wales, developed the eighth family therapist coding system. Derived from the Developing Interactive Skills Category System used by the British Air Transport and Travel Industry Training Board, the Cardiff system consists of 15 mutually exclusive categories that target the in-therapy verbal behavior of family therapists. In the first and only observational investigation of co-therapist behavior to date, Dowling (1979) used her system in a primarily descriptive study of five experienced family therapists as they interacted in various co-therapist combinations in the treatment of nine families.

Sampling three whole sessions from the beginning, middle and end of each case (only one interview could be obtained for two of the nine cases), Dowling found that the therapists spent one-third of the therapy time (23 hours) intervening into the family system. The following five categories were "highly used": Enlarging, Integrating, Pointing Out, Eliciting and Proposing. In contrast, the following categories were "rarely used": Open (self-disclosure), Disagreeing, Bringing In, Defending/Attacking and Shutting Out.

To evaluate the "consistency" of each therapist's behavior with different co-therapists, Dowling used Kendall's coefficient of concordance. She found a high degree of stylistic consistency for each therapist (.62 to .85) in terms of the rank order of his/her use of the categories. "However, it was found that although the order remains the same, the amount of time they spend operating within a certain category does vary according to co-therapist, as a result of the complementarity function" (p. 189).

Using the 15-category system as a self-report device, Dowling (1979) asked her therapists to rank order the categories "to make a profile of a co-therapist with whom they would feel most comfortable" (p. 189). The following were listed as more desirable: Pointing Out, Bringing In, Proposing, Open, Enlarging and Disagreeing. The presence in this list of behaviors that were "rarely used" (Bringing In, Open and Disagreeing) offers support for the complementary hypothesis that "therapists tend to look for certain behaviors in a co-therapist that they do not practice to a high degree themselves" (p. 190). The therapists also revealed a high degree of agreement as to the behavioral characteristics desired in a co-therapist.

Refining her analysis, Dowling evaluated co-therapist preference in terms of different family (client) types, and found that the following were rated as highly desirable for all families: Supporting, Bringing In and Eliciting. In contrast, Disagreeing, Defending/Attacking and Shutting Out were rated as "least desirable." Dowling did not attempt to account for the fact that "Disagreeing" was rated as "desirable" in the general co-therapist preference data, and as "undesirable" in the family type data. Since the rank orders were so similar for the different family types, Dowling was unable to conclude that there were specific behavior patterns that her therapists preferred for specific types of families.

The final part of Dowling's study concerns the accuracy with which therapists perceive their own behavior. Comparing each therapist's observed use of the categories with his or her self-description, Dowling found no correlation between the two sets of data for four of her five experienced therapists. The only therapist with a significant Spearman rho was Dowling, who participated as a subject in her own study. She attributed the accuracy of her own perceptions to the fact that she was more familiar with the coding system than any of the other therapists. "The implication is that in order for therapists to become more accurate in their perception of their own behavior, they have to practice the recognition and categorization of their interventions" (p. 193).

Seen as a pilot investigation of family and co-therapist behavior, Dowling's (1979) study generated some interesting findings. She found that each of her therapists had a consistent trans-contextual (context = co-therapist) behavioral profile, and that they also had fairly high agreement about the types of behaviors that were desirable and undesirable in a co-therapist (independent of family type). Contrary to her prediction, Dowling also found that experienced therapists were not very accurate perceivers and/or describers of their own behavior, a finding which raises questions about the validity or accuracy of self-report data.

Due to several methodological problems, these findings must all be regarded as highly tentative. The foremost problem with this research is the lack of reliability data. Dowling was the only coder in her study and she did not evaluate the intrarater (or interrater) reliability of her ratings. Therefore, it is impossible to evaluate the extent to which the findings (and/or lack of them) derive from real differences or similarities in the subject sample, or from the poor reliability of the data.

Another problem concerns the fact that Dowling was both a subject and the sole coder in her study. This multi-role involvement in the study, coupled with the lack of reliability data, makes it impossible to rule out the possibility that experimental bias may have influenced the findings. Additional problems involve the small N, the minimal use of comparative statistics, as well as Dowling's failure to specify the scoring unit to which the coding system was applied.

The last point about this study revolves around the relationship between its findings and the findings from Rice et al.'s self-report studies on co-therapy. Together, these studies constitute the existing research on co-therapist behavior in the family field. Unfortunately, due to population (both therapist and family), instrument and procedure differences, the results of the two research efforts cannot be compared.

Family Therapist Behavior: A Summary. As this review has indicated, process research focusing on the behavior of the family therapist has not produced a clear or consistent body of substantive findings. Eight coding systems have been developed to study the therapist's behavior. The three coding systems developed by the Montreal Group have produced a mixed body of findings. Positive findings have derived from the FTIS-I, although the strongest results have come from the FTIS-II. Unfortunately, due to the Montreal Group's use of the STFTS as a

method for generating raw process data, it is impossible to evaluate the extent to which their findings can be generalized to real therapy therapist behavior. Concerning the McMaster-Northwestern Group, the results of the initial study with the FTBS were encouraging, but of limited generalizability. The reliability and validity of the FTCS, the most sophisticated and complex therapist coding system developed to date, are in the process of being evaluated. The results of the University of Utah Group's initial study (Alexander et al., 1976) with their eight ordinal scales were intriguing, but the methodological limitations of the study (pretherapy process ratings) hindered the extent to which the findings could be generalized to actual, intherapy behavior. The results of the Brigham Young Group's research (Allred and Kersey, 1977) have not supported the validity of the AIAC as a measure of family therapist behavior. Finally, due to several methodological problems, the Cardiff Group's findings, although interesting, must be regarded as highly tentative.

Despite the lack of consistency and clarity in most of these results, the extant research on family therapist behavior has opened some important methodological pathways. At this early time in the field's development, negative or nonsignificant results can be used to rule out or modify systems or procedures that do not appear to be valid or productive. Understanding the pitfalls and limitations of such systems or procedures can save the researcher time and energy in developing or selecting those that will meet his needs. Various strengths and weaknesses of a number of the methodological features of the systems and studies that have been discussed will be examined in greater detail below.

In the last analysis, because of the relatively little research that has been done with the above-mentioned systems, all of the results derived from them must be viewed with caution. The validity and reliability of a coding system cannot stand or fall on the results of one or two initial studies. More research needs to be done before any definitive conclusions can be drawn.

Direct Observation Measures: Family (patient) behavior

Eight coding systems have been used to study the behavior of the family members during family therapy. These systems and the results of the studies in which they have been used will be reviewed in this section. The first three systems that will be examined were designed to complement three of the family therapist coding systems that were discussed in the preceding section.

The Montreal Group. To complement their Drive/Interpretation therapist coding system, the Montreal Group created a nominal scale to code the "underlying affective content" of the family members' verbal statements during family therapy sessions (Guttman et al., 1972). Based on Rado's (1958) theory of affective expression, their coding system consists of the following three mutually exclusive code categories: *Emergency* (E). *Welfare* (W), and *Neutral* (N). E statements deal with "emergency" emotions like anger, fear, guilt, depression and grief. W statements deal with "welfare" emotions like pleasure, love, joy, happiness and liking. The N category was "used only when underlying affective content could not be attributed to a statement" (Guttman et al., 1972). The overall interrater reliability of the three category system was adequate (74%), although the reliabilities of the individual code categories ranged from 50% to 90%.

In the only test of the validity of the three-category system, Postner et al. (1971) failed to find any relationship between the three categories and family therapy outcome. The only findings that did emerge from that study related solely to the process of therapy. As therapy progressed, family members 1) spoke less to the therapist and more to each other, and 2) expressed more welfare feelings to each other.

As with their therapist D-I findings, Postner et al.'s family findings were not impressive. Considering the large number of variables studied, their few significant results do not support the validity of their three-category system. However, the lack of family findings may derive from the methodological limitations of Postner et al.'s study, as opposed to the invalidity of the system. Firm validity conclusions must await more methodologically adequate research with the E/N/W system.

The University of Utah Group. In conjunc-

tion with their eight (ordinal) scale therapist coding system, Alexander et al. (1976) used a two-category nominal scale to analyze the quality of the family members' communication during family therapy sessions. This scale derives from Gibb's (1961) work with small ad hoc groups and characterizes communication as either *Defensive* or *Supportive*. Defensive communications involve verbal and paralinguistic behaviors "that are threatening or punishing to others and reciprocally invite and produce defensive behaviors in return" (Alexander et al., 1976, p. 9). Alexander's coding manual for this system specifies the following Defensive subcategories which are used as coding guides rather than actual code categories: judgmental-dogmatism, control and strategy, indifference, and superiority. Supportive communications decrease anxiety, clarify communication and stimulate positive interactions. Alexander's Supportive subcategories are genuine information-seeking/giving, spontaneous problem-solving, empathic understanding, and equality. In an experimental (nontherapy) task situation, the Supportive-Defensive (S-E) system revealed differences between the interaction patterns of delinquent and nonclinical ("normal") families (Alexander, 1973).

Alexander et al.'s (1976) process-outcome study has been the only attempt to date to use the S-D system to study in-therapy family behavior. For each of the 21 families in that study, three 15-minute audiotaped samples were coded with the S-D system. The three samples respectively represented the first portion of the initial family therapy session, the last portion of that session and the first portion of the next-to-last session (since four families dropped out after one session, the last sampling point yielded only 17 samples). In this study each code category was made into an ordinal scale with the four following scale points: 1) never occurring; 2) occurring infrequently; 3) occurring often; and 4) "constituting almost all the behavior expressed by that person" (Alexander et al., 1976, p. 10). The ordinal scale ratings were based on the rate judgments of trained coders. The reliability of the coders' ratings, based on 12 reliability probes during the actual coding of the data, was quite high (91% agreement). The data analysis for this study relied on the Family S/D ratio, a statistic in which the numerator and denominator were based on the sum of the communications on each dimension divided by the number of family members (1976, p. 10).

Alexander et al. found a relationship between outcome and Family S/D scores from the next-to-last session. The families with better outcomes had higher S/D ratios—they were more supportive to each other at the end of therapy. No relationships emerged between outcome and family scores from either (early vs. late) of the initial session samples. These findings were interpreted as reflecting the effects of intervention (as opposed to initial family differences). On the basis of these encouraging results, coupled with the positive findings from Alexander's earlier family interaction study (1973), the S-D system appears to have discriminant (types of families and outcomes) validity.

The Brigham Young University Group. Two of the the the ten code categories of Allred's Interaction Analysis of Counselors (AIAC) focus on the client's verbal behavior, characterizing it as either Works or Resists. The other eight AIAC code categories focus on the behavior of the therapist (nos. 1 to 7) or the therapist-client (family member) interaction (no. 10).

The results of the AIAC research, presented and summarized by Allred and Kersey (1977), were discussed in the previous section on family therapist behavior. Unfortunately, Allred and Kersey did not specifically discuss the findings on the two AIAC client code categories, focusing instead on ratio scores that mix therapist and client behaviors. Therefore, it is impossible to separately evaluate the validity of Works and Resists. As mentioned previously the only formal research on the AIAC has focused on the concurrent validity of the instrument. The results of that research have not supported the validity of the AIAC.

Heckel. Building on Salzberg's (1962) group therapy research, Heckel (1972) developed a coding system to analyze the in-therapy verbal behaviors of group therapy patients. Using the patient speech as the scoring unit, his system consists of two separate scales. The first one scores each patient speech in one of three topic categories: 1) environmental responses dealing with "nonrelevant subjects"; 2) personal responses dealing with personal problems; and

3) group responses dealing with other patients' problems and/or group matters. Each patient speech can be scored on as many of the following 11 categories of the second scale as are applicable: 1) therapist-directed responses; 2) negative interaction responses; 3) initiating activity; 4) seeking information; 5) giving information; 6) seeking opinion; 7) giving opinion; 8) elaborating; 9) summarizing and testing; 10) evaluating and diagnosing; and 11) group building (Heckel, 1975). Heckel reported an overall interrater reliability coefficient for both scales of .86.

Using these scales, Heckel (1975) compared the in-therapy verbal responses of 27 family therapy outpatients (six families) and 23 group therapy (three groups) outpatients at two points (second and eighth sessions) in co-therapy.[15] At both sample points, the family therapy patients had lower percentages on five variables: environmental; personal; therapist-directed; elaborating; and group building. They had higher percentages at both points on four variables: group; negative; seeking information and opinion (a combined variable); and giving information and opinion (another combined variable). At the second session, the family therapy patients did more summarizing and at the eighth session they did more evaluating than the group therapy patients. The general picture that emerged is

that the family, even in distress, is a highly developed group with levels of cohesion and interaction not found in stranger groups. They waste little time in warm up and irrelevant comments either at the beginning of therapy or in later sessions as indicated by the low levels of environmental responding. Their need to involve themselves with the therapist appears less, and their ability to respond on a group interaction level is markedly different from the stranger group (Heckel, 1975, p. 255).

Additional, the data suggest that the familiarity of the family members allows them to spend less time elaborating and group building and more time being negative (less socially "desirable") than the group members. The overall impres-

---

[15] Heckel (1975) did not specify the size of his summarizing unit, e.g. the amount of data sampled from each session, or his data format (audiotape, transcript, etc.).

sion is that the family members "get down to business" more quickly. Heckel was particularly impressed by "the highly reactive and quick movement" that his therapists found "when working with families as opposed to traditional stranger therapy groups" (1975, p. 257).

The large number of significant findings (over 75%) reported by Heckel (1975) suggests that his scales have adequate discriminant validity. However, because Heckel did not control for therapist and/or patient differences, the differences that his scales picked up cannot be clearly or directly tied to the different treatment modalities (family versus group). The differences can only be attributed with any certainty to the different therapist-patient-modality "packages."

De Chenne. Coming out of an individually-oriented client-centered tradition, Klein et al. (1970) developed the Experiencing (EXP) Scale "for evaluating the quality of a patient's self-involvement in psychotherapy directly from tape recordings or typescripts of the therapy session" (p. 1). This seven-point ordinal scale measures the extent to which the patient's "ongoing, bodily, felt flow of experiencing is the basic datum of his awareness and communications about himself" (1970, p. 1). The EXP scale has been one of the most well-designed and thoroughly researched instruments for studying patient process in the field of psychotherapy research. A number of different studies over the past ten years have demonstrated the predictive and discriminant validity of the EXP Scale in individual psychotherapy research (Kiesler, 1973).

In the first attempt to date to apply the EXP scale to family therapy, De Chenne (1973) compared spouse responses to their mates and to the therapist in nine conjoint marital therapy sessions (with nine different therapists and couples). With one rater (the "best" of four in pretraining) scoring every spouse response in each session, De Chenne's analysis used both mean and peak EXP scores. Despite the fact that the mean EXP level of spouse-following-spouse statements was significantly lower than the mean of spouse-following-therapist statements (as predicted), De Chenne questioned the validity of this finding because the mean difference was only .15. He commented that "Even among the best raters, the reliability of scoring would

not allow a meaningful distinction of .15 of a scale stage" (1973, p. 213).[16] This study's strongest finding was that the peak EXP level of the spouse-following-spouse statements was lower (one whole scale point; p < .001) than the peak level of the spouse-following-therapist statements. De Chenne interpreted this finding as indicating that "each spouse is involved in one experiential 'system' with the therapist and another with the spouse" (1973, p. 213), and that the difference between the systems is most apparent in peak as opposed to mean EXP scores.

De Chenne's study supports the validity of the EXP scale as a measure of patient process in conjoint marital therapy. However, his results must be viewed with caution, in that the relevance and/or meaning of the distinction the EXP scale was able to make in his study is unclear. Nevertheless, De Chenne's results are suggestive and hopefully will lead to further evaluation of the EXP Scale as a process instrument in family therapy research.

Winer. Attempting to operationalize Bowen's (1966, 1978) concept of "differentiation of self," Winer (1971) developed the Change (C) Ratio. Generated by the "qualified pronoun count," the C Ratio is based on the number of "differentiated 'I' " statements made by family members during therapy, divided by the number of "we," "our" and "us" statements. Derived from a sentence by sentence analysis of every speech, a C Ratio is computed for each patient. This statistic rests on the assumption that the higher the C Ratio, the greater the degree of differentiation of self from the "undifferentiated family ego mass" (Bowen, 1966, p. 355).

In an exploratory study, Winer (1971) evaluated changes in the degree of "differentiation" in four married couples that were in group treatment over a three-and-a-half-year period with Murray Bowen. At the time of the study, none of the couples had terminated therapy. Coded samples consisting of the "first two or three available, complete clear recordings" were compared with "the three most recent sessions" (1971, p. 246). Winer predicted that the average

---

[16] This finding was further weakened by the fact that the mean EXP levels of the two types of statements were positively and significantly correlated.

C Ratio from the "first two or three" sessions would be less than one, and that the average C Ratio from the last three sessions would be greater than one. The C Ratios from six of the eight patients supported the first prediction, whereas the C Ratios from all eight supported the second one. Additionally, Winer discovered that

In early sessions, the husband-wife C Ratio response was extremely similar, showing almost a mirror pattern. Recent sessions show widely varying response patterns within each couple. This unlooked-for finding may confirm the usefulness of the qualified pronoun count as a tool to measure change, for it suggests that change takes place not only in terms of increased C Ratio, but also in terms of reduced homogeneity of response between couples (1971, p. 247).

Winer's results can be viewed as very preliminary evidence in support of the discriminant validity of the C Ratio. Her hypotheses were not tested statistically and no reliability data were reported for the fairly complicated unitization procedure or for the actual scoring (pronoun identification) process. The number of subjects in the study was very small and it was not clear whether the average C Ratios for the "pre" and "post" sessions were based on the same number of observations. The results cannot be generalized beyond the eight patients and their therapy group with Murray Bowen. Until the construct (the extent to which the C Ratio measures "differentiation") and predictive (the extent to which it is related to outcome) validities of the C Ratio have been evaluated, it is impossible to disregard the possibility that the changes that Winer noted represent nothing more than relatively superficial linguistic shifts (as opposed to "deeper" psychological ones). Clearly, Winer's (1971) pilot data need to be followed up on with more extensive and rigorous research to formally test the reliability of the qualified pronoun count and the validity of the C Ratio.

Zuk. Hypothesizing that *laughter in family therapy* disguises feelings and/or reflects anxiety, Zuk, Boszormenyi-Nagy, and Heiman (1963) examined the frequency of family member laughter in 13 taped sessions from the treatment of a family with a schizophrenic daughter. They found considerable variability in the reliability with which different family members' laughter could be rated. Based on data from one session, judges had the greatest difficulty (79% agreement) rating the patient's laughter (which sounded like "wheezing, sniffling or even crying") and the least difficulty (100% agreement) rating father's.

Zuk et al. (1963) explored the effect of time (session quarter) and person (who speaks to whom) on laughter frequency. In terms of time, they found a number of differences within and across the laughter patterns of the family members. Mother and father had the highest laughter frequencies in the first 15 minutes (quarter) of the 13 sessions, whereas the schizophrenic daughter had the highest frequency in the third quarter. The person-laughter results were only reported descriptively: Forty-seven percent of mother's laughter occurred when her husband was talking to another participant; 78% of the father's laughter occurred when he was talking to someone else; and 49% of the daughter's laughter occurred when the therapist was addressing her parents.

Zuk et al. interpreted their results in terms of various theories of anxiety or tension management. Unfortunately, the lack of empirical data on the laughter-anxiety link makes it impossible to evaluate the validity of their interpretation of the findings. Undoubtedly, laughter means different things and/or functions in different ways for different people in different contexts. Therefore, a unitary interpretation of laughter behavior (laughter = anxiety) is too reductionistic. Zuk et al.'s study clearly demonstrates systematic variations in laughter frequency in one family in therapy. However, the meaning of these variations can only be clarified with more research focusing on the validity (meaning and/or relevance) of laughter frequency in family therapy.

The Wynne Group. As a pioneer in the family therapy field, Lyman Wynne has devoted his research career to studying the families of schizophrenics. His "core" hypothesis has been that the individual patient's thought disorder reflects a stylistically similar "transactional thought disorder" which is revealed in his family's communication patterns (Wynne, 1972). Relying on a predictive design, most of Wynne's research has attempted to determine the extent to which a judge (or judges) could predict the type of disturbance in a family's offspring from listening to excerpts of the family's interaction in response to a structured, projective task in a laboratory setting (Singer and Wynne, 1965). However, in two very exploratory studies (Morris and Wynne, 1965; Palombo, Merrifield, Weigert, Morris and Wynne, 1967) Wynne's predictive method was applied to the verbal behavior (audiotapes and transcripts) of family members during family therapy sessions.

Morris and Wynne (1965) tested a judge's ability to predict the nature of a young adult's illness after listening to "sanitized" (all diagnostic clues and significant interaction with the patient were deleted) excerpts from his family's treatment. On a sample of eight families, the judge was able to predict, at a better than chance level, the global diagnoses of the patients, as well as their forms of thinking (amorphous, nixed, fragmented and non-schizophrenic). In this study, the judge used three "predictor" variables as guides in making his predictions. Two of these variables, Family Role Structure and Parental Styles of Expressing Affect, were not systematically operationalized. However, the third "predictor" variable, Parental Styles of Handling Attention and Communicating, was operationalized with an Attention Scale that derived from Singer and Wynne's work.

The Attention Scale enumerated ten ways in which families disrupt their attentional focus during family therapy. It is "composed of steps from undifferentiated, amorphous thought toward focal attention" (Morris and Wynne, 1963, p. 34). The scale goes from "undirected attention" (category one) through "disorganized disruptions of attention" (category three) to "overfocusing of attention" (category ten), and has both nominal and ordinal features. A family member receives a score of zero (none noted) to five (predominant or pervasive) in each of the ten scale categories.

The Attention Scale and the other two predictor variables were not used statistically. Instead, Morris and Wynne's judge used them as guides to examine the family therapy interaction prior to making his prediction. Palombo et al. (1967) basically replicated Morris and Wynne's

study, but instead of one judge they used three. They found that the three judges, after considerable training, were able to accurately predict the nature of the offspring's psychopathology. To determine the usefulness of the Attention Scale in the prediction process, Palombo et al. asked their three judges to evaluate its utility. They found mixed results and concluded that the judges' "training in the schema was a valuable and effective, if not necessary or sufficient, condition for the success of their predictions" (1967, p. 409).

These two studies (Morris and Wynne, 1965; Palombo et al., 1967) must be viewed as exploratory rather than confirmatory research. They demonstrate that it is possible for trained judges to reliably and accurately predict the nature of an inpatient's illness from listening to excerpts of family therapy sessions with his family. Additionally, their presentation of the Attention Scale and their attempt to apply it to the process of family therapy represent one of the first attempts in the field to operationalize one aspect of the patient's process during family therapy. Unfortunately, they did not evaluate the interrater reliability of the Attention Scale as applied to family therapy process, nor did they statistically relate the Attention Scale ratings to their criterion variables. They did attempt to highlight some of the factors that may have been involved in the prediction process, but they did not systematically assess the extent to which these factors accounted for the variance in their judges' predictions. Surprisingly and disappointingly, these two studies represent the only forays of Wynne's research group into the process of family therapy.

Family (Patient) Behavior: A Summary. As with the family therapist behavior studies, the research on the behavior of the family members during family therapy has not produced a clear or consistent body of results. Eight coding systems have been used to study the in-therapy behavior of family members. All eight of these systems focus exclusively on verbal behavior[17] and most have adequate reliability. The results

---

[17] Actually, Zuk et al.'s (1963) laughter research does not strictly deal with verbal behavior, as laughter can also be classified as a type of paralinguistic behavior.

of the studies that have been done with these systems are summarized below.

Using the Montreal Group's category system (E/N/W), Postner et al. (1971) did not find any relationship between the three code categories and family therapy outcome. Their only significant result, which was somewhat puzzling in light of their lack of process-outcome findings, was that, as therapy progressed, family members expressed more Welfare affect to each other. With their two category S-D system, Alexander et al. (1976) found that families with better outcomes had higher S/D ratios (were more supportive) at the end of therapy. Because Allred and Kersey (1977) did not report their results with the two AIAC client code categories independently of their therapist code category results, it was impossible to evaluate their validity. The three above-mentioned systems were used to complement each research group's family therapist coding system.

The following five client or family member systems were used independently of family therapist coding systems. Employing his two-scale (three and 11 categories respectively) group therapy coding system, Heckel (1975) found many differences between the in-therapy behaviors of group and family therapy clients. The general picture that emerged from Heckel's study was that the family therapy clients, in relation to the group therapy clients, interacted more with each other and less with the therapist and were less polite and more open and straightforward with each other. Using Klein et al.'s (1970) seven-point, ordinal Experiencing Scale, De Chenne (1973) found that spouse-following-therapist statements reflected higher peak levels of experiencing than the spouse-following-spouse statements in marital therapy. Winer (1971) found that, over the course of a marital therapy group, the average C Ratio (I/We) of six of the eight clients in the group shifted from less than to greater than one. She interpreted this finding as reflecting a change in the "degree of differentiation" of the marital partners. Studying a portion of one family's sessions in therapy, Zuk (1963) found that the frequency of laughter varied both within and across family members. Lastly, Morris and Wynne (1963) and Palombo et al. (1967) used the Attention Scale to facilitate their judges' predictions about the nature of an offspring's psychopathology after listening to excerpts from his family's therapy sessions.

The body of this review highlighted important methodological problems and/or limitations with most if not all of the client system studies. Generally, the methodological quality of these studies has been poor, and their scope has been very limited. However, the major problem with this body of research is that, for the most part, only one substantive study has been done with each of the eight systems. Leads have been explored and not followed up. As with the therapist systems, no single study, regardless of its quality or scope, can establish or fail to establish the validity and/or reliability of a coding system. More research needs to be done with each system before any firm conclusions can be drawn about its validity, feasibility, or utility. The research on family member behavior that has been reviewed should be considered as pilot or exploratory research. As such, each system and study represent the beginning of a path into a largely uncharted territory.

A puzzling phenomenon is that, with few exceptions, family therapy researchers dealing with family member behavior in therapy have not availed themselves of the experience and knowledge gained by researchers in the related field of family interaction research. This research area grows out of the larger field of social interaction or small group research, and involves the application of coding systems to family behavior in response to structured tasks in a laboratory or "natural" (non-therapy) setting. The research in this area has been extensively reviewed several times within the last decade (Framo, 1972; Jacob, 1975; Riskin and Faunce, 1972), and a wide variety of well-designed and researched coding systems have been developed (Gottman, 1978; Hops, Wills, Patterson, and Weiss, 1971; Mishler and Waxler, 1968; Patterson, Ray, Shaw and Cobb, 1969; Riskin and Faunce, 1968, 1970a, 1970b).

In general, the family interaction researchers have not applied their methods to the study of family behavior in therapy, perhaps because the therapy setting, and particularly the intrusive presence of the family therapist, represent uncontrolled sources of variance in family behavior that are not present in the laboratory or natural setting. An additional factor is that a fair number of the family interaction researchers are behaviorists, and have developed family therapy programs that rely minimally, if at all, on conventional family therapy sessions (Gottman, 1978; Hops et al., 1971; Patterson et al., 1969). The University of Utah Group, Alexander et al. (Alexander, 1973; Alexander et al., 1976) and Wynne's Group (Morris and Wynne, 1965; Palombo et al., 1967) represent the only researchers who have done work in both areas, applying their respective scales (S-D and Attention) to family interaction in both experimental and therapeutic settings. Hopefully more researchers will apply the knowledge and systems of the family interaction field to the in-therapy behavior of family members.

This review of the research on the in-therapy behavior of the family has highlighted the fact that this research area is so young and undeveloped that clear trends or patterns of findings have not yet emerged. However, in reviewing this research, an incipient trend can be discerned. The first three family member coding systems that were discussed all contain what might be referred to as a positive and a negative category. The positive categories in the systems are Welfare, Supportive, and Works, and the complementary negative categories are, respectively, Emergency, Defensive and Resists. A number of coding systems that have been developed in the family interaction area also include positive and negative categories which are labeled as such (Bugental, Love, Kaswan, and April, 1971; Gottman, 1978; Riskin and Faunce, 1968, 1970a, 1970b). The extent to which all of the positive categories and all of the negative categories actually target similar phenomena has not been tested empirically, and it may well be that they are measuring different things. However, the ubiquity of the positive/negative distinction in family coding systems implies a certain face validity. Insofar as process researchers indicate what they consider to be important and/or useful by including it in their coding systems, family behavior researchers clearly consider positive/negative to be *a* if not *the* critical distinction.

Symmetrical Systems. Psychotherapy coding systems can be characterized as either complementary or symmetrical (Watzlawick, Beavin

and Jackson, 1967, pp. 68-69). The systems that have been reviewed so far are complementary in that they are based on the use of different systems and/or categories for the therapist and clients. In contrast, several researchers (Scheflen, 1966; Benjamin, 1977, 1979) have developed symmetrical systems that apply the same systems and categories to the behavior of the therapist and clients.[18]

The two symmetrical systems that will be discussed are more than psychotherapy or family therapy coding systems. Actually, they are models or systems for analyzing human interaction that have been applied to the process of family therapy. Neither of these systems was designed explicitly to study family therapy (or any kind of psychotherapy). Each embodies a comprehensive model of human behavior that can be used to elucidate and analyze virtually any kind of human interaction. Additionally, both systems attempt to identify the underlying form or structure of human behavior and, as such, constitute structural models (Gardner, 1972).

Scheflen. Scheflen's (1966, 1973) *context analytic approach* to process analysis derives from communication theory (Bateson, 1972; Birdwhistell, 1970) and cybernetics (Miller, 1965; Wiener, 1961). Of the two symmetrical approaches, Scheflen's is the least "psychological" and most ethnographic. As much as possible, context analysis eschews theoretical assumptions and technical terminology, and attempts to "get back to the study of behavior itself" (Scheflen, 1973, p. 7). It entails an intensive, detailed description of every discernible (to the participants) behavior (verbal and kinesic) of every individual within a group during a transaction. After behaviors are identified, context analysts

examine the relations of one behavior to another and these to a third until we have identified all of the

---

[18] The researcher's choice of a symmetrical or complementary system depends on his/her theory of psychotherapy, and in particular the role of the psychotherapist. For instance, complementary systems derive from a theory that conceives of the client and therapist roles as distinct, whereas symmetrical systems derive from a theory that minimizes role distinctions.

behavioral elements that constitute a single, defined subsystem of behavior or change (1973, p. 8).

Subsequently, these "defined subsystems" are integrated into larger interpersonal or transactional units.

Context analysis of a transaction can begin at any organizational or system (individual, dyadic, triadic, etc.) level. Scheflen prefers to unitize his transactions on the basis of postural shifts or "positions." Thus, initially, behaviors are categorized according to kinesic form. Adding together and integrating positions, transactional patterns or structures are derived that are particular to the participants in a given transaction. The isolated positions and the integrated patterns or structures that emerge out of a given transaction are equivalent to nominal code categories. However, in contrast to the other symmetrical system (Benjamin, 1977, 1979) and the other coding systems that have been examined, these nominal categories can change with different participants and/or different transactions. As such, the specific categories that context analysts use to describe and analyze a transaction do not constitute a transcontextual coding system. In essence, each transaction generates the terms or categories of its own analysis.

Scheflen (1973) applied his method to the description and analysis of a single psychotherapy session with an adolescent schizophrenic girl, her mother and two well-known co-therapists (Carl Whitaker and Thomas Malone).[19] Since Scheflen's method eschews experimental methodology and statistical analysis, the data it generates are entirely descriptive. The session analysis results were complex and varied. An example of his findings was that the participants assumed ten positions during the session: 1) explaining; 2) passive protesting; 3) listening; 4) questioning; 5) contending; 6) accusing; 7) defending; 8) intervention; 9) resigning; and 10) tactile contacting. This finding means that whenever a participant shifted from one of the above-mentioned activities, he discernibly shifted his/her position. Many additional findings were reported about the session at both higher (more macroscopic) and

lower (more microscopic) levels of organization.

To be accurate, Scheflen does not offer a coding system but a method of analysis that derives a specific coding system or group of nominal categories at each system level from a particular transaction. The critical element of his approach is his method, not the content it generates. The great benefit of his approach is that it is without a doubt the least reductionistic process analysis method. It does minimal violence to the integrity and uniqueness of a given transaction. Its greatest deficit is the complexity and sophistication of the method. It involves great amounts of time, video and sound equipment, as well as considerable expertise on the part of the investigator(s). From the relatively narrow perspective of the psychotherapy researcher, another drawback to this approach is the lack of a transcontextual coding system that can be applied across different psychotherapeutic situations. This deficit limits the extent to which the knowledge derived from context analysis can be employed in training psychotherapists (and particularly family therapists) and in generating transcontextual or even context specific psychotherapeutic "laws."

Benjamin. Benjamin (1974, 1977, 1979) developed and refined a *structural analytic model* that deals with both interpersonal and intrapsychic functioning. Structurally, her model derives from earlier models developed by Leary (1957) and Schaefer (1965). In terms of psychological content, Benjamin's model draws primarily from client-centered therapy (Rogers, 1951, 1957) and secondarily from psychoanalytic theories of development (i.e., Erikson, 1959; Freud, 1964; Mahler, 1968).

This complex model is based on the Chart of Social Behavior, a diagram that consists of three planes or surfaces. The first and top plane, labeled *Other*, identifies 36 parentlike behaviors of another person directed toward the self, e.g., Friendly listen, Punish, Ignore, etc. The second and middle plane, *Self*, delineates 36 complementary childlike "responses of the self to the other" (Benjamin, 1979, p.5), e.g., Openly disclose, Appease, Wall-off, etc. These two surfaces constitute the Interpersonal planes of the chart and represent complementary, dyadic interpersonal relationships. The third and bottom plane, *Introject*, "describes the intrapsychic ef-

---

[19] Actually, the total project reported in Scheflen's (1973) book involved ten sessions. However, the book focused primarily on the first session.

fect when the self focuses on the self, i.e., turns the behaviors of the other inward onto the self. Prototypically, the Introject plane describes the result of turning Parental behaviors onto the Self" (Benjamin, 1979, p. 5). This intrapsychic surface of the model similarly consists of 36 "internal" or "covert" behaviors such as Explore, Vengeful self-punish, Fantasy, etc.

Benjamin's model is one of the most highly integrated and coordinated approaches to process analysis. Each of the three planes is organized around two theoretically orthogonal dimensions or axes. On each plane the horizontal axis represents affiliation and the vertical axis interdependence. Opposite behaviors are found at the poles of each axis. For instance, on the Other plane, Endorse Freedom is juxtaposed to Manage, Control on the interdependence axis, whereas Tender Sexuality is juxtaposed to Annihilating Attack on the affiliation axis. These axes divide each plane into four quadrants. Each quadrant in turn is divided into nine perimeter points at ten degree intervals. Each perimeter point identifies a specific behavior (4 × 9 = 36). Moving counterclockwise on the perimeter of the Other plane from Tender Sexuality (3 o'clock) to Endorse Freedom (12 o'clock), the subjective quality of the nine behaviors changes in the direction of the approaching pole, e.g., from Warmly Welcome through Show Empathic Understanding to Encourage Separate Identity. The nine steps in each quadrant of each plane are related to nine "tracks" that deal with various psychological variables like Approach-Avoidance (Track 1), Attachment (Track 3) and Identity (Track 8).

Each plane of Benjamin's model is analogous to a distinct 36-category interval coding scale.[20] Each of the 108 behaviors in her model is identified with a three digit number. The first digit indicates the plane (1 = other, 2 = Self, and 3 = Introject), the second digit targets the quadrant of the plane (I-IV), and the third digit identifies the track within the quadrant (0-8) to which any particular behavior belongs. The theoretical core of Benjamin's model is expressed

through her system's ability to permit identification of the *opposite* (Friendly Listen-115 and Accuse, Blame-135), the *complement* (Friendly Listen-115 and Openly Disclose, Reveal-215) and the antithesis or *antidote* (the opposite of the complement, e.g., Accuse, Blame-135 and Openly Disclose, Reveal-215) of specific behaviors (1979, pp. 7-8).

Benjamin's system can be used in a variety of ways. As a research instrument,[21] it was designed initially to be used as a self-report measure that relied on questionnaires filled out by the participants in a transaction. Benjamin (1977) used the system in this way within an N of 1 format to describe and analyze the three-year therapy of a single family. In this study, the chart was used to illuminate family dynamics, to generate a treatment plan, to delineate changes during therapy, to analyze resistance and to identify movement toward therapeutic goals. In a more recent study, Benjamin (1979) also used the chart as a self-report measure to operationalize a variety of key and heretofore hard-to-capture transactional concepts in the family therapy field (entrapment, pamper-overindulge, and double-bind).

In her more recent study (1979) Benjamin illustrated the use of the chart as an observational measurement system for classifying transactions between the therapist and client in the family-oriented psychotherapy of a young professional woman. Preliminary evidence indicates that coders could reliably (product-moment correlations of .92 and .88) rate videotaped interview behavior in terms of the eight quadrants in the two interpersonal planes (Other and Self).

Benjamin has developed a theoretically sophisticated, complex, dynamic and multi-purpose system for analyzing a wide variety of interpersonal and intrapsychic transactions. Her two efforts to apply the system to family interaction and family therapy (1977, 1979) have illustrated with case examples several of the ways her system can be used as a process measure. In terms of the system's use as an observational instrument, a number of critical methodological

---

[20] These scales are characterized as interval scales because the scale points (categories) are conceptually equidistant (10 degrees). These scales (or planes) represent the only interval scales that have been developed in the field of psychotherapy process research.

---

[21] Additionally, its dynamic quality (identification of opposites, etc.) gives it great potential as a training-supervision framework.

issues have yet to be addressed, which leaves the scoring procedure unclear. For instance, what is the scoring unit for the system and is each act in a transaction analyzed on each plane? Similarly, can an act be scored with more than one behavior from a plane at the same time, i.e., are the code categories on a scale mutually exclusive?

The potential of Benjamin's model as a family therapy process research instrument has just begun to be tapped. Hopefully, the pathways that Benjamin has already opened up with her system will be further explored and additional pathways opened up as more research with the system emerges.

Family Therapy Process Research: A Summary

The preceding section has reviewed most, if not all of the extant quantitative research on the process of family therapy. This research has approached family therapy process with both self-report and direct observation access strategies. By far the bulk of research in the field has used the latter strategy. In terms of focus, the research has either taken a complementary position and attended to the therapist and/or family members with different code systems or categories, or adopted a symmetrical position and attended to the therapist and family members with the same system. Most research has derived from the complementary position.

All of the research in the area can be characterized as exploratory. In fact, most of it constitutes pilot research. A considerable variety of process analysis systems has been developed and tested in one or two studies that were of poor to mediocre methodological quality. A coherent body of findings has not yet emerged. What the field clearly needs at this point is persistence. Researchers need to follow through with more studies of their own and each other's coding systems. This is the only way that a coherent and meaningful body of knowledge can be accumulated. The leads exist—they need to be pursued.

FAMILY THERAPY PROCESS RESEARCH: METHODOLOGICAL ISSUES

This section identifies and explores a number of important methodological issues that must be confronted in doing or evaluating family therapy process research. The sequence of issue examination in this section corresponds roughly to the sequence in which the researcher encounters these issues in attempting to describe and analyze the process of family therapy. This section is divided into two parts. The first focuses on variable selection and instrumentation. The second deals with issues of research design and data analysis. As appropriate, examples will be drawn from the preceding literature review to illustrate the ways in which the various issues have been handled. Additionally, a variety of methodological and clinical research possibilities will be suggested as different research issues are examined.

Kiesler (1973) devoted a chapter of his book to a discussion of methodological issues in psychotherapy process research. This chapter (1973, pp. 27-68) is a good companion piece to this section. However, Kiesler's chapter was written from the perspective of individual psychotherapy. In contrast, this section explores the methodology of psychotherapy process research from the perspective of the family therapy process researcher. This section rests on the assertion that the predominant, individually-oriented psychotherapy process research methology must be modified (or expanded) to accommodate the unique theoretical and pragmatic features of family therapy.

Variable Selection and Instrumentation

Variable selection—What to study?

The first problem that confronts the family therapy process researcher is the overwhelming amount of data embodied in the process of family therapy. Essentially, the initial task is to focus on some relevant aspects(s) of this "data mass," to reduce it to manageable proportions. In other words, one must decide which variable(s) to study and which to ignore.

The variables that have been or can be studied in family therapy process research can be located at various points on an abstractness continuum. The more abstract variables tend to be referred to as concepts, constructs or dimensions, whereas the less abstract and more concrete ones tend to be clearly behavioral. For instance, the therapist coding system developed by Alexander et al. (1976) targets relatively abstract constructs like Affect-behavior integration, Warmth and Directiveness. This is also the case with Klein et al.'s (1970) client coding system that deals with the concept of Experiencing. These relatively abstract variables can be juxtaposed to the highly concrete ones targeted by Chagoya et al.'s (1974) FTIS (Asks questions, Gives task, etc.) and Pinsof's (1979) FTCS (Negative Emotion-NE/Communication-C/Now-N/, etc.).

Highly abstract variables are subject to unintentional multidimensionality—a situation in which the variable may contain a number of unspecified subvariables that must be theoretically and methodologically "untangled" and differentiated. Similarly, the more abstract the variable, the greater the amount of inference necessary to rate and study it. Both of these related problems can reduce the construct validity (and reliability) of an abstract variable, making it difficult to know exactly what the variable represents.

As Kiesler (1973) suggested, these problems can be ameliorated by having a clear conceptualization of the variable or construct to be studied.[22] The variable should derive from an explicit, theoretical framework that permits generation of hypotheses about the way the variable might behave in different research situations. This theoretical framework facilitates hypothesis formation about the way the variable interacts with other pertinent variables. Thus, as well as clarifying the variable itself, the researcher needs to clarify its theoretical or multivariate context.

Selecting such a "clear variable" is important because "it is intimately related to the resolution of other methodological problems" (Kiesler, 1973, p. 31). The foremost "methodological problem" concerns operationalizing the variable so that it can be measured (or coded). The clearer the theoretical variable, the easier it operationalizes. For example, if a concept such as empathy is considered to have verbal, paralinguistic and kinesic components, separate instruments (scales) can be found or created to measure each component. If the components of a construct like therapist empathy are undifferentiated, they cannot be operationalized and the construct will be unintentionally multidimensional. A number of researchers consider this to be the case with Rogers' (1957) presentation of the concept of empathic understanding and Truax's (1961; Truax and Carkhuff, 1967) attempt to operationalize it with his Accurate Empathy (AE) Scale (Caracena and Vicory, 1969; Kiesler et al., 1967). The validity and feasibility of operational measures (scales) relate primarily to the quality of conceptualization involved in clarifying the construct from which the measures derive.

In contrast to abstract variables, highly concrete variables target discrete behaviors and are easy to operationalize. However, they are subject to the problem of interpretation and relevance. They are easy to measure, but it is hard to know what they mean. This problem is exemplified by Zuk et al.'s (1963) laughter research discussed above. Systematic variations in laughter frequency were noted, but their meaning was unclear.

As with the more abstract variables, this problem can be ameliorated by "nesting" a concrete variable within a differentiated hypothesis framework. Such a framework should permit identification of a variety of clinical hypotheses about the variable's behavior in different research situations and in relationship to its multivariate context. In terms of laughter, if one hypothesizes that it functions to mask negative feelings, one would predict that as negative feelings emerge in family therapy, the frequency of laughter will increase. The more specific the hypotheses about a variable (and its multivariate context), the easier it is to meaningfully interpret the findings it generates.

The critical point is that no matter where one starts on the abstractness continuum, the amount of conceptual work that goes into clarifying a variable and its context is directly related to the validity and feasibility of research about the variable. Whether one works down (toward concrete operationalization) with an abstract variable, or up (toward abstract relevance and meaning) with a concrete one, conceptual clarity and specificity are essential.

---

[22] This discussion portrays the research process as if it involved a single variable. This univariate focus is purely for clarity's sake, and should not obscure the fact that many process researchers deal with multiple variables.

Instrumentation—How to study it?

Once a variable has been selected, the researcher must decide how to study or measure it. As a result of clarifying the variable, avenues of operationalization should be apparent. Initially, the process researcher must decide what kinds of client (family member) and/or therapist behaviors (cues) characterize the variable. In doing so, the behavioral channels (verbal, paralinguistic and kinesic) that carry or express the cues must be identified and the access strategies must be decided upon. Once the actors (family members and/or therapist), cues, channels and modes of access have been considered, a system for measuring or coding the variable must be created or selected from existing systems.

General criteria for coding systems

Family therapy coding systems can be comparatively evaluated on a number of general criteria or characteristics.

Reconstructivity. Coding or rating involves abstracting out certain characteristics of the phenomenon that is coded. This abstraction process reduces the phenomenon to one or more of the code category or scale points of the coding system in question. These code data constitute the "abstracted phenomenon." Reconstructivity refers to the ability of the coding system to permit clinically meaningful reconstruction, from the code data, of the specific behaviors or experiences from which they were abstracted. Coding systems that are low in reconstructivity do not permit the research consumer (in this case family therapists and family therapy researchers) to develop a clear, meaningful picture of the clinical entity that was rated. In terms of therapist behavior, a minimally reconstructive system would not permit the consumer to know what the therapist actually did in a particular transaction. It might allow him to know how it was done (well or poorly), or how much of a particular dimension or variable was present in the behavior (Warmth, Humor, etc.), but it would not let him know *what* it was.

The most highly reconstructive family therapy process instrument is Pinsof's (1979b) FTCS, a system that was explicitly designed to be reconstructive. That system consists of multiple (nine) nominal scales. In general, single-scale (univariate) systems tend to be low in reconstructivity. This also appears to be the case with many ordinal (as opposed to nominal) scales.

Reconstructivity increases the specificity of a coding system. Additionally, it increases the extent to which the system can be used to train therapists for the specificity question. Such training involves teaching clinicans to identify critical client (family member) behaviors and to perform critical interventions in the contexts in which the coding system has shown them to be effective.

Obviously, no feasible coding system will ever permit "total" reconstruction of every family or therapist behavior/experience.

Reconstructivity is always partial. However, the greater the reconstructive ability of a coding system, the greater its clinical specificity and relevance, which increases that system's ability to deal with the specificity question (Pinsof, 1979b, p. 9).

Modality-System Fit. This criterion deals with the extent to which a psychotherapy process measurement system fits, accommodates or describes the unique theoretical and pragmatic features of the psychotherapeutic modality to which it is applied. Many of the coding systems reviewed in the preceding section were designed to fit individual psychotherapy or counseling. These systems ignore certain critical aspects of family therapy process. The foremost pragmatic feature that distinguishes family therapy (from individual therapy in particular) is that usually more than one family member is present at the interview. In terms of the therapist, this means that he can talk directly to one or more family members simultaneously. Additionally, the therapist can directly modify family transactional patterns in the interview.[23] In terms of family behavior, multiple clients mean that many different kinds of behavior can be occurring simultaneously.

On a theoretical level, family therapy rests on a conceptual foundation derived from general

---

[23] Pinsof's (1979b) FTCS is the only system developed to date that identifies to whom the therapist is speaking. The direct modification of family behavior in the interview, as well as being encompassed by the FTCS, is also dealt with by Pinsof's FTBS (1979a) and Chagoya et al.'s (1974) TFIS.

systems theory (Bertalanffy, 1968; Buckley, 1968). The implications of this perspective for psychotherapy research (both process and outcome) have hardly been explored. Another distinctive conceptual feature of family therapy (in contrast to individual and group therapy) is that it is clearly designed to deal directly with intimate, familial behavior/experience (love, sex, conflict, discipline, etc.) between the clients (family members). An additional feature of family therapy is that, conceptually, the target of therapy is not only the individual client, but the family system.

The more a coding system fits a particular therapeutic modality, the greater its reconstructivity and specificity. Fit also becomes important when coding system data are used for training therapists. In light of the preceding discussion, it would seem unwise to base a family therapy training program on research data derived from instruments that were not designed to fit family therapy. This is not to say that such instruments cannot be helpful in developing family therapy training programs, but only that, in themselves, they are not sufficient.

Orientation-System Fit. Each of the major psychotherapeutic modalities (individual, group and family) contains various orientations and schools. Within individual psychotherapy, the predominant orientations have been psychoanalytic, behavioral and client-centered. As this book attests, similar and additional orientations characterize the field of family therapy. This criterion deals with the extent to which a coding or measurement system fits the (allegedly) unique features of distinctive orientations or schools within a therapeutic modality. The more universal or comprehensive a coding system, the more it is designed to identify and differentiate distinct features of specific, within-modality orientations.

Of the coding systems examined in the preceding review, only Chagoya et al.'s (1974) FTIS and Pinsof's (1979) FTCS were explicitly designed to distinguish characteristic features of a variety of family therapy orientations. These or other comprehensive systems (to be developed) could be used to systematically evaluate the extent to which therapist behavior differs across family therapy orientations (Structural,

Strategic, Behavioral, Psychoanalytic, etc.). If differences emerge, these systems could also be used to find out whether they "make a difference" (are differentially effective).

Exhaustiveness. This fourth and last criterion concerns the ability of a measurement system to code, in a meaningful (not an "other") category, every intelligible therapist and/or client behavior. This criterion is particularly relevant to observational systems that use nominal (as opposed to ordinal) scales. Exhaustiveness is important for at least three reasons. First, it increases the specificity and meaningfulness of coding system data by providing a complete picture of the subject's behavior. Secondly, exhaustive systems code the entire stream of therapist and/or client behavior, which is a prerequisite to sequential behavior analysis, a data analysis approach that is becoming increasingly important in the field of psychotherapy process research. The third reason is that exhaustiveness prohibits coders from prematurely terminating the coding process by forcing them to actively categorize every statement. The presence of an "Other" category in non-exhaustive systems frequently permits the coders to "dump" problematic behaviors into that category without having to think them through and classify them in more descriptive, "active" categories. Exhaustive systems keep coders "on their toes." Most of the nominal scale coding systems that were reviewed above are exhaustive.

Specific System Criteria. In addition to the four general criteria presented above, family therapy process analysis systems can be evaluated or compared on a variety of specific or micro-methodological criteria.[24]

Scale Type. Measurement systems consist of one or more scales. Most of the scales that have been applied to the process of family therapy (and psychotherapy in general) are either nominal or ordinal. Selection of a particular type of

---

[24] Most of the following discussion on instrumentation focuses primarily on the issues and problems involved in the use of direct observation measures, as opposed to self-report instruments.

scale depends on a number of factors, the foremost of which is the kind of variable to be studied. Continuous variables, such as Warmth (Alexander et al., 1976) and Experiencing (Klein et al., 1970), are operationalized most appropriately with ordinal scales, "which subsume a set of points that describe varying degrees of the dimension being observed" (Kiesler, 1973, p. 35). Discontinuous or discrete variables, such as Drive (Postner et al., 1971), Support (Pinsof, 1979a), Giving Opinion (Heckel, 1975), and Overfocusing of Attention (Morris and Wynne, 1965), are scaled most appropriately with nominal scales or what Kiesler calls "category systems" (1973, p. 35). In contrast to the quantitative differences between ordinal scale points, nominal scale points (or categories) differ qualitatively. Assigning discrete behaviors to separate categories, the essence of nominal scaling, can be based on any kind of qualitative difference. Behaviors can be categorized according to function, structure, content, etc.

Ordinal scales are subject to certain problems, the first of which is lack of specificity. Frequently, ordinal scales are used to measure relatively abstract or nonspecific[25] variables. Subsequently, if the variable has not been adequately clarified, the scale may, like the variable, be unintentionally multidimensional. If this is the case, it becomes very difficult to know what the scale is actually measuring. Furthermore, it makes it difficult to know the specific client and/or therapist behaviors that the coders use as rating cues to make their scale ratings. Such a lack of behavioral specificity hinders identification (in particular for training purposes) of what the ordinal scale actually codes. To avoid this pitfall, the scale points of ordinal scales need to behaviorally anchored by specifying the cue behaviors that define them.

The second major problem with ordinal scales is that they reflect the evaluative positions (or biases) of their developers, and are subsequently more subject to coder bias. With most ordinal scales, a particular score is not only higher or lower, but also implicitly "better" or

"worse." For instance, with Alexander et al.'s (1976) therapist Warmth scale and Klein et al.'s (1970) client Experiencing scale, a higher score is clearly more desirable than a lower one. Thus, with ordinal scales, the coder characterizes and evaluates simultaneously, whereas with most nominal scales the coder solely characterizes or categorizes. Removing evaluation from the coding or rating process minimizes the likelihood that the coder's response will influence the ratings.[26]

The major problem that can afflict nominal scales is lack of specificity. For instance, Sigal et al.'s failure to find significant results in their studies with their two-category D-I Scale (Postner et al., 1971) can be attributed, at least in part, to the global quality of the two code categories. Coding the entire spectrum of therapist verbal behavior with just two code categories meant that each category included many different types of interventions. The therapist's behavior could change radically over the course of therapy, but if the change involved an increase in one type of intervention and a comparable decrease in the frequency of another intervention that belonged to the same category, the changes would cancel each other. This would result in no change in the score of the code category that encompassed the two interventions, and might lead to the erroneous conclusion that the therapist's behavior had not changed at all. This lack of specificity with nominal scales can be remedied by making the scale more molecular and differentiating.

Increasing the molecularity of a nominal scale involves adding more categories to the scale. Usually it is done to increase scale validity, particularly discriminant validity. The risk or trade-off in attempting to increase validity by adding code categories is a loss in reliability. Every time the number of options open to the coder increases, the likelihood of coder error also increases. This is the process researcher's dilemma—gain in validity or meaning versus a loss in simplicity and reliability. The issue that

---

[25] A number of psychotherapy researchers have asserted that the so-called nonspecific variables (Caring, Attention, Warmth, etc) are more related to outcome than the specific ones (Transference Interpretation, Reflection, etc.) (Frank, 1973).

[26] An additional problem with ordinal scales concerns their statistical accessibility. Although this appears to be changing, historically, the analysis of ordinal scale data has been confined to the realm of non-parametric statistics. The more powerful parametric statistical procedures could only be applied to nominal or interval scale data.

continually confronts the process researcher is whether a potential methodological loss (like lowered reliability) is worth the substantive gain.

An example of this dilemma concerns coding the therapist, and involves

what to do with categories that are scored so infrequently as to render measurements of reliability almost impossible yet which may turn out to be critical categories in terms of producing change or in discriminating between therapeutic techniques (J. Sigal, 1978, personal communication).

For instance, Pinsof (1979a) found that his FTBS category Refocus (R) differentiated his condition-groups as predicted. However, in the reliability sample for that study (six 15-minute samples from six different sessions), Refocus only occurred once. To some extent, this problem can be remedied by using larger reliability samples and/or by pre-selecting or generating samples in which the code behavior occurs more frequently (Gottman and Markman, 1978, p. 45). However, the basic dilemma remains—is the relevance gain worth the methodological loss? This dilemma can only be resolved on a case by case basis, in terms of the researcher's goals and constraints.

Similarly, the type of scale (ordinal versus nominal) that is selected or created should fit the research questions and theoretical variables chosen for empirical investigation. Both types of scales have their assets and deficits, and can only be evaluated in relation to the tasks and variables in question. With molecular nominal scales, it is generally easier to pinpoint the actual behaviors being rated, but it is impossible to rate degrees of the variable as one can with ordinal scales. Regardless of the type of scale ultimately used, the specificity of the scale is probably the most critical determinant of its validity and usefulness.[27]

Unitization. Unitization relates primarily to observational coding systems, and involves de-

lineating the behavioral units or samples to which the system will be applied. Drawing on the work of other process researchers, Kiesler (1973) identifies three types of hierarchically integrated units of which the process researcher needs to be aware: the scoring unit, the contextual unit, and the summarizing unit. The *scoring unit* is "the specific segment of the content that is characterized by placing it in a given category" (Kiesler, 1973, p. 38). The *contextual unit* surrounds the scoring unit and sets the limits on the amount of data that the coder can consider in assigning a scoring unit to a category or scale level. The *summarizing unit* "is the group of scoring units about which some statement is made, or the unit in terms of which quantification is performed" (Kiesler, 1973, p. 39). In a typical study, the scoring unit might be the speech (everything one person says between the utterances of one or more other people), the contextual unit might be the preceding and successive speeches, and the summarizing unit might be a 15-minute interview segment. Generally, the scoring unit is the most critical of the three, because it is the data segment that is directly targeted by the coding system and coder.

Pinsof (1979a, 1979b) has explored the use of various scoring units. Most coding systems use fixed scoring units like the sentence or speech. In his FTBS study, Pinsof (1979a) used

a new type of scoring unit called the therapist "statement" which varies according to the code category to which it is assigned. For instance, the statement, "You're looking pretty angry," would be itself be coded as an Affect-Now (AN), whereas the statement "You're looking pretty angry since your wife began to express her doubts about your relationship," would be coded as a Sequence-Now (SN). The structurally more complex SN code supersedes or takes priority over the simpler, less inclusive AN code (pp. 5-6).

The flexible therapist statement was intended to maximize the clinical sensitivity and validity of the FTBS by operationally recognizing the fact that therapist interventions are sized differentially, i.e., they come in different sizes. In attempting to increase the validity of the FTBS, Pinsof ran the risk of jeopardizing FTBS reliability. The flexible scoring unit complicated cod-

---

[27] Certain types of coding systems combine ordinal and nominal scales. For instance, the Attention Scale (Morris and Wynne, 1965) used by Wynne's research group consists of ten nominal code categories that are each rated with a five-point ordinal scale.

ing by forcing the coder to simultaneously unitize and categorize.

In analyzing the FTBS reliability data, Pinsof found "that approximately one-third of the coder disagreements involved unitization errors in which one coder rated a statement that the other coder failed to differentiate from other statements" (1979a, p. 10). In fact, the interrater reliability of the FTBS increased ten percentage points when the unitization errors were deleted from the reliability analysis. These reliability data indicated that the flexible scoring unit had markedly reduced the reliability of the FTBS.

In developing the FTCS, Pinsof (1979b) attempted to reduce the complexity of the coding task by moving from a flexible unit to a fixed one. However, to maintain the same clinical sensitivity that the flexible therapist statement provided, Pinsof used three distinct hierarchically integrated scoring units. The nine scales of the FTCS focus on different dimensions or aspects of the therapist's verbal behavior. In developing the FTCS, it became apparent that the variables targeted by the scales functioned at different levels of abstraction.

Rather than use the same scoring unit for all nine scales, which would have forced certain scales to work at a level of abstraction that was not suited to the variable they targeted, Pinsof (1979b) permitted each scale to work at its own "best" level by delineating multiple scoring units:

The TOPIC Scale (#1) uses the smallest scoring unit—the verb. The INTERVENTION, TEMPORAL ORIENTATION, TO WHOM, INTERPERSONAL STRUCTURE, SYSTEM MEMBERSHIP, ROUTE and GRAMMATICAL FORM Scales (Nos. 2-8) use the intermediate size scoring unit—the main or independent clause and its attendant subordinate or dependent clauses. The EVENT RELATIONSHIP Scale (#9) uses the largest FTCS scoring unit—the speech (Pinsof, 1979b, p. 13).

In a further effort to separate unitization and categorization, and thereby reduce the complexity of the coding process, Pinsof (1979b) advocated pre-unitization of the data (transcripts) by a unitization coder. Thus, the FTCS coder receives a pre-unitized transcript which he subsequently codes with each of the nine scales.

The delineation of scoring units can be based on a variety of factors. The simplest and most clear-cut basis for unitization is grammatical form. Most observational process researchers have used some type of grammatical unit like the phrase, sentence or speech. Another more complicated and perhaps more meaningful basis for unitization involves the delineation of clinical units like the intervention or operation. Such units would probably have to be flexible, which raises all of the same problems that Pinsof (1979a) confronted with his flexible therapist statement.

So far, this discussion has focused on the delineation of verbal channel units. The only researcher in the family therapy process area that has explicitly dealt with nonverbal or kinesic units is Scheflen (1973). His search for natural units has lead him to focus on "positions" delineated by distinct "postural shifts." Other potential bases for kinesic units are gaze direction and head nods (Dittman, 1972) or shifts in distinctive facial expressions (Ekman, Friesen, and Ellsworth, 1972).

The important point in selecting scoring units (as well as contextual and summarizing units) is that the units should fit the variables to be studied as well as the scales that will be used to study them. Another critical point is that, in reporting their research, process investigators must specify their units. As the literature review indicated, a number of researchers even failed to report what kind of scoring unit they used. Since process results are at least in part a function of the type of units used, the research consumer needs to know what kind of unit was used with a particular system in a particular study in order to comparatively evaluate the results of that study.[28]

Data Format. The third specific system criterion or characteristic concerns the format of the data to which the system will be applied. The researcher must decide on the medium (format) through which the raw data (family and therapist behavior/experience) will be presented to the coders. Should the raw data be presented via audiotape, videotape and/or transcripts? As

---

[28] An interesting and important methodological study might compare the effects (on results) of using different units with the same coding system and the same raw data.

with most methodological issues, this decision can only be made in relation to the research questions, theoretical variables, coding systems and research constraints (cost, etc.) in question. If one is primarily interested in variables characterized by kinesic behaviors, videotape is clearly the medium of choice. In contrast, if one is primarily interested in stylistic variables characterized by paralinguistic behavior (Rice, 1965), audiotape is the best choice. The choice of a medium is not so clear-cut when the behaviors characterizing the variable are verbal; videotape, audiotape or transcripts can be used.

A critical data format issue concerns *channel isolation*. Clearly, videotape provides the most information of any format. However, this can be a mixed blessing. If one is primarily interested in verbal channel variables and has coders use videotape, it is impossible to evaluate the extent to which the coders' ratings might be contaminated by information from the kinesic and paralinguistic channels, both of which are available on videotape. Going to audiotape still leaves the possibility of paralinguistic contamination. Transcripts are the least contaminated medium, in that they isolate the verbal or linguistic channel. Ideally, in rating kinesic variables, the audio portion of the videotape should be deleted to prevent paralinguistic and verbal contamination of the ratings.

Channel isolation permits the researcher to maximize the likelihood that the coders are rating what they are supposed to be rating. It is designed to highlight just the specific medium that conveys the information targeted by the measurement system. This increases the validity and specificity of the coding system, as well as the researcher's ability to know exactly what is being studied.

A related problem concerns coding systems, such as Alexander et al.'s (1976) eight therapist scales, that target "mixed" variables that are both verbal and nonverbal (Warmth, Humor, etc.). Alexander et al.'s (1976) ratings with the scales were based on live observation of their therapists during training sessions. In that situation or with videotape (the appropriate medium for such mixed scales), with a mixed variable, it is impossible to identify the specific cues that the coders are using to make their ratings. Channel isolation is not useful with a mixed variable, unless the variable has been conceptually differentiated enough to permit separate scales to be found or developed to measure its kinesic, paralinguistic and verbal cues. Gottman's (1978) Couples' Interaction Scoring System (CISS) is one of the few examples of such a differentiated, multi-channel system in the family field, but it has never been applied to the process of family therapy.

Coders. The fourth and last specific system variable to be discussed concerns the coders that apply the system to the study data. Unfortunately, many process researchers, particularly in the family therapy field, fail to specify a number of important characteristics about their coders and the way in which they were trained to use their system.

The level of clinical expertise or understanding required of a coder to use a coding system is seldom mentioned in process research reports. Nobody in the family therapy process field has empirically examined the effects on scale ratings of using coders with different levels of expertise. If one could demonstrate no significant differences between coders at different levels, the use of naive coders would result in considerable economic savings (Kiesler, 1973). However, one must also remember the only thing better about clinically unsophisticated coders is their cost. That a sophisticated and complex process analysis system, such as Benjamin's (1979) structural model or Pinsof's (1979) FTCS, requires a relatively sophisticated coder does not reduce the value or usefulness of the system. In the other sciences, progress has usually been accompanied by a need for increasingly sophisticated personnel to implement new technologies.

The primary therapeutic modality (individual, family, etc.) that a clinician-coder practices and believes in and the orientation within the modality (psychoanalytic, behavioral, etc.) together constitute that person's "clinical orientation." Most, if not all psychotherapy (and family therapy) process researchers fail to specify the clinical orientation of their coders. None of them has empirically examined the effects of coder orientation on the results generated by their systems. Determining the effects of coders with different orientations reveals information about the modality-and-orientation-system-fit of a coding system. It can help to delineate a system's operational range.

If process researchers mention anything about their coders, it is usually the amount of training they received in how to use the system. According to Kiesler (1973), the amount of training that coders require can be used to indicate the amount of inference demanded by the coding task, or the clarity-unclarity of the code definitions. It may also be a function of the complexity of the coding system. The type of training that the coders received is as important to know as the total amount. Unfortunately, the effects of different coder training procedures on coding system results have not been investigated to date.[29]

Since most researchers have failed to mention these coder factors in reporting their research, it is impossible to even begin evaluating their effects on the research results. As uncontrolled, potentially confounding factors, level of clinical expertise, clinical orientation, and the amount and quality of coder training could account for some of the inconsistent findings generated by the same or similar systems in different studies with different sets of coders. Additionally, the failure to investigate the effects of these coder factors makes it very difficult for researchers to begin accumulating information about the kinds of coders and training that maximize or minimize coding system performance.

Variable Selection and Instrumentation: A Summary. In addition to examining various issues concerning the selection of theoretical variables, this section has also explored four general and four specific criteria that can be used to design and evaluate systems for measuring those variables. A number of major themes have surfaced repeatedly throughout this section. The first is that in selecting variables and in choosing or creating measurement systems, the researcher should be cognizant of the extent to which they accommodate the unique theoretical and pragmatic realities of family therapy. A second major theme is the need for clarity and specificity in variable identification and operationalization. Without clarity and specificity it is impossible to know what is actually being studied.

A third theme concerns what might be called methodological congruence. This refers to the prescription that a measurement system, and all of its general and specific characteristics, should "fit" or be appropriate to the variables and research questions under consideration. The process researcher is continually exposed to a variety of methodological dilemmas or trade-offs that involve giving up something (such as high reliability) for something else (increased validity). The concept of methodological congruence provides a general framework for resolving these dilemmas—the option should be chosen that is most congruent with the researcher's variables and questions.

The fourth and last major theme involves reporting. A constant refrain throughout the discussion of the four specific system criteria was that family therapy process researchers do not adequately report critical characteristics of their instruments and procedures. This makes it very difficult to comparatively evaluate studies, and also inhibits the development of a coherent body of methodological information that can be used by other process researchers.

Research design and data analysis

This section focuses primarily on evaluating various research strategies that have been or could be used to evaluate the reliability and validity of family therapy process coding systems. Additional research design and data analysis issues will also be examined.

Reliability.[30] There are basically two types of reliability that are relevant to process coding systems. The first and most critical type, interrater reliability, deals with the extent to which

---

[29] *Editor's Note.* Also note that the choice of rating vantage point, e.g., trained judges vs. patients vs. therapists, must be considered very carefully, and the decision made must be consistent with the theory from which the dimension under study derives. For example, decades and hundreds of studies of the client-centered "conditions" of empathy, warmth and genuineness have used trained (non-participant) judges for evaluating therapists on these qualities, despite the fact that only patient ratings of these variables are theoretically meaningful (Gurman, 1977).

[30] This discussion only focuses on the reliability of direct observation (as opposed to self-report) measures.

two or more raters agree in their assignment of behaviors to levels within an ordinal scale or to categories within a nominal scale. Most family therapy process researchers have reported the interrater reliabilities of their coding systems.

In contrast, Pinsof (1979a) has been the only family therapy process researcher to deal with the second type, intrarater reliability. This type of reliability deals with the extent to which a coder agrees with himself when coding the same data at two different times. Theoretically, if intrarater reliability is low, interrater reliability should also be low, although the reverse is not necessarily true. In developing a new coding system, intrarater reliability data can be crucial. If adequate intrarater reliability can be attained, even in the face of low interrater reliability, it means that at least the process analysis system can be learned and applied consistently. In such a situation, low interrater reliability only means that the coders did not share the same understanding. In contrast, low intrarater and low interrater reliabilities together suggest that a measurement system cannot be acquired and applied consistently, and that its development potential is very limited.

In general, process researchers only investigate the reliability of their scoring process. Kiesler made the point that with coding systems that involve scoring units that are not easily delineated, it is "important to distinguish between the reliability of the unitization process and of the scoring process" (1973, p. 52). Separation of these two reliabilities is crucial in the development of a process analysis system, because it facilitates identification of the factors that might be contributing to low reliability. Pinsof (1979a) separately examined unitization and scoring reliabilities and found that the FTBS reliability increased markedly when unitization errors were deleted from the analysis. This finding played a critical role in the development of the scoring units for the FTCS (Pinsof, 1979b).

Reliability Statistics. Kiesler (1973) commented that "different problems and different statistics are involved in assessing reliability for nominal (category systems) and ordinal (dimensional rating) scales" (p. 53). With ordinal scales, researchers have used a variety of correlation coefficients. However, for nominal scales, as-

sessing reliability is actually more complex than for ordinal scales.

Certain individual therapy researchers (Dollard and Auld, 1959; Kiesler, 1973) questioned the utility of using the simplest nominal scale reliability statistic—proportion of agreement. They rightly point out that it does not adjust for chance or "marginal" agreement. For instance, if two coders are using a three category system like the Montreal Group's (Postner et al., 1971) E/N/W client scale, on the basis of chance alone (assuming that scoring units are assigned to each category with equal frequency), the coders should agree approximately one-third of the time. A proportion of agreement score of .75 for such a system is not comparable to a similar figure for Heckel's (1975) 11 category client system.

In an effort to improve on the crude proportion of agreement statistic, Dollard and Auld (1959) and Dittes (1959) suggest the use of Kendall's *tau*, which

unlike the percentage of agreement measure, is not inflated by the possibility of hitting on similar categorizations by chance. With *tau* this chance level of agreement has, so to speak, been subtracted out (Dittes, 1959, p. 343).

A more recent statistic, Cohen's (1960) k (kappa), not only takes into account the category base rate, but also accounts for the frequency with which the coders actually use each category (marginal rates). The statistical significance of a k score in relation to marginal base rates can easily be computed, and Cohen has even developed a way to compute maximum k, a measure of a nominal scale's reliability potential.

Another problem with reliability statistics has to do with the origin of the data used to compute the index. Frequently, process researchers report that their coders were trained to a criterion level and then coded the study data. This procedure rests on a conception of reliability as a static or fixed phenomenon, rather than as a variable that fluctuates in response to other coder, training, time, system and data variables.

This stable characteristic conception of reliability is becoming increasingly untenable in the light of the evidence on the stability of reliability scores. Exploring reliability with Patterson et al.'s family interaction coding system, Reid (1970) found that "following training, the absence of monitoring produced abrupt decreases in observer reliability" (Patterson, Cobb, and Ray, 1972, p. 27). Truax and Carkhuff (1967, p. 45) reported considerable variation in AE reliability indices from a number of different studies. The evidence suggests that one cannot assume that once coders have been trained to a criterion level, their reliability will stay at that level as they code the study data, or that two sets of coders will use the same instrument with the same interrater reliability.

It is essential to measure the actual reliability with which a given set of coders applied a coding system to a specific set of data. The ideal sampling format uses repeated measurements of interrater reliability throughout a coding project. This format requires considerable (if not total) overlap in the coders' assignments. Of course, the coders should be blind as to which of their coding assignments overlap.

The evidence also suggests that retraining sessions may be helpful at various points during coding, to maintain the level of reliability. The retraining sessions can be on a fixed schedule or on a flexible "need" schedule that is based on determining the points at which reliability "drift" has exceeded a lower limit. Patterson et al. (1972) used such "booster sessions" to maintain their coders' reliability level.

Applicability Range—Subject Differences. Another characteristic of most process analysis systems is that they can be used very reliably with certain subjects (therapists and/or clients), whereas with other subjects reliability levels drop dramatically. Zuk et al. (1963) found large variations in the reliability with which their coders rated the laughter of the different members of a single family. Most coding systems are maximally applicable and reliable with certain types of subjects. In fact, reliability may be one of the best indicators of the extent to which a coding system fits or is appropriate to a certain subject population.

Unfortunately, most process researchers have not investigated the applicability range of their process analysis systems. The information gained from such an analysis can facilitate system modification, theory refinement, and the delineation of the contexts within which specific variables and coding systems function effectively.

Reliability Levels—How Much Is Enough? Every process researcher struggles with the issue of determining an acceptable reliability level—how much is enough? This can be done statistically with an index like Cohen's (1960) k, which permits significance testing to determine the extent to which a score deviates from chance agreement (marginal rates). However, a relatively low k (.40) score can differ significantly (p < .05) from chance, yet still fall far below conventionally acceptable levels (.80 = .90).

The section on methodological issues has repeatedly stressed the process researcher's dilemma—high reliability and coding system simplicity seem to be positively related, whereas both seem to be negatively related to system validity. Along these lines, Gottman and Markman (1978) noted:

There may thus be some sense in which favoring global systems which produce high levels of reliability may produce observations of low validity. We may need to concentrate on producing observation systems that optimize both reliability and validity rather than doing the job sequentially, that is, first insisting that reliability is arbitrarily in the 80 to 90% range and then assessing validity (p. 47).

The research goal thus becomes a quest for the optimum reliability-validity mix—the point at which the system is reliable enough to accomplish its validity task.

The use of arbitrary reliability levels does not make methodological sense. In fact, the use of such a criterion could result in the demise of a potentially useful process analysis system. Acceptable reliability levels can only be determined in relationship to the validity demands placed on a coding system. A relativistic, task-specific approach to reliability places the primary emphasis on validity. Thus, if significant validity findings emerge from a system with conventionally low reliability scores, the validity findings suggest that the coding system is reliable enough to accomplish the task at hand. From this perspective, the research question becomes "reliable enough for what?"

Validity. The validity of a process analysis

system deals with two broad areas: the extent to which the system or scale measures what it purports to measure, and secondly, the extent to which whatever it is measuring is relevant. These areas focus respectively on the internal and external validity of the coding system.[31] Internal validity is particularly relevant to ordinal scaling systems that are measuring relatively abstract variables or dimensions. It is less relevant with highly differentiated nominal scaling systems that target discrete types of behavior. Since this latter type of system is measuring behaviors as opposed to constructs, it tends to have greater internal face validity. External validity is critical with both types of scaling systems.

A variety of research strategies can be used to establish the validity (internal or external) of a coding system. These strategies correspond to what has been called discriminant, predictive and construct validity.

Discriminant Validity. One way to establish the external validity of a measure is to test its ability to make a variety of distinctions between groups that are known to differ on theoretically important variables. For instance, one can test a system's ability to differentiate therapists with different levels of experience or expertise. (Pinsof, 1979a), or a system's ability to differentiate orientations within a therapeutic modality. Other distinctions may involve discriminating therapist behavior in different contexts (Pinsof, 1979a) and at different points in treatment (Sigal et al., 1977).

Predictive Validity. Predictive validity concerns the extent to which a variable or instrument can be used to predict behavior/experience on another variable. Within the field of psychotherapy research, the most common strategy for establishing the predictive validity of a process measure has been to examine the relationship between the scores it generates and the outcome of treatment. Within the field of family therapy process research, Alexander et al. (1976), Postner et al. (1971) and Sigal et al. (1979) have

been the only researchers to systematically evaluate the predictive validity of their instruments. Only Alexander et al. and Sigal et al. found any relationship between their process measures and outcome.

Generally, in talking about predictive validity in psychotherapy research, one assumes that a variable should predict the outcome of treatment. Treatment outcome is considered the foremost criterion variable in predictive studies. From a process research perspective, this means that a researcher should be able to demonstrate that whatever he is measuring in therapy should make a difference in terms of what goes on outside of therapy. This is considered the ultimate test of a measure's external validity.

However, another type of outcome can be considered—the immediate outcome of an intervention. Most interventions are designed to have an immediate impact on the client system. For instance, a family therapist may direct a family member to speak directly to another family member in the session. The desired immediate or "proximal" outcome of such an intervention would be for the family member to speak directly to the other family member. The ideal long-term or "distal" outcome of such an intervention would be for the level of spontaneous, direct interaction in the family to increase.

Unfortunately, the whole area of proximal outcome has hardly been explored within the field of psychotherapy research, and it has not been investigated at all by family therapy researchers. As a result of all the intervening variables, the methodological distance between an intervention and a distal outcome is far greater than the distance between an intervention and a proximal outcome.[32] This reduced distance increases the likelihood of finding clear and consistent predictive validity results. If family therapy researchers could identify the likelihood with which a particular intervention would produce a particular proximal outcome, the speci-

---

[31] Historically (Campbell and Stanley, 1963), these terms have been applied to experiments. In contrast, in this context, they are being applied to the experimental instruments or measures.

[32] *Editors' Note*. Note that Pinsof's distinction here between "proximal" and "distal" outcomes of therapeutic intervention is quite different from the distinction, made in the next chapter, between "mediating" and "ultimate" treatment goals and outcomes. Pinsof's terms emphasize change on a *temporal* dimension, while the distinction we make in the next chapter is one of the psychological *level* of treatment outcomes.

ficity question would be one step closer to being answered.

Construct Validity. Of the three specific types of validity being discussed, construct validity is the only one that deals exclusively with the internal validity of a measurement system. It targets the extent to which a scale measures what it was designed to measure. Generally, construct validity is most applicable to ordinal scales that measure continuous constructs or dimensions.

Allred's research with the AIAC (Allred and Kersey, 1977) represents the sole attempt within the field of family therapy research to formally test the construct validity of an instrument. Within the family interaction field, Turk and Bell (1972) applied a number of different *Power* measures to the same data, and found little correlation between the measures, which called into question the construct validity of all of them. That type of methodological research is particularly critical with ordinal process measures, in that it can lead to further clarification of what they are measuring. Such research also facilitates comparison of results from studies that used similar measures.

Family Therapist Behavior: The Problem of Stimulus Heterogeneity. In classical experimental design, when testing for differences between subjects, each subject should ideally be exposed to the same experimental stimulus. In family interaction research, for instance, the behavior of different types of families (distressed versus non-distressed; schizophrenic versus neurotic, etc.) is evaluated by exposing the families to a standard stimulus such as Strodtbeck's (1951) Revealed Difference Technique. If differences emerge between types of families, the use of a standard stimulus controls for the rival hypothesis that the differences derive from stimulus heterogeneity.

Family therapy process researchers who are studying family therapist behavior must also control for stimulus heterogeneity. For instance, in comparing the behavior of psychoanalytic and behavioral family therapists, if each therapist in the study works with a different family, one cannot dismiss the possibility that

the group differences may be due to differences in the families the therapists treated. This problem can be dealt with most effectively through random assignment of families and therapists. Unfortunately, random assignment usually involves considerable administrative reorganization in most clinics and, even more importantly, raises serious ethical issues.[33]

The other alternative is to standardize the in-therapy behavior of family members. Sigal et al. (1973, 1977, 1979) pioneered this area with their STFTS, a simulated therapy situation in which the therapist responds to a family on videotape. However, Sigal et al. (1973, 1977) did not find any consistent correlation between the real therapy verbal behavior of family therapists and their responses to the STFTS, which calls into question the extent to which STFTS findings can be generalized to "real" therapist behavior. Nevertheless, the correlation that Sigal et al. (1979) found between STFTS data (analyzed with their FTIS-II) and outcome "suggests that a correlation between simulated and real situations is not a necessary condition for obtaining standardizable measures that will predict outcome of family therapy" (J. Sigal, personal communication, 1979). It is only a necessary condition for elucidating the process of family therapy.

Tucker and Pinsof (1979) tackled the problem of stimulus heterogeneity by using actors who were trained to interact with each other as disturbed family members. Family therapy trainees conducted regular initial interviews with an actor family before and after one year in the family therapy training proam at the Center for Family Studies/Family Institute of Chicago. The data from this project are currently in the process of being analyzed. Impressionistic results have been quite positive, with both actors and therapist-subjects commenting that the experience "felt real." Also, the actors had no problem staying in role for the 50-minute interview. Pinsof is in the process of evaluating the extent to which therapist verbal behavior differs in re-

---

[33.] *Editors' Note.* The ethical problems inherent in random assignment can, however, be minimized a great deal by the use of a "treatment on demand" cell in the design. See the next chapter in this *Handbook* for a discussion of this design strategy.

sponse to the actor family (a flexible standard stimulus) and a similar real family.

Data Analysis. All extant nominal scale family therapy process research has focused on the frequencies or proportions of particular behaviors (code categories) that occur within a given time period. Typically, these behaviors are summed and averaged across various time periods (samples) and subjects, producing what Mishler and Waxler (1975) refer to as "aggregate analyses."

This data analysis approach is not consistent with a number of core assumptions that underlie most family or systems therapies. For instance, aggregate analysis overlooks the fact that "social interaction is patterned and organized through time" (Mishler and Waxler, 1975, p. 17) Additionally, it assumes that the meaning of an act is independent of the context in which it occurs, a proposition that has been directly attacked by family (Auerswald, 1968, 1971; Watzlawick et al., 1967) and systems theorists (Bateson, 1972; Buckley, 1968).

To remedy the problems inherent in aggregate analysis, a number of family interaction and psychotherapy researchers (Gottman and Bakeman, 1979; Hertel, 1972; Mishler and Waxler, 1975; Raush, 1965, 1972) within the last 15 years have advocated the sequential analysis of family interaction and the process of psychotherapy. Such analysis attempts to delineate the patterning of behavior over time and examines "the contingent relations between acts in sequence" (Mishler and Waxler, 1975, p. 19).

Three approaches to the sequential analysis of social interaction have been developed—Markov chain, information and lag sequential analysis. Markov chain (Patterson, 1976; Raush, 1972) and information analysis (Attneave, 1959; Mishler and Waxler, 1975) are complementary approaches to the analysis of stochastic or probabilistic processes. The most basic statistic in both approaches is the conditional (or transitional) probability coefficient. Markov chain analysis targets the relationship between specific consecutive acts in the behavior stream, whereas information analysis targets the amount of information, structure or stereotypy in the stream as a whole. In relation to each other, Markov chain analysis provides a molecular and behaviorally specific interaction analysis, whereas information theory offers a molar analysis of the interactive process.

Lag sequential analysis (Sackett, 1977) represents the third approach and, of the three, embodies the most sophisticated method of specific sequence detection. It is a variant of Markov chain analysis, but is not bound by the Markov property which understands the probability of a given (consequent) event as solely a function of the immediately antecedent event. Gottman, Markman, and Notarius (1977) used lag sequential analysis to study marital interaction in distressed and nondistressed couples and found various sequential patterns that differentiated the couples.

Sequential analysis offers family therapy process researchers a powerful tool for analyzing the therapeutic process. It allows for the identification of therapist operations (chains of interventions) and permits identification of the interaction context in which a given event or series of events occurs. Ultimately, it provides a framework for the identification of probabilistic "laws" on which a science of family therapy can be based.

Research Design and Data Analysis: A Summary. This section has made a number of key points concerning strategies for establishing the reliability and validity of family therapy process measures, for overcoming the problem of stimulus heterogeneity in family therapist studies, and for statistically analyzing nominal process data. In terms of validity and reliability, the latter should be the handmaiden of the former. Additionally, reliability indices should be based on repeated measures taken at various times while the study data are being coded, and they should take into consideration the base or marginal hit rates of the system in question. In terms of validity, and in particular predictive validity, process researchers need to explore the whole realm of proximal or process outcomes. In relation to the problem of stimulus heterogeneity, the use of actor families holds considerable promise. In order to bring their data analysis procedures into line with the conceptual reality of family or systems therapy, process researchers should avail themselves of the techniques of sequential interaction analysis. This approach facilitates identification of process patterns and probabilistic laws.

CONCLUDING COMMENTS

This chapter has attempted to fulfill a number of tasks. The first task was to make a case for process research in the family therapy field. The second was to review the relatively small amount of family therapy process research that has been done to date. More than reviewing the substantive findings of that body of research (which were relatively few), the purpose of that literature review was to delineate the research pathways that have begun to penetrate the terrain of family therapy process, a terrain which Nathan Epstein, in a personal discussion with the author, called a "jungle." The third task was the examination of a variety of methodological issues that must be dealt with by family therapy process researchers. This task also inolved providing a framework for the conduct of process research within the family therapy field.

What is clear from this chapter is that the field of family therapy process research has hardly been explored. A clear and consistent body of knowledge (both substantive and methodological) has not yet emerged. Family therapy process researchers must build upon the research that has already been done, transforming the above mentioned pathways into distinct roads. The beginnings are there—they need to be developed. Hopefully, this chapter can function as both a stimulus and guide to that development.

REFERENCES

Alexander, J. F. Defensive and supportive communications in normal and deviant families. *Journal of Consulting and Clinical Psychology*, 1973, *40*, 223-231.

Alexander, J. F., & Barton, C. Behavioral systems therapy with delinquent families. In: D.H.L. Olson (Ed.), *Treating Relationships*. Lake Mills, Ia.: Graphic, 1976.

Alexander, J., Barton, C., Schiavo, R.S., & Parsons, B.V. Systems-behavioral intervention with families of delinquents: Therapist characteristics, family behavior and outcome. *Journal of Consulting and Clinical Psychology*, 1976, *44*, 656-664.

Alexander, J., & Parsons, B. Short-term behavioral intervention with delinquent families: Impact on family proc-

ess and recidivism. *Journal of Abnormal Psychology*, 1973, *81*, 219-255.

Allred, G. H., & Kersey, F. L. The AIAC, A design for systematically analyzing marriage and family counseling: A progress report. *Journal of Marriage and Family Counseling*, 1977, *3*, 17-25.

Ansbacher, H. L., & Ansbacher, R. R. *The Individual Psychology of Alfred Adler*. New York: Basic Books, 1956.

Attneave, F. *Applications of Information Theory to Psychology*. New York: Holt, Rinehart and Winston, 1959.

Auerswald, E. H. Interdisciplinary versus ecological approach. *Family Process*, 1968, *7*, 202-215.

Auerswald, E. H. Family change and the ecological perspective. *Family Process*, 1971, *10*, 3, 263-280.

Bales, R. F. *Interaction Process Analysis*. Cambridge, Mass.: Addison-Wesley Press, Inc., 1950.

Bateson, G. *Steps to an Ecology of Mind*. New York: Ballantine Books, 1972.

Beels, C. C., and Ferber, A. Family therapy: A view. *Family Process*, 1969, *8*, 280-318.

Beels, C. C., Ferber A. What family therapists do. In: A. Ferber, M. Mendelson, & A. Napier, (Eds.), *The Book of Family Therapy*. Science House, Inc., 1972.

Benjamin, L. S. Structural analysis of social behavior. *Psychological Review*, 1974, *81*, 392-425.

Benjamin, L. S. Structural analysis of a family in therapy. *Journal of Consulting and Clinical Psychology*, 1977, *45*, 391-406.

Benjamin, L. S. Structural analysis of differentiation failure. *Psychiatry*, 1979, *42*, 1-23.

Bergin, A. The evaluation of therapeutic outcomes. In: A. Bergin & S. Garfield, (Eds.) *Handbook of Psychotherapy and Behavior Change: An Empirical Analysis*. New York: John Wiley and Sons, Inc., 1971.

Bergin, A., & Garfield, S. (Eds.) *Handbook of Psychotherapy and Behavior Change: An Empirical Analysis*. New York: John Wiley and Sons, Inc., 1971.

Bertalanffy, L. von. *General System Theory: Foundations, Development, Applications*. New York: George Braziller, 1968.

Birdwhistell, R. *Kinesics and Context: Essays on Body Motion Communication*. Philadelphia: University of Pennsylvania Press, 1970.

Bowen, M. The use of family theory in clinical practice. *Comprehensive Psychiatry*, 1966, *7*, 345-374.

Bowen, M. *Family Therapy in Clinical Practice*. New York: Jason Aronson, Inc., 1978.

Buckley, W. *Modern Systems Research for the Behavioral Scientist: A Sourcebook*. Chicago: Aldine Publishing Co., 1968.

Bugental, D., Love, L., Kaswan, J., & April, C. Verbal-nonverbal conflict in parental messages to normal and disturbed children. *Journal of Abnormal Psychology*, 1971, 77, 6-10.

Campbell, D., & Stanley, J. *Experimental and Quasi-experimental Designs for Research*. Chicago: Rand McNally and Co., 1963.

Caracena, P. F., & Vicory, J. R. Correlates of phenomenological and judged empathy. *Journal of Counseling Psychology*, 1969, *16*, 510-515.

Chagoya, L., Presser, B., & Sigal, J. J. *Family therapists intervention scale-I*. Unpublished manuscript, Institute of Community and Family Psychiatry, Jewish General Hospital, Montreal, 1974.

Cleghorn, J., & Levin, S. Training family therapists by setting instructional objectives. *American Journal of Orthopsychiatry*, 1973, *43*, 439-446.

Cohen, J. A. coefficient of agreement for nominal scales.

Educational and Psychological Measurement, 1960, *20*, 37-46.

De Chenne, T. K. Experiential facilitation in conjoint marriage counseling. *Psychotherapy: Theory, Research and Practice*, 1973, *10*, 212-214.

DiLoreto, A. O. *Comparative Psychotherapy: An Experimental Analysis*. Chicago: Aldine-Atherton, Inc., 1971.

Dittes, T.E. Previous studies bearing on content analysis of psychotherapy. In Dollar, T. and Auld, F. *Scoring Human Motives: A Manual*. New Haven, Conn.: Yale University Press, 1959.

Dittman, A. T. *Interpersonal Messages for Emotion*. New York: Springer Publishing Co., Inc., 1972.

Dollard, J., & Auld, F. *Scoring Human Motives: A Manual*. New Haven, Conn.: Yale University Press, 1959.

Dowling, E. Co-therapy: A clinical researcher's view. In: S. Walrond-Skinner, (Ed.) *Family and Marital Therapy*. London: Routledge and Kegan Paul, 1979.

Dreikurs, R. *Adlerian Family Counseling: A Manual for Counseling Centers*. Eugene, Oregon: University of Oregon Press, 1959.

Duncan, S. Jr., & Fiske, D. W. *Face-to-Face Interaction: Research, Methods and Theory*. Hillsdale, New Jersey: Lawrence Erlbaum Associates, Publishers, 1977.

Ekman, P., Friesen, W. V., & Ellsworth, P. *Emotion in the Human Face: Guidelines for Research and an Integration of Findings*. New York: Pergamon Press, Inc., 1972.

Epstein, N. B., & Bishop, D. S. Position-paper—family therapy: State of the art—1973, *Canadian Psychiatric Association Journal*, 1973, *18*, 175-183.

Epstein, N. B., Bishop, D. S. & Levin, S. The McMaster Model of family functioning, *Journal of Marriage and Family Counseling*, 1978, *4*, 19-31.

Erikson, E. H. *Identity and the Life Cycle*. New York: International Universities Press, 1959.

Ferber, A., Mendelsohn, M., & Napier, A. *The Book of Family Therapy*. New York: Science House, Inc., 1972.

Framo, J. (Ed.) *Family Interaction: A Dialogue between Family Researchers and Family Therapists*. New York: Springer Publishing Inc., 1972.

Frank, J. *Persuasion and Healing: A Comparative Study of Psychotherapy*. (Rev. Ed.) Baltimore: Johns Hopkins University Press, 1973.

Freud, S. *An Outline of Psycho-analysis*. In: Standard Ed. Complete Psychological Works, Vol. 23; London: Hogarth, 1964.

Gardner, H. *The Quest for Mind: Piaget, Levi-Straus and the Structuralist Movement*. New York: Random House, 1972.

Garfield, S. L., & Bergin, A. E. Therapeutic conditions and outcome. *Journal of Abnormal Psychology*, 1971, *77*, 108-114.

Garfield, S. L., & Bergin, A. E. (Eds.) *Handbook of Psychotherapy and Behavior Change: An Empirical Analysis*. (2nd Ed.) New York: John Wiley and Sons, 1978.

Gibb, J. R. Defensive communications, *Journal of Communications*, 1961, *3*, 141-148.

Glass, G. V., & Smith, M. L., *Meta-Analysis of psychotherapy outcome studies*. Paper presented at the Society for Psychotherapy Research, San Diego, 1976.

Gottman, J. *Couples interaction scoring system (CISS): Coding manual*. Unpublished manuscript. Dept. of Psychology, University of Illinois, Champaign, Ill., 1978.

Gottman, J., & Bakeman, R. The sequential analysis of observational data. In: Lamb, M., Soumi, S., & Stephenson, G. (Eds.) *Social Interaction Analysis*. Madison: University of Wisconsin Press, 1979.

Gottman, J. M. and Markman, H. J. Experimental designs of psychotherapy research. In: S. L. Garfield & A. E. Bergin (Eds.) *Handbook of Psychotherapy and Behavior Change: An Empirical Analysis*. New York: John Wiley and Sons, 1978, pp. 23-62.

Gottman, J., Markman, H., & Notarius, C. The topography of marital conflict: A sequential analysis of verbal and non-verbal behavior, *Journal of Marriage and Family*, 1977, *39*, 461-477.

Gurman, A. S. Marital therapy: Emerging trends in research and practice. *Family Process*, 1973, *12*, 45-54.

Gurman, A. S., & Kniskern, D. P. Research on marital and family therapy: Progress, perspective and prospect. In: S. L. Garfield and A. E. Bergin, (Eds.) *Handbook of Psychotherapy and Behavior Change: An Empirical Analysis*. (2nd Ed.) New York: John Wiley and Sons, 1978.

Gurman, A. S., & Razin, A. M. (Eds.) *Effective Psychotherapy: A Handbook of Research*. New York: Pergamon Press, 1977.

Guttman, H. A., Spector, R. M., Sigal, J. J., Epstein, N. B., & Rakoff, V. Coding of affective expression in conjoint family therapy. *American Journal of Psychotherapy*, 1972, *26*, 185-194.

Heckel, R. V. Predicting role flexibility in group therapy by means of a screening scale. *Journal of Clinical Psychology*, 1972, *28*, 570-573.

Heckel, R. V. A comparison of process data from family therapy and group therapy. *Journal of Community Psychology*, 1975, *3*, 254-257.

Hertel, R. K. Application of stochastic process analysis to the study of psychotherapeutic processes. *Psychological Bulletin*, 1972, *77*, 421-430.

Hollis, F. Explorations in the development of a typology of casework treatment. *Social Casework*, 1967a, *48*, 335-341.

Hollis, F. The coding and application of a typology of casework treatment. *Social Casework*, 1967b, *48*, 489-497.

Hollis, F. A profile of early interviews in marital counseling. *Social Casework*, 1968a, *49*, 35-43.

Hollis, F. Continuance and discontinuance in marital counseling and some observations on joint interviews. *Social Casework*, 1968b, *49*, 167-174.

Hops, H., Wills, T. A., Patterson, G. R., & Weiss, R. L. *Marital interaction coding system*. Unpublished manuscript. University of Oregon, 1971.

Jacob, T. Family interaction in disturbed and normal families: A methodological and substantive review. *Psychological Bulletin*, 1975, *82*, 33-65.

Kersey, F. L. *An exploratory factorial validity study of Allred's interaction analysis for counselors*. Unpublished masters thesis, Brigham Young University, 1976.

Kiesler, D. J. *The Process of Psychotherapy: Empirical Foundations and Systems of Analysis*. Chicago: Aldine Publishing Co., 1973.

Kiesler, D. J., Mathieu, P. L., & Klein, M. H. A summary of the issues and conclusions. In: C. R. Rogers, E. T. Gendlin, D. J. Kiesler & C. B. Truax (Eds.) *The Therapeutic Relationship and its Impact: A Study of Psychotherapy with Schizophrenics*. Madison: Psychiatric Institute, Bureau of Audio Visual Instruction, 1970, 2 vols.

Leary, T. *Interpersonal Diagnosis of Personality*. New York: Ronald Press, 1957.

Lewis, M., & Rosenblum, L. H. (Eds.) *The Effect of the Infant on its Caregiver*. New York: John Wiley and Sons, 1974.

Luborsky, L., Singer, B., & Luborsky, L. Comparative studies of psychotherapies. *Archives of General Psychiatry*,

1975, *32*, 995-108.

Mahler, M. *On Human Symbiosis and the Vicissitudes of Individuation*, Vol. 2. New York: International Universities Press, 1968.

Mayerovitch, J. *A reliability study of a new system for coding family therapists' verbalizations*. Unpublished masters thesis. Western Michigan University, Kalamazoo, Michigan, 1972.

Miller, J. G. Living systems—basic concepts. *Behavioral Science*, 1965, *10*, 193-411.

Mishler, E., & Waxler, N. *Interaction in Families*. New York: John Wiley and Sons, 1968.

Mishler, E., & Waxler, N. The sequential patterning of interaction in normal and schizophrenic families. *Family Process*, 1975, *14*, 17-50.

Mitchell, K. M., Bozarth, J. D., & Krauft, C. C. A reappraisal of the therapeutic effectiveness of accurate empathy, non-possessive warmth and genuineness. In: A. S. Gurman and A. M. Razin (Eds.) *Effective Psychotherapy: A Handbook of Research*. New York: Pergamon Press, 1977.

Morris, G. O., & Wynne, L. C. Schizophrenic offspring and parental styles of communication: A predictive study using excerpts of family therapy recordings. *Psychiatry*, 1965, 28 19-44.

Olson, D. H. L. (Ed.) *Treating Relationships*. Lake Mills, Ia.: Graphic, 1976.

O'Mahoney, M. T. *The marital therapy session report*. Unpublished manuscript. 1978, Institute of Psychiatry, Northwestern Memorial Hospital, Chicago, Ill., 60611.

Orlinsky, D. E., & Howard, K. I. *Varieties of Psychotherapeutic Experience: Multivariate Analyses of Patients' and Therapists' Report*. New York: Teachers College Press, 1975.

Orlinsky, D. E., & Howard, K. I. The relation of process to outcome in psychotherapy. In S. L. Garfield and A. E. Bergin (Eds.) *Handbook of Psychotherapy and Behavior Change: An Empirical Analysis*. (2nd Ed.) New York: John Wiley and Sons, 1978.

Palombo, S. R., Merrifield, J., Weigert, W., Morris, G. O., & Wynne, L. C. Recognition of parents of schizophrenics from excerpts of family therapy interviews. *Psychiatry*, 1967, *30*, 405-412.

Paolino, T. J., and McCrady, B. S. (Eds.) *Marriage and Marital Therapy: Psychoanalytic, Behavioral and Systems Theory Perspectives*. New York: Brunner/Mazel, 1978.

Patterson, G. R. The aggressive child: Victim and architect of a coercive system. In: E. J. Mash, L. A. Hamerlynck & L. C. Handy (Eds.) *Behavior Modification and Families*. New York: Brunner/Mazel, 1976, 267-316.

Patterson, G. R., Cobb, J. A., & Ray, R. A social-engineering technology for retraining the families of aggressive boys. In: H. Adams & L. Unikel, (Eds.) *Georgia Symposium in Experimental Clinical Psychology, Vol. II*. Springfield, Ill.: Charles Thomas Publisher, 1972.

Patterson, G. R., Ray, R. S., Shaw, D. A., & Cobb, J. A. *Manual for coding of family interactions*. Unpublished paper, Oregon Research Institute and University of Oregon, 1969.

Pinsof, W. M. *Truax's accurate empathy scale: A critical review of the research*. Unpublished paper, Center for Family Studies, Department of Psychiatry, Northwestern University Medical School, Chicago, 1976.

Pinsof, W. M. The family therapist behavior scale (FTBS): Development and evaluation of a coding system. *Family Process*, 1979a, *18*, 4, 451-461.

Pinsof, W. M. *The Family Therapist Coding System (FTCS) Coding Manual*. Center for Family Studies, Department of Psychiatry, Northwestern University Medical School, Chicago, 1979b.

Postner, R. S., Guttman, H., Sigal, J., Epstein, N. B., & Rakoff, V. Process and outcome in conjoint family therapy. *Family Process*, 1971, *10*, 451-474.

Presser, B. G., Sigal, J. J., Mayerovitch, J., & Chagoya, L. *Individual differences in family therapists' style: A coding system and some results*. Paper presented at the annual meeting of the Canadian Psychological Association, Windsor, Ontario, Canada, 1974.

Rado, S. From the metaphysical ego to the bio-cultural action-self. *Journal of Psychology*, 1958, *46*, 279-290.

Rappoport, J. and Chinsky, M. J. Accurate empathy: Confusion of a construct. *Psychological Bulletin*, 1972, 77, 400-404.

Raush, H. L. Interaction sequences. *Journal of Personality and Social Psychology*, 1965, *2*, 487-499.

Raush, H. L. Process and change: A markov model for interaction. *Family Process*, 1972, *2*, 275-298.

Reid, J. B. Reliability assessment of observation data: A possible methodological problem. *Child Development*, 1970, *41*, 1143-1150.

Rice, D. G., Fey, W. F., & Kepecs, J. G. Therapist experience and "style" in co-therapy. *Family Process*, 1972, *11*, 1-12.

Rice, D. G., Gurman, A. S., & Razin, A. M. Therapist sex, style and theoretical orientation. *Journal of Nervous and Mental Disease*, 1974, *159*, 413-421.

Rice, D. G. Razin, A. M., & Gurman, A. S. Spouses as cotherapists: Variables and implications for patient-therapist matching. *Journal of Marriage and Family Counseling*, 1976, *2*, 55-62.

Rice, L. N. Therapist's style of participation and case outcome. *Journal of Consulting Psychology*, 1965, *29*, 1-5-160.

Riskin, J., & Faunce, E. E. *Family interaction scales scoring manual*. Unpublished manuscript, Mental Research Institute, Palo Alto, 1968.

Riskin, J., & Faunce, E. E. Family interaction scales, I: Theoretical framework and method. *Archives of General Psychiatry*, 1970a, *22*, 504-512.

Riskin, J. & Faunce, E. E. Family interaction scales III. Discussion of methodology and substantive findings, *Archives of General Psychiatry*, 1970b Vol. 22, pp. 527-537.

Riskin, J., & Faunce, E. E. An evaluative review of family interaction research. *Family Process*, 1972, *11*, 365-456.

Rogers, C. R. *Client-Centered Therapy*. Boston: Houghton-Mifflin, Co., 1951.

Rogers, C. R. The necessary and sufficient conditions of therapeutic personality change. *Journal of Consulting Psychology*, 1957, 21, 95-103.

Rogers, C. R., Gendlin, E. T., Kiesler, D. J., & Truax, C. B. *The Therapeutic Relationship and its Impact: A Study of Psychotherapy with Schizophrenics*. Madison: University of Wisconsin Press, 1967.

Sackett, G. P. A taxonomy of observational techniques and a theory of measurement. In: G. P. Sackett & H. C. Haywood, (Eds.) *Observing Behavior: Data Collection and Analysis Methods*. Baltimore: University Park Press, 1977.

Sackett, G. P., & Haywood, H. C. (Eds.) *Observing Behavior: Data Collection and Analysis Methods*. Baltimore: University Park Press, 1977.

Sager, C. J., & Kaplan, H. S. *Progress in Group and Family Therapy*. New York: Brunner/Mazel, 1972.

Salzberg, H. C. Effects of silence and redirection on verbal responses in group psychotherapy. *Psychological Reports*, 1962, *11*, 455-461.

Sanders, J. P. *A study in counselor evaluation scale validation: An exploratory examination of naive counselors' scores on Allred's interaction analysis for counselors with selected scores on the Strong Vocation Interest Blank.* Unpublished master's thesis, Brigham Young University, 1974.

Schaefer, E. S. A configurational analysis of children's reports of parent behavior. *Journal of Consulting Psychology*, 1965, *29*, 552-557.

Scheflen, A. E. Natural history method in psychotherapy: Communicational research. In: L. A. Gottschalk & A. H. Auerbach, (Eds.) *Methods of Research in Psychotherapy.* New York: Appleton-Century-Crofts, 1966.

Scheflen, A. E. *Communicational Structure: Analysis of a Psychotherapy Transaction.* Bloomington and London: Indiana University Press, 1973.

Shapiro, R. Therapist attitudes and premature termination in family and individual therapy. *Journal of Nervous and Mental Disease*, 1974, *159*, 101-107.

Shapiro, R., and Budman, S. Defection, termination, and continuation in family and individual therapy. *Family Process*, 1973, *12*, 55-67.

Sigal, J. J., Guttman, H. A., Chagoya, L., and Lasry, J. C. Predictability of family therapists' behavior. *Canadian Psychiatric Association Journal*, 1973, *18*, 199-202.

Sigal, J. J., Lasry, J. C., Guttman, H., Chagoya, L., and Pilon, R. Some stable characteristics of family therapists' interventions in real and simulated therapy sessions. *Journal of Consulting and Clinical Psychology*, 1977, *45*, 23-26.

Sigal, J. J., Presser, B. G., Woodward, C. W., Santa-Barbara, J., Epstein, N. B., & Levin, S. *Therapists' interventions in a simulated family as predictors of outcome in family therapy.* Unpublished manuscript. Institute of Community and Family Psychiatry, Jewish General Hospital, Montreal, 1979.

Singer, M. T., & Wynne, L. C. Thought disorder and family relations of schizophrenics, IV: Results and implications. *Archives of General Psychiatry*, 1965, *12*, 201-212.

Sloane, R. B., Staples, F. R., Cristol, A. H., Yorkston, N.J. & Whipple, K. *Psychotherapy versus Behavior Therapy.* Cambridge: Harvard University Press, 1975.

Strodtbeck, F. Husband and wife interaction over revealed differences. *American Sociological Review*, 1951, *16*, 468-473.

Tomm, K. M., & Wright, L. M. Training in family therapy: Perceptual, conceptual and executive skills. *Family Process*, 1979, *18*, 227-250.

Tripp, R. M. *An exploratory study of Allred's interaction analysis for counselors: The relationship of naive counselors' scores on the AIAC to their scores on selected scales of the MMPI.* Unpublished master's thesis, Brigham Young University, 1975.

Truax, C. B. A scale for the measurement of accurate empathy. *Psychiatric Institute Bulletin*, Wisconsin Psychiatric Institute, University of Wisconsin, 1961, *1* (12).

Truax, C. B., & Carkhuff, R. R. *Toward Effective Counseling and Psychotherapy: Training and Practice.* Chicago: Aldine Publishing Co., 1967.

Tucker, S. J. & Pinsof, W. M. *The evaluation of family therapy training.* Research in progress, Center for Family Studies, Department of Psychiatry, Northwestern University Medical School, Chicago, 1979.

Turk, J. L., & Bell, N. W. Measuring power in families *Journal of Marriage and the Family*, 1972, *34*, 215-222.

Walrond-Skinner, S. (Ed.) *Family and Marital Therapy.* London: Routledge and Kegan Paul, 1979.

Watson, W. *An exploratory study of Allred's interaction analysis for counselors: The relationship of selected AIAC ratio scores to Truax accurate empathy scale scores.* Unpublished master's thesis. Brigham Young University, 1975.

Watzlawick, P., Beavin, J. H., & Jackson, D. D. *Pragmatics of Human Communication: A Study of Interactional Patterns, Pathologies, and Paradoxes.* New York: W. W. Norton, 1967.

Wells, R. A. & Dezen, A. E. The results of family therapy revisited: The non-behavioral methods. *Family Process*, 1978, *17*, 251-274.

Wells, R. A., Dilkes, T. C., & Trivelli, N. The results of family therapy: A critical review of the literature. *Family Process*, 1972, *11*, 189-208.

Wiener, N. *Cybernetics.* (2nd Ed.). Cambridge, Mass.: M.I.T. Press, 1961.

Winer, L. R. The qualified pronoun count as a measure of change in family psychotherapy. *Family Process*, 1971, *10*, 243-248.

Wynne, L. Communication disorders and the quest for relatedness in families of schizophrenics. In: C. J. Sager & H. S. Kaplan (Eds.) *Progress in Group and Family Therapy.* New York: Brunner/Mazel, 1972.

Zuk, G. H. *Family Therapy: A Triadic Based Approach.* New York: Behavioral Publications, Inc., 1971.

Zuk, G. H., Boszormenyi-Nagy, I., & Heiman, E. Some dynamics of laughter during family therapy. Originally printed in *Family Process*, 1963, *2*, 302-314. Reprinted in G. H. Zuk, (Ed.) *Family Therapy: A Triadic Based Approach.* New York: Behavioral Publications, Inc., 1971.

EDITORS' REFERENCE

Gurman, A. S. The patient's perception of the therapeutic relationship. In: A. S. Gurman & A. M. Razin (Eds.), *Effective Psychotherapy: A Handbook of Research.* New York: Pergamon, 1977.

CHAPTER 20

Family Therapy
Outcome Research:
Knowns and Unknowns

Alan S. Gurman, Ph.D. and

David P. Kniskern, Psy.D.

We shall not cease from exploration
And the end of all our exploring
Will be to arrive where we started
And know the place for the first time.
　　　　　　　　　　—T.S. Eliot

In the last decade, the rate of growth of research on the outcomes of marital and family therapy has been astounding. Consider some crude indices of this growth. In 1972, Wells et al. published the first review of outcome studies in the family area, and could identify only 13 relevant reports, with a total sample of 290; a year later, Gurman (1973b), offering the first broad review of the results of marital therapy, identified 15 studies totaling 726 cases. Only five years later, Gurman and Kniskern (1978a) presented the most comprehensive analysis of outcome research in marital and family therapy to date and were able to examine over 200 reports, with a total *N* approaching 5,000.

The enormous increase in the number of empirical studies in the field has been dramatically paralleled by, and perhaps even outstripped by,

the rate at which *reviews* of this outcome research have accumulated. As of mid-1979, we were able to locate 32 such reviews, ranging from reviews of the entire field (e.g., Gurman and Kniskern, 1978a), to reviews of subdomains of the field such as nonbehavioral family therapies (e.g., Wells and Dezen, 1978a), behavioral marriage therapy (e.g., Jacobson, 1979; Jacobson and Martin, 1976), group marital (e.g., Gurman, 1971) and family (Benningfeld, 1978; Strelnick, 1977) therapy, to highly specialized areas, such as marital enrichment programs (Gurman and Kniskern, 1977) and marital communication skill-training (Birchler, 1979). In addition, there have appeared two reviews addressing family therapy training (Kniskern and Gurman, 1979; Liddle and Halpern, 1978). Table 1 lists these reviews and identifies the scope of each review. In addition, some of these reviews already have elicited some very lively and provocative debates (Gurman and Knudson, 1978; Gurman and Kniskern, 1978c, 1978d; Gurman, Knudson, and Kniskern, 1978; Jacobson and Weiss, 1978; Stanton and Todd, 1980; Wells and Dezen, 1978a, 1978b).

TABLE 1
A Decade in the Growth and Development of
Reviews of Family Therapy Research

Author	Date	Cumulative Frequency By Year	Scope[a]
Lebedun	1970	1	Marital group counseling
Gurman	1971		Group marital therapy
		3	
Patterson	1971		Behavioral family therapy
Wells et al.	1972	4	Family therapy (excluding behavioral)
Gurman	1973b	5	Marital therapy
Beck	1975		Marital counseling
Greer and D'Zurilla	1975		Behavioral marriage therapy
		9	
Gurman	1975a		Marital therapy
Kniskern	1975		Family therapy
Patterson et al.	1976		Behavioral marriage therapy
Jacobson and Martin	1976	12	Behavioral marriage therapy
Steinglass	1976		Family therapy of alcoholism
Gurman and Kniskern	1977		Marital enrichment programs
		14	
Strelnick	1977		Multiple family group therapy
Bennigfeld	1978		Multiple family therapy
DeWitt	1978		Family therapy (excluding behavioral)
Gurman and Kniskern	1978a		Marital and family therapy, divorce therapy
Gurman and Kniskern	1978b		Deterioration in marital and family therapy
Gurman and Kniskern	1978c		Behavioral marriage therapy
		23	
Jacobson	1978		Marital therapy
Liddle and Halpern	1978		Family therapy training
Luber	1978		Marital communication skills training and contingency contracting models
Wells and Dezen	1978a		Family therapy (excluding behavioral)
Birchler	1979		Marital communication skills
Gurman and Kniskern	1979		Marital and family therapy
Jacobson	1979	31	Behavioral marriage therapy
Kniskern and Gurman	1979		Family therapy training
Masten	1979		Family therapy for childhood disorders
Patterson and Fleischman	1979		Behavioral family intervention
Stanton	1979		Family treatment of drug abuse
Williams and Miller	1979		Marital therapy (a review of reviews)
Pinsof	1981	32	Family therapy process research

[a]The appearance of the unqualified descriptors "family therapy" or "marital therapy" indicates the review of empirical studies of *all* family or marital treatment methods, respectively. Reviews limited to specific areas, or excluding only certain areas, are indicated by other descriptors.

At the present time, we believe that there is no need or justification for further detailed reviews of the outcome literature. There is no need because, despite the increasing frequency of relevant outcome studies, the accretion of knowledge from such studies over any period of less than about five years is unlikely to be sufficient to have a significant impact on either research methodology or clinical practice.[1] There is no current justification for such reviews since what is needed, in our opinion, is not a re-mastication of what already has been digested, but a re-direction and re-focus toward identifying what needs to be studied in the future, and toward the identification of the clinically most relevant questions needing answers. Unless this future-oriented *pre*view is accomplished, we will continue to see the wasteful accumulation of tremendously overlapping, non-additive reviews of virtually the same literature (e.g., DeWitt, 1978; Gurman and Kniskern, 1978a; Wells and Dezen, 1978a).

Thus, in this chapter, we will not painstakingly study the reports we have already examined carefully elsewhere (Gurman and Kniskern, 1977, 1978a, 1978b) or the several dozen reports appearing since our previous publications in this area. Our propensity to be the "curators and connoisseurs of the relationship between family therapy and psychotherapy research" (Taggart, 1978, p. 109) will not be exercised by additional archival activity in this chapter. We will largely eschew our role as the "chroniclers of and gatekeepers" for the field (Jacobson and Weiss, 1978, p. 149) in favor of a new role, that of family therapy research cartographers. Like good fron-

---

[1.] This is obviously an arbitrary position, yet it seems to be consistent with the rate at which important research knowledge about psychotherapy tends to accumulate (cf. Garfield and Bergin, 1978).

tiersmen, we will leave a clearly marked trail of the path that has already been traveled so that we and the reader know our point of departure. In a sense, then, in this chapter we will adopt the role of both historians and mapmakers. A colleague of ours[2], in discussing the goals of psychotherapy with trainees, often reminds them that, "If you don't know where you're going, you probably won't get there." To this, we would add that if you don't know where you are, it is hard to know how far you are from where you want to be, and that if you don't know where you have come from, you may end up walking around in circles.

Our goal in this chapter, then, is to summarize (not review) what we believe has been learned from family therapy outcome research in order to specify what we still do not know and need to know. We also will address, selectively, some crucial issues involved in how researchers could most profitably go about trying to answer the many unanswered and unaddressed questions that face the practitioners of family therapy.

Moreover, we will attempt to address empirical questions and issues from the clinician's vantage point, while addressing clinicians' concerns from an empirical perspective. This notion initially may confuse some readers, since it suggests viewing "x" in the context of "y," while also viewing "y" in the context of "x." This appears not to be logically possible since "x" and "y" cannot simultaneously be both the object and subject of our analysis. On the other hand, if one takes the position, as we do, that clinical concerns and empirical concerns are not antagonistic, but are, in fact, synergistic and *should* be indistinguishable, then the apparent dilemma is immediately resolved. Finally, since the overriding emphasis of this *Handbook* is explicitly clinical, we will not belabor the common fundamental research design issues that any family therapy researcher must attend to, although some of these will necessarily be addressed in our summary of the research literature and in our attempt to write a flexible script for family therapy outcome research over the next decade or so. For the reader who chooses to study more closely these methodological issues applied specifically to family therapy re-

search, we suggest the reading of the publications cited in Table 2. Additional noteworthy discussion of important design issues in psychotherapy research in general are: Outcome Evaluation—Bergin and Lambert (1978), Kazdin and Wilson (1978a), Strupp and Hadley (1977); Experimental Design—Gottman and Markman (1978), Mahoney (1978); Analogue Designs—Kazdin (1978b), Kazdin and Wilson (1978b); Single Case Methodology—Hersen and Barlow (1976), Kazdin (1978a), Kratochwill (1978); Placebo Groups—O'Leary and Borkovec (1978); Expectancies—Wilkins (1973, 1977).

THE OUTCOME OF THE FAMILY THERAPIES

If all the evidence as you receive it leads to but one conclusion . . . don't believe it!

—Molière

As this *Handbook* demonstrates, there is no unitary family therapy. Rather, there are numerous family and marital therap*ies*, with both overlapping and clearly divergent assumptions about the nature of psychopathology, necessary treatment goals, and the routes to effective therapeutic change. Moreover, unlike the field of individual behavior therapy, in which attempts have been made to automate treatment and eliminate the need for a therapist (e.g., Biglan, Villwock & Wick, 1979), to our knowledge no one has yet suggested such a possibility in treating disturbed families. The practice of family therapy requires the presence of a family therapist. While such a reminder may seem patronizingly obvious, a good deal of the outcome research in family therapy has been conducted as if this were not the case (Gurman, 1978a, 1978b; Gurman and Kniskern, 1978d). That is, such research is often carried out without regard for examining the effects of therap*ists* independently of, or in interaction with, the effects of treatments *qua* treatments, and thus are subject to the criticism of having implicitly endorsed one or more "uniformity myths" (Kiesler, 1971) about psychotherapy. Klein and Gurman (1980) have articulated some of the major conceptual and clinical problems engendered in such research strategies.

---

[2] Richard J. Thurrell, M.D.

TABLE 2

Major Discussions of Methodological Issues
in Family Therapy Outcome Research

Author	Date	Focus
Coché	1978	Research issues unique to the study of family therapy outcomes
Gale	1979	Relationship of family theory to family therapy research
Gurman and Klein	1980	Outcome evaluation and the treatment of women in marital and family therapy
Gurman and Kniskern	1977	Outcome criteria and common design deficiencies in study of marital enrichment programs
Gurman and Kniskern	1978a	Outcome criteria in marital and family therapy, especially issues of different perspectives on change, levels of assessment, and selection of appropriate family subsystems for evaluation
Gurman and Kniskern	1978d	Outcome criteria in family therapy
Jacobson	1978	Outcome criteria in marital therapy, common design considerations
Jacobson	1979	Design issues particularly relevant to teasing out active ingredients in behavioral marriage therapy
Malouf and Alexander	1976	Family therapy research in applied settings, especially community clinics
O'Leary and Turkewitz	1978	Common methodological errors in marital therapy research
Pinsof	1981	Family therapy process research
Rosman	1977	Outcome criteria in family therapy
Wells and Dezen	1978a	Common design issues and deficiencies in family therapy research; outcome criteria
Wells et al.	1972	General discussion of the use of major experimental designs in family therapy research
Williams and Miller	1980	Design criteria in marital therapy research

Thus, as we now begin to summarize what we have learned, or think we have learned, about the efficacy of the family therapies, it is essential to bear in mind the following considerations:

(a) In general, it is impossible to disentangle treatment effects from therapist effects in the studies done to date.
(b) The treatments that have been studied have almost never followed "pure" applications of given treatment models.
(c) With infrequent exceptions, it is impossible to be certain just what specific treatment interventions have actually been used, since treatment operations have almost never been described in detail.

Thus, given these and other sources of heterogeneity of actual treatment interventions (i.e., what therapists do, regardless of what they say they do, or are expected to do within a given school of therapy), we cannot be very certain of the meaning or specific practical implications of many of these research results. Nonetheless, in several areas of this literature, the results are so consistent that they seem to us to point to clinically meaningful trends (Gurman and Kniskern, 1978a). To facilitate an understanding of both the clinical relevance and limitations of existing outcome research, we will pose and respond to a number of questions about the efficacy of the family therapies.

How Effective are the Family Therapies?

There are two major approaches to answering this question. The first addresses the issue of whether receiving any of the family therapies (under any clinical conditions) is more effective than receiving no (formal) treatment at all. Our position on this question has changed very little since our earlier review (Gurman and Kniskern, 1978a). We believe that the existing evidence from controlled studies of nonbehavioral marital and family therapies, viewed admittedly broadly, suggests that such treatments are often effective beyond chance. Our evaluation of the positiveness of these results is somewhat more favorable to family therapies than is the evaluation of Wells and Dezen (1978a), whose review both we (Gurman and Kniskern, 1978d) and others (Stanton and Todd, 1980) have critiqued elsewhere. Our assessment of the status of results emerging from controlled studies of nonbehavioral marital therapies is also more optimistic than that of Jacobson (cf. Gurman, 1978c; Gurman, Knudson and Kniskern, 1978; Jacobson, 1978; Jacobson and Weiss, 1978).

Our assessment of the effects of behavioral family therapies (e.g., Patterson, 1971) as compared to no treatment is also quite positive. There is accumulating evidence (e.g., Cole and Morrow, 1976; Karoly and Rosenthal, 1977; Reisinger, Frangia and Hoffman, 1976), however, that focal operant treatment strategies are quite insufficient when serious marital difficulties coexist with deviant child behavior. In a related context, Matthews et al. (1977) have demonstrated how severe marital conflict may interfere with the otherwise often effective behavior therapy of agoraphobia through exposure treatment. Moreover, many of the best designed studies of the outcomes of behavioral family therapy have involved clinical interventions that are difficult to classify as owing their technical rationale predominantly to social learning theory (e.g., Alexander and Parsons, 1973; Alexander et al., 1976).

Behavioral marriage therapy research has shown what we consider (Gurman, 1978c; Gurman and Kniskern, 1978a) to be rather impressive gains with mildly or moderately distressed couples, but there is somewhat less persuasive evidence of the power of these methods with severely distressed couples or with couples with one (or two) severely disturbed individuals. While at least one major proponent of behavioral marriage therapy (Jacobson, 1978, 1979; Jacobson and Weiss, 1978) thinks rather positively of the results of controlled outcome studies in this area, we are struck by their frequent methodological inadequacies (Gurman, 1977a; Gurman and Kniskern, 1978c) and the questionable relevance of many of their outcome measures for clinical practice (Gurman and Kniskern, 1978a; Gurman and Klein, 1980a, 1980b).

Selected issues about control groups

Despite the logical power of controlled treatment studies, we need to recognize that there

are at least three very important caveats to be considered in conducting such experimental investigations. First, there is no such thing as a true control group. It has been well documented in individual psychotherapy research (cf. Bergin and Lambert, 1978) that supposedly "untreated" patients rather often get themselves "treated," whether by the local bartender, a close friend, or even by another professional therapist (outside the research protocol). We see no reason to suspect that this is not also the case in pathological marital and family situations, e.g., the couple whose relationship has been emotionally dead for years may arrange implicitly that one or both partners have an extramarital affair to break up their pseudo-mutual impasse. In the end, then, what we really have in many, if not most, supposedly "controlled" outcome studies are comparative studies. The only problem, and it is a significant one, is that under such naturalistic life conditions we do not know with what our formal treatment has been unintentionally compared!

A second matter in the use of untreated control groups is that while researchers usually do their best to match treated and "untreated" families according to variables either known or suspected to be relevant to outcome, naiveté may prevail. Consider, for example, the family whose adolescent son has just been arrested for setting fires, or the spouses who have almost killed each other during their tenth argument this week. Even if they do not seek help elsewhere while in our "untreated" condition, do we really believe that people who are willing to wait for our research design to offer treatment represent the same clinical phenomena as those families with whom they are "matched" on such mundane variables as years married, number of children, educational level, etc.? We are amazed how often good clinicians can delude themselves about such issues when they put on their laboratory jackets and take out their probability tables. We agree with Myers (1972) that, "in practice we expect the experimenter to use his brains as well as his F ratios to draw inferences" (p. 169). These comments, of course, are especially relevant for studies using a no-treatment control condition.

A third issue confronting the use of control groups, whether no-treatment or wait-list controls, is that of research ethics, and is loaded with emotional and political concerns. For example, what are the ethics of telling 20 families with anorexic daughters who may be near death that, if they want treatment at Clinic X, they will have to wait four months while 20 other anorexic families receive treatment? Of course, these families are free to refuse to take part in the study, but that is hardly a sufficient resolution of the dilemma. Placebo controls offer an alternative but are plagued with additional ethical difficulties (O'Leary and Borkovec, 1978).

In fact, there is an alternative for the family therapy researcher who wants to keep his/her control families *essentially* untreated (formally, that is), yet still not arouse the wrath and scorn of local human subjects committees. A control procedure known as "treatment on demand" (TOD) was recently developed in the Boston-New Haven collaborative studies of the psychotherapy of depression (DiMascio and Klerman, 1977) and is now in use in similar research at the University of Wisconsin (Klein, Greist, Gurman, and Van Cura, 1978). In this approach, the appropriate number of families or couples would be randomly assigned to the TOD control group. Unlike standard wait-list or placebo control groups, however, each family would have access to a therapist in the study pool *on demand*, i.e., at their initiative. In the research protocol, such visits would be severely limited in number and possibly in length, e.g., in a study in which initially treated families might receive 12 sessions, TOD families might be limited to one half-hour session per month, if they are to remain (in terms of data analyses) in the control condition. If a family demanded more frequent meetings with their therapist, i.e., exceeded the limit on the total number of meetings established in the research protocol, they would be dropped from the TOD cell and be replaced by another (randomly assigned) family. They would continue to be treated according to usual clinical considerations, and to be followed by the research project, as long as they continued their consent. Thus, the investigator who was simply comparing family therapy "X" with no treatment would potentially then have four treatment conditions: 1) family therapy "X"; 2) TOD remainers, i.e., those families who never requested treatment; 3) TOD partial remainers, i.e., those families who requested therapy visits but did not exceed the protocol limit; and 4) TOD dropouts, i.e., those families who exceeded the protocol limit. Differences among groups 2, 3 and 4, independent of their clinical outcomes, would offer a rich source of post-hoc information relevant to the formulation of hypotheses about family therapy dropouts and to the design of future empirical studies. Moreover, such a control procedure is unlikely to arouse significant ethical concern, since treatment is immediately available to all families in the control condition.[3] Finally, such a design strategy is much less likely than traditional control strategies to accumulate absolute dropouts, i.e., those who sever all contact with the research team. Thus, TOD probably offers the closest approximation to a "true" no-treatment condition that has yet emerged in psychotherapy outcome research, and has much greater appeal than alternative procedures to both administrators of mental health services and to nonresearcher practicing clinicians.

What percentage of families receiving family therapy improve?

The second way of addressing the broad question about the effectiveness of the family therapies is to examine the rates (percentages) of treated couples and families who improve during treatment. Note that we say "during" treatment, not "because of" treatment. Fewer than a dozen controlled family therapy outcome studies also report the percentage of families/couples improved, so that we must turn, for a limited answer to this question, to uncontrolled single-group studies. Summarizing across all the studies providing such information, we have found (Gurman and Kniskern, 1978a) an improvement rate of roughly two-thirds. Specifically, our analysis showed 61% of marital cases improved, and 73% of family cases improved. Actually, these marital results are somewhat deflated because they include studies of the treatment of marital problems with individual psychotherapy. With these cases excluded, the rate of improved mar-

---

[3.] In fact, using this procedure, it is often true that therapists are *more* available to families than in many overloaded clinical settings.

ital therapy cases increases to 65%.[4]

Does the developmental level of the identified patient disciminate among family therapy outcomes?

To date, no controlled studies of this question exist. The data from uncontrolled investigations reveal a trend toward better outcome when the identified patient is a child or adolescent (71% improved) than when the identified patient is an adult (65% improved) (Gurman and Kniskern, 1978a). Existing data do not allow a further discrimination between the outcomes of family therapy for child vs. adolescent identified patients.

Do patients ever worsen as the result of family therapies?

There is a good deal of both clinical and empirical evidence (Gurman and Kniskern, 1978a, 1978b) of the occurrence of deterioration or "negative effects" in marital and family therapies, both behavioral and nonbehavioral. Since only a small amount of this evidence derives from controlled studies, family therapies cannot be implicated, with certainty, to have caused such worsening. Still, the apparent frequency of such negative effects (5-10%) is so similar to those documented in the practice of individual and group psychotherapy (Bednar and Lawlis, 1971; Bergin and Lambert, 1978; Lambert, Bergin, and Collins, 1977) and there is such a clearly emerging clinical picture of the conditions which heighten the chances of deterioration (Gurman and Kniskern, 1978b), that it seems quite unlikely that the harmful effects of family therapies that have been documented have appeared merely because of inadequate sampling or related methodological shortcomings. To date, then, we know little about the deterioration-inducing components of family therapies *qua* treatment methods, but a good deal more about the sort of family therapist who increases the chances of negative therapeutic effects. In a capsule description of the deterioration-in-

ducing family therapist, Gurman and Kniskern (1978b) note that

The available evidence points to a composite picture of deterioration in marital-family therapy being facilitated by a therapist with poor relationship skills who directly attacks "loaded" issues and family members' defenses very early in treatment, fails to intervene in or interpret intrafamily confrontation in ongoing treatment, and does little to structure and guide the opening of therapy or to support family members. Such a style is even more likely to be countertherapeutic with patients who have weak ego-defenses or feel threatened by the nature or very fact of being in treatment (p. 14).

Which Family Therapies Are Most Effective?

> *Whenever many different remedies are proposed for a disease, it usually means that we know very little about the disease, which is also true of a . . . (remedy) when it is vaunted as a panacea or cure-all for many diseases.*
>
> —Garrison

This question cannot, of course, be meaningfully answered in the form in which we have posed it above, that is, the form in which it is most often asked. Despite the extravagant, even grandiose, claims made at times by certain leaders in the family therapy field about the universal (sic) applicability and efficacy of their approaches, there can be little doubt that, while publicly entertaining such fantasies may have proselytizing value, such assertions are entirely unsubstantiated and have a probability of being realized that approaches zero. The well-worn, but still salient, reminder that the ultimate empirical *and* clinical question is, "What treatment for what problem? (with what therapists, etc., etc.)," takes us in a very different direction. In this section, we will summarize our current assessment of which marital and family therapies seem to be most effective or promising in general, which effective treatment components have been identified within given therapeutic methods, and what specific therapies seem most efficacious for certain relatively well-defined clinical problems.

1) Among the marital therapies that are not explicitly behavioral (e.g., Jacobson, Chapter

---

[4] Of course, such data tell us virtually nothing about the effective treatment components. Still, they do serve the useful *political* purpose of establishing at least a crude empirical basis for the continued practice and teaching of marriage and family therapy.

15) or exclusively symptom-focused (e.g., Sluzki, 1978), but which have many common characteristics (Gurman, 1978c) and can be summarily described as pragmatic psychodynamic therapies (e.g., Sager, Chapter 3), conjoint treatment clearly is the method of choice (Gurman and Kniskern, 1978a). Conjoint group therapy seems rather potent as well. On the other hand, collaborative and concurrent treatments (cf. Green, 1965) have received little support and appear to be on the wane in any case (Gurman, 1973a).

2) Individual psychotherapy for the treatment of marital problems has a noteworthy poor record of positive outcomes and a strikingly high rate of negative outcomes. Gurman and Kniskern (1978a) found only a 48% improvement rate for such treatment, but a rate of deterioration (11.6%) that doubled that (5.6%) found in all other marital treatment formats combined (Gurman and Kniskern, 1978b), all of which have in common that both spouses receive treatment.[5]

3) Behavioral marriage therapy appears to be about as effective for minimally-moderately distressed couples as nonbehavioral methods (Jacobson, 1978, 1979), though it must be emphasized that behavioral and nonbehavioral studies often employ rather different outcome criteria. Neither behavioral nor psychodynamic marital therapy has accumulated much empirical support in the treatment of severely distressed marriages.

4) The only treatment ingredients that have received consistently positive empirical support as facilitating the outcomes of marital therapies, apparently regardless of the general mode of such therapies (cf. Gurman, 1975b; Jacobson, 1979), are those that increase couples' communication skills (Birchler, 1979; Gurman and Kniskern, 1977, 1978a; Jacobson, 1978, 1979). In fact, at this point, it is defensible to argue that increased communication skills, however they are achieved, are a sine qua non of effective

marital therapy. Lest this position be misunderstood, we are not, however, arguing that improved communication skills are *sufficient* for positive outcomes in most cases, or that these data ipso facto support the efficacy of intervention programs that are entirely limited to a focus on enhancing communication skills (cf. Gurman and Kniskern, 1977).

5) There is tentative evidence, reviewed by Jacobson (1978), that marital therapy, especially in a group context, may be at least an effective adjunct treatment for couples with an alcoholic spouse (also see Gurman and Kniskern, 1978a).

6) Despite the widespread public awareness of conjoint sex therapy for couples, and the frequent professional ballyhoo about treatment effectiveness, the number of well controlled studies in the area is few, and most studies are plagued with methodological inadequacies (Gurman and Kniskern, 1978a; Jacobson, 1978). Nonetheless, conjoint, behaviorally-oriented therapies for sexual dysfunction have received significant empirical support and should be considered the treatment of choice for such problems, especially when severe nonsexual marital problems do not exist. Referring again to conclusion 4, above, it should be recalled that communication training is a routine component of all directive sex therapy programs.

7) Family therapies of several modes are at least as effective as and probably more effective than many commonly offered treatments (e.g., individual psychotherapy) for problems that clearly involve marital and/or family conflict.

8) Family therapies are often more effective than individual psychotherapy even for problems that are not presented as interpersonal and which often are presented as individualized or intrapsychic.

9) At present, no conclusive assessment can be made of the general comparative efficacy of behavioral vs. other marital and family treatment methods. Such studies are nearly non-existent.

10) Structural family therapy (Minuchin, 1974) thus far has received very encouraging empirical support for the treatment of certain childhood and adolescent psychosomatic symptoms, i.e., anorexia (Minuchin et al., 1975, 1978; Rosman et al., 1976) and asthma (Minuchin et al., 1975), and adult drug addiction (Stanton and Todd,

---

[5.] In many lectures we have given, we have frequently been asked (usually by defenders of the psychoanalytic faith) whether these results could have been biased by a disproportionate representation in individual treatment of patients whose spouses refused to take part in conjoint therapy. We know of no evidence that would confirm this suspicion. In fact, most relevant studies (cf. Gurman and Kniskern, 1978a) either used random assignment to individual and conjoint conditions or were based on *therapists'* recommendations for individual treatment.

1976, 1978). For ethical reasons which seem methodologically insurmountable (Gurman and Kniskern, 1978a), no controlled treatment trials have been conducted with families with psychosomatic children, yet the clinical results at both termination and follow-up are extremely impressive. At the moment, structural family therapy should be considered the family therapy treatment of choice for these childhood psychosomatic conditions and, to our knowledge, it is the most empirically supported psychotherapy approach of *any* sort for these conditions. The studies of structural family therapy with drug addicts are among the very best controlled outcome studies in the entire research literature on family therapy, existing inaccurate critiques of those studies (Wells and Dezen, 1978a) notwithstanding (Stanton and Todd, 1980).[6]

11) Operantly oriented behavioral family therapy (e.g., Patterson, 1971) appears quite effective for changing the frequency of selected intrafamily childhood behaviors, e.g., aggressiveness, especially when marital conflict is not severe (Gordon and Davidson, Chapter 14; Patterson, 1975).

12) The "systems-behavioral" family therapy of Alexander et al. (now formally called "functional family therapy"—see Barton and Alexander, Chapter 11) at the University of Utah (Alexander and Barton, 1976; Alexander and Parsons, 1973), which incorporates both interventions derived from social learning theory and interventions based on family systems theories, has accumulated impressive outcomes in the treatment of families with adolescents involved in soft juvenile delinquency.

13) Despite increasing clinical sophistication on the part of marital and family therapists regarding the psychology of the divorce process (e.g., Kressel and Deutsch, 1977), there is essentially no empirical evidence that procedures referred to broadly as "divorce counseling/ therapy" lead to positive outcomes (Gurman and Kniskern, 1978a).

---

6. While the Philadelphia Child Guidance Clinic studies of psychosomatic conditions have not included untreated control groups, they may be considered quasi-experimental studies in that most patients served as their own controls by virtue of having received a great deal of other treatment prior to entry into structural therapy.

What Factors Make Family Therapies More Effective?

Aside from treatment factors *qua* type of treatment, e.g., behavioral, structural, etc., three major sources of possible variables exist that may influence the results of marital and family therapies: other treatment factors, patient/family factors, and therapist factors. Here we summarize our current state of relative (cf. Garfield and Bergin, 1978; Gurman and Razin, 1977) ignorance about such variables (Gurman and Kniskern, 1978a).

Treatment Factors

1) The length of therapy, whether measured as total elapsed time or as total treatment sessions, has infrequently been studied in relation to outcome. The evidence to date suggests that brief time-limited treatments and other brief treatments (arbitrarily defined here as up to 20 sessions, or about 4-5 months) are, in general, probably equal in effectiveness to lengthier family therapies.

2) Which family members are involved in treatment seems to exert a powerful effect, especially regarding the involvement of the father in family therapies (also note the significance of the inclusion of both spouses in treating marital problems, discussed earlier). The father's presence clearly improves the odds of good outcomes in many situations. The reader is cautioned, however, that insufficient data exist to support any assertions about the necessity of always including two or more generations in the treatment of marital or family dysfunction.

3) The use of various apparatuses in family therapy, e.g., videotape, electromechanical signaling devices, while offering fertile ground for future research, has not yet been convincingly demonstrated to improve therapeutic outcomes.

Patient-Family Factors

1) For a small number of specific diagnostic categories (i.e., adolescent psychosomatic problems, certain childhood behavior problems, soft delinquency, drug abuse, alcoholism, sexual dysfunction), there currently exist marital or family therapies which appear to lead to good to excellent therapeutic outcomes. For the re-

mainder of the vast array of common psychiatric problems, e.g., depression, anxiety, the psychoses, etc., there is little to no evidence of the efficacy of any marital or family therapy.

2) In addition, there is no evidence currently available about the treatment of choice for various categories of *couples* or *families*, e.g., enmeshed, pseudo-mutual, above and beyond the appearance of identified patient symptoms in certain family "types" (e.g., Minuchin et al., 1975).

3) Few markers of family interaction style have been found to predict treatment responsiveness (Stanton et al., 1979). Of course, little study in this domain has emerged. Thus far, low authoritarianism, openness to disagreement, low coercion and competitiveness, and low role traditionality seem to have moderately positive mediating effects on outcome. As is often the case in psychotherapy, it appears that in family therapy, too, the rich get richer and the poor suffer most from inflation.

4) A number of family constellation variables and family demographic characteristics have been studied as predictors of treatment outcome, and have shown unreliable relationships to therapeutic effectiveness. These include: intact vs. single-parent families, family constellation, family size, identified patient birth order and age, length of marriage, and parental educational level. Coché (1978) has struck an important note about the complexities of establishing constellational classifications. She notes, e.g., that "families having an adolescent can refer to a widower with an only child, parents with eight children ages 11-20, or a divorced mother with three children ages one, three and 13" (p. 10).

Therapist Factors

1) Therapist experience level in family therapy has been shown to bear an uncertain relationship to treatment outcomes. Some data suggest, however, that experience level *differences* between co-therapists may weaken therapeutic effectiveness.

2) To date, there are no persuasive data that support the oft-asserted superiority of co-therapy over therapy done by a single therapist.

3) There exists an accumulating empirical literature supporting the relationship between treatment outcome and a therapist's relationship skills. This literature suggests that it is generally important for the marital-family therapist to be active and to provide some structure to early interviews, but not to confront tenuous family defenses very early in treatment. Excesses in this direction are among the main contributors to premature termination and to negative therapeutic outcomes (Gurman and Kniskern, 1978b). A reasonable mastery of technical skills may be sufficient to prevent worsening or to maintain pretreatment functioning in very difficult cases, but more refined relationship skills are necessary to yield truly positive outcomes in marital-family therapy. Moreover, the impact of such relationship skills is not limited to more affectively and intrapsychically-oriented treatment, but is equally salient in behavioral treatment (Alexander et al., 1976; Gurman and Kniskern, 1978a; Jacobson, Chapter 15).

Some Reflections on Past Research and Recommendations for Future Uncontrolled Studies of Family Therapy Outcome

As noted at the outset of this chapter, the recent generation of reviews of the literature on the outcomes of family therapy indeed has been impressive. Among these reviews, two (Jacobson, 1978; Wells and Dezen, 1978a) are of particular importance here, since their authors have shown some fundamental disagreement with some of our conclusions about the empirical status of family therapies, summarized (and updated since Gurman and Kniskern, 1978a) above. The basic point on which Jacobson (1978) and Wells and Dezen (1978a) disagree with the present authors involves the methodological adequacy of a number of the studies on which we have based our assessments of the efficacy of certain family therapies, especially those that are not behaviorally-oriented. The issue does not involve disagreement about the methodological adequacy of specific studies, but rather addresses the matter of whether such studies, which we agree are deficient, can be instructive nonetheless.

Thus, Jacobson (1978) has written that uncontrolled clinical studies (which form only *part* of the basis for our conclusions) are "from a scientific standpoint . . . of limited utility, since they neither objectively demonstrate the efficacy of their procedures nor further understanding of the mechanisms by which such positive changes might come about" (p. 396). Furthermore, Jacobson (1978) has argued, "these reports do not qualify as scientific investigations" (p. 403). In a similar spirit of what we recently called "technolatry and methodolatry" (Gurman and Kniskern, 1978d), Wells (1977) argues that it is "self-deceptive" to believe that a series of logically flawed studies (e.g., uncontrolled single-group studies) can "converge" (our term: Gurman and Kniskern, 1978a, p. 845) toward any useful conclusions.

Our response to the critiques offered by our colleagues is, simply, that they are correct on methodological grounds, but that they have used the wrong criterion for judging the *usefulness* of such research findings. We certainly do not endorse the view that family therapy researchers should treat methodological issues casually, and, in fact, have proposed explicit guidelines for evaluating the adequacy of research in this field (Gurman and Kniskern, 1978a). Nevertheless, we believe that, like love, methodological adequacy is not enough. If research on family therapy is to have clinical impact, then inferences about the efficacy of our treatments must also be characterized by *logical* adequacy. Thus, the logic behind our broad conclusion (Gurman and Kniskern, 1978a) of the overall efficacy of nonbehavioral family therapies can be elaborated as follows. First, as noted above, in reaching this conclusion, we have not relied solely on the results of uncontrolled studies. Second, even the results of poorly controlled studies are *entirely consistent* with those of better quality (in keeping with the same trend in individual psychotherapy research). Third, the results of uncontrolled studies of nonbehavioral marital and family treatments suggest the same broad conclusions about both general effectiveness *and* comparative effectiveness across the three levels (uncontrolled single group, uncontrolled comparative, and controlled studies) of design sophistication noted by Wells (1977; Wells and Dezen, 1978a; Wells et al. 1972) himself. Finally, as we have noted elsewhere (Gurman and Kniskern, 1978a), "largely positive results emerge on the basis of a *wide variety of*

criteria, on change measures from a *number of evaluative perspectives*, for *many types of marital and family problems*, from therapy conducted by *clinicians of all the major therapeutic disciplines*, and in therapy carried out in a *number of treatment settings*" (p. 845, emphasis added).

It is on these bases, not on the basis of uncritical acceptance of the results of uncontrolled studies, that we have concluded that these *patterns* of results imply the consistency and power of an underlying, converging clinical phenomenon that overrides issues of the design quality of individual studies. The logical rationale for this position is that the outright rejection of single studies because of design flaws is wasteful of significant data that, though ambigous in their own right, can be informative when viewed in the context of dozens of other studies. In contrast, note Jacobson's (1978) comments that the results of uncontrolled studies "may be more a function of *therapist-shared perceptions* than of actual client improvement" (p. 403 emphasis added), and that, "perhaps (couples) therapists are *predisposed* to perceive a certain percentage of their clients as improved, *regardless of actual change* occurring in therapy. *Clients might cooperate* in this endeavor by creating the *impression* of better functioning . . ." (p. 403, emphasis added). These comments strike us as remarkably inferential, coming as they do from the pen of a behavior therapist. In our view, Jacobson's position would require the operation of an unconscious process that entangles both patients and their therapists, and which cuts across temporal and geographic boundaries in a most startling manner. Even in our most psychodynamic moments (e.g., Gurman and Knudson, 1978; Gurman et al., 1978), we could not seriously consider the existence of such a collective collusion aimed toward denying the impotence of any therapy method.

Moreover, the attempted "objectivity" of which our critics speak so highly is itself elusive (cf. Wells and Dezen, 1978a; Stanton and Todd, 1980), and may reflect a measure of "self-deception" (Wells, 1977) that is as pernicious and deserving of scrutiny as are the purportedly repeated collusive denials of the therapists and patients who have been studied in the reports which we continue to find clinically meaningful.

Thus, for example, Stanton and Todd (1980) recently performed a content analysis of the evaluative statements made by Wells and Dezen (1978a) about specific studies in their review of nonbehavioral family therapy. The degree of positive evaluation was correlated with the design quality and level of sophistication of the studies reviewed by Wells and Dezen. Stanton and Todd concluded, "None of the statistical correlations were positive and half of them were significantly negative, a result which is completely opposite to what would be expected. This indicates that Wells and Dezen have introduced biases into their review in the form of *undue praise of many uncontrolled studies and inordinate criticism of more sophisticated and better-designed research*" (emphasis added). Like beauty, empirical elegance is unreliable in the eye of the scolder!

Uncontrolled Studies and the Process of Discovery in Family Therapy. Moreover, there is a more specific purpose to which uncontrolled single-group studies can be put. For example, even Jacobson (1978) has acknowledged that such reports may "generate hypotheses which can later be tested in controlled investigations" (p. 403). We concur with Jacobson's view, but would extend it considerably. To us, it is questionable whether the field of family therapy is yet advanced enough to engage *all* its empirical efforts at verification. Rather, we believe that the field is still sufficiently in flux that empirical research oriented toward *discovery* rather than verification is also in order. This kind of discovery process is not especially well served by tightly controlled investigation. On the contrary, thoughtful study of family therapy in uncontrolled designs can be enormously profitable for this end. For example, Bentovim (Bentovim and Kinston, 1978; Kinston and Bentovim, 1978) at the Hospital for Sick Children in London, following the lead of Malan (1963, 1976), has begun a series of investigations of brief focal family therapy aimed at assessing psychodynamic improvement on an individualized case basis, and Campbell (1979), working at the Tavistock Clinic in London, has begun an uncontrolled study of the effects of the identified (child) patient's "distance-regulating behavior" in the family, therapist interventions to modify

such regulation, and treatment outcome.

Comparative and Controlled Studies of Family Therapy Outcome

In this section, we will not belabor the methodological intricacies of conducting comparative and controlled studies of (family) therapy outcome, since these are familiar and have been considered at length elsewhere (e.g., Gottman and Markman, 1978; Mahoney, 1978). Rather, we will briefly consider some as yet unresolved issues in conducting such studies, and will enumerate some priorities for research on the outcomes of the family therapies. We will also nominate a small number of important specific questions that require answering, and the answering of which we think will have potential for immediate practical clinical benefit.

Comparative Study of Family Therapies. There is a serious political danger in the comparative study of the family therapies. Family therapy is still so new and represents, as shown throughout this *Handbook*, such a challenge to most traditional views of psychopathology and psychotherapy, that much of the energy of the field has gone toward establishing its conceptual and professional legitimacy in the mental health field at large. As a result, convictions about the efficacy of particular methods of family therapy have been largely based on devotion to a small number of charismatic figures in the field, at times bordering on professional cultism. The resulting danger is that there now exists within the field a perceptible competitiveness, apparently geared toward establishing single treatment methods and models as universally superior within the broad scope of the family therapies. Clearly, continued activity of this sort can only be destructive to the field as a whole. Since we do not believe it is possible for any family therapy method to be universally, or even nearly so, superior to other methods, we would strongly encourage the refocusing of empirical energies toward common problems. We believe that the field of family therapy is now politically, conceptually and technically solid enough to be able to lay aside at least some internal competitive struggles, and to begin to address questions of the comparative utility of different methods in ways that will serve the interests of patients, rather than of proselytizing clinicians. With this perspective in mind, we would encourage researchers to consider especially carefully two major issues in the comparative study of the family therapies.

First, the comparative study of two or more treatment methods is virtually useless unless a specific patient population has been well defined. The outcome question in comparative studies is always of the form, "Which of the treatment methods under study is more (or most) effective for *this* specific clinical situation?" We refer here to clinical "situations" rather than to "disorders," since there are several available methods for defining and selecting a family population for study. This can be accomplished via identification of family interaction styles held in common, regardless of presenting complaints (e.g., Cambell, 1979), by identification of developmental and/or constellational similarities (e.g., Gartner et al., 1978), by limiting samples to those presenting specific complaints or symptoms (e.g., Minuchin et al., 1975, 1978) at the individual or interactional level, or by limiting samples on the basis of traditional psychiatric nosology applied to the identified patient.

Many, if not most, family therapists will be likely to revolt against the latter two options, especially the last option, finding such a strategy grossly antagonistic to the widely shared beliefs within the field about the conceptual and clinical adequacy of individual diagnosis. This predictable response notwithstanding, it is clear that diagnostic procedures at a family system level are so poorly developed as to currently preclude routine sample definition with such strategies. In addition, and particularly because of the preceding consideration, there is no existing empirical evidence that sample selection based on identified patient diagnosis precludes the development of effective, specifically applied family treatment methods. Thus, one of the major methodological issues confronting family therapy research, the resolution of which will have practical impact, follows logically from the above considerations. Specifically, in terms of applying various explicitly defined treatment methods to particular clinical situations, what is lost and what is gained by adopting different strategies

of defining a patient population for study?

In addition, of course, comparative family studies are only useful to the extent to which they also specify the actual treatment operations used by therapists. We will comment further on this issue in our discussion of controlled studies of family therapy outcome.

A second major issue in the design of comparative studies also needs to be addressed. Comparative studies of different treatment methods do not, of course, require an untreated control group. That is, one may ask whether treatment A is superior to treatment B for problem X without also asking whether either treatment is superior to no treatment. Ultimately, it would seem ideal to ask both questions within the same study. Still, practical and ethical considerations often work against the feasibility of such a design. Moreover, comparative studies that do not include an untreated group can still answer questions with enormous practical payoff. In designing comparative studies of family therapy outcome, attention must be paid to the use to which the findings may be put. For example, in certain settings, such as community mental health centers, the range of therapist skills may be limited, say, to a small number of specific family therapy methods, e.g., operant management techniques and structural family therapy. Given ethical and local political concerns about creating no-treatment groups in the face of rising demand for family treatment services, the former forces may predominate design considerations. Thus, if, at clinic X, treatments A and B are the only family methods available to the staff in treating some commonly seen problem C, it may be quite sufficient, for local policymaking purposes, to determine the relative impact of A and B on C, without attending to the question of whether A or B are superior to no treatment. But the issue here is not only, "What is the question being asked?" but also, "*How* and *by whom* will the findings be used?" The typical board of directors of a public clinic is unlikely to withdraw all family therapy services if, as in our scenario, treatments A and B, the only ones available at clinic X, are found to be no more effective than no treatment for problem C. On the other hand, given a high demand for service, a finding that treatment A is clearly superior to treatment B is a good deal more likely to have administrative impact. Even in the face of increasingly influential consumerism in the delivery of mental health services, the public generally shows more concern that they receive the best available treatment than that they only receive treatments whose efficacy per se has been reliably and repeatedly documented. While such a stance may horrify certain academicians, we believe that such a relativistic position is quite justified, under the sorts of common organizational constraints we have described.

There are three specific, clinically relevant, comparative study issues, which cut across theoretical orientations, that we think deserve immediate research attention.

1) Under what conditions of practice within any family treatment method does *co-therapy* yield clinical outcomes that are superior to therapy done by solo therapists, and does even this superiority (if found) justify the continued practice of co-therapy in terms of broader, extratherapeutic considerations, such as treatment efficiency and financial cost (to both patient and service provider)?

2) In what ways do varying treatment elements, within a given method of family therapy, influence the rate of *dropouts* and of *premature termination*? Gurman and Kniskern (1978a, 1978b) have identified several factors that seem to operate in this process across family treatment methods, but little is currently known about the factors influencing this phenomenon *within* different treatment methods.

3) Our final candidate for a high priority comparative study issue that is not school-specific may seem nearly sacrilegious to family therapy purists. Since we do not believe that conjoint family therapy of any sort is always the treatment of choice for psychological problems (cf. Garfield and Bergin, 1978), we conclude that the comparative study of specific conjoint family treatment methods with efficacious methods of psychotherapy, whether individual or other unit of treatment, is absolutely essential. We would especially endorse the comparative study of family therapies with individual therapies which have already received encouraging empirical support in the treatment of specific disorders, e.g., cognitive therapy (Beck et al., 1979) for the treatment of depression, and exposure therapy (Marks, 1978) for the treatment of agoraphobia. We want to be clear that in making such a recommendation we are not motivated by the all too common politicized desire to "outdo" traditional, individually focused therapies. Rather, since successful treatments have already been developed for the treatment of a small number of important, common and specific clinical syndromes, the issue at hand is whether any currently available marital or family therapy methods can, while at least matching effectiveness with these individual methods, demonstrate reliably positive impact on psychological dimensions and criteria not addressed directly by individual therapy methods. More concretely, for example, why should any family therapy be used to treat mild to moderate depression since there already exists a frequently effective treatment for this disorder, unless such a therapy can be shown to be equally effective on, say, symptomatic criteria, and superior on other criteria, e.g., prevention of relapse, lowered incidence of depression in other family members, etc.? If a given method of family therapy were shown to be equally effective on symptomatic criteria, but not on other dimensions, that family therapy method's applicability to the treatment of depression would need to be seriously questioned, since treating a marital dyad or entire nuclear family may be significantly less cost-effective than treating the "identified patient" alone.

Controlled Studies.

1) A very important development in the design and conduct of psychotherapy outcome studies has occurred in the last few years. More and more, there has been emphasis on explicating the independent variable by designing explicit *treatment manuals* for therapists which specify the nature and sequence of therapist interventions and allow a check on whether the therapist adheres to the treatment model. As Gelder (1978) has said, "There is very little point in studying a treatment which another person cannot reproduce." The most impressive implementation of this strategy to date has been the manual for the cognitive therapy of depression (Beck et al., 1979). Further evidence of the impact of this trend toward developing explicit treatment manuals is shown in the editorial pol-

icy of at least two journals (*Cognitive Therapy and Research* and *Journal of Applied Behavior Analysis*) of refusing to publish studies of treatment for which such a formal elaboration of actual interventions is not available. Unfortunately, such criteria are not currently employed by any family therapy journals.

We strongly encourage the development of such treatment manuals for the practice of marital and family therapies. Our prediction is, however, that the possibility of creating useable manuals will vary widely across different family therapy methods. For example, it should be much easier to write such manuals for behavioral family therapy than for experiential approaches, such as that of Whitaker and Keith (Chapter 6). Indeed, rather explicit operationalization of therapeutic procedures already exists in the areas of behavioral marriage therapy (Jacobson, Chapter 15), sex therapy (Heiman, LoPiccolo, and LoPiccolo, Chapter 16), marital and family enrichment (L'Abate, Chapter 17) and operant child management (Gordon and Davidson, Chapter 14). Systems-behavioral family therapy (Barton and Alexander, Chapter 11), Bowen therapy (Kerr, Chapter 7), strategic therapy (Stanton, Chapter 10), structural therapy (Aponte and VanDensen, Chapter 9), and other brief, symptom-focused therapies (e.g., Bodin, Chapter 8) should pose only slightly more difficulty in this regard, while psychodynamically-oriented approaches (e.g., Framo, Chapter 4; Sager, Chapter 3; Skynner, Chapter 2) present considerably greater challenges in this realm.

Indeed, a most provocative and perplexing problem is raised by the possibility (indeed, in our minds, likelihood) that to attempt to carry out some family therapies, such as that of Whitaker and his colleagues, according to an explicit treatment manual would effectively destroy the method! Still, we believe that at least certain broad intervention principles can be explicated even within such approaches, and that the chapter in this *Handbook* by Whitaker and Keith represents a major first step in this direction.

Finally, we would like to raise a related question which has not yet been addressed empirically in any psychotherapy research circles. That is, does therapist adherence to a treatment manual in any way *impede* the practice of psychotherapy? Our own clinical and supervisory experience suggests that it often does have such inhibiting effects, especially for relatively inexperienced clinicians, but whether these side-effects override the advantages of explicating treatment operations, and when, and for whom, remain to be investigated.

2) A closely related issue is that, to date, most of the major methods of marital and family therapy have gone almost entirely unstudied in outcome research (cf. Gurman & Kniskern, 1978a). A major research priority for the family therapy field, then, should be to concentrate on family treatment methods that already have had widespread clinical and training impact. Among these methods we would include: Bowen therapy, contextual therapy, object-relations approaches, and paradoxical and strategic therapies.

3) Among the family therapies that have received encouraging empirical support, we would encourage component analysis of the effective, i.e., essential, treatment ingredients. For example, structural family therapy for the treatment of anorexia nervosa almost routinely includes operant strategies, yet the relative contributions to outcome of these behavioral techniques and of techniques that are more specific to the model (cf. Aponte and Van Deusen, Chapter 9; Minuchin et al., 1975) have yet to be determined. Two instructive illustrations of this issue have appeared in the study of behavioral methods. For example, Jacobson's (1979) research has led to a serious questioning of the necessity, in behavioral marriage therapy, of the use of contingency contracting, which until only recently was viewed as a technical sine qua non within that approach (e.g., Weiss, 1975). Similarly, Alexander's group (cf. Chapter 11) has accumulated persuasive evidence that in the treatment of families with juvenile delinquents, therapist mastery of behavioral technology is not sufficient for positive outcomes, but must be accompanied by certain specific therapist relationship skills.

4) Beyond everyday lay experience and speculative clinical lore, very little is known about the natural history of marital and family dysfunction and conflict. Advances in this area have been made in the study of the psychological sequelae of the divorce process (cf. Kaslow, Chapter 18), but scientific knowledge of the course of most other common family problems

lags far behind. The study of naturalistic processes of marital and family change and of homeostasis is not only fascinating in its own right, but would provide a more substantive basis for the comparison of the effects of professional treatment.

5) Replication of marital and family therapies that have yielded encouraging outcome results is sorely needed. Of particular importance is the need to address the generalizability of positive results obtained in previous studies. Klein and Gurman (1977) and Kniskern and Gurman (1979) have raised the question of whether the outcomes documented in a setting in which a particular method of treatment was developed would generalize beyond the "parent setting" to other treatment settings. For example, even the repeated demonstrations of the efficacy of structural family therapy described earlier in this chapter do not logically preclude the possibility that the use of the same methods might be considerably less effective at Family Institute X than at the Philadelphia Child Guidance Clinic, even given expert and thorough training in these methods at Institute X. If a treatment method is very effective either across the board or for very specific disorders *only* in the setting in which it originated, or if it is substantially less effective in other clinical settings, the power of the method per se would need to be seriously questioned.

The point, here, then, is that even the most apparently effective family therapies must not be assumed to be powerful across clinical settings. The possibility of the influence of setting-effects on the outcome of family therapy is an enormously significant one, given the charisma that has characterized so many leaders in the family therapy movement, and the cultism that has so often characterized their followers.

6) The manner of public reporting of the results of controlled family therapy studies, and of uncontrolled comparative studies as well, must also change. Much too often, results presented on the basis of group statistics obscure valuable information contained within an investigator's data. We totally agree with Garfield's (1977) recommendation that beyond the usual reporting of mean (group) change in studies of treatment outcome, two additional data be presented: the standard deviations of the change

measures used, and a frequency distribution showing how many cases improved, at specified levels, on each outcome criterion. We would add a third additional dimension for reporting, i.e., *within* cases, how many show improvement on how many criteria, and on what criteria? For example, it might be found and reported that in a sample of 20 treated families, evaluated on three criteria, two showed negative change on criteria *a* and *c*, and no change on criterion *b*; five showed positive change on criterion *a* only, and no change on *b* or *c*; nine showed positive change on criteria *a* and *b*, and no change on *c*; and four showed positive change on all three criteria. The superior potential clinical meaningfulness and utility of such data over group means alone are self-evident.

Therapist, Patient and (Other) Treatment Factors

Among the many treatment factors (beyond those specific to given family therapy methods) that impinge on the process and outcome of treatment, we identify three that are of particular importance across theoretical orientations, and which we recommend as high priority matters for empirical study within this realm. The first involves the setting in which treatment occurs, and the others involve temporal considerations.

Kinney et al. (1977) recently provided some interesting results about the outcomes of therapists' entering the homes of families in crisis for extended periods of time to prevent one or more family members from being placed in group homes, foster homes, or other institutional care. Results indicated successful prevention of outside placement for 121 of 134 family members at a savings of over $2,300 per client, compared to projected placement costs. While the intensity of therapist activity and availability was confounded with the location of intervention in this study, the clinical results are encouraging. In particular, they raise the question of when family therapy and other family-oriented interventions are best carried out outside a therapist's consultation room. Home-based treatments are not unique to the Kinney et al. project, of course, having received considerable attention from behavior therapists (e.g., Patterson, 1971) and other family therapists (e.g., Speck and Attneave, 1973).

As noted above, the design of the Kinney et al. (1977) study was confounded by its failure to control the intensity of therapist involvement with their families in crisis. This factor of therapist involvement relates directly to another issue, that of treatment intensity, or what we call *treatment density*, that is, the amount of treatment time per calendar time. This issue has been a predominant consideration in crisis intervention and was a major factor behind the development of multiple impact therapy (MacGregor et al., 1964). Beyond the uncontrolled study of the MacGregor et al. (1964) group, the matter of family therapy density has never been studied, and the effects of variations therein have never been investigated with this factor serving as an independent variable, although at least one such study is now underway (Schneider, 1979). Given the limited periods of total elapsed time that characterize most marital and family therapies (Gurman, 1978c; Gurman and Kniskern, 1978a), it would be quite instructive to learn whether increasing levels of treatment density facilitates clinical outcomes.

Finally, and closely related to the issue of treatment density, two other temporal factors seem especially worthy of investigation. These both involve *treatment length*. First, there is the obviously important question of the effects of length as measured by total number of treatment sessions (especially, of typical one- to one-and-a-half hour periods). The second dimension involves the frequency (e.g., once a week vs. biweekly) of treatment sessions (with session length and total number of sessions held constant). Again, given the current lack of evidence (Gurman, and Kniskern, 1978a) that lengthier treatments (measured by number of sessions) are generally superior to briefer or to time-limited treatments, the practical clinical question should be addressed as to whether the temporal *distribution* of sessions has a reliable impact on treatment outcome, and in what specific clinical situations.

Patient-Family Factors

Beyond the existing evidence that a small number of specific family therapy methods have offered promising results for the treatment of specific disorders (e.g., structural family therapy for anorexia nervosa), we know very little about other "patient" factors that predict outcome. We say "patient" factors because we wish to include under this term *both* individual variables in the identified patient and in other family members and interactional and systemic variables. As noted earlier, we think the major research priority in this area is to determine the relative influence on family therapy outcome of individual vs. interpersonal variables. To that recommendation, we would add that the additive and interactional (in the statistical sense) effects of these two categories of independent variables are equally deserving of high priority status for research in this domain.

Therapist Factors

Elsewhere, we have thoroughly examined what is currently known about the influence of therapist variables on family therapy outcome (Gurman, 1978a, 1978b; Gurman and Kniskern, 1978a, 1978b, 1978d, 1979). Partly on the basis of those reviews, which were summarized earlier in this chapter, we give high priority to the future study of the following issues involving therapist variables.

1) While the field of psychotherapy at large has often been roundly condemned, in part, for too frequently (sic) studying the outcomes of treatment as practiced by relatively inexperienced clinicians (e.g., Meltzoff and Kornreich, 1979), we think this concern is totally misguided, in general, and especially in family therapy. The usual rationale for this critical stance toward the study of therapy done by relative neophytes is that to accurately gauge the upper limits of influence of psychotherapy, it must be studied under conditions approximating its ideal practice. To wit, the argument goes, if very experienced therapists cannot obtain positive outcomes (in general, or with specific methods), then it is foolhardy and meaningless to inquire about the effectiveness of more junior clinicians. This position is quite illogical, since it is an unanswered empirical question as to whether inexperienced therapists, on the average, are any more or less likely to obtain positive outcomes using methods that are ineffective in the hands

of more seasoned clinicians.

Moreover, since family therapy is still such a young field, it still numbers relatively few highly experienced therapists, despite the recent membership growth spurts of major professional organizations such as the American Association for Marriage and Family Therapy (which had approximately 7,600 members as of mid-1979). The implication of this is obvious: Most marital and family therapy is being practiced, indeed taught, by relatively inexperienced clinicians. Thus, if one wants to learn about the effectiveness of most of the family therapies, one virtually cannot not study relative neophytes. But beyond this pragmatic consideration, we take the position that there *should* be study of such young family therapists if for no other reason (but we think it is a good one) than that there will always be neophyte practitioners in the field, and we need to know about their effectiveness as much as we need to know about the effectiveness of family therapy masters, and probably more so.[7]

Thus, we hope to have disabused researchers of their excessive concerns about obtaining samples of experienced family therapists as a guiding principle in their design protocols. Of course, further study of the specific effects of varying therapist experience levels is also in order, especially if tied to an elucidation of the particular ways in which different experience levels are manifest in overt in-session therapist behavior (cf. Auerbach and Johnson, 1977). Given the paucity of research on training in the field (Kniskern and Gurman, 1979), such studies could be quite helpful.

2) Just as different patients and families require different treatments, some family therapies are more effective in the hands of some therapists than in the hands of others. As Skynner and Skynner (1978) recently quipped, we need "different thinks for different shrinks." It is difficult to practice any family therapy method without confronting the "personal spill" (Coché, 1978) of one's own private past and present family experience into the treatment enterprise. Future efforts would be wisely directed toward

identifying the best matches between family therapist personality factors and particular methods and strategies of intervention. For example, we would predict that strong preference for a "take charge" and orderly personal style would be a much better "match" with structural family therapy and with behavioral methods than with more experiential methods, such as that of Whitaker and Keith (Chapter 6). Increasing specification of these maximal pairings between therapist personal style and treatment method would offer important practical benefit for curriculum development in family therapy training, perhaps especially in the planning of flexible sequences of such training exposures and experiences (Kniskern and Gurman, 1979).

3) As noted earlier in this chapter, co-therapy is an area loaded with controversy and mostly devoid of data (Roman and Meltzer, 1977) in the family therapy field. For example, Haley (1976) asserts with passion his uncompromising belief in the wastefulness and irrelevance of the practice, while Whitaker and Keith (Chapter 6), with equal fervor, argue that co-therapy is almost always a necessity. Obviously, the issue is not so absolute. The necessity (read: improved effectiveness) of co-therapists clearly varies as a function of factors about which we can only now speculate (e.g., severity of the presenting problem, felt therapist comfort), but about which we need unambiguous data. For example, the working style of a highly directive therapist (e.g., Haley) might well be compromised by the presence of a co-therapist, while the therapeutic power of self-disclosure of other therapists (e.g., Whitaker) might render them too personally vulnerable to be effective in the absence of a co-therapist. As a further illustration of the non-empirical basis for prevailing decisions about the wisdom of co-therapy, we can cite the practices of family therapists at the Tavistock Clinic in London. While sharing a common psychodynamic (object-relations theory) conceptual heritage, therapists in the Department for Children and Parents rarely employ co-therapy, while therapists working in the Department for Adolescents almost always use co-therapists (Campbell, 1979)!

4) Finally, we would strongly encourage the further study and specification of therapist relationship skills that affect treatment outcome.

---

7. In addition, the *longitudinal* study of the development of family therapy skill and clinical effectiveness would be enormously informative for training purposes.

The work of Alexander and his colleagues (Chapter 11) is clearly the model to be emulated thus far. More focally, we would like to see attention directed toward two issues in this realm. First, what therapist relationship skills are potent for both better (cf. Gurman and Kniskern, 1978a) and for worse (cf. Gurman and Kniskern, 1978b) *across* different methods of family therapy? Second, what therapist relationship skills are uniquely salient *within* different treatment methods? We believe it is extremely important that these questions be addressed, lest much of family therapy evolve into a technology without a soul, which we fear may be on the not too distant horizon (cf. Gurman and Kniskern, 1978d and Wells and Dezen, 1978a, 1978b; also, cf. Gurman and Knudson, 1978; Gurman et al., 1978, and Jacobson and Weiss, 1978).

Relationship Factors in Family Therapy: Some Further Thoughts. Consider the complexity of "relationship factors" in family therapy, especially as contrasted with individual psychotherapy. In individual psychotherapy, there is one physical dyad. We say "physical" dyad, because there are also present the dyadic relationships between the therapist and the patient's father, the therapist and the patient's mother, the patient and the therapist's father, mother, etc., that operate symbolically. There are also the transferential and countertransferential dyads between the patient and the therapist as his father/mother, the therapist and the patient as his son-daughter, etc. If we confine our observation to immediately observable relationships, however, there is but one. Now, consider a common family therapy context, a married couple and two co-therapists. Here, we have six dyads, four triads, and one tetrad. Bring in the couple's two children and we now have *fifteen* dyads, *twenty* triads, etc. These clusters of persons are all in relationships. *Which* relationships shall we examine?

To ease our task a bit, we may identify the three relationship *categories* in the above therapy scenario, i.e., patient-patient, patient-therapist, and therapist-therapist. The relationships among and between family members, of course, are those which we are trying to change, whereas the other relationship categories are those we try to use to effect change in the family

relationship system. We have considered co-therapy issues earlier in this chapter and elsewhere (Gurman, 1978a, 1978b, 1978d; Gurman and Kniskern, 1978a). Here, we would like to add a few brief thoughts about a conceptual context in which we may view the operation of therapist-patient relationship factors and which addresses their impact across varying methods of family treatment.

While we have criticized the recent rise in family therapy of what we call "technolatry," i.e., the worship of therapeutic technology at the expense of more subtle relationship variables (Gurman and Kniskern, 1978d; Gurman and Knudson, 1978; Gurman et al., 1978), it is clear, on both clinical and empirical grounds, that therapist relationship skills reflect only a part of the necessary attributes of the effective family therapist. One of the major deficiencies of examining these relationship factors in ways familiar in the study of individual psychotherapy (e.g., by focusing on a therapist's empathy and warmth) is that many schools of family therapy, e.g., structural, behavioral, strategic, while employing (though not always fostering) such "traditional" relationship dimensions, also rely heavily on the social engineering of family transactions.

We point out the obvious here in order to raise a meta-issue about the issue. That is, under what *structural* conditions of psychotherapy, and under what *technical* conditions of psychotherapy, should we logically expect traditional sorts of therapist relationship skills to make a significant clinical difference? Particularly important are some basic differences between individual therapy and family therapy. For example, the therapist may systematically deemphasize his leadership role and emphasize relationships within the family. Indeed, many family therapists avoid interpretation of their position in the family. At other times, even though the therapist may intend to emphasize his/her relations with the family, the family itself may choose to deemphasize the therapist. For example, the family may constructively extrude the therapist and proceed to work rather independently, so that the therapist allows this process to continue, or the family may become pleased with its own curative powers and try to exclude the parental figure of the therapist.

In addition, family therapy may produce dangers different from individual therapy that require the therapist to be much more than, e.g., empathic, warm and genuine. The family may become quite vicious in its treatment of some family members, or one member may show problems or behaviors that are very frightening to the family. In these situations, the family therapist may need to demonstrate rather forceful qualities if the treatment situation is to remain viable. If these types of problems are recurrent, the family therapist may need to repeatedly demonstrate these forceful qualities, and *these* qualities may become the most important conditions he/she can provide for family members.

Conversely, how may family therapy approximate individual therapy, such that traditional therapist relationship skills become more central? First, of course, the therapist may focus on family-therapist relations, as noted earlier. Second, the family may defend its position and its individual members by idealizing the therapist. Third, the family may not present the dangers that, as noted, are more likely to demand other kinds of therapist attributes and skills. In these ways, something like individual therapy may characterize the family treatment situation and lead, under empirical scrutiny, to confirmation of the central role of many of the same therapist relationship skills that are often operative in individual psychotherapy (cf. Gurman and Razin, 1977).

This discussion should also suggest why the overt delineation of patient and therapist roles may be more important in family therapy than in individual psychotherapy and why it may be a necessary precondition for the operation of certain therapist relationships skills. Unless or until the family is sufficiently controlled by an emerging common treatment vocabulary, ritual and intellectual belief about how therapy works and how the family works, the therapist is unlikely to be able to assume a role as a good empathic father or mother. He or she will need to expend considerable effort in managing other aspects of the treatment situation and, as a result, be less available for relations with each individual in the family, thus obviously diminishing the impact of such modes of relating, at least for certain periods or stages of the development of a working therapeutic alliance.

Each family member may enter therapy viewing the problem in different terms. Arguments, fights and power-plays may result from efforts to force other family members to adopt one's viewpoint. The therapist may, by offering a different and unaligned view, allow family members to mutually adopt a common framework and vocabulary as a starting point for change. In individual therapy, the therapist can more easily adopt the patient's framework as the basis for initiating a therapeutic alliance.

As therapy progresses, the therapist may need to become more flexible and allow the family to develop its own vocabulary and pattern of interaction. This change may involve a rejection of attitudes, beliefs and values held in common with the therapist early in treatment. Therapist rigidity at the time of this "recalibration" may interfere with or prevent the family from developing its own way of operating. The result may be a stalemate or a late termination.

Whether the above model will, in fact, yield predictions that will stand up well under empirical scrutiny is not our main concern. Rather, we have outlined our thinking about *one* different way to view the operation of relationship skills in family therapy in the hope that it will provoke others to think, and investigate creatively these aspects of the process and outcome of family therapy.

THE CRITERION PROBLEM IN FAMILY THERAPY OUTCOME RESEARCH

The road is not the road,
The road is how you walk it.
—Juan Ramon Jimènez

If the field of family therapy in particular, and psychotherapy in general, had as many effective treatments to offer as it has had fruitless, adversarial debates about the "right" criteria to use to measure therapeutic change, few of our patients would leave our offices without marked improvement. In this final section, we will attempt to avoid assiduously a further contribution to such "discussions," which typically emerge as monologues rather than as the dialogues for which they were intended. Rather, we will leave it to others to continue the practice of disguising deeply held personal ideologies in the garb of pseudo-mutual proclamations. We will not attempt to endorse the superior wisdom that some think inheres in the emphasis on specific criteria of change. As Malouf and Alexander (1976) have emphasized, it is difficult to specify outcome criteria that are appropriate for family therapy research in general because "any measure of effectiveness is highly related to the theoretical orientation or practical needs of the investigator and must be evaluated within the investigator's own context" (p. 64). We will, however, set forth and elaborate our view of the major conceptual and clinical domains that, we assert, any family therapy investigator should consider thoughtfully in the design of a study of treatment outcome.[8] Consistent with the explicit intent and scope of this chapter, we will not address the many basic methodological and statistical matters that must be thought through in planning such research, as these have been adequately presented elsewhere (e.g., Gottman and Markman, 1978; Mahoney, 1978; O'Leary and Borkovec, 1978; O'Leary and Turkewitz, 1978).

The Nature of Therapeutic Goals and Their Relationship to Assessing Change

As seen throughout this *Handbook,* the nature of treatment goals that characterize the manifold models and methods of family therapy varies tremendously in terms of their specificity, focus, breadth and depth. A distinction among levels of treatment goals that is rarely addressed explicitly by these models, yet which is crucial for understanding the clinical meaning of the outcome criteria used in research studies, is that between *mediating* and *ultimate* goals. Parloff (1976) draws the distinction between these levels of therapeutic goals:

Mediating goals are those which reflect the clinician's assumptions regarding the necessary steps and stages through which a patient must progress if the treatment is to be effective. These goals represent the postulated enabling or intermediate conditions which will permit the attainment of the ultimate goals. The ultimate goals of psychotherapy must, however, go beyond such hypothesized mediating variables as inferences regarding the resolution of neurotic con-

flicts, growth . . . enhancing the communicational systems, etc. (p. 317).

For example, mediating goals could include problem specification, clarification of individual wants in a relationship, the modification of communication patterns, the detriangulation of an index child patient from marital conflict, and redefinition or reframing of the behavior of one or more family members. Ultimate goals could include, e.g., increased role flexibility, reestablishment of generational boundaries, increased self-esteem, decreased unconscious collusion, and increased intimacy. In our view, the failure of researchers and clinicians alike to make this distinction between mediating and ultimate goals is the primary factor (professional politics aside) accounting for disagreements about the appropriateness and/or sufficiency of specific outcome criteria put forth by different treatment models and research investigations. As a result, therapists, researchers and even (perhaps, particularly!) reviewers of outcome research routinely draw clinically weak comparative conclusions about the efficacy of different family therapy methods. It is like pitting the successful midsummer repair of an automobile engine malfunction against a family's enjoyment of their summer vacation (where use of the family car seems to be required), and asking, "which is better?" Neither is "better." But they certainly are qualitatively different. Moreover, the second condition is likely to be contingent upon the first. Thus, their relationship is sequentially specific. Note that the proper repair of the automobile's malfunction does not require (necessarily lead to) the enjoyment of the subsequent journey, but that the journey could not begin without adequate mechanical correction (assuming the family cannot steal, borrow, rent or buy another automobile).

We know of no empirical study in which the degree of achievement of both mediating goals *and* the ultimate goals facilitated by their achievement have been assessed. The logical (and clinically self-deceptive) errors thus committed explicitly, or not precluded implicitly, in interpreting the results of all family therapy outcome studies to date fall into two categories. First, the investigator (or the consumer of a research study) may argue (or infer) that since

---

[8] These suggestions, of course, inevitably reflect *our* personal and conceptual biases. It cannot be otherwise.

mediating goals were achieved, the conceptually linked ultimate goals must have been reached or will be reached eventually, after treatment has ended. Second, the investigator (or consumer) may argue (or infer) that since a specific ultimate goal was achieved, the logically linked mediating goals must have been achieved. The first conclusion is deficient on both logical grounds (cf. repair of the automobile does not guarantee a pleasant vacation) and on empirical grounds (cf. the family has not actually been asked whether their vacation was pleasant). The second conclusion is faulty in that it is based on the absence of any demonstration that the intermediate steps purportedly required to have been achieved have even been attended to, much less mastered (cf. knowing with certainty that the family's vacation was pleasant does not disallow the possibility that they may have decided, at the last minute, to fly to their destination).

Thus, we believe it essential to family therapy outcome research, on both logical and clinical grounds, (a) that the distinction between mediating and ultimate treatment goals be kept in clear focus, and (b) that studies of treatment outcome include measures of both categories of goal achievement. Furthermore, we see no reason to assume that when mediating goals have been achieved, the achievement of ultimate goals must follow closely in time. Rather, the latter outcomes may be temporally quite distant "sleeper effects" (Rosman, 1977, p. 7). The need for multiple follow-ups in family therapy outcome studies is thus essential, for this reason, in addition to its more common purpose of determining the durability of changes manifest at the end of treatment.

The Modification of Therapeutic Goals and Its Relationship to Assessing Change

In addition to the above considerations, it is absolutely necessary, though rarely addressed in treatment outcome research (cf. Klein et al., 1979), that changes in treatment goals during the course of therapy be accommodated by the research design. These changes may involve either the specific content nature of the goals aimed for, the relative importance of multiple goals, or both. For example, a couple may enter therapy in order to stop or to decrease their fighting about the division of household tasks, and after several sessions agree that their mutual sexual inhibitions are of much greater concern to them than their initial complaints. They may or may not continue to desire to change their household management problems. In either case, it would be important that assessment of outcome at termination (and follow-up) address both their household management and their sexual interaction. Moreover, the couple might have also addressed, from the outset of therapy, or later, two other recurrent, central problems, and they might be asked to reach a consensus on the rank-ordering of the importance of each of these problems to their relationship, so that differential weighting of the amount and direction of change in each of their four target areas could be accomplished.

Assessment of family therapy outcome is made more relevant to clinical practice when both initial treatment goals *and* emerging treatment goals are addressed in the evaluation of change.

Individualized "versus" Standardized Measures

The preceding discussion clearly reveals our belief in the importance of tailoring treatment goals to specific cases, and implementing the necessary research design considerations to allow evaluation of change on these case-tailored measures. Good examples of the use of individually tailored outcome measures in family therapy research can be found in Campbell (1979), Feldman (1978), Schneider (1979), and Santa-Barbara (1975). The tailoring of outcome assessment to individual cases at times is pitted "against" the use of core batteries, as though the two represented warring religions. Thus, two major research methodologists (Gottman and Markman, 1978) recently wrote that

The "core concept" battery is a step backward in psychotherapy research for it continues to view therapy and change as uniform concepts. Change measures ought to be geared to what it is that a therapeutic program plans to accomplish; it makes as much sense to use the core battery to evaluate psychotherapy as it does to measure improvement in reading compre-

hension following treatment for sexual dysfunction (p. 43, emphasis added).

What such researchers often fail to understand is that core batteries of across-study standardized outcome measures were never intended to comprise the *sole* outcome criteria for *any* treatment study. The major, and significant, virtue of core batteries is that they allow for at least partial between-study comparability that otherwise would occur largely by chance. As Waskow (1975), one of the editors of the first volume (Waskow and Parloff, 1975) to make specific recommendations for the contruction of a core battery for outcome research (in individual psychotherapy), makes clear, standardized "core" change indices are *never* sufficient to the evaluative task facing researchers.

Our view on the advisability of core batteries is adamantly middle-of-the-road. We are not opposed in principle to the notion of a core battery, yet we are not terribly optimistic about the chances of a single effective core battery ever being realized. Thus, our view is quite different from that of Gottman and Markman (1978), and more in line with that of Bergin and Lambert (1978), whose major hesitation in endorsing the core battery idea derives from their pessimism about the probability of consensus ever being reached among researchers. Our own pessimism is based on four considerations. First, most leaders of the family field are still addicted to proselytizing, with the result that more allegiance is paid to charismatic personalities than to a common goal of empirical scrutiny. Second, family therapies have clearly made a major impact on the conceptualization and treatment of psychopathology, but the struggles of family approaches to be accepted by the therapeutic community at large may not allow sophisticated scientific examination within the family field until the boundary battles outside the field are resolved or at least tempered. Third, even if researchers and clinicians could agree on the core dimensions requiring assessment, there are major prolems to be encountered in selecting the measures for these dimensions. Among the more than 100 instruments for the assessment of marital and family interaction recently categorized by Cromwell et al. (1976), many require either extensive or expensive apparatus, tremendous investments of time in their administration, or both. Moreover, the reliability and validity of most of these measures have not yet been demonstrated.

Finally, one of the most serious deficiencies in the family field is that researchers have largely failed to develop useful and valid measures of most of the core theoretical constructs (e.g., "pseudo-mutuality," "enmeshment," "collusion," "triangulation") that have become reified among clinicians. Before spawning dozens of instruments to assess newly emerging dimensions of marital and family interactions, it would be more useful for researchers, in active collaboration with clinicians, to begin to operationalize the salient dimensions of the major theories of marital-family therapy that have already had a tremendous influence on thousands of practitioners. Moreover, measures need to be used that are not only conceptually sound, but also meaningful to clinicians and families, lest family therapy researchers evolve a "system" unto themselves that is divorced from clinical application.

On the other hand, it should be emphasized that core battery advocates may simply have been asking the wrong question, "Can there be constructed a battery of outcome measures that can be usefully applied across treatment studies?" A more optimistic and refined version of this question might yield greater payoff, as Bergin and Lambert (1978) suggest. That is, the development of a *series* of core batteries, each of which is centered on a specific clinical problem or on logical classes of problems, might yield great empirical and clinical benefits. The best example to date of such an effort is contained in the recently funded, multi-million dollar, six-year collaborative National Institute of Mental Health (NIMH) study of the treatment of major depressive disorders (NIMH, 1978). In that research program, several research centers are following identical research protocols, including the use of a core set of outcome measures developed by the investigators at the participating institutions. We suspect that analogous efforts in the family therapy field are but a matter of time. It seems clear to us that it is the collaborative nature of research programs such as that directed by the NIMH that will allow the development of useful core batteries that are offered for the study of the treatment of specific disorders.

Finally, we would like to make one additional, very specific recommendation to family therapy researchers.

We believe it is encumbent upon researchers that, in addition to the use of measures of obvious interest to the particular treatments under study, they also include among their outcome measures variables that are central to theoretical orientations *other* than those reflected in the treatment methods being evaluated. To illustrate the enriching potential of such an approach, Gurman (1978c) has asked,

Would it not be provocative and exciting to find, for example, that behavioral negotiation-training and contracting procedures (with couples) produce significant increases in differentiation of self, or that the working-through of the transference in marital therapy yields significant positive changes in a couple's ability to problem-solve constructively? (p. 553)

As Garfield (1977) has succinctly stated the issue, "If we fully open our eyes to what is actually occurring we may find that there are other things going on which are of potential importance but which are overlooked because of preconceived conceptual blinders" (p. 11).

Some Considerations and Propositions for the Choice of Units, Vantage Points and Levels in Assessing Change

In addition to the basic questions confronting a researcher in his/her choice of outcome criteria for a particular investigation, other significant issues must be addressed. While only a few of these issues are unique to family therapy research (Gurman and Kniskern, 1978a, 1978b), they all are, nonetheless, crucial in the design of clinically and conceptually sound studies of family therapy outcome.

What units should be assessed?

In our view, since marital-family therapy frequently, though not universally, seeks to improve the functioning of all family members and their intrafamily interactions, it is imperative that change be assessed routinely at the individual, dyadic, and system levels. Obviously,

the number of possible loci of change rapidly increases as the system size increases (e.g., in a four-member family there are four individuals, six dyads, four triads, and one family system). Since it will often not be practical to measure change in all possible family subunits, priorities must be established to guide the selection of subunits to be assessed. We propose a tentative model, shown in Table 3, that we believe provides these needed guidelines.

We assert that family units I, II, and III, the Identified Patient, the Marriage, and the Total System, which in some cases is equivalent to the marriage, are the minimal units for assessment and must be examined in any marital/family therapy outcome study, regardless of the family constellation or treatment context. This position, originally set forth in Gurman and Kniskern (1978a), is similar to, but a good deal more specific than that of DeWitt (1978), who takes the more general stance that change should be measured at both the identified patient and systemic levels.

Units IV to VII represent other family units on two dimensions: same versus other generation relative to the identified patient, and individual versus relationship functioning. These four family units are listed in order of their importance for the assessment of change in marital/family therapy from unit IV (Same Generation of IP: Individual), which we consider most important, to unit VII (Cross-Generation of IP: Relationship), which we consider least important. Although we recognize that other therapists and researchers may question our decision, we have based our schema for priorities on the belief that dysfunctional families have strong morphostatic characteristics that will tend to negate system change and that could produce symptoms in other family members and/or relationships.

We would argue that a higher level of positive change has occurred when improvement is evidenced in systematic (total family) or relationship (dyadic) interactions than when it is evidenced in individuals alone (note that we make the assumption, to be discussed below, that individual change can occur without system change). This is true whether the individual is the identified patient, an individual of the same generation as the identified patient, or an in-

TABLE 3

A Priority Sequence for Assessing Therapeutic Change in Couples and Families

		Treatment Context and Family Constellation				
		Family Therapy I: Child as Identified Patient		Family Therapy II: Parent as Identified Patient	Marital Therapy: Spouse/Parent as Identified Patient	
Familial Unit of Assessment		Family With More Than One Child	One-Child Family		Marriage with child(ren)	Childless Marriage
I.	Identified patient (IP)	IP child	IP child	IP parent	IP spouse	IP spouse
II.	Marriage	Marriage	Marriage	Marriage	Marriage	Marriage
III.	Total system	Family	Family	Family	Family	(Marriage)
IV.	Same generation of IP: individual	IP's siblings	--	Non-IP spouse	Non-IP spouse	Non-IP spouse
V.	Cross-generation of IP: individual	Each parent	Each parent	Each child	Each child	--
VI.	Same generation of IP: relationship	Ip child and non-IP child (ren)	--	(Marriage)	(Marriage)	(Marriage)
VII.	Cross-generation of IP: relationship	Parents and IP child: child 1 = IP	Parents and IP child	Child(ren) and IP parent	(Parents and child(ren), i.e., Family)	--
		Parents and non-IP child(ren)	(Parents and IP child)	Children and non-IP parent	(As above)	--

Note: Parentheses indicate that this familial unit has already been accounted for at earlier level of assessment priority. Blank spaces indicate that assessment of this familial unit is logically impossible.

dividual of the cross-generation relative to the identified patient. In addition, more positive change can be said to have occurred when improvement is noted on a total system level than on a single relationship level which, in turn, reflects more profound change than that achieved by any single individual or even by a series of individuals. Thus, a low level of family flexibility, adaptability, and change is manifest when symptomatic behavior decreases in the identified patient and appears in another individual of the same generation (family unit IV). Based on clinical experience and theories of family interaction and pathology, we contend that change is "better" when such a shift occurs either across generations in another individual (unit V), or, better yet, in a relationship (units VI and VII). That is, individual change does not logically require system change, but stable system change

does require individual change and relationship change, and relationship change requires individual change.

In this sense, it is "better" for deterioration to occur at a total system level than on a single relationship level which, in turn, is "better deterioration" than that lodged in any one individual. Deterioration in any family subunit, of course, is undesirable, but removal of a single individual or a single relationship from the system-regulating "scapegoat" position and the emergence of symptomatic behavior at a different level of interactional experience may be necessary in order for the total treatment unit to acknowledge the dysfunctional nature of the marital or family system. Our schema is designed to insure that the worst sort of deterioration will be the most likely to be detected. Deterioration in families must be assessed before therapy termination so that steps can be taken to return these deteriorated units to a healthier level of functioning. Since the overwhelming majority of studies of marital and family therapy have been of short duration (Gurman and Kniskern, 1978a), it is quite possible that some proportion of the cases of deterioration in marital-family therapy that we have documented (Gurman and Kniskern, 1978b) may, in fact, have reflected such an intermediate stage of the therapeutic process. If therapy had been of longer duration, some of these couples and families might have "worked through" this intermediate stage to an improved level of functioning. In this context, it should be clear that, in marital-family therapy, deterioration is not necessarily the opposite of improvement. In fact, "deterioration" could be viewed by the therapist as an important *mediating* goal of treatment. Empirical study of the occurrence of therapy-induced deterioration in couples and families would be of major theoretical and practical value.

Routine consideration of these multiple familial units for assessing therapeutic change would have an additional advantage, that of evaluating whether there are different rates of change in different family subsystems. For example, as Todd (1978) has suggested, marital interaction patterns may change more slowly than many childhood behaviors.

Identified patient status as an outcome criterion: A pivotal issue

The posttreatment symptomatic status of the identified patient (IP) in family therapy cannot be ignored. Obviously, not all courses of family therapy, and probably fewer courses of marital therapy, are initiated by the family's (or others') presentation of *one* family member as psychiatrically symptomatic. Still, such is the case in many family therapies, especially (but not only) those that are initially child- or adolescent-centered. In addition to the inherent meaningfulness of assessing change in terms of patients' stated complaints, inclusion of measures of IP status after therapy has other advantages. First, in many cases, the IP's symptoms are rather straightforwardly defined, hence, relatively easy to measure and, therefore, allowing rather high

levels of reliability and validity. Second, since there needs to be some consensus for family members, therapists, and researchers alike as to what should comprise the relevant outcome dimension(s) in each case, IP symptoms "are at least a common denominator, even if all the investigators agree that they stand for something else" (Rosman, 1977, p. 5).

Still, IP symptomatic status is extremely problematic when used as the sole change criterion. Although the use of a single outcome criterion of any sort severely weakens the usefulness of a given study, the sole use of IP status as a change index raises special concerns. First, it avoids confronting the issues involved in differentiating between mediating and ultimate treatment goals, as discussed earlier in this chapter. Similarly, it precludes study of the changing of goals that emerge during treatment, as previously discussed. Third, and of most theoretical importance, the use of IP symptomatic status as the sole outcome criterion allows absolutely no conclusions to be drawn about change at the (family) system level. All clinical models of family functioning and of family therapy offer rather explicit statements about the role of the IP in the complex matrix of family interactions. For example, Rosman (1977), who is associated with structural family therapy, has argued that, ". . . while the symptom improvement is an outcome measure of major importance, it is also *instrumental in facilitating other outcome possibilities*" (p. 6), such as changes in family interaction patterns. Such a view is hardly unique to structural family therapists, yet it is rare to find *demonstrations* of such facilitation of broader family change in the research literature. Unfortunately, it is quite common to find empirically unsubstantiated *assertions* of such interrelatedness. Since there exists, in our opinion, overwhelming evidence (e.g., Garfield and Bergin, 1978) that individuals *can* change in significant ways without therapeutic attention to marital or family issues, the question arises, what is the range of relationships between IP change and system change? For example, can important family interaction patterns change without a resulting change in the IP? Under what conditions? Can significant IP change occur with only minimal consequent impact on the family as a system, or on other family subunits, e.g., the marital relationship (when a child is the IP)? What is the aggregate outcome value of positive IP change and co-occurring negative change in other individuals, or in other relationships, e.g., marital? When are the latter two situations the result of excessive, imbalanced focusing on the IP, and when are they the result not of a misplaced focus, but of an incomplete treatment? Under what specific IP and family interaction conditions is IP change enhanced (or impeded) by a focus on non-IP family units? Questions such as these are of enormous practical significance since their answers would allow greater specification than is now possible of both the proper focus and sequencing of clinical interventions on a case-tailored basis.

From what vantage points should change be assessed?

Just as multidimensional criteria are a necessity in studying the outcomes of the family therapies (Gurman and Kniskern, 1978a, 1978b; Wells and Dezen, 1978a), assessment of change from multiple *perspectives* is also required. It is increasingly being recognized that it is difficult to achieve consensus on outcome measures deriving from different vantage points. For example, therapists' judgments about the process (Gurman, 1977b) and outcome (Mintz, 1977) of psychotherapy can be routinely expected to show only low correlation with the views of patients and external judges. Fiske (1975) has argued persuasively that since a source of data is not a measuring instrument, attempts to eliminate disagreement among rating sources and reduce what is usually considered error variance are futile. Fiske (1975, p. 20) argues:

A source of data yields observations from a distinctive role providing distinctive experience. When an observer representing a source makes judgments about the complex variables of interest to current psychotherapeutic theory, he is actually processing his own experience . . . Nearly exact agreement can be obtained only from inanimate measuring instruments or from observers functioning like instruments.

Fiske also notes (p. 23) that, "instead of seeking to minimize (differences in perceptions), researchers should seek to identify the unique components of the perceptions and judgments from each source."

In studying the treatment of relationships, researchers must attend to the unique perceptions of both "insiders" and "outsiders" (Cromwell et al., 1976; Olson, 1974) of the family system. Olson (1974) considers an "insider" to be "a person in a relationship who is able to provide information on both his own feelings and behavior and his perceptions of the others with whom he has a relationship," while an "outsider" is a person "who serves as a participant or external observer of interaction between other individuals." We, like Framo (1965), view the reporter's frame of reference somewhat differently from Olson, in that we do not consider the marital/family therapist to be an observer (i.e., an "outsider"). The family therapist does not ultimately remain within the family system, but during the process of treatment he/she is at times as much a part of the family dynamics as is any member of the family being helped (Minuchin, 1974; Whitaker, 1975). Thus, although the family therapist is only temporarily an "insider" of the family system, he/she is always an "insider" of the treatment system.

We suggest that in deciding on the perspective from which change in marital/family therapy should be assessed, researchers must consider two dimensions: the perceiver's insideness-outsideness relative to the *treatment system* and the degree of inference involved in making a given judgment. In decreasing order of insideness, we see the following potential evaluative sources: family members, therapist(s), therapy supervisors, significant others, trained judges making inferential assessments (e.g., family members' individuation), objective observers recording noninferential public events (e.g., smiles, self-reference statements), and computers and machines doing likewise (e.g., voice-activated apparatus to record speech duration).

Before considering the various levels of inference involved in selecting outcome criteria, we would like to offer some observations about the role of patient and therapist "insiders" in evaluating family treatment outcome. First, we, like many others (e.g., Jacobson, 1978; Wells & Dezen, 1978a), think that the *sole* use of any given perspective in assessing treatment outcome is indefensible on both methodological and clinical grounds. Despite the nearly universal agreement among psychotherapy researchers on the need for multiperspective assessment of change, the family therapy research literature is seriously marred by the very frequent use of only single evaluative source. For example, of the approximately 200 studies of family therapy we have reviewed elsewhere (Gurman and Kniskern, 1978a), more than 50% employed only one evaluative perspective.

Secondly, we disagree with many of our colleagues about the value of patient- and therapist-derived outcome measures. Ross (1978), for example, argues that since "Change in the child's behavior is . . . sought by influencing the behavior of key adults in the child's environment . . . parent-gathered observational data or parental judgments of the child's behavior may be grossly confounded and their use as criteria for measuring outcome is highly questionable" (p. 4). Ross' position is quite consistent with that of Jacobson (1978), who distinguishes between self-reported change and "actual" change (p. 400) in marital therapy. "Actual" change purportedly can only be based on "objective" indices, such as behavior counts. But just what is "actual" change? Following Fiske's (1975) argument, such "objective changes" are no more real than those based on patient reports. They are, of course, different, but they certainly do not deserve the label of superiority often assigned to them, despite the problems of validity involved in self-report measures. Indeed, "objective" indices are the best sources of assessment from certain theoretical perspectives, e.g., behavioral. But they are not inherently better than indices based on patients' and therapists' subjective judgments. Any measure that is valid, reliable, and theoretically meaningful is useful in assessing family therapy outcome. Gottman and Markman (1978) express our position well: "The critical question . . . is not whether or not self-reports are better or worse than behavior observation measures, but under what condition both kinds of measures can best be used as outcome measures" (p. 43). For example, Gottman and Markman emphasize that increasing the situational specificity of items in self-report measures greatly enhances their validity and meaningfulness. It is ironic that researchers who reject patient reports of change often do accept patients' initial complaints and expressions of suffering for both clinical and research purposes.

The therapist is also an "insider" to the family treatment process whose judgments about treatment outcome have often been disparaged because of the "bias" presumed to be inherent in such judgments. While we do not doubt the existence of such biases, we would remind the reader that they may turn in the directions of either overestimating change (i.e., face-saving dissonance reduction) or underestimating change (e.g., self-imposed demands for profound personality transformation). In any case, certain instrumentation procedures and statistical methods (e.g., Mintz, 1977) can overcome a good deal of the difficulty caused by therapist bias. Unyielding adversaries of the use and usefulness of therapist outcome ratings fail to appreciate that psychotherapists offer a uniquely informed perspective on clinical change, which should be sought to be understood rather than impulsively dismissed. For example, Gurman and Kniskern (1978a), reviewing the results of behavioral marital and family therapy, noted the rarity of studies in which the therapist's view of change was considered, and concluded that, "It is as if the implicit message were that despite the therapist's assumed expertise as a change-agent, he or she offers no uniquely valuable perspective in assessing clinical change!" (p. 852).

Finally, we believe it is a myth that there exist any criteria for assessing the outcomes of family therapy that are truly "objective." Even with the least inferential of indices, the choice of content has to have been made by people. As our recent theoretical critiques of behavioral marriage therapy (Gurman and Knudson, 1978; Gurman et al., 1978) showed, even criteria that satisfy the most "objective" of behavioral researchers have profound implicit value-laden and ideological underpinnings (Gurman and Klein, 1980a, 1980b).

As noted above, not only must the degree of perceiver insideness-outsideness to the treatment system be considered, but also the level of inference involved in making given evaluative judgments. Table 4 defines the nature of information obtained at various inferential levels of assessing therapeutic change in family therapy, and suggests the ideal judges for each level of inference.

The degree of inference involved in a given judgment increases from simple behavior counts (Level I) to system properties and individual psychodynamics (Level VI). Not all levels are

TABLE 4
Levels of Inference in Assessing Family Therapy Outcome

Level	Information Obtained	Illustration	Best Judge/Source
Ia.	Simple behavior counts	Frequency of interruptions, verbal assents, topic shifts	Machine or trained orjective observers
b.	Performance on clinically relevant, non-familial objective criteria	School grades, hospitalization, police arrest history	Institutional records
II.	Perceived family interaction patterns	Reciprocity, conflict-resolution, decision-making	Trained observers
III.	Behavioral self-reports, individually or interactionally focused	Sexual Interaction Inventory, Spouse Observation Checklist	Family members
IV.	Nonbehavioral self-report, intrapersonally focused	MMPI, Eysenck Personality Inventory	Family members
V.	Nonbehavioral report of self in relationship to others (and/or vice versa)	Marital satisfaction, various communication inventories	Family members
VIa.	Individual psychodynamics or personality structure	Rorschach, TAT	Expert judge
b.	Family psychodynamics	Collusion	Therapist or expert (professional judge)
c.	Inferred family system properties	Enmeshment, pseudo-mutuality	Therapist or expert (professional judge)

meaningfully or economically assessed by all possible sources. For example, highly inferential dimensions are best judged by the therapist providing treatment or by expert professional judges, whereas simple behavior counts could be accomplished by a variety of people, but to use the therapist for this purpose would be, at least, financially wasteful. Finally, it should be obvious that it is much more difficult to measure validly and reliably Level VI variables than variables at lower levels of inference.

Some Meta-Criteria for Evaluating the Outcomes of the Family Therapies

> Statistics are like bikinis: what they reveal is suggestive, what they conceal, vital.
>
> —Paul Watzlawick

In addition to the preceding conceptual and measurement considerations involved in evaluating the effectiveness of the family therapies, there are several broader criteria that are sig-

nificant as well. Since the majority of these have been addressed in detail elsewhere (see, especially, Garfield, 1977; Kazdin and Wilson, 1978a, 1978b; Wells and Dezen, 1978a), here we will discuss them only briefly.

Patient-related criteria

As noted earlier in this chapter, the statistical mean on a given criterion for a group of patients may conceal more than it reveals. In this regard, we recommend that the following additional dimensions be included in future reports of the outcomes of family therapy:

1) Evidence that in-therapy treatment effects have generalized to the world outside therapy.

2) Evidence of the posttreatment durability of the gains achieved. A one-year follow-up should be considered minimal.

3) The proportion of cases which show improvement, no change, and deterioration, presented separately for each criterion.

4) The breadth of treatment effects, reported as the number of criteria on which each *case*

shows improvement, no change, and deterioration, presented as a frequency distribution.

5) Evidence (beyond the statistical significance of changes in group means) of the clinical importance of the changes achieved by families and by individual family members. In this regard, particular attention should be paid to the documentation of treatment effects that are sensitive to women's issues and feminist values, and which do not implicitly reinforce existing sex-role stereotypes (cf. Gurman and Klein, 1980a, 1980b).

Treatment efficiency criteria

Patient/family change is not the only criterion on which treatment efficacy can be based. Criteria related to the efficiency, as well as efficacy, of treatment also need to be considered.

1) The degree of patient/family *compliance* with the treatment(s) offered serves as a useful partial index of therapeutic efficiency. If, for example, treatment A achieves consistently superior outcomes to treatment B in the therapy of problem X, yet accumulates a dropout rate several times greater than that accruing to B, arguments favoring the superiority of A would need careful qualification and reevaluation. Thus, if the rate of families remaining in treatment A were sufficiently low, the general value of offering this treatment could be questioned on the basis of its limited applicability to large numbers of distressed families.

2) The *disseminability* of a treatment method is another important index of therapeutic efficiency. For example, if treatments C and D are of equal power in terms of patient-related change criteria, yet C can be administered (with no loss of therapeutic effectiveness) to groups of couples or families, then C would have an important leg up over D in terms of this dimension of efficiency.

3) The *duration* of therapy, measured in terms of total treatment hours and/or total elapsed time of treatment, is an obvious efficiency-related criterion to be considered in the complex matrix of factors leading to judgments about the outcomes of the family therapies. Given equivalent therapeutic outcomes, generalizability of treatment effects, and durability of those effects, briefer therapies should be judged superior to longer-term methods.

4) The *degree of family involvement* required to achieve particular therapeutic ends also needs to be incorporated into a far-reaching assessment of family therapy outcome. Thus, for example, equivalent therapeutic outcomes achieved for the treatment of a given clinical problem would demonstrate quite different efficiencies if treatment E required the active involvement of both parents and children, while treatment F required only parental involvement.

5) *Patient costs, both financial and psychological* also need to be considered in determining treatment efficiency. Direct monetary costs, of course, are influenced enormously by the cost of therapist training and the disseminability of the method, e.g., M.A. level therapists will charge lower fees than their M.D. or Ph.D. colleagues, and group therapies almost always cost patients less (per session) than treatment given to one couple or family at a time. Moreover, treatments of equal clinical outcome are probably not of equivalent general value if one extracts a much higher emotional toll (to achieve the same outcome result) from patients than the other.[9]

6) As just noted, the *costs of therapist training* constitute a significant contribution to direct patient costs. To date, we are aware of no empirical evidence that nonprofessional family therapists, either as a group or under special circumstances, are able to achieve clinical outcomes that match those of professionally trained therapists. Were this outcome equivalence to obtain, even for a restricted number and range of clinical problems, nonprofessionally delivered treatments for those specific difficulties would be preferred.

7) Finally, and of special concern to family therapists, there is a very serious need to evaluate the *developmental impact* of different family and marital therapies. This impact takes three forms: (a) the impact of therapeutic outcomes on the mid- and long-range development of the children who are the identified patients and are treated directly by family therapy;

---

[9]Of course, an "emotional toll" can be extracted at both ends of a continuum of affectivity. For example, treatment methods that implicitly endorse repression of feelings can be as "costly" and detrimental as those that require a great deal of overt emotional expression.

(b) the impact on children not directly treated, as in conjoint marital therapy; and (c) the impact of treatment in both of the preceding contexts on the children of the children treated directly or indirectly in the present. Evaluation of this third level of developmental impact would require research programs that extend over a 10-to-20-year period. While such research projects would demand extraordinary financial and programmatic support, not to mention investigative dedication, such studies, in our view, would offer the possibility of demonstrating the most profound and far-reaching effects of the family therapies that is possible.

CODA: RESEARCH ON TRAINING IN FAMILY THERAPY

All of the considerations involved in designing studies on the outcomes of marriage and family therapy and reviews of the evidence of treatment effectiveness in this field will be of minimal value if our gradually accumulating knowledge and increasing methodological sophistication do not translate into direct implications for the training of future marital-family therapists. Moreover, research efforts need to be directed specifically to the process and outcomes of family therapy training methods. While the experientially based literature on family therapy training and supervision is enormous (Liddle and Halpern, 1978), we must acknowledge and underline the field's collective *empirical* ignorance about this domain. Indeed, there now exists no research evidence that training experiences in marital-family therapy in fact increase the effectiveness of clinicians (Kniskern and Gurman, 1979). Recently, we examined the current models of family therapy training (Kniskern and Gurman, 1979), proposed a methodology for the evaluation of training programs, and suggested a number of specific questions and issues requiring empirical study in four areas: the selection of family therapy trainees, and the outcomes of the three major methods of family therapy training—didactic, supervisory and experiential. In addition to our own notions about what constitute the most salient and practical questions regarding the effects of training in family therapy, the curious and motivated reader will find a panoramic host of additional training-relevant questions addressed, implicitly at least, in each of the clinical chapters of this *Handbook*.

In conclusion, the field of family therapy is a rapidly growing one by any standard used to assess such activity. Specialized training programs are being developed in many locations around the world, and more existing psychotherapy service and training centers and clinics are involving family therapy in their overall training program. Now is the time to begin to integrate empirical study of the training process with empirical study of the outcomes of family therapies themselves, so that the next generation of family therapists can benefit fully from our advances in both realms, rather than blindly repeating our clinical and training errors.

REFERENCES

Alexander, J. & Barton, C. Behavioral systems therapy with delinquent families. In: D.H.L. Olson (Ed.), *Treating Relationships*. Lake Mills, Ia.: Graphic, 1976.

Alexander, J., Barton, C., Schiavo, R.S. & Parsons, B.V. Therapist characteristics, family behavior and outcome. *Journal of Consulting and Clinical Psychology*, 1976, *44*, 656-664

Alexander, J. & Parsons, B. Short-term behavioral intervention with delinquent families: Impact on family process and recidivism. *Journal of Abnormal Psychology*, 1973, *81*, 219-225.

Auerbach, A. & Johnson, M. Research on the therapist's level of experience. In: A. Gurman & A. Razin (Eds.), *Effective Psychotherapy: A Handbook of Research*. New York: Pergamon, 1977.

Beck, A.T., Rush, A.J., Emery, G. & Shaw, B. *Cognitive Therapy of Depression*. New York: Guilford, 1979.

Beck, D.F. Research findings on the outcomes of marital counseling. *Social Casework*, 1975, *56*, 153-181.

Bednar, R.L. & Lawlis, G.F. Empirical research in group psychotherapy. In: A.E. Bergin and S.L. Garfield (Eds.), *Handbook of Psychotherapy and Behavior Change*. New York: Wiley, 1971.

Benningfeld, A.B. Multiple family therapy systems. *Journal of Marriage and Family Counseling*, 1978, *4*, 25-34.

Bentovim, A. & Kinston, W. Brief focal family therapy when the child is the referred patient: I - Clinical. *Journal of Child Psychology and Psychiatry*, 1978, *19*, 1-12.

Bergin, A.E. & Lambert, M.J. The evaluation of therapeutic outcomes. In: S.L. Garfield & A.E. Bergin (Eds.), *Handbook of Psychotherapy and Behavior Change*, Second edition. New York: Wiley, 1978.

Biglan, A., Villwock, C. & Wick, S. The feasibility of a computer controlled program for the treatment of test anxiety. *Journal of Behavior Therapy and Experimental Psychiatry*, 1979, *10*, 47-50.

Birchler, G.R. Communication skills in married couples. In: A.S. Bellack & M. Hersen (Eds.), *Research and Practice in Social Skills Training*. New York: Plenum, 1979.

Campbell, D. Personal communication, 1979.

Coché, J.M. *The uniqueness of family therapy outcome research: Critical research issues*. Paper presented at the Society for Psychotherapy Research, Toronto, June, 1978.

Cole, C. & Morrow, W.R. Refractory parent behaviors in behavior modification training groups. *Psychotherapy*, 1976, *13*, 162-169.

Cromwell, R., Olson, D. & Fournier, D. Diagnosis and evaluation in marital and family counseling. In: D.H.L. Olson (Ed.), *Treating Relationships*. Lake Mills, Ia.: Graphic, 1976.

DeWitt, K.N. The effectiveness of family therapy: A review of outcome research. *Archives of General Psychiatry*, 1978, *35*, 549-561.

DiMascio, A. & Klerman, G. *An appropriate control group for psychotherapy research in depression*. Paper presented at the Society for Psychotherapy Research, Madison, WI, June, 1977.

Feldman, L. *Problem change assessment*. Research in progress, Northwestern University Medical School, 1978.

Fiske, D.W. *A source of data is not a measuring instrument*. *Journal of Abnormal Psychology*, 1975, 84, 20-23.

Framo, J.L. Systematic research on family dynamics. In: I. Boszormenyi-Nagy & J. Framo (Eds.), *Intensive Family Therapy*. New York: Harper and Row, 1965.

Gale, A. Problems of outcome research in family therapy. In: S. Walrond-Skinner (Ed.), *Family and Marital Psychotherapy: A Critical Approach*. London: Routledge & Kegan Paul, 1979.

Garfield, S.L. *Some reflections on the nature of psychotherapy*. Presidential Address, Society for Psychotherapy Research, Madison, WI, June, 1977.

Garfield, S.L. & Bergin, A.E. *Handbook of Psychotherapy and Behavior Change*, Second edition. New York: Wiley, 1978.

Gartner, R.B., Fulmer, R.H., Weinshel, M. & Goldklank, S. The family life cycle: Developmental crises and their structural impact on families in a community mental health center. *Family Process*, 1978, *17*, 47-58.

Gelder, M. *Some priorities for research in psychotherapy*. Paper presented at the Society for Psychotherapy Research, Toronto, June, 1978.

Glick, I, & Kessler, D. *Marital and Family Therapy*. Second Edition. New York: Grune and Stratton, 1980.

Gottman, J.M. & Markman, H.J. Experimental designs in psychotherapy research. In: S. Garfield & A. Bergin (Eds.), *Handbook of Psychotherapy and Behavior Change*. Second edition. New York: Wiley, 1978.

Greene, B.L. *The Psychotherapies of Marital Disharmony*. New York: Free Press, 1965.

Greer, S.E. & D'Zurilla, T.J. Behavioral approaches to marital discord and conflict. *Journal of Marriage and Family Counseling*, 1975, *1*, 299-315.

Gurman, A.S. Group marital therapy: Clinical and empirical implications for outcome research. *International Journal of Group Psychotherapy*, 1971, *21*, 174-189.

Gurman, A.S. Marital therapy: Emerging trends in research and practice. *Family Process*, 1973, *12*, 45-54. (a)

Gurman, A.S. The effects and effectiveness of marital therapy: A review of outcome research. *Family Process*, 1973, *12*, 145-170. (b)

Gurman, A.S. Some therapeutic implication of marital therapy research. In: A.S. Gurman & D.G. Rice (Eds.), *Couples in Conflict: New Directions in Marital Therapy*. New York: Aronson, 1975. (a)

Gurman, A.S. Couples' facilitative communication skill as a dimension of marital therapy outcome. *Journal of Marriage and Family Counseling*, 1975, *1*, 163-174. (b)

Gurman, A.S. Behavioral marriage therapy and the current empirical scene. *Association for the Advancement of Behavior Therapy Newsletter*, 1977, *4*(6), 18. (a)

Gurman, A.S. The patient's perception of the therapeutic relationship. In: A.S. Gurman & A. Razin (Eds.), *Effective Psychotherapy: A Handbook of Research*. New York: Pergamon, 1977. (b)

Gurman, A.S. *Relationship factors in marital and family therapy*. Paper presented at the Minnesota Conference on Psychotherapy and Behavior Change, Minneapolis, October, 1978. (a)

Gurman, A.S. *Does the family therapist matter in family therapy?* Paper presented at the Society for Psychotherapy Research, Toronto, June, 1978. (b)

Gurman, A.S. Contemporary marital therapies: A critique and comparative analysis of psychoanalytic, behavioral and systems theory approaches. In: T.J. Paolino & B.S. McCrady (Eds.), *Marriage and Marital Therapy*. New York: Brunner/Mazel, 1978. (c)

Gurman, A.S. *The future of family therapy research: If the road is how you walk it, we'd better watch our step*. Keynote Address, Southeastern Symposium on the Family, Blacksburg, VA, April, 1978. (d)

Gurman, A.S. & Klein, M.H. The treatment of women in marital and family conflict: Recommendations for outcome evaluation. In: A. Brodsky & R. Hare-Mustin (Eds.), *Research on Psychotherapy with Women*. New York: Guilford, 1980(a).

Gurman, A.S. & Klein, M.H. Women and behavioral marital therapy: An unconscious male bias? *Women: Counseling, Therapy and Mental Health Services*, 1980, *1*, in press. (b)

Gurman, A.S. & Kniskern, D.P. Enriching research on marital enrichment programs. *Journal of Marriage and Family Counseling*, 1977, *3*, 3-11.

Gurman, A.S. & Kniskern, D.P. Research on marital and family therapy: Progress, perspective and prospect. In: S. Garfield & A. Bergin (Eds.), *Handbook of Psychotherapy and Behavior Change*, Second edition. New York: Wiley, 1978. (a)

Gurman, A.S. & Kniskern, D.P. Deterioration in marital and family therapy: Empirical, clinical and conceptual issues. *Family Process*, 1978, *17*, 3-20. (b)

Gurman, A.S. & Kniskern, D.P. Behavioral marriage therapy: II. Empirical perspective. *Family Process*, 1978, *17*, 139-148. (c)

Gurman, A.S. & Kniskern, D.P. Technolatry, methodolatry and the results of family therapy. *Family Process*, 1978, *17*, 275-281 (d)

Gurman, A.S. & Kniskern, D.P. The outcomes of family therapy: Implications for training and practice. In: G. Berenson & H. White (Eds.), *Annual Review of Family Therapy*, 1978 New York: Human Sciences Press, 1979.

Gurman, A.S. & Knudson, R.M. Behavioral marriage therapy: I. A psychodynamic-systems analysis and critique. *Family Process*, 1978, *17*, 121-138.

Gurman, A.S., Knudson, R.M. & Kniskern, D.P. Behavioral marriage therapy: IV. Take two aspirin and call us in the morning. *Family Process*, 1978, *17*, 165-180.

Gurman, A.S. & Razin, A.M. *Effective Psychotherapy: A Handbook of Research*. New York: Pergamon, 1977.

Haley, J. *Problem-Solving Therapy*. San Francisco: Jossey-Bass, 1976.

Hersen, M. & Barlow, D.H. *Single-case Experimental Designs: Strategies for Studying Behavior Change*. New York: Pergamon, 1976.

Jacobson, N.S. A review of the research on the effectiveness of marital therapy. In: T.L. Paolino & B.S. McCrady (Eds.), *Marriage and Marital Therapy*. New York: Brunner/Mazel, 1978.

Jacobson, N.S. Behavioral treatments for marital discord: A critical appraisal. In: M. Hersen, R.M. Eisler & P.M. Miller (Eds.), *Progress in Behavior Modification*, Vol. 7. New York: Academic Press, 1979.

Jacobson, N.S. & Martin, B. Behavioral marriage therapy: Current status. *Psychological Bulletin*, 1976, *83*, 540-556.

Jacobson, N.S. & Weiss, R.L. Behavioral marriage therapy: III. The contents of Gurman et al. may be hazardous to our health. *Family Process*, 1978, *17*, 149-164.

Karoly, P. & Rosenthal, M. Training parents in behavior modification: Effects on perceptions of family interactions and deviant child behaviors. *Behavior Therapy*, 1977, *8*, 406-410.

Kazdin, A.E. Methodological and interpretive problems of single-case experimental designs. *Journal of Consulting and Clinical Psychology*, 1978, *46*, 629-642. (a)

Kazdin, A.E. Evaluating the generality of findings in analog therapy research. *Journal of Consulting and Clinical Psychology*, 1978, *46*, 673-686. *(b)*

Kazdin, A.E. & Wilson, G.T. Criteria for evaluating psychotherapy. *Archives of General Psychiatry*, 1978, *35*, 407-416. (a)

Kazdin, A.E. & Wilson, G.T. *Evaluation of Behavior Therapy*. Cambridge, MA: Ballinger, 1978. (b)

Kiesler, D.J. Experimental designs in psychotherapy research. In: A. Bergin & S. Garfield (Eds.), *Handbook of Psychotherapy and Behavior Change*. New York: Wiley, 1971.

Kinney, J.M., Madsen, B., Fleming, T. & Haapala, D.A. Homebuilders: Keeping families together. *Journal of Consulting and Clinical Psychology*, 1977, *45*, 667-673.

Kinston, W. & Bentovim, A. Brief focal family therapy when the child is referred patient: II. Methodology and results. *Journal of Child Psychology and Psychiatry*, 1978, *19*, 119-143.

Klein, M.H., Greist, J.H., Gurman, A.S. & Van Cura, L. *The psychotherapy of depression*. Research in progress, University of Wisconsin Medical School, 1978.

Klein, M.H. & Gurman, A.S. *A proposal for collaborative research on the psychotherapy of depression*. Invited paper, National Institute of Mental Health, 1977.

Klein, M.H. & Gurman, A.S. Actual and reality: Some clinical implications of experimental designs for behavior therapy of depression. In: L.P. Rehm (Ed.) *Behavior Therapy for Depression*. New York: Plenum, 1980.

Kniskern, D.P. *Research prospects and perspectives in family therapy*. Paper presented at the Society for Psychotherapy Research, Boston, June, 1975.

Kniskern, D.P. & Gurman, A.S. Research on training in marriage and family therapy: Status, issues and directions. *Journal of Marital and Family Therapy*, 1979, *5*, 83-94.

Kratochwill, T.R. *Single-Subject Research: Strategies for Evaluating Change*. New York: Academic Press, 1978.

Kressel, K. & Deutsch, M. Divorce therapy: An in-depth survey of therapists' views. *Family Process*, 1977, *16*, 413-444.

Lambert, M. Bergin, A. & Collins, J. Therapist-induced deterioration in psychotherapy. In: A. Gurman & A Razin (Eds.), *Effective Psychotherapy: A Handbook of Research*. New York: Pergamon, 1977.

Lebedun, M. Measuring movement in group marital counseling. *Social Casework*, 1970, *51*, 35-43.

Liddle, H. & Halpern, R. Family therapy training and supervision: A comparative review. *Journal of Marriage and Family Counseling*, 1978, *4*, 77-98.

Luber, R.F. Teaching models in marital therapy: A review and research issue. *Behavior Modification*, 1978, *2*, 77-91.

MacGregor, R. Ritchie, A., Serrano, A., Schuster, F.P., McDonald, E.C. & Goolishian, H.A. *Multiple Impact Therapy with Families*. New York: McGraw-Hill, 1964.

Mahoney, M.J. Experimental methods and outcome evaluation. *Journal of Consulting and Clinical Psychology*, 1978, *46*, 660-672.

Malan, D. *A Study of Brief Psychotherapy*. London: Tavistock, 1963.

Malan, D. *The Frontier of Brief Psychotherapy*. New York: Plenum, 1976.

Malouf, J.L. & Alexander, J.F. Family therapy research in applied community settings. *Community Mental Health Journal*, 1976, *12*, 61-71.

Marks, I. Behavioral psychotherapy of adult neurosis. In: S. Garfield & A. Bergin (Eds.), *Handbook of Psychotherapy and Behavior Change*, Second edition, New York: Wiley, 1978.

Masten, A.S. Family therapy as a treatment for children: A critical review of outcome research. *Family Process*, 1979, *18*, 323-336.

Matthews, A., Teasdale, J., Munby, M., Johnston, D. & Shaw, P. A home-based treatment program for agoraphobia. *Behavior Therapy*, 1977, *8*, 915-924.

Meltzoff, J. & Kornreich, M. *Research in Psychotherapy*. Chicago: Atherton, 1970.

Mintz, J. The role of the therapist in assessing psychotherapy outcome. In: A.S. Gurman & A. Razin (Eds.), *Effective Psychotherapy: A Handbook of Research*. New York: Pergamon, 1977.

Minuchin, S. *Families and Family Therapy*. Cambridge, Mass.: Harvard University Press, 1974.

Minuchin, S., Baker, L., Rosman, B., Liebman, R., Milman, L. & Todd, T. A conceptual model of psychosomatic illness in children. *Archives of General Psychiatry*, 1975, *32*, 1031-1038.

Minuchin, S., Rosman, B.O. & Baker, L. *Psychosomatic Families*. Cambridge, MA: Harvard University Press, 1978.

Myers, J.L. *Fundamentals of Experimental Design*. Second edition. Boston: Allyn & Bacon, 1972.

National Institute of Mental Health. *Announcement: Psychotherapy of Depression Collaborative Program*. Washington, D.C., NIMH, December 1978.

O'Leary, K.D. & Borkovec, T.D. Conceptual, methodological and ethical problems of placebo groups in psychotherapy research. *American Psychologist*, 1978, 33, 821-830.

O'Leary, K.D. & Turkewitz, H. Methological errors in marital and child treatment research. *Journal of Consulting and Clinical Psychology*, 1978, *46*, 747-758.

Olson, D.H. *Insiders' and outsiders' view of relationships: Research strategies*. Paper presented at the Symposium on Close Relationships. University of Masschusetts, 1974.

Parloff, M.B. The narcissism of small differences—and some big ones. *International Journal of Group Psychotherapy*, 1976, *26*, 311-319.

Patterson, G.R. Behavioral intervention procedures in the classroom and in the home. In: A.E. Bergin and S.L. Garfield (Eds.), *Handbook of Psychotherapy and Behavior Change*. New York: Wiley, 1971.

Patterson, G.R. The aggressive child: Victim and architect of a coercive system. In: E.J. Mash, L.A. Hamerlynck, and L.C. Handy (Eds.), *Behavior Modification and Families*. New York: Brunner/Mazel, 1976.

Patterson, G.R., Weiss, R.L. & Hops, H. Training of Marital Skills. In: H. Leitenberg (Ed.), *Handbook of Behavior Modification and Behavior Therapy*. New York: Prentice-Hall, 1976.

Patterson, G.R. & Fleischman, M. Maintenance of treatment effects: Some considerations concerning family systems and follow-up data. *Behavior Therapy*, 1979, *10*, 168-173.

Pinsof, W. Family therapy process research. In: A. Gurman & D. Kniskern (Eds.), *Handbook of Family Therapy*. New York: Brunner/Mazel, 1981.

Reisinger, J.J., Frangia, G.W. & Hoffman, E.H. Toddler management training: Generalization and marital status. *Journal of Behavior Therapy and Experimental Psychiatry*, 1976, 7, 335-340.

Roman, M. & Meltzer, B. Co-therapy: A review of current literature. *Journal of Sex and Marital Therapy*, 1977, *3*, 63-77.

Rosman, B. *Outcome and other criteria in the evaluation of family therapy*. Paper presented at the American Orthopsychiatric Association Meeting, New York, October, 1977.

Rosman, B.L., Minuchin, S., Liebman, R. & Baker, L. Input and outcome of family therapy in anorexia nervosa. In: J.L. Claghorn (Ed.), *Successful Psychotherapy*. New York: Brunner/Mazel, 1976.

Ross, A.O. *Child behavior therapy: Reflections on a review*. Paper presented at the Society for Psychotherapy Research, Toronto, June, 1978.

Santa-Barbara, J. *The role of goal attainment scaling in the evaluation of family therapy outcome*. Paper presented at the Goal Attainment Scaling Conference, Minneapolis, 1975.

Schneider, T. Personal communication, 1979.

Skynner, A.C.R. & Skynner, P. *Systems, families and therapy*. Paper presented at the American Association of Marriage and Family Counselors Meeting, Houston, October, 1978.

Sluzki, C.E. Marital therapy from a systems theory perspective. In: T.J. Paolino & B.S. McCrady (Eds.) *Marriage and Marital Therapy*. New York: Brunner/Mazel, 1978.

Speck, R.V. & Attneave, C.L. *Family Networks*. New York: Pantheon, 1973.

Stanton, M.D. Some outcome results and aspects of structural family therapy with drug addicts. In: D. Smith, S. Anderson, M. Buxton, T. Chung, N. Gottlieb & W. Harvey (Eds.), *A Multicultural View of Drug Abuse*. Cambridge, MA: Schenkman, 1978.

Stanton, M.D. Family treatment approaches to drug abuse problems: A Review. *Family Process*, 1979, *18*, 251-280.

Stanton, M.D. & Todd, T.C. *Structural family therapy with heroin addicts: Some outcome data*. Paper presented at the Society for Psychotherapy Research, San Diego, June, 1976.

Stanton, M.D. & Todd, T.C. A critique of the Wells and Dezen review of non-behavioral family therapy outcome studies. *Family Process*, 1980, *19*, 169-176.

Stanton, M., Todd, T., Stier, F., Van Deusen, J., Marder, L., Rosoff, R., Seaman, S. & Skibinski, E. *Family characteristics and family therapy of heroin addicts: Final report, 1974-1978*. Submitted to the National Institute on Drug Abuse (Grant No. R01-DA-1119) by the Philadelphia Child Guidance Clinic, 1979.

Steinglass, P. Experimenting with family treatment approaches to alcoholism, 1950-1975: A review. *Family Process*, 1976, *15*, 97-124.

Strelnick, A.H. Multiple family group therapy: A review of the literature. *Family Process*, 1977, *16*, 307-326.

Strupp, H.H. & Hadley, S.W. A tripartite model of mental health and therapeutic outcomes: With special reference to negative effects in psychotherapy. *American Psychologist*, 1977, *32*, 187-196.

Taggart, M. Abstracts. *Journal of Marriage and Family Counseling*, 1978, *4*, 109.

Todd, T. *Methodological problems in outcome research*. Paper presented at the Society for Psychotherapy Research, Toronto, June, 1978.

Waskow, I.E. Fantasied dialogue with a researcher. In: I.E. Waskow & M.B. Parloff (Eds.), *Psychotherapy Change Measures*. Rockville, MD: National Institute of Mental Health, 1975.

Waskow, I.E. & Parloff, M.B. *Psychotherapy Change Measures*. Rockville, MD: National Institute of Mental Health, 1975.

Weiss, R.L. Contracts, cognition and change: A behavioral approach to marriage therapy. *Counseling Psychologist*, 1975, *5*, 15-26.

Wells, R.A. Tempests, teapots (and research design): Rejoinder to Stanton and Todd. *Family Process*, 1980. *19*, 177–178.

Wells, R.A. Discussion. Panel presented at the American Orthopsychiatric Association Meeting, New York City, April, 1977.

Wells, R.A. & Dezen, A.E. The results of family therapy revisited: The nonbehavioral methods. *Family Process*, 1978, *17*, 251-274. (a)

Wells, R.A. & Dezen, A.E. Ideologies, idols (and graven images?): Rejoinder to Gurman and Kniskern. *Family Process*, 1978, *17*, 283-286. (b)

Wells, R.A. Dilkes, T. & Trivelli, N. The results of family therapy: A critical review of the literature. *Family Process*, 1972, 7, 189-207.

Whitaker, D.A. A family therapist looks at marital therapy. In: A.S. Gurman and D. Rice (Eds.), *Couples in Conflict: New Directions in Marital Therapy*. New York: Aronson, 1975.

Wilkins, W.W. Expectancy of therapeutic gain: An empirical and conceptual critique. *Journal of Consulting and Clinical Psychology*, 1973, *40*, 69-77.

Wilkins, W.W. Expectancies in applied settings. In: A.S. Gurman & A. Razin (Eds.), *Effective Psychotherapy: A Handbook at Research*. New York: Pergamon, 1977.

Williams, A.M. & Miller, W.R. Evaluation and Research in marital therapy. In: G.P. Sholevar (Ed.), *Marriage in a Family Affair: Textbook of Marriage and Marital Therapy*, New York: Spectrum, 1980.

Subject Index

Name Index